Lecture Notes in Computer Science　10961

Commenced Publication in 1973
Founding and Former Series Editors:
Gerhard Goos, Juris Hartmanis, and Jan van Leeuwen

More information about this series at http://www.springer.com/series/7407

Osvaldo Gervasi · Beniamino Murgante
Sanjay Misra · Elena Stankova
Carmelo M. Torre · Ana Maria A. C. Rocha
David Taniar · Bernady O. Apduhan
Eufemia Tarantino · Yeonseung Ryu (Eds.)

Computational Science and Its Applications – ICCSA 2018

18th International Conference
Melbourne, VIC, Australia, July 2–5, 2018
Proceedings, Part II

 Springer

Editors
Osvaldo Gervasi ⓘ
University of Perugia
Perugia
Italy

Beniamino Murgante ⓘ
University of Basilicata
Potenza
Italy

Sanjay Misra ⓘ
Covenant University
Ota
Nigeria

Elena Stankova ⓘ
Saint Petersburg State University
Saint Petersburg
Russia

Carmelo M. Torre ⓘ
Polytechnic University of Bari
Bari
Italy

Ana Maria A. C. Rocha ⓘ
University of Minho
Braga
Portugal

David Taniar ⓘ
Monash University
Clayton, VIC
Australia

Bernady O. Apduhan
Kyushu Sangyo University
Fukuoka shi, Fukuoka
Japan

Eufemia Tarantino ⓘ
Politecnico di Bari
Bari
Italy

Yeonseung Ryu ⓘ
Myongji University
Yongin
Korea (Republic of)

ISSN 0302-9743   ISSN 1611-3349 (electronic)
Lecture Notes in Computer Science
ISBN 978-3-319-95164-5   ISBN 978-3-319-95165-2 (eBook)
https://doi.org/10.1007/978-3-319-95165-2

Library of Congress Control Number: 2018947453

LNCS Sublibrary: SL1 – Theoretical Computer Science and General Issues

Printed on acid-free paper

This Springer imprint is published by the registered company Springer International Publishing AG
part of Springer Nature
The registered company address is: Gewerbestrasse 11, 6330 Cham, Switzerland

Preface

These multiple volumes (LNCS volumes 10960–10964) consist of the peer-reviewed papers presented at the 2018 International Conference on Computational Science and Its Applications (ICCSA 2018) held in Melbourne, Australia, during July 2–5, 2018.

ICCSA 2018 was a successful event in the International Conferences on Computational Science and Its Applications (ICCSA) conference series, previously held in Trieste, Italy (2017), Beijing, China (2016), Banff, Canada (2015), Guimaraes, Portugal (2014), Ho Chi Minh City, Vietnam (2013), Salvador, Brazil (2012), Santander, Spain (2011), Fukuoka, Japan (2010), Suwon, South Korea (2009), Perugia, Italy (2008), Kuala Lumpur, Malaysia (2007), Glasgow, UK (2006), Singapore (2005), Assisi, Italy (2004), Montreal, Canada (2003), and (as ICCS) Amsterdam, The Netherlands (2002) and San Francisco, USA (2001).

Computational science is a main pillar of most current research and industrial and commercial activities and it plays a unique role in exploiting ICT innovative technologies. The ICCSA conference series has been providing a venue to researchers and industry practitioners to discuss new ideas, to share complex problems and their solutions, and to shape new trends in computational science.

Apart from the general tracks, ICCSA 2018 also included 33 international workshops, in various areas of computational sciences, ranging from computational science technologies, to specific areas of computational sciences, such as computer graphics and virtual reality. The program also featured three keynote speeches.

The success of the ICCSA conference series, in general, and ICCSA 2018, in particular, is due to the support of many people: authors, presenters, participants, keynote speakers, session chairs, Organizing Committee members, student volunteers, Program Committee members, International Advisory Committee members, International Liaison chairs, and people in other various roles. We would like to thank them all.

We would also like to thank Springer for their continuous support in publishing the ICCSA conference proceedings and for sponsoring some of the paper awards.

July 2018

David Taniar
Bernady O. Apduhan
Osvaldo Gervasi
Beniamino Murgante
Ana Maria A. C. Rocha

Welcome to Melbourne

Welcome to "The Most Liveable City"[1], Melbourne, Australia. ICCSA 2018 was held at Monash University, Caulfield Campus, during July 2–5, 2018.

Melbourne is the state capital of Victoria, and is currently the second most populous city in Australia, behind Sydney. There are lots of things to do and experience while in Melbourne. Here is an incomplete list:

- Visit and experience Melbourne's best coffee shops
- Discover Melbourne's hidden laneways and rooftops
- Walk along the Yarra River
- Eat your favourite food (Chinese, Vietnamese, Malaysian, Italian, Greek, anything, ... you name it)
- Buy souvenirs at the Queen Victoria Market
- Go up to the Eureka, the tallest building in Melbourne
- Visit Melbourne's museums
- Walk and enjoy Melbourne's gardens and parks
- Visit the heart-shape lake, Albert Park Lake, the home of the F1 Grand Prix
- Simply walk in the city to enjoy Melbourne experience
- Try Melbourne's gelato ice cream

Basically, it is easy to live in and to explore Melbourne, and I do hope that you will have time to explore the city of Melbourne.

The venue of ICCSA 2018 was in Monash University. Monash University is a member of Go8, which is considered the top eight universities in Australia. Monash University has a number of campuses and centers. The two main campuses in Melbourne are Clayton and Caulfield. ICCSA 2018 was held on Caulfield Campus, which is only 12 minutes away from Melbourne CBD by train.

The Faculty of Information Technology is one of the ten faculties at Monash University. The faculty has more than 100 full-time academic staff (equivalent to the rank of Assistant Professor, Associate Professor, and Professor).

I do hope that you will enjoy not only the conference, but also Melbourne.

David Taniar

---

[1] The Global Liveability Report 2017, https://www.cnbc.com/2017/08/17/the-worlds-top-10-most-livable-cities.html

Organization

ICCSA 2018 was organized by Monash University (Australia), University of Perugia (Italy), Kyushu Sangyo University (Japan), University of Basilicata (Italy), and University of Minho, (Portugal).

Honorary General Chairs

Antonio Laganà	University of Perugia, Italy
Norio Shiratori	Tohoku University, Japan
Kenneth C. J. Tan	Sardina Systems, Estonia

General Chairs

David Taniar	Monash University, Australia
Bernady O. Apduhan	Kyushu Sangyo University, Japan

Program Committee Chairs

Osvaldo Gervasi	University of Perugia, Italy
Beniamino Murgante	University of Basilicata, Italy
Ana Maria A. C. Rocha	University of Minho, Portugal

International Advisory Committee

Jemal Abawajy	Deakin University, Australia
Dharma P. Agrawal	University of Cincinnati, USA
Marina L. Gavrilova	University of Calgary, Canada
Claudia Bauzer Medeiros	University of Campinas, Brazil
Manfred M. Fisher	Vienna University of Economics and Business, Austria
Yee Leung	Chinese University of Hong Kong, SAR China

International Liaison Chairs

Ana Carla P. Bitencourt	Universidade Federal do Reconcavo da Bahia, Brazil
Giuseppe Borruso	University of Trieste, Italy
Alfredo Cuzzocrea	University of Trieste, Italy
Maria Irene Falcão	University of Minho, Portugal
Robert C. H. Hsu	Chung Hua University, Taiwan
Tai-Hoon Kim	Hannam University, South Korea
Sanjay Misra	Covenant University, Nigeria
Takashi Naka	Kyushu Sangyo University, Japan

Rafael D. C. Santos	National Institute for Space Research, Brazil
Maribel Yasmina Santos	University of Minho, Portugal

Workshop and Session Organizing Chairs

Beniamino Murgante	University of Basilicata, Italy
Sanjay Misra	Covenant University, Nigeria
Jorge Gustavo Rocha	University of Minho, Portugal

Award Chair

Wenny Rahayu	La Trobe University, Australia

Web Chair

A. S. M. Kayes	La Trobe University, Australia

Publicity Committee Chairs

Elmer Dadios	De La Salle University, Philippines
Hong Quang Nguyen	International University (VNU-HCM), Vietnam
Daisuke Takahashi	Tsukuba University, Japan
Shangwang Wang	Beijing University of Posts and Telecommunications, China

Workshop Organizers

Advanced Methods in Fractals and Data Mining for Applications (AMFDMA 2018)

Yeliz Karaca	IEEE
Carlo Cattani	Tuscia University, Italy
Majaz Moonis	University of Massachusettes Medical School, USA

Advances in Information Systems and Technologies for Emergency Management, Risk Assessment and Mitigation Based on Resilience Concepts (ASTER 2018)

Maurizio Pollino	ENEA, Italy
Marco Vona	University of Basilicata, Italy
Beniamino Murgante	University of Basilicata, Italy
Grazia Fattoruso	ENEA, Italy

Advances in Web-Based Learning (AWBL 2018)

Mustafa Murat Inceoglu	Ege University, Turkey
Birol Ciloglugil	Ege University, Turkey

Bio- and Neuro-inspired Computing and Applications (BIONCA 2018)

Nadia Nedjah   State University of Rio de Janeiro, Brazil
Luiza de Macedo Mourell State University of Rio de Janeiro, Brazil

Computer-Aided Modeling, Simulation, and Analysis (CAMSA 2018)

Jie Shen   University of Michigan, USA
Hao Chen   Shanghai University of Engineering Science, China
Youguo He   Jiangsu University, China

Computational and Applied Statistics (CAS 2018)

Ana Cristina Braga   University of Minho, Portugal

Computational Geometry and Security Applications (CGSA 2018)

Marina L. Gavrilova   University of Calgary, Canada

Computational Movement Analysis (CMA 2018)

Farid Karimipour   University of Tehran, Iran

Computational Mathematics, Statistics and Information Management (CMSIM 2018)

M. Filomena Teodoro   Lisbon University and Portuguese Naval Academy,
                       Portugal

Computational Optimization and Applications (COA 2018)

Ana Maria Rocha   University of Minho, Portugal
Humberto Rocha   University of Coimbra, Portugal

Computational Astrochemistry (CompAstro 2018)

Marzio Rosi   University of Perugia, Italy
Dimitrios Skouteris   Scuola Normale Superiore di Pisa, Italy
Albert Rimola   Universitat Autònoma de Barcelona, Spain

Cities, Technologies, and Planning (CTP 2018)

Giuseppe Borruso   University of Trieste, Italy
Beniamino Murgante   University of Basilicata, Italy

Defense Technology and Security (DTS 2018)

Yeonseung Ryu   Myongji University, South Korea

Econometrics and Multidimensional Evaluation in the Urban Environment (EMEUE 2018)

Carmelo M. Torre	Polytechnic of Bari, Italy
Maria Cerreta	University of Naples Federico II, Italy
Pierluigi Morano	Polytechnic of Bari, Italy
Paola Perchinunno	University of Bari, Italy

Future Computing Systems, Technologies, and Applications (FISTA 2018)

Bernady O. Apduhan	Kyushu Sangyo University, Japan
Rafael Santos	National Institute for Space Research, Brazil
Shangguang Wang	Beijing University of Posts and Telecommunications, China
Kazuaki Tanaka	Kyushu Institute of Technology, Japan

Geographical Analysis, Urban Modeling, Spatial Statistics (GEO-AND-MOD 2018)

Giuseppe Borruso	University of Trieste, Italy
Beniamino Murgante	University of Basilicata, Italy
Hartmut Asche	University of Potsdam, Germany

Geomatics for Resource Monitoring and Control (GRMC 2018)

Eufemia Tarantino	Polytechnic of Bari, Italy
Umberto Fratino	Polytechnic of Bari, Italy
Benedetto Figorito	ARPA Puglia, Italy
Antonio Novelli	Polytechnic of Bari, Italy
Rosa Lasaponara	Italian Research Council, IMAA-CNR, Italy

International Symposium on Software Quality (ISSQ 2018)

Sanjay Misra	Covenant University, Nigeria

Web-Based Collective Evolutionary Systems: Models, Measures, Applications (IWCES 2018)

Alfredo Milani	University of Perugia, Italy
Clement Leung	United International College, Zhouhai, China
Valentina Franzoni	University of Rome La Sapienza, Italy
Valentina Poggioni	University of Perugia, Italy

Large-Scale Computational Physics (LSCP 2018)

Elise de Doncker	Western Michigan University, USA
Fukuko Yuasa	High Energy Accelerator Research Organization, KEK, Japan
Hideo Matsufuru	High Energy Accelerator Research Organization, KEK, Japan

Land Use Monitoring for Soil Consumption Reduction (LUMS 2018)

Carmelo M. Torre   Polytechnic of Bari, Italy
Alessandro Bonifazi   Polytechnic of Bari, Italy
Pasquale Balena   Polytechnic of Bari, Italy
Beniamino Murgante   University of Basilicata , Italy
Eufemia Tarantino   Polytechnic of Bari, Italy

Mobile Communications (MC 2018)

Hyunseung Choo   Sungkyunkwan University, South Korea

Scientific Computing Infrastructure (SCI 2018)

Elena Stankova   Saint-Petersburg State University, Russia
Vladimir Korkhov   Saint-Petersburg State University, Russia

International Symposium on Software Engineering Processes and Applications (SEPA 2018)

Sanjay Misra   Covenant University, Nigeria

Smart Factory Convergence (SFC 2018)

Jongpil Jeong   Sungkyunkwan University, South Korea

Is a Smart City Really Smart? Models, Solutions, Proposals for an Effective Urban and Social Development (Smart_Cities 2018)

Giuseppe Borruso   University of Trieste, Italy
Chiara Garau   University of Cagliari, Italy
Ginevra Balletto   University of Cagliari, Italy
Beniamino Murgante   University of Basilicata, Italy
Paola Zamberlin   University of Florence, Italy

Sustainability Performance Assessment: Models, Approaches and Applications Toward Interdisciplinary and Integrated Solutions (SPA 2018)

Francesco Scorza   University of Basilicata, Italy
Valentin Grecu   Lucia Blaga University on Sibiu, Romania
Jolanta Dvarioniene   Kaunas University, Lithuania
Sabrina Lai   Cagliari University, Italy

Advances in Spatio-Temporal Analytics (ST-Analytics 2018)

Rafael Santos   Brazilian Space Research Agency, Brazil
Karine Reis Ferreira   Brazilian Space Research Agency, Brazil
Joao Moura Pires   New University of Lisbon, Portugal
Maribel Yasmina Santos   University of Minho, Portugal

Theoretical and Computational Chemistry and Its Applications (TCCA 2018)

M. Noelia Faginas Lago | University of Perugia, Italy
Andrea Lombardi | University of Perugia, Italy

Tools and Techniques in Software Development Processes (TTSDP 2018)

Sanjay Misra | Covenant University, Nigeria

Challenges, Trends and Innovations in VGI (VGI 2018)

Beniamino Murgante | University of Basilicata, Italy
Rodrigo Tapia-McClung | Centro de Investigación en Geografia y Geomática Ing
| Jorge L. Tamay, Mexico
Claudia Ceppi | Polytechnic of Bari, Italy
Jorge Gustavo Rocha | University of Minho, Portugal

Virtual Reality and Applications (VRA 2018)

Osvaldo Gervasi | University of Perugia, Italy
Sergio Tasso | University of Perugia, Italy

International Workshop on Parallel and Distributed Data Mining (WPDM 2018)

Massimo Cafaro | University of Salento, Italy
Italo Epicoco | University of Salento, Italy
Marco Pulimeno | University of Salento, Italy
Giovanni Aloisio | University of Salento, Italy

Program Committee

Kenny Adamson | University of Ulster, UK
Vera Afreixo | University of Aveiro, Portugal
Filipe Alvelos | University of Minho, Portugal
Hartmut Asche | University of Potsdam, Germany
Michela Bertolotto | University College Dublin, Ireland
Sandro Bimonte | CEMAGREF, TSCF, France
Rod Blais | University of Calgary, Canada
Ivan Blečić | University of Sassari, Italy
Giuseppe Borruso | University of Trieste, Italy
Ana Cristina Braga | University of Minho, Portugal
Yves Caniou | Lyon University, France
José A. Cardoso e Cunha | Universidade Nova de Lisboa, Portugal
Rui Cardoso | University of Beira Interior, Portugal
Leocadio G. Casado | University of Almeria, Spain
Carlo Cattani | University of Salerno, Italy
Mete Celik | Erciyes University, Turkey
Alexander Chemeris | National Technical University of Ukraine KPI, Ukraine
Min Young Chung | Sungkyunkwan University, South Korea

Florbela Maria da Cruz Domingues Correia	Polytechnic Institute of Viana do Castelo, Portugal
Gilberto Corso Pereira	Federal University of Bahia, Brazil
Carla Dal Sasso Freitas	Universidade Federal do Rio Grande do Sul, Brazil
Pradesh Debba	The Council for Scientific and Industrial Research (CSIR), South Africa
Hendrik Decker	Instituto Tecnológico de Informática, Spain
Frank Devai	London South Bank University, UK
Rodolphe Devillers	Memorial University of Newfoundland, Canada
Joana Matos Dias	University of Coimbra, Portugal
Paolino Di Felice	University of L'Aquila, Italy
Prabu Dorairaj	NetApp, India/USA
M. Irene Falcao	University of Minho, Portugal
Cherry Liu Fang	U.S. DOE Ames Laboratory, USA
Florbela P. Fernandes	Polytechnic Institute of Bragança, Portugal
Jose-Jesus Fernandez	National Centre for Biotechnology, CSIS, Spain
Paula Odete Fernandes	Polytechnic Institute of Bragança, Portugal
Adelaide de Fátima Baptista Valente Freitas	University of Aveiro, Portugal
Manuel Carlos Figueiredo	University of Minho, Portugal
Maria Antonia Forjaz	University of Minho, Portugal
Maria Celia Furtado Rocha	PRODEB–PósCultura/UFBA, Brazil
Paulino Jose Garcia Nieto	University of Oviedo, Spain
Jerome Gensel	LSR-IMAG, France
Maria Giaoutzi	National Technical University, Athens, Greece
Arminda Manuela Andrade Pereira Gonçalves	University of Minho, Portugal
Andrzej M. Goscinski	Deakin University, Australia
Sevin Gmïgmï	Izmir University of Economics, Turkey
Alex Hagen-Zanker	University of Cambridge, UK
Malgorzata Hanzl	Technical University of Lodz, Poland
Shanmugasundaram Hariharan	B.S. Abdur Rahman University, India
Eligius M. T. Hendrix	University of Malaga/Wageningen University, Spain/The Netherlands
Tutut Herawan	Universitas Teknologi Yogyakarta, Indonesia
Hisamoto Hiyoshi	Gunma University, Japan
Fermin Huarte	University of Barcelona, Spain
Mustafa Inceoglu	EGE University, Turkey
Peter Jimack	University of Leeds, UK
Qun Jin	Waseda University, Japan
A. S. M. Kayes	La Trobe University, Australia
Farid Karimipour	Vienna University of Technology, Austria
Baris Kazar	Oracle Corp., USA
Maulana Adhinugraha Kiki	Telkom University, Indonesia
DongSeong Kim	University of Canterbury, New Zealand

Taihoon Kim	Hannam University, South Korea
Ivana Kolingerova	University of West Bohemia, Czech Republic
Rosa Lasaponara	National Research Council, Italy
Maurizio Lazzari	National Research Council, Italy
Cheng Siong Lee	Monash University, Australia
Sangyoun Lee	Yonsei University, South Korea
Jongchan Lee	Kunsan National University, South Korea
Clement Leung	Hong Kong Baptist University, Hong Kong, SAR China
Chendong Li	University of Connecticut, USA
Gang Li	Deakin University, Australia
Ming Li	East China Normal University, China
Fang Liu	AMES Laboratories, USA
Xin Liu	University of Calgary, Canada
Savino Longo	University of Bari, Italy
Tinghuai Ma	NanJing University of Information Science and Technology, China
Luca Mancinelli	Trinity College Dublin, Ireland
Ernesto Marcheggiani	Katholieke Universiteit Leuven, Belgium
Antonino Marvuglia	Research Centre Henri Tudor, Luxembourg
Nicola Masini	National Research Council, Italy
Eric Medvet	University of Trieste, Italy
Nirvana Meratnia	University of Twente, The Netherlands
Alfredo Milani	University of Perugia, Italy
Giuseppe Modica	University of Reggio Calabria, Italy
Josè Luis Montaña	University of Cantabria, Spain
Maria Filipa Mourão	IP from Viana do Castelo, Portugal
Laszlo Neumann	University of Girona, Spain
Kok-Leong Ong	Deakin University, Australia
Belen Palop	Universidad de Valladolid, Spain
Marcin Paprzycki	Polish Academy of Sciences, Poland
Eric Pardede	La Trobe University, Australia
Kwangjin Park	Wonkwang University, South Korea
Ana Isabel Pereira	Polytechnic Institute of Bragança, Portugal
Maurizio Pollino	Italian National Agency for New Technologies, Energy and Sustainable Economic Development, Italy
Alenka Poplin	University of Hamburg, Germany
Vidyasagar Potdar	Curtin University of Technology, Australia
David C. Prosperi	Florida Atlantic University, USA
Wenny Rahayu	La Trobe University, Australia
Jerzy Respondek	Silesian University of Technology, Poland
Humberto Rocha	INESC-Coimbra, Portugal
Alexey Rodionov	Institute of Computational Mathematics and Mathematical Geophysics, Russia

Jon Rokne	University of Calgary, Canada
Octavio Roncero	CSIC, Spain
Maytham Safar	Kuwait University, Kuwait
Chiara Saracino	A.O. Ospedale Niguarda Ca' Granda - Milano, Italy
Haiduke Sarafian	The Pennsylvania State University, USA
Marco Paulo Seabra dos Reis	University of Coimbra, Portugal
Jie Shen	University of Michigan, USA
Qi Shi	Liverpool John Moores University, UK
Dale Shires	U.S. Army Research Laboratory, USA
Inês Soares	University of Coimbra, Portugal
Takuo Suganuma	Tohoku University, Japan
Sergio Tasso	University of Perugia, Italy
Ana Paula Teixeira	University of Trás-os-Montes and Alto Douro, Portugal
Senhorinha Teixeira	University of Minho, Portugal
Parimala Thulasiraman	University of Manitoba, Canada
Carmelo Torre	Polytechnic of Bari, Italy
Javier Martinez Torres	Centro Universitario de la Defensa Zaragoza, Spain
Giuseppe A. Trunfio	University of Sassari, Italy
Toshihiro Uchibayashi	Kyushu Sangyo University, Japan
Pablo Vanegas	University of Cuenca, Ecuador
Marco Vizzari	University of Perugia, Italy
Varun Vohra	Merck Inc., USA
Koichi Wada	University of Tsukuba, Japan
Krzysztof Walkowiak	Wroclaw University of Technology, Poland
Zequn Wang	Intelligent Automation Inc., USA
Robert Weibel	University of Zurich, Switzerland
Frank Westad	Norwegian University of Science and Technology, Norway
Roland Wismüller	Universität Siegen, Germany
Mudasser Wyne	SOET National University, USA
Chung-Huang Yang	National Kaohsiung Normal University, Taiwan
Xin-She Yang	National Physical Laboratory, UK
Salim Zabir	France Telecom Japan Co., Japan
Haifeng Zhao	University of California, Davis, USA
Kewen Zhao	University of Qiongzhou, China
Fabiana Zollo	University of Venice Cà Foscari, Italy
Albert Y. Zomaya	University of Sydney, Australia

Reviewers

Afreixo Vera	University of Aveiro, Portugal
Ahmad Rashid	Microwave and Antenna Lab, School of Engineering, Korea
Aguilar José Alfonso	Universidad Autónoma de Sinaloa, Mexico
Albanese Valentina	Università di Bologna, Italy
Alvelos Filipe	University of Minho, Portugal
Amato Federico	University of Basilicata, Italy
Andrianov Serge	Institute for Informatics of Tatarstan Academy of Sciences, Russia
Antunes Marília	University Nova de Lisboa, Portugal
Apduhan Bernady	Kyushu Sangyo University, Japan
Aquilanti Vincenzo	University of Perugia, Italy
Asche Hartmut	Potsdam University, Germany
Aslan Zafer	Istanbul Aydin University, Turkey
Aytaç Vecdi	Ege University, Turkey
Azevedo Ana	Instituto Superior de Engenharia do Porto, Portugal
Azzari Margherita	Universitá degli Studi di Firenze, Italy
Bae Ihn-Han	Catholic University of Daegu, South Korea
Balci Birim	Celal Bayar Üniversitesi, Turkey
Balena Pasquale	Politecnico di Bari, Italy
Balucani Nadia	University of Perugia, Italy
Barroca Filho Itamir	Instituto Metrópole Digital da UFRN (IMD-UFRN), Brazil
Bayrak §sengül	Haliç University, Turkey
Behera Ranjan Kumar	Indian Institute of Technology Patna, India
Bimonte Sandro	IRSTEA, France
Bogdanov Alexander	Saint-Petersburg State University, Russia
Bonifazi Alessandro	Polytechnic of Bari, Italy
Borruso Giuseppe	University of Trieste, Italy
Braga Ana Cristina	University of Minho, Portugal
Cafaro Massimo	University of Salento, Italy
Canora Filomena	University of Basilicata, Italy
Cao Yuanlong	University of Saskatchewan, Canada
Caradonna Grazia	Polytechnic of Bari, Italy
Cardoso Rui	Institute of Telecommunications, Portugal
Carolina Tripp Barba	Universidad Autónoma de Sinaloa, Mexico
Caroti Gabriella	University of Pisa, Italy
Ceccarello Matteo	University of Padova, Italy
Cefalo Raffaela	University of Trieste, Italy
Cerreta Maria	University Federico II of Naples, Italy
Challa Rajesh	Sungkyunkwan University, Korea
Chamundeswari Arumugam	SSN College of Engineering, India
Chaturvedi Krishna Kumar	Patil Group of Industries, India
Cho Chulhee	Seoul Guarantee Insurance Company Ltd., Korea

Choi Jae-Young	Sungkyunkwan University, Korea
Choi Kwangnam	Korea Institute of Science and Technology Information, Korea
Choi Seonho	Seoul National University, Korea
Chung Min Young	Sungkyunkwan University, Korea
Ciloglugil Birol	Ege University, Turkey
Coletti Cecilia	University of Chieti, Italy
Congiu Tanja	Università degli Studi di Sassari, Italy
Correia Anacleto	Base Naval de Lisboa, Portugal
Correia Elisete	University of Trás-Os-Montes e Alto Douro, Portugal
Correia Florbela Maria da Cruz Domingues	Instituto Politécnico de Viana do Castelo, Portugal
Costa e Silva Eliana	Polytechnic of Porto, Portugal
Cugurullo Federico	Trinity College Dublin, Ireland
Damas Bruno	LARSyS, Instituto Superior Técnico, Univ. Lisboa, Portugal
Dang Thien Binh	Sungkyunkwan University, Korea
Daniele Bartoli	University of Perugia, Italy
de Doncker Elise	Western Michigan University, USA
Degtyarev Alexander	Saint-Petersburg State University, Russia
Demyanov Vasily	Heriot-Watt University, UK
Devai Frank	London South Bank University, UK
Di Fatta Giuseppe	University of Reading, UK
Dias Joana	University of Coimbra, Portugal
Dilo Arta	University of Twente, The Netherlands
El-Zawawy Mohamed A.	Cairo University, Egypt
Epicoco Italo	Università del Salento, Italy
Escalona Maria-Jose	University of Seville, Spain
Falcinelli Stefano	University of Perugia, Italy
Faginas-Lago M. Noelia	University of Perugia, Italy
Falcão M. Irene	University of Minho, Portugal
Famiano Michael	Western Michigan University, USA
Fattoruso Grazia	ENEA, Italy
Fernandes Florbela	Escola Superior de Tecnologia e Gestão de Braganca, Portugal
Fernandes Paula	Escola Superior de Tecnologia e Gestão, Portugal
Ferraro Petrillo Umberto	University of Rome "La Sapienza", Italy
Ferreira Fernanda	Escola Superior de Estudos Industriais e de Gestão, Portugal
Ferrão Maria	Universidade da Beira Interior, Portugal
Figueiredo Manuel Carlos	Universidade do Minho, Portugal
Fiorini Lorena	Università degli Studi dell'Aquila, Italy
Florez Hector	Universidad Distrital Francisco Jose de Caldas, Colombia
Franzoni Valentina	University of Perugia, Italy

Freitau Adelaide de Fátima Baptista Valente	University of Aveiro, Portugal
Gabrani Goldie	Bml Munjal University, India
Garau Chiara	University of Cagliari, Italy
Garcia Ernesto	University of the Basque Country, Spain
Gavrilova Marina	University of Calgary, Canada
Gervasi Osvaldo	University of Perugia, Italy
Gioia Andrea	University of Bari, Italy
Giorgi Giacomo	University of Perugia, Italy
Giuliani Felice	Università degli Studi di Parma, Italy
Goel Rajat	University of Southern California, USA
Gonçalves Arminda Manuela	University of Minho, Portugal
Gorbachev Yuriy	Geolink Technologies, Russia
Gordon-Ross Ann	University of Florida, USA
Goyal Rinkaj	Guru Gobind Singh Indraprastha University, India
Grilli Luca	University of Perugia, Italy
Goyal Rinkaj	GGS Indraprastha University, India
Guerra Eduardo	National Institute for Space Research, Brazil
Gumgum Sevin	İzmir Ekonomi Üniversitesi, Turkey
Gülen Kemal Güven	Istanbul Ticaret University, Turkey
Hacızade Ulviye	Haliç Üniversitesi Uluslararas, Turkey
Han Longzhe	Nanchang Institute of Technology, Korea
Hanzl Malgorzata	University of Lodz, Poland
Hayashi Masaki	University of Calgary, Canada
He Youguo	Jiangsu University, China
Hegedus Peter	University of Szeged, Hungary
Herawan Tutut	Universiti Malaysia Pahang, Malaysia
Ignaccolo Matteo	University of Catania, Italy
Imakura Akira	University of Tsukuba, Japan
Inceoglu Mustafa	Ege University, Turkey
Jagwani Priti	Indian Institute of Technology Delhi, India
Jang Jeongsook	Brown University, Korea
Jeong Jongpil	Sungkyunkwan University, Korea
Jin Hyunwook	Konkuk University, Korea
Jorge Ana Maria, Kapenga John	Western Michigan University, USA
Kawana Kojiro	University of Tokio, Japan
Kayes Abu S. M.	La Trobe University, Australia
Kim JeongAh	George Fox University, USA
Korkhov Vladimir	St. Petersburg State University, Russia
Kulabukhova Nataliia	Saint-Peterburg State University, Russia
Kumar Pawan	Expert Software Consultants Ltd., India
Laccetti Giuliano	Università degli Studi di Napoli, Italy
Laganà Antonio	Master-up srl, Italy
Lai Sabrina	University of Cagliari, Italy

Laricchiuta Annarita	CNR-IMIP, Italy
Lazzari Maurizio	CNR IBAM, Italy
Lee Soojin	Cyber Security Lab, Korea
Leon Marcelo	Universidad Estatal Península de Santa Elena – UPSE, Ecuador
Lim Ilkyun	Sungkyunkwan University, Korea
Lourenço Vanda Marisa	University Nova de Lisboa, Portugal
Mancinelli Luca	University of Dublin, Ireland
Mangiameli Michele	University of Catania, Italy
Markov Krassimiri	Institute for Information Theories and Applications, Bulgaria
Marques Jorge	Universidade de Coimbra, Portugal
Marvuglia Antonino	Public Research Centre Henri Tudor, Luxembourg
Mateos Cristian	Universidad Nacional del Centro, Argentina
Matsufuru Hideo	High Energy Accelerator Research, Japan
Maurizio Crispini	Politecnico di Milano, Italy
Medvet Eric	University of Trieste, Italy
Mengoni Paolo	Università degli Studi di Firenze, Italy
Mesiti Marco	Università degli studi di Milano, Italy
Millham Richard	Durban University of Technology, South Africa
Misra Sanjay	Covenant University, Nigeria
Mishra Anurag	Helmholtz Zentrum München, Germany
Mishra Biswajeeban	University of Szeged, Hungary
Moscato Pablo	University of Newcastle, Australia
Moura Pires Joao	Universidade Nova de Lisboa, Portugal
Moura Ricardo	Universidade Nova de Lisboa, Portugal
Mourao Maria	Universidade do Minho, Portugal
Mukhopadhyay Asish	University of Windsor, Canada
Murgante Beniamino	University of Basilicata, Italy
Nakasato Naohito	University of Aizu, Japan
Nguyen Tien Dzung	Sungkyunkwan University, South Korea
Nicolosi Vittorio	University of Rome Tor Vergata, Italy
Ogihara Mitsunori	University of Miami, USA
Oh Sangyoon	Ajou University, Korea
Oliveira Irene	University of Trás-Os-Montes e Alto Douro, Portugal
Oluranti Jonathan	Covenant University, Nigeria
Ozturk Savas	The Scientific and Technological Research Council of Turkey, Turkey
P. Costa M. Fernanda	University of Minho, Portugal
Paek Yunheung	Seoul National University, Korea
Pancham Jay	Durban University of Technology, South Africa
Pantazis Dimos	Technological Educational Institute of Athens, Greek
Paolucci Michela	Università degli Studi di Firenze, Italy
Pardede Eric	La Trobe University, Australia
Park Hyun Kyoo	Petabi Corp, Korea
Passaro Tommaso	University of Bari, Italy

Pereira Ana	Instituto Politécnico de Bragança, Portugal
Peschechera Giuseppe	University of Bari, Italy
Petri Massimiliano	Università di Pisa, Italy
Pham Quoc Trung	Ho Chi Minh City University of Technology, Vietnam
Piemonte Andrea	Università di Pisa, Italy
Pinna Francesco	Università degli Studi di Cagliari, Italy
Pinto Telmo	University of Minho, Portugal
Pollino Maurizio	ENEA, Italy
Pulimeno Marco	University of Salento, Italy
Rahayu Wenny	La Trobe University, Australia
Rao S. V.	Duke Clinical Research, USA
Raza Syed Muhammad	Sungkyunkwan University, South Korea
Reis Ferreira Gomes Karine	National Institute for Space Research, Brazil
Reis Marco	Universidade de Coimbra, Portugal
Rimola Albert	Autonomous University of Barcelona, Spain
Rocha Ana Maria	University of Minho, Portugal
Rocha Humberto	University of Coimbra, Portugal
Rodriguez Daniel	The University of Queensland, Australia
Ryu Yeonseung	Myongji University, South Korea
Sahni Himantikka	CRISIL Global Research and Analytics, India
Sahoo Kshira Sagar	C. V. Raman College of Engineering, India
Santos Maribel Yasmina	University of Minho, Portugal
Santos Rafael	KU Leuven, Belgium
Saponaro Mirko	Politecnico di Bari, Italy
Scorza Francesco	Università della Basilicata, Italy
Sdao Francesco	Università della Basilicata, Italy
Shen Jie	University of Southampton, UK
Shintani Takahiko	University of Electro-Communications, Japan
Shoaib Muhammad	Sungkyunkwan University, South Korea
Silva-Fortes Carina	ESTeSL-IPL, Portugal
Singh V. B.	University of Delhi, India
Skouteris Dimitrios	SNS, Italy
Soares Inês	INESCC and IPATIMUP, Portugal
Sosnin Petr	Ulyanovsk State Technical University, Russia
Souza Erica	Universidade Nova de Lisboa, Portugal
Stankova Elena	Saint-Petersburg State University, Russia
Sumida Yasuaki	Kyushu Sangyo University, Japan
Tanaka Kazuaki	Kyushu Institute of Technology, Japan
Tapia-McClung Rodrigo	CentroGeo, Mexico
Tarantino Eufemia	Politecnico di Bari, Italy
Tasso Sergio	University of Perugia, Italy
Teixeira Ana Paula	Universidade Católica Portuguesa, Portugal
Tengku Adil	La Trobe University, Australia
Teodoro M. Filomena	Lisbon University, Portugal
Tiwari Sunita	King George's Medical University, India
Torre Carmelo Maria	Polytechnic of Bari, Italy

Torrisi Vincenza	University of Catania, Italy
Totaro Vincenzo	Politecnico di Bari, Italy
Tran Manh Hung	Institute for Research and Executive Education, Vietnam
Tripathi Aprna	GLA University, India
Trunfio Giuseppe A.	University of Sassari, Italy
Tóth Zoltán	Hungarian Academy of Sciences, Hungary
Uchibayashi Toshihiro	Kyushu Sangyo University, Japan
Ugliengo Piero	University of Torino, Italy
Ullman Holly	University of Delaware, USA
Vallverdu Jordi	Autonomous University of Barcelona, Spain
Valuev Ilya	Russian Academy of Sciences, Russia
Vasyunin Dmitry	University of Amsterdam, The Netherlands
Vohra Varun	University of Electro-Communications, Japan
Voit Nikolay	Ulyanovsk State Technical University, Russia
Wale Azeez Nurayhn	University of Lagos, Nigeria
Walkowiak Krzysztof	Wroclaw University of Technology, Poland
Wallace Richard J.	Univeristy of Texas, USA
Waluyo Agustinus Borgy	Monash University, Australia
Westad Frank	CAMO Software AS, USA
Wole Adewumi	Covenant University, Nigeria
Xie Y. H.	Bell Laboratories, USA
Yamauchi Toshihiro	Okayama University, Japan
Yamazaki Takeshi	University of Tokyo, Japan
Yao Fenghui	Tennessee State University, USA
Yoki Karl	Catholic University of Daegu, South Korea
Yoshiura Noriaki	Saitama University, Japan
Yuasa Fukuko	High Energy Accelerator Research Organization, Korea
Zamperlin Paola	University of Florence, Italy
Zollo Fabiana	University of Venice "Cà Foscari", Italy
Zullo Francesco	University of L'Aquila, Italy
Zivkovic Ljiljana	Republic Agency for Spatial Planning, Belgrade

Sponsoring Organizations

ICCSA 2018 would not have been possible without the tremendous support of many organizations and institutions, for which all organizers and participants of ICCSA 2018 express their sincere gratitude:

Springer International Publishing AG, Germany
(http://www.springer.com)

Monash University, Australia
(http://monash.edu)

University of Perugia, Italy
(http://www.unipg.it)

University of Basilicata, Italy
(http://www.unibas.it)

Kyushu Sangyo University, Japan
(www.kyusan-u.ac.jp)

Universidade do Minho, Portugal
(http://www.uminho.pt)

Keynote Speakers

New Frontiers in Cloud Computing for Big Data and Internet-of-Things (IoT) Applications

Rajkumar Buyya[1,2]

[1] Cloud Computing and Distributed Systems (CLOUDS) Lab,
The University of Melbourne, Australia
[2] Manjrasoft Pvt Ltd., Melbourne, Australia

Abstract. Computing is being transformed to a model consisting of services that are commoditised and delivered in a manner similar to utilities such as water, electricity, gas, and telephony. Several computing paradigms have promised to deliver this utility computing vision. Cloud computing has emerged as one of the buzzwords in the IT industry and turned the vision of "computing utilities" into a reality.

Clouds deliver infrastructure, platform, and software (application) as services, which are made available as subscription-based services in a pay-as-you-go model to consumers. Cloud application platforms need to offer

1. APIs and tools for rapid creation of elastic applications and
2. a runtime system for deployment of applications on geographically distributed computing infrastructure in a seamless manner.

The Internet of Things (IoT) paradigm enables seamless integration of cyber-and-physical worlds and opening up opportunities for creating newclass of applications for domains such as smart cities. The emerging Fog computing is extending Cloud computing paradigm to edge resources for latency sensitive IoT applications.

This keynote presentation will cover:

a. 21st century vision of computing and identifies various IT paradigms promising to deliver the vision of computing utilities;
b. opportunities and challenges for utility and market-oriented Cloud computing,
c. innovative architecture for creating market-oriented and elastic Clouds by harnessing virtualisation technologies;
d. Aneka, a Cloud Application Platform, for rapid development of Cloud/Big Data applications and their deployment on private/public Clouds with resource provisioning driven by SLAs;
e. experimental results on deploying Cloud and Big Data/Internet-of-Things (IoT) applications in engineering, and health care, satellite image processing, and smart cities on elastic Clouds;

f. directions for delivering our 21st century vision along with pathways for future research in Cloud and Fog computing.

Short Bio Dr. Rajkumar Buyya is a Redmond Barry Distinguished Professor and Director of the Cloud Computing and Distributed Systems (CLOUDS) Laboratory at the University of Melbourne, Australia. He is also serving as the founding CEO of Manjrasoft, a spin-off company of the University, commercializing its innovations in Cloud Computing. He served as a Future Fellow of the Australian Research Council during 2012-2016. He has authored over 625 publications and seven text books including "Mastering Cloud Computing" published by McGraw Hill, China Machine Press, and Morgan Kaufmann for Indian, Chinese and international markets respectively. He also edited several books including "Cloud Computing: Principles and Paradigms" (Wiley Press, USA, Feb 2011).

He is one of the highly cited authors in computer science and software engineering worldwide (h-index = 117, g-index = 255, 70,500 + citations). Dr. Buyya is recognized as a "Web of Science Highly Cited Researcher" in both 2016 and 2017 by Thomson Reuters, a Fellow of IEEE, and Scopus Researcher of the Year 2017 with Excellence in Innovative Research Award by Elsevier for his outstanding contributions to Cloud computing.

Software technologies for Grid and Cloud computing developed under Dr. Buyya's leadership have gained rapid acceptance and are in use at several academic institutions and commercial enterprises in 40 countries around the world. Dr. Buyya has led the establishment and development of key community activities, including serving as foundation Chair of the IEEE Technical Committee on Scalable Computing and five IEEE/ACM conferences. These contributions and international research leadership of Dr. Buyya are recognized through the award of "2009 IEEE Medal for Excellence in Scalable Computing" from the IEEE Computer Society TCSC.

Manjrasoft's Aneka Cloud technology developed under his leadership has received "2010 Frost & Sullivan New Product Innovation Award". He served as the founding Editor-in-Chief of the IEEE Transactions on Cloud Computing. He is currently serving as Co-Editor-in-Chief of Journal of Software: Practice and Experience, which was established over 45 years ago. For further information on Dr. Buyya, please visit his cyberhome: www.buyya.com.

Approximation Problems for Digital Image Processing and Applications

Gianluca Vinti

Department of Mathematics and Computer Science,
University of Perugia, Italy

Abstract. In this talk, some approximation problems are discussed with applications to reconstruction and to digital image processing. We will also show some applications to concrete problems in the medical and engineering fields. Regarding the first, a procedure will be presented, based on approaches of approximation theory and on algorithms of digital image processing for the diagnosis of aneurysmal diseases; in particular we discuss the extraction of the pervious lumen of the artery starting from CT image without contrast medium. As concerns the engineering field, thermographic images are analyzed for the study of thermal bridges and for the structural and dynamic analysis of buildings, working therefore in the field of energy analysis and seismic vulnerability of buildings, respectively.

Short Bio Gianluca Vinti is Full Professor of Mathematical Analysis at the Department of Mathematics and Computer Science of the University of Perugia. He is Director of the Department since 2014 and member of the Academic Senate of the University. Member of the Board of the Italian Mathematical Union since 2006, member of the "Scientific Council of the GNAMPA-INdAM "(National Group for the Mathematical Analysis, the Probability and their Applications) since 2013, Referent for the Mathematics of the Educational Center of the "Accademia Nazionale dei Lincei" at Perugia since 2013 and Member of the Academic Board of the Ph.D. in Mathematics, Computer Science, Statistics organized in consortium (C.I.A.F.M.) among the University of Perugia (Italy), University of Florence (Italy) and the INdAM (National Institute of High Mathematics).

He is and has been coordinator of several research projects and he coordinates a research team who deals with Real Analysis, Theory of Integral Operators, Approximation Theory and its Applications to Signal Reconstruction and Images Processing.

He has been invited to give more than 50 plenary lectures at conferences at various Universities and Research Centers. Moreover he is author of more than 115 publications on international journals and one scientific monography on "Nonlinear Integral Operators and Applications" edited by W. de Gruyter. Finally he is member of the Editorial Board of the following international scientific journals: Sampling Theory in Signal and Image Processing (STSIP), Journal of Function Spaces and Applications, Open Mathematics, and others and he holds a patent entitled: "Device for obtaining informations on blood vessels and other bodily-cave parts".

Contents – Part II

Workshop Computational and Applied Statistics (CAS 2018)

Workshop Computational Geometry and Security Applications (CGSA 2018)

Workshop Computational Movement Analysis (CMA 2018)

Workshop Computational Mathematics, Statistics and Information Management (CMSIM 2018)

Workshop Computational Optimization and Applications (COA 2018)

Workshop Computational Astrochemistry (CompAstro 2018)

Workshop Advanced Methods in Fractals and Data Mining for Applications (AMFDMA 2018)

Numerical and Analytical Investigation of Chemotaxis Models

Günter Bärwolff[(✉)] and Dominique Walentiny

Technische Universität Berlin, Institute of Mathematics,
Straße des 17. Juni 136, 10623 Berlin, Germany
baerwolf@math.tu-berlin.de

Abstract. The Keller-Segel system is a linear parabolic-elliptic system, which describes the aggregation of slime molds resulting from their chemotactic features. By chemotaxis we understand the movement of an organism (like bacteria) in response to chemical stimulus, for example attraction by certain chemicals in the environment.

In this paper, we use the results of a paper by Zhou and Saito to validate our finite volume method with respect to blow-up analysis and equilibrium solutions. Based on these results, we study model variations and their blow-up behavior numerically.

We will discuss the question whether or not conservative numerical methods are able to model a blow-up behavior in the case of non-global existence of solutions.

Keywords: Chemotaxis model · Blow-up phenomenon
Finite volume method

1 Introduction

In this paper, we will study models for chemotaxis, commonly known as the Keller-Segel system.

It describes the movement of cells, specifically the Dictyostelium discoïdeum, which is a species of soil-living amoeba, often referred to as slime mold. The Keller-Segel system, named after the American physicist Evelyn Fox Keller and the American mathematician Lee Aaron Segel, consists of an elliptic and a parabolic partial differential equation coupled with initial and homogeneous Neumann boundary conditions [10,11]. The Neumann boundary conditions imply that there is no flow through the boundary of the domain, meaning that there are no cells leaving or entering the system. Both boundary and initial conditions are needed in order to find a solution to the Keller-Segel system. The mere question of the solvability of such a system in general is very challenging and stands in focus of current research [3]. Additionally, it is difficult to state an universal method to solve partial differential equations. The finite volume method is used because of its conservation properties [1,5].

© Springer International Publishing AG, part of Springer Nature 2018
O. Gervasi et al. (Eds.): ICCSA 2018, LNCS 10961, pp. 3–18, 2018.
https://doi.org/10.1007/978-3-319-95165-2_1

If a solution of a system of partial differential equations becomes pointwise larger and larger until it eventually becomes infinite in finite time, we speak of numerical blow-up. The cell aggregation of the system is counterbalanced by diffusion, but if the cell density is sufficiently large, the chemical interaction dominates diffusion and may lead to finite-time blow-up of the cell density [13]. This behavior is often referred to as the most interesting feature of the Keller-Segel equations [8,9].

2   Chemotaxis and Keller-Segel System

For a wide description of the Chemotaxis/Keller-Segel model and extensive explanations and derivations of the models, we refer to the thesis [16] and the review paper [7].

In its original form, the Keller-Segel system consists of four coupled reaction-advection-diffusion equations [11]. These can be reduced under quasi-steady-state assumptions to a model for two unknown functions u and v which will form the basis for our study. With an appropriate non-dimensionalisation and some very natural assumptions starting from the original Keller-Segel system, we get the following systems of partial differential equations:

$$
\begin{aligned}
u_t &= \nabla \cdot (D\nabla u - \chi u \nabla v) \\
0 &= \nabla^2 v + u - v
\end{aligned}
\tag{1}
$$

and

$$
\begin{aligned}
u_t &= \nabla \cdot (D\nabla u - \chi u \nabla v) \\
v_t &= \nabla^2 v + u - v.
\end{aligned}
\tag{2}
$$

(1) and (2) are the so-called minimal models with the density of the cellular slime molds u, the concentration of the chemical substance/attractant v and the diffusion coefficient of cell D.

The important term in the equation for u,

$$
\Phi_{\text{chemo}} = \chi u \nabla v,
$$

is the chemotactic flux (see Müller et al. [12]) where χ, the chemotactic sensitivity, depends on the density of the attractant.

Both (1) and (2) are considered in a bounded domain $\Omega \in \mathbb{R}^d$, $d = 1, 2, 3$. The mathematical models are closed by zero flux boundary conditions (homogeneous Neumann) on $\Gamma = \partial\Omega$ and initial conditions $u(x,0) = u_0(x)$ and $v_0(x,0) = v_0(x)$ (only necessary for (2)).

The first substantial mathematical analysis of the Keller-Segel model was performed by Gajewski and Zacharias [6] introducing a Lyapunov function for the system (2). All other mathematical investigations of Keller-Segel systems followed the ideas of [6]. As a result of the analysis, global existence of solutions in the sub-critical case were shown.

Extensive mathematical and numerical analysis of the minimal Keller-Segel system (1) can be found in the paper of Zhou and Saito [17].

The Keller-Segel system admits several a priori estimates which reflects the basic modeling assumptions that have been mentioned above: the solution remains positive

$$u(t, x) > 0 \tag{3}$$

and the total mass is conserved

$$\int_\Omega u(t, x)\mathrm{d}x = \int_\Omega u_0(x)\mathrm{d}x =: m^0, \tag{4}$$

which imply the conservation of the L^1 norm:

$$\|u(t)\|_{L^1(\Omega)} = \|u_0\|_{L^1(\Omega)}, \quad t \in [0, T].$$

2.1   Variations of the Minimal Keller-Segel System

From the view of mathematical biology, it is interesting to consider modifications of the standard Keller-Segel system. Roughly, the mathematical meaning of the modifications is a regularisation. This leads to different behavior of the solutions and in some cases blow-up effects can be suppressed.

In this paper, we will discuss and numerically analyse the following models.

Signal-dependent sensitivity models

Consideration of signal-dependent sensitivity leads to the receptor model

$$u_t = \nabla \cdot (D\nabla u - \frac{\chi u}{(1 + \alpha v)^2}\nabla v)$$
$$v_t = \nabla^2 v + u - v, \tag{5}$$

and the logistic model

$$u_t = \nabla \cdot (D\nabla u - \chi u\frac{1 + \beta}{v + \beta}\nabla v)$$
$$v_t = \nabla^2 v + u - v. \tag{6}$$

For $\alpha \to 0$, model (5) tends to the minimal model (2), and for $\beta \to \infty$, the model (6) approaches the minimal model.

Density-dependent sensitivity models

For the volume-filling model

$$u_t = \nabla \cdot (D\nabla u - \chi u(1 - \frac{u}{\gamma})\nabla v)$$
$$v_t = \nabla^2 v + u - v, \tag{7}$$

we get the minimal model by $\gamma \to \infty$. Another type of a density-dependent sensitivity model is given by

$$u_t = \nabla \cdot (D\nabla u - \chi u\frac{1}{1 + \epsilon u}\nabla v)$$
$$v_t = \nabla^2 v + u - v, \tag{8}$$

where $\epsilon \to 0$ leads to the minimal model.

Signal and cell kinetics models

The nonlinear signal kinetics model reads as

$$u_t = \nabla \cdot (D\nabla u - \chi u \nabla v)$$
$$v_t = \nabla^2 v + \frac{u}{1 + \Psi u} - v \qquad (9)$$

and approximates the minimal model for $\Psi \to 0$. The cell kinetics model is of the form

$$u_t = \nabla \cdot (D\nabla u - \chi u \nabla v) + ru(1 - u)$$
$$v_t = \nabla^2 v + u - v \qquad (10)$$

and in the limit of zero growth $r \to 0$, it leads to the minimal model.

3 Finite Volume Scheme

We will next determine the terms which are necessary for the construction of the finite volume method. We will then present a linear finite volume scheme and take a look at the conservation laws.

We will follow the notation described in [17] and [5]. Let Ω be a convex polygonal domain in $\mathbb{R}$. First, we will define a very important notion following Eymard et al. [5]:

Definition 1 (Admissible mesh). *Let Ω be an open bounded polygonal subset of $\mathbb{R}$, $d = 2$ or $d = 3$. An admissible finite volume mesh of Ω, denoted by $\mathcal{T}$, is given by a family of control volumes, which are open polygonal convex subsets of Ω, a family of subsets of $\overline{\Omega}$ contained in hyperplanes of $\mathbb{R}^d$, denoted by $\mathcal{E}$ (these are edges (two-dimensional) or sides (three-dimensional) of the control volumes), with strictly positive $(d - 1)$-dimensional measure, and a family of points of Ω denoted by $\mathcal{P}$ satisfying the following properties (in fact, we shall denote, somewhat incorrectly, by $\mathcal{T}$ the family of control volumes):*

(i) The closure of the union of all the control volumes is $\overline{\Omega}$, $\overline{\Omega} = \bigcup_{K \in \mathcal{T}} \overline{K}$.

(ii) For any $K \in \mathcal{T}$, there exists a subset $\mathcal{E}_K$ of $\mathcal{E}$ such that $\partial K = \overline{K} \backslash K = \bigcup_{\sigma \in \mathcal{E}_K} \overline{\sigma}$. Furthermore, $\mathcal{E} = \bigcup_{K \in \mathcal{T}} \mathcal{E}_K$.

(iii) For any $(K, L) \in \mathcal{T}^2$ with $K \neq L$, either the $(d - 1)$-dimensional Lebesgue measure of $\overline{K} \cap \overline{L}$ is 0 or $\overline{K} \cap \overline{L} = \overline{\sigma}$ for some $\sigma \in \mathcal{E}$, which will then be denoted by $K|L$.

(iv) The family $\mathcal{P} = (x_K)_{K \in \mathcal{T}}$ is such that $x_K \in \overline{K}$ (for all $K \in \mathcal{T}$) and, if $\sigma = K|L$, it is assumed that $x_k \neq x_L$, and that the straight line $\mathcal{D}_{K,L}$ going through x_K and x_L is orthogonal to $K|L$.

(v) For any $\sigma \in \mathcal{E}$ such that $\sigma \subset \partial\Omega$, let K be the control volume such that $\sigma \in \mathcal{E}_K$. If $x_K \notin \sigma$, let $\mathcal{D}_{K,\sigma}$ be the straight line going through x_K and orthogonal to σ, then the condition $\mathcal{D}_{K,\sigma} \cap \sigma \neq \emptyset$ is assumed; let $y_\sigma = \mathcal{D}_{K,\sigma} \cap \sigma$.

Let $\mathcal{T}$ be an admissible mesh. As defined above, an element $K \in \mathcal{T}$ is called control volume. We introduce the neigborhood of $K \in \mathcal{T}$:

$$\mathcal{N}_K := \{L \in \mathcal{T} \mid \overline{L} \cap \overline{K} \neq \emptyset\}.$$

Let $K|L$ (or $\sigma_{K,L}$) denote the common edge $\overline{L} \cap \overline{K}$ of control volumes K and L. We introduce the set of interior (resp. boundary) edges inside Ω (resp. on Γ):

$$\mathcal{E}_{\text{int}} = \{K|L \mid \forall K \in \mathcal{T}, \forall L \in \mathcal{N}_K\},$$
$$\mathcal{E}_{\text{ext}} = \mathcal{E} \setminus \mathcal{E}_{\text{int}}.$$

For every control volume K, let P_K (or denoted by x_K) be the control point. And the segment $\overline{P_K P_L}$ is perpendicular to $K|L$ for all $K \in \mathcal{T}$, $L \in \mathcal{N}_K$.
Set

$$d_{K,L} := \text{dist}(P_K, P_L), \qquad \tau_{K,L} := \frac{m(K|L)}{d_{K,L}}, \quad K, L \in \mathcal{T},$$
$$d_{K,\sigma} := \text{dist}(P_K, \sigma_{K,\Gamma}), \qquad \tau_{K,\sigma} := \frac{m(\sigma_{K,\Gamma})}{d_{K,\sigma}}, \quad \tau_{K,\sigma} \in \mathcal{E}_{\text{ext}}.$$

Here, $m(\mathcal{O}) = m_{d-1}(\mathcal{O})$ denotes the $(d-1)$-dimensional Lebesgue measure of $\mathcal{O} \subset \mathbb{R}^{d-1}$.
Note that

$$\tau_{K,L} = \tau_{L,K},$$

which means that it does not make any difference whether we consider the neighbor L of control volume K or the neighbor K of control volume L.

We will now introduce a linear finite volume scheme in order to discretise the Keller-Segel system.

3.1 Linear Finite Volume Scheme

An important issue of the discretisation of the Keller-Segel system is the handling of the convective terms. Upon computing a convection-diffusion problem, there often occur problems when the convective term gets by far bigger than the diffusion term. In our example, when the cell density is very large, the cell aggregation outbalances diffusion. To handle this, an upwind scheme is used [15]. The error of the upwind scheme is of order $\mathcal{O}(h)$, however, the physics of the system is better reproduced than by use of the central difference quotient. Especially in convection dominated cases like drift diffusion, instead of simple upwind schemes, Scharfetter-Gummel approximations are used. They control the order of approximation between one and two, depending on the convection velocity.

We set the function space X_h for the discrete solution (u_h, v_h):

$$X_h = \text{span}\{\phi_K \mid K \in \mathcal{T}\},$$

where ϕ_K is the characteristic (or indicator) function of K ($\phi_K = 1$ in K, $\phi = 0$ otherwise). With the assumptions on the mesh from above, we define the discrete

$W^{1,p}$ semi-norm for $u_h \in X_h$:

$$|u_h|_{1,p,\mathcal{T}}^p = \sum_{K|L\in\mathcal{E}_{\text{int}}} \tau_{K,L} d_{K,L}^{2-p} |u_K - u_L|^p, \quad \text{for } p \in [1,\infty), \qquad (11)$$

$$|u_h|_{1,\infty,\mathcal{T}} = \max_{K|L\in\mathcal{E}_{\text{int}}} \frac{|u_K - u_L|}{d_{K,L}}. \qquad (12)$$

We further set the discrete $W^{1,p}$ norm for X_h: For any $u_h \in X_h$,

$$\|u_h\|_{1,p,\mathcal{T}} := |u_h|_{1,p,\mathcal{T}} + \|u_h\|_p.$$

For $u_h \in X_h$ and $K \in \mathcal{T}$, we set $u_K = u_h(P_K)$. Given the initial condition

$$u_h^0 \in X_h, \quad u_h^0 \geq 0,$$

$$\int_\Omega u_h^0 dx = \sum_{K\in\mathcal{T}} m(K)u_K^0 \equiv \theta > 0, \qquad (13)$$

we state the finite volume scheme for the Keller-Segel system (1):
Find $(u_h^n, v_h^n) \in X_h \times X_h$ for $n \in \mathbb{N}_+$, such that:

$$\sum_{L\in\mathcal{N}_K} \tau_{K,L}(v_K^{n-1} - v_L^{n-1}) + m(K)v_K^{n-1} = m(K)u_K^{n-1}$$

$$\Leftrightarrow \sum_{L\in\mathcal{N}_K} \frac{m(K|L)}{d_{K,L}}(v_K^{n-1} - v_L^{n-1}) + m(K)v_K^{n-1} = m(K)u_K^{n-1}, \qquad (14)$$

which is the discrete to the elliptic equation

$$-\Delta v + v = u,$$

and

$$m(K)\partial_{\tau_n} u_K^n + \sum_{L\in\mathcal{N}_k} \tau_{K,L}(u_K^n - u_L^n)$$

$$+ \sum_{L\in\mathcal{N}_k} \tau_{K,L} \left[(Dv_{K,L}^{n-1})_+ u_K^n - (Dv_{K,L}^{n-1})_- u_L^n \right] = 0$$

$$\Leftrightarrow m(K)\frac{u_K^n - u_K^{n-1}}{\tau_n} + \sum_{L\in\mathcal{N}_k} \frac{m(K|L)}{d_{K,L}}(u_K^n - u_L^n)$$

$$+ \sum_{L\in\mathcal{N}_k} \frac{m(K|L)}{d_{K,L}} \left[\max(v_L^{n-1} - v_K^{n-1}, 0)u_K^n - \max(-(v_L^{n-1} - v_K^{n-1}), 0)u_L^n \right] = 0, \qquad (15)$$

which is the discrete to the parabolic equation

$$u_t = \Delta u - \nabla \cdot (u\nabla v),$$

using implicit Euler for the time discretisation. For the parabolic v-equation of (2), we also use the implicit Euler method, as in the case of the parabolic u-equation.

Here, $w_+ = \max(w, 0)$, $w_- = \max(-w, 0)$, hence following the technique of an upwind approximation, and

$$Dv_{K,L} = v_L - v_K \text{ for } v_h \in X_h, \quad Dv_{K,\sigma} = 0 \text{ for } \sigma \in \mathcal{E}_{\text{ext}}.$$

In the scheme, $\tau > 0$ is the time-step increment, $t_n = \tau_1 + \cdots \tau_n$, and $\partial_{\tau_n} u_K^n$ is the backward Euler difference quotient approximating to $\partial_t u(t_n)$, which is defined by

$$\partial_{\tau_n} u_K^n = \frac{u_K^n - u_K^{n-1}}{\tau_n}.$$

For the modified models (5)–(10), we have the more general equations

$$u_t = \nabla \cdot (D\nabla u - \varphi(u, v)u\nabla v) \quad \text{and} \quad v_t = \Delta v + \psi(u)u - v. \qquad (16)$$

Finally, for (16), we have to modify the discretisation (15) by inserting a factor $\varphi(u_L^{n-1}, v_L^{n-1})$. In other words, we perform a linearisation.

3.2 Conservation Laws

We consider the Keller-Segel system (1). The solution (u, v) satisfies the conservation of positivity

$$u(x, t) > 0, \quad (x, t) \in \bar{\Omega} \times [0, T], \qquad (17)$$

and the conservation of total mass

$$\int_\Omega u(x, t)\mathrm{d}x = \int_\Omega u_0(x)\mathrm{d}x, \quad t \in [0, T], \qquad (18)$$

which imply the conservation of the L^1 norm.

Remark 1. The value of $\|u_0\|_{L^1(\Omega)}$ plays a crucial role in the blow-up behavior and global existence of solutions, as we will see in Theorem 3.

The conservation properties (17) and (18) are essential requirements and it is desirable that numerical solutions preserve them when we solve the Keller-Segel system by numerical methods.

In the following, we will state some important theorems when working with conservation laws. For the proofs, we refer to the paper [17] and the thesis [16].

Theorem 1 (Conservation of total mass). *Let $\{(u_h^n, v_h^n)\}_{n \geq 0} \subset X_h$ be the solution of the finite volume scheme (14–15). Then we have*

$$(v_h^n, 1) = (u_h^n, 1) = (u_h^0, 1), \quad \forall n \geq 0. \qquad (19)$$

Theorem 2 (Well-posedness and conservation of positivity). *Let $u_h^0 \geq 0$, $u_h \not\equiv 0$. Then (14)–(15) admits a unique solution $\{(u_h^n, v_h^n)\}_{n \geq 0} \subset X_h \times X_h$, such that $u_h^n > 0$ for $n \geq 1$ and $v_h^n > 0$ for $n \geq 0$.*

3.3 Discrete Free Energy

As mentioned before, the L^1 conservation (which follows from the conservation of positivity and the conservation of total mass) is an important feature of the Keller-Segel system. Another important feature of the Keller-Segel system is the existence of free energy. By free energy we understand the energy in a physical system that can be converted to do work. It is desirable that the numerical solution preserves both these properties.

For the free energy

$$W(u(t), v(t)) = \int_\Omega (u \log u - u) dx - \frac{1}{2} \int_\Omega uv dx, \qquad (20)$$

one can show the important energy inequality. The free energy is expressed as

$$\frac{d}{dt} W(u(t), v(t)) \le 0, \quad t \in [0, T].$$

In the following, we will discuss a discrete version of the energy equality (20). For the solution $\{(u_h^n, v_h^n)\}_{n \ge 0}$ of the finite volume scheme (14)−(15), we set

$$H_h^n := \sum_{K \in \mathcal{T}} m(K)(u_K^n \log u_K^n - u_K^n). \qquad (21)$$

For any internal edge $K|L \in \mathcal{E}_{\text{int}}$, we set

$$\tilde{u}_{K,L}^n = \frac{u_K^n - u_L^n}{\log u_K^n - \log u_L^n}, \quad \text{for } u_K^n \ne u_L^n. \qquad (22)$$

Let $\tilde{u}_{K,L}^n = u_K^n$, if $u_K^n = u_L^n$. Then there exists $s_{K,L}^n \in [0, 1]$ such that

$$\tilde{u}_{K,L}^n = s_{K,L}^n u_K^n + (1 - s_{K,L}^n) u_L^n. \qquad (23)$$

Analogous to the energy function $W(u, v)$, we define the discrete energy function

$$W_h^n = H_h^n - \frac{1}{2} \sum_{K \in \mathcal{T}} m(K) u_K^n v_K^n.$$

However, we can not obtain the inequality $\partial_{\tau_n} W_h^n \le 0$. Instead of that, we have the following estimate on $\partial_{\tau_n} W_h^n$. For the discrete energy W_h^n, we have the inequality

$$\partial_{\tau_n} W_h^n \le - \sum_{K|L \in \mathcal{E}_{\text{int}}} \tau_{K,L} \left| \frac{Du_{K,L}^n}{\sqrt{\tilde{u}_{K,L}^n}} - Dv_{K,L}^{n-1} \sqrt{\tilde{u}_{K,L}^n} \right|^2$$

$$- \frac{\tau_n}{2} \left[\sum_{K \in \mathcal{T}} |\partial_{\tau_n} v_K^n|^2 + \sum_{K|L \in \mathcal{E}_{\text{int}}} \tau_{K,L} |\partial_{\tau_n} (Dv_{K,L}^n)|^2 \right] + C_h(u_h^n, v_h^n),$$

where $C_h(u_h^n, v_h^n)$ is defined by

$$
C_h(u_h^n, v_h^n) :=
$$
$$
-\sum_{K|L \in \mathcal{E}_{\text{int}}} \tau_{K,L} \left[(Dv_{K,L}^{n-1})_+^2 (1 - s_{K,L}^n)(u_K^n - u_L^n) + (Dv_{K,L}^{n-1})_-^2 s_{K,L}(u_L^n - u_K^n) \right],
$$

and it admits the estimate:

$$
|C_h(u_h^n, v_h^n)| \le Ch \, |u_h^n|_{1,\infty,\mathcal{T}} \, |v_h^n|_{1,2,\mathcal{T}} \, .
$$

Here, $s_{K,L}^n$ satisfies (23) and $|\cdot|_{1,p,\mathcal{T}}$ is defined by (11) and (12).

Thus, the finite volume scheme conserves the energy inequality in the above noted sense.

4   Numerical Blow-Up

When organisms, such as the amoeba Dictyostelium discoïdeum, secrete an attracting chemical and move towards areas of higher chemical concentration, this leads to aggregation of organisms. The cell aggregation is counterbalanced by diffusion, in particular by the use of the upwind type approximation. However, if the cell density is sufficiently large, the chemical interaction dominates the diffusion and this may lead to finite-time blow-up of the cell density.

This blow-up phenomenon, or chemotactic collapse, can never occur in one dimension, which was shown in [17]. In two dimensions, it can occur if a total cell number on Ω is larger than a critical number but it can never occur for the total cell number on Ω less than the critical number [2,4]. We will focus on the two-dimensional case, shortly discuss some important properties of the system before turning to the finite volume scheme. Throughout this section, we will distinguish between the conservative and non-conservative system and derive the finite volume scheme for both, using Cartesian coordinates.

4.1   Two-Dimensional System

We consider the finite volume scheme with mesh $\mathcal{T}$:

$$
-L = x_{\frac{1}{2}} < x_{1+\frac{1}{2}} < \cdots < x_{N+\frac{1}{2}} = L,
$$

where $0 < N \in \mathbb{N}$ is the number of control volumes, $h = \frac{2L}{N}$ is the uniform mesh size in both directions. We set

$$
u_{i,j}^0 = u_0(x_i, y_j), \quad i = 1, \ldots, N, \; j = 1, \ldots, M.
$$

Let $(u_{i,j}^n, v_{i,j}^n)$ be the approximation of $(u(t_n, x_i, y_j), v(t_n, x_i, y_j))$. With the obvious notations for the forward and backward difference quotients

$$
\nabla_x u^n = \frac{u_{i+1,j}^n - u_{i,j}^n}{h}, \quad \nabla_{\bar{x}} u^n = \frac{u_{i,j}^n - u_{i-1,j}^n}{h},
$$

we formulate the finite volume scheme for the minimal Keller-Segel system. It is to find

$$u^n = (u^n_{i,j})^{N,M}_{i,j=1}, \quad v^n = (v^n_{i,j})^{N,M}_{i,j=1}$$

for $n = 1, 2, ..., J$, such that

$$-\nabla_x \nabla_{\bar{x}} v^n_{i,j} - \nabla_y \nabla_{\bar{y}} v^n_{i,j} + v^n_{i,j} = u^{n-1}_{i,j},$$

$$\partial_\tau u^n_{i,j} - \nabla_x \nabla_{\bar{x}} u^n_{i,j} - \nabla_y \nabla_{\bar{y}} u^n_{i,j} + \frac{\chi}{h} convup(\nabla v, u) = 0,$$

$$v^n_{0,j} = v^n_{1,j}, \ v^n_{i,0} = v^n_{i,1}, \ v^n_{0,N} = v^n_{0,N+1}, \ v^n_{N,0} = v^n_{N+1,0},$$

$$u^n_{0,j} = u^n_{1,j}, \ u^n_{i,0} = u^n_{i,1}, \ u^n_{0,N} = u^n_{0,N+1}, \ u^n_{N,0} = u^n_{N+1,0}.$$

with the upwind-discretisation

$$convup(\nabla v, u) = [\max(\nabla_x v^n, 0) + \max(-\nabla_{\bar{x}} v^n, 0)]u^n_{i,j}$$
$$+[\max(\nabla_y v^n, 0) + \max(-\nabla_{\bar{y}} v^n, 0)]u^n_{i,j}$$
$$- \max(-\nabla_x v^n, 0)u^n_{i+1,j} - \max(\nabla_{\bar{x}} v^n, 0)u^n_{i-1,j}$$
$$- \max(-\nabla_y v^n, 0)u^n_{i,j+1} - \max(\nabla_{\bar{y}} v^n, 0)u^n_{i,j-1}$$

where $\tau > 0$ is the time-step increment and $\{u^0_{ij}\}^{N,M}_{i,j=1} \geq 0$ and not identically zero.

Blow-Up Behavior

Theorem 3 (2D Blow-Up). *In $\mathbb{R}^2$, assume $\int_{\mathbb{R}^2} |x|^2 u_0(x) \mathrm{d}x < \infty$.*

(i) (Blow-up) When the initial mass satisfies

$$m^0 := \int_{\mathbb{R}^2} u_0(x) \mathrm{d}x > m_{crit} := 8\pi$$

then any solution to the Keller-Segel system (1) becomes a singular measure in finite time.

(ii) When the initial data satisfies

$$\int_{\mathbb{R}^2} u_0 |log(u_0(x))| \mathrm{d}x < \infty \quad and \quad m^0 := \int_{\mathbb{R}^2} u_0(x) \mathrm{d}x < m_{crit} := 8\pi,$$

there are weak solutions to the Keller-Segel system (1) satisfying the a priori estimates

$$\int_{\mathbb{R}^2} u \left[|\ln(u(t))| + |x|^2 \right] \mathrm{d}x \leq C(t), \quad \|u(t)\|_{L^p(\mathbb{R}^2)} \leq C(p, t, u^0)$$

for $\|u_0\|_{L^p(\mathbb{R}^2)} < \infty, \ 1 < p < \infty$.

The mathematical interest here is to prove existence with an energy method rather than direct estimates based on Sobolev inequalities. For the proof, we refer to [14] or [16].

Remark 2. In general bounded domains, with no-flux boundary conditions, the critical mass is 8π because blow-up may occur on the boundary which intuitively acts as a reflection wall.

Properties of the System. In order to consider the blow-up solution, the moment is introduced:

$$M_2(t) = \int_\Omega u(x,t)|x|^2 \mathrm{d}x = 2\pi \int_0^L u(r,t)r^3 \mathrm{d}r, \qquad (24)$$

which, with $\theta = \int_\Omega u_0 \mathrm{d}x$, satisfies

$$\frac{d}{dt}M_2(t) \le 4\theta - \frac{1}{2\pi}\theta^2 + \frac{1}{\pi L^2}\theta M_2(t) + \frac{1}{2e\pi}\theta^{\frac{3}{2}} M_2(t)^{\frac{1}{2}}. \qquad (25)$$

This implies that if $\theta > 8\pi$ and $M_2(0)$ is sufficiently small, we then have

$$\frac{d}{dt}M_2(t) < 0, \quad t > 0, \qquad (26)$$

which means that $M_2(t) \to 0$ at some time $t = t_b$. Since $u > 0$ and $\int_\Omega u(x,t) = \theta$, the function u actually blows up in finite time t_b. We call t_b the blow-up time.

We aim to show the discrete version of inequality (25). For $n = 1, \dots, J$, we have

$$\frac{M_2^n - M_2^{n-1}}{\tau} \le \frac{4\theta}{2\pi} - \left(\frac{\theta}{2\pi}\right)^2 + C_1\theta M_2^{n-1} + C_2\theta^{\frac{3}{2}}\sqrt{M_2^{n-1}} + C_3 h\theta^2, \qquad (27)$$

where C_1, C_2, C_3 are independent of h, θ and M_2^{n-1}.

We should mention that (27) is not satisfied for the conservative scheme introduced above.

4.2 Non-conservative Finite Volume Scheme

We will now consider the numerical scheme without conservation of positivity but satisfying (27). With the above defined notations, we obtain this so-called non-conservative scheme by replacing the conservative discretised parabolic equation by

$$\partial_\tau u_{i,j}^n - \nabla_x \nabla_{\bar{x}} u_{i,j}^{n-1} - \nabla_y \nabla_{\bar{y}} u_{i,j}^{n-1}$$
$$+\frac{\chi}{h}(\nabla_x v_{i,j}^{n-1} u_{i,j}^n + \nabla_y v_{i,j}^{n-1} u_{i,j}^n + \nabla_{\bar{x}} v_{i,j}^{n-1} u_{i-1,j}^n + \nabla_{\bar{y}} v_{i,j}^{n-1} u_{i,j-1}^n) = 0. \qquad (28)$$

We will now state that (27) is satisfied for the non-negative solution of the non-conservative scheme. In view of (27), for $\theta > 8\pi$ and sufficiently small M_2^0, M_2^n decreases by n. When M_2^n approaches 0, we have

$$\frac{M_2^n - M_2^{n-1}}{\tau} \approx \frac{4\theta}{2\pi} - \left(\frac{\theta}{2\pi}\right)^2.$$

Theorem 4. *For the non-conservative scheme introduced above, let J be the largest time step such that $(u_h^n, v_h^n) \ge 0$, for any $1 \le n \le J$. Then we have the moment inequality*

$$\frac{M_2^n - M_2^{n-1}}{\tau} \le \frac{4\theta}{2\pi} - \left(\frac{\theta}{2\pi}\right)^2 + C_1\theta M_2^{n-1} + C_2\theta^{\frac{3}{2}}\sqrt{M_2^{n-1}} + C_3 h\theta^2,$$

where C_1, C_2, C_3 are independent of h, θ and M_2^{n-1}.

5   Numerical Examples

In order to verify the theoretical results, we conducted various numerical simulations. We implemented the presented finite volume schemes using Python. The model and used parameters can be found in the figure captions. For the simulations, we used the conservative scheme.

We consider $\Omega = (0,1)^2$ and use a direction equidistant discretisation with $1 < N \in \mathbb{N}$, $h = \frac{1}{N-1}$ and $\tau = \tau_n = 0.2h$, $N = 41$ and $N = 61$. As initial conditions, we use

$$u = 1, \quad v = 1 + 0.1 \exp(-10((x-1)^2 + (y-1)^2))$$

on Ω. In all examples, we reached the steady state (global existence of the solution), as can be seen in Figs. 1, 2 and 3. The solutions were grid-independent.

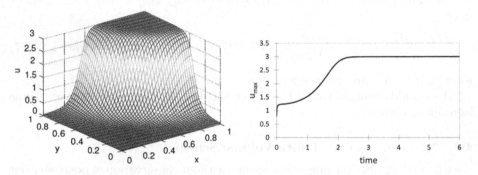

Fig. 1. Cell density (left) and cell density peak evolution (right) for problem (7), using $D = 0.1, \chi = 5.0, \gamma = 3.0$ (steady state)

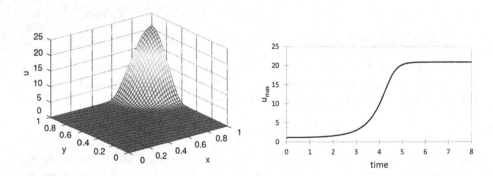

Fig. 2. Cell density (left) and cell density peak evolution (right) for problem (8), using $D = 0.1, \chi = 5.0, \epsilon = 1.0$ (steady state)

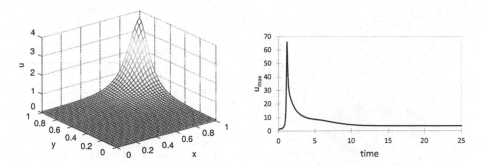

Fig. 3. Cell density (left) and cell density peak evolution (right) for problem (10), using $D = 0.1, \chi = 5.0, r = 0.25$ (steady state)

With the same setting, we define the function

$$W_{(x_0,y_0)} = \frac{M}{2\pi\theta} \exp\left(-\frac{(x - x_0)^2 + (y - y_0)^2}{2\theta}\right),$$

where $(x_0, y_0) \in (0, 1)^2$, $M = 6\pi$, $\theta = \frac{1}{500}$ and choose the initial function

$$u_0 = W_{(\frac{1}{3},\frac{1}{3})} + W_{(\frac{1}{3},\frac{2}{3})} + W_{(\frac{2}{3},\frac{1}{3})} + W_{(\frac{2}{3},\frac{2}{3})}. \tag{29}$$

We also consider a non-symmetric situation given by the initial function

$$u_0 = \frac{1}{3}W_{(\frac{1}{3},\frac{2}{3})} + \frac{1}{2}W_{(\frac{1}{3},\frac{1}{3})} + W_{(\frac{2}{3},\frac{2}{3})}. \tag{30}$$

The initial mass is $24\pi > 8\pi$ and $11\pi > 8\pi$, respectively and thus, we expect the solutions to blow up in finite time.

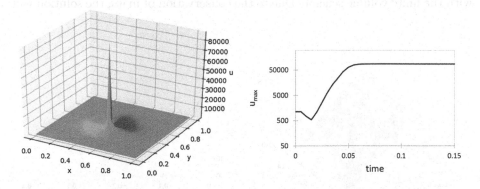

Fig. 4. Cell density (left) and cell density peak evolution (right) for problem (1) with initial data (29), using parameters $D = 0.1, \chi = 1$ (approximation of blow-up)

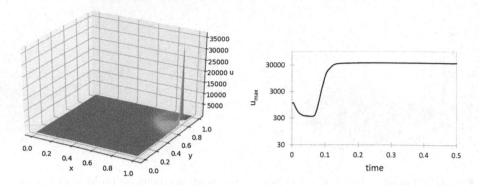

Fig. 5. Cell density (left) and cell density peak evolution (right) for problem (1) with initial data (30), using parameters $D = 1, \chi = 1$, (approximation of blow-up)

Let then $\Omega = (-0.5, 0.5)^2$. We consider the initial value

$$u_0 = 40 \exp\left(-10(x^2 + y^2)\right) + 10, \tag{31}$$

where $\|u_0\|_1 \approx 21.93 < 8\pi$. Therefore the solution will not blow up. With the same setting but the initial data

$$\begin{aligned} u_0 = &100 \exp\left(-\frac{x^2 + y^2}{0.04}\right) + 60 \exp\left(-\frac{(x - 0.2)^2 + y^2}{0.05}\right) \\ &+ 30 \exp\left(-\frac{x^2 + (y - 0.02)^2}{0.05}\right), \end{aligned} \tag{32}$$

where $\|u_0\|_1 \approx 26.26 > 8\pi$.

Remark 3. Note that it is only possible to approximate the blow-up behavior with the finite volume scheme. Due to the conservation of mass, the solution will

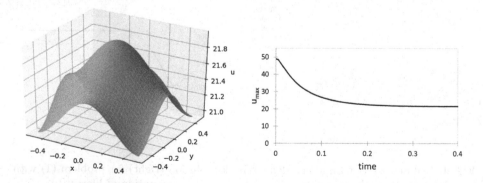

Fig. 6. Cell density (left) and cell density peak evolution (right) for problem (1) with initial data (31), using parameters $D = 0.1, \chi = 1$ (steady state)

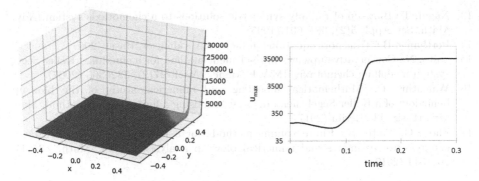

Fig. 7. Cell density (left) and cell density peak evolution (right) for problem (1) with initial data (32), using parameters $D = 0.1, \chi = 1$ (approximation of blow-up)

never become infinite in time. The possible maximum of the cell density depends on the used discretisation. Thus, with a very fine discretisation near the corner $(x, y) = (1, 1)$ a good approximation of the blow-up behavior is possible, as can bee seen in Figs. 4, 5 and 7.

References

1. Ascher, U.M.: Numerical methods for evolutionary differential equations. Society for Industrial and Applied Mathematics (SIAM), Philadelphia (2008)
2. Blanchet, A., Dolbeault, J., Perthame, B.: Two-dimensional Keller-Segel model: Optimal critical mass and qualitative properties of the solutions. Electron. J. Differ. Equ. **2006**, 33 (2006)
3. Cho, C.-H.: A numerical algorithm for blow-up problems revisited. Numer. Algorithms **75**(3), 675–697 (2017)
4. Dolbeault, J., Perthame, B.: Optimal critical mass in the two dimensional Keller-Segel model in R^2. C. R. Math. Acad. Sci. Paris **339**(9), 611–616 (2004)
5. Eymard, R., Gallouët, T., Herbin, R.: Finite volume methods. In: Handbook of numerical analysis, Vol. 7: Solution of equations in $\mathbb{R}^n$ (Part 3). Techniques of scientific computing, pp. 713–1020. Elsevier, Amsterdam (2000)
6. Gajewski, H., Zacharias, K.: Global behaviour of a reaction-diffusion system modelling chemotaxis. Math. Nachr. **195**, 77–114 (1998)
7. Hillen, T., Painter, K.J.: A user's guide to PDE models for chemotaxis. J. Math. Biol. **58**(1–2), 183–217 (2009)
8. Horstmann, D.: Aspekte positiver Chemotaxis. Univ. Köln, Köln (1999)
9. Jäger, W., Luckhaus, S.: On explosions of solutions to a system of partial differential equations modelling chemotaxis. Trans. Am. Math. Soc. **329**(2), 819–824 (1992)
10. Keller, E.F., Segel, L.A.: Initiation of slime mold aggregation viewed as an instability. J. Theor. Biol. **26**(3), 399–415 (1970)
11. Keller, E.F., Segel, L.A.: Model for chemotaxis. J. Theor. Biol. **30**(2), 225–234 (1971)
12. Müller, J., Kuttler, C.: Methods and models in mathematical biology. Springer, Deterministic and stochastic approaches. Berlin (2015)

13. Nagai, T.: Blow-up of radially symmetric solutions to a chemotaxis system. Adv. Math. Sci. Appl. **5**(2), 581–601 (1995)
14. Perthame, B.: Transport equations in biology. Birkhäuser, Basel (2007)
15. Saito, N.: Conservative upwind finite-element method for a simplified Keller-Segel system modelling chemotaxis. IMA J. Numer. Anal. **27**(2), 332–365 (2007)
16. Walentiny, D.: Mathematical modeling and numerical study of the blow-up behaviour of a Keller-Segel chemotaxis system using a finite volume method. Master's thesis, TU Berlin (2017)
17. Zhou, G., Saito, N.: Finite volume methods for a Keller-Segel system: discrete energy, error estimates and numerical blow-up analysis. Numer. Math. **135**(1), 265–311 (2017)

Methodological Approach to the Definition of a Blockchain System for the Food Industry Supply Chain Traceability

Rafael Bettín-Díaz[(✉)], Alix E. Rojas[(✉)], and Camilo Mejía-Moncayo[(✉)]

Universidad EAN, Bogotá, Colombia
{rbettind4339,aerojash,cmejiam}@universidadean.edu.co

Abstract. In this paper, we present a novel methodology to integrate the Blockchain technology in the food industry supply chain to allow traceability along the process and provide the ultimate customer with enough information about the origin of the product to make an informed purchase decision. This methodology gathers the best practices in marketing, process engineering and the technology itself, alongside with the authors' experience during its application in the organic coffee industry in the Colombian market. The Authors extracted the best out of the best practices and made it simple for anyone interested in its uses and application. The result is a simple and easy methodology that suits any product, supply chain, and required system configurations; due to its versatility and adaptability.

Keywords: Blockchain · Process · Traceability · Supply chain

1 Introduction

According to the World Health Organization (WHO), "people are now consuming more foods high in energy, fats, free sugars or salt/sodium, and many do not eat enough fruit, vegetables and dietary fiber such as whole grains" [1]. Additionally, with the growing demand in the fitness market, in line with NIELSEN "consistent with consumers' rating of the importance of attributes, sales of products with natural and organic claims have grown 24% and 28%, respectively, over the two-year period" [2]. With this information, we can appreciate how vital has become for people to change its eating habits. Specifically, in Colombia people tend to look for food with local ingredients, natural and organic alternatives[1] which makes us think about the current state of the transformation process that experience food across the value chain, since its plantation until its placement on a supermarket shelf. In Colombia, the government has delivered some regulation around the production of organic products [3,4]; however, concerning

---

[1] Nielsen Global Survey on Health and Wellness. 3rd semester of 2014.

© Springer International Publishing AG, part of Springer Nature 2018
O. Gervasi et al. (Eds.): ICCSA 2018, LNCS 10961, pp. 19–33, 2018.
https://doi.org/10.1007/978-3-319-95165-2_2

execution, we are very late, most of the natural stores have not certification whatsoever. Ultimate customers only trust people's goodwill when they talk about the organic origin of a product and, the final customer is not aware of the roots of the food they are paying for. Here is where technology comes in; we have always experienced technology in different scenarios that have helped us generate some improvement in the way we perceive or do things on a daily basis, even technology has changed how we do businesses. The Blockchain is what we call a disruptive technology, thus, overturns the traditional business model, which makes it much harder for an established firm to embrace[2]. A clear example of this is the e-mail, it replaced the postal office service, this has been more vivid for recent generations, nevertheless, no matter the age, people look for a laptop with Internet to send a letter [5].

In this context, this research pursues the integration of the Blockchain technology with the supply chain in the organic food industry in the Colombian market. It seeks to decentralize the information, provide trust among all participants, trace the data along the supply chain [6,7], and discover a new range of opportunities for applications that can provide the ultimate customer with information beyond a supermarket label. This will help validate its scope as part of a business process, keeping in mind that the Blockchain technology at this point of its development cannot be called itself a new methodology for process improvement, optimization or automation [8–10]. In the final stage of this research, with this integration, the Blockchain technology, and the process as it is, we will provide a methodological approach for its implementation in any supply chain. This document begins with a brief review of Blockchain and its main characteristics, it also covers the foundations of the supply chain, followed by the presentation of the methodological approach for its implementation and the final conclusions.

2   Blockchain

According to [6], cited by [5], "in its most precarious form, is the public ledger of all Bitcoin transactions that have been executed; but, since its conception, the Blockchain has evolved further than the platform for storage financial transactions managed by a cryptocurrency". The Blockchain is like a database, it is a way of storing records of value and transactions [7]. In general matters, that last sentence explains very quickly and, in simple words, the aim of Blockchain. However, the technology goes further than a shared database; a Blockchain is essentially a distributed database of records, we can also call it a public ledger of transactions or even digital events that have been executed and shared among participating parties (nodes). In the general ledger each transaction is verified by consensus of a majority of the participants in the Network, and once entered, the information cannot be erased, modified or altered [11].

---

[2] Definition taken from Cambridge Dictionary.

2.1 How Does a Blockchain Works?

Blockchain may have been born because of Bitcoin, and nowadays it is used as the underlying technology for any cryptocurrency and its transactions. But, it goes beyond that, due to its architecture, it gives the participants the ability to share a ledger that is updated, through peer-to-peer replication, every time a transaction occurs, it means that each participant (node) in the network acts as both a publisher and a subscriber.

To make this simple each node can receive or send transactions to other nodes, and the data is synchronized across the network as it is transferred [12]. The transactions on the network would look like this: Where subject A wants to transfer a digital asset to subject B, for this case, it is electronic cash, most known as a cryptocurrency, which underlying technology is Blockchain. Once subject A creates the transaction it is broadcasted to all the nodes connected to the network with many other transactions that were made at the same period. This is represented online as a block; at this point, in order to certify the validity of this transaction, different mathematical algorithms are being resolved, these were used in the first place to encrypt the digital signature that was used to send the transaction; each node will work on finding a proof-of-work, that can take up to 10 min approximately, once they have found it, the block is broadcasted to the network and other nodes would only accept the block if all the transactions in it are valid. Once this is verified and approved by all the nodes connected, the block is added to the Chain, this whole process is known as mining; in the end, subject B can see the transaction reflected on its side.

2.2 Key Elements of a Blockchain Architecture

- Nodes: It refers to a participant of the network.
- Hash functions: "these functions are a mathematical algorithm that takes some input data and creates some output data" [13], this means that a hash function will take an input of any length and will have an output of a fixed length.
- Proof-of-work: It is a consensus mechanism that allows each Blockchain connected node to keep transactions secure and reach a tamper-resistant agreement [14].
- Mining: This refers to adding new blocks of records (transactions) to the public ledger of Blockchain.
- Timestamp Server: It proves that the data must have existed at the time, obviously, to get into the hash [15].

2.3 Characteristic of a Blockchain Network

According to [6,7], cited by [5], we are going to emphasize the most important benefits and disadvantages of the Blockchain technology:

Benefits:

- Compared to existing technologies of record keeping and common databases, transparency is one of the most significant improvements of Blockchain.
- No intermediaries involved during the process, whether it is used as record keeping or data transfer.
- It uses a decentralized network, which reduces the possibility of hacking, downtime system or loss of data.

All of the above, in conjunction, create trust among participants of the network, which is one of the principal characteristics. Allowing participants that have never even met before transacting one another with the confidence that this technology provides.

- It provides security through traceability. All data entered or registered on the Blockchain cannot be mutable, altered or changed, which allows a clear record from the very start of any transaction. It means a Blockchain can be easily auditable.
- The Blockchain provides multiple uses, almost any kind of asset can be recorded on it. Different industries, like retail, are already developing applications based on Blockchain.
- The technology is pretty accessible, no need for significant investments, nor complex infrastructures. There are already platforms based on Blockchain like Ethereum[3] that will allow us to create Decentralized Applications (dApps[4]).
- Reduced cost of maintaining a big network of multiple ledgers can be avoided by using Blockchain and its one-single ledger to keep records of all the transactions across companies.
- Being distributed has one more benefit, it increases the transaction speed. By removing all the intermediaries and everyone can audit and verify the information recorded on the Blockchain.

Challenges:

- Usually, Blockchain networks are public, which provides lack of security, when talking about a financial Blockchain. In a Blockchain public network everyone will be able to see everyone's transactions and balances. It is safe to say that, there are also private Blockchains, which can be used in processes like supply chain.
- Public and private keys,[5] in Blockchain provides the user with the capacity of making transactions of any kind, depending on the type of Blockchain network uses. Hence, once it loses any of the two keys (public or private) it

---

[3] Is a Blockchain platform that is public and has a programmable transaction functionality [16].

[4] Are applications that run on a P2P network of computers rather than a single computer (blockchainhub.net, n.d.).

[5] It is like the username and passwords that most people use as identifiers in any other application.

loses everything, and there is no way to recover it, and people will have to write down such sensible information which reflects the security concerns in the industry.

- Even though decentralization is something why this technology excels, it may be one of the reasons why its adoption can take longer, since no single organization has control over the Blockchain.
- The Blockchain network still has scalability issues; currently, the Bitcoin platform can support up to 7 transactions per second, this is way below the average amount of transactions the visa network is capable of handling per second.
- Trust is a big deal regarding transactions between parties; nevertheless, the uses of a Blockchain network is related to cryptocurrencies, and there is a lack of trust in people to use digital cash.
- Because it is a recent technology, people are trying to understand how it works, its uses and applications. Likewise, as financial-transaction services are the most commonly used by Blockchain networks people are afraid of the ledgers being public.
- Regulation of governments and bank institutions will be an issue that will face the Blockchain technology along the way.
- Integration with existing legacy systems is one of the critical points of the technology, especially for bank institutions, due to the cost of migration and replacing systems.

Most of its disadvantages are a result of the natural cause of the state of its development. Something particular about it, is the constant evolution by being immersed in an everyday-changing environment, regarding content, application, development, and researchers to determine more applicability and provide industries with a wide range of uses. But, the counterpart is its benefits, nobody planned for this technology to be so disruptive, even though, the direction is clear, this will revolve many industries. Few people know in detail all about the technology, this is not a lethal threat to sectors, but, they need to know how to work with innovation and use it for growth. There is one thing to keep in mind, right now there's a hype with this technology, that will continue maybe for the next decade, but, the real focus is on the strategic applications and uses that can contribute to real development. Here is important to take an in-depth look at what this technology has to offer and what is needed to adopt it.

3   Supply Chain

Christopher [17], stated that the "supply chain objective refers to processes and activities that produce value in the form of products and services in the hands of the ultimate consumer". It can be used as an objective of the supply chain management, and for this research, the added value is one of the essential ingredients of the whole process. Currently, the general supply chain management process, no matter the perspective, offers no information to the final consumer.

As seen in the definition above, the process foundations relays on the communication and integration of a set of actors that manufacture or produce a good or a service. This particular definition is linked with the objective of this paper, due to the importance of providing valuable information to the ultimate consumer and being an essential piece of the chain as maintaining trust along the process and create trust during purchasing as one of the leading pillars of [18]. Also, it is important to point out the definition of the Council of Supply Chain Management professionals [19], but mostly, this statement, "starting with unprocessed raw materials and ending with the final customer using the finished goods, the supply chain links many companies together".

In the food industry, this is merely raw material, that needs to be transformed or processed to deliver a finished good to the final consumer. In between the entire process, there are different actors, some of the participants of the supply chain according to [20], cited by [5], are (a) Producers or manufacturers, organizations that make a product; this can include the transformation of raw material or the production of finished goods; (b) Distributors, are mostly known as wholesalers; (c) Retailers, manage stock inventory and sell in smaller quantities to the general public; (d) Customers or consumers, may be the end user of a product who buys the product in order to consume it; (e) Service or goods providers are organizations that provide services to producers, distributors, retailers, and customers.

The competitiveness of the food industry would thus be the ability to sell products that, in one hand, meet demand requirements (price, quality, and quantity) and, at the same time, ensure profits over time that enable the companies to do well economically, develop their business and thrive [21].

Therefore, there is a constant, the customer that demands better products due to its sophisticated taste; this change necessarily obligates the industry to adapt very quickly to these changes and respond accordingly. The structural adjustment of the food sector is therefore linked to consumer preferences, which have an increasing impact on the industry as a result of income developments, shifts in the population structure and new lifestyles. Other essential impact that influence the food sector is globalization, liberalization of world trade and agricultural markets and the emergence of new markets from Central and Eastern Europe all the way to India and China. Finally, significant shifts and changes in technology, including information technology have led to new products and methods to organize the supply chain [21].

For this research, this is a Cold Chain, in which the hygienic safety of food depends largely on the respect of the cold chain, throughout all stages of storage and transport among the producer, carrier, distributor, and the consumer. Traceability, is a crucial concern to all participants and stakeholders in the food chain, this mainly refers to the ability to trace, throughout all stages of production, processing and distribution, the path of a food product, a food feed, a food-producing animal or a substance to be incorporated or even possibly incorporate it into a food product or a food feed [22]. It can also provide support for public health and help authorities determine the causes of contamination or help the companies reassure customers and increase competitiveness on the market through sales and market share. Finally, we have the quality challenge; this is an essential concept in the food industry, the compliance certification attests that a non-alimentary and unprocessed food or agricultural product complies with specific characteristics or previously set rules concerning the production, packaging or origin [22].

4 Supply Chain Meets Blockchain

Today many large industries are taking advantage of the Blockchain main characteristics such as immutability, traceability, and security to boost their business and overcome the counterfeit issues that have affected millions of brands over decades. A 2017 study from the Global Financial Integrity Organization (GFI) estimates the global trade value of counterfeit- and pirated goods to generate between US 923 billion to US 1.13 trillion annually. With this number increasing every day, it becomes imperative to adopt new technologies that make more efficient the whole process; some companies around the globe like, Unilever and FedEx, are using Blockchain to make more efficient the supply chain for some of their products; for Unilever this means, "the company hopes its strategy will build trust with consumers, who may be willing to pay a premium for a sustainably-sourced product" [23]; while FedEx, "is explicitly delving into creating uniform logistics standards for Blockchain applications across the industry" [24]. Therefore, it becomes relevant the proposal for a methodology that would help to meet business needs for the Colombian market in such an important industry, as it is the coffee industry.

4.1 The Application of Blockchain over the Supply Chain

For the integration between Blockchain and Supply chain, this research proposes to develop a methodological approach and a practical view to understand the generalities of this methodology. In summary, Fig. 1 shows four layers to understand the development of this methodology; The first one has to do with the product definition, where is important to gather as much as information about it, such as the characteristics and processes associated to its production. Then, we have the process, knowing the actors, and a detailed definition or characterization of the process to produce the product, according to the definition made earlier following these steps. After that, comes the information layer, where business rules, assets, and the information flow layout have to be defined; it's important to note that for this Data Flow Diagram (DFD) it is essential to consider the definitions made related to product characteristics, that is the information that will add more value to system. At last, the technology layer, which is where definitions are made about the platform to be used for the deployment of the Blockchain according to the process and the descriptions made.

As we present this methodological approach, we are going to showcase a practical use, for the Colombian coffee Supply Chain that will be explained accordingly in the following steps.

26   R. Bettín-Díaz et al.

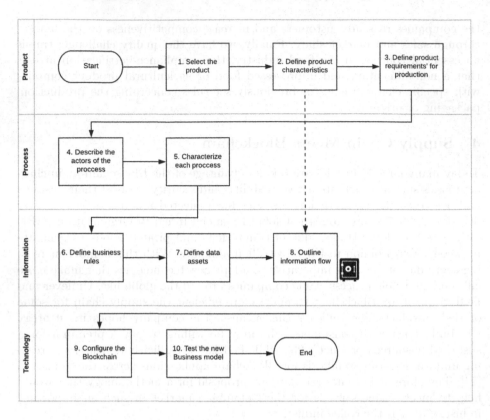

Fig. 1. Methodology summary for Blockchain applicability

1. **Select the product:** As simple as it may seem, the nature of the product to be selected will define in a significant proportion the scope of the architecture to be developed, at the level of understanding processes, operations and the different components that are part of the product's identity. At this point, it is recommended to know about the industry or productive sector of the product you are selecting to work with.
2. **Product characteristics:** A product is defined as a set of fundamental attributes united in an identifiable way [25]. Based on product design methodologies, in this stage, we seek to describe all the characteristics associated with the product selected, as shown in the Fig. 2. The detail in the definition of these characteristics is important because the meaning of the supply chain and all the processes immersed in it, for the elaboration of this, will depend on them.
3. **Requirements for production:** A fundamental part of the definitions to be made, is to consider all the requirements that are necessary to obtain the product, these are technical, functional, legal, and regulatory. As a fundamental part of this implementation, that seeks to generate interaction among

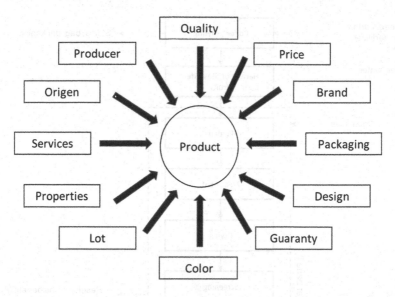

Fig. 2. Product characteristics

different parties, it is that the information for all processes, for everyone involved, is available.

4. **Actors of the process:** It is necessary within the initial characterization made for the value chain, in this case, the supply chain, to identify the primary entities that generate or add value to the final product. These are fundamental items in this definition because they are the locations where the information is born, where the processes and the central points for the interconnection of the processes are developed, see Fig. 3. For this research, the supply chain in the coffee industry was created considering the most important actors [26].

5. **Unit operations and processes:** For each actor there will be unitary operations and processes that will shape each one of the characteristics defined for the product. Knowing in detail what these are, the components of each one of them and the process that occurs in them will provide us with relevant

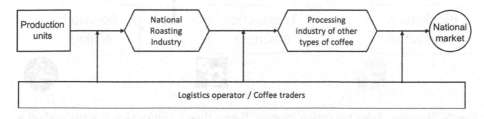

Fig. 3. Actors in the supply chain for the Colombian coffee industry. Depending on the objective of the project, this chain may be longer or shorter; this is a representation of the main actors of the coffee industry in Colombia.

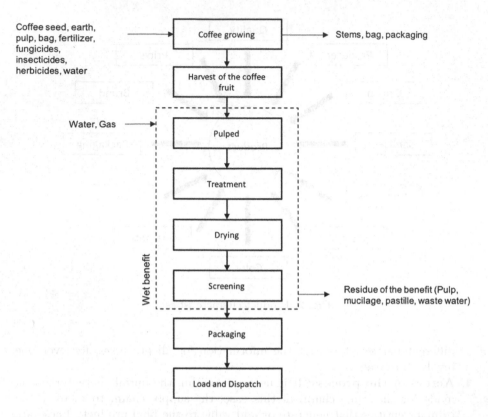

Fig. 4. Productive Units Process. It shows how the process of coffee harvesting is made in a traditional farm in Colombia; this process ends with a wet benefit packed and ready to sell to the manufacturers that produce different types of coffee.

and sufficient information to know what information should be extracted from that operation. These processes can be detailed thought a BDF (Block Diagram Flow) or BFPD (Block Flow Process Diagram) according to [27]. See Fig. 4.

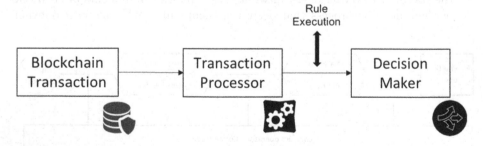

Fig. 5. Business Rules Execution Process. Every time a transaction is generated on a Blockchain, this goes through a transaction processor which will execute rules if defined and decide.

6. **Business rules:** In a Blockchain, this will help you to apply rules anytime you process a transaction. In this case, a transaction can be a purchase, a sale, a payment, even a control point along the process chain. As it is shown in Fig. 5, once a transaction is stored in the Blockchain, a transaction processor will validate the rules for that specific transaction, and if applicable, it will decide what to do with it, depending on its configuration.

   "The process also covers reviewing the rules, registering agreement between the parties, testing the rules on transaction data, simulating scenarios to understand their business impact, and storing them in a secure and transparent way. In addition, the same attention must be applied to data models and the business domain models they represent. The parties also must define how rules are governed: who can define rules, who can deploy rules, and the processes for changing rules" [28].

7. **Digital asset:** "Digital asset is a floating claim of a particular service or good ensured by the asset issuer, which is not linked to a particular account and is governed using computer technologies and the Internet, including asset issuance, the claim of ownership, and transfer" [29]. That being said, a Digital asset, for this particular case, are the documents that will allow the transaction to be valid. For each process in the supply chain there will be several assets that are going to be needed to make this a successful process; however, it will depend on the amount of transactions required for the specific system.

8. **Information flow:** Using Data Flow Diagram [30] will help you to understand how the information interacts across processes. For this, it is necessary to have an accurate definition of the assets and the data involved in each process. This will create the transactions on the Blockchain, as shown in Fig. 6; where we have the information defined, the process where that information is processed, and the outcome for the Blockchain.

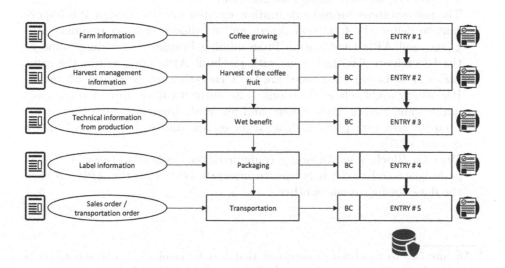

Fig. 6. Productive units information flow chart

9. **Configure the Blockchain:** First of all, it is imperative to define what kind of Blockchain you need and its technological architecture as defined by [31]. For example, a private Blockchain will only allow a few nodes connected to the network to transact with the information and use the ledger, in this kind of networks participant are very limited on what they can do, unlike a public Blockchain, that allows anyone to see or send transactions and actively participate in the process [32,33].

Then, it is necessary to select the most suitable consensus mechanism for the specific scenario, some of them are, proof of work [15], proof of stake [34], proof of activity [35], proof of luck [36], among others. This should be chosen in conjunction with the Blockchain platform to be used in the network; there are many of them out there, some of the most popular platforms are (in alphabetic order): BigChainDB, Corda, Credits, Domus Tower Blockchain, Elements Blockchain Platform, Ethereum, HydraChain, Hyperledger Fabric, Hyperledger Iroha, Hyperledger Sawtooth Lake, Multichain, Openchain, Quorum, Stellar and Symbiont Assembly [37,38]; according to the authors' experience, here are some of the parameters to take into consideration to validate which platform suits your business model the best: (a) Maturity, this refers to how long this platform has been in the market, its support model and documentation, (b) Easy of development, depending on your development skills, this point is of importance to consider, (c) Confirmation time, this will much depend on the consensus mechanism, this is why these two must be evaluated together, and (d) Privacy between nodes, as explained before some platform will allow you to configure public or private networks, this is according to the specific type of network for your business model.

The parameters that needs to be configure will vary depending on the platform, some of them can be changed during run-time but some cannot, this is a very crucial step during configuration.

The last two steps during configuration are, user interface design, it is important to define the front end design and to choose the programming language, and APIs (Application Programming Interface[6]) building; some of the Blockchain platforms come with pre-built APIs but, mainly, the categories of APIs you would need are for: Generating key pairs and addresses, Performing audit related functions, Data authentication through digital signatures and hashes, Data storage and retrieval, Smart-asset life-cycle management issuance, payment, exchange, escrow and retirement and Smart contracts [37].

Once the Blockchain platform is configured, the application (user front end) is designed and ready, it is time to integrate both with the APIs, to have the data flowing to one another.

---

[6] An interface to a software component that can be invoked at a distance over a communications network using standards-based technologies [39].

10. **Test the new business model:** Based on the objective of the project and the definition made for the Blockchain system, it is recommended before going live to define a set of tests. It should include, unit tests, to ensure each component of the complete architecture is working as expected; and integrated tests, to verify the flow along the Blockchain architecture. It is important to consider for these test scenarios, definitions such: participants, permissions, assets and transactions and the outcome expected for each one of those tests.

5 Conclusions

Blockchain technology may have the capacity to revolutionize businesses through a more transparent, secure, and decentralize system, by generating trust among participants. With this research arose the potential and opportunity to develop a methodology to integrate this technology with the processes along the supply chain that would help, in this case, provide the ultimate customer with the tools to make an informed purchase decision. As a result, the authors propose a step by step methodology that it is easy to follow and implement for any product, and it is scalable for other processes different to the supply chain; due to the central principle of its developments, which is to validate various elements that will add value to meet the objectives of the project.

Based on this methodological approach, the authors adopted the best marketing practices regarding product development; process engineering, which helps to understand the life cycle of the product along the entire supply chain, from raw material to finished products. Finally, the technology itself, which is not the purpose of this document; however, a fundamental guide is presented to develop a project from start to finish. It should be noted that anyone who wants to apply this methodology must have the knowledge related to the industry, the processes involved and the product to know what the result of this exercise will be concerning information that will travel to the Blockchain. The authors know the application of this technology has some specific requirement regarding the socio-cultural environment, such as IT infrastructure, which can be difficult for some of the participants; but, this obstacle needs to be overcome with governmental policies and education, which is not in the context of this article.

Additionally, during the research process, the authors have envisioned different applications for this methodology, that can be used to design a certification system based on Blockchain, by automatically gather required information across the process which will make it easy to audit and track for all participants involved. This scenario will use a centralized network to safeguard the information, which is controlled by a certification authority.

Finally, this is one of the many other methodologies that can be used to adopt Blockchain into a process, either financial, logistics, or any other of the value chain. But, due to the infancy of the technology is not easy to get there and find the perfect way to do it. The authors will continue investigating and improving this approach as the technology evolves.

References

1. WHO: World Health Oorganization: Healthy diet (2015)
2. Nielsen: We are what we eat: Healthy eating trends around the world. Technical report, NIELSEN (2014)
3. Ministerio de Agricultura y Desarrollo Rural: Reglamento para la producción primaria, procesamiento, empacado, etiquetado, almacenamiento, certificación, importación y comercialización de Productos Agropecuarios Ecológicos (2008)
4. Ministerio de Agricultura y Desarrollo Rural: Resolución número (148) (2004)
5. Bettín-Díaz, R.: Blockchain, una mirada a la descentralización de las transacciones y de la información. SISTEMAS **93**(102), 52–59 (2017)
6. Swan, M.: Blueprint for a New Economy, 1st edn. O'Reilly Media Inc., United States of America (2015)
7. Gates, M.: Blockchain: Ultimate guide to understanding blockchain, bitcoin, cryptocurrencies, smart contracts and the future of money. 1st edn. (2017)
8. Milani, F., García-Bañuelos, L., Dumas, M.: Blockchain and Business Process Improvement (2016)
9. Tapscott, D., Tapscott, A.: The impact of the blockchain goes beyond financial services. Harvard Business Review, May 2016
10. Jerry, C.: Making blockchain ready for business (2016)
11. Crosby, M., Nachiappan Pattanayak, P., Verma, S., Kalyanaraman, V.: BlockChain Technology Beyond Bitcoin. Sutardja Center for Entrepreneurship & Technology Technical Report, Berkeley Univesity of California, p. 35 (2015)
12. Gupta, M.: Blockchain for Dummies. John Wiley & Sons Inc., Hoboken (2017)
13. Sean: If you understand Hash Functions, you'll understand Blockchains (2016)
14. Icahn, G.: BLOCKCHAIN: The Complete Guide To Understanding Blockchain Technology. Amazon Digital Services LLC (2017)
15. Nakamoto, S.: Bitcoin: A Peer-to-Peer Electronic Cash System, p. 9 (2008)
16. Bresett, M.: Ethereum: What You Need to Know about the Block Chain Based Platform (2017)
17. Christopher, M.: Logistics; Supply Chain Management, 4th edn. Pearson, New Jersey (2011)
18. Hacker, S.K., Israel, J.T., Couturier, L.: Building Trust in Key Customer Supplier Relationships. The performance Center and SatisFaction Strategies, p. 10 (1999)
19. Council of Supply Chain Management Professionals: Supply Chain Management Definitions and Glossary (2013)
20. Hugos, M.: Essentials of Supply Chain Management. 2nd edn. John Wiley & Sons, Inc., Hoboken (2006)
21. Turi, A., Goncalves, G., Mocan, M.: Challenges and competitiveness indicators for the sustainable development of the supply chain in food industry. Procedia Soc. Behav. Sci. **124**(Suppl. C), 133–141 (2014)
22. Hua, A.V., Notland, J.S..: Blockchain enabled Trust and Transparency in supply chains, NTNU School of Entrepreneurship, 37 p. (2016). https://doi.org/10.13140/RG.2.2.22304.58886
23. Kapadia, S.: Unilever taps into blockchain to manage tea supply chain — Supply Chain Dive (2017)
24. Das, S.: FedEx Turns to Blockchain to 'Transform the Logistics Industry' (2018)
25. Stanton, W.J., Etzel, M.J., Walker, B.J.: Fundamentos del Marketing, 14th edn., vol. 14th. McGraw-Hill, Mexico (2007)

26. García, R.G., Olaya, E.S.: Caracterizacioón de las cadenas de valor y abastecimiento del sector agroindustrial del cafcè. Cuad. Adm. Bogotaá (Colombia) **19**, 197–217 (2006)
27. Turton, R., Bailie, R.C., Whiting, W.B., Shaeiwitz, J.A.: Analysis, Synthesis and Design of Chemical Processes, 3rd edn. Pearson Education Inc., Boston (2009)
28. Mery, S., Selman, D.: Make your blockchain smart contracts smarter with business rules. © Copyright IBM Corporation 2017, p. 21 (2017)
29. BitFury Group: Digital Assets on Public Blockchains (2016)
30. Tao, Y., Kung, C.: Formal definition and verification of data flow diagrams. J. Syst. Softw. **16**(1), 29–36 (1991)
31. Wu, H., Li, Z., King, B., Miled, Z.B., Wassick, J., Tazelaar, J.: A distributed ledger for supply chain physical distribution visibility. Information, Switzerland (2017)
32. O'Leary, D.E.: Configuring blockchain architectures for transaction information in blockchain consortiums: the case of accounting and supply chain systems. Intell. Syst. Account. Financ. Manag. **24**(4), 138–147 (2017)
33. Lai, R., LEE Kuo Chuen, D.: Blockchain - from public to private. In: Handbook of Blockchain, Digital Finance, and Inclusion, vol. 2, pp. 145–177. Elsevier (2018)
34. Siim, J.: Proof-of-Stake Research Seminar in Cryptography
35. Bentov, I., Lee, C., Mizrahi, A., Rosenfeld, M.: Proof of activity: extending Bitcoin's proof of work via proof of stake. ACM SIGMETRICS Perform. Eval. Rev. **42**(3), 34–37 (2014)
36. Milutinovic, M., He, W., Wu, H., Kanwal, M.: Proof of Luck: an Efficient Blockchain Consensus Protocol (2017)
37. Nagpal, R.: 17 blockchain platforms - a brief introduction - Blockchain Blog - Medium
38. g2crowd: Best Blockchain Platforms Software in 2018 — G2 Crowd
39. 3scale: What is an aPi?

Implementation Phase Methodology for the Development of Safe Code in the Information Systems of the Ministry of Housing, City, and Territory

Rosa María Nivia⒟, Pedro Enrique Cortés⒟, and Alix E. Rojas⁽✉⁾⒟

Universidad EAN, Bogotá, Colombia
{rniviabe1625,pcortess2651,aerojash}@universidadean.edu.co

Abstract. In the modern age of the Internet and information technology, information security in terms of software development has become a relevant issue for both public and private organizations. Considering the large budget that the nation must invest to prevent and repair computer attacks, the development of secure software in the Ministry of Housing, City, and Territory –MHCT– became a need that must be solved from the area of technology. Since information is the most important asset of any organization, it is essential to generate information systems with high levels of security, integrity, and reliability. We propose a methodology for the development of secure code, with the necessary procedures and indications to prevent possible attacks to information security and aimed at covering the development phase in the process of creating information systems for the MHCT. This is a specific methodology that was raised from different methodologies that address this problem, which we compared and evaluated based on different criteria that are relevant in the MHCT.

Keywords: Security code development methodology
Information system · Good practices
Ministry of Housing City and Territory

1 Introduction

During the last decade, the development of secure software has not had the required relevance, causing unauthorized access to processed information. This lack of security seriously affects the integrity, availability, and confidentiality of the information, and increases its risk of loss. Colombia registers as the third country in Latin America with the most impact in 2016, showing Information Technology Security as a weakness instead of a strength [11], is constantly subject to cyber attacks, to which public entities are not exempt.

© Springer International Publishing AG, part of Springer Nature 2018
O. Gervasi et al. (Eds.): ICCSA 2018, LNCS 10961, pp. 34–49, 2018.
https://doi.org/10.1007/978-3-319-95165-2_3

Another factor that infers in this problem is the fact that there is no security guarantee of the information in the organizations. Approximately 80% of the organizations do not have an Information Security Management System, supported by the ISO 27001 standard [18], reason why they do not have documented strategies that may be approved and supported directly by the top management, additionally, there is no risk management plan at the technological and information systems level.

According to the fraud and cyber crime survey in Colombia which reveals that the incidence of economic cyber crime in companies that operate in Colombia in 2011, was 65% and in 2013 it grew to 69%. The economic damage caused by these frauds and cyber crimes in Colombia in 2011 amounted to approximately 950 Million USD and in 2013 the figure grew to 3,600 Million USD [21].

A high percentage of the types of fraud perpetrated were due to the vulnerabilities identified in the information systems, this is how the attacks are increasing and mainly are presented on the applications, due to the fact that information security is not taken into account [16]. For the development of secure code in order to mitigate risks such as authentication and execution with high privileges [22]. Web applications have become vulnerable applications, due to the strong and extensive use of Internet and additionally because they are always exposed on the network. Most of these attacks are Cross Site Scripting and SQL Injection. The cause of these attacks is the lack of security in the development of the programs, due to the fact that the majority of developers do not have knowledge of what is a secure code, they do not know the tools that allow them to protect the code, and they are not it demands that they use them, therefore they do not know how to program safely [16]. According to [23] "The cost of unsafe software in the global economy is seemingly incommensurable". In June 2002, the US National Standards Institute (NIST) published a study on the costs of unsafe software for the US economy due to inadequate software testing. Interestingly, they estimate that a better testing infrastructure could save a third of these costs, or about $22 billion a year [29].

In accordance with the above, it is necessary to create a methodology to generate secure code, as well as offer tools for the development of secure applications, which allow to evaluate and maintain the secure code over time and train developers in processes and techniques of information security, in order to offer customers secure and high-quality applications. The project must address the issue of security testing, and static code analyzers, which allow to measure the load of the components associated with the development, to establish potential bottlenecks in the applications. The project will not only be focused on evaluating and showing the methodologies of development of safe code existing in the market and tools currently used in the safe development, but also in making a formal proposal of how to implement them in the MHCT in the cases in which on-site software is developed or a software house is contracted to develop information systems.

2   Background

The Ministry of Housing, City, and Territory (MHCT by its abbreviation in English) is the head of the housing sector in Colombia. Its main objective is to achieve, within the framework of the law and its powers, to formulate, adopt, direct, coordinate, and execute public policy, plans, and projects in territorial and urban planned development in the country, the consolidation of the system of cities, with efficient and sustainable land use patterns, considering housing access and financing conditions, and the provision of public services for drinking water and basic sanitation (Table 1).

The MHCT is a public order entity at the national level, whose purpose is developing a comprehensive housing policy to strengthen the existing model, and generating social interest housing programs and projects, free housing programs, and projects to access housing through programmed savings, additionally to water and basic sanitation projects [28].

The information systems –IS– of the MHCT are a fundamental component to carry out its mission and enable the strategy to achieve its strategic objectives and offer its products and services to the country. Among the most important information systems of the MHCT that operate missionary issues are (see Fig. 1):

- The Investment System in Drinking Water and Basic Sanitation (SINAS by its abbreviation in Spanish)
- The Integral Management and Evaluation System (SIGEVAS by its abbreviation in Spanish)
- IS for the projects of the Vice MHCT of Drinking Water and Sanitation
- IS for the Registration of Urban Licenses.
- IS for Sub-Division for the Input of Health care Products and Various Goods (SISPV by its abbreviation in Spanish)
- IS for projects of the Vice MHCT of Housing and Information System adopted by the former National Institute for Social Interest Housing and Urban Redevelopment (INURBE by its abbreviation in Spanish)
- IS for the management of housing subsidies

None of the above in the MHCT has the development of a secure code that would allow the use of methodologies and/or good security practices during its Systems Development life cycle (SDLC), which entails putting the processed information at risk in these information systems.

Understanding Secure Code as the code tested to resist attacks against the integrity, confidentiality, and availability of information in a proactive way. With the application of techniques to generate secure code, it is expected that after suffering attacks, applications are not affected and continue to provide the service.

In addition to the afore mentioned, the MHCT requires the development of information systems that allow integrating information from both the housing sector and the water and sanitation sector, in order to have information supplies to formulate public policies on housing issues and potable water, however, the information systems of the MHCT are developed in different programming

Table 1. Products and services offered by the MHCT

Housing	Drinking water and basic sanitation
Housing Program 100% subsidized: aimed at Colombians who live in extreme poverty and have no chance of accessing a housing loan with market offers. The goal of the government through the MHCT is to deliver 100,000 homes, and thus contribute to the creation of employment and poverty reduction in the country	Basic Water and Sanitation Program - Departmental Water Plan: achieve a comprehensive combination of resources and the implementation of efficient and sustainable schemes in the provision of public utilities for drinking water and basic sanitation
"Mi Casa Ya" Housing Program - Savers: aimed at middle class Colombians, who according to their income, are given subsidies so that they can pay the initial payment and the mortgage loan	Basic Water and Sanitation Program - "Todos por el Pacífico": build aqueduct and sewerage systems in the municipalities of the Pacific region of the country linked to the program and thus ensure the provision of services that ensure the sustainability of the investment
"Mi Casa Ya" Housing Program - Initial Fee: aimed at Colombians who have incomes of two to maximum four minimum wages, the MHCT will subsidize the initial installment of your home, with a value exceeding seventy CLMMW (current legal monthly minimum wage) and a value less than or equal to one hundred thirty-five CLMMW	Water and Basic Sanitation Program - Rural Projects: the objective is to give special importance in the provision of water supply and basic sanitation in rural areas, and in this way try to reduce the great difference compared to the supply indicatorsin urban areas
"Mi Casa Ya" Housing Program - Interest Rate Subsidy: aimed at Colombians who have an income of maximum eight SMLMV, who do not own a home in the country and who have not been beneficiaries at any time with the subsidy at the interest rate	Basic Water and Sanitation Program - Connect with the Water: through intradomiciliary and residential connections, promote access to public utilities for water supply and sewerage
	Basic Water and Sanitation Program - Connect with the Water: through intradomiciliary and residential connections, promote access to public utilities for water supply and sewerage

languages, which makes their integration difficult, consequently creating policies for the new developments to use the standards that have been defined, however, there is no methodology available that allow to have information systems developed in secure code. The security of the information systems is fundamental both for the MHCT and for the country in general, since these contribute to social

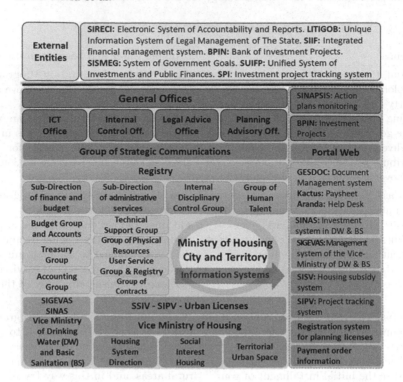

Fig. 1. Functional areas and information systems of the MHCT

equity and the quality of life of Colombians, promoting access to urban housing, drinking water, and to basic sanitation. In the light of all this, the MHCT requires having a methodology that allows the development of secure information systems. That is why it is worth asking: Does implementing a methodology for the development phase of secure code in the MHCT of Housing, City, and Territory, serve as a guide to establish protection mechanisms and compile a set of recommendations as part of the organizational strategy in information security? The methodology for the development of the secure code that will be created for the MHCT of Housing, City, and Territory will bear the name Methodology for the Development of Secure Code of the MHCT of Housing, City, and Territory (DCS-MHCT by its abbreviation in Spanish).

For all the above, the MHCT requires having a methodology that allows the development of secure information systems. That is why it is worth asking: implement a methodology for the development phase of Secure Code in the MHCT, serve as a guide to establish protection mechanisms and have a set of recommendations to guide them as a of the parts of the organizational strategy in information security?.

The methodology for the development of the secure code of the MHCT that will be created will have the name DCS-MHCT Methodology, which are the initials of the Methodology for the Development of Secure Code of the MHCT.

It is a current concern of the MHCT the lack of "a Methodology to implement the phase of the Development of Secure Code", in a high percentage the developments of information systems do not include the generation of secure code, nor do they involve methodologies for development of secure code in the different phases from the analysis to the start-up; this generates very high risks for the MHCT when it comes to deploying new information systems.

3 Analysis and Comparison of the Main Methodologies for the Development of Secure Code

After defining the problem, we identified the needs and requirements regarding security in the Ministry's information systems. This information was useful to define criteria to evaluate the methodologies to develop a safe code, which should be compared and evaluated in this investigation. In a first phase, we selected a group of methodologies focused on the development of the secure code, to then select a smaller and easier to use group of methodologies, whose methodologies were strongly aligned with the Ministry's requirements. There are several methodologies for developing secure code presents some examples of traditional cascade methodologies, agile and extreme development, and unified rational process [13]. The intention with the development of this project is neither to point to a particular safe code development methodology, nor to provide certain guidelines that conform to a specific methodology. Instead, the methodologies most used in the medium will be analyzed to finally present a model of development of safe code that is practical and useful to be used by engineers specialized in the development of information systems for the MHCT where the secure code is taken into account.

Before starting to develop secure code, the first thing to do is a risk analysis [12]. First, we identify which are the critical assets of the entity that are part of the information flow of the software and are involved in the development process or that are somehow going to be exposed in the application and then identify which are the possible threats that they can exploit the vulnerabilities of these assets [10]. The main threat, or source of danger, is often a cybercriminal who exploits vulnerabilities to launch attacks using different malicious agents.

The software is exposed to 2 general categories of threats: Threats during development: a software engineer can sabotage the program at any point in its development. Threats during the operation: an internal or external aggressor tries to sabotage the system. According to [5] "Many of the defects related to software security can be avoided if developers are better equipped to recognize the implications of their design and implementation possibilities."

During the risk analysis process it is necessary to prioritize them, with the aim of defining which are the most critical and, in this way, achieve a classification that allows to define the order in that must be attended to and identify where to invest the most effort or money to mitigate the associated risk [4,19]. Below are some of the main methodologies used in the development of secure code.

3.1   Definition Criteria for Assessment

In this phase of the project, an analysis was made of the different methodologies, techniques and academic proposals related to the development of a secure code, to identify advantages and disadvantages of each, especially from the point of view of the needs and context of the Ministry.

One of the main objectives of the project is that the methodology and guidance generated in the project is aligned with the reality of the Ministry of Housing, City and Territory, in such a way that its application generates a high value for the fulfillment of the mission of the Ministry and to achieve its vision, taking into account the priorities identified, the existing processes, the tools available to the Ministry and the resources currently available to the Ministry for the development of information systems and for information security. The key aspects that were taken into account are described below, and Table 2 shows the summary of the criteria and the associated rubric to evaluate the methodologies.

Table 2. Summary evaluation criteria

Qualification criteria			
Key aspects	Low	Medium	High
Strategic alignment	Does not contain elements of strategic alignment - organizational	It contains some elements of alignment but the impact to the entity is not clear	The alignment with the organization and its impact on the organization is clear
Adoption of the industry	There are no references of adoption in the industry	There are references of adoption in the industry	References of successful adoption in the industry are found
Maturity levels	Does not have levels of maturity	Maturity levels are implicitly defined	Maturity levels are explicitly defined
Low resources	It requires high resources	It requires few resources, but it does not focus on the main thing	It is simple, requires few resources, It's practical and focuses on the main thing
Digital government alignment	Does not meet or meet only one requirement	It meets two or three requirements	It meets more than three requirements

Strategic Alignment. The methodology proposed in the project contains a guideline that allows the security requirements to be prioritized according to the specific needs of the Ministry at that time. Another issue that it hopes to resolve is that by applying the methodology, it can provide feedback to senior managers on the impact or benefits of the Ministry's security requirements.

Adoption of Industry. The selected methodology must have been tested in the industry, and know in advance the positive and negative results in real organizations, in such a way that risks are identified at an early stage when adopting specific practices of the methodology.

Maturity Levels. Starting to implement a methodology with a very high level of maturity can lead to a culture shock that prevents appropriation. The main objective of this third criterion is to adopt a methodology with an initial level of maturity, so that cultural changes, the transfer of knowledge, the appropriation of resources and tools, among others, can be assimilated incrementally.

Low Resources. The methodology must use the minimum possible resources due to the national austerity policy, therefore, it is very important to identify methodologies that are applicable to small development groups, that do not require specialized training, that focus on what is most important, and that allows to define requirements in a practical and agile way.

Digital Government Alignment. The methodology proposed in the project contains a guideline that allows the security requirements to be prioritized according to the specific needs of the Ministry at that time. Another issue that it hopes to resolve is that by applying the methodology, it can provide feedback to senior managers on the impact or benefits of the Ministry's security requirements.

Support in the Current Platform. The Ministry of ICT, has defined within the Digital Government Manual, the ICT component for management, which seeks to make the information be used in a better way in state entities, for its analysis, effective administrative management, and decision making [27]. So that this criterion seeks that the selected methodologies cover the aspects defined in the guidelines LI.SIS20, LI.SIS21, LI.SIS22, and LI.SIS23 of the Digital Government. These guidelines say that The Management of Information Technologies and Systems must:

- LI.SIS20: have quality plans for the software components of their information systems. This Quality Plan must be part of the software development process.
- LI.SIS21: consider the requirements of the institution, the functional and technical restrictions, and the attributes of quality in the design of the information systems.
- LI.SIS22: incorporate those security components for the treatment of information privacy, the implementation of access controls, as well as information integrity and encryption mechanisms.
- LI.SIS22: take into account mechanisms that ensure the historical record in order to maintain the traceability of the actions carried out by the users.

3.2 Evaluation of Methodologies and Preliminary Results

First, there will be a brief tour of different methodologies that exist today in the field of computer security. The main methodologies that were considered are listed below (Table 3).

- SEI: As part of the SEI CERT initiative to develop secure coding standards, the SEI has published coding standards in several languages such as C, C++, java and Perl [3].
- ISO 27034-1: The ISO in 2011 published the international standard ISO/IEC 27034 as part of the ISO2700 series of standards on information security, which defines in general terms the concepts and generalities of how The security of applications in organizations should be addressed under the framework of an Information Security Management System [17].
- APPLE: It is a guide developed by Apple mainly aimed at developers of applications on Macintosh and iOS devices, in which the main software vulnerabilities are presented and the forms of programs to avoid them are defined. Additionally, it has two appendices, the first is a checklist of the main security features that every application should have. And the second appendix provides a guide to the security aspects that should be taken into account when you have software developed by third parties [1].
- OWASP: The OWASP foundation was established in 2001 as a non-profit organization, aims to provide information about the security of applications independently, without commercial purposes, practical and cost-effective [8]. The foundation supports several projects all focused on the security of the applications, the most known project of the foundation is the OWASP Top

Table 3. Valuation of the methodologies based on the criteria

Criteria	Valued methodologies								
	SEI	ISO 27034-1	Apple	OWASP	WASC	SANS	NIST	MS	Gary MG
Strategic alignment	Low	High	Low	High	Low	Med	High	Med	Med
Digital government alignment	High	High	Med	High	Low	Med	High	High	Med
Adoption of industry	Med	Med	Low	High	Med	Med	High	High	High
Low resources	High	Low	High	High	Low	Med	Low	Med	High
Madurity levels	High	Low	High	High	Low	High	Low	Low	High
Support	Med	High	Med	High	Low	High	Low	High	High

Ten of which there is a candidate version to be issued in 2017, which describes the 10 most critical risks for the security of the Web applications [31]. This Top Ten has allowed to prioritize the security efforts in the vulnerabilities of the applications that have been most exploited in organizations and that have caused the most damage to them. Another important project of the foundation that is relevant to the project is the OWASP SAMM (Software Assurance Maturity Model), which is a framework for defining objectives to establish the security of applications in an organization, depending on the specific risks of the same, the tolerance to the risk and the available resources [33]. There is also another project called OWASP Secure Coding Practices, which has generated a 17-page guide to the most important practices in the development of secure software, without taking into account a specific technology or language [30]. This is complemented by the .NET project, which contains 59 pages of information on information security in the .NET platform, specifically for software developers [32].

- WASC: It is a document whose last update was in 2011 that makes a compendium of the threats and weaknesses that can lead to the commitment of a web page. This document was made focused on developers, security professionals and software quality assurance. It defines at which stage of the development cycle it is most likely that each vulnerability will be introduced into the software, whether in the design, in the implementation or in the deployment. The 171-page document includes a clear description and examples of coding in multiple languages of 34 different types of attacks, and 16 different vulnerabilities [2].
- SANS: SANS publishes a poster with the most relevant information of its applications security courses, in the November 2016 version, it proposes a checklist of good practices in software safe development in topics such as error handling and logs, data protection, configurations, authentication, session management, handling of inputs and outputs, and access control. On the second page of the poster, it suggests a secure applications program comprised of four components, design, testing, correction, and governance. It also includes good practices in DevOps and mobile applications [7].
- NIST: It is the national institute of standards and technology of the United States of America, which maintains a series of publications specialized in information security called the SP800 series, so that the agencies of the country adopt good practices in information security in all areas of it. The publication defines how to address the aspects of information security in the software development cycle (SDLC), from planning to the disposal or registration of the information system [20, 29].
- Microsoft (MS): Microsoft as one of the world's leading software developers, has recognized for several years the importance of addressing information security requirements in all phases of the software development cycle. As part of the strategy to improve software security, Microsoft has developed several projects and initiatives, one of which is the Security Development Lifecycle [14], which guides developers to incorporate security into the cycle processes of life of software development in organizations. Microsoft also published a

book about its SDLC [15], in which all the phases of the SDLC and implementation recommendations in the companies are described in a detailed and practical way. Another of the important resources developed by Microsoft are the coding guides [26], which present the recommendations of secure coding in .NET language. This resource for secure coding is within the framework of security recommendations for the .NET framework [25].

- Gary McGraw: He is one of the main authors on Cybersecurity issues and specifically in the area of secure software development, founder of the company Cigital, which maintains the BSIMM project [6], which defines a maturity model in application security and periodically performs a benchmark of maturity in approximately 95 software development firms. In 2006 he published the book Software Security: Building Security [24], which became a bet-seller and a must in the area of secure application development. The focus of the McGraw methodology is to address the specific security issues within the software development cycle (Systems Development Life Cycle - SDLC) in high relevance points, which the author calls Security Touchpoints.

It has been decided to analyze these methodologies because they are internationally recognized and are very close to the requirements that have been established for the project. Most of these methodologies are developed by communities that constantly meet to establish what improvements and changes require to keep them updated and improve their functionality. Several of them are oriented to the management of the entire life cycle of the development of secure software and have tools that require a license for their use. These methodologies are the most used by the big corporations in the world and by the software factories. Additionally, the methodologies that will be analyzed have been sufficiently proven to take them into account in a comparative analysis that any private company or government institution intends to do. Finally, it can be said that these methodologies have provided sufficient documentation for them to be studied, tested and used by teams specialized in software development, which has given them recognition in the market as the most used experts, for these reasons they have been selected for the analysis.

4   The DCS-MHCT Methodology

The DCS-MVCT methodology is an acronym in Spanish that translates Development of Secure Code for the Ministry of Housing, City and Territory. In the definition of the general framework of the DCS-MVCT methodology, the models of OWASP, Gary McGraw and SDL of Microsoft were considered. And the objective of this methodology is to ensure that the source code and the information managed through the MHCT information systems are secure.

Figure 2 shows the phase of the SDLC in which the methodology is focused, which corresponds to the programming or development of the code. According to the results obtained to propose the best alternative that should be used in the development of information systems for the MHCT, and therefore, adopted by software developers, internal or external to the Ministry.

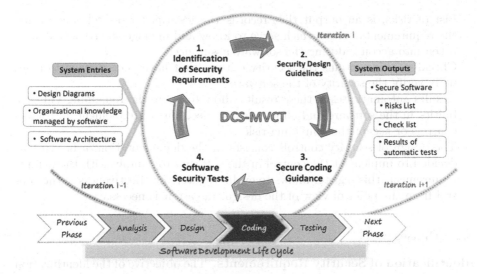

Fig. 2. The DCS-MHCT methodology diagram

This methodology is composed of four phases, which are aligned with a software development cycle and in each of the phases defines the suggested security elements, so that in the end the developed software can be considered safe. In the first phase, security requirements are analyzed; in the second, the requirements are transferred to specific software design components; in the third, the specific requirements are codified and in the fourth phase, the tests that verify the security controls established in the software are performed. Each of the parts that make up the methodology will be detailed in the next sections.

4.1 Inputs and Outputs

To ensure that the methodology can be followed, the following artifacts are wanted:

- Software architecture, which should describe the main components of the software, and how they relate to each other.
- Software design diagrams, use case diagrams, data flow diagrams and any other type of diagram that allows knowing how information flows through the software and the components that will integrate it.
- The knowledge of the information managed by the software is essential to determine the relevant impacts that the commitment of security in the software can have.

Once the first iteration of the methodology is completed, it is expected to have the following artifacts:

- Secure software, which would be the main objective of the methodology, that the developed software mitigate the risks that the information may have from its design, coding and implementation.

– List of risks, is an output that records the identified risks relevant during the requirements phase, which serve to know and manage the risks that were taken into account during the software assurance.
– Checklist, this contains the security criteria that have been defined to manually verify the security of the software.
– Results automatic tests, these results allow to know the remaining vulnerabilities in the software and allow to make decisions to implement additional controls or accept the remaining risk.
– The design of security controls consists in the documentation of how it was decided to implement the control in the software to comply with the defined requirement, this register allows to evaluate later the effectiveness of the control from the point of view of the design, in case it is necessary.

4.2   Phases

Identification of Security Requirements. The objective of the identification phase of security requirements is to define the security requirements that the information system must have based on a risk analysis. The architecture risk analysis should be composed of two macro activities, which can be done in parallel [24]: (1) Analysis of resistance to attacks, and (2) Analysis of ambiguity. The analysis of resistance to attacks consists mainly in identifying weaknesses in the software that can be used by an attacker, the defined approach to address this activity, is to perform checks through checklists. The analysis of ambiguity aims to identify new risks that have not been previously documented in a checklist and that requires the evaluation of personnel with experience in the software and in the general architecture of the system to be developed.

Security Design Guidelines. Since the requirements of the previous phase are delivered in the form of a risk checklist, this phase is in charge of defining the controls that reduce the security risks. For this phase, a risk assessment committee should be formed, to which the treatment options can be presented, so that the committee will approve the decisions on how the security controls will be implemented in the software. This committee must analyze each of the risks identified in the previous phase and must define, for each risk reported, the security requirements in the software that are more convenient and viable for the Ministry.

Secure Coding Guidelines. The person in charge of software development and coding must analyze the documented security requirements and understand them in order to define how to implement them in the software. The following general and specific recommendations include the most important controls to be taken into account in software coding and serve as the basis for defining and coding the software in a secure manner.

Software Security Test. In the last phase, it is verified that the identified security requirements and good safe development practices have been effectively implemented in the software. Ideally this activity should be done by the developer to verify that he fulfilled all the requirements. In this phase it contemplates three perspectives, the first one is the manual review through a checklist that contains the security requirements that were defined in the design stage and the good security practices implemented in the coding stage. The second perspective is the automatic review of the software through a tool that reviews the security from the source code and the configuration of the software, for this methodology due to the context of the Ministry it is proposed to use the function of code analysis included in the framework of ASP.NET development, which can be found under the menu "Analyze" in the option "Configure Code Analysis for Website" and in the selection of rules select the integrated rules "Security Rules". The third perspective is the dynamic automatic review of the software through a vulnerability analysis tool, in this methodology it is proposed to use the free OWASP ZAP tool.

The development of the DCS-MVCT Methodology, included processes focused on the improvement of security during the development of secure code. The use of the methodology adjusted to the needs of the Ministry is necessary to mitigate and avoid attacks that, although they are minimal, must be endured, causing loss of time and some setbacks. In this case, the best methodology is one that adapts to the needs of the Ministry and the context of the information systems to be developed. When the Ministry contracts an external development, it must demand the use of the DCS-MVCT Methodology implemented in the entity, to be applied during the development of the information systems, to guarantee the security of the software.

5 Conclusions

After a review of the general literature on academic and technical proposals of the different components of the existing methodologies regarding the subject of safe code, a thorough analysis was carried out and nine of the most known methodologies in the market were selected, because they all count with many of the necessary requirements for this project, such as easy adoption of the industry, a high level of maturity, applicability to the programming language and technological platform of the MHCT, and the use of the least possible resources. Taking into account that the need for a quick and easy application, in addition to its adaptation to the changing structure of the data model and software development in the MHCT, in the DCS-MHCT Methodology, different types of formats were created to define the criteria that has to be taken into account during the different tests performed to verify the quality, usability, and compliance with the objectives of the secure code developed in the MHCT.

According to the experience acquired during the development of this project, we detected that the security in the applications must be considered from the beginning of the development of the code, and mainly from the phase of requirements elicitation, because repairing the security holes when the application is finished and probably in production can be very expensive, even in some cases when the applications are too robust and large, it is cheaper to do them again than to repair errors in programming, design, and security holes. Unfortunately, organizations still see security as a cost and not as an added value that provides prestige and reliability for internal and external users.

The security in the information systems of the MHCT of Housing, City, and Territory has become a transversal element that must be immersed in each phase during the life cycle of software development. Hackers are prepared to go a step further in planning new attacks on organizations. If they continue to develop the software in the traditional way, it is concluded that the information systems will go to production with untreated vulnerabilities, gap that will be exploited by the attackers, exploiting those vulnerabilities that could be avoided using a methodology such as the one that has been developed in this project.

Defining and applying the DCS-MVCT Methodology in the Ministry brings important benefits such as: managing the security of the new information systems developed in the Ministry, carrying out the necessary tests before going out to production and making the programmers aware of the use of the methodology for the development of secure software.

References

1. Apple Computer Inc.: Secure Coding Guide (2016)
2. The Web Application Security Consortium: The WASC Threat Classification v2.0 (2011)
3. Standards, SEI CERT Coding: Obtenido de Software Engineering Institute - Carnegie Mellon University, 24 de abril de (2017)
4. Bijay, K., Jayaswal, P.C.: Design for Trustworyhy Software. Pearson (2007)
5. Brito, C. J.: Metodologías para desarrollar software seguro (2013)
6. BSIMM Initiative: BSIMM Framework (2017)
7. SANS: What Works in Application Security (2016)
8. Curphey, Mark - OWASP: A Guide to Building Secure Web Applications - The Open Web Application Security Project (2005)
9. Deloitte: Encuesta de Seguridad Mundial. USA: Deloitte Survey (2007)
10. Williams, J. OWASP Foundation: The Open Web Application Security Project (2008)
11. Forero, R.A.: Dinero. Obtenido de Amenazas cibernéticas y la vulnerabilidad de nuestro negocio (2016)
12. Glass, R.L.: Building Quality Software. Prentice Hall, Upper Saddle River, New Jersey (1992)
13. Munassar, N.M.A., Govardhan, A.: A comparison between five models of software engineering. Int. J. Comput. Sci. Issues 5, 95–101 (2010)
14. Microsoft Corporation: The Security Development Lifecycle Developer Starter Kit (2017)
15. Howard, M., Lipner, S.: The Security Development Lifecycle, vol. 8. Microsoft Press a Division of Microsoft Corporation, Redmond (2006)
16. Huseby, S.H.: Innocent Code - A Security Wake-Up Call for Web Programmers. Wiley, London (2004)

17. International Organization for Standarization and International Electrotechnical Commission: ISO/IEC 27034-1 Application Security - Overview and Concepts. ISO (2011)
18. ISO/IEC, I.: ISO. ISO/IEC 27001:2013 - Information technology - Security Techniques - Information security management systems. ISO/IEC (2013)
19. Jhohn Viega, G.M.: Building Secure Software. Pearson, Indianapolis (2001)
20. Kissel, R.: Security Considerations in the System Development Life Cycle. NIST Special Publication, Technical report, National Institute of Standards and Technology (2008)
21. ISACA.: Encuesta de Fraude y Cibercrimen en Colombia. Bogota (2013)
22. Florez, H., Sanchez, M., Villalobos, J.: A Catalog of Automated Analysis Methods for Enterprise Models. Springer, New York (2016). https://doi.org/10.1186/s40064-016-2032-9
23. McConnel, S.: Code Complete: A Practical Handbook of Software Construction, 2nd edn. Microsoft Press, Redmond (2004)
24. McGraw, G.: Software Security: Building Security in. Addison Wesley, Boston (2006)
25. Microsoft Corp.: Microsoft Security Development Lifecycle (SDL) - Process Guidance (2012)
26. Microsoft Corp.: Improving Web Application Security: Threats and Countermeasures (2017)
27. MINTIC: Conoce la estrategia de gobierno en línea (2017)
28. Minvivienda: Misión y Visión del Ministerio de Vivienda (2017)
29. National Institute of Standards and Technology: Security Considerations in the System Development Life Cycle (2008)
30. OWASP Foundation: OWASP Secure Coding Practices - Quick Reference Guide (2015)
31. OWASP Foundation: The Open Web Application Security Project (2015)
32. OWASP Foundation: OWASP.NET Project (2016)
33. OWASP Foundation: OWASP SAMM Project (2017)

Cryptanalysis and Improvement of an ECC-Based Authentication Protocol for Wireless Sensor Networks

Taeui Song[1], Dongwoo Kang[2], Jihyeon Ryu[1], Hyoungshick Kim[3], and Dongho Won[4(✉)]

[1] Department of Platform Software, Sungkyunkwan University, 2066 Seobu-ro, Jangan-gu, Suwon-si, Gyeonggi-do 16419, Korea
{tusong,jhryu}@security.re.kr
[2] Department of Electrical and Computer Engineering, Sungkyunkwan University, 2066 Seobu-ro, Jangan-gu, Suwon-si, Gyeonggi-do 16419, Korea
dwkang@security.re.kr
[3] Department of Software, Sungkyunkwan University, 2066 Seobu-ro, Jangan-gu, Suwon-si, Gyeonggi-do 16419, Korea
hyoung@skku.edu
[4] Department of Computer Engineering, Sungkyunkwan University, 2066 Seobu-ro, Jangan-gu, Suwon-si, Gyeonggi-do 16419, Korea
dhwon@security.re.kr

Abstract. The Internet of Things is the interconnection of devices that exchange collected data with each other through the internet using electronics, software, and sensors. Wireless sensor network is used extensively in implementation of the Internet of Things system. With the increasing use of them, many researchers have focused on the security in wireless sensor network environment. In 2016, Wu et al. proposed a user authentication protocol for wireless sensor network, claiming it was secure from various types of attacks. However, we found out that their scheme has some vulnerabilities to the user impersonation attack, and the denial of service attack. In order to overcome these problems, we review Wu et al.'s protocol and propose an improved protocol based on their protocol. Then, we show that our proposed protocol is more secure than other authentication protocols for wireless sensor network.

Keywords: Authentication · Internet of Things
Elliptic curve cryptography · Wireless sensor network

1 Introduction

The Internet of Things(IoT) means the technology that connects objects to other objects by embedding sensors and communication units in objects. As information and communication technology develops, the IoT is expanding everywhere fast. Nowadays, it is widely used in most fields including home appliances, traffic, construction, and healthcare system. Wireless sensor network(WSN) plays an

© Springer International Publishing AG, part of Springer Nature 2018
O. Gervasi et al. (Eds.): ICCSA 2018, LNCS 10961, pp. 50–61, 2018.
https://doi.org/10.1007/978-3-319-95165-2_4

important role in the IoT by facilitating remote data collection. In general, there are three different kinds of participants in WSN: the sensors, the gateway and users. The sensors which are deployed in some objects and areas collect information from the environment. They have limited power and resources. The gateway acts as a communication bridge between the sensors and users. All sensors are registered in the gateway and the gateway manages the sensors for the security of the network. For this reason, a user who wants to get information from a particular sensor has to register in the gateway where the sensor is registered. After registering in the gateway, the user connects to the gateway and establishes a session key with the sensor through the gateway. In this process, the user must be authenticated to access to the sensor. If the authentication process is successful, the user can obtain information collected by the sensor. Initially, WSN was composed of homogeneous sensors, so there were some difficulties in collecting different kinds of information. However, recently, heterogeneous sensors are used in WSN instead of homogeneous sensors. Because of these sensors, it became possible to gather a variety of information and as a result WSN can be used in various fields. With the increasing use of WSN, security threats to WSN are also growing exponentially year after year. Since there are confidential and sensitive information among the data collected by diverse kinds of sensors, including private and military information, the security of WSN is considered the most important issue. If malicious people steal and misuse critical information, it leads to huge losses. Therefore, in order to keep information safe, access to sensors must be restricted to authorized personnel only. That is to say, all entities must achieve mutual authentication in WSN. For this reason, many researchers have presented several kinds of user authentication protocols for WSN such as RSA-based, smart card-based, and elliptic curve cryptography(ECC)-based protocols.

In 2004, Watro et al. [13] suggested an authentication protocol for wireless sensor network using RSA. Also, Wong et al. [14] proposed a password-based protocol for WSN using hash function in 2006. In 2009, Das [4] found out that an attacker could impersonate sensors in Watro et al.'s protocol and Wong et al.'s protocol was susceptible to the stolen verifier attack and many logged in users with the same log-in id threat. After analyzing Wong et al.'s protocol, Das presented a smart card-based authentication protocol improving Wong et al.'s. Unfortunately, Das's protocol was also shown to be susceptible to the forgery attack and the insider attack later on. In order to fix these problems, Chen and Shih [2], He et al. [5] and Khan and Alghathbar [7] proposed improvements of Das's protocol. However, some security problems were founded in their protocols. For example, Chen and Shih's protocol could not block the replay attack and the forgery attack and He et al.'s protocol could not provide user anonymity as well as mutual authentication. Furthermore, Vaidya et al. [12] found out that Khan and Alghathbar's protocol suffered from the stolen smart card attack, the forgery attack and the node capture attack. Then, they suggested an improved two factor user authentication protocol.

In 2011, Yeh et al. [17] presented the first ECC-based user authentication protocol for WSN but it had some drawbacks including lack of mutual authentication and forward security. To overcome the vulnerabilities of Yeh et al.'s protocol, Shi and Gong [10] proposed a new user authentication protocol for WSN using ECC in 2013. Later on, Choi et al. [3] pointed out that Shi and Gong's protocol was susceptible to the sensor energy exhausting attack, the session key attack, and the stolen smart card attack. Then they proposed improvements of Shi and Gong's protocol. In 2014, Turkanović et al. [11] presented a user authentication protocol for heterogeneous ad hoc WSN in which a user can access to a sensor directly. Afterward, Amin and Biswas [1] found out that Turkanović et al.'s protocol could not block the stolen smart card attack, the off-line password guessing attack and the user impersonation attack. Moreover, they claimed that Turkanović et al.'s protocol was not appropriate for WSN because the power consumption of the sensor was high in Turkanović et al.'s protocol. In order to solve these vulnerabilities, they presented a new protocol for WSN but it was pointed out that their protocol was also vulnerable to the user, a gateway, and sensor forgery attacks by Wu et al. [16].

In 2014, Hsieh and Leu [6] found out that Vaidya et al.'s protocol was susceptible to the insider attack and the password guessing attack. Also, they proposed an improved protocol based on Vaidya et al.'s. Nevertheless, Hsieh and Leu's protocol still had some problems defending against the off-line guessing attack, the insider attack, the sensor capture attack and the user forgery attack. Hence, Wu et al. [15] suggested a new authentication protocol for WSN and argued that their protocol could overcome the common security problems. However, recently, we found out that Wu et al.'s protocol is not secure against the user forgery attack and the denial of service attack.

In this paper, we review Wu et al.'s protocol and point out that their protocol is vulnerable to the user impersonation attack and the denial of service attack. After illustrating its vulnerabilities, we propose a secure ECC-based authentication protocol for WSN.

The remainder of the paper is organized as follows. First, in Sect. 2, we introduce elliptic curve cryptography which is applied to Wu et al.'s protocol and our protocol. Then, we review Wu et al.'s protocol in Sect. 3 and analyze their protocol in Sect. 4. Our protocol and the security analysis of it are presented in Sects. 5 and 6. Finally, we conclude the paper in Sect. 7.

2   Preliminaries

Before reviewing Wu et al.'s protocol, we explain elliptic curve cryptography which is used in Wu et al.'s and our protocols.

2.1   Elliptic Curve Cryptography

In 1985, Koblitz [8] and Miller [9] suggested the cryptography system using the elliptic curve independently. Although ECC uses a small key size compared to other public key cryptography such as RSA and ElGamal, it provides a similar level of security as them.

The elliptic curve is expressed by the equation $y^2 = x_3 + ax + b \bmod p$ over a prime finite field F_p, where $a, b \in F_p$ satisfying $4a^3 + 27b^2 \neq 0 \bmod p$. There are three problems related to ECC: Elliptic Curve Discrete Logarithm Problem(ECDLP), Elliptic Curve Computational Diffie-Hellman Problem(ECCDHP), and Elliptic Curve Decisional Diffie-Hellman Problem(ECDDHP).

- ECDLP: Given two points P and Q in G, it is difficult to find $x \in Z_q^*$ such that $Q = xP$, where xP is P added to itself x times using the elliptic curves operation.
- ECCDHP: Given two points xP and yP in G, where $x, y \in Z_q^*$, it is difficult to compute xyP in G.
- ECDDHP: For $x, y, z \in Z_q^*$, given three points xP, yP and zP in G, it is hard to decide whether $zP = xyP$.

3   Review of Wu et al.'s Protocol

There are four phases in Wu et al.'s protocol: initialization, registration, login and authentication and password change. The notations used in this paper are summarized in Table 1.

Table 1. Notations and their meanings

Notation	Meaning
p, q	Large prime numbers
$E(F_p)$	A finite field F_p on the elliptic curve E
G	A subgroup of $E(F_p)$ with order q
P	The generator of G
U_i, ID_i, PW_i	The $i-th$ user with his identity and password
S_j, SID_j	The $j-th$ sensor with its identity
GW, gs	The gateway and its secret key
SK_u, SK_s	The session keys formed by the user and the sensor
$\mathcal{A}$	The attacker
$h(\cdot), h_1(\cdot)$	The hash function
$\oplus$	The exclusive-or operation
$\|$	The concatenation operation

3.1   Initialization

First, GW generates a group G of elliptic curve points on the elliptic curve E. Then, GW chooses a secret key gs and two hash functions.

3.2 Registration

User Registration

1. U_i picks his or her identity ID_i and password PW_i, and generates a random nonce N_1. Next, U_i computes $TP_i = h(N_1 \parallel PW_i)$ and $TI_i = h(N_1 \parallel ID_i)$ and sends $\{TP_i, TI_i, ID_i\}$ to GW through a secure channel.
2. After getting the registration message from U_i, GW computes $PV_i = h(ID_{GW} \parallel gs \parallel TI_i) \oplus TP_i$ and $IV_i = h(TI_i \parallel gs) \oplus TI_i$. Then GW stores ID_i in its database, stores (PV_i, IV_i, P, p, q) into the smart card and sends it to U_i.
3. Finally, U_i stores $NV_i = h(ID_i \parallel PW_i) \oplus N_1$ into the smart card received from GW.

Sensor Registration

1. S_j sends its identity SID_j to GW through a secure channel.
2. GW computes $ss_j = h(SID_j \parallel gs)$ and transmits it to S_j. Then, SID_j and ss_j are stored in S_j.

3.3 Login and Authentication

1. U_i puts his or her smart card in a device and inputs ID_i and PW_i. The smart card calculates $N_1 = NV_i \oplus h(ID_i \parallel PW_i)$, $TI_i = h(N_1 \parallel ID_i)$ and $TP_i = h(N_1 \parallel PW_i)$ using the values stored in it.
2. U_i selects random nonces $\alpha \in [1, q-1]$, N_2 and N_3, and chooses the sensor S_j. Then, the smart card calculates $TI_i^{new} = h(N_2 \parallel ID_i)$, $UC_1 = PV_i \oplus TP_i \oplus N_3$, $UC_2 = \alpha P$, $UC_3 = IV_i \oplus TI_i \oplus TI_i^{new} \oplus h(N_3 \parallel TI_i)$, $UC_4 = h(N_3 \parallel TI_i^{new} \parallel UC_2) \oplus ID_i$ and $UC_5 = h(ID_i \parallel TI_i \parallel TI_i^{new} \parallel SID_j)$. Next, it sends the login request message $LM_1 = \{TI_i, SID_j, UC_1, UC_2, UC_3, UC_4, UC_5\}$ to GW.
3. After getting the login request message from U_i, GW calculates $N_3 = UC_1 \oplus h(ID_{GW} \parallel gs \parallel TI_i)$, $TI_i^{new} = UC_3 \oplus h(TI_i \parallel gs) \oplus h(N_3 \parallel TI_i)$ and $ID_i = UC_4 \oplus h(N_3 \parallel TI_i^{new} \parallel UC_2)$. If ID_i is not in its database or $UC_5 \neq h(ID_i \parallel TI_i \parallel TI_i^{new} \parallel SID_i)$, the process is terminated. If not, GW calculates $ss_j = h(SID_j \parallel gs)$ and $GC_1 = h(TI_i \parallel SID_j \parallel ss_j \parallel UC_2)$. Then it transmits $LM_2 = \{TI_i, SID_j, UC_2, GC_1\}$ to S_j.
4. S_j verifies SID_j and $GC_1 \stackrel{?}{=} h(TI_i \parallel SID_j \parallel ss_j \parallel UC_2)$. If the verification is successful, S_j selects random nonce $\beta \in [1, q-1]$ and calculates $SC_1 = \beta P$, $SC_2 = \beta UC_2$, $SK_s = h_1(UC_2 \parallel SC_1 \parallel SC_2)$, $SC_3 = h(TI_1 \parallel SID_j \parallel SK_s)$ and $SC_4 = h(ss_j \parallel TI_i \parallel SID_j)$. After that, $LM_3 = \{SC_1, SC_3, SC_4\}$ is sent to GW.
5. GW verifies $SC_4 \stackrel{?}{=} h(ss_j \parallel TI_i \parallel SID_j)$. If it is correct, GW calculates $GC_2 = h(ID_{GW} \parallel gs \parallel TI_i^{new}) \oplus h(TI_i^{new} \parallel N_3)$, $GC_3 = h(TI_i^{new} \parallel gs) \oplus h(TI_i \parallel N_3)$ and $GC_4 = h(ID_i \parallel TI_i \parallel TI_i^{new} \parallel SID_j \parallel GC_2 \parallel GC_3 \parallel N_3)$. Finally, $LM_4 = \{SC_1, SC_3, GC_2, GC_3, GC_4\}$ is sent to U_i.

6. After verifying $GC_4 \overset{?}{=} h(ID_i \parallel TI_i \parallel TI_i^{new} \parallel SID_j \parallel GC_2 \parallel GC_3 \parallel N_3)$ received from GW, U_i calculates $UC_6 = \alpha SC_1$ and $SK_u = h_1(UC_2 \parallel SC_1 \parallel UC_6)$. Then U_i verifies $SC_4 \overset{?}{=} h(TI_i \parallel SID_j \parallel SK_u)$. If it holds, the smart card calculates $NV_i^{new} = N_2 \oplus h(ID_i \parallel PW_i)$, $PV_i^{new} = GC_2 \oplus h(N_2 \parallel PW_i) \oplus h(TI_i^{new} \parallel N_3)$ and $IV_i^{new} = GC_3 \oplus TI_i^{new} \oplus h(TI_i \parallel N_3)$. Lastly, it changes (NV_i, PV_i, IV_i) into $(NV_i^{new}, PV_i^{new}, IV_i^{new})$.

3.4 Password Change

1. U_i puts his or her smart card in a device and enters ID_i and PW_i. Then, the smart card calculates $N_1 = NV_i \oplus h(ID_i \parallel PW_i)$, $TI_i = h(N_1 \parallel ID_i)$ and $TP_i = h(N_1 \parallel PW_i)$.
2. U_i chooses random nonces N_4 and N_5, and computes $TI_i^{new} = h(N_4 \parallel ID_i)$, $UC_7 = PV_i \oplus TP_i \oplus N_5$, $UC_8 = IV_i \oplus TI_i \oplus TI_i^{new} \oplus h(N_5 \parallel TI_i)$, $UC_9 = ID_i \oplus h(N_5 \parallel TI_i^{new})$ and $UC_{10} = h(ID_i \parallel TI_i \parallel TI_i^{new} \parallel N_5)$. After the calculation, U_i sends the message $CM_1 = \{TI_i, UC_7, UC_8, UC_9, UC_{10}\}$ to GW.
3. GW calculates $N_5 = UC_7 \oplus h(ID_{GW} \parallel gs \parallel TI_i)$, $TI_i^{new} = UC_8 \oplus h(TI_i \parallel gs) \oplus h(N_5 \parallel TI_i)$ and $ID_i = UC_9 \oplus h(N_5 \parallel TI_i^{new})$ first. Next, it verifies whether ID_i is in its database and checks $UC_{10} \overset{?}{=} h(ID_i \parallel TI_i \parallel TI_i^{new} \parallel N_5)$. If the verification is successful, GW computes $GC_5 - h(ID_{GW} \parallel gs \parallel TI_i^{new}) \oplus h(TI_i^{new} \parallel N_5)$, $GC_6 = h(TI_i^{new} \parallel gs) \oplus h(TI_i \parallel N_5)$ and $GC_7 = h(ID_i \parallel N_5 \parallel TI_i \parallel TI_i^{new} \parallel GC_5 \parallel GC_6)$. Then, $CM_2 = \{GC_5, GC_6, GC_7\}$ is sent to U_i.
4. U_i verifies $GC_7 \overset{?}{=} h(ID_i \parallel N_5 \parallel TI_i \parallel TI_i^{new} \parallel GC_5 \parallel GC_6)$. If it holds, U_i can input a new password PW_i^{new}. Next, the smart card calculates $TP_i^{new} = h(N_4 \parallel PW_i^{new})$, $PV_i^{new2} = GC_5 \oplus h(TI_i^{new} \parallel N_5) \oplus TP_i^{new}$, $IV_i^{new2} = GC_6 \oplus h(TI_i \parallel N_5) \oplus TI_i^{new}$ and $NV_i^{new2} = h(ID_i \parallel PW_i^{new}) \oplus N_4$. Finally, (NV_i, PV_i, IV_i) are replaced with $(NV_i^{new2}, PV_i^{new2}, IV_i^{new2})$.

4 Cryptanalysis of Wu et al.'s Protocol

4.1 User Impersonation Attack

In Wu et al.'s protocol, when an attacker $\mathcal{A}$ registers his account, he or she can get the smart card which contains the values of PV_A, IV_A, NV_A, P, p and q. With his or her identity, password and the smart card, $\mathcal{A}$ can impersonate other legal users. We illustrate the process below.

1. An attacker $\mathcal{A}$ gets the values of PV_A, IV_A, NV_A, P, p, and q from his smart card, and computes $N_{A1} = NV_A \oplus h(ID_A \parallel PW_A)$, $TI_A = h(N_{A1} \parallel ID_A)$ and $TP_A = h(N_{A1} \parallel PW_A)$.
2. $\mathcal{A}$ guesses arbitrary identity ID^*.

3. $\mathcal{A}$ selects random nonces $\alpha \in [1, q-1]$, N_{A2}, N_{A3}, and the sensor SID_j which he or she wants to connect, computes $TI_A^{new} = h(N_{A2} \parallel ID_A)$, $UC_{A1} = PV_A \oplus TP_A \oplus N_{A3}$, $UC_{A2} = \alpha P$, $UC_{A3} = IV_A \oplus TI_A \oplus TI_A^{new} \oplus h(N_{A3} \parallel TI_A)$, $UC_{A4} = h(N_{A3} \parallel TI_A^{new} \parallel UC_{A2}) \oplus ID^*$ and $UC_{A5} = h(ID_A \parallel TI_A \parallel TI_A^{new} \parallel SID_j)$ and sends $LM_{A1} = \{TI_A, SID_j, UC_{A1}, UC_{A2}, UC_{A3}, UC_{A4}, UC_{A5}\}$.

4. GW computes $N_{A3} = UC_{A1} \oplus h(ID_{GW} \parallel gs \parallel TI_A)$, $TI_A^{new} = UC_{A3} \oplus h(TI_A \parallel gs) \oplus h(N_{A3} \parallel TI_A)$, $ID^* = UC_{A4} \oplus h(N_{A3} \parallel TI_A^{new} \parallel UC_{A2})$ and checks if ID^* is in its database. If there is a match, $\mathcal{A}$ can impersonate the legal user whose identity is ID^*. Although ID^* is different from ID_A which is used to compute TI_A, GW cannot find out it.

4.2 Denial of Service Attack

In Wu et al.'s protocol, a smart card does not check the validity of password entered. That means that even if a user inputs incorrect password, the process continues until GW checks its validity. It leads to the denial of service attack as well as unnecessary waste of resources. The process is illustrated below.

1. An attacker $\mathcal{A}$ puts his or her smart card in a device, enters his identity ID_A and incorrect password PW_A^*, and calculates $N_{A1}^* = NV_A \oplus h(ID_A \parallel PW_A^*)$, $TI_A^* = h(N_{A1}^* \parallel ID_A)$ and $TP_A^* = h(N_{A1}^* \parallel PW_A^*)$.

2. $\mathcal{A}$ selects random nonce $\alpha[1, q-1]$, N_{A2}, and N_3, picks the sensor S_j, computes $TI_A^{new} = h(N_{A2} \parallel ID_A)$, $UC_{A1}^* = PV_i \oplus TP_A^* \oplus N_3$, $UC_{A2} = \alpha P$, $UC_{A3}^* = IV_A \oplus TI_A^* \oplus TI_A^{new} \oplus h(N_{A3} \parallel TI_A^*)$, $UC_{A4}^* = h(N_{A3} \parallel TI_A^{new} \parallel UC_{A2}) \oplus ID^*$ and $UC_{A5}^* = h(ID_A \parallel TI_A^* \parallel TI_A^{new} \parallel SID_j)$, and sends incorrect message $LM_{A1} = \{TI_A^*, SID_j, UC_{A1}^*, UC_{A2}, UC_{A3}^*, UC_{A4}^*, UC_{A5}^*\}$.

3. GW computes $N_{A3} = UC_{A1}^* \oplus h(ID_{GW} \parallel gs \parallel TI_A^*)$, $TI_A^{new*} = UC_{A3}^* \oplus h(TI_i^* \parallel gs) \oplus h(N_{A3}^* \parallel TI_A^*)$, $ID_A^* = UC_{A4}^* \oplus h(N_{A3}^* \parallel TI_A^{new*} \parallel UC_{A2})$ and checks if ID_A^* is in its database and $UC_{A5} \overset{?}{=} h(ID_A^* \parallel TI_A^* \parallel TI_i^{new*} \parallel SID_j)$. Since UC_{A5}^* does not match with UC_{A5}, GW terminates the process in this phase.

If an attacker $\mathcal{A}$ sends a large of incorrect messages as discussed above, the gateway GW will process the messages over and over. Eventually, it will cause GW to be paralyzed by draining GW's resources.

5   The Proposed Authentication Protocol

To overcome the security drawbacks of Wu et al.'s protocol, we propose an improved protocol based on Wu et al.'s protocol. Our protocol consists of four phases like Wu et al.'s.

5.1   Initialization

This phase is the same as the initialization phase in Wu et al.'s protocol.

5.2   Registration

User Registration

1. U_i picks his or her identity ID_i and password PW_i. After that, U_i selects a random nonce N_1 and calculates $TP_i = h(N_1 \parallel PW_i)$ and $TI_i = h(N_1 \parallel ID_i)$. Then, $\{TP_i, TI_i, ID_i\}$ is sent to GW.
2. GW computes $PV_i = h(ID_{GW} \parallel gs \parallel TI_i) \oplus TP_i$ and $IV_i = h(TI_i \parallel ID_i \parallel gs) \oplus TI_i$, and stores ID_i in its database. Also, GW issues a smart card containing (PV_i, IV_i, P, p, q) and sends it to U_i.
3. After getting the smart card from GW, U_i computes $NV_i = h(ID_i \parallel PW_i) \oplus N_1$ and $V_i = TP_i \oplus TI_i \oplus N_1$, and stores result values into the smart card.

Sensor Registration. There is no difference between this phase and the sensor registration phase in Wu et al.'s protocol.

5.3   Login and Authentication

1. U_i puts his or her smart card in a device and inputs ID_i and PW_i. Then, the smart card computes $N_1 = NV_i \oplus h(ID_i \parallel PW_i)$, $TI_i = h(N_1 \parallel ID_i)$ and $TP_i = h(N_1 \parallel PW_i)$.
2. The smart card verifies $V_i \overset{?}{=} TP_i \oplus TI_i \oplus N_1$. If the verification is successful, U_i selects random nonces $\alpha \in [1, q-1]$, N_2, N_3 and the sensor S_j.
3. The smart card computes $TI_i^{new} = h(N_2 \parallel ID_i)$, $UC_1 = PV_i \oplus TP_i \oplus N_3$, $UC_2 = \alpha P$, $UC_3 = IV_i \oplus TI_i \oplus TI_i^{new} \oplus h(N_3 \parallel TI_i)$, $UC_4 = h(N_3 \parallel TI_i^{new} \parallel UC_2) \oplus ID_i$ and $UC_5 = h(ID_i \parallel TI_i \parallel TI_i^{new} \parallel SID_j)$, and sends the login request message $LM_1 = \{TI_i, SID_j, UC_1, UC_2, UC_3, UC_4, UC_5\}$ to GW.
4. GW computes $N_3 = UC_1 \oplus h(ID_{GW} \parallel gs \parallel TI_i)$, $TI_i^{new} = UC_3 \oplus h(TI_i \parallel ID_i \parallel gs) \oplus h(N_3 \parallel TI_i)$ and $ID_i = UC_4 \oplus h(N_3 \parallel TI_i^{new} \parallel UC_2)$. Next, GW checks the validity of ID_i and $UC_5 \overset{?}{=} h(ID_i \parallel TI_i \parallel TI_i^{new} \parallel SID_i)$. If it holds, GW calculates $ss_j = h(SID_j \parallel gs)$ and $D_1 = h(TI_i \parallel SID_j \parallel ss_j \parallel UC_2)$ and sends $LM_2 = \{TI_i, SID_j, UC_2, GC_1\}$ to S_j.
5. S_j verifies SID_j and $GC_1 \overset{?}{=} h(TI_i \parallel SID_j \parallel ss_j \parallel UC_2)$. If it fails, the process is terminated. Otherwise, S_j picks random nonce $\beta \in [1, q-1]$ and computes $SC_1 = \beta P$, $SC_2 = \beta UC_2$, $SK_s = h_1(UC_2 \parallel SC_1 \parallel SC_2)$, $SC_3 = h(TI_1 \parallel SID_j \parallel SK_s)$ and $SC_4 = h(ss_j \parallel TI_i \parallel SID_j)$. Then, it transmits $LM_3 = \{SC_1, SC_3, SC_4\}$ to GW.
6. GW checks $SC_4 \overset{?}{=} h(ss_j \parallel TI_i \parallel SID_j)$. If the verification is successful, GW calculates $GC_2 = h(ID_{GW} \parallel gs \parallel TI_i^{new}) \oplus h(TI_i^{new} \parallel N_3)$, $GC_3 = h(TI_i^{new} \parallel gs) \oplus h(TI_i \parallel N_3)$ and $GC_4 = h(ID_i \parallel TI_i \parallel TI_i^{new} \parallel SID_j \parallel GC_2 \parallel GC_3 \parallel N_3)$. Finally, it sends $LM_4 = \{SC_1, SC_3, GC_2, GC_3, GC_4\}$ to U_i.
7. After getting the message from GW, U_i verifies $GC_4 \overset{?}{=} h(ID_i \parallel TI_i \parallel TI_i^{new} \parallel SID_j \parallel GC_2 \parallel GC_3 \parallel N_3)$ first. If it is wrong, the smart card stops the process. If not, the smart card calculates $UC_6 = \alpha SC_1$ and $SK_u = h_1(UC_2 \parallel$

$SC_1 \parallel UC_6$), and verifies $SC_4 \overset{?}{=} h(TI_i \parallel SID_j \parallel SK_u)$. If it is successful, the smart card computes $NV_i^{new} = N_2 \oplus h(ID_i \parallel PW_i)$, $PV_i^{new} = GC_2 \oplus h(N_2 \parallel PW_i) \oplus h(TI_i^{new} \parallel N_3)$ and $IV_i^{new} = GC_3 \oplus TI_i^{new} \oplus h(TI_i \parallel N_3)$. Lastly, (NV_i, PV_i, IV_i) are changed into $(NV_i^{new}, PV_i^{new}, IV_i^{new})$.

5.4 Password Change

1. U_i puts his or her smart card in a device and enters ID_i and PW_i. After that, the smart card calculates $N_1 = NV_i \oplus h(ID_i \parallel PW_i)$, $TI_i = h(N_1 \parallel ID_i)$ and $TP_i = h(N_1 \parallel PW_i)$.
2. The smart card computes $TP_i \oplus TI_i \oplus N_1$ and checks if the result value is equal to V_i stored in the smart card. If it is correct, the smart card ask U_i to input a new password PW_i^{new}.
3. After U_i inputs PW_i^{new}, the smart card calculates $TP_i^{new} = h(N_1 \parallel PW_i^{new})$, $PV_i^{new} = PV_i \oplus TP_i \oplus TP_i^{new}$, $NV_i^{new} = h(ID_i \parallel PW_i^{new}) \oplus N_1$ and $V_i^{new} = TP_i^{new} \oplus TI_i \oplus N_1$. Lastly, the smart card changes (PV_i, NV_i, V_i) into $(PV_i^{new}, NV_i^{new}, V_i^{new})$.

6 Cryptanalysis of the Proposed Protocol

In this section, we explain our proposed protocol is secure against various types of attacks. Table 2 shows the comparison of security properties between our protocol and other ECC-based protocols.

Insider attack. In user registration phase, a user submits $TI_i = h(N_1 \parallel PW_i)$ to GW. There is no way that an insider attacker guesses PW_i without knowing the value of N_1. Therefore, our proposed protocol can block the insider attack.

Table 2. The comparison of security properties

Attack and security property	Wu et al.	Shi and Gong	Choi et al.	Ours
Resistant to the insider attack	✓	✓	✓	✓
Resistant to the off-line password guessing attack	✓	×	×	✓
Resistant to the user impersonation attack	×	×	×	✓
Resistant to the gateway forgery attack	✓	✓	✓	✓
Resistant to the denial of service attack	×	✓	✓	✓
Resistant to the replay attack	✓	✓	✓	✓
Resistant to the sensor capture attack	✓	✓	✓	✓
Provide user anonymity	✓	×	×	✓
Provide mutual authentication	✓	✓	✓	✓
Resistant to session key leakage	✓	✓	✓	✓

Off-line password guessing attack. An attacker $\mathcal{A}$ can get the values of (PV_i, IV_i, NV_i) from U_i's smart card and eavesdrop the messages $\{LM_1^{old}, LM_2^{old}, LM_3^{old}, LM_4^{old}\}$ from the last session. $\mathcal{A}$ guesses ID_i and PW_i and calculates $TI_i^* = h(NV_i \oplus h(ID_i^* \parallel PW_i^*) \parallel ID_i^*)$ and $TP_i^* = h(NV_i \oplus h(ID_i^* \parallel PW_i^*) \parallel PW_i)$ by using the equation $N_1 = NV_i \oplus h(ID_i \parallel PW_i)$. $\mathcal{A}$ can also get the equations $UC_1^{old} = PV_i \oplus h(NV_i \oplus h(ID_i^* \parallel PW_i^*) \parallel PW_i) \oplus N_3$ and $UC_4^{old} = h(N_3 \parallel h(NV_i \oplus h(ID_i^* \parallel PW_i^*) \parallel ID_i^*) \parallel UC_2^{old})$. N_3 is absolutely necessary to get PW_i from the equations that $\mathcal{A}$ obtained. However, $\mathcal{A}$ can get N_3 only if he has the value of gs which is the secret key of the gateway. It is impossible for $\mathcal{A}$ to obtain gs so he or she cannot conduct the off-line password guessing attack.

User impersonation attack. Suppose that $\mathcal{A}$ tries to impersonate legal user using his or her own identity, password and smart card. $\mathcal{A}$ guesses other user's identity ID_i and uses it to calculate $UC_4 = h(N_3 \parallel TI_A^{new} \parallel UC_2) \oplus ID_i$. Also, he or she computes UC_1, UC_2, UC_3 and UC_5 and transmits the login request message to GW. After getting the login request message from $\mathcal{A}$, GW computes $ID_i = UC_4 \oplus h(N_3 \parallel TI_A^{new} \parallel UC_2)$, $TI_A^{new*} = UC_3 \oplus h(TI_A \parallel ID_i \parallel gs) \oplus h(N_3 \parallel TI_A)$. Then, GW checks $UC_5 \stackrel{?}{=} h(ID_i \parallel TI_A \parallel TI_A^{new*} \parallel SID_j)$. However, the verification check fails because $TI_A^{new*} = UC_3 \oplus h(TI_A \parallel ID_i \parallel gs) \oplus h(N_3 \parallel TI_A)$ which is calculated by GW is different from the original $TI_A^{new} = h(TI_A \parallel ID_A \parallel gs)$. It means that the user impersonation attack cannot succeed in our protocol.

Gateway forgery attack. To forge the gateway, $\mathcal{A}$ needs gs because gs is used to compute the values in messages to be sent to SID_j and U_i. However, $\mathcal{A}$ cannot obtain gs so our proposed protocol can block the gateway forgery attack.

Denial of service attack. $\mathcal{A}$ might conduct the denial of service attack by inputting the wrong identity or password and sending the wrong message to the gateway repeatedly. However, in the proposed protocol, the smart card verifies the identity and password entered before transmitting the login request message to the gateway. Therefore, even if $\mathcal{A}$ inputs the wrong identity or password continuously to paralyze the gateway, it never affects the gateway.

Replay attack. Suppose that $\mathcal{A}$ eavesdrops the previous login request message $\{TI_i, SID_j, UC_1, UC_2, UC_3, UC_4, UC_5\}$ and transmits the same login message to the gateway. After that, the gateway computes GC_1 and sends the message M_2 which is the same as the previous M_2. However, the sensor choose a new random nonce β and computes new SC_1 and SC_2 using β. Therefore, although $\mathcal{A}$ conducts replay attack using the previous login message, he or she cannot get the session key unless he or she knows the α which is used to calculate UC_2.

Sensor capture attack. Even if $\mathcal{A}$ gets SID_j and its secret number ss_j, $\mathcal{A}$ cannot obtain secret numbers of other sensors because there is no direct correlation between ss_j and ss_k of other sensor k. It means our protocol can prevent the sensor capture attack.

User anonymity. In our protocol, TI_i is used in the login and authentication phase instead of ID_i. Moreover, it is changed after every authentication phase. Therefore, even if $\mathcal{A}$ gets TI_i, $\mathcal{A}$ cannot get ID_i from TI_i and cannot trace the user's activities.

Mutual authentication. In our proposed protocol, U_i, GW and SID_j can authenticate each other by checking the messages from other party. First, GW verifies the login request message from U_i by checking whether UC_5 is correct. Next, SID_j also verifies the message from GW by checking whether GC_1 is correct. Then, GW checks SC_4 which is sent by SID_j is correct to authenticate SID_j. Finally, U_i authenticates GW by checking GC_4. Through these verification processes, our protocol can provide the mutual authentication.

Session key leakage. Although $\mathcal{A}$ can get the values of UC_2 and SC_1 by eavesdropping the messages between legal entities, $\mathcal{A}$ cannot calculate the session key because it is impossible to obtain SC_2 from UC_2. It means our protocol is secure against session key leakage.

7   Conclusion

In this paper, we reviewed Wu et al.'s ECC-based authentication protocol for WSN and showed that their protocol is vulnerable to the user impersonation attack and the denial of service attack. In order to overcome the security weaknesses of it, we suggested an improved ECC-based authentication protocol. Also, we verified that our proposed protocol can block various types of attacks and it is more secure than other ECC-based authentication protocols by analyzing protocols.

Acknowledgments. This research was supported by Basic Science Research Program through the National Research Foundation of Korea(NRF) funded by the Ministry of Education (NRF-2010-0020210).

References

1. Amin, R., Biswas, G.: A secure light weight scheme for user authentication and key agreement in multi-gateway based wireless sensor networks. Ad Hoc Netw. **36**, 58–80 (2016)
2. Chen, T.H., Shih, W.K.: A robust mutual authentication protocol for wireless sensor networks. ETRI J. **32**(5), 704–712 (2010)
3. Choi, Y., Lee, D., Kim, J., Jung, J., Nam, J., Won, D.: Security enhanced user authentication protocol for wireless sensor networks using elliptic curves cryptography. Sensors **14**(6), 10081–10106 (2014)
4. Das, M.L.: Two-factor user authentication in wireless sensor networks. IEEE Trans. Wirel. Commun. **8**(3), 1086–1090 (2009)
5. He, D., Gao, Y., Chan, S., Chen, C., Bu, J.: An enhanced two-factor user authentication scheme in wireless sensor networks. Ad hoc Sens. Wirel. Netw. **10**(4), 361–371 (2010)

6. Hsieh, W.B., Leu, J.S.: A robust user authentication scheme sing dynamic identity in wireless sensor networks. Wirel. Pers. Commun. **77**(2), 979–989 (2014)
7. Khan, M.K., Alghathbar, K.: Cryptanalysis and security improvements of two-factor user authentication in wireless sensor networks. Sensors **10**(3), 2450–2459 (2010)
8. Koblitz, N.: Elliptic curve cryptosystems. Math. Comput. **48**(177), 203–209 (1987)
9. Miller, V.S.: Use of elliptic curves in cryptography. In: Williams, H.C. (ed.) CRYPTO 1985. LNCS, vol. 218, pp. 417–426. Springer, Heidelberg (1986). https://doi.org/10.1007/3-540-39799-X_31
10. Shi, W., Gong, P.: A new user authentication protocol for wireless sensor networks using elliptic curves cryptography. Int. J. Distrib. Sens. Netw. **9**(4), 730831 (2013)
11. Turkanović, M., Brumen, B., Hölbl, M.: A novel user authentication and key agreement scheme for heterogeneous ad hoc wireless sensor networks, based on the Internet of Things notion. Ad Hoc Netw. **20**, 96–112 (2014)
12. Vaidya, B., Makrakis, D., Mouftah, H.T.: Improved two-factor user authentication in wireless sensor networks. In: 2010 IEEE 6th International Conference on Wireless and Mobile Computing, Networking and Communications (WiMob), pp. 600–606. IEEE (2010)
13. Watro, R., Kong, D., Cuti, S.F., Gardiner, C., Lynn, C., Kruus, P.: TinyPK: securing sensor networks with public key technology. In: Proceedings of the 2nd ACM workshop on Security of Ad Hoc and Sensor Networks, pp. 59–64. ACM (2004)
14. Wong, K.H., Zheng, Y., Cao, J., Wang, S.: A dynamic user authentication scheme for wireless sensor networks. In: IEEE International Conference on Sensor Networks, Ubiquitous, and Trustworthy Computing, 2006, vol. 1, pp. 244–251. IEEE (2006)
15. Wu, F., Xu, L., Kumari, S., Li, X.: A privacy-preserving and provable user authentication scheme for wireless sensor networks based on Internet of Things security. J. Ambient Intell. Humaniz. Comput. **8**(1), 101–116 (2017)
16. Wu, F., Xu, L., Kumari, S., Li, X., Shen, J., Choo, K.K.R., Wazid, M., Das, A.K.: An efficient authentication and key agreement scheme for multi-gateway wireless sensor networks in IoT deployment. J. Netw. Comput. Appl. **89**, 72–85 (2017)
17. Yeh, H.L., Chen, T.H., Liu, P.C., Kim, T.H., Wei, H.W.: A secured authentication protocol for wireless sensor networks using elliptic curves cryptography. Sensors **11**(5), 4767–4779 (2011)

Optimization of the Choice of Individuals to Be Immunized Through the Genetic Algorithm in the SIR Model

Rodrigo Ferreira Rodrigues[1,2], Arthur Rodrigues da Silva[1,2],
Vinícius da Fonseca Vieira[1,2], and Carolina Ribeiro Xavier[1,2(✉)]

[1] Department of Computer Science, Universidade Federal de
São João Del Rei - UFSJ, São João Del Rei, Brazil
[2] Graduate Program in Computer Science, Universidade Federal de
São João Del Rei - UFSJ, São João Del Rei, Brazil
carolinaxavier@ufsj.edu.br

Abstract. Choosing which part of a population to immunize is an important and challenging task when fighting epidemics. In this paper we present an optimization methodology to assist the selection of a group of individuals for vaccination in order to restrain the spread of an epidemic. The proposed methodology is to build over the SIR (Susceptible/Infected/Recovered) epidemiological model combined to a genetic algorithm. The results obtained by the application of the methodology to a set of individuals modeled as a complex network show that the immunization of individuals chosen by the implemented genetic algorithm causes a significant reduction in the number of infected ones during the epidemic when compared to the vaccination of individuals based on a traditionally studied topological property, namely, the PageRank of individuals. This suggests that the proposed methodology has a high potential to be applied in real world contexts, where the number of vaccines is reduced or there are limited resources.

Keywords: Genetic algorithm · SIR epidemiological model
Optimization in complex networks · Vaccination

1 Introduction

Vaccination is the most effective method in the prevention of infectious diseases [6]. Only in December 2017 more than 1.4 million vaccines were sent to Nigeria to prevent yellow fever, demonstrating the importance of vaccination in combating epidemics. Despite its benefits, several vaccination difficulties are still found, such as limited financial resources and the difficulty of total vaccination of a target population.

Epidemiological models are widely studied in the literature for the analysis and simulation of epidemic behaviors and, among them, the SIR model stands out for its simplicity of use and great accuracy in the simulations. Although the

O. Gervasi et al. (Eds.): ICCSA 2018, LNCS 10961, pp. 62–75, 2018.
https://doi.org/10.1007/978-3-319-95165-2_5

ability in modeling the infection dynamics of an epidemic, the original model does not consider the relationships and contact between individuals, and it is interesting to use a variation of the original model, because its dynamics are based on complex networks [12]. Infection, in the context of complex networks based SIR model, occurs through the contact of individuals taking into account variables such as the probability of infection or immunity of an individual.

Choosing individuals to be vaccinated can be understood as a problem of seed choices in a problem of maximizing influence on social networks. In order to define the optimal group of individuals to be vaccinated so that the epidemic spreads less, it would be necessary to test all possible combinations of individuals, characterizing such problem in the class of NP-hardness [9] problems.

Among the various optimization heuristics, genetic algorithms are one of the most important ones due to their low consumption of computational resources, their ease of implementation and satisfactory final results. In this sense, this work proposes a methodology for an efficient solution of the optimization problem of selecting a group of individuals to be vaccinated. The proposed methodology is to apply a genetic algorithm to SIR epidemiological model in order to determine which individuals are most suitable for vaccination in a resource-limited environment to restrain the spread of epidemic.

This paper is organized as follows. Section 2 presents some works from the literature related to the proposed methodology. Section 3 introduces the concepts of complex networks. Section 4 introduces the concepts of epidemiological models and describes the SIR epidemiological model. In Sect. 5 the concept of genetic algorithms is presented. Section 6 presents the proposed methodology. Section 7 presents the results obtained by the performed experiments and some discussion. Section 8 presents a conclusion on this work and points out future directions.

2   Related Work

Some works can be found in the literature aiming to choose a small subset of individuals in a network that maximizes the global reach in the network. The propagation models considered by the authors to model the spreading process are varied as well as the contexts of such works ranging from social influence to epidemiological control.

Chen et al. [4] propose a method of influence maximization considering Linear Threshold model [8]. They proposed a scalable algorithm for directed acyclic graphs (LDAG) applying Linear Threshold model for networks with millions of nodes and edges, obtaining good results when compared to other works from the literature [9].

Newman presents in [12] a study on the behavior of epidemics in social networks. The work shows how a large class of standard epidemiological models can be solved in several types of networks. In order to test the model, Newman simulates how a sexually transmitted disease behaves in a network using the SIR model. The model reflected well the transmission of the disease and the results were satisfactory according to the authors.

Bucur and Iacca [3] explore the problem of maximizing influence in social networks by using genetic algorithms and demonstrate how the use of simple genetic operators makes it possible to find viable solutions of high power of influence equal to or better than other heuristics known. Furthermore, it is observed that GA surprisingly provides less costly solutions over greedy algorithms.

3   Complex Networks

A network can be defined as a set of nodes or vertices linked by edges [1]. Complex networks are networks with non-trivial topological features (such as connection patterns between their elements that are not purely regular nor purely random). These resources do not occur in simple networks, such as random graphs, but in real systems modeling. Complex networks can be classified according to statistical properties such as the degree distribution and the agglomeration coefficient [2].

Within the classifications are the small world networks, proposed by Watts and Strogatz [16]. In this mathematical model, it is described the behavior of a complex network in which most of the connections are established between the nearest nodes, behaving like a small world. In this type of network, the average distance between any two nodes does not exceed a small number of nodes.

3.1   PageRank

Proposed by Page et al. [13], PageRank measures the importance of a page by counting the quantity and quality of links pointing at it.

In the calculation of PageRank, the internet is traveled as a network, where each node represents a page and each edge represents a reference from one page to another. A link to a page counts as a "vote". The metric assigns a value to each node of the network. The higher this value, the greater the importance of this node in the network. From the point of view of network theory, PageRank is a centrality metric and is generally used to measure the level of influence of a node in the network.

4   Epidemiological Models

Epidemiological models describe in a simplified way the dynamics of epidemic transmission. Such models can be divided into two categories, stochastic and deterministic. Stochastic models estimate the likelihood of infections (usually in small populations), allowing random variation of their inputs during the course of their execution [15]. In deterministic models, the population (usually large) is subdivided into groups where each group represents a stage of the epidemic. The dynamics of such groups are described by differential equations.

Due to the different dynamics during an epidemic, such as the arrival of new susceptible individuals, there are different models that include such variables, such as MSIR and SIS models, all based on the SIR model.

4.1 SIR Epidemiological Model

Developed by Kermack and McKendrick [10], this model considers a fixed population and divides it into 3 groups:

- Susceptible: Individuals who may be contaminated by other individuals.
- Infected: Infected individuals who may infect other susceptible individuals.
- Recovered: Individuals who have been infected but have recovered (or died). They are resistant to the epidemic and can not infect or be infected.

This model follows an unidirectional flow between the 3 groups. Each group represents a stage where an individual or group of individuals find themselves in relation to the epidemic. The migration dynamics between groups can be seen in Fig. 1, where each individual passes through the 3 stages following the order indicated by the arrows. It is worth emphasizing that the individual can only belong to only one group at a time.

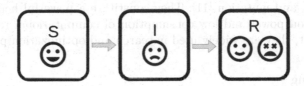

Fig. 1. Representation of the flow of individuals between the groups in the SIR model. (Color figure online)

The SIR model in its original form does not consider the interaction between the individuals, it only describes the size of each group at a time instant t and establishes how the functions of transitions between the groups are.

4.2 SIR's Mathematical Model

Considering $N = S(t) + I(t) + R(t)$ as a fixed population, Kermack and McKendrick describe the density of the Susceptible, Infected and Recovered group, respectively, at a time t through the following differential equations [10]:

$$\frac{dS}{dt} = -\beta SI, \tag{1}$$

$$\frac{dI}{dt} = \beta SI - \gamma I, \tag{2}$$

$$\frac{dR}{dt} = \gamma I, \tag{3}$$

where β is either the contact speed or infection of the disease and γ the average rate of recovery/death.

4.3   SIR Model over Networks

In addition to the differential equations model, the SIR model can also be implemented through a network [1]. In this way, each node in the network represents an individual in the population and each edge between individual represents an interpersonal contact, through which the epidemic can be transmitted.

At each iteration, the neighbors of an infected node are infected following a certain probability, represented by the probability of infection β. In addition, infected individuals also recover themselves following a probability, represented by the likelihood of recovery γ. In addition to the mathematical model, the network version also influences the spread of the epidemic.

5   Genetic Algorithm

Genetic algorithms (GA) are a subclass of evolutionary algorithms. GAs use techniques inspired by the theory of evolution, such as natural selection, heredity, recombination, and mutation [11]. They constitute a powerful heuristic due to their abstraction power and low consumption of computational resources, and due to this fact, they are widely used in search and optimization problems.

5.1   Modeling

Based on the natural selection process proposed by Darwin and Wallace in [5], it is assumed that in a population made up of individuals with diverse characteristics, individuals who are more adapted to the environment are more likely to perpetuate their characteristics through the process of reproduction. In this regard, for such simulation, genetic algorithms are modeled as follows:

- Gene: Features that compose an individual, usually assume either binary or positive integer values.
- Chromosome or Individual: Set of genes or characteristics, represents a solution for the problem to be solved by GA.
- Population: Set of chromosomes or solutions to be tested for the proposed problem.

5.2   Basic Operations

The genetic algorithm subjects the population to 4 steps at each generation:

- **Evaluation**: Through an evaluation function, each individual (or solution) is evaluated and a score (fitness) is assigned to it.
- **Parent Selection**: At this step a set of individuals is selected to cross their genes. Individuals with a higher score are more likely to be selected. This step can be performed in various ways such as roulettes, tournaments or even randomly.

- **Crossover**: From the set of selected parents, two parents are drawn and the crossing of their genes is performed, one of the crossing types used is the n-points crossing. The number of crossing points can be chosen according to the problem to be solved. This process is repeated until a new population of the original population size is obtained. The Fig. 2 represents the cross between two parents represented by the blue and red colors with a dashed line indicating the cut-off point. The resulting children are made up of half the genes from each parent. This stage is very important because it isn't only responsible for combining solutions, but also for producing even better solutions, guaranteeing the intensification of the search.
- **Mutation**: With the new population generated, the mutation stage is aimed at the exploration for new solutions. This process prevents the algorithm from getting stuck in optimal local solutions, preventing it from becoming stagnant. The mutation occurs randomly and with a low probability of occurrence. Its process is simple, the algorithm runs through its population, and for each gene of each individual it is generated a random number. If this number reaches the mutation threshold, the current gene value is changed to a valid random value.

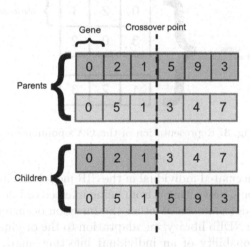

Fig. 2. One point crossing in genetic algorithm.

These 4 steps are repeated until the maximum number of defined generations is reached. For each generation, new individuals are generated from parents of the current generation who presented good solutions to the problem, thus causing a convergence for a group of individuals who are candidates for the solution at the end of the process.

6   Methodology

In order to model the spreading of diseases in small world networks, i.e., networks where any individual can be reached by any other with a small number of hops, the networks in this work were generated considering Watts-Strogatz model for small-world networks [16]. With this consideration, the experiment environment for the proposed methodology can be analogous to real world contexts, where it is well known that this phenomenon naturally occurs.

The Watts-Strogatz networks considered for the experiments were generated by NetworkX [7], a widely used library for generating and analysing complex networks. For the execution of the SIR model, the NDlib [14] library was used due to its efficiency and simplicity of use.

In the GA model created, the size of the chromosome is the number of available vaccines and consequently, a chromosome represents the individuals that will be vaccinated in the simulated scenario. Moreover, each gene of a chromosome represents a vertex from the network. In this way, each chromosome represents a set of nodes which will be vaccinated in the network and the solution represents a set of individuals which reduce the impact of an epidemic. The representation of the GA population is illustrated by Fig. 3.

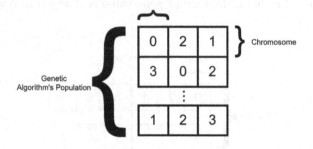

Fig. 3. Representation of the GA's population.

To simulate a vaccinated individual in the SIR model, the individual is moved to the recovered group, preventing it from being infected or infecting another one.

Due to the non-determinism of either the infection occurrence or recovery of an individual in the NDlib library, an adaptation to the original implementation was made. The probability of an individual infecting another individual was set as fixed for a complete execution of GA, however, random and different for each individual. Such decision was necessary because randomness in the SIR model significantly impacts its output, making it impracticable to investigate the behavior of the GA in the proposed methodology.

6.1   The Algorithm

Initially the algorithm loads the relations between the individuals from a text file and generates the corresponding graph, where each vertex represents an individual and the existence of an edge between two individuals represents the contact between them. After that, the genetic algorithm is started with a random population, where the genes of each chromosome can assume values v, where v $\geq$ 0 and v $\leq$ (population size of the graph - 1). Then the iterations of the genetic algorithm begin, and such iterations are terminated when the genetic algorithm reaches a fixed number of generations.

With each generation of the genetic algorithm, its population is crossed chromosome by chromosome, and each chromosome is evaluated using the SIR model. The result of the evaluation is the number of infected individuals obtained for that configuration. Such result will be the fitness value of the chromosome.

Evaluating a GA's chromosome means to execute the SIR model by moving the associated individuals of the chromosome into the recovered group. This action changes the dynamics of infections so that we can test which individuals make the epidemic spread less. The SIR model of each test is performed until all individuals in the infected or recovered group reach 0, with no further chances of infection. After all chromosomes are evaluated, the genetic algorithm advances one generation, performing all the steps described in Sect. 5.

When the genetic algorithm reaches the fixed number of generations, we will have a set of chromosomes where each one contains a set of individuals that cause the epidemic to spread less. The chromosome with the best fitness (fewer infected individuals) is considered as solution to the problem.

7   Results and Discussions

In order to evaluate the proposed methodology, three networks with different sizes (500, 1000 and 2000 nodes) were generated considering the Watts-Strogatz model for small-world networks. The created algorithm was executed 100 times for each scenario and the initial configuration is presented in the Table 1.

Table 1. Initial configuration of the algorithm.

Network	Initial number of infected	Number of vaccines	GA's generations
watts_strogatz_500	25	25	100
watts_strogatz_1000	50	50	100
watts_strogatz_2000	100	100	100

At the end of the 100 executions, some analysis can be performed considering the individuals' selection frequency in the set of individuals to be vaccinated, as presented in Figs. 4, 5 and 6, respectively for the networks with 500, 1000 and 2000 nodes (watts_strogatz_500, watts_strogatz_1000 and watts_strogatz_2000). The horizontal axis represents the number of times in which the individuals are considered for the vaccinated subset, while the vertical axis represent the number of individuals considered at each bin.

The results observed in Figs. 4, 5 and 6 indicate that, despite their sizes, the networks present a similar behavior, where many individuals were selected few times for vaccination and few individuals were selected many times for vaccination, as expected in a seed-choice problem.

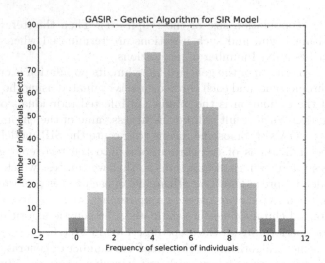

Fig. 4. Watts_strogatz_500 network graph.

In order to facilitate the interpretation of the data, a sample of the 15 most-selected individuals by the algorithm, considering all executions for each of the 3 networks, was collected. From these samples, 3 bipartite graphs, represented by the Figs. 7, 8 and 9 were constructed. The nodes on the left side of the figures (yellow nodes) are sorted from the sample by their PageRank [13] and the nodes on the right side (purple nodes) are sorted by the number of times they were selected for vaccination. The edges that connect the two columns of nodes are used to highlight the placement of the same individual in the two columns.

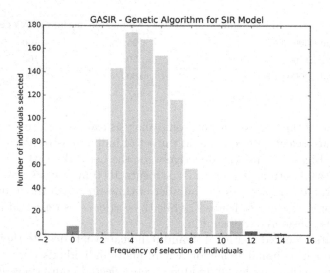

Fig. 5. Watts_strogatz_1000 network graph.

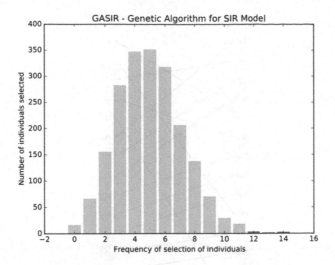

Fig. 6. Watts_strogatz_2000 network graph.

It is observed that even poorly-ranked individuals by PageRank, some of them were selected for vaccination with a high frequency. Considering that the dynamics of the epidemic has some randomness, the appearance of these individuals more than once indicates that it probably plays an important role in the

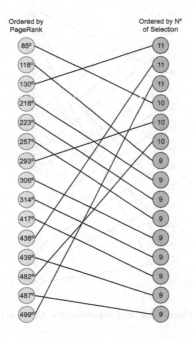

Fig. 7. Relation between PageRank and selection for the watts_strogatz_500 network.

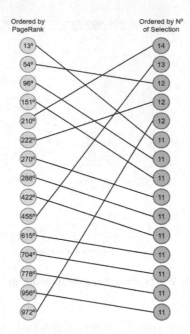

Fig. 8. Relation between PageRank and selection for the watts_strogatz_1000 network.

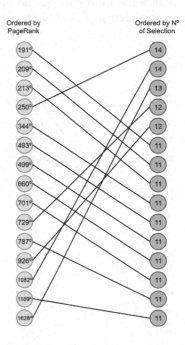

Fig. 9. Relation between PageRank and selection for the watts_strogatz_2000 network.

transmission of the epidemic and carrying out its vaccination will cause it to play a "barrier" role, changing the way the epidemic spreads.

The convergence of GA to the watts_strogatz_500, watts_strogatz_1000 e watts_strogatz_2000 networks can be seen in the Figs. 10, 11 and 12 respectively. The lines indicate the number of infected during the GA generations: the green one indicates the best convergence, the red one indicates the worst, and the blue one indicates the average case.

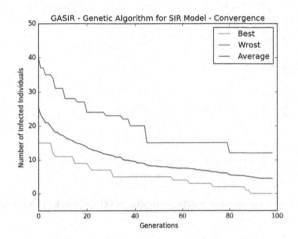

Fig. 10. GA's convergence for watts_strogatz_500 network. (Color figure online)

As it can be seen in the Fig. 10 which represents the network watts_strogatz_500, in the best case, it is noted that the algorithm initially manages to contain the epidemic for the total of 10 individuals, reaching none infected at the end of the process in a network of 500 individuals.

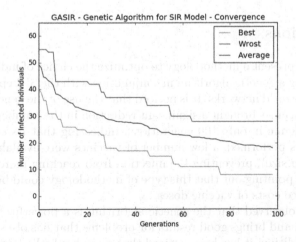

Fig. 11. GA's convergence for watts_strogatz_1000 network. (Color figure online)

As can be seen in the Fig. 11 which represents the network watts_strogatz_1000, in the best case, the algorithm initially manages to contain the epidemic for the total of 40 individuals, ending with 10 infected individuals in a total network of 1000 ones.

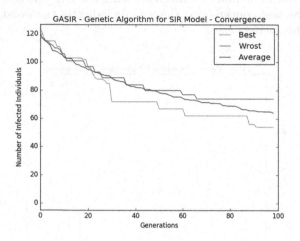

Fig. 12. GA's convergence for watts_strogatz_2000 network. (Color figure online)

As can be seen in the Fig. 12 which represents the watts_strogatz_2000 network, that contains 2000 individuals, in the best case the number of infected fell from 120 to just over 60 individuals, indicating that the epidemic was contained, early in the algorithm, to 6% of the population and reaching just over 3% at the end of the process.

A significant reduction in the number of infected individuals is observed, even in the worst cases of GA convergence.

8   Conclusions

In this work we present a methodology to optimize the choice of individuals to be immunized using a genetic algorithm in conjunction with the SIR epidemiological model on small-world networks. It is noticed that the use of the genetic algorithm to choose the vaccines brought a significant reduction in the number of infections during the epidemic in only 100 generations, indicating that its convergence is fast. In the tests performed, a low number of vaccines were available (5% of the total population size), preventing the infection from reaching more than 95% of the population, pointing out that this type of methodology could be used in case of need to reduce costs of vaccine doses.

It has been observed that the genetic algorithm is a powerful tool, has easy implementation and brings good results for problems that has objective function unknown. In addition, it has been noticed that an individual's PageRank on the network does not necessarily reflect on its selection for vaccination, pointing out that such a measure would not necessarily bring good results if used for the random selection of individuals for vaccination. For future studies, it may be investigated how AG calibration may influence the choice of subjects to be immunized.

References

1. Barabási, A.L.: Network Science. Cambridge University Press, Cambridge (2016)
2. Boccaletti, S., Latora, V., Moreno, Y., Chavez, M., Hwang, D.U.: Complex networks: structure and dynamics. Phys. Rep. **424**(4–5), 175–308 (2006)
3. Bucur, D., Iacca, G.: Influence maximization in social networks with genetic algorithms. In: Squillero, G., Burelli, P. (eds.) EvoApplications 2016. LNCS, vol. 9597, pp. 379–392. Springer, Cham (2016). https://doi.org/10.1007/978-3-319-31204-0_25
4. Chen, W., Yuan, Y., Zhang, L.: Scalable influence maximization in social networks under the linear threshold model. In: 2010 IEEE 10th International Conference on Data Mining (ICDM), pp. 88–97. IEEE (2010)
5. Darwin, C., Wallace, A.: On the tendency of species to form varieties; and on the perpetuation of varieties and species by natural means of selection. Zool. J. Linn. Soc. **3**(9), 45–62 (1858)
6. Control of the Centers for Disease Control and Prevention, et al.: A CDC framework for preventing infectious diseases. Sustaining the essentials and innovating for the future. CDC, Atlanta (2011)
7. Hagberg, A., Schult, D., Swart, P.: NetworkX library developed at the Los Alamos national laboratory labs library (DOE) by the university of California (2004). https://networkx.lanl.gov
8. Kempe, D., Kleinberg, J., Tardos, É.: Maximizing the spread of influence through a social network. In: Proceedings of the Ninth ACM SIGKDD International Conference on Knowledge Discovery and Data Mining, pp. 137–146. ACM (2003)
9. Kempe, D., Kleinberg, J., Tardos, É.: Influential nodes in a diffusion model for social networks. In: Caires, L., Italiano, G.F., Monteiro, L., Palamidessi, C., Yung, M. (eds.) ICALP 2005. LNCS, vol. 3580, pp. 1127–1138. Springer, Heidelberg (2005). https://doi.org/10.1007/11523468_91
10. Kermack, W.O., McKendrick, A.G.: A contribution to the mathematical theory of epidemics. Proc. Roy. Soc. Lond. A: Math. Phys. Eng. Sci. **115**, 700–721 (1927)
11. Mitchell, M.: An Introduction to Genetic Algorithms. MIT press, Cambridge (1998)
12. Newman, M.E.: Spread of epidemic disease on networks. Phys. Rev. E **66**(1), 016128 (2002)
13. Page, L., Brin, S., Motwani, R., Winograd, T.: The pagerank citation ranking: Bringing order to the web. Tech. rep, Stanford InfoLab (1999)
14. Rossetti, G., Milli, L., Rinzivillo, S., Sîrbu, A., Pedreschi, D., Giannotti, F.: NDlib: a python library to model and analyze diffusion processes over complex networks. Int. J. Data Sci. Analytics **5**, 1–19 (2017)
15. Trottier, H., Philippe, P.: Deterministic modeling of infectious diseases: theory and methods. Internet J. Infect. Dis. **1**(2), 3 (2001)
16. Watts, D.J., Strogatz, S.H.: Collective dynamics of 'small-world' networks. Nature **393**(6684), 440–442 (1998)

RUM: An Approach to Support Web Applications Adaptation During User Browsing

Leandro Guarino de Vasconcelos[1]([✉]), Laércio Augusto Baldochi[2],
and Rafael Duarte Coelho dos Santos[1]

[1] National Institute for Space Research, Av. dos Astronautas, 1758,
Sao Jose dos Campos 12227-010, Brazil
leandro.guarino@lit.inpe.br, rafael.santos@inpe.br
[2] Federal University of Itajuba, Av. BPS, 1303, Itajuba 37500-903, Brazil
baldochi@unifei.edu.br
http://www.inpe.br

Abstract. In order to fulfill the needs and preferences of today's web users, adaptive Web applications have been proposed. Existing adaptation approaches usually adapt the content of pages according to the user interest. However, the adaptation of the interface structure to meet user needs and preferences is still incipient. In addition, building adaptive Web applications requires a lot of effort from developers. In this paper, we propose an approach to support the development of adaptive Web applications, analyzing the user behavior during navigation, and exploring the mining of client logs. In our approach, called RUM (Real-time Usage Mining), user actions are collected in the application's interface and processed synchronously. Thus, we are able detect behavioral patterns for the current application user, while she is browsing the application. Facilitating its deployment, RUM provides a toolkit which allows the application to consume information about the user behavior. By using this toolkit, developers are able to code adaptations that are automatically triggered in response to the data provided by the toolkit. Experiments were conducted on different websites to demonstrate the efficiency of the approach to support interface adaptations that improve the user experience.

Keywords: User behavior analysis · Web usage mining
Adaptive web applications

1 Introduction

Currently the Web is pervasive in everyday life. It is hard to imagine modern life without e-commerce, e-government, home banking, news portals, video streaming and other services available on the Web. As more and more people rely on these services, more data is generated, making the Web larger each day. In such a large hyperspace, it is easy to feel lost during navigation.

© Springer International Publishing AG, part of Springer Nature 2018
O. Gervasi et al. (Eds.): ICCSA 2018, LNCS 10961, pp. 76–91, 2018.
https://doi.org/10.1007/978-3-319-95165-2_6

In order to fulfill the needs of modern Web users, applications need to present the right content at the right time [1]. Thus, to anticipate the user's needs, it is paramount to get knowledge about her. Therefore, analyzing the user's behavior in web applications is becoming more relevant.

Ten years ago, Velasquez and Palade [1] stated that future web applications would be able to adapt content and structure to fulfill user's needs. However, after a decade, this is not a reality in most web applications. Adapting content is becoming more common, specially because companies have found the opportunity to profit by presenting personalized ads to web users. However, the adaptation of the interface is still incipient in order to meet user's needs and preferences.

By analyzing the behavior of users while interacting with applications, it is possible to acquire information that allows understanding their needs and preferences. Therefore, it is paramount to record the details regarding the user's interaction with the application, which is done using logs. Web applications can provide two types of logs: server logs and client logs.

In order to reveal the user's behavior expressed in logs, they must be processed. Web Usage Mining (WUM) techniques have been proposed in order to extract knowledge from logs. By exploiting this knowledge, it is possible to write applications that are able to customize the user's experience. For this reason, WUM is an important tool for e-marketing and e-commerce professionals. This paper presents an approach that explores the processing of client logs to support the construction of adaptive web applications. Called RUM (Real-time Usage Mining), our approach logs the user's interaction in order to (i) support the remote and automatic usability evaluation in web applications and (ii) detect user's behavior patterns in these applications.

By leveraging our previous work on usability evaluation [2,3], RUM provides a service that evaluates the usability of tasks performed by users while they browse web applications. This service allows the detection of users who might have been having difficulties to accomplish tasks. Thus, during user's browsing, the application may consume the result of the usability evaluation, allowing the developer to code interface adaptations that are triggered whenever an usability problem is detected.

The detection of behavior patterns is performed by exploring an automated knowledge discovery process in the collected logs. User profiles may then be associated to the detected patterns, which allows the developer to code profile-based adaptations. Therefore, when a pattern associated to a profile is detected, the application is able to adapt its interface in order to fulfill the user's needs and preferences.

In order to facilitate the adoption of the RUM approach, we implemented a toolkit that encapsulates its services. The main goal of TAWS (Toolkit for Adaptive Web Sites) is to reduce the coding effort to develop adaptive web applications. By using TAWS, developers have transparent access to services that collect and analyze logs, perform usability evaluation of tasks and execute the knowledge discovery in the collected logs. Thus, the developer put effort only to code actions for adaptation that may be triggered in response to the data provided by the toolkit.

We performed two experiments to evaluate our approach. The first aimed to demonstrate how developers may benefit from our usability evaluation service in order to code adaptive applications that aid users who are experiencing difficulties to accomplish tasks. The second experiment exploited the automated knowledge process provided by RUM to support the identification of usage patterns, which were used to adapt the applications in order to improve the user's experience. The two experiments provided good results, showing that RUM is effective to support the development of adaptive web applications.

This paper is organized as follows. Section 2 describes the previous work that motivated the development of the RUM approach. Section 3 presents the RUM approach, detailing its architecture and its main features. On Sect. 5, we present the experiments performed to evaluate the effectiveness of our approach to support the construction of adaptive web applications through detecting behavioral patterns. Section 6 compares and contrasts RUM to similar work reported in the literature. Finally, on Sect. 7 we summarize the contributions of our approach.

2   Previous Work

The World Wide Web presents a clear structural pattern in which websites are composed of a collection of pages that, in turn, consist of elements such as hyperlinks, tables, forms, etc., which are usually grouped by particular elements such as DIV and SPAN. By exploring this pattern, and considering that interface elements are typically shared among several pages, we proposed COP [2], an interface model that aims to facilitate the definition of tasks.

The main concepts in COP are Container, Object, and Page. An object is any page element that the user may interact with, such as hyperlinks, text fields, images, buttons, etc. A container is any page element that contains one or more objects. Finally, a page is an interface that includes one or more containers.

Besides exploiting the fact that containers and objects may appear in several pages, the COP model also exploits the similarities of objects and containers within a single page. In any given page, an object may be unique (using its id) or similar to other objects in terms of formatting and content. The same applies to containers: a container may be identified in a unique way, or it may be classified as similar to other containers, but only in terms of formatting.

The COP model was the foundation for the development of USABILICS [2], a task-oriented remote usability evaluation system. USABILICS evaluates the execution of tasks by calculating the similarity among the sequence of events produced by users and those previously captured by evaluators. By using USABILICS, evaluators may benefit from the COP model to define generic tasks, thus saving time and effort to evaluate tasks. The usability evaluation approach provided by USABILICS is composed of four main activities: task definition, logging, task analysis, and recommendations.

1. **Task definition.** USABILICS provides a task definition tool called Usa-Tasker [2], which allows developers to define tasks by simply interacting with the application's GUI. UsaTasker provides a user-friendly interface for the management of tasks, where the evaluator can create (record), view, update and delete tasks. For recording a task, all that is required is to use the application as it is expected from the end user. While the evaluator surfs the application interface, she is prompted with generalization/specialization options, as specified by the COP model.
2. **Logging.** Our solution exploits a Javascript client application that recognizes all page elements using the Document Object Model (DOM) and binds events to these elements, allowing the logging of user interactions such as mouse movements, scrolling, window resizing, among others. Events generated by the pages of the application, such as *load* and *unload* are also captured. Periodically, the client application compresses the logs and send them to a server application.
3. **Task analysis.** We perform task analysis by comparing the sequence of events recorded for a given task and the corresponding sequence captured from the end users' interactions. The similarity between these sequences provides a metric of efficiency. The percentage of completeness of a task provides a metric of effectiveness. Based on these parameters, we proposed a metric for evaluating the usability of tasks called the usability index [2].
4. **Recommendations.** USABILICS is able to identify wrong actions performed by end users and the interface components associated to them. By analyzing a set of different tasks presenting low usability, we found out that wrong actions are mainly related to hyperlink clicks, to the opening of pages, to the scrolling in pages and the interaction with forms. We defined six recommendations for fixing these issues. An experiment [2] showed that, by following our recommendations, developers were able to improve the usability of web applications.

A restriction of the USABILICS tool was the inability to define and analyze tasks on mobile devices, such as smartphones and tablets. To address this limitation, we developed a tool called MOBILICS [3], which extends the main modules of USABILICS in order to support the usability evaluation of mobile web applications.

Both the USABILICS and MOBILICS tools perform the usability evaluation after users finish their interactions. However, detecting users' difficulties during browsing is essential to help them achieve the desired goals in the web application. Therefore, these previous research have motivated the development of the approach presented in this paper.

3 The RUM Approach

The RUM approach was planned to provide information regarding the user's behavior in web applications. To achieve this goal we designed a modular architecture to provide facilities for logging, storing, processing and analyzing client logs. Figure 1 depicts RUM's architecture, which is organized in five modules:

1. **Log collection:** collects and stores the user's actions performed in the application's interface;
2. **Task analysis:** provides the remote and automatic usability evaluation during navigation; it evaluates tasks previously defined by the application specialist;
3. **Automated KDD:** detects behavior or usage patterns exploring the navigation history of past users;
4. **Knowledge repository:** stores and processes the detected behavior patterns, using parameters provided by the application specialist;
5. **Services:** listens to requests from the web application, providing information regarding the user's behavior during navigation.

In Fig. 1, the arrows depict the data flow among modules and the numbers on arrows indicate the flow sequence. Initially, as illustrated by arrow 1, the Logging module detects the user's actions on the application's interface, considering the specificities of the input device (desktop, tablet, smartphone). Following, as depicted by arrows 2 and 3, the detected actions are converted to logs in order to be processed by the Task Analysis and Automated KDD modules.

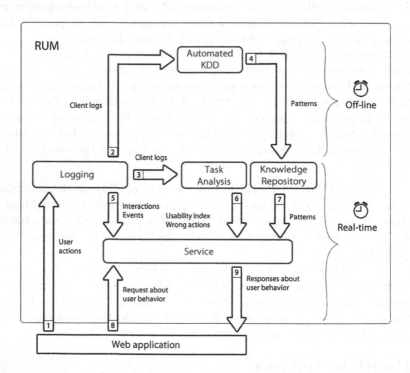

Fig. 1. Architecture of the RUM approach

The detected behavior patterns feed the Knowledge Repository module (arrow 4), which is responsible for defining the relevance of each pattern.

As the user's behavior changes over time, this module is responsible for managing patterns accordingly.

While the user is browsing, the web application may interact with the Service module to request information regarding the user's actions (arrow 8). Based on this information, preprogrammed interface adaptations may be triggered. Arrow 9 depicts the response for a given request. Possible responses are the last actions of the current user (arrow 5), the result of the usability evaluation during navigation (arrow 6), and the behavior patterns performed by the active user (arrow 7).

The details of each module of RUM's architecture are presented in depth in the following subsections.

3.1   Log Collection

The Logging module is responsible for organizing the collected logs as a directed graph containing two types of nodes: (i) interaction nodes and (ii) user action nodes. An interaction node represents the user's session in the web application and, therefore, contains general information regarding the whole session, such as initial time, final time, used browser and operational system. On the other hand, action nodes store the actions performed by the user on the application's interface, including mouse actions, scrolling, touch events, etc. The following sections present the Task Analysis module and the knowledge discovery automated process.

3.2   Task Analysis

In our previous work, we proposed a task-based approach for the automatic and remote usability evaluation of web applications. In order to evaluate our approach, we developed a tool called USABILICS, which performs the automatic and remote usability evaluation in desktop-based web applications [2]. We then evolved our tool to support the usability evaluation of mobile web applications, i.e., applications designed to execute on mobile devices, such as smartphones and tablets [3].

USABILICS performs usability evaluation asynchronously, after gathering and storing the logs of several users. In the current research, we leveraged this previous work in order to analyze the usability of the user *while* she is performing a task.

The goal of the usability evaluation in RUM is to provide information regarding the current user's interactions, as soon as it detects users that are facing difficulties to perform tasks. When struggling users are detected, interface adaptations may be triggered to support them.

As RUM aims at supporting the construction of adaptive web applications, the task analysis module performs the usability evaluation during navigation, in contrast to USABILICS, which performs the evaluation asynchronously. While the user browses the application, an algorithm compares the user's navigational path to optimal paths previously recorded by the application specialist. This way, it is possible to detect when the user starts and finishes a given task. As soon as the algorithm detects the execution of a task, it is possible to provide information regarding the user's interaction, such as (i) the task that is being performed; (ii) the usability index of the task being executed or already executed; and (iii) the wrong actions executed while performing a task. The application developer may explore this information to write adaptations in order to support users facing difficulties to perform tasks.

The definition of tasks is not feasible or relevant for all web applications. In informational websites, for instance, a single action – or a slight number of actions – may represent a task. In a news portal, different paths may lead to the same article. Also, there are recreational web applications in which tasks are not clearly defined. To support adaptations in these applications, RUM offers a module that performs knowledge discovery in logs, which works in tandem with another module, the Knowledge Repository. Both modules are presented in the following section.

3.3 Knowledge Discovery in Logs

The Knowledge Discovery in Databases (KDD) is a well-established field of study and has proven to be effective to extract knowledge from databases. The RUM approach exploits KDD techniques to discover usage patterns in client logs.

Users in web applications present different needs and preferences, i. e., various user's behaviors. The KDD process in RUM aims to detect sequential patterns and association rules using attributes associated with the user's behavior.

The KDD process usually presents a set of steps, starting with the selection of the data to be processed and ending with the knowledge extracted from this data. Following, we present the steps in RUM's KDD process. The first four are automated processes.

Selection: In the first step of the process, attributes that characterize the user's behavior was chosen. For the selection of the attributes, the user's actions that indicate a decision, the actions that precede a decision and the structure of the Web pages were observed in different Web applications.

When using touch-based devices, users interact by rolling the screen vertically and reaching links that enable features or take them to other pages. During the interaction, different users perform tasks at distinct time intervals. Also, their ability with touch devices should also be observed. For example, inexperienced users on these devices tend to operate them more slowly, while users who use them more frequently usually perform more actions in a short time. In addition to the experience with mobile devices, the experience with the web application itself also influences the decisions and the browsing time of the user. We also noted that impatient users usually perform actions faster and, consequently, access more pages.

The result of this analysis was the selection of eight attributes that can be retrieved from the logs: interaction time, amount of clicks (touches), amount of scrolling actions, average time interval between the scrolling actions, maximum page area covered by the user, clicked links, visited pages, and amount of other actions.

From these attributes, four datasets are produced:

1. **Dataset "ClickedLinks":** contains boolean attributes that represent the clicked links in each interaction;
2. **Dataset "ProfileRules":** contains nominal attributes that represent value classes of each attribute: session duration, number of clicks, number of scrolling actions, average time interval between the scrolling actions, number of actions performed (events), maximum area viewed by the user and number of visited pages;
3. **Dataset "ProfileRulesByPage":** combines the attributes of datasets *ClickedLinks* and *ProfileRules* to reduce the granularity in extracting sequential patterns, to find more accurate sequences between pages;
4. **Dataset "TimeByPage":** contains nominal attributes that represent the clicked links in each interaction and the interaction time between clicks.

To find sequential patterns in datasets *ClickedLinks*, *ProfileRulesByPage* and *TimeByPage*, And extract the relation between the attributes of the dataset *ProfileRules*, the association rules technique was chosen. In the first three datasets, the existence of the transactional data model, in which there is a precedence relation between the instances, leads to the use of this technique. The reason for choosing the method for the dataset *ProfileRules* is the ability of the algorithms to detect associative patterns between attributes of the instances.

Preprocessing and Transformation: In this step, attributes are extracted from logs, and noisy data is eliminated. In addition, a program performs the transformation of the selected attribute set into nominal and binary attributes, which will be processed to allow the identification of sequential patterns and association rules.

Mining: In the fourth step, the transformed data is used as input in mining algorithms, according to the goals of each set of selected attributes.

Interpretation and Evaluation: In the last step, the applications specialist defines user's profiles for the web application. Following, she associates the detected patterns to the defined profiles, discarding patterns considered irrelevant. Moreover, the specialist may associate a given action to one or more patterns, allowing this action to be triggered when a user performs its associated pattern. It is important to notice that these actions are implemented by the application developer. Therefore, the role of RUM is to inform the web application about the occurrence of an action defined by the application specialist. By using this flexible approach, RUM may be adapted to any web application.

The knowledge discovery process is periodically executed, feeding RUM's Knowledge repository module with the detected patterns. The role of this module is to manage patterns using an incremental procedure. When a new pattern is detected, it is compared to patterns already known. If the new pattern already belongs to the repository, its priority is raised. In the other hand, if the new pattern is equivalent to a pattern previously discarded by the specialist, then this pattern is also discarded. By ranking patterns continuously, the knowledge repository module is able to deal with the change of behavior that happens over time. Therefore, patterns that stop being executed get low priority and, eventually, are discarded. Once a new pattern is stored in the knowledge repository module, it is ready to be compared to the navigation of an active user.

Following, we discuss the Service module, which aims to make the facilities provided by RUM available as services to web applications.

3.4 Service Module: Analyzing the User's Behavior Synchronously

The main feature of RUM's approach is the ability to analyze the user behavior while she is browsing the application. This synchronous support is provided by the Service module, which is responsible for providing the facilities provided by RUM as a set of services.

The service module provides to the web application: (i) the actions performed by the active user; (ii) the usability index and the wrong actions of any task of the application; and (iii) the patterns performed by the active user. By exploiting this information, the application developer is able to write code to adapt the application, solving usability issues, or adapting the application according to user needs and preferences.

In order to support the adoption of the RUM approach by web developers, we implemented TAWS – Toolkit for Adaptive Web Sites.

4   Implementation of the TAWS Toolkit

TAWS encapsulates log collection, processing, and analysis of user's behavior, reducing the effort of the application developer. An important feature of TAWS is the ease of deployment in any Web application, regardless of the resources used in the software development stage, because it relies on standard Web development technologies.

To provide scalability from small to large Web applications, TAWS is based on a distributed architecture, and its implementation includes relational and non-relational databases, data mining libraries and strategies to optimize the collection and processing of client logs.

In TAWS' architecture, the data structures of different database technologies are integrated. For the storage and manipulation of logs, the toolkit uses a NoSQL database for graphs, Neo4J. The results of task analysis and automated KDD process are stored in a document database, MongoDB.

In TAWS, this RUM module was implemented based on Web services, establishing communication between the Web application and the modules that process and analyze the logs. Thus, the information provided by the Web service feeds the Web application to support adaptations preprogrammed by the developer.

During browsing, the TAWS Web service receives requests from the Web application and, asynchronously, performs queries in the Log Collection, Task Analysis, and Knowledge Repository modules. For example, if the application requires the pages visited by the active user, the Web service performs a query on the real-time database of the Log collection mechanism. If there is a request about the behavior patterns executed by the active user, the Web service compares the user's actions to usage patterns stored in the Knowledge Repository.

For requests, the Web application uses a library, called *jUsabilics*. This library sends requests to the TAWS Web service asynchronously. After the Web service processes the request, TAWS returns the information queried to the Web application.

In Sect. 5, we present experiments for building adaptive Web applications using the RUM approach, which includes examples of using the *jUsabilics* library.

5   Experiments and Results

Modern Web applications are not only composed of simple HTML pages to display text. Web applications currently offer the user a variety of interactive features that make it easier to navigate, such as search boxes and links that load content asynchronously. In this scenario, the demonstration of the RUM approach requires Web applications with different user profiles.

Therefore, we conducted two experiments on different Web applications. In the first experiment [4], reported in Sect. 5.1, the purpose was to exploit usability evaluation during navigation in order to support users facing difficulties to accomplish tasks. In the second experiment, discussed in Sect. 5.2, the objective was to trigger adaptations at the interface consuming the results of pattern detection during user browsing.

5.1   Task Analysis During Browsing to Support Adaptive Web Applications

To demonstrate the effectiveness of the RUM approach on usability evaluation, we performed an experiment [4] with the challenge of improving the usability of a website during user's browsing. The goal of this experiment was to verify if the RUM approach is able to provide relevant information about the user's behavior during browsing, i.e. while the user is performing a task. Therefore, in this experiment, there is the integration of task analysis during browsing and the usage of the library *jUsabilics*.

By exploiting the services provided by the *jUsabilics* library, the application may request information regarding the usability index and the execution of wrong actions by the active application user. This way, it is possible to code adaptations in order to support users that are struggling to perform a task. The experiment described in [4] presented the results of an adaptation triggered during navigation in order to assist users to perform the task of buying an online course. The study showed that the performed adaptation reduced the number of wrong actions and improved the usability index when the user was having trouble to perform the task.

Task analysis covers many aspects of a Web application, but there is a need to understand user behavior even when he/she is not performing a task. For this, a second experiment was conducted to demonstrate pattern detection during browsing, consuming the results of the KDD module and Knowledge Repository.

5.2 Adaptive Web Application Based on Patterns of User Behavior

On some websites, there are well-defined user's profiles because there are usually specific content for each profile. At the National Institute for Space Research (INPE/Brazil), the most visited website provides information about the weather in Brazil and is called Center for Weather Forecasting and Climate Studies (CPTEC). According to information provided by the website developers, there are more than 2 million visits per month, resulting from a variety of user profiles, such as researchers, journalists and students, as well as the general public. On the CPTEC website, there is a specialized area on Weather (tempo.cptec.inpe.br), which provides technical and non-technical information on weather forecasting in the different regions of the Brazilian territory.

For ordinary citizens, the website offers the weather forecast by city, where the user can search for a city using a form. Moreover, the main website page shows the forecast for the Brazilian state capitals and towns where there are airports.

Daily, CPTEC meteorologists update on the website the result of different analyses, such as surface synoptic chart analysis, analysis of the satellite image from Brazil, analysis of maximum and minimum temperatures for the state capitals and analysis of the weather conditions for each region of Brazil. These resources are directed to researchers and journalists. For researchers interested in CPTEC data, weather information is available for the researcher to perform his synoptic analysis.

This experiment was conducted in partnership with the developers of the CPTEC website. Initially, TAWS was deployed on the site to gather user's interactions. For this, TAWS was hosted on a cloud server similar to the one used in the first experiment, with Linux operating system, Ubuntu Server distribution 14.04 64-bits, 2 GHz processor, 2 GB RAM Memory, and 40 GB hard drive.

In the first phase of the experiment, a sample of 60,664 sessions was collected from several devices, detecting more than 3.6 million events. With the collected logs, the automated KDD module became operational for the extraction of patterns. A feature of the Weather website is the existence of a single page that loads content dynamically, like many modern Web applications. Thus, between sets of attributes specified in Sect. 3, it was selected the set *ClickedLinks* for the experiment, which contains the links clicked on each interaction, to detect sequential patterns. This set was chosen with the purpose of analyzing how the user interacts with the central area of the page, which contains the links *Synoptic Analysis*, *Satellite*, *Weather Conditions*, *Maximum Temperature*, *Minimum Temperature*, and links for each region of Brazil.

Due to the innovation of the method proposed in this research, we decided to schedule a meeting with the website developers, who are experts on the site and know the different user's profiles and all the content available to the public. In this session, the patterns detected by the *toolkit* were presented for them. Sixty-six related sequences were identified, representing user's sequential patterns. A subset of these sequences is shown in Table 1.

Table 1. Example of the sequential patterns detected in logs of the website

Priority	Pattern
1	Weather Conditions, Maximum Temperature, Minimum Temperature, Satellite
2	Synoptic Analysis, Maximum Temperature, Minimum Temperature
3	Weather Conditions, Minimum Temperature, Satellite, Southeast
4	Weather Conditions, Maximum Temperature, Satellite
5	Weather Conditions, Minimum Temperature, Satellite

In a group, the specialists analyzed the sequences to infer the relation between each sequence and the known user's profiles. After the analysis, five actions for adaptation were associated with certain sequences selected by the specialists. The following list relates the actions for adaptation and the patterns associated with them. The actions chosen for adaptation aim to meet the specific profiles of researchers who access the CPTEC website. According to the specialists' point of view, they associate the detected patterns to the behavior of scientists, so this profile was chosen for adaptation.

1. Recommending "Do your Synoptic Analysis": Synoptic Analysis, Technical Bulletin
2. Recommending "Weather forecast for Brazilian semi-arid": Weather Conditions, Midwest, North, Northeast
3. Recommending to visit the subdomain "Observational data": Synoptic Analysis, Weather Conditions, Minimum Temperature, Satellite, Southeast
4. Recommending the new website about Satellite data: Weather Conditions, Minimum Temperature, Satellite, Southeast
5. Recommending the subdomain about "Numerical Weather Forecast": Brazil, Weather Conditions, Satellite

Since the patterns were associated with actions, TAWS has deployed again on the website to trigger actions. In the background, a script was implemented to measure acceptance of the suggested adaptations to the user.

On the website, the only implementation effort for the developer is a script to receive from the TAWS the patterns detected during navigation and trigger the preprogrammed adaptations.

In the second phase of the experiment, 86,070 interactions and more than 3 million user actions were collected. During the interactions, TAWS operated with all modules, from collection to detection of patterns selected from the Knowledge Repository. Adaptations were triggered as soon as the patterns were detected. Table 2 shows the results for each suggested adjustment, detailing how many times each one appeared to users and how many times they clicked. The ratio between the number of clicks and the number of views was called user's acceptance rate. We may observe that the pattern related to Numerical Weather Forecast was the most frequent, with 164 occurrences. However, the action that had the highest acceptance rate was the work on the Satellite page, resulting in 38.5% acceptance.

Table 2. Results of adaptations

Action for adaptation	Number of views	Clicks	Acceptance rate
1 (Synoptic Analysis)	82	21	26,0%
2 (Brazilian Semi-arid)	27	4	13,7%
3 (Observational data)	51	1	1,6%
4 (Satellite)	142	55	**38,5%**
5 (Numerical weather forecast)	**164**	33	20,1%
Total	466	114	24%

The experiment on the website tempo.cptec.inpe.br is considered satisfactory for evaluation of pattern detection during browsing. The results show that the adaptations were displayed 466 times (0.5% about the number of interactions in the analyzed period). It is important to emphasize that the adaptations selected by the experts were directed to specific profiles of researchers, who do not represent the majority of the users of the website. For example, in the same period, 7% of users (6,182) accessed the site to search the weather forecast for a particular city through the search form. Therefore, it is observed that there is a significantly larger volume of interested citizens on the website than researchers. According to experts, one factor that motivates researchers to access the site is the occurrence of a particular meteorological event, which did not occur during the experiment period.

The results of the experiment show that the RUM approach can detect patterns during browsing. Considering the adaptations suggested by the experts, there are improvements to be made. The hypotheses are that the patterns associated by the specialists with the actions need to be refined. However, the result shows that 114 users (24%) accepted the recommendations during browsing.

6 Related Work

Web user's behavior analysis has been investigated with different aims in the last decade. Serdyukov [5], for instance, explores behavioral data for improving the search experience, while other works exploit this type of analysis to improve data visualization [6], log mining [7] and to provide statistical analysis of user's data. The literature also reports works targeted specifically to certain kinds of web applications, such as e-learning [8].

Peska et al. [9] proposed a PHP component called UPComp that allows the usage of user preferences to support recommendations. UPComp is a standalone component that can be integrated into any PHP web application. Our toolkit, on the other hand, exploits a Javascript code that can be embedded in any web application, not only Web applications written in PHP.

Apaolaza et al. [10] developed a tool that is easily deployable in any web application and transparently records data regarding the user's actions in web pages. Differently, from RUM, the goal of this tool is to enhance the user's accessibility in web applications. Also, it does not support any analysis during navigation.

Thomas presented LATTE [7], a software tool that extracts information from the user's interactions and correlates patterns of page views to user's actions. These patterns can help Web developers to understand where and why their sites are hard to navigate.

Similarly to the TAWS toolkit, Google Analytics provides an API[1] that allows a web application to consume data in real time about the active user, such as the used browser, viewed pages, etc. Besides providing this same data, our toolkit also allows the web application to consume information regarding the usability of the application, such as user's wrong actions and the usability index of tasks. Moreover, our tool also detects behavioral patterns performed by the current user.

Abbar et al. [11] developed an approach that performs the analysis of the user's actions synchronously. However, the analysis is conducted on the content accessed by the user, unlike our approach, which analyzes user's actions performed on the application's user interface. The approach of Abbar et al. is targeted to support news websites, and its goal is to recommend relevant articles to the user during navigation.

Mobasher et al. [12] conducted research for creating adaptive websites with the recommendation of URL from the analysis of the user's active session. Khonsha and Sadreddini [13] proposed a framework to support the personalization of web applications. Their approach mines both the user logs and the content of the website, aiming to predict the next request for pages. None of these works provides a way to consume the analysis results synchronously in order to allow the adaptation of the interfaces during navigation.

---

[1] https://developers.google.com/analytics/devguides/reporting/realtime/v3/.

7 Conclusions

On the Web, analyzing user's behavior through logging has become increasingly important because of the need to build applications that fit the needs of each user. The motivation for this comes down to a question: "If people are different why do we make the same website for all individuals?"

The essence of the RUM approach is the mining of client logs to extract patterns of behavior. Such patterns are analyzed by the application specialist, in order to select the consistent patterns for the characterization of user's profiles. Patterns selected by the expert are compared during navigation with user's actions, and when they are detected, adaptations preprogrammed by the developer are triggered.

A significant contribution of this research is the ability to implement the approach in any Web application, through the TAWS toolkit. Thus, any Web application can become adaptive consuming information generated by RUM during the user's navigation.

The development of the RUM approach generated important contributions for research related to the analysis of user's behavior and the construction of adaptive Web applications, among which we highlight:

- The definition of the attribute sets for the knowledge discovery process of client logs, which can be applied to different contexts and scenarios of Web applications. With these attributes, the most important aspects of user's behavior are contemplated;
- The automated KDD process, which allows the application to learn user's behavior over time, detecting new patterns and discarding patterns that are no longer relevant;
- The usability evaluation during navigation, which contributes to the detection of usability problems while the user navigates, and therefore this allows to assist and maintain it on the website;
- Pattern detection during navigation, which gives the expert the ability to configure actions for adaptation to be triggered during user's interaction. These actions can help user's interaction or recommend relevant content.
- The TAWS toolkit, which implements the approach efficiently using strategies to optimize processing from log collection to detection of patterns during navigation;
- The *jUsabilics* library, which reduces the implementation effort in the Web application to consume user's behavior information.

References

1. Velasquez, J.D., Palade, V.: Adaptive Web Sites: A Knowledge Extraction from Web Data Approach, vol. 170. IOS Press (2008)
2. Vasconcelos, L.G., Baldochi, Jr., L.A.: Towards an automatic evaluation of web applications. In: SAC 2012: Proceedings of the 27th Annual ACM Symposium on Applied Computing, pp. 709–716. ACM, New York (2012)

3. Goncalves, L.F., Vasconcelos, L.G., Munson, E.V., Baldochi, L.A.: Supporting adaptation of web applications to the mobile environment with automated usability evaluation. In: Proceedings of the 31st Annual ACM Symposium on Applied Computing, SAC 2016, pp. 787–794. ACM, New York (2016)
4. Vasconcelos, L.G., Santos, R.D.C., Baldochi, L.A.: Exploiting client logs to support the construction of adaptive e-commerce applications. In: Proceedings of the 13th International Conference on e-Business Engineering, ICEBE 2016, Macau, China, pp. 164–169 (2016)
5. Serdyukov, P.: Analyzing behavioral data for improving search experience. In: Proceedings of the 23rd International Conference on World Wide Web. WWW 2014 Companion, Republic and Canton of Geneva, Switzerland, International World Wide Web Conferences Steering Committee, pp. 607–608 (2014)
6. Khoury, R., Dawborn, T., Huang, W.: Visualising web browsing data for user behaviour analysis. In: Proceedings of the 23rd Australian Computer-Human Interaction Conference, OzCHI 2011, pp. 177–180. ACM, New York (2011)
7. Thomas, P.: Using interaction data to explain difficulty navigating online. ACM Trans. Web 8(4), 24:1–24:41 (2014)
8. Kuo, Y.H., Chen, J.N., Jeng, Y.L., Huang, Y.M.: Real-time learning behavior mining for e-learning. In: Proceedings of the 2005 IEEE/WIC/ACM International Conference on Web Intelligence, pp. 653–656, September 2005
9. Peska, L., Eckhardt, A., Vojtas, P.: Upcomp - a PHP component for recommendation based on user behaviour. In: Proceedings of the 2011 IEEE/WIC/ACM International Conferences on Web Intelligence and Intelligent Agent Technology, WI-IAT 2011, vol. 03, pp. 306–309. IEEE Computer Society, Washington, DC (2011)
10. Apaolaza, A., Harper, S., Jay, C.: Understanding users in the wild. In: Proceedings of the 10th International Cross-Disciplinary Conference on Web Accessibility, W4A 2013, pp. 13:1–13:4. ACM, New York (2013)
11. Abbar, S., Amer-Yahia, S., Indyk, P., Mahabadi, S.: Real-time recommendation of diverse related articles. In: Proceedings of the 22nd International Conference on World Wide Web, WWW 2013, pp. 1–12. ACM, New York (2013)
12. Mobasher, B., Cooley, R., Srivastava, J.: Creating adaptive web sites through usage-based clustering of URLs. In: Proceedings of the 1999 Workshop on Knowledge and Data Engineering Exchange (KDEX 1999), pp. 19–25 (1999)
13. Khonsha, S., Sadreddini, M.: New hybrid web personalization framework. In: 2011 IEEE 3rd International Conference on Communication Software and Networks (ICCSN), pp. 86–92, May 2011

Gini Based Learning for the Classification of Alzheimer's Disease and Features Identification with Automatic RGB Segmentation Algorithm

Yeliz Karaca[1]($\boxtimes$), Majaz Moonis[2], Abul Hasan Siddiqi[3], and Başar Turan[4]

[1] University of Massachusetts Medical School, Worcester, MA 01655, USA
yeliz.karaca@ieee.org
[2] Department of Neurology and Psychiatry, University of Massachusetts Medical School, Worcester, MA 01655, USA
moonism@ummhc.org
[3] School of Basic Sciences and Research, Sharda University, Noida 201306, India
siddiqi.abulhasan@gmail.com
[4] IEEE, Junior Member, Istanbul, Turkey
basar.turan@ieee.org

Abstract. Magnetic Resonance Image segmentation is the process of partitioning brain data, which is regarded as a highly challenging task for medical applications, particularly in Alzheimer's Disease (AD). In this study, we have developed a new automatic segmentation algorithm which can be seen as a novel decision making technique that can help diagnose decision rules studying magnetic resonance images of the brain. The proposed work consist of a total of five stages: (i) the preprocessing stage that involves the use of dilation and erosion methods via gray-scale MRI for brain extraction (ii) the application of multi-level thresholding using Otsu's method with a threshold value of ($\mu_i > 15$ pixels) to determine the RGB color segment values (iii) the calculation of area detection (RGB segment scores) by applying our newly proposed automatic RGB Color Segment Score Algorithm to the predetermined RGB color segments (iv) creating the AD_dataset using the pixels of the lesion areas calculated via MR imaging (v) the post-processing stage that involves the application of Classification and Regression Tree (CART) algorithm to the AD_dataset. This study aims at contributing to the literature with the decision rules derived from the application of CART algorithm to the calculated RGB segment scores using our newly proposed automatic RGB Color Segment Score Algorithm in terms of the successful classification of AD.

Keywords: Diagnostics · Segmentation · Decision tree
Alzheimer Diseases

© Springer International Publishing AG, part of Springer Nature 2018
O. Gervasi et al. (Eds.): ICCSA 2018, LNCS 10961, pp. 92–106, 2018.
https://doi.org/10.1007/978-3-319-95165-2_7

1   Introduction

Generally speaking, Multidimensional Digital Image Processing (MDIP) is regarded as an area that has been attracting a lot of considerable interest in today's world and currently it can clearly be said that it works very closely with the realm of medicine. With computer techniques, MDIP of physical build are to be studied and adapted accordingly in order to aid with process of envisaging the obscure diagnostic characteristics which tend to be otherwise troublesome to analyze using planar imaging approaches [1–3]. Image segmentation is regarded as a technique with two fundamental purposes. Firstly, it aims to disintegrate the image into multiple sections to work on. In not so complicated situations, the surroundings are controlled adroitly in order to make it possible to extract solely the sections to be analyzed. Cluster formation approaches are not only one of the most intriguing areas, but also ones that focus on particle aggregation. Sometimes works tend to support the fact that core features of particle aggregation tend to be closely related with Cluster Morphology Analysis (CMA) [4].

Alzheimer's Disease (AD), which is a widespread type of mental deterioration, is observed in people as they get older in time. The signs and symptoms of AD can vary greatly such as difficulty in remembering recent events, problems with language, disorientation, behavior and mood swings. There are minimum 30 million AD patients in the world today. Whats more, as life expectancy increases gradually, there will be three times more people with AD by 2050 [1]. As a result of the aforementioned boost in AD cases, the detection of efficient biomarkers and curing people who display the early symptoms of AD is of importance [5–7].

More and more researchers seem to focus on the use of Magnetic Resonance Imaging in AD related work as it has a rather non-invasive, quite accessible, great spatial resolution and enhanced contrast amongst soft tissues [8]. Recently, various Magnetic Resonance Imaging biomarkers have been suggested in dividing AD patients into groups at diverse phases of the illness [8 10]. A considerable number of computational neuroimaging papers have given a lot of attention to anticipating people with a potential of having AD by making use of MRI, Chupin et al. [11], Klöppel et al. [12], Cuingnet et al. [13], Davatzikos et al. [14] with automatic segmentation and classification. Recently, image processing methods based the classification of Alzheimers Disease has been studied by Cheng et al. [15] with Cascaded Convolutional Neural Network, Zhu et al. [16] using regression methods, Zhang et al. [17], multi-modal multi-task learning method, Liu et al. [18], deep learning, Morra et al. [19] and Support Vector Machines ADA Boost algorithm.

In this study, the classification of MRI hidden diagnosis tends to have realized the pixels (R segment score, G segment score, B segment score) in lesion areas using the necessary image processing techniques. The current study aims to present a novel MRI-based technique as to detect potential AD patients by using computational algorithms for MRI analysis. Compared to studies with the intention of early diagnosis of AD in the literature, this study [11–19] is thought to make a difference with the calculation of RGB segment scores (area detection) via the application of our newly proposed automatic RGB Color Segment Score Algorithm to RGB Color segments (greater than threshold value (pixels)). Our proposed approach entails a number of stages combining certain concepts into a consistent system for the classification of Alzheimer's Disease in three core areas namely preprocessing, segmentation, and post-processing: (i) Gray scale MRI for the preprocessing stage which entails dilation and erosion using data from AD (MRIs of 5 individuals with Alzheimers Disease) and NC (MRIs of 5 Normal Control group) for brain extraction (ii) the calculation of the area detected (RGB segment scores) by applying our newly proposed algorithm (automatic RGB Color Segment Score Algorithm) to predetermined RGB segments via multi-level thresholding using Otsu's method (iii) creating the AD-dataset using the pixels of the lesion areas (R segment score, G segment score, B segment score) calculated via MR imaging (iv) the post-processing stage that involves the application of Classification and Regression Tree (CART) algorithm to the AD-dataset. This study relies on a combination of Classification and Regression Tree (CART) algorithm and our newly proposed automatic Red Green Blue (RGB) segmentation algorithm by via multi-level thresholding using Otsu's method.

In this study, for the first time in the literature, RGB segment scores (area detection) have been calculated via the application of our newly proposed automatic RGB Segment Score Algorithm to RGB color segments (greater than threshold value (pixels)) of the MR images that belong to the AD patients. This paper aims to contribute to the literature in terms of the successful classification of Alzheimer's Disease through the application of CART algorithm to RGB segment scores.

The content of this study can be summarized in three distinct parts. The following section describes the materials and methods. Section 3 presents experimental results for the proposed processing stages namely preprocessing, segmentation, and post-processing with the help of CART algorithm. Finally, Sect. 4 concludes this work by outlining some future research directions.

2   Materials and Methods

2.1   Materials

We have worked on a total number of 10 MRIs, which belong to the members of the Alzheimer Disease group (AD (5)) as well as Normal Control group (NC (5)), which have obtained from the Open Access Series of Imaging Studies (OASIS). The general public has been given access to OASIS by the Alzheimers Disease Research Center at Washington University and Dr. Randy Buckner of the Howard Hughes Medical Institute (HHMI) at Harvard University [20] in order to diagnose the administration of the algorithm images gathered from OASIS.

2.2   Methods

In this study, we have tried to provide some potential contributions. We have introduced the data from MRI which is relatively a novel segmentation hidden diagnostic attributes (pixels). The MR images, used in this study, belong to 5 individuals with Alzheimer's Disease (AD) and 5 Normal Control (NC). Our proposed method is a multi step procedure for the classification of Alzheimer's Disease (AD) and Normal Control (NC). Our proposed method is reliant on the steps specified below:

(i) Preprocessing stage: Of the morphological image processing methods, dilation and erosion have been selected in order to conduct brain extraction from the gray-scale MR images that belong to 5 individuals with Alzheime's Disease (AD) and 5 Normal Control (NC).

(ii) RGB segmentation stage: The RGB color segmentation values with the threshold value of ($\mu_i > 15$ pixels) have been determined via multi-level thresholding using Otsu's method. Through the application of our newly proposed automatic RGB Color Segment Score Algorithm (see Fig. 5) to the RGB color segments, area detection (RGB segment scores) has been calculated. And with the help of the pixels in the lesion areas calculated using (R segment score, G segment score, B segment score) the MRIs, AD_dataset has been created.

(iii) Post-processing stage: The decision rules are obtained by applying the CART algorithm to AD_dataset for a successful classification of AD.

Computations and figures have been obtained by Matlab environment.

Basics of Image Processing and Analysis. *Morphological Image Processing(MIP)* is a group of non-linear operations on the physical form or morphology of characteristics in any given image. Dilation of an image f by a structuring element s (denoted $g = f \oplus s$) yields a brand-new binary imaging $g = f \oplus s$ with the images in every position (x, y) of a structuring element's origin where the structuring element s hits input image. The erosion of a gray scale image f by a structuring element s denoted $f \ominus s$ that yields a brand-new binary image $f \ominus s$ with the images in every position (x, y) of a structuring element's origin at which that structuring element s fits the input image [21]. Given a grayscale image f and structuring element B, dilation and erosion can be defined as in Eqs. 1 and 2 below.

Here, (x, y) and (s, t) are the coordinate sets of the images f and B, respectively.

$$f \oplus s = max\left\{f(x - s, y - t) + (s,t)|(x - s), (y - t) \in D_f; (s,t) \in D_b\right\} \quad (1)$$
$$f \ominus s = min\left\{f(x + s, y + t) - (s,t)|(x + s), (y + t) \in D_f; (s,t) \in D_b\right\} \quad (2)$$

Histogram Matching. Histogram Matching forces the intensity distribution of an image to match the intensity distribution of a target [21]. It is a generalization of histogram equalization. The latter transforms an input image into an output image with equally many pixels at every gray level (i.e. a flat histogram) and is solved using the following point operation [21] as Eq. 3.

$$g^* = QP\left[g\right] \quad (3)$$

where g is the input image, g^* is the image with a flat histogram, and P is the cumulative distribution function. Let the histogram of an image g be denoted by $H_g(q)$ as a function of gray level $q \in Q$. The cumulative distribution function p of the images. g is as Eq. 4.

$$P[g] = 1/|g| \int_0^Q H_g(q)\, dq \tag{4}$$

Given Eq. 4, the problem of matching the histogram of an image g with the desired histogram of the image g^0 is solved as follows [21] (see Eq. 5).

$$g^0 = P^{-1}[P[g]] \tag{5}$$

In Eq. 5, the histogram matching involves two concatenated point operations, where P^{-1} is the inverse function of P. Practically the cumulative distribution function and its inverse function are discrete, which could be implemented using lookup tables [21].

In this study, of all the morphological image processing methods, dilation and erosion have been applied to the MR images in order to conduct brain extraction using gray scale MR images of 5 AD patients and 5 NC individuals.

Segmentation. Segmentation divides any given image into disjoint similar regions, where all the pixels of the same class are ought to have some common characteristics. Our study, in which a brand-new algorithm segments regions in an image, is based on determining the seed regions of that image. Subcategories of segmentation are namely manual, semi-automatic, and fully-automatic [22]. In this study, segmentation based on Magnetic Resonance Imaging (MRI) data is an essential part as well as time-consuming manual task performed by medical experts [23], [24]. Automatizing the procedure tends to be quite difficult due to the many different types detected in the tissues amongst various cases and in multiple situations showing some resemblance with the normal tissues. Magnetic Resonance Imaging is a leading technique that tends to provide rich information about the anatomy of the soft-tissues in humans. Numerous brain detection and segmentation approaches to distinguish from Magnetic Resonance Imaging are available. These methods are analyzed pinpointing the benefits as well as obstacles they hold in terms of AD diagnosis as well as its successful segmentation. Additionally, the uses of Magnetic Resonance Imaging detection together with segmentation in diverse processes are explained.

If the domain of an image is shown with I, the segmentation issue is to choose the groups $S_k \subset I$ all of which stand for the whole image I. Therefore, the groups that form segmentation are obliged to correspond to Eq. 6.

$$I = \bigcup_{k=1}^K S_k \tag{6}$$

If $S_k \cap S_j \neq \emptyset$ for $k \neq j$, and each S_k is connected. Segmentation approach identifies the groups which match specific anatomical structures as well as areas of interest in that image. If areas do not have to be connected, determining groups are named as pixel classification and groups themselves are named classes. Pixel classification in preference to classical segmentation is generally

a precious target when it comes to medical images, especially when disassoci-
ated regions of the same tissue demands identification. The thresholding, region
based, edge based, deformable models and classification methods are some of
the existing segmentation techniques. These methods are grouped as supervised
and unsupervised approaches. Approaches based on brain segmentation seem to
be divided based on different principles [23–26].

Multilevel Thresholding Method. Any given image is a 2D gray-scale intensity
function that holds N pixels with gray-scale s from 0 to $L-1$. Let I stand for
a gray-scale image with gray-scales as Eq. 7.

$$\Omega = \{r_i, i = 0, \cdots, L-1 | r_0 < r_1 < r_{L-1}\} \tag{7}$$

The goal of MTM is to separate the pixels of the image in m classes $C_1...C_m$
by setting the threshold $T_1...T_{m-1}$. Thus C_1 incorporates all pixels with gray-
scale $T_0 < r_k < T_1$, class contains all pixels in terms of $T_1 < r_k < T_2$ so on. Pay
attention to the maximum gray-scale $r_{L-1} + 1 = L$ is in class C_m at all times.
Thresholds T_0 and T_m are not calculated; they are described as 0 and L in the
same order as first mentioned.
    Imagine we have $m-1$ thresholds $\mathbf{T} = T_1...T_{m-1}$, in which $r_0 < T_1 < ... <$
$T_{m-1} \leq r_{L-1}$. Let $T_0 = r_0, T_m = r_{L-1} + 1$ an m-partition of Ω is as described
in Eq. 8.

$$C_1 = \{r_k | r_k \in \Omega, i = 0, ..., T_{i-1} < r_k < T_i\}, i = 1, ..., m \tag{8}$$

For every component, class mean is as Eq. 9.

$$\mu_i = \sum_{r_k = T_{i-1}}^{T_{i-1}} h_{r_k} \tag{9}$$

In this study, the most meaningful optimum threshold value in pixel values
of MR images of 5 AD, 5 NC individuals, in which RGB segments are calculated,
is calculated in Eq. 9 as $\mu_i > 15$ pixels. Through Multi-level thresholding using
Otsu's method, RGB color segmentation values with threshold values (pixels)
have been determined. Our newly proposed automatic RGB color segment scor-
ing algorithms were applied to the specified RGB color segments in order to
calculate the area detection (RGB segment scores).

Classification and Regression Tree Algorithm. CART algorithm can be
used for building both Classification and Regression Decision Trees. The impurity measure needed in constructing a decision tree in CART algorithm is Gini
Index. The decision tree built by CART algorithm is always a binary decision
tree [27].

$$Gini(D) = 1 - \sum_{i=1}^{m} p_i^2 \tag{10}$$

p_i is the possibility the dataset in D and is a part of class C_i. It can be assessed
by $|C_{i,D}|/|D|$. We calculate the total over m classes [28]. The Gini index regards
a binary split for each of the attributes. If A is a discrete valued attribute with
v distinct values. $a_1, a_2, ..., a_v$ occurs in D. If one wants to determine the best

binary split on A. It should be through the analysis of all the possible subsets that can be generated using the known values of A. Each subset S_A is considered to be a binary test for A attribute of the form $A \in S_A$. For a dataset, this analysis will yield satisfying result if the value of A is one of the values included in S_A. If A has v possible values then there will be 2^v possible subsets. The attribute that has the minimum Gini index or one that boosted the reduction in impurity tends to be selected as the splitting attribute.

3   Experimental Results

3.1   Proposed Model for Automatic RGB Color Segmentation

In this study, the proposed automatic MRI segmentation for significant attributes (pixels) is divided into three main stages as can be seen Fig. 1: (i) preprocessing, (ii) our newly proposed automatic RGB Color Segment Score Algorithm and (iii) post-processing with CART algorithm decision rules about AD and NC.

In this study, Fig. 1 shows the pipeline of our method that proposes the automatic hidden diagnostic significant attributes (pixels) segmentation for both AD and NC groups. The layout represents that the MRI has initially been preprocessed in order to yield accurate level of intensity in homogeneity. After preprocessing, RGB color segments (with a threshold value of (pixels)) have been subjected to our newly proposed automatic RGB Color Segment Score Algorithm in order to calculate RGB segment scores. Afterwards, these calculated segment scores of AD and NC groups are extracted in order to attain decision rules through CART algorithm and delivered as class label (AD/NC).

Preprocessing. The preprocessing of MRI data is a challenging issue in terms of segmentation due to the bias present in the resulting scan. In this study, the preprocessing steps applied to the MRI dataset are namely histogram matching, binarization, dilation and erosion, respectively, in order to perform brain extraction from the patient's gray scale MR images. The results obtained for a sample MR image in the data set to which the preprocessing steps are applied are shown in Fig. 2.

Figure 2 shows the representation of (a) to MRI data. Histogram of original MRI: MR image of the patient, calculated by gray-scale histogram (see Fig. 2(b)). Binary MRI: Binarization is applied for contrast enhancement of the pixels in the gray-scale MR image (see Fig. 2(c)). Cleaned MRI: For calculation of the pixels in the lesion areas (R segment score, G segment score, B segment score) in the binary MRI, the regions around the skull are calculated by the image dilation method (see Fig. 2(d)). Erosion Binary MRI: On the MR image, areas outside the skull periphery are colored in white by erosion (see Fig. 2(e)). Skull Stripped MRI: In the image, which is attained by subtracting the MR image obtained from erosion (see Fig. 2(e)) from the MR image obtained from dilation (see Fig. 2(d)), brain extraction (see Fig. 2(f)) is conducted via the Binary Image (see Fig. 2(c)).

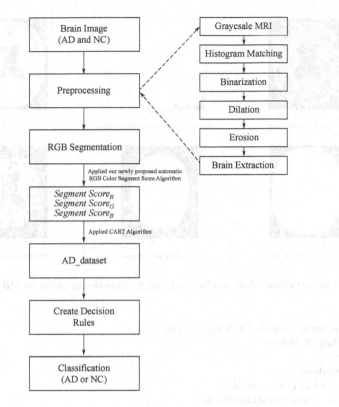

Fig. 1. Pipeline of our method (Classification of the AD_dataset with the application of our newly proposed RGB segmentation algorithm through CART algorithm).

Newly Proposed Automatic RGB Color Segment Score Algorithm. In this study, the following steps have been followed in order to calculate the RGB segment scores (pixels) in the lesion areas on the gray-scale MR images obtained from the preprocessing steps (see Fig. 1). (i) Multi level thresholding using Otsu's method is applied to the MR images (5 AD, 5 NC), and RGB color segments larger than the threshold value ($\mu_i > 15$ pixels) are determined (see Fig. 3). RGB segment scores are calculated through the application of our newly proposed automatic RGB Color Segment Score Algorithm to RGB color segments (with the threshold value of ($\mu_i > 15$ pixels) (see Fig. 3).

Step 1: In the gray-scale MR imaging (5 AD, 5 NC) with threshold value of ($\mu_i > 15$ pixel), RGB color segment scores ($Score_R(i), Score_G(i), Score_B(i)$) are calculated (see Eq. 11).

$$Score_R(i) = \sqrt{Area(i) \times Perimeter(i)}$$
$$Score_G(i) = \sqrt{Area(i) \times Perimeter(i)} \qquad (11)$$
$$Score_B(i) = \sqrt{Area(i) \times Perimeter(i)}$$

100   Y. Karaca et al.

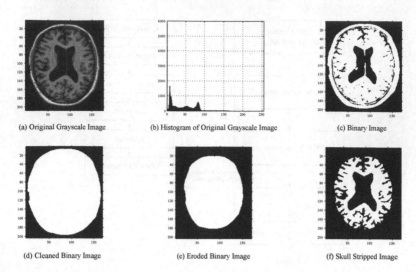

(a) Original Grayscale Image   (b) Histogram of Original Grayscale Image   (c) Binary Image

(d) Cleaned Binary Image   (e) Eroded Binary Image   (f) Skull Stripped Image

Fig. 2. Brain extraction obtained by applying preprocessing steps to MRI data of AD patients.

Input: Gray-Scale MR Image($n = i{\times}j$)
Output: Dataset

Method:
(1) **while** (i is to *row*) **do**{
(2)   **while** (j is to *column*) **do**{
(3) $Score_R$ (i), $Score_G$ (i), $Score_B$ (i)   (see Eq. 11)
(4)   Total $Score_R$ (i), Total $Score_G$ (i), Total $Score_B$ (i) (see Eq. 12)
(5)   Segment $Score_R$ (i), Segment $Score_G$ (i), Segment $Score_B$ (i) (see Eq. 13)
(6)}}

Fig. 3. Our newly proposed automatic RGB Color Segment Score Algorithm.

In the sample gray-scale MR image, which belongs to an AD patient, with the threshold value of ($\mu_i > 15$ pixel), Red(R) segment pixel is calculated as $Score_R(i)$ (see Fig. 4).

Step 2: $TotalScore_R(i), TotalScore_G(i), TotalScore_B(i)$ are calculated using the results obtained from $Score_R(i), Score_G(i), Score_B(i)$ (see Eq. 12).

$$TotalScore_R(i) = \sum_{i=0}^{n} Score_R(i)$$
$$TotalScore_G(i) = \sum_{i=0}^{n} Score_G(i) \qquad (12)$$
$$TotalScore_B(i) = \sum_{i=0}^{n} Score_B(i)$$

Step 3: $SegmentScore_R(i), SegmetScore_G(i), SegmentScore_B(i)$, are obtained with the help of $TotalScore_R(i), TotalScore_G(i), TotalScore_B(i)$ (see Eq. 13).

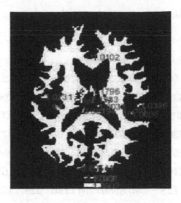

Fig. 4. In the gray-scale MR image, which belongs to an AD patient, Red (R) segment pixel is calculated as $Score_R(i)$. (Color figure online)

$$SegmentScore_R(i) = \sqrt{TotalScore \times n}$$
$$SegmentScore_G(i) = \sqrt{TotalScore \times n} \quad\quad (13)$$
$$SegmentScore_B(i) = \sqrt{TotalScore \times n}$$

In this study, the reason why we tend to propose this new automatic RGB Color Segment Score Algorithm [11–19] is that it is different from other segmentation algorithms in the literature for the fact that it not only determines the RGB color segmentation values with threshold value of ($\mu_i > 15$ pixels) by applying multi-level thresholding using Otsu's method to MR images of AD and NC individuals, but also when applied to the predetermined RGB color segments, it makes it possible to calculate (Eqs. 11, 12 and 13) the area detection (pixels in lesion areas calculated from the MR images (R segment score, G segment score, B segment score)).

At the end of these in Steps (1–3), the area covered by the lesions in the MR images, which belong to the AD and NC individuals, of the suggested new automatic RGB Color Segment Score Algorithm is calculated.

AD_dataset (see Table 1) is created with the pixels (R segment score, G segment score, B segment score) in lesion areas calculated based on the MR images of AD and NC individuals.

In order to successfully classify AD disease, decision rules have been obtained by applying CART algorithm to AD_dataset.

Creating Decision Rules with CART Algorithm. For the successful classification of AD disease, CART Classification and Regression Tree (CART) algorithm is applied to AD_dataset obtained from application of proposed new automatic RGB Color Segment Score Algorithm and decision rules are obtained. It is finally used to evaluate the segmentation score results of AD_dataset ($SegmentScore_R(i)$, $SegmetScore_G(i)$, $SegmentScore_B(i)$). The steps pertaining to the application of CART algorithm to the Segment Score can be seen in Fig. 5.

Table 1. AD-dataset obtained from the application of the proposed new automatic RGB Color Segment Score Algorithm.

ID	$SegmentScore_R$	$SegmentScore_G$	$SegmentScore_B$	Class
1	529.493127351501	356.053363167986	249.153328423716	NC
2	449.679506444335	410.363141454810	326.279636681542	NC
3	193.736071433081	637.614636819160	255.093749959439	NC
4	437.392517265366	355.013264186805	208.827759073036	NC
5	320.697772012526	669.978299345067	345.295953497784	NC
6	237.163436077104	436.909179802421	243.716358914598	AD
7	236.469923941728	590.898674611140	228.744570309022	AD
8	225.161853285334	449.600179456343	138.655755194015	AD
9	271.286526580267	1016.03389100160	193.831426322260	AD
10	339.624096967731	581.260590915557	391.403076239609	AD

Input: AD_dataset
Output: AD or NC

Method:
(1) **while** (*k* is to 10*)* **do**{
(2)   **while** (*l* is to 3) **do**{
(3)   //RGB *Segment Score* dataset is split into AD or NC
(4)   **for each** pixel in the *Segment Score* dataset the average of median and the value following the median is calculated
(5)   //the Gini value of the pixel in the dataset
(6)   //generating the Decision tree rules belonging to the dataset

$$Gini(D) = 1 - \sum_{j-1}^{m} p_j^2$$

(7)   //forming of the dataset based on the decision tree rules
(8)}}}

Fig. 5. Obtaining decision rules for AD and NC with the application of CART algorithm.

Following the classification of the AD-dataset trained with CART algorithm.

Step 1: A best split account is created for the creation of decision trees from the attributes in AD-dataset ($SegmentScore_R$, $SegmetScore_G$, $SegmentScore_B$) applied to the CART algorithm.

Step (2–6): The values of the decision trees and of the attributes ($SegmentScore_R$, $SegmetScore_G$, $SegmentScore_B$) are calculated.

Step (7–8): The decision tree obtained by applying the Classification and Regression Tree (CART) algorithm to AD-dataset (see Table 1) is shown in Fig. 6.

The decision rules (Rule 1, Rule 2 and Rule 3) obtained by applying the CART algorithm to AD_dataset are given below.

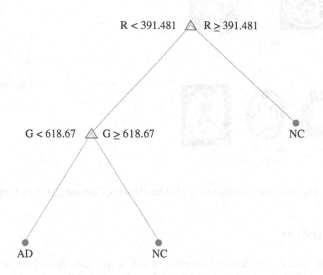

Fig. 6. CART algorithm graph based on AD_dataset.

Rule 1: IF $SegmentScore_R \geq 391.481$ **THEN** Class is **NC**

Rule 2: IF $SegmentScore_R < 391.481$ **AND** $SegmentScore_G \geq$ 618.67 **THEN** Class is **NC**

Rule 3: IF $SegmentScore_R < 391.481$ **AND** $SegmentScore_G <$ 618.67 **THEN** Class is **AD**

In order to determine the class of the MR image of a new patient, the application steps of the preprocessing, segmentation and post-processing operations in the Test MR image are given below (see Fig. 7(a–c)). The RGB segment scales in the test MR image are calculated (see Eq. 11, Eq. 12, and Eq. 13).

$SegmentScore_R(i) = 121.463432864132$
$SegmentScore_G(i) = 434.204150277899$
$SegmentScore_B(i) = 218.134874132034$

The calculated RGB segment scores ($SegmentScore_R$, $SegmetScore_G$, $SegmentScore_B$) are applied to the decision tree obtained from AD_dataset (see Fig. 6). As a result of this application (Rule 3), the class is designated as Alzheimer's Disease (AD) (see Fig. 7).

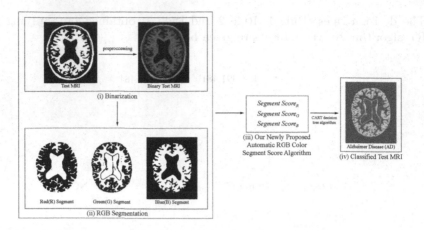

Fig. 7. The flow of classification of Alzheimer's Disease(AD) in test data.

4   Conclusion

In the present study, we have devised a novel approach based on segmentation and computational methods of MRI mining for AD. The ultimate aim of this paper is to propose a brand-new approach in Alzheimer's Disease MRI with the use of RGB color segments via multi-level thresholding using Otsu's method. This study is intended to get our newly proposed automatic RGB Color Segment Score Algorithm outcomes with appearance and spatial consistency. This study is proposed in three stages all of which engage in the process of training the AD and NC classifiers. In the first level of preprocessing, the image is applied to the brain detection. Thence the training dataset (AD_dataset) is obtained with the help of our newly proposed automatic RGB Color Segment Score Algorithm. In the second step, the training process is executed with the decision rules for AD and NC. Finally, test results are evaluated for the proposed system. Overall, the successful classification of Alzheimer's Disease has been the central focus of this study. With this in mind, our newly proposed automatic RGB Color Segment Score Algorithm has been of immense help in terms of calculating the RGB segment scores to which CART algorithm is applied. Thereupon, the decision rules are obtained, which we envisage that it is going to make a valuable contribution to the existing literature.

References

1. Beham, M.P., Gurulakshmi, A.B.: Morphological image processing approach on the detection of tumor and cancer cells. In: 2012 International Conference on Devices, Circuits and Systems (ICDCS), pp. 350–354 (2012)
2. Mayasi, Y., Helenius, J., McManus, D.D., Goddeau, R.P., Jun-OConnell, A.H., Moonis, M., Henninger, N.: Atrial fibrillation is associated with anterior predominant white matter lesions in patients presenting with embolic stroke. J. Neurol. Neurosurg. Psychiatry **89**(1), 6–13 (2018)

3. Karaca, Y., Cattani, C., Moonis, M., Bayrak, Ş.: Stroke subtype clustering by multifractal bayesian denoising with Fuzzy C Means and K-Means algorithms. Complexity **2018**, 1–15 (2018)
4. McKhann, G., Drachman, D., Folstein, M., Katzman, R., Price, D., Stadlan, E.M.: Clinical diagnosis of Alzheimer's disease report of the NINCDSADRDA work groupunder the auspices of department of health and human services task force on Alzheimer's disease. Neurology **34**(7), 939–939 (1984)
5. Khachaturian, Z.S.: Diagnosis of Alzheimer's disease. Arch. Neurol. **42**(11), 1097–1105 (1985)
6. Dubois, B., Feldman, H.H., Jacova, C., DeKosky, S.T., Barberger-Gateau, P., Cummings, J., Delacourte, A., Galasko, D., Gauthier, S., Jicha, G., Meguro, K.: Research criteria for the diagnosis of Alzheimer's disease: revising the NINCD-SADRDA criteria. Lancet Neurol. **6**(8), 734–746 (2007)
7. Salvatore, C., Castiglioni, I.: A wrapped multi label classifier for the automatic diagnosis and prognosis of Alzheimers disease. J. Neurosci. Methods **302**, 55–65 (2018)
8. Gad, A.R., Hassan, N.H., Seoud, R.A.A., Nassef, T.M.: Automatic machine learning classification of Alzheimer's disease based on selected slices from 3D magnetic resonance imagining. Age **67**, 10–5 (2017)
9. Vemuri, P., Gunter, J.L., Senjem, M.L., Whitwell, J.L., Kantarci, K., Knopman, D.S., Bradley, F.B., Ronald, C.P., Jack Jr., C.R.: Alzheimer's disease diagnosis in individual subjects using structural MR images: validation studies. Neuroimage **39**(3), 1186–1197 (2008)
10. Chupin, M., Grardin, E., Cuingnet, R., Boutet, C., Lemieux, L., Lchricy, S., Benali, H., Garnero, L., Colliot, O.: Fully automatic hippocampus segmentation and classification in Alzheimer's disease and mild cognitive impairment applied on data from ADNI. Hippocampus **19**(6), 579–587 (2009)
11. Kloppel, S., Stonnington, C.M., Chu, C., Draganski, B., Scahill, R.I., Rohrer, J.D., Fox, N.C., Jack Jr., C.R., Ashburner, J., Frackowiak, R.S.: Automatic classification of MR scans in Alzheimer's disease. Brain **131**(3), 681–689 (2008)
12. Cuingnet, R., Gerardin, E., Tessieras, J., Auzias, G., Lehricy, S., Habert, M.O., Chupin, M., Benali, H., Colliot, O.: Alzheimer's disease neuroimaging initiative. automatic classification of patients with Alzheimer's disease from structural MRI: a comparison of ten methods using the ADNI database. Neuroimage **56**(2), 766–781 (2011)
13. Davatzikos, C., Fan, Y., Wu, X., Shen, D., Resnick, S.M.: Detection of prodromal Alzheimer's disease via pattern classification of magnetic resonance imaging. Neurobiol. Aging **29**(4), 514–523 (2008)
14. Cheng, D., Liu, M.: Classification of Alzheimer's disease by cascaded convolutional neural networks using PET images. In: Wang, Q., Shi, Y., Suk, H.-I., Suzuki, K. (eds.) MLMI 2017. LNCS, vol. 10541, pp. 106–113. Springer, Cham (2017). https://doi.org/10.1007/978-3-319-67389-9_13
15. Zhu, X., Suk, H.I., Lee, S.W., Shen, D.: Canonical feature selection for joint regression and multi-class identification in Alzheimer's disease diagnosis. Brain Imaging Behav. **10**(3), 818–828 (2016)
16. Zhang, D., Shen, D.: Alzheimer's disease neuroimaging initiative: multi-modal multi-task learning for joint prediction of multiple regression and classification variables in Alzheimer's disease. NeuroImage **59**(2), 895–907 (2012)
17. Liu, S., Liu, S., Cai, W., Pujol, S., Kikinis, R., Feng, D.: Early diagnosis of Alzheimer's disease with deep learning. In: 2014 IEEE 11th International Symposium on Biomedical Imaging (ISBI), pp. 1015–1018 (2014)

18. Zhang, Y., Wang, S., Sui, Y., Yang, M., Liu, B., Cheng, H., Sun J., Jia, W., Phillips, P., Gorriz, J. M.: Multivariate approach for alzheimers disease detection using stationary wavelet entropy and predator-prey particle swarm optimization. J. Alzheimer's Dis. 1–15 (2017, preprint)
19. http://www.oasis-brains.org/
20. Rother, C., Minka, T., Blake, A., Kolmogorov, V.: Cosegmentation of image pairs by histogram matching-incorporating a global constraint into mrfs. In: 2006 IEEE Computer Society Conference on Computer Vision and Pattern Recognition, vol. 1, pp. 993–1000 (2006)
21. Prastawa, M., Bullitt, E., Ho, S., Gerig, G.: A brain tumor segmentation framework based on outlier detection. Med. Image Anal. **8**(3), 275–283 (2004)
22. Pal, N.R., Pal, S.K.: A review on image segmentation techniques. Pattern Recogn. **26**(9), 1277–1294 (1993)
23. Kurugollu, F., Sankur, B., Harmanci, A.E.: Color image segmentation using histogram multithreshing and fusion. Image Vis. Comput. **19**(13), 915–928 (2001)
24. Zhang, Y., Wang, S., Phillips, P., Dong, Z., Ji, G., Yang, J.: Detection of Alzheimer's disease and mild cognitive impairment based on structural volumetric MR images using 3D-DWT and WTA-KSVM trained by PSOTVAC. Biomed. Sig. Process. Control **21**, 58–73 (2015)
25. Kumar, N., Alam, K., Siddiqi, A.H.: Wavelet transform for classification of EEG signal using SVM and ANN. Biomed. Pharmacol. J. **10**(4), 2061–2069 (2017)
26. Crawford, S.L.: Extensions to the CART algorithm. Int. J. Man-Mach. Stud. **31**(2), 197–217 (1989)
27. Sathyadevi, G.: Application of CART algorithm in hepatitis disease diagnosis. In: 2011 International Conference on Recent Trends in Information Technology (ICRTIT), pp. 1283–1287 (2011)

Classification of Erythematous - Squamous Skin Diseases Through SVM Kernels and Identification of Features with 1-D Continuous Wavelet Coefficient

Yeliz Karaca[1](✉), Ahmet Sertbaş[2], and Şengül Bayrak[3]

[1] University of Massachusetts Medical School, Worcester, MA 01655, USA
yeliz.karaca@ieee.org
[2] Department of Computer Engineering, İstanbul University, 34000 İstanbul, Turkey
asertbas@istanbul.edu.tr
[3] Department of Computer Engineering, Haliç University, 34000 İstanbul, Turkey
bayraksengul@ieee.org

Abstract. Feature extraction is a kind of dimensionality reduction which refers to the differentiating features of a dataset. In this study, we have worked on ESD_Data Set (33 attributes), composed of clinical and histopathological attributes of erythematous-squamous skin diseases (ESDs) (psoriasis, seborrheic dermatitis, lichen planus, pityriasis rosea, chronic dermatitis, pityriasis rubra pilaris). It's aimed to obtain distinguishing significant attributes in ESD_Data Set for a successful classification of ESDs. We have focused on three areas: (a) By applying 1-D continuous wavelet coefficient analysis, Principle Component Analysis and Linear Discriminant Analysis to ESD_Data Set; w_ESD Data Set, p_ESD Data Set and l_ESD Data Set were formed. (b) By applying Support Vector Machine kernel algorithms (Linear, Quadratic, Cubic, Gaussian) to these datasets, accuracy rates were obtained. (c) w_ESD Data Set had the highest accuracy. This study seeks to identify deficiencies in literature to determine the distinguishing significant attributes in ESD_Data Set to classify ESDs.

Keywords: Wavelet Analysis · Feature extraction · Cubic kernel
Classification

1 Introduction

Classification methods, which are formed on machine learning, help with the decision making process in various fields of health care such as prognosis, diagnosis, screening, etc. Producing accurate results is very important in classifiers particularly in the field of medicine. A large number of false negatives in screening boosts the possibility of patients not receiving the care they seek. Dimensionality reduction as a preprocessing phase to machine learning is efficient in getting rid of unnecessary as well as inessential data, which tends to boost learning accuracy

© Springer International Publishing AG, part of Springer Nature 2018
O. Gervasi et al. (Eds.): ICCSA 2018, LNCS 10961, pp. 107–120, 2018.
https://doi.org/10.1007/978-3-319-95165-2_8

as well as enabling us to better comprehend the end results. Researchers have come up with a great number of methods in the field of machine learning and dimensionality reduction [1–3].

Erythemato-squamous skin diseases (ESDs) are commonplace dermatological diseases which can be seen in 2–3% of people worldwide [4]. ESDs include six groups of diseases which have similar psoriasis signs as well as symptoms such as redness (erythema) that results in the loss of cells (squamous) (see more on that [4–9]). ESD diseases are namely psoriasis, seborrheic dermatitis, lichen planus, pityriasis rosea, chronic dermatitis as well as pityriasis rubra pilaris. These diseases seem to have in common not only the medical characteristics of erythema as well as scaling, but also a lot of histopathological attributes. We still do not know for sure what really leads to these kinds of diseases but we highly suspect that hereditary and environmental factors may be the key players for patients of different age groups [7]. The differential diagnosis of ESD tends to be a big challenge in dermatology since it confides in analysing characteristics gathered from the analyses of not only the clinical but also histopathological ones [5], which in the end urge us to have a meticulous examination and understanding to have a much more accurate analysis.

The idea of technology in the field of medicine is an induction motor which focuses on the decision features of the ESDs and may later help diagnose people with the potential of some type of ESDs. To analyse ESD, we have some quantitative machine learning models such as multilayer perceptron neural networks [10], support vector machines [11], neurofuzzy inference system [12], decision trees [13], genetic algorithm [14], and K-means algorithm [15] to help with the decision-making process. In literature, there have been a number of studies that have identified the significant attributions of ESD diseases in recent years and classified them with machine learning based classification techniques such as Xie et al. [16] hybrid feature selection method with SVM, Abdi et al. [17] Particle Swarm Optimization with SVM algorithm, Polat et al. [13] k-NN based weighted preprocessing with decision trees, Ozcift et al. [19] Bayesian Network feature selection with genetic algorithm.

We have a more comprehensive and through method than any other study conducted with ESD_Data Sets [16–19], considering the scale of 366 (patients with any of the 6 types of ESD diseases clinical as well as histopathological datasets); namely from psoriasis, seborrheic dermatitis, lichen planus, pityriasis rosea, chronic dermatitis, as well as pityriasis rubra pilaris. Identifying subgroups of ESDs have been quite laborious. Furthermore, of all the papers done so far on various kinds of analyses with respect to the ESDs dataset, none of them has related attributes through the feature extraction methods with SVM kernels (Linear, Quadratic, Cubic, and Gaussian) algorithms applied for classification. Hence, these methods have been carried out to distinguish significant attributes that belong to the people for the classification of 6 subgroups of ESDs. We have gained distinguishing significant attributes from 1-D Continuous wavelet coefficient analysis, Principle Component Analysis (PCA), Linear Discriminant Analysis (LDA) datasets (w_ESD, p_ESD, l_ESD). The classification of the datasets has been based on SVM kernels (Linear, Quadratic, Cubic, and Gaussian) algorithms. w_ESD Data Set has worked better than other datasets of ESDs. Considering all these former studies, ours is much more exhaustive in terms of the ESDs Data Sets gathered from 1-D Continuous Wavelet analysis; in fact, there is hardly any study that is similar to this one in terms of SVM kernels classification algorithms.

The outline of this study constitutes four main sections: Part 2 sheds light on the data as well as the methods of ESD. Part 3 focuses on certain experimental results and Part 4 produces the conclusion.

2   Data and Methods

2.1   Patient Details

In this study, we have worked with the Data Set (ESD_Data Set) that comprises of the clinical as well as histopathological attributions of ESD disease diagnosed patients based on psoriasis (111), seborrheic dermatitis (60), lichen planus (72), pityriasis rosea (49), chronic dermatitis (52), and pityriasis rubra pilaris (see Table 1). The ESD_Data Set consists of 33 attributes.

Table 1. ESD_Data Set description.

Number of ESD	Attributes	Data size
Psoriasis (111) Seborrheic Dermatitis (60) Lichen Planus (72) Pityriasis Rosea (49) Chronic Dermatitis (52) Pityriasis Rubra Pilaris (20)	**Clinical Attributes** (erythema, scaling, definite borders, itching koebner phenomenon, polygonal papules, follicular papules, oral mucosal involvement, knee and elbow involvement, scalp involvement, family history, Age (linear)) **Histopathological Attributes** (melanin incontinence, eosinophils in the infiltrate, PNL infiltrate, fibrosis of the papillary dermis, exocytosis acanthosis, hyperkeratosis, parakeratosis, clubbing of the rete ridges, elongation of the rete ridges, thinning of the suprapa pillary epidermis, spongiform pustule, munro microabcess, focal hypergranulosis, disappearance of the granular layer, vacu olisation and damage of basal layer, spongiosis, saw-tooth ap pearance of retes, follicular horn plug, perifollicular, parakeratosis, inflammatory monoluclear inflitrate, band-like infiltrate)	366×33

The ESD_Data Set was gathered from the UC Irvine Machine Learning Repository [20].

2.2   Methods

The purpose of this paper is to identify the distinguishing significant attributes in the successful classification of ESD diseases.

Here are the steps that our technique depends on:

(a) Out of the feature extraction methods, 1-D continuous wavelet coefficient analysis (w_ESD Data Set), Principle Component Analysis (p_ESD Data Set) and Linear Discriminant Analysis (l_ESD Data Set) have been applied to the ESD_Data Set (33 attributes) and based on the results, datasets have been created by identifying the distinguishing significant attributes of ESD.

(b) Support Vector Machines kernel algorithms (Linear, Quadratic, Cubic, Gaussian) have been applied to the ESD_Data Set, w_ESD Data Set, p_ESD Data Set and l_ESD Data Set that have been generated from significant attributes and also ESD diseases (psoriasis, seborrheic dermatitis, lichen planus, pityriasis rosea, chronic dermatitis, as well as pityriasis rubra pilaris) were classified. And from there on, the results obtained from the classification accuracy rates have been compared.

(c) Based on the classification of the accuracy rate results, discriminating significant attributes have been identified in the classification of ESD diseases.

Computations and figures were obtained by Matlab environment.

1-D Continuous Wavelet Coefficient Analysis. Spectrum analysis of the signals is done by Fourier transformation first introduced in the field of signal processing; features can be defined in the frequency domain [21].

$$X(w) = F\{x(t)\} = \int_{-\infty}^{\infty} x(t)e^{-jwt}dt \tag{1}$$

$$x(t) = F^{-1}\{X(w)\} = \frac{1}{2\pi}X(w)e^{jwt}dw \tag{2}$$

In the Fourier transform equation, the $x(t)$ sign is multiplied by the complex multiplier over the entire time interval. As a result, the $X(w)$ Fourier coefficients are calculated.

In continuous wavelet transform, the ψ wavelet function in the whole time interval of the signal is the sum of scale and attribute multiplication. From the calculations of continuous wavelet coefficient analysis, wavelet coefficients are obtained based on the scale and position of the function. Each coefficient, multiplied by the accurately scaled as well as shifted wavelet, forms the wavelet components of the original signal.

What wavelet transform mathematically means is:

$$W(a,b) = \frac{1}{\sqrt{a}} \int_{-\infty}^{\infty} x(t).\psi\overline{\left(\frac{t-b}{a}\right)}dt \tag{3}$$

$$W(a,b) = x(t)\overline{\psi_{a,b}}(t)dt \tag{4}$$

as shown in the equations above. In these equations keeping $a > 0, b \in \Re$ in mind, a is the scaling parameter; b is the transformation one; $x(t)$ symbol, ψ is the wavelet function (mother wavelet), and $W(a,b)$ symbol indicates continuous wavelet transform [21–23].

Wavelet Analysis below shows the 33 attributes (see Table 1) with the help of continuous wavelet transform Eq. 3 in which the scaling as well as shift attributes are as:

- b = ESD_Data Set samples (see Table 1),
- For all the analyses c = 32, frequency = 0.5 were taken.

In this study, discriminating significant attributes have been determined by applying the attributes found in the 1-D continuous wavelet coefficient analysis to the ESD_Data Set (see Table 1).

Principle Component Analysis. PCA can be defined as a statistical calculation which benefits from an orthogonal transformation to turn a group of observations of potentially correlated variables into a group of linearly uncorrelated ones called principal components. The number of principal components is less than or equal to that of original attributes. In the transformation, the first principal component has the largest variance [24] and each component that follows in return has the highest variance under the constraint that it's orthogonal to the prior ones. The principal components can be defined as orthogonal since they are the eigenvectors of the covariance matrix that is regarded as symmetrical. Principle Component Analysis is regarded as a delicate one bearing in mind the relative scaling of the original attributes [24,25]. When ESD_Data Set (366×33) p is defined as, $w_k = (w_1, ..., w_p)_k$, line vector X_i and new basic component scores are expressed as $t_i = (t_1, ..., t_k)_i (p > k)$.

The first basic component is taken based on Eq. 5.

$$t_{k(i)} = x_i.w_k \tag{5}$$

Linear Discriminant Analysis. LDA variance analysis and regression analysis are a linear combination that calculates correlated attributes [26–28]. LDA is closely related to Principal Component Analysis (PCA) as well as factor analysis. Because these methods of analysis are linear combinations that try to represent the best data between attributes. The difference of LDA from PCA is that it acts as a model amongst the data in various classifications. As it can be seen in this study, Fisher's discriminant, which represents classifications in data sets with more than two classes, uses subspace [26]. C is the average of classes, i.e., μ_i and its covariance value is Σ. The changes in classifications are calculated based on Eqs. 6 and 7 and $\vec{w}$.

$$\sum_b = \frac{1}{C} \sum_{i=1}^{C} (\mu_i - \mu)(\mu_i - \mu)^T \tag{6}$$

The symbol $\vec{w}$ is the eigenvector of $\Sigma^{-1}\Sigma_b$ that classifies the eigenvalues within the dataset.

$$S = \frac{\vec{w}^T \sum_b \vec{w}}{\vec{w}^T \sum \vec{w}} \tag{7}$$

If $\Sigma^{-1}\Sigma_b$ is diagonal, then the eigenvectors amongst the properties of classes $C - 1$ spread in the subspace. Thus, the significant attributes in the dataset are selected (see more information [27]).

Support Vector Machines. The Support Vector Machine (SVM) algorithm is linearly separable. It creates a linear model by matching input space to a kernel space [29].

SVM algorithm can be applied where there are problems with classification and regression. The basis of the regression technique is to mirror the character of the training data as close to reality as possible and to find a linear discriminant function based on statistical learning theory. Kernel functions are used in the classification of datasets with multiple classes [3].

In the SVM algorithm, the two conditions that can be encountered in Fig. 1 are that the data are either linearly separable or linearly non-separable. In situations where the information cannot be linearly parted, nonlinear classifiers are alternative to linear classifiers. In this context, the nonlinear feature space calculates the linear classifiers in Eq. 8 by transforming the $x \in R^n$ observation vector to a vector z in space with a higher order. The feature space of this z vector is denoted by F. In this case, θ is expressed as $z = \theta_x$ by matching with $R^n \longrightarrow R^F$ [31,32].

$$x \in R^n \to z(x) = [a_1, \theta_1(x), K, a_n, \theta_n(x)^T] \in R^F \tag{8}$$

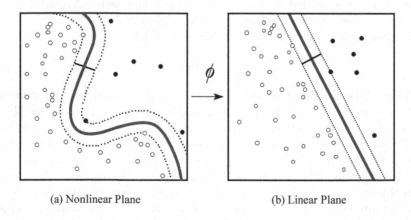

(a) Nonlinear Plane   (b) Linear Plane

Fig. 1. An example of nonlinear-linear plane for the multiclass Support Vector Machine algorithm [29].

When nonlinear separability is considered, the samples in the training set cannot be linearly separated in the initial input space. In such cases, the SVM transforms from the initial input space into a high-dimensional fea-ture space, which is easily classified linearly with the aid of the non-linear mapping function. Thus, instead of finding the product values of all values repeatedly using the kernel functions, it directly replaces the value in the kernel function, allowing the value of the attribute space to be found. Nonlinear transformations can be performed by means of a kernel function (Eqs. 9, 10, 11) mathematically expressed as $K(x_i, x_j) = \phi(x)\phi(x_j)$ in support vector machines, thus allowing linear discrimination of the data at high dimension [29–31].

$$Quadratic\ Kernel : K = (x_i, x_j) = \tanh(x_i, x_j - \delta) \tag{9}$$

$$Cubic\ Kernel : K(x_i, x_j) = (x_i.x_j + 1)^d \tag{10}$$

$$Gaussian\ Radial\ Basis\ Function\ Kernel : K(x_i, x_j) = e^{-\|x_i, x_j\|^2 / 2\sigma^2} \tag{11}$$

Support Vector Machine kernel algorithms (Linear, Quadratic, Cubic, Gaussian) are to be applied to the ESD_Data Set, w_ESD Data Set, p_ESD Data Set and l_ESD Data Set, which are generated from distinguishing significant attributes and then the results of the accuracy ratios of ESD diseases (psoriasis, seborrheic dermatitis, lichen planus, pityriasis rosea, chronic dermatitis, as well as pityriasis rubra pilaris) will be compared.

3   Results and Discussion

In this part of the study, the sections on which feature selection methods are applied to identify the distinguishing significant attributes in the ESD_Data Set are: 3.1 Analysis of 1-D Continuous Wavelet Coefficient, 3.2 Analysis of Principle Component Analysis, 3.3 Analysis of Linear Discriminant Analysis, and finally in Sect. 3.4 Classification of Analysis Results with SVM Kernels Algorithms, the results of the accuracy ratios have been compared by applying SVM kernel (Linear, Cubic, Quadratic, Gaussian) algorithms to ESD_Data Set, w_ESD Data Set, p_ESD Data Set and l_ESD Data Set.

3.1   Analysis of 1-D Continuous Wavelet Coefficient

In this part of our study, the 1-D Continuous Wavelet method (db4, level 5) has been applied to distinguish significant attributes in the ESD_Data Set (33 attributes) to classify ESD diseases.

For the classification of ESD diseases, 1-D continuous wavelet coefficients analysis has been applied to identify discriminant significant attributes in the ESD_Data Set (33 attributes). The results of only 2 of the distinguishing significant attributes in the classification of ESD diseases obtained from the analysis results of the 1-D continuous wavelet coefficients method are given in Fig. 2 as an example.

Figure 2. 1-D Continuous Wavelets Coefficient for six ESD diseases based on (Exocytosis, Perifollicular parakeratosis), (Acanthosis, Band Like Infiltrate) Level 1, Db4, Level 5 (a) psoriasis (b) seborrheic dermatitis (c) lichen planus (d) pityriasis rosea (e) chronic dermatitis (f) pityriasis rubra pilaris (mesh funttion peaks(25)).

In this study, we have chosen the number of the biggest selected coefficients by typing for psoriasis is 111, seborrheic dermatitis is 60, lichen planus is 72, pityriasis rosea is 49, chronic dermatitis is 52, as well as pityriasis rubra pilaris is 20.

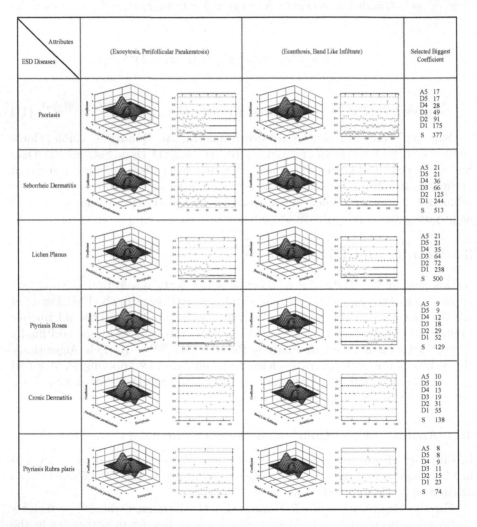

Fig. 2. 1-D Continuous Wavelets Coefficient for six ESD diseases based on (Exocytosis, Perifollicular parakeratosis), (Acanthosis, Band Like Infiltrate) Level 1, Db4, Level 5 (a) psoriasis (b) seborrheic dermatitis (c) lichen planus (d) pityriasis rosea (e) chronic dermatitis (f) pityriasis rubra pilaris (mesh funttion peaks(25)).

Fig. 2.(a) = cwt (Exocytosis – Perifollicular parakeratosis, 1:111, 'db4'), c = cwt (Acanthosis – Band Like Infiltrate, 1:111, 'db4'),

Fig. 2.(b) = cwt (Exocytosis – Perifollicular parakeratosis, 1:60, 'db4'), c = cwt (Acanthosis – Band Like Infiltrate, 1:60, 'db4'),

Fig. 2.(c) = cwt (Exocytosis – Perifollicular parakeratosis, 1:72, 'db4'), c = cwt (Acanthosis – Band Like Infiltrate, 1:72, 'db4'),

Fig. 2.(d) = cwt (Exocytosis – Perifollicular parakeratosis, 1:49, 'db4'), c = cwt (Acanthosis – Band Like Infiltrate, 1:49, 'db4'),

Fig. 2.(e) = cwt (Exocytosis – Perifollicular parakeratosis, 1:52, 'db4'), c = cwt (Acanthosis – Band Like Infiltrate, 1:52, 'db4'),

Fig. 2.(f) = cwt (Exocytosis – Perifollicular parakeratosis, 1:20, 'db4'), c = cwt (Acanthosis – Band Like Infiltrate, 1:20, 'db4').

In this study, through the application of the 1-D continuous wavelet coefficient analysis to identify discriminating significant attributes in the ESD Disease subgroups spongiosis, scaling, perifollicular parakeratosis, itching, inflammatory mononuclear infiltrate, hyperkeratosis, exocytosis, family history, disappearance of the granular layer, band like infiltrate, age (linear), w_ESD Data Set (364 × 11) has been generated.

3.2   Analysis of Principle Component Analysis

For the classification of ESD diseases, the principle component analysis method has been applied to determine distinguishing significant attributes in the ESD_Data Set (33 attributes).

In the classification of ESD diseases, the distinguishing significant attributes obtained from the Principal Component Analysis results are given in Fig. 3.

In this study, as it is shown in Fig. 3, the eigenvalue proportion is (eigenvalue > 1.035741). In this study, p_ESD Data Set (364 × 7) has been generated by applying principle component analysis to determine distinguishing significant attributes in ESD diseases subgroups, erythema, scaling, definite borders, itching, koebner phenomenon, polygonal papules and follicular papules.

Axis	Eigen value	Difference	Proportion (%)	Histogram	Cumulative (%)
1	9.260674	3.755320	27.24 %		27.24 %
2	5.505354	2.419046	16.19 %		43.43 %
3	3.086308	0.846414	9.08 %		52.51 %
4	2.239894	0.907509	6.59 %		59.09 %
5	1.332385	0.118770	3.92 %		63.01 %
6	1.213615	0.177874	3.57 %		66.58 %
7	1.035741	0.071086	3.05 %		69.63 %

Fig. 3. Significance of Principle Components eigenvalue table for ESD diseases.

3.3   Analysis of Linear Discriminant Analysis

In this part of the study, Linear Discriminant Analysis (p-value) has been applied to determine the distinguishing significant attributes in the ESD_Data Set to classify ESD diseases.

Distinguishing significant attributions of the classification of ESD diseases obtained from the analysis results of the Linear Discriminant Analysis method are given in Table 2 in detail.

In this study, the p-value proportion is (p-value > 0.1) as can be seen Table 2.

Table 2. LDA Manova for ESD diseases.

Attribute	Psoriasis	Seborrheic dermatitis	Lichen planus	Pityriasis rosea	Chronic dermatitis	Pityriasis Rubra pilaris	F	p-value
erythema	5.571822	4.699528	6.88451	4.110099	4.615916	4.601627	0.85663	0.510573
definite borders	2.037993	1.412595	0.120835	1.537588	−0.593959	1.09093	1.50705	0.187093
knee and elbow	1.636899	0.968546	−1.517619	0.367415	0.264721	3.573973	1.25602	0.282755
involvement scalp involvement	−2.711616	−1.592607	−3.347544	−1.336666	−1.810216	0.147586	0.73855	0.595026
melanin incontinence	−4.48415	−4.335425	6.025482	−4.499411	−0.594979	−2.354991	1.56134	0.170568
acanthosis	2.620522	3.329435	4.574563	3.012223	4.31715	2.596219	0.67361	0.643734
parakeratosis	0.670815	1.133956	4.3317	1.801834	1.208169	−0.507087	1.78154	0.116115
spongiform pustule	−0.004005	−1.433042	2.103908	−0.985003	−1.01946	−2.546682	1.02	0.405755
vacuolisation and damage of basal layer	2.780006	1.573019	13.172675	1.439153	1.183298	−0.245328	1.39494	0.225696
follicular horn plug	−5.217326	−2.293482	−3.512712	−3.007532	1.586379	−6.725457	0.78108	0.563903
Age (linear)	0.218138	0.184332	0.211421	0.176372	0.161891	0.082617	0.94448	0.452286

In this study, we have used linear discriminant analysis to determine the distinguishing significant attributes of ESD diseases in ESD_Data Set erythema, definite borders, knee as well as elbow involvement, scalp involvement, melanin incontinence, acanthosis, parakeratosis spongiosis, follicular horn plug, Age (linear) attributes were obtained and l_ESD Data Set (364×11) have been created.

3.4   Classification of Analysis Results with SVM Kernels Algorithms

Results of the classification accuracy rates gathered through applying SVM Kernels (Linear, Quadratic, Cubic, Gaussian) algorithms to the ESD_Data Set (364×33), w_ESD Data Set (364×11), p_ESD Data Set (364×7), and l_ESD Data Set (364×11) It is calculated according to the 5-fold cross validation method (see Table 3).

Table 3. SVM kernels (Linear, Quadratic, Cubic, Gaussian) accuracy rates for ESD_Data Set, w_ESD Data Set, p_ESD Data Set, l_ESD Data Set.

Data Sets/SVM Kernels	Linear	Quadratic	Cubic	Gaussian
ESD_Data Set (364 × 33)	77%	75.1%	**77.3%**	77%
w_ESD Data Set (364 × 11)	96.7%	97%	**97.3%**	96.4%
p_ESD Data Set (364 × 7)	85.4%	**86.3%**	85.2%	85.4%
l_ESD Data Set (364 × 11)	81.7%	82%	80.1%	**83.3%**

In order to classify the ESD diseases, the SVM kernels (Linear, Quadratic, Cubic, Gaussian) have respectively been applied to the data sets (ESD_Data Set: 364 × 33, w_ESD Data Set: 364 × 11, p_ESD Data Set: 364 × 7, l_ESD Data Set: 364 × 11) and the confusion matrices of the most successful accuracy rates obtained (see Table 3) are given in Fig. 4.

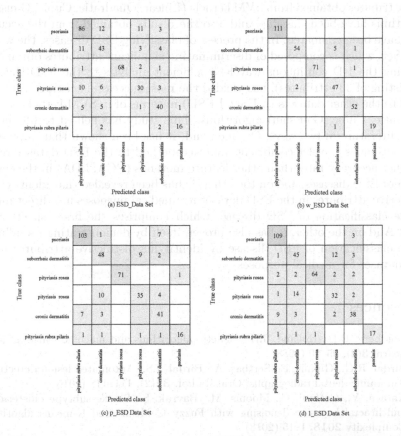

Fig. 4. The most successful accuracy rate SVM kernels confusion matrix for (a) ESD_Data Set, (b) w_ESD Data Set, (c) p_ESD Data Set, (d) l_ESD Data Set.

The most successful accuracy rates acquired of the SVM kernels Confusion Matrix are as follows: for the ESD_Data Set (see Fig. 4(a)) it is Lichen Planus skin disease via Cubic Kernel algorithm, for the w_ESD Data Set (see Fig. 4(b)) it is Psoriasis skin disease via Cubic Kernel algorithm, for the p_ESD Data Set (see Fig. 4(c)) it is Lichen Planus skin disease via Quadratic kernel algorithm and finally for the l_ESD Data Set (see Fig. 4(d)) it is Psoriasis skin disease via Gaussian Kernel algorithm.

4   Conclusion

This study aims to identify distinctive attributes in the ESD_Data Set (33 attributes) to successfully classify ESD diseases. Through the application of feature extraction methods (1-D continuous wavelet coefficients, PCA, LDA) to the ESD_Data Set consisting of 364 individuals with ESD, the Data Sets (w_ESD Data Set, p_ESD Data Set, l_ESD Data Set) generated by distinguishing significant attributes obtained from SVM kernels (Linear, Quadratic, Cubic, Gaussian) algorithms have been classified and also the results obtained from the accuracy rates have been compared. In the process of classifying ESD diseases, the w_ESD Data Set, which is composed of discriminating significant attributes obtained by applying the 1-D continuous wavelet coefficient analysis to the ESD_Data Set (consisting of 33 attributes), has yielded the most successful accuracy rate compared to the other datasets (p_ESD, l_ESD) in terms of in SVM kernels (Linear, Quadratic, Cubic, Gaussian) algorithms. This study has helped to fill the gap in the literature in two ways. On one hand, it has been shown that applying of 1-D continuous wavelet coefficient analysis method to the ESD dataset results in higher accuracy rates than other feature methods (PCA, LDA) in the classification of ESD diseases, and on the other, it has been revealed that identifying of distinctive attributes in the ESD dataset for medical purposes has direct impact on the classification of ESD disease, which comprises the first aspect of our study. And on the other, it has also proven itself by demonstrating its influence of the classification of ESD disease by identifying distinctive attributes in the ESD dataset for medical purposes.

References

1. Goldberg, D.E., Holland, J.H.: Genetic algorithms and machine learning. Mach. Learn. **3**(2), 95–99 (1988)
2. Birdal, R.G., Gümüş, E., Sertbaş, A., Birdal, I.S.: Automated lesion detection in panoramic dental radiographs. Oral Radiol. **32**(2), 111–118 (2016)
3. Karaca, Y., Cattani, C., Moonis, M., Bayrak, Ş.: Stroke subtype clustering by multifractal bayesian denoising with Fuzzy C Means and K-means algorithms. Complexity **2018**, 1–15 (2018)
4. Griffiths, W.A.D.: Pityriasis rubra pilaris. Clin. Exp. Dermatol. **5**(1), 105–112 (1980)

5. Kim, G.W., Jung, H.J., Ko, H.C., Kim, M.B., Lee, W.J., Lee, S.J., Kim, D.W., Kim, B.S.: Dermoscopy can be useful in differentiating scalp psoriasis from seborrhoeic dermatitis. Br. J. Dermatol. **164**(3), 652–656 (2011)
6. Elic, R., Durocher, L.P., Kavalec, E.C.: Effect of salicylic acid on the activity of betamethasone-17, 21-dipropionate in the treatment of erythematous squamous dermatoses. J. Int. Med. Res. **11**(2), 108–112 (1983)
7. Krain, L.S.: Dermatomyositis in six patients without initial muscle involvement. Arch. Dermatol. **111**(2), 241–245 (1975)
8. Marzano, A.V., Borghi, A., Stadnicki, A., Crosti, C., Cugno, M.: Cutaneous manifestations in patients with inflammatory bowel diseases: pathophysiology, clinical features, and therapy. Inflamm. Bowel Dis. **20**(1), 213–227 (2013)
9. Ziemer, M., Seyfarth, F., Elsner, P., Hipler, U.C.: Atypical manifestations of tinea corporis. Mycoses **50**(s2), 31–35 (2007)
10. Bonerandi, J.J., Beauvillain, C., Caquant, L., Chassagne, J.F., Chaussade, V., Clavere, P., Desouches, C., Garnier, F., Grolleau, J.L., Grossin, M., Jourdain, A.: Guidelines for the diagnosis and treatment of cutaneous squamous cell carcinoma and precursor lesions. J. Eur. Acad. Dermatol. Venereol. **25**(s5), 1–51 (2011)
11. Baxt, W.G.: Use of an artificial neural network for data analysis in clinical decision-making: the diagnosis of acute coronary occlusion. Neural Comput. **2**(4), 480–489 (1990)
12. Ubeyli, E.D., Güler, I.: Automatic detection of erythemato-squamous diseases using adaptive neuro-fuzzy inference systems. Comput. Biol. Med. **35**(5), 421–433 (2005)
13. Polat, K., Güneş, S.: A novel hybrid intelligent method based on C4. 5 decision tree classifier and one-against-all approach for multi-class classification problems. Expert Syst. Appl. **36**(2), 1587–1592 (2009)
14. Guvenir, H.A., Demiröz, G., Ilter, N.: Learning differential diagnosis of erythemato-squamous diseases using voting feature intervals. Artif. Intell. Med. **13**(3), 147–165 (1998)
15. Ubeyli, E.D., Doğdu, E.: Automatic detection of erythemato-squamous diseases using k-means clustering. J. Med. Syst. **34**(2), 179–184 (2010)
16. Xie, J., Wang, C.: Using support vector machines with a novel hybrid feature selection method for diagnosis of erythemato-squamous diseases. Expert Syst. Appl. **38**(5), 5809–5815 (2011)
17. Abdi, M.J., Giveki, D.: Automatic detection of erythemato - squamous diseases using PSO - SVM based on association rules. Eng. Appl. Artif. Intell. **26**(1), 603–608 (2013)
18. Polat, K., Güneş, S.: The effect to diagnostic accuracy of decision tree classifier of fuzzy and k-NN based weighted pre-processing methods to diagnosis of erythemato-squamous diseases. Digit. Signal Proc. **16**(6), 922–930 (2006)
19. Ozcift, A., Gulten, A.: Genetic algorithm wrapped Bayesian network feature selection applied to differential diagnosis of erythemato-squamous diseases. Digit. Signal Proc. **23**(1), 230–237 (2013)
20. Asuncion, A., Newman, D.: UCI machine learning repository (2007)
21. Wickerhauser, M.V.: Adapted Wavelet Analysis from Theory to Software. IEEE Press, New York (1994)
22. Karaca, Y., Aslan, Z., Cattani, C., Galletta, D., Zhang, Y.: Rank determination of mental functions by 1D wavelets and partial correlation. J. Med. Syst. **41**(2), 1–10 (2017)
23. Flandrin, P.: Wavelet analysis and synthesis of fractional Brownian motion. IEEE Trans. Inf. Theory **38**(2), 910–917 (1992)

24. Jolliffe, I. T.: Principal component analysis and factor analysis. In: Principal Component Analysis, pp. 115–128. Springer (1986)
25. Wood, F., Esbensen, K., Geladi, P.: Principal component analysis. Chemometr. Intel. Lab. Syst **2**(1987), 37–52 (1987)
26. Izenman, A.J.: Linear discriminant analysis. In: Modern Multivariate Statistical Techniques, pp. 237–280 (2013)
27. Mika, S., Ratsch, G., Weston, J., Scholkopf, B., Mullers, K.R.: August. Fisher discriminant analysis with kernels. In: Proceedings of the 1999 IEEE Signal Processing Society Workshop Neural Networks for Signal Processing IX, pp. 41–48 (1999)
28. Altman, E.I., Marco, G., Varetto, F.: Corporate distress diagnosis: comparisons using linear discriminant analysis and neural networks (the Italian experience). J. Bank. Financ. **18**(3), 505–529 (1994)
29. Hearst, M.A., Dumais, S.T., Osuna, E., Platt, J., Scholkopf, B.: Support vector machines. IEEE Intell. Syst. Appl. **13**(4), 18–28 (1998)
30. Karaca, Y., Zhang, Y., Cattani, C., Ayan, U.: The differential diagnosis of multiple sclerosis using convex combination of infinite kernels. CNS Neurol. Disord. Drug Targets (Formerly Current Drug Targets-CNS & Neurological Disorders) **16**(1), 36–43 (2017)
31. Scholkopf, B., Smola, A.J.: Learning with Kernels: Support Vector Machines, Regularization, Optimization, and Beyond. MIT Press, Cambridge (2001)
32. Karaca, Y., Hayta, Ş.: Application and comparison of ANN and SVM for diagnostic classification for cognitive functioning. Appl. Math. Sci. **10**(64), 3187–3199 (2016)

ANN Classification of MS Subgroups with Diffusion Limited Aggregation

Yeliz Karaca[1(✉)], Carlo Cattani[2], and Rana Karabudak[3]

[1] University of Massachusetts Medical School, Worcester, MA 01655, USA
yeliz.karaca@ieee.org
[2] Engineering School, DEIM, University of Tuscia, 01100 Viterbo, VT, Italy
cattani@unitus.it
[3] Department of Neurology, Hacettepe University, 06100 Ankara, Turkey
rkbudak@hacettepe.edu.tr

Abstract. In Diffusion Limited Aggregation (DLA), the procedure in which substances blend irrevocably to produce dendrites, is idealised. During this process, the slowest phase tends to be the diffusion of substance to aggregate. This study focuses on the procedure where substances enduring a random walk because of Brownian motion cluster together to form aggregates of such particles. Magnetic Resonance Image (MRI) is one of the methods used for identifying nervous system chronic disorders. MS_ dataset, comprised of MR images belonging to patients with one of the MS subgroups, was used in this study. The study aims at identifying the homogenous and self-similar pixels that the regions with lesions are located by applying the DLA onto the patients' MR images in line with the following steps: (i) By applying the Diffusion Limited Aggregation (DLA) algorithm onto the MS_dataset (patients' MRI) the regions with the lesion have been identified. Thus, DLA_MS dataset has been generated. (ii) Feed Forward Back Propagation (FFBP) and Cascade Forward Back Propagation (CFBP) algorithms, two of the artificial neural network algorithms, have been applied to the MS_dataset and DLA_MS dataset. MS subgroups have been classified accordingly. (iii) Classification Accuracy rates as obtained from the application of FFBP and CFBP algorithms on the MS_dataset and DLA_MS dataset have been compared. Having been done for the first time, it has been revealed, through the application of ANN algorithms, how the most significant pixels are identified within the relevant dataset through DLA.

Keywords: Diffusion limited aggregation · Multifractal technique
Stochastic · MRI

1 Introduction

Cluster formation models are topics that have been studied at length in the literature. A core task in this field of research tends to be the particle aggregation process analyses. Some studies claim that key features of the procedures

© Springer International Publishing AG, part of Springer Nature 2018
O. Gervasi et al. (Eds.): ICCSA 2018, LNCS 10961, pp. 121–136, 2018.
https://doi.org/10.1007/978-3-319-95165-2_9

tend to be stringently related with the cluster morphology. It is thought that in the creation of the DLA cluster with substances that contain various forms of alteration of aggregation, procedures can play a role in the changes regarding the morphology of the DLA. The current paper analyses the creation of DLA groups of substances that are of numerous sizes. This study also reveals that the aggregates gained as a result of the method create an angle selection instrument about dendritic growth which effects shielding effect of DLA edge and also impacts clusters' fractal aspect.

Multiple sclerosis (MS) is that affects the central nervous system (CNS). It is characterized by inflammation, demyelination and axonal degenerative changes. MS usually begins between the ages of 20 and 40, affecting women two to three times [1]. 85%–90% of the patients have a relapsing course from onset characterized by neurological symptoms associated with areas of CNS inflammation. More than half of untreated patients transit to a phase of gradual worsening over the course of two decades [2,3]. Progressive forms of MS can be present as the initial disease course (primary progressive MS) in approximately 10%–15% of the patients [4,5]. The incidence of MS varies across regions, with rates as high as 8–10 new cases per 100,000 in high latitudinal regions [6,7]. Current estimates put forth that over 700,000 people are affected in Europe, with over 2.5 million cases worldwide [8], which represent a significant burden in terms of impact on quality of life, societal costs and personal expenses [9,10].

In the current study, we have dealt with the dataset of individuals who have the diagnosis of Multiple Sclerosis disease with the following subgroups: Relapsing Remitting MS, Secondary Progressive MS or Primary Progressive MS in the current study. About 25% of MS patients tends to have Relapsing-Remitting MS. It resembles the benign type during the first period, and full recovery is observed following the attacks. Full or almost full recovery periods are at stake following the acute attacks. No progression is seen in the disease in between the intervals of the attacks [10–13]. Secondary Progressive MS (SPMS) has an onset that resembles the Relapsing-Remitting MS (RRMS) subgroup. Following an early period that approximately lasts 5–6, it manifests a secondary progression. Following a period with attacks and recoveries, the number of the attacks diminishes and the improvement is little. The disability gradually increases as well [11–14]. In the Primary Progressive MS (PPMS) improvement is not reported in general and there is a slow or rapid progression of the disorder [15]. MRI data tend to be amongst the significant information pertaining to the people who suffer from this disease. We can classify the data may be into main categories as shown below.

Lately, there has been a growing interest in the fractal and multifractal analyses. As for literature concerning this case in point, Fazzalari et al. [16] studied the fractal dimension for trabecular bone, while Esgiar et al. [17] did the fractal analysis to be able to detect colonic cancer. Goldberger et al. [18] studied the chaos and fractals for human physiology, and Cross [19] carried out the study concerning the fractals for pathology. In addition to these studies, fractal based Electromyography analysis was dealt with by Arjunan et al. [20], and fractal analysis for DNA data as handled by Galich et al. [21] emphasized the importance of fractal and multifractal methods in terms of information analyses. It is acknowledged that the multifractal methods are the right characteristics descriptors in procedures related to MS cases [22–28]. On the other hand, it has also been observed that there exists an absence in subject matter as well as in the literature in terms of research that handle blended procedures of numeric information, multifractal methods and machine learning techniques.

This method of ours is more complete and broader as our current study is comprehensive when compared with other studies that have been carried out with regard to the dataset [22–28] in literature, taking into account the dimension of 9 (the number of patients with 3 different MS subgroups MRI data). The 3 different MS subgroups are RRMS, SPMS, PPMS as mentioned above. The classification of the subgroups of MS is a remarkable challenge in its own term. In addition, all research performed on many different kinds of analysis on the MS-dataset, not any work has been reported yet, related to the MRI through multifractal technique of FFBP and CFBP algorithms applied for clustering purposes. Therefore, multifractal DLA algorithm has been applied for the identification of homogenous and self-similar pixels that belong to the patients for the classification of three MS subgroups. We obtained homogenous and self-similar pixels (a single seed particle) from multifractal technique dataset (DLA_MS dataset). This dataset is classified using the FFBP and CFBP algorithms. As a result, it has been observed that DLA_MS dataset has yielded a better classification than the MS-dataset of MS subgroups. When compared with the studies aforementioned, this study of ours is a comparative one with comprehensive features because the MS datasets as gathered from the multifractal technique have been applied for the first time in literature for the FFBP as well as CFBP classification algorithms.

The organization of the paper can be summarized as: Part 2 is about materials as well as methods of MS. Part 3 gives information about the experimental results. Finally, Part 4 shares the conclusions regarding this study, outlining some suggestions for the future research.

2 Materials and Methods

2.1 Data

This study is concerned with the MRI data of the MS subgroup patients from Hacettepe University (Ankara, Turkey) Neurology and Radiology Department. The MS subgroup adheres to the McDonald criteria [14]. The MRI that belong to patients aged 18–65 who received definitive diagnosis of MS with the subgroups of RRMS(3), PPMS(3) and SPMS(3) 18–65 are used in this study. The MRI has the resolution of 256 × 256 and the MRI have been gathered using a 1.5 T device (Magnetom, Siemens Medical Systems, Erlangen, Germany).

Magnetic Resonance Imaging. Magnetic Resonance Imaging (MRI) is a sensitive methods in order to detect the chronic diseases of the nervous system [15, 22].

MRI is capable of revealing the damaged tissue regions or regions with inflammation on the central nervous system.

2.2 Methods

We have provided two potential contributions in this study, first of which is that we introduced a relatively novel multifractal technique that calculates the homogenous and self-similar data from MS_ dataset. We also proposed the use of MS_dataset and homogenous and self-similar MS_dataset (DLA_MS dataset) to be trained with FFBP as well as CFBP algorithms in terms of classifying and also to enhance the success level of classification of the subgroups of MS. The technique is based on several stages given as you can see in the following bullet points:

(a) Multifractal technique DLA algorithm was applied to the MS_dataset to identify the MS_dataset significant homogenous and self-similar.
(b) The DLA_MS dataset obtained from MS_dataset and multifractal technique DLA algorithm (DLA_MS dataset) were classified by the application of FFBP and CFBP algorithms.
(c) The comparisons of datasets (MS_dataset, DLA_MS dataset) were carried out with the FFBP and CFBP algorithms in regards to the classification accuracies. Figures as well as computations have been gathered through by Matlab and FracLab.

Diffusion Limited Aggregation. Diffusion-Limited Aggregation (DLA) can be defined as a mechanism which describes the irrevocable growth of fractal aggregates in which diffusion is the dominant transport. The cluster is created starting with a static seed particle in a DLA simulation. Afterwards, another particle is launched from a certain distance and diffuses through the space with Brownian motion [29–33]. If the walker particle comes across and finds a particle in the middle of its trajectory, it will face a collision and subsequently stick to the particle. Following this sticking, the two particles generate a static cluster. At that moment, a new particle is launched and the process is repeated. The simulation comes to an end when the cluster reaches the desired number of particles. The basic algorithm of the off-lattice DLA process is depicted in Fig. 1.

The simulation has an important aspect and that is to define a collision between the walker and any of the particles constituting the cluster. The walker cannot take the normal step of size L, represented by the red line since it experiences a collision with the particle in the cluster. Rather, it will take a step of size L_{hit}. To know if there will be a collision between the walker and a particle in the cluster L_{hit} is required to be computed [31]. In line with Eq. 1.

$$\alpha = x_p - (x_0 + L_{hit} \cdot \cos(\alpha))$$
$$\alpha = y_p - (x_0 + L_{hit} \cdot \sin(\alpha))$$

(1)

Here, α is the angle of the future step. Following the collision, the distance between the particles is equal to the particle diameter α_p.

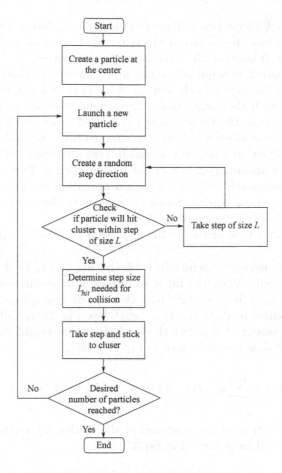

Fig. 1. Flow chart of the multifractal DLA algorithm [31].

The data structure is simple in the square lattice case; it serves to have an image (two-dimensional array of integers of) size $n \times n$, in which n represents the maximum size that is aimed to be attained [32, 33].

As for this current study, the MR images of the MS patients with the RRMS, SPMS, PPMS Subgroups have the resolution of 256×256, in which $n = 256$ (a single seed particle) is the maximum size that is aimed to be reached ($x_p = 256$, $y_p = 256$). ($L_{hit} = 10000$).

ANN Algorithms. ANN algorithms were inspired and modelled by biological neural networks about the interrelatedness of the neurons in the human nervous systems of the human brain [34]. ANN algorithms solve problems via the use of sample data as well as supervised learning. Feed Forward Back Propagation as well as Cascade Forward Back Propagation algorithms are two of the supervised learning ANN algorithms.

Feed Forward Back Propagation Algorithm. Multilayer Perceptron (MLP) is an ANN system that has a feed forward which includes one or more than one hidden layer being in use in-between the input as well as output layers. In multi-layered networks, information is acquired by the input layer (x). Through operations conducted within the network, the output value that forms in the output layer (d) is compared with the target value. Error value that forms in-between the value found as well as the target value is updated in order to lessen weights. Hence, the error value of each system is subtracted from the updated operations of the previous layer in the systems which have multitude of hidden layers. In addition, the learning operation of the system for the learning of the data is repeated. Consequently, weight correction operation starts with the weight reliant on the output and the operation endures up to the point when the input level is attained in the reverse order [34, 35].

The general structure of the FFBP algorithm is described in the six steps below:

Step 1: The network architecture of the algorithm is defined and the weights are included. When the input examples with m-dimension is entered, $x_i = [x_1, x_2, ..., x_m]^T$ is seen. Likewise, the output examples desired with n-dimension is specified by $d_k = [d_1, d_2, ..., d_n]^T$ (see Fig. 2). x_i values, the output values of the neurons in i^{th} layer(n), the total input that would come to a neuron in j layer is applied as it can be seen in Eq. 2 [36, 37].

$$net_j = \sum_{i=1}^{m} w_{ji}.x_i \quad \text{(from } i. \text{ node to } j. \text{ node)} \quad (2)$$

Step 2: The output of the j neuron in the hidden layer (transfer function output) is calculated as presented in Eq. 3.

$$y_i = f_j(net_j), \quad j = 1, 2, ..., J \quad (3)$$

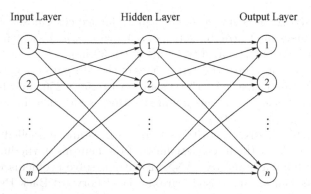

Fig. 2. FFBP algorithm general network structure.

Step 3: The total input that will come to k neuron in the output layer is calculated in line with Eq. 4.

$$net_k = \sum_{j=1}^{J} w_{kj} \cdot y_j \tag{4}$$

Step 4: The calculation of the non-linear output of a k neuron in the output layer is performed as in Eq. 5.

$$o_k = f_k(net_k), \quad k = 1, 2, ..., n. \tag{5}$$

Step 5: The output that is gained from the network is compared with the actual output as well as e_k error is computed.

$$e_k = (d_k - o_k) \tag{6}$$

Step 6: d_k and o_k denote the target of any k neuron in the output layer and the outputs obtained from the network, respectively. The weights that have been obtained from the output layer are updated. The total square error is calculated as in Eq. 7 for every example,

$$E = \frac{1}{2} \sum_k (d_k - o_k)^2 \tag{7}$$

For the classification of the MS Subgroups, FFBP algorithm was applied to the MS_dataset $(256 \times 256 \times 9)$ and DLA_MS dataset $X = (x_1, x_2, ..., x_{256 \times 256 \times 9})$.

Cascade Forward Back Propagation Algorithm. Cascade Forward Back Propagation (CFBP) algorithm can be likened to the FFBP algorithm. One single dissimilarity is related to the link in- between the neurons on the input layer, hidden layer as well as the output layers. Cells which tend to be subsequent of one another are connected and training is performed in this fashion. It is possible to apply the training process at two or more levels [38–41] (see Fig. 3 below).

We will provide an overview for the methodology utilized in the learning process that has been conducted here.

Step 1: Initialize the weights with small random values.
Step 2: For every combination (p_q, d_q) in the learning sample:

- Propagate the entries p_q forward through the neural network layers:

$$a^0 = p_q; a^k = f^k(W^k a^{k-1} - b^k), \quad k = 1, ..., m \tag{8}$$

- Back propagate the sensitivities through the neural network layers:

$$\begin{aligned} \delta^M &= -2F'^M(n^M)(d_q - a^M) \\ \delta^k &= F'^k(n^k)(W^{k+1})^T \delta^{k+1}, \quad k = M-1, ..., 1 \end{aligned} \tag{9}$$

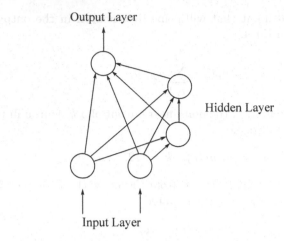

Fig. 3. The general structure of the CFBP algorithm.

- Modify the weight as well as biases:

$$\Delta W^k = -\eta \delta^k (a^{k-1})^T, \quad k = 1, ..., M$$
$$\Delta b^k = -\eta \delta^k, \quad k = 1, ..., M \tag{10}$$

Step 3: If the stopping criteria are fulfilled, then stop; otherwise, if they are not attained, they permute the presentation order of the combination based on the learning input data and start Step 2 over.

For the classification of the MS Subgroups, CFBP algorithm was applied to the MS_dataset $(256 \times 256 \times 9)$ and DLA_MS dataset $X = (x_1, x_2, ..., x_{256 \times 256 \times 9})$.

3   Experimental Results

The experimental results are comprised of three main parts: 3.1 Analysis of DLA handles the application of DLA algorithm flow chart steps (see Fig. 1) on the MS_dataset that constitutes the MRI of patients with MS Subgroups of RRMS, SPMS or PPMS. By this application, the DLA_MS dataset was obtained that include the significant homogenous and self-similar pixels. 3.2. Analysis of ANN has the application of FFBP and CFBP on the DLA_MS dataset respectively. 3. Results of ANN algorithm part provides the comparison of the accuracy results for the classification performances of FFBP and CFBP algorithms after their application on the DLA_MS dataset.

3.1   Analysis of Diffusion Limited Aggregation

In the first stage of the study, the flow chart application steps (see Fig. 1) of DLA algorithm was applied to the MS_dataset that is comprised of the MRI

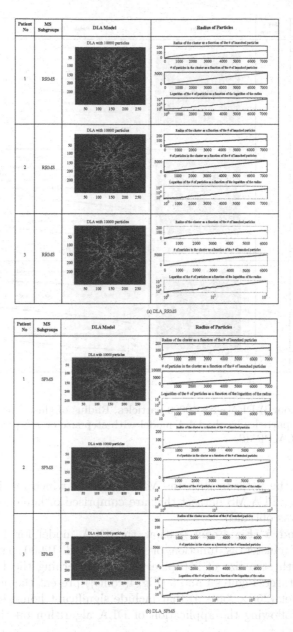

Fig. 4. DLA with 10000 particles, Radius of cluster as function of the launched 10.000 particles by the DLA model with step size of 256 pixel points radius of cluster, (a) DLA_RRMS (b) DLA_SPMS.

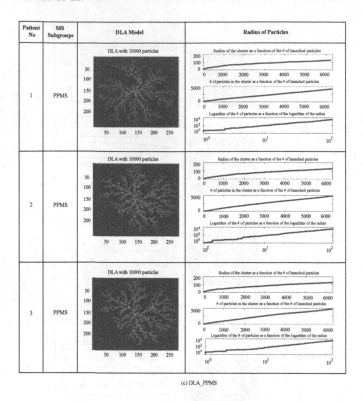

(c) DLA_PPMS

Fig. 5. (Fig. 4 (cont.)) DLA with 10000 particles, Radius of cluster as function of the launched 10.000 particles by the DLA model with step size of 256 pixel points radius of cluster, (c) DLA_PPMS.

that belong to the patients with the MS Subgroups which are RRMS, SPMS or PPMS. Thus, DLA_MS dataset that are comprised of homogenous and self-similar pixels was obtained.

Figures 4 and 5 (Fig. 4(cont.)) show the DLA model for 10000 particles and Radius of cluster as function of the launched 10000 particles by the DLA model with step size of 256 pixel points concerning the RRMS, SPMS, PPMS MRI dataset. Figures 4 and 5 (Fig. 4(cont.)) present the obtaining of the MS_DLA dataset ($256 \times 256 \times 9$) that include significant homogenous and self-similar pixels following the application of DLA algorithm on the MS_dataset ($256 \times 256 \times 9$).

3.2   Analysis of ANN Algorithms

In this study, the MRI images of the patients with RRMS(3), SPMS(3), PPMS(3) are used, comprising the MS_dataset (see Fig. 6(a)).

In this part, which is the second stage of the study, there is the obtaining of the DLA_MS dataset (see Fig. 6(b)) that is comprised of significant homogenous

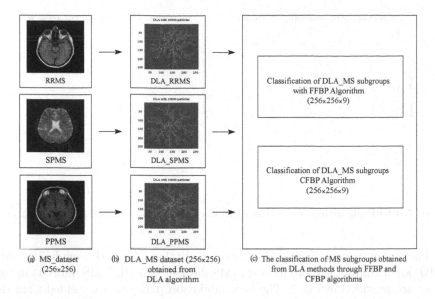

Fig. 6. The classification of DLA_MS dataset, obtained by the application of DLA method on the MS_dataset, through the use of FFBP and CFBP algorithms.

and self-similar pixels as obtained from the application of DLA algorithm to the MS_dataset. FFBP and CFBP algorithms (see Fig. 6(c)) were applied to the MS_dataset and DLA_MS dataset for the classification of the subgroups of MS (see Fig. 6).

Application of the FFBP and CFBP algorithms on the DLA_MS dataset in the following sections.

Application of Feed Forward Back Propagation Algorithm. The common parameters that produce the most accurate rates in terms in classifying MS_dataset and DLA_MS dataset with FFBP algorithm are provided in Table 1.

The performance graph obtained from the DLA_MS dataset and MS_dataset classification through the FFBP algorithm for the MS Subgroups is provided in Fig. 7.

Table 1. FFBP algorithm network properties.

Network properties	Values
Training Function	Levenberg Marquardt (trainlm)
Adaption Learning Function	Learngdm
Performance Function	Mean Squared Error (MSE)
Transfer Function	Tansig
Epoch Number	1000
Hidden Layer Neuron Number	10

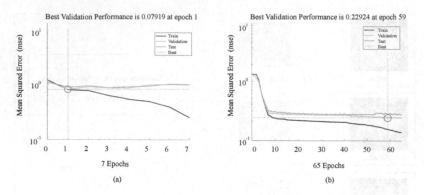

Fig. 7. FFBP algorithm performance graph (a) DLA_MS dataset (b) MS_dataset.

The Mean Square Error (MSE) values obtained from the modelling with FFBP algorithm for the two datasets (MS_dataset and DLA_MS dataset) in this study are provided in Fig. 7. The best validation performance yielded from the training procedure of FFBP algorithm with 65 epoch for the DLA_MS dataset is 0.07919 (see Fig. 7(a)). The best validation performance as obtained from the training procedure of FFBP algorithm with 7 epoch for the MS_dataset is 0.2292 (see Fig. 7(b)). According to the best validation performance result (see Fig. 7), calculated regarding the FFBP Algorithm, the classification accuracy rate of the DLA_MS dataset proves to be better than that of the MS_dataset.

Application of Cascade Forward Back Propagation Algorithm. The common parameters that produce the most accurate rates in the classification of the MS_dataset and DLA_MS dataset with CFBP algorithm are provided in Table 2.

Table 2. Properties for the CFBP algorithm network.

Network Properties	Values
Training Function	Levenberg Marquardt (trainlm)
Adaption Learning Function	Learngdm
Performance Function	Mean Squared Error (MSE)
Transfer Function	Tansig
Epoch Number	1000
Hidden Layer Neuron Number	10

The performance graph obtained from the DLA_MS dataset and MS_dataset classification through the CFBP algorithm for the MS Subgroups is provided in Fig. 8.

The Mean Square Error (MSE) values obtained from the modelling with CFBP algorithm for the two datasets (MS_dataset and DLA_MS dataset) in

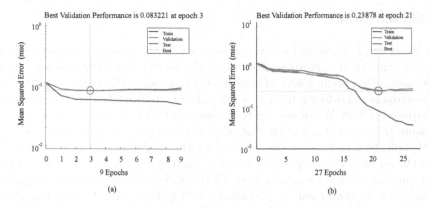

Fig. 8. CFBP algorithm performance graph (a) DLA_MS dataset (b) MS_dataset.

this study are provided in Fig. 8. The best validation performance yielded from the training procedure of CFBP algorithm with 9 epoch for the DLA_MS dataset is 0.08322 (see Fig. 8(a)). The best validation performance as obtained from the training procedure of CFBP algorithm with 27 epoch for the MS_dataset is 0.2387. (see Fig. 8(b)). According to the best validation performance result (see Fig. 8), calculated regarding the CFBP Algorithm, the classification accuracy rate of the DLA_MS dataset proves to be better than that of the MS_dataset.

The accuracy rate for the training procedure through the modelling by FFBP and CFBP network regarding the MS_dataset and DLA_MS dataset is presented in Table 3.

The Results of Artificial Neural Networks Classification. The results of the accuracy rates for the MS subgroup classification as obtained from FFBP and CFBP algorithms, applied to the MS_dataset and DLA_MS dataset are provided in Table 3.

Table 3. DLA_MS dataset, MS_dataset classification accuracy rates with FFBP and CFBP algorithms.

Data Sets	FFBP	CFBP
DLA_MS dataset (256 × 256)	92.10%	91.70%
MS_dataset (256 × 256)	77.08%	76.20%

According to the MS subgroup classification results as obtained from this study (see Table 3) are 92.1% and 91.7% for the FFBP and CFBP algorithms, respectively. They are applied on the DLA_MS dataset comprised of significant homogenous and self-similar pixels. The classification accuracy rates of the MS Subgroups with FFBP and CFBP algorithms through the DLA_MS dataset proved to be better respectively 15.02%, 15.5% compared to the MS_dataset.

4   Conclusion

This paper tends to extend earlier research with a novel approach proposed in MS core captions in regards to MRI through the use of multifractal technique. The classification performance of multifractal technique (DLA algorithm) for the MS subgroups regarding a total of 9 MS patients' dataset has been provided in a comparative way. When our study is compared with the other studies in the literature [22–28], it is seen that first of all there is no pixel point constraint for the classification of 3 subgroups of MS. Another point is that it is possible to select the significant homogenous and self-similar pixels through the multifractal technique. Last but not least, common FFBP and CFBP algorithms are applied to the datasets comprised of significant pixel points. FFBP algorithm yields the best result for overlapped dataset and it proves to be comparatively better than CFBP algorithm. Applying multifractal technique as well as FFBP and CFBP algorithms to MRI information gathered from pixel points of people who have three MS Subgroups was a first. Last but not least, the multifractal DLA algorithm application used in our study has proven to be a lot better when it is compared with the other relevant methods and techniques.

References

1. Noseworthy, J.H., Lucchinetti, C., Rodriguez, M., Weinshenker, B.G.: Multiple sclerosis. New Engl. J. Med. **343**, 938–952 (2000)
2. Confavreux, C., Vukusic, S.: Natural history of multiple sclerosis: a unifying concept. Brain **129**, 606–616 (2006)
3. Weinshenker, B.G., Bass, B., Rice, G.P.A., Noseworthy, J., Carriere, W., Baskerville, J., Ebers, G.C.: The natural history of multiple sclerosis: a geographically based study. I. Clinical course and disability. Brain **112**, 133–146 (1989)
4. Miller, D.H., Leary, S.M.: Primary-progressive multiple sclerosis. Lancet Neurol **6**, 903–912 (2007)
5. Poser, C.M., Paty, D.W., Scheinberg, L., McDonald, W.I., Davis, F.A., Ebers, G.C., Johnson, K.P., Sibley, W.A., Silberberg, D.H., Tourtellotte, W.W.: New diagnostic criteria for multiple sclerosis: guidelines for research protocols. Annal. Neurol. **13**(3), 227–231 (1983)
6. Kingwell, E., Zhu, F., Marrie, R.A., Fisk, J.D., Wolfson, C., Warren, S., Profetto - McGrath, J., Svenson, L.W., Jette, N., Bhan, V., Yu, B.N., Elliott, L., Tremlett, H.: High incidence and increasing prevalence of multiple sclerosis in British Columbia, Canada: findings from over two decades (1991–2010)
7. Grytten, N., Aarseth, J.H., Lunde, H.M., Myhr, K.M.: A 60- year follow-up of the incidence and prevalence of multiple sclerosis in Hordaland County. Western Norway. J. Neurol. Neurosurg. Psychiatry **87**, 100–105 (2016)
8. Browne, P., Chandraratna, D., Angood, C., Tremlett, H., Baker, C., Taylor, B.V., Thompson, A.J.: Atlas of Multiple Sclerosis 2013: a growing global problem with widespread inequity. Neurology **83**, 1022–1024 (2014)
9. Kobelt, G., Thompson, A., Berg, J., Gannedahl, M., Eriksson, J.: New insights into the burden and costs of multiple sclerosis in Europe. Mult. Scler. **23**, 179–191 (2017)

10. Stawowczyk, E., Malinowski, K.P., Kawalec, P., Mocko, P.: The indirect costs of multiple sclerosis: systematic review and meta-analysis. Expert Rev. Pharmacoecon Outcomes Res. **15**, 759–786 (2015)
11. Kurtzke, J.F.: Rating neurologic impairment in multiple sclerosis: an expanded disability status scale (EDSS). Neurology **33**(11), 1444–1444 (1983)
12. Dendrou, C.A., Fugger, L., Friese, M.A.: Immunopathology of multiple sclerosis. Nature Rev. Immunol. **15**(9), 545 (2015)
13. Karaca, Y., Osman, O., Karabudak, R.: Linear modeling of multiple sclerosis and its subgroups. Turkish J. Neurol. **2**, 7–12 (2015)
14. Thompson, A.J., Banwell, B.L., Barkhof, F., Carroll, W.M., Coetzee, T., Comi, G., Correale, J., Fazekas, F., Filippi, M., Freedman, M.S., Fujihara, K.: Diagnosis of multiple sclerosis: 2017 revisions of the McDonald criteria. The Lancet Neurology (2017)
15. Lublin, F.D., Reingold, S.C.: Defining the clinical course of multiple sclerosis results of an international survey. Neurology **46**(4), 907–911 (1996)
16. Fazzalari, N.L., Parkinson, I.H.: Fractal dimension and architecture of trabecular bone. J. Pathol. **178**(1), 100–105 (1996)
17. Esgiar, A.N., Naguib, R.N., Sharif, B.S., Bennett, M.K., Murray, A.: Fractal analysis in the detection of colonic cancer images. IEEE Trans. Inf. Technol. Biomed. **6**(1), 54–58 (2002)
18. Goldberger, A.L., Amaral, L.A., Hausdorff, J.M., Ivanov, P.C., Peng, C.K., Stanley, H.E.: Fractal dynamics in physiology: alterations with disease and aging. Proc. Natl. Acad. Sci. **99**(suppl. 1), 2466–2472 (2002)
19. Cross, S.S.: Fractals in pathology. J. Pathol. **182**(1), 1–8 (1997)
20. Arjunan, S.P., Kumar, D.K.: Fractal based modelling and analysis of electromyography (EMG) to identify subtle actions. In: 29th Annual International Conference of the IEEE Engineering in Medicine and Biology Society, pp. 1961–1964, August 2007
21. Galich, N.E.: Complex networks, fractals and topology trends for oxidative activity of DNA in cells for populations of fluorescing neutrophils in medical diagnostics. Phys. Procedia **22**, 177–185 (2011)
22. Esteban, F.J., Sepulcre, J., de Mendizbal, N.V., Goi, J., Navas, J., de Miras, J.R., Bejarano, B., Masdeu, J.C., Villoslada, P.: Fractal dimension and white matter changes in multiple sclerosis. Neuroimage **36**(3), 543–549 (2007)
23. Diniz, P.R.B., Murta-Junior, L.O., Brum, D.G., de Araujo, D.B., Santos, A.C.: Brain tissue segmentation using q-entropy in multiple sclerosis magnetic resonance images. Braz. J. Med. Biol. Res. **43**(1), 77–84 (2010)
24. Reishofer, G., Koschutnig, K., Enzinger, C., Ebner, F., Ahammer, H.: Fractal dimension and vessel complexity in patients with cerebral arteriovenous malformations. PloS One **7**(7), e41148 (2012)
25. Lahmiri, S., Boukadoum, M.: Automatic brain MR images diagnosis based on edge fractal dimension and spectral energy signature. In: 2012 Annual International Conference of the IEEE Engineering in Medicine and Biology Society (EMBC), pp. 6243–6246 (2012)
26. Takahashi, T., Murata, T., Omori, M., Kosaka, H., Takahashi, K., Yonekura, Y., Wada, Y.: Quantitative evaluation of age-related white matter microstructural changes on MRI by multifractal analysis. J. Neurol. Sci. **225**(1), 33–37 (2010)
27. Karaca, Y., Cattani, C.: Clustering Multiple Sclerosis subgroups with multifractal methods and Self-Organizing Map algorithm. Fractals **25**(04), 1740001 (2017)

28. Esteban, F.J., Sepulcre, J., de Miras, J.R., Navas, J., de Mendizbal, N.V., Goi, J., Quesada, J.M., Bejarano, B., Villoslada, P.: Fractal dimension analysis of grey matter in multiple sclerosis. J. Neurol. Sci. **282**(1), 67–71 (2009)
29. Karaca, Y., Cattani, C., Moonis, M., Bayrak, Ş.: Stroke subtype clustering by multifractal bayesian denoising with Fuzzy C Means and K-means algorithms. Complexity **2018**, 1–15 (2018)
30. Kramers, H.A.: Brownian motion in a field of force and the diffusion model of chemical reactions. Physica **7**(4), 284–304 (1940)
31. Turkevich, L.A., Scher, H.: Occupancy-probability scaling in diffusion-limited aggregation. Phys. Rev. Lett. **55**(9), 1026 (1985)
32. Lee, J., Stanley, H.E.: Phase transition in the multifractal spectrum of diffusion-limited aggregation. Phys. Rev. Lett. **61**(26), 2945 (1988)
33. Tolman, S., Meakin, P.: Off-lattice and hypercubic-lattice models for diffusion-limited aggregation in dimensionalities 28. Phys. Rev. A **40**(1), 428 (1989)
34. Wang, S.C.: Artificial neural network. In: Interdisciplinary Computing in Java Programming, pp. 81–100. Springer, Boston (2003)
35. Schalkoff, R.J.: Artificial Neural Networks. McGraw-Hill, New York (1997)
36. Johansson, E.M., Dowla, F.U., Goodman, D.M.: Backpropagation learning for multilayer feed-forward neural networks using the conjugate gradient method. Int. J. Neural Syst. **2**(04), 291–301 (1991)
37. Svozil, D., Kvasnicka, V., Pospichal, J.: Introduction to multi-layer feed-forward neural networks. Chemom. Intell. Lab. Syst. **39**(1), 43–62 (1997)
38. Goyal, S., Goyal, G.K.: Cascade and feedforward backpropagation artificial neural networks models for prediction of sensory quality of instant coffee flavoured sterilized drink. Can. J. Artif. Intell. Mach. Learn. Pattern Recogn. **2**(6), 78–82 (2011)
39. Lashkarbolooki, M., Shafipour, Z.S., Hezave, A.Z.: Trainable cascade-forward backpropagation network modeling of spearmint oil extraction in a packed bed using SC-CO2. J. Supercrit. Fluids **73**, 108–115 (2013)
40. Karaca, Y., Hayta, Ş.: Application and comparison of ANN and SVM for diagnostic classification for cognitive functioning. Appl. Math. Sci. **10**(64), 3187–3199 (2016)
41. Karaca, Y., Bayrak, Ş., Yetkin, E.F.: The classification of Turkish economic growth by artificial neural network algorithms. In: International Conference on Computation Science and its Applications, pp. 115–126 (2017)

Workshop Advances in Information Systems and Technologies for Emergency Management, Risk Assessment and Mitigation Based on the Resilience Concepts (ASTER 2018)

Geo-environmental Study Applied to the Life Cycle Assessment in the Wood Supply Chain: Study Case of Monte Vulture Area (Basilicata Region)

Serena Parisi[1]([⊠]), Maria Antonietta De Michele[2],
Domenico Capolongo[2], and Marco Vona[3]

[1] Progen S.r.l.s., P.le Vilnius, 27, 85100 Potenza, PZ, Italy
parisiserena80@gmail.com
[2] Department of Earth and Geoenvironmental Sciences, University of Bari,
Bari, Italy
m.demichele10@studenti.uniba.it,
domenico.capolongo@uniba.it
[3] School of Engineering, University of Basilicata, Potenza, Italy
marco.vona@unibas.it

Abstract. The present work was carried out in the context of the research project entitled "LIFE CYCLE ASSESSMENT (LCA): ANALYSIS OF SUS-TAINABILITY IN THE WOOD SUPPLY CHAIN OF BASILICATA REGION" ITALY. The work had as main objective the identification of the fundamental geo-environmental factors of Mount Vulture forested areas of the Basilicata region, which directly or indirectly affect the quality and quantity of forest areas, for a detailed analysis of certified raw materials used in the sustainable building. The survey, with appropriate skills provides a optimal study of the life cycle (LCA), which analyzes the into and out material flows, energy and emissions at all stages of the product, "from cradle to grave". For feedback LCA, it was used a new environmental indicator, represented by the Water Footprint (WF) which was calculated by means of CROPWAT version 8.0 Software. The results show that most of the Water Footprint associated with the raw material, in the wood supply chain, is attributable to the growth stage of forest types present in the Mount Vulture area. Obviously, this study focused on the initial phase of an extensive research project and has provided the information required for the next application of LCA in the sustainability analysis.

Keywords: Life Cycle Assessment · Monte Vulture · Water footprint
Sustainability analysis

1 Introduction

Taking into account the evolving eco-sustainability scenarios, the product/service certifications are increasingly required; in the case under examination for wood and derivatives products, environmental certifications are required for forest management, for wood products and derivatives. The main objective of the work was the identification of the fundamental geological, geomorphological, lithological, climatic and pedological factors of a sample area of the Basilicata region (Monte Vulture), characterized by forest coverings, which directly or indirectly influence the quality and quantity of the wood types, for a detailed analysis of certified raw materials, for use in eco-sustainable construction. It's in this sense that, the role of the geologist can find relevant applications about environmental studies. In fact, a detailed survey with appropriate skills, ensures a life cycle analysis (LCA) that detects the incoming and outgoing flows of the raw material, energy and emissions in all production phases. The analysis of the data obtained from the last mapping of the Italian network LCA (Life Cycle Analysis) (http://www.reteitalianalca.it/) chapter [1], places Basilicata among the last regions on the national territory, which uses this methodology as a tool for analyzing territorial management systems and wood supply chain. For this reason Basilicata was chosen as an experimental laboratory for the analysis of the life cycle of different wood types used in sustainable construction. In recent years, the wooden construction system is increasingly growing, thanks to the use of wood as a high performance structural material. Basilicata is a region rich in wooded areas that cover about 355.409 hectares. This resource represents a wealth, both for the environment and for the regional wood industry. The first step to start a sustainable forest management is the in-depth knowledge of the "forest resource". The study of the geological characteristics of the areas, where forest coverings are present, is important for an understanding of the factors that most influence the quality of the raw materials and also the certified quality of the final products. The present work has aimed to identify the distribution, type and quantity of the wood materials. To this end, the development of an integrated tool, necessary for the sustainable management of forest resources, combining territorial databases and territorial information systems (GIS), was of fundamental importance.

1.1 Life Cycle Assessment Methodology (LCA)

Before explaining the specific objectives of the work, it is necessary to introduce the usefulness of the Life Cycle Assessment methodology, used to evaluate the environmental impacts of the wood supply chain. The analysis of the life cycle is an assessment that arises as a result of the growing attention, by public and private subjects, to energy issues, climate change, water resource, land use and to the environmental sustainability of production processes. In this new approach it is necessary to associate the production process of the various products and services with a correct estimate of the environmental impacts that the process entails; this evaluation can be carried out through a Life Cycle Assessment (LCA). This method allows determining and quantifying the energy and environmental loads in the different phases of the production cycle. The LCA methodology also focuses on the water resource used at all stages of the production process. The fundamental aspect of this tool is the ability to evaluate the impacts of a product in a complete way, considering all the associated environmental aspects. In the LCA context, however, the water aspect and the impacts determined by its use are underestimated. This lack is probably caused by the fact that the LCA has developed mainly in the context of industrial processes that have few dependence on water resources, with respect to the production of agro-food products. It is in this context that the present study aimed at emphasizing the role of water resources and its environmental impact on the calculation of the LCA in the sustainability analysis of the wood supply chain. The used approach has allowed assessing and estimating the water impact in the sustainability evaluation of the wood supply chain of the Monte Vulture area. Therefore, through the LCA, the environmental effects on the consumption of water resources for the production cycle are quantified, using appropriate impact indicators.

1.2   Water Footprint Methodology for Evaluating and Managing Water Sustainability

LCA assessments are comparing with a new environmental indicator: the Water Footprint (WF). The WF is an indicator that quantifies the appropriation by man, of the available global fresh water, referring not only to the volume of water consumed, but also to the type and location of its use. The WF of a company is the total direct and indirect volume of utilized water, necessary to support all activities. For the WF calculation of a company we refer to the methodology presented by Gerbens-Leenes and Hoekstra [2]. The present work has focused on the geological and hydrogeological data which can provide fundamental information on environmental indicator assessments such as WF. A fundamental difference between the WF and the Life Cycle Analysis is that, while the result of the LCA is measured directly in CO_2 equivalent, the WF measures the impacts, according to the hydrogeological situation of the basin. Therefore, the WF of a product is not constant and precisely, for this reason, the year to which the data used for the WF calculation, must always be specified. The adopted method is the same one proposed by the WF Network. In this paper we will present a specific case study developed by going back to the Basilicata wood sector of the sample area represented by the Monte Vulture area. In conclusion have been identified the relevant geological variables that directly influence the choice of a type of wood, in terms of quality and quantity, in the use of the same in eco-sustainable building. The calculation software used to determine the Water Footprint is the CROPWAT developed by the United Nations Food and Agriculture Organization (FAO, 2009) [3], which is based on the method described by Allen [4]. The CROPWAT model calculates: *crop water requirement* (CWR) during the whole growing period in particular climatic conditions; *effective precipitation* during the same period; *irrigation requirements* (irrigation scheduling). This model is more effective when climate data obtained from representative pluviometric stations or from CLIMWAT (FAO 1993) [5] are available.

2   Study Area

2.1   Geology and Hydrogeology

The choice of the Monte Vulture sector as a study area is to be related to multiple factors. Considered, the strong multidisciplinary nature of the study, many factors have influenced the choice of the territorial context, among which, the large amount of available data, in terms of geological, hydrogeological, climate characters and land use data. In addition, the area of Monte Vulture is characterized by geomorphological, geological, climatic, pedological aspects, as well as diversity in terms of forest cover, useful for the application, at the local level, of the methodology for assessing the new environmental indicator, represented by Water Footprint (WF). Monte Vulture is an isolated cone (1320 m a.s.l.) shaped strato-volcano of Quaternary age, close to the western portion of the *Bradanic foredeep* on the northeastern sector of the Basilicata region (Italy) (Fig. 1). Volcanic activity took place between middle Pleistocene and Upper Pleistocene (Brocchini et al. [6]; Buettner et al. [7]). The volcanic products consist of 700 m of dominantly undersaturated silica pyroclastic deposits and subordinate lava flows arranged in radial banks with respect to the summit of the Monte Vulture (Schiattarella et al. [8]; Serri et al. [9]; Giannandrea et al. [10]). In the peripheral sectors of the volcanic structure, fluvio-lacustrine deposits from Pliocene to lower Pleistocene age, with intercalations of pyroclastic layers, are present (Fiumara di Atella Super-synthems, Giannandrea et al. [11] Fig. 1). Monte Vulture basin represents one of the most important aquifer systems of southern Italy, mainly constituted of pyroclastic and subordinate lava flow layers, with different permeabilities which locally give rise to distinct aquifer layers. The principal hydrogeological complexes are volcanic products, with high-medium permeability values composed mainly of pyroclastic deposits and subordinate lava flows, which are the principal host aquifer rocks (Fig. 2). Flow direction and rates are controlled by the properties of the rock matrix and also by the existing fracture network. The bedrock units are the marly-clayey complex, the calcareous-marly complex and arenaceous-conglomeratic-clayey showing less permeability. The different permeabilities of the volcanic products, fluvio-lacustrine deposits and the sedimentary bedrock are show in the hydrogeological map (Fig. 2).

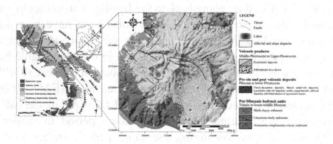

Fig. 1. On the left, sketch geological map of the central-southern Italy (from Bonardi et al.). On the right geological setting of Mt. Vulture area (base geological map by Giannandrea et al. modified [10]). The geological map is provide in Gauss-Boaga, Zone Est coordinates, using the Roma Datum of 1940, by Parisi et al. [12].

In agreement with UNESCO/FAO [13], the study area is characterized by a temperate Mediterranean climate, with moderately hot summers and cold winters. The investigated sector shows a mean annual rainfall amount of about 750 mm y-1 (data based on observations from 1964 to 2006, Hydrographic Service of Civil Engineers of Puglia Region) with a maximum amount of rainfall from November to February (Parisi et al. [12]). The maximum rainfall amounts are associated to the highest altitudes of the

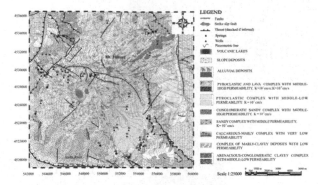

Fig. 2. Hydrogeological map of the study area. The map and the location data are provided in UTM Zone 33 coordinates, using the European Datum of 1950. Geology base map by Giannandrea et al. [10] by Parisi et al. [12].

study area. The estimated average annual precipitation amount of about 850–650 mm y-1 and a potential evapotranspiration of about 580 mm y-1. The annual average temperature for the Vulture area is about 13 °C (data from 1964 to 2006), with a maximum from July to August (22 °C) and a minimum between December and February ($\sim$5 °C) (Parisi et al. [10],).

2.2   Land Use and Pedology

This section describes the pedological provinces and their characteristics, with regard to the spatial and altimetry distribution of the origin and nature, land use and its vegetation, about the study area. This information was fundamental for data input of the CROPWAT 8.0 software [3], used to determine the WF indicator. The investigated area is characterized by the presence of four pedological provinces described below. The *pedological province 9*: Soils of the volcanic structure of the Monte Vulture; *pedological province 8*: Soils of the fluvio-lacustrine basins and the internal alluvial plains; *pedological province 7*: Soils of the central massifs with a irregular morphology; *pedological province 6*: Soils of central massifs with a steep morphology. Each of these provinces is characterized by the presence of different forest coverings. This characteristic lends itself to the achievement of the objectives, as well as, to the application of the Life Cycle Assessment (LCA) methodology for the evaluation of the water impact indicator represented by the Water Footprint. The thematic map, shown below, highlights the presence of different forest categories, digitized and archived in a geo-database appropriately implemented for this work. The forest categories cover areas with different geological, geomorphological and altitude features, with various local climatic characteristics (microclimate) in terms of rainwater rates, recorded by existing pluviometric stations in the area (Fig. 3). In details, the area has been divided into 4 sub-areas, corresponding to the pluviometric stations coverage, calls respectively: Monticchio Bagni A1 (North West sector); Melfi A2 (North Est sector); Rapolla A3 (South Est sector); Atella A4 (South sector); Castel Lagopesole, A5 (South West sector).

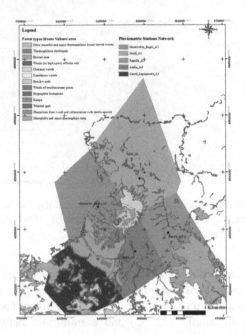

Fig. 3. Forest types map of the Monte Vulture area.

3 Methodology and Data Collection

The Water Footprint (WF) is an indicator that allows the calculation of water consumption, taking into account both direct and indirect uses. The WF of a product is defined as the total volume of fresh water used directly and indirectly to produce the product itself and it is evaluated considering the use of water in all phases of the production chain.

3.1 Water Footprint Calculation Method

The WF consists of three components: blue, green and gray water footprint (Hoekstra [2]). This is a peculiar characteristic of the WF methodology as it allows to distinguish between the different types of water and therefore to evaluate separately also the impacts that are connected.

Blue Water Footprint

The global resources of blue water consist in surface and groundwater and the blue water footprint is the volume of fresh water that is consumed to produce the goods and services consumed by an individual or a community. The final use of the blue water refers to one of the following four cases:

(1) evaporation of water;
(2) water that is incorporated into the product;

(3) water does not return to the same water catchment area, for example water returns to another river basin or to the sea;

(4) water is not returned in the same period, for example water is taken during a period of a dryness period and is returned in a wet period.

The blue water footprint in a process step is calculated as follows:

$$WF_{proc,blu} = Evaporation + Storage + Release flow$$

Green Water Footprint

The Green Water Footprint is the volume of rainwater consumed during the production process. The green WF is an indicator of the human use. Measure the part of evaporated rainwater, and therefore is no longer available for nature. Green water refers to precipitation which does not recharge groundwater, but is stored in the ground in the form of moisture or in any case remains temporarily on the surface or within the vegetation. In the end, this part of the precipitation evaporates or transpires through the plants. Green water is considered important for the growth of crops and forests because it can be a productive growth factor. However, it should be noted that not all of the green water can be consumed by crops because there will always be evaporation of the soil and because not all periods of the year and areas are suitable for the growth of crops and/or forests. The green water footprint in a process phase is equal to:

$$WF_{proc,green} = Evaporation + Storage$$

Gray Water Footprint

This component is an indicator of the pollution degree of fresh water associated with a process phase, and therefore of treatment in the specific case of the raw materials. It is defined as the volume of fresh water that is required to be able to assimilate the load of pollutants in order to maintain water quality standards. The gray water footprint of a process step is calculated as follows:

$$WF_{grey} = \frac{L}{C_{max} - C_{nat}} \ (volume/time)$$

Where C_{max} is the maximum acceptable concentration, and C_{nat} is the natural concentration of the receiving body.

3.2   Acquisition and Analysis of Input Data

For the calculation of the WF components, the published and unpublished data deriving from the PhD thesis of Parisi [14], referring to the 2007 hydrogeological year, were taken into account.

Input Climatic data

Temperature (C°), humidity (%), wind (km/day), solar exposure (hours), relative to the rainfall stations existing in the study area, have been considered. The obtained data were put in the CROPWAT 8.0 calculation software. The area has been divided, according to the coverage of the pluviometric stations network into 5 sub-areas, as before explained. The input data were georeferenced for the subsequent mapping phase to determine Water Footprint values. In detail, with the CROPWAT 8.0 Software have been also calculated the Radiation (Rad in $MJ/m^2/day$) and Evaporation (ET_0 in mm/day), values. ET_0 was calculated considering the option (Penman - Monteith Calcultion).

Input Pluviometric data

In terms of average monthly precipitation (mm), referred to a hydrogeological year.

Input Crop data

The data included in the FAO CROPWAT 8.0 software [3], related to the forest types identified in the study area, coming from professional and bibliography sources, because the database of the software did not provide indications about the following parameters: *Crop coefficient* (Kc); *Rooting depth* (m); *Critical depletion fraction*; *Yield response factor* (Ky); *Crop height* (m).

Input Soil data

The input data, about the soil types characterizing the study area, have been get from the regional portal of the Basilicata Region RSDI (http://rsdi.regione.basilicata.it/webGis/gisView.jsp). The parameters taken into account are: *Total Evailable Soil Moistore*; the *Maximum rain infiltration rate*; *Maximum rooting depht*; *Initial soil moisture depletion* and *Initial availabe soil moisture*.

For the meaning of the values and parameters, please refer to the CROPWAT 8.0 Software Manual [3].

4 Results and Discussion

4.1 Calculation of the Water Footprint in the Monte Vulture Area: CROPWAT Method

The total volume of water used to produce an agricultural and/or forest crop (crop water use, m^3/yr) is calculated as follows:

$$CWU_{[c]} = CWR_{[c]} \cdot \frac{Production_{[c]}}{Yeld_{[c]}}$$

where CWR is the *Crop Water Requirement*, measured at the field level (m^3/ha), *Production* is the total volume of crop production (ton year) and *Yeld* is the yield of the crop defined as the volume of production of a culture c by area of production unit (ton/ha). CWR is defined as the total amount of water needed for the evapotranspiration of a crop, from sowing to harvest and in a specific climate regime. The assumption underlying this calculation and the CWR model is that there are no water restrictions due to rain or irrigation, and the plant growth conditions are optimal. The water needs of the crops are calculated with the accumulation of data for the culture c and a given period d.

$$CWR_{[c]} = 10 \cdot \sum_{d=1}^{lp} ET_c[c, d]$$

Where, $CWR_{[c]}$ is the water requirement for the crop (m^3/hectare); ETc [c, d] is the daily evapotranspiration of the culture for the entire growth period (mm/day).

Alternatively, it can be estimated by means of a model based on empirical formulas. The classical reference model for calculating ET_C is the Penman - Monteith, according to the method recommended by FAO (Allen et al. [4]). The direct measurement of a plant's evapotranspiration is expensive and unusual. In general, evapotranspiration is estimated indirectly, using a model that uses data of the climate, soil and crop characteristics as data input.

4.2 Calculation of the Crop Water Requirement with the CROPWAT Model

The water need of the crops is the water necessary for the evapotranspiration, under ideal growth conditions, measured from sowing to harvest. Ideal conditions occur when soil water, thanks to rain or irrigation, does not limit plant growth and crop yield. The daily evapotranspiration of the cultures is obtained by multiplying the reference evapotranspiration with the crop coefficient (crop) Kc. The equation used to determine the ET_c for the present study is:

$$ET_{[c]} = Kc_{[c]} \cdot ET_0$$

$Kc_{[c]}$ and ET_0 were introduced in the previous section, where the calculation methods were illustrated. The reference evapotranspiration ET_0, is the evapotranspiration rate from a reference surface, with water availability. The only factors that influence ET_0 are climate parameters. ET_0 expresses the evaporation power in the atmosphere in a specific position and in a period of the year not considering the characteristics of the crops and soil factors. Kc on the other hand depends exclusively by the variety of forest type, climate and crop growth.

Green Water Footprint

As introduced in the section on the Water Footprint calculation method, the Water Footprint consists of three components: blue, green and gray water footprint (Hoekstra [4]).

$$WF_{prodotto} = WF_{blue} + WF_{green} + WF_{grey}$$

The ET_{green} is calculated as the minimum between, the effective precipitation of the entire growing period of the plant and the calculated CWR.

$$ET_{green} = \min\left(CWR, P_{eff}\right)$$

$$CWU_{green} = 10\sum\nolimits_{d=1}^{\lg p} ET_{green}$$

Effective precipitation (P_{eff}) is part of the total amount of precipitations that is retained from the soil so that it is potentially available to meet crop water needs. It is often less than the total precipitation because not all rainfall can be available for cultivation practices, for example due to runoff or infiltration (Dastane, 1978). The type of soil is a parameter to assess the amount of water retained within the soil. In the study case, having rainfall data directly inputted in the calculation software, the real P_{eff} was determined.

Blue Water Footprint

The evapotranspiration of blue water (ET_{blue}), is assumed equal to the minimum value between the actual irrigation flow and the water flow required for irrigation.

$$ET_{blue} = \min\left(IR, I_{eff}\right)$$

Effective irrigation is the part of water supplied for irrigation that is stored as moisture in the soil and available for evaporation of the plant. Irrigation requirement (IR) is calculated as the difference between crop water requirement and effective precipitation. The irrigation requirement is zero if the effective rainfall is larger than the crop water requirement. This means:

$$IR = \max(0, CWR - P_{eff})$$

The calculation carried out by CROPWAT, can be implemented by calculating the irrigation required by the plant based on the information about climate and culture parameters derived from the database implemented in this work.

Each period of plant growth has a different irrigation request and a different effective irrigation. The total value of the blue and green water footprint is calculated by adding the water flow rates measured in mm/day for the duration (in days) of the growth period. In our case IR (irrigation requirement) was found to be null, since the effective rainfall is higher than the crop water requirement (CWR). This means that in this case ET_{blue} is equal to zero.

Gray Water Footprint

The gray component of the Water Footprint for shrub growth (WFproc, gray, m3/ton) is calculated as the demand for the chemical rate per hectare (AR, kg/ha) multiplied by the leaching fraction (a) divided by the difference between the maximum acceptable concentration (C_{max}, kg/m^3) and the natural concentration for the considered pollutant (C_{nat} kg/m^3) and then divided by crop yield (Y, ton/ha). Gray WF in agriculture is inversely proportional to the amount of rainfall. Therefore, a smaller dilution water corresponds to the more intense precipitations. Being the study extended to the forest areas and not to the singular crops the gray component of WF cannot be considered because they are natural forest types set on the reliefs and valleys according to specific climatic characteristics (in terms of microclimate, altitudinal, pedological and exposure of the slopes). From the undertaken study it can be said that the values of the Water Footprint are due only to the green component. The WF data were uploaded to the GIS platform for better understand the spatial distributions of the obtained results.

From the analysis of the results, it can be said that the water requirement remains the same but obviously depending on the geographical position in terms of altitude, the type of forest and therefore the micro climate, the portion of the water requirement satisfied by the rainfall varies, as well as the part satisfied by irrigation. The water footprint is not constant and varies according to the season, the climatic conditions and the type of rainfall. Adding the results of each phase, we obtain the total value of the WF associated with the supply of raw materials, such as wood. The final result shows that the total WF associated with the product is given only by the green type WF contribution. The results in term of ET_{green} are shown in Fig. 4.

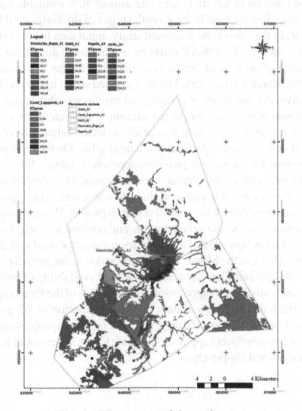

Fig. 4. ET_{green} map of the study area.

5 Conclusions

The evaluation of the impact of water footprints, associated with consumer products, until now had been limited to the characterization of the results (Ridoutt and Pfister [15]). In the present study, carried out as part of the research project entitled "LIFE CYCLE ASSESSMENT (LCA): SUSTAINABILITY ANALYSIS IN THE BASILICATA WOOD SUPPLY CHAIN", we went beyond the characterization phase for the impact assessment, using indexes impact measures proposed by researchers in the LCA field (Pfister [16]). The method provides indices that are a function of the geographical position in which the water footprints are located along the entire product chain. This also made it possible to evaluate the representativeness of these indices in relation to the water footprint calculated for the wood supply chain. Starting from the primary data it was highlighted in the calculation phase of the indicator, as the volumes of precipitation water for the growth of the forest types present in the study area, are almost 50% available for evapotranspiration, and therefore directly used in the growth stages of the considered forest covering type. In particular, in the case of the presented study, input data for the calculation of the Water Footprint with the CROPWAT software are not available in the literature. This represents an ounce of strength of the study undertaken for the first time in a territorial context such as the Monte Vulture area. The investigated sector in fact, is characterized by a rich in forest diversity and types of pedological provinces. This is due to the fact that there is not yet a unique reference for the calculation of the water footprint and therefore many studies give up the source of their data or leave out the calculation of the impression and consider their contribution to the final result negligible. On the contrary, in this study an explicit calculation was carried out, providing a precise reference for the used data. This constitutes an added value to the obtained results, since the calculations are made on precise and therefore comparable and reproducible references. The opportunity to carry out a pilot study was provided by the present research project. Water Footprint evaluation highlight critical points and future developments and confirm its strengths. The results of the Water Footprint show how most of the water footprint associated with the raw material in the wood supply chain, of the Monte Vulture area is due to the growth phase of different forest type, such as Oaks and Chestnut woods. The high availability of precipitation water allows to completely satisfy the evapotranspiration requests of the forest types. The results show that the agricultural WF is given only by the contribution of WFgreen. Obviously this study involved the initial phase of a large research project in progress and provided the necessary data for the subsequent application of Life Cycle Assessment in the analysis of sustainability in the wood supply chain.

References

1. Life Cycle Analysis. http://www.reteitalianalca.it/
2. Gerbens-Leenes, P.W., Hoekstra, A.Y.: The water footprint of energy from biomass: a quantitative assessment and consequences of an increasing share of bio-energy in energy supply. Ecol. Econ. **68**, 1052–1060 (2008)
3. FAO, 2009 FAO: CLIMWAT 2.0 database, Food and Agriculture Organization, Rome, Italy. www.fao.org/nr/water/infores_databases_climwat.html. 85

4. Allen, J.A.: Virtual water: A strategic resource, global solutions to regional conflicts. Groundwater **36**(4), 545–546 (1998)
5. FAO 1993: CLIMWAT for CROPWAT: a climatic database for irrigation planning and management. Irrigation and Drainage, Paper No. 49, FAO, Rome. http://www.fao.org
6. Brocchini, D., La Volpe, L., Laurenzi, M.A., Principe, C.: Storia evolutiva del Monte Vulture, vol. 12. Plinius (1994)
7. Buettner, A., Principe, C., Villa, I.M., Brocchini, D.: Geocronologia 39Ar -40Ar del Monte Vulture. In: Principe, C. (a cura di) La Geologia del Monte Vulture. Regione Basilicata. Dipartimento Ambiente, Territorio e Politiche della Sostenibilità. Grafiche Finiguerra, Lavello, pp. 73–86 (2006)
8. Schiattarella, M., Di Leo, P., Beneduce, P., Giano, S.I.: Quaternary uplift vs tectonic loading: a case study from the Lucanian Apennine, southern Italy. Quatern. Int. **101–102**, 239–251 (2003)
9. Serri, G., Innocenti, F., Manetti, P.: Magmatism from mesozoic to present: petrogenesis, time-space distribution and geodynamic implications. In: Vai, G.B., Martini, I.P. (eds.) Anatomy of an Orogen: the Apennines and Adjacent Mediterranean Basins, pp. 77–103. Springer, Dordrecht (2001). https://doi.org/10.1007/978-94-015-9829-3_8
10. Giannandrea, P., La Volpe, L., Principe, C., Schiattarella, M.: Carta geologica del Monte Vulture alla scala 1:25.000. Litografia Artistica Cartografica, Firenze (2004)
11. Giannandrea, P., La Volpe, L., Principe, C., Schiattarella, M.: Unità stratigrafiche a limiti inconformi e storia evolutiva del vulcano medio-pleistocenico di Monte Vulture (Appennino meridionale, Italia). Boll. Soc. Geol. Ital. **125**, 67–92 (2006)
12. Parisi, S., Paternoster, M., Kohfahl, C., Pekdeger, A., Meyer, H., Hubberten, H.W., Spilotro, G., Mongelli, G.: Groundwater recharge areas of a volcanic aquifer system inferred from hydraulic, hydrogeochemical and stable isotope data: Mount Vulture, southern Italy. Hydrogeol. J. (2011). https://doi.org/10.1007/s10040-010-0619-8
13. UNESCO/FAO: Carte bioclimatique de la Zone Méditerrané (1963)
14. Parisi, S.: Hydrogeochemical tracing of the groundwater flow pathways in the Mont Vulture volcanic aquifer system (Basilicata, southern Italy). Ph.D. thesis, p. 314 (2010)
15. Ridoutt, B.G., Eady, S.J., Sellahewa, J., Simons, L., Bektash, R.: Water footprinting at the product brand level: case study and future challenges. J. Clean. Prod. **17**(13), 1228–1235 (2009)
16. Pfister, S., Hellweg, S.: The water "shoesize" vs. footprint of bioenergy. Proc. Natl. Acad. Sci. **106**(35), E93–E94 (2009)

A Preliminary Method for Assessing Sea Cliff Instability Hazard: Study Cases Along Apulian Coastline

Roberta Pellicani[✉] ⓘ, Ilenia Argentiero ⓘ, and Giuseppe Spilotro ⓘ

Department of European and Mediterranean Cultures,
University of Basilicata, Matera, Italy
{roberta.pellicani, ilenia.argentiero,
giuseppe.spilotro}@unibas.it

Abstract. The instability processes of sea cliffs are the result of the influence of different hazard factors that depends mainly on the coastal morphology. For this reason, the hazard associated to instability processes affecting cliffs can be carried out by means of different methodological approaches. In particular, the presence of a beach at the cliff toe, which dampens the impulsive impact of sea waves and reduces the marine processes of erosion on the cliff, allows to analyze it as a generic rocky slope with same morphology and identical geo-structural characters. Among different stability methods, heuristic approaches can provide a preliminary evaluation of the stability conditions of cliffs and a zonation of the cliff portions most susceptible to instability phenomena. In presence of fractured, anisotropic and discontinuous rocky cliffs, the stability analyses through a deterministic approach are difficult to be performed. This paper presents a procedure to assess the stability conditions of three rocky cliffs located along the Apulia coast based on a heuristic slope instability system, the Slope Mass Rating (SMR) of Romana (1985). This model was used to individuate the most unstable areas on the cliff walls, mostly prone to rockfall hazard. This procedure is particularly useful, as can address more detailed study on the cliff portions most susceptible to block detachment.

Keywords: Sea cliff · Instability · Hazard · Slope Mass Rating method

1 Introduction

The instability processes of sea cliffs, in most cases, are the result of their morpho-evolutional dynamic. Several factors affect the hazard of sea cliffs and their identification is essential to evaluate the relevant aspects of instability phenomena (size, frequency or return time, time between the first measurable events and the parossistic event) and the risk mitigation strategies. The factors, affecting intrinsically the stability of cliffs, are therefore those typical of hillslopes, such as the lithological, stratigraphic, structural and morphological (slope and aspect of the wall, etc.) settings and the hydrogeology and the mechanical properties of the rocky mass [1, 2]. However, the external factors are represented by impact of sea waves, currents and tides, as well as meteorological agents, the biological activity of marine micro and macro organisms

© Springer International Publishing AG, part of Springer Nature 2018
O. Gervasi et al. (Eds.): ICCSA 2018, LNCS 10961, pp. 152–165, 2018.
https://doi.org/10.1007/978-3-319-95165-2_11

and, finally, by human activities [3]. The influence of different hazard factors on the whole instability process depends on the coastal morphology, i.e. lower cliffs are more affected by the sea actions, while coastal morphologies more similar to hillslopes are mostly subject to the effects of the subaerial processes, depending on the lithological and stratigraphic structure of the cliff [4]. In this scenario, an essential role is assumed by the presence or absence of the marine platform at the coast toe and, where present, by its morphology [5]. In fact, only the presence of a shallow platform could dampen the impulsive impact of waves to the cliff, reducing the marine processes of erosion and retreat of the cliff. In the same way, the presence of a beach at cliff toe reduces the impact of the waves, producing a lower incidence of wave motion on the evolutional dynamic of the cliff. In this case, the instability processes of the cliff walls are attributable exclusively to the subaerial processes and, therefore, in the context of a stability analysis of the cliffs with beach at the toe, the wall can be treated as a generic rock slope of the same morphology and with identical geo-structural characters. As the morphology of cliffs changes, it is different not only the methodological approach for spatial hazard (susceptibility) assessment, but the overall level of risk associated and therefore the degree of attention and mitigation actions of the potential risk. Indeed, the possible detachment of a rocky block from a plunging cliff involves a degree of loss on a certain element at risk generally lower than a potential collapse from a cliff with beach at the toe. For these reasons, in assessing the hazard associated to sea cliffs instability, the first factor to be considered is the morphology of the coastline, because it is the guideline for the choice of the forecast model and, consequently, of the predisposing factors to be implemented.

In the national and international literature there are numerous contributions related to the hazard (or susceptibility) evaluation procedures. The main methodological approaches vary from empirical or statistical techniques, preferably applied on a regional scale, to deterministic approaches (numerical modelling), mainly used in local-level susceptibility analyses with a limited number of parameters. Concerning rocky slope instability, regional studies are generally aimed to produce hazard maps in GIS environment, by creating and overlapping basic thematic layers representing the distribution in the study area of the factors considered significant for the instability process [6]. Deterministic approaches, including numerical modelling methods (i.e. Finite Element Method – FEM, Finite Difference Method – FDM, Boundary Element Method – BEM, Distinct Element Method – DEM) allow to perform advanced modelling of the failure mechanisms through sophisticated calculation codes [7]. Nevertheless, the implementation of the complex stress-strain relations of the material requires to know in depth the study domain (geometry, morphological, structural and hydrogeological structure of the cliff, strength and deformability parameters of rocky mass), available only through an accurate in situ surveys. The stability analysis of a rock mass, fractured and karstfied, anisotropic and discontinuous from a geomechanical and geostructural point of view, makes a deterministic approach difficult. In the absence of detailed input data, the methodological approach that should be adopted for a preliminary study of the stability conditions of cliffs must necessarily be based on a series of spatial correlations between the geometric, geomechanical and geostructural parameters characterizing the rock mass to achieve a geomechanical parameterization and zoning of the area and the relative susceptibility to instability phenomena.

In this paper, a procedure to assess the stability conditions of cliffs is presented. The methodological approach, carried out on three rocky cliffs located along the Apulia coast, is based on a heuristic slope instability system, the Slope Mass Rating (SMR) of Romana [8]. This model was used to individuate the most unstable areas on the cliff walls, mostly prone to rockfall hazard, starting from the estimation of geometric, structural and mechanical features of the rocky mass. This procedure is particularly useful, as can addressed more detailed study on the cliff portions most susceptible to block detachment.

2 Methodology

In order to obtain a classification of the rocky mass quality and to individuate the potential failure mechanisms along the cliff face, the Rock Mass Rating (RMR) system of Bieniawski [9] and Markland's [10] test were, respectively, carried out. These analyses need the knowledge of several parameters on rock material and discontinuities, obtainable from a geomechanical characterization of the rock masses, to be performed along scan lines, aimed to collect data about: number of joints families, dip and dip direction of each discontinuities, compressive strength of rock material, Rock Quality Designation (RQD) values, spacing between discontinuities, persistence, roughness and aperture of the joints, type and nature of the filling material, hydraulic conditions and weathering conditions of discontinuities. The geomechanical survey has been executed according to ISRM standards [11]. The RMR characterization was performed by assigning the values summarized in Table 1 to the several rocky mass parameters and by summing them. The quality class of rocky mass, as well as other mechanical parameters, was deduced from the overall value of RMR index, as shown in Table 2. The kinematic analysis has been carried out using the Markland's (1972) test, in order to analyze the potential failure mechanisms. In general, the kinematic analysis, which is purely geometric, examines which modes of failure are possible in a jointed rock mass, without consideration of the forces involved [12]. The stability conditions of rock slopes are strongly influenced by the geostructural features of the rock mass. Therefore, a correct evaluation of the trend of discontinuities within the rock mass in relation to the slope orientation is crucial for the identification of falling paths of potentially unstable boulders [13, 14]. The Markland's test differentiates the sliding along one plane (planar sliding) from the sliding along the line of intersection of two joints (wedge sliding) and from the toppling. In particular, angular relationships between discontinuities (dip and dip direction) and slope surfaces (slope angle and aspect) were applied to determine the potential and modes of failures. The geomechanical data, i.e. RMR index and joint orientation properties, were subsequentely used for evaluating the spatial distribution of SMR index (Romana 1985) on the rock walls of cliffs. The Slope Mass Rating (SMR) system is a heuristic slope instability model [15–17], which has been applied in order to individuate the most unstable areas on the rocky faces, which are potential block detachment areas.

The SMR index is generally obtained, by modifying the RMR index (Bieniawski 1989) through four adjustment factors, three depending on the relationship between

Table 1. Rock mass classification parameter values of Bieniawski [9].

Parameters			Value ranges						
1	Compressive strength of rock material	Point load strength index (MPa)	> 10	10–4	4–2	2–1	Not Applicable		
		Uniaxial compressive strength (MPa)	> 250	250–100	100–50	50–25	25-5	5 - 1	< 1
	Rating		**15**	**12**	**7**	**4**	**2**	**1**	**0**
2	RQD (%)		100–90	90–75	75–50	50–25	< 25		
	Rating		**20**	**17**	**13**	**8**	**3**		
3	Spacing of joints (m)		> 2	2–0,6	0,6–0,2	0,2–0,06	< 0,06		
	Rating		**20**	**15**	**10**	**8**	**5**		
4	Conditions of joints		Very rough surfaces, Not continuous, No separation, Unweathered wall rock	Slightly rough surfaces, Separation < 1 mm, Slightly weathered wall rock	Slightly rough surfaces, Separation < 1 mm, Highly weathered wall rock	Slickensided surfaces or gouge < 5 mm thick or separation 1-5 mm Continuous	Soft gouge > 5 mm thick or separation > 5 mm Continuous		
	Rating		**30**	**25**	**20**	**10**	**0**		
5	Groundwater	Inflow per 10 m tunnel length (l/min)	None	< 10	10–25	25–125	> 125		
		Ratio (joint water pressure)/(major principal stress)	0	< 0,1	0,1–0,2	0,2–0,5	> 0,5		
		General conditions	Completely dry	Damp	Wet	Dripping	Flowing		
	Rating		**15**	**10**	**7**	**4**	**0**		

Table 2. RMR classification of Bieniawski [9]: RMR values, rock quality class, average stand-up time, cohesion and friction angle of rock mass.

$RMR_{'79\,-'89}$	0-20	21–40	41-60	61-80	81-100
Class	V	IV	III	II	I
Quality	Very poor	Poor	Discrete	Good	Ottima
Average stand-up time	30 min. for 1 m span	10 h for 2.5 m span	1 week for 5 m span	1 year for 8 m span	20 years for 15 m span
c' (MPa)	< 0,10	0,10–0,20	0,20–0,30	0,30–0,40	> 0,40
φ' (°)	< 15°	15°–25°	25°–35°	35°–45°	> 45°

joint and slope orientation and one factor related to the excavation method, through the following equation:

$$SMR = RMR_{1989} + (F_1 \times F_2 \times F_3) + F_4 \tag{1}$$

where: RMR_{1989} is the Rock Mass Rating by Bieniawski [9]. F_1 reflects the parallelism between joint (α_j) and slope (α_s) face strikes. F_2 refers to joint dip angle (β_j) in failure planar mode and the plunge of the intersection line of two discontinuities (β_i) in the

Table 3. Values of adjustment factors: F1, F2, F3 in relation to joint and slope orientations and for different failure modes; F4 for different methods of excavation (Romana 1985 [8])

Adjustment factors Failure modes*		Orientation classes				
		Very favourable (very low failure probability)	Favourable	Fair	Unfavourable	Very unfavourable (very high failure probability)
P/W	$\alpha|_{j/i}$-$\alpha_s|$	>30°	30°–20°	20°–10°	10°–5°	< 5°
T	$\alpha|_j$-α_s-180|					
F_1		0.15	0.40	0.70	0.85	1.00
P/W	$\beta_{j/i}$	< 20°	20°–30°	30°–35°	35°–45°	>45°
T	β_j					
(P/W) F_2		0.15	0.40	0.70	0.85	1.00
(T) F_2		1.00	1.00	1.00	1.00	1.00
P/W	$\beta|_{j/i}$-$\beta_s|$	>10°	10°–0°	0°	0–(–10°)	<-10°
T	$\beta|_{j/i}$ + $\beta_s|$	< 110°	110°–120°	>120°	–	–
F_3		0	–6	–25	–50	–60
F_4		Natural slopes	Presplitting	Smooth blasting	Blasting or mech. excavation	Deficient blasting
		15	10	8	0	–8

*P: Planar sliding; W: Wedge sliding; T: Toppling.
α_s: dip direction of slope; $\alpha_{j/i}$: dip direction of joint or intersection line of two joints.
β_s: dip of slope; $\beta_{j/i}$: dip of joint or intersection line of two joints.

failure wedge mode. F_3 reflects the relationship between the dip of joints (β_j) and the slope angle of rock faces (β_s). F_4 is related to the method of slope excavation; for natural slopes, the value of F_4 is 15. In Table 3 the values of adjustment factors F_1, F_2 and F_3 for different failure modes (planar sliding, wedge sliding and toppling) are listed. The SMR index ranges between 0 and 100 and is subdivided into five classes of instability (Table 4). On the basis of the SMR index, a spatially distributed classification of unstable areas on the rock walls of cliffs has been obtained, taking into account the quality of the rock mass (through the RMR index) and the spatial relationships between the discontinuities and the orientation of the rock faces. These most unstable areas have been considered as potential rockfall detachment areas and used as input release areas for the subsequent numerical simulation of the rockfall trajectories. This method does not consider the marine erosion factors, in particular the wave impact effect. For this reason, it was applied to cliffs characterized by the presence of a beach at the toe.

Table 4. Description of SMR and stability classes with the corresponding potential failure mode and suggested stabilization measures.

Class n.	V	IV	III	II	I
SMR values	0-20	21-40	41-60	61-80	81-100
Description	Very bad	Bad	Normal	Good	Very good
Stability	Completely unstable	Unstable	Partially stable	Stable	Completely stable
Failures	Big planar or soil-like or circular	Planar or big wedges	Planar along some joints or many wedges	Some blocks	No failure
Support	Reexcavation	Corrective	Systematic	Occasional	None

3 Cliffs of Apulia and Study Cases

The Apulia region is characterized by a relevant extension of coasts, about 900 km, of which about 25% (210 km) is represented by cliffs, both plunging cliffs and cliffs with beach at the toe (Fig. 1).

Most of the cliffs in Apulia are located along the coastline of the Gargano promontory; in this area they extend almost continuously from Rodi Garganico to Manfredonia and there are both plunging cliffs and cliffs with beach. Moving further south along the Apulian coastline, the cliffs are present near the city of Trani and Bisceglie. Although this stretch of coastline is classifiable as a cliff, due to the more modest heights it is not comparable in height to the Gargano cliffs. Along the southern coastline of Bari there are significant stretches of cliffs, particularly along the coastline of the territory of Polignano a Mare. The territory of Brindisi is also characterized by stretches of cliffs with not very high heights; they are located all along the coastline called "Costa Merlata" due to the continuous alternation of small bays and headlands.

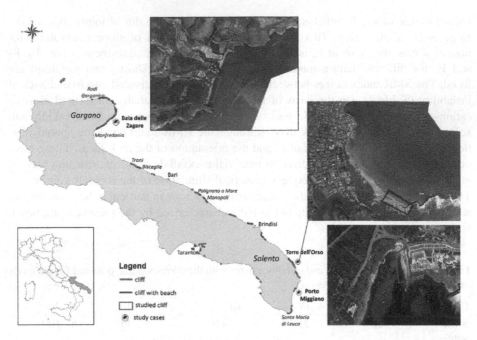

Fig. 1. Distribution of cliffs along the coastline of Apulia region, with localization of the three study cases (Baia delle Zagare, Torre dell'Orso and Porto Miggiano) and orthophotos of the analyzed cliff treats.

There are also stretches of plunging cliffs and cliffs with sandy and pebble beaches at the toe both in the north and in the south of the city of Brindisi.

The Salento coastline is characterized by different stretches of cliffs, mainly on the Adriatic side rather than on the Ionian one. Indeed, there are plunging cliffs and cliffs with beach at the toe along the coastline from San Foca to San Andrea, passing through Torre dell'Orso, where the cliffs reach even more considerable heights. They are also present in the Otranto territory, where a part of the inhabited area is placed on vertical cliffs. Other important cliffs of Salento are located at south of Santa Cesarea Terme near Porto Miggiano and also along the coastal stretch, which runs for about 6 km in length, starting from Gagliano del Capo up to Santa Maria di Leuca. Also on the Ionian side there are coastal stretches classified as plunging cliffs and cliffs with sandy beach at the toe, which however presents a linear development much more limited than the stretches of cliffs facing the Adriatic Sea. Finally, cliffs are also present in the ionian arch of Taranto, they are cliffs with a height much lower than those described above and border the perimeter of the Mar Grande and continue south of Taranto, resulting in a succession of beautiful pocket beaches.

In the following paragraphs, the procedure for assessing the propensity to instability of the cliff has been applied to three case studies, specifically Baia delle Zagare, Torre dell'Orso and Porto Miggiano. For these study cases, a spatially distributed classification of unstable areas on the rocky walls has been obtained, on the basis of the SMR index, taking into account the quality of the rock mass (through the RMR index) and the spatial relationships between the discontinuities and the orientation of the rock faces. This analysis was carried out in 2010 during a study on the cliffs of Apulia region.

3.1 Baia delle Zagare

The near coastline of Baia delle Zagare (Gargano area, Fig. 1) is characterized by a wide variety of morphologies, including limestone cliffs, conglomerates, wide beaches, suspended valleys, bays, coves and minor forms. The cliff of Baia delle Zagare has essentially a linear development, interspersed with headlands and the outlet of two river valleys where the pebble beach reaches its maximum width (Figs. 1 and 2a). In the stretches of cliffs not protected from beach at the toe, the signs of instability are more evident, with open fractures, presence of blocks detached from the rock wall, etc. (Fig. 2b). Characteristic is the presence of two stacks in the central part of the bay, one of which also has a marine arch (Fig. 2c). The study was conducted on a stretch of coast where the cliff has a pebble beach at the toe, is about 20–30 m high and consists of a single lithology, namely limestone densely fractured with flint nodules and bands.

Fig. 2. Photos of Baia delle Zagare coastline (a), of an unstable block bordered by an open fracture (b) and of stacks (c).

These are in decimetric dip-slope strata interspersed with flint bands of similar thickness. At places the orientation of the layers appears chaotic because it is affected by slump.

In order to define the characteristics of the discontinuities and the overall quality of the rock mass, geomechanical surveys were carried out along two scan lines, in the most accessible portion of cliff walls. A total of 25 discontinuities have been detected. The kinematic analyses, conducted using the Markland test (1972), have identified as possible instability mechanism only the planar sliding along some planes of discontinuity in both the scan lines. The evaluation and classification of parameters related to the intact rock and the discontinuities, according to RMR of Bieniawski allowed to define as discrete the quality of rocky mass along both the scan lines. The instability zonation along the rocky faces, according to the SMR model, highlighted two main unstable areas in both the scan lines and a secondary, in extension, zone partially instable within the S1 scan line (Fig. 3).

Fig. 3. Zonation of SMR instability classes along Baia delle Zagare cliff.

3.2   Torre dell'Orso

The morphology of the near coastline of Torre dell'Orso site is characterized by the presence of cliffs interspersed with a wide sandy bay with a width of 30–40 meters and a length of 750 m (Fig. 1). The cliffs show evident signs of rockfall for most of the cases occurred with the mechanism of cracking by erosion at the toe and toppling. Indeed, rocky blocks of various sizes, which can reach several cubic meters of volume, are almost always at the toe of the cliffs, and in general the signs left on the walls by the instability phenomena are clearly visible; in most of it there are main scarps and collapsed blocks (Fig. 4).

The cliff in the studied stretch is, in the Torre dell'Orso area, one of the sites most affected by instability phenomena. Indeed, there are large rocky volumes on the sandy beaches due to rockfall and toppling phenomena. The studied cliff is near the Cave of San Cristoforo and consists of calcarenite. It is about 12–15 m high and has a sandy beach at the toe. In order to define the characteristics of rocky mass and discontinuities, geomechanical surveys were carried out along a scan line (S1), in the most accessible portion of cliff walls. A total of 23 discontinuities have been detected. The instability mechanisms identified by the Markland test are the toppling and the planar sliding on some discontinuity planes.

Fig. 4. Photos of unstable portions of Torre dell'Orso cliff.

The RMR classification of rocky mass allowed to define as discrete the quality of rocky walls. The instability zonation, according to the SMR model, highlighted two main unstable areas in both the scan lines and a stable area within them (Fig. 5).

Fig. 5. Zonation of SMR instability classes along Torre dell'Orso cliff.

3.3 Porto Miggiano

The third study case, near the Porto Miggiano village, consists of a cliff with a height varying between 20 and 25 m. A man-made platform is present at the toe. The products of instability, consisting of calcarenite blocks of variable dimensions detached by the cliff walls, occupy a narrow band that borders the cliff and are partially or completely submerged (Fig. 1). The studied cliff is characterized by two overlapped levels of calcarenite of different age and consistency, with marl intercalations and averagely fractured. The instability process is characterized by three components: (i) processes of continental origin; (ii) presence of karstic levels and karstic-marine caves at sea level standstills; (iii) processes of marine origin, mainly due to the impulsive transfer of wave energy. Along the east side wall of the Porto Miggiano inlet, 11 scan lines were made for a total length of about 112 m distributed as follows: S1–S7 starting from the beach, on the outcrop of Calabrian calcarenite; S8–S11 on the outcrop of Tyrrhenian calcarenite (Fig. 6).

Fig. 6. Zonation of SMR instability classes along the eastern side wall of Porto Miggiano cliff.

A number of 110 discontinuities were detected. The Markland test highlighted planar sliding, wedge sliding and toppling as potential instability kinematics along some joints. The mapping of the potential instability was limited to the accessible portions of the cliff on which it was possible to carried out the geomechanical survey, namely up to a height of about 2 m from the platform. At places, the stability zonation has been extended to heights greater than 2 m based on the persistence of the discontinuities detected. Further potentially unstable portions have been qualitatively identified by visual analysis. The results are shown in Fig. 6. The cliff walls along the east side of inlet are mainly partially stable or unstable.

4   Discussion and Conclusion

Concerning Baia delle Zagare, the discrete geomechanical characteristics of the rocky mass and the distribution and orientation of discontinuities do not appear to determine particular instability conditions. However, the thick stratification of limestone with dip-slope flint, although of low angle, in relation to the orientation of cliff walls leads to potential instability. Furthermore, evident signs of previous and in progress instability

Fig. 7. Detachment of blocks from the cliff of Baia delle Zagare: (a) photo before the event with highlighted elements at risks, (b) photo after the event, (c) SMR modeling results with localization of the detachment [photos by Antonello Fiore].

are visible in correspondence of the promontories and the stretches of cliffs not protected from the beach at the toe. On the latter the actions of the sea storms, especially in winter, determine the widening of fractures and the fall of blocks as evidenced by the "monolith" and other detached blocks in the northern section of the bay (Fig. 2).

Also the calcarenite cliff of Torre dell'Orso, in the studied section, shows fair geomechanical characteristics of the rocky mass due to the high value of the RQD index (massive calcarenite) and the high joint spacing. Nevertheless, the accumulations at the cliff toe highlight the susceptibility of the cliff to instability and, in this regard, the kinematic analysis has shown propensity to toppling and sliding of blocks along a surface. The SMR stability analysis also highlighted areas of potential instability.

Along Porto Miggiano previous and potential instability conditions were highlighted. These derive from the presence of numerous fractures, sub-vertical and persistent, some with non-matching extremities, which also define blocks of large dimensions classifiable as unstable. Moreover, the presence of an artificial platform at the cliff toe is ineffective for the purposes of protection from the wave actions especially during sea storms.

Finally, the effectiveness and usefulness of the proposed procedure is confirmed by a rockfall event occurred at Baia delle Zagare in 2011, after these analyses, in a zone of the studied cliff where the rocky face was inclined in counterslope due to the presence at the toe of an erosion line (Fig. 7a, b). This event, although the area affected by instability was not too wide, could have determine high risk condition for the habitual presence of people. This instability event is important because it represents a validation of SMR model results, as the detachment zone is comprised in the area classified as unstable (Fig. 7c).

References

1. Budetta, P., Galietta, G., Santo, A.: A methodology for the study of the relation between coastal cliff erosion and the mechanical strength of soils and rock masses. Eng. Geol. **56**, 243–256 (2000)
2. Dipova, N.: Preliminary assessment on the modes of instability of the Antalya (SW-Turkey) coastal cliff. Environ. Earth Sci. **59**, 547–560 (2009)
3. Pellicani, R., Miccoli, D., Spilotro, G., Gallipoli, M.R., Mucciarelli, M., Bianca, M.: Dynamic response of a rocky cliff under the sea wave pulse: a study along the Adriatic coast of Polignano (Apulia, Italy). Environ. Earth Sci. **73**(10), 6243–6257 (2015). https://doi.org/10.1007/s12665-014-3848-7
4. Bezerra, M.M., Moura, D., Ferreira, O., Taborda, R.: Influence of wave action and lithology on sea cliff mass movements in Central Algarve Coast, Portugal. J. Coast. Res. **27**(6A), 162–171 (2011)
5. Andriani, G.F., Walsh, N.: Rocky coast geomorphology and erosional processes: a case study along the Murgia coastline South of Bari, Apulia - SE Italy. Geomorphology **87**(3), 224–238 (2007)
6. Dorren, L.K.A., Seijmonsbergen, A.C.: Comparison of three GIS-based models for predicting rockfall runout zones at a regional scale. Geomorphology **56**, 49–64 (2003)
7. Agliardi, F., Crosta, G.: High resolution three-dimensional numerical modelling of rockfalls. Int. J. Rock Mech. Min. Sci. **40**, 455–471 (2003)

8. Romana, M.: New adjustment rating for application of Bieniawski classification to slopes. In: International Symposium on Role of Rock Mechanics, Zacatecas, pp. 49–53 (1985)
9. Bieniawski, Z.T.: Engineering Rock Mass Classifications, p. 25. Wiley, New York (1989)
10. Markland, J.T.: A useful technique for estimating the stability of rock slopes when the rigid wedge sliding type of failure is expected. Imperial College Rock Mechanics Research Report No. 19, p. 10 (1972)
11. ISRM: Suggested method for the quantitative description of discontinuities in rock masses. In: Brown, E.T. (ed.) Rock Characterization Testing and Monitoring, pp. 3–52. Pergamon, Oxford (1981)
12. Gupta, V., Tandon, R.S.: Kinematic rockfall hazard assessment along a transportation corridor in the Upper Alaknanda valley, Garhwal Himalaya, India. Bull. Eng. Geol. Environ. 74(2), 315–326 (2014). https://doi.org/10.1007/s10064-014-0623-7
13. Ghosh, S., Gunther, A., Carranza, E.J.M., Van Westen, C.J., Jetten, V.G.: Rock slope instability assessment using spatially distributed structural orientation data in Darjeeling Himalaya (India). Earth Surf. Process. Landf. 35(15), 1773–1792 (2010)
14. Barlow, J., Gilham, J., Ibarra Cofrã, I.: Kinematic analysis of sea cliff stability using UAV photogrammetry. Int. J. Remote Sens. 38, 2464–2479 (2017). https://doi.org/10.1080/01431161.2016.1275061
15. Budetta, P.: Assessment of rockfall risk along roads. Nat. Hazard Earth Syst. Sci. 4, 71–81 (2004)
16. Marchetti, D., Avanzi, G.A., Sciarra, N., Calista, M.: Slope stability modelling of a sandstone cliff south of Livorno (Tuscany, Italy). Risk Anal. 6, 321–333 (2008). https://doi.org/10.2495/risk080321. WIT Trans. Inf. Commun. 39
17. Pellicani, R., Spilotro, G., Van Westen, C.J.: Rockfall trajectory modeling combined with heuristic analysis for assessing the rockfall hazard along the Maratea SS18 coastal road (Basilicata, Southern Italy). Landslides 13(5), 985–1003 (2016). https://doi.org/10.1007/s10346-015-0665-3

Groundwater Recharge Assessment in the Carbonate Aquifer System of the Lauria Mounts (Southern Italy) by GIS-Based Distributed Hydrogeological Balance Method

Filomena Canora[(✉)] , Maria Assunta Musto, and Francesco Sdao

School of Engineering, University of Basilicata, Potenza, Italy
{filomena.canora, francesco.sdao}@unibas.it,
mari.mst91@libero.it

Abstract. The carbonate aquifer system of the northern sector of the Lauria Mounts, located in the southern-western part of the Basilicata region (southern Italy), represents a strategic hydrostructure of the Lucanian Apennines for its groundwater resources. Several springs exploited and not, characterized by important groundwater discharges, drain the aquifer system. In recent decades the demand of freshwater is rising in relation to the population needs, land use change and climate variations, rendering water availability in the future uncertain. For these reasons, intensive actions are being done to ensure the effective protection and quantification of the available groundwater resources. In this perspective, the assessment of the aquifer recharge is the starting point for the correct definition of the available groundwater resources, aimed at the delineation of the proper protection and adequate management of these resources. In this study the application of the inverse hydrogeological water balance method to assess the potential aquifer recharge distributed in the hydrogeological basin, has been carried out based on a GIS procedure. The hydrogeological characterization and the groundwater recharge assessment of the carbonate hydrostructure result to be essential to define integrated actions and strategies for groundwater effective protection and sustainable management.

Keywords: Groundwater recharge · Inverse hydrogeological balance
GIS procedure

1 Introduction

Sustainable social and economic development is widely dependent on water resources. However, assurance of the good quality water in sufficient quantities to satisfy the demand of a constantly changing society represents the main challenge of the 21st century [1]. Nowadays the water demand has become more pressing and the consumption for the development of large urban concentrations, the intensive irrigation areas and the industrial use, have made the rationalization and protection of water resources a primary issue. In many regions, the water quantity and quality are potentially strongly affected by many natural and anthropogenic factors such as climate

© Springer International Publishing AG, part of Springer Nature 2018
O. Gervasi et al. (Eds.): ICCSA 2018, LNCS 10961, pp. 166–181, 2018.
https://doi.org/10.1007/978-3-319-95165-2_12

change, overexploitation, and human activities. Groundwater represents an important freshwater resource, especially for drinking use, that can only be managed through the hydrogeological characterization of the aquifers and the definition of their potentialities and quality.

In Basilicata region extensive fractured and karst carbonate hydrostructures due to their peculiar geostructural features and hydrogeological conditions are characterized by the presence of a considerable number of springs. Many of these springs have a remarkable and constant groundwater discharges, therefore, the determination of the amount of water resource potentially exploitable is a necessary datum for the hydrogeological characterization of the system.

The accurate groundwater recharge assessment has a primary importance for implementing a sustainable integrated management of groundwater resources for water supply purposes. The effective management of groundwater resources requires the understanding of the hydrological processes and the estimation of magnitude of hydrogeological balance parameters essential to estimate the potential aquifer recharge under the given climate conditions.

In the last decades, several actions are defined intensively for the quantification and the correct safeguarding of the available groundwater. In this perspective, the aquifer active recharge represents the starting point for a correct definition of the available resources and in the delineation of the protection actions.

This study was conducted to assess the groundwater recharge in the carbonate aquifer system of the Lauria Mounts northern sector (southern Italy) by GIS-based spatially distributed inverse hydrogeological balance method [2, 3]. Geographic information systems (GIS) based approach is widely used tool to analyse and elaborate environmental data, and the analysis stands out because of it allows for parameterisation and processing large datasets and it yields the explicit results.

2 Study Area

The morphostructure of the Lauria Mounts northern sector, geographically located in the southern-western part of the Basilicata region along the Calabrian-Lucanian border, constitutes an important carbonate hydrostructure drained by several springs with huge discharges. It extends in the EW direction from Lauria to Castelluccio villages and includes the mountains of Serra Tornesiello (1185 m), Castello Starsia (1387 m), Serra Rotonda (1285 m), La Spina Mount (1652 m) and Zaccana Mount (1580 m).

The morphostructure is bounded to the N by the watershed of the Sinni River, to the NE by the Torrente Peschiera, to the E from the urban areas of Castelluccio Superiore and Castelluccio Inferiore. In SE sector by the Mercure River basin the carbonate massif is bordered, in the southern sector by the Valico Prestieri and Fosso Mancosa, to the SW by Serra La Nocara, to the W by Lauria urban area and the lower part of the Torrente Caffaro tributary of the Noce River (Fig. 1).

The geographic location of the study area, immediately inside the imposing Apennine Chain, that rise along the Tyrrhenian coast, has a strongly impact on climate factors. The sea confers its beneficial effect to the climate that results substantially mild, despite the mountainous character of the territory. The average annual precipitation,

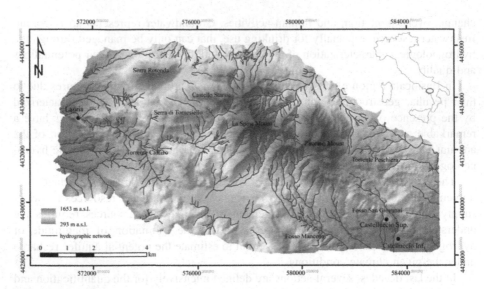

Fig. 1. Geographic location of the study area with elevation map and hydrographic network

always very high, is about 1550 mm. The annual typical mediterranean rainfall regime involves very rainy winters and dry summers. The maximum monthly precipitation value is recorded in December, the minimum in July. The thermic regime is essentially characterized by the maximum of about 23 °C in summer that always occurs in the months of July - August and the minimum of about 6.5 °C in winter. The average annual temperature is instead of about 14 °C.

3   Geological and Hydrogeological Setting of the Lauria Mounts

3.1   Geological Features of the Study Area

The morphostructure oriented in the WNW-SSE direction is located to the west of the Mercure basin, which separates the carbonate structure from the neighbouring mountains of the Pollino Chain [4].

The Lauria Mounts, characterized by a significant geological-structural complexity, represent a high-structural consisting of the Meso-Cenozoic calcareous-dolomitic succession, referable to the Alburno-Cervati-Pollino Unit [5], constituting the monoclinals of the Calabrian-Lucanian border, confined by the Miocene clayey-marly flysch (Fig. 2).

The tectonic setting of the Lauria Mounts derives from the activity of the quaternary faults on the Pliocene contraction structure. The transcurrent deformation, active from the Superior Pliocene, whose faults are subsequently reactivated in the extensional system [6, 7], produces a complex structural pattern [8]. Structural studies on the Castrovillari [6], Mercure [9] and Morano Calabro basins [10] made it possible to place

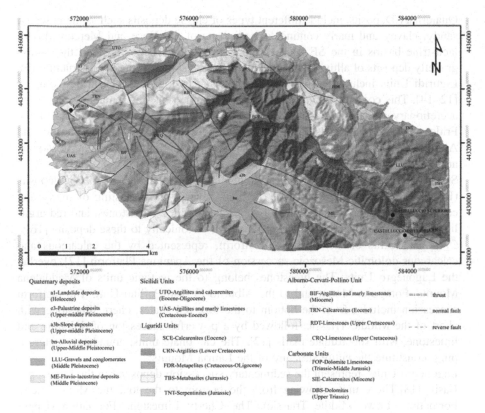

Quaternary deposits

- al-Landslide deposits (Holocene)
- e3-Palustrine deposits (Upper-middle Pleistocene)
- a3b-Slope deposits (Upper-middle Pleistocene)
- bn-Alluvial deposits (Upper-Middle Pleistocene)
- LLU-Gravels and conglomerates (Middle Pleistocene)
- ME-Fluvio-lacustrine deposits (Middle Pleistocene)

Sicilidi Units

- UTO-Argillites and calcarenites (Eocene-Oligocene)
- UAS-Argillites and marly limestones (Cretaceous-Eocene)

Liguridi Units

- SCE-Calcarenites (Eocene)
- CRN-Argillites (Lower Cretaceous)
- FDR-Metapelites (Cretaceous-OLigocene)
- TBS-Metabasites (Jurassic)
- TNT-Serpentinites (Jurassic)

Alburno-Cervati-Pollino Unit

- BIF-Argillites and marly limestones (Miocene)
- TRN-Calcarenites (Eocene)
- RDT-Limestones (Upper Cretaceous)
- CRQ-Limestones (Upper Cretaceous)

Carbonate Units

- FOP-Dolomite Limestones (Triassic-Middle Jurassic)
- SIE-Calcarenites (Miocene)
- DBS-Dolomites (Upper Triassic)

thrust

normal fault

reverse fault

Fig. 2. Geo-lithological Map of the Lauria Mounts northern sector

a time constraint to the transcurrent activity, which is still present during the Sicilian, while the extensional tectonic, still active, develops starting from the passage between the Lower and Middle Pleistocene.

The tectonic structures oriented approximately N120° are particularly important, as responsible for the genesis and evolution of many quaternary basins, including those present in the Calabrian-Lucanian border [7].

The carbonate morphostructure is bordered by high-angle transcurrent and extensional faults that generated a series of depressions filled by the quaternary continental deposits and by the Miocene terrigenous sediments [4].

The study area presents the Apennine trend fault system with N120 ± 10° orientation and systematically distributed fault systems oriented NS, N30-50° and N160°, generally in association with thrusts and folds (Fig. 2).

Carbonate successions are bounded to the north by an important thrust front with N-NE vergence, produced by the translational tectonics that led the Liguridi and Sicilidi Units to overlap on the Carbonate Units of the Apennine Platform, on the Lagonegro Units and on the Apula Platform Units [11].

Different stratigraphic-structural units, recognized in the southern Apennines, are present in the Lauria Mounts structure [5] (Fig. 2):

- Quaternary Deposits, include different types of clastic deposits such as the gravelly, sandy, clayey and marly continental sediments of the Noce and Mercure fluvio-lacustrine basins in the SE zone of the Lauria Mounts structure and the sandy-gravelly deposits of alluvial fans located along the slopes of the hydrostructure [9];
- Liguridi Units include the basinal turbiditic succession of the Liguride Complex [12–14]. This complex (Cretaceous-Oligocene) represents the remaining part of an accretionary wedge, subsequently distinguished in the two tectonic units of the Frido and Silentina Units [5, 15], and includes the Crete Nere, Saraceno and Albidona Formations. This succession is present at the limits of the Lauria Mounts area.
- Sicilidi Units, made up of marly, calcareous-clayey and arenaceous-pelitic deposits (Upper Cretaceous-Oligocene); the Torbido River Unit, consisting of marly and calcilutite limestone with nodules of chert, calcarenites, sandstones, and red argillites (Middle-Oligocene Eocene) stands above tectonically to these deposits [16];
- Carbonate Units of the Apennine Platform, represented by the calcareous and calcareous-dolomitic Mesozoic succession of the Apennine Platform [17], overlay the Lagonegro Units. The limestones belong to the tectonic units of Maddalena Mounts, Foraporta Mount and to the Alburno-Cervati-Pollino Unit. The platform succession includes from the bottom to the top: red shales, chert, limestone with chert of the Middle Triassic, followed by a powerful succession of dolomite and limestone, with subordinate marls [17]. The carbonate units, abundantly outcropping, constitute the entire structure of the Lauria Mounts;
- Lagonegro Units, represent the sedimentary succession deposited in the Lagonegro Basin [18].These units showing from the bottom to the top: the Monte Facito Formation (Lower-Middle Triassic). The Cherty Limestone Formation (Upper Triassic). The Siliceous Schists Formation (Cretaceous-Jurassic) and the Galestri Formation (Jurassic Superior) [11, 15, 19, 20]. The Lagonegro Units outcrop only along the northern external margins of the Lauria Mounts structure.

3.2 Hydrogeological Characterization of the Aquifer System

The evident geostructural peculiarities condition the complex hydrogeological structure, the groundwater flow directions and the emergencies of the springs. The geometry of the carbonate hydrostructure consists of two separated aquifers with different hydrogeological and hydrodynamic characteristics, bordered laterally by major faults, and characterized by subsurface boundaries that define the different groundwater flow directions: the Lauria and the La Spina - Zaccana aquifers, both characterized by the presence of important springs representing a strategic water resource for the area and Basilicata region [21] (Fig. 3). Numerous other emergencies with smaller groundwater amounts are present in the entire study area.

The groundwater flow directions, conditioned by different factors such as the rock fracturing degree, the karst activity and the presence of the basal dolomite complex at the south-eastern part of the aquifer system, essentially occurs in two preferential directions prevailing NE-SW and NW-SE, in the direction of the areas where the major springs emerge. The hydrostructure presents different hydrogeological complexes, having distinct lithological and hydraulic features (Fig. 4):

Fig. 3. Hydrogeological Map showing the Lauria Aquifer (red line) and La Spina - Zaccana Aquifer (blue line) with relative permeability classes and the springs location (Color figure online)

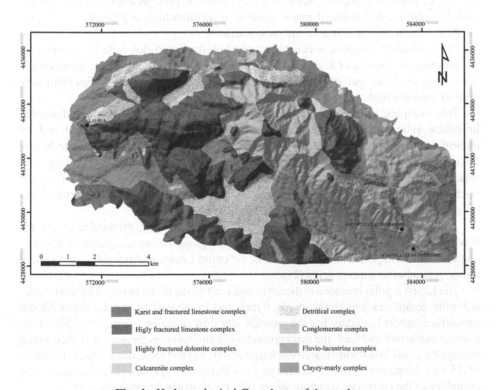

Fig. 4. Hydrogeological Complexes of the study area

The Clayey-marly complex, constituted by the pelagic and chaotic sequences of varicoloured clays, marls and marly limestone belonging to the Sicilidi and Lagonegresi Units and by the structurally complex quartzites, clays and marls referable to the Frido Unit, has a very low degree of relative permeability. These formations play an important hydrogeological role, border the carbonate hydrostructure and create the limit of permeability of groundwater emergencies conditions. The hydraulic conductivity can be estimated $<10^{-9}$ m/s [22].

The Fluvio-lacustrine complex includes clays, marly clays, layered clayey marls with sandy layers and a succession of polygenic conglomerates with an abundant sandy matrix. It is characterized by a medium-low degree of relative permeability and by the quaternary deposits of the Mercure basin, borders the carbonate hydrostructure along its southern boundary.

The Conglomerate complex, characterized by a medium degree of relative permeability, outcrops in the south-eastern part of the investigated area and consists of massive or poorly layered conglomerates and breccias, discreetly cemented. This complex presents a discrete groundwater circulation fed by the carbonate complexes.

The Detrital complex, constituted by heterogeneous conglomerates and gravels with different cementation, with a medium degree of relative permeability. This hydrogeological complex includes the detrital and clastic deposits that constitute the alluvial fans and the debris cones. The hydraulic conductivity presents values between 10^{-7} m/s and 10^{-5} m/s [22].

The Calcarenite complex, made of a succession of grey well-layered calcarenites with frequent intercalations of marls, presents a medium-high degree of relative permeability due to the presence of the rock fractures.

The Carbonate complex is constituted the limestone and dolomite. Depending on the presence or absence of karst forms, the fracturing state, the hydraulic conductivity is between 10^{-2} m/s and 10^{-4} m/s [22] and the relative permeability varies from very high to medium-high.

This complex can be divided into three subcomplexes: the karst and fractured limestone subcomplex with developed karst effects (dolines and cavities) and an intense fracturing state, with a very high degree of relative permeability; the highly fractured limestone subcomplex, affected by an intense and pervasive fracturing with spaced and unfilled fractures that confer a high degree of relative permeability; the fractured dolomite subcomplex, characterized by limestones with spaced fractured and by a medium-high degree of relative permeability.

The groundwater flow in the La Spina – Zaccana aquifer, predominantly in the NW-SE direction, feeds the San Giovanni springs group (mean discharge of 450 l/s), one of the most important water resource in the entire Lucanian Apennines, and several minor groundwater emergencies [21].

The Lauria aquifer bounded to the north and west by the thrust between the carbonate-dolomite complexes and clayey-marly flysch and to the east by the La Spina Mount subsurface aquifer boundary has the groundwater flow direction oriented NE-SW in the entire substructure and feeds the main groundwater emergencies represented by the major spring of Caffaro Mandarino (mean discharge of 810 l/s) and the Caffaro (mean discharge of 25 l/s), Montepesco (mean discharge of 4 l/s) minor springs [21], located to the boundary of the carbonate structure where the clayey-marly deposits outcrop.

4   Data and Methodologies

The aquifer recharge can be estimated using direct methods that describe the mechanism of water percolation from the soil to the aquifer or indirect methods that permit the estimation of the effective infiltration trough the analysis of the topographic, hydrogeological and climate variables. The inverse hydrogeological water balance method is an indirect methodology consisting in the calculation of effective infiltration, considering climate data, such as rainfall and temperature, and topographic and hydrogeological parameters, such as altitude and the characteristics of the hydrogeological complexes present in the basin that host groundwater [3, 23].

This method implemented in GIS allows the spatial distribution of the effective infiltration rate (potential recharge of the aquifer) in the well-identified hydrogeological basin on the basis of geo-structural and hydrogeological data. The methodological approach provides the area discretized in square cells, whose the size is defined according to the extension of the domain and to the quality and quantity of the available data. Furthermore, the geological and hydrogeological map (in shapefile format) and the DTM (Digital Terrain Model) of the study area must be available.

To proceed with the elaboration of the hydrogeological balance terms it is necessary the georeferencing and the digitalization of the thematic maps and the georeferenced location of the pluviometric and thermometric stations present within the territory of interest and/or immediately adjacent. Subsequently, the spatial processing of the precipitation and temperature involves the selection and reconstruction of the historical data series for sufficiently long and homogeneous period to include long-term variations of the climate data.

The water balance equation supplies the mean annual evaluation of the individual variables provided by the expression (1) in which the system inputs are equal to the outputs, in the considered reference period (2000–2016):

$$P = ET_r + I + R \tag{1}$$

where:

P indicates the precipitation (mm); ET_r the amount of actual evapotranspiration (mm); R the direct runoff (mm) and I is the effective infiltration (mm) that can be considered as the active groundwater recharge.

The analysis proceeds with the calculation of the monthly and annual averages of the pluviometric and thermometric data collected for each station and the determination of the corrected average annual temperatures (Tc) as a function of precipitation.

The spatial distribution in the hydrogeological basin of thermo-pluviometric parameters (precipitation and corrected temperature) is performed starting from the data of thermo-pluviometric stations and the definition of the relative linear regression functions depending on altitude. The altitude in each cell is defined by the DTM.

Monthly temperature data were used to estimate the average annual corrected temperature (T_c) at each thermometric station using (2):

$$T_c = \sum_{i=1}^{N} P_i T_i / P \tag{2}$$

where:

P_i is the average monthly precipitation (mm); T_i indicates the temperature (°C) of the i-th month and P is the average annual precipitation of the reference period (mm).

These values are useful to estimate the real evapotranspiration and the effective precipitation.

The estimation of actual evapotranspiration (ETr) was performed using the Turc's formula [24] (3):

$$ET_r = \frac{P}{\sqrt{0,9 + \left(\frac{P}{300 + 25*T_c + 0,05*T_c^3}\right)^2}} \tag{3}$$

where:

ET_r is the average annual actual evapotranspiration (mm); P the average annual precipitation (mm); T_c is the average annual corrected temperature (°C) function of the precipitation.

The effective rainfall (P_e), in mm/y, evaluated as the difference between precipitation (P) and actual evapotranspiration (ET_r), represents the sum of two aliquots: the effective infiltration (I) and the direct runoff (R) (4):

$$Pe = P - ET_r = R + I \tag{4}$$

where:

P indicates the mean annual precipitation (mm); ET_r the amount of mean annual actual evapotranspiration (mm); R the direct runoff (mm) and I the effective infiltration (mm) The identification of the potential infiltration coefficient (χ) is a function of the hydrogeological complexes present in the area of interest.

The effective infiltration was calculated based on effective rainfall (Pe) values and potential infiltration coefficients by using (5):

$$I = Pe \times \chi \tag{5}$$

where:

I indicates the mean annual effective infiltration (mm); Pe indicates the mean annual effective precipitation (mm); χ is the potential infiltration coefficient (dimensionless).

The value of the potential infiltration coefficient is also function of specific characteristics of the present carbonate lithologies such as fracturing and karst processes which strongly influence the rock permeability. Ultimately, the spatially distributed value of effective infiltration and direct runoff are defined. The term of effective infiltration is considered contributes to the recharge of the aquifer, therefore the sum of this term related to the whole area of interest provides the value of the potential active recharge.

The direct runoff rate, i.e. the flow rate on the topographic surface is a part of the effective rainfall is calculated indirectly as the difference between the effective rainfall and the effective infiltration.

The procedure implemented and performed through the support of the QGIS results to be easy and reliable, permits the implementation of a complex relational geodatabase that allows the processing of the thematic maps and informative layers related to the different components of the inverse hydrogeological water balance as well as the interpretation and synthesis of the data.

5 Results and Discussion

To assess the potential aquifer recharge (i.e. effective infiltration) of the hydrogeological basin, the estimation of the water budget components was conducted by means of the inverse hydrogeological water balance approach.

The inverse hydrogeological balance procedure has been applied in GIS environment to elaborate the numerical spatially distributed water balance components and finally the quantitative estimation of the average annual effective infiltration (active recharge), considering the multiannual historical series of climate data [23]. The daily precipitation and air temperatures series for the period from 2000 to 2016 were collected from the Regional Civil Protection Agency database, in 4 thermo-pluviometric stations (Trecchina, Lagonegro, Maratea and Nemoli stations) located in the proximity of the study area. The thermo-pluviometric data analysis permits the determination of the mean annual spatial distribution of the precipitation and temperature measured in individual climate stations.

The collected data and thematic layers were implemented in Quantum GIS (QGIS) software. The study area has been discretized in grid cells 20 m × 20 m and the hydrogeological balance parameters have been calculated for each cell.

In order to assess the spatial distribution of the average annual precipitation values on the entire hydrogeological basin, each punctual station was elaborated through a statistical analysis using a method that considers a linear regression as function of altitude P = f(q) (6):

$$P\,(mm) = 0.9255 \times q\,(m\ a.s.l.) + 1025.2\,(r2 = 0.9815) \tag{6}$$

In GIS, in each cell 20 m × 20 m using the linear regression equation the specific precipitation P = f(q) was defined and interpolated to obtain the spatial distribution of the average annual precipitation related to the reference period from 2000 to 2016, on the entire study basin (Fig. 5).

In the same way as the precipitation, the average annual corrected temperature was defined by the Eq. (2), correlated with the altitude by a linear regression Eq. (7) and interpolated to obtain the spatial distribution (Fig. 6):

Fig. 5. Spatial distribution of the average annual precipitation

Fig. 6. Spatial distribution of the average annual corrected temperature

$$T(°C) = -0.0078 \times q\,(\text{m a.s.l.}) + 14.779\,(r^2 = 0.9082) \qquad (7)$$

To evaluate the actual evapotranspiration the Turc's formula was applied [24]. Its reliability is confirmed by numerous studies executed in the Mediterranean basins and European areas [2, 25] (Fig. 7).

Fig. 7. Spatial distribution of the average annual actual evapotranspiration defined by the Turc empirical formula

The effective rainfall represents the sum of two aliquots: the effective infiltration and the direct runoff (Fig. 8).

Fig. 8. Spatial distribution of the average annual effective precipitation related to the reference period from 2000 to 2016

The variation of the effective precipitation (P_e) has allowed to obtain the contribution of the effective infiltration adopting the potential infiltration coefficients (χ) (Table 1), in related to the different hydrogeological complexes in the entire hydrogeological basin. The infiltration capacity, in fact, depends on many factors such as outcropping lithologies, soil textures, rock fracturing, karst processes etc., expressed by the definition of the potential infiltration coefficients [2, 23, 26].

Table 1. Potential infiltration coefficients of the hydrogeological complexes present in the study area

Hydrogeological Complex	χ
Karst and fractured limestone complex	0.85
Highly fractured limestone complex	0.80
Highly fractured dolomite complex	0.75
Calcarenite complex	0.70
Detritical complex	0.50
Conglomerate complex	0.50
Fluvio-lacustrine complex	0.30
Clayey-marly complex	0.20

The potential infiltration coefficient has been assigned to each identified hydrogeological complex, it considers the characteristics of the aquifer system, the permeability of the complexes belonging to the study domain and referring to the values of literature [27] (Table 1).

The effective infiltration was calculated based on effective rainfall (Pe) values and potential infiltration coefficients. The interpolation of the data gives back its spatial distribution on the hydrogeological basin (Fig. 9).

The direct runoff rate, i.e. the flow rate on the topographic surface, was assessed indirectly as the difference between the effective rainfall and the effective infiltration.

The inverse hydrogeological water balance application, using GIS, provides the distribution of all hydrogeological water balance variables in the hydrogeological basin. These values are relative to the reference period of observations 2000–2016 (Table 2).

The hydrostructure of the Lauria Mounts northern sector presents an area extension of about 60 km^2 and an mean annual direct precipitation of about 1540 mm/y, for the period from 2000–2016. The average annual water amount of the precipitation is divided into a real evapotranspiration value equal to 506.3 mm/y, which considering the potential infiltration coefficient relative to the single hydrogeological complexes, provide an effective infiltration rate equal to 724.6 mm/y.

The annual groundwater potential active recharge estimated for the entire hydrogeological basin gives a the total volume equal to 1379 l/s, which is in agreement with the outflows data of the numerous springs present in the basin such as Caffaro, Caffaro-Mandarino, Arena Bianca, Montepesco and San Giovanni, whose the total discharges are quantifiable in about 1470 l/s. The comparison between of the estimated active recharge with the average discharges rate presents an error equal to 6%, less than 10%,

Fig. 9. Spatial distribution of the average annual effective infiltration evaluated respect the reference period from 2000 to 2016

Table 2. Average annual water amount of the inverse hydrogeological balance components

Variable	mm/y	l/s
Direct Precipitation (P)	1540	2929
Actual Evapotranspiration (ET$_r$)	506.3	963
Effective Infiltration (I)	724.6	1379
Direct Runoff (R)	309.1	587

therefore, the inverse water balance can be considered effective [27]. The inverse hydrogeological balance method applied to the aquifer system of Lauria Mountains confirms that the input and output terms are in equilibrium.

The aquifer active recharge amount plays an important role to obtain an adequate groundwater resources management, that probably will be strongly conditioned considering future climate trends.

6   Conclusions

The inverse hydrogeological water balance method proposed in this paper to assess the groundwater recharge is based on a GIS procedure starting from geological, hydrogeological, topographic and available metereological data. This procedure, relatively simple to apply, allows to implement and elaborate large datasets. The advantage of applying the inverse hydrogeological balance methodology in GIS, consists in the spatially distributed analysis of the climate data, topographic and hydrogeological conditions on groundwater recharge. This GIS approach proves to be very useful in the estimation of the effective infiltration (aquifer recharge), and can be used to improve quantitative sustainable groundwater protection. Moreover, implemented structure in GIS with the parameters as attribute tables has demonstrated interesting aspects. The procedure involves some steps where it is necessary to provide available external inputs and the functions used are implemented in GIS software packages. All calculations can be performed both in raster and in vector data. Considering the reliability of the proposed approach in the investigated area, based on GIS technology, we consider it objective, very useful in the potential recharge estimation of the aquifers and repeatable in other hydrogeological contexts.

References

1. Eden, S., Lawford, R.G.: Using science to address a growing worldwide water dilemma for the 21st Century. In: Lawford, et al. (eds.) Water: Science, Policy and Management. Water Resources Monograph 16. Publisher AGU (2003)
2. Civita, M.: L'infiltrazione potenziale media annua nel massiccio del Matese (Italia Meridionale). In: Atti 2° Convegno Internazionale sulle Acque Sotterranee, pp. 129–142, Palermo (1973)
3. Civita, M., De Maio, M.: Average ground water recharge in carbonate aquifers: a gis processed numerical model. Sciences et techniques de l'environnement. Mémoire hors-série, pp. 93–100 (2001)
4. Gioia, D., Schiattarella, M.: Caratteri morfotettonici dell'area del Valico di Prestieri e dei Monti di Lauria (Appennino Meridionale). Il Quat. Ital. J. Quat. Sci. 19(1), 129–142 (2006)
5. D'Argenio, B., Pescatore, T., Scandone, P.: Schema geologico dell'Appennino meridionale (Campania e Lucania). In: Atti del convegno "Moderne vedute sulla geologia dell'Appennino". Quad. Acc. Naz. Lincei 183, 49–72 (1973)
6. Russo, F., Schiattarella, M.: Osservazioni preliminari sull'evoluzione morfostrutturale del bacino di Castrovillari (Calabria settentrionale), Studi Geol. Camerti, vol. spec., 1992/1, pp. 271–278 (1992)
7. Schiattarella, M.: Quaternary tectonics of the Pollino Ridge, Calabria-Lucania boundary, Southern Italy. In: Holdsworth, R.E., Strachan, R.A., Dewey, J.F. (eds.) Continental Transpressional and Transtensional Tectonics, vol. 135, pp. 341–354, Geological Society, London, Spec. Publ. (1998)
8. Turco, E., Maresca, R., Cappadona, P.: La tettonica plio-pleistocenica del confine calabro-lucano: modello cinematico. Mem. Soc. Geol. It. 45, 519–529 (1990)
9. Schiattarella, M., Torrente, M.M., Russo, F.: Analisi strutturale ed osservazioni morfostratigrafiche nel bacino del Mercure (confine calabro-lucano). Il Quaternario 7, 613–626 (1994)
10. Perri, E., Schiattarella, M.: Evoluzione tettonica quaternaria del bacino di Morano Calabro (Catena del Pollino, Calabria settentrionale). Boll. Soc. Geol. It. 116, 3–15 (1997)
11. Patacca, E., Scandone, P.: Geology of the Southern Apennines. Boll. Soc. Geol. It. Special Issue 7, 75–119 (2007)
12. Ogniben, L.: Schema introduttivo alla geologia del confine calabro-lucano. Mem. Soc. Geol. It. 8, 435–763 (1969)
13. Knott, S.D.: The Liguride Complex of Southern Italy – a Cretaceous to Paleogene accretionary wedge. Tectonophysics 142, 217–226 (1987)

14. Knott, S.: Structure kinematics and metamorphism in the Liguride Complex, Southern Apennine. Italy. J. Struct. Geol. **16**, 1107–1120 (1994)
15. Scandone, P.: Studi di geologia lucana: Carta dei terreni della serie calcareo-silico-marnosa e note illustrative. Boll. Soc. Natur. Napoli **81**, 255–300 (1972)
16. Bonardi, G., Amore, F.O., Ciampo, G., De Capoa, P., Miconnet, P., Perrone, V.: Il Complesso Liguride Auct.: stato delle conoscenze e problemi aperti sulla sua evoluzione pre-appenninica ed i suoi rapporti con l'Arco Calabro. Mem. Soc. Geol. It. **41**, 17–35 (1988)
17. Mostardini, F., Merlini, S.: Appennino centro meridionale. Sezioni geologiche e proposta di modello strutturale. Mem. Soc. Geol. It. **35**, 177–202 (1986)
18. Scandone, P.: The preorogenic history of the Lagonegro basin (southern Apennines). In: Squyres, C. (ed.) "Geology of Italy", The Earth Sciences Society of the Libyan Arab Republic, pp. 305–315 (1975)
19. Scandone, P.: Studi di geologia lucana: la serie calcareo-silico-marnosa e i suoi rapporti con l'Appennino calcareo. Bollettino Società Naturalisti in Napoli **76**, 1–175 (1967)
20. Marsella, E.: I terreni lagonegresi tra San Fele e la Val d 'Agri. Evoluzione tettonico-sedimentaria (Trias superiore-Giurassico). Tesi di Dottorato in Geologia del Sedimentario, Univ. Napoli (1988)
21. Landsystem: Piano di Risanamento delle Acque della Regione Basilicata – Censimento dei corpi idrici. Regione Basilicata (1987)
22. Sdao, F., D'Ecclesiis, G.: Idrogeologia dei Monti di Lauria (Basilicata). Atti del 3° Convegno Nazionale Protezione e Gestione Acque Sotterranee per il III Millennio, Quaderni di Geologia Applicata, vol. 2, pp. 175–183, BOLOGNA: Pitagora Ed., Parma, ottobre (1999). ISBN 9788837111496
23. Civita, M.: Idrogeologia Applicata e Ambientale. CEA, Milano, 794 pp. (2005)
24. Turc, L.: Calcul du bilan de l'eau évaluation en fonction des précipitations et des températures. IAHS Publ **37**, 88–200 (1954)
25. Santoro, M.: Sulla applicabilità della formula di Turc per il calcolo della evapotraspirazione effettiva in Sicilia. Istituto di Idraulica della Università di Palermo (1970)
26. Manfreda, S., Sdao, F., Sole, A.: In hydrogeological water balance in carbonate hydro-structure. In: Proceedings of 2nd IASWE/WSEAS International Conference on Water Resources, Hydraulics & Hydrology (WHH 2007), pp. 216–222 (2007)
27. Celico, P.: Prospezioni idrogeologiche; Liguori, Napoli, Italy, 1-536, 8820713314 (1988)

Workshop Advances in Web Based Learning (AWBL 2018)

Course Map: A Career-Driven Course Planning Tool

Sarath Tomy$^{(\boxtimes)}$ and Eric Pardede

La Trobe University, Melbourne, VIC 3086, Australia
{s.tomy,e.pardede}@latrobe.edu.au

Abstract. Student success has become one of the primary indicators of higher education quality. Universities expect students to be more independent in making decisions about their course and subjects. However, students are less likely to make the best choices when they lack meaningful information. The task of subject selection is very complex and require multiple considerations on the value of the content, skills, time and workload. Choosing inappropriate subjects make the student think that their chosen course is wrong for their desired career. This article introduces a tool to assist students in planning their course with respect to labour market opportunities, technical skills and time. The online dashboard tool that shows the relationship among course, skills and career help students by providing a clarity on what is expected of them, what skills they need to develop, how they need to learn, progress and succeed. The interactive dashboards help students to effectively manage their studies and provide more personalized learning experience.

Keywords: Course planning · Student dashboard · Student success

1 Introduction

The motivation to enter university education is generally perceived to be to study a specific discipline in depth, to gain a degree, get a higher qualification and thus get a good job [1]. However, the successful transition of students into higher education is now generally regarded as a longer, more complex process than 'induction' [2]. A critical issue is related to a student's sense of belonging. Students are less likely to make the best course choices when they lack meaningful information and the opinions they obtain may provide inaccurate information [3]. The choice of course is driven by the expectation of acquiring a job where knowledge gained during education will be applied [4, 5].

Prior to every semester, students make a series of interdependent selection, choosing the specific academic subjects that will comprise their study course in the next term. Universities expect students to be more independent in making decisions about their course and subjects. However, many students have difficulty adjusting to university teaching methods and expectations. The task of subject selection is very complex and require multiple considerations on the value of the content, skills, time and workload. They have to decide what is important to them with regards to their career interests, personal academic goals, and their schedule.

O. Gervasi et al. (Eds.): ICCSA 2018, LNCS 10961, pp. 185–198, 2018.
https://doi.org/10.1007/978-3-319-95165-2_13

Lack of accurate initial information leads to unrealistic expectations regarding the amount of work and time involved in university study [6]. Time allocated to some of the subjects might be inappropriate or can cause schedule overlapping [7]. Sometimes they select subjects without considering its prerequisites and therefore they are not allowed to take the advanced subjects in the following semesters [6]. The fact is that students always do not have the information on how the skills gained through the subjects are aligned and how it can help in getting their chosen career which led them to choose an inappropriate mix of subjects in each semester [8]. However, choosing inappropriate modules of subjects make the student think that their chosen course is wrong for their desired career. Students face unmet expectations which lead to career-related anxiety if the chosen field of education does not lead to the chosen occupation. Career-related anxiety is a predictor of academic persistence [9].

Decisions on choosing subjects can have great influence on students' future career opportunities because early decisions can determine later choices. This paper proposes a course planning framework that connects course, skills and career by analyzing the data gathered from educational environments and career advertisements. These dimensions were selected because they aligned with the purposes and outcomes of student success in higher education. The framework is implemented as a software application using text mining and data analytics to assist students in better selection and management of subjects with respect to the anticipated careers. The paper examines the effectiveness of the application by evaluating its functionalities from the perspective of the prime beneficiaries of graduate employability: students, employers and universities, and by comparison with the existing models with respect to academic preparedness, efficient academic workload management and core skill development. The research will add to the already existing body of literature on student success. The research could also serve as a stepping stone to further research on other aspects of student satisfaction and retention.

The rest of the paper is organized as follows. Section 2 provides an overview about the related works focusing on models and tools for efficient management of course and workload. Section 3 details the development of the proposed course planning tool. The data collection and implementation is also discussed in this section. Section 4 illustrates the application user interface dashboards. Section 5, discusses the effectiveness of the application by evaluating its functionalities. The conclusion of this paper and future work in this research area are discussed in the last section.

2   Literature Review

There are several works attempt to provide methods for students to manage their course and workload. Hsu et al. [10] investigates student satisfaction from the perspective of alumni and proposed a decomposed alumni satisfaction model which provides strategic management maps to identify areas for continuous improvement. They found that course design needs the most attention and it should be relevant to the real-world opportunities to work.

Bennett et al. [11] proposed a model of course provision in higher education in terms of the knowledge and skill outcomes planned for and taught, by connecting five elements: disciplinary content knowledge, disciplinary skills, workplace awareness, workplace experience and generic skills. Warren [12] identifies three forms to support employability in curriculum development: separate, semi-integrated and integrated curriculum models and argues that the combination of the semi-integrated and integrated models of curriculum are more effective to succeed at university. Elliott and Shin [13] state academic support, classroom technology, and out-of-the-classroom experiences influence students' academic satisfaction.

Other than the theoretical models, many educational institutions are using practical methods and tools for students to manage their course and workload. For example, the National University of Singapore provides a timetable builder and knowledge platform, NUSMods to prepare students to plan their timetable and manage their workload [14]. The University of Arizona developed an interactive course planning system, Smart Planner for navigating course options and optimizing the route to a degree by providing them with a visual presentation of their current academic status and future path [15]. Many other universities including California state university use this as academic planning tool [16]. On the other hand, many universities provide resources for managing time and task, planning semester and assignment in the form of videos, word and pdf files [17, 18].

The available tools in universities, such as subject enrolment systems and learning management systems, support students to manage their learning in relation to already chosen subjects within a progression period. But they do not assist students to plan their entire course with respect to their career or help students understand how the skills that they learn from a course can help them to embark on a career [5].

3   Proposed Course Planning Tool

Better academic preparedness and understanding of the type of learning that is required to succeed at university are important considerations in student retention [6]. A clear understanding of academic path from first year onwards can contribute students to make meaningful sense of their choice by enabling them to construct relationships amongst their career aspirations and their studies. Students who choose a major specifically associated with a career choice are less likely to leave university before completing a degree [6]. Moreover, there is a potential for better academic performance and the student's anticipated success influences persistence and subsequent achievement of course objectives [3].

Students need to understand themselves and about the working environment, they are going to enter in order to empower them to enter and succeed in their wider lives [9]. So it is important for establishing an evidence-based approach to assist them in navigation through their academic journey with purpose and clarity. The planning and management of course by utilizing the real world information increase their motivation which will increase their comprehension and excitement for the curriculum.

3.1   Course Planning Framework

Our approach is based on the DOTS model [19], the traditional model of career planning by slightly modifying the elements based on the context of course planning. It aims to assist students in subject selection and career options around a four-concept approach which consists of self-awareness, opportunity awareness, decision learning and transition learning. Self-awareness refers to the help that is given to students to understand themselves, their choices, skills, abilities, interest, time and responsibilities. Opportunity awareness aims to help students to understand the range of career opportunities that exist in the world of work they are going to enter with demands, rewards and strategies. Decision learning aims to help students understand how to make considered choices of academic subjects and plan options in relation to anticipated skills and careers. Transition learning aims to help students the effective management of the implementation of the considered choices in terms of skill, time and prepared for the transitions from university education to the world of work [9, 20].

The 'Course Map' framework shown in Fig. 1 illustrates the interaction between opportunity awareness, decision learning, self-awareness and transition learning through career, skills and course component. The career component consists of three elements: core career options, career details and future scope which aims to address the opportunity awareness concept. It is widely accepted that if students select courses with a genuine motivation to succeed and can foresee personal or career benefits resulting from the completion, they are more likely to complete their studies [5]. The decision learning concept addressed by the skills component by mapping the subject-specific skills from the subjects within a course with the job-specific skills required in the job description.

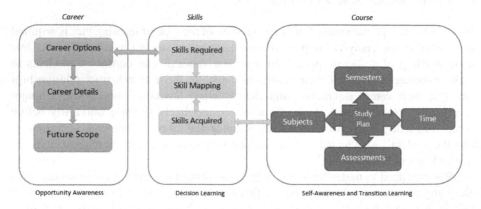

Fig. 1. Course map framework

A study conducted by Hernández-March et al. [21] found that the competencies employers value the most in graduates are technical field-specific knowledge and interpersonal skills. As the skills element interlinks the subjects and careers and provides information on how each subject relates to each different career option, this will help to avoid issues such as students changing courses or dropping out of university, to a large extent. The course component aims to manage the course efficiently by addressing the self-awareness and transition learning concept. It provides a structured study plan which consists of combined information on the interaction between subjects, semesters, time and assessments.

3.2 Course Planning Data Collection and Implementation

As a starting point of the demonstration of our model, we utilize two different courses (Bachelor of Computer Science and Master of Information Technology) from an Australian university.

At first, the course data is collected from the course guides and stored in the database. Then we extract the skills, assessment methods and details for each subject taught within that course and store them in the database. In the second stage, the data on skills with matching job positions are extracted from career advertising websites including seek.com.au, au.indeed.com using specific keywords relating to the skills and job details from acs.org.au, onetonline.org and joboutlook.gov.au. In the data pre-processing step, the raw data is processed and filtered using R libraries and stored it in the database. The skills are then extracted to create a skill mapping taxonomy for information technology domain with the help of domain expert. The skills with the related skills are then stored in the database.

The platforms reviewed in this section use the web as a delivery channel for the information. So our proposed model is built as dashboards in HTML Web pages using PHP with a MySQL database running with Apache server. All the data analysis and text processing are done using R. For generating visualizations and validations, we use JavaScript, jQuery and Ajax.

4   Course Planning Tool User Interface

The application user interfaces of interactive dashboards are designed to provide in-depth understanding and management of courses and a more personalized learning experience. The application user interface provides information for students about their course, subjects, career, workload and assessments. The following subsections provide more details on each of the components in our model.

4.1   Career Component Interface

For students to make a considered decision about their career, it is essential that they understand the opportunities that are available to them in relation to their career of interest [1]. The career options component shown in Fig. 2 presents relevant information on career options, job trends and salary scales with respect to their chosen study area in Australia, as currently, this study concentrates on the Australian context.

The career details interface navigates from the career options and provides advanced visualization and details about the selected career. It is designed to assist students to understand possible career options and help them to make more informed choices based on the domain area. The employment level, work styles, description,

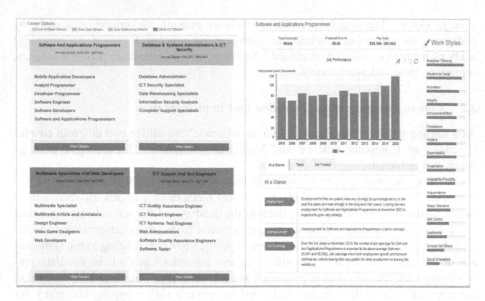

Fig. 2. Career component interface – career options (left) and career details (right)

responsibilities and tasks associated with this role are presented. This section also displays different job positions and how they perform over the years in terms of openings. The career trends along with the projected growth and pay scales will give students an idea of the prospect of the career option.

4.2 Course Component Interface

According to Elliot and Healy [22] student satisfaction results when actual performance meets or exceeds the student's expectations. The course interface as shown in Fig. 3 helps students to plan prepare and engage in their studies. Students need to understand what they are going to do in the course they have enrolled or intend to enrol. They should have a clear picture on the subjects available in each semester, the subjects that need pre-requisites, and the core subjects of their course. The overall availability of subjects in their academic journey helps them to get an overview of the entire course. Along with the course structure, it also provides options to select their area or stream to specialize. According to the chosen stream, in the interface, the subjects will be projected with a different colour which can assist students in choosing the subjects depending on the career they like to pursue.

4.3 Subject Component Interface

The subject interface is mainly designed to provide in-depth information regarding a subject. Figure 4 shows a typical screenshot of this section. The subject credit points, teaching period, description, and suggested time to spend is displayed in this section. It

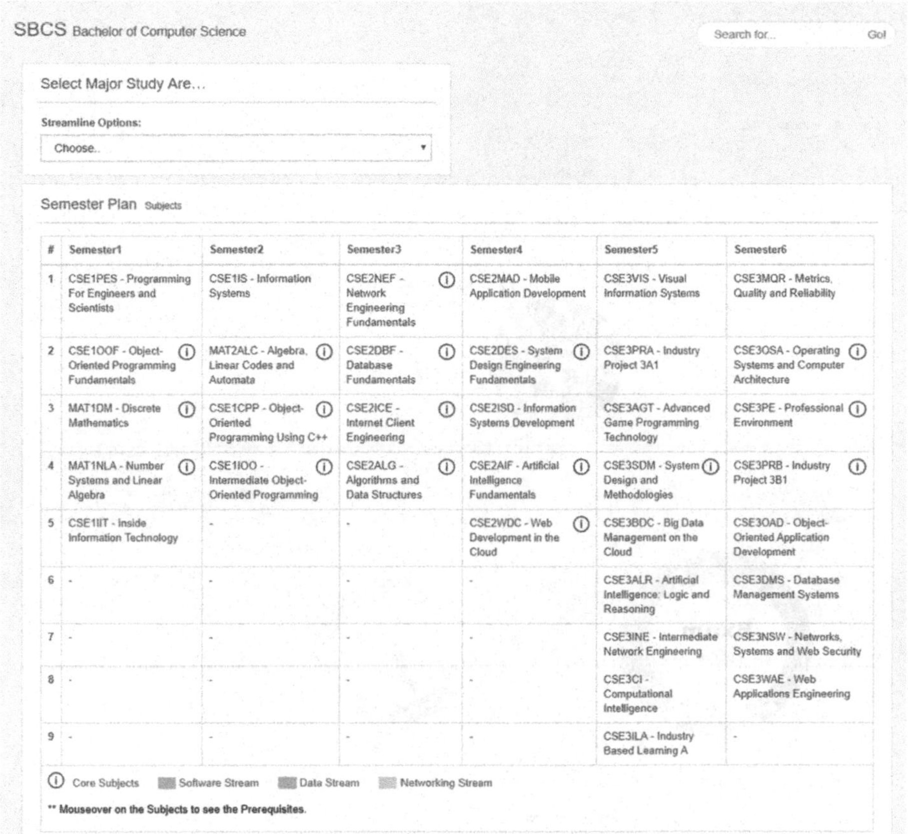

SBCS Bachelor of Computer Science   Search for..   Go!

Select Major Study Are…

Streamline Options:
Choose..   ▼

Semester Plan Subjects

#	Semester1	Semester2	Semester3	Semester4	Semester5	Semester6
1	CSE1PES - Programming For Engineers and Scientists	CSE1IS - Information Systems	CSE2NEF - Network Engineering Fundamentals (i)	CSE2MAD - Mobile Application Development	CSE3VIS - Visual Information Systems	CSE3MQR - Metrics, Quality and Reliability
2	CSE1OOF - Object-Oriented Programming Fundamentals (i)	MAT2ALC - Algebra, Linear Codes and Automata (i)	CSE2DBF - Database Fundamentals	CSE2DES - System Design Engineering Fundamentals (i)	CSE3PRA - Industry Project 3A1	CSE3OSA - Operating Systems and Computer Architecture (i)
3	MAT1DM - Discrete Mathematics (i)	CSE1CPP - Object-Oriented Programming Using C++ (i)	CSE2ICE - Internet Client Engineering	CSE2ISD - Information Systems Development	CSE3AGT - Advanced Game Programming Technology	CSE3PE - Professional Environment (i)
4	MAT1NLA - Number Systems and Linear Algebra (i)	CSE1IOO - Intermediate Object-Oriented Programming (i)	CSE2ALG - Algorithms and Data Structures	CSE2AIF - Artificial Intelligence Fundamentals (i)	CSE3SDM - System Design and Methodologies (i)	CSE3PRB - Industry Project 3B1 (i)
5	CSE1IIT - Inside Information Technology	-	-	CSE2WDC - Web Development in the Cloud (i)	CSE3BDC - Big Data Management on the Cloud	CSE3OAD - Object-Oriented Application Development
6	-	-	-	-	CSE3ALR - Artificial Intelligence: Logic and Reasoning	CSE3DMS - Database Management Systems
7	-	-	-	-	CSE3INE - Intermediate Network Engineering	CSE3NSW - Networks, Systems and Web Security
8	-	-	-	-	CSE3CI - Computational Intelligence	CSE3WAE - Web Applications Engineering
9	-	-	-	-	CSE3ILA - Industry Based Learning A	-

(i) Core Subjects   ■ Software Stream   ■ Data Stream   ■ Networking Stream
** Mouseover on the Subjects to see the Prerequisites.

Fig. 3. Course component interface

also provides interactive graduate capabilities and intended learning outcomes based on the hard skills of this subject.

Based on the competence level some students are good at certain types of assessment. Research argues that students who have a clear understanding of the assessment process and expectations have higher confidence levels which result in good academic scores [23]. The assessments methods and the subject importance relevant to the chosen stream is also shown in this section. The suggested time to spend for each assessment specific to each subject help students to plan and prepare their assessment tasks earlier in order to help them from the risk of dropping out due to poor academic performance [7].

4.4   Semester Planner

Time management and good planning allow students to spread their workload throughout the semester rather than respond reactively to assignment deadlines which can often coincide at the same time. Efficient time management equips students to

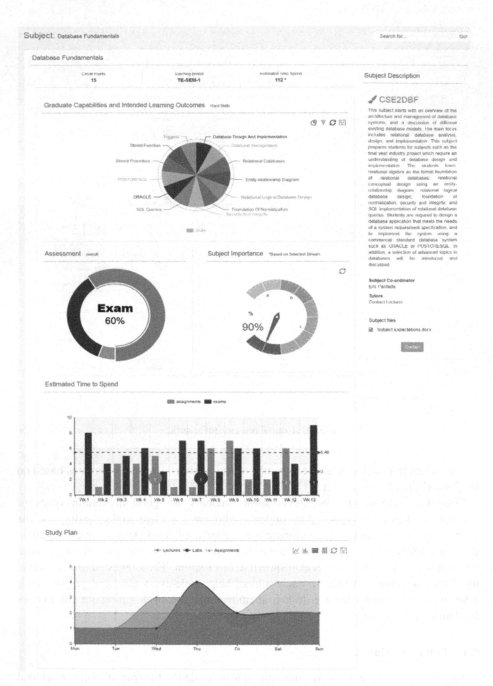

Fig. 4. Subject component interface

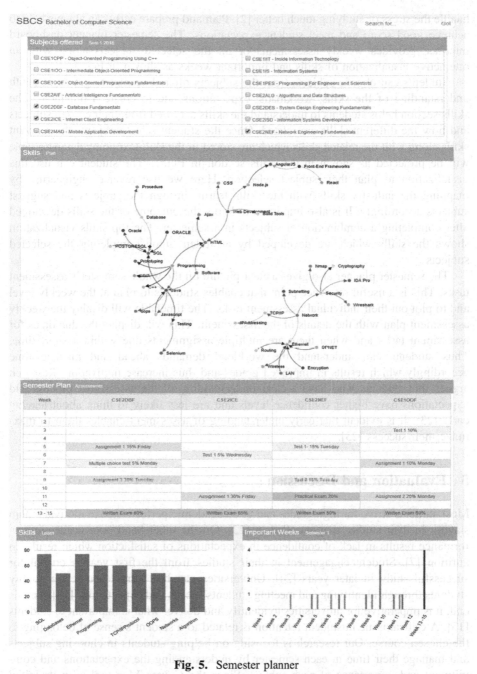

Fig. 5. Semester planner

handle the stress of studying much better [2]. Plan and prepare early can always help to achieve good score and meet student expectations. The semester planner dashboard interface provides weekly assessments of all the selected subjects along with an interactive visualization of skills and important weeks as shown in Fig. 5.

Students can choose subjects from the subjects offered section to get an in-depth understanding of the skills, workloads, expectations and to create a timetable. The skills section helps students to understand the skills acquired from their chosen subjects and how the different skills are related. Once the student select subjects, the relevant skills along with the related skills which are stored in the skill taxonomy database table will be projected as shown in the skills section in Fig. 5. The student can use this visualization to plan their subject selection. Here we use reverse engineering by mapping the industry skills with the skills learnt through the subjects and suggest subjects accordingly. It is also important to know the outcome of the skills developed after completing a combination of subjects in a semester. The top skills visualization shows the skills which are developed by a student upon completing the selected subjects.

The semester planner also gives a clear picture on the whole semester's assessment tasks. This is a useful reference point that enables students to plan at the weekly level and to plot out their individual assessment tasks. The timetable will display the weekly assessment plan with the details of the assessment. This will display the due dates for assessment tasks and when there are multiple assignments due within a short time. Thus students can understand the workload demands ahead and manage time accordingly which results in improved grades and thus increase motivation. Research argues that students who have a clear understanding of the assessment process and expectations have higher confidence levels and are less likely to think about leaving early [23]. It is evident that early understanding of assessment enables them to maximize their success [23].

5   Evaluation and Discussion

Most students strive for high grades and good academic performance to motivate them staying in their studies they enrolled in [22]. On the other hand poor academic performance results in lack of confidence in expectations of satisfaction which results in attrition [7]. Student engagement in their studies from the first year is crucial for successful study in later years [24]. Universities can best attract and retain quality students through identifying and meeting students' needs and expectations [13]. To this end, it is imperative for universities to identify and deliver what is important to students [13]. A critical issue in student retention is related to a student's sense of belonging to the chosen course. Our research is focusing on helping students in choosing subjects and manage their time in each semester by understanding the expectations and commitment and importance of each subject. Since the Course Map tool is in its initial development stage as a course planning tool, this study examines the effectiveness of the model by evaluating its functionalities in alignment with the prime beneficiaries of student satisfaction and retention – students and universities. We also compare our proposed tool with existing models and systems in the area of course planning and academic workload management.

5.1   Evaluation with Prime Beneficiaries

From students' perspective, this is a tool to assist them to plan and manage their course. Most students do not know how much study time and effort they need to spend on a subject. Inability to manage time and workload demands make students fall behind and they have become students at risk. So it is important that they can allocate enough time for each subject in each semester when preparing their personal timetable. Early planning and preparation help students to achieve good grades and meet student expectations. The tool guides students to choose a course with respect to their desired career, allocate their time, choose subjects based on the skills they want to develop, understand their assessments and deadlines in advance, visualize how the skills developed in each subject contribute to each career option in their chosen stream and obtain clarity on their career path.

As the prime motivation for students to engage in university study is to secure employment, the clarity of career path through skill mapping helps students to better understand the subjects and make informed decisions. The career component enables students to clearly understand particular career paths. It does not only provide in-depth information on the skills and competencies required of graduates in each career position, it also provides crucial information on the future scope of these careers with relevant figures and tables. An awareness of job opportunities in different sectors is also important for students as these can act as motivators when choosing specific courses and subjects [7].

Motivation is important for academic achievement [7]. Early planning and preparation can help students achieve good results and improve their motivation [4]. Students need to understand what they are studying in their course and their assessment tasks in order to plan early. The semester planner is designed to help students better understand the subjects they are studying within a course. This is important when they are planning their subjects and semesters early so that they can obtain a complete idea of what they are going to study each semester. Moreover, because this information is presented in a graphical and interactive way, it can provide students with a bigger picture of their academic track by helping them visualize the outcome of their choices.

From a university perspective, this is a mean for improving student retention, success and employability. Student satisfaction is the key factor for universities to survive, remain competitive and grow. As the tool provides a clear explanation on how each course or degree relates to each different career option, this will assist students to make the right choice based on their desired career pathway, which in turn, improves student satisfaction with their course and thus contributes to their success. This will help to avoid issues such as students changing courses or dropping out of university, to a large extent. Moreover, this tool will help in the design of curriculum which reflects the job market by monitoring the skills required in the labour market and mapping them with the skills offered by the subjects within a course. Furthermore, it will increase graduate employability which will increase the overall reputation of the university.

5.2   Comparison with Existing Models

Universities invest great efforts in guiding students through the selection process to reach optimal decisions in their specific course choices [12]. However, most existing models and tools failed to provide an effective support system in assisting students to plan their entire course by better academic preparedness, efficient academic workload management and core skill development. Research shows that better academic preparedness, efficient academic workload management and core skill development can successfully lead to student success [4, 5, 23, 25, 26]. We compare our model with the existing models in terms of these three parameters as shown in Table 1. In comparison with other models, our Course Map application provides better academic preparedness, efficient academic workload management and improved core skill development.

Table 1. Comparison with existing models

Model	References	Model type	Academic preparedness	Academic workload management	Core skill development
Alumni satisfaction model	[10]	Conceptual model	Yes	No	No
Course provision	[11]	Theoretical model	No	No	Yes
Integrated curriculum models	[12]	Theoretical model	No	No	Yes
NUSMods	[14]	Practical application	Yes	Yes	No
Smart planner	[15]	Practical application	Yes	Yes	No
Academic skills	[17, 18]	Resource files	Yes	Yes	No
Course map		Conceptual model and practical application	Yes	Yes	Yes

6   Conclusion

The transition to university learning is challenging for the majority of students [23]. Prior to every semester, students need to go through the subject selection process. These subject choices are important because this determines their future career decisions. Students want to choose their subjects based on the workforce outcomes of graduates, but without a true navigational system, the process is mostly guesswork. Universities must understand students' needs in order to motivate them to achieve their goals [10]. It is important that students are informed about the outcomes of their course throughout their academic journey to motivate them to achieve their goals. Researchers suggest that students' career aspirations need to be nurtured and supported with appropriate and relevant information [27, 28]. The main reason students withdraw from their course is that they feel that their chosen course was wrong.

The article discusses conditions that influence institutional effectiveness in reducing dropout and proposed a course mapping tool to manage their courses based on the four concept of DOTS model- self-awareness, opportunity awareness, decision learning and transition learning. The tool provides dashboards for students to plan, prepare and engage in their studies which can be integrated into their online learning management platform. The interactive user interfaces show the relationship among course, skills and career help by providing students with clarity about what is expected of them, what skills they need to develop, how they need to learn, how to progress and succeed. The combined knowledge of both the skills students developed and how they relate to their potential career path helps to build confidence, a positive attitude towards learning and successful engagement with the course. Thus, a student's future aspirations can be strongly nurtured.

In this paper, we have focused mainly on the Information Technology domain with limited available data. In the future, the application will be improved by collecting more data from different disciplines. The system will be further improved by adding automated weighted scheme using text mining to the skill taxonomy. We have evaluated the functionalities of our model with the support of literature. As an ongoing project, survey with end users is currently under preparation to evaluate the framework and the application.

References

1. Dacre Pool, L., Sewell, P.: The key to employability: developing a practical model of graduate employability. Education+Training **49**, 277–289 (2007)
2. Brooman, S., Darwent, S.: Measuring the beginning: a quantitative study of the transition to higher education. Stud. High. Educ. **39**, 1523–1541 (2014)
3. Pass, M.W., Mehta, S.S., Mehta, G.B.: Course selection: student preferences for instructor practices. Acad. Educ. Leadersh. J. **16**, 31 (2012)
4. Shury, J., Vivian, D., Turner, C., Downing, C.: Planning for success: graduates' career planning and its effect on graduate outcomes. Department for Business, Innovation and Skills (2017)
5. Crosling, G., Heagney, M., Thomas, L.: Improving student retention in higher education: improving teaching and learning. Aust. Univ. Rev. **51**, 9–18 (2009)
6. Bowles, A., Fisher, R., McPhail, R., Rosenstreich, D., Dobson, A.: Staying the distance: students' perceptions of enablers of transition to higher education. High. Educ. Res. Dev. **33**, 212–225 (2014)
7. Kori, K., Pedaste, M., Altin, H., Tõnisson, E., Palts, T.: Factors that influence students' motivation to start and to continue studying information technology in Estonia. IEEE Trans. Educ. **59**, 255–262 (2016)
8. Greenbank, P.: Career decision-making: 'I don't think twice, but it'll be all right'. Res. Post Compuls. Educ. **19**, 177–193 (2014)

9. McIlveen, P., Brooks, S., Lichtenberg, A., Smith, M., Torjul, P., Tyler, J.: Career development learning frameworks for work-integrated learning. In: Billett, S., Henderson, A. (eds.) Developing Learning Professionals. Professional and Practice-based Learning, vol. 7. Springer, Dordrecht (2011). https://doi.org/10.1007/978-90-481-3937-8_9

10. Hsu, S.-H., Wang, Y.-C., Cheng, C.-J., Chen, Y.-F.: Developing a decomposed alumni satisfaction model for higher education institutions. Total Qual. Manag. Bus. Excell. **27**, 979–996 (2016)

11. Bennett, N., Dunne, E., Carré, C.: Patterns of core and generic skill provision in higher education. High. Educ. **37**, 71–93 (1999)

12. Warren, D.: Curriculum design in a context of widening participation in higher education. Arts Humanities High. Educ. **1**, 85–99 (2002)

13. Elliott, K.M., Shin, D.: Student satisfaction: an alternative approach to assessing this important concept. J. High. Educ. Policy Manag. **24**, 197–209 (2002)

14. National University of Singapore. https://nusmods.com/timetable. Accessed 05 Mar 2018

15. University of Arizona Smart Planner. https://uaccess.arizona.edu/safiles/smartplanner/story_html5.html?lms=1. Accessed 05 Mar 2018

16. California State University Smart Planner. http://www.csuchico.edu/em/ENews/F14/smartplanner.shtml. Accessed 05 Mar 2018

17. The University of Melbourne Academic Skills. http://services.unimelb.edu.au/academicskills/all_resources#study-skills. Accessed 05 Mar 2018

18. University of New South Wales Academic Skills. https://student.unsw.edu.au/skills. Accessed 05 Mar 2018

19. Law, B., Watts, A.G.: Schools, Careers and Community. Church Information Office, London (1977)

20. Watts, A.: Careers education in higher education: principles and practice. Br. J. Guid. Couns. **5**, 167–184 (1977)

21. Hernández-March, J., Martín del Peso, M., Leguey, S.: Graduates' skills and higher education: the employers' perspective. Tert. Educ. Manag. **15**, 1–16 (2009)

22. Elliott, K.M., Healy, M.A.: Key factors influencing student satisfaction related to recruitment and retention. J. Mark. High. Educ. **10**, 1–11 (2001)

23. Thomas, L.: Building Student Engagement and Belonging in Higher Education at a Time of Change, vol. 100. Paul Hamlyn Foundation (2012)

24. Krause, K.L., Coates, H.: Students' engagement in first-year university. Assess. Eval. High. Educ. **33**, 493–505 (2008)

25. Schertzer, C.B., Schertzer, S.M.: Student satisfaction and retention: a conceptual model. J. Mark. High. Educ. **14**, 79–91 (2004)

26. Clemes, M.D., Gan, C.E., Kao, T.-H.: University student satisfaction: an empirical analysis. J. Mark. High. Educ. **17**, 292–325 (2008)

27. Wiseman, J., Davies, E., Duggal, S., Bowes, L., Moreton, R., Robinson, S., Nathwani, T., Birking, G., Thomas, L., Roberts, J.: Understanding the changing gaps in higher education participation in different regions of England. Department for Business, Innovation and Skills (2017)

28. Lay-Hwa Bowden, J.: What's in a relationship? Affective commitment, bonding and the tertiary first year experience–a student and faculty perspective. Asia Pac. J. Mark. Logist. **25**, 428–451 (2013)

A Learner Ontology Based on Learning Style Models for Adaptive E-Learning

Birol Ciloglugil[1]($\boxtimes$)(iD) and Mustafa Murat Inceoglu[2](iD)

[1] Department of Computer Engineering, Ege University,
35100 Bornova, Izmir, Turkey
birol.ciloglugil@ege.edu.tr
[2] Department of Computer Education and Instructional Technology,
Ege University, 35100 Bornova, Izmir, Turkey
mustafa.inceoglu@ege.edu.tr

Abstract. Learning style models are used as indicators of individual differences of learners based on observations during learning processes. Numerous learning style models have been developed to model the individual differences of learners. Among these models, Felder-Silverman, Honey-Mumford and Kolb learning style models are the most-widely used ones in the literature. Learning style models are frequently used to provide personalization in adaptive e-learning systems. On the other hand, with the advancements on Semantic Web technologies in the last decade, ontologies have been used to represent domain knowledge and user information in the e-learning field, too. Ontological learner models have been developed and learners have been modeled based on their individual differences, usually based on their learning styles. In this regard, we examined how learning style models have been modeled with ontologies in different adaptive e-learning systems for personalization. Then, we proposed a learner modeling ontology based on three learning style models; Felder-Silverman, Honey-Mumford and Kolb; for personalized e-learning. Initial usage of the proposed learner ontology in a multi-agent based e-learning system is also discussed with current limitations and future work directions.

Keywords: Learning styles · Semantic web · Ontology
Adaptive E-Learning · Personalization

1 Introduction

Learners have different individual needs, objectives and preferences that affect their learning processes [1]. Adaptive e-learning systems keep track of the individual differences of learners and provide them personalized learning materials based on these individual differences [2,3]. Thus, adaptive e-learning systems have two main components at the center of their designs; learner models and learning material models. In order to match learners with the most suitable

© Springer International Publishing AG, part of Springer Nature 2018
O. Gervasi et al. (Eds.): ICCSA 2018, LNCS 10961, pp. 199–212, 2018.
https://doi.org/10.1007/978-3-319-95165-2_14

learning materials, learners and learning materials should be modeled with some common standards [4].

Learner models are essential sources for personalization in e-learning systems. Personalization aims to recommend the most suitable learning materials to learners based on their learning characteristics [1]. Personalization can be based on learner's prior knowledge, motivation level, objectives and preferences [2]. Learning style models are also frequently used in adaptive e-learning systems to model individual differences of learners for personalization purposes [5–7]. In this study, we focused on learning style models and examined the most-widely used three models in the literature [5–8]; Felder-Silverman [9], Honey-Mumford [10] and Kolb [11].

IEEE LOM (Learning Object Metadata) [12] and SCORM (Sharable Content Object Reference Model) [13] are the most widely used representation standards for learning materials. Learning materials are packaged with SCORM standard as learning objects to increase reusability. Learning objects have metadata about their content that are usually defined by IEEE LOM metadata standard. Thus, in order to provide standardization and increase re-usability, learning materials are generally stored in learning object repositories as learning objects by using IEEE LOM and SCORM standards [14].

Semantic Web technologies and ontologies are used for knowledge representation in various domains [15]. They make it possible for data representation models to be available to various e-learning systems [14]. Thus, these systems can share their learner models, learning material models and other domain information with each other. This increases the re-usability of the learner and domain models among different systems, and therefore, provides new solutions for interoperability of different e-learning systems [16]. Learning objects and learning style models have been modeled by using ontologies in various systems [17–23]. A review on ontology usage in e-learning systems that focuses on metadata modeling of learning objects, especially with the IEEE LOM standard is presented by [14]. A review of learner modeling with ontologies based on learning style models is provided by [16].

Agent technology has been applied in the e-learning field to provide multi agent systems (MAS) based e-learning systems [24]. There are various efforts to provide MAS based e-learning systems in the literature [18,23,25–28]. Some of the application areas for agents include; pedagogical agents for personal recommendations to learners, harvester agents collecting appropriate learning materials for learners and monitoring agents keeping track of the interaction among learners and the system to provide interventions if needed. In MAS based e-learning systems, agents interact with learning resources and learner models that are part of their environment [26,27]. Agents can organize how to store, search and retrieve learning materials for other agents and/or learners [28]. Multi agent systems are generally used together with Semantic Web technologies [15,24]. E-learning systems that utilize both technologies include [18,23,28].

In this paper, we proposed an ontological learner model based on the three most-commonly used learning style models in the literature; Felder-Silverman,

Honey-Mumford and Kolb. The proposed learner model has a relatively simple design, yet the main contribution of it lies on its flexibility for combining different learning style models and examining the relationships between these learning style models. Most of the studies in the literature use a single learning style model [1,3,17,18,22,23,25] or a combination of two models [19,21]. Our approach provides a foundation to observe the interaction among the three learning style models currently modeled in the learner ontology, based on learner behaviors in the e-learning system.

The proposed learner model is initially used as part of a multi agent based e-learning system presented by [28]. The MAS based e-learning system [28] exploits an e-learning environment model based on Agents and Artifacts (A&A) Metamodel [29] and is implemented by using CArtAgO (Common Artifact infrastructure for Agent Open environment) framework [30]. The adaptive e-learning environment architecture proposed in [28] uses the learner model proposed in this study and adds personalization support to the environment model presented in [26].

The rest of the paper is organized as follows; Sect. 2 introduces the learning style concept and the learning style models used in the proposed learner model. Section 3 discusses related work by examining how learning styles are modeled in adaptive e-learning systems with ontologies. Section 4 addresses modeling of the learner ontology proposed in this paper to support personalization. Section 5 elaborates on how the proposed ontology is utilized as part of the MAS based e-learning system in [28]. Finally, Sect. 6 concludes the paper by addressing current limitations and future work directions.

2 Learning Style Models

Learning style models are commonly used in adaptive e-learning systems for modeling the way the students learn. Keefe (1979) defines learning styles as "the characteristic cognitive, affective and physiological behaviors that serve as relatively stable indicators of how learners perceive, interact with and respond to the learning environment" [31].

There are more than 70 learning style models in the literature [32]. However, Felder-Silverman learning style model (FSLSM) [9], Honey and Mumford learning style model [10] and Kolb's Experiential Learning Theory [11] are three of the most-widely used learning style models in the literature [5–8]. The relationships between learning materials represented as learning objects and learners modeled with their learning styles in adaptive e-learning systems are reviewed by [4,21]. These relationships provide the foundation to offer personalized e-learning solutions. For example, a personalization approach based on FSLSM to match learners with learning objects is proposed in [33] by using these relationships.

2.1 Kolb

Kolb learning style model is based on the "Experiential Learning Theory" [11] that models the learning process of learners. "Experiential Learning Theory" views the learning process as a four-stage loop and states that the learners need four abilities for efficient learning; "Concrete Experience Abilities", "Reflective Observation Abilities", "Abstract Conceptualization Abilities" and "Active Experimentation Abilities". These four abilities form two dimensions in a polarized manner; "Concrete" / "Abstract" and "Active" / "Reflective". According to Kolb learning style model, based on these dimensions, learners are categorized in four subclasses; "Convergers", "Divergers", "Assimilators" and "Accomodators".

2.2 Honey-Mumford

Honey-Mumford learning style model [10] is based on Kolb's "Experiential Learning Theory" [11]. Thus, the categorization of Honey-Mumford is similar to Kolb's classification. Subclasses of Honey-Mumford learning style model are given with the subclass they correspond to in Kolb's model in parenthesis as; "Activist" (Kolb's "Accomodators"), "Theorist" (Kolb's "Assimilators"), "Pragmatist" (Kolb's "Convergers") and "Reflector" (Kolb's "Divergers").

2.3 Felder-Silverman

Felder-Silverman Learning Style Model (FSLSM) [9] is a four-dimensional model, where learners are modeled with "Sensing" / "Intuitive", "Visual" / "Verbal", "Active" / "Reflective" and "Sequential" / "Global" dimensions based on the way they perceive, receive, process and understand information, respectively. The Index of Learning Styles (ILS) [34] is a ready to use scale to determine learning style of learners with FSLSM.

ILS consists of 44 questions in total, as there are 11 questions for each dimension. The questions in ILS scale provide two options that are graded as +1 or −1, respectively. Therefore, the total ILS score of a learner is an odd number in the interval [−11,+11]. If a learner's score for a FSLSM dimension is in the interval [−3,3], than the learner has a balanced learning style for that dimension. If the score is in the interval [−7,−5] or [5,7], than the learner has a moderate preference for one pole of that dimension. Finally, if the score is in the interval [−11,−9] or [9,11], the learner has a stronger tendency for one pole of that dimension.

Since there are numerous learning style models, during their development phases, some models are inspired by and/or directly take some of their dimensions from other learning style models. Thus, dimensions of some models may intersect with each other. For example, the information processing dimension of Felder-Silverman learning style model (Active/Reflective) is derived from Kolb's Experiential Learning Theory. Since Honey-Mumford learning style model is also based on Kolb's Experiential Learning Theory, their Activist and Reflector categories are closely related to Active/Reflective dimension of FSLSM [21].

Felder-Silverman Learning Style Model is the most widely used model [5–8], that is also recommended as the most suitable model to be used in adaptive e-learning systems [8]. Therefore, students are modeled by using Felder-Silverman

Learning Style Model in many studies in the literature [16]. This is the main reason for focusing on this model in the learner ontology presented in this paper.

3 Related Work

Semantic Web technology and ontologies are frequently used in the e-learning domain [35]. Ontology-based representations of learners and learning resources have been developed and used in different adaptive e-learning systems [14,16]. Students, teachers, institutions, learning materials and other components of adaptive e-learning systems are represented semantically by using ontologies [17–23]. Different learning style models are also modeled with ontologies as part of the student/learner models in adaptive e-learning systems [18,19,21–23]. As mentioned earlier, both learners and learning resources should be modeled in e-learning systems to provide meaningful recommendations to learners [4]. Therefore, learners, learning resources or both of them can be modeled based on learning styles in ontologies.

In this section, we focused on studies that explicitly described the ontological structure of their learner models with learning styles and analyzed semantic representations of learning style models in adaptive e-learning systems. However, it should be noted that, with less dimensions and poles to model, Honey-Mumford and Kolb have relatively simple ontology designs compared to Felder-Silverman learning style model. Even though there are systems like [19,20] using Honey-Mumford or Kolb learning style models, none of the systems we examined explicitly showed how they modeled these learning style models in ontologies. Therefore, in this section we could only examine how Felder-Silverman learning style model is modeled with ontologies.

A domain ontology that describes learning materials for personalization in educational systems is presented in [17]. Their ontology supports learning styles with FSLSM, however the emphasis is on hardware and software features of the devices required to display the learning resources. In this ontology, learning resources are represented with the "Resource" class which has three object properties that establish relations with; (a) the "Course" class to define the courses the resource is included in, (b) the "Concept" class to indicate the concepts the resource describes, and (c) the "ResourceDescription" class to describe the learning resource. The "ResourceDescription" class has five datatype properties (location, language, description, interactivity type and difficulty level) and five object properties that describe relations with; (a) the "Author"s it is created by, (b) the "Keyword"s it has, (c) the "Objective"s it helps to achieve, (d) the "LearningStyle" it has and (e) the "Device"s it requires. The "LearningStyle" class has four datatype properties represented with integer values that correspond to dimensions of FSLSM (active-reflective, sensing-intuitive, visual-verbal, sequential-global).

A domain ontology and a multi-agent based e-learning system architecture that supports re-estimating students' learning styles during the courses they take to provide better personalization is presented by [18]. Their domain ontology, which can be seen in Fig. 1, is based on [17]. However, [18] omitted the "Device" related components, because they concentrated on working with PCs only. The ontology presented by [17] describes learning resources that compose a course and supports learning styles of resources. [18] modified and added some classes and relations to the domain ontology. The "Learner" class was added to the domain ontology as learners are important actors of adaptive e-learning systems. The "Learner" class has nine datatype properties (full name, date of birth, sex, phone number, email, level of study, year of study, work status and performance) and three object properties that describe relations with; (a) the "Competence (Objective)"s the learner has, (b) the "Course"s the learner takes, and (c) the "LearningStyle" the learner has.

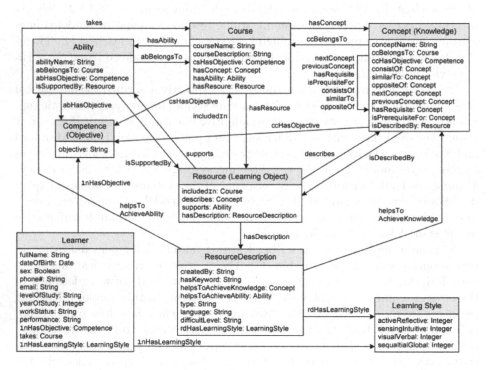

Fig. 1. General layout of the domain ontology proposed in [18].

[18] models learning styles of students with FSLSM and the "LearningStyle" class is defined the same way as the domain ontology of [17]. However, the additions of "Learner" class and "lnHasLearningStyle" object property of the "Learner" class provide a significant contribution. With the "lnHasLearningStyle" object property of the "Learner" class and the "rdHasLearningStyle" object property of the "ResourceDescription" class, learning styles are included in the descriptions of both learners and learning resources. Using these two object properties together helps the implementation of personalization in adaptive

e-learning systems [4]. Hence, learning resources that fit the best to a learner can be adaptively delivered [33].

"LearningStyleTheory" class is incorporated in [19]'s ontology to support more than one learning style models. [19] demonstrated the multiple learning style theory support of its domain ontology with only one dimension of "FSLSM" and "Kolb". However, no explicit detail is given on how they modeled Kolb learning style model in their ontology.

The main advantage of representing different learning style models in domain ontologies is the flexibility of selecting which learning style and/or dimension is more adequate to the type of recommendation being applied by the adaptive e-learning system. In the ontology we proposed, we extended the learning style models support of [19] to three most-widely used models; "FSLSM", "Honey-Mumford" and "Kolb"; and made it possible to work with all dimensions of these learning style models. However, providing personalization based on each learning style model is a challenging task on its own and supporting a combination of different models requires meticulous pedagogical research.

4 The Proposed Learner Ontology

During the development phase of the proposed learner ontology, we used Protege (http://protege.stanford.edu) as ontology development environment, OWL (Web Ontology Language) as ontology language and HermiT (http://hermit-reasoner. com) as a reasoner to check the consistency of our ontology.

Learners should be modeled based on their individual differences and preferences to provide personalization. Learning style models are one of the most-commonly used and efficient sources for personalization that represent information on how learners can achieve better learning performances based on their strengths and weaknesses at learning. Therefore, the focus of the learner modeling in this paper is on learning style models. In this regard, three most-widely used learning style models in the literature (Felder-Silverman, Honey-Mumford and Kolb) are modeled in the learner ontology developed for this study. The proposed ontological learner model is illustrated in Fig. 2.

"Learner" class is at the center of the developed ontology. Learners are represented with the "Learner" class which has three object properties that establish relations with; (a) the "PersonalInfo" class to define the personal information of the learner, (b) the "Education" class to indicate the educational background of the learner, and (c) the "LearningStyle" class to describe the learning style information of the learner. Every "Learner" individual should have personal information in the ontology represented as a "PersonalInfo" individual. The "PersonalInfo" class has datatype properties such as name, surname and username. Moreover, "Learner" individuals can be connected to zero or more "Education" and "LearningStyle" individuals.

Educational information of learners are modeled by the courses students take and the concepts related to these courses. The "Education" class is connected to the "Course" class with the "takesCourse" object property. Individuals of the

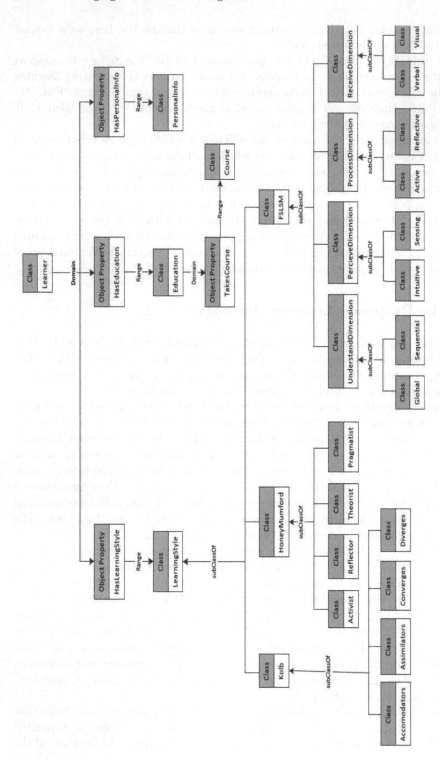

Fig. 2. The proposed ontological learner model.

"Education" class can take zero or more "Course"(s). Each "Course" can cover zero or more "Concept"(s). We developed an example "Digital Logic Design" course individual in the ontology and designed its concepts based on the concepts determined by [36] for Digital Logic Design courses; "Boolean Algebra", "Logic Gates", "Number Systems", "Gate-Level Minimization", "Combinational Functions and Circuits", "Arithmetic Functions and Circuits", "Sequential Circuits", "Register and Counters", "Finite-State Machines", "Computer Architecture", "Hardware Description Languages", "Implementation Technologies" and "Memory Systems".

Class hierarchy of the developed learner ontology, that depicts the subclass relations of learning styles, is given in Fig. 3. As the main focus of our ontology, learning styles information of learners are modeled with the "LearningStyle" class that can be represented with zero or more of its three subclasses. These subclasses correspond to the learning style models covered in this paper; "Felder-Silverman", "Honey-Mumford" and "Kolb". "Kolb" learning style class has four subclasses; "Convergers", "Divergers", "Assimilators" and "Accomodators". The subclasses of "Honey-Mumford" learning style class are; "Activist", "Theorist", "Pragmatist" and "Reflector". "Felder-Silverman" has four subclasses for its dimensions; "PerceiveDimension", "ReceiveDimension", "ProcessDimension" and "UnderstandDimension". Each dimension also

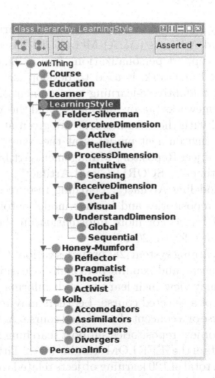

Fig. 3. Class hierarchy of the developed learner ontology.

has two subclasses indicating the learning style of the learners for that dimension; "Sensing" and "Intuitive" for "PerceiveDimension", "Visual" and "Verbal" for "ReceiveDimension", "Active" and "Reflective" for "ProcessDimension" and "Sequential" and "Global" for "UnderstandDimension".

After the design and development of the learner ontology, individuals of the designed classes have been created for the queries of the personalization approaches to operate on. Since learners can be modeled with zero to three learning style models in our ontology, the individuals are created to have zero to three learning styles information, too.

By modeling three learning style models in the learner ontology, we provided the ontological infrastructure to support personalization based on these learning styles. We focused on the components related to personalization during the design phase of the ontology. Thus, educational information such as university, faculty, department, educational year and curriculum, that are not used for personalization purposes, are not modeled in the ontology. This decision is made to include only the necessary components in the ontology, and to have a simpler learner model [37].

5   Exploiting the Learner Ontology in a MAS Based E-Learning System

The proposed ontology is utilized by the MAS based e-learning system [28] that extends the Agents and Artifacts (A&A) Metamodel based e-learning environment model in [26] to support personalization. Jason [38], a BDI (Belief Desire Intention) based agent framework, is used to develop [28]. Architecture of the A&A Metamodel based adaptive e-learning environment [28] is given in Fig. 4. Agent development frameworks (Jason and Jadex) and the MAS based e-learning applications developed with these frameworks are given at the left hand side of Fig. 4. The e-learning environment model is at the center containing five artifact types; "Learning Object Repository Management Artifact", "Local Learning Object Repository Artifact", "SCORM Cloud Artifact", "Personalization Artifact" and "Learner Modeling Artifact". Learning resources that are located in two different types of repositories and learner model ontologies can be seen at the right hand side of Fig. 4. For more information on the components of the architecture readers can refer to [26–28].

The MAS based e-learning system [28] provides various GUIs for users to login, select course and/or concept, and examine personalized learning paths. After a successful login, learners may view their learning style information, the courses they take and the concepts of a selected course. Learners may request a personalized learning path for a course or a concept of a selected course. Artifacts responsible for accessing the learning object repositories support searching learning objects with three metadata elements of the IEEE LOM standard; "1.2 Title", "1.4 Description" and "1.5 Keywords". A total of 120 learning objects related to Digital Logic Design course have been developed and stored in learning object repositories to test the personalization features of the MAS based e-learning system [28].

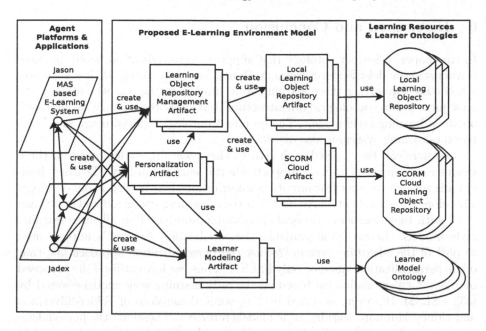

Fig. 4. Architecture of the Agents and Artifacts Metamodel based adaptive e-learning environment proposed in [28] that utilizes the proposed ontology.

Two of the five artifact types given in Fig. 4 are related to providing personalization. "Learner Modeling Artifact"s are in charge of the learner modeling related operations such as login, queries about courses taken by students and learning styles of learners. This artifacts use the proposed ontology for performing these operations to provide basic services for personalization. "Personalization Artifact"s are responsible for providing personalized learning paths to learners by using the operations presented by the "Learner Modeling Artifact"s. The MAS based e-learning system [28] includes "Personalization Artifact"s that apply the personalization approach proposed in [33], which is based on Felder-Silverman learning style model.

As stated in Section 2.3, Active/Reflective dimension of FSLSM and Honey-Mumford learning style model's Activist and Reflector categories are closely related to each others. There are some IEEE LOM metadata elements ("5.1 Interactivity Type" and "5.3 Interactivity Level") that can be used to provide personalization for both FSLSM and Honey-Mumford learning style models [21]. The personalization approach proposed in [33] already uses the aforementioned IEEE LOM metadata elements for personalization. Therefore, the personalization approach implemented in [33] implicitly supports personalization based on Honey-Mumford learning style model. However, it should be noted that this is a partial support and more detailed relations between other IEEE LOM metadata elements and Honey-Mumford learning style model should be investigated.

6 Discussion and Conclusion

In this paper, a learner ontology that supports personalization based on three learner style models; Felder-Silverman, Honey-Mumford and Kolb; has been presented. By supporting three learning style models in the learner ontology, we have provided the ontological infrastructure that supports personalization based on these learning style models. The proposed ontology's initial usage in a MAS based e-learning system is also discussed.

Learners can be modeled with zero to three learning styles based on three learning style models currently supported in the learner ontology. "Learner" individuals with up-to-three learning styles information already exist in our ontology. Therefore, "Personalization Artifact"s of the e-learning system offered in [28] can work with these learners to provide personalization based on all three learning style models. However, the available "Personalization Artifact"s implemented as part of the e-learning system [28] use the personalization approach [33] that offers personalization based on only FSLSM. Thus, we have utilized the proposed ontology for personalization based on the only learning style model covered by [33]; FSLSM. However, as stated by [21], some dimensions of Felder-Silverman and Honey-Mumford learning style models intersect. Therefore, the personalization approach in [33] implicitly covers Honey-Mumford learning style model in a partial way. With addition of new relations, Honey-Mumford learning style model can be supported relatively easily.

For future work, it is planned to extend the personalization support of the MAS based e-learning environment [28] by designing new "Personalization Artifact"s based on the other learning style models that are already modeled in the proposed learner ontology; "Kolb" and "Honey-Mumford". Moreover, new personalization approaches based on more than one learning style models can be designed as future work. This can pave the way to investigate the relationships between different learning style models.

References

1. Essalmi, F., Ayed, L.J.B., Jemni, M., Kinshuk, Graf, S.: A fully personalization strategy of e-learning scenarios. Comput. Hum. Behav. **26**(4), 581–591 (2010)
2. Ciloglugil, B., Inceoglu, M.M.: User modeling for adaptive e-learning systems. In: Murgante, B., Gervasi, O., Misra, S., Nedjah, N., Rocha, A.M.A.C., Taniar, D., Apduhan, B.O. (eds.) ICCSA 2012. LNCS, vol. 7335, pp. 550–561. Springer, Heidelberg (2012). https://doi.org/10.1007/978-3-642-31137-6_42
3. Sangineto, E., Capuano, N., Gaeta, M., Micarelli, A.: Adaptive course generation through learning styles representation. Univ. Access Inf. Soc. **7**(1–2), 1–23 (2008)
4. Ciloglugil, B.: A Review of the Relationship between Learning Styles and Learning Objects for Adaptive E-Learning. In: International Conference on Computer Science and Engineering, UBMK 2016, pp. 514–518 (2016)
5. Akbulut, Y., Cardak, C.S.: Adaptive educational hypermedia accommodating learning styles: a content analysis of publications from 2000 to 2011. Comput. Educ. **58**(2), 835–842 (2012)

6. Truong, H.M.: Integrating learning styles and adaptive e-learning system: current developments, problems and opportunities. Comput. Hum. Behav. **55**, 1185–1193 (2015)
7. Ozyurt, O., Ozyurt, H.: Learning style based individualized adaptive e-learning environments: content analysis of the articles published from 2005 to 2014. Comput. Hum. Behav. **52**, 349–358 (2015)
8. Ciloglugil, B.: Adaptivity based on felder-silverman learning styles model in e-learning systems. In: 4th International Symposium on Innovative Technologies in Engineering and Science, ISITES 2016, pp. 1523–1532 (2016)
9. Felder, R.M., Silverman, L.K.: Learning and teaching styles in engineering education. Eng. Educ. **78**(7), 674–681 (1988)
10. Honey, P., Mumford, A.: The Manual of Learning Styles. Peter Honey, Maidenhead (1982)
11. Kolb, D.A.: Experiential Learning: Experience as the Source of Learning and Development. Prentice-Hall, Englewood Cliffs, New Jersey (1984)
12. IEEE-LOM, IEEE LOM 1484.12.1 v1 Standard for Learning Object Metadata - 2002 (2002). http://grouper.ieee.org/groups/ltsc/wg12/20020612-Final-LOM-Draft.html. Accessed 10 Mar 2018
13. SCORM 2004: 4th Edition (2009). http://scorm.com/scorm-explained/technical-scorm/content-packaging/metadata-structure/. Accessed 10 Mar 2018
14. Ciloglugil, B., Inceoglu, M.M.: Ontology usage in e-learning systems focusing on metadata modeling of learning objects. International Conference on New Trends in Education, ICNTE 2016, pp. 80–96 (2016)
15. Berners-Lee, T., Hendler, J., Lassila, O.: The Semantic Web. Sci. Am. **284**(5), 34–43 (2001)
16. Ciloglugil, B., Inceoglu, M.M.: Learner modeling with ontologies based on learning style models. In: The 12th International Computer & Instructional Technologies Symposium, ICITS 2018, Izmir, Turkey, 2–4 May 2018. (accepted)
17. Gascuena, J.M., Fernandez-Caballero, A., Gonzalez, P.: Domain ontology for personalized e-learning in educational systems. In: Sixth International Conference on Advanced Learning Technologies, ICALT 2006, pp. 456–458. IEEE (2006)
18. Dung, P.Q., Florea, A.M.: An architecture and a domain ontology for personalized multi-agent e-learning systems. In: Third International Conference on Knowledge and Systems Engineering, KSE 2011, pp. 181–185, IEEE (2011)
19. Valaski, J., Malucelli, A., Reinehr, S.: Recommending learning materials according to ontology-based learning styles. In Proceedings of the 7th International Conference on Information Technology and Applications, ICITA 2011, pp. 71–75 (2011)
20. Kurilovas, E., Kubilinskiene, S., Dagiene, V.: Web 3.0-Based personalisation of learning objects in virtual learning environments. Comput. Hum. Behav. **30**, 654–662 (2014)
21. Essalmi, F., Ayed, L.J.B., Jemni, M., Kinshuk, Graf, S.: Selection of appropriate e-learning personalization strategies from ontological perspectives. Interact. Des. Architecture(s) Journal - IxD&A **9**(10), 65–84 (2010)
22. Yarandi, M., Jahankhani, H., Tawil, A. R. H.: A personalized adaptive e-learning approach based on semantic web technology. Webology 10(2), (2013). Art-110
23. Rani, M., Nayak, R., Vyas, O.P.: An ontology-based adaptive personalized e-learning system, assisted by software agents on cloud storage. Knowl.-Based Syst. **90**, 33–48 (2015)

24. Ciloglugil, B., Inceoglu, M.M.: Developing adaptive and personalized distributed learning systems with semantic web supported multi agent technology. In: 10th IEEE International Conference on Advanced Learning Technologies, ICALT 2010, Sousse, Tunesia, 5–7 July 2010, pp. 699–700. IEEE Computer Society (2010)
25. Sun, S., Joy, M., Griffiths, N.: The use of learning objects and learning styles in a multi-agent education system. J. Interact. Learn. Res. **18**(3), 381–398 (2007)
26. Ciloglugil, B., Inceoglu, M.M.: Exploiting agents and artifacts metamodel to provide abstraction of e-learning resources. In: 17th IEEE International Conference on Advanced Learning Technologies, ICALT 2017, Timisoara, Romania, 3–7 July 2017, pp. 74–75. IEEE (2017). https://doi.org/10.1109/ICALT.2017.130
27. Ciloglugil, B., Inceoglu, M.M.: An agents and artifacts metamodel based e-learning model to search learning resources. In: Gervasi, O., Murgante, B., Misra, S., Borruso, G., Torre, C.M., Rocha, A.M.A.C., Taniar, D., Apduhan, B.O., Stankova, E., Cuzzocrea, A. (eds.) ICCSA 2017. LNCS, vol. 10404, pp. 553–565. Springer, Cham (2017). https://doi.org/10.1007/978-3-319-62392-4_40
28. Ciloglugil, B., Inceoglu, M.M.: An adaptive e-learning environment architecture based on agents and artifacts metamodel. In: 18th IEEE International Conference on Advanced Learning Technologies, ICALT 2018, Mumbai, India, 9–13 July 2018. (accepted)
29. Ricci, A., Piunti, M., Viroli, M.: Environment programming in multi-agent systems: an artifact-based perspective. Auton. Agents Multi-Agent Syst. **23**(2), 158–192 (2011)
30. Ricci, A., Viroli, M., Omicini, A.: CArtA gO: A framework for prototyping artifact-based environments in MAS. In: Weyns, D., Parunak, H.V.D., Michel, F. (eds.) E4MAS 2006. LNCS (LNAI), vol. 4389, pp. 67–86. Springer, Heidelberg (2007). https://doi.org/10.1007/978-3-540-71103-2_4
31. Keefe, J.: Student learning styles: Diagnosing and describing programs. National Secondary School Principals, Reston VA (1979)
32. Coffield, F., Moseley, D., Hall, E., Ecclestone, K.: Should We Be Using Learning Styles? What Research Has to Say to Practice. Learning and Skills Research Centre/University of Newcastle upon Tyne, London (2004)
33. Ciloglugil, B., Inceoglu, M.M.: A felder and silverman learning styles model based personalization approach to recommend learning objects. In: Gervasi, O., Murgante, B., Misra, S., Rocha, A.M.A.C.M.A.C., Torre, C.M.M., Taniar, D., Apduhan, B.O.O., Stankova, E., Wang, S. (eds.) ICCSA 2016. LNCS, vol. 9790, pp. 386–397. Springer, Cham (2016). https://doi.org/10.1007/978-3-319-42092-9_30
34. Felder, R.M., Soloman, B.A.: Index of Learning Styles questionnaire (1997). http://www.engr.ncsu.edu/learningstyles/ilsweb.html
35. Kardan, A.A., Aziz, M., Shahpasand, M.: Adaptive systems: a content analysis on technical side for e-learning environments. Artif. Intell. Rev. **44**(3), 365–391 (2015)
36. Spivey, G.: A taxonomy for learning, teaching, and assessing digital logic design. In: 37th Annual Conference on Frontiers In Education Conference-Global Engineering: Knowledge Without Borders, Opportunities Without Passports, FIE 2007, pp. F4G–9. IEEE (2007)
37. Noy, N., McGuinness, D.L.: Ontology development 101. Stanford University, Knowledge Systems Laboratory (2001)
38. Bordini, R.H., Hübner, J.F., Wooldridge, M.: Programming multi-agent systems in AgentSpeak using Jason, vol. 8. Wiley, Chichester (2007)

Workshop Bio and Neuro Inspired Computing and Applications (BIONCA 2018)

Simulating Cell-Cell Interactions Using a Multicellular Three-Dimensional Computational Model of Tissue Growth

Belgacem Ben Youssef[(✉)]

College of Computer and Information Sciences,
Department of Computer Engineering, King Saud University, Riyadh, Saudi Arabia
BBenyoussef@ksu.edu.sa

Abstract. We report simulation results describing cell-cell interactions using a versatile computational model to simulate the growth of multicellular tissues employing a discrete approach based on cellular automata. In particular, we present results of cell collision and aggregation for three cell populations each having its own division and motion characteristics based on experimental data. The developed model allows us to study the tissue growth rates and population dynamics of different populations of migrating and proliferating mammalian cells in a mixed and segmented seeding distribution. In this regard, the model assumes that nutrient and growth factor concentrations remain constant in space and time. Cell migration is modeled using a discrete-time Markov chain approach. Both heterotypic and homotypic cell-cell interactions play important roles in cell and tissue functions. The temporal evolution of the frequency of cell collision and aggregation and their relations to other variables that quantify some of the dynamics of cell populations can be predicted by this model for different cell seeding distributions.

Keywords: Cell collision · Cell aggregation · 3D model
Multicellular tissue growth · Cellular automata

1 Introduction

Each year, millions of surgical procedures are performed to relieve patients who are affected by tissue loss, due to burns and injuries, or organ failure. Operations treating patients using tissue reconstruction and organ transplantation have been highly successful. However, the number of patients treated by these therapies is small due to the limited number of donors available. Hence, the primary focus of tissue engineering is the growth of three-dimensional tissues with proper structure and function. Tissue engineers combine knowledge from the areas of biochemistry, medical sciences, and engineering to develop bioartificial tissue substitutes or to induce tissue remodelling in order to repair, replace, or enhance tissue functions [1].

© Springer International Publishing AG, part of Springer Nature 2018
O. Gervasi et al. (Eds.): ICCSA 2018, LNCS 10961, pp. 215–228, 2018.
https://doi.org/10.1007/978-3-319-95165-2_15

Natural tissues are multicellular and have a specific three-dimensional architecture. This structure is supported by the extracellular matrix (ECM). The ECM often has the form of a three-dimensional network of cross-linked protein strands. In addition to determining the mechanical properties of a tissue, the ECM plays many important roles in tissue development. Biochemical and biophysical signals from the ECM modulate fundamental cellular activities, including adhesion, migration, proliferation, differentiation, and programmed cell death [10]. Recent studies of biomaterials have provided ways to manipulate some of these cellular activities through the use of targeted fabrication or modification of bioartificial scaffolds [11].

Tissue engineers grow bioartifical tissue substitutes by reproducing the structural components of naturally grown tissues. However, tissue growth is a complex process affected by many contributing factors such as the type of cells, initial seeding densities, spatial distribution of the seed cells and the culture conditions [5,6]. The dynamic process for generating cellularized tissue substitutes can be described as follows:

- A small tissue sample is harvested from the patient or donor.
- Cells are isolated, cultured and seeded into a three-dimensional scaffold with the proper structure and surface properties. The scaffold may contain growth factors to induce and maintain the proper differentiated cellular function.
- The cells migrate in all directions and proliferate to populate the scaffold. Cell migration speeds and proliferation rates are controlled by the surface properties and morphology of the scaffold. Bioactive agents may also be used to regulate cell migration and proliferation.
- The bioartificial tissue substitute is implanted in the patient.

Scaffold properties, cell activities like adhesion or migration, and external stimuli that modulate cellular functions are among the many factors that affect the growth rate of tissues. Therefore, the development of bio-artificial tissue substitutes involves extensive and time-consuming experimentation. The availability of computational models with predictive abilities may greatly speed up progress in this area.

This research focuses on the development of computational models to simulate the growth of three-dimensional tissues consisting of more than one cell type. Our contributions in this paper deal with the use such models to study the dynamics of cell-cell interactions. The success of models that describe the dynamic behaviour of cell populations, however, will depend on our ability to accurately describe the collision and aggregation of different cell types in various seeding environments.

2   Related Work

Various modeling approaches have been used to simulate the population dynamics of proliferating cells. Early attempts to model cell population growth were limited to nonmotile cells and the study of contact inhibition phenomena on the proliferation of anchorage-dependant endothelial cells. These early models considered nonmotile cells proliferating in two dimensions, or on microcarriers [9]. In disregarding cell locomotion, the cell growth rates in these early models were restricted by the effects of contact inhibition. Further research work showed the importance of cell motility and cell-cell interaction in describing the cell proliferation rates [4]. Any comprehensive model for tissue growth must consider these processes and account for the growth factors that regulate their rates. Later, Ben Youssef et al. in [7] developed the first three-dimensional cellular automata model for tissue growth. This work also utilizes a Markov chain approach to model the trajectories of migrating cells and is focused primarily on the study of a single population of proliferating and migrating cells [2]. It forms the basis for our model here.

3   Modeling of Cell Collision and Aggregation

To model our biological system, we focused our attention on four cellular processes: cell division, cell migration, cell collision, and cell aggregation. The first two processes are described elsewhere [2]. The latter two are described in the next two sections, respectively. These four processes are illustrated in Fig. 1. For example, mother cell 1, at the top left of the cellular space, migrates downwards, and divides into two daughter cells. These two daughter cells, in this scenario, move around until they encounter each other, at which time aggregation occurs. If one of these daughter cells moves away and encounters a cell of a different type (type 2), then collision occurs.

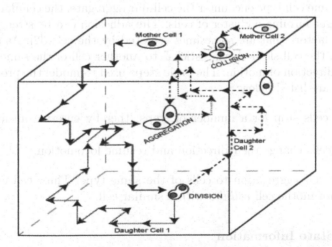

Fig. 1. An illustration showing the persistent random walk of two mother cells of different types (1 and 2) during their division cycle. The two daughter cells move away from each other and may aggregate or collide with other cells

3.1 Cell Collision

Mammalian cells move in a certain direction for some period of time and, then, they turn and migrate in another direction. Cell collision occurs when a cell moving in a certain direction encounters another cell of a different type in its path. When a cell of one type collides with a cell of a different type, the cell slows down for a period of time and then changes its direction. The duration of time a cell stays in the stationary state after a cell collision is based on its type [3]. Once the cell is ready to resume its motion, it migrates in a new direction. The modeling steps used in the cell collision process are described below:

– The cell stops for a number of steps.
– The cell changes its direction and resumes motion.

In this model, cell collisions can occur either when a cell is moving in a given direction, or when a cell is changing its direction and encounters another cell of a different type.

3.2 Cell Aggregation

Cell aggregation is a feature of tissue formation that allows the binding of cells of the same type. It is this specific grouping of cells that enables the tissue to perform its intended purpose. Cell aggregation is the combination of two cellular functions: cell-to-cell recognition and cell adhesion. The self-recognition quality lets cells identify cells of the same type. When cells of the same type encounter each other, they adhere to one another and form a cellular aggregate [1]. As more cells of the same cell type encounter the cellular aggregate, the cellular aggregate becomes larger forming a cluster of cells. The adhesion can be strengthened by aggregation factors that are sometimes secreted by the cells [2]. As a result of aggregation, the cell slows down, "sticks" to another cell of the same type, and changes its direction of motion. The basic steps used to model the process of cell aggregation are listed below:

– The two cells stop for a number of steps, thereby entering an aggregation state.
– The two cells change their direction and resume locomotion.

We limit cell aggregation to cells of the same type. Thus, cell aggregation occurs when a motile cell *collides* with a similar cell.

3.3 Cell State Information

To characterize a heterotypic cell-cell interaction, our model uses a collision stationary state (denoted by $l = 0$). If a cell c collides with another cell of a different type, cell c stops moving and enters what is known as the collision stationary state. It remains in that state for a defined period equal to its expected waiting time, $E(T_0)$. When $E(T_0)$ expires, cell c can move away in a randomly assigned direction.

In the case of a homotypic cell-cell interaction, we added a second stationary state (denoted by $l = 7$). Two colliding cells of the same cell type will enter the aggregation state and stick together for a defined period equal to $E(T_7)$. The value of $E(T_7)$ indicates the likelihood for the cells to form multicellular aggregates. When a cell collides with another cell of the same type, that is already in the aggregation state, then the first cell will enter the aggregation state and both cells will reset their persistence counters to $E(T_7)/\Delta t$. Once this waiting time has expired, the two cells can move away in randomly assigned directions.

The state of a cell takes values from the following set of eight digit integer numbers: $\Omega = \{klmnpqrs | k, l, m, n, p, q, r, \text{and } s \in \mathbb{N}\}$, where k is the cell type. The direction of motion is identified by the direction index l. When l is equal to 0, the cell is in the collision stationary state. When the value of l ranges from 1 to 6, it represents one of six directions the cell is currently moving in (east, north, west, south, above, and below). If it is equal to 7, it enters an aggregation stationary state where it "sticks" to another cell of the same type potentially forming cellular aggregates. The digits mn denote the persistence counter. It is the time remaining until the next change in the direction of cell movement. The cell phase counter is represented by the digits $pqrs$. The cell phase counter is the time remaining before the cell divides.

3.4   Initial Conditions

Three cell populations are used to simulate cell collision and aggregation. Each of these three cell populations, referred to as cell population 1, cell population 2 and cell population 3, has its own division and migration characteristics. The division time distributions for these three cell populations are given in Table 1. For example, this table shows that for cell population 1, 64% of the living cells have division times between 12 and 18 h, 32% of the living cells have division times between 18 and 24 h, and 4% of the living cells have division times between 24 and 30 h. Furthermore, cells from population 1 are considered to be fast-moving cells that migrate at 10 µm/h while cells from population 2 are moderately fast-moving cells migrating at a speed of only 2 µm/h and cells from population 3 are slow moving cells migrating at 0.5 µm/h.

3.5   Cell Seeding Topology

In this study, we consider an initial cell seeding topology, known as uniform topology. This topology was chosen for its applicability to experimental research conducted in laboratories whereby cells are randomly seeded in the cellular space. This topology simulates the migration and proliferation of cells in a sparsely and uniformly seeded environment with the objective of simulating tissue regeneration. With such a cell seeding topology, we have associated two types of cell distributions as described below.

1. Segmented Distribution. Here, each cell type is seeded in a separate area of the cellular space. During the simulation, cells can migrate freely and can enter areas that were originally designated for a particular type of cell during the initial cell seeding. Figure 2(a) shows an example of a segmented distribution in the case of uniform seeding topology of three cell types. The seeding density indicates the percentage of sites occupied by cells at the start of the simulation.

2. Mixed Distribution. The other seeding distribution associated with this cell seeding topology is the mixed distribution. Here, the different cell types are seeded together in a random order according to the cell topology. Figure 2(b) shows the mixed distribution of three cell types in the uniform seeding topology.

Table 1. Cell division time distributions for the three cell populations

Division Time Interval (hrs)	Cell Population 1	Cell Population 2	Cell Population 3
[12, 18)	64%	0%	4%
[18, 24)	32%	64%	32%
[24, 30)	4%	32%	64%
[30, 36)	0%	4%	0%

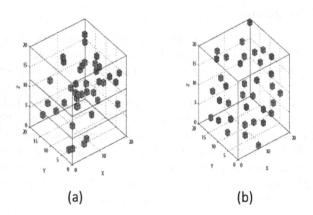

(a)   (b)

Fig. 2. An example of a uniform seeding topology using three cell populations in (a) a segmented and (b) a mixed distribution. In each case, a seeding density of 0.5% is used in a $20 \times 20 \times 20$ cellular array

3.6 Dynamics of Cell-Cell Interactions

At the start of each simulation, the cellular space is seeded with a total number of seed cells equal to N_0. These seed cells migrate and proliferate in the cellular array based on the cellular automata rules to simulate the dynamic process of tissue growth [8]. After some time t, $N_c(t)$ sites of the cellular automaton are occupied by cells. Eventually, some cells may become contact inhibited. This takes place when a cell is completely surrounded by other cells. The total number of completely surrounded cells at time t is given below by $N_s(t)$:

$$N_s(t) = \sum_{i=1}^{n} N_{s_i}(t) = N_{s_1}(t) + N_{s_2}(t) + \ldots + N_{s_n}(t) \tag{1}$$

where $N_{s_i}(t)$ is the number of completely surrounded cells of cell type i at time t and n is the number of cell types. Thus, the fraction of completely surrounded cells, denoted by $\psi(t)$, can thus be computed. This is the fraction of cells in the cellular space that can not move or divide. It is given by:

$$\psi(t) = \frac{N_s(t)}{N_c(t)} = \sum_{i=1}^{n} \psi_i(t) \tag{2}$$

with,

$$\psi_i(t) = \frac{N_{s_i}(t)}{N_c(t)}, \tag{3}$$

where $\psi_i(t)$ is the fraction of completely surrounded cells of cell type i. In addition, the frequency of cell-cell interactions, which reflects the total number of cell-cell interactions for a given cell per simulation step Δt, is provided by:

$$F_c(t) = \frac{\text{Total number of cell-cell interactions in } [t, t + \Delta t]}{N_c(t) \times \Delta t}. \tag{4}$$

It follows that $F_c(t)$ yields the sum of the number of cell collisions, or *heterotypic* cell interactions, and the number of cell aggregations, also known as *homotypic* cell interactions.

We also define the cell heterogeneity measure for cell population i, denoted by H_i, as the ratio of the initially seeded number of cells from population i to that from all the three cell populations. The ratio H_i is given by:

$$H_i = \frac{\text{Number of seed cells from population } i}{\text{Total number of seed cells from all populations}}. \tag{5}$$

Thus, $\sum_{i=1}^{n} H_i = 1$. In our simulations, we used $H_1 = H_2 = H_3 = \frac{1}{3}$. That is, there are equal numbers of seed cells from all three populations in the cell seeding density.

4   Simulation Results and Discussion

The simulation results presented herein were obtained using a $240 \times 240 \times 240$ cellular array, a 99.99% confluence parameter, and average waiting times of 2 h for the six directional states and 1 h each for the aggregation state and the collision state, respectively. For the segmented distribution, we used a "fast-slow-moderate" cell seeding combination. Here, we initially restricted the placement of fast cells in the first segment followed by the slow moving cells in the second then the moderate ones in the last segment. Figure 3 shows two-dimensional cell population profiles at four different time instants along the z dimension of the cellular grid using an initial seeding density of 0.5%. Fast moving cells are depicted in blue (or dark grey), moderate ones in green (or light grey), and the slow ones in red (or regular grey). The figure illustrates the diffusion level of fast moving cells into the cellular space. Due to space limitations, we only report results for the "fast-slow-moderate" cell seeding combination of the segmented distribution. The reader is referred to [12] for additional information.

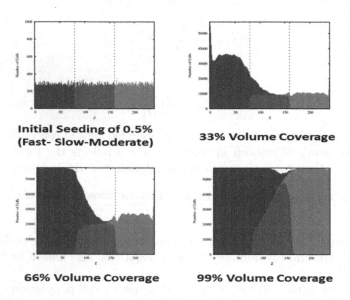

Fig. 3. Cell population profiles at four time instants along the z-axis for the "fast-slow-moderate" cell seeding combination of the segmented distribution. Blue or dark grey represents fast cells; red or regular grey represents slow cells; green or light grey represents cells with moderate speed (Color figure online)

4.1   Segmented Uniform Distribution

Figures 4, 5 and 6 show the temporal evolution of the frequency of cell-cell interactions for cell population 1, cell population 2, and cell population 3, respectively. Cells with faster speeds generate a higher frequency of cell-cell interactions when compared with cells having moderate speeds. Homotypic cell interactions constitute the largest component of cell-cell interactions for all three cell populations. For cells with higher speeds, the corresponding peak takes place sooner in time, around day number 5, compared to about 2.5 days later for the other two cell

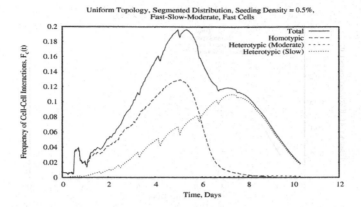

Fig. 4. The temporal evolution of the frequency of cell-cell interactions and its components for cell population 1 (fast cells)

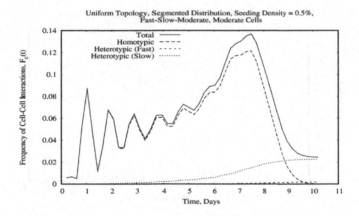

Fig. 5. The temporal evolution of the frequency of cell-cell interactions and its components for cell population 2 (cells with a moderate speed)

populations. Cells moving at high speeds tend to reach far empty spaces in segments that were initially seeded with cells of lower speeds yielding an increase in their cell interactions. The next largest component is the result of cell interactions with cells from the neighboring segment for cells from populations 1 and 2 since they were seeded in the two end segments, respectively. For cells from population 3, which were seeded initially in the middle segment, they generated more cell interactions with cells from population 1 than those from population 2 due to the higher motility of the former and their diffusion in nearby sites, which creates more opportunities for cell-cell interactions.

Figure 7, which shows how the fraction of surrounded cells evolves over time, corroborates this observation and depicts the fact that cells with higher motility also possess higher fractions of surrounded cells resulting in faster overall volume coverage and higher tissue growth rate.

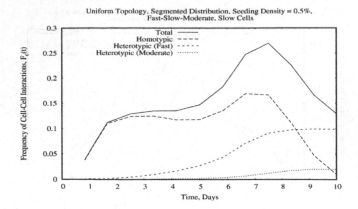

Fig. 6. The temporal evolution of the frequency of cell-cell interactions and its components for cell population 3 (slow cells)

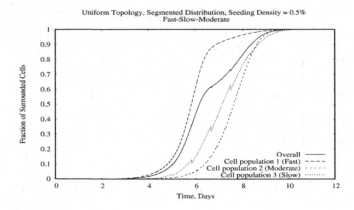

Fig. 7. The temporal evolution of the total fraction of surrounded cells and its three components for the segmented distribution using the "fast-slow-moderate" cell seeding combination

4.2   Mixed Uniform Distribution

Figures 8, 9 and 10 show the frequency of cell-cell interactions versus time for populations 1, 2, and 3, respectively. Here, the impact of increasing cell speeds on increasing the frequency of cell-cell interactions is manifest in a clear way. Peak values of 0.53, 0.285, and 0.24 are obtained for the frequency of cell-cell interactions of the three cell populations, respectively. In addition, the impact of cell interactions with cells of a different type becomes the dominant factor as cell population speeds increase from slow to moderate then fast. In this regard, we notice that cell collisions increase much more rapidly than cell aggregations from day 3 to day 7 highlighting the impact of contact inhibition between different cell types.

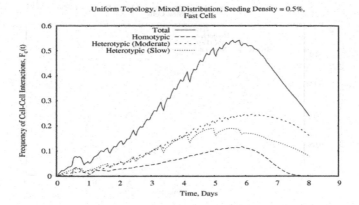

Fig. 8. The temporal evolution of the frequency of cell-cell interactions and its components for cell population 1 (fast cells) in the mixed seeding distribution

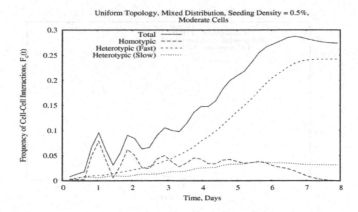

Fig. 9. The temporal evolution of the frequency of cell-cell interactions and its components for cell population 2 (cells with a moderate speed) in the mixed seeding distribution

Figure 11 displays the temporal evolution of the total fraction of surrounded cells and its components. Due to the nature of the mixed distribution, the fraction of surrounded cells for cell population 3 (slow cells) is the largest due to its low motility and an increase of the effect of contact inhibition from cells of other types. This impact is shown in Fig. 10. This figure displays the frequency of cell interactions for the slow population. After 4.5 days, the frequency of heterotypic cell interactions is larger than the homotypic kind for cell population 3. The latter has been decreasing for a while whereas the other two types keep increasing until nearly day 7.

226   B. B. Youssef

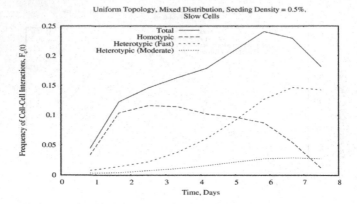

Fig. 10. The temporal evolution of the frequency of cell-cell interactions and its components for cell population 3 (slow cells) in the mixed seeding distribution

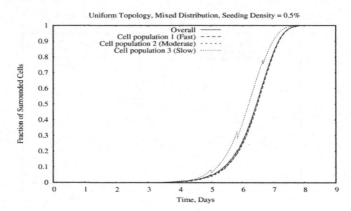

Fig. 11. The temporal evolution of the total fraction of surrounded cells and its three components when using a mixed cell-seeding distribution

5   Conclusion

In this paper, we presented simulation results for cell collision and cell aggregation obtained using a three-dimensional computational model for multicellular tissue growth. When employing three types of cell populations with different migration speeds and division time distributions, our simulations showed that faster moving cells yield an increase in the frequency of their cell-cell interactions for both cell seeding distributions. It appears that the frequency of cell-cell interactions may depend at least primarily on the dynamics of the cell populations present in the cellular space. Including other seeding arrangements of cells in the segmented distribution will be needed to further elucidate this phenomenon.

Throughout these results, we noted that a rapid increase in the fraction of surrounded cells is accompanied by a fast decrease in the frequency of cell-cell interactions (see results starting from day 6 till confluence). Moreover, the segmented uniform distribution yielded a smaller overall frequency of cell-cell interactions for the population of fast cells. In the case of the population of slow-moving cells, nearly similar peak values for the overall frequency of cell-cell interactions were obtained by both cell seeding distributions (0.27 vs. 0.24). However, in the segmented distribution, the slow cells mostly stay bunched together in their original segment as depicted by the consistently high frequency of homotypic cell interactions. In the mixed distribution, their heterotypic interactions with the fast cells become dominant due to the rapid movement of the latter to nearby sites whose neighborhoods were mostly occupied by the former. These conclusions may have important implications for the design of experiments that can test the efficacy of cell heterogeneity and cell seeding distributions designed to enhance or minimize the frequency of cell-cell interactions in a tissue growth environment.

Acknowledgments. The author would like to acknowledge the support for this research from the Research Centre in the College of Computer & Information Sciences and the Deanship of Scientific Research at King Saud University.

References

1. Palsson, B.O., Bhatia, S.N.: Tissue Engineering. Pearson Prentice Hall, Upper Saddle River (2004)
2. Ben Youssef, B.: A visualization tool of 3-D time-varying data for the simulation of tissue growth. Multimed. Tools Appl. **73**(3), 1795–1817 (2014)
3. Chang, L., Gilbert, E.S., Eliashberg, N., Keasling, J.D.: A three-dimensional, stochastic simulation of biofilm growth and transport-related factors that affect structure. Micro-biology **149**(10), 2859–2871 (2003)
4. Cickovski, T.M., et al.: A framework for three-dimensional simulation of morphogenesis. IEEE ACM T. Comput. Biol. Bioinform. **2**(4), 273–288 (2005)
5. Drasdo, D., Jagiella, N., Ramis-Conde, I., Vignon-Clemental, I.E., Weens, W.: Modeling steps from benign tumor to invasive cancer: examples of intrinsically multiscale problems. In: Chauviere, A., Preziosi, L., Verdier, C. (eds.) Cell Mechanics: From Single Scale-Based Models to Multiscale Modeling. pp. 379–416. CRC Press, Boca Raton (2010)
6. Majno, G., Joris, I.: Cells, Tissues, and Disease: Principles of General Pathology. Oxford University Press, New York (2004)
7. Ben Youssef, B.: A parallel cellular automata algorithm for the deterministic simulation of 3-D multicellular tissue growth. Cluster Comput. **18**(4), 1561–1579 (2015)
8. An, G., Mi, Q., Dutta-Moscato, J., Vodovotz, Y.: Agent-based models in translational systems biology. Wiley Interdiscip. Rev. **1**(2), 159–171 (2009)
9. Azuaje, F.: Computational discrete models of tissue growth and regeneration. Brief. Bioinform. **12**(1), 64–77 (2011)
10. Palsson, E.: A three-dimensional model of cell movement in multicellular systems. Future Gener. Comp. Sy. **17**(7), 835–852 (2001)

11. Liu, X., Ma, P.: Polymeric scaffolds for bone tissue engineering. Ann. Biomed. Eng. **32**(3), 477–486 (2004)
12. Youssef, B.B.: Visualization of spatial patterns of cells using a 3-D simulation model for multicellular tissue growth. In: Proceedings of the 4th IEEE International Conference on Multimedia Computing and Systems (ICMCS 2014), pp. 367–374, Marrakech, Morocco (2014)

Workshop Computer Aided Modeling, Simulation, and Analysis (CAMSA 2018)

Vulnerability of Pugu and Kazimzumbwi Forest Reserves Under Anthropogenic Pressure in Southeast Tanzania

Guy Boussougou Boussougou[1(✉)], Yao Télesphore Brou[2],
and Patrick Valimba[3]

[1] UMR ESPACE-DEV (UAG, UM2, UR), University of La Réunion,
40 Avenue de Soweto, 97410 Saint Pierre, France
guyboussougou@yahoo.fr
[2] UMR ESPACE-DEV (UAG, UM2, UR), University of La Réunion,
15 Avenue René Cassin, 97744 Saint Denis, France
[3] Engineering and Technology, University of Dar Es Salaam, PO. Box 35176,
Dar Es Salaam, Tanzania

Abstract. Located in the eastern part of Tanzania, coastal zones are recognized as hotspots of global biodiversity. But for several years now, they have been subjected to many pressures of a natural and human nature. Forest degradation occurs mainly in protected areas close to cities. Thus, the two forest reserves of Pugu and Kazimzumbwi are the most threatened forests on the Tanzanian coast. Thus, this study is intended to assess the expansion of vulnerability around reserves under anthropogenic pressures using multi-criteria analysis and bio-physical and socio-economic data. The results of the multi-criteria analysis show that the risk of forest degradation remains very high in the eastern part of the reserves due to the proximity of the towns of Pugu and Kisarawe. There is also the import share of the proximity of communication axes such as the main road to the east of the reserves and the railroad to the north in the vulnerability process.

Keywords: Multi-criteria analysis · Anthropogenic pressure
Pugu and kazimzumbwi forest reserve

1 Introduction

Population growth, agricultural production, livestock expansion, bush fires and charcoal use are having a negative impact on coastal forests in East Africa [1]. Indeed, the East African forests rich in natural resources are increasingly subject to human pressures (population growth, poverty, weak institutions…) combined with climate change [2–5]. Between 2000 and 2012, deforestation caused the loss of about 6 million hectares of forest in East Africa [1]. In Tanzania, this loss amounts to 1990300 ha [6]. The areas most affected by degradation are areas rich in natural resources. This is particularly the case in coastal areas or the eastern mountain arc recognized as hotspots of global biodiversity [7]. Forest degradation is more intense near major cities, such as the Pugu and Kazimzumbwi forest reserves in the peri-urban areas of Dar Es Salaam.

© Springer International Publishing AG, part of Springer Nature 2018
O. Gervasi et al. (Eds.): ICCSA 2018, LNCS 10961, pp. 231–240, 2018.
https://doi.org/10.1007/978-3-319-95165-2_16

These two forests are among the most disturbed coastal natural forests in Tanzania due to the combination of human activities induced by cities, mainly agriculture, timber harvesting and pole cutting.

Faced with the degradation of forest landscapes in the said reserves [8], it is necessary to identify the most impacting vulnerability factors in the environment.

So the question is, how can we locate and spatialize the highest pressure zones around protected areas? The hypothesis formulated states that there is strong pressure due to human activities on the forest reserves of Pugu and Kazimzumbwi resulting in their vulnerability. The objective of this study is to assess the spatial vulnerability of the environment in relation to the criteria that favour the settlement of populations around forest reserves. This work is organized as follows: presentation of the study site, data and treatment methods and finally analysis of the results and discussion.

2 Study Area

The Pugu and Kazimzumbwi forest reserves are part of Tanzania's coastal protected areas. These are remnants of an ancient large forest cover area belonging to the Zanzibar-Inhambane section of the Guinean and Congolese Plant Geographical Region [9]. They are located in the peri-urban area of Tanzanian town Dar es Salaam. Despite their limited size, these forests are internationally recognized as "hotspots" of the diversity of endemism [10]. Both reserves are located on the border between the Pwani region and Dar Es Salaam and belong to the Kisarawe district. The geographical coordinates are respectively: 6°55' S-7°02' S; 39°02 E-39°04' E and 6°55' S-7°02' S; 39°02 E-39°04' E (Fig. 1). Their altitude varies between 120 and 280 m and is approximately 20 to 25 km from the town of Dar Es Salaam (accessible by land). The area of forest reserves is 7856,928 ha (2423.38 ha for Pugu and 5433,548 ha for Kazimzumbwi).

3 Data and Methods

3.1 Data

Locating and spatializing pressure zones requires a certain amount of data. The data retained in this work are: the roadmaps were downloaded from the OSM site, the watercourse and railway were digitized on the topographic map of Tanzania (United Republic of Tanzania, 1978), the elevations and slopes derived from the numerical terrain model (SRTM at 90 m) (http://dwtkns.com/srtm/). The data on land use classes comes from the SPOT 6 image processing of 2015 using the object-oriented classification method used in Boussougou's thesis work [11] (Guy Boussougou, 2017).

In this study, remote sensing is used as an essential means of updating spatially referenced map data, including roads, urban areas and constraint zones that prohibit population settlement within the Pugu and Kazimzumbwi forest reserves.

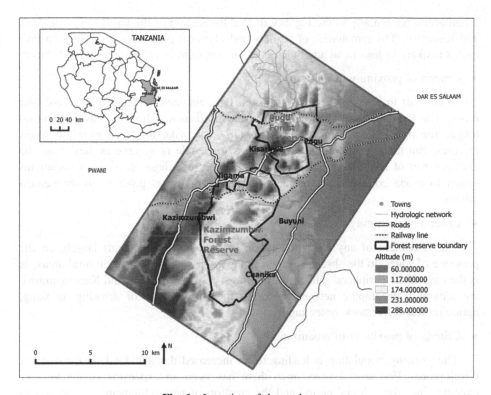

Fig. 1. Location of the study area

3.2   Methods

The methodological approach of this study is essentially based on a multi-criteria analysis combining remote sensing data and GIS.

Modelling data that may influence the presence or absence of one population at one location relative to another is complex. In this type of problem, we are often confronted with decision-making situations of a multi-criteria nature. The most important step for data modeling is the identification of the different criteria (factors and constraints) that can be taken into account in the multi-criteria analysis. Criteria were selected through field surveys and validated by resource persons (maintenance guide in 2015). Thus, seven (7) factors were selected for our work: roads, railways, watercourses, urban centre, urban spot, altitude and slopes. Constraints are the obstacles that prevent human settlement in one place. In our case, it is essentially the boundaries of reserves that constitute a legal barrier to settlement. All the selected vectorial data is transformed into raster data and then the DISTANCE function of the IDRISI software is applied. The description of each criteria is presented above:

- Proximity criteria for the road network

A large part of the population is located around the main lines of communication. These roads enable people to buy agricultural products and sell them in the nearest urban areas, particularly in the big city of Dar Es Salaam or the small towns of Pugu and Kisarawe. The remoteness of farmers and charcoal producers from the transport routes is likely to lead to an additional cost for transport in proportion to the distance.

• Criteria of proximity to railways

In contrast to roads, the railway network has remained unchanged since colonial times. The Pugu station, which has long been used as a station for travellers, is no longer functional. The trains using these railways make no stops near the forest reserves. But these roads provide easy access to people on-reserve as they cross the northern part of the reserves. Illegal coal producers use these channels of communication to evade control. They use motorcycles to transport products to the nearest villages.

• Criteria of proximity to watercourse

The settlement of any rural population in a given area depends largely on the presence of water. In the absence of a drinking water supply network in rural areas, as is the case in the peripheral villages of the forest reserves of Pugu and Kazimzumbwi, the natural hydrographic network becomes the only source of drinking, cooking, agricultural and livestock water supply.

• Criteria of proximity to urbanization

The growing population is leading to an increased demand for land for housing development. For several years now, there has been an expansion of the villages existing since the colonial period and the creation of new settlements. Urban sprawl around protected areas is stopped by the presence of forest reserve boundaries. Nevertheless, the proximity of the houses around the reserves facilitates the penetration of the populations inside the reserves. The stain built here was extracted from the land use map of the SPOT 6 image of June 2015 in the Boussougou thesis in 2017.

• Criteria of proximity to the urban centre

The urban centres of cities located near forest reserves are places where the majority of forest products are sold: timber (beds, chairs…), poles for construction, medicinal plants, charcoal, which constitutes almost 90% of the population's energy [12]. The proximity of the latter allows farmers or sellers to easily sell their products without too much transport cost. This is why we consider this factor. The urban centres here are the villages on the immediate periphery of the reserves: Pugu, Kazimzumbwi, Vigama, Masika, Buyuni, Kisarawe.

• Slope criteria

The slope of the terrain is an important parameter to be taken into account when modelling the population distribution. Hilly areas with steep slopes are less conducive to settlement and agriculture. The "slope" variable is an endogenous data that is derived directly from the SRTM. The 90-m SRTM is used here because it is the finest numerical terrain model in our study area. Slopes were obtained using the slope function of the Arcgis software.

- Altitude criteria

The altimetry of the area must also be taken into account in the spatial distribution of populations. Indeed, populations will tend to settle in low areas to protect themselves from bad weather conditions (e.g. cyclone passage). The same is true for cultivated areas, which will be more in the valleys than at the tops of the hills. This may explain the abundant forest in the hills of the reserves.

- Constraint

The constraints mainly concern the limits of reserves, which constitute a legal obstacle to the settlement of the population. In our case study, the only real constraint that limits populations to settle in the forest reserves of Pugu and Kazimzumbwi remains the limits of these reserves. Despite these limitations, some populations still try to settle there, but have their facilities destroyed by the authorities. Today, the law has become stricter and those apprehended may face high fines or even imprisonment. The only buildings on the reserves are the Mikani Primary School and teaching accommodations in the Pugu Reserve and the military base north of the Kazimzumbwi Reserve.

3.2.1 Multi-criteria Evaluation and Weighting of Criteria

After determining the overall criteria for the presence of a population in one place rather than another, we proceeded with the weighted linear approach [13]. This method is performed using IDRISI's MCE function, which represents the procedure for combining criteria in the form of Eq. (1):

$$C = SX_iW_i * PC_j \qquad (1)$$

Where C is the composite index, X_i is the value of factor i, W_i is the weight of each factor and C_j is the value of constraint j.

However, it is important to remember that for this method to work, the different scales of measurement must be standardized for each factor. For this purpose, all factors were expressed in a range from 0 to 255. Thus, the maximum value (255) represents the best evaluation and thus the best place according to the criterion considered.

For the weighting of criteria, we used the so-called pair comparison approach developed by Saaty [14] in the context of the decision-making process called AHP (Analytical Hierarchy Process). This technique is programmed in the IDRISI software with the WEIGHT function. This function is used to determine the relative weights for a group of factors in a multi-criteria evaluation. Weights are determined from a series of comparisons by pairs of factors according to their importance in determining suitability to produce standardized weighting coefficients with a sum of 1. These weights can then be used to weight the factors in a linear weighting combination using the EMC function.

This step is very delicate and requires the intervention of decision-makers (maintenance guide) to assign a coefficient to each factor. Therefore, for each pair of possible factors, an evaluation is introduced in a coupled matrix. The weights are then determined from the principal eigenvector of the evaluation matrix. For our study, we used the values presented in Table 1.

Table 1. Criteria weighting matrix for multi-criteria analysis

	Road	Railways	Urban	Urban centre	Slope	Altitude	Watercourse
Road	1						
Railways	1/3	1					
Urban	1/5	5	1				
Urban centre	1	2	2	1			
Slope	2	5	5	2	1		
Altitude	3	5	5	3	2	1	
Watercourse	1	3	2	2	1	1/3	1

The weighting values are calculated using the WEIGHT function. This function also makes it possible to assess the consistency of judgments a posteriori using the ICO (overall consistency index). The latter measures proximity to coherent judgments. According to Saaty [14], if the ICO is greater than 0.1, the evaluation matrix should be re-evaluated.

The general methodology of the study is presented in the digram above (Fig. 2):

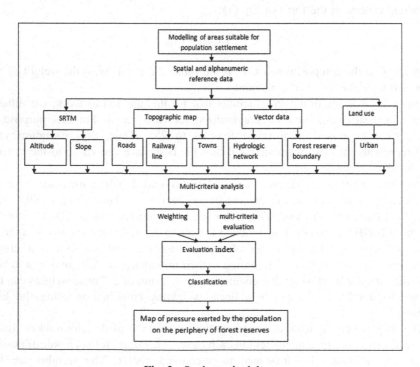

Fig. 2. Study methodology

4 Result and Discussions

First, the weight of all factors is presented in Table 2. The overall consistency index (ICO) here is 0.06, which expresses a satisfactory consistency of the judgements.

Table 2. Criteria weighting matrix for multi-criteria analysis

Criterias	Weight
Road	0.2012
Railways	0.0687
Urban	0.3172
Urban centre	0.0969
Slope	0.1376
Altitude	0.1388
Watercourse	0.0396
Overall Indices of Consistency	0.06 < 0.1

Analysis of this result reveals the primary impact of proximity to homes (32%) and roads (20%). Elevations and slopes also play a role in the settlement of populations with 13.88% and 13.76% respectively. Railways, urban centres and rivers play a minor but not negligible role. They contribute 9%, 7% and 3% respectively to the settlement of the study area's populations.

In a second step, all these factors made it possible to establish the anthropogenic pressure map of the study area on the basis of the multi-criteria analysis (Fig. 3). We then identified four (4) areas of human pressure: (1) very sensitive, (2) sensitive, (3) moderately sensitive and (4) not very sensitive. The mapping analysis shows that the most vulnerable area (very sensitive) to degradation by human influence is in the eastern part around the major cities (Chanika Buyuni, Pugu and Kisarawe) along the main roads. This makes forest reserves particularly sensitive in their eastern parts and also on their immediate periphery. This analysis is consistent with the previous analysis showing the strong influence of residential and road proximity on modelling. Overall, it can be observed that the forest reserves of Pugu and Kazimzumbwi are globally under human pressure as a whole, starting from very sensitive to moderately sensitive areas. There are some areas of low sensitivity to human pressures in the western part of the study area, Kazimzumbwi Reserve and north of the Pugu Reserve.

Linking the pressure map with the land cover map of 2015 and altitude (SRTM, 90 m), allows us to see that the very sensitive zones correspond to areas of high urbanization (large villages: Pugu, Kazimzumbwi, Byuni and Chanika). Sensitive areas correspond to areas of low urbanisation, crops and savannahs. It is also noted that the topography of the area is a barrier to the settlement of populations in certain areas. These include areas with elevations above 200 m, which correspond to areas that are not very sensitive to human pressure.

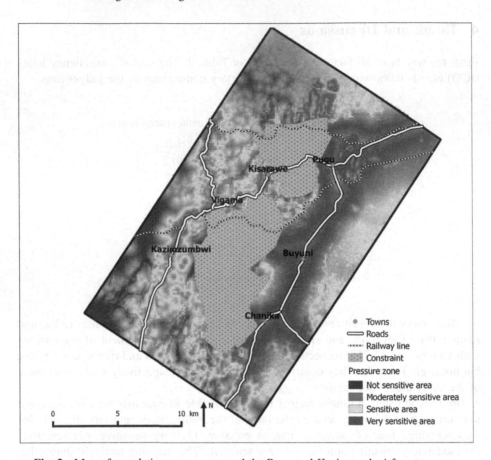

Fig. 3. Map of population pressure around the Pugu and Kazimzumbwi forest reserves

The multi-criteria analysis based on the weighted linear method, using seven (7) criteria and the constraint map, produced an anthropogenic pressure map around the Pugu and Kazimzumbwi forest reserves. Both reserves are very vulnerable to human pressures, especially in their eastern parts.

The multi-criteria analysis approach has also been used in several countries in Africa such as vory Coast for the determination of potential solid waste disposal sites in Abidjan district [15], in Burkina Faso for the identification of areas conducive to market gardening in the city of Ouagadougou [16]. However, this approach remains very delicate in its implementation. Its robustness and reliability depend on the accuracy of the criteria taken into account during the modelling process and their weighting. The slightest underestimation in the weighting of a major factor may cause a bias in the quality of the expected outcome [17].

This method nevertheless provides a good basis for decision making by managers of the two forest reserves of Pugu and Kazimzumbwi by showing the areas most exposed to the phenomenon of forest degradation linked to human practices. Faced with this document, decision-makers and planners could define the first priority intervention actions in the short term.

5   Conclusion

This study highlighted the importance of anthropogenic factors (communication axis, urbanization) and biophysical factors (altitude, slope) in the vulnerability of two forest reserves in southeast Tanzania. The results show that human pressure on the forest reserves of Pugu and Kazimzumbwi is generally moderate. However, the risk of forest degradation remains very high in the eastern part of the reserves close to the big cities. Indeed, the most vulnerable areas are those located near major roads and urban centres such as the towns of Pugu and Kisarawé. Identified degradation indicators are axes on which protected area managers can rely to improve resource management and reduce degradation of forest landscapes. This will in the long term reduce the vulnerability of the Pugu and Kazimzumbwi forest reserves.

Acknowledgement. This article is taken from Guy Boussougou Boussougou's thesis defended in 2017 in subparts 3.2 and 3.3 of chapter 3.

References

1. Living forests report: chapter 5_saving forests at risk. WWF, Gland, Switzerland, pp. 31–32 (2015)
2. Strömquist, L., Backéus, I.: Integrated landscape analyses of change of miombo woodland in tanzania and its implication for environment and human livelihood. Geogr. Ann. Ser. A Phys. Geogr. **91**(1), 31–45 (2009)
3. Holden, S.: Century of technological Change and deforestation in the miombo Woodlands of northern Zambia. In: Angelsen, A., Kaimowitz, D. (eds.) Agricultural Technologies and Tropical Deforestation. CAB International, Wallingford (2001)
4. Bandyopadhyay, S., Shyamsundar, P., Baccini, A.: Forests, biomass use and poverty. Ecol. Econ. **70**, 2461–2471 (2011)
5. WWF miombo ecoregion Programme: Miombo Ecoregion "Home of the Zambezi": Conservation Strategy 2011–2020, Harare, Zimbabwe (2012)
6. Hansen, M.C., et al.: Science **342**, 850–853 (2013)
7. Bugess, N.D., Cordeiro, N., Doggart, N., Fjeldså, J., Howell, K.M., Kilahama, F., Loader, S. P., Lovett, J.C., Mengon, M., Moyer, D., Nashanda, E., Perkin, A., Stanley, W.T., Stuart, S.: The biological importance of the Eastern Arc Mountains of Tanzania and Kenya. Biol. Cons. **134**, 209–231 (2007)
8. Mdemu, M., Kashaigili, J.J., Lupala, J., Levira, P., Liwenga, E., Nduganda, A., Mwakapuja, F.: Dynamics of land use and land cover changes in the Pugu and Kazimzumbwi Forest Reserves, pp. 71–72 (2012)

9. White, F.: The vegetation of Africa. A descriptive memoir to accompany the UNESCO/AETFAT/UNSO vegetation map of Africa. Natural Resources Research XX. Unesco Paris, 356 p. (1983)

10. Howell, K.M.: Pugu Forest Reserve: biological values and development. Af. J. Ecol **19**, 73–81 (1981). https://doi.org/10.4000/vertigo.5356. http://faostat.fao.org/default.aspx

11. Boussougou Boussougou, G.: Vulnérabilité des paysages forestiers en relation avec les activités humaines et la variabilité climatique en Tanzanie : Analyse prospective des dynamiques de l'occupation du sol des réserves forestières de Pugu et de Kazimzumbwi. Géographie. Université de la Réunion, pp. 109–112 (2017)

12. URT: The National Energy Policy. United Republic of Tanzania (2015)

13. Daoud, B.H.: Intégration de l'analyse multicritère dans les systèmes d'information géographique : développement d'un prototype MapInfo-Electre. Thèse de magister, Centre national des techniques spatiales, Arzew (Algérie), 93 p. (1997)

14. Saaty, T.L.: A scaling method for priorities in hierarchical structures. J. Math. Psychol. **15**, 234–281 (1977)

15. Kouamé, K.J., Deh, S.K., Anani, A.T., Jourda, J.P., Biemi, J.: Gestion des déchets solides dans le District d'Abidjan (Sud de la Côte d'Ivoire): Apports d'un SIG et des méthodes d'analyse multicritère. In: Conférence francophone ESRI, Versailles de 10 au 11 octobre 2007

16. Kêdowide, C.M.G.: Modélisation géomatique par évaluation multicritère pour la prospection de sites d'agriculture à Ouagadougou. VertigO – La revue en sciences de l'environnement **10** (2), 20 (2010). http://vertigo.revues.org/10368

17. Bensaïd, A., Barki, M., Talbi, O., Benhanifia, K., Mendas, A.: L'analyse multicritère comme outil d'aide à la décision pour la localisation spatiale des zones à fortes pression anthropique: le cas du département de Naama en Algérie. Revue Télédétection **7**(1), 359–371 (2007)

Formal Reasoning for Air Traffic Control System Using Event-B Method

Abdessamad Jarrar[(✉)] and Youssef Balouki

Computing, Imaging and Modeling of Complex Systems Laboratory,
Faculty of Sciences and Technologies of Settat, University Hassan First,
Settat, Morocco
Abdessamad.jarrar@gmail.com

Abstract. We present a formal modeling and verification of Air Traffic Control system (ATC) for airspace management. This system assists air traffic controllers by visualizing aircrafts in the airport vicinity. In such a critical-safety system, the use of robust formal methods that assure bugs absence is highly required. Therefore, we use a formalism of discrete transition systems based on abstraction and refinement along proof obligations. These proofs ensure the consistency of the system by mean of invariants preservation and deadlock freedom. The first guarantee that all invariants hold permanently and thus provide a handy solution for bugs absence verification. The second prove that the system runs forever to avoid deadlock. This modeling and proving enable us to establish that the system is, relatively to some criteria, correct by construction.

Keywords: Formal method · Event-B · Air traffic management
Platform RODIN · Refinement patterns

1 Introduction

Air traffic management is one of the most complex critical-safety problems. This management is provided by controllers located in a control tower. Many tools were developed to assist controllers to do their job. However, we cannot ensure that these tools will not stop working at a certain moment due to some design errors. Therefore, we develop formal modeling of an assisting system for air traffic management in airport airspace. This work has two purposes; the first one is to provide a well structured model to be used in future systems. And the second purpose is to be used for reverse engineering by comparing the resulting model with the current systems to improve them and avoid future problems. According to our research, this work is one of the first formal modeling of the ATC system considering taking off and landing at the same time. Few works presented a formal modeling of takeoff procedure [15, 16], and others presented landing system [17]. However, we see that formalizing taking off and landing separately ignore the fact that these operations occur in the same airport and share the same runways. Therefore, they must be modeled together.

We model the system functional and non-functional requirements. The functional requirements specify the behavior of the system, whereas, the non-functional requirements specify some other properties such as security and safety requirements.

We formalize these requirements using event-B, which is a formal method for software and system design. We use Event-B for two reasons: the first is that it is based on a refinement. Refinement means creating an abstract model of the system and then enriching it in successive steps, each step contains more details about the real system until we get a final concrete model that contain all the elements of the system. Furthermore, refinement makes modeling easier than trying to model the whole system at once. The second reason is that it is based on a mathematical language which allows proving system correctness. During development, we establish proofs called proofs obligations. These proofs are established to ensure the correctness of each model before and after refinement. The most important proofs are invariants preservation that guarantees that all invariants are obeyed during the system life time. Also, we ensure that the system will never come to a deadlock state, thus, we establish additional proofs called deadlock freedom. The combination of these proofs provides a resulting correct by construction system [23].

The rest of the paper is structured as follows. Section 2 gives some background on formal methods and validation tools that we use. The main content of the paper is in Sect. 3 describing our approach to develop the air traffic control system along three models. The first one includes the essence of air traffic management. The second presents how the system schedules taking off and landing aircrafts. Section 4 presents proof statistics that was generated by Rodin platform. Finally, we conclude in Sect. 5.

2   Background

2.1   Related Works

To avoid unwanted delay in flights at the airports during the departure and arrival process of aircrafts, [16] paper presents a step by step modeling process for the departure of the aircrafts. The methodology used for this modeling process is VDM++ which is an object oriented model based formal approach. This method ensures the safety and correctness by identifying errors at early stages of systems designing. It also provides extremely valuable solution of problem and also improves the confidence of the quality of the software. However, this work lack of analysis and the modeling presented is very abstract which limits its applicability.

In a similar work [15], the author develops a formal specification the procedure of aircrafts take-off using VDM-SL and graph theory. This formal specification of graph-based model, taxiways, aircrafts, runways and controllers is provided in static part of the model. The state space analysis describing take-off algorithms is provided by defining optimal paths and possible operations in dynamic model expediting the departure procedure. The model is developed by a series of refinements following the stepwise development approach. Although this work presents a detailed specification of the departure procedure but it requires further investigation to real-time management which is a major factor in the departure procedure.

In the other hand, [17] introduces a formal modeling of aircraft landing system. This work considered as a benchmark for techniques and tools dedicated to the verification of behavioral properties of landing system. However, it neglects the procedure of landing which must be taken into consideration to ensure system safety and focus more on the mechanical system.

In this work, we aim to present a formal modeling and verification of an ATC system considering aircrafts departure and landing side by side. This modeling ensure the consistency between the two procedures, However, we see that formalizing taking off and landing separately ignore the fact that these operations occur in the same airport and share the resources (runways, airport airspace, etc.). Therefore, they must be modeled together.

2.2 Formal Methods

The failure of software and hardware in critical systems may leads to the loss of lives and resources. This encourages many scientists to develop methods to reduce the risk of failure; in these cases, formal methods can be subject of a handy solution. These methods were originally developed for specifying and verifying the correct behavior of software and hardware systems, as well as for synthesis of such systems [1]. Modeling a system using a formal method and prove system correctness require mathematical knowledge and accuracy. In some cases, it require a lot of time to completely model a complex system. However, the strong assurance of bugs' absence is very important especially in safety-critical systems such as air traffic management.

There a variety of formal methods available:

- Hoare logic is a formal method for reasoning on computer programs correctness [2].
- Petri nets theory allows a system to be modeled by Petri net which is a mathematical representation of the system. Analysis of Petri net reveals important information about the structure and the behavior of the system [3].
- LOTOS is a specification language that sees the system as a set of processes which interact and exchange data with each other and with their environment [4].
- The Z language is a specification language based on predicates. The specification of invariants and the specification of operations have the form of a predicate [5].
- The B method (development of the Z language) is a method of software development based on an abstract machine notation used in the development of computer software (B language) [6].
- Event-B is a formal method for software and system design. This method is based on refinement and proof obligations, which ensures a strong assurance of bugs' absence [7]. Also, it is possible to translate Event-B/Rodin project to an executable code [18].

2.3 Event-B

In event-B, a system is developed in successive. We start with a very abstract model called initial model, and then we refine it to get a more concrete models. These models are made up of contexts and machines. Contexts are the static parts of models; they are presented in term of sets, constants and axioms, whereas, machines are the dynamic part of models. In a machine, variables describe the current status of a system; these statuses are constrained by invariants. Invariants are the necessary properties that must be preserved during system function. Statuses transitions are described by events, which are a set of actions. Each action changes the value of certain variable. Events may have some necessary conditions to be triggered; these conditions are called guards. The figure below illustrates the process of development in event-B (Fig. 1):

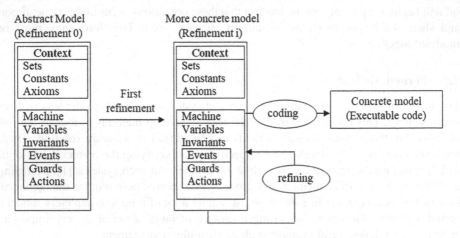

Fig. 1. Process of developement in Event-B

To ensure system correctness, some properties must be proved. These proofs are called proof obligations. They include invariants preservation, which ensure that all invariants are permanently obeyed during system function. They include also deadlock freedom to ensure that the system will never be in a status where no guard is verified, which means no event can be trigger. Most of these proofs are done automatically by means of the platform Rodin. Rodin is a tool that supports the application of the Event-B formal method. It provides core functionality for syntactic analysis and proof-based verification of Event-B models [8]. In some cases, Rodin may need to be manually guided to prove some properties. This is done by indicating some hypotheses that Rodin must consider. These hypotheses may be ignored by Rodin because he sees that it is not needed for the desired proof. In other cases, we add hypothesis and then Rodin prove the desired property; after that we prove separately the added hypothesis.

3 Development

In this section, we present our approach to develop the Air traffic control system. This development is designed progressively by starting with an abstract model and integrating more details in the following steps (refinement). The initial model captures the essence of traffic management and the different elements taken into consideration. The refined model introduces the scheduling method used during taking off and landing. This scheduling method assigns priority of taking off using FCFS (First Comes First Served) and the priority for landing based on deadline monotonic [19]. Moreover, this system gives the highest priority to emergency situations such as medical and terroristic threats.

Our model is based on one runway. However, this model maximizes the use of one runway to land and takeoff aircrafts while maintaining deadlines as much as possible.

3.1 Initial Model: An Abstract Model of the Landing Process

In this initial model, we introduce the essence of ATC system and the different components taken into consideration. The first component is the runway which is, according to the International Civil Aviation Organization ICAO, a rectangular area on a land aerodrome prepared for the landing and takeoff of aircrafts. Runways are equipped with lights indicating their status; these lights are called RunWays Status Lights RWSL. The RWSL system was developed by the Federal Aviation Administration FAA to improve air crew and vehicle operator situational awareness. These lights are embedded in the pavement of runways and taxiways and turn red when it is not safe to enter for a certain reason. In this paper, we develop a system for ATC to manage aircrafts traffic in the vicinity of the airport airspace. Hence, we are not interested in the taxiways and the traffic on the ground. We model only status lights of the runway due to its relation to the airspace traffic management [9].

Our first model is made up of two parts: static part and dynamic part [7]. The static part is called context and contains carrier sets, constants and associated axioms, whereas the dynamic part (called machine) contains variables, invariants and events. In the first context, we introduce the carrier set *RW_STATUSES* corresponds to the possible statuses of the runway *{available, unavailable}* (*axm1*), as for *RWL_STATUSES* represents runway lights statuses *{ON, OFF}* (*axm2*). We present also *AIRCRAFTS* set denoting all possible aircrafts that might exist in the airport vicinity currently in the past or even in the future, and we axiomatize that it is finite (*axm3*). Additionally, we define various types of aircrafts as a carrier set *TYPES*, and these types are also finite (*axm4*).

For each aircraft in the radar range, a significant status is associated. We propose these statuses to help controllers to distinguish between aircrafts landing, taking off, entering airport, waiting for landing clearance, etc. When an aircraft enter the aircraft vicinity, the status *blocked* is assigned to it. If the aircraft intend to land, it fly toward the VOR area (Very high frequency omni directional radio range) to be qualified to get landing clearance. At this stage, the system assigns to the aircrafts *readyL* status, which means that it is ready for landing. After getting landing clearance, it is assigned to *landing* state until finishing landing and passengers' departure; and then it is considered in *TerminatedL* status. Likewise, an aircraft in the runway, after passengers' arrival, is considered ready to takeoff and being assigned to *readyT* status. Immediately upon takeoff clearance confirmation, it is considered in *takingoff* status. Finally, the aircraft leave out the VOR and return to *blocked* status until getting out of the airport radar range [10, 11, 19]. We express these statuses as elements of a carrier set called *STA-TUSES* (*axm5*). The figure below illustrates this process and the different statuses (Fig. 2):

To summarize, the first context is made up of: four sets (RW_STATUSES, RWL_STATUSES, AIRCRAFTS, and STATUSES), ten constants (Available, Unavailable, ON, OFF, Blocked, ReadyL, Landing, TerminatedL, ReadyT, and

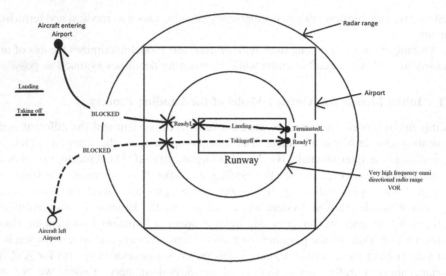

Fig. 2. Aircrafts landing/taking off statuses

TakingOff), and five axioms (axm1, axm2, axm3, and axm4). This is expressed as shown in the following box:

AXIOMS
axm1 : partition(RW_STATUSES,{available},{unavailable})
axm2 : partition(RWL_STATUSES,{ON},{OFF})
axm3 : finite(AIRCRAFTS)
axm4 : partition(STATUSES, {Blocked}, {ReadyL}, {Landing}, {TerminatedL}, {ReadyT}, {TakingOff})

In the dynamic part (machine), we introduce two variables *curr_RW_status* and *curr_RWL_status* denoting respectively the current statuses of the runway and runway lights (whereas, *RW_STATUS* and *RWL_STATUS* represent all the possible statuses). These two variables are defined by means of two invariants *inv1* and *inv2*. *Inv1* defines *curr_RW_status* as an element of the *RW_STATUS*, which means that *curr_RW_status* may equal *available* or *unavailable*. Likewise, *curr_RWL_status* is an element of *RWL_STATUS*.

In order to ensure the traffic safety in the runway, the status lights are turned ON whenever the runway is unavailable. However, taxiways intersect the runway at many points and therefore vehicles must be aware of the runway usage. These lights help to determine when it is not safe to proceed into or across the runway. Although, the RWSL does not act as a substitution of the ATC clearance, which means that vehicle should not enter the runway without a controller clearance even if the RWSL have gone out. We model this by means of equivalence between the RWST and runway status (*inv3*). We introduce also a subset of *AIRCRAFTS* called *aircrafts_in_airport* denoting the set of aircrafts in the airport (*inv4*).

As mentioned before, the system associates to each aircraft in the radar range a significant status. Therefore, we introduce a variable *statusof* associating to each aircraft its status formalized as a total function from *aircrafts_in_airport* to the set *AIRCRAFTS* (*inv5*) [20, 21]. We define variables and invariants of the initial model as follows:

INVARIANTS:

inv1 : *curr_RW_status* ∈ *RW_STATUS*

inv2 : *curr_RWL_status* ∈ *RWL_STATUS*

inv3 : *curr_RW_status=unavailable* ⇔ *curr_RWL_status=ON*

inv4 : *aircrafts_in_airport* ⊆ *AIRCRAFTS*

inv5 : *statusof* ∈ *aircrafts_in_airport→ STATUSES*

After defining all variables and invariants of the first machine, we present the different machine statuses transactions described by events. Firstly, we have to define what happen at the beginning. For this purpose, we define the INITIALISATION event that corresponds to the initial statuses of the system. We assume initially that the runway is available, runway lights are off, there are not aircrafts in the airport, and no aircraft status is assigned.

Beside the initialization event, we introduce eight more events: Entering_Radar_ Range, Entering_VOR, Start_Landing, Terminating_Landing, Takeoff_Preparing, Start_takingoff, Terminating_takingoff, and Airport_Departing. The Entering_Radar_ Range trigger when an aircraft enter the range of the airport radar range. An entering aircraft must be added to the set of aircrafts in the airport (aircrafts_in_airport) and assigned to the Blocked status. However, during carrying out proofs obligation for different events, we discovered that some guards are needed for each event. For the Entering_Radar_Range event, two guards are needed to be added: the first ensure that the entering aircraft is effectively a well defined aircraft and known by the system. The second guard guarantees that it is not an element of the aircrafts_in_airport set. Similarly, the Entering_VOR is the event associated to an aircraft entering the VOR. This event assign to an aircraft the status Ready under the condition that it is an element of the air-crafts_in_airport set, and it was in Blocked status. Moreover, the Start Landing event trigger whenever an aircraft get landing clearance. To get that clearance, it must have been in the VOR (which means in Ready status) and an element of the aircrafts_in_airport. Furthermore, the runway must be currently available and the runway lights must be OFF. After the aircraft landing and passengers' departure, the Terminating_Landing event triggers indicating the end of landing process by assigning the aircraft to the status TerminatedL. Therefore, freeing the runway and turning runway's lights off.

The Takeoff_Preparing event trigger when an aircraft is ready to take off. This means that the aircraft previously finished its landing (it is in TerminatedL status). This event assigns to the aircraft the status ReadyL. After finishing take off preparation, the aircraft get take off clearance. The event triggered at this stage is Start_takingoff; this event allocate the runway for the aircraft and turn lights on under the condition that the runway is not reserved by another aircraft. Afterward, the aircraft terminates taking off and leaves the VOR to returns to the first status Blocked. The event corresponds to this is Terminating_takingoff; this event has two guards: the first ensures that the aircraft is an element of the aircrafts_in_airport set, and the second is that it is in Takingoff status. Finally, the Airport_Departing event triggers indicating that the aircraft is leaving the radar range thus removing it from aircrafts_in_airport. Moreover, the status of the aircraft is deleted by remove it from the total function statusof [22]. We formalize the events of the initial model in the following boxes:

Start_Landing

ANY
  aircraft
WHERE
  grd1 : aircraft ∈ aircrafts_in_airport
  grd2 : statusof(aircraft) = ReadyL
  grd3 : curr_RW_status = available
  grd4 : curr_RWL_status = OFF
THEN
  act1 : statusof(aircraft) := Landing
  act2 : curr_RW_status := unavailable
  act3 : curr_RWL_status := ON
END

Terminating_Landing

ANY
  aircraft
WHERE
  grd1 : aircraft ∈ aircrafts_in_airport
  grd2 : statusof(aircraft) = Landing
THEN
  act1 : statusof(aircraft) := TerminatedL
  act2 : curr_RW_status := available
  act3 : curr_RWL_status := OFF
END

Takeoff_Preparing

ANY
  aircraft
WHERE
  grd1 : aircraft ∈ aircrafts_in_airport
  grd2 :   statusof(aircraft) = TerminatedL
THEN
  act1 : statusof(aircraft) := ReadyT
END

Start_takingoff

ANY
  aircraft
WHERE
  grd1 : aircraft ∈ aircrafts_in_airport
  grd2 : statusof(aircraft) = ReadyT
  grd3 : curr_RW_status = available
  grd4 : curr_RWL_status = OFF
THEN
  act1 : statusof(aircraft) := TakingOff
  act2 : curr_RW_status := unavailable
  act3 : curr_RWL_status := ON
END

Terminating_takingoff

ANY
  aircraft
WHERE
  grd1 : aircraft ∈ aircrafts_in_airport
  grd2 : statusof(aircraft) = TakingOff
THEN
  act1 : statusof(aircraft) := Blocked
  act2 : curr_RW_status := available
  act3 : curr_RWL_status := OFF
END

Airport_Departing

ANY
  aircraft
WHERE
  grd1 : aircraft ∈ aircrafts_in_airport
  grd2 : statusof(aircraft) = Blocked
THEN
  act1 :aircrafts_in_airport :=
       aircrafts_in_airport \ {aircraft}
  act2 : statusof := {aircraft} ⩤ statusof
END

3.2 Refinement: Introducing Scheduling Methods

In this refinement, we present how the system manages aircrafts taking off and landing. Therefore, we need to define some additional variables and invariants. The first variable is deadline which is a total function from the aircrafts_in_airport set to some natural number. The second is a set for aircrafts ready to take off denoted ready_to_take-off_aircrafts. We present also another variable that refer to the moment that an aircraft became ready to land. Finally, we introduce a set for aircrafts requiring urgent landing due to a certain issue.

INVARIANTS

inv1 : deadline ∈ aircrafts_in_airport → N

inv3 : ready_to_takeoff_aircrafts ⊆ aircrafts_in_airport

inv2 : the_ready_to_takeoff_moment ∈ ready_to_takeoff_aircrafts → N

inv4 : ∀A·(A∈ready_to_takeoff_aircrafts ⇒ A∈aircrafts_in_airport ∧ statusof(A)=ReadyT)

The currently used method for aircrafts taking off is FCFS where aircrafts take off in the order that they are ready. We formalize this by introducing firstly a set of aircrafts ready to take off and a total function returning for each aircraft the moment it is ready to take off. These moments are associated at the same time aircrafts are associated to the *readyL* status. This is done during the takeoff_preparing event in addition to adding the aircraft to the ready_to_takeoff_aircrafts set. Once having these data about aircrafts, the system adopt the FCFS scheduling for giving take off clearance by means of the following guards in the start_takingoff event:

---

grd5 : ∀A· A∈aircrafts_in_airport ⇒ statusof(A)≠TakingOff

grd6 : ∀A· A∈ready_to_takeoff_aircrafts ⇒
        the_ready_to_takeoff_moment(A)≥ the_ready_to_takeoff_moment(aircraft)

The first guard requires that there is no other aircraft using the runway to take off. The second one ensures that the aircraft that will get take off clearance is the one with the minimum ready to take off moment (the one has been ready to take off first). Finally, we delete information about the aircraft after give it landing clearance by means of the following two actions:

---

act4 : ready_to_takeoff_aircrafts := ready_to_takeoff_aircrafts \ {aircraft}

act5 : the_ready_to_takeoff_moment := {aircraft} ◁ the_ready_to_takeoff_moment

---

Similarly to the take off process, the currently used method for aircraft landing is FCFS [9, 12]. This method has two advantages: it is easy to implement and it also minimizes the number of aircraft deviations. However, it has a major drawback, the aircraft with a low landing speed may affect the landing of others faster ones. Therefore, the global landing duration of aircrafts is increased. Also, FCFS does not offer more flexibility to air traffic controllers [12, 13]. These limitations have encouraged us to use a new approach based on real-time scheduling algorithm such as Deadline Monotonic (DM) [14]. This approach assigns priority to aircrafts with the shortest deadline which offers an effective method for meeting deadlines as much as possible. However, maintaining deadlines respected is not always possible. In some cases, the sum of some high priority aircrafts landing durations is greater than the deadline of an aircraft with a lower priority. In this situation, we have two choices: the first is to proceed landing even if that some aircrafts will not respect their deadlines (note that we still optimizing deadlines respecting) [11]. The second is to prevent the aircraft from entering VOR and redirect it to another runway. This choice is up to controller to decide, the system will only notify him.

As we based landing process on DM scheduling, the landing priority go to the aircraft with the lowest deadline; the exception is emergency cases. However, the emergency landing request means that a threat may affect passenger safety, and safety come first. Therefore, the emergency cases have the highest priority. Additionally, the runway should be available for landing; this means that there is no other aircraft currently using it. This is formalized as guards in the start_landing event as follows:

> grd5 :   ∀A· A∈aircrafts_in_airport ⇒ statusof(A)≠Landing
> grd6 :   ((deadline(aircraft)=min({dl |∃A· A∈aircrafts_in_airport ∧ statusof(A)=ReadyL ∧ dl=deadline(A)})) ∧ Urgents=∅) ∨ aircraft∈Urgents

4   Proving Model Correctness

In this section, we use RODIN to prove that our model is correct. We present below the table of statistics proofs generated by RODIN:

This table measures the size of proofs generated including automatic and manual proofs. Note that there are many proof obligations in the first refinement due to the introduction of scheduling management. In order to guarantee the correctness of this scheduling process, various invariants must be established. Moreover, our formal model introduces management functions such as sigma, min, deadline and average landing durations. According to this report, we conclude that RODIN inference prover was able to establish 91% of proofs, which makes the task of modeling and proving easier (Table 1).

Table 1. Rodin report

Element name	Total	Auto	Manual
Air traffic control	125	114	11
Initial context	5	5	0
First refinement context	9	9	0
Initial machine	45	42	3
First refinement machine	66	58	8

5 Conclusion

We have presented a formal specification and verification of an air traffic control system using a formal method. We have started with an initial model that captures the essence of traffic management and the different elements taken into consideration. The first refinement introduces the scheduling method used during taking off and landing. The process presented in this work is based on FCFS during taking off and on Deadline monotonic during landing.

Because of environmental, political and geographical constraints, capacity cannot be easily increased by building new airports or runways. Therefore, our model is based on one runway. In future work, we can improve our model by considering the case of several runways in the same airport and several airports.

References

1. Audsley, N.C., Burns, A., Wellings, A.J.: Deadline monotonic scheduling theory and application. Control Eng. Pract. **1**(1), 71–78 (1993)
2. Hoare, C.A.R.: An axiomatic basis for computer programming. Commun. ACM **12**(10), 576–580 (1969)
3. Peterson, J.L.: Petri nets, computing surveys. ACM Comput. Surv. **9**(3), 223–252 (1977)
4. Bolognesi, T., Brinksma, E.: Introduction to the ISO specification language LOTOS. Comput. Netw. ISDN Syst. **14**(1), 25–59 (1987)
5. Spivey Oriel, J.M.: Understanding Z: A Specification Language and its Formal Semantics. Cambridge University Press, New York, NY, USA ©ISBN: 0-521-33429-2 (1988)
6. Hoang, T.S., Kuruma, H., Basin, D., Abrial, J.R.: Developing topology discovery in Event-B. Sci. Comput. Program. **74**(11–12), 879–899 (2009)
7. Abrial, J.-R.: Modeling in Event-B: System and Software Engineering. Cambridge University Press, New York (2010)
8. Rodin, C., Jastram, M., Butler, M.: User's Handbook (2011)
9. Pinol, H., Beasley, J.E.: Scatter search and bionomic algorithms for the aircraft landing problem. Eur. J. Oper. Res. **171**(2), 439–462 (2006)
10. Yu, S.P., Cao, X.B., Zhang, J.: A real-time schedule method for aircraft landing scheduling problem based on cellular automation. Appl. Soft Comput. **11**(4), 3485–3493 (2011)
11. Su, W., Abrial, J.-R.: Aircraft landing gear system: approaches with Event-B to the modeling of an industrial system. In: Boniol, F., Wiels, V., Ait Ameur, Y., Schewe, K.-D. (eds.) ABZ 2014. CCIS, vol. 433, pp. 19–35. Springer, Cham (2014). https://doi.org/10.1007/978-3-319-07512-9_2
12. Wilhelm, N.C.: An anomaly in disk scheduling: a comparison of FCFS and SSTF seek scheduling using an empirical model for disk accesses. Commun. ACM **19**(1), 13–17 (1976)
13. Schmid, U., Blieberger, J.: Some investigations on FCFS scheduling in hard real time applications. J. Comput. Syst. Sci. **45**(3), 493–512 (1992)
14. Jin, J., Nahrstedt, K.: QoS specification languages for distributed multimedia applications: a survey and taxonomy. IEEE Multimed. Mag. **11**(3), 1–10 (2004)
15. Zafar, N.A.: Formal specification and analysis of take-off procedure using VDM-SL. Complex Adapt. Syst. Model. **5**(5), (2016)

16. Yousaf, S., Zafar, N.A., Khan, S.A.: Formal analysis of departure procedure of air traffic control system. In: 2010 2nd International Conference on Software Technology and Engineering (ICSTE), vol. 2 (2010)
17. Méry, D., Singh, N.K.: Modeling an aircraft landing system in Event-B. In: Boniol, F., Wiels, V., Ait Ameur, Y., Schewe, K.-D. (eds.) ABZ 2014. CCIS, vol. 433, pp. 154–159. Springer, Cham (2014). https://doi.org/10.1007/978-3-319-07512-9_12
18. Méry, D., Kumar Singh, N.: EB2J : Code generation from Event-B to Java. In: SBMF - Brazilian Symposium on Formal Methods, São Paulo, Brazil (2011)
19. Jarrar, A., Balouki, Y., Gadi, T., Chougdali, S.: Modeling aircraft landing scheduling in Event B. In: Noreddine, G., Kacprzyk, J. (eds.) ITCS 2017. AISC, vol. 640, pp. 127–142. Springer, Cham (2018). https://doi.org/10.1007/978-3-319-64719-7_12
20. Jarrar, A., Bellasri, O., Chougdali, S., Balouki, Y.: Formal specification and verification of transmission control protocol. In: Proceedings of the 2nd International Conference on Computing and Wireless Communication Systems, p. 30. ACM (2017)
21. Jarrar, A., Gadi, T., Balouki, Y.: Modeling the internet of things system using complex adaptive system concepts. In: Proceedings of the 2nd International Conference on Computing and Wireless Communication Systems, p. 22. ACM (2017)
22. Jarrar, A., Balouki, Y., Gadi, T.: Formal specification of QoS negotiation in ODP system. Int. J. Electric. Comput. Eng. 7(4), 2045 (2017)
23. Belhaj, H., Balouki, Y., Bouhdadi, M., El Hajji, S.: Using event B to specify QoS in ODP enterprise language. In: Working Conference on Virtual Enterprises, pp. 478–485. Springer, Berlin, Heidelberg (2010)

A Multiscale Finite Element Formulation for the Incompressible Navier-Stokes Equations

Riedson Baptista[1,2(✉)] ⓘ, Sérgio S. Bento[1,2] ⓘ, Isaac P. Santos[1,2] ⓘ,
Leonardo M. Lima[1] ⓘ, Andrea M. P. Valli[1] ⓘ, and Lucia Catabriga[1] ⓘ

[1] High Performance Computing Lab, Federal University of Espírito Santo,
Vitória, ES, Brazil
{riedson.baptista,sergio.bento,isaac.santos}@ufes.br,
lmuniz@ifes.edu.br, {avallic,luciac}@inf.ufes.br
[2] Department of Applied Mathematics, Federal University of Espírito Santo,
São Mateus, ES, Brazil

Abstract. In this work we present a variational multiscale finite element method for solving the incompressible Navier-Stokes equations. The method is based on a two-level decomposition of the approximation space and consists of adding a residual-based nonlinear operator to the enriched Galerkin formulation, following a similar strategy of the method presented in [1,2] for scalar advection-diffusion equation. The artificial viscosity acts adaptively only onto the unresolved mesh scales of the discretization. In order to reduce the computational cost typical of two-scale methods, the subgrid scale space is defined using bubble functions whose degrees of freedom are locally eliminated in favor of the degrees of freedom that live on the resolved scales. Accuracy comparisons with the streamline-upwind/Petrov-Galerkin (SUPG) formulation combined with the pressure stabilizing/Petrov-Galerkin (PSPG) method are conducted based on 2D benchmark problems.

Keywords: Finite element method · Multiscale formulation
Navier-Stokes equation · Incompressible flow problems

1 Introduction

Many phenomena of scientific and engineering interest are modeled by the Navier-Stokes equations, composed by momentum and continuity equations with velocity field and pressure as the unknowns. Since the pressure is an unknown in the momentum equations but not in the continuity equation, the discretization must satisfy the Ladyzhenskaya-Babuska-Brezzi (LBB) condition [3]. This condition makes a relation between pressure and velocity approximation that increases the number of degrees of freedom, making the solution of the linear system more costly. Because of that, most finite element techniques and computations reported in the past three decades are based on stabilized formulations.

© Springer International Publishing AG, part of Springer Nature 2018
O. Gervasi et al. (Eds.): ICCSA 2018, LNCS 10961, pp. 253–267, 2018.
https://doi.org/10.1007/978-3-319-95165-2_18

Another source of numerical difficulty is due to the presence of the nonlinear convective term. High Reynolds number flows are convection dominated and stabilization techniques, such as Streamline-Upwind/Petrov-Galerkin(SUPG) [4,5] or Galerkin-Least-Squares (GLS) [6], must be used to avoid non-physical oscillation.

The most well known stabilized finite element formulations for incompressible flows are based on the SUPG [4] and the pressure-stabilizing/Petrov–Galerkin (PSPG) [5] formulations. In general, they prevent numerical instabilities in solving problems with high Reynolds or Mach numbers and shocks or thin boundary layers, as well as when using equal-order interpolation functions for velocity and pressure. Generally, the stabilization methods need to define parameters that involves a measure of the local length scale (also known as "element length") and other parameters such as the element Reynolds and Courant numbers. Those parameters have attracted a significant attention and research in the computational fluid dynamics community in the last three decades, once there is no universal formula to define them.

In the mid 1990s the multiscale variational methodology (Variational Multiscale - VMS) was introduced by Hughes in [7] as a technique to model the subgrid scales in the solution of partial differential equations, especially the advective-dominated transport equation. Since then, some multiscale methods have been developed for incompressible flow problems as in [8–10]. Nonlinear multiscale variational methods have been developed in the last decade of which we highlight a couple of parameter-free methods: the NSGS (Nonlinear Subgrid Stabilization method) [1,2] and the DD (Dynamic Diffusion method) [11,12] to solve advection dominated transport problems; and the NMV (Nonlinear Multiscale Viscosity) method [13,14] to solve the system of compressible Euler equations.

In this paper we present a nonlinear multiscale parameter-free method to solve incompressible flow problems, named NSGS-NS method. As the NSGS method, the basic idea is to add a nonlinear artificial viscosity only onto the unresolved mesh scales of the discretization where the amount of artificial viscosity depends on the residual of the equation on each element. The nonlinear artificial viscosity added to the numerical formulation is made adaptively, leading to a self-adaptive methodology. We evaluate the accuracy of the formulation through numerical studies, comparing it with the SUPG/PSPG method.

The remainder of this work is organized as follows. Section 2 briefly addresses the governing equations and the variational multiscale formulation. Numerical experiments are conducted in Sect. 3 to show the behavior of the new multiscale finite element method for a manufactured problem with the known exact solution and 2D benchmark problems for incompressible flow problems. Section 4 concludes the paper.

2   The NSGS-NS Multiscale Finite Element Method

Let Ω be an open domain in $\mathbb{R}^2$ with a piecewise regular boundary Γ. The set of incompressible stationary Navier-Stokes equations is given as

$$(u \cdot \nabla)u - 2\nu\nabla \cdot \varepsilon(u) + \nabla p = f, \quad \text{in} \quad \Omega, \tag{1}$$

$$\nabla \cdot u = 0, \quad \text{in} \quad \Omega, \tag{2}$$

where u and p denote velocity and kinematic pressure, ν is the kinematic viscosity, f is a body force, and $\varepsilon(u)$ is the strain rate tensor defined as $\varepsilon(u) = \frac{1}{2}(\nabla u + (\nabla u)^T)$. A set of appropriate boundary conditions is added to Eqs. (1) and (2).

To define the finite element discretization, we consider a triangular partition T_h of the domain Ω into n_{el} elements, where $\Omega = \bigcup_{e=1}^{n_{el}} \Omega_e$ and $\Omega_i \cap \Omega_j = \emptyset$, $i,j = 1,2,\cdots,n_{el}, i \neq j$. The approximation spaces are decomposed into a direct sum of a resolved (grid) scale space and an unresolved (subgrid) scale space. We define

$$\mathcal{U}_h = \{\mathbf{u}_h \in [H^1(\Omega)]^2; \mathbf{u}_h|_{\Omega_e} \in [\mathbb{P}_1(\Omega_e)]^2, \mathbf{u}_h = \mathbf{g} \quad \text{on} \quad \Gamma_g\}$$

as the discrete resolved (coarse) scale space for velocity in which $\mathbb{P}_1(\Omega_e)$ represents the set of first order polynomials in Ω_e and H^1 is the Hilbert space [15]. Here, the small-scale space is defined using bubble functions to reduce the computational cost typical of two-scale methods. By denoting $\psi_b \in H_0^1(T)$ as the bubble function defined in each element, we define

$$\mathcal{U}_B = \{\mathbf{u}_B \in [H_0^1(\Omega)]^2; \mathbf{u}_B|_{\Omega_e} \in [span(\psi_B)]^2, \forall \Omega_e \in T_h\}$$

as the subgrid (fine) scale space. We also need to define the resolved and the subgrid scale spaces for pressure,

$$\mathcal{P}_h = \{p_h \in H^1(\Omega); p_h|_{\Omega_e} \in \mathbb{P}_1(\Omega_e), \int_\Omega p_h \, d\Omega = 0\},$$

$$\mathcal{P}_B = \{p_B \in H_0^1(\Omega); p_B|_{\Omega_e} \in span(\psi_B), \forall \Omega_e \in T_h\}.$$

We introduce an additional discrete space for velocity, $\mathcal{U}_E$, such that the decomposition $\mathcal{U}_E = \mathcal{U}_h \oplus \mathcal{U}_B$ holds, Fig. 1. For pressure, we define the discrete space $\mathcal{P}_E = \mathcal{P}_h \oplus \mathcal{P}_B$ as the direct sum of the spaces $\mathcal{P}_h$ and $\mathcal{P}_B$ defined before. The bubble basis function is defined here as the simple cubic polynomial function,

$$\psi_B(\mathbf{x}) = 27N_1^e(\mathbf{x})N_2^e(\mathbf{x})N_3^e(\mathbf{x}), \tag{3}$$

where N_i^e represents the local shape function associated with node $i = 1,2,3$.

The numerical formulation presented in this work follows the framework of the variational multiscale methodology, decomposing the variational problem into two sub-problems, as described in [16]: one associated to the resolved (or coarse) scales and the other associated to the unresolved (or fine) ones.

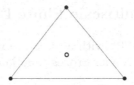

Fig. 1. $\mathcal{U}_E$ Representation: • stands for $\mathcal{U}_h$ nodes (grid) and ○ stands for $\mathcal{U}_B$ nodes (subgrid).

The inclusion of the fine scales influence stabilizes the solution. In a similar way to the NSGS method [1,2], we add to the numerical formulation a residual-based nonlinear operator only onto the unresolved scales.

The NSGS-NS method for solving the incompressible Navier-Stokes equations consists of finding $\boldsymbol{u}_E = \boldsymbol{u}_h + \boldsymbol{u}_B \in \mathcal{U}_E$ and $p_E = p_h + p_B \in \mathcal{P}_E$, with $\boldsymbol{u}_h \in \mathcal{U}_h$, $\boldsymbol{u}_B \in \mathcal{U}_B, p_h \in \mathcal{P}_h$ and $p_B \in \mathcal{P}_B$, such that

$$\int_\Omega \boldsymbol{w}_E \cdot (\boldsymbol{u}_E \cdot \nabla \boldsymbol{u}_E - \boldsymbol{f})\, d\Omega + 2\nu \int_\Omega \boldsymbol{\varepsilon}(\boldsymbol{w}_E) : \boldsymbol{\varepsilon}(\boldsymbol{u}_E)\, d\Omega$$

$$- \int_\Omega p_E \nabla \cdot \boldsymbol{w}_E\, d\Omega + \sum_{e=1}^{nel} \int_{\Omega_e} \nabla \boldsymbol{w}_B : (\delta_B \nabla \boldsymbol{u}_B)\, d\Omega = 0 \qquad (4)$$

$$\int_\Omega q_E \nabla \cdot \boldsymbol{u}_E\, d\Omega = 0 \qquad (5)$$

$\forall \boldsymbol{w}_E = \boldsymbol{w}_h + \boldsymbol{w}_B \in \mathcal{V}_E$ and $\forall q_E = q_h + q_B \in \mathcal{P}_E$ with $\boldsymbol{w}_h \in \mathcal{V}_h, \boldsymbol{w}_B \in \mathcal{U}_B$, $q_h \in \mathcal{P}_h$ and $q_B \in \mathcal{P}_B$, where $\mathcal{V}_E = \mathcal{V}_h \oplus \mathcal{U}_B$ with $\mathcal{V}_h = \{\boldsymbol{w}_h \in [H^1(\Omega)]^2; \boldsymbol{w}_h|_{\Omega_e} \in [\mathbb{P}_1(\Omega_e)]^2, \boldsymbol{w}_h = \boldsymbol{0}$ on $\Gamma\}$. Here, the amount of artificial viscosity δ_B is calculated on the element-level by

$$\delta_B(\boldsymbol{u}_h, p_h) = \begin{cases} \dfrac{h}{2} \dfrac{\|R(\boldsymbol{u}_h, p_h)\|}{\|\nabla(\boldsymbol{u}_h, p_h)\|}, & \text{if } \|\nabla(\boldsymbol{u}_h, p_h)\| > 0; \\ 0, & \text{otherwise.} \end{cases} \qquad (6)$$

where $\| \cdot \|$ is the Euclidean norm, $R(\boldsymbol{u}_h, p_h) = (\boldsymbol{u}_h \cdot \nabla)\boldsymbol{u}_h - 2\nu \nabla \cdot \boldsymbol{\varepsilon}(\boldsymbol{u}_h) + \nabla p_h + \nabla \cdot \boldsymbol{u}_h - \boldsymbol{f}$ is the residue of the problem associated to the resolved scales on Ω_e and h is the local length scale proposed in [17]. Observe that the numerical formulation (4)–(5) is nonlinear due to the convective term $\boldsymbol{u}_E \cdot \nabla \boldsymbol{u}_E$ and the operator

$$\sum_{e=1}^{nel} \int_{\Omega_e} \nabla \boldsymbol{w}_B(\boldsymbol{u}_h, p_h) : (\delta_B(\boldsymbol{u}_h, p_h) \nabla \boldsymbol{u}_B)\, d\Omega$$

added to the unresolved scales of the Galerkin formulation. To handle the nonlinearities of the numerical model, we use a Picard method. Thus, if the superscript c denotes a previous nonlinear iteration, $\boldsymbol{u}^c = \boldsymbol{u}_h^c + \boldsymbol{u}_B^c$, $\delta_B^c = \delta_B(\boldsymbol{u}_h^c, p_h^c)$ and exploiting the linearity of the weighting function slot, the weak problem can be decomposed into a sequence of two linearized sub-problems as follows.

The linearized coarse-scale sub-problem:

$$\int_\Omega \boldsymbol{w}_h \cdot (\boldsymbol{u}^c \cdot \nabla(\boldsymbol{u}_h + \boldsymbol{u}_B) - \boldsymbol{f}) \, d\Omega + 2\nu \int_\Omega \boldsymbol{\varepsilon}(\boldsymbol{w}_h) : \boldsymbol{\varepsilon}(\boldsymbol{u}_h + \boldsymbol{u}_B) \, d\Omega$$

$$- \int_\Omega (p_h + p_B) \nabla \cdot \boldsymbol{w}_h \, d\Omega = 0 \qquad (7)$$

$$\int_\Omega q_h \nabla \cdot (\boldsymbol{u}_h + \boldsymbol{u}_B) \, d\Omega = 0 \qquad (8)$$

The linearized fine-scale sub-problem:

$$\int_\Omega \boldsymbol{w}_B \cdot (\boldsymbol{u}^c \cdot \nabla(\boldsymbol{u}_h + \boldsymbol{u}_B) - \boldsymbol{f}) \, d\Omega + 2\nu \int_\Omega \boldsymbol{\varepsilon}(\boldsymbol{w}_B) : \boldsymbol{\varepsilon}(\boldsymbol{u}_h + \boldsymbol{u}_B) \, d\Omega$$

$$- \int_\Omega (p_h + p_B) \nabla \cdot \boldsymbol{w}_B \, d\Omega + \sum_{e=1}^{nel} \int_{\Omega_e} \nabla \boldsymbol{w}_B : (\delta_B^c \nabla \boldsymbol{u}_B) \, d\Omega = 0 \qquad (9)$$

$$\int_\Omega q_B \nabla \cdot (\boldsymbol{u}_h + \boldsymbol{u}_B) \, d\Omega = 0 \qquad (10)$$

A heuristic scaling of the continuity equation is considered to approximate the fine-scale pressure [9, 18] as

$$p_B = -\tau_{LSIC} \nabla \cdot \boldsymbol{u}_h \qquad (11)$$

where $\tau_{LSIC} = \sqrt{\nu^2 + (\|\boldsymbol{u}_h\| h/2)^2}$ is the Least-Squares on Incompressibility Constraint (LSIC) parameter defined in [8]. As a consequence, Eq. (10) does not have to be considered – in other words, q_B will be null.

Applying the standard finite element approximation on each scale, Eqs. (7)–(9), we arrive at the following local system of algebraic equations,

$$\begin{bmatrix} K_{hh} & N_{hB} & G_{hh} \\ N_{Bh} & K_{BB} & G_{Bh} \\ G_{hh}^T & G_{hB} & 0 \end{bmatrix} \begin{bmatrix} U_h \\ U_B \\ P_h \end{bmatrix} = \begin{bmatrix} F_h \\ F_B \\ 0 \end{bmatrix}, \qquad (12)$$

where U_h, P_h and U_B are the nodal values of the unknowns $\boldsymbol{u}_h$, p_h and $\boldsymbol{u}_B$ on each element Ω_e. The local matrices and vectors in Eq. (12) are defined by:

$$K_{hh} : \int_{\Omega_e} \boldsymbol{w}_h \cdot (\boldsymbol{u}^c \cdot \nabla \boldsymbol{u}_h) \, d\Omega + 2\nu \int_{\Omega_e} \boldsymbol{\varepsilon}(\boldsymbol{w}_h) : \boldsymbol{\varepsilon}(\boldsymbol{u}_h) \, d\Omega$$

$$+ \int_{\Omega_e} (\nabla \cdot \boldsymbol{w}_h)(\tau_{LSIC} \nabla \cdot \boldsymbol{u}_h) \, d\Omega,$$

$$N_{hB} : \int_{\Omega_e} \boldsymbol{w}_h \cdot (\boldsymbol{u}^c \cdot \nabla \boldsymbol{u}_B) \, d\Omega, \quad N_{Bh} : \int_{\Omega_e} \boldsymbol{w}_B \cdot (\boldsymbol{u}^c \cdot \nabla \boldsymbol{u}_h) \, d\Omega$$

$$G_{hh} : -\int_{\Omega_e} p_h \nabla \cdot \boldsymbol{w}_h \, d\Omega, \quad G_{hh}^T : \int_{\Omega_e} q_h \nabla \cdot \boldsymbol{u}_h \, d\Omega,$$

$$K_{BB} : 2\nu \int_{\Omega_e} \varepsilon(\boldsymbol{w}_B) : \varepsilon(\boldsymbol{u}_B) \, d\Omega + \int_{\Omega_e} \nabla \boldsymbol{w}_B : (\delta_B^c \nabla \boldsymbol{u}_B) \, d\Omega,$$

$$G_{Bh} : - \int_{\Omega_e} p_h \nabla \cdot \boldsymbol{w}_B \, d\Omega, \quad G_{hB} : \int_{\Omega_e} q_h \nabla \cdot \boldsymbol{u}_B \, d\Omega,$$

$$F_h : \int_{\Omega_e} \boldsymbol{w}_h \cdot \boldsymbol{f} \, d\Omega, \quad F_B : \int_{\Omega_e} \boldsymbol{w}_B \cdot \boldsymbol{f} \, d\Omega. \tag{13}$$

Performing a static condensation of the unknowns $\boldsymbol{u}_B$ at each element, the linear system of Eq. (12) can be written in terms of nodal unknowns U_h and P_h as follows

$$\begin{bmatrix} M_{11} & M_{12} \\ M_{21} & M_{22} \end{bmatrix} \begin{bmatrix} U_h \\ P_h \end{bmatrix} = \begin{bmatrix} F_1 \\ F_2 \end{bmatrix}, \tag{14}$$

where

$$M_{11} = K_{hh} - N_{hB}[K_{BB}]^{-1}N_{Bh},$$
$$M_{12} = G_{hh} - N_{hB}[K_{BB}]^{-1}G_{Bh},$$
$$M_{21} = G_{hh}^T - G_{hB}[K_{BB}]^{-1}N_{Bh},$$
$$M_{22} = -G_{hB}[K_{BB}]^{-1}G_{Bh},$$
$$F_1 = F_h - N_{hB}[K_{BB}]^{-1}F_B,$$
$$F_2 = -G_{hB}[K_{BB}]^{-1}F_B.$$

In other words, the fine-scale space of the unknown is condensed onto the resolved scale degrees of freedom, resulting in the local linear system (14) involving only U_h and P_h. The nonlinear convergence of the Picard method is checked for the resolved scale degrees of freedom, under a given prescribed relative tolerance, tol_{nl}, and a maximum number of nonlinear iterations ($itmax_{nl}$). The resulting linear systems are solved by GMRES with incomplete factorization (ILU) preconditioners.

3   Numerical Experiments

In the experiments, we consider a manufactured problem with a smooth known exact solution and two well-known 2D benchmark problems for incompressible flow problems: the "lid-driven cavity" and the "backward-facing step". Our multiscale methodology is compared to the SUPG/PSPG presented in [17,19]. First, we numerically evaluate the convergence rates of NSGS-NS and SUPG/PSPG approximations in $L^2(\Omega)$ norm for a problem with a smooth known solution. Next, we compare the numerical solution obtained by the two methods with the results presented in [20] for the "lid-driven cavity" problem and with experimental results [21] for the "backward-facing step" problem.

We define a relative tolerance in the Picard iterations equal to $tol_{nl} = 10^{-3}$ and a maximum number of nonlinear steps equal to $itmax_{nl} = 1000$. The resulting linear systems are solved by GMRES method with 45 vectors to restart,

tolerance equals 10^{-12} with incomplete factorization (ILU) preconditioners –
ILU(0) for the first problem and ILU(10) for the second and third problems.
The domains are discretized considering meshes generated by the Gmsh software [22] and the tests were performed on a machine with an Intel Core i5-6200U 2.3 GHz × 4 processor with 8 GB of RAM and Ubuntu 16.04 operating
system.

3.1   Problem with the Exact Solution

For the first numerical experiment, the model is very simple. We verify the
capability of our method to accurately represent the flow and we calculate the
convergence rates. The experiment was introduced in [23] for Stokes flow and
also studied in [24,25]. The analytic solution for this problem is defined by the
smooth velocity $\boldsymbol{u} = (x^2(1-x)^2(2y-6y^2+4y^3), (1-y)^2(-2x+6x^2-4x^3))^T$ and
pressure $p = x^2 - y^2$, defined on the unit square $\Omega = (0,1) \times (0,1)$ with viscosity
$\nu = 0.01$. The velocity field is divergence free and satisfies the no-slip condition,
$\boldsymbol{u} = 0$, on the boundary $\partial\Omega$. The body force $\boldsymbol{f}$ is constructed considering the
exact solution applied in Eq. (1).

The approximate solutions are computed for a sequence of five uniform
meshes with 4×4, 8×8, 16×16, and 32×32 cells with two linear triangular elements in each cell. The convergence of the NSGS-NS numerical solutions
can be observed in Fig. 2 for the velocity profiles in both directions. The errors
in the L^2-norm associated with NSGS-NS and SUPG/PSPG methods for the
velocity are plotted against mesh size on a log-log scale in Fig. 3. The same convergence rates are obtained for both methods - around 1.5 - that is obtained for
stabilized methods in general [26]. We obtain approximate slopes of 1.47 and
1.51 for NSGS-NS and SUPG/PSPG methods respectively, as it can be seen in
Fig. 3.

3.2   The Lid-Driven Cavity Flow

The lid-driven cavity problem has long been used as a standard benchmark for
the incompressible Navier-Stokes equations. Figure 4 shows the problem description and the unstructured triangular mesh with 3721 nodes and 7200 elements
used in the experiments. The flow is driven by applying a unit tangential velocity
on the top surface of a two-dimensional square domain, with Dirichlet boundary conditions on all sides. The pressure is prescribed to be zero at the center
of the cavity. As a result of the moving side at the top of the cavity, a recirculation region is developed that bears a primary vortex in the middle of the
cavity. Depending on the Reynolds number, additional secondary vortices may
appear in the corners of the cavity, see Fig. 5 for $Re = 1000$ and $Re = 5000$. Our
results show excellent agreement with the high accuracy experiments presented
in [20].

The quality of NSGS-NS and SUPG/PSPG approximate solutions can be
better observed in Fig. 6 for the velocity profiles along vertical and horizontal

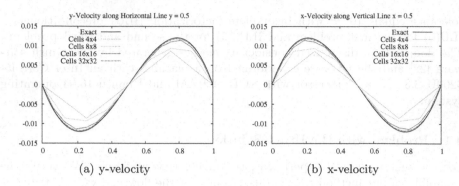

Fig. 2. The NSGS-NS solutions for the Stokes flow using a sequence of uniform meshes: (a) vertical velocity for $y = 0.5, 0 \leq x \leq 1$ and (b) horizontal velocity for $x = 0.5, 0 \leq y \leq 1$.

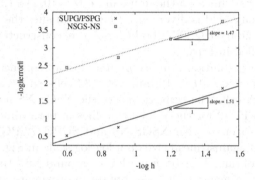

Fig. 3. Velocity convergence rates for the problem with exact solution in the L^2-norm.

lines through the geometric center. The NSGS-NS method is in excellent agreement with the experiments presented by [20] ("Reference" in the figure), for $Re = 1000$ and $Re = 5000$. We can also observe that the SUPG/PSPG method do not present good solutions when the Reynolds number increases. These results indicate that the NSGS-NS method is able to handle this highly complex problem and yield a quite satisfactory solution.

Table 1 shows the computational performance of both methods in terms of number of nonlinear iterations (NL_{iter}), number of linear GMRES iterations ($GMRES_{iter}$) and CPU time in seconds (CPU_{time}). For the mesh with 3721 nodes, NSGS-NS needs more nonlinear iterations - and larger CPU time – than the SUPG/PSPG, although NSGS-NS solutions are much better. When we refine the mesh the SUPG/PSPG solutions improve, as shown in Fig. 7, but the CPU time increases significantly, due to the increase in the size of the resulting linear system. Furthermore, even for the most refined mesh used in this example the SUPG/PSPG method could not exceed the excellent results obtained with the NSGS-NS approach. Figure 8 shows the nonlinear evolution of the residual

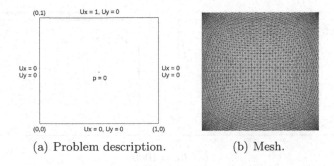

(a) Problem description.   (b) Mesh.

Fig. 4. Lid-driven cavity problem description and mesh.

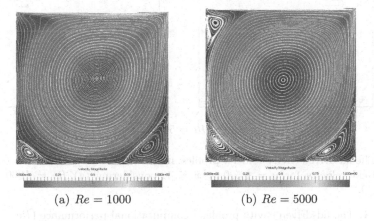

(a) $Re = 1000$ (b) $Re = 5000$

Fig. 5. Lid-driven cavity: NSGS-NS solutions (a) $Re = 1000$ and (b) $Re = 5000$.

force in the Euclidean norm for both methods and $Re = 1000$ and $Re = 5000$. As observed in Table 1 for $Re = 5000$, the residual curves confirm that SUPG/PSPG converges faster than NSGS-NS with a smaller number of nonlinear iterations.

3.3 The Backward Facing Step Flow

The study of backward facing step flows performs an important branch of fundamental fluid mechanics. It consists of a fluid flowing into a straight channel which abruptly widens on one side. Numerical results obtained using a wide range of methods can be found in [10,21,27]. When the fluid flows downstream, it produces a recirculation zone on the lower channel wall, and for sufficiently high Reynolds it also produces a recirculation zone farther downstream on the upper wall. Figure 9 shows the problem description, the boundary conditions and the triangular mesh with 1131 nodes and 2010 elements used in all experiments.

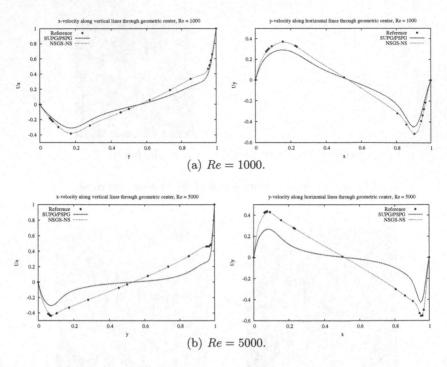

(a) $Re = 1000$.

(b) $Re = 5000$.

Fig. 6. The lid-driven cavity velocity profiles: horizontal velocity for $x = 0.5, 0 \leq y \leq 1$ and vertical velocity for $y = 0.5, 0 \leq x \leq 1$, considering (a) $Re = 1000$ and (b) $Re = 5000$.

Table 1. The lid-driven cavity problem: computational performance ($Re = 5000$).

Methods	NL_{iter}	$GMRES_{iter}$	CPU_{time}
NSGS-NS: 3721 nodes	58	2330	17.08
SUPG/PSPG: 3721 nodes	30	751	7.09
SUPG/PSPG: 14641 nodes	28	1005	33.15
SUPG/PSPG: 58081 nodes	35	2711	275.12

The basic characteristics of this experiment are well illustrated in Figs. 10(a), (b) and (c), respectively, for Reynolds numbers equal 100, 500 and 805. The figures show only the part of the computational domain that contains all the essential features ($6 < x < 30$). The streamlines shown in Fig. 10 show that, for $Re = 100$, the flow widens immediately behind the step and an eddy is formed. When viscosity is further reduced ($Re = 500$ and $Re = 805$), the main flow is drawn downward, causing it to separate from the upper boundary and leading to the formation of a second eddy. Note that the first eddy increases in size when the Reynolds number increases ($Re = 500$ to $Re = 805$).

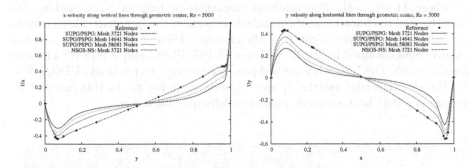

Fig. 7. The lid-driven cavity problem using SUPG/PSPG for $Re = 5000$: horizontal velocity for $x = 0.5, 0 \le y \le 1$ and vertical velocity for $y = 0.5, 0 \le x \le 1$.

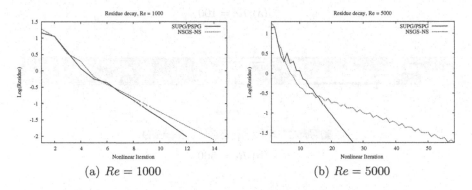

(a) $Re = 1000$ (b) $Re = 5000$

Fig. 8. Residue of the lid-driven cavity problem for $Re = 1000$ and $Re = 5000$.

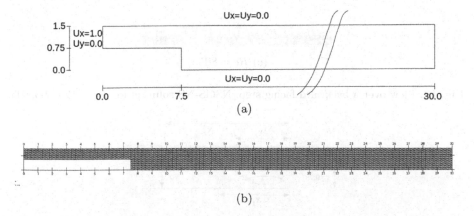

Fig. 9. Flow over a backward facing step: (a) problem domain and (b) finite element mesh (1131 nodes and 2010 elements).

Figure 11 shows the dimensionless characteristic lengths x_1, x_2 and x_3, frequently used to characterize the simulation result of this problem. Those lengths are normalized by the height H of the channel. Table 2 compares the physical experiments obtained in [21,27] with the SUPG/PSPG and NSGS-NS methods for $Re = 805$. The NSGS-NS method presents better solution than SUPG/PSPG for the characteristic lengths x_1 and x_2, but worse for x_3. In this experiment, we can say that both methods present satisfactory solutions.

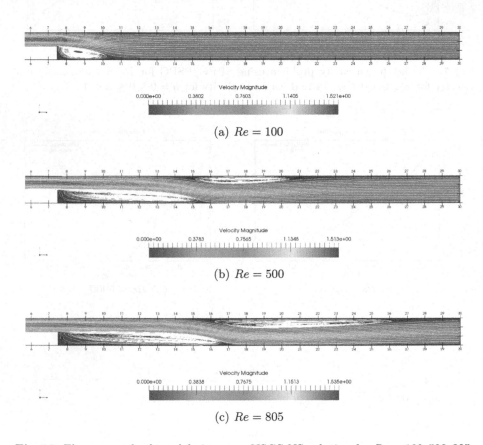

(a) $Re = 100$

(b) $Re = 500$

(c) $Re = 805$

Fig. 10. Flow over a backward facing step: NSGS-NS solution for $Re = 100, 500, 805$.

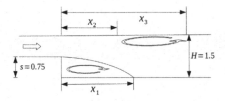

Fig. 11. Flow over a backward-facing step - characteristic lengths.

Table 2. Flow over a backward-facing step: characteristic lengths, $Re = 805$

Re = 805	x_1/H	x_2/H	x_3/H
Lee, T., and D. Mateescu	6.45	5.15	10.25
SUPG/PSPG Method	5.47	4.33	11.47
NSGS-NS Method	6.33	5.56	12.67

4 Conclusions

We presented a variational multiscale finite element method for solving the incompressible Navier-Stokes equations, named NSGS-NS method. The method consists of adding an artificial viscosity, through a residual-based nonlinear operator, acting only onto the fine (subgrid) scale of the discretization, yielding a parameter-free consistent method. The subgrid scale space is defined by using bubble functions, to reduce the computational cost of typical two-scale methods. Performing a static condensation, the small scale space of the unknown is condensed onto the resolved (grid) scale degrees of freedom. The methodology leads to a nonlinear scheme, which is solved by an iteration-lagging procedure only for the finite element grid.

Our multiscale finite element method is compared to the SUPG/PSPG approach presented in [17,19]. Convergence rate in the $L2$-norm is obtained for our method, which are similar to those obtained with the SUPG/PSPG stabilization technique. With two 2D benchmark problems, we illustrate the robustness of the NSGS-NS method showing its behavior using piecewise linear triangular elements enriched by bubbles with structured and unstructured grids. The numerical experiments demonstrated that the solutions obtained with our nonlinear variational multiscale method is comparable with those obtained with the SUPG/PSPG method in both benchmark problems: lid-driven cavity and the backward-facing step. We highlight that for the lid-driven cavity problem the NSGS-NS method yields much better solutions.

References

1. Santos, I.P., Almeida, R.C.: A nonlinear subgrid method for advection-diffusion problems. Comput. Methods Appl. Mech. Eng. **196**, 4771–4778 (2007)
2. Santos, I.P., Almeida, R.C., Malta, S.M.C.: Numerical analysis of the nonlinear subgrid scale method. Comput. Appl. Math. **31**(3), 473–503 (2012)
3. Brezzi, F.: On the existence, uniqueness and approximation of saddle-point problems arising from lagrangian multipliers. ESAIM: Math. Model. Numer. Anal. - Modélisation Mathématique et Analyse Numérique **8**(R2), 129–151 (1974)
4. Brooks, A.N., Hughes, T.J.R.: Streamline Upwind/Petrov-Galerkin formulations for convection dominated flows with particular emphasis on the incompressible Navier-Stokes equations. Comput. Methods Appl. Mech. Eng. **32**, 199–259 (1982)
5. Hughes, T., Tezduyar, T.: Finite element methods for first-order hyperbolic systems with particular emphasis on the compressible Euler equations. Comput. Methods Appl. Mech. Eng. **45**, 217–284 (1984)

6. Hughes, T.J., Franca, L.P., Hulbert, G.M.: A new finite element formulation for computational fluid dynamics: Viii. The Galerkin/Least-Squares method for advective-diffusive equations. Comput. Methods Appl. Mech. Eng. **73**(2), 173–189 (1989)
7. Hughes, T.J.R.: Multiscale phenomena: Green's functions, the Dirichlet-to-Neumann formulation, subgrid scale models, bubbles and the origins of stabilized methods. Comput. Methods Appl. Mech. Eng. **127**(1–4), 387–401 (1995)
8. Codina, R., Blasco, J.: Analysis of a stabilized finite element approximation of the transient convection-diffusion-reaction equation using orthogonal subscales. Comput. Vis. Sci. **4**, 167–174 (2002)
9. Lins, E.F., Elias, R.N., Guerra, G.M., Rochinha, F.A., Coutinho, A.L.G.A.: Edge-based finite element implementation of the residual-based variational multiscale method. Int. J. Numer. Methods Fluids **61**(1), 1–22 (2009)
10. Masud, A., Khurram, R.: A multiscale finite element method for the incompressible Navier–Stokes equations. Comput. Methods Appl. Mech. Eng. **195**(13–16), 1750–1777 (2006)
11. Arruda, N.C.B., Almeida, R.C., Carmo, E.G.D.: Dynamic diffusion formulations for advection dominated transport problems. Mecánica Computacional **29**, 2011–2025 (2010)
12. Valli, A.M., Almeida, R.C., Santos, I.P., Catabriga, L., Malta, S.M., Coutinho, A.L.: A parameter-free dynamic diffusion method for advection-diffusion-reaction problems. Comput. Math. Appl. **75**(1), 307–321 (2018)
13. Bento, S.S., Barbosa, P.W., Santos, I.P., de Lima, L.M., Catabriga, L.: A nonlinear finite element formulation based on multiscale approach to solve compressible Euler equations. In: Gervasi, O., Murgante, B., Misra, S., Borruso, G., Torre, C.M., Rocha, A.M.A.C., Taniar, D., Apduhan, B.O., Stankova, E., Cuzzocrea, A. (eds.) ICCSA 2017, Part VI. LNCS, vol. 10409, pp. 735–743. Springer, Cham (2017). https://doi.org/10.1007/978-3-319-62407-5_55
14. Bento, S.S., de Lima, L.M., Sedano, R.Z., Catabriga, L., Santos, I.P.: A nonlinear multiscale viscosity method to solve compressible flow problems. In: Gervasi, O., Murgante, B., Misra, S., Rocha, A.M.A.C., Torre, C., Taniar, D., Apduhan, B.O., Stankova, E., Wang, S. (eds.) ICCSA 2016, Part I. LNCS, vol. 9786, pp. 3–17. Springer, Cham (2016). https://doi.org/10.1007/978-3-319-42085-1_1
15. Brenner, S.C., Scott, L.R.: The Mathematical Theory of Finite Element Methods. Texts in Applied Mathematics. Springer, New York (2002). https://doi.org/10.1007/978-1-4757-3658-8
16. Hughes, T.J., Feijóo, G.R., Mazzei, L., Quincy, J.B.: The variational multiscale method-a paradigm for computational mechanics. Comput. Methods Appl. Mech. Eng. **166**(1–2), 3–24 (1998)
17. Tezduyar, T.E.: Adaptive determination of the finite element stabilization parameters. In: Proceedings of the ECCOMAS Computational Fluid Dynamics Conference, September 2001
18. Calo, V.M.: Residual-based multiscale turbulence modeling: finite volume simulations of bypass transition. PhD thesis, Stanford University (2005)
19. Elias, R.N., Coutinho, A.L.G.A., Martins, M.A.D.: Inexact Newton-type methods for non-linear problems arising from the SUPG/PSPG solution of steady incompressible Navier-Stokes equations. J. Braz. Soc. Mech. Sci. Eng. **26**, 330–339 (2004)
20. Ghia, U., Ghia, K., Shin, C.: High-Re solutions for incompressible flow using the Navier-Stokes equations and a multigrid method. J. Comput. Phys. **48**(3), 387–411 (1982)

21. Lee, T., Mateescu, D.: Experimental and numerical investigation of 2-D backward-facing step flow. J. Fluids Struct. **12**(6), 703–716 (1998)
22. Geuzaine, C., Remacle, J.F.: Gmsh: A 3-D finite element mesh generator with built-in pre- and post-processing facilities. Int. J. Numer. Methods Eng. **79**(11), 1309–1331 (2009)
23. Johnson, C., Pitkäranta, J.: Analysis of some mixed finite elements related to reduced integration. Technical report, Chalmers University of Technology and University of Goteborg (1980)
24. Carey, G., Krishnan, R.: Penalty approximation of stokes flow. Comput. Meths. Appl. Mech. Eng. **35**, 169–206 (1982)
25. Valli, A., Coutinho, A., Carey, G.: Control strategies for timestep selection in finite element simulation of incompressible flows and coupled heat and mass transfer. Technical report, COPPE - Federal University of Rio de Janeiro (2001)
26. Tobiska, L., Verfürth, R.: Analysis of a streamline diffusion finite element method for the stokes and Navier–Stokes equations. SIAM J. Numer. Anal. **33**(1), 107–127 (1996)
27. Armaly, B.F., Durst, F., Pereira, J., Schönung, B.: Experimental and theoretical investigation of backward-facing step flow. J. Fluid Mech. **127**, 473–496 (1983)

A Self-adaptive Approach
for Autonomous UAV Navigation
via Computer Vision

Gabriel Fornari[1](✉) ⓘ, Valdivino Alexandre de Santiago Júnior[1] ⓘ,
and Elcio Hideiti Shiguemori[2] ⓘ

[1] Instituto Nacional de Pesquisas Espaciais, Avenida dos Astronautas, 1758,
Jardim da Granja, São José dos Campos, SP 12227-010, Brazil
{gabriel.fornari,valdivino.santiago}@inpe.br
[2] Instituto de Estudos Avançados, Trevo Coronel Aviador José Alberto Albano do
Amarante, 1, Putim, São José dos Campos, SP 12228-001, Brazil
elcio@ieav.cta.br

Abstract. In autonomous Unmanned Aerial Vehicles (UAVs), the vehicle should be able to manage itself without the control of a human. In these cases, it is crucial to have a safe and accurate method for estimating the position of the vehicle. Although GPS is commonly employed in this task, it is susceptible to failures by different means, such as when a GPS signal is blocked by the environment or by malicious attacks. Aiming to fill this gap, new alternative methodologies are arising such as the ones based on computer vision. This work aims to contribute to the process of autonomous navigation of UAVs using computer vision. Thus, it is presented a self-adaptive approach for position estimation able to change its own configuration for increasing its performance. Results show that an Artificial Neural Network (ANN) presented the best performance as an edge detector for pictures with buildings or roads and the Canny extractor was better at smooth surfaces. Moreover, our self-adaptive approach as a whole shows gain up to 15% if compared with non-adaptive methodologies.

Keywords: Unmanned Aerial Vehicles · Computer vision
Autonomous navigation · Self-adaptive

1 Introduction

It is undeniable that Unmanned Aerial Vehicles (UAVs) are now part of human life. Also called drones, the UAVs emerged in 1916 as flying bombs [8]. Today, different sizes and shapes of drones are built and used for services that encompasses inspection, surveillance, environmental monitoring, cargo transportation and attacks on ground targets [11].

UAVs can be manually and remotely operated by radio control, but can also be autonomous. When a UAV is autonomous, its control system must be able

O. Gervasi et al. (Eds.): ICCSA 2018, LNCS 10961, pp. 268–280, 2018.
https://doi.org/10.1007/978-3-319-95165-2_19

to guide and navigate without human intervention. The most common approach of navigating is using GPS (Global Positioning System), but, given intrinsic problems with this system, such as signal failure in GPS denied environments and malicious attacks, new approaches have been emerging as alternatives, such as the one based on computer vision [1,11].

In this approach, the information provided by cameras is used to compute the position of the UAV. Although it has certain advantages, such as low cost, low weight and low power consumption considering some UAV models, the approach faces other problems, such as luminosity effects, land coverage and sensor resolution [1]. Within this area, several works propose the use of different methodologies and image processing algorithms to safely and correctly compute the position of the UAV without using GPS. Although some of them propose data fusion for improving performance, none of them presents the idea of adeptness.

Organisms immersed in dynamic environments may have adaptation as an essential advantage for their survival. Dynamic operating environments have characteristics that can not be controlled and that can constantly and quickly change. In such environments, the need of an organism change its own behavior may improve its performance. In the scientific literature, this process is called from different names, such as self-adaptive systems [13], autonomic computing [10], and Dynamically Reconfigurable Systems (SRDs) [7,16].

In this sense, this work presents a new self-adaptive methodology for autonomous navigation of UAVs based on computer vision. The approach, called Machine Learning for Autonomous Unmanned aerial Vehicle via computer Vision (MLAUVV), is able to configure itself according to different environments, choosing the most suitable image processing algorithms.

This paper is structured as follows. Section 2 discusses studies related to the area of computer vision applied to UAVs. Section 3 presents in detail the proposed methodology. Section 4 presents the main results and analysis based on such results. Concluding remarks are in Sect. 5.

2   Related Work

The research in navigation based on computer vision applied to UAVs has started in the nineties of the last century [3]. Since then, lots of works have proposed several kinds of solutions based on computer vision to solve different kinds of problems, e.g. obstacle detection, landing and target tracking. Two surveys present several discussions about computer vision algorithms applied to UAVs [1,11]. Here, the focus will be studies related to pose estimation of UAVs using vision-based systems.

One way of estimating the position of the UAV is through Simultaneous Localization And Mapping (SLAM), which aims to build a map of the environment and, at the same time, estimate the position of the robot. To do that, the robot should return several times to the starting point in order to reduce drift errors, which can be a problem when low endurance drones are used in large environments [15].

Other pose estimation techniques are visual odometry [4,6] and template matching [3,15,20]. The major difference between them is that the former computes the relative position and the latter the absolute position. The relative position is calculated based on overlapped images taken by the UAV, while the absolute position is estimated comparing the UAV image with a reference image (e.g., a satellite image). Below, some papers that use these techniques are discussed.

In [6], visual odometry and template matching techniques were fused together in order to reduce error. As the reliability of odometry decreases on large distances due to small errors caused by relative displacements of successive images, template matching is used to compensate the error. Besides that, Digital Elevation Model (DEM) and high resolution images were used as input information. The algorithm to perform the matching was Normalized Cross Correlation (NCC) and Robust-Oriented Hausdorff Measure (ROHM).

Based on the idea of [6], Conte and Doherty use visual odometry and template matching as an alternative to GPS [4]. The template matching algorithm for odometry was the Kanade-Lucas-Tomasi (KLT), a feature extractor-based method. The template matching is composed by Sobel edge extractor and cross correlation. Since cross correlation is sensitive to rotation and scale changes, Inertial Sensors (INS) onboard the aircraft were fused using Kalman Filter and used to correct the orientation and scale of the images. In another paper [5], the authors improve their methodology by changing some algorithms, such as cross correlation for NCC, and removing Sobel edge extractor before correlation.

In [20], the Phase Correlation (PC) algorithm is tested and compared with NCC and Mutual Information (MI). The authors claim that the PC algorithm presents better results due to its illumination-invariant feature, which is able to ignore the luminance effects between images. The goal of this work is more related to the advantages of the PC algorithm rather than UAV navigation.

In [3], the authors present a new way to perform the correlation between the UAV image and the reference image by using Scale Invariant Feature Transform (SIFT) and RANdom SAmple Consensus (RANSAC). The main advantage of the SIFT algorithm over cross correlation is its scale and rotation invariance. Again, the focus of the paper is more related to the problem of matching images instead of proposing a complete methodology for UAV navigation.

In [14], the authors present a matching algorithm based on class histograms and classified reference maps. The UAV images are segmented and classified by a neural network into grass, asphalt, and house. Based on the classified image, histograms are computed and compared to histograms obtained from the reference images. The authors claim that the methodology is invariant to rotation but not to scale and also that the impact of luminosity is reduced.

The Simulated Annealing meta-heuristic is used to enhance the results estimated by template matching and INS in [15]. The first is computed using Zero-mean Normalized Cross Correlation (ZNCC) between a UAV image and a reference image, and the last is obtained from sensors onboard the aircraft.

All such previous studies do not present a self-adaptive approach to select the most suitable computer vision algorithms according to environmental conditions. For example, information given by DEMs will be useless in flat regions, as well as optical sensors will not work well during the night. In this sense, this work proposes a self-adaptive approach, which is able to change the current running algorithm aiming to increase performance. Although the approach is general and can be used combining different techniques, in this work the template matching is explored observing its performance under the change of land covers.

3   Self-adaptive Approach for Autonomous UAV Navigation

The self-adaptive approach proposed in this work, called MLAUVV, is based on Rice's abstract model for algorithm selection [17]. His model is based on one question: given a whole set of algorithms, which one will best solve a given problem under specific circumstances? Thus, five topics, called by Rice "spaces", should be used to outline the problem of algorithm selection and hence answer the proposed question. The relationship between them are shown in Fig. 1. Furthermore, these spaces are here defined in the context of autonomous navigation via computer vision. More specifically, within the context of template matching based on optical images.

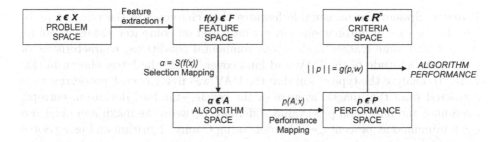

Fig. 1. Abstract model proposed by John Rice explaining the problem of algorithm selection. Adapted from [17].

Problem Space: the set of instances of a problem class. The problem chosen in this work is to estimate the position (latitude and longitude) during the flight of the UAV using only template matching. More specifically, the problem can be stated as finding the correct matching between the reference image and the captured image. One instance of this problem would be all the information gathered by the UAV sensors at an instant of time, which include the UAV image.

Algorithm Space: the set of algorithms that can be used to tackle the problem. In this paper, the template matching methodology was chosen (see [2,4]).

Thus, two different filters (average and Gauss) and three edge extractors (Canny [18], Sobel [18] and a Neural Network [2]) were selected to compare their performances based on the works [2,4]. To compute the matching, the normalized cross correlation algorithm was elected.

Performance Space: the set of possible performance metrics. In this work, the euclidean distance between the estimated position and the GPS position was chosen. Figure 2 shows how the error is computed.

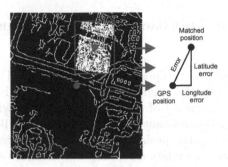

Fig. 2. Error calculation between the position given by the GPS and the position given by the template matching.

Feature Space: the measurable features that characterize the selected problem. In the case of autonomous navigation based on computer vision, it can be divided into some classes, such as environmental conditions, characteristics of the sensor, attitude of the UAV and land cover, being the latter chosen in this work. To analyze the type of soil that the UAV was flying over, 8 properties were extracted from the images: average of the pixels, standard deviation, entropy, maximum and minimum pixel value, difference between the maximum pixel and the minimum one, percentage of borders using Canny algorithm and using Sobel algorithm.

Criteria Space: a set of weights to adjust the relative importance of the performance metrics. In this work, there is only one performance metric, so this space is not needed.

Based on Rice's abstract model, the next step is to test all algorithms to realize about their performances. Once each algorithm has its own performance calculated for an instance of the problem (see Performance Mapping in Fig. 1), the Selection Mapping must be able to correctly link a given instance to its best algorithm. To do that, the use of machine learning techniques is proposed; two in particular: neural networks and Bayes networks. Finally, the machine learning techniques can be used to select new instances of the problem maximizing the performance of the overall system.

Now, the self-adaptive approach can be summarized in Fig. 3. In this work, the features of the problem are properties of the image captured by the UAV.

Based on these properties, an already trained machine learning technique, which can be a Bayes network or a neural network, is able to decide which algorithm is better given the current position of the UAV. After the decision, this approach chooses the best algorithm (filter and edge detector) to estimate the UAV position.

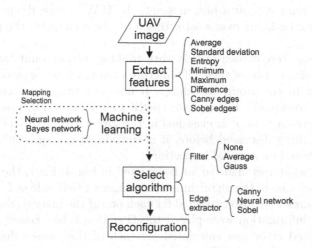

Fig. 3. The MLAUVV approach based on Rice's abstract model and machine learning techniques.

4 Evaluation

In order to verify the proposed self-adaptive methodology, tests using real UAV flight data were performed. The data used in this work was obtained by an airplane and a UAV. The airplane provided the reference image that covers the area of civil contingency agency in Revinge, Sweden. It depicts an area of approximately $1\,km^2$ and has spatial resolution of $0.5\,m/pixel$. The UAV flew in a portion of the same area, covering a small part of the reference image. The flight was done by a Yamaha R-MAX at a velocity of $3\,m/s$ at approximately $60\,m$ above the ground. The camera was fixed in a gimbal and adjusted to point nadir. The captured images have resolution of 288×360 pixels and spatial resolution of approximately $0.12\,m/pixel$ width and $0.11\,m/pixel$ height.

Based on Rice's model, each image (instance of the problem) has its best algorithm. Initially, a mapping was done in which each image pointed to a specific algorithm. The problem was then to train a classifier able to correctly link each instance to a given algorithm. Then, instead of adopting one algorithm per image, one algorithm was adopted for a set of images.

Now, Rice's abstract model (see Sect. 3) can be applied in order to train the machine learning techniques again. The only thing that will change is the performance metric because now it should consider a certain amount of images instead of only one. It is important to note that the best algorithm will be chosen for a group of images and not anymore for single ones. It means that the best algorithm can be one for a single image but another for the entire group. The new performance metric chosen was the accumulated error, calculated by summing the error of each separate picture of a given class.

Since the UAV takes pictures while moving, it is expected that the ground changes over time, e.g., at a first moment, the UAV can be flying over a house but later it can be flying over a lake. Based on these changes, the pictures were grouped.

Four groups were chosen in this work tanking into account the presence of buildings, roads or none of them. If a picture presents a house or other building, it is classified in the group "building". If not, but presents a crossroad, it is classified as "crossroad". If the picture neither shows a building nor a crossroad but if it presents a road, it is classified in the group "road". If the picture does not show anything discussed before, it is considered as "smooth". The images were chosen based on a visual inspection.

Basically, what was made so far is depicted in Fig. 4. First, the error of each picture for each one of the algorithms was computed (left side of Fig. 4). Besides that, the features were also extracted for each one of the images (right side of the Fig. 4). Both information were placed together in a table. Based on the table, the accumulated error was calculated for each of the classes discussed above (building, crossroad, road and smooth).

Table 1 shows the accumulated error for each algorithm. As can be seen, the best algorithm for the classes building, crossroad and road is the same and is composed by the average filter and the neural network edge extractor. On the other hand, the algorithm composed of no filter and the Canny edge extractor claims to be the best in the class smooth.

Table 1. Accumulated error of the 9 algorithms for each class of images.

Algorithm			Accumulated error (m)			
Id	Filter	Edge	Building	Crossroad	Smooth	Road
1	Gauss	Canny	3290	4393	6455	5047
2	Gauss	Neural network	4955	4551	7587	4407
3	Gauss	Sobel	1495	1066	7708	4085
4	Average	Canny	3159	4393	6419	5043
5	Average	Neural network	569	462	6708	3331
6	Average	Sobel	1435	1092	7680	3543
7	None	Canny	3684	4592	5930	5129
8	None	Neural network	929	985	6882	3728
9	None	Sobel	1867	1767	7809	4210

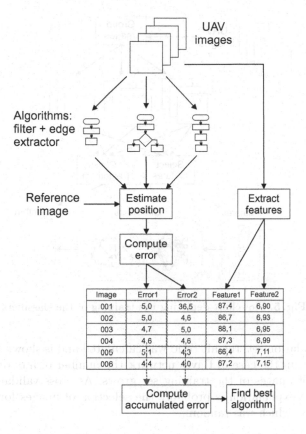

Fig. 4. Flowchart depicting the steps developed to elect the best algorithm.

Based on the results of Table 1, it is possible to choose the best algorithm for a certain performance metric and to train machine learning techniques. These steps are depicted in Fig. 5. First, the images were splitted according to the classes defined previously. For each class, the algorithm with best performance, i.e., with the smallest error was selected. Finally, the classifiers were trained using the features extracted from the pictures.

In this work, 520 images were selected and grouped into the four classes described above. The images were splitted into two groups, being the first used for validation of the classifiers and composed by 30% of the original amount of images and the second used for training, being composed by the remaining amount (70%). Using only images from the second group, the training was made through cross correlation for the whole group (70%), and for 50% and 30% of the original amount of pictures.

The architecture of the Bayes network [12] was built using a genetic algorithm while its conditional probabilities were built with the simple estimator. Among other configurations, the Multilayer Perceptron (MLP) [9] trained with 21 neurons in the hidden layer presented better accuracy in the classification.

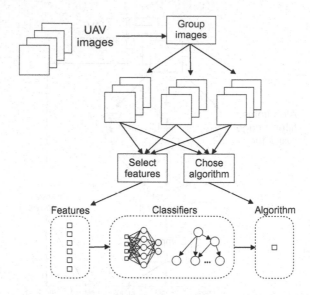

Fig. 5. Flowchart depicting the training of the classifiers.

Using the validation set, the hit ratio was calculated and is shown in Table 2. As it can be seen, in the case of Bayes network the number of hits decreases when the number of images of the training set grows. As cross validation had been used here, the explanation is probably the selection of images for training and validation sets, which was random.

Table 2. Percentage of Bayes network and multilayer perceptron hits.

Classifier	% of hits		
	30% of training	50% of training	70% of training
Bayes network	97.44%	97.44%	95.51%
Multilayer perceptron	98.08%	98.08%	98.08%

In order to understand the impact of the self-adaptive approach on a path traveled by the UAV, the steps depicted in Fig. 3 were followed. To do that, a hypothetical route was created using the 30% of the images not engaged in the training. The classifiers decided which algorithm should be used for each image based on its features. The time taken for choosing the algorithm is composed by the time of classification plus time of feature extraction. Running on a Intel i7 notebook, the time taken to classify one image was approximately 0.03 s. Figure 6 shows the error related to each picture using both classifiers, Bayes network and MLP, over 4 different terrains. It is interesting to note that, sometimes, due to incorrect classifications, one classifier has better result than the other (e.g., image number 31 of Fig. 6).

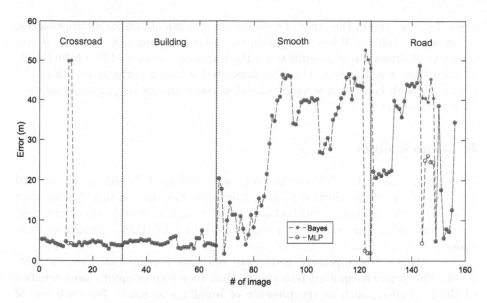

Fig. 6. The error related to each image for both classifiers, Bayes network and MLP. The vertical black line is used split the different image classes.

Table 3. Accumulated error of the 9 algorithms and the adaptive approach.

Algorithm	Filter	Edge extractor	Accumulated error (m)
1	Gauss	Canny	5547
2	Gauss	Neural network	6502
3	Gauss	Sobel	4337
4	Average	Canny	5478
5	Average	Neural network	3248
6	Average	Sobel	4150
7	None	Canny	5614
8	None	Neural network	3785
9	None	Sobel	4706
Adaptive	Bayes 70%		3114
Adaptive	Perceptron 70%		2776

Observing Fig. 6, it is important to notice that the algorithm composed by average filter and Neural Network edge extractor presented good results when the land cover has a building or a crossroad. When the surface present only a road, even choosing the best algorithm (average filter + Neural Network), the error is too high. The same thing occurs when the surface is smooth.

At this point, it would be interesting to compare the results of the self-adaptive approach and the non adaptive approach. To do this, the accumulated error, i.e., the sum of the error of each image, was calculated for all approaches, as shown in Table 3. When comparing the adaptive approach with the 9 non adaptive algorithms it is possible to see the improvement of up 15% of the result. Besides that, the Bayesian classifier presented a worse performance than the neural network because it wrongly classified some images (e.g., images number 11 and 12 of Fig. 6).

5   Conclusions

In this work, the MLAUVV methodology was presented. Based on the original problem of algorithm selection proposed by John Rice and on machine learning techniques, the presented methodology aims to automatically chose the best algorithm within the context of navigation control for UAVs using computer vision.

To validate this approach, tests were performed using data from a UAV flight. The data was splitted into classes that took into account characteristics of the land cover, such as the presence of buildings or roads. For each one of these classes the best algorithm, composed by a filter and an edge extractor, was chosen. A MLP and a Bayesian network were trained in order to classify the images in their respective classes. In the end, the results obtained using the adaptive approach were compared to the results using non adaptive approaches. An improvement of 15% was reached. Furthermore, for the set of images and the set of algorithms explored in this work, the algorithm composed by average filter and Neural Network edge extractor was set as the best when the land cover has a building, a crossroad or a road. When the surface is smooth, the best algorithm is composed by the Canny edge extractor and no filter.

As future work, four topics will be explored in ore detail. First, new filters and edge extractors will be added, such as the median filter and partial area effect [19]. Further work will be done concerning machine learning techniques, and Support Vectors Machines and Decision Trees are the next goals in this topic. New performance metrics will also be explored, such as processing time and memory use of the algorithms. Finally, new tests will be performed using data from other flights.

Acknowledgments. The authors would like to thank José Renato Garcia Braga for its collaboration and discussions during the development of this work and to Department of Computer and Information Science (IDA) of Linköpings Universitet for providing the images used in this work. Gabriel Fornari would like to acknowledge the scholarship provided by CNPq under the process number $140694/2016 - 1$. This work is partially supported by the Swedish Research Council (VR) Linnaeus Center CADICS, ELLIIT, and the Swedish Foundation for Strategic Research (CUAS Project, SymbiK-Cloud Project).

References

1. Al-Kaff, A., Martín, D., García, F., de la Escalera, A., María Armingol, J.: Survey of computer vision algorithms and applications for unmanned aerial vehicles. Expert Syst. Appl. **92**, 447–463 (2018). https://doi.org/10.1016/j.eswa.2017.09. 033

2. Braga, J.R.G., Velho, H.F.C., Conte, G., Doherty, P., Shiguemori, E.H.: An image matching system for autonomous UAV navigation based on neural network. In: 2016 14th International Conference on Control, Automation, Robotics and Vision (ICARCV), pp. 1–6. IEEE, November 2016. https://doi.org/10.1109/ICARCV. 2016.7838775

3. Cesetti, A., Frontoni, E., Mancini, A., Ascani, A., Zingaretti, P., Longhi, S.: A visual global positioning system for unmanned aerial vehicles used in photogrammetric applications. J. Intell. Robot. Syst. **61**(1–4), 157–168 (2011). https://doi. org/10.1007/s10846-010-9489-5

4. Conte, G., Doherty, P.: An integrated UAV navigation system based on aerial image matching. In: 2008 IEEE Aerospace Conference, pp. 1–10. IEEE, March 2008. https://doi.org/10.1109/AERO.2008.4526556

5. Conte, G., Doherty, P.: Vision-based unmanned aerial vehicle navigation using georeferenced information. EURASIP J. Adv. Sig. Process. **2009**(1), 387308 (2009). https://doi.org/10.1155/2009/387308

6. Sim, D.-G., Park, R.-H., Kim, R.-C., Lee, S.U.: Integrated position estimation using aerial image sequences. IEEE Trans. Pattern Anal. Mach. Intell. **24**(1), 1–18 (2002). https://doi.org/10.1109/34.982881

7. Ferguson, S., Siddiqi, A., Lewis, K., de Weck, O.L.: Flexible and reconfigurable systems: nomenclature and review. In: ASME Design Engineering Technical Conferences, Design Automation Conference, Las Vegas, NV, Paper No. DETC2007/DAC-35745, pp. 1–15 (2007)

8. Filho, P.F.F.S.: Automatic landmark recognition in aerial images for the autonomous navigation system of unmanned aerial vehicles. Ph.D. thesis, Instituto Tecnológico de Aeronáutica (2016)

9. Hagan, M.T., Demuth, H.B., Beale, M.H.: Neural Network Design, vol. 2. Springer, London (2014)

10. Huebscher, M.C., McCann, J.A.: A survey of autonomic computingdegrees, models, and applications. ACM Comput. Surv. **40**(3), 1–28 (2008). https://doi.org/10. 1145/1380584.1380585

11. Kanellakis, C., Nikolakopoulos, G.: Survey on computer vision for UAVs: current developments and trends. J. Intell. Robot. Syst. Theory Appl. **87**(1), 141–168 (2017). https://doi.org/10.1007/s10846-017-0483-z

12. Kotsiantis, S.B.: Supervised machine learning: a review of classification techniques. Informatica **31**, 249–268 (2007). https://doi.org/10.1115/1.1559160

13. Krupitzer, C., Roth, F.M., Vansyckel, S., Schiele, G., Becker, C.: A survey on engineering approaches for self-adaptive systems. Pervasive Mob. Comput. **17**(PB), 184–206 (2015). https://doi.org/10.1016/j.pmcj.2014.09.009

14. Lindsten, F., Callmer, J., Ohlsson, H., Tornqvist, D., Schon, T.B., Gustafsson, F.: Geo-referencing for UAV navigation using environmental classification. In: 2010 IEEE International Conference on Robotics and Automation, pp. 1420–1425. IEEE, May 2010. https://doi.org/10.1109/ROBOT.2010.5509424

15. Liu, X., Wang, H., Fu, D., Yu, Q., Guo, P., Lei, Z., Shang, Y.: An area-based position and attitude estimation for unmanned aerial vehicle navigation. Sci. China Technol. Sci. **58**(5), 916–926 (2015)

16. Lyke, J.C., Christodoulou, C.G., Vera, G.A., Edwards, A.H.: An introduction to reconfigurable systems. Proc. IEEE **103**(3), 291–317 (2015). https://doi.org/10.1109/JPROC.2015.2397832
17. Rice, J.R.: The algorithm selection problem. Adv. Comput. **15**(C), 65–118 (1976). https://doi.org/10.1016/S0065-2458(08)60520-3
18. Szeliski, R.: Computer Vision, Texts in Computer Science, vol. 5. Springer, London (2011). https://doi.org/10.1007/978-1-84882-935-0
19. Trujillo-Pino, A., Krissian, K., Alemán-Flores, M., Santana-Cedrés, D.: Accurate subpixel edge location based on partial area effect. Image Vis. Comput. **31**(1), 72–90 (2013). https://doi.org/10.1016/j.imavis.2012.10.005
20. Wan, X., Liu, J., Yan, H., Morgan, G.L.: Illumination-invariant image matching for autonomous UAV localisation based on optical sensing. ISPRS J. Photogramm. Remote Sens. **119**, 198–213 (2016). https://doi.org/10.1016/j.isprsjprs.2016.05.016

An Agent Based Model for Studying the Impact of Rainfall on Rift Valley Fever Transmission at Ferlo (Senegal)

Python Ndekou Tandong Paul[1(✉)], Alassane Bah[2], Papa Ibrahima Ndiaye[3], and Jacques André Ndione[4]

[1] Department of Mathematics and Computer Science,
Cheikh Anta Diop University, Dakar, Senegal
pppython@yahoo.fr
[2] ESP, Department of Mathematics and Computer Science,
Cheikh Anta Diop University, Dakar, Senegal
alassane.bah@gmail.com
[3] Department of Mathematics, Alioune Dione University, Bambey, Senegal
papaibra.ndiaye@uadb.edu
[4] Centre de suivi Ecologique, Dakar, Senegal
jacques-andre.ndione@cse.sn

Abstract. In this paper, we created a conceptual model UML (unified modelling language) showing interactions between animals, mosquitoes, environment, and climate factors. The UML static model was used to build an agent-based model that helps to study the impact of rainfall variability on the number of infected hosts after the outbreak of Rift valley fever. Several simulations were done on the multi-agent CORMAS platform. The different results showed continued growth in infections during the rainy season. A sensitivity analysis taking into account the delayed rains and dry spells have allowed us to know a clear vision about the rate of infected animals due to the rainfall variability. This work defines a framework for studying the impact of climatic changes on vector-borne diseases.

1 Introduction

Rift valley Fever is a disease transmitted by Aedes vexans or Culex poicilipes mosquitoes. This disease cannot be eradicated without the expertise of epidemiologists taking into account climate factors. For a better understanding of mechanisms of outbreak and propagation, the modeling of local and global transmission should be made for the further study of this disease. A brief overview has been done on recent studies that have shown that: In the 2000s, a study on the existence of vector-borne diseases has led to first isolate the pathogen agent of Rift Valley fever [1,2] in Ferlo. The environmental hypothesis has been the subject of multiple studies with the use of remote sensing data as an indicator of viral activity in Kenya [3,9]. In 2005, Mondet et al. [4,5] have shown links between

© Springer International Publishing AG, part of Springer Nature 2018
O. Gervasi et al. (Eds.): ICCSA 2018, LNCS 10961, pp. 281–290, 2018.
https://doi.org/10.1007/978-3-319-95165-2_20

rainfall and population dynamics of Aedes vexans arabiensi vectors. Ndione et al. [6] presented the impact of the temporary ponds on the transmission dynamics of the Rift valley fever [6,18] in Ferlo. The Variability of climatic factors [8] (seasons, rainfall) is a determining factor on the transmission of vector-borne diseases [4–7]. Nowadays, several scientific studies have contributed to show the impact of variability on the rainy seasons [10,20] and the intensity of daily rainfall on the transmission and the emergence of this disease. Recently, several results of modeling [23] have shown links between water ponds dynamics, rainfall events, abondance of mosquitoes and the dynamic of RVF transmission. The spacio-temporal distribution of rainfall events and water ponds explains the high number of mosquitoes during rainy season [24]. The population dynamics of Rift Valley Fever vectors, Aedes vexans Meigen and Culex poicilipes were studied in northern Senegal by [25]. They showed that Rainfall periodicity can be seen as a key factor controlling Aedes vexans population abundance and rainfall had no impact on the high number of Culex mosquitoes. Multi-agent systems have been the subject of numerous publications in the field of health and biomedicine. Calabretto et al. proposed [12] an agent based model to characterize patients undergoing treatment by hospital pharmacists in order to avoid side effects related to medication administration in patients. Riano et al. [13] proposed a multi-agent model to assist in the management units welcoming palliative care of patients with high-risk health conditions. In 2003, Triola et al. [14] helped to implement the MAS (multi-agent system) in simulations of infections in intensive care units. The agent-based models were used for the study of vector-borne diseases in several respects: the impact of herd mobility in the dynamics of transmission of RVF was approached by Paul et al. [15]. Sensitivity analysis of the impact of seasonal variability has not been the aimed of the previous studies by Python Ndekou T. Paul et al. [15] so we found it useful to take into account because the life cycle of mosquitoes depends on the intensity of rainfall during the rainy season. The review of the literature allowed us to notice that several studies have contributed to the explaining of the phenomena of transmission of the RVF [16] but very few have used multi-agent models of which their strong point is the use of local interactions [17]. This article, in the context of the implementation of new control strategies against vector-borne diseases in developing countries, provides a new approach for agent-based modeling integrating rainfall variability. The aim of the integration of rainfall variability in the model is to study their impact on the Rift Valley fever transmission at Ferlo (Senegal) in the long and short term.

2   Presentation of the Ferlo Area

Ferlo is located in the north of Senegal and extends from the valley of Senegal River. The study was conducted between the months of June and September during the year 2013. The climate of the Ferlo region is characterized by two main seasons: a dry season and a rainy season. The mean annual rainfall there is mainly provided by squall lines, and ranges from 300 mm to 500 mm [22]. During the summer monsoon, a large quantity of small and temporary water ponds are thus formed, leading to an environment favoring in the breeding and hatching of mosquitoes including Aedes vexans and Culex poicilipes associated with the RVF [11,22]. In the Ferlo region, water ponds are widely distributed.

3   Description of an Agent Based Model

The UML model shows interactions between animals, mosquitoes, water ponds (Fig. 1). It allows us to identify the following principal agents. Host agents, Mosquito agents, water pond agents and Climate agent. All mosquito agents live within water ponds. During the rainy season, host agents move to water ponds when they are in search of the water. Each host agent use the method searchWater() to find a water pond. When each mosquito is in contact with one host, it uses the method bitehost() to bite the host by using the probability of the biting. Mosquito Agent must search Host Agent to have a blood meal for the fertilization of eggs. Host Agent must move within Pond Agent to have water to drink. Water Pond Agent changes its physiological state at each time as the function of the rainfall coming from the Climate Agent.

Water Pond Agent

The water pond agent is the central element of the outbreak and transmission of RVF. It is the meeting place for the animals that are in search of water to drink and mosquitos that must take a blood meal to fertilize their eggs. The dynamics of Water Pond agents depends on climatic factors. Interactions between Water Pond agents and Climate agents have a great impact on the life cycle of Aedes vexans mosquitos. Each Water Pond agent performs two major functions: a filling function according to the water pond, and a water loss function. The filling function is ensured by the rain that falls directly on the ponds and also water runoff from elsewhere. The water loss function is provided by the phenomenon of evaporation, infiltration and water consumption by the animal herds. The Infiltration essentially depends on the kind of soil, resulting from the soil permeability.

Behaviors of Water Pond Agent

The behaviors of each Water pond agent are described by the computer program. The methods used by each Water pond agent are listed as follows: initPont( ) is a method allowing to initialize the parameter values, waterClimate( ) is a method allowing to update the climatic parameters, waterDynamic( ) is a method allowing to compute at each step of simulation the quantity of water within the pond taking into account the water loss (infiltration, runoff, evaporation).

Mosquito Agent

The mosquito life cycle is composed of four distinct phases: egg, larva, pupa and adult [21]. Each Mosquito agent has the following attributes: physioState indicates the physiological state (egg, larva, pupa and adult) of the mosquito.

Behaviors of Mosquito Agents

The behaviors of each mosquito agent are described by the following methods: biteHost( ) is a method allowing to sting the host and take the blood meal. It is during that sting that the host can be infected, SearchingHost( ) is a method allowing to look for the host in the vicinity of the water pond, layEgg( ) is a method allowing to lay eggs. Each mosquito agent is in direct interaction with Water Pond agents and Host agents. The Water Pond agent serves as a habitat while the Host agent allows to have a blood meal.

Host Agent

Animals like cattle, sheep, camels and goats are infected by Aedes mosquitos during the rainy season from June to October each year. Each of these animals is modeled by the Host agent. Each host agent has the following attributes: physioState indicates the physiological state of the host, sanitaryState indicates the healthy state of the host (healthy, infected and infecting), mobilityDegree indicates its degree of mobility specifying the maximum distance from which each host agent can found a water pond.

Behaviors Host Agents

Each Host agent interacts with mosquito agents. The host agent has the following methods: searchWater( ) is the method that allows it to identify a water pond, WaterConsumption( ) is a method that allows it to consume water, MovePond( ) is a method that allows it to move in a water pond by using a degree of mobility, Healthdynamic( ) is a method that allows to update its sanitary state.

Climate Agent

The climate agent is characterized by the daily temperature, daily humidity and daily precipitation. The Climate agent has the following attributes:temperature indicates de daily temperature of the day, humidity indicates the daily humidity of the day, precipitation: indicates the daily precipitation of the day.

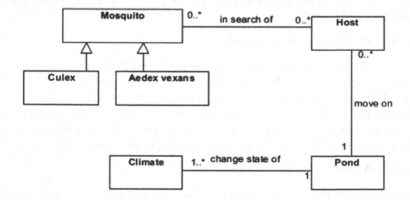

Fig. 1. UML model of interactions between hosts, mosquitos, water pond and climate factors

4   Experimental Description

In the CORMAS [19] platform of the modelling, each simulation is done in 365 steps corresponding to 365 days of the year. The simulation is organized as follows: (a) the first part is to initialize the virtual environment and create the different agents that will be in interactions. (b) The second part is to use the original data of rainfall during the year 2013. (c) The last part consists in analyzing the sensitivity analysis of rainfall. The results from these sensitivity analyses will be used to make comparative studies to assess changes in the infected host rates.

5   Experimental Results

To perform the simulations, the following data are used: a grid of 10 square kilometers (Fig. 2) corresponding to the study of the spread of Rift Valley fever. A herd of 100 sheeps among which 9% are infected, 80% of infected eggs, 20 empty water ponds at the beginning of the simulation and 20 animal's settlement. The rainfall data corresponding to the different seasons (wet and dry) are used in the simulation of 365 days corresponding to 365 simulation steps; here a step corresponds to a day. All mosquitos at the beginning of the simulations are in the form of eggs that go through six months of dry seasons before hatching as soon as the first rains. Different agents are randomly placed in the environment at the beginning of the simulation. Only hosts move to the water ponds, the mosquitos in this model do not leave the water ponds. For the first simulation, the rainfall data corresponding to the seasons in terms of reality are used to produce the results, and then a sensitivity analysis is made on changes in precipitation in the months that precede the rainy season and after the rainy season. A sensitivity analysis was also made on a dry spell in October. The following results are obtained: (Fig. 3) shows the evolution of the percentage of infected hosts, based on the number of days during the dry season and the rainy season in 2013. (Fig. 4) shows respectively the percentage of infected hosts, then a curve showing the impact of one-month delay of the rainy season on the cumulative number of infected hosts. (Fig. 5) shows the impact of the shift of the end of the rainy season from two months on the transmission dynamics of the RVF in the Ferlo region. (Fig. 6) shows the impact of variability in the percentage of infected hosts with the inclusion of a dry spell in October. All simulations show an infection rate of 9% for all of the dry season before the rainy season.

6   Discussion

Modeling and simulation of local interactions between animals and mosquitoes help to measure effectively the percentage of hosts infected with the Rift Valley Fever in Ferlo (Senegal). The observations that the existence of mosquitoes and the growth in the number of infected animals depend on the presence of rain are proven by the simulation conducted over a period of one year [26]. Indeed,

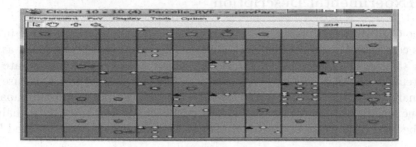

Fig. 2. Overview of the screen shot of the step 204 (the 204th day of a year of simulation) showing the Host agents in yellow, the Vector agents in red, Settlement agents in black, water pond agents in blue and yellow shaded. (Color figure online)

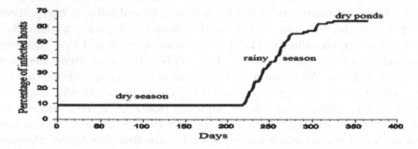

Fig. 3. The curve shows the percentage of hosts that have infected during the simulation. We have taking into account to the climate data of 2013 in the region of Ferlo (Senegal). In this context, the rainy season begins in July and ends in December.

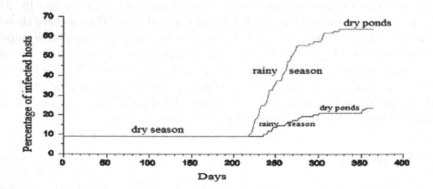

Fig. 4. The curves show the shift that occurs when the rainy season is delayed by one month (zero rainfall in July) corresponding to a sensitivity analysis of daily rainfall during the first month of the rainy season.

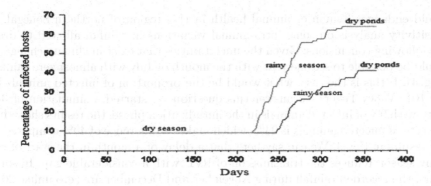

Fig. 5. The curves show the shift that occurs when the rainy season is shortened to two months (zero precipitation in November and December) corresponding to a sensitivity analysis of daily rainfall during the last month of the rainy seasons.

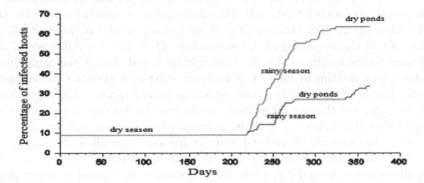

Fig. 6. The curves show the shift that occurs when you have a break in rainfall (precipitation void) corresponding to a sensitivity analysis of the daily rainfall for the entire month of October.

the results in (Fig. 3) show a vision of evolution cases of the Rift Valley fever in three phases related to intra-annual seasonal rainfall variations. The first phase shows a constant trend rate of 9% of the disease during the 6-month dry season. The second phase shows a growth in the number of infected hosts due to the presence of rainfall between the months of July to October, with a few days of rain between the months of November and December. The third phase presents a new a constant situation of the number of infected hosts equaling 64% due to the presence of drought that forced to the drying of water ponds. This dryness leads to a shutdown of the mosquito life cycle process. The simulation results in Fig. 3 show the impact of the changing seasons [28] on the transmission dynamics of rift valley fever in Ferlo. During the rainy season, the number of days in a month rains may vary. This change impacts on the duration of eggs hatching, impacts on the transition of larvae to pupae and impacts on the emergence of larvae to adult mosquitoes. The birth of thousands of mosquitoes with high infection rates would endanger human or animal health in this region of northern Senegal. A sensitivity analysis on some intra-annual variations in rainfall allowed to draw the following conclusions: Given the uncertainties that exist in climate change, it would be possible to see one year with the month of July with almost zero rainfall (Fig. 4). If this is the case, what would be the proportion of infected animals by the Rift Valley Fever? To answer this question we started a simulation of 365 steps with 9% of infected animals in the initialization phase, the results show that the rate of infected animals is 24%, which makes a difference of 40% compared to the results in Fig. 3. We can say here that a delay of a month in the start of the rainy season reduces the transmission of RVF with a considerable gap. In some years, the recorded rainfall during November and December are zero unlike 2013 where there were five days of low intensities. A simulation of 365 days in this case allows us to obtain 41% of infected (Fig. 5) animals, which makes a difference of 33% from the results in (Fig. 3). In general, during the month of October, the number of rainy days sometimes exceeds five days, but we realize that in some years, this number tends to 0. Therefore making a simulation over the year 2013 with a dry spell in October (Fig. 6), we get about 34% of infected animals against 9% at the beginning of the simulation. There is a net difference of 30% compared to the results of (Fig. 3). It should be noted that at the beginning of the dry season starting in January, mosquitoes exist only as eggs. Comparing the results in cases when there is a delay of one month of rains on the beginning of rainy seasons, and the case when there are no rains in November and December, we note that the number of infected animals when there is a delay of rains is inferior to the number of infected animals for zero rainfall in November and December. This is justified by the fact that the development cycle of the adult mosquitoes also takes a delay, while at the beginning of November, water ponds are already full of mosquitoes that are capable of infecting animals [26]. The using of agent based model in this work is justified by the fact that it is possible to know the forecast in terms of number of infected hosts depending on seasonal, monthly or even daily rainfall variations [27].

7   Conclusion

For assessing the risk of transmission in terms of infection rate of animals in the region of Ferlo contacts between animals and infected mosquitoes were modeled by an agent-based model, taking into account rainfall variability. Several simulations of 365 steps each allowed to say: Check the number of infected hosts in the water ponds during the rainy season would lead to significantly reduce the onset and spread of the Rift valley fever in Ferlo (Senegal). The number of infected hosts is dictated by the duration of the rainfall seasons. In an artificial environment, we studied the impact of rainfall variability on the transmission of RFV. The results confirm the fact that the number of infected hosts grows considerably during the rainy season. We also noted that after the end of the rainy season, the number of infections continues to grow, because the ponds are filled with water and will evaporate for some time during the dry season. It has been found that a delay of the start of the rains would give low rates of infections compared to an anticipation of the dry season. A dry spell significantly reduced the number of infected hosts, but the rate is still higher than the number of infected in cases where there is an anticipation of the dry season. The control of dry spells can also control the disease. The agent-based model developed as part of this article provides a basic platform to predict in long-and short-term the number of infections, and finally set plans to fight against this disease. With this model, we can simulate all suspected cases of fluctuation in intra-annual rainfall variations. The agent-based model is a powerful tool to represent the spatio-temporal dynamics of mosquito-animal interactions by taking into account the behavior of the latter and all that regulates their development cycle and existence. The developed model as part of this article provides a platform to better understand the mechanisms of transmission and emergence of the rift valley fever in Ferlo Senegal with all possible sensitivity analysis aspects.

References

1. Fontenille, D., Traore-Lamizana, M., Diallo, M., Thonnon, J., Digoutte, J.P., Zeller, H.G.: New vectors of Rift Valley Fever in West Africa. Emerg. Infect. Dis. 4(2), 289–93 (1998)
2. Traore-Lamizana, M., Zeller, H.G., et al.: Isolations of West Nile and Bagaza viruses from mosquitoes (Diptera: Culicidae) in central Senegal (Ferlo). J. Med. Entomol. 31(6), 934–8 (1994)
3. Ndione, J.-A., Diop, M., Lacaux, J.-P., Gaye, A.T.: Variabilité intra-saisonnière de la pluviométrie et émergence de la fièvre de la vallée du rift (FVR) dans la vallée du fleuve Sénégal: nouvelles considérations. Climatologie 5, 83–97 (2008)
4. Linthicum, K.J., Assaf, A., Compton, J.T., Kelley, P.W., Myers, M.F., Peters, C.J.: Climate and satellite indicators to forecast Rift Valley Fever epidemics in Kenya. Science 285, 397–400 (1999)
5. Mondet, B., Diaite, A., Fall, A.G., Chevalier, V.: Relations entre la pluviométrie et le risque de transmission virale par les moustiques: cas du virus de la Rift Valley Fever (RVF) dans le Ferlo (Senegal). Environnement, Risques et Santé 4, 125–129 (2005)
6. Ndione, J.A., Lacaux, J.P., Toure, Y., Vignolles, C., Fontanaz, D., Lafaye, M.: Mares temporaires et risques sanitaires au Ferlo: contribution de la teledetection pour l'étude de la fievre de la vallee du rift entre août 2003 et janvier 2004. Secheresse 20(1), 153–160 (2009)
7. Colwell, R.R.: Global climate and infectious disease: the cholera paradigm. Science 274(5295), 2025–2031 (1996)
8. Colwell, R.R., Patz, J.A.: Climate, Infectious Disease and Health. American Academy of Microbiology, Washington, DC (1998)
9. Ndione, J.-A., Besancenot, J.-P., Lacaux, J.-P., Sabatier, Ph.: Environnement et épidémiologie de la fievre de la vallee du Rift (FVR) dans le bassin inferieur du fleuve Senegal. Environnement, Risques et Sante 2, 1–7 (2003)
10. McMichael, A., Woodruff, R., Hales, S.: Climate change and human health: present and future risks. Lancet 367, 859 (2006)
11. Koenraadt, C.J.M., Githeko, A.K., Takken, W.: The effects of rainfall and evapotranspiration on the temporal dynamics of Anopheles gambiae s.s. and Anopheles arabiensis in a Kenyan village. Acta Trop 90, 141–153 (2004)

12. Calabretto, J-P., Couper, D., Mulley, B., Nissen, M., Siow, S., Tuck, J.: Agent support for patients and community pharmacists. In: Proceedings of the 35th Annual Hawaii International Conference on System Sciences (HICSS- 35.02), p. 153b, January 2002
13. Riano, D., Prado, S., Pascual, A., Martin, S.: A multi-agent system model to support palliative care units. In: Proceedings of the 15th IEEE Symposium on Computer-Based Medical Systems (CBMS 2002), p. 35, June 2002
14. Triola, M.M., Holzman, R.S.: Agent-based simulation of nosocomial transmission in the medical intensive care unit. In: Proceedings of the 16th IEEE Symposium on Computer-Based Medical Systems (CBMS 2003), p. 284, June 2003
15. Paul, P.N.T., Bah, A., Ndiaye, P.I., Ndione, J.A.: An agent-based model for studying the impact of herd mobility on the spread of vector-borne diseases: the case of Rift Valley Fever (Ferlo Senegal). Open J. Model. Simul. 2, 97–111 (2014)
16. Sow, A., Faye, O., Ba, Y., Diallo, D., Fall, G., Faye, O., et al.: Widespread Rift Valley Fever emergence in Senegal in 2013–2014. Open Forum Infect. Dis. 3(3) (2016). https://doi.org/10.1093/ofid/ofw149PMCID. ofw149. Published online 21 July 2016. PMC5047427
17. Himeidan, Y.E., Kweka, E.J., Mahgoub, M.M., El Rayah, E.A., et al.: Recent outbreaks of Rift Valley Fever in East Africa and the Middle East. Front. Public Health 2, 169 (2014)
18. Lacaux, J.P., Tourre, Y.M., Vignolles, C., Ndione, J.A., Lafaye, M.: Classification of ponds from high-spatial resolution remote sensing: application to Rift Valley Fever epidemics in Senegal. Remote Sens. Environ. 106, 66–74 (2007). https://doi.org/10.1016/j.rse.2006.07.012
19. Bousquet, F., Bakam, I., Proton, H., Le Page, C.: Cormas: common-pool resources and multi-agent systems. In: Pasqual del Pobil, A., Mira, J., Ali, M. (eds.) IEA/AIE 1998. LNCS, vol. 1416, pp. 826–837. Springer, Heidelberg (1998). https://doi.org/10.1007/3-540-64574-8_469
20. Koenraadt, C.J., Paaijmans, K.P., Githeko, A.K., Knols, B.G., Takken, W.: Egg hatching, larval movement and larval survival of the malaria vector Anopheles gambiae in desiccating habitats. Malar. J. 2, 20 (2003)
21. http://healthstaff.blogspot.com/p/life-cycle-of-aedes-mosquito.html
22. Bop, M., Amadou, A., Seidou, O., Kébé, C.M.F., Ndione, J.A., Sambou, S., Sanda, I.S.: Modeling the hydrological dynamic of the breeding water bodies in Barkedji's zone. J. Water Resour. Prot. 6, 741–755 (2014)
23. Porphyre, T., Bicout, D.J., Sabatier, P.: Modelling the abundance of mosquito vectors versus flooding dynamic. Ecol. Model. 183, 173–181 (2005)
24. Ndione, J.-A., Besancenot, J.-P., Lacaux, J.-P., Sabatier, Ph.: Environnement et épidémiologie de la fiàvre de la vallée du Rift (FVR) dans le bassin inférieur du fleuve Sénégal. Environnement, Risques et Santé 2, 1–7 (2003)
25. Ba, Y., Diallo, D., Fadel Kebe, C.M., Dia, I., Diallo, M.: Aspects of bioecology of two Rift Valley Fever virus vectors in Senegal (West Africa): Aedes vexans and Culex poicilipes (Diptera: Culicidae. J. Med. Entomol. 42(5), 739–750 (2005)
26. Davies, F.G., Linthicum, K.J., James, A.D.: Rainfall and epizootic Rift Valley Fever. Bull. World Health Organ. 63(5), 941–3 (1985)
27. Anyamba, A., Linthicum, K.J., Tucker, C.J.: Climate-disease connections: Rift Valley Fever in Kenya. Cad Saude Publica 17(Suppl), 133–140 (2001)
28. Martin, V., Chevalier, V., Ceccato, P., Anyamba, A., De Simone, L., Lubroth, J., de La Rocque, S., Domenech, J.: The impact of climate change on the epidemiology and control of Rift Valley Fever. Rev. Sci. Tech. 27(2), 413–26 (2008)

Workshop Computational and Applied Statistics (CAS 2018)

Implementation of Indonesia National Qualification Framework to Improve Higher Education Students: Technology Acceptance Model Approach

Dekeng Setyo Budiarto[1(✉)], Ratna Purnamasari[1], Yennisa[1],
Surmayanti[2], Indrazno Siradjuddin[3], Arief Hermawan[4],
and Tutut Herawan[4,5,6]

[1] Department of Accounting, Universitas PGRI Yogyakarta, Yogyakarta,
Indonesia
dekengsb@upy.ac.id
[2] Universitas Putra Indonesia (YPTK), Padang, Indonesia
[3] State Polytechnic of Malang, Malang, Indonesia
[4] Universitas Teknologi Yogyakarta, Yogyakarta, Indonesia
[5] Universitas Negeri Yogyakarta, Yogyakarta, Indonesia
[6] AMCS Research Center, Yogyakarta, Indonesia

Abstract. In order to face the global competition, graduates' competence is nowadays problem faced by many higher learning institutions. This study is aimed to test students' competence using the Technology Acceptance Model (TAM) framework. It tests the effect of perceived usefulness (PU) and perceived ease of use (PEU) on behavior intention to use (BIU) and student' competence. The data used is a primary data that was collected by distributing questionnaire to 128 students who use e-learning. The samples were selected using the convenience sampling method. The data obtained was evaluate both by reliability and validity tests, while the hypothesis was tested using multiple regression. The result shows that PU and PEU have significant effect on BIU, and furthermore BIU has significant effect on student' competence (cognitive, affective, and psychomotor). It provides theoretical contribution that technology utilization can improve student' competence.

Keywords: Perceived usefulness · Behavioral intention to use
Cognitive · Affective · Psychomotor

1 Introduction

To create graduates with knowledge, attitude, skills, and competence is the responsibility of university as administrator of education. President Regulation No. 8 of 2012 on the Indonesian National Qualification Framework (*Kerangka Kualifikasi Nasional* Indonesia-KKNI) mandates university to organize education in order to create graduates who have abilities in accordance with the level of competence needed. Graduates' competence can be measured using three indicators: cognitive competence

© Springer International Publishing AG, part of Springer Nature 2018
O. Gervasi et al. (Eds.): ICCSA 2018, LNCS 10961, pp. 293–304, 2018.
https://doi.org/10.1007/978-3-319-95165-2_21

(knowledge), affective (attitude), and psychomotor (skill) [1]. This study is conducted to understand student' competence through the utilization of information technology (e-learning) using the Technology Acceptance Model (TAM) framework. Information technology and information system have the same terminology [2], so in this study technology/information system will be referred to as information technology (IT).

TAM developed by Davis [3] is behavioral concept referring to technology users. Studies in the implementation of TAM are highly interesting because (1) the literature review of TAM only identifies its technological aspect; (2) even though TAM is very popular, this concept needs to be developed according to the changes in the environment [4]. Several researchers have used the TAM framework in various areas such as consumer behavior [5–7]; employees' behavior in non-profit organizations [8, 9] and employees' behavior in manufacturing companies [10]. Other studies have proved that the concept of TAM affects information system users' performance [11, 12]. This study is interesting because the TAM concept to test the students' competence in the implementation of KKNI is still limited.

According to previous studies Lee *et al.* [13]; Peslak *et al.* [14], perceived usefulness (PU), perceived ease of use (PEU), and behavior intention to use (BIU) are the constructs of TAM. PU is used to assess the benefit of a new technology that will be used. Somebody will accept a new technology if they feel that technology is beneficial [6]. PEU is an important factor for people when they want to choose a new technology. When a technology is user-friendly it will increase people's trust and improved user convenience [7]. Besides PU and PEU, Behavioral intention to use has a strong effect on people so that they try to improve their ability by utilizing the technology [12].

Besides explaining the relationship among several constructs in TAM, this study also explains the effect of TAM on student' performance who utilize e-learning. In this study, student' performance is measured using three competences according to the Bloom taxonomy: cognitive, affective, and psichometric [15]. Therefore, the aim of this study is to test the effect of PU and PEU on BIU, as well as testing the effect of BIU on student' competence who use e-learning. This study will provide benefit in the development of e-learning and theory testing related with TAM.

The rest of this paper is organized as follows. Section 2 describes the theoretical framework. Section 3 describes hypothesis development. Section 4 presents methodology and data analysis. Section 5 presents results and discussion. Finally, the conclusion of this work is described in Sect. 6.

2 Theoretical Framework

2.1 Technology Acceptance Model

One of the most important models in analyzing IT implementation is Technology Acceptance Model (TAM). This model developed by Davis [3] explains that IT users will decide to accept a new technology by considering several constructs which consist of PU, PEU, and BIU [6]. Perceived usefulness is defined as the prospective users subjective probability that using a specific application system will increase their job performance within an organizational context. Usefulness is also defined as a total value a user perceives from using an innovation [7, 16]. The PEU is defined as the degree to which the prospective user expects the target system to be free of effort [3, 14]. The BIU is defines as the actual usage of gives information system and therefore determines technology acceptance [9]. The main mechanism underlying perceived usefulness is effort decreasing and the core mean underlying PEU are system design and features [17, 18].

2.2 Competence

President Regulation No 8 of 2012 on KKNI is a framework of competence and qualification hierarchical arrangement that will be able to reconcile, equalize, and integrate education, vocational training, and job experience field in order to provide recognition on work competence according to job structure in various sectors. Students' ability/performance in this case is a combination of cognitive, affective, and psychomotor domains [19]. Cognitive competence consists of behavior that emphasizes intellectual aspects such as knowledge and thinking ability. This domain consists of six levels [20, 21]: (1) knowledge, (2) comprehension, (3) application, (4) analysis (understanding and elaboration), (5) synthesis (integration), and (6) evaluation (appraisal). In the context of university students, cognitive competence is define as student's ability in academic field which represented by their grade point. A high grade point is an indicator used to understand the level of students comprehension on the courses that they have taken. The affective domain is about values, attitudes and behaviors. It includes, in a hierarchy, an ability to listen, to respond in interactions with others, to demonstrate attitudes or values appropriate to particular situations, to demonstrate balance and consideration, and at the highest level, to display a commitment to principled practice on a day-to-day basis, alongside a willingness to revise judgment and to change behavior in the light of new evidence [22–24]. In the context of university students, the affective competence shows the ability in conveying ideas in a group setting and their discipline so that they can be accepted in an environment.

The psychomotor domain is concerned with motor skills or actions and the performance that these produce and 'embrace coordinated physical movements evaluated in terms of time, precision and technique' [23, 25, 26]. In its context, university students use this domain when they perform a presentation. Students who have a high psychomotor ability will have a good attitude when they do a presentation, or presenting the paper systematically and answering the questions clearly. Based on several study results and on definition explained above, a study model is presented in Fig. 1.

3 Hypothesis Development

3.1 Perceived Usefulness and Behavioral Intention to Use

In order to increase competitiveness, universities can implement technology, because IT implementation can benefits organizations [13, 27]. Because of that, the user perception and understanding of IT is the most effective way and is a very important factor in understanding the benefit of a technology [28]. PU reflects how strong somebody's trust is in trying to utilize the technology. Somebody will have certain expectations on the IT benefit and will decide to use it [29]. The result from previous studies [4, 7, 9]

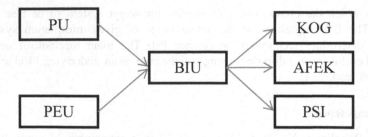

Fig. 1. Relationship between independent variables and dependent variable

explain that PU affects BIU: the higher the user's level of trust, the higher the BIU to use IT. Based on the results of the above-mentioned studies, the hypothesis is proposed as follows:

Hypotheses 1: PU has a significant effect on BIU

3.2 Perceived Ease of Use and Behavioral Intention to Use

TAM is a framework of model used to predict and explain the behavior in using technology [9]. Besides PU, PEU is also an antecedent that may affect people's willingness to adopt a technology [3, 13]. The end user of IT will feel that a technology is easy or hard to use. Before utilizing a new technology the prospective user will learn the excellence and try new technology before deciding to adopt it [10]. The organization will swiftly accept and implement a technology that is easy to use. A prospective user will not choose complex technology, but he will choose the technology that is easy to use. The easier the technology, the more likely it is to be used more often [4, 7, 8, 13, 18, 30]. Based on the result, the hypothesis is proposed as follows:

Hypotheses 2: PEU has a significant effect on BIU

3.3 Behavioral Intentions to Use and Competence

Prior research suggests that individual technology acceptance level may effect the learning performance outcome when activities are conducted through information technology. Although the current research stream is ultimately interested in performance as a key outcome of use, intentions are relevant to understand how the individual's reactions might affect the performance [12]. Besides that, Goodhue and Thompson [31] explain that technology will affect the individual's performance if the technology is put to a good use and to support the work. The other research from Yu and Yu [32] found evidence that IT implementation is related with people's performance. People behavior were represented with the intensity of using the technology has a potential to increase their performance [10, 11]. Based on the description above the hypothesis is proposed as follows:

Hypotheses 3a: behavioral intention to use affects the cognitive competence
Hypotheses 3b: behavioral intention to use affects the affective competence
Hypotheses 3c: behavioral intention to use affects the psychomotor competence

---

4 Research Method

4.1 Research Sample and Data Collection Method

The samples in this study are 128 university students from semester 2, 4, and 6 of the Accounting Department who have utilized e-learning. The samples are divided into three groups of courses taught by three lecturers. This study uses non probability sampling (convenience) method in selecting the samples. The sampling technique allows researchers to select samples based on the convenience [33]. Many studies investigating TAM use the convenience sampling. Furthermore, this technique is used to ensure a better response rate in a short period of time [9]. This study employs two approaches to gather the data, questionnaire and observation. The Questionnaire was selected because it questionnaire method is an effective tool to collect large amount of data in a within short period of time [18, 34]. The questionnaire was distributed to the students to measure the implementation of TAM through e-learning. To assess students' competence on cognitive, affective, and psychomotor dimensions, the lecturers performed an observation.

4.2 Operationalization of Variables

Students' competence is measured using three constructs: cognitive, affective, and psychomotor dimensions. Cognitive competence shows students' ability/performance during their study. Referring to previous studies [12, 35] the cognitive construct is measured using students grade point, (1–4 point) drawn from university database. The affective competence is measured using 6 items using the indicator from Miller [23] and Winkel [36]: (1) receiving; (2) responding; (3) value; (4) organization; (5) characterization; and (6) valuing. The psychomotor competence consists of movement and physical coordination, including perception, readiness, reaction, and creativity. The psychomotor competence is measured using 5 questions with the indicators from Winkel [36]: (1) perception; (2) set; (3) response; (4) mechanism; and (5) origination. The PU is measured using 5 question items adopted from Davis [3], Anormaliza et al. [4] with the following indicators: (1) speed of learning process; (2) performance improvement; (3) ease of use; (4) user effectiveness; and (5) user productivity. The PEU is measured using five question items adopted from Davis [3] Alharbi and Drew [9] with 6 question items with the following indicators: (1) perceived ease; (2) perceived experience; and (3) flexibility. BIU is measured using three question items adopted from Davis [3], Alharbi and Drew [9] with the following indicators: (1) intention; (2) prediction; and (3) plan of information system usage. In this study, the responses for point '4' scale for affective and psychomotor items are treated as one category called 'strongly agree'. While, point '1' are treat as one category called 'strongly disagree'.

4.3   Data Analysis Method

Validity and reliability testing of instruments is performed before the data are analyzed. Validity is tested using product-moment correlation with 5% probability. Reliability testing is performed using Cronbach's Alpha with a minimum threshold of 0.6. The gathered data is analyzed using multiple linear regression analysis to find the effect of each variable. The model fit testing is performed using F-test, while the hypothesis testing is performed using a t-test with significance level of 5%. The coefficient of determination is employed to find the strength of relationship between the independent variables and the dependent variable. The hypothesis testing is performed using following regression models:

$$BIU = \alpha + \beta_1.PU + \beta_2.PEU + e \tag{1}$$

$$KOG = \alpha + \beta_3.BIU + e \tag{2}$$

$$AFEK = \alpha + \beta_4.BIU + e \tag{3}$$

$$PSI = \alpha + \beta_5.BIU + e \tag{4}$$

Model 1 is used to test the first hypothesis (H_1) and second the hypothesis (H_2) with BIU as dependent variable, and PU and PEU as independent variable. Model 2, model 3, and model 4 are used to test the third hypothesis (H_3a; H_3b; H_3c) with KOG (cognitive competence), AFEK (affective competence), and PSI (psychomotor competence) as dependent variables and BIU as independent variable.

5   Results and Discussion

The objective of this study was to identify the factors of the behavioral concept of technology users related to students' competences based on empirical analysis. Because the factors referring to technology users' behavior can be identified by measuring students' perceptions, this study selected the students and surveyed them for the purpose of this research. The survey research method is very useful in collecting data from a large number of individuals in a relatively short period of time and at lesser cost [37]. Hence, for the current study, the questionnaire survey was chosen for data collection (See Appendix). This study is based on responses from 128 students from PGRI University Yogyakarta. Based on the results from questionnaires filling (See Table 1) we have 35 (27.3%) male respondents and 93 (72.7%) female respondents. 28.1% are in semester 2, 39.1% are in semester 4, and 32.8% are in semester 6. Based on the

Table 1. Respondents' Demographics

Demographics	Total	Percentage
Gender		
Male	35	27.3%
Female	93	72.7%
Semester		
Semester 2	36	28.1%
Semester 4	50	39.1%
Semester 6	42	32.8%
Usage Frequency		
<10 times (low)	30	23.4%
10–20 times (moderate)	46	35.9%
>20 times (high)	52	40.6%

frequency of usage, 40.6% use e-learning 20 times or more, 35.9% respondents use e-learning 10–20 times, and 23.4% respondents use e-learning <10 times. The results of questionnaire distribution is presented in respondents' demographics in Table 1.

5.1   Validity and Reliability Testing

Validity testing is performed to test the extent to which the instrument can be used as a measuring tool. In this study, validity testing is performed by reviewing the p value in the result of correlation testing using Pearson product-moment. The Pearson correlation is calculates between each item of the questionnaire and the total score. the instrument is valid if $p < 0.05$. Reliability testing is performed to test the extent to which the instrument will generate similar results if re-testing is performed, or showing the consistence of answer from time to time. In this study instrument reliability is tested using Cronbach's Alpha. The instrument is reliable if Cronbach's Alpha > 0.6 [38]. Based on the results of validity and reliability testing (Table 2) we can explain that all instruments were less than < 0.01; thus we can conclude that all instruments are valid. The Cronbach Alpha value of PU is 0.666; PEU of 0.734; BIU of 0.604; AFEK of 0.620; and PSI of 0.602. Based on the testing results, all variables have a Cronbach's Alpha value > 0.6 (all instruments are reliable).

The results of mean value testing on competency are presented at Table 3. The mean value for cognitive competency is on the range 2.96–3.36. The mean value for the affective competency is on the range of 3.04–3.35, while the mean value for the psychomotor competency is on the range of 2.91–3.18. These results mean that the mean value of the high-frequency users of e-learning is higher than that of low-frequency users. However, these results are needed further in-depth study.

5.2   Hypotheses Testing

The analysis results (Table 4) show that all hypotheses proposed in this study are supported. Based on Table 4 we can be explain that PU has a positive effect on BIU (p-value = 0.045, β = 0.256) (hypothesis 1 is supported). PEU has a positive effect on

Table 2. Validity and reliability testing

Variable	Instruments	Pearson correlation	Cronbach' Alpha
Perceived usefulness (PU)	Speed of learning process	0.726**	0.666
	Performance improvement	0.707**	
	Ease of use	0.408**	
	User effectiveness	0.667**	
	User productivity	0.730**	
Perceived ease of use (PEU)	Perceived ease	0.788**	0.734
	Perceived clear and understandability	0.511**	
	Perceived skillful	0.805**	
	Perceived flexibility	0.444**	
	Perceived easiness of usage	0.522**	
	Perceived experience	0.816**	
Behavioral intention to use (BIU)	Intention of using the information system	0.759**	0.604
	Prediction of using the information system	0.742**	
	Plan of using the information system	0.746**	
Affective (AFEK)	Receiving	0.677**	0.620
	Responding	0.542**	
	Value	0.490**	
	Organization	0.662**	
	Characterization	0.574**	
	Valuing	0.575**	
Psychometric (PSI)	Perception	0.585**	0.602
	Set	0.632**	
	Response	0.722**	
	Mechanism	0.650**	
	Origination	0.509**	

**significant at $p < 1\%$

Table 3. Mean rating of competency

Frequency	Cognitive		Affective		Psychomotor	
	Mean	S. Dev.	Mean	S. Dev.	Mean	S. Dev.
<10 times (low)	2.96	0.235	3.04	0.330	2.91	0.300
10–20 times (moderate)	3.23	0.226	3.22	0.356	3.13	0.452
>20 times (high)	3.36	0.179	3.35	0.353	3.18	0.425

BIU (p-value = 0.009, β = 0.366) (hypothesis 2 is supported). BIU has a positive effect on KOG (p-value = 0.004, β = 0.250) (hypothesis 3a is supported). The testing for hypothesis 3b generates a R^2 value of 0.065 significant at 0.004 (hypothesis 3b is supported), while for hypothesis 3c the R^2 value is 0.034 significant at 0.037 (hypothesis 3c is supported).

Table 4. Hypothesis Testing

	Coef β	Sig (t test)	Sig (F test)	R2/Adj R2	Result
PU → BIU	0.256	0.045*	0.000**	0.317/0.306	Supported
PEU → BIU	0.366	0.009**			Supported
BIU → KOG	0.250	0.004**	0.004**	0.063/0.055	Supported
BIU → AFEK	0.255	0.004**	0.004**	0.065/0.058	Supported
BIU → PSI	0.184	0.037*	0.037*	0.034/0.026	Supported

**significant at $p < 1\%$, *significant at $p < 5\%$

Even though Lee *et al.* [13] stated that a person who considers a technology too easy and simple will probably not help in improving performance, however this study provides different evidence. This study results proves that PU has a significant effect on BIU, which is consistent with the study results by [4, 9, 29]. This shows that PU of e-learning will improve the behavior in using e-learning. In line with the concept of TAM, which states that the benefits of PU felt by somebody when implementing technology has a big contribution to IT user. Even if somebody believes that IT is highly beneficial, but feels that the IT is hard to use, then the benefit of implementing it does not match with the improvement of performance [3]. Because of that, individuals will tend to utilize IT if they feel that the technology is easy to use and can assist them in performing a better work [7].

6 Conclusion and Future Work

This study has presented the implementation of Indonesia national qualification framework to improve higher competences of education students by using the technology acceptance model (TAM). The result of this study have proven that the implementation of a technology/information system can improve users' competence, thus very beneficial for organization development. The results of hypothesis testing showed that PU and PEU have a significant effect on BIU. Besides that, BIU also affects information system users' competence. The result of this study proves that universities can implement TAM in the field of information system development. For students, this study implies that their perceived understanding on technology is a very important factor in improving their competence. Universities as education administrators must be able to choose the proper technology, easy to understand, and easy to be used because proper technology may decrease costs [13] and improve effectiveness and efficiency [18]. Technology users' behavior also implies for the organization (university) because the organization can try new methods in developing e-learning [18] by implementing the differentiated strategies based on technology and thus create various innovation opportunities, both for products and services [29].

The limitations and suggestions proposed in this study are: firstly, the researcher conducted a size power test, and the results suggest that the sample size should be increased, as a higher sample size would help draw a more general conclusion [9]. Secondly, this study only tests the implementation of TAM and students' competence in using e-learning; future studies can elaborate the theory of end-user computer satisfaction (EUCS) because a technology that is easy to use and beneficial will affect users' satisfaction [14]. Thirdly, PU and PEU of e-learning depend on individual expectation and can change according to their experience in using the IT [13, 39] compatibility is connected on the fit of technology with prior experiences of users' [10]. Because of this reason, next studies can test respondents' competence based on their experience in using technology/information system. The regression models (model 1, 2, 3) have low of R^2 value. The suggestion for future researchers who are interested in developing the concept of technology adoption would be using the Partial Least Squares (PLS) [40], which can simultaneously test the relationship among variables.

Appendix

Questionnaire for students	
No	Behavioral intention to use
1	I intend to use e-learning in the next semester
2	I predict that I would use e-learning in the next semester
3	I plan to use e-learning in the next semester
No	Perceived usefulness
4	Using e-learning would enable me to accomplish tasks more quickly
5	Using e-learning would make it easier to do my job
6	Using e-learning would improve my job performance
7	Using e-learning in my job would increase my productivity
8	Using e-learning would enhance my effectiveness on the job
No	Perceived ease of use
9	I feel that using e-learning would be easy for me
10	I feel that my interaction with e-learning would be clear and understandable
11	I feel that it would be easy to become skillful at using e-learning
12	I would find e-learning to be flexible to interact with
13	It would be easy for me to get e-learning to do what I want to do
14	I feel that my ability to determine e-learning ease of use is limited by may lack of experience
Questionnaire for teachers	
No	Affective
15	Actively provides idea in group
16	Defends the idea
17	Seriously does all of assignments
18	Accepts recommendations and suggestions
19	Behaves with discipline
20	Accepts the decisions
No	Psychomotor
21	Ability in using tools for serving a presentation

(continued)

(continued)

Questionnaire for students	
No	Behavioral intention to use
22	Ability in arranging material
23	Level of speed in doing the assignments
24	Behavior in doing a presentation
25	Ability in analyzing and answering the questions

References

1. Rahyubi, H.: Teori-teori belajar dan aplikasi pembelajaran motorik; Deskripsi dan tinjauan kritis, Cetakan ke 2, Penerbit Nusa Media, Bandung (2014)
2. Budiarto, D.S.: Accounting information systems (AIS) alignment and non-financial performance in small firm. Int. J. Comput. Netw. 6(2), 15–25 (2014)
3. Davis, F.D.: Perceived usefulness, perceived ease of use, and user acceptance of information technology. MIS Q. 13(3), 319–339 (1989)
4. Anormaliza, R., Sabate, F., Viejo, G.: Evaluating student acceptance level of e-learning system. In: Proceeding of ICERI 2015, Seville, Spain: pp. 2393–2399 (2015)
5. Constantiou, I.D., Mahnke, V.: Consumer behavior and mobile TV service: do men differ from women in their adoption intentions? J. Electr. Commer. Res. 11(2), 127–139 (2010)
6. Cclik, H.E., Yilmaz, V.: Extending the technology acceptance model for adoption of e-shopping by consumer in turkey. J. Electr. Commer. Res. 12(2), 152–164 (2011)
7. Talukder, M., Quazi, A., Sathye, M.: Mobile phone banking usage behavior: an Australian perspective. Australas. Acc. Bus. Financ. J. 8(4), 83–100 (2014)
8. Lane, M., Stagg, A.: University staff adoption of i pads: An empirical study using an extended Technology Acceptance Model. Australas. J. Inf. Syst. 18(3), 53–73 (2014)
9. Alharbi, S., Drew, S.: Using the technology acceptance model in understanding academics behavioral intention to use learning management systems. Int. J. Adv. Comput Sci. Appl. 5(1), 143–155 (2014)
10. Veloo, R., Masood, M.: Acceptance and intention to use the i-learn system in an automotive semiconductor company in the northern region of Malaysia. Procedia Soc. Behav. Sci. 116, 1378–1382 (2014)
11. Lucas Jr., Hendry, C., Spitler, V.K.: Technology use and performance: a field study of broker workstation. Decis. Sci. 30(2), 291–311 (1999)
12. Buche, M.W., Davis, L.R., Vician, C.: Does technology acceptance affect e-learning in a non-technology intensive course. J. Inf. Syst. Educ. 23(1), 42–50 (2012)
13. Lee, Y., Hsieh, Y., Hsu, C.N.: Adding innovation diffusion theory to the technology acceptance model: supporting employee intentions to use e-learning systems. Educ. Technol. Soc. 14(4), 124–137 (2011)
14. Peslak, A., Ceccucci, W., Bhatnagar, N.: Analysis of the variables that affect frequency of use and time spent on text messaging. Issues Inf. Syst. 13(1), 361–370 (2012)
15. Athanassiou, N., McNett, J.M., Harvey, C.: Critical thinking in the management classroom: Bloom's Taxonomy as a learning tool. J. Manag. Educ. 27(5), 553–555 (2003)
16. Kim, H., Chan, H., Gupta, S.: Value-based adoption of mobile internet: an empirical investigation. Decis. Support Syst. 43(1), 111–126 (2007)
17. Moore, T.: Toward an integrated model of it acceptance in healthcare. Decis. Support Syst. 53, 507–516 (2012)

18. Al-Adwan, Al-Adwan, A., Smedley, J.: Exploring students acceptance of e-learning using technology acceptance model in Jordanian universities. Int. J. Educ. Dev. Inf. Commun. Technol. **9**(2), 4–18 (2013)
19. Rovai, A.P., Wighthing, M.J., Baker, J.D., Grooms, L.D.: Development of an instrument to measure perceived cognitive, affective, psychomotor learning in traditional and virtual classroom higher education setting. Internet High. Educ. **12**(1), 7–13 (2009)
20. Bloom, B.S.: Taxonomy of educational objectives: the classification of educational goalss. Longmans, Green, New York (1956)
21. Adams, N.E.: Bloom's taxonomy of cognitive learning objectives. J. Med. Libr. Assoc. **103** (3), 151–153 (2015)
22. Shepard, K.: Higher Education for Sustainability: Seeking affective learning outcomes. Int. J. Sustain. High. Educ. **9**(1), 87–98 (2008)
23. Miller, C.: Improving and enhancing performance in the affective domain of nursing students: insights from the literature for clinical educators. Contemp. Nurse **35**(1), 2–17 (2010)
24. Cazzell, M., Rodriguez, A.: Qualitative analysis of student beliefs and attitudes after an objective structured clinical evaluation: implications for affective domain learning in undergraduate nursing education. J. Nurs. Educ. **50**(12), 711–714 (2011)
25. Gunther, M., Alligood, M.R.: A discipline-specific determination of high quality nursing care. J. Adv. Nurs. **38**(4), 353–359 (2002)
26. Merritt, R.D.: The psychomotor domain: Research Starter Education. Great Neck Publishing, NY (2008)
27. DeRouin, R.E., Fritzsche, B.A., Salas, E.: E-learning in organizations. J. Manag. **31**(6), 920–940 (2005)
28. Lau, S.H., Woods, P.: An investigation of user perception and attitudes toward learning object. Br. J. Edu. Technol. **39**(4), 685–699 (2008)
29. Averdung, A., Wagenfuehrer, D.: Consumers acceptance, adoption and behavioral intention regarding environmentally sustainable innovations. E3 J. Bus. Manag. Econ. **2**(3), 98–106 (2011)
30. Ong, C.S., Lai, J.Y., Wang, Y.S.: Factors affecting engineers acceptance of asynchronous e-learning systems in high-tech companies. Inf. Manag. **14**, 795–804 (2004)
31. Goodhue, D., Thompson, R.L.: Task-technology fit and individual performance. MIS Q. **19**(2), 213–236 (1995)
32. Yu, T.K., Yu, T.Y.: Modeling the factors that affect individuals' utilization of online learning systems: an empirical study combining the task technology fit model with the theory of planned behavior. Br. J. Edu. Technol. **41**(6), 1003–1017 (2010)
33. Zikmund, W.G.: Business research methods. The Dryden Press, Oak Brook (2000)
34. Saunders, M., Lewis, P., Thornhill, A.: Research methods for business student, 5th edn. Person Education Limited, UK (2009)
35. Davis, L.R., Johnson, D.L., Vician, C.: Technology-mediated learning and prior academic performance. Int. J. Innov. Learn. **2**(4), 386–401 (1995)
36. Winkel, W.S.: Psikologi pengajaran, Edisi Lima belas, Penerbit Media Abadi, Yogyakarta (2012)
37. Lee, E., Choi, Y.: A study of the antecedents and the consequences of social network service addition: a focus on organizational behaviors. Glob. Bus. Financ. Rev. **20**(2), 83–93 (2015)
38. Hair, J.R., William, C., Barry, J., Rolph, E.A.: Multivariate data analysis, 7th edn. Prentice Hall, Pearson (2010)
39. Venkatesh, V., Davis, F.D.: Assessing it usage: the role of prior experience. Manag. Inf. S. Q. **19**(4), 561–570 (2000)
40. Budiarto, D.S., Rahmawati, Prabowo, M.A.: Accounting information systems alignment and SMEs performance: A literature review. Int. J. Manag. Econ. Soc.Sci. **4**(2), 58–70 (2015)

Convergence Analysis of MCMC Methods for Subsurface Flow Problems

Abdullah Mamun[1], Felipe Pereira[1], and Arunasalam Rahunanthan[2(✉)]

[1] Department of Mathematical Sciences, University of Texas at Dallas, Richardson,
TX 75080, USA
{axm148730,luisfelipe.pereira}@utdallas.edu
[2] Department of Mathematics and Computer Science, Central State University,
Wilberforce, OH 45384, USA
aRahunanthan@centralstate.edu

Abstract. In subsurface characterization using a history matching algorithm subsurface properties are reconstructed with a set of limited data. Here we focus on the characterization of the permeability field in an aquifer using Markov Chain Monte Carlo (MCMC) algorithms, which are reliable procedures for such reconstruction. The MCMC method is serial in nature due to its Markovian property. Moreover, the calculation of the likelihood information in the MCMC is computationally expensive for subsurface flow problems. Running a long MCMC chain for a very long period makes the method less attractive for the characterization of subsurface. In contrast, several shorter MCMC chains can substantially reduce computation time and can make the framework more suitable to subsurface flows. However, the convergence of such MCMC chains should be carefully studied. In this paper, we consider multi-MCMC chains for a single–phase flow problem and analyze the chains aiming at a reliable characterization.

Keywords: MCMC · Convergence analysis · Subsurface flow

1 Introduction

The primary source of uncertainty in predictive simulations of subsurface flows is the lack of information about the coefficients of the governing partial differential equations. Here we focus on the characterization of rock absolute permeability by addressing an ill-posed inverse problem consisting in determining an ensemble of permeability fields that are consistent with field measurements of fluid fractional flow curves in a few wells. We consider a Bayesian framework using a Markov

F. Pereira—The research by this author is supported in part by the National Science Foundation under Grant No. DMS 1514808, a Science Without Borders/CNPq-Brazil grant and UT Dallas.

A. Rahunanthan—The research by this author is supported by the National Science Foundation under Grant No. HRD 1600818.

© Springer International Publishing AG, part of Springer Nature 2018
O. Gervasi et al. (Eds.): ICCSA 2018, LNCS 10961, pp. 305–317, 2018.
https://doi.org/10.1007/978-3-319-95165-2_22

Chain Monte Carlo (MCMC) method for reconstructing permeability fields and we aim at sampling from the posterior distribution of the characteristics of the subsurface. A computationally expensive step in this method consists in the evaluation of the likelihood, which involves solving systems of partial differential equations with permeability fields as input parameters. There are two difficulties that one has to overcome for an effective posterior exploration in a practical period of time: the cost of fine grid, forward-in-time numerical simulations and the sequential nature of the MCMC.

Parallel versions of MCMC have been developed, and there are two different lines of work: One could run multiple MCMC chains simultaneously in parallel [7] or, alternatively a pre-fetching strategy could be applied to just one MCMC chain [1]. Some of the authors and their collaborators have investigated carefully the pre-fetching technique for porous media flows [8]. Here we focus on a careful investigation of the convergence of multiple MCMCs. We consider a simple subsurface problem, the tracer injection in an aquifer, and we take advantage of state-of-the-art hardware, a GPU cluster, to address the expensive simulations associated with the MCMCs.

This paper is organized as follows. The physical and mathematical modeling of the problem at hand is discussed in Sect. 2. The Karhunen–Loève expansion for the effective parametrization of uncertainty appears in Sect. 3. The Bayesian approach for quantifying uncertainty in permeability fields is presented in Sect. 4. In Sect. 5 the theory we need to assess the convergence of MCMC algorithms is carefully explained. In the numerical experiments in Sect. 6 our main results are presented. Section 7 contains our conclusions.

2   Modeling

We consider a square-shaped subsurface aquifer Ω with a heterogeneous permeability field. The aquifer contains a spill well at one of the corners through which tracer-tagged (or contaminated) water is discharged. We model the transport of the contaminant in terms of a tracer flow problem, in that the concentration of the contaminant does not affect the underlying velocity field. The aquifer is equipped with two monitoring wells, one of which is placed along the diagonal and opposite to the spill well. The other monitoring well is positioned at the center of one of the two sides that enclose the previous monitoring well at the corner (Fig. 1). The pore space is filled with the fluid. The governing equations for the tracer flow problem are given by Darcy's law along with mass conservation:

$$\nabla \cdot \boldsymbol{v} = 0, \quad \text{where} \quad \boldsymbol{v} = -\frac{k}{\mu}\nabla p, \quad \boldsymbol{x} \in \Omega, \tag{1}$$

and

$$\phi(\boldsymbol{x})\frac{\partial c}{\partial t} + \nabla \cdot (c\boldsymbol{v}) = 0, \tag{2}$$

where $\boldsymbol{v}$, c and k represent the Darcy flux, the concentration of the contaminant and the absolute permeability, respectively. The symbols ϕ and μ denote respectively the porosity of the reservoir and the viscosity of the fluid. The porosity, which is one of the two important physical properties of rocks in determining flow patterns, is taken to be a constant (for simplicity) throughout the whole domain.

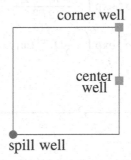

Fig. 1. Physical model of the problem.

In order to characterize the (unknown) permeability field we will consider data in a form of tracer fractional flow curve that is given by

$$F(t) = 1 - \frac{\int_{\partial\Omega_{\text{out}}} v_n c \, dl}{\int_{\partial\Omega_{\text{out}}} v_n \, dl}, \tag{3}$$

where $\partial\Omega_{\text{out}}$ and v_n denote the boundary of the discharged region and the normal component of the velocity field, respectively. The non-dimensional time is symbolized by t which is measured in Pore Volume Injected (PVI) and this PVI is calculated as

$$\text{PVI} = \int_0^T V_p^{-1} \int_{\partial\Omega_{\text{out}}} v_n \, dl \, d\tau, \tag{4}$$

where the total pore volume of the reservoir is denoted by V_p and T stands for the time interval during which the contaminant spill occurred. The coupled system (1) and (2) of PDEs is solved numerically on GPU devices applying an operator splitting technique [13,14]. The three wells in the computational domain are modeled with proper boundary conditions.

3 The Karhunen–Loève Expansion

For computational efficiency, the present study requires a reduction of the extraordinarily large dimension of uncertainty space describing the permeability field. Accordingly, the Karhunen–Loève expansion (KLE) [10,16] accomplished through proper parametrization of the uncertainty space is employed to achieve the desired dimension. Moreover, a standard assumption in the area of geostatistics is to model the permeability field to follow a log-normal distribution [5], i.e.,

$\log [k(\boldsymbol{x}, \omega)] = Y^k(\boldsymbol{x}, \omega)$, where $\boldsymbol{x} \in \Omega \subset \mathbf{R}^2$ and ω represents the random element in the probability field. In addition, $Y^k(\boldsymbol{x}, \omega)$ is a field possessing Gaussian distribution with the covariance function

$$R(\boldsymbol{x}_1, \boldsymbol{x}_2) = \sigma_Y^2 \exp\left(-\frac{|x_1 - x_2|^2}{2L_x^2} - \frac{|y_1 - y_2|^2}{2L_y^2}\right)$$

$$= \sigma_Y^2 \exp\left(-\frac{1}{2}|\boldsymbol{L}^{-1}(\boldsymbol{x}_1 - \boldsymbol{x}_2)|^2\right), \tag{5}$$

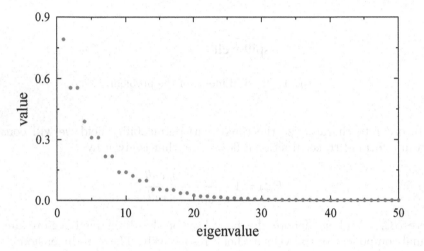

Fig. 2. Eigenvalues of the KLE for the Gaussian covariance with $L_x = L_y = 0.2$ and $\sigma_Y^2 = 4$.

where L_x and L_y are the correlation lengths of $\boldsymbol{L} = \mathrm{diag}(L_x, L_y)$ in x- and y-direction, respectively and $\sigma_Y^2 = E[(Y^k)^2]$. We consider $Y^k(\boldsymbol{x}, \omega)$ as a second–order stochastic process and $E[(Y^k)^2] = 0$. Thus, $Y^k(\boldsymbol{x}, \omega)$ can be expanded as a series with respect to a given arbitrary orthonormal basis $\{\varphi_i\}$ in L^2 as

$$Y^k(\boldsymbol{x}, \omega) = \sum_{i=1}^{\infty} Y_i^k(\omega)\varphi_i(\boldsymbol{x}), \tag{6}$$

with

$$Y_i^k(\omega) = \int_\Omega Y^k(\boldsymbol{x}, \omega)\varphi_i(\boldsymbol{x})d\boldsymbol{x} \tag{7}$$

being functions of random variable. Furthermore, the basis functions $\{\varphi_i\}$ satisfying

$$\int_\Omega R(\boldsymbol{x}_1, \boldsymbol{x}_2)\varphi_i(\boldsymbol{x}_2)d\boldsymbol{x}_2 = \lambda_i\varphi_i(\boldsymbol{x}_1), \quad i = 1, 2, ..., \tag{8}$$

make Y_i^k uncorrelated, and $\lambda_i = E[(Y_i^k)^2] > 0$. Thereby, the assumption $\theta_i^k = Y_i^k/\sqrt{\lambda_i}$ allows θ_i^k to satisfy $E(\theta_i^k) = 0$ and $E(\theta_i^k \theta_j^k) = \delta_{ij}$, and hence

$$Y^k(\boldsymbol{x}, \omega) = \sum_{i=1}^{\infty} \sqrt{\lambda_i} \theta_i^k(\omega) \varphi_i(\boldsymbol{x}) \simeq \sum_{i=1}^{N_k} \sqrt{\lambda_i} \theta_i^k \varphi_i(\boldsymbol{x}). \tag{9}$$

The expansion (9) is called the KLE in which the eigenvalues are assumed to be ordered so that $\lambda_1 \geq \lambda_2 \geq \cdots$. On the other hand, the basis functions $\varphi_i(\boldsymbol{x})$ in the above KLE are deterministic and sort out the spatial dependence of the permeability field. The scalar random variables θ_i^k represent the uncertainty in the expansion and only the leading order terms with respect to the magnitude of λ_i are kept to get most of the energy of the stochastic process $Y^k(\boldsymbol{x}, \omega)$.

4   Bayesian Inference

The Bayesian framework is introduced in this section to sample the permeability field, which is our problem of interest. We do this sampling conditioned on the available fractional flow data F_m from the conditional distribution $P(\psi|F_m)$, where the field ψ represents the vector $\boldsymbol{\theta}^k$ containing the random coefficients in KLE, i.e., $\psi = [\boldsymbol{\theta}^k]$. Bayes' theorem gives

$$\pi(\psi) = P(\psi|F_m) \propto P(F_m|\psi)P(\psi), \tag{10}$$

where the forward solution of the governing equations is required to get the likelihood function $P(F_m|\psi)$. The prior distribution of ψ is given by $P(\psi)$ in (10) and the normalizing constant is disregarded because of the iterative updating procedure. Additionally, the likelihood function is assumed to follow a Gaussian distribution [6]

$$P(F_m|\psi) \propto \exp\left(-(F_m - F_\psi)^\top \Sigma (F_m - F_\psi)\right), \tag{11}$$

where the known permeability k and porosity ϕ are employed for solving the forward problem to get the simulated fractional flow curve F_ψ. The covariance matrix is denoted by $\Sigma = \boldsymbol{I}/2\sigma_F^2$, where $\boldsymbol{I}$ is the identity matrix and σ_F^2 is a precision parameter.

The Metropolis-Hasting MCMC is used to sample the permeability field from the posterior distribution. The goal of MCMC is to create a Markov Chain, which has the stationary distribution $\pi(\psi)$. An instrumental distribution $q(\psi_p|\psi)$, where ψ represents the previously accepted state/parameters in the chain, is used to propose $\psi_p = [\boldsymbol{\theta}_p^k]$ at every iteration. The forward problem is then solved to determine the acceptance probability,

$$\alpha(\psi, \psi_p) = \min\left(1, \frac{q(\psi|\psi_p)P(\psi_p|F_m)}{q(\psi_p|\psi)P(\psi|F_m)}\right), \tag{12}$$

i.e., ψ_p is accepted with probability $\alpha(\psi, \psi_p)$.

5   Convergence Analysis of the MCMC Algorithm

There are several diagnostics [3,4,11] for monitoring the convergence of an MCMC algorithm. A common approach is to start multiple MCMC chains from different initial conditions and to measure when these sequences mix together sufficiently. At convergence, these chains should come from the same distribution, which is determined by comparing the variance and mean of each chain to those of the combined chains. Two most commonly used convergence measures are the Potential Scale Reduction Factor (PSRF) and its multivariate extension (MPSRF). Brooks and Gelman [2] showed that the monitoring PSRF takes into account only a subset of parameters and one may not achieve the right conclusion. On the other hand, MPSRF incorporates the convergence information of all the parameters and their interactions. Thus, MPSRF is a better strategy for checking the convergence of a high-dimensional problem. This method works as follows.

Let us consider the number of parameters be equal to N (in our case $N = 20$) and the vector $\boldsymbol{\theta}^k$ contains these parameters. Let us have m chains with n posterior draws of $\boldsymbol{\theta}^k$ in each chain and $\boldsymbol{\theta}_i^{kt}$ represents the generated value at iteration t in chain i. Then, the posterior variance-covariance matrix in higher dimensions is estimated by

$$\widehat{\mathbf{V}} = \frac{n-1}{n}\mathbf{W} + \left(1 + \frac{1}{m}\right)\frac{\mathbf{B}}{n}, \tag{13}$$

where

$$\mathbf{W} = \frac{1}{m(n-1)}\sum_{i=1}^{m}\sum_{t=1}^{n}\left(\boldsymbol{\theta}_i^{kt} - \bar{\boldsymbol{\theta}}_{i.}^{k}\right)\left(\boldsymbol{\theta}_i^{kt} - \bar{\boldsymbol{\theta}}_{i.}^{k}\right)', \tag{14}$$

and

$$\mathbf{B} = \frac{n}{m-1}\sum_{i=1}^{m}\left(\bar{\boldsymbol{\theta}}_{i.}^{k} - \bar{\boldsymbol{\theta}}_{..}^{k}\right)\left(\bar{\boldsymbol{\theta}}_{i.}^{k} - \bar{\boldsymbol{\theta}}_{..}^{k}\right)' \tag{15}$$

denote the within and between-chain covariance matrix, respectively. Here $\bar{\boldsymbol{\theta}}_{i.}^{k}$ and $\bar{\boldsymbol{\theta}}_{..}^{k}$ represents the respective mean within and between the chain. The MPSRF is determined from n iterations of the MCMC algorithm after discarding first few iterations as a burn-in.

In this case, the comparison of the pooled variance to the within-chain variance requires us to compare the matrices $\widehat{\mathbf{V}}$ and $\mathbf{W}$. Brooks and Gelman [2] summarized this comparison with the maximum root statistic, which gives the maximum scale reduction factor (R^p) of any linear projection of $\boldsymbol{\theta}^k$. The estimate

R^p of MPSRF is defined by

$$
\begin{aligned}
R^p &= \max_a \frac{a'\widehat{\mathbf{V}}a}{a'\mathbf{W}a} \\
&= \max_a \frac{a'\left[\frac{n-1}{n}\mathbf{W} + \left(1 + \frac{1}{m}\right)\frac{\mathbf{B}}{n}\right]a}{a'\mathbf{W}a} \\
&= \frac{n-1}{n} + \left(\frac{m+1}{m}\right)\max_a \frac{a'Ba/n}{a'\mathbf{W}a} \\
&= \frac{n-1}{n} + \left(\frac{m+1}{m}\right)\lambda_1,
\end{aligned}
$$

where λ_1 is the largest eigenvalue of the positive definite matrix $\mathbf{W}^{-1}\mathbf{B}/n$. Notice that the "scale reduction factor" applies to $\sqrt{R^p}$. Thus we can write

$$
\text{MPSRF} = \sqrt{\left(\frac{n-1}{n} + \left(\frac{m+1}{m}\right)\lambda_1\right)}. \tag{16}
$$

Clearly, if the vector θ^k comes from the same posterior distribution, then under the assumption of equal means between sequences, $\lambda_1 \to 0$. Therefore, MPSRF goes to 1.0 for a reasonably large n and draws the convergence of the chains.

As in [2] we define the Potential Scalar Reduction Factor (PSRF) as follows:

$$
\text{PSRF}_p = \sqrt{\frac{\text{diag}(\widehat{\mathbf{V}})_p}{\text{diag}(\mathbf{W})_p}}, \text{where } p = 1, 2, ...N. \tag{17}
$$

where all the PSRF's should be closer to 1 for a convergence of the chains. Moreover,

$$
\widehat{R}^{\max} \leq \widehat{R}^{\text{p}}, \tag{18}
$$

where $\widehat{R}^{\text{p}}$ is the MPSRF defined in (16), applied to the vector of parameters, θ^k and $\widehat{R}^{\max}$ denotes the maximum of the univariate PSRF values.

6   Numerical Studies

In this section the simulations of the tracer flow problem in an aquifer with a heterogeneous permeability field as shown in (Fig. 3) are discussed and the corresponding numerical results are presented. The domain of the study contains a spill well and two monitoring wells and their positions were indicated in Sect. 2. Both the contaminant and the fluid inside the aquifer have the same viscosity. We consider that the uncontaminated aquifer is initially saturated by the fluid, i.e., $c(x, t = 0) = 0$. The contaminated water enters the aquifer at the rate of one pore-volume every 5 years.

The precision σ_F^2 in the likelihood function (11) representing the measurement errors must be fixed a priori [9]. Moreover, the smaller value of σ_F^2 produces the better sampled fractional flow curves. Accordingly, in the current analysis,

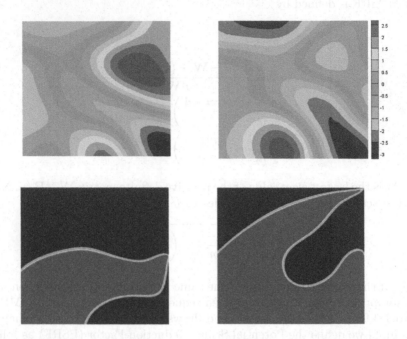

Fig. 3. Top: Left to right the permeability (in log) distributions of the underlying field at 15000 and 20000 accepted proposals, respectively. Bottom: Left to right the contaminant concentration plots at $t = 0.4$ PVI and $t = 0.9$ PVI, respectively.

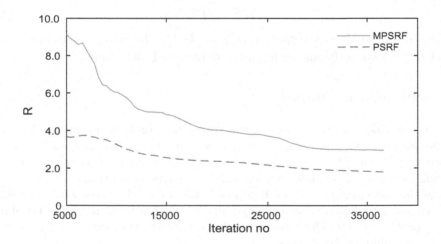

Fig. 4. The maximum of the PSRF's and the MPSRF.

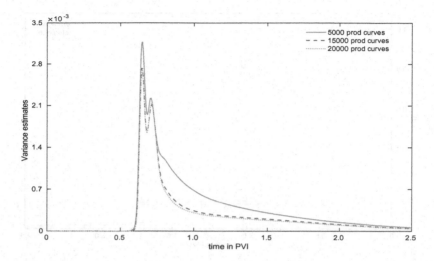

Fig. 5. Variance of fractional flow curves for 5000, 15000 and 20000 samples from each chain for the center well.

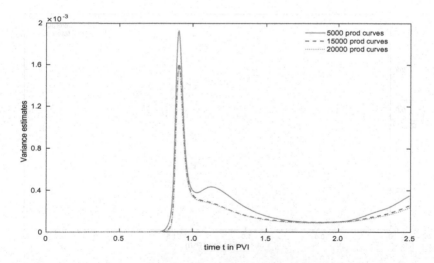

Fig. 6. Variance of fractional flow curves for 5000, 15000 and 20000 samples from each chain for the corner well.

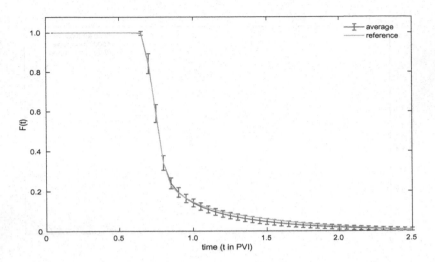

Fig. 7. Average fractional flow curve with error bars (within one standard deviation) and the reference fractional flow curve for the center well.

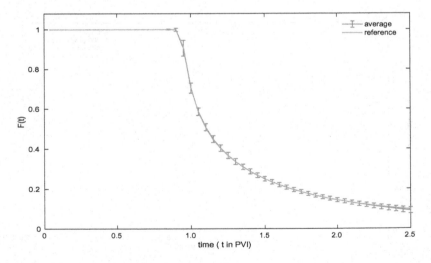

Fig. 8. Average fractional flow curve with error bars (within one standard deviation) and the reference fractional flow curve for the corner well.

we consider $\sigma_F^2 = 10^{-4}$. On the other hand, we take the correlation length $L_x = L_y = 0.2$ and variance $\sigma_Y^2 = 4$ for KLE in (9). Figure 2 reveals that the eigenvalues decay very fast for these values and the first twenty eigenvalues in the KLE should be enough. We use a fine grid of size 128×128 in our simulations. The random walk sampler is set as $\theta_p^k = \beta\,\theta^k + \sqrt{1 - \beta^2}\,\epsilon$, where θ^k is the previously accepted proposal, θ_p^k is the current proposal, β is a tuning parameter and ϵ is a $\mathcal{N}(0, 1)$-random variable. We take $\beta = 0.95$ in our study.

In the Bayesian MCMC, we solve the forward problem until 2.5 PVI and the fractional flow curves are recorded for the accepted profiles in the MCMC chain. All the accepted profiles produce a very similar set of fractional flow curves. For this reason, we aggregate the results of the forward problem to get the average fractional flow curves.

We run six MCMC chains with different initial values. We examine the values of PSRF's and the multivariate measures (MPSRF) for the vector θ^k consisting of twenty parameters of those chains. Figure 4 shows the maximum of the individual PSRF's and MPSRF. The graph confirms that the maximum of the PSRF's is bounded above by the MPSRF as indicated in (18). Figure 4 also gives an indication that the maximum of the PSRF's may get closer to one while the simulations continue, and the same could be said about the MPSRF. Thus, we can say that the six chains mix well and get closer to the convergence.

Figures 5 and 6 show the variances of the fractional flow curves for the center and corner wells, respectively. The variances are computed by taking 5000, 15000 and 20000 fractional flow curves from each chain. The variance curves for 15000 and 20000 look very similar. Thus, it is sufficient to aggregate a maximum of 15000 fractional flow curves to get a reliable estimate of the ensemble uncertainty. However, Fig. 4 shows that we need more MCMC iterations to achieve the statistical convergence.

Figures 7 and 8 show the average fractional flow curves and error bars within one standard deviation, which are computed using 15000 samples from each chain, and the reference fractional flow curves for the center and corner well, respectively. They show that, as expected, the ensemble average fractional flow curves recover the reference solution within one standard deviation.

7   Conclusions

We considered a Bayesian statistical approach to characterize the permeability field with data from a linear transport problem (the tracer flow) in the subsurface. In this approach, we need to compute the likelihood function for each proposal in an MCMC method that is computationally very expensive. It often limits the applicability of the Bayesian framework to such problems. In this paper, we investigated the statistical convergence of a multi-MCMC approach, which can make the Bayesian framework more attractive for subsurface characterization. We determined that the rigorous convergence criterion may require more than 35000 MCMC samples from each chain for a convergence within a stochastic space of dimension 20. We also showed that the primary quantity of interest for porous media flow applications (the standard deviation associated with fractional flow curves) can, in fact, be accurately estimated with about 15000 samples from each chain. Thus, this finding makes MCMC methods more attractive for subsurface flow problems. The authors intend to further investigate faster MCMC procedures (such as, e.g., [12,15]) along the lines of the work described here.

Acknowledgments. The authors would like to thank the Department of Mathematics and Computer Science of the Central State University for allowing to run the MCMC simulations on the NSF-funded CPU-GPU computing cluster.

References

1. Brockwell, A.: Parallel Markov Chain Monte Carlo simulation by pre-fetching. J. Comput. Graph. Stat. **15**(1), 246–261 (2006)
2. Brooks, S., Gelman, A.: General methods for monitoring convergence of iterative simulations. J. Comput. Graph. Stat. **7**, 434–455 (1998)
3. Brooks, S., Roberts, G.: Convergence assessments of Markov Chain Monte Carlo algorithms. Stat. Comput. **8**, 319–335 (1998)
4. Cowles, M.K., Carlin, B.: Markov Chain Monte Carlo convergence diagnostics: a comparative review. J. Am. Stat. Assoc. **91**, 883–904 (1996)
5. Dagan, G.: Flow and Transport in Porous Formations. Springer, Heidelberg (1989). https://doi.org/10.1007/978-3-642-75015-1
6. Efendiev, Y., Hou, T., Luo, W.: Preconditioning Markov Chain Monte Carlo simulations using coarse-scale models. SIAM J. Sci. Comput. **28**(2), 776–803 (2006)
7. Ginting, V., Pereira, F., Rahunanthan, A.: Multiple Markov Chains Monte Carlo approach for flow forecasting in porous media. Procedia Comput. Sci. **9**, 707–716 (2012)
8. Ginting, V., Pereira, F., Rahunanthan, A.: A prefetching technique for prediction of porous media flows. Comput. Geosci. **18**(5), 661–675 (2014)
9. Lee, H., Higdon, D., Bi, Z., Ferreira, M., West, M.: Markov random field models for high-dimensional parameters in simulations of fluid flow in porous media. Technical report, Technometrics (2002)
10. Loève, M.: Probability Theory. Springer, Berlin (1977). https://doi.org/10.1007/978-1-4684-9464-8
11. Mengersen, K.L., Robert, C.P., Guihenneuc-Jouyaux, C.: MCMC convergence diagnostics: a review. In: Bernardo, M., Berger, J.O., Dawid, A.P., Smtith, A.F.M. (eds.) Bayesian Statistics, vol. 6, pp. 415–440. Oxford University Press, Oxford (1999)
12. Neal, R.M.: MCMC Using Hamiltonian Dynamics. Chapman and Hall/CRC Press, Boca Raton (2011)
13. Pereira, F., Rahunanthan, A.: Numerical simulation of two-phase flows on a GPU. In: 9th International Meeting on High Performance Computing for Computational Science (VECPAR 2010), Berkeley, June 2010
14. Pereira, F., Rahunanthan, A.: A semi-discrete central scheme for the approximation of two-phase flows in three space dimensions. Math. Comput. Simul. **81**(10), 2296–2306 (2011)

15. Vrugt, J.: Markov Chain Monte Carlo simulation using the DREAM software package: theory, concepts, and MATLAB implementation. Environ. Model. Softw. **75**, 273–316 (2016)
16. Wong, E.: Stochastic Processes in Information and Dynamical Systems. McGraw-Hill, New York (1971)

Weighting Lower and Upper Ranks Simultaneously Through Rank-Order Correlation Coefficients

Sandra M. Aleixo[1][(✉)] and Júlia Teles[2]

[1] CEAUL and Department of Mathematics, ISEL – Instituto Superior de Engenharia de Lisboa, IPL – Instituto Politécnico de Lisboa, Rua Conselheiro Emídio Navarro, 1, 1959-007 Lisbon, Portugal
`sandra.aleixo@adm.isel.pt`
[2] CIPER and Mathematics Unit, Faculdade de Motricidade Humana, Universidade de Lisboa, Estrada da Costa, 1499-002 Cruz Quebrada – Dafundo, Portugal

Abstract. Two new weighted correlation coefficients, that allow to give more weight to the lower and upper ranks simultaneously, are proposed. These indexes were obtained computing the Pearson correlation coefficient with a modified Klotz and modified Mood scores. Under the null hypothesis of independence of the two sets of ranks, the asymptotic distribution of these new coefficients was derived. The exact and approximate quantiles were provided. To illustrate the value of these measures an example, that could mimic several biometrical concerns, is presented. A Monte Carlo simulation study was carried out to compare the performance of these new coefficients with other weighted coefficient, the van der Waerden correlation coefficient, and with two non-weighted indexes, the Spearman and Kendall correlation coefficients. The results show that, if the aim of the study is the detection of correlation or agreement between two sets of ranks, putting emphasis on both lower and upper ranks simultaneously, the use of van der Waerden, signed Klotz and signed Mood rank-order correlation coefficients should be privileged, since they have more power to detect this type of agreement, in particular when the concordance was focused on a lower proportion of extreme ranks. The preference for one of the coefficients should take into account the weight one wants to assign to the extreme ranks.

Keywords: Monte Carlo simulation · Rank-order correlation
Weighted concordance · Signed Klotz scores · Signed Mood scores
van der Waerden scores

1 Introduction

The Spearman's rank order correlation [20] and Kendall's tau [9] coefficients are widely used to evaluate the correlation, which is equivalent to assess the concordance, between two sets of ranks. Nevertheless, in some cases the agreement

© Springer International Publishing AG, part of Springer Nature 2018
O. Gervasi et al. (Eds.): ICCSA 2018, LNCS 10961, pp. 318–334, 2018.
https://doi.org/10.1007/978-3-319-95165-2_23

should be evaluated differently depending on the location of the ranks to which we intend to give more weight. Indeed, in many practical situations the focus is on the evaluation of agreement among the lower (respectively, upper) ranks, being the disagreement in the remaining ranks negligible. Several coefficients have been proposed to assess the agreement in these situations. Most of them were obtained computing the Pearson correlation coefficient based on weighted scores. This is the case of top-down correlation coefficient [8], which uses the Savage scores [18]. Maturi and Abdelfattab [12] also proposed a weighted rank correlation that weigh the ranks by w^r, where w could assume any value in the interval $]0, 1[$ and r is the rank of observation. Pinto da Costa and Soares [14] and Pinto da Costa et al. [15] proposed two new weighted rank correlation coefficients, in which the weights express the distance between the two ranks through a linear function of them, giving more importance to the upper ranks rather than the lower ones. Other coefficients, that are based on different approaches, have been proposed, such as, the weighted Kendall's tau statistics [19], the Blest's correlation coefficient [1], and the symmetric version of Blest index [5].

While it is true that these indexes are of great relevance, it is also quite important to have available coefficients that allow to give more weight to the lower and upper ranks simultaneously, i.e., coefficients that emphasize the agreement in both extremes of the rankings but not in the center [8]. Some weighted correlation coefficients can be applied in this sense depending on the way the data were ranked. For example, Pinto da Costa et al. [15] in an application to microarray data, used the r_{W2} coefficient to give more weight to the smallest and largest gene expression values, adapting the ranks assignment. However, the van der Waerden correlation coefficient [7,8], also known as Gaussian rank correlation coefficient [2], enables to put more weight in the lower and upper ranks simultaneously using a different strategy, through the plug-in of the van der Waerden scores in the Pearson correlation coefficient formula. Following this idea, in this paper, two new weighted rank correlation coefficients, that allow to put more weight in the most extreme ranks, are proposed. These indexes, that will be defined in the next section, were obtained computing the Pearson correlation coefficient with modified Klotz and modified Mood scores.

The relevance of the issues related to concordance is undoubted due to the widespread use of these measures in several areas, such as medicine, sports and anthropometry. The importance of this topic in medicine is emphasized by the number of articles that annually appear in statistical journals [22]. Despite this finding, the weighted rank concordance topic has been somewhat forgotten, even though its usefulness in several biometrical fields where the concordance on the extreme ranks could be of primordial importance. In many cases, the extreme ranks match with people belonging to risk groups for several diseases. So, when evaluating agreement between two different instruments, methods, devices, laboratories, or observers, the focus in the lower and upper ranks is an important issue. For example, when one wants to evaluate the agreement between two methods of assessing platelet aggregation [23], besides the use of non-weighted measures of agreement, it may be also important to have coefficients that put the focus on the extreme ranks, since they can be associated with individuals that

have thrombocytopenia (a number of platelets lower than normal) or thrombocy-
tosis (a number of platelets higher than normal). A further use of the weighted
rank-order correlation coefficients, that emphasizes both the lower and upper
ranks, is the evaluation of agreement between the ranks resulting from people's
preferences. Indeed, when humans state their preferences, their top and lower
choices are more important and accurate than intermediate ones. This is what
happens in an example of Gould and White [6], where people are asked to rank
their preferences for a fixed number of places on several maps, and it was noted
that it was very simple to rank the places they like and dislike very much, but
there are a number of areas in the middle to which they are indifferent.

The remainder of paper is organized in six sections. Two new rank-order
correlation coefficients, that weight lower and upper ranks simultaneously, are
shown in Sect. 2. In Sect. 3, Gaussian limit distribution of these coefficients is
derived. In Sect. 4, exact and approximate quantiles are listed. An illustrative
example is presented in the Sect. 5. The simulation study results are shown in
Sect. 6, and in Sect. 7 the discussion and conclusions are drawn.

2   Rank-Order Correlation Coefficients to Weigh the Lower and Upper Ranks Simultaneously

The aim of this study is to propose new correlation coefficients that are more
sensitive to agreement at both extremes simultaneously. The idea behind them
is the computation of Pearson correlation coefficient with scores that put more
weight in lower and upper ranks at once, giving them the same importance.

Suppose that n subjects are ranked by two observers producing two sets of
ranks. Let R_{ij} represents the rank assigned to the jth subject by the ith observer,
for $i = 1, 2$ and $j = 1, \ldots, n$. The van der Waerden scores [24],

$$W_{ij} = \Phi^{-1}\left(\frac{R_{ij}}{n+1}\right),$$

are an example of scores that put more weight at both extremes simultaneously.
In this paper, two other scores with similar characteristics are defined: the signed
Klotz scores,

$$SK_{ij} = sign\left(R_{ij} - \frac{n+1}{2}\right)\left(\Phi^{-1}\left(\frac{R_{ij}}{n+1}\right)\right)^2,$$

based on Klotz scores [10], and the signed Mood scores,

$$SM_{ij} = sign\left(R_{ij} - \frac{n+1}{2}\right)\left(R_{ij} - \frac{n+1}{2}\right)^2,$$

adapted from Mood scores [13], where $sign(x) = 1$ if $x \geq 0$, and $sign(x) = -1$ otherwise. For instance, in the case $n = 5$, associated to the vector of
ranks $(1, 2, 3, 4, 5)$, the scores are as follows: $(-0.967, -0.431, 0, 0.431, 0.967)$

for the van der Warden scores; $(-0.935, -0.186, 0, 0.186, 0.935)$ for the signed Klotz scores; $(-4, -1, 0, 1, 4)$ for the signed Mood scores. An example of these three types of scores, for $n = 20$, is presented in Sect. 5. To better understand the behavior of these scores, they are plotted for sample sizes $n = 5, 10, 15, 20, 30, 50, 100, 200, 500$ in Fig. 1. Considering the fact that the range of values of the signed Mood scores are quite different from the range of values of the other scores, the plotted scores were the standardized ones. It can be seen that the three types of scores have different behaviors, being signed Klotz scores those who give more weight to the most extreme ranks. Although the van der Waerden and the signed Mood scores assign similar weights to the extremes ranks, it can be seen that, for smaller sample sizes, the van der Waerden scores give less weight to the extreme ranks than the signed Mood scores, while for higher sample sizes the opposite occurs.

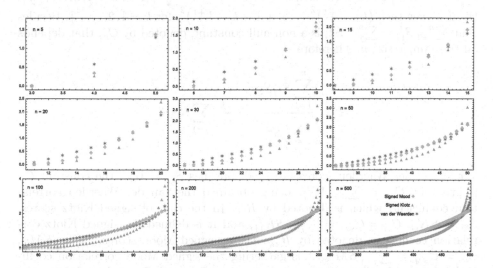

Fig. 1. Graphics of standardized van der Waerden, signed Klotz and signed Mood scores, for several sample sizes.

To simplify the presentation of the van der Waerden and the new coefficients, consider that S_{ij} denotes a generic score, associated to the rank that was awarded by the ith observer to the jth subject, for $i = 1, 2$ and $j = 1, 2, \ldots, n$. The score S_{ij} can be the van der Waerden score W_{ij}, the signed Klotz score SK_{ij}, or the signed Mood score SM_{ij}. We will assume that there are no ties among the variables being ranked. Without loss of generality, the rank-order correlation coefficients, that put more weight on the lower and upper ranks simultaneously, are represented by R_S and can be defined by

$$R_s = \cfrac{n \sum_{j=1}^{n} S_{1j}S_{2j} - \sum_{j=1}^{n} S_{1j} \sum_{j=1}^{n} S_{2j}}{\sqrt{n \sum_{j=1}^{n} S_{1j}^2 - \left(\sum_{j=1}^{n} S_{1j}\right)^2} \sqrt{n \sum_{j=1}^{n} S_{2j}^2 - \left(\sum_{j=1}^{n} S_{2j}\right)^2}}.$$

For any one of the three scores, one has that $\sum_{j=1}^{n} S_{1j} = \sum_{j=1}^{n} S_{2j} = 0$. In the case of van der Waerden and signed Klotz scores: (i) if n odd then $\Phi^{-1}\left(\frac{k}{n+1}\right) = -\Phi^{-1}\left(\frac{n+1-k}{n+1}\right)$, for $k = 1, 2, \ldots, \lfloor\frac{n}{2}\rfloor$, and $\Phi^{-1}\left(\frac{(n+1)/2}{n+1}\right) = \Phi^{-1}\left(\frac{1}{2}\right) = 0$; (ii) if n even then $\Phi^{-1}\left(\frac{k}{n+1}\right) = -\Phi^{-1}\left(\frac{n+1-k}{n+1}\right)$, for $k = 1, 2, \ldots, \frac{n}{2}$. For the signed Mood scores: (i) if n odd then $\left(k - \frac{n+1}{2}\right)^2 = \left(n + 1 - k - \frac{n+1}{2}\right)^2$, for $k = 1, 2, \ldots, \lfloor\frac{n}{2}\rfloor$; (ii) if n even then $\left(k - \frac{n+1}{2}\right)^2 = \left(n + 1 - k - \frac{n+1}{2}\right)^2$, for $k = 1, 2, \ldots, \frac{n}{2}$. Besides that $\sum_{j=1}^{n} S_{1j}^2 = \sum_{j=1}^{n} S_{2j}^2$ is a non null constant, denoted by C_s, that depends on the sample size n. Therefore

$$R_s = \frac{\sum_{j=1}^{n} S_{1j}S_{2j}}{\sum_{j=1}^{n} S_{1j}^2} = \frac{1}{C_s} \sum_{j=1}^{n} S_{1j}S_{2j}.$$

When van der Waerden scores are used, one has $S_{ij} = W_{ij}$, the constant C_s is given by $C_W = \sum_{j=1}^{n} W_{1j}^2$, being obtained the van der Waerden correlation coefficient, which is denoted by R_W. In the case of signed Klotz scores, $S_{ij} = SK_{ij}$, $C_s = C_{SK} = \sum_{j=1}^{n} SK_{1j}^2$, and it is defined the signed Klotz correlation coefficient, denoted by R_{SK}. Using signed Mood scores, $S_{ij} = SM_{ij}$, $C_s = C_{SM} = \sum_{j=1}^{n} SM_{1j}^2$, it is gathering the signed Mood correlation coefficient, denoted by R_{SM}. The coefficients R_W, R_{SK} and R_{SM} take values in the interval $[-1, 1]$. For example, with the two vectors of ranks $(1, 4, 3, 2, 5)$ and $(1, 3, 2, 4, 5)$ one obtains $R_W = 0.75$, $R_{SK} = 0.94$ and $R_{SM} = 0.91$, while in case of Spearman and Kendall's tau coefficients the correlations are $R_{Sp} = 0.70$ and $R_\tau = 0.60$, respectively.

3   The Coefficients Asymptotic Distributions

In this section, the asymptotic distributions of R_W, R_{SK} and R_{SM} are derived, under the null hypothesis of independence between the two sets of rankings. The null hypothesis of independence implies that all permutations of ranks $(R_{11}, R_{12}, \ldots, R_{1n})$ paired with ranks $(R_{21}, R_{22}, \ldots, R_{2n})$ are equally likely. The three correlation coefficients have the same asymptotic distribution, so it can be stated the following result:

Theorem 1. *Considering the null hypothesis of independence in the rankings, then* $\mathbb{E}\left(R_s\right) = 0$, $Var\left(R_s\right) = \frac{1}{n-1}$ *and the statistic* $\sqrt{n-1}\,R_s$ *has asymptotic standard normal distribution.*

Proof. Given $a\left(R_{1j}\right) = S_{1j}/\sqrt{C_s}$ and $a\left(R_{2j}\right) = S_{2j}/\sqrt{C_s}$, it is possible to write R_s as a linear rank statistic:

$$R_s = \frac{\sum_{j=1}^{n} S_{1j} S_{2j}}{C_s} = \sum_{j=1}^{n} \frac{S_{1j}}{\sqrt{C_s}} \frac{S_{2j}}{\sqrt{C_s}} = \sum_{j=1}^{n} a\left(R_{1j}\right) a\left(R_{2j}\right).$$

So, under the null hypothesis of independence between the two sets of rankings, attending to Theorem V.1.8 in Hájek and Šidák [7], the distribution of R_s is asymptotically normal with $\mathbb{E}\left(R_s\right) = 0$ and $Var\left(R_s\right) = \frac{1}{n-1}$, for $n \to +\infty$ (see details in Appendix A1).

4   Exact and Approximate Quantiles

The exact quantiles of R_W, R_{SK} and R_{SM}, for $n = 3(1)10$, are listed in Table 3 (in Appendix A2), and the approximate quantiles for larger n, namely for $n = 11(1)20$ and $n = 30(10)100$, are shown in Table 4 (in Appendix A2). The exact quantiles were easily obtained generating all possible permutations of ranks, and the straightforward procedure is to fix one permutation for the first sample of ranks and to calculate the values of correlation coefficients under all equally likely permutations of ranks of the other sample [21]. The approximate quantiles were obtained by Monte Carlo simulation with 100,000 replicates for each n. The simulations to obtain exact and approximate quantiles were made using package *combinat* [3] of the R software, version 3.0.2. [16].

5   Example

To illustrate the utility of these two new rank-order correlation coefficients, we will consider a set of 20 pairs of ranks, $\{(R_{1j}, R_{2j}), j = 1, \ldots, 20\}$, that are listed in Table 1 and displayed in Fig. 2. Despite the first and the last three ranks

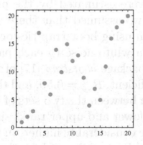

Fig. 2. Scatter plot of the 20 pairs of ranks.

Table 1. Pairs of ranks (R_{1j}, R_{2j}), $j = 1, \ldots, 20$ and the corresponding van der Waerden, signed Klotz and signed Mood scores.

R_{1j}	R_{2j}	W_{1j}	W_{2j}	SK_{1j}	SK_{2j}	SM_{1j}	SM_{2j}
1	1	−1.67	−1.67	−2.78	−2.78	−90.25	−90.25
2	2	−1.31	−1.07	−1.71	−1.14	−72.25	−56.25
3	3	−1.07	−1.31	−1.14	−1.71	−56.25	−72.25
4	17	−0.88	0.88	−0.77	0.77	−42.25	42.25
5	8	−0.71	−0.30	−0.51	−0.09	−30.25	−6.25
6	6	−0.57	−0.57	−0.32	−0.32	−20.25	−20.25
7	14	−0.43	0.43	−0.19	0.19	−12.25	12.25
8	10	−0.30	−0.06	−0.09	0.00	−6.25	−0.25
9	15	−0.18	0.57	−0.03	0.32	−2.25	20.25
10	12	−0.06	0.18	0.00	0.03	−0.25	2.25
11	13	0.06	0.30	0.00	0.09	0.25	6.25
12	9	0.18	−0.18	0.03	−0.03	2.25	−2.25
13	4	0.30	−0.88	0.09	−0.77	6.25	−42.25
14	7	0.43	−0.43	0.19	−0.19	12.25	−12.25
15	5	0.57	−0.71	0.32	−0.51	20.25	−30.25
16	11	0.71	0.06	0.51	0.00	30.25	0.25
17	16	0.88	0.71	0.77	0.51	42.25	30.25
18	18	1.07	1.67	1.14	2.78	56.25	90.25
19	19	1.31	1.31	1.71	1.71	72.25	72.25
20	20	1.67	1.07	2.78	1.14	90.25	56.25

are in total agreement, there is a substantial disagreement in what concerns the remaining ranks, that were obtained through a permutation of the numbers 4 to 17. The van der Waerden, the signed Klotz and the signed Mood scores associated with the two sets of ranks are presented in Table 1.

Spearman, Kendall's tau, van der Waerden, signed Klotz and signed Mood rank-order correlation coefficients were calculated for these data. The 95% bootstrap confidence intervals were estimated by the percentile method, based on 100, 000 samples [4]. Since we assumed that there are no ties among the variables being ranked but when using bootstrap ties occur, we applied a smoothed bootstrap adding a gaussian white noise to each pair of resampled ranks. The results, obtained using the package *bootstrap* [17] of R software, are displayed in Table 2. The Spearman coefficient, $R_{S_p} = 0.59$, and the Kendall's tau, $R_\tau = 0.45$, show a moderate correlation between the two sets of ranks. When the rank-order coefficients, that weigh the lower and upper ranks simultaneously, were applied, the values of correlations are considerably higher. In the case of van der Waerden coefficient, the correlation is $R_W = 0.70$, and for the other coefficients, that put

Table 2. Rank-order correlation coefficients and 95% bootstrap confidence intervals.

Coefficient	Correlation	95% C.I.
Spearman	0.594	(0.086, 0.902)
Kendall's tau	0.453	(0.074, 0.811)
van der Waerden	0.700	(0.258, 0.911)
Signed Klotz	0.910	(0.619, 0.984)
Signed Mood	0.805	(0.425, 0.958)

even more weight in the extreme ranks, the correlation coefficients reach values that reveal higher agreement patterns, $R_{SK} = 0.91$ and $R_{SM} = 0.81$, for the signed Klotz and the signed Mood rank-order correlations, respectively.

6   Simulation Study

A Monte Carlo simulation study was carried out to assess the performance of the two new weighted correlation coefficients, and to compare their performance with the ones attained by the well-known Spearman's rank-order and Kendall's tau correlation coefficients, and with the van der Waerden correlation coefficient. The simulations were made using the R software.

The data generation scheme was similar to the one followed by Legendre [11]. A n-dimensional vector of standard random normal deviates was generated producing the first group of observations. These observations were sorted in ascending order. To obtain the second group of n observations: (i) random normal deviates with zero mean and a suitable chosen standard deviation σ were added to the values of the first group of observations, for $i = 1, \ldots, [np]$ and $i = n - [np] + 1, \ldots, n$ (i.e., for the observations with the most extreme ranks in the first sample), (ii) random normal deviates with zero mean and standard deviation σ were generated, for $i = [np] + 1, \ldots, n - [np]$ (i.e., for the observations with the intermediate ranks in the first sample), with $0 < p < 1$. The ranks of each one of these two groups of observations are the correlated samples of ranks that were considered.

The way the data were simulated allows to obtain samples of ranks in which the correlation in the lower and upper ranks are higher than in the intermediate ranks. The values considered for σ enable to evaluate the performance of coefficients for several intensities of agreement (the lower values of σ correspond to higher degrees of agreement). The two values assigned for the proportion of ranks that were correlated, $p = 0.25$ and $p = 0.1$, allow to compare the performance of the coefficients in a scenario where the concordance was focused on a higher proportion of extreme ranks (scenario 1), with a scenario in which the concordance was targeted for a lower proportion of extreme ranks (scenario 2).

In this simulation study, 60 simulated conditions were evaluated, attending to possible combinations of p ($p = 0.1, 0.25$), n ($n = 20, 30, 50, 100, 200, 500$) and σ ($\sigma = 0.25, 0.5, 1, 3, 5$). In each simulated condition, 10,000 replications were run in order to: (i) obtain the mean and standard deviations of simulated Spearman, Kendall's Tau, van der Waerden, signed Klotz and signed Mood rank-order correlation coefficients; (ii) estimate the power of each coefficient by the percentage of rejected null hypotheses, when testing whether the underlying population concordance coefficient is greater than zero, at 5% significance level.

The simulation results concerning the means and standard deviations of the rank-order correlation coefficients are given in Table 5 (in Appendix A2), while the corresponding powers are shown in Table 6 (in Appendix A2). Following, the most relevant results presented in these tables were analyzed. As expected, the correlation coefficients means estimates and the powers of all indexes in scenario 1 are higher than the respective values attained in scenario 2 (for the same n and σ). This is due to the higher percentage of ranks that are in agreement in scenario 1. For both scenarios, it can be observed that for higher degrees of agreement (smaller values of σ), the means of correlation coefficients estimates, as the respective powers are, obviously, higher than for smaller degrees of agreement (i.e. higher values of σ).

Generally, in both scenarios, the correlation coefficients means and the powers are higher for the three weighed coefficients when compared with the other two non-weighed. Nevertheless, this difference is more evident in scenario 2. It can be further noted that, in scenario 1, for higher degrees of agreement, the means estimates of signed Klotz and signed Mood correlation coefficients and its powers are similar and slightly higher than van der Waerden correlations. Globally, in scenario 2, the means estimates and the powers of signed Klotz coefficients are higher than the respective values for the other two weighted rank-order coefficients; this is more meaningful specially for the higher degrees of agreement.

In scenario 1, for the higher intensities of agreement ($\sigma = 0.25, 0.50, 1$), the five coefficients have high powers for all sample sizes, and for the lower intensities of agreement ($\sigma = 3, 5$), the powers are at least acceptable only for the higher sample sizes. It was considered that, a power is acceptable if its value is around 80%, and it is considered good beyond 90%. In scenario 2, for the higher intensities of agreement ($\sigma = 0.25, 0.50, 1$) and higher sample sizes, the five coefficients have really good powers. For the higher intensities of agreement and smaller sample sizes, while in scenario 1 the powers are quite good for all correlation coefficients, in scenario 2 the powers are quite good only for weighted rank-order correlation coefficients, except for R_W in the case $n = 20$ in which the power is acceptable. For lower degrees of agreement (higher values of σ), in the case of higher proportion ($p = 0.25$) of correlated ranks, the power of non-weighted correlations are similar (sometimes higher) than weighted correlations. Actually, the pairs of rank vectors that result from this combination of parameters have identical levels of correlation in the extremes as in the middle, yielding similar powers for weighted and non-weighted correlation coefficients.

In what concerns type I error rate, Monte Carlo simulations, based on $10,000$ replications, that was done with data obtained from two independent vectors of standard random normal deviates, revealed that the empirical type I error rates were close enough to nominal significance level of 0.05, when testing whether the underlying population concordance coefficient is greater than zero. These results were omitted since they are not essential.

7 Discussion and Conclusions

The two new rank correlation coefficients presented in this paper, signed Klotz and signed Mood, as well as van der Waerden correlation coefficient, have the benefit of putting more weight in lower and upper ranks simultaneously. The behavior of these three coefficients was evaluated, through the comparison with the widely used non-weighted Spearman's rank-order correlation and Kendall's tau coefficients. Other purpose of this paper was to assess whether signed Klotz and signed Mood correlation coefficients can bring an added value in the evaluation of rank concordance, when the objective is to put more emphasis on lower and upper ranks simultaneously. To accomplish this purpose, in Sect. 5 was presented an example, which can be adapted to several situations in biometrical fields, and in Sect. 6 a Monte Carlo simulation study was performed.

In the example that was considered, the first and the last three ranks are in total agreement, but there is a disagreement in the remaining ranks. The values obtained for the three weighed coefficients are considerably higher than for the non-weighed coefficients, moreover the correlations of the two proposed weighted coefficients, which put even more weight in extreme ranks, are the highest.

Based on the simulation study results, it can be stated that, when it is important to emphasize the agreement in lower and upper ranks simultaneously, it should be used one of the weighted correlations coefficients, van der Waerden, signed Klotz or signed Mood, depending on the weight which one wants to give to the extreme ranks. Being the purpose to put more weight on a lower proportion of the most extreme ranks, signed Klotz correlation coefficient should be preferred.

The two proposed weighted rank-order correlation coefficients, as well as van der Warden coefficient, enable the detection of agreement between two sets of ranks, in situations not detected by non-weighted coefficients, namely where the agreement was focused in both extremes of the rankings and what happens in the central ranks is not so important. In some cases this is the purpose of the study and the choice of a weighted rank-order correlation coefficient is obvious. In other situations, the use of two types of correlation coefficients, weighted and non-weighted, can be advantageous, enabling a better understanding of the phenomenon under investigation.

Acknowledgments. Research was partially sponsored by national funds through the Fundação Nacional para a Ciência e Tecnologia, Portugal – FCT, under the projects PEst-OE/SAU/UI0447/2011 and UID/MAT/00006/2013.

A Appendix

A1 Mean and Variance of R_s

Indeed, under the null hypothesis of independence of the two sets of rankings $((R_{11}, R_{12}, \ldots, R_{1n})$ and $(R_{21}, R_{22}, \ldots, R_{2n}))$, the expected value of R_s is zero:

$$\mathbb{E}(R_s) = \mathbb{E}\left(\frac{1}{C_s}\sum_{j=1}^{n} S_{1j}S_{2j}\right) = \frac{1}{C_s}\sum_{j=1}^{n}\mathbb{E}(S_{1j}S_{2j}) = \frac{n}{C_s}\mathbb{E}(S_{1j})\mathbb{E}(S_{2j}) = 0.$$

In fact, the expected values of each one of the variables S_{ij}, with $i = 1, 2$ and $j = 1, \ldots, n$, is zero, since it is an expected value of a function of a discrete uniform variable in n points, X_{ij}, with probability function $f_{X_{ij}}(x) = \frac{1}{n}$, i.e.,

$$\mathbb{E}(S_{ij}) = \mathbb{E}(g(X_{ij})) = \sum_{j=1}^{n}g(x)f_{X_{ij}}(x) = \frac{1}{n}\sum_{j=1}^{n}s_{ij} = 0.$$

Note that for the van der Waerden and for the signed Klotz correlation coefficients one has $X_{ij} = \frac{R_{ij}}{n+1}$, but while $g(X_{ij}) = \Phi^{-1}(X_{ij})$ in van der Waerden case, $g(X_{ij}) = sign\left(R_{ij} - \frac{n+1}{2}\right)\left(\Phi^{-1}(X_{ij})\right)^2$ for the signed Klotz. In the case of signed Mood correlation coefficient, $X_{ij} = R_{ij} - \frac{n+1}{2}$ and $g(X_{ij}) = sign(X_{ij})X_{ij}^2$.

In what concerns the variance of R_s, under the null hypothesis of independence between the two sets of rankings, one has:

$$Var(R_s) = Var\left(\frac{1}{C_s}\sum_{j=1}^{n}S_{1j}S_{2j}\right) = \frac{1}{C_s^2}Var\left(\sum_{j=1}^{n}S_{1j}S_{2j}\right). \tag{1}$$

As a matter of fact,

$$Var\left(\sum_{j=1}^{n}S_{1j}S_{2j}\right)$$
$$= nVar(S_{1j})Var(S_{2j}) + n(n-1)Cov(S_{1j}, S_{1k})Cov(S_{2j}, S_{2k})$$
$$= n(Var(S_{1j}))^2 + n(n-1)(Cov(S_{1j}, S_{1k}))^2.$$

Attending to the fact that

$$Var(S_{1j}) = \mathbb{E}(S_{1j}^2) - \mathbb{E}^2(S_{1j}) = \mathbb{E}(S_{1j}^2) = \sum_{j=1}^{n}(g(x))^2 f_{X_{ij}}(x) = \frac{C_s}{n}$$

and, considering the joint probability function of the random sample (X_{1j}, X_{1k}), $f_{(X_{1j}, X_{1k})}(x_{1j}, x_{1k}) = \frac{1}{n(n-1)}$, for $j \neq k$ and $j, k = 1, \ldots, n$, then

$$Cov(S_{1j}, S_{1k}) = \mathbb{E}(S_{1j}S_{1k}) - \mathbb{E}(S_{1j})\mathbb{E}(S_{1k}) = \mathbb{E}(S_{1j}S_{1k}) = \mathbb{E}(g(X_{1j})g(X_{1k}))$$
$$= \sum_{j \neq k}g(x_{1j})g(x_{1k})f_{(X_{1j}, X_{1k})}(x_{1j}, x_{1k}) = \frac{1}{n(n-1)}\sum_{j \neq k}s_{1j}s_{1k}$$
$$= \frac{1}{n(n-1)}\left[\left(\sum_{j=1}^{n}s_{1j}\right)^2 - \sum_{j=1}^{n}s_{1j}^2\right] = -\frac{C_s}{n(n-1)}.$$

Therefore

$$Var\left(\sum_{j=1}^{n} S_{1j}S_{2j}\right) = n\left(Var\left(S_{1j}\right)\right)^2 + n(n-1)\left(Cov\left(S_{1j}, S_{1k}\right)\right)^2$$

$$= n\left(\frac{C_S}{n}\right)^2 + n(n-1)\left(-\frac{C_S}{n(n-1)}\right)^2 = \frac{C_S^2}{n-1}. \quad (2)$$

Finally, from Eqs. (1) and (2), it follows that $Var\left(R_s\right) = \frac{1}{n-1}$.

A2   Tables

Table 3. Exact quantiles of R_W, R_{SK}, and R_{SM}

n	.90	.95	.975	.99	.995	.999	.9999
van der Waerden coefficients							
3	1	1	1	1	1	1	1
4	.7760	0.8338	1	1	1	1	1
5	.6858	.7889	.8727	.9173	1	1	1
6	.6021	.7293	.8013	.8723	.9501	1	1
7	.5507	.6649	.7611	.8453	.8791	.9398	1
8	.5070	.6214	.7094	.7942	.8430	.9171	.9755
9	.4711	.5833	.6682	.7539	.8030	.8846	.9507
10	.4423	.5501	.6335	.7189	.7696	.8551	.9274
Signed Klotz coefficients							
3	1	1	1	1	1	1	1
4	.5899	.9837	1	1	1	1	1
5	.5954	.7024	.9442	.9811	1	1	1
6	.5667	.6505	.8899	.9623	.9705	1	1
7	.5237	.6281	.7899	.9105	.9396	.9895	1
8	.4916	.5985	.7128	.8422	.9025	.9497	.9932
9	.4587	.5663	.6628	.7930	.8574	.9253	.9839
10	.4331	.5393	.6302	.7487	.8174	.8991	.9662
Signed Mood coefficients							
3	1	1	1	1	1	1	1
4	.6098	.9756	1	1	1	1	1
5	.6176	.7426	.9132	.9706	1	1	1
6	.5646	.6864	.8274	.9406	.9547	1	1
7	.5357	.6531	.7602	.8673	.9031	.9796	1
8	.4974	.6133	.7033	.8063	.8604	.9247	.9865
9	.4661	.5763	.6610	.7585	.8150	.8983	.9689
10	.4394	.5447	.6281	.7185	.7745	.8658	.9419

Table 4. Approximate quantiles of R_W, R_{SK}, and R_{SM}.

n	.90	.95	.975	.99	.995	.999	.9999
	van der Waerden coefficients						
11	.4186	.5214	.6024	.6874	1	1	1
12	.3960	.4962	.5772	.6606	.7126	.8048	.8883
13	.3789	.4758	.5529	.6345	.6861	.7754	.8508
14	.3648	.4569	.5341	.6111	.6600	.7520	.8374
15	.3529	.4420	.5141	.5918	.6412	.7373	.8165
16	.3388	.4256	.5007	.5782	.6275	.7192	.8141
17	.3275	.4143	.4838	.5594	.6124	.6897	.7936
18	.3152	.3975	.4677	.5438	.5938	.6863	.7622
19	.3087	.3908	.4570	.5316	.5771	.6569	.7384
20	.2991	.3788	.4431	.5148	.5599	.6460	.7352
30	.2399	.3062	.3624	.4235	.4644	.5369	.6505
40	.2069	.2625	.3099	.3670	.4019	.4737	.5669
50	.1828	.2343	.2782	.3276	.3602	.4264	.4963
60	.1660	.2137	.2529	.2969	.3276	.3877	.4614
70	.1567	.2003	.2371	.2785	.3070	.3663	.4300
80	.1453	.1863	.2206	.2603	.2879	.3403	.4157
90	.1358	.1745	.2078	.2438	.2702	.3226	.3826
100	.1288	.1657	.1963	.2312	.2563	.3088	.3557
	Signed Klotz coefficients						
11	.4121	.5144	.6006	.7126	1	1	1
12	.3923	.4914	.5768	.6757	.7480	.8480	.9205
13	.3725	.4709	.5551	.6495	.7161	.8142	.8815
14	.3575	.4530	.5342	.6300	.6920	.7899	.8957
15	.3502	.4404	.5169	.6052	.6594	.7735	.8550
16	.3355	.4261	.5041	.5892	.6462	.7625	.8522
17	.3239	.4124	.4866	.5701	.6261	.7261	.8281
18	.3114	.3974	.4711	.5557	.6086	.7162	.8113
19	.3074	.3884	.4598	.5394	.5905	.6968	.8061
20	.2973	.3776	.4457	.5250	.5731	.6771	.7788
30	.2381	.3055	.3635	.4283	.4734	.5695	.6693
40	.2053	.2637	.3141	.3718	.4132	.5006	.5805
50	.1817	.2334	.2811	.3330	.3698	.4429	.5202
60	.1650	.2119	.2536	.3007	.3356	.3996	.5002
70	.1555	.1992	.2368	.2820	.3135	.3696	.4492
80	.1440	.1848	.2199	.2629	.2922	.3577	.4256
90	.1352	.1740	.2091	.2479	.2743	.3331	.4020
100	.1278	.1649	.1978	.2347	.2623	.3126	.3731

(continued)

Table 4. (*continued*)

n	.90	.95	.975	.99	.995	.999	.9999
Signed Mood coefficients							
11	.4178	.5169	.5981	.6864	1	1	1
12	.3963	.4940	.5730	.6611	.7125	.8127	.8939
13	.3778	.4741	.5488	.6336	.6853	.7780	.8802
14	.3633	.4544	.5313	.6107	.6580	.7553	.8564
15	.3539	.4412	.5124	.5877	.6394	.7372	.8262
16	.3386	.4254	.4995	.5767	.6204	.7201	.8181
17	.3273	.4134	.4835	.5596	.6060	.6925	.7998
18	.3159	.3986	.4658	.5416	.5910	.6811	.7760
19	.3090	.3901	.4555	.5297	.5757	.6594	.7508
20	.2997	.3786	.4427	.5122	.5592	.6422	.7396
30	.2396	.3057	.3603	.4243	.4642	.5341	.6302
40	.2059	.2628	.3102	.3648	.4031	.4780	.5688
50	.1828	.2334	.2785	.3292	.3607	.4211	.5055
60	.1666	.2130	.2522	.2961	.3263	.3880	.4680
70	.1564	.2001	.2372	.2786	.3071	.3622	.4259
80	.1458	.1862	.2207	.2598	.2887	.3443	.4043
90	.1366	.1740	.2074	.2439	.2698	.3204	.3812
100	.1288	.1649	.1969	.2312	.2568	.3055	.3551

Table 5. Mean (standard deviation) of Spearman, Kendall's Tau, van der Waerden, signed Klotz, and signed Mood correlation coefficient estimates, for two scenarios: on the left, the concordance was targeted for a higher proportion ($p = 0.25$) of extreme ranks, and on the right, the concordance was focused on a lower proportion ($p = 0.1$) of extreme ranks.

n	σ	Scenario 1 ($p = 0.25$)					Scenario 2 ($p = 0.1$)				
		R_{Sp}	R_τ	R_W	R_{SK}	R_{SM}	R_{Sp}	R_τ	R_W	R_{SK}	R_{SM}
20	0.25	.81(.06)	.67(.08)	.86(.05)	.92(.05)	.91(.04)	.38(.15)	.28(.13)	.48(.13)	.71(.08)	.55(.11)
	0.5	.75(.09)	.59(.10)	.79(.08)	.83(.09)	.83(.08)	.37(.16)	.27(.13)	.46(.14)	.66(.11)	.52(.13)
	1	.58(.15)	.43(.13)	.61(.14)	.62(.16)	.63(.14)	.29(.19)	.21(.14)	.36(.18)	.47(.19)	.39(.18)
	3	.25(.21)	.18(.16)	.26(.21)	.26(.22)	.27(.21)	.13(.22)	.09(.16)	.15(.22)	.18(.23)	.16(.22)
	5	.15(.22)	.11(.16)	.16(.22)	.16(.23)	.17(.22)	.08(.23)	.05(.16)	.09(.23)	.11(.23)	.10(.23)
30	0.25	.86(.04)	.71(.05)	.89(.03)	.93(.04)	.94(.02)	.42(.12)	.31(.10)	.54(.09)	.76(.05)	.59(.08)
	0.5	.79(.07)	.62(.07)	.82(.06)	.84(.07)	.85(.06)	.41(.12)	.29(.10)	.52(.10)	.72(.08)	.57(.10)
	1	.60(.12)	.45(.10)	.63(.11)	.63(.13)	.65(.11)	.33(.14)	.23(.11)	.40(.14)	.52(.15)	.43(.14)
	3	.26(.17)	.18(.12)	.28(.17)	.27(.17)	.28(.17)	.14(.18)	.10(.13)	.17(.18)	.19(.19)	.17(.18)
	5	.16(.18)	.11(.13)	.17(.18)	.16(.18)	.17(.18)	.09(.18)	.06(.13)	.10(.18)	.12(.19)	.10(.18)
50	0.25	.83(.03)	.67(.04)	.88(.02)	.94(.03)	.93(.02)	.45(.09)	.32(.07)	.58(.07)	.80(.03)	.63(.06)
	0.5	.77(.05)	.60(.05)	.82(.04)	.85(.06)	.85(.04)	.44(.09)	.31(.07)	.56(.07)	.76(.05)	.60(.07)
	1	.60(.09)	.43(.07)	.63(.08)	.64(.10)	.65(.09)	.35(.11)	.25(.08)	.44(.10)	.56(.12)	.46(.10)
	3	.26(.13)	.18(.09)	.28(.13)	.27(.14)	.28(.13)	.15(.14)	.11(.09)	.18(.14)	.21(.14)	.19(.14)
	5	.16(.14)	.11(.09)	.17(.14)	.16(.14)	.17(.14)	.10(.14)	.07(.10)	.11(.14)	.13(.14)	.12(.14)
100	0.25	.86(.02)	.70(.03)	.90(.01)	.95(.02)	.94(.01)	.47(.06)	.34(.05)	.61(.04)	.83(.02)	.65(.04)
	0.5	.79(.03)	.61(.04)	.84(.03)	.86(.04)	.87(.03)	.46(.06)	.33(.05)	.59(.05)	.79(.03)	.62(.04)
	1	.61(.06)	.44(.05)	.65(.06)	.65(.07)	.67(.06)	.37(.08)	.26(.06)	.46(.07)	.59(.08)	.48(.07)
	3	.27(.09)	.18(.06)	.29(.09)	.27(.10)	.29(.09)	.16(.10)	.11(.07)	.19(.10)	.22(.10)	.20(.10)
	5	.17(.10)	.11(.07)	.18(.10)	.17(.10)	.18(.10)	.10(.10)	.07(.07)	.12(.10)	.13(.10)	.12(.10)
200	0.25	.86(.01)	.70(.02)	.91(.01)	.95(.01)	.95(.01)	.48(.04)	.35(.03)	.63(.03)	.85(.01)	.66(.03)
	0.5	.80(.02)	.62(.02)	.84(.02)	.86(.03)	.87(.02)	.47(.04)	.33(.03)	.60(.03)	.80(.02)	.64(.03)
	1	.62(.04)	.45(.04)	.66(.04)	.65(.05)	.67(.04)	.38(.05)	.26(.04)	.48(.05)	.60(.06)	.49(.05)
	3	.27(.06)	.18(.04)	.29(.06)	.27(.07)	.29(.06)	.17(.07)	.11(.05)	.20(.07)	.23(.07)	.20(.07)
	5	.17(.07)	.11(.05)	.18(.07)	.17(.07)	.18(.07)	.10(.07)	.07(.05)	.12(.07)	.14(.07)	.12(.07)
500	0.25	.86(.01)	.70(.01)	.91(.01)	.95(.01)	.95(.01)	.48(.03)	.35(.02)	.64(.02)	.86(.01)	.67(.02)
	0.5	.80(.01)	.62(.02)	.85(.01)	.87(.02)	.87(.01)	.47(.03)	.34(.02)	.62(.02)	.81(.02)	.64(.02)
	1	.62(.03)	.45(.02)	.66(.02)	.66(.03)	.67(.02)	.38(.03)	.27(.02)	.49(.03)	.61(.04)	.50(.03)
	3	.27(.04)	.18(.03)	.29(.04)	.27(.04)	.29(.04)	.17(.04)	.12(.03)	.21(.04)	.23(.05)	.21(.04)
	5	.17(.04)	.11(.03)	.18(.04)	.17(.04)	.18(.04)	.11(.04)	.07(.03)	.13(.04)	.14(.05)	.13(.04)

Table 6. Powers (%) of Spearman, Kendall's Tau, van der Waerden, signed Klotz, and signed Mood correlation coefficients, for two scenarios: on the left, the concordance was targeted for a higher proportion ($p = 0.25$) of extreme ranks, and on the right, the concordance was focused on a lower proportion ($p = 0.1$) of extreme ranks.

n	σ	Scenario 1 ($p = 0.25$)					Scenario 2 ($p = 0.1$)				
		R_{Sp}	R_τ	R_W	R_{SK}	R_{SM}	R_{Sp}	R_τ	R_W	R_{SK}	R_{SM}
20	0.25	100.00	100.00	100.00	100.00	100.00	51.99	53.83	79.31	99.94	93.04
	0.50	99.84	99.78	99.95	99.93	99.96	49.35	51.00	73.53	97.62	86.18
	1	90.08	89.71	93.36	92.58	94.51	33.79	34.69	47.40	70.48	55.32
	3	28.80	28.25	30.98	29.84	32.39	13.51	13.18	15.55	19.36	16.69
	5	16.44	16.04	17.45	17.25	18.11	9.65	9.40	10.59	12.12	11.07
30	0.25	100.00	100.00	100.00	100.00	100.00	83.60	83.42	99.41	100.00	99.99
	0.50	100.00	100.00	100.00	100.00	100.00	79.75	79.58	97.87	99.94	99.29
	1	98.80	98.79	99.30	98.90	99.50	56.68	58.01	76.62	90.81	82.00
	3	42.16	42.19	45.14	42.14	46.27	18.72	18.97	22.62	27.84	23.63
	5	22.39	22.58	23.59	21.98	23.86	11.56	11.54	12.86	15.47	13.61
50	0.25	100.00	100.00	100.00	100.00	100.00	99.29	98.73	100.00	100.00	100.00
	0.50	100.00	100.00	100.00	100.00	100.00	98.76	98.01	100.00	100.00	100.00
	1	99.94	99.93	99.98	99.98	99.97	85.64	85.60	96.64	99.16	97.62
	3	58.94	59.07	63.73	60.51	65.55	28.21	28.39	35.39	43.78	36.94
	5	29.66	30.00	32.80	30.92	33.37	16.27	16.43	19.83	23.42	20.77
100	0.25	100.00	100.00	100.00	100.00	100.00	100.00	100.00	100.00	100.00	100.00
	0.50	100.00	100.00	100.00	100.00	100.00	100.00	100.00	100.00	100.00	100.00
	1	100.00	100.00	100.00	100.00	100.00	99.50	99.40	99.99	100.00	100.00
	3	86.76	86.72	90.65	86.97	91.48	49.92	50.20	62.60	70.05	64.00
	5	52.07	52.19	56.34	51.54	57.02	26.27	26.16	32.85	38.23	33.77
200	0.25	100.00	100.00	100.00	100.00	100.00	100.00	100.00	100.00	100.00	100.00
	0.50	100.00	100.00	100.00	100.00	100.00	100.00	100.00	100.00	100.00	100.00
	1	100.00	100.00	100.00	100.00	100.00	100.00	100.00	100.00	100.00	100.00
	3	99.09	99.11	99.63	99.04	99.65	77.95	77.97	89.81	93.75	90.01
	5	77.06	77.17	82.60	76.25	83.27	42.23	42.41	54.35	59.85	54.88
500	0.25	100.00	100.00	100.00	100.00	100.00	100.00	100.00	100.00	100.00	100.00
	0.50	100.00	100.00	100.00	100.00	100.00	100.00	100.00	100.00	100.00	100.00
	1	100.00	100.00	100.00	100.00	100.00	100.00	100.00	100.00	100.00	100.00
	3	100.00	100.00	100.00	100.00	100.00	98.90	98.91	99.87	99.96	99.90
	5	98.38	98.35	99.40	98.40	99.51	77.45	77.47	88.56	91.58	89.07

References

1. Blest, D.C.: Rank correlation - an alternative measure. Aust. N. Z. J. Stat. **42**, 101–111 (2000)
2. Boudt, K., Cornelissen, J., Croux, C.: The Gaussian rank correlation estimator: robustness properties. Stat. Comput. **22**(2), 471–483 (2012)
3. Chasalow, S.: combinat: combinatorics utilities. R package version 0.0-8. (2012). http://CRAN.R-project.org/package=combinat

4. Efron, B., Tibshirani, R.J.: An Introduction to the Bootstrap. Chapman and Hall, New York (1993)
5. Genest, C., Plante, J.F.: On Blest's measure of rank correlation. Can. J. Stat. **31**, 35–52 (2003)
6. Gould, P., White, R.: Mental Maps, 2nd edn. Routledge, London (1986)
7. Hájek, J., Šidák, Z.: Theory of Rank Tests. Academic Press, New York (1972)
8. Iman, R.L., Conover, W.J.: A measure of top-down correlation. Technometrics **29**, 351–357 (1987)
9. Kendall, M.G.: A new measure of rank correlation. Biometrika **30**, 81–93 (1938)
10. Klotz, J.: Nonparametric tests for scale. Ann. Math. Stat. **33**, 498–512 (1962)
11. Legendre, P.: Species associations: the Kendall coefficient of concordance revisited. J. Agric. Biol. Environ. Stat. **10**, 226–245 (2005)
12. Maturi, T., Abdelfattah, E.: A new weighted rank correlation. J. Math. Stat. **4**, 226–230 (2008)
13. Mood, A.M.: On the asymptotic efficiency of certain nonparametric two-sample tests. Ann. Math. Stat. **25**, 514–522 (1954)
14. Pinto da Costa, J., Soares, C.: A weighted rank measure of correlation. Aust. N. Z. J. Stat. **47**, 515–529 (2005)
15. Pinto da Costa, J., Alonso, H., Roque, L.: A weighted principal component analysis and its application to gene expression data. IEEE/ACM Trans. Comput. Biol. Bioinform. **8**(1), 246–252 (2011)
16. R Core Team: R: a language and environment for statistical computing. R Foundation for Statistical Computing, Vienna, Austria (2013). http://www.r-project.org/
17. S original, from StatLib and by Rob Tibshirani. R port by Friedrich Leisch: bootstrap: Functions for the Book "An Introduction to the Bootstrap". R package version 2015.2 (2015). http://CRAN.R-project.org/package=bootstrap
18. Savage, I.R.: Contributions to the theory of rank order statistics – the two-sample case. Ann. Math. Stat. **27**, 590–615 (1956)
19. Shieh, G.S.: A weighted Kendall's tau statistic. Stat. Prob. Lett. **39**, 17–24 (1998)
20. Spearman, C.: The proof and measurement of association between two things. Am. J. Psychol. **15**, 72–101 (1904)
21. Sprent, P., Smeeton, N.C.: Applied Nonparametric Statistical Methods, 4th edn. Chapman and Hall/CRC, Boca Raton (2007)
22. Teles, J.: Concordance coefficients to measure the agreement among several sets of ranks. J. Appl. Stat. **39**, 1749–1764 (2012)
23. Tóth, O., Calatzis, A., Penz, S., Losonczy, H., Siess, W.: Multiple electrode aggregometry: a new device to measure platelet aggregation in whole blood. Thrombosis Haemost. **96**, 781–788 (2006)
24. van der Waerden, B.L.: Order tests for the two-sample problem and their power. In: Proceedings of the Koninklijke Nederlandse Akademie van Wetenschappen, Series A, vol. 55, pp. 453–458 (1952)

A Cusp Catastrophe Model
for Satisfaction, Conflict, and Conflict
Management in Teams

Isabel Dórdio Dimas[1,2]([✉]) [iD], Teresa Rebelo[3,4] [iD], Paulo Renato Lourenço[3,4] [iD],
and Humberto Rocha[5,6] [iD]

[1] ESTGA, Universidade de Aveiro, 3750-127 Águeda, Portugal
idimas@ua.pt
[2] GOVCOPP, Universidade de Aveiro, 3810-193 Aveiro, Portugal
[3] IPCDVS, Universidade de Coimbra, 3001-802 Coimbra, Portugal
[4] FPCEUC, Universidade de Coimbra, 3000-115 Coimbra, Portugal
{terebelo,prenato}@fpce.uc.pt
[5] CeBER and FEUC, Universidade de Coimbra, 3004-512 Coimbra, Portugal
hrocha@mat.uc.pt
[6] INESC-Coimbra, 3030-290 Coimbra, Portugal

Abstract. Teams are now a structural feature in organizations, and
conflict, which is recognized as an inescapable phenomenon in the team
context, has become an area of increased research interest. While the
literature shows contradictory results regarding the impact of conflicts
on teams, the strategies used to manage them have shown that can help
to explain the differentiated effects of conflict situations. Adopting a
nonlinear dynamic system perspective, this research tests a cusp catastrophe model for explaining team members' satisfaction, considering the
roles of conflict and of conflict management. In this model, the conflict
type is the asymmetry variable and conflict-handling strategies are the
bifurcation variables. The sample is composed of 44 project teams, and
data was collected at two points (half-way through and at the end of
the project). The presence of a cusp catastrophe structure in the data
was tested through both the dynamic difference equation modeling approach, which implements the least squares regression technique, and the
indirect method, which uses the maximum likelihood estimation of the
parameters. The results suggest that the cusp model is superior to the
linear model when the bifurcation variables are passive strategies, while
less clear results were found when active strategies are considered. Thus,
the findings show a tendency for a nonlinear effect of passive strategies
on members' satisfaction. Accordingly, this study contributes to the literature by presenting passive conflict-handling strategies in a bifurcation
role, which suggests that beyond a certain threshold of the use of these
kind of strategies, teams might oscillate between two attractors.

Keywords: Cusp model · Nonlinear analysis · Teams · Satisfaction

© Springer International Publishing AG, part of Springer Nature 2018
O. Gervasi et al. (Eds.): ICCSA 2018, LNCS 10961, pp. 335–350, 2018.
https://doi.org/10.1007/978-3-319-95165-2_24

1   Introduction

Modern organizations, more than at any other time in history, rely on groups as a way of structuring their activities. The belief that the use of groups is related to improvements in terms of quality, performance and innovation has led to the proliferation of this strategy of organizing the work [1]. Assuming that teams are created with the aim of generating value for the organization, a significant part of the research developed in this area has been trying to identify the conditions that contribute to team effectiveness (e.g., [2,3]). Team effectiveness is a multi-dimensional construct that integrates several dimensions, ranging from criteria more related to the task system of the team, such as performance or innovation, to criteria that concern the affective system of the team, like the quality of the group experience or satisfaction [4,5].

According to Hackman [4], team effectiveness can be evaluated through three different dimensions: (a) the degree to which the team's results meet, or exceed, the standards of quantity and quality of those who receive, review, and/or use it; (b) the extent to which social processes within the team maintain, or enhance, the ability of the group to work together in the future; and (c) the degree to which the group experience satisfies the social needs of its members, contributing to an increase in well-being and development. In the present paper, our focus is on the processes that influence team members' satisfaction, which is in line with the third dimension of Hackman's three dimensional approach [4]. Satisfaction with the team can be defined as an affective response from members to the team, to its characteristics and to the way it functions [6,7]. Although organizational teams are created, essentially, with the purpose of achieving task results, their ability to meet the emotional and social needs of their members is extremely important since it affects the functioning of the whole system. Indeed, the literature shows that members' satisfaction with the team may influence team performance [8], as well as team members' willingness to continue to work together in the future [9].

Despite the many advantages associated with the presence of teams in the organizational setting, teamwork can also pose some challenges to individuals and organizations [10]. When individuals are gathered in teams, they have to interact with each other in order to perform the tasks. This interdependence, while being one of the strengths of working in groups, opens the way to dis-agreements and discussions that are inescapable phenomena in the team con-text. Accordingly, conflict emerges as a central topic to be studied in order to understand the dynamics, functioning and effectiveness of teams [11]. Conflict can be defined as a disagreement that is perceived as creating tension by at least one of the parties involved in an interaction [12].

Over the years, researchers have been trying to clarify the consequences of conflict on team outcomes (e.g., [12–14]). Much of this research distinguishes between two types of conflict: task conflict, which encompasses disagreements among team members regarding the work being performed, and affective con-flict, which is related to situations of tension between team members caused by differences in terms of personality or values [15]. Although, theories argue that, when conflict is focused on the task, can have positive outcomes, these positive effects have been largely elusive [12,16]. In fact, empirical results consistently report a negative impact of intragroup conflict on team effectiveness (e.g., [12,13,16]). When the outcome considered is team member's satisfaction, results tend to be even more consistent. Indeed, even if a conflict might be positive for task results because team members gain information about different opinions and perspectives [15], individuals who engage in conflict situations feel frustration and irritation and tend to be less satisfied with their team [13].

To understand the effects of intragroup conflict on team results, particularly on team members' satisfaction, we have to consider the way team members handle conflict situations. At the intragroup level, conflict management strategies describe the responses of team members to conflict situations [11]. Although several frameworks exist for classifying conflict management strategies (e.g., [17–19]), most of them are based on a two-dimensional typology: one dimension encompasses the extent to which one wants to pursue one's interests (concern for self) and the other dimension concerns the extent to which one wants to fulfill the interest of the other party involved in the interaction (concern for others). From the combination of these two dimensions, five conflict-handling strategies emerge, of which the most studied are: integrating (high concern for self/high concern for others), dominating (high concern for self/low concern for others), avoiding (low concern for self/low concern for others) and obliging (low concern for self/high concern for others) [20]. Integrating and dominating are both active strategies of handling conflict. While integrating is a cooperative approach and dominating is a competitive one, when parties adopt these strategies act in an assertive way in order to attain the desired goals. They are in control of their own actions and they try to influence the outcomes obtained from the conflict situation [21,22]. Avoiding and obliging are passive strategies of managing conflict: when individuals adopt avoiding or obliging strategies to handle conflict situations, they are giving up on their own interests and they behave as passive recipients of their counterpart's actions and initiatives [21,23].

Previous studies have tried to clarify how particular ways of managing intragroup conflict influence team effectiveness (e.g., [24,25]). Integrating has been reported as the most constructive way of handling conflict and evidence has been found for its positive effect on team members' satisfaction [11,13]. However, handling conflict through a collaborative approach may not always be an appropriate strategy. Indeed, previous studies found that certain conflict situations are difficult to settle to mutual satisfaction and being cooperative and understanding in this kind of situations is unlikely to solve the problem, contributing to its escalation [25,26]. Moreover, integrating is a strategy that consumes time and energy and detracts the team from the task, threatening the ability of the team to achieve its results [25]. This is particularly important when the frequency of conflict is too high. Dominating, in turn, being a win-lose strategy, has been related to negative consequences, such as poor performance and poor levels of satisfaction [13,27,28]. However, although much of the literature presents the dominating strategy as a non-effective way of facing a conflict situation, there is also some empirical evidence for the positive consequences of dominating for effectiveness (e.g., [29]). These results are in line with the conflict management contingency approach [18], which assumes that the appropriateness of each conflict-handling strategy depends on the circumstances. Concerning passive strategies of conflict management, the results are even more inconclusive. Indeed, although some studies suggest that adopting a passive strategy of conflict management might be an effective way of handling some kinds of conflict [25], others suggest that the lack of controls in the results obtained that characterizes this kind of strategy tends to increase strain and frustration [21] generating dissatisfaction in the teams.

In the traditional teamwork research literature, low levels of consensus like the one reported above are common. Actually, discrepancies like these ones appear and have been, mainly, treated as irregularities because the linear and reductionist approach is not able to capture the complexity of teams [30–32]. In order to understand the dynamic nature of teams, one should adopt perspectives and methods that recognize the nonlinear nature of the relationships between team inputs, processes and outcomes [33]. Accordingly, the central aim of the present paper is to examine team members' satisfaction from a nonlinear dynamical system (NDS) perspective taking into account the role played by conflict and conflict management.

The NDS approach is the study of how complex processes unfold over time and is sometimes known as chaos theory or complexity theory [34]. One branch of complexity science, catastrophe theory, which is based on nonlinear modeling methods, enables the analysis of discontinuous, abrupt changes in dependent variables resulting from small and continuous changes in independent variables [35]. Cusp catastrophe theory, the most commonly used in team research, describes change between two stable states of the dependent variable (i.e., order parameter) and two independent variables (i.e., control parameters) [36]. The possibility of modeling discontinuous changes, richly describing the phenomenon under consideration [37], is one advantage of this approach that can contribute to the development of the knowledge about the complex relationships between conflict, conflict management and satisfaction.

The purpose of the present paper is to test a cusp model in the data, which is summarized in Fig. 1. Members' satisfaction is considered the dependent variable or the order parameter, which is influenced by intragroup conflict and conflict management. Based on the literature presented above, it is expected that intragroup conflict will maintain a negative and stable relationship with members' satisfaction, because the higher the level of task and affective conflict within the team, the lower the level of satisfaction of the members with the team. Thus, members' satisfaction is considered as the asymmetry variable in the cusp model since this type of parameter is related to the order parameter in a consistent pattern [37]. Conflict management, in turn, is a potential candidate for a bifurcation parameter, inasmuch as it could lead the group system to a sudden change in level of satisfaction. Hence, the inconsistent pattern of results concerning the relationship between conflict-handling strategies and satisfaction might be a clue for the presence of a nonlinear relationship still unknown. A certain amount of each of the conflict-handling strategies might be beneficial, allowing the group to manage the conflict situations in an effective way, leading, consequently, to positive feelings towards the group. However, a high frequency of use of each of the strategies mentioned might be dysfunctional: active strategies might contribute to an escalation of conflict, with negative consequences for team results, while passive strategies might lead to an increase in the levels of frustration, jeopardizing the levels of satisfaction. Consequently, conflict-handling strategies is a potential candidate for a bifurcation parameter, since it might lead team members to a sudden change in level of satisfaction.

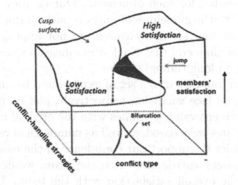

Fig. 1. A three-dimensional display of the cusp catastrophe response surface of members' satisfaction as a function of type of conflict (asymmetry) and conflict-handling strategies (bifurcation).

2 Materials and Methods

2.1 Sample

A longitudinal study was conducted in which we surveyed project teams from technological and engineering programs of one Portuguese university. These undergraduate programs are organized in a Project-Based Learning (PBL) environment. Within this framework, students are asked to develop, in small groups (between three and six members), real-life challenges that are presented to them as projects. Students have one semester to develop their projects and, when needed, professors can guide them, acting as facilitators.

Data was collected in a meeting with each team at two points in the semester: at the middle of the academic semester (T1) and at the end of the semester (T2), before the public presentation of the work developed. At T1 participants were asked about what had happened in the team since the beginning of the group until the moment they filled in the questionnaire and at T2 students were asked to evaluate the group according to what had happened since the previous data collection. Forty-four project groups participated in the data collection. Teams had, on average, four members (SD = 0.9), with a mean age of 24 years

(SD = 6.5), 88% were male, 78% were full time students and most of them (55%) were attending the third year of the program (31% were attending the first year and the remaining the second year).

2.2   Measures

In the present study, all constructs under study (i.e., members' satisfaction with the team, intragroup conflict and conflict management) were measured through single-item measures and VAS (Visual Analogue Scales). In the case of conflict and conflict management since they are multidimensional constructs, a single-item measure was created for each dimension. Our decision to use this kind of measures is in line with the guidelines of authors such as Roe, Gockel and Meyer [38], which state that multi-item measures are not appropriate for capturing change in groups over time and that single-item measures and graphic scales are suitable alternatives in longitudinal studies.

All measures were submitted to a set of experts and to three pilot studies for estimating content and face validities, respectively, and no problems have been identified [39]. Convergent validity studies with the original multi-item measures on which these measures were based, as well as nomological validity studies, were also conducted in order to support our confidence in the measures used [40, 41].

To measure members' satisfaction with the team, we developed one single-item that assesses the overall satisfaction with the team. The development of this item was based on the Gladstein's Global Satisfaction Scale [42], which is composed of three items. Participants were asked to mark on a VAS, from 0 (very dissatisfied) to 10 (very satisfied), the degree of satisfaction, or dissatisfaction, with the team, at the two data collection points.

To measure intragroup conflict, two items were developed based on the 9-item scale by Dimas and Lourenço [13]: one item for assessing task conflict and the other one for measuring affective conflict. Participants were asked, at T1, to mark on a VAS, from 0 (never) to 10 (always), the frequency of the occurrence of tension related to the way the work should be performed (task conflict) and to differences of personality or values between members (affective conflict).

To measure conflict management, four single-item measures were developed based on the ROCI-II multi-item scale [43]. Participants were asked to mark on a VAS, from 0 (never) to 10 (always), the frequency of adopting each of the four conflict management strategies in order to handle conflict situations, from the beginning of the project to the data collection point (T1).

2.3   Data Analysis

Mathematically, the cusp model is expressed by a potential function $f(y)$:

$$f(y/a, b) = ay + \frac{1}{2}by^2 - \frac{1}{4}y^4. \tag{1}$$

Equation (1) represents a dynamical system, which is seeking to optimize some function [44, 45]. Setting the first derivative of the Eq. (1) to zero, it results in the Eq. (2), which represents the three-dimensional equilibrium response surface of the cusp model:

$$\frac{\delta f(y)}{\delta y} = 0 \Leftrightarrow -y^3 + by + a = 0, \tag{2}$$

where a is the asymmetry factor and b is the bifurcation factor.

In the present research design, the teams began to work at time T0 (not measured), while two measurements were carried out at the middle of teams' life (T1) and at the end of the teams' life (T2). These two measures in time facilitate the application of the dynamic difference equation modeling approach, which implements least squares regression techniques [46]. According to this method all variables were transformed to z scores corrected for location and scale:

$$z = \frac{y - \lambda}{s}, \tag{3}$$

where λ is the minimum value of y and the scale s is the ordinary standard deviation. The specific equation to be tested for a cusp catastrophe model is:

$$\delta z = z_2 - z_1 = b_1 z_1^3 + b_2 z_1 CHS + b_3 C + b_4 \tag{4}$$

where z is the normalized behavioral variable, while C and CHS are the normalized asymmetry (conflict) and the bifurcation (conflict-handing strategies), respectively. The nonlinear model is tested against its linear alternatives, from which the most antagonistic is the pre/post model:

$$z_2 = b_1 CHS + b_2 C + b_3 z_1 + b_4. \tag{5}$$

For both models, z_1 is team members' satisfaction at T1 while at T2 is z_2 and $b_i, i = 1, \ldots, 4$ are the model's parameters to be determined by least squares regression.

In order to test the nonlinear hypothesis that a cusp catastrophe is appropriate model to describe satisfaction, the regression equation (4) should account for a larger percent of the variance in the dependent variable than the linear alternatives. In addition, the coefficients of both the cubic and the product terms in Eq. (4) must be statistically significant.

Moreover, additional calculations were carried out with the indirect method, which implements the cusp pdf and uses maximum likelihood estimation of the parameters [47]. The calculations are performed in R cusp package. In this method, the statistical evaluation model fit was based on pseudo-R^2 statistics for the cusp models and on AIC, AICc and BIC indices (Akaike's criterion, Akaike's criterion corrected for small samples and Bayes's information criterion, respectively). Also the likelihood ratio chi-square was used in order to compare the fit of the cusp models and the linear regression models [37]. In addition, the presence of a cusp catastrophe is established by the statistical significance of its coefficients.

Table 1. Means, standard deviations, and intercorrelations of study variables.

	Mean	SD	1	2	3	4	5	6	7	8
1. Task conflict T1	2.91	1.95	–	–	–	–	–	–	–	–
2. Affective conflict T1	2.24	2.05	.69**	–	–	–	–	–	–	–
3. Avoiding T1	3.99	1.79	.27*	.26*	–	–	–	–	–	–
4. Integrating T1	7.66	1.32	−.28*	−.32*	.20	–	–	–	–	–
5. Obliging T1	5.93	1.32	−.40*	−.26*	−.05	.32*	–	–	–	–
6. Dominating T1	2.51	1.44	.51**	.59**	.42**	−.18	−.10	–	–	–
7. Satisfaction T1	7.25	2.20	.05	−.04	.12	.47**	.02	−.06	–	–
8. Satisfaction T2	7.64	1.72	−.18	−.07	−.13	.20	.01	−.06	.45**	–

Note: **p < .01, *p < .05.

Table 2. The difference model estimated by least squares regression: slopes, standard errors and t-tests for cusp and the linear control. Integrating as bifurcation variable.

Model	Variable name	R^2	B	SEB	β	t
Pre/Post		.27*				
z_1	Satisfaction		0.52	0.16	.52	3.34**
b	Integrating		0.08	0.17	−.08	−0.48
a	Task conflict		−0.34	0.19	.34	−1.73[†]
a	Affective conflict		0.16	0.19	.16	0.84
Cusp 1		.27*				
z_1^3	Satisfaction		−0.07	0.03	−.36	−2.52*
b	Integrating		0.22	0.22	.22	1.59
a	Task conflict		−0.30	−0.29	−.29	−1.51
a	Affective conflict		0.23	.22	.22	1.17

Note: **p < .01, *p < .05, †p < .10.

3 Results

As the unit of analysis in the present study was the group rather than the individual, members' responses were aggregated to the team level for further analyses. In order to justify the aggregation of the team level constructs (conflict type and conflict-handling strategies), the ADM index [48] was used. The average ADM values obtained for task conflict, affective conflict, integrating, dominating, avoiding and obliging were, respectively, 1.13 (SD = 0.87), 0.99 (SD = 0.88), 1.0 (SD = 0.93), 1.27 (SD = .85), 1.7 (SD = 1.09), 1.26 (SD = 0.87). Since all the values were below the upper-limit criterion of 2.0, team members' scores were aggregated, with confidence, to the team level.

Table 1 displays the means, standard deviations and correlations for all variables under study. Tables 2, 3, 4 and 5 shows the regression slopes, standard errors and t-tests for four cusp catastrophe models and their pre/post linear models. Table 2 shows the results for the difference model estimated by least

Table 3. The difference model estimated by least squares regression: slopes, standard errors and t-tests for cusp and the linear control. Dominating as bifurcation variable.

Model	Variable name	R^2	B	SEB	β	t
Pre/Post		.26*				
z_1	Satisfaction		0.48	0.14	.48	3.46**
b	Dominating		0.05	0.17	.05	0.26
a	Task conflict		−0.33	0.20	−.33	−1.70†
a	Affective conflict		0.16	0.21	.16	0.77
Cusp 1		.25*				
z_1^3	Satisfaction		−0.09	0.03	−.50	−2.93**
b	Dominating		−0.18	0.15	−.22	−1.14
a	Task conflict		−0.37	0.21	−.35	−1.79†
a	Affective conflict		0.22	0.21	.21	1.05

Note: **p < .01, *p < .05, †p < .10.

Table 4. The difference model estimated by least squares regression: slopes, standard errors and t-tests for cusp and the linear control. Obliging as bifurcation variable.

Model	Variable name	R^2	B	SEB	β	t
Pre/Post		.27*				
z_1	Satisfaction		0.48	0.14	.48	3,49**
b	Obliging		−0.10	0.15	−.10	−0.67
a	Task conflict		−0.37	0.20	−.37	−1.81†
a	Affective conflict		0.18	0.19	.18	0.95
Cusp 1		.47***				
z_1^3	Satisfaction		−0.11	0.02	−.59	−4.64***
b	Obliging		0.32	0.07	.54	4.29***
a	Task conflict		−0.35	0.17	−.34	−2.08*
a	Affective conflict		0.24	0.17	.23	1.42

Note: ***p < .001, **p < .01, *p < .05, †p < .10.

squares regression, with task and affective conflicts as asymmetry variables and integrating as a bifurcation variable. The cusp model and the pre/post linear explain a similar proportion of the variance ($R^2 = .27$), and, in the cusp model, only the cubic term is significant [t = −2.52, p < 0.05]. Table 3, in turn, shows the results for the difference model estimated by least squares regression, with task and affective conflicts as asymmetry variables and dominating as a bifurcation variable. Results revealed that the cusp model explains a smaller proportion of the variance ($R^2 = .25$) compared to the pre/post linear model ($R^2 = .26$). In the cusp model, the cubic term [t = −2.93, p < 0.01] and task conflict [t = −1.79, p < 0.10] were significant. Table 4 displays the model fit for the difference

344   I. D. Dimas et al.

Table 5. The difference model estimated by least squares regression: slopes, standard errors and t-tests for cusp and the linear control. Avoiding as bifurcation variable.

Model	Variable name	R^2	B	SEB	β	t
Pre/Post		.28*				
z_1	Satisfaction		0.50	0.14	.50	3.60**
b	Avoiding		−0.15	0.14	−.15	−1.08
a	Task conflict		−0.30	0.19	−.30	−1.56
a	Affective conflict		0.20	0.19	.20	1.05
Cusp 1		.29**				
z_1^3	Satisfaction		−0.08	0.03	−.45	−3.19**
b	Avoiding		−0.22	0.12	−.27	−1.87†
a	Task conflict		−.38	0.20	−.36	−1.91†
a	Affective conflict		0.26	0.20	.25	1.33

Note: **$p < .01$, *$p < .05$, †$p < .10$ (one-tailed).

Table 6. The cusp model estimated by maximum likelihood method: slopes, standard errors, Z-tests and model fit statistics for the cusp and the linear model. Members' satisfaction (T2–T1) as dependent variable, types of conflict as asymmetry variables and integrating as bifurcation variable.

Model		b	SEB	Z-value
Cusp 1				
w	Members' satisfaction	0.28	0.04	7.57***
a	Task conflict	−1.82	0.76	−2.39*
a	Affective conflict	0.69	0.82	0.85
b	Integrating	0.55	0.24	2.29*
Models' fit statistics				
Models	R^2	AIC	AICc	BIC
Linear model	.18	128.59	130.17	137.51
Cusp model	.20	128.25	131.36	140.74

Note: ***$p < .001$, *$p < .05$.

model estimated by least squares regression, with task and affective conflicts as asymmetry variables and obliging as a bifurcation variable. The cusp model is superior to the pre/post linear by explaining a larger portion of the variance ($R^2 = .47$), while the cubic term [$t = -4.64$, $p < 0.001$], the bifurcation [$t = 4.29$, $p < 0.001$] and the asymmetry task conflict [$t = -2.08$, $p < 0.05$] are statistically significant. Similarly, Table 5 gives the model fit for the difference model with task and affective conflicts as asymmetry variables and avoiding as a bifurcation variable. Results reveal that the cusp model is superior to the pre/post linear by explaining a larger proportion of the variance ($R^2 = .29$), while the cubic term [$t = -3.19$, $p < 0.01$], the bifurcation [$t = 1.87$, $p < 0.10$] and the asymmetry

Table 7. The cusp model estimated by maximum likelihood method: slopes, standard errors, Z-tests and model fit statistics for the cusp and the linear model. Members' satisfaction (T2–T1) as dependent variable, types of conflict as asymmetry variables and dominating as bifurcation variable.

Model		b	SEB	Z-value
Cusp 1				
w	Members' satisfaction	0.42	0.09	4.74***
a	Task conflict	−1.00	0.56	−1.78[†]
a	Affective conflict	0.41	0.68	0.61
b	Dominating	−1.51	2.68	−0.39
Models' fit statistics				
Models	R^2	AIC	AICc	BIC
Linear model	.08	133.88	135.46	142.80
Cusp model	.12	134.04	137.15	146.53

Note: ***p < .001, [†]p < .10 (one-tailed).

Table 8. The cusp model estimated by maximum likelihood method: slopes, standard errors, Z-tests and model fit statistics for the cusp and the linear model. Members' satisfaction (T2–T1) as dependent variable, types of conflict as asymmetry variables and obliging as bifurcation variable.

Model		b	SEB	Z-value
Cusp 1				
w	Members' satisfaction	0.45	0.07	6.14***
a	Task conflict	−0.69	0.47	−1.45*
a	Affective conflict	0.45	0.45	1.01
b	Obliging	−2.38	1.01	2.35*
Models' fit statistics				
Models	R^2	AIC	AICc	BIC
Linear model	.09	133.43	135.01	142.35
Cusp model	.11	128.25	134.19	143.57

Note: ***p < .001, *p < .05.

task conflict [t = −1.91, p < 0.10] are statistically significant. The above cusp analyses support the role of conflict management (in particular, avoiding and obliging) as bifurcations and exemplified the special role that they might have for team functioning.

In order to find further support for the cusp structure identified, the cusp model was also estimated by maximum likelihood method. Tables 6, 7, 8 and 9 show the slopes, standards errors, Z-tests and model fit statistics for the cusp and the linear model. Table 6 displays the estimated cusp model with types of conflict as the asymmetry variables and integrating as the bifurcation variable. As can

Table 9. The cusp model estimated by maximum likelihood method: slopes, standard errors, Z-tests and model fit statistics for the cusp and the linear model. Members' satisfaction (T2–T1) as dependent variable, types of conflict as asymmetry variables and avoiding as bifurcation variable.

Model		b	SEB	Z-value
Cusp 1				
w	Members' satisfaction	0.45	0.09	5.22***
a	Task conflict	−0.63	0.49	−1.28
a	Affective conflict	0.41	0.51	0.80
b	Avoiding	2.38	1.43	1.66[†]
Models' fit statistics				
Models	R^2	AIC	AICc	BIC
Linear model	.11	132.60	134.17	141.52
Cusp model	.10	129.09	132.21	141.58

Note: ***p < .001, [†]p < .10 (one-tailed).

be seen, the cusp model is superior to the linear one, although the difference is not significant ($\chi^2(2) = 4.34$ ns), and task conflict and integrating were both statistically significant. Table 7, in turn, gives the estimated cusp model with types of conflict as the asymmetry variables and dominating as the bifurcation variable. The cusp model was superior to the linear model but the difference was not statistically significant ($\chi^2(2) = 3.84$ ns). The role of dominating as a bifurcation variable was also not statistically significant. Table 8 displays the results for the cusp model with types of conflict as the asymmetry variables and obliging as the bifurcation variable. Results support the superiority of the cusp model when compared to the linear one. Indeed, the R^2 of the cusp model ($R^2 = .11$) was superior to the linear model ($R^2 = .09$), and the difference was significant ($\chi^2(2) = 6.35$, p < .05). Moreover, the estimates of fit AIC, AICc and BIC also recommend the superiority of the cusp model. The role of obliging as bifurcation was significant, as well as the role of task conflict as the asymmetry variable. Finally, Table 9 shows the estimated cusp model with types of conflict as the asymmetry variables and avoiding as the bifurcation variable. Although the role of avoiding as bifurcation was marginally significant, the linear model ($R^2 = .11$) was significantly superior ($\chi^2(2) = 7.50$, p < .05) to the cusp model ($R^2 = .10$).

Overall, results obtained with the difference model estimated by least squares regression and with the indirect model estimated by maximum likelihood method, go in the same direction, revealing the existence of a cusp structure in our data, where the role of task conflict as an asymmetry variable and of conflict management, in particular of the obliging strategy, is clearly supported.

4 Discussion and Conclusions

Teams have been theoretically conceived as complex, adaptive and dynamic systems: (a) *complex*, because they are entities embedded in a hierarchy of levels revealing complex behaviours; (b) *adaptive*, because they are continuously adapting to environmental changes; and (c) *dynamic*, due to their functioning being dependent both on the team's history and on its anticipated future [9,49]. Despite the general acceptance of teams as complex adaptive systems, the examples of empirical research that incorporate this conceptualization remain scarce [32]. The present paper intends to be a contribution to understanding the complexity of team dynamics, by studying members' satisfaction with the team from a nonlinear dynamic system perspective, taking into account the role played by conflict and conflict management.

With regard to intragroup conflict, in line with the literature [12,13], task conflict presented a negative linear effect on satisfaction, whereas the role of affective conflict was not significant. Because conflict generates tension and discomfort, it is not surprising that team members are less satisfied with being a part of teams where conflicts are very frequent. The non-significant relationship between affective conflict and satisfaction might be due to the fact that we are studying groups that are created to develop a task and, in consequence, the task system is the most prevalent [13].

Conflict-handling strategies act as bifurcation variables exhibiting a "moderating" role with nonlinear effects. As a result, sudden shifts between different modes of satisfaction (high or low) might occur, beyond a threshold value. From the conflict-management strategies that were studied, the role of passive strategies as bifurcation variables, in particular the strategy of obliging, was better supported by the data. Beyond a certain threshold of obliging, groups that have the same level of conflict might oscillate between two attractors, the modes of high and low satisfaction levels, respectively. A small variation in obliging leads the system to an area of unpredictability in terms of members' satisfaction. Thus, the present research contributes to the literature by presenting conflict management as a bifurcation, which might explain the discrepancies between findings about the relationship between passive strategies of conflict-handling and team effectiveness [21,25].

Another contribution of the present paper is the use of both the difference equation modeling approach, which implements the least squares regression technique, and the indirect method, which uses the maximum likelihood estimation of the parameters, in order to test the presence of a cusp model. By going in the same direction, the results found with the two methods reinforce the presence of a cusp structure in our data. Moreover, the results reveal that both the difference equation modeling approach and the indirect method are appropriate strategies to use with this kind of data.

The present study, supporting the nonlinear dynamics of conflict, conflict management and satisfaction, adds to the growing body of research that considers teams as complex adaptive and dynamic systems. Despite the contributions of our research, the present work also presents limitations. An important shortcoming of this study is the sample size, which does not allow the simultaneous testing of the four conflict-handling strategies as bifurcation within a cusp model. Moreover, our study is focused on a particular type of group: project groups composed of students. Future studies should replicate the present findings with different teams, such as organizational workgroups.

Acknowledgments. This work was supported by the Fundação para a Ciência e a Tecnologia (FCT) under project grants UID/MULTI/00308/2013 and POCI-01-0145-FEDER-008540.

References

1. Salas, E., Stagl, K.C., Burke, C.S.: 25 years of team effectiveness in organizations: research themes and emerging needs. Int. Rev. Ind. Organ. Psychol. **19**, 47–91 (2005)
2. Ilgen, D.R., Hollenbeck, J.R., Johnson, M., Jundt, D.: Teams in organizations: from input-process-output models to IMOI models. Annu. Rev. Psychol. **56**, 517–543 (2005)
3. Marks, M.A., Mathieu, J.E., Zaccaro, S.J.: A temporally based framework and taxonomy of team processes. Acad. Manag. Rev. **26**, 356–376 (2001)
4. Hackman, J.R.: The design of work teams. In: Lorsch, J. (ed.) Handbook of Organizational Behavior, pp. 315–342. Prentice Hall, Englewood Cliffs (1987)
5. Aubé, C., Rousseau, V.: Team goal commitment and team effectiveness: the role of task interdependence and supportive behaviors. Group Dyn. Theor. Res. Pract. **9**, 189–204 (2005)
6. Wiiteman, H.: Group member satisfaction: a conflict-related account. Small Group Res. **22**, 24–58 (1991)
7. Dimas, I.D., Lourenço, P.R., Rebelo, T.: Scale of satisfaction with the working group: construction and validation studies. Av. en Psicol. Latinoam. **36**, 197–210 (2018)
8. Lester, S.W., Meglino, B.M., Korsgaard, M.A.: The antecedents and consequences of group potency: a longitudinal investigation of newly formed work groups. Acad. Manag. J. **45**, 352–368 (2002)
9. Sundstrom, E., De Meuse, K.P., Futrell, D.: Work teams: applications and effectiveness. Am. Psychol. **45**, 120–133 (1990)
10. Aubé, C., Rousseau, V.: Counterproductive behaviors: group phenomena with team-level consequences. Team Perform. Manag. Int. J. **20**, 202–220 (2014)
11. DeChurch, L.A., Marks, M.A.: Maximizing the benefits of task conflict: the role of conflict management. Int. J. Confl. Manag. **12**, 4–22 (2001)
12. De Dreu, C.K.W., Weingart, L.R.: Task versus relationship conflict, team performance, and team member satisfaction: a meta-analysis. J. Appl. Psychol. **88**, 741–749 (2003)
13. Dimas, I.D., Lourenço, P.R.: Intragroup conflict and conflict management approaches as determinants of team performance and satisfaction: two field studies. Negot. Confl. Manag. Res. **8**, 174–193 (2015)
14. Shaw, J.D., Zhu, J., Duffy, M.K., Scott, K.L., Shih, H.A., Susanto, E.: A contingency model of conflict and team effectiveness. J. Appl. Psychol. **96**, 391–400 (2011)

15. Jehn, K.A.: A multimethod examination of the benefits and detriments of intragroup conflict. Adm. Sci. Q. **40**, 256 (1995)
16. De Wit, F.R.C., Greer, L.L., Jehn, K.A.: The paradox of intragroup conflict: a meta-analysis. J. Appl. Psychol. **97**, 360–390 (2012)
17. Deutsch, M.: The resolution of conflict: constructive and destructive processes. Am. Behav. Sci. **17**, 248 (1973)
18. Thomas, K.W.: Conflict and conflict management: reflections and update. J. Organ. Behav. **13**, 265–274 (1992)
19. Rahim, M.A.: A strategy for managing conflict in complex organizations. Hum. Relat. **38**, 81–89 (1985)
20. Kuhn, T., Poole, M.S.: Do Conflict management styles affect group decision making? Evidence from a longitudinal field study. Hum. Commun. Res. **26**, 558–590 (2000)
21. Dijkstra, M.T.M., de Dreu, C.K.W., Evers, A., van Dierendonck, D.: Passive responses to interpersonal conflict at work amplify employee strain. Eur. J. Work Organ. Psychol. **18**, 405–423 (2009)
22. van de Vliert, E., Euwema, M.C.: Agreeableness and activeness as components of conflict behaviors. J. Pers. Soc. Psychol. **66**, 674–687 (1994)
23. van de Vliert, E., Euwema, M.C., Huismans, S.E.: Managing conflict with a subordinate or a superior: effectiveness of conglomerated behavior. J. Appl. Psychol. **80**, 271–281 (1995)
24. Alper, S., Tjosvold, A., Law, K.S.: Conflict management, efficacy, and performance in organisational teams. Pers. Psychol. **53**, 625–642 (2000)
25. De Dreu, C.K.W., Van Vianen, A.E.M.: Managing relationship conflict and the effectiveness of organizational teams. J. Organ. Behav. **22**, 309–328 (2001)
26. Murnighan, J.K., Conlon, D.E.: The dynamics of intense work groups: a study of british string quartets. Adm. Sci. Q. **36**, 165–186 (1991)
27. Behfar, K.J., Peterson, R.S., Mannix, E.A., Trochim, W.M.K.: The critical role of conflict resolution in teams: a close look at the links between conflict type, conflict management strategies, and team outcomes. J. Appl. Psychol. **93**, 170–188 (2008)
28. Friedman, R.A., Tidd, S.T., Currall, S.C., Tsai, J.C.: What goes around comes around: the impact of personal conflict style on work conflict and stress. Int. J. Confl. Manag. **11**, 32–55 (2000)
29. Liu, J., Fu, P., Liu, S.: Conflicts in top management teams and team/firm outcomes. Int. J. Confl. Manag. **20**, 228–250 (2009)
30. Dimas, I.D., Rocha, H., Rebelo, T., Lourenço, P.R.: A nonlinear multicriteria model for team effectiveness. In: Gervasi, O., et al. (eds.) ICCSA 2016. LNCS, vol. 9789, pp. 595–609. Springer, Cham (2016). https://doi.org/10.1007/978-3-319-42089-9_42
31. Rebelo, T., Stamovlasis, D., Lourenço, P.R., Dimas, I., Pinheiro, M.: A cusp catastrophe model for team learning, team potency and team culture. Nonlinear Dyn. Psychol. Life Sci. **20**, 537–563 (2016)
32. Ramos-Villagrasa, P.J., Marques-Quinteiro, P., Navarro, J., Rico, R.: Teams as complex adaptive systems: reviewing 17 years of research. Small Group Res. **49**, 135–176 (2018)
33. Mathieu, J.E., Hollenbeck, J.R., van Knippenberg, D., Ilgen, D.R.: A century of work teams in the journal of applied psychology. J. Appl. Psychol. **102**, 452–467 (2017)
34. Guastello, S.J.: Nonlinear dynamics, complex systems, and occupational accidents. Hum. Factors Ergon. Manuf. **13**, 293–304 (2003)

35. Thom, R.: Structural Stability and Morphogenesis: An Outline of a General Theory of Models. W.A. Benjamim, Reading (1975)
36. Ceja, L., Navarro, J.: 'Suddenly I get into the zone': examining discontinuities and nonlinear changes in flow experiences at work. Hum. Relat. **65**, 1101–1127 (2012)
37. Escartin, J., Ceja, L., Navarro, J., Zapf, D.: Modeling workplace bullying using catastrophe theory. Nonlinear Dyn. Psychol Life Sci **17**, 493–515 (2013)
38. Roe, R.A., Gockel, C., Meyer, B.: Time and change in teams: where we are and where we are moving. Eur. J. Work Organ. Psychol. **21**, 629–656 (2012)
39. Santos, G., Costa, T., Rebelo, T., Lourenço, P.R., Dimas, I.: Desenvolvimento Grupal: uma abordagem com base na teoria dos sistemas dinâmicos não lineares - Construção/adaptação e validação de instrumento de medida [Group development: a nonlinear dynamical system approach – development/adaptation and validation of a measure]. In: Actas do VIII SNIP, Aveiro, Portugal (2013)
40. Vais, R.F.: Validade convergente, validade nomológica e fiabilidade de medidas de um só-item [Convergent validity, nomological validity and reliability of single-item measures]. Master Thesis, FPCE, University of Coimbra, Coimbra, Portugal (2014)
41. Melo, C.: Validade convergente, fiabilidade e validade nomológica de medidas de um só-item: interdependência de tarefa, team learning e satisfação [Convergent validity, reliability, and nomological validity of single-item measures: task interdependence, team learning and satisfaction]. Master Thesis, FPCE, University of Coimbra, Coimbra, Portugal (2015)
42. Gladstein, D.L.: Groups in context: a model of task group effectiveness. Adm. Sci. Q. **29**, 499–517 (1984)
43. Rahim, M.A.: A measure of styles of handling interpersonal conflict. Acad. Manag. J. **26**, 368–376 (1983)
44. Gilmore, R.: Catastrophe Theory for Scientists and Engineers. Wiley, New York (1981)
45. Poston, T., Stewart, I.: Catastrophe Theory and Its Applications. Dover Publications, New York (1978)
46. Guastello, S.J.: Managing Emergent Phenomena: Non-linear Dynamics in Work Organizations. Erlbaum, New Jersey (2002)
47. Grasman, R.P.P.P., van der Maas, H.L.J., Wagenmakers, E.-J.: Fitting the cusp catastrophe in R: a cusp package primer. J. Stat. Softw. **32**, 1–27 (2009)
48. Burke, M.J., Finkelstein, L.M., Dusig, M.S.: On average deviation indices for estimating interrater agreement. Organ. Res. Methods **2**, 49–68 (1999)
49. McGrath, J.E., Arrow, H., Berdahl, J.L.: The study of groups: past, present, and future. Pers. Soc. Psychol. Rev. **4**, 95–105 (2000)

Benefits of Multivariate Statistical Process Control Based on Principal Component Analysis in Solder Paste Printing Process Where 100% Automatic Inspection Is Already Installed

Pedro Delgado[1]([⊠]), Cristina Martins[1], Ana Braga[2]([iD]),
Cláudia Barros[2], Isabel Delgado[1], Carlos Marques[1],
and Paulo Sampaio[2]([iD])

[1] Bosch Car Multimedia Portugal SA, Apartado 2458, 4705-970 Braga, Portugal
pedro.delgado@pt.bosch.com
[2] ALGORITMI Centre, University of Minho, 4710-057 Braga, Portugal

Abstract. The process of printing and inspecting solder paste deposits in Printed Circuit Boards (PCB) involves a very large number of variables (more than 30000 can be found in 3D inspection of high density PCBs). State of the art Surface Mount Technology (SMT) production lines rely on 100% inspection of all paste deposits for each PCB produced. Specification limits for Area, Height, Volume, Offset X and Offset Y have been defined based on detailed and consolidated studies. PCBs with paste deposits failing the defined criteria, are proposed to be rejected.

The study of the variation of the rejected fraction over time, has shown that the process is not always stable and it would benefit from a statistical process control approach.

Statistical process control for 30000 variables is not feasible with a univariate approach. On one side, it is not possible to pay attention to such a high number of Shewhart control charts. On the other side, the very rich information contained in the evolution of the correlation structure would be lost in the case of a univariate approach.

The use of Multivariate Statistical Process Control based on Principal Component Analysis (PCA-MSPC) provides an efficient solution for this problem.

The examples discussed in this paper show that PCA-MSPC in solder paste printing is able to detect and diagnose disturbances in the underlying factors which govern the variation of the process. The early identification of these disturbances can be used to trigger corrective actions before disturbances start to cause defects. The immediate confirmation of effectiveness of the corrective action is a characteristic offered by this method and can be observed in all the examples presented.

Keywords: Multivariate Statistical Process Control
Principal Component Analysis · Solder Paste Inspection
Hotelling's T^2 · Squared Prediction Error · Variable contributions
Normal Operation Conditions

© Springer International Publishing AG, part of Springer Nature 2018
O. Gervasi et al. (Eds.): ICCSA 2018, LNCS 10961, pp. 351–365, 2018.
https://doi.org/10.1007/978-3-319-95165-2_25

1 Introduction

The solder paste printing together with 3D Solder Paste Inspection (3DSPI), constitute a key process in surface mount technology and reflow soldering production lines. Number of defects in the end of production line and reliability of Printed Circuit Boards (PCB) solder joints depend strongly on stable and well centred paste printing process.

In Bosch Car Multimedia Portugal, before 2008, the quality of this process was assured through the use of best practices defined in production guidelines, well trained and experienced team of line operators and process engineers, the use of top class machines and raw material, adequate preventive maintenance and regular machine capability evaluation.

From 2008 until 2017, the process was significantly improved by the introduction of 3DSPI: Area, Height, Volume, Offset X and Offset Y of each paste deposit are measured on all PCBs. It is a 100% inspection performed in-line by an automatic measuring system. Lower Specification Limit (LSL) and Upper Specification Limit (USL) for each type of variable were defined based on detailed studies of short term, long-term, within line and between line variations. Stable production periods of more than eight hours without defects after reflow soldering were taken as a starting point. Differences between paste deposit geometries and raw material types, were considered in the specification.

The introduction of 3DSPI was a key factor for quality improvement and cost reduction in Bosch Car Multimedia Portugal production lines. PCBs with high probability of failure in subsequent process phases, could then be rejected based on objective criteria.

The goal of the work presented in this paper is to confirm the following statements: Multivariate Statistical Process Control based on PCA (PCA-MSPC) is appropriate for monitoring processes where the number of variables can reach 30000; PCA-MSPC control charts do help in the identification of assignable causes of variation and contribute to stabilize the process; this framework can be installed and work efficiently in production lines with cycle times as low as twenty seconds; stability of processes where 100% automatic inspection is already installed can still be improved with multivariate statistical process control.

2 Solder Paste Printing and 3D Solder Paste Inspection

2.1 Process Description

In a SMT production line with reflow soldering, the first important step is paste printing. Solder paste deposits are accurately printed in PCB copper pads where electronic components will later on be placed by high speed and high accuracy pick and place machines. The PCB populated with electronic components placed on top of solder paste deposits, is then submitted to a reflow soldering process with a suitable temperature profile. Cycle times in SMT production lines can be as low as twenty seconds.

The required volume, position and shape of paste deposits is obtained through the use of a printing stencil with opening holes. An adequate amount of solder paste is placed on the top side of the stencil and pushed by a squeegee device in the direction of the PCB pads as illustrated in Fig. 1.

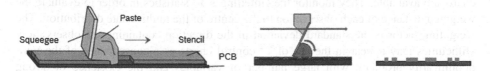

Fig. 1. Formation of solder deposits.

Most common stencil thicknesses are 150 μm, 125 μm and 112 μm. More than one thickness can be used in the same stencil.

The repeatability of this printing process depends on the correct configuration of different process parameters.

Known root causes of process variation are PCB fixation problems (the PCB must be well supported and stable during the printing process), machine alignment (conveyor, stencil and PCB support must be parallel) PCB warpage, machine printing speed, squeegee pressure, and many others.

Causes of variation are widely described by standardization entities, suppliers of printing machines and solder paste, as well as SMT electronic manufacturers. However, it is essential to know the exact degree in which these causes of variation are affecting Bosch Car Multimedia specific products and production lines.

Area, Height, Volume, Offset X and Offset Y of all deposits of all PCBs are measured by 3DSPI. PCBs with non-conform paste deposits will be rejected. This rejection of faulty PCBs protects subsequent processes and ultimately the client from receiving non-conform products. Another benefit is that historical data becomes available to process engineers who can use this information to evaluate and improve process stability and optimize performance.

2.2 Univariate and Multivariate Statistical Process Control

Even with 100% inspection and correct rejection of non-conform products, process stability is not guaranteed. The analysis of variation in the non-conform rate shows that solder paste printing process still shows some amount of instability. The need of a different kind of process control technique was identified. Detecting negative trends in an early phase and triggering preventive actions before the occurrence of defects, became the new goals (Reis and Gins 2017; Ferrer 2014; Reis and Delgado 2012).

The well-known features of Statistical Process Control (SPC) based on the distinction of stable versus unstable processes (common causes of variation versus assignable causes of variation) are the classical answer for stabilizing and optimizing processes. This is usually accomplished by monitoring overtime the distribution of a variable and checking that it has approximately constant location, spread and shape. Shewhart control charts and process capability indexes are the most widely used tools.

The classical approach analyses only one variable at a time. Correlations with other variables are not considered. It is immediately recognized that this approach is not feasible when thousands of variables have to be monitored (Montgomery 2009; Shewhart 1931).

When more than one variable have to be jointly evaluated, multivariate control charts are available. They monitor the Hotelling's T^2 statistics in order to evaluate the weighted distance of each observation to the centre of the multivariate distribution. The weighting factor is the standard deviation in the direction containing the observation. Difficulties may appear in the use of T^2 control charts as a consequence of the multicollinearity problem: with large number of variables and the existence of strong correlations, the inversion of the correlation matrix is difficult or not possible because it becomes ill-conditioned or singular (MacGregor and Kourti 1995; Montgomery 2009).

The chemical industry came up with a solution to this problem using a framework known as Multivariate Statistical Process Control based on PCA also referred to as PCA-MSPC (MacGregor and Kourti 1995; Nomikos and MacGregor 1995).

In a first step, the original hyperspace constituted by all the original variables, is rotated in a way that the new variables become aligned with orthogonal directions of maximum variance. The mathematical tool used is the eigenanalysis of the variance-covariance matrix (or the correlation matrix). This method provides a new axis system aligned with the main directions of variation. The transformed variables are ordered by the amount of variation explained. The direction of these new axis is given by the eigenvectors and the variance observed in each one of these directions is given by the eigenvalues. It was observed in many different fields of application that the underlying factors governing the observed variance tends to concentrate in a smaller number of main directions which are then called principal components (PC). The rotation in order to get a new set of orthogonal variables and the dimensionality reduction obtained by retaining only a smaller number of principal components, provides features which makes this framework very attractive for process control (Jackson 1991; Jolliffe 2002; Montgomery 2009; Wold et al. 1987). Some of those features are described in the following paragraphs.

Using a certain number of observations produced under stable conditions, a model can be built which describes the type of variation to be expected if no disturbances happen in the process. The stable period is known as Normal Operation Conditions period (NOC), training set or phase 1.

Model building and validation, the most computational demanding and time consuming part of this framework, can be made off-line and easily exported to an in-line process (Esbensen et al. 2002).

In order to export the model to the online monitoring engine, it is only necessary to export the mean values, the standard deviation values, the principal component loadings and control limits calculated for the chosen significance level. Mean and standard deviation are used for mean centring and unit variance scaling. Principal component loadings are the coefficients of the linear combinations which performs the PCA rotation and are the key to compute the scores, that is, the value of the original variables when represented in the new axis system.

T^2 statistics can easily be calculated in-line by summing the squared value of scores of each observation in each one of the retained principal component new axes. T^2

control chart can be used to monitor the distance of each observation to the centre of the model and monitor process stability in phase 2.

The stability of the correlation structure can also be monitored in phase 2 using a statistics known as Squared Prediction Error (SPE) or Q. A sudden modification of the correlation structure is indicated by a high value of Q.

The method is reversible: An observation vector in the original space can be transformed to the reduced dimensionality PCA sub-space. An observation represented in the PCA subspace can be converted back to the original variable space with a prediction error which depends on the number of principal components retained. This transformation can be made with simple matrix equations (MacGregor and Kourti 1995; Martins 2016).

A large number of numerical and graphical tools like score scatter plots, score timeline plots, loading plots, T^2 control charts, Q control charts and some others are available.

When a process disturbance is detected by T^2 or Q control charts, a process is available to compute which original variables have contributed more to this deviation. Intuitive contribution charts are also available.

Associated with each principal component, it is frequently possible to identify a physical meaning.

The installation of PCA-MSPC usually leads to early detection of process disturbances, faster diagnostics of root causes of process deviations, increased knowledge about the process and faster validation of effectiveness of corrective actions.

3 Model Building and Real Time Monitoring with PCA-MSPC

The installation of control charts involves two phases. In phase 1, samples are collected which are representative of the full range of acceptable products. Such period of time is usually referred to as Normal Operation Conditions period. Ideally, this period is centred close to nominal values, and the observed variance should be caused only by common causes of variation or other causes of variation which are intrinsic to the process and cannot be completely eliminated. In other words, production should be well centred and stable in NOC period (Montgomery 2009; Tracy et al. 1992).

Having a good model is a crucial element for an effective process control. In order to obtain a good model, it is necessary to select a sample which is representative of future acceptable production lots, exclude outliers and use cross validation to define the number of principal components to retain. Expertise in both PCA-MSPC and solder paste printing technologies is required for building models which will work correctly in production monitoring.

PCA models created in the scope of this work usually retain six principal components and explain approximately 50% to 60% of the observed variance as shown in Fig. 2.

In phase 2, also known as control phase, new observations are measured and compared to the model. The intention of the comparison is to decide if the differences can be explained by common causes of variation or if the differences observed can only

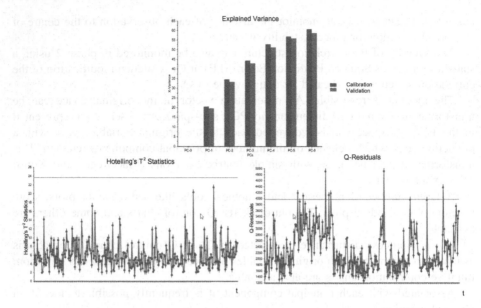

Fig. 2. Number of PC retained, explained variance, T^2 and Q residuals control charts in phase 1.

be explained assuming the occurrence of an assignable cause of variation (Montgomery 2009; Tracy et al. 1992).

The first level of this evaluation is made in a cockpit chart with control charts for T^2, Q and principal component scores. In this work, control limits are calculated for a significance level of 0,1%. If the cockpit char shows instability, then a deeper dive can be made through the contribution plots in order to identify the original variables affected by the previously detected disturbance.

In this work, the software used is The Unscrambler X Process Pulse II® from CAMO Software AS. The Unscrambler® is used to create the model (phase 1) and Process Pulse II® is used to monitor the process (phase 2).

The described set-up is able to detect the existence of assignable causes of variation like outliers, trends, oscillations or other unusual patterns. T^2 and Q act as summary statistics; timeline principal component scores provide some degree of diagnostic ability since they are frequently associated to a physical meaning; raw data and contribution plots show in detail which original variables contributed to the disturbance. Examples of such cockpit charts are shown in Figs. 3 and 4.

In raw data and contribution plots (Fig. 4), continuous black (or yellow) lines represent the mean values obtained in NOC period. Black (or yellow) dashed lines, represent minimum and maximum values observed in each variable in NOC period. If possible, more than 250 observations are used to build the model. Excluding abnormal circumstances, these black lines are expected to cover a zone of approximately three standard deviations away from the mean value. Blue lines, represent the current observation. The raw data plot can be graphed in the original variable scale or in mean

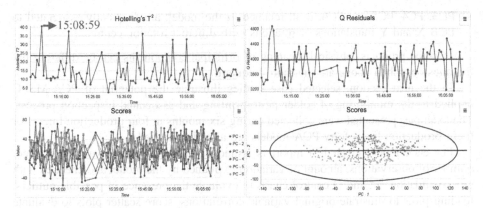

Fig. 3. Cockpit chart using The Unscrambler X Process Pulse II®.

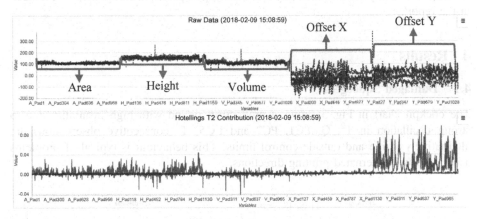

Fig. 4. Raw Data and Hotelling's T^2 contribution plots for PCB at 15:08:59 (X axis presents variable names A_Pad1-A_Pad1162, H_Pad1-H_Pad1162, V_Pad1-V_Pad1162, X_Pad1-X_Pad1162, Y_Pad1-Y_Pad1162). (Color figure online)

centred and unit variance scale. Area and Volume original units are percent points; Height, Offset X and Y are expressed in μm.

As shown in Fig. 3, PCB printed at 15:08:59 has high values of T^2 and Q. Contributions plot and raw data (Fig. 4) show high contributions for many Offset Y variables.

Studies made using information collected in NOC period (different production lines/products) have indicated that the physical meaning frequently associated with principal components are:

- PC1 associated to printing direction affecting mainly Offset Y and in a smaller degree Area, Height and Volume.
- PC2 associated with Area, Height and Volume influenced by PCB solder mask thickness, stencil cleaning cycle, machine parameters like squeegee pressure, printing speed, panel snap-off, stencil and squeegee wear-out and many others.

- PC3, PC4, PC5 and PC6, if all retained in the model, are frequently associated to PCB X and Y translations or rotations with different rotation centres.

In some products, physical meaning of principal components can be different but the ones described above are the more frequent.

In the next section, selected case studies illustrate the potential of PCA-MSPC applied to the monitoring of solder paste printing and associated inspection process. The examples presented were collected during six months in four production lines. For these production lines, forty PCA models are already installed.

For each model created, a report is issued containing process parameters used, number of observations, amount of variation explained by the model and checked with cross-validation, T^2 and Q control charts to evaluate the presence of possible outliers, loading plots to illustrate original variable correlations, score scatter plots to evaluate possible existence of clusters, score timeline plots to evaluate process stability. If existing and clearly documented, physical meaning of principal components is included in the report.

4   Results

4.1   Damaged Squeegees

The cockpit chart in Fig. 5 shows a production period with high instability due to strong oscillation in T^2, Q, PC1, PC2 and PC5. T^2 consecutive observations are alternatively inside and outside control limits. This behaviour is typical of problems associated with alternated printing directions.

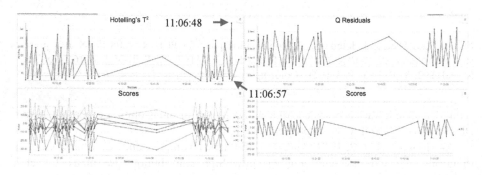

Fig. 5. Process instability associated to forward and backward printing direction.

Figures 6 and 7 shows raw data and contribution plots for two consecutive observations, the first being outside control limits and the second being inside control limits. The plots in Fig. 6 show excessive amount of paste visible in Height and Volume variables. It should be noted that not all Height and Volume variables are affected. The plots in Fig. 7 show that all variables are close to model centre.

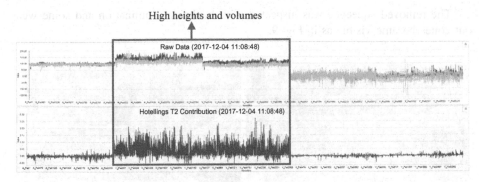

Fig. 6. Raw data and contribution plot for PCB 11:06:48 (X axis presents variable names A_Pad1-A_Pad3576, H_Pad1-H_Pad3576, V_Pad1-V_Pad3576, X_Pad1-X_Pad3576, Y_Pad1-Y_Pad3576).

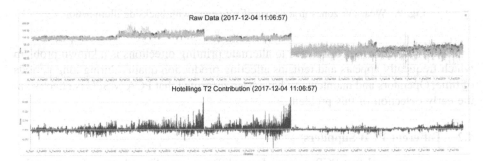

Fig. 7. Raw data and contribution plot for PCB 11:06:57 (X axis presents variable names A_Pad1-A_Pad3576, H_Pad1-H_Pad3576, V_Pad1-V_Pad3576, X_Pad1-X_Pad3576, Y_Pad1-Y_Pad3576).

When the problem is associated to printing direction, the squeegee is the most probable root cause. The squeegee was replaced at 11:15 and T^2, Q, PC1, PC2 and PC5 returned to a position closer to the model centre as can be confirmed in Fig. 8.

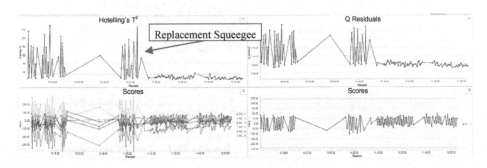

Fig. 8. Squeegee replaced at 11:15.

The removed squeegee was inspected with backside illumination and some wear out zones became visible as in Fig. 9.

Fig. 9. Wear out zones in a damaged squeegee with backside illumination.

Damaged squeegees associated to alternate printing directions is a known problem which frequently appears and remains affecting production quality during long periods of time. Operators and maintenance have been informed that PCA-MSPC is effective in the early detection of this problem.

4.2 Different PCB Suppliers

It is to be expected that PCB coming from different suppliers show different results. These differences, if not too large, are part of the variation which we cannot be avoided.

Figure 10 shows a production process where T^2 and PC1 show some deviation from the centre of the model. At approximately 15:09, T^2 and PC1 changed suddenly approaching the centre showing a stable process. Line operator informed that a new lot of raw PCBs was introduced in the line.

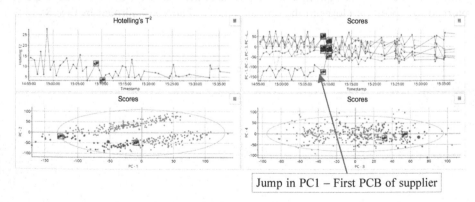

Jump in PC1 – First PCB of supplier

Fig. 10. T^2 and PC1 sudden change caused by PCBs from a different supplier.

In this particular case, PC1 physical meaning is the difference between supplier 1 and supplier 2. In order to double check this conclusion, the operator was asked to reintroduce in the line PCBs from supplier 1. As expected, T^2 and PC1 returned to the initial condition, as shown in Fig. 11.

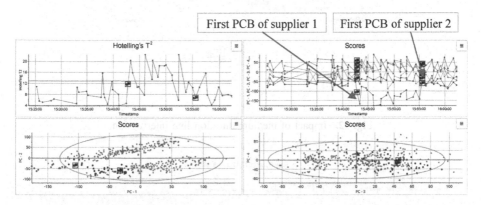

Fig. 11. Confirmation of different T^2 and PC1 results caused by different PCB suppliers.

If the difference from PCB suppliers is not too large, this assigned cause of variation can be accepted and included in the model. If it is too large, the inspection machine measurement program has to be adapted performing an operation called bare board teaching.

4.3   Impact of Production Line Interruptions of Small to Medium Duration

In this example, it was observed that the first PCB produced after two-hour production line stoppage shows decreased Volumes, Areas and Heights of paste.

Figure 12 shows stable production until around 06:00. The production line had interruptions until 8:00.

The PCB produced at 08:35:26 shows sudden change in T^2, Q and PC2 statistics. Raw data and contribution plot in Fig. 13 show high contribution from many Volume, Area and Height variables. This reduced amount of paste, was related to dried paste in some stencil openings caused by production line stoppage. The same pattern happened around 9:00 after an interruption of forty minutes.

Figure 14 shows raw data and contributions for the PCB produced at 08:47:54 with values close to the model centre.

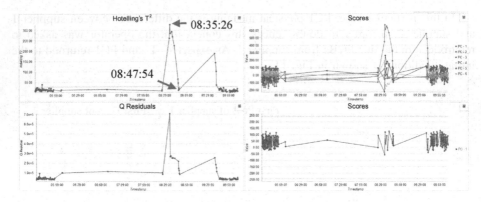

Fig. 12. Impact of medium duration line interruption.

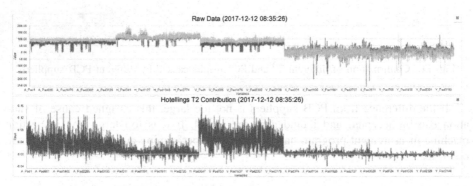

Fig. 13. Raw data and contribution plot after a medium duration line interruption. Note 0,16 maximum in contribution plot Y axis (X axis presents variable names A_Pad1-A_Pad3576, H_Pad1-H_Pad3576, V_Pad1-V_Pad3576, X_Pad1-X_Pad3576, Y_Pad1-Y_Pad3576).

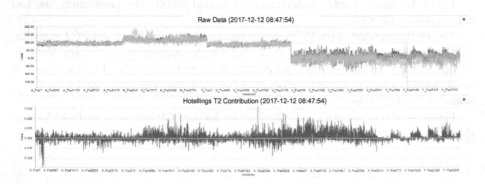

Fig. 14. Raw data and contribution plot for an observation close to model centre. Note 0,03 maximum in contribution plot Y axis (X axis presents variable names A_Pad1-A_Pad3576, H_Pad1-H_Pad3576, V_Pad1-V_Pad3576, X_Pad1-X_Pad3576, Y_Pad1-Y_Pad3576).

5 Quantification of Improvement

Process monitoring using PCA-MSPC was installed in production line 15 (SMT15) in March 2017. SMT15 was chosen as a pilot line because it runs high density PCBs. The installation of PCA models for products running in the line was made during March and April. Some optimizations were made and the new system was in full operation by the end of May. Process disturbances and their associated root causes were identified and corrected. The evolution of First Pass Yield (FPY) is shown in Fig. 15.

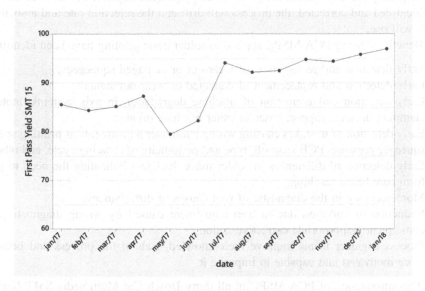

Fig. 15. First pass yield evolution in SMT15.

Due to the sustained improvement observed, the system has been recently installed in three additional production lines and will be extended to all thirty SMT lines until the end of 2018.

A process engineer specialized in PCA-MSPC and solder paste printing, will be in charge of a centralized performance monitoring. Every disturbance identified will be analysed and maintenance will introduce corrective actions when appropriate. Effectiveness of corrective actions, will also be confirmed immediately after the maintenance intervention.

In order to quantify the results obtained in eight months, a six sigma metrics is used. First Pass Yield (FPY) and Defects Per Million Opportunities (DPMO) are calculated and compared to six-sigma long term quality level of 5.4 DPMO.

The FPY is 0.97 as shown in Fig. 15, number of defect opportunities assumed for reference is 5000 (high density PCBs running in this line). The base error rate of the process is expressed in DPMO. The average number of Defects Per Unit (DPU) is $5000 \times$ DPMO $\times 10^{-6}$. The approximation given by the Poisson distribution, FPY $= e^{-DPU}$ provides an estimation of 6 DPMO. This is a very good result close to six sigma quality level of 5.4 DPMO.

6 Conclusions

When the number of variables to be controlled is very high (thousands or tens of thousands), 100% automatic inspection is important because it avoids that defective products reach further steps of the production process or the final client. It is to be underlined that this is a full automatic process made under control of a computer program at high speed and without human intervention. However, 100% automatic inspection is not enough to guarantee stable processes. Assignable causes of variation are frequently present without being identified by process engineers. If these causes are not identified and corrected, the process will drift and the rejection rate and associated costs will rise.

Benefits of using PCA-MSPC applied to solder paste printing have been identified:

- Early detection and replacement of wear-out or damaged squeegees;
- Early detection and replacement of damaged or wear-out stencils;
- Early detection and correction of machine degradation in axis systems, motors, clamping devices, support bases or other machine organs;
- Early detection of mistakes causing wrong parameter adjustments as printing speed, squeegee pressure, PCB snap-off, type and periodicity of cleaning cycle, and others;
- Early detection of differences in solder mask thickness indicating the need to perform bare board teaching;
- More accuracy in the diagnostic of root causes of disturbances;
- Reduction of variation due to over-adjustment caused by wrong diagnostic and consequent inappropriate corrective action;
- Process engineer teams improve their knowledge about the process and become more motivated and capable to improve it.

The introduction of PCA-MSPC in all thirty Bosch Car Multimedia SMT lines is the next step in the direction of better process monitoring, lower costs and improved quality.

Another important conclusion is that PCA-MSPC framework worked well with a number of variables as high as 30000 and a number of six principal components explaining an approximate value of 50% to 60% of total observed variance.

T^2 and principal component score control charts behave according the expectations and show good sensitivity and specificity. Q control charts show frequently stable values but out of the control limits calculated in phase 1.

One way to improve Q specificity, is to build the model using a sample that contains observations taken from lots produced in different days. A model build in this way is more representative of future production, Q statistics behaviour gets better but sensitivity of T^2 and principal component score statistics decreases slightly.

Future work will be done in order to improve Q specificity without degrading T^2 sensitivity.

Acknowledgements. This work has been supported by: European Structural and Investment Funds in the FEDER component, through the Operational Competitiveness and Internationalization Programme (COMPETE 2020) [Project n° 002814; Funding Reference: POCI-01-0247-FEDER-002814], COMPETE: POCI-01-0145-FEDER-007043 and FCT- (Fundação para a Ciência e Tecnologia) within the Project Scope: UID/CEC/00319/2013.

References

Esbensen, K.H., Guyot, D., Westad, F., Houmoller, L.P.: Multivariate data analysis: in practice: an introduction to multivariate data analysis and experimental design. In: Multivariate Data Analysis (2002)

Ferrer, A.: Latent structures-based multivariate statistical process control: a paradigm shift. Qual. Eng. **26**(1), 72–91 (2014)

Jackson, J.E.: A User's Guide to Principal Components. Wiley, New York (1991)

Jolliffe, I.T.: Principal Component Analysis, 2nd edn. Springer, New York (2002). https://doi.org/10.1007/b98835

MacGregor, J.F., Kourti, T.: Process analysis, monitoring and diagnosis, using multivariate projection methods. Chemom. Intell. Lab. Syst. **28**(1), 3–21 (1995)

Martins, C.: Controlo Estatístico Multivariado do Processo. Universidade do Minho (2016). in Portuguese

Montgomery, D.C.: Introduction to Statistical Quality Control, 6th edn. Wiley, New York (2009)

Nomikos, P., MacGregor, J.: Statistical Process Control of Batch Processes (1995)

Reis, M., Delgado, P.: A large-scale statistical process control approach for the monitoring of electronic devices assemblage. Comput. Chem. Eng. **39**, 163–169 (2012)

Reis, M., Gins, G.: Industrial process monitoring in the Big Data/Industry 4.0 era: from detection, to diagnosis, to prognosis. Processes **5**(3), 35 (2017)

Shewhart, W.A.: Economic Control of Quality of Manufactured Product. D. Van Nostrand Company, Inc., New York (1931). (Volume Republished in 1980 as a 50th Anniversary Commemorative Reissue by ASQC Quality Press)

Tracy, N.D., Young, J.C., Mason, R.L.: Multivariate control charts for individual observations. J. Qual. Technol. **24**(2), 88–95 (1992)

Wold, S., Geladi, P., Esbensen, K., Ohman, J.: Multi-way principal components and PLS analysis. J. Chemom. **1**, 41–56 (1987)

Multivariate Statistical Process Control Based on Principal Component Analysis: Implementation of Framework in R

Ana Cristina Braga[1]([✉])(iD), Cláudia Barros[1], Pedro Delgado[2],
Cristina Martins[2], Sandra Sousa[1], J. C. Velosa[2](iD), Isabel Delgado[2],
and Paulo Sampaio[1](iD)

[1] ALGORITMI Centre, University of Minho, 4710-057 Braga, Portugal
acb@dps.uminho.pt
[2] Bosch Car Multimedia Portugal SA, Apartado 2458, 4705-970 Braga, Portugal
Pedro.Delgado@pt.bosch.com

Abstract. The interest in multivariate statistical process control (MSPC) has increased as the industrial processes have become more complex.

This paper presents an industrial process involving a plastic part in which, due to the number of correlated variables, the inversion of the covariance matrix becomes impossible, and the classical MSPC cannot be used to identify physical aspects that explain the causes of variation or to increase the knowledge about the process behaviour.

In order to solve this problem, a Multivariate Statistical Process Control based on Principal Component Analysis (MSPC-PCA) approach was used and an R code was developed to implement it according some commercial software used for this purpose, namely the ProMV (c) 2016 from ProSensus, Inc. (www.prosensus.ca).

Based on used dataset, it was possible to illustrate the principles of MSPC-PCA.

This work intends to illustrate the implementation of MSPC-PCA in R step by step, to help the user community of R to be able to perform it.

Keywords: Multivariate Statistical Process Control (MSPC)
Principal Component Analysis (PCA) · Control charts
Contribution plots · R language

1 Introduction

Modern production processes have become more complex and now require a joint analysis of a large number of variables with considerable correlations between them [13].

With univariate statistical process control (SPC), it is possible to recognize the existence of assignable causes of variation and distinguish unstable processes from stable processes where only common causes of variation are present. The main SPC charts are Shewhart, CUSUM and EWMA charts. They are easy to use and enable to discriminate between unstable and stable processes. This way, it is possible to detect many types of faults and reduce the production of non-conform products [14].

Although SPC Shewhart charts were designed to control a single characteristic, if more than one characteristic is relevant to the process and these characteristics are independent, the use of those charts is still the right choice. However, a separate analysis of correlated variables may lead to erroneous conclusions.

Figure 1 describes a process with two quality variables (y_1, y_2) that follow a bivariate normal distribution and have a $\rho(y_1, y_2)$ correlation. The ellipse represents a contour for the in-control process; the dots represent observations and are also plotted as individual Shewhart charts on y_1 and y_2 vs. time. The analysis of each individual chart shows that the process appears to be in statistical control. However, the true situation is revealed in the multivariate y_1 vs. y_2, where one observation is spotted outside the joint confidence region given by the ellipse [10].

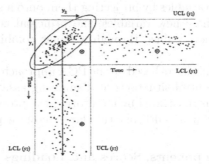

Fig. 1. The misleading nature of univariate charts (adapted from [10]).

When applying a multivariate statistical approach for monitoring the status of a process, a set of difficulties can be found. Some of them are listed in [11], as follows:

1. Dimensionality: large amounts of data, including hundreds or even thousands of variables (e.g. chemical industry);
2. Collinearity among the variables;
3. Noise associated with the measurement of process variables;
4. Missing data: the largest data sets contain missing data (sometimes up to 20%).

Thus, it is necessary to find methods to help overcome these difficulties.

In complex processes with a large number of variables (tens, hundreds or even thousands), another problem, associated with collinearity, should be considered: the inversion of the variance/covariance matrix to compute the distance of Hotelling's T^2 becomes difficult or even impossible (singular matrix). In such cases, the traditional multivariate approach must be extended and the principal component analysis (PCA) should be used in order to obtain new uncorrelated variables. This process is achieved through a spatial rotation, followed by a projection of the original data onto orthonormal subspaces [7].

The R language provides a flexible computational framework for statistical data analysis. R has several packages and functions to perform the PCA, and a recent one to perform the multivariate statistical quality control (MSQC) [18], but the sequence to perform MSPC-PCA is missing and hard to follow.

This study describes an R code that covers all the main steps of the MSPC-PCA in an industrial context. All computation implemented in R follows the procedures used by ProSensus Commercial Software, which deals with multivariate data analysis for a large number of variables.

The main packages used in this study were prcomp, psych, FactoMineR or pcaMethods.

2   Multivariate Statistical Process Control Based on PCA

The use of PCA aims to reduce the dimensionality of a dataset with a large number of correlated variables by projecting them onto a subspace with reduced dimensionality [8]. These new variables, the principal components (PCs), are orthogonal and can be obtained through a linear combination of the original variables [3].

Multivariate control charts based on the PCA approach provide powerful tools for detecting out of control situations or diagnosing assignable causes of variation. This function was illustrated by monitoring the properties of a low-density polyethylene produced in a multi-zone tubular reactor, as presented in [10].

2.1   Principal Components, Scores and Loadings

To perform PCA, consider a data set given by a matrix X, where n and p are, respectively, the number of observations (rows) and the process variables (columns). As a process can have different variables expressed in different units, before applying PCA, the variables are usually standardized by scaling them to zero mean and unit variance. The packages prcomp, pcaMethods (available in Bioconductor) and FactoMineR perform this kind of analysis.

2.2   Representation of the Observations in the Reduced Dimension PCA Model - Geometric Interpretation

The equation $T = P'X$ is interpreted as a rotation of the axis system composed of the original variables set X into a new axis system composed of the PCs.

As mentioned earlier, most of the variability in the original data is captured in the first m PCs. Thus, the previous equation for the full PCA model can be written for a new reduced dimension model [14]:

$$T_m = P'_m X \Rightarrow X = T_m P'_m + E = \sum_{i=1}^{m} t_i p'_i + E \tag{1}$$

where E is the residual matrix given by the difference between the original variables and their reconstruction using the reduced dimension PCA model.

The geometric interpretation of the previous equations is the projection of the original variables onto a subspace of dimension $m < p$ after the previously described rotation.

The concept is illustrated in Fig. 2, where a three-dimensional dataset is represented, as are its projection (scores) in a plane with two-dimensions (PC1 and PC2) [11].

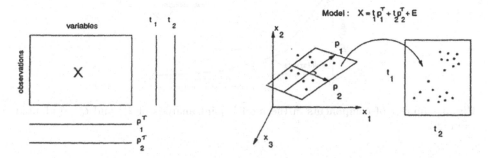

Fig. 2. PCA as a data projection method (source: [11]).

Four types of observation can be found with this projection of data:

1. "regular observations": in accordance with the PCA model defined;
2. "good leverage points": close to the PCA subspace but far from the center;
3. "orthogonal outliers": with a long orthogonal distance to the PCA subspace, but close to regular observations, when looking at their projection onto the PCA subspace;
4. "bad leverage points": with a long orthogonal distance and far from the regular observations [4].

2.3   Number of Principal Components

The number m of principal components retained to build the PCA model can be defined by using some of the following methods: the amount of variability explained by the PCA model (R^2), the Kaiser method, the scree plot, the broken stick or the cross-validation (Q^2) [8]. When used individually, none of these methods is definitive. Some commercial software packages specialized in MSPC, such as ProMV from ProSensus, use a joint analysis of R^2 and Q^2.

The percentage of variability (R^2) explained by the model is directly related to the number of principal components considered for the PCA model and can be computed by $100 \times (\sum_i^m \lambda_i / \sum_i^p \lambda_i)$ %, where λ_i corresponds to the eigenvalue for PCi [8].

The cross-validation (Q^2) describes the predictive ability of the proposed model and is based on the evaluation of prediction errors of the observations not used to build the model [21]. For the training data, the prediction error decreases as more components are added. However, for the testing data, i.e., observations that were not used to build the model, this error increases when too many components are used. This effect happens because the model is being over-fitted with noise. The number of components to be considered is the one with the smallest prediction error (Fig. 3).

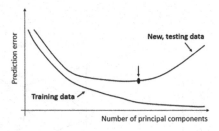

Fig. 3. Number of components in the model: joint analysis of R^2 and Q^2 (adapted from [2])

2.4 Multivariate Control Charts Based on PCA for Detecting Assignable Causes

Take into account that T^2 statistic is the weighted distance of an observation to the center of the PCA subspace, the weighting factor is the variation in the direction of the observation so T_m^2 can be computed as follows [10]:

$$T_m^2 = \sum_{i=1}^{m} \frac{t_i^2}{s_{t_i}^2} = \sum_{i=1}^{m} \frac{t_i^2}{\lambda_i} \tag{2}$$

The upper control limit for T^2, with $100(1-\alpha)\%$ confidence, is given by the F-distribution with m and $n-m$ degrees of freedom [10]:

$$UCL\left(T_m^2\right) = \frac{m\left(n^2-1\right)}{n\left(n-m\right)} F_{\alpha,m,n-m} \tag{3}$$

It can also be approximated by the chi-square distribution [15]:

$$UCL\left(T_m^2\right) = \chi_{m,\alpha}^2 \tag{4}$$

The square prediction error (SPE) or Q statistics is related to the variability in the PCA model and can be defined as the quadratic orthogonal distance [10]:

$$SPE = \sum_{j=1}^{p} \left(x_{new,j} - \hat{x}_{new,j}\right)^2 \tag{5}$$

Assuming that residuals follow a multivariate normal distribution, the upper control limit for the SPE chart can be computed using the following equation [6]:

$$UCL\,(SPE_\alpha) = \theta_1 \left[\frac{z_\alpha \sqrt{2\theta_2 h_0^2}}{\theta_1} + \frac{\theta_2 h_0\,(h_0 - 1)}{\theta_1^2} + 1 \right]^{1/h_0} \tag{6}$$

where, $h_0 = 1 - \frac{2\theta_1\theta_3}{3\theta_2^2}$, $\theta_i = \sum_{j=m+1}^{p} \lambda_j^i$ with $i = 1, 2, 3$ and z_α is the value of the standard normal distribution with level of significance α.

According to [17], an approximation of SPE, based on a weighted chi-square distribution, can be used, as follows:

$$UCL\,(SPE_\alpha) = \frac{\nu}{2b}\chi_{\frac{2b^2}{\nu},\alpha}^2 \tag{7}$$

where b is the sample mean and ν is the variance.

2.5 Diagnosing Assignable Causes

After detecting a faulty observation, the PCA model should be able to identify which variables contribute most to this situation.

Contribution plots were firstly introduced by [12] and decompose the fault detection statistics into a sum of terms associated with each original variable. Consequently, the variables associated with the fault should present larger contributions. This way, using contribution plots, it is possible to focus the attention on a small subset of variables, thus making engineer and operator diagnostic activities easier [9].

As there is no unique way to decompose these statistics, various authors have proposed different formulas to calculate the contributions [9]. Westerhuis et al. [20] discussed the contribution plots for both the T^2 and SPE statistics in the multivariate statistical process control of batch processes. In particular, the contributions of process variables to the T^2 are generalized to any type of latent variable model with or without orthogonality constraints. Alcala and Qin [1] assigned these contributions to three general methods: complete-decomposition, partial-decomposition and reconstruction-based contributions.

The contribution to T^2 of a variable x_j, for m PCs, is given by:

$$cont_j^{T^2} = x_j \sqrt{\sum_{i=1}^{m} \left(\frac{t_i}{s_{ti}} \right)^2 p_i^2} \tag{8}$$

The contribution to SPE of a variable x_j, for m retained PCs, is given by:

$$cont_j^{SPE} = e_j^2 \times sign(e_j) \tag{9}$$

where $e_j = x_j - \hat{x}_j = x_j - \sum_{i=1}^{m} t_i p_i$

2.6   Steps for Applying MSPC-PCA

To apply the MSPC-PCA it is necessary to follow the following steps:

(1) Collection of a sample representative of the normal operating conditions (NOC);
(2) Application of PCA: use of `prcomp` function in R, the standardization is included;
(3) Definition of the number of principal components to be retained: the `FactoMineR` package could be used to produce the same results of `prcomp` and we can chose directly the number of components as parameter in the function. Another way to perform PCA is `pcaMethods` that uses some measures for internal cross validation techniques;
(4) Interpretation of the model obtained: analysis of scores and loadings plots. To draw these graphs we use the package `ellipse` and `plot`;
(5) Identification of the physical meaning of each of the principal components, if existing;
(6) Plot control charts for T^2 and SPE defining the limits according to the equations;
(7) Interpretation of contributions plot and elimination of strong outliers.

3   Results

This section will present the scripts of R code for the R user community to be able to perform MSPC-PCA by following all the necessary steps described in Sect. 2.6. For each step an example of a dataset of a plastic part will be presented. The goal of this study was to identify which geometrical dimensions of this plastic parts had the highest variability.

All calculation methods used were implemented in R programming language. The most important packages and sections of the R codes were included for reference.

The plastic parts used in this study were selected from the same production batch on three different days (20 parts per day). The mold had two cavities and 86 geometrical dimensions, such as flatness, length, width and thickness, which were measured with a coordinate measuring machine. This dataset will be designated, in the R code, by `dataset`.

3.1   Model Summary

PCA is aimed to produce a small set of independent principal components, from a large set of correlated original variables. Usually, a smaller number of PCs explains the most relevant parts of variability in the dataset. The method used to decide the number of PCs to retain was the joint observation of two indicators: R^2, which is a quantification of the explained percentage of variation obtained directly with the eigenvalues; and Q^2, which measures the predictive ability of the model and is obtained through cross-validation.

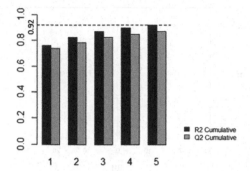

Fig. 4. Graphical result.

Table 1. Tabular result.

Comp	Cumulative R^2	Cumulative Q^2
PC1	0.7605	0.7418
PC2	0.8255	0.7755
PC3	0.8686	0.8043
PC4	0.8977	0.8253
PC5	0.9204	0.8387

R^2 can be computed by using the function `prcomp` included in the `stats` package of R, as follows:

```
acp<-prcomp(dataset,scale=T)
```

The `FactoMineR` package also provides a list of results for multivariate analysis methods, such as PCA, correspondence analysis or clustering [5].

In this work, cross-validation was obtained with the `pcaMethods` package. It provides a set of different PCA implementations, together with tools for cross-validation and visualization of the results [19]. The code used to perform the cross-validation was:

```
pc.Meth.sca.cv<-pca(scale(dataset), nPcs=5, method = 'svd',cv='q2')
plot(pc.Meth.sca.cv)
cv.tab<-as.data.frame(cvstat(pc.Meth.sca.cv))
```

Both indicators, R^2 and Q^2, suggested that five PCs were enough to explain the relevant part of the variability associated to the production process of the plastic part (Fig. 4 and Table 1). The total variation explained by the model with five components was approximately 92%.

3.2   Score Plots

Score plots are useful graphical analysis tools. Timeline score plots for a single PC are used to analyze time-related variation. Scatter plots of the combination of two PC scores are used to analyze the presence of clusters and how each observation is aligned with each one of the PCs. Observations that lie outside of the control limits may represent outliers. Score plots in this paper showed the control limits for 95% (dashed ellipse) and 99.7% (continuous ellipse).

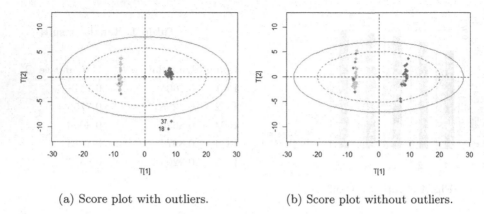

(a) Score plot with outliers.   (b) Score plot without outliers.

Fig. 5. Score plot for PC1/PC2.

Score plots can be obtained with the *ellipse* function, which creates the outline of a confidence region for two score variables [16]. Part of the R code used to obtain the score plots for PC1 and PC2 is the following:

```
a.acp<-acp$x[,1:2]
centros.acp<-colMeans(a.acp)
lcov.acp=solve(cov(a.acp))
lcov.acp
plot(ellipse(type = "chi",cov(acp$x[,c(1,2)]), level=0.95),
type="l", xlab= "T[1]", ylab="T[2]",col='red', lty=2,xlim=c(-28,28),ylim=c(-12,12)
points(centros.acp [1], centros.acp [2], pch=1)
abline(h=0,lty=2)
abline(v=0,lty=2)
points(ellipse(type = 'chi',cov(acp$x[,c(1,2)]), level=.997), col='red',type="l")
tipo.obs<-substr(abbreviate(amostra[,1]), start = 5,stop = 5)
tipo.obs
cores<- ifelse(tipo.obs=='1' ,"5", "2")
points(-acp$x[,c(1,2)], cex= 0.75, pch=10, col=cores)
text(x = -acp$x[18,1], y = -acp$x[18,2],labels = 18,cex = .8, pos = 2)
text(x = -acp$x[37,1], y = -acp$x[37,2],labels = 37,cex = .8, pos = 2)
```

By analyzing the score plots (Fig. 5), the physical meaning associated with the PCs retained can be identified. PC1 distinguishes two clusters corresponding to each one of two cavities in the mold; PC2, which explains approximately 6.5% of the variation, is highly influenced by observations 18 and 37, which are outliers. If these two observations are removed and the new model is built, then PC2 becomes influenced by parts warpage, which is present in both cavities and explains approximately 5%.

The percentages of the total variance explained by PC3, PC4 and PC5, 4.1%, 2.5% and 2.4%, reflect different machine adjustments or different machine/raw material conditions in the different production days. However, each one is so small that their effects were not further analyzed.

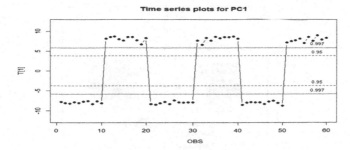

Fig. 6. Time series score plot for PC1.

The code used to perform the time line score (Fig. 6), for example, for PC1 was:

```
n<-nrow(amostra)
n
plot(1:n,-acp$x[,1],ylim = c(-12,12), main = "Time series plots for PC1",xlab = 'OBS',
ylab = 'T[1]')
lines(1:nrow(variaveis),-acp$x[,1],type="b",col='black',pch=19)
abline(h=-5.854,lty=1,col='red')
abline(h=-3.781,lty=2,col='red')
abline(h=5.854,lty=1,col='red')
abline(h=3.781,lty=2,col='red')
text(58,5.854, labels='0.997',pos = 3,cex=0.8,col='red')
text(58,3.781, labels='0.95',pos = 3,cex=0.8,col='red')
text(58,-5.854, labels='0.997',pos = 3,cex=0.8,col='red')
text(58,-3.781, labels='0.95',pos = 3,cex=0.8,col='red')
```

3.3 Loading Plots

Loading plots display the projection of the unit vector with the direction of each original variable in the new PCA axis system. When represented in a scatter plot, the variables that are strongly correlated with a PC create a small angle with this PC direction. The variables that are closer to the center of the plot are not relevant for explaining the variation associated with this PCs pair.

Part of the R code used to compute the loadings plot for PC1 and PC2 is:

```
load<-sweep(pca3$var$coord,2,sqrt(pca3$eig[1:ncol(pca3$var$coord),1]))
[,1:ncol(pca3$var$coord)]
plot(load.stand[,c(1,2)], xlim=c(-.2,.2),ylim=c(-.40,.40),xlab='PC1',ylab = 'PC2')
abline(h=0,lty=2)
abline(v=0,lty=2)
text(load.stand[,1],load.stand[,2],labels =colnames(dataset),cex=0.8, lwd=2,col="blue")
```

The loadings plot $PC1-PC2$, in Fig. 7, show the variables that are positively or negatively correlated with $PC1$, which is already known to represent the different cavities. The variables with high loadings in the $PC2$ are describing warpage, as already mentioned.

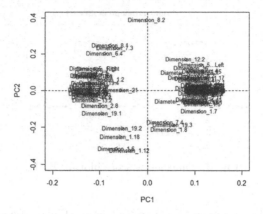

Fig. 7. Loadings plot $PC1 - PC2$.

3.4 Hotelling's T^2 Control Charts and Contributions Plot

T^2 indicates the distance from an observation to the center of the PCA subspace; it is a summary statistics calculated as the sum of squares of the scores of each observation in each one of the retained principal components. In the case of plotting only two-dimensions, all points in the ellipse have the same T^2 value and correspond to an upper limit (95% or 99.7%) estimated from the model.

The R code used for T^2 is the shown below and follows Eq. 2.

```
num.com <- 5
a.acp <- acp$x[,1:num.com]
centros.acp <- colMeans(a.acp)
lcov.acp = solve(cov(a.acp))
dm.acp <- rep(0,length(a.acp[,1]))
for(i in 1:length(a.acp[,1])){
dm.acp[i]=round(t(a.acp[i,]-centros.acp)%*%lcov.acp%*%(a.acp[i,]-centros.acp),3)
}
```

The upper limits (95% and 99.7%), according to Eq. 3, are computed by using the following code:

```
k<-num.com
n<-nrow(dataset)
cc.sw.UCL.997<-(k*(n+1)*(n-1))/(n*(n-k)) * qf(.997,k, n-k)
cc.sw.UCL.95<-(k*(n+1)*(n-1))/(n*(n-k)) * qf(0.95,k, n-k)
```

Using the dataset of a plastic part, the control charts for T^2 shown in Fig. 8 suggest that assignable causes of variation were associated with observations 18 and 37. Thus, a method that allows identifying the original variables associated with these assignable causes of variation is required. This method is the calculation of contributions.

Contribution plots are used to identify which variables contribute more to T^2 values. Observation 18 is further analyzed concerning their contributions to T^2. Since the effect observed in observation 18 is the same as in observation 37,

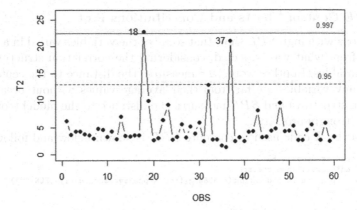

Fig. 8. Hotelling's T^2 control chart.

the contribution plots for observation 37 were not presented in this study. Part of the code used to perform the contribution plot to T^2 is (based on Eq. 8):

```
data <- matrix(NA, nrow=num.com, ncol=ncol(dataset))
for (i in 1:num.com){
num=round(t(a.acp[1,i]-centros.acp[i])%*%lcov.acp[i,i]%*%(a.acp[1,i]-centros.acp[i]),3)
data[1,]<-num%*%load[,i]^2
}
contr<-sqrt(colSums(data))*scale(dataset)[1,]
barplot(contrP,axes = T, ylim=c(-8,7),cex.axis = .9)
```

Considering the previous analyses related to loadings and scores, and the high contributions of the variables Dimension 1.12, Dimension 1.6, Dimension 8.2 and Dimension 7.3 and Dimension 8.1, as shown in Fig. 9, it can be concluded that this part has a problem of planeness (Dimensions 1.6 and 1.12) associated with a reduced thickness (Dimensions 8.1 and 8.2).

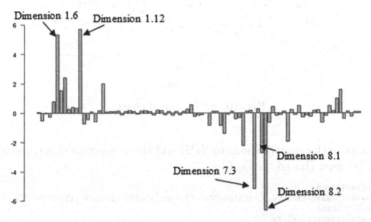

Fig. 9. Contribution Plot to Hotelling's T^2 for observation 18.

3.5 *SPE* Control Charts and Contributions Plot

Observations with high *SPE* show that some of the variables varied in a different direction from what was expected, considering the correlation structure of the original variables. In other words, T^2 measures the distance to the center of the model (many variables are far from their average values without breaking the correlation structure) and *SPE* measures the distance to the model (correlation structure strongly broken).

Part of the R code used to compute *SPE* is shown below and follows Eq. 5:

```
num.com.spe<-as.numeric(5)
a<-pca3$ind$coord[,1:num.com.spe]
load<-sweep(pca3$var$coord,2,sqrt(pca3$eig[1:ncol(pca3$var$coord),1]),FUN="/")
[,1:num.com.spe]
Ye<-a %*% t(load)
Qt<-rowSums((scale(dataset)-Ye)^2)
```

According to [6], the R code that should be used to perform the upper limits (95% and 99.7%) for *SPE* is the following (based on Eq. 6):

```
QCL99.7<-(var(Qt)/(2*mean(Qt)))*qchisq(p = .997,df = (2*mean(Qt)^2)/var(Qt))
QCL95<-(var(Qt)/(2*mean(Qt)))*qchisq(p = 0.95,df = (2*mean(Qt)^2)/var(Qt))
```

The control charts for *SPE* is illustrated in Fig. 10 and suggest that assignable causes of variation were associated with observation 28.

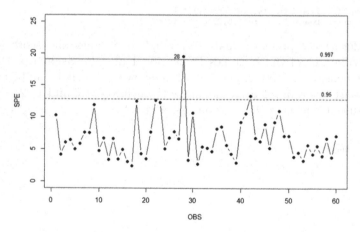

Fig. 10. *SPE* control chart.

To compute the contributions to *SPE* and the respective chart, the following code can be used (based on Eq. 9):

```
a<-pca3$ind$coord
load<-sweep(pca3$var$coord,2,sqrt(pca3$eig[1:ncol(pca3$var$coord),1]),FUN="/")
Ye<-a %*% t(load)
erros<-scale(variaveis)-Ye
CONT<- matrix(NA, nrow= nrow(dataset), ncol=ncol(dataset))
for(i in 1:nrow(erros)){
CONT[i,]<-sign(erros[i,])*erros[i,]*t(erros[i,])}
barplot(CONT[28,],axes = T,names.arg=colnames(dataset),ylim=c(-4,6),cex.axis = .9)
```

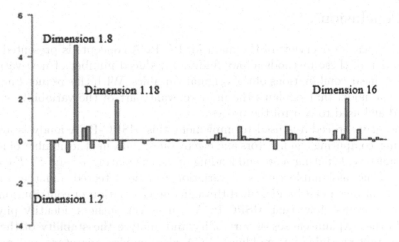

Fig. 11. Contributions Plot to SPE for observation 28.

In Fig. 11, variable Dimension 1.8, with a high contribution to SPE, does not show the usual variability associated with different cavities. In this observation, Dimension 1.8 has an increased value without being followed by other variables that should have a high correlation with it.

3.6   Raw Data: The Original Values of Dataset

Once the variables that contribute most to T^2 and SPE are detected, the original variables are analyzed to check which could contribute to a product malfunction.

Regarding the variables with high contributions in observation 18, raw data of the original variables show that they have values lower than what would be expected, as presented in Fig. 11 for variable Dimension 8.1. It was previously referred that observation 37 had the same effect as observation 18; this conclusion is confirmed by the raw data of variable Dimension 8.1, presented in Fig. 12.

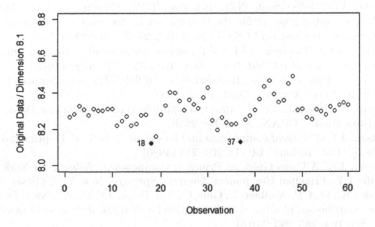

Fig. 12. Original values for variable Dimension 8.1.

4   Conclusions

In this paper, an overview of the main MSPC-PCA concepts is presented. The application of these methods allows finding a reduced number of new variables that are linear combinations of the original variables. With this reduced number of PCs, a model that explains the most relevant part of the variability can be created and used to control the process.

The main procedures used to implement this MSPC-PCA analysis are the following: computing eigenvectors and eigenvalues; choosing the number of model components; calculating score and loading plots; calculating T^2 and SPE control charts. Thus, assignable causes of variation can be detected and the original variables involved can be identified through the calculation of contributions.

These results show that MSPC-PCA can detect outliers, identify physical aspects that explain causes of variability and analyze the stability of the production process (injection molding). PCA also enables operators and process engineers to increase their knowledge about the way the process behaves and to identify the underlying factors which govern the variability of the process.

The use of the R programming language in an industrial example demonstrates the great potential of MSPC-PCA techniques in multivariate data analysis and multivariate statistical control of processes.

Acknowledgments. This work has been supported by: European Structural and Investment Funds in the FEDER component, through the Operational Competitiveness and Internationalization Programme (COMPETE 2020) [Project n° 002814; Funding Reference: POCI-01-0247-FEDER-002814], COMPETE: POCI-01-0145-FEDER-007043 and FCT - (Fundação para a Ciência e Tecnologia) within the Project Scope: UID/CEC/00319/2013.

References

1. Alcala, C.F., Qin, S.: Joe: Analysis and generalization of fault diagnosis methods for process monitoring. J. Process Control **21**, 322–330 (2011)
2. Aptula, A.O., Jeliazkovab, N.G., Schultzc, T.W., Cronina, M.T.D.: The better predictive model: high q2 for the training set or low root mean square error of prediction for the test set? QSAR Comb. Sci. **24**(3), 385–396 (2005)
3. Bharati, M.H., MacGregor, J.F.: Multivariate image analysis for real-time process monitoring and control. Ind. Eng. Chem. Res. **37**, 4715–4724 (1998)
4. Hubert, M., Rousseeuw, P.J., Branden, K.V.: ROBPCA: a new approach to robust. Am. Stat. Assoc. Am. Soc. Qual. **47**, 1 (2005)
5. Husson, F., Josse, J., Le, S., Mazet, J.: Multivariate Exploratory Data Analysis and Data Mining. CRAN, November 2016
6. Jackson, J.E.: Principal components and factor analysis: Part I - principal components. J. Qual. Technol. **14**(11), 201–213 (1980)
7. Jackson, J.E.: A Users Guide to Principal Components. Wiley, New York (1991)
8. Jolliffe, I.T.: Principal Component Analysis. Springer, New York (1986)
9. Van den Kerkhof, P., Vanlaer, J., Gins, G., Van Impe, J.F.M.: Analysis of smearing-out in contribution plot based fault isolation for Statistical Process Control. Chem. Eng. Sci. **104**, 285–293 (2013)

10. Kourti, T., MacGregor, J.F.: Process analysis, monitoring and diagnosis, using multivariate projection methods. Chemometr. Intell. Lab. Syst. **28**(1), 3–21 (1995)
11. MacGregor, J.F.: Using on-line process data to improve quality: challenges for statisticians. Int. Stat. Rev. **65**, 309–323 (1997)
12. MacGregor, J., Jaeckle, C., Kiparissides, C., Koutoudi, M.: Process monitoring and and diagnosis by multi block pls methods. AIChE J. **40**(5), 826838 (1994)
13. MacGregor, J.F., Yu, H., Muoz, S.G., Flores-Cerrillo, J.: Data-based latent variable methods for process analysis, monitoring and control. Comput. Chem. Eng. **29**, 1217–1223 (2005)
14. Martin, E.B., Morris, A.J., Zhang, J.Z.: Multivariate statistical process control charts and the problem of interpretation: A short overview and some applications in industry. System Engineering for Automation (1996)
15. Montgomery, D.C.: Introduction to Statistical Quality Control. Wiley, New York (2009)
16. Murdoch, D., Chow, E.D., Celayeta, J.M.F.: Functions for drawing ellipses and ellipse-like confidence regions. CRAN, April 2013
17. Nomikos, P., MacGregor, J.F.: Multivariate SPC charts for monitoring batch processes. Technometrics **31**(1), 41–59 (1995)
18. Santos-Fernandez, E.: Multivariate Statistical Quality Control Using R, vol. 14. Springer, New York (2013)
19. Stacklies, W., Redestig, H., Wright, K.: A collection of PCA methods. CRAN, February 2017
20. Westerhuis, J.A., Gurden, S.P., Smilde, A.K.: Generalized contribution plots in multivariate statistical process monitoring. Chemometr. Intell. Lab. Syst. **51**, 95–114 (2000)
21. Wold, S.: Cross-validatory estimation of the number of components in factor and principal components models. Technometrics **20**(4), 397–405 (1978)

Accounting Information System (AIS) Alignment and Non-financial Performance in Small Firm: A Contingency Perspective

Dekeng Setyo Budiarto[1]([⊠]), Rahmawati[2],
Muhammad Agung Prabowo[2], Bandi[2], Ludfi Djajanto[3],
Kristianto Purwoko Widodo[4], and Tutut Herawan[4,5,6]

[1] Department of Accounting, Universitas PGRI Yogyakarta,
Yogyakarta, Indonesia
dekengsb@upy.ac.id
[2] Faculty of Economics and Business, Universitas Sebelas Maret,
Surakarta, Indonesia
[3] Politeknik Negeri Malang, Malang, Indonesia
[4] Universitas Teknologi Yogyakarta, Yogyakarta, Indonesia
[5] Universitas Negeri Yogyakarta, Yogyakarta, Indonesia
tutut@uny.ac.id
[6] AMCS Research Center, Yogyakarta, Indonesia

Abstract. Accounting Information System (AIS) is very important for Small and Medium Enterprises (SMEs) because it can provide information for the owner in decision making. In line with the result of previous study, which find that AIS alignment is needed because it will affect company performance. This study aims to test the direct relationship and mediating relationship among three contingency variables of AIS alignment on non-financial performance. This study employs questionnaire with 87 SMEs owner in Yogyakarta region as samples. The results show that AIS sophisticated, owner commitment affect non-financial performance, either directly or mediated by AIS alignment. This study implies that AIS is very essential for SMEs to survive in a very competitive environme.

Keywords: Accounting information system · Alignment
Non-financial performance

1 Introduction

Previous researchers has try to explain the effect of information technology[1] (IT) implementation in Small and Medium Enterprises (SMEs) [1–4]. The study that investigates the implementation of IT in SMEs is very important Grande, [5] for the following reasons: first, there are differences between SMEs and large firm in IT adoption and

---

[1] Refers to previous study that found that accounting information system has the same terminology with Management Accounting System (MAS) Management Information System (MIS), accounting information system which is the part of information technology [15, 16].

© Springer International Publishing AG, part of Springer Nature 2018
O. Gervasi et al. (Eds.): ICCSA 2018, LNCS 10961, pp. 382–394, 2018.
https://doi.org/10.1007/978-3-319-95165-2_27

implementation [6]. Second, company needs a large sum of money to make a design, test, and implement IT Lim *et al.* [7], while the limitation in budget is the main problem faced by SMEs [8]. Third, even though SMEs owner realize that performance measurement is an important activity, however they may not use it properly [9]. The contingency perspective explains that organizational performance is affected by internal factors [10]. In line with the argument, Hussin *et al.* [11]; Ismail and King [12] explain that SMEs performance is affected by alignment between capacity and IT requirement. Furthermore, Ismail and King [13]; Al-Eqab and Ismail [14] prove that IT alignment is affected by organizational factors such as AIS sophisticated and owner commitment, and situational factor that is external IT expertise [11]. The SMEs need AIS sophisticated to face market competition [3], to facilitate the realization of objectives [17], provide flexibility in developing strategy, especially in facing consumers' demand [18]. Besides that, SMEs also need owner's commitment in implementing the IT; the more committed the owner, the implementation of technology will be easier [19]. The SMEs owner who have commitment will realize that IT is very important for SMEs to survive [20]. In addition to AIS sophisticated and owner commitment, external IT expertise becomes another important factor for SMEs in IT implementation [11]. Human resources limitedness makes external IT expertise is needed for SMEs because assistance from the experts in IT may decrease risk and facilitate and fasten IT implementation in SMEs [20, 21].

This study aims to test direct relationship between AIS sophisticated, owner commitment, external IT expertise, and non-financial performance, as well as the indirect relationship among the variables mediated by AIS alignment. This study results are important for SMEs owner so that they can plan and select the IT that meet their capacity and requirement. This study employs non-financial performance measurements because financial performance has a limitation that is it reports short-term performance and not a prediction for long-term performance [22]. Financial performance such as cost efficiency tends to push managers to commit moral hazard in order to maximize their profits [23]. Thus, to support and evaluate the success of organization, Harrison and Pole [24]; Choe [22] proposes the usage of non-financial performance measurement. Non-financial performance represented by service quality will leads to the increase in cost, thus reducing profitability [25]. However, non-financial performance measurement may provide several benefits such as quality improvement and faster delivery [16, 26, 27]. Zuriekat *et al.* [28] explain that the measurement of financial and non-financial performance has a different role in supporting company's operation. Financial measurement is more suitable to be used in organization that has multiple departments, but it will be harder to be implemented in SMEs [29].

The rest of this paper is organized as follow: Sect. 2 describes research proposed model and hypothesis development. Section 3 presents research model. Section 4 presents obtained results and following by discussion. Finally, Sect. 5 concludes this work.

2   Research Model and Hypotheses Development

This study is focused in SMEs in retail activities due to the difference in business type may affect IT implementation and performance [16]. Besides that, other studies have proved that non-financial performance in retail business can be assessed from service quality [30]. The factors that are likely to affects the implementation of IT in SMEs are AIS sophisticated, owner commitment, and external IT expertise. The Model of this study (Fig. 1) is a development from previous studies that explain the relationship between organizational factor and situational factor with IT alignment [11, 13, 14] as well as its effect on non-financial performance [22].

2.1   AIS Sophisticated and AIS Alignment

Company, regardless of its size, will face competition to protect its existence. To face the competition, SMEs must implement the technology [17]. In supporting managers' decision and increase the number of customers and market share, IT sophistication is needed by companies [2, 18]. One of SMEs' limitation lies on the limited number of employees; if not the nonexistence of employees; who can develop IT, thus it needs a sophisticated technology that can provide various information. IT sophisticated is very needed by SMEs to follow the change in demand from customers [15]. The other findings show that SMEs that have implementing the IT will be easier to acquire IT sophisticated [14, 31]. SMEs must take an action so that IT alignment can support organizational objectives, thus the implementation of IT will improve firm efficiency [8]. Company needs a good information system to support their daily activities and operation. The addition of information system will improve the flexibility so that the company will be stronger and easier in achieving its objectives [32]. Tuanmat and Malcolm [10] find the evidence that SMEs in Malaysia use AIS to support the changes in manufacturing technology in order to improve their performance. Estebanez [17] states that SMEs in service industry in Spain use IT more intensive and is very dependent on IT sophisticated. Due to these facts, even with various limitations, there is a growing numbers of SMEs that implement IT [11]. Based on the findings above, the hypothesis is proposed:

H1: AIS sophisticated significantly affects AIS alignment in SMEs

2.2   Owner Commitment and AIS Alignment

Generally, the manager who responsible on SMEs company operation is the owner [33]. Because of that, owner's commitment is a very important factor for SMEs in implementing IT. Ismail and King [1] explains that, in various cases, the implementation of IT in SMEs is still less efficient, thus owner commitment on IT development is needed, high commitment will facilitate the company in selecting the technology that fit with their needs.

Generally, SMEs do not have IT expert or IT department, thus the owner has a very important role in creating IT alignment [11, 17]. SMEs owner who understand the function of IT will try to choose the one that fit to avoid over investment [13]. Owner who

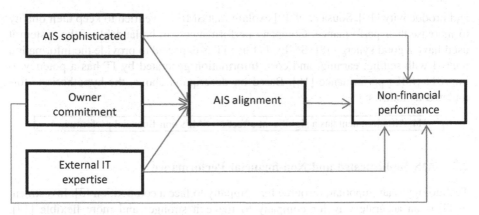

Fig. 1. The effect of AIS sophisticated, owner commitment, external IT expertise on AIS alignment and non-financial performance

has commitment in IT usage will make a good planning and evaluate IT usage in his company. Besides that, the success of SMEs is not assessed from company size only, but also can be viewed from the owner's capability in using IT [33]. Based on findings above, the hypothesis is formulated as follows:

> H2: owner commitment significantly affects AIS alignment in SMEs

2.3 External IT Expertise and AIS Alignment

One of SMEs limitations in IT implementation is the limited number of human resource who understands IT. This limitation makes the implementation process is less optimal [7]. Thong [33] explains that one of the success factors for SMEs in the implementation of IT is the cooperation between IT consultants with the owner in integrating the information system in the company. Finding from previous studies show that SMEs owner and external IT expertise is two success keys that affect the implementation of IT [11]. The SMEs owners argue that IT can be used in a long period of time, thus external IT expertise is only needed when a crash take place. However, external IT expertise is still needed because most SMEs have not implemented the IT appropriately. It is strengthen by Ismail and King [13] finding that proved that external IT expertise affects the implementation of IT in SMEs. Based on above findings, the hypothesis is proposed as follows:

> H3: External IT expertise significantly affects AIS alignment in SMEs

2.4 AIS Alignment and Non-financial Performance

The optimal implementation of IT will facilitate SMEs owner in managing their company so that they can compete more competitively because IT improvement is essential, even for a small company [17]. To face environmental uncertainty, several organizations have decided to invest in IT in the hope that it will improve the quality and productivity [10]. Sousa *et al.* [9] explain that SMEs have tried to keep their quality to increase their performance. Company performance will be laudable if the system it used have a good synergy [8]. SMEs that use IT is expected to provide the information related with selling, earning, and cost. Information generated by IT has a potency to improve SMEs performance [16]. Based on description above, the hypothesis is formulated as follows:

> H4: AIS alignment has a significant effect on SMEs non-financial performance

2.5   AIS Sophisticated and Non-financial Performance

Technology is an important resource for company to face a competition [3]. Investment in IT is an accurate way for company to make it stronger and more flexible [17]. Company will be able to respond quickly on customer's demand on qualified product as well as reducing its dependence on supplier through IT implementation [10]. Ismail and King [1] find evidence that SMEs that have information system that consistent with its needs have a better performance. Other studies, Soudani [32] finds evidence that AIS is very beneficial for SMEs and affecting organizational performance. Company needs IT to support its operation processes, an appropriate technology will support the company in achieving its objectives. In a large company, technology can be matched with requirement due to the existence of financial resource allocation. However, SMEs have a financial limitation, thus they have to choose an appropriate technology. Thus, to process daily transactions (selling and receivables) and monthly transactions (payroll and inventory calculations) SMEs need AIS that fit with its needs [16]. Based on above findings, the hypothesis is proposed:

> H5: AIS sophistication has a significant effect on SMEs non-financial performance

2.6   Owner Commitment and Non-financial Performance

Owner commitment on technology advancement has a big role for SMEs in the success of IT implementation, especially AIS. Owner who has got used to operate technology will find it easier to plan and evaluate the need of IT in their company [34]. Owner commitment on technological advancement will motivate the employees to participate and feel that they are the part of company information system development process. Employees' participation in IT development process can reduce the failure in technology implementation process [4]. Based on above findings, the hypothesis is proposed as follows:

> H6: owner commitment has a significant effect on SMEs non-financial performance

2.7   External IT Expertise and Non-financial Performance

Bledsoe and Ingram [7], Choe [22] develop a non-financial performance measurement that covers product quality, time for delivery, and customer's satisfaction. The improvement in quality and delivery speed is two problems that deemed very important for company. Technological congruence can ascertain that company can maintain its product quality. Finding from previous study Amidu et al. [20] explain that SMEs need external IT expertise to develop its technology, especially for process and transaction in accounting cycle. External IT expertise will be needed when SMEs are unable to overcome the problems related with IT failure. Due to that reason, in IT development process, external IT expertise participation is very important. Besides that, SMEs owners believe that the technology they develop can be used in a long-term period, while in reality IT need upgrade which usually performed by IT consultant [16]. Based on findings of the literatures, the hypothesis is proposed:

H7: External IT expertise has a significant effect on SMEs non-financial performance

3 Research Method

The population in this study is all owners of SMEs in retail sector and has implemented IT in Yogyakarta. Based on the data from Industrial, Trades, Cooperation, and SMEs Agency (Dinas Perindustrian, perdagangan, Koperasi dan UKM), the number of SMEs in Yogyakarta is 1,429. For the convenience purpose, this study only focused on Sleman, Bantul, Kulon Progo, Gunung Kidul regencies, and Yogyakarta city. This study is employ retail business only to ensure the homogeneity of data. This study use purposive sampling (non-probability sampling) as sampling technique, the technique in which the samples are selected based on certain characteristics [35]. The characteristics used by the researcher refer to the Act No 5/2008 on SMEs that is have maximum 2.5 billion rupiah in term of sales per year, have 5–19 employees for small enterprises and 20–99 employees for medium enterprises. Before the questionnaire distributed to the respondent prior tests on small business owners and students research, some questionnaires were drop from the questionnaires list.

In this study AIS alignment is a match between AIS capacity and AIS requirement. The AIS alignment is measured by multiplying all items in AIS capacity and AIS requirement. The AIS requirement and AIS capacity is measured with 12 question items developed by Ismail and King [1] with 4 point scale, in which point 1 for "very disagree" up to point 4 "very agree". The indicators for the question are: focus, orientation, time horizon, aggregation, timeliness, financial, non-financial, quantitative, and qualitative [13]. In this case, high alignment results from high ratings for an AIS requirement and high rating for AIS capacity. The AIS sophisticated are a sophistication of an application in providing information so that it can fulfill SMEs owner. AIS sophisticated are measured using 11 question items on accounting application and supporting application for office activities developed by [13]. The questionnaire uses 4 point scales, point 1 for "unimportant" up to point 4 "very important". The owner's commitment is owner's strong will to keep using technology because he believes that technology is important factor for his business development. Owner commitment is measured using 15 question items related with information needs, hardware and software selection, system implementation, and planning for future usage of IT. The questionnaire for this variable is adopted from Hussin et al. [11] and Ismail and King [12] with 4 point scale, point 1 for "low participation" up to point 4 for "high participation". Referring to Thong and Yap [36], external IT expertise is a person/company who assists SMEs in implementing IT, and oftentimes is a consultant/vendor who has an expertise in information system. The questionnaire for this variable consists of 5 question items related with external IT participation in hardware and software selection, training, and information system development. The questions are adopted from Ismail and King [1, 13] studies. The answer is stated in 4 point scales, point 1 for "do not participate" up to point 4 for "participate". Non-financial performance is measured using eight question items adopted from previous studies [22]. The answer is stated in 4 point scales, point 1 for "no information" up to point 4 "large information". The questions are related to the information about products failure/defects, product quality, number of returned products, number of defected supplies, lengths of cycle time from order to delivery and delivery.

4   Result and Discussion

This study is a survey study using questionnaire in data collection process. The sample is all owners of SMEs in Yogyakarta. The study is conducted in 4 months from January 1, up to May 30, 2015. The result of data from questionnaire is presented in the following Table 1:

Table 1. The result of returned questionnaire

Explanation	Quantity
(1)	(2)
The number of distributed questionnaire	= 300
The number of returned questionnaires	= 110
The number of defected/not meet the criteria questionnaire	= (23)
The number of questionnaires is able to analyzed	= 87

Based on Table 1 above, we can explain that there are 300 questionnaires sent to respondents. The questionnaires returned during the study are 110 questionnaires. Twenty three questionnaires cannot be processed further because of incomplete fillings. The usable questionnaires are 87 questionnaires with respond rate of 26%. The low response rate is due to the limited number of SMEs that have implemented IT. Besides that, this study only allocates four months to collect the data.

4.1   Results

An analysis of result by business classification of SMEs is presented in Table 2 and the level of IT adoption is presented in Table 3.

Validity testing is performed by reviewing the p value in the result of correlation testing using pearson product-momment. The Pearson correlation is calculates between each item of the questionnaire and the total score (total scores of AIS alignment). After the test of validity, for example is Table 4 (2 instrument X1.8 and X1.9 drop from the list), the next step is performing reliability testing. Based on Table 5, Cronbach alpha

Table 2. The classification of business

Classification	Region					Number of SMEs	Percentage
	Kota	Sleman	Bantul	Kulon Progo	Gunung Kidul		
Phone store	6	5	4	2	1	18	20.69
Drug store	2	3	3	2	0	10	11.49
Batik store	2	2	1	0	0	5	5.75
Accessories	2	4	1	0	0	7	8.05
Stationery	2	3	2	2	1	10	11.49
Minimarket	5	3	3	1	1	13	14.94
Spare part	2	2	3	0	0	7	8.05
Computer	7	3	4	3	0	17	19.54
Total	28	25	21	10	3	87	100

Table 3. Adoption level

Classification	Adoption level			Number of SMEs	Percentage
	Initiation	Diffusion	Integration		
Phone store	8	6	4	18	21.88
Drug store	10	-	-	10	12.50
Batik store	5	-	-	5	6.25
Accessories	7	-	-	7	9.38
Stationery	10	-	-	10	10.42
Minimarket	13	-	-	13	13.54
Spare part	7	-	-	7	8.33
Computer	10	5	2	17	17.71
Total	70	11	6	87	100

Table 4. Validity testing of X1 (AIS sophisticated)

	X1.1	X1.2	X1.3	X1.4	X1.5	X1.6	X1.7	X1.8	X1.9	X1.10	X1.11	Total
X1.1	1											
X1.2	0.320**	1										
X1.3	0.727**	0.351**	1									
X1.4	0.340**	0.567**	0.285**	1								
X1.5	0.954**	0.257*	0.748**	0.296**	1							
X1.6	0.316**	0.971**	0.304**	0.534**	0.271*	1						
X1.7	0.631**	0.310**	0.899**	0.213*	0.674**	0.303**	1					
X1.8	−0.111	−0.037	0.269*	0.400**	0.137	0.015	0.202	1				
X1.9	−0.061	0.143	0.175	0.048	0.086	0.164	0.067	0.483**	1			
X1.10	0.627**	0.246*	0.899**	0.198	0.670**	0.235*	0.942**	0.167	0.125	1		
X1.11	0.279**	0.490**	0.245*	0.937**	0.257*	0.472**	0.211*	0.482**	0.031	0.260*	1	
Total	0.747**	0.687**	0.757**	0.694**	0.731**	0.677**	0.740**	0.181	0.149	0.720**	0.675**	1

** Significant at $\alpha = 1\%$, * significant at $\alpha = 5\%$

Table 5. Reliability test

Variable	Number of Question	Cronbach Alpha	Explanation
(1)	(2)	(3)	(5)
AIS sophistication	9	0.892	Reliable
Owner commitment	13	0.871	Reliable
External IT expertise	5	0.793	Reliable
AIS Requirement	12	0.758	Reliable
AIS capacity	15	0.824	Reliable
Non-financial performance	7	0.816	Reliable

value for each variable is 0.892 for AIS sophistication; 0.871 for owner's commitment; 0.793 for external IT expertise; 0.758 for AIS requirement; 0.824 for AIS capacity; and 0.816 for non-financial performance. Reliability testing on all variables shows Cronbach alpha value greater than 0.6, this shows that all instruments are reliable and can be analyzed further.

This study uses three regression models to test the hypotheses. Model 1 is used to test hypothesis 1; hypothesis 2; hypothesis 3 with AIS alignment as dependent variable. Model 2 is used to test hypothesis 4 with non-financial performance as dependent variable. Model 3 is used to test hypothesis 5, hypothesis 6, and hypothesis 7 with non-financial performance as dependent variable. The results of hypotheses testing on the effect of AIS sophisticated, owner commitment, and external IT expertise on AIS alignment and non-financial performance is presented in Table 6.

Table 6 below shows the result for hypothesis 1, hypothesis 2, and hypothesis 3 which test the effect of AIS sophisticated, owner commitment, and external IT expertise on AIS alignment.

Table 6. Result of Regression Testing

Explanation	Model 1	Model 2	Model 3
	Coef. β (sig)	Coef. β (sig)	Coef. β (sig)
AIS sophisticated (x1)	0.334 (0.002)**		0.265 (0.009)**
Owner commitment (x2) External IT expertise (x3)	0.213 (0.041)* −0.038 (0.707)		0.250 (0.014)* 0.183 (0.072)
AIS alignment (Y)		0.382 (0.000)**	
F value	6.189 (0.001)*	14.495(0.000)**	0.000**
Adjusted R^2:	0.153	0.136	0.196

** Significant at $\alpha = 1\%$, * significant at $\alpha = 5\%$

The result of F-test shows F value of 6.189 with significant value of 0.001 and adjusted R^2 of 0.153. This shows that the independent variables can explain 15.3% of variation in dependent variable. The further testing on hypothesis 1 shows p value for AIS sophisticated of 0.002 (significant), owner's commitment has a significant effect on AIS alignment with p value of 0.041 (significant), external IT expertise has no a significant effect on AIS alignment with p value of 0.707 (not significant), thus hypothesis 1, 2 are supported while hypotheses 3 is rejected. Testing on model 2 acquires F value of 14.495 with p value < 0.001 (significant) and adjusted R^2 of 0.146. AIS alignment has a significant effect on non-financial performance with p value < 0.001 (significant). From the result of hypothesis testing we can conclude that AIS alignment has a significant effect on non-financial performance (hypothesis 4 is supported). Testing of model 3 acquires p value on AIS sophisticated of 0.009 (significant); owner commitment of 0.014 (significant); external IT expertise of 0.072 (not significant). From the results of testing on model 3 we can conclude that hypothesis 5, hypothesis 6 are supported while hypothesis 7 is rejected.

4.2 Discussion

This study results show several important findings that can be discussed. The first finding supports contingency theory as in Ismail and King [12] study that is AIS sophisticated, owner commitment affect AIS alignment. This finding is not surprising because previous study has proved that SMEs have tried to implement IT according to their needs [11]. The other results, Ismail and King [13] explain that SMEs in Malaysia that implement "analytical-based applications" find it easier to gain AIS alignment. The implementation of sophisticated technology will strengthen the company's position in the competition. Sophisticated technology will facilitate SMEs to perform accounting transaction such as selling, receivables, supplies, and payroll [17]. Furthermore, owner's commitment is an important factor in AIS implementation because owner has an important role in strategy planning for SMEs development [11]. Owner that understand the importance of technology is more prone to follow changes and make a good planning, thus technology can be implemented appropriately [6]. The adoption technology will provide accurate information as a base for decision making [12]. The last factor that affects AIS alignment is external IT expertise. With the limitation in human resource field, assistance from external parties, either consultant of government can help SMEs achieve better alignment, however using external IT expertise will increase SMEs cost. Second finding shows that most of the SMEs (80%) are in initiation level, which means that most of the SMEs have not utilize IT maximally, IT planning and control is still limited. Moreover, the SMEs in diffusion level (12%) and integration level (8%) are the SMEs that sell IT related commodities (computer store & phone store). This result provides an interesting material to be further studied, especially on owner's understanding on IT benefits. There are two possibilities related with this problem, first, the owner understand that IT is an important factor but do not implement it, and second, owner uses IT according to company's necessities to hold IT investment cost to minimum. The third finding, the direct effect of AIS sophisticated, owner commitment, and external IT expertise on non-financial performance (Fig. 2). This is quite surprising because previous study Budiarto, [16] find that AIS alignment

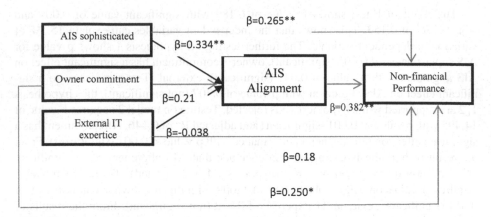

Fig. 2. The relationship between AIS sophisticated, owner commitment, external IT expertise, and non-financial performance.

is intervening variable that affects non-financial performance. This finding becomes a challenge for future studies to test the factors that affect SMEs performance.

Development in SMEs is not determined by its size but more on owner's role and ability in IT knowledge [33]. Owner must follow IT development and utilize IT optimally, especially for planning and strategy formulation [37]. SMEs owner that has a good understanding on technology will try to encourage their employees to participate in IT implementation, thus employees will feel that they become an important part in the company Dubihlela and Rundora [4] which in turn will improve their performance [31].

This study has several limitations that become a gap for future studies. The first limitation is this study proved that most of the SMEs are in initiation level where the owner has an excessive authority in IT implementation, this shows that IT has not implemented optimally in SMEs. Future research should study the IT implementation level further, because IT alignment relates with SMEs performance [1, 16]. The second limitation is this study does not test whether SMEs that selected as samples are private companies or family controlled companies. According to Chu [38], only small and family owned SMEs that have a better performance. The third limitation is the measurement of non-financial performance which only employs broad-scope, timelines, and aggregation indicator, without using integration indicator due to the SMEs selected as samples do not have division in their company. Future studies can develop the study samples to include SMEs with multiple divisions so that integration indicator can be implemented.

5   Conclusion

The analysis results show that all hypotheses proposed in this study are not supported. Besides having an effect on AIS alignment; situational factors and organizational factors also have a direct effect on non-financial performance. The testing on model 1 shows that AIS sophisticated, owner commitment has a significant effect on AIS alignment while external IT expertise has no significant effect on AIS alignment. This result is in line with [1, 11]. The testing on model 2 shows that AIS alignment has a significant effect on non-financial performance. This result is in line with [16]. The testing on model 3 shows that AIS sophisticated, owner commitment has a significant effect on non-financial performance while external IT expertise has no significant effect on non-financial performance. The result of testing on model 3 is in line with contingency theory explained by previous researchers [10].

References

1. Ismail, N.A., King, M.: The alignment of accounting and information systems in SMEs in Malaysia. J. Glob. Inf. Technol. Manag. **9**(3), 24–42 (2006)
2. Boulianne, E.: Revisiting fit between AIS design and performance with the analyzer strategic type. Int. J. Account. Inf. Syst. **8**, 1–16 (2007)
3. Isobe, T., Makino, S., Montgomery, D.: Technological capabilities and firm performance; the case of small manufacturing firms in Japan. Asia Pac. J. **25**, 413–428 (2008)
4. Dubihlela, J., Rundora, R.: Employee training, managerial commitment and the implementation of activity based costing; impact on performance of SMEs. Int. Bus. Econ. Res. J. **13** (1), 27–38 (2014)
5. Grande, E., Estebancz, R., Colomina, C.: The impact of accounting information systems (AIS) on performance measures: empirical evidence in Spanish SMEs. Int. J. Digit. Account. Res. **11**, 25–43 (2010)
6. Lee, S.M., Kim, J., Choi, Y., Lee, S.: Effect of IT knowledge and media selection on operational performance of small firm. Small Bus. Econ. **32**, 241–257 (2009)
7. Lim, H.D., Richardson, V.J., Smith, R.E.: A meta-analysis of the effect of IT investment on firm financial performance. J. Inf. Syst. **25**(2), 145–169 (2011)
8. Levy, M., Powel, P., Yetton: Contingent dynamics of IS strategic alignment in small & medium sized enterprises. J. Syst. Inf. Technol. **13**(2), 106–124 (2011)
9. Sousa, S.D., Aspinwall, E.M., Rodrigues, A.G.: Performance measure in English SMEs: survey result. Benchmarking Int. J. **13**(1/2), 120–134 (2006)
10. Tuanmat, Z., Smith, M.: The effect of change in competition, technology, and strategy on organizational performance in small and medium manufacturing companies. Asian Rev. Account. **19**(3), 208–220 (2011)
11. Hussin, H., King, M., Cragg, P.: IT alignment in small firm. Europ. J. Inf. Syst. **11**, 108–127 (2002)
12. Ismail, N.A., King, M.: Firm performance and AIS alignment in Malaysian SMEs. Int. J. Account. Inf. Syst. **6**, 241–259 (2005)
13. Ismail, N.A., King, M.: Factors influencing the alignment of accounting information systems in small and medium sized Malaysian manufacturing Firms. J. Inf. Syst. Small Bus. **1**(1–2), 1–20 (2007)
14. Al-Eqab, M., Ismail, N.A.: Contingency factors and accounting information system design in Jordanian companies. IBIMA Bus. Rev. **2011**, 1–13 (2011). Article ID 166128
15. Naranjo, D.: The role of sophisticated accounting system in strategy management. Int. J. Digit. Account. Res. **4**(8), 125–144 (2004)
16. Budiarto, D.S.: Accounting information system (AIS) alignment and non-financial performance in small firms. Int. J. Comput. Network **6**(2), 15–25 (2014)

17. Eztebanez, R., Grande, E., Colomina, C.: Information technology implementation: evidence in Spanish SMEs. Int. J. Account. Inf. Manag. **18**(1), 39–57 (2010)
18. Burca, S., Fynes, B., Brannick, T.: The moderating effect of information technology sophistication on service practice performance. Int. J. Oper. Prod. Manag. **26**(11), 1240–1254 (2006)
19. Lohman, J.M.: The legal and accounting side of managing a small business. Ingrams **26**(21) (2000)
20. Amidu, M., Effah, J., Abor, J.: E-Accounting practices among small & medium enterprises in Ghana. J. Manag. Policy Pract. **12**(4), 146–155 (2011)
21. Pulakanam, V., Suraweera, V.: Implementing accounting software in small business in New Zeland: an exploratory investigation. Account. Bus. Public Interes. **9**, 98–124 (2010)
22. Choe, J.M.: The organizational learning effect of management accounting information under advanced manufacturing technology. Europ. J. Inf. Syst. **11**, 142–258 (2002)
23. Tangen, S.: Performance measurement; from philosophy to practice. Int. J. Product. Perform. Manag. **53**(8), 726–737 (2004)
24. Harrison, S.P., Poole, M.: Customer-focused manufacturing strategy and the use of operations-based non-financial performance measures: a research note. Account. Organ. Soc. **22**(6), 557–572 (1997)
25. Tarigan, D.J., Deborah, C.W.: The relationship between non-financial performance and Financial Performance Using balance scorecard framework: a research in café and restaurant sector. Int. J. Innov. Manag. Technol. **3**(5), 614–618 (2012)
26. Miller, J.A.: Designing and implementing a new cost management systems. J. Cost Manag., 41–53 (1992). Winter
27. Bledsoe, N.L., Ingram, R.W.: Customer satisfaction through performance evaluation. J. Cost Manag., 43–50 (1997). Winter
28. Zuriekat, M., Rafat, S., Salah, A.: Participation in performance measurement systems and level of satisfaction. Int. J. Bus. Soc. Sci. **2**(8), 159–168 (2011)
29. Chow, C.W., Stede, W.A.: The use and usefulness of financial performance measures. Manag. Account. Q. **7**(3), 1–8 (2006). Spring
30. Ittner, C.D., David, F.L.: Are non-financial measure leading indicator of financial performance? an analysis of customer satisfaction. J. Account. Res. **36**, 1–36 (1990)
31. Woznica, J., Healy, K.: The level of information systems integration in SMEs in Irish manufacturing sector. J. Small Bus. Enterp. Dev. **16**(1), 115–128 (2009)
32. Soudani, S.N.: The usefulness of an accounting information system for effective organizational performance. Int. J. Econ. Financ. **4**(5), 136–144 (2012)
33. Thong, J.Y.L.: An integrated model of information systems adoption in small business. J. Manag. Inf. Syst. **15**(4), 187–214 (1999). Spring
34. Mostafa, R., Colin, W., Marian, V.: Entrepreneurial orientation, commitment to the internet and export performance in small and medium sized exporting firm. Int. J. Entrep. **3**, 291–302 (2006)
35. Zikmund, W.G.: Business Research Methods. The Dryden Press, Orlando (2000)
36. Thong, J.Y.L., Yap, C.S.: CEO characteristics, organizational characteristics, and information technology adoption in small business. Omega **23**(4), 429–442 (1995)
37. Dibrel, C., Davis, P.S., Craig, J.: Fueling innovation through information technology in SMEs. J. Small Bus. Manag. **46**(2), 203–218 (2008)
38. Chu, W.: The influence of family ownership on SME performance: evidence from public firms in Taiwan. Small Bus. Econ. **33**, 353–373 (2009)

Workshop Computational Geometry and Security Applications (CGSA 2018)

Algorithms of Laser Scanner Data Processing for Ground Surface Reconstruction

Vladimir Badenko[1]([✉]) [ID], Alexander Fedotov[1] [ID],
and Konstantin Vinogradov[2] [ID]

[1] Peter the Great St.Petersburg Polytechnic University,
Polytechnicheskaya 29, 195251 St.Petersburg, Russia
vbadenko@gmail.com, afedotov@spbstu.ru
[2] Saint-Petersburg State University, Universitetskaya Emb. 13B,
199034 St.Petersburg, Russia
kostyal495@mail.ru

Abstract. Laser scanning data processing is widely used to solve regional planning problems in a GIS environment including Digital Terrain Models (DTMs) analysis and ground surface reconstruction. Some gaps in algorithms for processing of raw laser scanning data during DTM creation are analyzed. Algorithms for filtration, triangulation and defragmentation of laser scanning point clouds are proposed. Advantages and disadvantages of the algorithms proposed are discussed. The proposed triangulation algorithm is used for defragmentation of laser scanning point clouds into semantic component parts. Defragmentation includes recognition of engineering objects and other objects of the terrain, and their delineation. The results of real problems' solutions described in the paper show the robustness of the proposed algorithms.

Keywords: Algorithm · Laser scanning data · Ground surface reconstruction
Triangulation · Digital Terrain Model

1 Introduction

Laser scanning technology is a widely used all over the world remote sensing technique for gathering spatial information [1]. Nowadays technologies based on laser scanning data have been used worldwide in a wide range of applications including Digital Terrain Models (DTMs) analysis, ground surface reconstruction, road management, urban modeling, heritage maintenance [2–6]. Corresponding types of laser scanning systems are divided into terrestrial, mobile and airborne [1, 2, 5, 7]. The main differences between the systems are the accuracy, the data acquisition solution and the covered area in one mission [8, 9]. During surveying the required distance from sensor to object is determined according the time delay (pulse method) or the phase shift (phase method) in laser signal reflected by object surface [1, 10, 11]. The result of laser scanning is a cloud of points, which is usually combined with photos [12]. Thus each records in a laser scanning point cloud (LSPC) (raw data) usually includes: three coordinates, an intensity of reflected signal and a color of point (R, G, B), that accurately describe the object being surveyed [13, 14].

© Springer International Publishing AG, part of Springer Nature 2018
O. Gervasi et al. (Eds.): ICCSA 2018, LNCS 10961, pp. 397–411, 2018.
https://doi.org/10.1007/978-3-319-95165-2_28

There are also many publications on the successful usage of LSPCs for DTMs creation taking into account that incorrect terrain information data affecting civil construction has become a major problem as it creates gaps in productivity [9, 15–18]. Extracting ground points from different LSPCs, which is referred to as data filtering, is extremely important for numerous geospatial applications and analyses [9, 19]. However, automatic filtering of ground points LSPC remains a challenging task [20–22]. In [15] the performance of eight filtering methods was evaluated. These methods were also divided according to their principle into 4 categories [9]: (1) the surface-based [12, 23–25] – this method creates a surface with a corresponding buffer zone; (2) the block-minimum [26] – this method classifies ground points on the assumption that the lowest point in a local neighborhood is a point on ground surface; (3) the slope-based [9, 21, 22, 27] – this method considers the slope between two near ground points to be less than a certain value; and (4) the clustering/segmentation method [28, 29]. One of the most popular models of ground surface for DTM is Delaunay triangulation, which provides the most qualitative and uniquely defined model (triangulation) [30]. At the same time, the usage of Delaunay triangulation is associated with a large expenditure of time and computer memory, which is a matter of actual importance for constructing a model from the big LSPC [14]. The task of DTM creation is one of the most urgent tasks of processing of laser scanning results despite the long history of the development of appropriate algorithms [3, 4, 23, 31–33].

Analysis of some gaps in algorithms for processing of raw laser scanning data for DTM creation is an objective of this paper. Some algorithms that can bridge the existing gaps are presented. The proposed hybrid algorithms include combination of different approaches. A triangulation algorithm can serve to defragment LSPCs into semantically different component parts. Defragmentation includes recognition of ground surface and engineering objects of the terrain, and their delineation. The results presented in the paper can serve as a basis for solving many civil engineering problems: not only such as creation of a DTM, but also can be useful for processing LSPCs during engineering survey of roads and existing buildings.

2 Materials and Methods

2.1 Filtration of Points Density

Here a point will be treated as a data structure ($a.x$, $a.y$ and $a.z$) that contains spatial coordinates and attribute information: color, time, intensity of the reflected laser signal measured, etc. The lexicographic order of sorting of points defines following relations between points a and b: $a > b$, $a < b$ or $a = b$. The lexicographic sorting order is specified by a function $F(a, b)$, which returns the result of comparison of two elements (points). This function returns the following values: $F(a, b) = -1$ if $a < b$; $F(a, b) = 1$ if $a > b$; $F(a, b) = 0$ if $a = b$. For the triangulation algorithm, various variants of the lexicographic comparison "x-y-z" or "y-x-z" can be used depending on the direction of "elongation" of a LSPC under discussion. Nevertheless, further only one order of lexicographic comparison will be considered: "x-y-z". An example of the sort function in the order of "x-y-z":

```
int comparePoint (Point a, Point b)
{
// sorting on x
    if (a.x < b.x) return -1;
    if (a.x > b.x) return  1;
// sorting on y
    if (a.y < b.y) return -1;
    if (a.y > b.y) return  1;
// sorting on z
    if (a.z < b.z) return -1;
    if (a.z > b.z) return  1;
// equal points
return 0;
}
```

If a container with hashing is used for sorting, then the values for x-y-z can be used successively for the hash function of key formation.

Further a filtration problem $OUT = F\ (IN)$ is considered. Here IN – is an original set of laser scanning points, F – is our filtration algorithm and OUT – is a result of filtration. OUT is a subset of IN. From the original set IN of points is needed to select such a subset of points $OUT \in IN$, that for all points of from OUT the following two conditions are fulfilled:

1. Conditions in the plane (for coordinates x and y):

$$|a.x - b.x| > eps \text{ and } |a.y - b.y| > eps, a \in OUT, b \in OUT \text{ and } OUT \in IN \quad (1)$$

Here, eps is a user's parameter that determines a value of the desired density of points. This filtering guarantees that there are no such points in the OUT subset that the distance between them is less than the value of eps. Therefore, the choice of the parameter eps value should be based on the analysis of a specific task and the experience of the user. It is possible also to set the condition (1) in the form:

$$\sqrt{(a.x - b.x)^2 + (a.y - b.y)^2} > eps, (a.x - b.x)^2 + (a.y - b.y)^2 > eps^2 \quad (2)$$

However, in terms of programming implementation (2) is less preferable, because for its implementation requires large computational costs without a tangible gain in quality.

2. Condition for height (for coordinate z).

From the subset Q, for any points of which the condition of identity is satisfied:

$$|a.x - b.x| < eps \text{ and } |a.y - b.y| < eps, a \in Q, b \in Q \text{ and } Q \in IN, \quad (3)$$

only one point is chosen $min\ (a.z)$ with minimal z value.

This solution of the filtration problem in such formulation is used primarily to ensure stability of a triangulation algorithm proposed further. The filtration algorithm is used to form a ground surface using a LSPC. It also can be used to reduce the number of points.

The filtration algorithm is implemented in two stages:

1. A set of laser scanning points is sorted by values of z coordinates.
2. All points are being included in a sorting container, which contains only unique values. The container can be a search binary tree or an associative container *set* from STL (Standard C++ Template Library).

For sorting at this stage, a following function is defined:

```
//Example of the lexicographic comparison function for
filtering in plane (x, y)
static float heps = eps / 2; // half
int filterPointXY(Point a, Point b)
{
    if (a.x < (b.x - heps)) return -1;
    if (a.x > (b.x + heps)) return 1;
    if (a.y < (b.y - heps)) return -1;
    if (a.y > (b.y + heps)) return 1;
    return 0;
}
```

It is not difficult to identify that for such comparison function the points a and b are considered to be equivalent (identical), if following condition is true:

$$|a.x-b.x| < eps \text{ and } |a.y-b.y| < eps. \tag{4}$$

During the second stage all non-unique (non-identical) points are ignored, except the first point. Since at the first stage the z sorting has already been performed, and the lowest points are the first in the container, it can be guaranteed that after the second stage the necessary subset of the bottom points has been created with the necessary lexicographical order. The actual range of filtration density d is within the following limits (Fig. 1):

$$eps < d \leq 2 * \sqrt{2} * eps \tag{5}$$

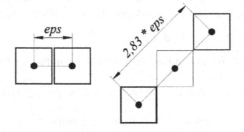

Fig. 1. Actual range of filtration density.

It should be taken into account that the proposed filtration for a set with the initial density of points significantly exceeding the value of *eps*, which is used in (1), ensures that the following condition is met: any adjacent points will be located no closer than the distance *eps* and not more than about *3 * eps* (Fig. 1). For estimation of an average value of the density of points, it is advisable to use the value *1.5 * eps*.

An alternative filtering variant was considered without performing the first stage. When a point is moving to a container, if there were "identical" points in the plane *(x, y)*, then a point with smaller coordinate *z* is chosen (Fig. 2).

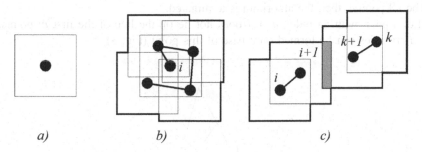

a)   b)   c)

Fig. 2. Migration of the filtering area.

This approach forms a smaller subset of filtered points than a subset of the first variant. This can be explained by the fact that the lowest point is not the first in the container, and the previous point-candidate for a lowest value has already supplanted some of the point-candidate (migration of "bottom" points and filtration zones). Figure 2a shows the point and the filtering zone of size *eps*. If, as a result of filtering, the minimum height is overridden, the filtering zone, which size can significantly exceed the original one, is migrated (Fig. 2b). Conflicts between filtering zones may also arise, which will result in the need to remove one of the conflicting zones (Fig. 2c). In general, for this algorithm, only the lower limit of the density range *eps* can be guaranteed, and the upper one is increased and cannot be reliably estimated.

The effectiveness of the first variant is that the preliminary sorting by *z* is done once for original LSPC, and in general, the filtration can be performed several times only on the second stage of filtration for different values of *eps*. It should be noted that this approach is easy to implement within the binary search tree, associative container *set* or for hash tables. In the case of hashing, the sorting order (for example, *x-y-z*) determines the order in which the composite index is generated for the hash function. The high sorting efficiency (in our case of filtering) within the binary search tree is determined by the fact that the search costs are determined by the function $O(log\ n)$, in contrast to the sequential search $O(n)$. Here *n* is the number of points in the original set.

2.2 Triangulation

Algorithms proposed here should be considered as a result of a compromise between the performance of the triangulation and the quality of the model. It is well known that the Delaunay triangulation provides building of a triangulation model which is the most qualitative, uniquely defined and invariant, in relation to the coordinate system. At the same time, the use of Delaunay triangulation is associated with a large expenditure of time and computer memory, which is a matter of actual importance for constructing a model from a LSPC.

As initial data for triangulation, a set of filtered points sorted in the plane (x, y), according to the proposed lexicographic order of sorting is considered. The process of triangulation involves the formation, at the initial stage, of a first face (triangle) of first 3 points, and then successively attaching remaining points. In fact, it is assumed that there is a real situation where first m points in the plane (x, y) lie on one line (and maybe all points), then the algorithm is terminated.

Let a point with an index $m + 1$ does not lie on the line of the first m points, so $m - 1$ triangles can be formed on a base of this point (Fig. 3).

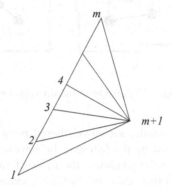

Fig. 3. A starting point set of triangulation

For any step of the triangulation the following 2 statements hold:

1. Outer edges of the triangulation form a convex boundary. This statement is obvious, since the starting set of triangles has a convex boundary. Any joining of a new point is also performed until the formation of a new convex boundary. At the same time, a new set of triangles joins to the triangulation (set *begin-end-i* in Fig. 4).
2. Any joining point lies outside the convex boundary of the triangulation. This condition is ensured as a result of the specified lexicographic sort order at the point filtration stage.

After each step of joining the point, optimization for the set of triangles *begin-end-i* is needed. Optimization is based on comparing two adjacent edges, where the length of their common edge is compared with the distance between unbound vertices (Fig. 5). An attempt to connect these unconnected vertices has been made. If, (1) the common edge and the test edge between the vertices intersect and, (2) the length of the test edge is shorter than the common edge, then a general quadrangle is rebuilding. The common edge is removed and a new edge replaces the test edge. Figure 5 illustrates the sequence of optimization steps. Here the dotted lines denote the segments to be compared.

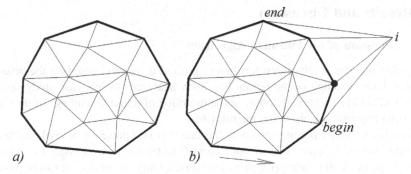

Fig. 4. One step of the triangulation algorithm

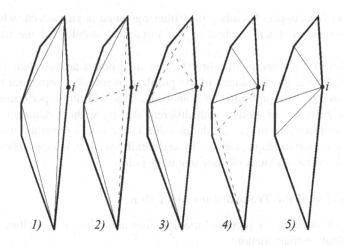

Fig. 5. Sequence of optimization steps: the dashed lines indicate the test edges to be compared.

It should be noted that the optimization is not performed to the full depth, and is limited to the edges incident to the vertex i. This serves to limit the optimization process on the principle of "minimal diagonal" and allows creating a surface model with a sufficient quality.

Therefore, the triangulation algorithm consists of two main steps:

1. Forming the starting set of triangles.
2. A cycle on a set of laser scanning points (excluding starting points):
    2.1. For an i-th point and the convex boundary, the search for the beginning and the end (*begin, end* in Fig. 3) of the new set of triangles is performed. The search begins at $i-1$ point, since it is lexicographically (but not geometrically) the closest point to i.
    2.2. Joining the triangles of the set of triangles *begin-end-i*.
    2.3. Optimization of triangles of the set of triangles *begin-end-i*.
    2.4. Change of convex boundary. Now it passes through the vertices *begin-end-i*.

3 Results and Discussion

3.1 Discussion of the Filtration Algorithm

Using this filtering an algorithm for direct "ground detection" based on the results of airborne laser scanning of the terrain has been analyzed. In this case study approximations of DTMs are strongly offset in the direction of removal (cutting) of protruding (elevated) fragments of the relief microforms.

Another difficulty is connected with the fact that in a presence of civil engineering structures and other objects that are not a part of the terrain, it is necessary to choose the value of *eps* exceeding their geometric dimensions. Only in this case, it can be assumed that the filtered set contains the relief points.

Some advantages of this filtering algorithm can be noted:

1. The lower (and upper) boundary of a filtering range is guaranteed, which allows taking into account and controlling the numerical stability of the triangulation algorithm.
2. From a set of measured points, directly measured points are selected. This is very important for the future solution of the problem of revealing structural relief lines, on the basis of its morphostructural analysis. This will allow performing composition (or merging) of meshes with different density without damaging the introduction of distortions in the calculations due to the filtering method used.
3. The method used has high productivity and flexibility. This is especially true during processing of large clouds of laser scanning points.

3.2 Discussion of the Triangulation Algorithm

Here are the features of the proposed triangulation algorithm, which allow us to construct a qualitative triangulation:

1. All search operations are performed on the outer boundary of the triangulation and do not depend on the number of its vertices and edges. Search is not performed across the entire border, but to the right and left of the lexicographically nearest point (the previous point). Even with optimization, adjacent faces are determined not from the search, but from an editable list of edges relationships. These search features determine high processing speed and linear cost growth with increasing number of source points.
2. Formation of triangulation develops in the positive direction of the X-axis (for sorting x-y-z, and for sorting by y-x-z - along the Y-axis) and over the entire width of the front. This makes it easy to split the model into fragments of a given size in the direction of triangulation. It should be noted that the implementation of the algorithm itself does not depend on the order of sorting *(x-y or y-x)*. The sorting order only affects the direction of triangulation. If the initial set of points has an oblong directionality, then the order of sorting is selected (according to the ratio of the sides of the bounding rectangle). Managing the order of sorting allows you to optimize the costs of implementing calculations.

3. Stability of the algorithm depends on the parameter, which is determined by the ratio of the density parameter to the width of the front of the triangulation $k = eps/R$. Here, R is the maximum possible distance between two lexicographically closest points. This value does not exceed the width of the front of the triangulation at its widest point. If the sort order x-y-z is used, then the triangulation develops in the positive direction of the X axis and the triangulation front is the maximum width along the Y axis. For a given value of eps, it is possible to estimate the maximum possible width of the triangulation front and predict the numerical stability of the computational process, and also recommend the sizes of the processed fragments.

There are also some disadvantages of the proposed algorithm that should be noted (in comparison with the Delaunay triangulation):

1. The algorithm is conditionally optimal in part of the geometry of triangles (faces). Optimization is performed at a limited depth. At the same time, a number of non-optimal faces on test calculations do not exceed 1–2%.
2. The algorithm is not invariant with respect to a coordinate system and a triangulation direction (sorting direction). When a triangulation direction is changed, new version of the surface model is created. It should be noted that the magnitude of these discrepancies is insignificant and fits into the number of non-optimal faces.

Despite the listed disadvantages, the advantages of this kind of triangulation for processing large data sets do not cause any doubts.

At this stage, the differences in quality between the Delaunay triangulation and the proposed approach do not have a significant effect on the process and the quality of the defragmentation (due to the high density of points). Nevertheless, productivity, in turn, differs by almost an order of magnitude. In the subsequent stages, during formation of final DTM, the Delaunay triangulation with constraints in the form of structural lines is used. However, here the density of the points and the size of the modeled fragments have been substantially reduced.

Comparison of dependence of calculation time of the triangulation vs. the number of initial points shows that the growth in costs in the Delaunay triangulation is determined by an almost quadratic dependence, and in proposed case almost linear dependence.

3.3 Application of the Algorithms Proposed

The proposed algorithm of triangulation of a LSPC cloud leads to a formation of a convex boundary. This does not always correspond to the real situation. However, removing edges of the outer border, which exceeds the length allowed by the user, allows solving this problem. Figure 6 shows an example of application of such algorithm modification. On the left is a triangulation without delineation with a convex outer boundary. On the right is the result of contouring with a non-convex outer boundary.

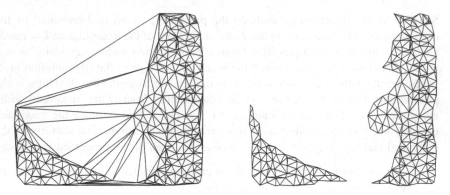

Fig. 6. Contouring of the convex boundary of a triangulation

The idea of such automatic contouring is based on an approach that implements the removal of edges of the outer border, the length of which is exceeded the user-defined value. This approach is implemented in the framework of the following algorithm:

1. A bi-directional list of edges of the outer boundary is formed (or taken directly from the triangulation proposed above).
2. For each edge, we calculate the weight (the edge length or the square of this distance).
3. Edges with weights are placed in the sorting container, where they are sorted in descending order of weights.
4. A cyclic procedure is performed:
   4.1. For the first edge (with the maximum length), a comparison is made with the user-defined value.
   4.2. If the length of the edge exceeds the allowable value, the edge is removed from the container, and instead of it two edges of the inner face are inserted, which rests on this edge. The internal face is marked as remote. Go to the beginning of the cycle.
   4.3. If the length is less than the tolerance, the cycle is ended.
5. The array of vertices of triangulation and face indices is being modified. As a result of this modification, the edges marked as deleted are deleted.

The method based on the use of triangulation models allows analyzing the connections of the nearest points, dividing the model into fragments and performing their topological analysis, visualizing the intermediate results in the form of surfaces. At the first stage, a surface is formed, which, as a result of transformations, smoothing and other possible procedures, is brought to a form that the user can recognize as the best approximation to the terrain. The proposed approach is based on such concepts as the boundary between adjacent faces and the "sloping" and "vertical" parts of the faces. To determine the characteristics of the face - "sloping" or "vertical", a comparison of the vertical excess and the maximum length of a facet edge projected onto a plane (or on the plane of an adjacent face) is used.

Let us there is an approach that uses the following formal functions:

$G(a)$ - function for edge a returns true if the edge is considered "flat" and false if the edge is vertical;

$F(a, b)$ - a function in which two adjacent edges a and b are compared, returns true if the boundary passes through the common edge ("fracture", etc.), and false otherwise.

Let there be a set of different variants of the function $G(a)$ and $F(a, b)$, and the user has the opportunity to select specific implementations for the computational process based on the visual analysis of the original surface and his own experience. This approach allows to implement various strategies for defragmenting the model.

Common for various defragmentation strategies is the following recursive algorithm for the development (expansion) of the boundary:

For a single edge, a conditional boundary is formed along its edges and on the basis of $F(a, b)$ an attempt is made to join adjacent edge. If a separate adjacent edge is not separated by a boundary, then the edge is included in this section and the boundary is modified (the edge is absorbed). If the boundary passes, then it is fixed, and then this edge is excluded from the analysis. As a result of the operation of such an algorithm, a bounded domain is obtained.

In Fig. 7 shows an example of such an area that has one external border (External Boundary - EB) and some finite number of internal areas (Internal Boundary - IB). Depending on the belonging to the external or internal border, it is possible to uniquely determine the hierarchy of relations between regions (fragments). Internal areas are also subject to defragmentation, and the results of dependencies between areas complement the hierarchy tree of objects.

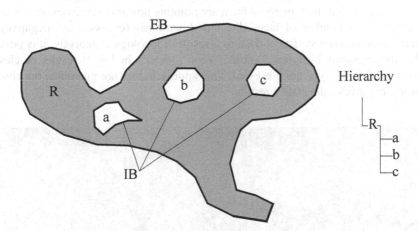

Fig. 7. A general representation of a bounded domain

This approach allows implementing various strategies for defragmenting models. Depending on belonging to the external or internal border, it is possible to uniquely determine the hierarchy of relations between regions (fragments). Internal areas are also subject to defragmentation, and the results of dependencies between areas complement the hierarchy tree of objects. Such a selection of the region is performed for all faces of the original surface, if they did not fall into any of the regions in the previous stage of defragmentation. Thus, entire investigated object is divided into regions (fragments) and a hierarchy tree of their relations (by nesting) is formed, which in turn serves as a basis for topological analysis of models (Fig. 8).

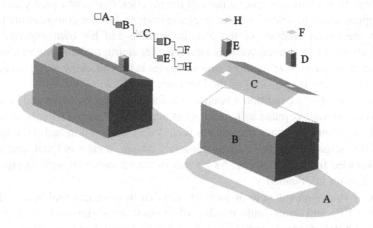

Fig. 8. Example of topological defragmentation of a civil structure

For each fragment, an array of additional statistical information is also formed. For example, for each external boundary of the region, a number of neighbor fragments is determined, as well as how many of them are pointing upwards (excesses are positive), and separately a number of faces directed downwards (excesses are negative). In general, based on such statistical data, as a result of topological analysis, it is possible to classify fragments by types: "earth", "roof", "wall". In Fig. 9 results of classify objects of the "roof" type are presented. This approach does not guarantee the absence of errors, but gives satisfactory results.

Fig. 9. Automatic classification of objects of the "roof" type (yellow) (Color figure online)

4 Conclusions

The task of the relief extraction and creation of its digital model is one of the most urgent tasks of processing the results of laser scanning. It should be recognized that in the process of formation of the main topographic products such as plans and maps, based on LSPC, significant progress has been achieved in the performance of field survey. Obviously, the weakest point in this technological cycle is the productivity of cameral work on the creation of topographic maps and plans. If the process of extraction of the topographic objects of the terrain from the photographs is technologically worked out, and has similar solutions in aerial photography, the process of creation of the digital model of relief is problematic enough. How to select a relief point from a LSPC? To solve this problem, different approaches are possible. The common thing for them is that all of them should be considered probabilistic, as there is no full guarantee that they all relate to the ground surface. Despite the existing morphological classification of the diversity of possible forms of relief, it is very difficult in a programmatic sense and automatic procedures are unlikely to be possible. In our opinion, it is advisable to talk about an automated solution. Automated solutions, in contrast to automatic solutions, are performed and managed with the direct participation of the user and can be considered as interactive.

It is planned to use various options for filtering points to highlight structural relief lines. Within the framework of the morphostructural analysis of the relief, there are algorithmic solutions for the allocation of structural relief lines over several DTMs constructed with different density of points (ref). The basic idea of such algorithms is that it is possible to construct a difference of two surfaces. For example, the first approximation of the surface relief with a density of points at $eps = 40$ m and the second surface is more dense - at $eps = 10$ m. Variations in the deviations of this difference surface from the plane (for example, in the distribution of the volume of the earthen mass, calculated by the method of trihedral prisms) determine the direction in which the position of the structural line can be refined purposefully or iteratively.

The results presented in the paper can serve as a basis for solving many civil engineering problems: not only for creation of a DTM, but also for processing laser scanning data during engineering survey of roads and existing building. There are no any assumptions on input point set, therefore the proposed method works on any type of LSPC. Automatically creating a quality DTM using raw laser scanning data in form of a point cloud is almost impossible. The proposed algorithms are another example of numerous techniques for refining and mapping the terrain. The proposed algorithms are successfully used by the authors to solve, for example, problems such as the development of measures to reduce flood damage and crop modelling, where an adequate ground surface reconstruction is important [34, 35]. The proposed approaches for DTM creation minimize needs for editing and increase the productivity of out-of-field works.

Acknowledgements. The research was supported by Ministry of Education and Science of Russia within the framework of the Federal Program "Research and Development in Priority Areas for the Development of the Russian the Science and Technology Complex for 2014-2020" (project ID RFMEFI58417X0025).

References

1. Puente, I., González-Jorge, H., Martínez-Sánchez, J., Arias, P.: Review of mobile mapping and surveying technologies. Measurement **46**(7), 2127–2145 (2013)
2. Guan, H., Li, J., Cao, S., Yu, Y.: Use of mobile LiDAR in road information inventory: a review. Int. J. Image Data Fusion **7**(3), 219–242 (2016)
3. Vosselman, G., Coenen, M., Rottensteiner, F.: Contextual segment-based classification of airborne laser scanner data. ISPRS J. Photogramm. Remote Sens. **128**, 354–371 (2017)
4. Dore, C., Murphy, M.: Current state of the art historic building information modelling. Int. Archiv. Photogramm. Remote Sens. Spat. Inf. Sci. **42**, 185–192 (2017)
5. Badenko, V., Zotov, D., Fedotov, A.: Hybrid processing of laser scanning data. In: E3S Web of Conferences – EDP Sciences, vol. 33, id.01047 (2018)
6. Badenko, V., Kurtener, D., Yakushev, V., Torbert, A., Badenko, G.: Evaluation of current state of agricultural land using problem-oriented fuzzy indicators in GIS environment. In: Gervasi, O., Murgante, B., Misra, S., Rocha, A.M.A.C., Torre, C., Taniar, D., Apduhan, Bernady O., Stankova, E., Wang, S. (eds.) ICCSA 2016. LNCS, vol. 9788, pp. 57–69. Springer, Cham (2016). https://doi.org/10.1007/978-3-319-42111-7_6
7. Kukko, A., Kaartinen, H., Hyyppä, J., Chen, Y.: Multiplatform mobile laser scanning: usability and performance. Sensors **12**(9), 11712–11733 (2012)
8. Tomljenovic, I., Höfle, B., Tiede, D., Blaschke, T.: Building extraction from airborne laser scanning data: an analysis of the state of the art. Remote Sens. **7**(4), 3826–3862 (2015)
9. Liu, X., Chen, Y., Cheng, L., Yao, M., Deng, S., Li, M., Cai, D.: Airborne laser scanning point clouds filtering method based on the construction of virtual ground seed points. J. Appl. Remote Sens. **11**(1), 016032 (2017)
10. Murphy, M., McGovern, E., Pavia, S.: Historic building information modelling–adding intelligence to laser and image based surveys of European classical architecture. ISPRS J. Photogramm. Remote Sens. **76**, 89–102 (2013)
11. Hichri, N., Stefani, C., De Luca, L., Veron, P., Hamon, G.: From point cloud to BIM: a survey of existing approaches. Int. Arch. Photogramm. Remote Sens. Spat. Inf. Sci. ISPRS Arch. **40**(5W2), 343–348 (2013)
12. Liu, X., Meng, W., Guo, J., Zhang, X.: A survey on processing of large-scale 3D point cloud. In: El Rhalibi, A., Tian, F., Pan, Z., Liu, B. (eds.) Edutainment 2016. LNCS, vol. 9654, pp. 267–279. Springer, Cham (2016). https://doi.org/10.1007/978-3-319-40259-8_24
13. Heo, J., Jeong, S., Park, H.-K., Jung, J., Han, S., Hong, S., Sohn, H.-G.: Productive high-complexity 3D city modeling with point clouds collected from terrestrial LiDAR. Comput. Environ. Urban Syst. **41**, 26–38 (2013)
14. Barazzetti, L.: Parametric as-built model generation of complex shapes from point clouds. Adv. Eng. Inform. **30**(3), 298–311 (2016)
15. Sithole, G., Vosselman, G.: Experimental comparison of filter algorithms for bare-Earth extraction from airborne laser scanning point clouds. ISPRS J. Photogramm. Remote Sens. **59**(1), 85–101 (2004)
16. Kobler, A., Pfeifer, N., Ogrinc, P., Todorovski, L., Oštir, K., Džeroski, S.: Repetitive interpolation: a robust algorithm for DTM generation from Aerial Laser Scanner Data in forested terrain. Remote Sens. Environ. **108**(1), 9–23 (2007)
17. Pirotti, F., Guarnieri, A., Vettore, A.: Ground filtering and vegetation mapping using multi-return terrestrial laser scanning. ISPRS J. Photogramm. Remote Sens. **76**, 56–63 (2013)
18. Kuzin, A.A., Kovshov, S.V.: Accuracy evaluation of terrain digital models for landslide slopes based on aerial laser scanning results. Ecol. Environ. Conserv. **23**(2), 908–914 (2017)

19. Tang, P., Huber, D., Akinci, B., Lipman, R., Lytle, A.: Automatic reconstruction of as-built building information models from laser-scanned point clouds: a review of related techniques. Autom. Constr. **19**(7), 829–843 (2010)
20. Gruszczyński, W., Matwij, W., Ćwiąkała, P.: Comparison of low-altitude UAV photogrammetry with terrestrial laser scanning as data-source methods for terrain covered in low vegetation. ISPRS J. Photogramm. Remote Sens. **126**, 168–179 (2017)
21. Xiong, L., Wang, G., Wessel, P.: Anti-aliasing filters for deriving high-accuracy DEMs from TLS data: a case study from Freeport. Tex. Comput. Geosci. **100**, 125–134 (2017)
22. Cățeanu, M., Arcadie, C.: ALS for terrain mapping in forest environments: an analysis of lidar filtering algorithms. EARSeL eProceedings **16**(1), 9–20 (2017)
23. Axelsson, P.: Processing of laser scanner data - algorithms and applications. ISPRS J. Photogramm. Remote Sens. **54**(2–3), 138–147 (1999)
24. Hu, H., Ding, Y., Zhu, Q., Wu, B., Lin, H., Du, Z., Zhang, Y., Zhang, Y.: An adaptive surface filter for airborne laser scanning point clouds by means of regularization and bending energy. ISPRS J. Photogramm. Remote Sens. **92**, 98–111 (2014)
25. Chen, C., Li, Y.: A robust method of thin plate spline and its application to DEM construction. Comput. Geosci. **48**, 9–16 (2012)
26. Pingel, T.J., Clarke, K.C., McBride, W.A.: An improved simple morphological filter for the terrain classification of airborne LIDAR data. ISPRS J. Photogramm. Remote Sens. **77**, 21–30 (2013)
27. Susaki, J.: Adaptive slope filtering of airborne LiDAR data in urban areas for digital terrain model (DTM) generation. Remote Sens. **4**(6), 1804–1819 (2012)
28. Yan, M., Blaschke, T., Liu, Y., Wu, L.: An object-based analysis filtering algorithm for airborne laser scanning. Int. J. Remote Sens. **33**(22), 7099–7116 (2012)
29. Lin, X., Zhang, J.: Segmentation-based ground points detection from mobile laser scanning point cloud. Int. Arch. Photogramm. Remote Sens. Spat. Inf. Sci. **40**(7), 99–102 (2015)
30. Masuda, H., He, J.: TIN generation and point-cloud compression for vehicle-based mobile mapping systems. Adv. Eng. Inform. **29**(4), 841–850 (2015)
31. Panholzer, H., Prokop, A.: Wedge-filtering of geomorphologic terrestrial laser scan data. Sensors **13**(2), 2579–2594 (2013)
32. Wei, Z., Ma, H., Chen, X., Liu, L.: An improved progressive triangulation algorithm for vehicle-borne laser point cloud. Int. Arch. Photogramm. Remote Sen. Spat. Inf. Sci. **42** (2W7), 929–933 (2017)
33. Yilmaz, M., Uysal, M.: Comparison of data reduction algorithms for LiDAR-derived digital terrain model generalisation. Area **48**(4), 521–532 (2016)
34. Fedorov, M.P., Maslikov, V.I., Badenko, V.L., Chusov, A.N., Molodtsov, D.V.: Reducing the risk of flooding by using hydro complexes distributed on the drainage basin. Power Technol. Eng. **51**(4), 365–370 (2017)
35. Badenko, V.L., Topaj, A.G., Yakushev, V.V., Mirschel, W., Nendel, C.: Crop models as research and interpretative tools. Sel'skokhozyaistvennaya Biologiya **52**, 437–445 (2017)

Molecular Structure Determination in the Phillips' Model: A Degree of Freedom Approach

Udayamoorthy Navaneetha Krishnan[1], Md Zamilur Rahman[1],
Asish Mukhopadhyay[1(✉)], and Yash P. Aneja[2]

[1] School of Computer Science, University of Windsor,
Windsor, ON N9B 3P4, Canada
asish.mukerji@gmail.com

[2] Odette School of Business, University of Windsor,
Windsor, ON N9B 3P4, Canada

Abstract. The Molecular Distance Geometry Problem (MDGP) is defined as the determination of the three-dimensional structure of a molecule using a subset of interatomic distances available. This is a special case of the problem of determining if a weighted graph can be embedded in a k-dimensional Euclidean space such the edge-weights are equal to the Euclidean distances between the corresponding embedded vertices. In the Phillips' model, a molecule is viewed as a chain of atoms, with a fixed bond length between two successive atoms, and the bond angle formed by three successive atoms also set to a fixed value. If $i, i+1, i+2$ and $i+3$ are the indices of four successive atoms, the torsion angle is the dihedral angle between the planes formed by the atoms $i, i+1, i+2$ and the atoms $i+1, i+2, i+3$. This angle is randomly chosen from a well-defined set. These choices fix the coordinates of the atoms, up to a rigid motion. In this paper, we propose a Degree of Freedom (DoF) approach to construct the atomic coordinates of a molecule in the framework of Phillips' model. In the DoF approach, we exploit the fact that n atoms in 3-space have $3n$ degrees of freedom, and each distance constraint reduces the degree of freedom by 1. In this approach, the torsion angles are not set. Instead, we exploit the fact if the distances from an atom with index i to atoms with indices $i - 1$ and $i - 2$ are known then the distance graph is chordal, allowing us to apply the Distance Matrix Completion Algorithm (DMCA) due to Zamilur et al. [1] to complete the remaining distances. Finally, the Stochastic Proximity Embedding (SPE) heuristic due to Agrafoitis [2] is used to determine the atomic coordinates.

Keywords: Molecular Distance Geometry · Phillips' model
Stochastic Proximity Embedding · Distance Matrix Completion

1 Introduction

Given a weighted graph $G = (V, E, w)$ on n vertices, $\{1, 2, 3, \ldots, n\}$, where $w : E \to R^+$ defines the edge weights, and a parameter k, the graph embedding

© Springer International Publishing AG, part of Springer Nature 2018
O. Gervasi et al. (Eds.): ICCSA 2018, LNCS 10961, pp. 412–424, 2018.
https://doi.org/10.1007/978-3-319-95165-2_29

problem seeks to determine if there exists an embedding of the vertices of G in a k-dimensional Euclidean space, R^k, such that the weight of an edge is equal to the Euclidean distance between the corresponding points in R^k. The problem can be formally defined thus:

Find $x_1, x_2, \ldots, x_n$ such that

$$||x_i - x_j|| = w(\{i, j\}), \tag{1}$$

where $\{i, j\} \in E$.

Saxe showed that the problem is strongly NP-complete [3].

An important special case of the above problem is the Molecular Distance Geometry Problem (MDGP). In this case, we have to determine the Cartesian coordinates $x_1 \ldots x_n \in R^3$ of the atoms of a molecule, given the distances between some pairs of atoms. This problem can be solved in linear time if exact distances between all pairs of atoms are available [4].

In reality, NMR technology yields only upper and lower bounds on the distances between some pairs of atoms for small molecules. Crippen and Havel proposed the EMBED algorithm to solve the problem despite this meagre and, often erroneous, data [5].

In this paper, we consider a simpler version of the MDGP: the structure of a protein molecule is assumed to be a polygonal chain in 3-dimensional space in the framework of Phillips' model. We introduce this model and other details in the next section.

2   Phillips' Model

In the Phillips' model [6], the artificial backbone of a protein molecule is conceived of as a chain of n atoms in $3d$-space (R^3) whose Cartesian coordinates are $x_1, \ldots, x_n$, $n \geq 4$.

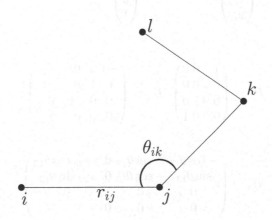

Fig. 1. Phillips' model explained

For each set of four consecutive atoms i, j, k, l,

- r_{ij}, the bond length, is the Euclidean distance between the atoms i and j.
- θ_{ik} is the bond angle corresponding to the relative position of the third atom, k with respect to the line containing the previous two atoms, i and j.
- ω_{il} is the torsion angle between the normals through the planes determined by the atoms i, j, k and j, k, l; this is thus the dihedral angle between these two planes.

The bond lengths and bond angles are set to their equilibrium values, viz. $r_{ij} = 1.526\text{Å}$ and $\theta_{ij} = 109.5°$ respectively, while the base torsion angle is set to one of three preferred values, viz., $60°, 180°$ and $300°$. The actual torsion angle values are seen as perturbations of the preferred torsion angle $60°, 180°$ and $300°$ and are generated by adding a random value from the set $\{\omega + i : i = -15°, ..., 15°\}$ to a randomly chosen preferred torsion angle ω. With the specifications of these three parameters, bond length, torsion and bond angles, we can determine the distances between all pairs of atoms and thus obtain instances for this restricted version of the Molecular Distance Geometry Problem.

The coordinates of the first three atoms are set in this manner. We fix the first atom at the origin of an orthogonal coordinate system. Thus $x_1 = (0,0,0)$. The second atom is positioned on the negative x-axis at a distance of r_{12} from the origin. Thus $x_2 = (-r_{12}, 0, 0)$; the third atom is fixed at $x_3 = (r_{23}cos(\theta_{13}) - r_{12}, r_{23}sin(\theta_{13}), 0)$. By setting the value of the torsion angle ω_{14}, the fourth atom in the chain is determined. Similarly, by setting the value of the torsion angle ω_{25} the fifth atom in the chain is determined, while by fixing the torsion angle ω_{36} the sixth atom in the chain is determined; and so on.

In general [6], the coordinates of the i-th atom $x_i = (x_{i1}, x_{i2}, x_{i3})$ are defined by the following matrix equations in homogeneous coordinates:

$$
\begin{pmatrix} x_{i1} \\ x_{i2} \\ x_{i3} \\ x_{i4} \end{pmatrix} = B_1 B_2 ... B_i \begin{pmatrix} 0 \\ 0 \\ 0 \\ 1 \end{pmatrix} \quad (i = 1, \ldots, n),
$$

where

$$
B_1 = \begin{pmatrix} 1 & 0 & 0 & 0 \\ 0 & 1 & 0 & 0 \\ 0 & 0 & 1 & 0 \\ 0 & 0 & 0 & 1 \end{pmatrix}, B_2 = \begin{pmatrix} -1 & 0 & 0 & -r_{12} \\ 0 & 1 & 0 & 0 \\ 0 & 0 & -1 & 0 \\ 0 & 0 & 0 & 1 \end{pmatrix},
$$

$$
B_3 = \begin{pmatrix} -\cos\theta_{13} & -\sin\theta_{13} & 0 & -r_{23}\cos\theta_{13} \\ \sin\theta_{13} & -\cos\theta_{13} & 0 & r_{23}\sin\theta_{13} \\ 0 & 0 & 1 & 0 \\ 0 & 0 & 0 & 1 \end{pmatrix}
$$

and for, $i \geq 4$,

$$B_i = \begin{pmatrix} -\cos\theta_{(i-2)i} & -\sin\theta_{(i-2)i} & 0 & -r_{(i-1)i}\cos\theta_{(i-2)i} \\ \sin\theta_{(i-3)i}\cos\omega_{(i-3)i} & -\cos\theta_{(i-2)i}\cos\omega_{(i-3)i} & -\sin\omega_{(i-3)i}r_{(i-1)i} & \sin\theta_{(i-2)i}\cos\omega_{(i-3)i} \\ sin\theta_{(i-2)i}\sin\omega_{(i-3)i} & -\cos\theta_{(i-2)i}\sin\omega_{(i-3)i} & \cos\omega_{(i-3)i}r_{((i-1)i)} & \sin\theta_{(i-2)i}\sin\omega_{(i-3)i} \\ 0 & 0 & 0 & 1 \end{pmatrix}$$

Once the Cartesian coordinates of all the atoms are determined, we calculate the complete distance matrix, representing the distances between all pairs of atoms of the molecular chain. In the next section, the complete distance matrix is used to test our Degree of Freedom approach.

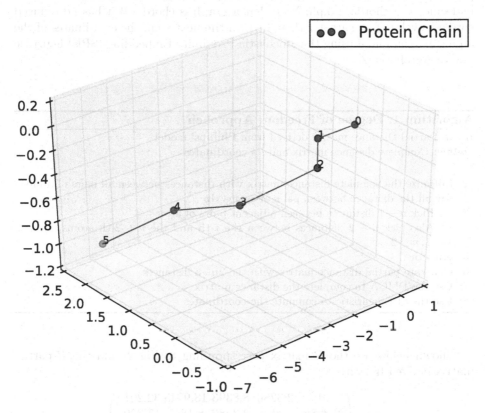

Fig. 2. Protein chain created using Phillips' model

3   The Degree of Freedom Approach

We begin with the simple observation that n atoms in $3d$-space have $3n$ degrees of freedom. A protein molecule in the Phillips' model has this number reduced to $2n+1$ in view if the $n-1$ distance constraints (equal to the number of bond lengths) between successive pairs of atoms. Since the position of first atom is fixed at the origin of coordinates, this is further reduced to $2n-2$. Furthermore,

$n - 2$ fixed bond angles add a further $n - 2$ distance constraints between the pairs of atoms j and $j + 2$, for $j = 1, \ldots, n - 2$. Thus we are left with only n degrees of freedom, or equivalently $n - 1$ distances remain unknown.

The following algorithm takes as input the complete distance matrix generated by the Phillips' model. We call this the R-matrix. From this matrix, a partial distance matrix, R-partial, is obtained by retaining only the distances selected by the above degree of freedom approach. This R-partial distance matrix is completed by a distance matrix completion approach proposed in [1]. This is possible because the distance graph on the vertex set (these are the atoms of our molecule) is a chordal graph. Note that a graph is chordal if it has no induced cordless cycles of size greater than 3 [7]. In the next step, the coordinates of the atoms are computed using the Stochastic Proximity Embedding (SPE) heuristic due to Agrafiotis [2].

Algorithm 1. Degree of Freedom Approach

Input: Partial Distance matrix derived from Phillips' model
Output: Complete distance matrix and its coordinates

1: Initialize the complete distance matrix with distances between all pairs of atoms
2: **for** all the distance between pairs of atoms **do**
3:   Pick $n - 1$ distances between adjacent pairs of atoms
4:   Also pick $n - 2$ distances between the i-th and the $i + 2$-th atoms, for $i = 1, \ldots, n - 2$
5: **end for**
6: Generate partial distance matrix with the $2n-3$ distances
7: Use the DMCA to complete the distance matrix
8: Use the SPE heuristic to compute the coordinates

Shown below are the R matrix corresponding to Fig. 2, and the R-partial matrix derived from it.

$$R = \begin{pmatrix} 0 & 2.3286 & 8.8393 & 18.9945 & 32.2019 \\ 2.3286 & 0 & 2.3286 & 8.1887 & 17.3396 \\ 8.8393 & 2.3286 & 0 & 2.3286 & 8.8393 \\ 18.9945 & 8.1887 & 2.3286 & 0 & 2.3286 \\ 32.2019 & 17.3396 & 8.8393 & 2.3286 & 0 \end{pmatrix} \quad (2)$$

$$R-\text{partial} = \begin{pmatrix} 0 & 2.3286 & 8.8393 & 0 & 0 \\ 2.3286 & 0 & 2.3286 & 8.1887 & 0 \\ 8.8393 & 2.3286 & 0 & 2.3286 & 8.8393 \\ 0 & 8.1887 & 2.3286 & 0 & 2.3286 \\ 0 & 0 & 8.8393 & 2.3286 & 0 \end{pmatrix} \quad (3)$$

4   Coordinates Computation Using SPE

Stochastic Proximity Embedding (SPE) is a heuristic proposed by Agrafoitis [2] as a faster alternative to the usual $O(n^2)$ Multi Dimensional Scaling (MDS), Principal Component Analysis (PCA) techniques used to recover the coordinates of n points from their mutual distances.

Let $R = [r_{ij}]$ be a partial or complete distance matrix corresponding to the true embedding of the points $P = \{p_1, p_2, \ldots, p_n\}$. The distance matrix $D = [d_{ij}]$ is obtained from an arbitrary embedding $P^a = \{p_1{}^a, p_2{}^a, \ldots, p_n{}^a\}$ in R^k.

The SPE heuristic has two cycles: the outer cycle is the learning cycle, and the inner cycle picks up pairs of points randomly from the set P^a and applies a Newton-Raphson root-finding style of correction to the current coordinates of the randomly picked pairs of points. The number of iterations of the algorithm is $C * S$, where C is the number of steps for the learning cycle, and S is the number of times a random pair of points is selected from the point set P^r. The parameters C and S are set so that $CS = o(n^2)$. The coordinates of the final generated point set is the output of SPE.

Algorithm 2. SPE [2]

Input: A random embedding of points in R^k
Output: Updated coordinates of the same points, consistent with the R-matrix

1: Initialize the coordinates of P^a
2: $k \leftarrow 1$
3: **while** $(k \leq C)$ **do**
4:     $l \leftarrow 1$
5:     **while** $(l \leq S)$ **do**
6:         Select a pair of points, p_i^a and p_j^a, at random and compute their distance $d_{ij} = \|p_i^a - p_j^a\|$.
7:         **if** $(d_{ij} \neq r_{ij})$ **then**
8:             $p_i^a \leftarrow p_i^a + \lambda \frac{1}{2} \frac{r_{ij} - d_{ij}}{d_{ij} + \epsilon}(p_i^a - p_j^a), \; \epsilon \neq 0$
9:             $p_j^a \leftarrow p_j^a + \lambda \frac{1}{2} \frac{r_{ij} - d_{ij}}{d_{ij} + \epsilon}(p_j^a - p_i^a), \; \epsilon \neq 0$
10:        **end if**
11:        $l \leftarrow l + 1$
12:    **end while**
13:    $\lambda \leftarrow \lambda - \delta\lambda$
14:    $k \leftarrow k + 1$
15: **end while**

The quality of the embedding produced by SPE is measured using the following stress function as described in [8].

$$S = \frac{\sum_{i<j} \frac{(d_{ij} - r_{ij})^2}{r_{ij}}}{\sum_{i<j} r_{ij}} \tag{4}$$

We applied SPE to the partial distance matrix, R-partial, of a protein molecule in the Philips model that was constructed using our degree of freedom approach (see 3). However, the molecular structure generated by SPE was not satisfactory, implying that SPE was not able to learn the distribution of the atoms.

As can be observed, the sample R-partial distance matrix produced by DoF approach has non-zero distance entries along two off-diagonals. We suspect this as a plausible reason for SPE not doing very well on the partial distance matrix, R-partial. To test the hypothesis that SPE is very sensitive to the spread of the points, particularly when this spread is along some direction, we carried out a small experiment. We ran SPE on the layout in the shape of the letter b shown in Fig. 3. Surprisingly, the points along the vertical line were not learnt as well as the rest of the points as can be seen from Fig. 4. A number of other experiments, not reported here, seem to confirm this hypothesis.

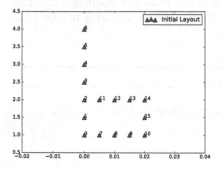
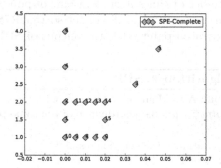

Fig. 3. Initial layout of b   **Fig. 4.** SPE layout of b

5   Distance Matrix Completion Approach

The distance graph corresponding to a distance matrix is a graph on the underlying points set, with an edge between two points if the distance between the two points is non-zero. Bakonyi and Johnson [9] showed that if the distance graph is chordal there exists a completion of the partial distance matrix to a complete distance matrix. Zamilur et al. [1] applied this idea to construct a 1-round algorithm for learning the locations of a set of points in the plane.

A brief description of this completion algorithm is this. We first compute a simplicial ordering of the vertices of the given chordal graph G. This simplicial ordering is exploited to add an edge at a time to construct a sequence of chordal graphs, ending with the complete graph [10]. For each selected edge, $[u, v]$, we find a maximal clique containing that edge. To find the maximal clique, we start with a clique containing two vertices of the given edge, and grow the current clique by adding a vertex v that is adjacent to every vertex in the current clique.

The distance matrix corresponding to this maximal clique is completed using the algorithm of Bakonyi and Johnson [9].

The Degree of Freedom approach takes $n-1$ and $n-2$ distances between the adjacent atoms and the atom next to the adjacent atom respectively. For the chosen distances, the resulting distance graph turned out to be chordal (see Fig. 5). This allows us to apply the Distance Matrix Completion algorithm to compute the distances between the remaining pairs of atoms. Once the distance matrix is completed, the $3d$ coordinates are computed using the SPE heuristic.

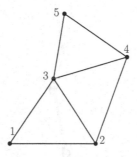

Fig. 5. Chordal Distance Graph

6   Experimental Results

The layout of a chain of 5 atoms (yellow disks in Fig. 6) was generated according to the Phillips' model. The R-matrix of the distances is as in Eq. 3. Their Cartesian coordinates, are:
$\{(0, 0, 0),(-1.526, 0, 0),(-2.8962, -0.6716,0),$
$(-3.9072, -0.3790, 0.4501),(-5.2984, 1.0028, -0.5148),(-6.3070, 2.0598, -0.9553)\}$,

listed in increasing order of the indices.

The same protein chain is also constructed in DoF model using DMCA + SPE with only $2n-3$ distances. The calculated coordinates are:
$\{(1.56433284, 0.57452693, -0.83311291),$
$(2.10220172, 0.50825107, -0.3995398),$
$(1.71776042, -0.1324179, -0.34579709),$
$(-3.696102, -0.03442974, 0.22117734),$
$(-5.14397621, -0.49209837, 0.37662301),$
$(-7.54421669, -0.4238319, 0.98064941)\}$.

These positions are shown as green disks. Visually, the two chains are seen to be near-identical, implying that in this case the DoF approach has worked successfully.

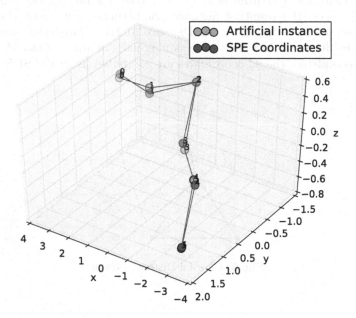

Fig. 6. Original protein chain Vs protein chain produced by DMCA + SPE (Color figure online)

7   MD-jeep with NMR Data

MD-jeep is a branch-and-prune based software developed by Mucherino et al. [11] to solve the Discretizable Molecular Distance Geometry Problem (DMDGP). The aim of DMDGP is to fix the position of an atom if the distance between that atom and three preceding atoms are known, assuming that a total order on the positions of all the atoms is available.

For an instance to qualify as a DMDGP problem, the following two assumptions must be satisfied for the weighted undirected graph $G = (V, E, w)$ corresponding to this instance.

– $\{1, 2, 3\} \in V$ should form a clique, and for each atom x_i the distance between three preceding and consecutive vertices must be known. In other words, weighted edges in the graph G exist connecting pairs of these vertices $(i - 1, i), (i - 2, i)$ and $(i - 3, i)$, where the weights are Euclidean distances.
– For each triplet of consecutive atoms, strict triangle inequality is satisfied by the corresponding distances.

Now with the positions of the three preceding atoms known, the intersection of three spheres (each centered at one of the preceding atoms in question and radius equal to the distance to the atom to be added) can be a circle or two points or one point only. The strict triangle inequality condition implies that the common intersection cannot be a circle for then the three preceding atoms would have to be linearly aligned. Thus it can occupy one of two possible positions. A binary tree data structure of possible positions of the atoms is maintained, and at every iteration the tree is expanded with the addition of two new positions. However, before adding a position to the binary tree, it is put through a feasibility test. This test checks if a potential position is consistent with other available distances. If the consistency test fails, then that position is not added to the tree and that the whole branch is pruned from the tree.

The pruning phase in the branch-and-prune algorithm reduces the size of the binary tree quickly, and the remaining branches are explored through an exhaustive search, which is not too expensive.

The MD-jeep software uses synthetic NMR data as input, created in a way to satisfy the assumptions made in the paper [12]. When all the assumptions are satisfied, the MD-jeep software with synthetic NMR data successfully generates a layout. A sample layout generated by MD-jeep is shown in Fig. 7.

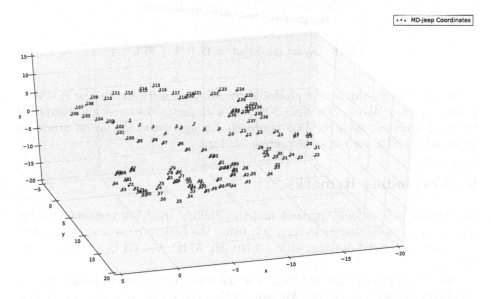

Fig. 7. MD-jeep coordinates

8   MD-jeep Vs. DMCA + SPE Using NMR Data

To compare our method (DMCA + SPE, with the degree of freedom approach),
we have used the synthetic NMR data that is part of the MD-jeep software
package. Note that the NMR data used here were generated by the authors of
MD-jeep to satisfy the assumptions required to solve an instance of DMDGP.

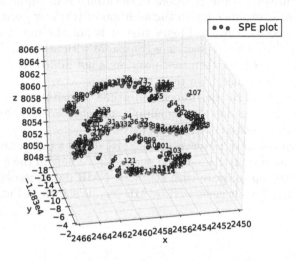

Fig. 8. Layout produced by DMCA + SPE

Figure 7 shows the layout produced by MD-jeep software for the synthetic
protein Id: 1crn. We used the same NMR file with partial distances and computed
the final structure, using our DoF approach. Figure 8 shows the layout produced
by DMCA + SPE for the same protein Id: 1crn.

9   Concluding Remarks

The Degree of Freedom Approach and the Phillips' model of instance creation
have been implemented in Python 2.7, using the basic numpy and scipy packages on a 64-bit HP desktop with a 3.70 GHz AMD A10 CPU, running under
Windows 8.1.

We should like to point out that as we increase the number of points DMCA
aborts due to numerical errors. We suspect that this is due to precision problems
arising out of floating-point calculations. We have circumvented this problem by
using the completed distances when DMCA aborts and then use these additional distances to complete the computation of the remaining distances using
SPE. This was done for an additional 10 point sets. For each set, we computed
the stress function as well as the cRMSD (this is the root-mean-square distance between two same-sized point sets) values to estimate the discrepancy
(see Table 1).

Table 1. cRMSD and the Stress function for various no. of points

No. of Points	cRMSD	Stress Function
5	0.092405002	0.015156232
6	0.370846601	0.009289248
7	1.609625109	0.03797316
8	0.824531356	0.004310616
9	0.780654964	0.002979685
10	0.616036684	0.002447328
11	2.434495218	0.033879593
12	1.235112879	0.001365694
13	2.849247676	0.021548734
14	0.94460547	0.000927799
15	3.935226235	0.021745748

References

1. Rahman, M.Z., Mukhopadhyay, A., Aneja, Y.P., Jean, C.: A distance matrix completion approach to 1-round algorithms for point placement in the plane. In: Gervasi, O., Murgante, B., Misra, S., Borruso, G., Torre, C.M., Rocha, A.M.A.C., Taniar, D., Apduhan, B.O., Stankova, E., Cuzzocrea, A. (eds.) ICCSA 2017. LNCS, vol. 10405, pp. 494–508. Springer, Cham (2017). https://doi.org/10.1007/978-3-319-62395-5_34
2. Agrafiotis, D.K.: Stochastic proximity embedding. J. Comput. Chem. **24**(10), 1215–1221 (2003)
3. Saxe, J.B.: Embeddability of weighted graphs in k-space is strongly NP-hard (1980)
4. Dong, Q., Wu, Z.: A linear-time algorithm for solving the molecular distance geometry problem with exact inter-atomic distances. J. Glob. Optim. **22**(1–4), 365–375 (2002)
5. Crippen, G.M., Havel, T.F., et al.: Distance Geometry and Molecular Conformation, vol. 74. Research Studies Press, Taunton (1988)
6. Phillips, A.T., Rosen, J.B., Walke, V.H.: Molecular structure determination by convex, global underestimation of local energy minima. Glob. Minimization Nonconvex Energy Funct. Mol. Conform. Prot. Fold. **23**, 181–198 (1995)
7. Golumbic, M.C.: Algorithmic Graph Theory and Perfect Graphs. Annals of Discrete Mathematics, vol. 57. North-Holland Publishing Co., Amsterdam (2004)
8. Agrafiotis, D.K., Bandyopadhyay, D., Yang, E.: Stochastic proximity embedding: a simple, fast and scalable algorithm for solving the distance geometry problem. In: Mucherino, A., Lavor, C., Liberti, L., Maculan, N. (eds.) Distance Geometry, pp. 291–311. Springer, New York (2013). https://doi.org/10.1007/978-1-4614-5128-0_14
9. Bakonyi, M., Johnson, C.R.: The euclidian distance matrix completion problem. SIAM J. Matrix Anal. Appl. **16**(2), 646–654 (1995)
10. Grone, R., Johnson, C.R., Sá, E.M., Wolkowicz, H.: Positive definite completions of partial hermitian matrices. Linear Algebr. Appl. **58**, 109–124 (1984)

11. Mucherino, A., Liberti, L., Lavor, C.: MD-jeep: an implementation of a branch and prune algorithm for distance geometry problems. In: Fukuda, K., Hoeven, J., Joswig, M., Takayama, N. (eds.) ICMS 2010. LNCS, vol. 6327, pp. 186–197. Springer, Heidelberg (2010). https://doi.org/10.1007/978-3-642-15582-6_34
12. Mucherino, A., Lavor, C., Liberti, L.: The discretizable distance geometry problem. Optim. Lett. **6**(8), 1671–1686 (2012)

An FPTAS for an Elastic Shape Matching Problem with Cyclic Neighborhoods

Christian Knauer, Luise Sommer$^{(\boxtimes)}$, and Fabian Stehn

Institute of Applied Computer Science, Universität Bayreuth, Bayreuth, Germany
{christian.knauer,luise.sommer,fabian.stehn}@uni-bayreuth.de

Abstract. In computational geometry, the elastic geometric shape matching (EGSM) problem class is a generalisation of the well-known geometric shape matching problem class: Given two geometric shapes, the 'pattern' and the 'model', find a *single* transformation from a given transformation class that, if applied to the pattern, minimizes the distance between the transformed pattern and the model with respect to a suitable distance measure.

In EGSM, the pattern is divided into subshapes that are transformed by a 'transformation ensemble', i.e., a set of transformations. The goal is to minimize the distance between the union of the transformed subpatterns and the model in object space as well as the distance between specific transformations of the ensemble. The 'neighborhood graph' encodes which translations should be similar.

We present a fully polynomial time approximation scheme (FPTAS) for EGSM instances for point sequences under translations with fixed correspondence where the neighborhood graph is a simple cycle.

Keywords: Computational geometry · Elastic shape matching
FPTAS · Approximation algorithm

1 Introduction

In classical geometric shape matching (GSM) problems, one is given a pattern P and a model Q, both from a class $\mathcal{S}$ of geometric shapes, along with a distance measure $d : \mathcal{S} \times \mathcal{S} \mapsto \mathbb{R}_0^+$. The task is to find a single transformation t from a given transformation class $\mathcal{T}$ acting on $\mathcal{S}$, so that $d(t(P), Q)$ is minimized.

Matching geometric shapes is a problem that occurs in many applications such as character recognition, logo detection, human-computer-interaction, etc., and in a variety of different scientific fields, e.g., robotics, computer aided medicine, drug design, etc., and thus has already received a considerable amount of attention. We refer to the survey papers by Alt et al. [1] and Veltkamp et al. [2] for an extensive overview.

Many *geometric registration problems* (where the task is to align two shapes in different coordinate systems), e.g., between the coordinate system of an operation theatre and the coordinate system of a $3D$-model of a patient acquired

© Springer International Publishing AG, part of Springer Nature 2018
O. Gervasi et al. (Eds.): ICCSA 2018, LNCS 10961, pp. 425–443, 2018.
https://doi.org/10.1007/978-3-319-95165-2_30

during a pre-operative MRI scan, can be modelled as a GSM instance by appropriately choosing S and d. There, the transformation that minimizes the distance between both geometric shapes is then used as the mapping from the pattern space into the model space.

In many applications, where local distortions and complex deformations may occur, such as soft tissue registrations, GSM problems are too restrictive because a single transformation is chosen to match the entire pattern to the model. To address this issue, GSM has been generalized to *elastic geometric shape matching* (EGSM), see [3,4]. Here, the pattern is partitioned into subshapes and instead of one single transformation, a so-called transformation ensemble is computed. Each subshape of the pattern is transformed by an individual transformation of the ensemble in order to minimize the distance between the transformed pattern and the model. Also, the 'consistency' of the ensemble is guaranteed by forcing the transformations acting on some neighboring subshapes of the pattern to be similar with respect to a suitable similarity measure for the class of transformations at hand. The dependencies between the transformations of an ensemble are encoded in a so-called neighborhood graph: The vertices are the transformations of the ensemble and an edge between two transformations enforces their similarity.

In [5], the authors considered several variants of this problem for different distance measures and graph families, including an algorithm that solves a variant of the problem for trees where only translations in a fixed direction are allowed in $O(n^2 \log n)$ time. In this paper, we focus on EGSM for point sequences under translations with fixed correspondence where the neighborhood graph is a simple cycle.

1.1   Problem Statement

In the following everything is stated in $\mathbb{R}^2$, $\|\cdot\|$ denotes the Euclidean norm and translations are represented by translation vectors. The following can also be extended to $\mathbb{R}^d$ for any $d \in \mathbb{N}$. Also, all index arithmetic is modulo n.

We consider the following variant of the elastic shape matching (ESM) problem introduced in [5]:

Problem 1. Given:

$$P = (p_0, \ldots, p_{n-1}) \text{ a sequence of points (the pattern) and}$$
$$Q = (q_0, \ldots, q_{n-1}) \text{ a sequence of points (the model).}$$

Find: A sequence of translations $T = (t_0, \ldots, t_{n-1})$, so that the function

$$\gamma(T, P, Q) := \max\{\max_{0 \le i < n} \|q_i - (p_i + t_i)\|, \max_{0 \le i < n} \|t_i - t_{i+1}\|\}$$

is minimized.

In other words, the goal is to find a sequence of translations $T = (t_0, \ldots, t_{n-1})$, so that p_i is matched to q_i and translated by t_i for all $0 \le i < n$

and maximum of all distances between successive elements of T in translation space and all distances between the translated points $(t_i + p_i)$ and q_i in model space is minimized. Measuring the distance of the points $(t_i + p_i)$ and q_i in model space is the same as measuring the distance of the points t_i and $q_i - p_i$ in translation space. This is why Problem 1 can be studied in translation space entirely:

Let $c_i := q_i - p_i$ for $0 \le i < n$ and $C := (c_0, \ldots, c_{n-1})$. The function $\gamma(T, P, Q)$ can be rewritten as

$$\gamma(T, C) := \max\{\max_{0 \le i < n} \|c_i - t_i\|, \max_{0 \le i < n} \|t_i - t_{i+1}\|\}.$$

We refer to translations in translation space (i.e. translations) simply as points. The neighborhood graph is given implicitly through the constraints on the translations, which form a simple cycle.

1.2 Basic Definitions

First, we introduce some notation:

Definition 1. *Let $c, u, v \in \mathbb{R}^2$ and $r > 0$.*

1. *$D_r(c)$ denotes the disk with radius r centered in c and $\partial D_r(c)$ denotes its boundary.*
2. *We define $I_r(c, u, v) := D_r(c) \cap D_r(u) \cap D_r(v)$.*

Definition 2. *For a given sequence $C = (c_0, \ldots, c_{n-1})$, we define $\delta^* := \min_T \gamma(T, C)$.*
  We call a sequence of points $T = (t_0, \ldots, t_{n-1})$ δ-admissible (for C), iff $\gamma(T, C) \le \delta$. A sequence, that is δ^*-admissible is called an optimal sequence. We will use the symbol T^* to denote an optimal sequence.
  A point t is called (δ, i)-admissible (for C), iff there is a δ-admissible sequence T so that $T = (t_0, \ldots, t_i = t, \ldots, t_{n-1})$.

Strictly speaking, δ^* and the concept of δ-admissibility depend on C, but since C is part of the input, we refrain from including C in the notation.

1.3 Previous Work and Our Contribution

In [5], the authors discussed several variants of EGSM problems, including an algorithm that solves a variant of the problem for trees where only translations in a fixed direction are allowed. In [6], we considered another a variant of the problem for trees under the L_1-, the L_∞-norm and under polygonal norms, and presented a polynomial time algorithm that gives a $(1 + \epsilon)$-approximation to the optimization variant of the same problem under the L_2-norm. However, there are no results regarding problem instances, where the neighborhood graph is a simple cycle. In particular, there is no literature, that deals with efficient exact or approximation algorithms for Problem 1 and we do not know, if the problem is NP-hard.

In this paper, we provide an FPTAS for Problem 1 and prove, that it computes a $(1 + \epsilon)$-approximation to δ^* in $O\left(\epsilon^{-1/2} \left(\log \epsilon^{-1}\right)^2 n^3 \log n\right)$ time or in $O\left(\left(\log \epsilon^{-1}\right) \epsilon^{-2} n^2 \log n\right)$ time for some $\epsilon > 0$.

2   The Algorithm

Observe, that there is a simple 3-approximation to δ^*:

Definition 3. *We define* $\delta^{(3)} := \gamma(C, C)$.

Lemma 1. C *gives a 3-approximation to* δ^*, *i.e.,* $\delta^{(3)} \leq 3\delta^*$.

Proof. The sequence C is $\delta^{(3)}$-admissible by construction. Consider an optimal sequence $T^* = (t_0^*, \ldots, t_{n-1}^*)$. Since $\|c_i - t_i^*\| \leq \delta^*$, $\|t_i^* - t_{i+1}^*\| \leq \delta^*$ and $\|c_{i+1} - t_{i+1}^*\| \leq \delta^*$, it follows that $\|c_i - c_{i+1}\| \leq 3\delta^*$ for all $0 \leq i < n$, and as a consequence

$$\delta^* = \gamma(T^*, C) \geq \frac{1}{3} \max_{0 \leq i < n} \|c_i - c_{i+1}\| = \frac{1}{3}\gamma(C, C) = \frac{1}{3}\delta^{(3)}.$$

$\square$

Lemma 1 is the basis for the construction of our FPTAS, since it implies, that every $(\delta^*, 0)$-admissible point lies within the disk $D_{\delta^{(3)}}(c_0)$. A simple way to get a $(1 + \epsilon)$-approximation to δ^* for some $\epsilon > 0$ is to sample t_0 from a dense enough ϵ_{grid}-grid (a grid where the distance between samples is at most ϵ_{grid}) that covers $D_{\delta^{(3)}}(c_0)$. We call the points of this grid *translation-samples*. Here, $\epsilon_{\mathrm{grid}} = \Theta\left(\epsilon\delta^{(3)}\right)$. We also sample the value δ of the objective function on the interval $[\frac{1}{3}\delta^{(3)}, \delta^{(3)}]$ with sample-distance $\epsilon_{\mathrm{obj}} = \Theta\left(\epsilon\delta^{(3)}\right)$. We call the samples on $[\frac{1}{3}\delta^{(3)}, \delta^{(3)}]$ *radius-samples*. We then test for every radius-sample δ, whether there exists a solution T' so that $\gamma(T', C) \leq \delta$ and a translation-sample is the ith component of T'. This test is a variant of a problem that has already been studied in [5], where the authors give an algorithm that solves this problem for paths and the case that only translations in a fixed direction are allowed in $O(n^2 \log n)$ time. We use a slightly modified version of this algorithm, see Sect. 3.3. Consequently, this simple FPTAS runs in $O\left(\epsilon^{-3} n^2 \log n\right)$ time.

This result can be improved in several ways. The first obvious improvement is to perform a binary search on $[\frac{1}{3}\delta^{(3)}, \delta^{(3)}]$, which improves the run-time to $O\left(\left(\log \epsilon^{-1}\right) \epsilon^{-2} n^2 \log n\right)$.

The second idea is based on Lemma 2 below, which says, that for every $\delta \geq \delta^*$, there is a δ-admissible sequence T containing a point t_i that lies on $\partial D_\delta(c_i)$ for some i. Consequently, we do not have to sample the whole disk $D_{\delta^{(3)}}(c_i)$ for the current radius-sample δ, but to only sample $\partial D_\delta(c_i)$. Unfortunately, there is no way to identify the disks (the c_i) with this property, hence it is no longer possible to pick an arbitrary disk and sample it, but we have to sample the boundary of all disks. This changes the run-time to $O\left((\log \epsilon^{-1}) \epsilon^{-1} n^3 \log n\right)$. Of course, this is only an improvement if $\epsilon^{-1} \gg n$. On the other hand, this strategy enables us to apply another modification: We can approximate each $\partial D_\delta(c_i)$ by a regular polygon with $O\left(\epsilon^{-1/2}\right)$ vertices. Due to the convexity of the problem, we can then perform a binary search on the edges of this polygon and get an FPTAS that runs in $O\left(\epsilon^{-1/2}\left(\log \epsilon^{-1}\right)^2 n^3 \log n\right)$ time. This gives us the following tradeoff between precision and input size:

Theorem 1. *We can compute a $(1+\epsilon)$-approximation to δ^* in $O\left((\log \epsilon^{-1}) \epsilon^{-2} n^2 \log n\right)$ time or in $O\left(\epsilon^{-1/2}\left(\log \epsilon^{-1}\right)^2 n^3 \log n\right)$ time.*

Since it is very clear how to implement the approximation when sampling the interior of $D_{\delta(3)}(c_0)$, we elaborate on the improvements of the second strategy.

Note that a suitable choice of ϵ strongly depends on the application as well as $\delta^{(3)}$, which is why we refrain from suggesting concrete choices of ϵ.

3   A Detailed Description

3.1   On (δ, i)-Admissible Points

The reason why it suffices to sample the boundaries of all disks rather than sampling the interior of one disk with a grid is, that any optimal solution T^* contains a *key-point*:

Definition 4. *A (δ^*, i)-admissible point t_i^* of $T^* = (t_0^*, \ldots, t_{n-1}^*)$ is called a key-point, iff $I_{\delta^*}(c_i, t_{i-1}^*, t_{i+1}^*) = \{t_i^*\}$ and $t_i^* \in \partial D_{\delta^*}(c_i)$.*

Lemma 2. *For every optimal sequence $T^* = (t_0^*, \ldots, t_{n-1}^*)$, there is an index $0 \le i < n$ so that t_i^* is a key-point.*

Before we can prove Lemma 2, we need consider certain characteristics of δ-admissible sequences $T = (t_0, \ldots, t_{n-1})$. Each of the points in T appears in exactly three of the constraints induced by $\gamma(T, C)$:

$$\begin{aligned} \|t_i - c_i\| &\le \delta, \\ \|t_i - t_{i-1}\| &\le \delta, \text{ and} \\ \|t_i - t_{i+1}\| &\le \delta. \end{aligned} \tag{1}$$

for all $0 \le i < n$. These constraints on t_i can be interpreted as disks of radius δ centered in t_{i-1}, t_{i+1} and c_i. Consequently t_i needs to lie in the common intersection $I_\delta(c_i, t_{i-1}, t_{i+1})$ of these three disks, see Figs. 1 and 2.

Proposition 1. *Let $T = (t_0, \ldots, t_{n-1})$ be a δ-admissible sequence. The set $I_\delta(c_i, t_{i-1}, t_{i+1})$ consists of exactly one point t_i iff one of the following cases holds:*

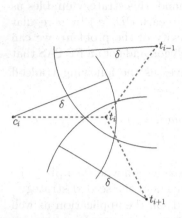

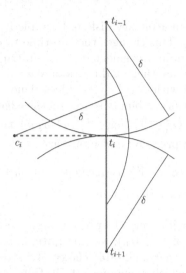

Fig. 1. The set $I_\delta(c_i, t_{i-1}, t_{i+1})$ is the intersection of $D_\delta(c_i)$, $D_\delta(t_{i-1})$ and $D_\delta(t_{i+1})$. The three constraints of (1) in which t_i appears, are visualised by fat line segments. They are not tight, which is indicated with dashed lines.

Fig. 2. The set $I_\delta(c_i, t_{i-1}, t_{i+1})$ consists of one point. The solid fat lines indicate tight constraints.

1. *The intersection of two of the three disks $D_\delta(c_i)$, $D_\delta(t_{i-1})$ and $D_\delta(t_{i+1})$ consists of one point, that in turn lies inside the third disk. Therefore t_i lies on the midpoint of the line segment between the centers of the first two disks, see Fig. 2. In this case we call t_i a segment-type point.*
2. *The intersection between any two of the three disks consists of more than one point, but the intersection of all three is one point and t_i lies in the interior of the triangle with vertices c_i, t_{i-1} and t_{i+1}. In this case, we call t_i a point-type point.*

Proof (Proposition 1). "$\Leftarrow$": trivial.

"$\Rightarrow$": The set $I_\delta(c_i, t_{i-1}, t_{i+1})$ is the intersection of three disks. Since $I_\delta(c_i, t_{i-1}, t_{i+1}) = \{t_i\}$, either the intersection of two of the three disks consists of only one point (which equals Part 1) or none of the intersections of two of three disks consists of one point, but the intersection of all three does. In the latter case, t_i is equally far from c_i, t_{i-1} and t_{i+1}, which implies that t_i is the circumcenter of the triangle with vertices c_i, t_{i-1} and t_{i+1}. Suppose t_i lies outside this triangle; this means that the triangle is obtuse. Let w.l.o.g. the obtuse angle be at c_i, so t_i and c_i are on opposing sides of the line segment $\overline{t_{i-1}t_{i+1}}$. Let t_i' be the midpoint of $\overline{t_{i-1}t_{i+1}}$ (so $t_i \neq t_i'$). Then t_i' is closer to c_i, t_{i-1} and t_{i+1} than t_i, which implies that t_i' is (δ, i)-admissible, so $t_i' \in I_\delta(c_i, t_{i-1}, t_{i+1})$, which is a contradiction. □

With this, we can now prove Lemma 2:

Proof (Lemma 2). Observe, that for every sequence $T = (t_0, \ldots, t_{n-1})$ and for all $0 \leq i < n$, the set $I_\delta(c_i, t_{i-1}, t_{i+1})$ is the intersection of three disks and thus has one of the following shapes:

1. The boundary of $I_\delta(c_i, t_{i-1}, t_{i+1})$ consists of three circular arcs that are connected by vertices. We call this shape *triangle-shape*.
2. The boundary of $I_\delta(c_i, t_{i-1}, t_{i+1})$ consists of two circular arcs that are connected by vertices. We call this shape *lens-shape*.
3. The set $I_\delta(c_i, t_{i-1}, t_{i+1})$ consists of one point. We call this shape *point-shape*.

Let $T^* = (t_0^*, \ldots, t_{n-1}^*)$ be an optimal sequence.

For the sake of contradiction, we assume that none of the constraints of (1) are tight for T^*. As a consequence, δ^* can be reduced by

$$\min \left(\min_{0 \leq i < n} \left(\delta^* - \|c_i - t_i^*\| \right), \min_{0 \leq i < n} \left(\delta^* - \|t_i^* - t_{i+1}^*\| \right) \right),$$

which is a contradiction. Consequently, every T^* contains at least one (δ^*, i)-admissible point that is involved in at least one tight constraint in (1).

Suppose that every point of T^* occurs in at most two tight constraints in (1) and that $I_{\delta^*}(i, t_{i-1}^*, t_{i+1}^*)$ has either triangle- or lens-shape for every index $0 \leq i < n$. Then the corresponding point lies either in the interior of $I_{\delta^*}(i, t_{i-1}^*, t_{i+1}^*)$ or on a circular arc (if it occurs in one tight constraint), on a vertex (if it occurs in two tight constraints) of the boundary of $I_{\delta^*}(i, t_{i-1}^*, t_{i+1}^*)$. Let t_i^* be a point of T^* that lies on the boundary of $I_{\delta^*}(i, t_{i-1}^*, t_{i+1}^*)$, and let t_i' be a point in the interior of $I_{\delta^*}(i, t_{i-1}^*, t_{i+1}^*)$. Then the sequence $(t_0^*, \ldots, t_{i-1}^*, t_i', t_{i+1}^*, \ldots, t_{n-1}^*)$ is optimal and $I_{\delta^*}(i, t_{i-1}^*, t_{i+1}^*)$ has either triangle- or lens-shape for all $0 \leq i < n$. Since this strategy can be applied to every point of T^* that occurs in up to two tight constraints, there is an optimal sequence so that none of its points occurs in a tight constraint, which is a contradiction.

Hence, T^* contains at least one point t_i^* so that $I_{\delta^*}(i, t_{i-1}^*, t_{i+1}^*) = \{t_i^*\}$ (t_i^* has point-shape). According to Proposition 1, t_i^* then is either a segment-type point (if it occurs in two tight constraints) or a point-type point (if it occurs in three tight constraints). One of the following two cases holds:

1. The point t_i^* is a segment-type point and $\|c_i - t_i^*\| = \delta^*$ is one of the two tight constraints, or t_i^* is a point-type point. Then, t_i^* lies on $\partial D_{\delta^*}(c_i)$ and hence is a key-point.
2. Case 2: For every t_i^* with $\{t_i^*\} = I_{\delta^*}(i, t_{i-1}^*, t_{i+1}^*)$ the following holds: t_i^* is a segment-type point and it lies on midpoint of the line segment $\overline{t_{i-1}^* t_{i+1}^*}$. If t_{i+1}^* or t_{i-1}^* occur in only one tight constraint (the constraint in which t_i^* occurs), both points can be shifted a little towards t_i^* so that $\|t_i^* - t_{i-1}^*\| < \delta^*$ and $\|t_i^* - t_{i+1}^*\| < \delta^*$. As a consequence, δ^* is not minimal, which is a contradiction. Hence $\{t_{i-1}^*\} = I_{\delta^*}(c_{i-1}, t_{i-2}^*, t_i^*)$ and $\{t_{i+1}^*\} = I_{\delta^*}(c_{i+1}, t_i^*, t_{i+2}^*)$. If either of them is a segment-type point and satisfies $\|t_j^* - c_j\| = \delta^*$ for one $j \in \{i - 1, i + 1\}$, or one of them is a point-type point, a point that lies on $\partial D_{\delta^*}(c_j)$ is found. If both points are segment-type points and $\|t_j^* - c_j\| < \delta^*$

for $j \in \{i-1, i+1\}$, t_{i-2}^* and t_{i+2}^* have to be analysed in the same manner. This strategy can be carried forward from point to point along C until one point-type point is found, or all points have been evaluated, which means that all of them are segment-type points. This implies that all $t_i^* \in T^*$ lie on a straight line and successive points have distance δ^*, which is a contradiction.

$\square$

To be precise, Lemma 2 contains more information than we need in order to prove that we can sample the boundaries of all disks instead of completely sampling one of the disks. The information that $I_{\delta^*}(i, t_{i-1}^*, t_{i+1}^*)$ consists of one point for at least one index i is required later in the arguments for Lemma 8.

3.2 On Approximating δ^*

There is at least one index $0 \le i < n$ for every $T^* = (t_0^*, \ldots, t_{n-1}^*)$, so that t_i^* is a key-point, which implies that $t_i^* \in \partial D_{\delta^*}(c_i)$. Since we have no way of determining the index i, so that t_i^* is a key-point, the boundaries of all disks have to be sampled in order to find a suitable approximation to t_i^*. Since we do not know the optimal radius δ^* either, we have to sample the boundary of all disks for dense enough radius-samples in $[\frac{1}{3}\delta^{(3)}, \delta^{(3)}]$. In order to verify that each binary search on $[\frac{1}{3}\delta^{(3)}, \delta^{(3)}]$ is successful, we have to prove that there actually is a sample-radius $\delta \in [\frac{1}{3}\delta^{(3)}, \delta^{(3)}]$ for all $0 \le i < n$, so that there is a (δ, i)-admissible point in $\partial D_\delta(c_i)$.

Lemma 3. *There is a $\delta^{(3)}$-admissible sequence $T = (t_0, \ldots, t_{n-1})$ so that every $(\delta^{(3)}, i)$-admissible point of T lies on $\partial D_{\delta^{(3)}}(c_i)$.*

Proof. Consider the $\delta^{(3)}$-admissible sequence C. If the sequence is shifted $\delta^{(3)}$-far in an arbitrary direction (e.g., $T := (t_0, \ldots, t_{n-1})$ with $t_i := c_i + (0, -\delta^{(3)})$ for all $0 \le i < n$), the sequence remains $\delta^{(3)}$-admissible and $t_i \in \partial D_{\delta^{(3)}}(c_i)$ for all $0 \le i < n$, see Fig. 3. $\square$

It is easy to see that Lemma 3 does not hold for every $\delta \ge \delta^*$, see Fig. 4.

Definition 5. *For every index i, let δ_i^* be the smallest value (not necessarily a radius-sample), so that there is a (δ_i^*, i)-admissible point $t_i \in \partial D_{\delta_i^*}(c_i)$.*

It follows from Lemma 3, that $\delta_i^* \le \delta^{(3)}$ for all $0 \le i < n$. In order to compute δ^* from the values $\delta_0^*, \ldots, \delta_{n-1}^*$, we need the following observation:

Lemma 4. *The following equation holds: $\delta^* = \min_{0 \le i < n} \delta_i^*$.*
Also, $\delta_i^* \in [\frac{1}{3}\delta^{(3)}, \delta^{(3)}]$ for all $0 \le i < n$.

Proof. Every δ_i^* meets the inequality $\delta_i^* \ge \delta^*$ and δ^* can not be smaller that the smallest of all δ_i^* due to Lemma 2. Hence, $\delta^* = \min_{0 \le i < n} \delta_i^*$. The second part of Lemma 4 follows from Lemma 3. $\square$

Consequently, in order to find δ^*, it suffices to compute δ_i^* for all $0 \le i < n$.

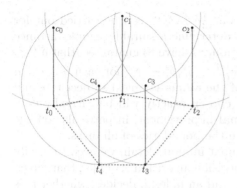 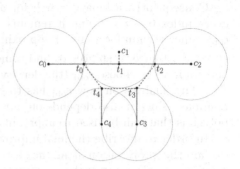

Fig. 3. Set T as constructed in the proof of Lemma 3 with tight constraints (solid fat lines) and constraints that are met with inequality (dashed fat lines).

Fig. 4. The same sequence C as in Fig. 3 and the sequence T, where t_1 can not lie on $\partial D_{\delta^*}(c_1)$. The tight constraints (solid fat lines) are δ^* long.

Definition 6. *Let $T^{(\epsilon)}$ be a solution so that $\delta^{(\epsilon)} := \gamma(T^{(\epsilon)}, C) \leq (1+\epsilon)\delta^*$. Let $t_i^{(\epsilon)}$ denote a $(1+\epsilon)$-approximation to a (δ_i^*, i)-admissible point t_i with $t_i \in \partial D_{\delta_i^*}(c_i)$. Let $\delta_i^{(\epsilon)}$ be the radius-sample of $t_i^{(\epsilon)}$.*

We already know, that $\delta_i^* \in [\frac{1}{3}\delta^{(3)}, \delta^{(3)}]$ for all i. In order to prove, that a binary search for δ_i^* on $[\frac{1}{3}\delta^{(3)}, \delta^{(3)}]$ works for every index i, we need one more characteristic of (δ, i)-admissible points.

Lemma 5. *Let $\bar{\delta} \geq 0$ be so that there is a $(\bar{\delta}, i)$-admissible point $t_i \in \partial D_{\bar{\delta}}(c_i)$. Then there is at least one (δ, i)-admissible point on $\partial D_{\delta}(c_i)$ for all $\delta \geq \bar{\delta}$.*

Proof. Let $\delta > \bar{\delta}$. Then the point t_i is (δ, i)-admissible, but does not lie on $\partial D_{\delta}(c_i)$. Also, there is a disk $D_{\delta - \bar{\delta}}(t_i)$ so that every point $t \in D_{\delta - \bar{\delta}}(t_i)$ is still (δ, i)-admissible, and by construction $\partial D_{\delta}(c_i)$ and $\partial D_{\delta - \bar{\delta}}(t_i)$ share exactly one point, see Fig. 5. $\qquad\square$

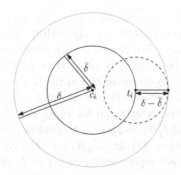

Fig. 5. The sets $\partial D_{\delta}(c_i)$ and $\partial D_{\delta - \bar{\delta}}(t_i)$ share exactly one point.

Consequently, a binary search for δ_i^* on $[\frac{1}{3}\delta^{(3)}, \delta^{(3)}]$ can be carried out for every index $0 \leq i < n$ and it remains to determine a suitable sample-distance ϵ_{obj}: Since we aim for a $(1 + \epsilon)$-approximation, we have to guarantee, that $\delta^{(\epsilon)} \leq (1 + \epsilon)\delta^*$. Hence, it suffices to find some $\delta_i^{(\epsilon)} \in [\delta_i^*, \delta_i^* + \epsilon\delta_i^*]$ for each $0 \leq i < n$ and we have to choose ϵ_{obj} (the density of the radius-samples) subject to ϵ and $\delta^{(3)}$. The analysis on how ϵ_{obj} has to be chosen exactly will be carried out in Lemma 8, since it also depends on our final improvement, in particular on the polygons that will be used to approximate the boundaries of all disks.

In order to describe the final improvement in more detail, we need to briefly explain the 'propagation along the path' decision algorithm $A1$ of [5], that, given a radius-sample δ, a translation-sample t_i and an index i, decides, whether t_i is (δ, i)-admissible.

3.3   An Algorithm for Paths

In Sect. 2, we mentioned, that due to the convexity of Problem 1, the run-time of the simple PTAS introduced in Sect. 2 can be improved by approximating the boundary of all disks by the boundary of a regular convex polygon and performing a binary search on the edges of that polygon. Then, for every sample-point t and sample-radius δ it is tested, if t is (δ, i)-admissible. For a given sequence C and index i there already exists an algorithm to test if a given point $t_i \in D_\delta(c_i)$ is (δ, i)-admissible: The point t_i is (δ, i)-admissible iff there are points $t_{i+1}, \ldots, t_{n-1}, t_0, \ldots, t_{i-1}$ so that all constraints encoded in $\gamma(T, C)$ are met. Solving this decision problem is the same as solving the following problem:

Problem 2. Given a sequence $C' = (c_1', \ldots, c_{n-1}')$, a point t and a parameter δ, is there a sequence $T' = (t_1', \ldots, t_{n-1}')$ with

$$
\begin{aligned}
\|c_j' - t_j'\| &\leq \delta \quad \text{for every } 1 \leq j < n, \\
\|t_j' - t_{j+1}'\| &\leq \delta \quad \text{for every } 1 \leq j < n - 1, \\
\|t - t_1'\| &\leq \delta \quad \text{and} \\
\|t_{n-1}' - t\| &\leq \delta ?
\end{aligned}
\tag{2}
$$

Here $c_j' := c_{i+j}$ and $t_j' = t_{i+j}$ for all $1 \leq j < n$, and $t = t_i$.

In [5] the authors introduced an algorithm, that solves Problem 2 in $O(n^2 \log n)$ time and space. We need to gain some insight on how this algorithm works and what the geometric properties of Problem 2 are in order to motivate and prove the correctness of the approach to approximate the boundaries of all disks mentioned above. Hence, we will now explain this algorithm in short with our notation and refer to [5] for more details.

Let $c_0' := t$, $c_n' := t$ and $I_j(t) := D_\delta(c_j')$, the set of points t_j' so that $\|t_j' - c_j'\| \leq \delta$ for $1 \leq j < n$. Let $I_0(t) := \{t\}$ and $I_n(t) := \{t\}$. We call the set $I_j(t)$ (or I_j in short) the *jth admissible region* and every $t \in I_j$ an *admissible point*. Note that every admissible region is convex. Let $S := (t = c_0', c_1', \ldots, c_{n-1}', t = c_n')$ be a sequence and $S_i := (c_0', \ldots, c_j')$ for $0 \leq j \leq n$.

The algorithm that decides whether there is a sequence T that satisfies (2) has an iterative structure. The basic idea is to propagate admissible points starting with $I_0 = t$ along S until c'_n is reached by appropriately merging the admissible regions of the successive points of S. Starting with I_1, the algorithm updates I_j to I'_j by replacing I_j with an adjusted set I'_j of admissible points until in the last step I_n is updated to I'_n. The jth and $(j-1)$th admissible region are merged into I'_j in such a way, that I'_j is not empty iff there is a set of points that

1. meets the similarity constraints of the points as imposed by sequence S_j and
2. guarantees that the Euclidean distance of the points that correspond to the points of S_j is at most δ.

Also, if $I'_j \neq \varnothing$, these points can be computed from $I'_0, \ldots, I'_j$.

To compute the set I'_j we proceed as follows: First, we *inflate* the region I'_{j-1} by δ which results in a set $I'^{\delta}_{j-1} := I'_{j-1} \oplus D_\delta$, where $\oplus$ denotes the Minkowski sum and D_δ is the disk with radius δ centered in the origin. The admissible region I'_j is given by $I'_j = I'^{\delta}_{j-1} \cap I_j$. This process is repeated until one of the following cases occurs:

1. There is an index j with $I'_j = \varnothing$ after the update:
   The process stops and NO is returned along with the tuple $(k(t_i), \mu(t_i))$, where $k(t_i)$ is the index of the first node that was not reached, and $\mu(t_i)$ is the Euclidean distance between the inflated version of the last non-empty admissible region and its succeeding admissible region.
2. I_n is updated and $I'_n \neq \varnothing$:
   The algorithm terminates and returns YES.

3.4 Approximating the Boundary of a Disk with a Polygon

The simplest approach that tests, if there is a $(1 + \epsilon)$-approximation to a key-point on $\partial D_\delta(c_i)$ is to pick $k = \Theta\left(\epsilon^{-1}\delta^{(3)}\right)$ suitably distributed translation-samples on $\partial D_\delta(c_i)$ and propagate all of them according to algorithm A1. In that way, $O(k)$ propagations (i.e., calls to algorithm $A1$) have to be carried out. This number can be reduced to $O(k^{1/2} \log k)$ by exploiting the convex structure of the admissible regions that occur during the propagation process: The main idea is to approximate $\partial D_\delta(c_i)$ by a regular polygon with $O(k^{1/2})$ vertices and to perform a binary search on each of its edges with a sample-distance that depends on ϵ and $\delta^{(3)}$.

At first, we will discuss how many vertices the inscribing polygon needs to have and what the minimum sample-rate for sample-points on each of the edges is on order to guarantee that for every point t on $\partial D_\delta(c_i)$ there is a sample point on the edges of the polygon that serves as a $(1 + \epsilon)$-approximation to t.

Definition 7. *Let $P_{\delta,p}(c_i)$ (or $P_\delta(c_i)$ in short) denote the inscribing regular polygon of $\partial D_\delta(c_i)$ with p vertices. By a slight abuse of notation, we identify $P_\delta(c_i)$ with its boundary, since we solely operate on the boundary of the polygons at hand. Also, let all such polygons be concentric.*

Lemma 6. *Let $p := \lceil 3^{1/4}\pi\epsilon^{-1/2}\rceil$ and let the edges of $P_\delta(c_i)$ be sampled with sample-distance ϵ_{edge} so that $\epsilon_{edge} \le \frac{1}{3}\delta^{(3)}\epsilon$. Then, there is a translation-sample $t \in P_\delta(c_i)$ for every point $u \in \partial D_\delta(c_i)$ so that $\|t - u\| \le \frac{1}{3}\delta^{(3)}\epsilon$.*

Proof. Let v and v' be two successive vertices of $P_\delta(c_i)$ and let e be the edge with endpoints v and v'. The points v, v' and c_i define an isosceles triangle with base e and apex angle $\alpha := 2\pi p-1$. The length of e can be estimated by using the Taylor series expansion of $\sin(\alpha/2)$ as

$$|e| = 2\delta \sin\left(\frac{\alpha}{2}\right) = 2\delta \sin\left(\frac{\pi}{p}\right) \le \frac{2\delta\pi}{p}.$$

The maximum distance between a point on $\partial D_\delta(c_i)$ and $P_\delta(c_i)$ is $\delta - |a|$, where a is the apothem of $P_\delta(c_i)$:

$$\delta - |a| = \delta - \delta\cos\left(\frac{\alpha}{2}\right) \le \delta\left(1 - \left(1 - \frac{\pi^2}{2p^2}\right)\right) = \delta\left(\frac{\pi^2}{2p^2}\right),$$

because the Taylor series expansion of $\cos\left(\frac{\alpha}{2}\right)$ can be estimated as $\cos(\alpha/2) \le (1 - \pi^2(2p^2)^{-1})$. Let the maximum distance between a point on $\partial D_\delta(c_i)$ and the closest translation-sample on $P_\delta(c_i)$ be named x. Since the maximum distance of a point on $\partial D_\delta(c_i)$ and $P_\delta(c_i)$ is $\delta - |a|$ and the samples that describe the edges of $P_\delta(c_i)$ have distance ϵ_{edge}, the application of Thales' theorem leads to

$$x^2 = (\delta - |a|)^2 + \left(\frac{\epsilon_{edge}}{2}\right)^2.$$

Since $\epsilon_{edge} \le \frac{1}{3}\delta^{(3)}\epsilon$, it follows that

$$x^2 \le \left(\frac{\delta\pi^2}{2p^2}\right)^2 + \left(\frac{\epsilon_{edge}}{2}\right)^2$$
$$= \frac{\delta^2\epsilon^2}{12} + \frac{\epsilon_{edge}^2}{4}$$
$$\le \frac{\delta^{(3)^2}\epsilon^2}{12} + \frac{(\epsilon\delta^{(3)})^2}{36} \le \left(\frac{1}{3}\epsilon\delta^{(3)}\right)^2$$
$$\Leftrightarrow x = \epsilon\frac{1}{3}\delta^{(3)}.$$

□

Strictly speaking, p depends on ϵ, but we refrain from including ϵ in the notation.

In the remainder, we will show, that the binary search among the samples on one edge of $P_\delta(c_i)$ can be carried out in $O\left(\log\epsilon^{-1}n^2\log n\right)$ time. Here $O\left(n^2\log n\right)$ is the time that is needed to carry out the propagation process for a single translation-sample t by algorithm A1. Since this approach builds on several properties of the tuple $(k(t), \mu(t))$ returned by algorithm A1, we have to introduce some of them first: The following lemma describes the dependency of the tuple on the translation-samples of one edge of $P_\delta(c_i)$.

Lemma 7. *Let* s *and* s' *be two* NO-*instances of algorithm* A1 *for a given radius-sample* δ, *i.e.*, $A1(s, \delta, i) = (\text{NO}, (k(s), \mu(s)))$ *and* $A1(s', \delta, i) = (\text{NO}, (k(s'), \mu(s')))$, *and let* $t \in \overline{ss'}$. *Then, either* $A1(t, \delta, i) = \text{YES}$, *or* $A1(t, \delta, i) = (\text{NO}, (k(t), \mu(t)))$. *In the latter case the tuple* $(k(t), \mu(t))$ *has the following properties:*

1. $k(t) \geq \min\{k(s), k(s')\}$,
2. *if* $k(t) = k(s) = k(s')$, *then* $\mu(t) \leq \max\{\mu(s), \mu(s')\}$.

Moreover, if $k(p) = k(s) = k(s')$ *for all points* $p \in \overline{ss'}$, *the function* $f \to [0, 1]$ *with* $x \mapsto \mu((1 - x)s + xs')$ *is strictly convex.*

In order to prove Lemma 7, we need one more observation:

Proposition 2. *Given two line segments* $\overline{ss'}$ *and* $\overline{uu'}$ *in the plane. If* $\|s - u\| \leq d$ *and* $\|s' - u'\| \leq d'$ *for* $d, d' \in \mathbb{R}^+$, *then for every point* $t_s \in \overline{ss'}$ *there is a point* $t_u \in \overline{uu'}$ *so that* $d_t := \|t_s - t_u\| \leq \max\{d, d'\}$ *and vice versa (Fig. 6).*

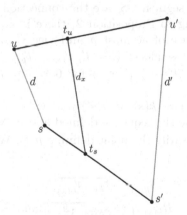

Fig. 6. Example of the quadrilateral considered in Proposition 2.

Proof. Every point $t_s \in \overline{ss'}$ can be expressed as $t_s = (1 - x)s + xs'$ for $x \in [0, 1]$. Choose $t_u = (1 - x)u + xu'$, then the following holds:

$$
\begin{aligned}
d_t = \|t_s - t_u\| &= \|(1 - x)s + xs' - ((1 - x)u + xu')\| \\
&= \|(1 - x)(s - u) + x(s' - u')\| \\
&\leq (1 - x)\|s - u\| + x\|s' - u'\| \\
&= (1 - x)d + xd' \leq \max(d, d').
\end{aligned}
$$

$\square$

With this, we can now prove Lemma 7:

Proof (Lemma 7). Let $C' = (c'_1, \ldots, c'_{n-1})$ with $c'_j := c_{i+j}$ for all $1 \leq j < n$.

Part 1: Let w.l.o.g. $k(s) \leq k(s')$. As mentioned in the description of the algorithm $A1$, $k(s)$ is the index of the first node that was not reached while propagating s. Of course, all nodes with smaller indices were reached. Suppose $s_{k(s)-1}$ is the point on $D_\delta(c'_{k(s)-1})$ that establishes $\mu(s)$, i.e., the point in $I_{k(s)-1}(s)$, that is closest to $D_\delta(c'_{k(s)})$. Then there is a sequence $(s = s_0, s_1, \ldots, s_{k-1})$ with $s_i \in D_\delta(c'_i)$ for $1 \leq i \leq k(s) - 1$ and $\|s_i - s_{i+1}\| \leq \delta$ for all $0 \leq i \leq k(s) - 2$. The point $s'_{k(s')-1}$ and the sequence $(s'_0, \ldots, s'_{k(s')-1})$ are defined in a similar way. We introduce the following notation for certain line segments:

$$S_i := \overline{s_i s'_i} \quad \text{for all } 0 \leq i \leq k(s) - 1,$$
$$R_i := \overline{s_i s_{i+1}} \quad \text{for all } 0 \leq i \leq k(s) - 2 \text{ and}$$
$$R'_i := \overline{s'_i s'_{i+1}} \quad \text{for all } 0 \leq i \leq k(s) - 2.$$

For all $0 \leq i \leq k(s) - 2$, the four line segments S_i, S_{i+1}, R_i and R'_i form a quadrilateral, where the two opposed sides R_i and R'_i have a length of at most δ. As illustrated in Fig. 7, the quadrilaterals are connected and form kind of a sequence where the line segments S_i are the connection between two successive quadrilaterals. According to Proposition 2, there is a point on S_{i+1} for every point on S_i with distance of at most δ and vice versa. Given Point $t \in S_0$, it follows that there is a sequence $(t = t'_0, t'_1, \ldots, t'_{k(s)-1})$ with $t'_i \in D_\delta(c'_i)$ for $1 \leq i \leq k(s) - 1$ and $\|t'_i - t'_{i+1}\| \leq \delta$ for $0 \leq i \leq k(s) - 2$. Hence $k(t) \geq \min\{k(s), k(s')\}$.

Part 2: Suppose $k(t) = k(s) = k(s')$ and w.l.o.g. $\mu(s) \geq \mu(s')$; also, let $(t = t'_0, t'_2, \ldots, t'_{k(s)-1})$ be the sequence defined above. Note, that $t'_{k(s)-1}$ lies on $S_{k(s)-1}$ and is not necessarily the point defining $\mu(t)$. We add one quadrilateral to the sequence:

$$S_{k(s)} := \overline{\bar{s}_{k(s)} \bar{s}'_{k(s)}},$$
$$R_{k(s)-1} := \overline{s_{k(s)-1} \bar{s}_{k(s)}} \text{ and}$$
$$R'_{k(s)-1} := \overline{s'_{k(s)-1} \bar{s}'_{k(s)}},$$

where $\bar{s}_{k(s)}$ is the point on $D_\delta(c'_{k(s)})$ with distance $\mu(s) + \delta$ to $s_{k(s)-1}$ and $\bar{s}'_{k(s)}$ is defined in a similar way. Again, $S_{k(s)-1}, S_{k(s)}, R_{k(s)-1}$ and $R'_{k(s)-1}$ form a quadrilateral, but this time, the two opposed sides have lengths $\mu(s) + \delta$ and $\mu(s') + \delta$. Due to Proposition 2, there is a point $\bar{t}'_{k(s)}$ on $S_{k(s)}$ with $\|t'_{k(s)-1} - \bar{t}'_{k(s)}\| \leq \max\{\mu(s) + \delta, \mu(s') + \delta\}$.

Now let $k(t) = k(s) = k(s')$ fo all points $t \in \overline{ss'}$ and let t be expressed as $t = (1 - x)s + xs'$. The sequence $(t = t'_0, \ldots, t'_{k(s)-1}, t'_{k(s)} = \bar{t}'_{k(s)})$ with $t'_i = ((1 - x)s_i + xs'_i)$ satisfies $t'_i \in D_\delta(c'_i)$, since every point t'_i is located on S_i and due to Proposition 2 two successive points have a distance of at most δ except for $t'_{k(s)-1}$ and $\overline{k(s)}_k$. As a consequence, we have:

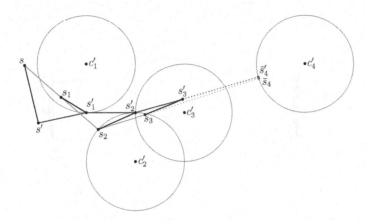

Fig. 7. The sequences $(s_0, \ldots, s_3, \bar{s}_4)$ and $(s'_0, \ldots, s'_3, \bar{s}'_4)$ form a sequence of quadrilaterals.

$$\mu(t) \leq \|t'_{k(s)-1} - \bar{t}'_{k(s)}\| - \delta$$
$$\leq (1-x)(\delta + \mu(s)) + x(\delta + \mu(s')) - \delta$$
$$= (1+x)\mu(s) + x\mu(s').$$

Since this holds for every choice of s and s' as well as every choice of $t \in \overline{ss'}$, Function f is convex.

Strictly speaking $\mu(t) < (1+x)\mu(s) + x\mu(s')$, because $S_{k(s)}$ is the chord of a disk and therefore the distance between $t'_{k(s)-1}$ and $\bar{t}'_{k(s)}$ is greater than the distance between $t'_{k(s)-1}$ and the disk that contains $\bar{t}'_{k(s)}$. □

Note, that Lemma 7 holds for any line segment contained in $D_\delta(c_i)$.

As a consequence of the convexity of function f, in order to test if there is a (δ, i)-admissible point on the line segment $\overline{ss'}$ (which means, that there is a point on $t \in \overline{ss'}$ so that the propagation of t with radius-sample δ is successful) a binary search can be carried out among the samples along the line segment $\overline{ss'}$.

The runtime depends on the number of sample-points that have to be evaluated, which is $O\left(\log \epsilon_{\text{edge}}^{-1}\right)$ for sample-rate ϵ_{edge}. Since every propagation takes $O(n^2 \log n)$ time, the procedure runs in $O\left(\log \epsilon_{\text{edge}}^{-1} n^2 \log n\right)$.

We already know from Lemma 6, that the length of an edge of $P_\delta(c_i)$ is at most $2\delta\pi p^{-1}$. With $\epsilon_{\text{edge}} \leq \frac{1}{3}\delta^{(3)}\epsilon$ and $p = \lceil 3^{1/4}\pi\epsilon^{-1/2} \rceil$, the number of translation-samples, that have to be propagated, is

$$\log\left(\frac{2\delta\pi}{\epsilon_{\text{edge}}p}\right) \leq \log\left(\frac{6\delta\pi\sqrt{\epsilon}}{\epsilon\delta^{(3)}\pi\sqrt[4]{3}}\right) \leq \log\left(\frac{1}{\sqrt{\epsilon}}\left(\frac{6}{\sqrt[4]{3}}\right)\right) \in O\left(\log\frac{1}{\sqrt{\epsilon}}\right), \quad (3)$$

which leads to a runtime of $O\left(\epsilon^{-1/2}\log \epsilon^{-1} n^2 \log n\right)$ in total for the evaluation of one polygon and a fixed radius-sample.

For technical reasons, we also need to state the following insight:

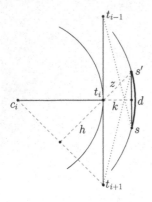

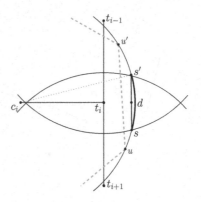

Fig. 8. The circular arc of $(\bar{\delta}, i)$-admissible points on $\partial D_{\bar{\delta}}(c_i)$ (fat) with line segments of length δ^* (solid fat lines) and $\bar{\delta}$ (dotted fat lines).

Fig. 9. $P_{\bar{\delta}}(c_i)$ (dashed fat lines), $D_{\bar{\delta}}(c_i)$ with edge $\overline{uu'}$ that intersects k.

Lemma 8. *Let $\bar{\delta} := \delta^* + \epsilon_{obj}$ and let s and s' be the endpoints of the circular arc of $(\bar{\delta}, i)$-admissible points on $\partial D_{\bar{\delta}}(c_i)$, then $\|s - s'\| \geq \epsilon_{obj}$.*

Let the sample-distance of the points on the edges of $P_{\bar{\delta}}(c_i)$ be $\epsilon_{edge} := \frac{\sqrt{3}}{12}\epsilon\delta^{(3)}$ and let $\epsilon_{obj} := \frac{\sqrt{3}}{12}\epsilon\delta^{(3)}$. Then there is a translation-sample on $P_{\bar{\delta}}(c_i)$ that is a $(1 + \epsilon)$-approximation to t_i^*.

Proof. There is exactly one (δ^*, i)-admissible point $t_i \in \partial D_{\delta^*}(c_i)$. Also, t_i lies inside the triangle defined by c_i, t_{i-1} and t_{i+1}, see Proposition 1, which implies, that either c_i and t_{i-1} or c_i and t_{i+1} lie on opposed sides of the tangent of $D_{\delta^*}(c_i)$ at t_i. If we increase δ^* by ϵ_{obj}, the intersection of $D_{\bar{\delta}}(t_{i-1})$ and $D_{\bar{\delta}}(t_{i+1})$ changes from just one point to a convex set in the shape of a lens. The circular arc of $(\bar{\delta}, i)$-admissible points on $\partial D_{\bar{\delta}}(c_i)$ is the intersection of this lens with $\partial D_{\bar{\delta}}(c_i)$ and a short geometric inspection shows that this circular arc (with endpoints s and s') is shortest, if the distance between t_{i-1} and t_{i+1} is $2\delta^*$ and both points lie on the tangent of $D_{\bar{\delta}}(c_i)$ at t_i.

Let $d := \overline{ss'}$, $h := \overline{\frac{1}{2}(c_i - t_{i+1}), t_i}$, $z := \overline{t_i s'}$ and $k := \overline{t_i, \frac{1}{2}(s - s')}$ (for a better understanding, see Fig. 8).

The application of Thales' theorem provides the following equations:

$$|h| = \frac{1}{\sqrt{2}}\delta^* \tag{4}$$

$$|z| = \sqrt{(\delta^* + \epsilon_{obj})^2 - |h|^2} - |h| \tag{5}$$

$$|k| = \sqrt{|z|^2 - \frac{1}{4}|d|^2}, \text{ and} \tag{6}$$

$$|k| = \sqrt{(\delta^* + \epsilon_{obj})^2 - \frac{1}{4}|d|^2} - \delta^*. \tag{7}$$

Squaring the Eq. (6)=(7) results in

$$|z|^2 - \frac{1}{4}|d|^2 = (\delta^* + \epsilon_{obj})^2 - \frac{1}{4}|d|^2 + (\delta^*)^2 - 2\delta^*\sqrt{(\delta^* + \epsilon_{obj})^2 - \frac{1}{4}|d|^2}.$$

Now Eq. (5) can be applied and both sides of the equation can be simplified:

$$\Leftrightarrow \left(\sqrt{(\delta^* + \epsilon_{obj})^2 - |h|^2} - |h|^2\right)^2 = (\delta^* + \epsilon_{obj})^2 + (\delta^*)^2 - 2\delta^*\sqrt{(\delta^* + \epsilon_{obj})^2 - \frac{1}{4}|d|^2}$$

$$\overset{(4)}{\Leftrightarrow} \sqrt{2}\sqrt{(\delta^* + \epsilon_{obj})^2 - \frac{1}{2}(\delta^*)^2} + \delta^* = 2\sqrt{(\delta^* + \epsilon_{obj})^2 - \frac{1}{4}|d|^2}.$$

Again, we square both sides of the equation and simplify the resulting terms:

$$\Leftrightarrow |d|^2 = 2(\delta^* + \epsilon_{obj})^2 - 2\sqrt{2}\delta^*\sqrt{(\delta^* + \epsilon_{obj})^2 - \frac{1}{2}(\delta^*)^2}.$$

Suppose $|d|^2 \geq \epsilon_{obj}{}^2$. Then

$$2(\delta^* + \epsilon_{obj})^2 - \epsilon_{obj}{}^2 \geq 2\sqrt{2}\delta^*\sqrt{(\delta^* + \epsilon_{obj})^2 - \frac{1}{2}(\delta^*)^2}$$

$$\Leftrightarrow 4(\delta^* + \epsilon_{obj})^4 - 4\epsilon_{obj}{}^2(\delta^* + \epsilon_{obj})^2 + \epsilon_{obj}{}^4 \geq 8(\delta^*)^2(\delta^* + \epsilon_{obj})^2 - 4(\delta^*)^4$$

$$\Leftrightarrow 12(\delta^*)^2\epsilon_{obj}{}^2 + 8\delta^*\epsilon_{obj}{}^3 + \epsilon_{obj}{}^4 \geq 0.$$

This holds for every $\delta^* \geq 0$ and $\epsilon_{obj} \geq 0$.

Since the maximum distance between a point on $P_{\bar{\delta}}(c_i)$ and the boundary $\partial D_{\bar{\delta}}(c_i)$ is smaller than ϵ_{obj}, one of the following two cases holds:

1. There is a vertex of $P_{\bar{\delta}}(c_i)$ that is located on the circular arc of $(\bar{\delta}, i)$-admissible points for $t_i \in \partial D_{\bar{\delta}}(c_i)$.
2. There is an edge of $P_{\bar{\delta}}(c_i)$ that intersects with k. Let the vertices of this edge be called u and u'.

If case 1 holds, then the vertex of $P_{\bar{\delta}}(c_i)$ on the circular arc gives a $(1 + \epsilon)$-approximation to t_i. If case 2 holds, then $\overline{uu'}$ and $I_{\bar{\delta}}(c_i, t_{i-1}, t_{i+1})$ intersect, see Fig. 9. The resulting line segment is shortest, if $\overline{uu'}$ is parallel to $\overline{t_{i-1}t_{i+1}}$; also, the line segments $\overline{t_{i-1}t_{i+1}}$ and d are parallel by construction. The intersection of $D_{\bar{\delta}}(t_{i-1})$ and $D_{\bar{\delta}}(t_{i+1})$ (the lens) is an axisymmetric convex object and $\overline{t_{i-1}t_{i+1}}$, which has length $2\epsilon_{obj}$, lies on its axis of symmetry. Hence, $|\overline{t_{i-1}t_{i+1}}| \geq |\overline{ab}| \geq |d|$ for every line segment $\overline{ab}$ that is parallel to $\overline{t_{i-1}t_{i+1}}$ and $\overline{ab}$ lies inside the vertical stripe within the lens that is bounded by $\overline{t_{i-1}t_{i+1}}$ and d, which is why the length of the line segment of (δ^*, i)-admissible points that lies inside $\overline{uu'}$ is at least ϵ_{obj} long. The sample-distance we use on the edges of $P_{\bar{\delta}}(c_i)$ is $\frac{\sqrt{3}}{12}\epsilon\delta^{(3)} < \frac{1}{3}\delta^{(3)}\epsilon$, which proves Lemma 8.   □

3.5 Description and Analysis of the Algorithm

We first describe the algorithm: At the start, the value of a 3-approximation to δ^* is computed in $O(n)$ time. Except for basic arithmetic operations, the algorithm consists of four nested loops: The first loop iterates over all of the n input points of the sequence C. For every such point a binary search for $\delta \in [\frac{1}{3}\delta^{(3)}, \delta^{(3)}]$ up to accuracy $\epsilon_{obj} = \frac{\sqrt{3}}{12}\delta^{(3)}\epsilon$ is carried out; this takes $O(\log \epsilon^{-1})$ steps. In each step of this binary search all $p = \lceil 3^{1/4}\pi\epsilon^{-1/2}\rceil \in O\left(\epsilon^{-1/2}\right)$ edges of $P_\delta(c_i)$ are inspected, and on each of them a binary search among $\frac{2\delta\pi}{\epsilon_{edge}} \in O\left(\frac{1}{\epsilon}\right)$ translation-samples is performed. Each translation-sample is propagated with algorithm A1 for paths, which takes $O(n^2 \log n)$ time per call. This gives a total runtime of $O\left(\epsilon^{-1/2}\left(\log \epsilon^{-1}\right)^2 n^3 \log n\right)$.

If $\delta^{(\epsilon)} < \delta^{(3)}$ is returned, it is valid since there was a translation-sample that has been propagated successfully and therefore is part of a $\delta^{(\epsilon)}$-admissible sequence T. This also means that the very translation-sample that establishes $\delta^{(\epsilon)}$ is propagated and together with the intermediate steps of the propagation gives a T, which then serves as a witness. If there was no successful propagation, $\delta^{(\epsilon)} = \delta^{(3)}$ is returned and we know from Lemma 1 that there is always a $\delta^{(3)}$-admissible sequence.

Now we analyse the precision of the algorithm: The precision of the binary search on δ is $\epsilon_{obj} < \frac{1}{3}\delta^{(3)}\epsilon$; also, all polygons are concentric by construction. If $P_\delta(c_i)$ and $P_{\delta+\epsilon_{obj}}(c_i)$ are two polygons with circumradii that differ by ϵ_{obj}, the distance between any point on $P_\delta(c_i)$ and the polygon $P_{\delta+\epsilon_{obj}}(c_i)$ is at most ϵ_{obj} and vice versa. Every edge of these two polygons is sampled with points of distance ϵ_{edge}, and with Thales' theorem it follows that for every translation-sample on $P_\delta(c_i)$ there is a translation-sample on $P_{\delta+\epsilon_{obj}}(c_i)$ with distance $\frac{1}{3}\delta^{(3)}\epsilon$ or less and vice versa. Combined with Lemma 6, we have that for every δ there is a translation-sample in $D_\epsilon(t_i)$ for every (δ, i)-admissible point $t_i \in \partial D_\delta(c_i)$. According to Lemma 8, one of the following two cases holds: Either there is at least one (δ, i)-admissible translation-sample on $P_\delta(c_i)$ for every $\delta \geq \delta^* + \frac{1}{3}\delta^{(3)}\epsilon$ so that the line segment of all (δ, i)-admissible points on one of the edges of this polygon is at least $\frac{1}{3}\delta^{(3)}\epsilon$ long, or one vertex of the polygon is a (δ, i)-admissible point and since all polygons are concentric, this vertex is (δ, i)-admissible for every $\partial D_\delta(c_i)$ with $\delta \geq \delta^*$. We consider the radius-samples $\bar{\delta}$, $\bar{\delta} + \epsilon_{obj}$ and $\bar{\delta} + 2\epsilon_{obj}$, where $\bar{\delta} := \delta^* + \zeta - \epsilon_{obj}$ for some $0 < \zeta < \epsilon_{obj}$. Since $\bar{\delta} < \delta^*$, none of the propagations for this δ are successful. A short analysis leads to $\bar{\delta} + \epsilon_{obj} < \delta^* + \epsilon_{obj} < \bar{\delta} + 2\epsilon_{obj} < \delta^* + \frac{1}{3}\delta^{(3)}\epsilon$.

Due to Lemma 8, this means, that for radius-sample $\bar{\delta} + 2\epsilon_{obj}$ the two endpoints of the circular arc of $(\bar{\delta} + 2\epsilon_{obj}, i)$-admissible points in $D_{\bar{\delta}+2\epsilon_{obj}}(c_i)$ have a distance of at least ϵ_{obj}, which is why there is at least one translation-sample on the inscribing polygon of this disk, that is propagated successfully and the algorithm returns $\delta^{(\epsilon)} = \bar{\delta} + 2\epsilon_{obj} < \delta^* + \frac{1}{3}\delta^{(3)}\epsilon < (1+\epsilon)\delta^*$ as the approximation to δ^*. Hence the algorithm computes a $(1 + \epsilon)$-approximation to δ^* for Problem 1.

It also returns a $(\delta^{(\epsilon)}, i)$-admissible point $t^{(\epsilon)}$ from which an $\delta^{(\epsilon)}$-admissible sequence $T^{(\epsilon)}$ can be computed in $O(n^2 \log n)$ time.

4   Conclusion

It is not known, if EGSM for point sets under translations is NP-hard, if the neighborhood graph is a simple cycle. However, the results provided in this paper give the first efficient technique to get a $(1 + \epsilon)$-approximation for EGSM instances under cyclic neighborhoods. At long sight, we believe this results to be the basis for the development of efficient approximation algorithms for different graph classes that contain cycles, e.g., graphs with given feedback vertex sets or bounded path- or treewidth.

References

1. Alt, H., Guibas, L.: Discrete Geometric Shapes: Matching, Interpolation, and Approximation. In: Handbook of Computational Geometry, pp. 121–153. Elsevier B.V. (2000)
2. Veltkamp, R.C., Hagedoorn, M.: State of the art in shape matching. In: Lew, M.S. (ed.) Principles of Visual Information Retrieval. Advances in Pattern Recognition, pp. 87–119. Springer, London (2001). https://doi.org/10.1007/978-1-4471-3702-3_4
3. de Berg, M., Cheong, O., van Kreveld, M., Overmars, M.: Computational Geometry: Algorithms and Applications, vol. 3. Springer-Verlag, Heidelberg (2008). https://doi.org/10.1007/978-3-540-77974-2
4. Besl, P.J., McKay, N.D.: A method for registration of 3-D shapes. IEEE Trans. Pattern Anal. Mach. Intell. **14**(2), 239–256 (1992). https://doi.org/10.1109/34.121791. http://portal.acm.org/citation.cfm?id=132022
5. Knauer, C., Stehn, F.: Elastic geometric shape matching for point sets under translations. In: Dehne, F., Sack, J.-R., Stege, U. (eds.) WADS 2015. LNCS, vol. 9214, pp. 578–592. Springer, Cham (2015). https://doi.org/10.1007/978-3-319-21840-3_48
6. Knauer, C., Sommer, L., Stehn, F.: Elastic geometric shape matching for translations under the Manhattan Norm. Comput. Geom. Theor. Appl. (2018). https://doi.org/10.1016/j.comgeo.2018.01.002

Workshop Computational Movement Analysis (CMA 2018)

The Computational Techniques for Optimal Store Placement: A Review

H. Damavandi[1], N. Abdolvand[1(✉)], and F. Karimipour[2]

[1] Department of Management, Faculty of Social Science and Economics,
Alzahra University, Tehran, Iran
N.Abdolvand@alzahra.ac.ir
[2] Department of Surveying and Geomatic Engineering, Faculty of Engineering,
University of Tehran, Tehran, Iran

Abstract. In today's world which is subject to an increasing number of stores and level of rivalry on a daily basis, decisions concerning a store's location are considered highly important. Over the years, researchers and marketers have used a variety of different approaches for solving the optimal store location problem. Like many other research areas, earlier methods for site selection involved the use of statistical data whereas recent methods rely on the rich content which can be extracted from big data via modern data analysis techniques. In this paper, we begin with assessing the historical precedent of the most accepted and applied traditional computational methods for determining a desirable place for a store. We proceed by discussing some of the technological advancements that has led to the advent of more cutting-edge data-driven methods. Finally, we extend a review of some of the most recent, location based social network data-based approaches, to solving the store site selection problem.

Keywords: Computational movement analysis
Location based social network data · Geo-marketing · Retail store location
Site selection

1 Introduction

Determining retail store popularity and studying the variables influencing it, has always been one of the hottest research topics noticed in many different scientific domains. From a marketing perspective, if retail store popularity from a target customer's point of view is what one is after, it can be controlled and even enhanced through accurate planning of the marketing mix elements. The marketing mix for production businesses was defined by Kotler as "a set of controllable marketing variables – product, price, place and promotion – that the firm can use to get a desired response from their target customers" (Rafiq and Ahmed 1992). Booms and Bittner (1981, pp. 47–51), later modified the marketing mix concept to better fit the marketing aspects of services by adding three new elements to the mix: process, physical evidence and participants. Accurate planning for the marketing mix elements includes making important decisions about a number of other factors. For example, planning for the "place" element, includes making decisions about factors like store location, distribution channels, accessibility,

© Springer International Publishing AG, part of Springer Nature 2018
O. Gervasi et al. (Eds.): ICCSA 2018, LNCS 10961, pp. 447–460, 2018.
https://doi.org/10.1007/978-3-319-95165-2_31

distribution network coverage, sales domains, inventory placement and transportation facilities. Store placement, especially for service providers and retail stores, has always been considered as one of the most important business decisions a firm can make, since it is a critical factor contributing to a business's overall chance for success. *"No matter how good its offering, merchandising, or customer service, every retail company still has to contend with three critical elements of success: location, location, and location"* (Taneja 1999, pp. 136–137). There are many different approaches to support decision making in case of retail store placement. Some of these approaches including relying on experience and the use of checklists, analogues and ratios have been around and used by marketing managers for many years (Hernández and Bennison 2005). Such techniques are favored by some managers since they require minimum levels of budget, technical expertise and data, yet their downfall lies in the high level of subjectivity in decision making and the fact that they are almost incompatible with GIS (Hernandez et al. 1998). Other techniques including approaches based on the central place theory, gravity models, the theory of minimum differentiation and data driven approaches such as feature selection are more computational and therefor need a higher level of expertise and resources, but at the same time offer a superior level of predictability and are not bound by a high amount of subjectivity.

In this paper, the main goal is to review the evolution of computational approaches to solving the retail store placement problem. Consequently, the principal contributions of this work can be listed as follows.

- An investigation of the origins and main principles of the most accepted theories that attempted to explain the relationship between location and store popularity and a review on some of the research that has been inspired by these theories over the past century.
- An exploration of the technological and scientific developments that led to the emergence of more data-driven and analytical approaches and an explanation of some of the challenges and advantages of using location based social network[1] data for site selection.
- A review of the LSBN-based feature selection frameworks proposed by a number of scientists over the past decade, an introduction to some of the most practical features they used to tackle the store placement problem and an assessment of the outcomes of their works.
- A discussion on the importance of accurate location placement and possible directions for future research on this subject.

2 Computational Techniques

Over the years, several theories have been proposed attempting to explain the circumstances of the effects of location on store popularity and success. While some of the traditional approaches such as the use of the central place theory, spatial interaction theory

---

[1] LSBN.

and the principal of minimum differentiation have been widely accepted and applied, they were mostly reliant on the use of statistical data, required high levels of specialty in terms of model building and they rely on unrealistic assumptions (Chen and Tsai 2016; Hernandez et al. 1998). On the other hand, recent technological advancements have led to the advent of new techniques based on the analysis of big data. Consequently, in this section, by considering a historical-methodological approach, we begin with a historical review of the most acknowledged traditional methods for site selection, proceed by discussing the developments that caused the emergence of new sources of data, hence the evolution of traditional methods into modern techniques and end with a methodological review of the new feature selection based approaches.

2.1 Traditional Methods

The question of placing chain stores across the network of a city in a way that optimizes the overall sales and customer attraction has been of interest to researchers, managers and other planning authorities for many years. Seventy-five years ago (in 1933), Walter Christaller proposed the central place theory while studying the central places in southern Germany. Although the significance of his theory was not appreciated until years later, according to Brown (1993), his theory became the basis for the retail planning policies of several countries. Around the same time, the spatial interaction theory (Reilly, 1929–1931) and the principle of minimum differentiation (Hotelling 1929) were introduced which together with the central place theory, shape the three main fundamental concepts in traditional retail location research (Litz 2014). Despite their shortcomings, including being normative and requiring a list of unrealistic assumptions, they still tend to attract a vast amount of academic attention (Brown 1993; Chen and Tsai 2016). Therefore, this section begins with a brief review of each of the aforementioned theories, continues with comparing the main goals, limitations and assumptions of them and ends with a review of some of the most significant papers inspired by the concepts of these theories.

The Central Place Theory

Scientists have tried to describe and characterize the regionalization of urban space in a hierarchical manner for almost a century now. *"A hierarchy emerges with respect to the types of relationships that exist given the cluster size, whether the cluster is a village, a town or a city"* (Arcaute et al. 2015; Berry et al. 2014). One of the most famous examples of this type of approach is the Central place hierarchies (Boventer 1969) introduced by Christaller (Arcaute et al. 2015). The origins of Christaller's central place theory dates back to 1933, when this German researcher first suggested that there is a reverse relationship between the demand for a product and the distance from the source of supply in a manner that leads to zero demand for distances farther than a certain range which is called the "range of a good". This theory is based on the importance of transportation costs for the customers and focuses on describing the number, spacing, size and functional composition of retail centers while assuming that all customers are rational decision makers, all sellers enjoy equivalent costs, free entry and fair pricing in a perfectly competitive market and shopping trips are single-purpose (Brown 1993).

The Principle of Minimum Differentiation

This theory was presented by Hotelling (Hotelling 1929), and focuses on the importance of a store's proximity to its main rivals and argues that distance from rivals is more important than distance from customers. Numerous researchers have tried to improve the principle of minimum differentiation ever since by considering variations in the basic underlying assumptions (Ali and Greenbaum 1977; Hartwick and Hartwick 1971; Lerner and Singer 1937; Nelson 1958; Smithies 1941). In 1958, based on Hotelling's theory, Nelson suggested that while suppliers of a given product or service are located near one another, demand rises (Litz 2014). Later, this theory was considered as the basis for multiple other approaches such as space syntax analysis (Hillier and Hanson 1984), natural movement (Hillier et al. 1993) and the multiple centrality assessment (Porta et al. 2009).

The Spatial Interaction Theory

Gravity models can be considered as the most distinguished and accepted solution to the retail store location problem for many years now. These models emphasize on a customer's perspective on availability and accessibility of a given store. The development of the first version of a gravity model was inspired in late 1930s by the work of Reilly, an American researcher (Kubis and Hartmann 2007). Reilly suggested that customers may make tradeoffs between the specific features and the overall attractiveness of a store's main product and the store's location (Litz 2014). Although the empirical tests demonstrated that under practical circumstances, the gravity model performs acceptably, there were also a number of researchers that argued that the variables used in the model, population and road distance, fail to perform well in some situations (Brown 1993; Huff 1962). Consequently, many researchers have tried to improve the gravity model by introducing more applicable and better performing variables into the model ever since. Wilson's model based on entropy-maximization and Huff's probabilistic potential model are two of the most accepted modified versions of Reilly's theory.

In 1967, Wilson introduced a model for spatial distribution (Wilson 1967) describing the flow of money from population centroids to retail centers (Wilson and Oulton 1983). In Wilson's model, survival of a retail center is dependent on its ability to compete for the limited amount of available resources (customers) (Piovani et al. 2017). Huff (1963, 1964) suggested that customers may prefer shopping areas based on their overall utility (Brown 1993). By dividing gravity models into two different general groups of qualitative and quantitative models and considering that quantitative models are again divided into two groups of deterministic and probabilistic models. While deterministic models usually calculate an estimation of accounting variables such as turnover or return on investment to present to marketing managers to decide upon, probabilistic models attempt to model the probability of a consumer that lives at location i to purchase products at location j and Huff's model is the perfect example of a probabilistic gravity model (Litz 2014) (Table 1).

A comparison of the Three Main Theories in Traditional Computational Site Selection

Table 1. Comparing the assumptions, revelations, goals and limitations of the central place theory, the theory of minimum differentiation and the spatial interaction theory

	The central place theory	The theory of minimum differentiation	The spatial interaction theory
Underlying assumptions	- All customers are distributed uniformly - All customers are rational decision makers - All sellers enjoy equivalent costs, free entry and fair pricing in a perfectly competitive market - All shopping trips are uniformly priced, equally feasible in various directions and single-purpose	- Demand is inelastic - Population density is uniform - Clustering is socially wasteful - Prices for similar goods are fixed	- The probability of the distribution of the trips that occur are proportional to the number of the states of the system which give rise to it - Group behavior is predictable on the basis of mathematical probability - Individuals are not willing to travel the same distances for all types of trips
Principal revelation	Proposes that there is a reverse relationship between the demand for a product and the distance from the source of supply	Argues that distance from rivals is more important than distance from customers	Suggests that customers may make tradeoffs between the features and the attractiveness of a store's main product and the store's location
Main goal	To describe and characterize the regionalization of urban space in a hierarchical manner	To assess the accessibility of a location within the network of a city	To demonstrate the gravitational forces that influence customer behavior
Limitations	- For the most part, the basic assumptions of this theory are unrealistic - It fails to consider the effects of product attributes such as cost and demand frequency	- Unrealistic assumptions about the market conditions and transportation costs - Failure to explain the clustering of firms and to acknowledge the positive effects of agglomerations	- Population and road distance (Original model's main variables) and other related parameters fail to perform well under certain circumstances - Inability to account for individual or small group behavior accurately

A Schematic Review of the Historical Trend of Some of the Research Advancements Made, Based on the Three Main Theories in Traditional Computational Site Selection

(Hotelling, 1929)	(Smithies,	(Hartwick &	(Drezner, 1982)	(Cardillo et al, 2006)
(Lerner & Singer,	1941)	Hartwick, 1971)	(Hillier & Hanson,	(Porta et al., 2009)
1937)	(Nelson, 1958)	(Ali & Greenbaum,	1984)	(Hehenkamp &
		1977)	(Aoyagi & Okabe,	Wambach, 2010)
		(Devletoglou, 1965)	1993)	(Fahui et al, 2014)
			(Hillier et al, 1993)	(Ottino-loffler et al,
			(Tabuchi, 1994)	2017)

• •

(Reilly,	(Warnts, 1957)	(Huff, 1963)	(Cadwallader,	(Xu & Liu, 2004)
1927)	(Voorhees, 1957)	(Harris, 1964)	1981)	(González-Benito et al,
		(Lakshmanan &	(Birkin, 1995)	2005)
		Hansen, 1965)	(Satani et al.,	(Teller & Reutterer,
		(Wilson, 1967)	1998)	2008)
		(Brunner & Mason,		(Suárez-Vega et al,
		1968)		2011)
		(Rushton, 1969)		(Li & Liu, 2012)

▬ ▬

(Christaller,	(Losch, 1940)	(Getis, 1963)	(Potter, 1981)	(Daniels, 2007)
1933)	(Berry & Garrison,	(Johnston, 1966)	(Mulligan,	(Nakamura, 2014)
	1958a)	(Johnston, 1968)	1987)	(Nogueira et al,
	(Berry & Garrison,	(Woldenberg,	(Bacon, 1991)	2014)
	1958b)	1968)		
		(Rushton, 1972)		
		(Davies, 1972)		

1920	1940	1960	1980	2000	2020

━━━ The central place theory

▬ ▬ ▬ The spatial interaction theory

• • • • • • The theory of minimum differentiation

2.2   The Emergence of LSBNs; Opportunities and Challenges

In the past decade, different factors like the advancements made in wireless communication technologies, the growing universal acceptance of location-aware technologies including mobile phones and smart tablets equipped with GPS[2] receivers, Sensors placed inside these devices, attached to cars and embedded in infrastructures, remote sensors transported by aerial and satellite platforms and RFID[3] tags attached to objects was complemented by the development of GIS[4] technologies to result in the availability of an increasing amount of data with content richness which can be exploited by analysts. With the emergence and growing popularity of social networks and location-aware services, the next step was combining these two technologies which resulted in the introduction of location based social networks (Kheiri et al. 2016). Since such networks act as a bridge establishing a connection between a user's real life and online activities (Kheiri et al. 2016), data obtained from them is considered among one of the most important resources of spatial data and presents a unique opportunity for researchers in business-related fields to precisely study consumer's behavioral patterns.

With the advancements mentioned above, the question of optimal store placement like many other scientific problems has entered a new era with fast, diverse and voluminous data, terms that are usually used to describe big data. The simplicity of capturing, recording and processing of data obtained from digital sources like LSBNs, is shaping a phenomenon which is being referred to as the fourth major scientific paradigm following empirical science describing natural phenomena, theoretical science using models and generalization, and computational science simulating complex systems (Miller and Goodchild 2016). Since optimal retail store placement clearly has a geographic nature, the introduction of LSBNs that are considered rich sources of geo-tagged data can be a rare and valuable opportunity for scientists and marketers. Consequently, Liu and his colleagues (Liu et al. 2015), introduced the term "social sensing" for describing the process and different approaches of analyzing spatial big data. The use of the term "sensing" in describing this process, represents two different aspects of such data. First, this kind of analog data can be considered as a complementary source of information for remote sensing data, because they can record the socio-economic characteristics of users whereas remote sensing data can never offer these kind of descriptive information. Second, such data follow the concept of Volunteered geographic information[5] (introduced by (Goodchild 2006)), meaning that every individual person in today's world can be considered as a sensor transmitting data as they move. However, like any other scientific advancement, the application of these new data sources is accompanied by a mixture of opportunities and challenges. For example, the small proportion of LSBN users in comparison to the overall retail store customers and the average age of these users which ranges from 15 to 30 years of old, may lead to some unwanted sampling errors (Lloyd and Cheshire 2017). Moreover, such data are naturally heterogeneous and

[2] Global Positioning System.
[3] Radio Frequency Identification.
[4] Geospatial Information Systems.
[5] VGI.

disrupted by noise and deviation. Therefore, using LSBN data should always include a pre-processing step including applying specific methods for eliminating noise and irrelevant data. For instance, in some cases, researchers consider eliminating duplicate check-ins and data related to users that only checked-in once, in order to get access to more homogenous and noise-free set of data (Kheiri et al. 2016).

Nevertheless, LSBN data offer vast opportunities as well. First of all, LBSN data offer high levels of temporal granularity in a worldwide scale and they can also be accessed really quickly (Lloyd and Cheshire 2017). Furthermore, LSBN data offer a more detailed description of geographic objects and spatial interactions despite the fact that they seem like weak sources of information at first. For example, two adjoining restaurants may be hard to distinguish based on traditional geotagged data, but in LSBNs, as they offer additional information such as venue classification, user generated comments and recommendations for popular venues, one can easily differentiate between adjacent venues (Kheiri et al. 2016). On the other hand, traditional data such as demographic, tax and land use data are recorded in standard spatial units and aggregation based on pre-assumed units may be subject to the famous modifiable aerial unit problem[6] error. Whereas in LSBNs, instead of defining venues inside traditional administrative boundaries, each venue is marked by the exact location in which it was built in (Zhou and Zhang 2016). Therefore, analyzing LSBN data and extracting meaningful and practical patterns from them may help businesses attract more customers and enhance their financial and operational outcomes (Papalexakis et al. 2011). Accordingly, Researchers in the past decade have focused some of their efforts on exploiting LSBN data to solve the retail store placement problem.

Other than one or two cases, most of the research using LSBN data for site selection, has taken advantage of the new advancements in feature selection. Based on the unique attributes and the type of information that can be retrieved from LBSN data, a number of features that influence retail store popularity are defined and then used to predict the popularity of given stores. Such techniques will be discussed in the next section.

2.3 LSBN Based Feature Selection Approaches

Using LSBN data as a source for defining a set of features in order to study the factors that influence retail store popularity is a rather new approach to solving the problem of store site selection. In 2013, Karamshuk and his colleagues (Karamshuk et al. 2013), presented a framework based on this approach for the first time. They attempted to assess the popularity of three different coffee shop and restaurant chains in New York city via data retrieved from the popular LSBN; Foursquare[7]. To accomplish this goal, they introduce a number of different features that capitalize upon the main characteristics of Foursquare data and then classify these features into two major groups; geographic and mobility features. Finally, they suggest two different approaches for using these features to assess the popularity of a given store: using each individual feature for popularity prediction and combining the features with a number of different

---

[6] MAUP.
[7] www.foursquare.com.

techniques, including a machine learning feature selection technique (RankNet algorithm). They compare the results obtained by these different approaches and conclude that using a combination of features using RankNet offers more accuracy. The accuracy level evaluation is based on the NDCG@k[8] approach which measures the percentage of accurately predicted popular stores in a list of "k" places by comparing the results to the actual popularity of stores.

Yu and his colleagues (2016), attempt to tackle another aspect of the store placement problem; choosing a shop-type from a list of candidate types for a given location. Based on the feature selection approach suggested by Karamshuk et al. they present a list of intended features for assessing the popularity of the candidate types of stores. They extract the needed information from two different LSBNs; Baidu[9] and Dianping[10]. In their framework, they utilize a matrix factorization technique to combine the selected features to recommend the best possible shop type (Popularity-wise) for a specific location. Finally, they evaluate the suggested framework by calculating its prediction accuracy and comparing it to the results of baseline methods including logistic regression, decision tree, SVM and Bayesian classification. Results suggest that the matrix factorization method is superior than baseline methods in terms of recommendation precision.

Wang and Chen (2016), propose a framework that forecasts the popularity a number of given candidates for a new restaurant specifically based on user generated reviews. They extract restaurant reviews on Yelp[11] to assess the prediction power of their framework which is based on the application of three different regression models (Ridge regression, support vector regression and gradient boosted regression trees) for feature combination. For performance evaluation, they use Rooted Mean Square Error[12] to test predictability precision, Spearman's rank correlation coefficient to measure the prediction accuracy relative to the ground-truth and Mean Average Precision[13] to evaluate ranking accuracy of relevant locations for a specific restaurant chain.

Rahman and Nayeem (2017), take advantage of a similar framework to the ones described before, to select a location for live campaigns. They exploit Foursquare data in order to compare the results of the direct use of features and a combination of features offered by a support vector machine regression, and demonstrate that the application of the regression model for feature selection offers more accuracy and better predictability (Table 2).

2.4   Discussion and Future Research

By investigating the related literature in retail store site selection, it is clear that while some researchers are still attempting to exploit the advantages of traditional theories in

---

[8] Normalized Discounted Cumulative Gain approach.

[9] www.Baidu.com.

[10] www.Dianping.com.

[11] www.Yelp.com.

[12] RMSE.

[13] MAP.

Table 2. A comparison between the features used in LSBN-based literature.

Features	Paper			
	(Karamshuk et al. 2013)	(Yu et al. 2016)	(Wang and Chen 2016)	(Rahman and Nayeem 2017)
Density	X	X	X	X
Entropy	X	X	X	X
Competitiveness	X	X	X	
Jensen's quality			X	
Area popularity	X			
Transition quality	X			
Incoming flow	X			
Transition density	X			
Distance to downtown		X		
Traffic accessibility		X		X
Complementaries		X		
Market attractiveness			X	
Market competitiveness			X	
The temporal signal				X

order to solve the question of finding an optimal location for stores, in the past years, a number of researchers have focused their work on presenting a more modern and data-driven framework that is built upon the idea of feature selection based on the information mined from LSBN data. Assessing the comparisons done in the later articles, between the results obtained from the direct use of defined features and using different techniques for feature combination, shows that exploiting different combination methods for feature selection offers more precision and accuracy than the use of direct features as prediction tools. Although Karamshuk et al. (Karamshuk et al. 2013) argued and proved that using a method of machine learning for feature selection may offer better results than some baseline methods such as regression models, the particular method they used (RankNet) is not considered state of the art as it does not take advantage of ensemble learning techniques in order to maximize the accuracy of feature selection. Moreover, there hasn't been a clear answer to the question of choosing the best possible approach out of the methods used for site selection in the recent papers. Hereupon, investigating and comparing the outcomes of different feature combination techniques including new approaches of ensemble machine learning, matrix factorization and different regression models in order to determine the best possible framework may be an interesting direction for future research.

3 Conclusion

For a retail store manager, one of the most complicated yet important decisions may be the determination and constant improving of the store placement strategy. Choosing the right location, inevitably effects the overall success or failure of a store. Hence, figuring out an optimal approach for making this important decision has been an interesting subject for researchers and managers over the years. The application of checklists, analogues, ratios and computational approaches based on the central place theory, gravity models and theory of minimum differentiation, are some of the traditional techniques that have been proposed by researchers and utilized by marketers to make better decisions considering a store's location over the past century (Brown 1993; Hernandez et al. 1998; Litz 2014).

In recent years, with the technological advancements made which led to the emergence of LSBNs, data retrieved from these networks has been noticed and exploited by researchers in many scientific fields, including marketing researchers looking for new data-driven approaches for optimal retail store placement. Despite the fact that LSBN data may force researchers to deal with a number of new challenges, the opportunities and advantages they offer seem too valuable to ignore. Therefore, researchers have tried to capitalize on the unique characteristics of LSBN data in the past years in order to present a new approach for solving the century-old question of optimal store placement, by defining a set of features and combining them using different algorithms. Although the results of the such researches can be deemed promising in terms of accuracy of prediction, there is still room to complete the presented frameworks by using new and improved data mining and machine learning algorithms and techniques for feature combination in order to achieve the best possible results.

References

Ali, M., Greenbaum, S.: A spatial model of the banking industry. J. Finan. **XXXII**(4), 1283–1303 (1977)

Aoyagi, M., Okabe, A.: Spatial competition of firms in a two dimensional bounded market. Reg. Sci. Urban Econ. **23**, 259–289 (1993)

Arcaute, E., Molinero, C., Hatna, E., Murcio, R., Vargas-ruiz, C., Masucci, A.P., Batty, M.: Cities and Regions in Britain through hierarchical percolation (2015)

Berry, B.J.L., Garrison, W.L., Berry, B.J.L., Garrison, W.L.: The functional bases of the central place hierarchy. Econ. Geogr. **34**(2), 145–154 (2014)

Birkin, M.: Customer targeting, geodemographics and lifestyle approaches. GIS for Bus. Serv. Plan. 104–138 (1995). https://www.amazon.com/Business-Service-Planning-Paul-Longley/dp/0470235101

Boventer, E.: Walter christaller's central places and peripheral areas: the central place theory in retrospect. J. Reg. Sci. **9**(1), 117–124 (1969)

Brown, S.: Retail location theory: evolution and evaluation Retail location theory: evolution and evaluation. Int. Rev. Retail Distrib. Consum. Res. **3**, 185–229 (1993)

Brunner, J.A., Mason, J.L.: The influence of time upon driving shopping preference. J. Mark. **32**(2), 57–61 (1968)

Booms, B.H., Bitner, M.J.: Marketing strategies and organization structures for service firms. In: Donnelly, J.H., George, W.R. (eds.) Marketing of Services, pp. 47–51. American Marketing Association, Chicago, IL (1981)

Cadwallader, M.: Towards a cognitive gravity model: the case of consumer spatial behaviour. Reg. Stud. 15(4), 37–41 (1981). https://doi.org/10.1080/09595238100185281

Cardillo, A., Scellato, S., Latora, V., Porta, S.: Structural properties of planar graphs of urban street patterns, pp. 1–8 (2006). https://doi.org/10.1103/PhysRevE.73.066107

Chen, L., Tsai, C.: Data mining framework based on rough set theory to improve location selection decisions: a case study of a restaurant chain. Tourism Manag. 53, 197–199 (2016)

Daniels, M.J.: Central place theory and sport tourism impacts, 34(2), 332–347 (2007). https://doi.org/10.1016/j.annals.2006.09.004

Devletoglou, N.E.: A dissenting view of duopoly and spatial competition. Economica 32(126), 140–160 (1965)

Drezner, Z.: Competitive location strategies for two facilities. Reg. Sci. Urban Econ. 12(4), 485–493 (1982). https://doi.org/10.1016/0166-0462(82)90003-5

González-Benito, Ó., Muñoz-Gallego, P.A., Kopalle, P.K.: Asymmetric competition in retail store formats: evaluating inter- and intra-format spatial effects. J. Retail. 81(1), 59–73 (2005). https://doi.org/10.1016/j.jretai.2005.01.004

Goodchild, M.F.: Citizens As Sensors: The World Of Volunteered Geography, pp. 1–15 (2006)

Harris, B.: A note on the probability. J. Reg. Sci. 5(2), 31–35 (1964)

Hartwick, J.M., Hartwick, P.G.: Duopoly in space. Can. J. Econ. 4(4), 485–505 (1971)

Hehenkamp, B., Wambach, A.: Survival at the center-the stability of minimum differentiation. J. Econ. Behav. Organ. 76(3), 853–858 (2010). https://doi.org/10.1016/j.jebo.2010.09.018

Hernandez, T., Bennison, D., Cornelius, S.: The organisational context of retail locational planning. GeoJournal 45, 299–300 (1998)

Hernández, T., Bennison, D.: The art and science of retail location decisions. Int. J. Retail Distrib. Manag. Emerald 28(8), 357–367 (2005)

Hillier, B., Hanson, J.: The Social Logic Of Space. Cambridge University Press (1984)

Hillier, B., Perm, A., Hanson, J., Grajewski, T., Xu, J.: Natural movement: or, configuration and attraction in urban pedestrian movement. Environ. Plan. B: Plan. Des. 20, 29–66 (1993)

Hotelling, H.: Stability in competition. Econ. J. 39(153), 41–57 (1929)

Huff, D.: A note on the limitations of intraurban gravity models. Land Econ. 38(1), 64–66 (1962)

Huff, D.: A probabilistic analysis of shopping center trade areas. Land Econ. 39(1), 81–90 (1963)

Huff, D.L.: Defining and estimating a trading area. J. Mark. 28, 34–38 (1964)

Karamshuk, D., et al.: Geo-Spotting: Mining Online Location-based Services for optimal retail store placement (2013)

Kheiri, A., Karimipour, F., Forghani, M.: Intra-urban movement pattern estimation based on location based social networking data. J. Geomat. Sci. Technol. 6(1), 141–158 (2016)

Kubis, A., Hartmann, M.: Analysis of location of large-area shopping centres, a probabilistic gravity model for the Halle–Leipzig Area. Jahrbuch F' Ur Regionalwissenschaft 27, 43–57 (2007). https://doi.org/10.1007/s10037-006-0010-3

Lakshmanan, J.R., Hansen, W.G.: A retail market potential model. J. Am. Inst. Plan. 31(2), 134–143 (1965). https://doi.org/10.1080/01944366508978155

Lerner, A.P., Singer, H.W.: Some notes on duopoly and spatial competition. J. Polit. Econ. 45(2), 145–186 (1937)

Li, Y., Liu, L.: Assessing the impact of retail location on store performance: a comparison of Wal-Mart and Kmart stores in Cincinnati. Appl. Geogr. 32(2), 591–600 (2012). https://doi.org/10.1016/j.apgeog.2011.07.006

Litz, R.A.: Does small store location matter? A test of three classic theories of retail location. J, Small Bus. Entrepreneurship, 37–41 (2014). https://doi.org/10.1080/08276331.2008. 10593436

Liu, Y., Liu, X., Gao, S., Gong, L., Kang, C., Zhi, Y., Chi, G.: Social sensing: a new approach to understanding our socioeconomic environments. Ann. Assoc. Am. Geogr. 37–41, May, 2015. https://doi.org/10.1080/00045608.2015.1018773

Lloyd, A., Cheshire, J.: Computers, environment and urban systems deriving retail centre locations and catchments from geo-tagged Twitter data. CEUS **61**, 108–118 (2017). https://doi.org/10.1016/j.compenvurbsys.2016.09.006

Miller, H., Goodchild.: Data-driven geography Data-driven geography. GeoJournal, August 2015. https://doi.org/10.1007/s10708-014-9602-6

Nakamura, D.: Social participation and social capital with equity and efficiency: an approach from central-place theory q. Appl. Geogr. **49**, 54–57 (2014). https://doi.org/10.1016/j.apgeog. 2013.09.008

Nelson, R.L.: The selection of retail locations. F.W. Dodge Corp., New York (1958)

Nogueira, M., Crocco, M., Figueiredo, A. T., Diniz, G.: Financial hierarchy and banking strategies : a regional analysis for the Brazilian case, pp. 1–18 (2014). https://doi.org/10.1093/cje/beu008

Ottino-loffler, B., Stonedahl, F., Wilensky, U.: Spatial Competition with Interacting Agents, pp. 1–16 (2017)

Papalexakis, E.E., Pelechrinis, K., Faloutsos, C.: Location Based Social Network Analysis Using Tensors and Signal Processing Tools (2011)

Piovani, D., Molinero, C., Wilson, A.: Urban retail dynamics : insights from percolation theory and spatial interaction modelling, pp. 1–11 (2017)

Porta, S., Strano, E., Iacoviello, V., Messora, R., Latora, V., Cardillo, A., Scellato, S.: Street centrality and densities of retail and services in Bologna, Italy **36**, 450–466 (2009). https://doi.org/10.1068/b34098

Rafiq, M., Ahmed, P.K.: Using the 7Ps as a generic marketing mix. Mark. Intell. Plan. **13**(9), 4–15 (1992)

Rahman, K., Nayeem, M.A.: Finding suitable places for live campaigns using location-based services, pp. 1–6 (2017)

Rushton, G.: Analysis of spatial behavior by revealed space preference. Annals. Assoc. Am. Geogr. **59**, 391–400 (1969)

Reilly, W.J.: Methods for the Study of Retail Relationships. University of Texas, Bureau of Business Research, Bulletin No. 2944, Austin (1929)

Satani, N., Uchida, A., Deguchi, A., Ohgai, A., Sato, S., Hagishima, S.: Commercial facility location model using multiple regression analysis. Science **22**(3), 219–240 (1998)

Smithies, A.: Optimum location in spatial competition. J. Polit. Econ. **49**(3), 423–439 (1941)

Suárez-Vega, R., Santos-Peñate, D.R., Dorta-González, P., Rodríguez-Díaz, M.: A multi-criteria GIS based procedure to solve a network competitive location problem. Appl. Geogr. **31**(1), 282–291 (2011). https://doi.org/10.1016/j.apgeog.2010.06.002

Tabuchi, T.: Two-stage two-dimensional spatial competition between two firms. Reg. Sci. Urban Econ. **24**(2), 207–227 (1994). https://doi.org/10.1016/0166-0462(93)02031-W

Taneja, S.: Technology Moves. In: Chain Store Age, pp. 136–137 (1999)

Teller, C., Reutterer, T.: The evolving concept of retail attractiveness: what makes retail agglomerations attractive when customers shop at them? J. Retail. Consum. Serv. **15**(3), 127–143 (2008). https://doi.org/10.1016/j.jretconser.2007.03.003

Voorhees, A.: Geography of Prices and Spatial Interaction (1957)

Wang, F., Chen, C., Xiu, C., Zhang, P.: Location analysis of retail stores in Changchun, China: a street centrality perspective. Cities **41**, 54–63 (2014). https://doi.org/10.1016/j.cities.2014.05.005

Wang, F., Chen, L.: Where to Place Your Next Restaurant? Optimal Restaurant Placement via Leveraging User-Generated Reviews, pp. 2371–2376 (2016)

Warnts, W.: Geography of prices and spatial interaction. In: Papers and Proceedings of the Regional Science Association, vol. 3 (1957)

Wilson, A.G.: A statistical theory of spatial distribution models. Transp. Res. **1**(3), 253–269 (1967)

Wilson, A.G., Oulton, M.J.: The corner-shop to supermarket transition in retailing: the beginnings of empirical evidence. Environ. Plan. A **15**, 265–274 (1983)

Xu, Y., Liu, L.: Gis Based Analysis of Store Closure : a Case Study of an Office Depot Store in Cincinnati, pp. 7–9, June 2004

Yu, Z., Tian, M., Wang, Z.H.U., Guo, B.I.N.: Shop-type recommendation leveraging the data from social media and location-based services. ACM Trans. Knowl. Discov. Data (TKDD) **11** (1), 1–21 (2016)

Zhou, X., Zhang, L.: Crowdsourcing functions of the living city from Twitter and Foursquare data, **406**, February 2016. https://doi.org/10.1080/15230406.2015.1128852

Contextual Analysis of Spatio-Temporal Walking Observations

K. Amouzandeh, S. Goudarzi, and F. Karimipour$^{(\boxtimes)}$

School of Surveying and Geospatial Engineering, College of Engineering,
University of Tehran, Tehran, Iran
{Amouzandeh.kimia,Samira.goodarzi.a,
fkarimipour}@ut.ac.ir

Abstract. Analysis of human movement data is becoming more popular in several applications. Particularly, analyzing sport movement data has been demanding. Most of the attempts made on this are, however, have focused on spatial aspects of the movement to extract some movement characteristics, such as positional pattern and similarities. This paper analyses walking observations to extract behavioural pattern of attributes (such as speed and heart rate) of a person to examine the effects of different contextual conditions on behavioural movement patterns. Particularly, experiments were conducted to explore the effect of day time, tiredness, and gender of the person on "movement parameter profiles". The key element of this research is projection of movement parameter profiles into an informative pattern that describes the behavioural movement pattern of a person. To illustrate the effect of different conditions, a simple distance function has been used to compare patterns considering the change of mentioned conditions. The results show that the gender of a person is among the contexts that considerably affect behavioural movement patterns in the case study.

Keywords: Movement observations · Movement Parameters Profile
Movement behavioural pattern · Spatiotemporal pattern · Walking

1 Introduction

Recent and emerging wearable technology which is incorporated into navigation systems and different sensors, have led to increases in the availability of various kinds of data for walking person. Thus, new exploratory tools and knowledge discovery techniques are required to extract meaningful information, discover interesting patterns, and explore the dynamic behaviour of moving objects in order to transform raw trajectory data into useful information to be used in reality interpretation and decision making [1]. Especially, analysis of movement observations, which contain information about the movement of each individual entity and the underlying mechanisms, are of great interest. These observations are key to the study and understanding of movement behaviour [2].

Today, with the emergence of new sensor technologies such as wearable sensors to measure parameters like heart rate and acceleration, a variety of movement parameters can be observed during movements. The development of analyzing techniques that are

© Springer International Publishing AG, part of Springer Nature 2018
O. Gervasi et al. (Eds.): ICCSA 2018, LNCS 10961, pp. 461–471, 2018.
https://doi.org/10.1007/978-3-319-95165-2_32

capable of exploiting these new sources of information thus appears to be a logical step forward for knowledge discovery from movement datasets [3]. In this case, in addition to the positional movement data, some set of ancillary observations that describe objects behavioural and cognitive proceeds are employed to study the behavioural movement patterns and their impacts on the target object [4].

It is essential for movement behaviour studies to take into consideration the so-called *movement parameters* (MPs), e.g. speed, acceleration, or direction, which are key to characterize the movement of objects [3]. For example, it is important to know about heartrate and speed patterns and their relationship with locational information such as slope for running or walking person in order to detect the persons' performance. In such cases, analyzing a persons' movement observations in terms of space (x, y, z) and time (t), through considering movement attributes of each person such as heartrate and contextual information (e.g. the environmental information such as temperature) will allow a better understanding of behavioural movement patterns and effect of different parameters on patterns as well.

This paper analyzes walking observations to extract behavioural pattern of attributes (such as speed and heart rate) of a person to examine the influence of different contextual conditions such as Gender of the person on behavioural movement patterns. For this, a segmentation approach is proposed to project the "Movement Parameter Profiles" into a pattern for analyzing changes in different movement attributes of each individual during walking in order to identify the effect of each personal context (e.g. gender of the person) and environmental context (e.g. day time, weather condition, etc.) on the movement patterns. A measure to assign distance value is then used to examine the effect of contexts on the movement. As expected, the results show that time series of each attribute for each person have a unique pattern describing the persons' movement behaviour, which changes in different contexts.

The reminder of this paper is organized as follows: Sect. 2 introduces the concepts of movement parameters, segmentation of movement data, and pattern comparison, which are the basis for the intended analysis of this paper. Section 3 introduces the proposed methodology of the research, whose implementation results are presented in Sect. 4. Finally, Sect. 5 concludes the paper and outlines directions for future work.

2   Preliminaries

Exploring human mobility behaviour is emerging into an interesting area of research, which requires extracting knowledge about the dynamic behaviour of people during doing different types of activities, and thus challenges developing new exploratory data analysis methods on various movement datasets. From a methodological standpoint, several research studies have contributed to introducing and developing methods for extracting movement patterns of different kinds of objects and comparing different patterns. This section specifically introduces the concepts of movement parameters, segmentation of movement data, and pattern comparison, which are needed for the intended analysis of this research.

2.1 Movement Parameters

Movement Parameters (MPs) are used to represent continuous process of movement. They are most commonly represented as a collection of spatial point objects with time while other parameters are stored as attributes.

For example, in Dodge et al. [5], Buchin et al. [6] and Laube et al. [7], movement parameters of a moving object such as heading, speed, acceleration, duration of movement, sinuosity, traveled path, displacement, and direction have been considered. Then, they presented some framework that segment and classify trajectories into sub trajectories based on any of these parameters to analyze movement behaviour of moving object.

Such descriptors are generated for characterizing the movement of an object. However, to the best of our knowledge, contextual information such as heartrate of the person, cadence and weather conditions have been barely considered in behavioural movement patterns.

2.2 Segmentation

In the study of movement, segmentation facilitates finding patterns and structures in movement data, and hence can help to understand the behaviour of moving objects [3]. Segmentation has been recently applied in several studies in the domain of moving object data analysis in order to extract homogenous characteristics for several purposes, such as indexing event and activity recognition along the geospatial life-lines of objects [8], and classification of movement data [9].

In particular, Chen et al. [10] proposed a novel representation of trajectories, called Movement Pattern Strings (MPS), which convert the trajectories into symbolic representations. Movement pattern strings encode both the movement direction and the movement distance information of the trajectories. Their experimental results show that MPSs are almost as effective as raw representation in classification and clustering tasks.

This paper employed segmentation to simplify the Movement Parameters Profile to investigate the effects of different contextual information on pro-files. We improved the segmentation method proposed in an earlier paper by Dodge et al. [3], which applies feature extraction techniques from map generalization and time series analysis in order to decompose trajectories into sequences of homogeneous movement characteristics. Buchin et al. [6] recently proposed a similar segmentation approach, which applies different criteria on MPs of objects (e.g. using ranges of speed or turning angle) on a continuous representation of trajectories.

2.3 Pattern Comparison

Differences between two signals are measured as the cost of transforming one sequence into another. Several movement similarity assessment methods are proposed on trajectories or Spatio-temporal signals (Chen et al. 2005; Vlachos et al. 2002a; Vlachos et al. 2002b). For instance, Little and Gu (2001) applied Dynamic Time Wrapping (DTW) on separate path and speed curves of trajectories. In order to simplify the process of similarity analysis, they applied a local geometric feature extraction technique using curvature information of the path and speed curves. Because of sensitivity of DTW to noise, shifts and scaling, Chen et al. (2005) introduced a novel distance function, called Edit Distance on Real sequence (EDR), to measure the similarity between two trajectories. On the other hand, Pelekis et al. [11] used locality in-between polylines (LIP), which relies on the area of the polygons formed between the intersection points created by the overlay of the two trajectories. In the same regards, Qi and Zheng [12] calculated similarity between trajectories by synthesizing shape difference and spatial distance. To achieve a more robust method, Sharif and Alesheikh [13] introduced a modified version of the dynamic time warping called context-based distance measure to contextually assess the multi-dimensional weighted similarities of commercial air planes trajectories. The results yielded the robustness of their method in quantifying the commonalities of trajectories and discovering movement patterns with 80% accuracy.

Most of the above studies are seeking for similarities between the geometric shape of the trajectories, or similarities between some Movement Parameter Profiles, which are all presented as a function of location and time (e.g. speed or tuning angle). They did not, however, consider contextual information of moving objects to analyze similarities between MP profiles. This concern has been partially taken into account by Dodge et al. (2012), where they have considered speed profile to compare speed patterns of moving objects. However, contextual information (such as environmental parameters or personal characteristics such as heart rate of the person at each tracking point) seems to be still ignored.

3 Research Methodology

In this paper, we analyze locational and contextual observations of a walking person to extract behavioural pattern of attributes of his/her in order to examine the influence of different conditions on behavioural movement patterns. Figure 1 illustrates the main steps of the research methodology, i.e.: (1) Construction of movement parameter profiles; (2) Segmentation and construction of the movement patterns; and (3) Pattern comparison.

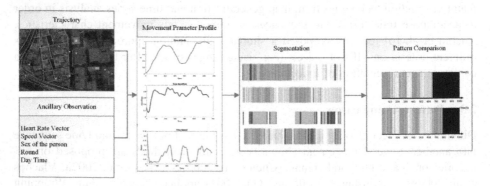

Fig. 1. Overview of the research methodology

When an object moves about in space, the evolution of its movement parameters can be seen as functions over time, which are called Movement Parameter Profiles (MPPs) by [9]. These profiles have some homogenous characteristics in all points and can describe the pattern of movement parameters of each individual object in a specific situation. In this paper, having constructed the MPPs from ancillary observations (e.g. heart rate and speed), a segmentation method is employed to extract local movement features of each movement parameter profile, which describes the movement pattern of a person through walking in a more informative way, and will be used later in comparison analysis.

3.1 Movement Parameter Profile

Movement Parameters (e.g. speed, acceleration, and heart rate) can be derived from trajectory of a moving person and thus describe their dynamic behaviour. In order to evaluate the movement behaviour inherent to the given trajectory data sets, various movement parameters can be computed for each point (fix) along a trajectory such as heart rate, speed, and acceleration [5, 7].

As suggested by Dodge et al. (2009), we constructed MPPs for walking observations through plotting their evolution over time (Fig. 2). Then, in order to compare them across persons, they were normalized to a common interval of [0, 1]. Constructing such profile for different movement parameters will exhibit different amplitude and frequency variations, hence giving clues to the underlying movement physics and behaviour.

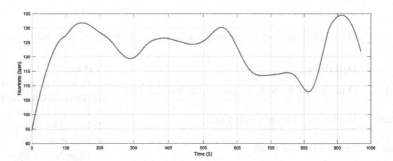

Fig. 2. An example of a movement parameter profile

3.2 Segmentation

To extract movement pattern from MPPs, a segmentation method based on Dodge et al. (2012) is employed. The segmentation process leads to a simplified, compressed representation of MPPs, which converts MP profiles derived from trajectories into three band binary representation. In other words, instead of using metric values of movement parameters, we characterize MPPs using 0 or 1, which denote a certain type of variation in movement parameters. In this representation, two important movement features are preserved to describe a point in the profiles:

(1) Amplitude of the point, which is measured by two characteristics: (a) direction of the point respect to the median line; and (b) deviation of the point from the median line of the profile, which yields an impression of the amplitude variation of a movement parameter over time and equates to its residual value from the median [9].

(2) Frequency, which is measured by sinuosity and is computed as a ratio of the distance ±k points along the profile to the length of the beeline connector centered at the point, as follow:

$$Sinuosity_{p,k} = \frac{\sum_{i=p-k}^{i=p+k-1} d_{i,i+1}}{d_{p-k,p+k}} \quad (1)$$

Note that the lag parameter (k) depends on the temporal granularity, spatial scale, as well as on the noise level of the observations. The sinuosity measure ranges from 1 (if profile points are collinear about the given point p) to infinity for a winding profile (i.e. a space filling curve) [9].

Having the three characteristics of direction of point, deviation and sinuosity quantified, we assigned red, green and blue band to them, respectively (Table 1). It provides a three-digit number for each point in MPP, which describe pixels in a column of segmentation result. The whole sequence of these pixels during walking is called Movement Parameter Pattern (MPPT). For instance, Fig. 3 represents the pattern of heart rate during walking. Here, the marked point is above the median line with low deviation and high sinuosity; thus, its value in the image space is "101", which is illustrated as magenta.

Table 1. Definition of the movement parameter pattern and their values

Band	Definition	Values
Red	Direction of the point respect to the median line	0: Below the median line
		1: Above the median line
Green	Deviation from the median line	0: Low Deviation
		1: High Deviation
Blue	Sinuosity of the point	0: Low Sinuosity
		1: High Sinuosity

3.3   Pattern Comparison

At the final step, the following equation is used to compare two MPPTs in order to measure the effect of contextual information on behavioural movement patterns.

$$D_{MPPT} = \sum_{b=1}^{3} \sum_{t=1}^{n} |MPPT_1(t)_b - MPPT_2(t)_b| \quad (2)$$

where MPPTi is the ith Movement Parameter Pattern, and b and t refer to band and time.

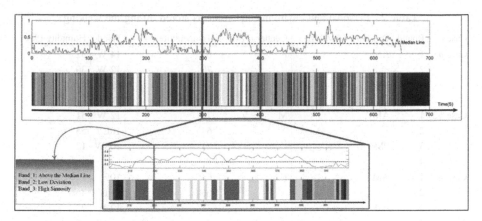

Fig. 3. Representation of a MPP and its corresponding MPPT

4   Implementation

We applied the proposed methodology to a sample walking data set. A predefined route (Fig. 4) was walked by four people. Positional data during the walking were collected by Garmin GPS Smartwatch. In addition, extra sensors collected the heart rate of the person and environmental parameters such as temperature, humidity, as well as wind direction and speed.

Fig. 4. The predefined path

Each person walked the route in two pair-rounds as follows: (a) In order to consider the level of tiredness, a pair of walking rounds were accomplished together, i.e. one exactly after the other (assuming that the person is more tired in the second round); (2) The above procedure was performed two times: one in the morning and one in the afternoon (in order to consider the possible day time effects). We also took the gender of the person into account (Table 2).

Table 2. Personal and environmental contexts stored during the walking

Case	Round	Day time (AM/PM)	Gender (F/M)	Temperature (°F)	Wind	Humidity (%)
Case #1	1	AM	F	64	14 W	32
	2			70	12 W	30
	3	PM		73	12 W	22
	4					
Case #2	1	AM	M	70	12 W	51
	2			64	10E	53
	3	PM		75	10SW	12
	4					
Case #3	1	AM	F	64	10E	56
	2			66	8NE	46
	3	PM		73	12 W	22
	4					
Case #4	1	AM	M	68	6NW	47
	2			64	7 W	52
	3	PM		73	12 W	24
	4					

Figure 5 illustrates example MPPs for speed, acceleration and heart rate. Moreover, MPPTs presented in Fig. 6 visually shows how the gender affect the variations of heartrate during the walking.

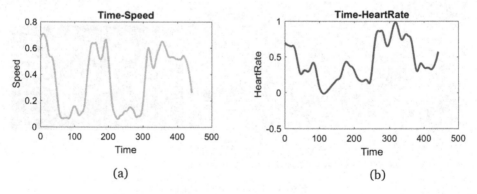

Fig. 5. Example MPPs for (a) speed and (b) heartrate

Having constructed the corresponding MPPTs for different cases for different parameters, we conducted several cross-examinations by calculating the DMPPT for different pairs of walking observations. Table 3 represents some examples of the calculated DMPPTs.

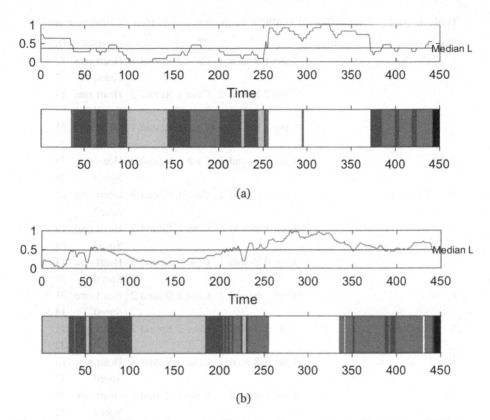

Fig. 6. Example MPPTs that shows the effect of gender on heart rate for (a) Men; (b)Women

According to Table 3, the following observations can be made:

- **Gender**: Items #1 and #2 respectively compare the same rounds of users (#1, #3) and (#2, #4) who have the same gender, while items #3 and #4 respectively compare the same rounds of users (#1, #2) and (#3, #4) with different genders. The results show that the DMPPT values for items #1 and #2 are significantly smaller that items #3 and #4, which may indicate that the effect of gender is considerable on the walking observations.
- **Tiredness**: Item #5 compares the first-morning and first-afternoon rounds of users #1 (female), while item #6 compares the morning-pair rounds of this user. This is the same for items #7 and #8, which belongs to user #2 (male). The corresponding DMPTs shows that the only significant changes occur in the heart rate and speed of the morning-pair of the male user (i.e. user #2), which arises the hypothesis that tiredness has more considerable effect on the performance of males.
- **Day time**: Items #9 and #11 respectively compares the morning-pair observations of users #3 (female) and #4 (male), while items #10 and #12 respectively compares the morning-afternoon observations of these users #3 (female) and #4 (male), which show no significant correlation between the day time and the calculated DMPTs.

Table 3. Some of the calculated DMPPTs to investigate the effect of different contexts

No.	Context to be investigated	1st case	2nd case	Parameter	D_{MPT}
1	Gender	Case 1 Round 1	Case 3 Round 1	Heart rate	12
				Speed	17
2		Case 2 Round 2	Case 4 Round 2	Heart rate	14
				Speed	16
3		Case 1 Round 1	Case 2 Round 1	Heart rate	31
				Speed	27
4		Case 3 Round 2	Case 4 Round 2	Heart rate	35
				Speed	28
5	Tiredness	Case 1 Round 1	Case 1 Round 3	Heart rate	18
				Speed	21
6		Case 1 Round 1	Case 1 Round 2	Heart rate	19
				Speed	15
7		Case 2 Round 1	Case 2 Round 3	Heart rate	14
				Speed	16
8		Case 2 Round 1	Case 2 Round 2	Heart rate	31
				Speed	14
9	Day time	Case 3 Round 1	Case 3 Round 2	Heart rate	15
				Speed	22
10		Case 3 Round 1	Case 3 Round 3	Heart rate	13
				Speed	31
11		Case 4 Round 1	Case 4 Round 2	Heart rate	26
				Speed	22
12		Case 4 Round 1	Case 4 Round 3	Heart rate	19
				Speed	24

5   Conclusion

This paper proposed an approach to represent the behavioural movement pattern people during walking through considering personal (e.g. heart rate and speed) and contextual information. We examined the influence of different contextual conditions such as gender, tiredness and day time on behavioural movement patterns. This was conducted by a segmentation approach to project the "movement parameter profiles" into a string pattern, and then a measure to assign a distance value was employed to examine the effect of different contexts on the movement.

The results derived from four case studies show that the effect of different contextual situations is dependent to many conditions and the approach have the potential to run the intended comparison. Drawing more concrete conclusions, however, needs more exploration on larger datasets and more complicated approaches. As part of our future work, we also intend to consider the effect of locational information such as slope in addition to contextual conditions on behavioural movement patterns.

References

1. Wang, J., Duckham, M., Worboys, M.: A framework for models of movement in geographic space. Int. J. Geogr. Inf. Sci. **30**(5), 970–992 (2016)
2. Dodge, S., et al.: Analysis of movement data. Int. J. Geogr. Inf. Sci. **30**(5), 825–834 (2016)
3. Dodge, S., Laube, P., Weibel, R.: Movement similarity assessment using symbolic representation of trajectories. Int. J. Geogr. Inf. Sci. **26**(9), 1563–1588 (2012)
4. Karimipour, F., et al.: Exploring spatio-temporal patterns in sport movement observations. In: Proceedings of the 13th International Conference on Location-Based Services (LBS) (2016)
5. Dodge, S., Weibel, R., Lautenschütz, A.-K.: Towards a taxonomy of movement patterns. Inf. Vis. **7**(3–4), 240–252 (2008)
6. Buchin, M., et al.: An algorithmic framework for segmenting trajectories based on spatio-temporal criteria. In: Proceedings of the 18th SIGSPATIAL International Conference on Advances in Geographic Information Systems. ACM (2010)
7. Laube, P., et al.: Movement beyond the snapshot–dynamic analysis of geospatial lifelines. Comput. Environ. Urban Syst. **31**(5), 481–501 (2007)
8. Yan, Z., Parent, C., Spaccapietra, S., Chakraborty, D.: A hybrid model and computing platform for spatio-semantic trajectories. In: Aroyo, L., Antoniou, G., Hyvönen, E., ten Teije, A., Stuckenschmidt, H., Cabral, L., Tudorache, T. (eds.) ESWC 2010. LNCS, vol. 6088, pp. 60–75. Springer, Heidelberg (2010). https://doi.org/10.1007/978-3-642-13486-9_5
9. Dodge, S., Weibel, R., Forootan, E.: Revealing the physics of movement: comparing the similarity of movement characteristics of different types of moving objects. Comput. Environ. Urban Syst. **33**(6), 419–434 (2009)
10. Chen, L., Özsu, M.T., Oria, V.: Symbolic representation and retrieval of moving object trajectories. In: Proceedings of the 6th ACM SIGMM International Workshop on Multimedia Information Retrieval. ACM (2004)
11. Pelekis, N., et al.: Similarity search in trajectory databases. In: 14th International Symposium on Temporal Representation and Reasoning. IEEE (2007)
12. Qi, L., Zheng, Z.: A measure of similarity between trajectories of vessels. J. Eng. Sci. Technol. Rev. **9**(1), 17–22 (2016)
13. Sharif, M., Alesheikh, A.A.: Context-awareness in similarity measures and pattern discoveries of trajectories: a context-based dynamic time warping method. GISci. Remote Sens. **54**(3), 426–452 (2017)

On Correlation Between Demographic Variables and Movement Behavior

R. Javanmard, R. Esmaeili, and F. Karimipour[✉]

School of Surveying and Geospatial Engineering, College of Engineering,
University of Tehran, Tehran, Iran
{reyhanejavanmard, roya.esmaeili, fkarimipour}@ut.ac.ir

Abstract. The importance of studying the behavior of people and the expansion of access to spatial data has led to development of activities related to study of movement of individuals as well as discovery of patterns and behavior of individuals for better use in urban planning and policymaking. Understanding the relationship between demographic variables and human movement as well as extraction of behavioral patterns is essential to assess different social issues such as locating infrastructures and city management, reducing traffic and structure of urban communities. This paper aims to explore a Swiss human movement sample dataset, called MDC, in order to discover the effect of demographic parameters on human movement patterns in Switzerland. The users' movement is characterized by area and shape index of the movements as the determinants of the activity space. The results declare that middle age users, females and people who work have more active mobility pattern, since they have higher area and shape index than users in other groups. Data analysis and comparison of results indicate that age and working are two decisive demographic factors for area and shape index of the activity space so they are useful for understanding some of the human's movement characteristics.

Keywords: Demographic variables · Movement behavior · Activity space

1 Introduction

Movement as "a change in the spatial location of the whole individual in time" is the result of complex states and behaviors of moving entities or processes [1]. Individuals' movements are measurable responses to the combination of internal states, physiological constraints, and environmental parameters [2], which control most of the essential behaviors of that entity or phenomena [3]. Therefore, it could be the base for analyzing the behavior of entities or movement phenomena in spatio-temporal spaces.

In recent years, movement of different entities and phenomena have been studied such as animals [4], taxis [5], football players [6], storms [7], and oil spills [8]. Humans movements has been specially investigated in this regards [9, 10]. Studying human movements and extraction of behavioral patterns is essential to assess different social issues. For example, understanding the way that people move, amount of their movement, and their internal interactions can lead to better understanding of different social issues such as spreading a special disease [11], locating infrastructures and city management, reducing traffic, and structure of urban communities [12].

In the past, most of the efforts to understand the human movement were based on questionnaires [13], which were low volume expensive data, and led to a time consuming, of limited efficiency, and non-repetitive process. For example, the U.S. national census produces a wealth of information on where hundreds of millions of people live and work, but this is carried out only once every 10 years [11]. In recent years, thanks to tracking devices (GPS, smartphones, geosensors, Radio Frequency Identification (RFID)), access to movement data has dramatically increased, in terms of volume, precision, and especially temporal resolution, which results in widespread study of moving object in a cheaper and more frequent manner [11]. Additionally, the emergence of Information and Communication Technology (ICT) such as cellphone and internet has increased the social interactions of people, which are captured through calls, emails and tweets [12]. This has led to increasing study of human movement and discovering the patterns and behavioral movement in order to use better in city management and planning.

In recent two decades, numerous researchers have studied human activity and their movement in their daily life. They showed that people in different socio-economic groups have heterogeneous behaviors [14] or, in other words, human movement is varying by gender, age, income, educational level, etc. [15]. For example, it has been reported that women travel more than men (specially toward non-work destinations), but in shorter distances [16]; income and educational level have important and positive influences on longer distance travels [17]; elderly people – more than 65 – travel less and in shorter distances than young people [18]; and employed people do long-term activities and the number of their travels is less than unemployed [19]. Furthermore, there has been evidences that elderly Chinese who live near their children have less and shorter distance travels than those who live alone [20]; low-income people in Chicago have less travels and in shorter distance [21]. Nevertheless, there is not considerable research on the relationship between mobility behavior and occupation and also how variables (age and occupation) are grouped are different in each study.

This paper aims to explore a Swiss human movement sample dataset called MDC[1] (more details in Sect. 2) in order to discover the effect of demographic variables on human movement patterns in Switzerland. The users' movement is characterized by area and shape index of the movements as the determinants of the activity space.

The rest of the paper is structured as follows: Sect. 2 introduces the MDC dataset in more details. Section 3 discusses the activity space of users' trajectory, as the concept employed to characterize the movements. Section 4 presents the research methodology and explores the correlation between the desired demographic variables and determinants of activity space. Finally, Sect. 5 concludes the paper.

---

[1] Mobile Data Challenge.

2 MDC Dataset

This research has been performed using the Mobile Data Challenge (MDC) dataset. In January 2009, Nokia Research Center Lausanne and its Swiss academic partners, IDIAP and EPFL, designed Lausanne Data Collection Campaign (LDCC) to create large-scale mobile data researcher sources [22]. Around 200 volunteers (38% male and 62% female) who live near Geneva Lake contributed in this project. Different types of data were recoded from the smart phones of volunteers, such as location (GPS), motion (accelerometer), proximity (Bluetooth), and communication (phone call and SMS logs) for a period of one year.

Among the 31 tables of the MDC database, the three following tables have been used in this paper (Fig. 1):

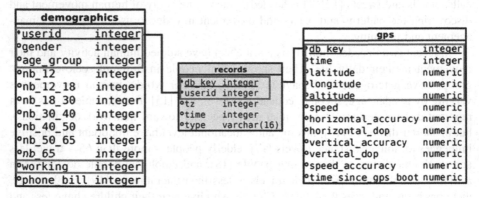

Fig. 1. The MDC tables used in this research.

- Demographic table, which includes age, gender and the occupation of users.
- GPS table, which contains the location (longitude, latitude, altitude) of users in every 5 s, and its related time.
- Records, which related the above two tables, through its *db-key* and *userid* fields.

The demographic variables of the dataset have been grouped into some groups, whose labels and value intervals are presented in Table 1.

3 Methodology

3.1 Activity Space

We deploy the *activity space* as a measure to characterize the users' mobility [23] – which is simply the environment or area within which the user moves. Activity space indicates dispersion of the places that user visits. It actually constructs a structure for the places visited by the user. Investigating the activity space helps to infer characteristics of the users' movement and understand the difference between their mobility behaviors.

Table 1. Labels of the grouping the demographic variables and their value intervals

Class	Labels and value intervals
Gender	1: female 2: male
Age	1: less than 16 years old 2: between 16 and 21 years old 3: between 22 and 27 years old 4: between 28 and 33 years old 5: between 33 and 38 years old 6: between 39 and 44 years old 7: between 45 and 50 years old 8: more than 50 years old
working	1: working full time 2: working part time 3: not currently working 4: studying full time 5: studying part time 6: housewife 7: retired 8: other

As Fig. 2 shows, there are three types of activity spaces, which are defined based on Standard Deviation Ellipse, Minimum Convex Polygon, and Daily Path Area [24]. The standard deviation ellipse is used in this research because the aim of the paper required the shape and direction of the activity space, which are considered by standard deviation ellipse. On the other hands, "activity space can be introduced based on ellipsoidal representation (e.g. standard deviational ellipse) or network representation (e.g., road networks)" [25]. As the geometrical characteristics of the activity space is required here, the ellipsoidal representation is used.

Finally, in order to identify the characteristics of the activity space, the following determinants have been employed:

Area: It indicates the extent of the activity space [26], and is used to infer the dispersion of the visited locations [27]. The area of the standard deviation ellipsoid is calculated as follow:

$$area = \pi ab. \tag{1}$$

where a is the semi major axis and b is semi minor axis of the ellipsoid.

Shape index: It is intuitively known that people move more frequently between their life's pegs (e.g., home, workplace, etc.), which directly influences the shape of the activity space. Thus, in the worst case, the activity space would be a straight line. The shape index is used here to understand "how much the activity space of users' trajectories deviates from this straight line" [25]. The shape index is calculated as follow:

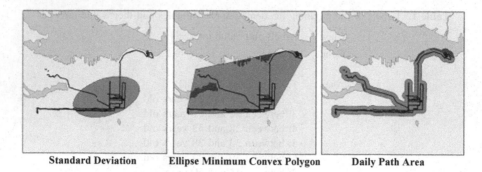

| Standard Deviation | Ellipse Minimum Convex Polygon | Daily Path Area |

Fig. 2. Three types of activity spaces [24].

$$shape\_index = 1 - \sqrt{1 - (\frac{b}{a})^2}. \tag{2}$$

3.2 Exploring the Correlation Between Demographic Variables and Movement Behavior

To determine the relationship between demographic variables and human's mobility, the deviation ellipse is used, whose area and shape index are considered as the determinants of the activity space.

In the first step, the center of the activity space must be determined. Among several approaches, the arithmetic mean of the coordinates weighted according to their frequency of being visited is considered as the center of the activity space, which are usually near to the users' home (Fig. 3) [27].

Moreover, the semi major (a) and semi minor arises (b) of the ellipse are calculated through the covariance matrix of the coordinates:

$$\sigma_x^2 = \frac{1}{n}\sum_{i=1}^{n}(x_i - \bar{x})^2. \tag{3}$$

$$\sigma_y^2 = \frac{1}{n}\sum_{i=1}^{n}(y_i - \bar{y})^2. \tag{4}$$

$$\mathrm{cov}(x,y) = \sum_{i=1}^{n}\frac{(x_i - \bar{x})(y_i - \bar{y})}{n}. \tag{5}$$

$$\Sigma = \begin{bmatrix} \sigma_x^2 & \sigma_{xy} \\ \sigma_{xy} & \sigma_y^2 \end{bmatrix}. \tag{6}$$

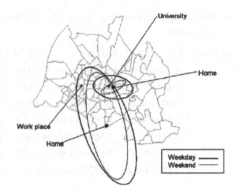

Fig. 3. Deviational ellipse and its arithmetic mean, which is near the home location [27]

The semi arises a and b can now be calculated from the Eigen vectors of the covariance matrix. Having the semi arises calculated, the area and shape index for each user are computed using the Eqs. 1 and 2, which are examined against demographic variables of age, gender and occupation.

4   Results

4.1   Relationship Between Age and Determinants of the Activity Space

In the MDC dataset, the users have been classified into 8 groups based on their age (Table 1). The first group were, however, removed here from the dataset, because in Switzerland, people below the age 18 (which belong to this group) "are considered as no capacity or with limited capacity for civil conduct in the legal system and their activity patterns may partially reflect the wills of their legal guardians (i.e., parents) instead of their own, therefore appearing to be more randomly distributed" [25]. The average and standard deviation of the area and shape index of the users were calculated for each group (Table 2).

Figure 4 demonstrates a correlation between age and area of the activity space. As expected, the higher is the age of the people, the greater is the area of their activity space, until they reach the age group 4. People aged 28 to 33 have the largest activity space area, which indicates that people in this age group have the most dispersion in their visited locations and are the most likely group to travel farther away. However, for people older than this age group, as the age increases, the activity space area gradually gets smaller and consequently old people tend not to travel far away.

In addition, analysis of the standard deviation of the activity space area for each age group shows that younger people not only have larger activity space areas, but also the value of their activity space areas have higher standard deviations, which means that they have a greater variation in the mobility behavior. In opposite, for people older than age group 4, as the age of people increases, the values of their activity space areas become close to each other, which indicates a more similar behavior among the elderly people.

Table 2. The average and standard deviation of the area and shape index of the activity spaces of the users based on their age groups

Age	Num_users	Avg[a] area	Std[b] area	Avg SI[c]	Std SI
2	13	1159691531	1548801618	0.1987	0.1481
3	56	1145495109	1227359219	0.1333	0.101
4	49	1480716658	1695331110	0.1289	0.1196
5	20	856463418	876613710	0.1954	0.1496
6	13	932192035	746671590	0.1803	0.1713
7	2	640557803	519549850	0.0523	0.0285
8	2	435634914	442231182	0.0757	0.019

[a]Average
[b]Standard deviation
[c]Shape index

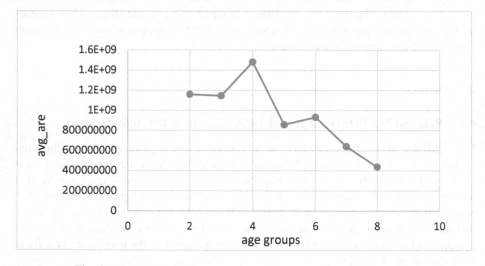

Fig. 4. The correlation between age and the area of the activity space

On the other hand, a correlation between age and shape index is observable (Fig. 5). This determinant increases as the age increases; and the highest shape index belongs to the age group 5 (age between 33 and 38), indicating that users' activity space in this age group have the highest deviation from the straight line. However, as the age increases the deviation tend to diminish. Hence, old people are more likely to travel just between the pegs of their life e.g. their home and workplace.

Moreover, analyzing the standard deviation of shape index for each group indicates that the less is the age, the greater is the standard deviation of the shape index, and the greater is the variety of human mobility behavior. Older people have smaller standard deviation of shape index, which represents the low variety in mobility behavior and, consequently, more similar behavior.

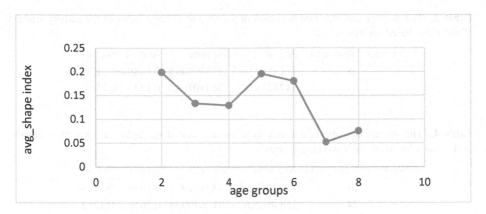

Fig. 5. The correlation between age and the shape index of the activity space.

4.2 Relationship Between Gender and Determinants of Activity Space

The MDC dataset is also classified based on the users' gender (Table 1). The parameters of the activity spaces mentioned in Sect. 4.1 are calculated for both classes, which demonstrate a correlation between gender and the mobility patterns of people (Table 3). It depicts that men have slightly larger activity space area and shape index than women. Many variables may also affect the activity space area and shape index according to their gender e.g. owning a personal car, job status, household size, and so on [28, 29].

There are previous studies confirming that women have shorter trip distance and smaller area of activity space [29, 30]. In many articles, this has been interpreted as household responsibility hypothesis, which declares that "women tend to take on more household and childcare responsibilities" [20, 31, 32]. Furthermore, women's low income causes short commuting since they cannot afford long commuting distances [33]. Job opportunities play an important role in the length of the commuting (activity space area). It is usually assumed that due to the evenly distributed job opportunities for women, they can find a job in the vicinity of their home, so their commuting distance will be shorter than men's [34, 35]. Another reason could be that "women encounter more space–time fixity than men because their activities are pegged around these fixities" [20].

On the other hand, according to Table 3, the value of men's activity space areas and shape indexes have slightly higher standard deviation, which indicates that they have greater variations in the mobility behavior.

4.3 Relationship Between Occupation and Determinants of Activity Space

According to users' classification based on their occupation in the MDC dataset (Table 1), activity spaces' parameters mentioned in previous sections are calculated (Table 4).

Table 3. The average and standard deviation of the area and shape index of the activity spaces of the users based on their gender

Gender	Num_users	Avg area	Std area	Avg SI	Std SI
1	58	1115559213	1225399405	0.1489	0.1139
2	97	1178738480	1364801645	0.1547	0.1438

Table 4. The average and standard deviation of the area and shape index of the activity spaces of the users based on their working groups

Working	Num_users	Avg area	Std area	Avg SI	Std SI
1	84	1284465015	1333871933	0.1679	0.1429
2	14	1583012661	2019640938	0.1656	0.1713
3	7	489493735	248725109	0.1363	0.0779
4	41	1056143333	1101882146	0.1305	0.1095
6	5	286988940	73794936	0.15783	0.0808

Table 4 indicates that the smallest area of the activity space belongs to the working group 6 (housewives). It can be attributed to the fact that housewives have responsibilities for house and kids (see household responsibility hypothesis mentioned in the previous sections), hence they travel shorter distances but more frequently so their activity space area is small. Moreover, although they have the smallest area but their shape index is not the smallest one, but it is larger than students and people who do not work. It is because of the fact that housewives have frequent responsibilities, but students mostly travel from home to school and conversely, and there are not great varieties in their visited places. Furthermore, unemployed people have small activity space area and shape index. It is because unemployed people are mostly either kids or old, and consequently they do not travel far away. Their shape index is also low, which means that they behave similarly.

Workplace of people may be far from their home and they also have free time after work to go to different places. Consequently, activity space area and shape index of employed people will be high.

On the other hand, people of the part-time job group have larger area than full-time job people. Full time students have the least shape index. A dominant theoretical explanation is that they most of the times commute between home and school, and thus do not have lots of free time to visit new places. Finally, Table 4 shows that the higher is the value of the activity space area, the higher is its standard deviation, which means that they have greater variations in the mobility behaviour.

5   Conclusions

This paper discusses the relationship between some demographic factors (i.e., age, gender and occupation) and movement behavior. For this, the dataset at hand was classified based on the desired demographic factors, and the determinants of the activity space (i.e., area and shape index) of each group were compared. In all cases, except gender, a significant relationship was observed to some extent. These promising results motivate more research on increasing movement data provided by devices such as GPS, smartphones, geosensors, etc., which can lead to better understanding of the way people move, amount of their movement, and their internal interactions in order to study different social issues such as spreading a special disease, locating infrastructures and city management, reducing traffic, and structure of urban communities; Nevertheless, the results of this paper may vary across different countries because of difference in culture, city size, infrastructures and so on. Thus, further analysis is required in other regions with consideration of more variables.

References

1. Dodge, S.: From observation to prediction: the trajectory of movement research in GIScience. Advancing geographic information science: the past and next twenty years, p. 123 (2015)
2. Gurarie, E., Andrews, R.D., Laidre, K.L.: A novel method for identifying behavioural changes in animal movement data. Ecol. Lett. 12(5), 395–408 (2009)
3. Madon, B., Hingrat, Y.: Deciphering behavioral changes in animal movement with a 'multiple change point algorithm-classification tree' framework. Front. Ecol. Evol. 2, 30 (2014)
4. Wang, Y., et al.: A new method for discovering behavior patterns among animal movements. Int. J. Geogr. Inf. Sci. 30(5), 929–947 (2016)
5. Bogorny, V., Wachowicz, M.: A framework for context-aware trajectory. In: Cao, L., Yu, P. S., Zhang, C., Zhang, H. (eds.) Data Mining for Business Applications, pp. 225–239. Springer, Boston (2009). https://doi.org/10.1007/978-0-387-79420-4_16
6. Dawson, B., et al.: Player movement patterns and game activities in the Australian Football League. J. Sci. Med. Sport 7(3), 278–291 (2004)
7. Dodge, S., Laube, P., Weibel, R.: Movement similarity assessment using symbolic representation of trajectories. Int. J. Geogr. Inf. Sci. 26(9), 1563–1588 (2012)
8. Afenyo, M., Veitch, B., Khan, F.: A state-of-the-art review of fate and transport of oil spills in open and ice-covered water. Ocean Eng. 119, 233–248 (2016)
9. Förster, A., et al.: On context awareness and social distance in human mobility traces. In: Proceedings of the Third ACM International Workshop on Mobile Opportunistic Networks. ACM (2012)
10. Siła-Nowicka, K., et al.: Analysis of human mobility patterns from GPS trajectories and contextual information. Int. J. Geogr. Inf. Sci. 30(5), 881–906 (2016)
11. Becker, R., et al.: Human mobility characterization from cellular network data. Commun. ACM 56(1), 74–82 (2013)
12. Toole, J.L., et al.: Coupling human mobility and social ties. J. R. Soc. Interface 12(105), 20141128 (2015)
13. Yamamoto, T., Kitamura, R.: An analysis of time allocation to in-home and out-of-home discretionary activities across working days and non-working days. Transportation 26(2), 231–250 (1999)
14. Wang, D., Cao, X.: Impacts of the built environment on activity-travel behavior: are there differences between public and private housing residents in Hong Kong? Transp. Res. Part A Policy Pract. 103, 25–35 (2017)

15. Feng, J.: The influence of built environment on travel behavior of the elderly in urban China. Transp. Res. Part D Transp. Environ. **52**, 619–633 (2017)
16. Roorda, M.J., et al.: Trip generation of vulnerable populations in three Canadian cities: a spatial ordered probit approach. Transportation **37**(3), 525–548 (2010)
17. Páez, A., et al.: Elderly mobility: demographic and spatial analysis of trip making in the Hamilton CMA. Canada. Urban Stud. **44**(1), 123–146 (2007)
18. Giuliano, G., Narayan, D.: Another look at travel patterns and urban form: the US and Great Britain. Urban Stud. **40**(11), 2295–2312 (2003)
19. Wang, D., Chai, Y., Li, F.: Built environment diversities and activity–travel behaviour variations in Beijing, China. J. Transp. Geogr. **19**(6), 1173–1186 (2011)
20. Feng, J., et al.: Elderly co-residence and the household responsibilities hypothesis: evidence from Nanjing. China. Urban Geog. **36**(5), 757–776 (2015)
21. Ureta, S.: To move or not to move? Social exclusion, accessibility and daily mobility among the low-income population in Santiago. Chile. Mobilities **3**(2), 269–289 (2008)
22. Laurila, J.K., et al.: The mobile data challenge: Big Data for mobile computing research. In: Pervasive Computing (2012)
23. Lu, X., et al.: Approaching the limit of predictability in human mobility. Scientific reports, 3, p. srep02923 (2013)
24. Hirsch, J.A., et al.: Generating GPS activity spaces that shed light upon the mobility habits of older adults: a descriptive analysis. Int. J. Health Geogr. **13**(1), 51 (2014)
25. Yuan, Y.: Characterizing Human Mobility from Mobile Phone Usage. University of California, Santa Barbara (2013)
26. Newsome, T.H., Walcott, W.A., Smith, P.D.: Urban activity spaces: Illustrations and application of a conceptual model for integrating the time and space dimensions. Transportation **25**(4), 357–377 (1998)
27. Schönfelder, S., Axhausen, K.W.: Activity spaces: measures of social exclusion? Transp. Policy **10**(4), 273–286 (2003)
28. Kawase, M.: Changing gender differences in commuting in the Tokyo metropolitan suburbs. GeoJournal **61**(3), 247–253 (2004)
29. Crane, R.: Is there a quiet revolution in women's travel? revisiting the gender gap in commuting. J. Am. Plan. Assoc. **73**(3), 298–316 (2007)
30. Scheiner, J.: Social inequalities in travel behaviour: trip distances in the context of residential self-selection and lifestyles. J. Transp. Geogr. **18**(6), 679–690 (2010)
31. Hanson, S., Hanson, P.: Gender and urban activity patterns in Uppsala, Sweden. Geographical Review, pp. 291–299 (1980)
32. Turner, T., Niemeier, D.: Travel to work and household responsibility: new evidence. Transportation **24**(4), 397–419 (1997)
33. Fanning Madden, J.: Why women work closer to home. Urban Stud. **18**(2), 181–194 (1981)
34. Hanson, S., Johnston, I.: Gender differences in work-trip length: explanations and implications. Urban Geogr. **6**(3), 193–219 (1985)
35. Hanson, S., Kominiak, T., Carlin, S.: Assessing the impact of location on women's labor market outcomes: A methodological exploration. Geogr. Anal. **29**(4), 281–297 (1997)

Workshop Computational Mathematics, Statistics and Information Management (CMSIM 2018)

Relating Hyperbaric Oxygen Therapy and Barotraumatism Occurrence: A Linear Model Approach

M. Filomena Teodoro[1,2]([✉]) [iD], Sofia S. Teles[1], Marta C. Marques[3], and Francisco G. Guerreiro[4]

[1] CINAV, Portuguese Naval Academy, Portuguese Navy,
Base Naval de Lisboa, Alfeite, 2810-001 Almada, Portugal
maria.alves.teodoro@marinha.pt
[2] CEMAT - Center for Computational and Stochastic Mathematics,
Instituto Superior Técnico, Lisbon University,
Avenida Rovisco Pais, n. 1, 1048-001 Lisboa, Portugal
[3] Medicine Faculty, Lisbon University,
Av. Professor Egas Moniz,
1600-190 Lisboa, Portugal
[4] CMSH, Centro de Medicina Subaquática e Hiperbárica, Portuguese Navy,
Azinhaga dos Ulmeiros, 1649-020 Lisboa, Portugal

Abstract. Hyperbaric oxygen therapy is a therapeutic modality that allows an increase of perfusion of O_2 in tissues reducing edema and tissue hypoxia, aiding the treatment of ischemia and infection [1,2]. Some complications of this therapy can happen, the middle ear barotraumatism is the most frequent.

The objectives of this study are to determine incidence and severity and to identify predictors of risk for barotraumatism of the middle ear in a large population of patients undergoing routine hyperbaric oxygen therapy.

This work studied the clinical characteristics of 1732 patients who underwent treatment at the Portuguese Navy's Center for Underwater and Hyperbaric Medicine between 2012 and 2016, in order to better characterize this issue with regard to incidence, severity and recurrence such as age, sex, clinical indication for hyperbaric oxygen therapy, personal history of allergic rhinitis and symptomatology of nasal obstruction at the time of the occurrence. Several statistical techniques such as analysis of variance and generalized linear models were applied.

Keywords: Hyperbaric oxygen therapy
Barotraumatism occurrence · Middle ear · Risk factors
General linear models

1 Introduction

Hyperbaric oxygen therapy (HBOT) is a therapeutic modality consisting of the intermittent administration of 100% oxygen within a chamber under pressure conditions above sea level pressure ($1\ ata^1$), allowing an increase of perfusion of O_2 in the tissues. Consequently, there exists a reduction in edema and tissue hypoxia, aiding the treatment of ischemia and infection [1,2]. Between several complications, middle ear barotrauma (BTOM) is the most frequent but its incidence, risk factors and severity are not yet well known.

This work started in [4,5], where the clinical characteristics of 1732 patients who underwent treatment at the Portuguese Navy's Center for underwater and hyperbaric medicine (HMCS) between 2012 and 2016 were studied, in order to better characterize this problem with regard to incidence, severity and recurrence, as well as to identify possible risk factors such as age, sex, clinical indication for HBOT, personal history of allergic rhinitis, and symptomatology of nasal obstruction at the time of the occurrence.

There was an incidence of 8.3% with BTOM between patients. Most of occurrences were unilateral 62%, the remaining 21% cases were bilateral. BTOM occurred in the first 3 sessions in 36% of cases and 44% in up to 5 sessions.

The recurrence rate was 28%. There were constructed statistical models so one could get the statistical significant relations between gender, personal clinical history and BTOM. Some risk factors were identified. An approach by analysis of variance [22] and general least squares (GLM) is still ongoing [6,7]. The results are promising but their analysis still need to be completed.

The outline of this work consists in four sections. Section 2 describes some adopted methodology and data collecting rules. In Sect. 3 a study group and a control group of 142 and 150 individuals respectively were selected and a preliminary statistical analysis is done. In last Section, we make some discussion and get some conclusions.

2   Background

2.1   A Historical Note

The development of Hyperbaric Medicine is closely linked to the History of Diving Medicine. The adverse physiological consequences of staying in an underwater environment led to the multiple medical applications of gas therapy in Modern Medicine [8]. It is impossible to determine the exact origin of the Occupational Diving [1,8]. In Ancient Greece, Plato and Homer report the trade in sea sponges. The diving, without the aid of equipment (limited to 30 m), would be current practice at this time [1]. As for the development and use of diving equipment, the first reference, which appears in a manuscript of the century. XIII, is attributed to Alexander the Great. In 320 A.C., this one dove inside a barrel of glass, at the

---

[1] The *ata* unit (atmosphere absolute) is used in place of atmosphere (*atm*) to indicate that the pressure shown is the total ambient pressure of the system, compared to vacuum, being calculated or measured. For example, for underwater pressures, a pressure of 3.1 *ata* would mean that the 1 *atm* of the air above water is included in this value and the pressure due to water would total 2.1 *atm*. Adapted from definition in [3].

Strait of Bosphorus. At this point, Aristotle already describes the perforation of the tympanic membrane in divers (possibly by barotraumatism) [1,8]. Around the year 1500, Leonardo Da Vinci designed several inventions for application in the dive, but none was developed. In 1616 was designed the first Bell of Dive, by Frank Kessler [1]. This consisted of a rigid mechanical structure of negative buoyancy. Four years later, the Dutchman Cornelius Drebbel develops a Diving Bell with an atmospheric air source and uses caustic soda as a carbon dioxide absorber, thus allowing the air support in an underwater environment. It is also in the seventeenth century that the Principle of Pascal and Boyle's Law are published, as well as the first use of compressed air in the treatment of diseases. In 1662 (before the discovery of oxygen), Henshaw used by the first time a chamber of compressed air, which he called "Domicilium". There he manipulated the pressure and temperature conditions to "aid digestion, facilitate respiration and detoxification, and thus prevent most pulmonary diseases." It was only in 1834 that the hyperbaric environment was used again in medical practice when the Frenchman Junod constructed a hyperbaric chamber (2-4 ATA) and used it to treat pulmonary diseases. [1] In 1841, Triger reports two cases of decompression sickness in minerals as well as the occurrence of otalgia during compression. In other reports, Triger reports that swallowing relieved otalgia. From 1860, several treatment centers began to appear in Europe (the Netherlands, Switzerland, United Kingdom, Italy, Russia, Austria, among others) and the first hyperbaric chamber was built in Canada. In 1878 is published "The Press Barométrique" by Paul Bert [9]. This work reports the main effects of HBOT, toxic effects on living organisms and the risk of seizures. It is also suggested to use normobaric oxygen in the treatment of decompression sickness. The toxic effect of oxygen in the Central Nervous System was later called the "Paul Bert Effect". Shortly afterwards, Scotsman Lorrain Smith describes the effect of oxygen in the lungs. [2,8] In 1937, Behnke and Shaw first used hyperbaric oxygen in the treatment of decompression sickness [8], but it was only in 1967 that the United States Undersea and Hyperbaric Medical Society (UHMS) [10], and in 1971 the European Underwater Baromedical Society (EUBS) was created in Europe with the aim of contributing to the advancement of science in the field of underwater and hyperbaric medicine and related disciplines; to provide a forum for scientific communication between individuals and groups whose professional activity concerns aspects of diving and/or hypobaric, hyperbaric and hyperoxic environment; to disclose factual and scientifically correct information related to Underwater and Hyperbaric Medicine [11].

3 Data

This study resulted from a collaboration between the Faculty of Medicine of the University of Lisbon and the Center of Underwater and Hyperbaric Medicine of the Portuguese Navy. This was an observational retrospective study designed for patients undergoing routine hyperbaric oxygen therapy in the period from 1 January 2012 to 31 December 2016. All patients receiving treatments in urgency arrangements during the period from 1 January 2012 to 31 December 2016 were excluded from the study.

All patients underwent ORL assessment and tympanogram before initiating treatment, as well as subjects undergoing OTHB teaching session, where the Valsalva and Toynbee maneuvers were taught and alerted to alarm signs and symptoms complications. Only patients who had at least one type A tympanogram of the Jerger system[2] [14] started therapy. All tympanograms with pressure within the maximal tympanic cavity between -99 and $+99$ daPa and type A tympanogram according to the Jerger Classification were considered "Normal", the rest being considered "abnormal". In all sessions, a nurse specialized in HBOT was present who assists the patients, if they show difficulty in equalizing. If a patient manifested otologic symptoms, this occurrence was recorded in the book of nursing cases and the patient was then submitted to a new tympanogram and ENT evaluation.

Patients underwent a therapeutic protocol consisting of daily HBOT sessions, each session lasting 100 min and being exposed to a pressure of 2.5 *ata*. The session begins with a 10 min compression phase, followed by a 75 min treatment phase and a 15 min. decompression phase. The treatment phase is further divided into two 35 min periods, intervals for a 5 min period in which patients breathe air. In the compression and decompression phases patients breathe air.

The clinical records of all patients who showed BTOM-compatible symptoms (auditory discomfort, otalgia, ear filling sensation, hearing loss, tinnitus and otorrhagia) were analyzed and clinical data were recorded on: Age, Gender, Clinical Indication for OTHB (sudden deafness; sonotrauma; otitis externa; diabetic ischemia; chronic arterial disease; mandibular osteorradionecrosis; others).

Symptomatology of acute nasal obstruction at the time of the occurrence referred to by the patient, since this may cause intraluminal blockage of the tube and cause tubal dysfunction (symptomatology referenced in the patient's record or case, written by the doctor who consulted Post-BTOM).

Personal history considered to be at risk for chronic nasal obstruction such as previous diagnosis of allergic rhinitis and some habitual medication that is related to an increased risk of medically induced non-allergic rhinitis.

---

[2] "The classification system for tympanograms commonly used today was developed by Liden [12] and Jerger [13]. There are three main types of tympanograms: A, B, and C. Type A tympanograms look like a teepee, and indicate a normal middle ear system, free of fluid or physiological anomalies which would prevent the admittance of sound from the middle ear into the cochlea. Type B tympanograms are a flat line, which is consistent with middle ear pathology, such as fluid or infection behind the ear drum. In some cases, these tympanograms are seen when there is a hole in the ear drum; the difference lies in the ear canal volume: a larger ear canal volume indicates a perforation in the ear drum. Type C tympanograms are still shaped like a teepee, but are shifted negatively on the graph. This indicates negative pressure in the middle ear space, often consistent with sinus or allergy congestion, or the end-stages of a cold or ear infection."

Regarding BTOM, it was analyzed: location (right, left or bilateral ear); severity of lesion; recurrence rate; pressure in the middle ear after BTOM (tympanogram after BTOM).

Randomly, a group of 150 patients from the target population who did not suffer BTOM during their treatment were selected. The clinical characteristics were compared and statistical analysis was performed in order to compare and identify risk factors between the two groups.

The level of BTOM can be done using the Teed modified classification. Severity Rating of Middle Ear Barotraumatism, proposed initially by Wallace Teed (an American diver during World War II) in [15], and modified by Haiden and Harris in [16,17], is a classification for the severity of this lesion which considers a scale with six levels from degree 0 until degree 5 is considered. The levels are defined in Table 1 and illustrated in Fig. 1.

Table 1. Modified Teed classification: gravity of BTOM.

Scale level	Description
0	Symptomatology without otological signs
1	Diffuse hyperemia and tympanic membrane retention
2	Light hemorrhage within the tympanic membrane
3	Significant hemorrhage within the tympanic membrane
4	Outstanding and dark tympanic membrane
5	Free haemorrhage in the middle ear, with tympanic perforation, bleeding visible inside or outside the external auditory canal

In [18,19] we can find a simpler description of the same scale classification.

4 Empirical Application

Summarizing the data, a study group and a control group of 142 and 150 individuals respectively were selected. The first step organizes the data and get some simple measures by descriptive statistic techniques and performs some intermediate level techniques, e.g, proportion tests, independence tests, etc.

In a preliminary data analysis and taking into account the non-quantitative nature of some involved variables, were calculated measures of association, nonparametric Spearmann correlation coefficient, nonparametric test of Friedman for paired samples, etc.

In Fig. 2 is summarized the control group age versus and study group age of the selected 178 participants. Control group and study group present a minimum

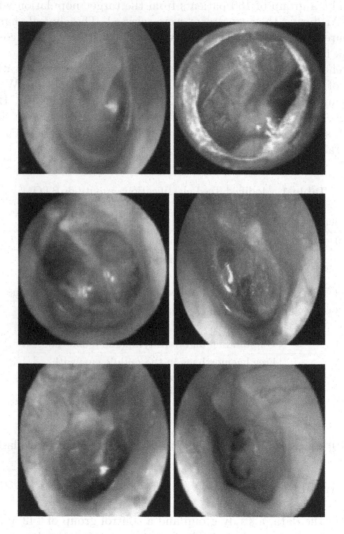

Fig. 1. Barotraumatism Classification (modified Teed). Levels 0, 1, 2, 3, 4, and 5 (from left to right and top to bottom). Top left: Normal Otoscopy level 0, source [21]; Top Right: Barotraum level 1, source [20]; Middle left: Barotraum level 2, source [21]; Middle right: Barotraum level 3, source [20]; Bottom left: Barotraum level 4, source [21]; Bottom right: Barotraum level 5, source [21]

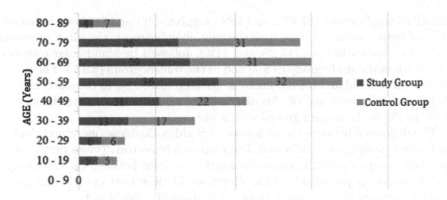

Fig. 2. Control group age versus and study group age.

and maximum age of 10 and 83 years, with a mean age of 55.05 and 55.36 respectively. Both groups present identical distribution of ages ($p-value = 0.80$).

The study group was composed of 70 men and 72 women, the control group being composed of 94 men and 56 women. The distribution per gender and group are statistically different ($p - value = 0.025$).

Clinical indication for hyperbaric oxygen therapy can occur due several diseases. It was registered the number of patients per HBOT indication. Such indication is displayed in Fig. 3.

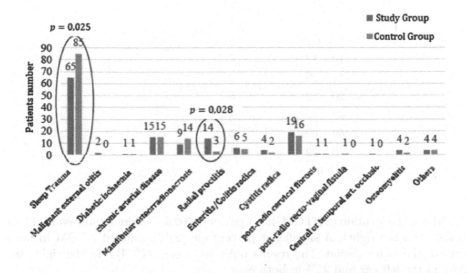

Fig. 3. Number of patients per HBOT prescription.

The most prevalent clinical indication in both groups was sudden deafness (45% and 57% in the study group and control group, respectively), followed by radicular complications (31.47% and 18%, respectively) and Diabetic ischaemia (10% in both groups). Among radiographic complications, the most prevalent was cystitis radica in both (13.2% and 11%), followed by mandibular osteorradionecrosis in the study group (9.8%) and in the control group (3.3%). The prevalence of rheumatoid arthritis is similar in both groups (4.2% in the study group). Therefore, the prevalence of the diagnosis of mandibular osteorradionecrosis (9.8% to 2% in the control group) stands out.

The difference between the diagnoses of Sudden Deafness (more prevalent in the control group, $p = 0.025$) and Jaw Osteorradionecrosis (more prevalent in the study group, $p = 0.028$) was statistically significant between the two groups. The difference in prevalence of the diagnoses of rickettsial cystitis and radial proctitis between the two groups was not statistically significant.

The characterization of BTOM between the patients is described in Table 2 taking account the incidence and number of therapeutic sessions until BTOM occurs. Considering all 1732 patients, 143 presented BTOM; the incidence of BTOM patients was around 8.3%. Only 41% of patients had their complete details recorded in clinical process. From the data that were collected (see Table 2), the BTOM occurred in the first three sessions in 36% of cases (of which 19% during the first session) and in 44% of cases up to five sessions.

Table 2. Number of sessions at the time of BTOM occurrence.

Number of sessions	Number of patients
0 – 3	21
4 – 5	5
6 – 9	9
10 – 14	5
15 – 29	3
20 – 29	6
39 – 49	3
50 – 69	5
70 – 99	1
>100	1

About the location of BTOM, most patients (62%) suffered unilateral BTOM (mostly on the right). A significant percentage (21%) suffered BTOM in both ears in the same session. The results obtained were: 34% BT in the right ear, 28% in the left ear and 21% in both ears.

The BTOM gravity, given the number of unilateral, bilateral recurrent BTOM's, amounts to a total of 208 ears BTOM is displayed in Table 3 and Fig. 4. Almost most were classified as grade 1 Teed Rating (30%). About 20% of the analyzed ears had a degree equal to or greater than 3 in this classification. The number of BTOM ears of each grade (see) was as follows in Table 3. About

50% of BTOM ears are classified in first four levels; Mostly 20% of BTOM ears have more serious (classified as 4 or 5). In 57 (27%) of BTOM's was not possible to classify due not being described in process (or the doctor has registered or not the patient has decided to be seen by a specialist outside CMSH).

Table 3. BTOM gravity considering modified Teed classification.

Grade	Percentage of BTOM ears
0	5.77
1	30.00
2	17.00
3	9.13
4	9.61
5	1.44

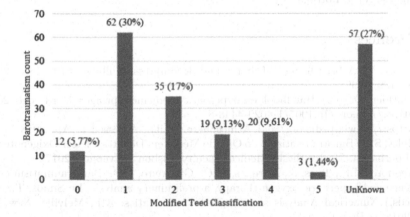

Fig. 4. Gravity of BTOM. Teed modified classification

With the described data we have obtained models by general linear model approach. Such models have been analyzed and tested but the study is still going on.

5 Results and Final Remarks

OTHB is an effective and safe medical therapy. Correct teaching of active equalization maneuvers and careful monitoring during the first sessions can greatly reduce the incidence of BTOM. In the CMSH of the Portuguese Navy there was an incidence of BTOM of 8.3%, being, in the great majority, of low gravity.

The risk of recurrence should be taken into account, and some patients should therefore take prophylactic medication for the remaining duration of treatment. The objectives of this study were to determine the incidence and severity, as well as to identify possible risk factors for barotraumatism of the middle ear in a large population of patients undergoing HBOT. Some GLM models were obtained so we could identify some risk factors. For example, with some simple models, Female gender, diagnosis of osteorradionecrosis of the mandible and personal history of allergic rhinitis were identified (statistically significant) as risk factors. No significant relationship was found between age, remaining clinical indications, risk medication and changes in tympanogram performed prior to initiation of treatment. This part of study is still going on, we are validating some models. Also, we intend to apply some more complex statistical techniques such as mixed models. A detailed analysis of these results will be described in an extended version of the present article.

Acknowledgements. This work was supported by Portuguese funds through the *Center for Computational and Stochastic Mathematics* (CEMAT), *The Portuguese Foundation for Science and Technology* (FCT), University of Lisbon, Portugal, project UID/Multi/04621/2013, and *Center of Naval Research* (CINAV), Naval Academy, Portuguese Navy, Portugal.

References

1. Acott, C.: A brief history of diving and decompression illness. SPUMS J. **29**(2), 98–109 (1999)
2. Mathieu, D. (ed.): Handbook on hyperbaric medicine. Springer, Dordrecht (2006). https://doi.org/10.1007/1-4020-4448-8
3. https://en.wikipedia.org/wiki/Atmosphere_(unit) . Accessed 17 Apr 2018
4. Teles, S.: O Barotraumatismo do Ouvido Médio em Doentes a Fazer Oxigenoterapia Hiperbárica. Master thesis, Medical Faculty, Lisbon University (2017)
5. Teodoro, M.F., Teles, S., Marques, M.C., Guerreiro, F.G.: Barotraumatism occurrence and hyperbaric oxygen therapy, a preliminary analysis. In: Simos, T., et al. (eds.) Numerical Analysis and Applied Mathematics. AIP, Melville, New York (2018, in Press)
6. Nelder, J.A., Wedderburn, R.W.M.: Linear models. J. R. Stat. Soc. **35**, 370–384 (1972)
7. Turkman, M.A., Silva, G.: Modelos Lineares Generalizados da teoria a prática. Sociedade Portuguesa de Estatística, Lisboa (2000)
8. Jain, K.K.: Textbook of Hyperbaric Medicine, 6th edn. Springer Nature, Cham (2017). https://doi.org/10.1007/978-3-319-47140-2
9. Bert, P.: La pression barométrique: recherches de physiologie expérimentale. G. Masson, Paris (1878)
10. Chandler, D.: Undersea and Hyperbaric Medical Society 1967–2007: A History of 40 Years. Undersea and Hyperbaric Medical Society, North Palm Beach (2007)
11. Davis, E.: The foundations for today's future. Diving Hyperb. Med. J. **41**(3), 118–120 (2011)
12. Liden, G.: The scope and application of current audiometric tests. J. Laryngol. Otol. **83**, 507–520 (1969)

13. Jerger, J.F.: Clinical experience with impedence audiometry. Arch. Otolaryngol. **92**, 311–324 (1970)
14. https://www.audiologyonline.com/ask-the-experts/common-types-of-tympanograms-361. Accessed 17 Apr 2018
15. Teed, R.: Factors producing obstruction of the auditory tube in submarine personnel. US Navy Med. Bull. **42**, 293–306 (1944)
16. Haines, H.L., Harris, J.D.: Aerotitis media in submariners. Ann. Otol, Rhinol. Laryngol. **55**, 347–371 (1946)
17. Harris, J.: The Ear and Hearing in Aquatic and Dysbaric Environments. Report no. 746, Naval Submarine Medical Reasearch Laboratory, Bureau of Medicine and Surgery, New London (1973)
18. Beuerlein, M., Nelson, R.N., Welling, D.B.: Inner and middle ear hyperbaric oxygen-induced barotrauma. Laryngoscope **107**(10), 1350–1356 (1997)
19. Fijen, V.A., Westerweel, P.E., Jan, P., Van Ooij, A.M., Van Hulst, R.A.: Tympanic membrane bleeding complications during hyperbaric oxygen treatment in patients with or without antiplatelet and anticoagulant drug treatment. Diving Hyperb. Med. J. **46**(1), 22–25 (2016)
20. Mathiew, J., Marroni, D., Kot, A.: 10th European consensus conference on hyperbaric medicine: recommendations for accepted and non-accepted clinical indications and practice of hyperbaric oxygen treatment. Diving Hyperb. Med. J. **47**(1), 24–32 (2017)
21. Hamilton-Farrell, M., Bhattacharyya, A.: Barotrauma. Injury **35**(4), 359–370 (2004)
22. Tamhane, A.C., Dunlop, D.D.: Statistics and Data Analysis: From Elementary to Intermediate. Prentice Hall, New Jersey (2000)

A Rule-Based System to Scheduling and Routing Problem in Home Health Care Services

Eduyn López-Santana(✉) , Germán Méndez-Giraldo ,
and José Ignacio Rodriguez Molano

Universidad Distrital Francisco José de Caldas, Bogotá, Colombia
{erlopezs, gmendez, jirodriguez}@udistrital.edu.co

Abstract. This paper studies the problem of knowledge acquisition to classify scheduling and routing problems in health care services. We use Knowledge Based Expert System based in a three rule-based system (RBS) to determine the technique to solve the problem for a heath care service problem. The first identify the type of scheduling problem according with scheduling, routing and routing-scheduling problems. With the results, a second RBS identifies the performance measures. And finally, a third RBS determines the best solution techniques to solve the problem. We present an application of home health care problem to identify how solve the problem.

Keywords: Rule-based system · Routing · Scheduling · Service system
Home health care

1 Introduction

Lopez-Santana et al. [1] review the scheduling problems in service systems and present a structure of a general Knowledge Based Expert System (KBES) to solve it. The scheduling problem consists in a decision-making process related with the allocation of resources to perform a set of tasks in a specific planning horizon subject several operational constraints such capacity or unavailability of resources, due dates, priorities, cancelations, among others to optimize one or more objectives, [2].

The proposed KBES by [1] is supported in two sub-KBES. The first one is a service systems classification component (SSCC) applied to International Standard of Industrial Classification (ISIC) system [3]. The proposed scheme considers the variables associated with customers, the system and the characteristics of the outputs to determine this information under the industry, section and division to which it belongs. On the other hand, the rules system is systematic and hierarchical because it must first determine the sector to which it belongs economic activity, with this result and other attributes to determine the section, and finally with these two additional results determine the division. This result is useful for companies to determine their classification and for entities that consolidate information for statistical purposes. The second one is a task scheduling component (TSC) that allows identifying the scheduling problem (or problems). After, it

© Springer International Publishing AG, part of Springer Nature 2018
O. Gervasi et al. (Eds.): ICCSA 2018, LNCS 10961, pp. 496–508, 2018.
https://doi.org/10.1007/978-3-319-95165-2_35

selects the best solution technique (or techniques) and setting the input data, parameters, outputs and performance measure to solve the problem.

This paper aims to apply the proposed KBES in a specific heath service system known as Home Health Care (HHC). The HHC is an alternative way to the traditional hospitalization which consists in delivering medical, paramedical and social services to patients at their homes rather than in a hospital [4, 5].

The remainder of this document is organized as follows. Section 2 presents a brief description of scheduling problem in service systems. Section 3 shows rule-based system to identify the scheduling problem and suggest a solution technique from the proposed notation. Section 4 presents the results in the HHC example. Finally, some conclusions are presented in Sect. 5 with future lines of research.

2 Scheduling Problem in Service Systems

2.1 Service Systems

Service systems could be defined as a set of service providers (resources) and set of service customers working together to coproduce value (flow control) in complex value

Table 1. Differences between manufacturing and service systems.

Features	Manufacturing systems	Services systems
Goods	Physical products, durable	Intangible, perishable
Inventory of goods	Allowed	No allowed
Demand	The demand could be postponed	The demand cannot be postponed
Contact with customers	Generally, is during the sale process	Generally, is during the service generation
Time response to demand	Lead Time	Customer tolerance, patience function
Location (Place)	Not necessarily close to the customer	Several: ranging from *in situ* to remote
Quality measurement	There are objective characteristics of the products	May be subjective and difficult
Consumption and production time	Are not given simultaneously	Are given simultaneously
Capacity lacks	Generate inventory or delays	Generate queues or dropouts
Resources	The resource are machines that operates automatized or by a human resource	The use of machines the for service is often less important than the employment of people
Ownership	The ownership of a product is transferred to the customer	The ownership of a product is not transferred to the customer

networks where providers and customers might be individuals, firms, government agencies, or any organization of people and technologies [3, 6]. In addition, service can be defined as the application of competences for the benefit of another [7] and a solution and a customer's experience that satisfy her or his wishes [8]. Service systems is as a set of activities performed by resources (machines and people) to meet the needs or desires of people through the transformation of the initial state of any of the customer's resources [9]. According with [1], Table 1 summarizes the main differences between manufacturing and service systems and given the notations used to represent the scheduling problems lack the several characteristics as ownership, coproduction, etc.

We propose a notation that consists in three fields $C/R/F$, where C is the Customer, R is the Resources and F is the Flow Control. Figure 1 presents our proposed notation over the good-dominant and service-dominant logic views proposed by [7]. Figures 2, 3 and 4 show the fields and its groups and variables with the defined outputs for each one.

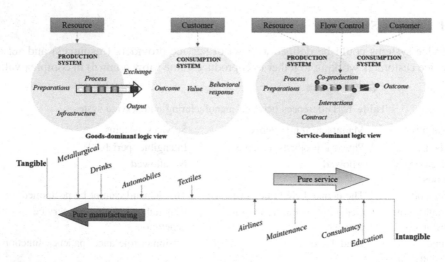

Fig. 1. Representation of the proposed notation for manufacturing and service systems

In pure manufacturing systems the production and consumption systems are separated, while in pure service system both production and consumption systems are related by the interactions and coproduction. Our notation represents this behavior as Flow Control. Figure 1 present some examples of systems for the variable Type of need with its outputs Intangible and Tangible to understand the differences between manufacturing and service systems.

2.2 Scheduling Problem

The general scheduling problem consists in finding the best sequence to perform a number of jobs in a number of machines (or resources) in order to optimize a one or more objective functions [10]. This problem is typically NP-hard and thus is difficult to

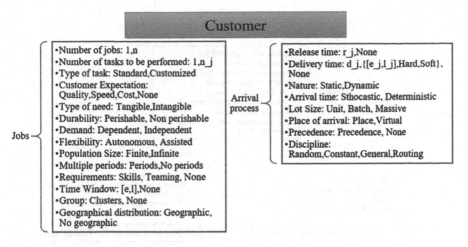

Fig. 2. Customer field of proposed notation for a service system

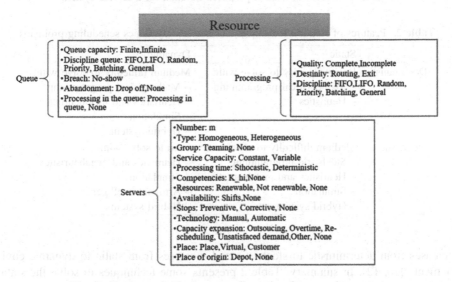

Fig. 3. Resource field of proposed notation for a service system

find an optimal solution since the computation time increases exponentially with the problem size [10].

The scheduling problems can be classified in deterministic and stochastic problems. In deterministic case, the information about processing times, release date, due dates, capacity, among others has a constant value while in stochastic case the information has a stochastic variability [10]. Another classification consists in static and dynamic scheduling [11]. If the jobs arrive simultaneously and all resources and all information are available at beginning of planning horizon, then the scheduling problem is said to be static. If jobs arrive intermittently and the resources are subject to several kinds of perturbations, the problem is dynamic. The complexity to solve the scheduling problem

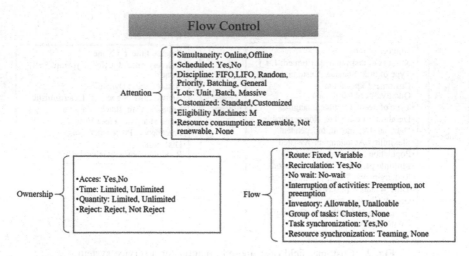

Fig. 4. Flow control field of proposed notation for a service system

Table 2. Features of solution techniques to static and dynamics scheduling problems

	Static	Dynamic
Deterministic	Relatively easy to solve with: – Mathematical programming – Heuristics	Medium difficulty to solve with: – Mathematical programming – Heuristics and metaheuristics – Simulation – Hybrid systems
Stochastic	Medium difficulty to solve with: – Stochastic programming – Heuristics and metaheuristics – Simulation – Hybrid systems	Hard to solve with: – Heuristics and metaheuristics – Simulation – Artificial intelligence – Hybrid systems

increases from deterministic to stochastic and increases from static to dynamic environments [10, 12]. In summary, Table 2 presents some techniques to solve the static and dynamics scheduling problems. Many of real-world scheduling problems in service systems are categorized in stochastic and dynamic environments [11, 13] thus it is hard to solve since the complex nature of services.

In the field of knowledge-based expert systems there are several applications in scheduling problems. Kusiak and Chen [14] discussed applications of ES in manufacturing planning and scheduling. They describe some expert systems applied in several manufacturing environments applying rules and frames. Jr. et al. [15] present an expert system to scheduling in job shop problems. They developed an ES that produce a specific schedule for the problem according to a procedure mathematically proven to provide a satisfactory and often optimal solution, given the criteria for the problem. The authors used a simulation model to test the effectiveness of a selected technique with respect to the chosen performance measure. Kusiak [16] presents a knowledge-based systems (KBS) to scheduling in automated manufacturing system. His KBS contains a heuristic algorithm that selected and execute the best algorithm of a set of scheduling problems. Mendez et al. [17] present an ES to scheduling in job shop problems. Their approach selects the best algorithm to solve the scheduling problem according with the features of the specific problem. Chen [18] states a self-adaptive agent-based fuzzy-neural system to solve a scheduling problem in a wafer fabrication factory. Their results improve the performance of scheduling jobs in the simulated wafer fabrication factory, especially with respect to the average cycle time and cycle time standard deviation.

3 The KBES to Scheduling Problems

López-Santana et al. [1] presents a general framework of an knowledge based expert system to solve the scheduling problem in service systems [2]. Figure 5 shows the framework with two inputs, a service system classification component (SSCC) described in [3] and the task scheduling component (TSC) described here. The SSCC consists in a classification system for the International Standard Industrial Classification (ISIC) system in the Colombian context, also to classify according to economy sector as Services, Manufacturing and Primary proposed by the authors for the section level and division level. Additionally, it is taken as instances for database-level Group, i.e. in total has 249 instances for the selection of rules.

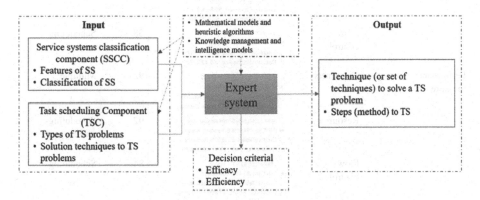

Fig. 5. General framework of a KBES to scheduling in service systems (source: [1])

The knowledge base consists in a set of 12 attributes: Coproduction, Dependence, Accumulation, Technology, Property, Simultaneity, Flexibility, Nature, Durability, Place, Scheduled and Standardization. The inference engine was made with an algorithm to generate tree C4.5 using the entropy information measure. The attributes were modeled using a knowledge acquisition model based in a non-linear optimization and an adaptive neuro-fuzzy inference system (ANFIS) approach (for details see [3]). The set of characteristics are defined in Table 3.

Table 3. List of characteristics (R_a)

r	Characteristic	r	Characteristic	r	Characteristic
1	Presence	12	Initial waiting time	22	Personalization
2	Behavior	13	Space	23	Appearance
3	Continuity	14	Cost of storage	24	Complementary products
4	Abandonment	15	Using machines/equipment	25	Knowledge
5	Operation	16	Using people	26	Consumption
6	Autonomy	17	Interaction	27	Place
7	Influence	18	Beneficiary	28	Displacement
8	Storage	19	Permission	29	Activity program
9	Storage time	20	Commercialization	30	Resource Scheduling
10	Anticipation	21	Virtual	31	Standardization
11	Wait time				

Table 4. Results of TSC applied of HHC system

Stage	Field	Result	# rules	Selected
Scheduling problem	Customers	○ J48 Acc.: 83,13% Sch&Rou ◉ PART Acc.: 84,94% Sch&Rou ○ DecisionTable Acc.: 76,10% Sche ○ DecisionStump Acc.: 66,87% Sch&Rou	45	Scheduling and routing
	Resource	○ J48 Acc.: 74,70% Sche ◉ PART Acc.: 75,90% Sche ○ DecisionTable Acc.: 65,86% Sche ○ DecisionStump Acc.: 59,64% Sche	44	Scheduling
	Flow control	○ J48 Acc.: 71,29% Sche ◉ PART Acc.: 76,10% Sche ○ DecisionTable Acc.: 63,05% Sche ○ DecisionStump Acc.: 55,42% Sche	38	Scheduling
Performance measure	Customers	○ J48 Acc.: 67,27% Scheduling ◉ PART Acc.: 71,49% Multiple ○ DecisionTable Acc.: 43,78% Recursos ○ DecisionStump Acc.: 30,12% General	92	Multiple
	Resource	○ J48 Acc.: 60,64% Scheudling-Routing ◉ PART Acc.: 64,06% Scheudling-Routing ○ DecisionTable Acc.: 36,55% Recursos ○ DecisionStump Acc.: 27,31% Scheduling	92	Scheduling-routing
	Flow control	○ J48 Acc.: 56,83% Recursos ◉ PART Acc.: 63,45% Scheduling ○ DecisionTable Acc.: 39,56% Recursos ○ DecisionStump Acc.: 27,31% Scheduling	84	Scheduling
Solution technique	Customers	○ J48 Acc.: 61,65% Optimization ◉ PART Acc.: 76,71% Sthocastic ○ DecisionTable Acc.: 54,62% Optimization ○ DecisionStump Acc.: 54,02% Optimization	88	Stochastic
	Resource	○ J48 Acc.: 55,22% Optimization ◉ PART Acc.: 71,29% Optimization ○ DecisionTable Acc.: 55,42% Optimization ○ DecisionStump Acc.: 54,02% Optimization	71	Optimization
	Flow control	○ J48 Acc.: 54,62% Optimization ◉ PART Acc.: 71,49% Optimization ○ DecisionTable Acc.: 57,03% Optimization ○ DecisionStump Acc.: 54,02% Optimization	86	Optimization

Figure 6 shows the TSC proposed. The TSC consists in a classification system for according with the scheduling problems in services systems. Figure 7 shows the methodology of three phases to build the rule-based system from the general framework of Fig. 6. The phase 1 is the knowledge acquisition in order obtain the knowledge base. The knowledge base consists in to determine the set of variables for each field the notation presented in Sect. 3. We use the set of attributes and characteristics determined by [3]. However, some variables are not related with the attributes or characteristics, then a survey are performed to determine all variables.

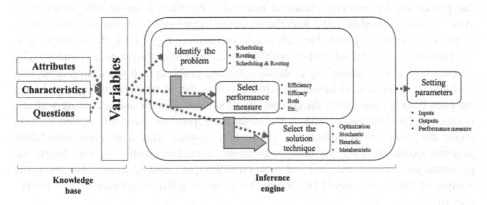

Fig. 6. General structure of the proposed rule-based system to scheduling for service systems.

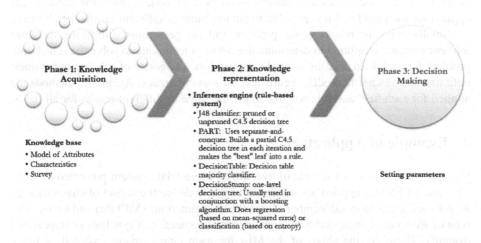

Fig. 7. Methodology to build a rule-based system.

The phase 2 uses as inference engine four methods to get the rules: J48 classifier, PART, Decision Table and Decision Stump. J48 consists in generating a pruned or unpruned C4.5 decision tree based in Entropy measure [19]. PART is a method that use separate-and-conquer strategy. It builds a partial C4.5 decision tree in each iteration and makes the "best" leaf into a rule. Decision Table consists in determining the class for building and using a simple decision table majority classifier. And, Decision Stump consist in using conjunction with a boosting algorithm, it does regression (based on mean-squared error) or classification (based on entropy) and the missing values are treated as a separate value. These methods were built in WEKA and the compared with the percentage of correctly classified instances. We have a set of 498 instances to classify with our method [20]. With the results of knowledge base, the inference engine works in waterfall way with three rule-based system (see Fig. 6). Firstly, we begin with the identification of the scheduling problem for each field of the proposed notation. The output consists in a scheduling problem, a routing problem or a scheduling & routing problem. It is possible to obtain the equal problem for all fields or different problems for each field because given the complexity of service systems and according with the notation defined in Figs. 1 and 2, the customer represents the consumption system, while the resources represents the production system, thus a different scheduling problem could be arise for these subsystems according with [20] and hence the problem, performance measure and solution technique could be hybrid. However, the analyst of the system could be chosen the same or different according with his/her expertise.

Once the problem is determined, we apply the second inference engine to determine the performance measure. For the example, we consider as performance measures a general classification: efficiency, effectiveness, both or none. Again, the methods are applied for each field and it is possible to get the same or different results for all fields.

Finally, with the results of the problem and the performance measure, the third inference engine is applied to determine the solution technique to solve the scheduling problem for each field. For the example, we use four categories of solution techniques: optimization, stochastic models, heuristics and metaheuristics. Again, the methods are applied for each field and it is possible to get the same or different results for all fields.

4 Example of Application

We apply our KBES to a sample of five workers in a HHC system presented by [21]. The first KBES was applied according with [3], we define the subset of characteristics R_a for each attribute a, the number of membership functions (MF) denoted by m_r. The type of MFs (μ_r) correspond to triangular (trimf), general bell (gbelmf) or trapezoidal (trapmf). These are the shape of the MFs for each characteristic modeled as fuzzy number.

Figure 8 presents the results of SSCC for a sample of 5 organizations. In addition, we present the reference value of model developed in [3, 22] and the average of the sample. In the sample, there is a consensus for all attributes except dependence, place and flexibility which as a small deviation 0.81, 1.10 and 0.64 respectively. Respect to reference value, attributes as nature, durability, coproduction, property and simultaneity

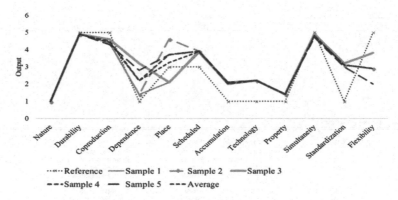

····=··Reference   ——Sample 1   —●—Sample 2   ═══Sample 3
---•Sample 4   ── Sample 5   ---Average

Fig. 8. Results of SSCC applied of HHC system

are too closed. In addition, place and scheduled attributes have a small deviation. However, the rest of attributes have big differences respect to reference value. With these results we need to update the knowledge base to our KBES learn with this new information. The classification obtained is as service, section Q, and division 86.

One of the most important decision in planning home health care services is the routing of caregivers, which means to decide in which sequence each caregiver will visit patients assigned to him/her [23]. There have been several research studies aimed at solve HHC routing problem, for instance in [24] was designed a support decision system for routing health operators using a heuristic procedure. The problem can be viewed as a combination of staff rostering problem and vehicle routing problem (VRP) [25]. Then, the problem is classified as workforce and routing problem.

Figure 9 presents the designed interfaces for knowledge acquisition and the inference engines. These ones were designed in Java and using Weka.

Table 4 summarizes the results of the TSC applied for the example. For the scheduling problem, in customer field, we obtain a scheduling and routing problem. For other fields, we obtain the scheduling problem as result. For the performance measure, our method identifies multiples criterion for the customers, scheduling-routing criterions for the resources, and the scheduling criteria for the flow control. These results suggest a multi objective model according that balance the customers satisfaction and the resources utilizations. Finally, for the solution technique, in the customer field, we obtain stochastic as solution technique. For the resources and flow control, we get optimization as results. Respect to solution techniques, there are applications of Mixed integer programming, branch and bound, dynamic programming, column generation and set partitioning problem, as is stated in [26] as common exact methods in the literature. On the other hand simulation and multi-agent systems has also been used for solving allocation and scheduling processes as seen in [27].

According with [16, 21], we take into account constraints as time windows of the patients, caregivers skills, caregivers working time, precedence (a prior visit of another staff member) and multiple depots. For the HHC problem is selected a multi-agent approach for solving dynamically the caregivers' routing problem. The multi-agent approach uses a multi-objective mixed integer model to make the routing which is

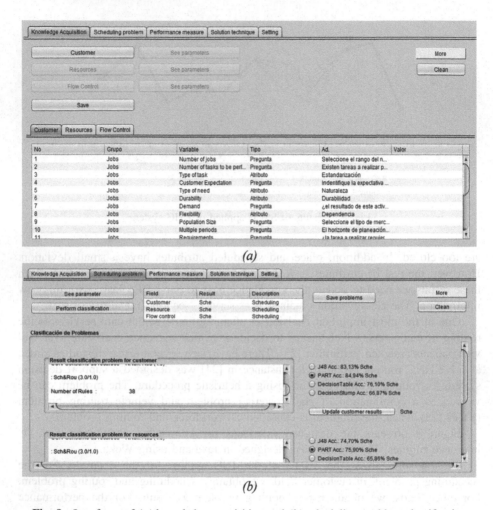

Fig. 9. Interfaces of *(a)* knowledge acquisition and *(b)* scheduling problem classification

updated by the agents when a new request appears presented in [26]. The mathematical model aims to minimize the time travelled as well as the delay in the arrival time at the patients' locations, considering caregivers' skills, patients' priority in their attention, caregivers' working time and caregivers' departure and arrival locations.

5   Conclusions

This paper reviews the scheduling problems in service systems and presents a structure of a rule-based system to identify the type of scheduling problem, the performance measure and the solution technique. The literature of scheduling problems in service system is scarce and the notations for scheduling problems were designed mainly to manufacturing applications. Thus, we propose a new notation that involves the characteristics of service system in three fields: customers, resources and flow control.

Our notation states a set of variables that allows to proposed rule-based system identify the scheduling problems between a set of possibilities defined as scheduling, routing or scheduling and routing. We use different classifiers to build the rules such as: J48, Decision Stump, PART; and Decision Table. In similar way, the performance measure is identified and then the solution technique. Our rule-based system is flexible because it is possible to choose the suggested output or another one. This characteristic allows growing up our knowledge base.

In the presented example of our KBES to HHC system, we obtain the setting of the input parameter to classify the service system and it is proposed a scheduling technique selection to solve the problem according with the classical method in the literature reviews. As result, we selected a multi-agent approach for solving dynamically the caregivers' routing problem, this approach uses a mixed integer programming model to route the caregivers to serve the patients' needs.

This work generates possible future development lines, one of which is the validation of results with a set of real companies and improving the database of information. Another possible line consists to explore other methods of numerical ratings that involves imprecision, for instance using fuzzy logic.

References

1. López-Santana, E.R., Méndez-Giraldo, G.A.: A knowledge-based expert system for scheduling in services systems. In: Figueroa-García, J.C., López-Santana, E.R., Ferro-Escobar, R. (eds.) WEA 2016. CCIS, vol. 657, pp. 212–224. Springer, Cham (2016). https://doi.org/10.1007/978-3-319-50880-1_19
2. Lopez-Santana, E.R., Castro, S.J.B., Giraldo, G.A.M.: Modelo metodológico para programación de tareas en sistemas de servicios: un enfoque de ingeniería de software. Redes de Ingeniería 7, 55–66 (2016). https://doi.org/10.14483/udistrital.jour.redes.2016.1.a07
3. López-Santana, E.R., Méndez-Giraldo, G.A.: A non-linear optimization model and ANFIS-based approach to knowledge acquisition to classify service systems. In: Huang, D.-S., Han, K., Hussain, A. (eds.) ICIC 2016. LNCS (LNAI), vol. 9773, pp. 789–801. Springer, Cham (2016). https://doi.org/10.1007/978-3-319-42297-8_73
4. Benzarti, E., Sahin, E., Dallery, Y.: A literature review on operations management based models developed for home health care services, Paris (2010)
5. Yalcindag, S., Matta, A., Sahin, E.: Operator assignment and routing problems in home health care services. In: IEEE International Conference on Automation Science and Engineering (CASE), pp. 329–334 (2012). https://doi.org/10.1109/CoASE.2012.6386478
6. Spohrer, J., Maglio, P.P., Bailey, J., Gruhl, D.: Steps toward a science of service systems. Computer 40, 71–77 (2007). https://doi.org/10.1109/MC.2007.33
7. Vargo, S.L., Lusch, R.F.: Service-dominant logic: continuing the evolution. J. Acad. Mark. Sci. 36, 1–10 (2008). https://doi.org/10.1007/s11747-007-0069-6
8. Spohrer, J.C., Demirkan, H., Krishna, V.: Service and science. In: Demirkan, H., Spohrer, J., Krishna, V. (eds.) Service Science: Research and Innovations in the Service Economy. Springer, Boston (2011). https://doi.org/10.1007/978-1-4419-8270-4_18
9. Pinedo, M.L.: Planning and Scheduling in Manufacturing and Services. Springer, New York (2005). https://doi.org/10.1007/978-1-4419-0910-7

10. Pinedo, M.L.: Scheduling: Theory, Algorithms, and Systems. Springer, Cham (2016). https://doi.org/10.1007/978-1-4614-2361-4
11. Pinedo, M., Zacharias, C., Zhu, N.: Scheduling in the service industries: an overview. J. Syst. Sci. Syst. Eng. **24**, 1–48 (2015). https://doi.org/10.1007/s11518-015-5266-0
12. Conway, R.W., Maxwell, W.L., Miller, L.W.: Theory of Scheduling. Addison Wesley, New York (1967)
13. Ouelhadj, D., Petrovic, S.: A survey of dynamic scheduling in manufacturing systems. J. Sched. **12**, 417–431 (2009). https://doi.org/10.1007/s10951-008-0090-8
14. Kusiak, A., Chen, M.: Expert systems for planning and scheduling manufacturing systems. Eur. J. Oper. Res. **34**, 113–130 (1988). https://doi.org/10.1016/0377-2217(88)90346-3
15. Johnson Jr, L.M., Dileepan, P., Sen, T.: Knowledge based scheduling systems: a framework. J. Intel. Manuf. **1**, 117–123 (1990). https://doi.org/10.1007/BF01472508
16. Kusiak, A.: KBSS: a knowledge-based system for scheduling in automated manufacturing. Math. Comput. Model. **13**, 37–55 (1990). https://doi.org/10.1016/0895-7177(90)90369-X
17. Méndez, G., Álvarez, L., Caicedo, C., Malaver, M.: Sistema experto para la programación de producción-investigación y desarrollo de un prototipo. Universidad Distrital Francisco José de Caldas, Colombia (2013)
18. Chen, T.: A self-adaptive agent-based fuzzy-neural scheduling system for a wafer fabrication factory. Expert Syst. Appl. **38**, 7158–7168 (2011). https://doi.org/10.1016/j.eswa.2010.12.044
19. Quinlan, J.R.: C4.5: Programs for Machine Learning. Morgan Kaufmann Publishers Inc., San Francisco (1993)
20. López-Santana, E.: Review of scheduling problems in service systems, Bogotá (2018)
21. López-Santana, E.R., Espejo-Díaz, J.A., Méndez-Giraldo, G.A.: Multi-agent approach for solving the dynamic home health care routing problem. In: Figueroa-García, J.C., López-Santana, E.R., Ferro-Escobar, R. (eds.) WEA 2016. CCIS, vol. 657, pp. 188–200. Springer, Cham (2016). https://doi.org/10.1007/978-3-319-50880-1_17
22. López-Santana, E., Méndez-Giraldo, G.: Proposal for a rule-based classification system for service systems. In: Proceedings of Fifth International Conference on Computing Mexico-Colombia and XV Academic Conference on Artificial Intelligence, Cartagena, pp. 1–8 (2015)
23. Yalcindag, S., Matta, A., Sahin, E.: Human resource scheduling and routing problems in home health care context: a literature review. In: 37th Conference on Operational Research Applied to Health Services (ORAHS), Cardiff, pp. 1–34 (2012)
24. Begur, S., Miller, D.M., Weaber, J.: An integrated spatial decision support system for scheduling and routing home health care nurses, pp. 35–48. Institute of Operations Research and Management Science (1997)
25. Yuan, Z., Fügenschuh, A.: Home Health Care Scheduling: A Case Study, Hamburg (2015)
26. López-Santana, E., Espejo-Díaz, J., Méndez-Giraldo, G.: Modelo de programación entera mixta para programación y ruteo en cuidado a la salud domiciliaria considerando la promesa de servicio. In: III Congreso Internacional de Industria y Organizaciones – "Gestión de Cadenas de Abastecimiento en un Mundo Cambiante", Cali, pp. 1–8 (2016)
27. Wahaishi, A.M., Aburukba, R.O.: An agent-based personal assistant for exam scheduling. In: World Congress on Computer and Information Technology (WCCIT), pp. 1–6. IEEE, Sousse (2013)

Kalman Filtering Applied to Low-Cost Navigation Systems: A Preliminary Approach

José Vieira Duque[1], Victor Plácido da Conceição[1] ⓘ,
and M. Filomena Teodoro[1,2](✉) ⓘ

[1] CINAV, Portuguese Naval Academy, Portuguese Navy, Base Naval de Lisboa,
Alfeite, 2810-001 Almada, Portugal
{vieira.duque,placido.conceicao,maria.alves.teodoro}@marinha.pt
[2] CEMAT - Center for Computational and Stochastic Mathematics,
Instituto Superior Técnico, Lisbon University,
Avenida Rovisco Pais, n. 1, 1048-001 Lisboa, Portugal

Abstract. The development of the technology in the last decades, and
in particular of the navigation and positioning systems, with the appearance of the Micro-Electro-Mechanical Systems (MEMS) allowed solutions of positioning and navigation low-cost. The objective of this work
is the construction of a low-cost positioning solution for small sailboats.
Kalman filtering is used to process data from an MEMS inertial sensor
and a GPS receiver on small sailing vessels. The validation of the work
is done by comparing the results obtained by the low-cost system with
those obtained by higher precision systems.

Keywords: Systems of navigation and positioning · Kalman filters
Low-cost · Small vessels

1 Introduction

The development of technology has been a constant in modern times. Navigation
and positioning systems were no exception to the rule. With the emergence of
Micro-Electro-Mechanical Systems (MEMS) it has become possible to reduce
the size and cost of these systems [1–3]. The integration of MEMS and Global
Positioning Sytem (GPS) (INS/GPS) inertial systems has allowed the creation
of low-cost navigation and positioning solutions. This technology has become so
accessible that, if a few years ago, they were only part of leading edge systems,
nowadays they are present in almost all existing smartphones.

Due to its dimensions and costs, it is difficult to install conventional navigation systems in small boats, this work intends to give an answer to this problem
using a technique widely used as a tool of excellence in signal processing, the
Kalman filters (KF), see, for example [4,5]. In some cases, Kalman et al. [6] have
described the Kalman filtering, where signal processing is based on stochastic

models, estimation and control [7,8]. In order to create a low-cost positioning solution that is applied to small sailboats, this work, based on the different KF approaches described in [9], uses a properly adjusted KF capable of merging data from a MEMS inertial sensor and a GPS receiver. The system presents a solution that allows to know the position and speed of the boat and its atitude in the three main axes, yaw, pitch and roll.

Data collection is not yet complete. In order to validate the results, filtered data obtained from the low-cost system are compared with data derived from higher precision systems. The analysis of results is still taking place, using some of the collected data, we have evidence of promising results. We have evidence of promising results.

The outline of this work consists in four sections. Section 2 describes some notes about Inertial Navigation Systems (INS) and Global Positioning Systems (GPS). In Sect. 3 we present some details about Kalman filtering. The empirical application is done in Sect. 4, where are described the selected equipments to get the data and how the experiment was implemented. In last Section, we do some final remarks.

2   Preliminaries

2.1   Inertial Navigation Systems

INS are so called because their operation is based on Newton's 1st Law, the Law of Inertia. It was at 17th century that the English physicist Isaac Newton introduced, for the first time in history, the concepts of inertia and acceleration. According to Newton, a body at rest tends to remain at rest, whereas a body with uniform motion tends to remain in uniform motion if the resultant F of the external forces applied to the system is null. In its 2nd Law, Newton proved that, in an inertial frame, the force F is directly proportional to the acceleration a of a given body, where the mass m of the body is the constant of proportionality ($F = ma$).

From the moment that it is possible to know the value of the acceleration it becomes possible, through the mathematical integration in order to the time, to know the speed and the displacement of a certain body. In order to know the value of the acceleration, it is necessary to use a device called an accelerometer (device that measures the acceleration of a body). However, if we only know the acceleration of a body, we cannot describe its motion correctly. In a complementary way, the measure of some angles is important, so a gyroscope (instrument that allows to measure the rotational movement of a body) is also considered. Joining gyroscopes and accelerometers in the same system, it becomes possible to know how the reference variable in relation to which the acceleration is being measured varies. When the inition position and initial velocity are known, the velocity and displacement can be obtained integrating the acceleration once and twice respectively. The two sensors are the basis of the Inertial Measurement Units (IMU). The magnetometer, a non inertial sensor, is often part of the most IMU. The magnetometer measures the intensity of the magnetic surrounding field improving the capacity of the IMU. The usual IMU constitution is: three accelerometers, three gyroscopes, one pair per orthogonal axis, one magnetometer. In some cases IMU includes more sensors, for example, for temperature.

INS's have some advantages when compared to other navigation systems:

- They are completely autonomous, do not have to send or receive any type of signal;
- Position and speed indication are continuous;
- They can be used in all weather conditions;
- Navigation information can be obtained for any Latitude, even in Polar regions.

However, INS's also have some disadvantages to their's use:

- Position and velocity information degrade over time;
- The equipment must be aligned at the beginning of each mission. This task is very complicated when the system is in motion or when it is in latitudes above 75°;
- High performance equipment is much expensive.

2.2 Global Positioning Sytem

The GPS is perhaps the best known of satellite positioning systems. This system started to be developed by the government of the United States of America in the middle of 1960, with the objective of locating the American submarines carrying nuclear missiles [10]. This technology, which initially had only six satellites, has undergone significant improvements over the years and is now composed of a network of twenty-four satellites that orbit the Earth at approximately 20000 km of altitude. The GPS was developed to be applied exclusively for military purposes, but the US government has decided to facilitate its use for civil purposes and has become the most widely used satellite positioning system in the world (see Fig. 1).

The system, which was only fully operational in 1993, consists of three components: space, control and user:

- Space segment: comprises the satellites broadcasting radiosignals to both control and users segments. Satellite's signals provide both ranging codes and navigation data messages.
- Control segment: consists of a network of ground stations whose function is to monitor and control the orbits of the satellites, to check the quality of the signal they transmit and calibrate the satellite clocks.
- User segment: consists of a GPS receiver that uses the information transmitted by the satellites to compute the (three-dimensional) position of the user.

The basic principle of GPS operation is relatively simple. The receiver needs to be receiving signals from at least four satellites to calculate the distance to these satellites. In order for the receiver to be able to compute the distance to the satellite, it needs to know the propagation speed of the signal and the time

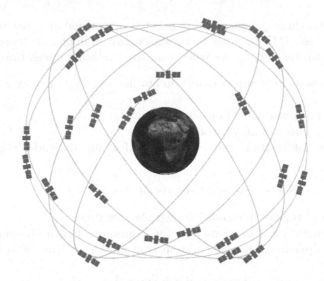

Fig. 1. Constellation of GPS satellites. Source: Adapted from [11]

the signal took to make the satellite - receiver path. The propagation velocity of the signal, in theoretical terms, would be approximately 300 000 km/s, which corresponds to the propagation velocity of electromagnetic waves (EM) in the vacuum. However the terrestrial atmosphere can not be compared to vacuum the speed of MS propagation varies either geographically or temporally. To address this problem, ground stations are responsible for taking measurements of the atmosphere, providing global models that allows the estimation of the delays and consequently the propagation speed of the signal. Knowing the propagation velocity of the signal and knowing the time, the receiver calculate the distance given by *distance = time × velocity*.

When the receiver computes the distance to the satellite, it is in a position placed in a sphere whose radius, centered on that satellite, is the distance from the receiver to the satellite. When the receiver calculates the distance to a second satellite, it obtains a second sphere that will intersect the first one in two points (see Fig. 2). In order to know in which of the points is necessary to calculate a third distance to a third satellite (see Fig. 3). The fourth satellite is used detrmine the receiver clock offset from system time and synchronize the time between the satellites and the receiver, significantly increasing the accuracy of the calculated position.

3   Kalman Filter

In 1960, engineer Rudolf Kalman published an article [4,6] in which he presented a new method of linear filtration. This method uses measurements of independent variables and the associated noise to filter the system signal and predict its next state through the use of statistical techniques. This new method introduced by Kalman in early sixty decade came to be known as Kalman Filter (KF) and

Fig. 2. Calculation the distance of two satellites

had its first use aboard the spacecraft navigation computers of the APOLLO project. The Kalman Filter is one of the most applied methods for tracking and estimation due to its simplicity, optimality, tractability and robustness [12].

Accordingly with Kay [8], KF can be seen as a sequential minimum mean square error (MMSE) estimator of a signal with noise. This signal is described by a state (or dynamical) model. When the errors are Gaussian distributed, the KF conduces to an optimal MMSE estimator; if the errors are not Gaussian distributed, the estimator still is a linear MMSE estimator.

The KF allows the fusion of several sensors according to the precision of each one. Through the construction and analysis of a matrix of errors (noise), the algorithm is able to decide not only what or which sensors to use to obtain the desired value at any moment, but also give more weight to the calculated estimate or to the value measured by the sensors. Some conditions are necessary for KF to be applied. The system in question is supposed linear and the error is supposed to be white Gaussian noise. Often, a real problem does not meet these conditions, being necessary to make some approximations, otherwise it would be quite complex to treat these problems mathematically. To model non-linear systems, the extended Kalman filter (EKF) was introduced, where non-linear models are linearized (first order approach) so the usual KF can be applied. According with the authors[1] of [12], the EKF is often hard to implement. As an

---

[1] The authors of [12] resume in a single paragraph the description of KF approach "...The Kalman Filter (KF) is one of the most widely used methods for tracking and estimation due to its simplicity, optimality, tractability and robustness. However, the application of the KF to nonlinear systems can be difficult. The most common approach is to use the Extended Kalman Filter (EKF) which simply linearizes all nonlinear models so that the traditional linear Kalman filter can be applied. Although the EKF (in its many forms) is a widely used filtering strategy, over thirty years of experience with it has led to a general consensus within the tracking and control community that it is difficult to implement, difficult to tune, and only reliable for systems which are almost linear on the time scale of the update intervals....".

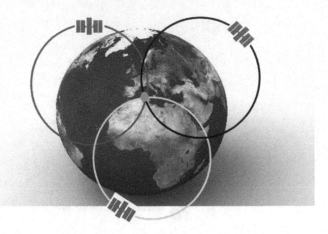

Fig. 3. GPS triangulation

alternative, they have proposed a new approach for highly nonlinear problems, with a performance at least equal to the EKF, with no linearization step and the error can have non-Gaussian behavior. This proposal takes advantage of prediction and correction steps, including between the first and the second usual steps a new one, where is used the unscented transform, conducing to the unscented Kalman filter (UKF).

Reminding that present work focuses on "low cost navigation systems", we reinforce the idea of Leccadito, M [13], a low-cost navigation system has some constraints. First you have to be able to work with the frequency of 50 Hz which is the frequency at which some sensors work, for example a GPS device. Second, low cost systems have less capacity for data storage and processing which limits the functions that can be used. Finally, must be paid attention to the language that is used, since a more complex computational language requires a processing capacity which is not possible. Leccadito, M [13] proposed that the algorithm should be developed as simply as possible so that the program can run and does not become a problem rather than a solution.

Summarizing, the KF allows to obtain approximate values and errors. Considering that this algorithm was not designed to be of high precision, but to allow a fusion of values obtained from the low cost sensors, the associated errors shall be negligible.

3.1   Some Kalman Filter Applications

A wide number of KF applications can be found easily in literature, for example, a less recent publication [5] described several applications from the beginning of the eighties. For the accomplishment of this work, we describe several previous works which have as central theme the use of KF in similar applications.

In 2009 Kaniewski and Kazubek [14] used a KF-based sensor fusion algorithm to construct a Heading Reference System (HRF) capable of integrating a navigation system based on the principle of Dead Reckoning (DR). They used the KF algorithm to merge data from an electronic magnetic compass and gyroscope, combining the information of the two sensors and, in each state, produce an estimate, as close as possible, of the actual value. The authors observed that KF played a very important role in the fusion of the data because it combined the ability to remain stable in the time of the magnetic compass with the short-term precision of the gyroscope.

In 2011 Xavier [17] applied the KF to correct data from a Radio-Frequency Identification (RFID) system where several RFID receivers capable of calculating the position of an object, given a reference, were used. The obtained values were subject to several interferences, a KF was able to reduce the errors of the signal. The author concluded that the KF application conduced to favorable results when compared with similar experiments without using KF approach.

In 2013 a KF-based sensor fusion algorithm was developed by Leccadito [13]. The author aimed to use low-cost IMU sensors to create an Attitude Heading Reference System (AHRS) capable of being integrated into the Unmanned Aerial Vehicle (UAV). In this work only inertial sensors, accelerometers, gyroscopes and magnetometers were used. Without the support of external corrections, the centrifugal forces present in the accelerometer measurements were filtered by a low complexity KF algorithm to integrate and correct the data of the sensors, while a low cost microprocessor was running.

Recently, Li and his colleagues [18] stated that the error drift problem used only IMU MEMS systems with a KF approach, developing what they called the KHD method. This method was used to solve the problem of Indoor positioning. Since the vast majority of Global Navigation Satellite System (GNSS) systems have little or no signal coverage inside buildings, it becomes necessary to use different equipment to achieve a positioning system. In this case, the authors used IMU MEMS sensors, and merged their data using a KF-based fusion algorithm to achieve a better heading estimation. The authors concluded that the KHD method besides being able to correct the heading data can still inhibit the effect of accumulation of the error in obtaining the position.

A few examples of the use of KF in recent years were provided. The KF used especially in sensor fusion algorithms was taken into consideration once these approach has increased substantially in last years due several causes, namely due the development of autonomous systems increasingly small and cheap. These systems require good navigation and positioning capabilities. They use low cost equipment which, when integrated by algorithms such as KF, are able to present very precise results, taking into account the quality/price ratio.

3.2   Kalman Filter Scheme

We can find the description of KF applied at numerous distinct areas due to its simplicity of implementation and for being an optimal estimator when the data is affected by with Gaussian noise. In [15], one of the most cited references about

KF, we find a short and simple approach about this theme. The KF algorithm works in two distinct steps, one of prediction followed by one of correction. As the name implies, in the prediction step the algorithm produces an estimate of the state of the system $x \in \Re^n$ in the next instant k using the state information in the recent past $k-1$ by minimizing the mean square error of the parameters estimators. In the correcting step, the filter uses the measurements obtained using the sensors to correct the calculated estimate and also to improve the estimation for the next state taking into account the error of the first estimate, as can be seen in Fig. 4.

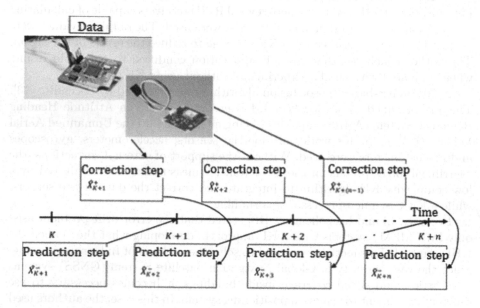

Fig. 4. Kalman filter structure

The KF algorithm is composed of a set of equations. It is necessary to know each of them in order to be able to understand the algorithm as a whole. Since KF is a mathematical algorithm, its principle is always the same. However, the terminology of the equations varies from author to author.

In this paper, it will be described in the most simpler way to be perceived. It is important to note that KF even though it has the filter name is also an estimator. Estimator that works recursively, that is to say that the previously estimated state $x_{(k-1)}$ is an input variable(s) for the state x_k that we are estimating. It has also been mentioned that the filter works in two distinct stages, the one of prediction and the one of correction. In order to not mislead it is necessary to mention that some authors use a priori terminology, to refer to the prediction step and a posteriori, when referring to the correction step. This terminology is used taking into account that the prediction step is performed a priori to know the values, z_k, measured by the equipment that are only known in the correction stage, a posteriori. This terminology is accompanied, in some cases, by the "−" sign to designate the variables that are calculated a priori, of the measures observed, [16,17].

Before we see how the estimator works, it is necessary to formulate the problem. We know that the KF will produce an estimate $\hat{x}_k$ of a state vector x at the instant k.

We can define the state transition equation by Eq. (1)

$$x_k = Ax_{k-1} + Bu_{k-1} + w_{k-1}, \tag{1}$$

where x_{k-1} is the value of the previous state, A is the transition matrix that characterizes the motion and B is the control matrix (relates the optimal control input and the state); u_k is a control signal and finally, w is the process noise.

Notice that Eq. (1) models the state x is a discrete time model, a linear stochastic difference equation, that is coupled with the measurement Eq. (2) given by

$$z_k = Hx_k + v_k, \tag{2}$$

where H is the matrix containing the measured values and v_k is the noise of the measurements. The Eq. (2) relates the state x_k with the measurent z_k. It is important to recall that the process is a estimation process, so will always have associated errors. These errors are taken into consideration so the algorithm improve estimation quality. That is why in the equation of propagation of the state Eq. (1), and in the equation of the measures Eq. (2) appear the associated errors w and v respectively, allowing to model the process.

After finding the main KF equations we need to define the equation(s) that will estimate the system. For each instant k of the system, we want to find the best estimate $\hat{x}$ of our signal x in the sense of the estimate that minimizes the mean square error of the estimated parameters. The iterative process is defined firstly by Eqs. (3) and (4) that correspond the prediction stage, transition from instant $k-1$ to instant k,

$$\hat{x}_k^- = A\hat{x}_{k-1} + Bu_{k-1}, \tag{3}$$

$$\hat{P}_k^- = A\hat{P}_{k-1} + Q, \tag{4}$$

where $\hat{x}_k^-$ is the value of the priori estimate of the state (signal) x at time k, $\hat{P}_k^-$ and Q are, respectively, the priori matrix of covariance of the state estimator $\hat{x}_k^-$ and the covariance matrix of the noise of process.

The equations of the iterative process that correspond to the correction step, are given by Eqs. (5–7)

$$G_k = \hat{P}_k^- H^T (H\hat{P}_k^- H^T + R)^{-1}, \tag{5}$$

$$\hat{x}_k = \hat{x}_k^- + G_k(z_k - \hat{x}_k^-), \tag{6}$$

$$\hat{P}_k = (I - G_kH)\hat{P}_k^-, \tag{7}$$

where G_k is the Kalman Gain matrix. It is important to note that, at this stage, the values of the state and its covariance matrix are corrected. To calculate the

Kalman Gain G_k, given by Eq. (5), it is necessary to know the priori covariance matrix P of the state vector, defined in Eq. (4). Finally, $\hat{x}_k$ is the value of the posteriori estimate of the state x at time k. Also, the covariance matrix of the state vector is corrected in Eq. (7), obtaining the posteriori $\hat{P}_k$. R is the covariance of the measurement noise error.

Notice that the computation of Kalman Gain is a key point of the whole algorithm. This matrix enables the KF algorithm to "learn" in each iteration it makes. The quality of the desired estimate depends on the number of iterations performed by the algorithm. Of course, all this depends on other factors such as initialization of the variables referring to the previous state and obtaining the matrices R and Q. The initialization step is the most complex of the algorithms, because when the first iteration is performed, the variables of the past state are not known, so it is necessary to assign covariance values of the errors, as well as the past estimation. The value of the previous state estimate is not a big problem, to this variable should be assigned a value, as close as possible, to the expected value. For its part the variable P is much more complicated to initialize. Obtaining the initial error covariance matrix of the sensors R is relatively simple to obtain, since the errors of the sensors can be known by, for example, comparing the data with other systems. The problem is when one has to initialize the error covariance matrix of the Q system, since it is much more difficult to estimate the error of the process.

Notice that the KF algorithm assumes linearity, that the process noise and measurement noise, w and v respectively, are white Gaussian noise, and each other are independents. These assumptions are reproduced in following equations. Equations (8–10) concern the white noise properties

$$E[w_k w_i^T] = \begin{cases} Q_k, i = k \\ 0, \quad i \neq k, \end{cases} \tag{8}$$

$$E[v_k v_i^T] = \begin{cases} R_k, i = k \\ 0, \quad i \neq k, \end{cases} \tag{9}$$

$$E[w_k] = 0; \quad E[v_i] = 0; \quad E[w_k v_i^T] = 0, \quad \forall k, i. \tag{10}$$

Equations (11) and (12) concern the Gaussian distribution of the process error

$$W \cap N(O, Q) \tag{11}$$

and the measurement error

$$V \cap N(O, R). \tag{12}$$

respectively.

These assumptions can shape the good performance of the KF, for example, if the process is strongly nonlinear or the error distribution is not Gaussian, other filters already referred previously shall be considered, e.g. the extended Kalman filter or the unscented Kalman filter.

4   Empirical Application

4.1   Equipment

This work is intended to be applied in small sailing vessels. It is important to know the dynamics of these boats since, besides their propulsion being with the wind, they are also of small dimensions. These characteristics make their behavior to present some differences when compared to other type of vessels. These necessary details will be explained later on.

One of the constraints of this work is the use of low cost sensors. After consultation of a large number of publication about sensors and related equipments, for example [20–26], the choice within the various types of existing sensors, it was decided as first option to resort to those available at the Naval Research Center, which are now presented.

The inertial sensor used to perform this study was the *Motion Position Unit* (MPU) 6050. This sensor obeys to the design constraints, availability and price. The choice of this sensor was mainly due to the fact that it had already been used in previous projects. In literature, stands out the work presented in [19], where the same sensor was applied. The MPU 6050, plus a temperature sensor that has not been used, consists of an accelerometer and MEMS gyroscope, each with three axes, which makes a total of six degrees of freedom. To integrate the accelerometer and gyroscope data, the MPU 6050 has a digital motion processor or Digital Motion Processor (DMP). This equipment has an analogue/digital converter for each of the channels. With this capability the MPU can take accelerometer and gyroscope readings on each of the axes simultaneously. Communication between the MPU 6050 and other devices, for example a microprocessor, is done through the I2C protocol.

After some research on sensor integration and low-cost GPS, the choice fell on GPS NEO 6M. This GPS module comprises two distinct parts. One consisting in an integrated processor capable of converting the raw data, into friendly user data, such as position and speed. The other being an antenna capable of picking up the signal sent by the satellites. The choice of this sensor did not fully comply with the proposed requirements. The GPS modules that were available besides being older, required another type of technical knowledge that is not dominated by the author. Thus, this module was purchased respecting the low cost restriction. Similarly to the MPU 6050, this GPS module also has I2C communication capability, which greatly simplifies its integration.

In order to facilitate the integration of the sensors, a microcontroller was used. Among the several possible options, and given the limitations imposed, two hypotheses remained, Raspberri Pi and Arduino. Both Raspberry Pi and Arduino are available in a number of different configurations, the former having more computing power and more memory capacity than the latter. However the Arduino has better communication facilities, with the sensors in question, and its programming is simpler and more intuitive. Both microcontrollers are low cost, and Arduino is cheaper. This fact can be explained by the greater capacity that the Raspberry Pi presents. The microcontrollers are both programmable and the Arduino has its own software, while Raspberry is open source and can even run the Linux operating system. The microcontroller chosen for this work was the Arduino. Although it has less processing capacity and memory, it has a greater ease of connection with the sensors and, it is reasonable to choose the least complex.

4.2   Implementation

One of the objectives of this work is to create an attitude measurement system for a light sailing vessel. We searched in literature similar approaches to get some indications how to proceed. An interesting work was found in [27]. For the creation of this system the Arduino Mega microcontroller was used to read and process the data acquired by the MPU 6050. Although the Arduino is easy to program, has good data acquisition and processing capabilities, its graphical interface lags behind other softwares as far as data analysis is concerned. To address this problem, we used the Matlab^2 tool to develop an algorithm model that uses simulated data, but allows a more careful analysis of the capabilities of the adopted filter. Initially we started by creating a simple algorithm that worked at one dimension. This model, although out of phase with the reality of the problem under study, allows us to have a very realistic perception of how FK works the data.

Subsequently, an algorithm was developed that, in addition to filtering the acceleration value, is also able to predict velocity and displacement. In order for the filter to be able to project velocity and position values through acceleration, it is necessary to use the kinematics equations. We can describe the motion of a body knowing only its acceleration in the case of non-existence of oscillations.

We can see some of the performed simulations in Fig. 5, where Kalman filter was applied to a simulated signal plus noise, presented in [28].

Through these equations, once applied to each of the axes, X, Y and Z, it is possible to know how a body moves in its three axes. Although in some cases the FK can be applied to all three axes simultaneously, in this case it was decided to apply the FK separately to each of the axes. In practice, this translates into the application of three identical FKs on different axes. Although this option may cause a greater delay the computational effort and the complexity of the algorithm are significantly lower. In order for the FK to be applied it is necessary to define, in addition to the initial conditions, the state transition equation and the equation of means. For the state transition equation it is necessary to define the state vector and the way it evolves with the system. Thus, the state vector X was defined, and since we want to know the velocity and the displacement through the acceleration, the matrix A was obtained. We can see in Fig. 6 the estimates of acceleration with real data. To complete this work, We need to perform and test the Kalman filter program relatively to hight precision sensors. Complete the treatment of collected data is determinant to go on the next stage:

---

^{2} MATLAB and Statistics Toolbox Release 2012b, The MathWorks, Inc., Natick, Massachusetts, United States.

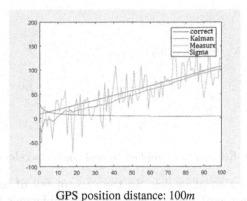

GPS position distance: 100*m*

GPS position distance:1000*m*

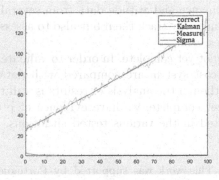

GPS position distance: > 1000*m*

Fig. 5. Kalman filter applied to a simulated signal plus noise. Top: GPS position distance: 100 m; Middle: GPS position distance:1000 m; Bottom: GPS position distance: >1000 m

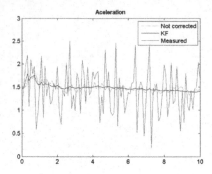

Fig. 6. Kalman filter applied to real signal (acceleration).

the statistical validation of models. In the case of fail of imposed hypotheses (linearity, whit noise, etc) may be necessary to implement the EFK or UFK. The results suggest that the present approach is a good contribution to the solution of low cost navigation positioning.

5   Final Remarks

In order to create a low-cost positioning solution that is applied to small sailboats, this work, based on the different KF approaches, uses a properly adjusted KF capable of merging data from a MEMS inertial sensor and a GPS receiver. The system shall presents solution that allows to know the position and speed of the boat and its atitude in the three main axes, yaw, pitch and roll. The efficiency of the data acquisition algorithm by merging data from different sensors (accelerometer and gyroscope) with different tolerances and performance requirements was not tested yet because data collection is still going on. This study is essential to accurately measure performance and atitude data from several small sailboats during races, in order to not only track them but also to assess the effectivenness of manoveuring strategies.

Data collection is not yet complete. In order to validate the results, the data obtained by the low-cost system are compared with data obtained by higher precision systems. Although the analysis of results is still taking place partially using the data not yet complete, we have evidence of promising results. The filter reacts as expected in the various tested situations, with different signal disturbances.

Acknowledgements. This work was supported by Portuguese funds through the *Center for Computational and Stochastic Mathematics* (CEMAT), *The Portuguese Foundation for Science and Technology* (FCT), University of Lisbon, Portugal, project UID/Multi/04621/2013, and *Center of Naval Research* (CINAV), Naval Academy, Portuguese Navy, Portugal.

References

1. Prime Faraday Partnership's: An Introduction to MEMS (Micro-electromechanical Systems). Prime Faraday Partnership's, Loughborough University, Loughborough (2002). http://www.amazon.co.uk/exec/obidos/ASIN/1844020207. Accessed 21 Apr 2018

2. What is MEMS Technology? (n.d.). https://www.mems-exchange.org/MEMS/what-is.html. Accessed 28 Feb 2018

3. Ganssle, J.: A Designers Guide to MEMS Sensors. Convergence Promotions LLC, Rhode Island (2012). https://www.digikey.com/en/articles/techzone/2012/jul/a-designers-guide-to-mems-sensors. Accessed 28 Feb 2018

4. Kalman, R.E.: A new approach to linear filtering and prediction problems. J. Basic Eng. **82**(1), 35–45 (1960). https://doi.org/10.1115/1.3662552

5. Sorenson, H.W. (ed.): Kalman Filtering: Theory and Application. IEEE Press, New Jersey (1985)

6. Kalman, R.E.: New methods in wiener filter theory. In: Bogdanoff, J.L., Kozin, F. (eds). Proceedings of the First Symposium on Engineering Application of Random Function Theory and Probability. John Wiley & Sons, New York (1963)

7. Maybeck, P.S.: Stochastic Models, Estimation and Control, vol. 1. Academic Press, New York (1979)

8. Kay, S.M.: Fundamentals of Statistical Signal Processing. Estimation Theory. Prentice Hall, New Jersey (1993)

9. Brown, R.G., Hwang, Y.C.: Introduction to Random Signals and Applied Kalman Filtering: With MATLAB Exercises, 4th edn. John Wiley & Sons, New Jersey (2012)

10. Mai, T.: Global Positioning System History (2012). https://www.nasa.gov/directorates/heo/scan/communications/policy/GPS_History.html. Accessed 1 March 2018

11. Mai, T.: Global Positioning System (2014). https://www.nasa.gov/directorates/heo/scan/communications/policy/GPS.html. Accessed 1 March 2018

12. Julier, S.J., Uhlmann, J.K.: New extension of the Kalman filter to nonlinear systems. In: Kadar, I. (ed.) Signal Processing, Sensor Fusion, and Target Recognition, VISPIE Proceedings 3068 (1997)

13. Leccadito, M.: A Kalman Filter Based Attitude Heading Reference System Using a Low Cost Inertial Measurement Unit. Master thesis, Virginia Commonwealth University, Richmond (2013). https://doi.org/10.2514/6.2015-0604

14. Kaniewski, P., Kazubek, J.: Integrated system for heading determination. Acta Phys. Pol. A **116**(3), 325–330 (2009). https://doi.org/10.12693/APhysPolA.116.325

15. Welch, G., Bishop, G.: An introduction to Kalman filter. Technical report TR 95–041, North Carolina University, Chappel Hill (2006)

16. Abreu, P.H., Xavier, J., Silva, D.C., Reis, L.P., Petry, M.: Using Kalman filters to reduce noise from RFID location system. Sci. World J. (2014). id 796279

17. Xavier, J.: Aplicação do Filtro de Kalman na correcção de dados provenientes de um sistema de Localização baseado em RFID. Master thesis, Faculdade de Engenharia da Universidade do Porto, Portugal (2011)

18. Li, X., Wang, J., Liu, C.: Heading estimation with real-time compensation based on Kalman filter algorithm for an indoor positioning system. ISPRS Int. J. Geo-Inf. **5**(6), 98 (2016). https://doi.org/10.3390/ijgi5060098

19. Oliveira, W.d.S., Gonçalves, E.N.: Implementação em c: filtro de kalman, fusão de sensores para determinação de ângulos. ForScience: Revista Científica Do IFMG **5**(3), e00287 (2017). http://www.forscience.ifmg.edu.br/forscience/index. php/forscience/article/view/287. Accessed 21 April 2018
20. Ring laser gyroscope—Britannica.com (2016). https://www.britannica.com/ technology/ring-laser-gyroscope. Accessed 19 February 2018
21. Fraden, J.: Handbook of Modern Sensors Physics, Designs, and Applications, 4th edn. Springer-Verlag, New York (2010). https://doi.org/10.1007/978-1-4419-6466-3
22. Llorente, A.: Acelerómetro y giroscopio MEMS (2014). https://www. industriaembebidahoy.com/acelerometro-y-giroscopio-mems/. Accessed 1 March 2018
23. Sampaio, C.: Medição de vibrações em equipamentos e/ou estruturas usando sensores low cost. Medição de vibrações, pp. 1–41 (2015)
24. Titterton, D.H., Weston, J.L.: Strapdown Inertial Navigation Technology. 2nd edn, Progress in Astronautics and Aeronautics Series, vol. 207. American Institute of Aeronautics and Astronautics, Reston (2004)
25. Wagner, J.F., Trierenberg, A.: The origin of the gyroscope: the machine of bohnenberger. Bull. Sci. Instrum. Soc. **107**, 10–17 (2010)
26. Wilson, J.S. (ed.): Sensor Technology Handbook. Elsevier, Burlington (2005). https://doi.org/10.1016/B978-075067729-5/50054-9
27. Cardeira, B.M.S.C.: Arquitecturas para Navegação Inercial/GPS com Aplicação a Veículos Autónomos. Master thesis, Instituto Superior Técnico, Lisboa (2009)
28. Duque, J.V., Conceição, V.P., Teodoro, M.F.: Filtragem de Kalman aplicada a sistemas de navegação de baixo custo. In: Ferreira, C. et al. (eds.) XXV Jornadas de Classificação e Análise de Dados, Proceedings of JOCLAD 2018 (2018). ISBN: 978-989-98955-4-6

A Two-Phase Method to Periodic Vehicle Routing Problem with Variable Service Frequency

Eduyn López-Santana[1]([✉]) [ID], Carlos Franco[2] [ID],
and Germán Méndez Giraldo[1] [ID]

[1] Universidad Distrital Francisco José de Caldas, Bogota, Colombia
{erlopezs,gmendez}@udistrital.edu.co
[2] Universidad del Rosario, Bogota, Colombia
carlosa.franco@urosario.edu.co

Abstract. This paper presents a method to solve the periodic vehicle routing problem with service frequency. The problem consists in finding a set of paths for a crew of vehicles to deliver products or services to a set of customers in a discrete planning horizon subject to constraints as vehicle capacity, distance-time constraints, time windows, and the variable demand that implies a not defined frequency. Our method solves iteratively two mixed integer programming models. The first one assigns customers to be visited on the planning horizon. The second finds paths to visit the customers for each period. However, in case of non-feasibility a set of rules modify the allocation and the process starts again until the solution is obtained. We present an example to illustrate the method.

Keywords: Vehicle routing · Optimization · Service frequency

1 Introduction

Service systems consist of activities that are offered using human or mechanical power in order to satisfy people's needs or wishes [1], also consist of a set of interacting resources provided by the customer and the provider [2]. Service systems are becoming a strategic area of scientific research from multidisciplinary approaches as an academic community of Service Science or Service Science Management and Engineering [3, 4].

In many real-world service systems exists a decision-making process related with the allocation of resources to perform a set of tasks in a specific planning horizon subject several operational constraints such capacity or unavailability of resources, due dates, priorities, cancelations, among others in order to optimize one or more objectives [5]. This work focusses on the problem of scheduling a set of resources that perform the service operations on the customer sites in a planning horizon where not all customers need to be served on each period. The customers are geographically distributed; thus, the resources need to be routing subject to several operational constraints as capacity, maximum length of a path, time windows among others.

© Springer International Publishing AG, part of Springer Nature 2018
O. Gervasi et al. (Eds.): ICCSA 2018, LNCS 10961, pp. 525–538, 2018.
https://doi.org/10.1007/978-3-319-95165-2_37

The novelty of our proposed approach consists in the integration of service models with scheduling and routing models. The Periodic Vehicle Routing Problems (PVRP) is a family of np-hard problems in which a company has a set of vehicles and needs to deliver products or services to a set of customers in a planning horizon where not all customers need delivery on each day. This problem has two sub-problems: (1) Customers must be assigned to days on the planning horizon guaranteeing the frequency of service requested; (2) Routes must be constructed for each vehicle and each day subject to operational constraints, like maximum length of time or distance travelled.

In addition, it is common the use a set of schedules previously generated to ensure the frequency of service requested e.g. two or three times per week, as a parameter of the problem so the selection of the best schedules meets the assignment of customers to days. In this paper, we present an alternative way to solve the PVRP without using a set of initial schedules. Our method consists in solving iteratively two mixed integer programming (MIP) models to build a unique set of visits in the planning horizon.

The remainder of this document is organized as follows. Section 2 presents a brief description of problem. Section 3 describes our proposed method. Section 4 presents an example of application of our method. Finally, some conclusions are presented in Sect. 5 with future lines of research.

2 Problem Statement and Literature Review

We consider a complete and directed network $G = (N, A)$, where the set $N = \{0\} \cup N_C$ is a set of customers and depot, node $\{0\}$ denotes the depot and $N_C = \{1, \ldots, n\}$ the set of customers. The set A represents the connections (i, j) between nodes $i, j \in N$. Let $K = \{1, \ldots, K\}$ be a discrete set of time periods. Each customer $i \in N_C$ has a total demand P_{ik}. A homogeneous fleet of vehicles $V = \{1, \ldots, m\}$, with capacity Cap_{kv} is available to perform the service. To satisfy the customers demand a distribution plan must be defined, indicating the quantity of product to be delivered to each customer at each period and there is a minimum frequency of service f_i for each customer. A cost $c_{ij} \geq 0$ is associated with each arc $(i, j) \in A$ and is paid every time a vehicle traverses the arc, and a cost Cv_{ik} of visits a customer i on period k, a cost Cf_i for the lack units respect a desired quantity Q_i^*, and a cost Ce_i to exceeds the desired quantity Q_i^*.

The problem consists of finding the quantity to be delivered to each customer at each period that, together with the set of routes that satisfy customer demands at the end of the horizon planning, minimize the total assignment and routing costs.

The literature on PVRP and its variants come from the 70's, initially with the work of Beltrami and Bodin [6] who proposed a heuristic approach solving the problem of waste collection. Rusell and Igo [7] proposed and tested several heuristics to obtain approximate solutions for the waste collection problem. Christofides and Beasley [8], presented a heuristic algorithm based on an initial choice for delivery days, followed by an information exchange with the purpose of minimizing the cost of distribution, and Tan & Beasley [9] presented a heuristic algorithm for solving the PVRP based on the work of Fisher and Jaikumar [10].

Since 2000 several researches have been developed on PVRP, it is worth noting the work of Drummond et al. [11] using an asynchronous parallel metaheuristics and

Mourgaya and Vanderbeck [12] presenting an algorithm based on column generation. Several extensions on PVRP have been found in the literature. Cordeau et al. [13] implemented the tabu search heuristic for solving the PVRP including multiple depots (MDPVRP). Hadjiconstantinou and Baldacci [14] solved a maintenance problem as a MDPVRP. Time windows were worked by Cordeau et al. [15] using a unified tabu search algorithm. Francis et al. [16] implemented a service choice variable and presented several heuristics for its solution.

In the literature, several feasible visit schedules are constructed beforehand and correspond to an input parameter of the model, subtracting flexibility to the supplier in the decision process and increasing the solution time. This lack evidenced, encourage this research focusing in the construction of the visit schedule adding flexibility in different ways (variable demand, deconsolidating load and use of non-regular days) and getting faster solutions.

3 Proposed Method

The method consists in an iterative two-phase system presented by [17]: in phase 1 customers are assigned to days of the planning horizon guaranteeing the vehicle capacity by Assignment Model, in phase 2 the Routing Model is used to get the paths for each day, when there is non-feasibility on routing model, some procedures (Exit Rule and Ending Inventory Rule) are run and a problematic customer is found and reassigned in phase 1. While a path cannot be constructed, then the Exit Rule is used to find the customer to be moved, the assignment must be made again, so the method ends when all customers are allocated in the planning horizon and feasible routes are designed for each day. Table 1 describes the method.

3.1 Phase 1: The Assignment Model

The Assignment Model is a mixed integer programming (MIP) model designed with the purpose of setting load to be transported and customers to days over the planning horizon, so the schedule is constructed. This is done by minimizing the total of visit and penalty costs designed to satisfy the minimum number of visits for each customer and add flexibility to the system. More visits than necessary could happen which means a better customer service and still a better total system cost. The MIP considers capacity of vehicles and balance equations satisfying the demand of customers by cost interaction.

We use three costs on the objective function which are explained following: Visit Cost represents the cost that the supplier must pay for activities related to the service of the customer like working hours, fixed and insurance costs; transportation costs are not considered here. Penalty costs are divided in two, Excess and Missing. Missing cost represents a penalty for serving the customer before he noticed and means a wrong use of his capacity. Excess cost represents lateness in the service so there is a violation on the agreement and problems on capacity or missing raw material, gets customer in trouble, for this reason penalty must be higher than missing cost. As we introduce a fictitious day, Excess Cost is used to punish the ending inventory left by transporter.

Table 1. Algorithm to solve the PVRP with variable frequency service

1	Set periods = {1,2, ..., t}, Nodes = {0,1,2, ..., n}
2	k ∈ days, i ∈ Nodes
3	**While** (k<t)
4	Solve **Assignment Model** (CV$_{ik}$).
5	**For** k = 1 to t-1
6	Solve **Routing Model** for k
7	**If** (**Routing Model** is not feasible)
8	Run **Exit Rule.**
9	t=1, **break for** Iteration happens.
10	**End-If**
11	**End-For**
12	**End-While**
13	**While** (k = t)
14	Solve **Routing Model** for t
15	**If**(**Routing Model** is not feasible)
16	Run **Ending Inventory Rule.**
17	**Else**
18	**Break.**
19	**End-If**
20	**End-While**
21	**End**

It's important to highlight that we introduce a concept named Wished Quantity to Transport. It represents the load that supplier must transport for providing a high service level. This parameter is important because it is compared against the units hold by the customer and the objective is they get as equal as possible. In addition, it represents the maximum level of inventory that the customer can store, or the minimum level of product required, depending of the problem context.

Sets

- I: Set of customers indexed in i.
- K: Set of periods (days) indexed in k. ($k + 1$ is fictitious day used only when ending inventory is necessary).
- V: Set of vehicles indexed in v.

Parameters

- Cv_{ik}: Visit cost to customer i on day k.
- Cf_i: Missing unit cost regarding to Wished Quantity to Transport of customer i.
- Ce_i: Excess unit cost regarding to Wished Quantity to Transport of customer i.
- P_{ik}: Demand of customer i on period k.
- M: Large positive number.
- Q_i^*: Wished Quantity to Transport for customer i.
- Cap_{kv}: Transport capacity of vehicle k on day v.
- II_i: Beginning inventory over the planning horizon of customer i.

Decision Variables

- $X_{ik} = \begin{cases} 1 & \text{if customer } i \text{ is served on day } k \\ 0 & \text{otherwise} \end{cases}$

- $Y_{ikv} = \begin{cases} 1 & \text{if customer } i \text{ is served on day } k \text{ by vehicle } v \\ 0 & \text{otherwise} \end{cases}$

- Uf_{ik}: Missing units regarded to Wished Quantity to Transport of customer i on day k.

- Ue_{ik}: Excess units regarded to Wished Quantity to Transport of customer i on day k.

- f_i: Service frequency of customer i on the planning horizon.

- I_{ik}: Inventory units accumulated to the end of day k and customer i.

- Qr_{ikv}: Units to be move to or from customer i on day k by vehicle v.

Model.

$$\min \sum_{i \in I} \sum_{k \in K} (Cv_{ik} * X_{ik} + Cf_i * Uf_{ik} + Ce_i * Ue_{ik}) + \sum_{i \in I} Ce_i * I_{k(t-1)} \quad (1)$$

Subject to:

$$\sum_{k \in K|k \neq |t|} X_{ik} = f_i \quad \forall i \in I \quad (2)$$

$$f_i \geq 1 \quad \forall i \in I \quad (3)$$

$$I_{io} = II_i \quad \forall i \in I \quad (4)$$

$$P_{ik} + I_{ik-1} - \sum_{v \in V} Qr_{ikv} = I_{ik} \quad \forall i \in I, \forall k \in K \quad (5)$$

$$I_{ik} \leq m(1 - X_{ik}) \quad \forall i \in I, \forall k \in K \quad (6)$$

$$Qr_{ikv} \leq mY_{tkv} \quad \forall i \in I, \forall k \in K, \forall v \in V \quad (7)$$

$$Uf_{ik} - Ue_{ik} = Q_i^* X_{ik} - \sum_{v \in V} Qr_{ikv} \quad \forall i \in I, \forall k \in K \quad (8)$$

$$\sum_{i \in I} Qr_{ikv} \leq Cap_{kv} \quad \forall k \in K, \forall v \in V \quad (9)$$

$$\sum_{v \in V} \sum_{k \in K} Q_{ikv} = \sum_k P_{ik} + II_i \quad \forall i \in I \quad (10)$$

$$Qr_{ikv} \leq \min(Cap_{kv}) \forall i \in I, k \in K, v \in V \quad (11)$$

$$X_{ik} = \sum_{v \in V} Y_{ikv} \quad \forall i \in I, \forall k \in K \quad (12)$$

$$\begin{aligned} Uf_{ik}, Ue_{ik}, I_{ik}, X_{ik} \geq 0 \quad \forall i \in I, \forall k \in K \\ Qr_{ikv}, Y_{ikv} \geq 0 \quad \forall i \in I, \forall k \in k, v \in V \end{aligned} \quad (13)$$

The objective function (1) represents the overall cost of visiting all customers and penalization customers including the ending inventory cost when it happens. Constraints (2) records the visit frequency for each customer and Constraints (3) establishes that the customer must be served at least once (except on fictitious day). Constraints (4) sets initial inventory if it is the case. Constraints (5) represents the balance of the units in the system, if they are transported inventory gets null, otherwise units are storage until next day, so in Constraints (6) inventory variable takes value when there is no visit on customer i, and in (7) the variable is positive not restricted if customer gets serve. Constraints (8) registers excess or missing units regarding to Wished Quantity to Transport when customer gets service. Constraints (9) guarantees capacity constrains in vehicles, Constraints (10) demand and initial inventory must be fulfilled and (11) limits the maximum number of units that can be transported to top vehicle capacity. Constraints (12) makes sure that customer is visited by only one vehicle and finally Constraints (13) are non-negative constraints.

There are some considerations around this model that must be notified: a customer must be served only once in a day, I_{it} and Qr_{itv} are mutually exclusive (Constraints 6 and 7), which means that if one gets value the other mandatory is null; total cost (which is it is the interaction of Visit and Penalty Costs) must have concavity behavior so there is a minimum point desirable to make transportation and vehicle assignment doesn't influence the route construction, it is only with the purpose of guaranteeing feasibility.

3.2   Phase 2: The Routing Model

After setting the visit schedule, routes are constructed for each period of the planning horizon by solving any routing problem; we present the Capacitated Vehicle Routing Problem with Time Windows (CVRP-TW) in similar way of [18, 19].
Sets

- N: set of nodes (customers and depot).
- V: set of vehicles.
- A: set of arcs (i,j).
- N_c: set of customers; $N_c = N \setminus \{0\}$.

Parameters

- C_{ij}: cost associated of arc $(i,j) \in A$.
- d_i: demand of customer i.
- Cap_v: vehicle capacity of vehicle v.
- a_i: lower bound of the time window of customer i.
- b_i: upper bound of time window of customer i.
- t_{ij}: travel time from node i to node j.
- ts_i: service time at customer i.

Decision Variables

- $X_{ijv} = \begin{cases} 1, & \text{if vehicle v travers arc } (i,j) \\ 0 & \text{in otherwise} \end{cases}$
- S_{iv}: start time of service at customer i for vehicle v.

Model

$$min \sum_{(i,j)\in A} \sum_{v\in V} C_{ij}X_{ijv} \tag{14}$$

$$\text{Subject to:} \tag{15}$$

$$\sum_{v\in V} \sum_{j\in\{A\setminus i\}} X_{ijv} = 1 \quad \forall i \in N_c \tag{16}$$

$$\sum_{v\in V} \sum_{j\in\{A\setminus i\}} X_{jiv} = 1 \quad \forall i \in N_c \tag{17}$$

$$\sum_{v\in V} \sum_{j\in A} X_{0jv} \leq |V| \tag{18}$$

$$\sum_{v\in V} \sum_{i\in A} X_{i0v} \leq |V| \tag{19}$$

$$\sum_{i\in Nc} d_i \sum_{j\in N} X_{ijv} \leq Cap_v \quad \forall v \in V \tag{20}$$

$$\sum_{i\in N} x_{ihv} = \sum_{j\in N} x_{hjv} \quad \forall h \in Nc, v \in V \tag{21}$$

$$s_{iv} \geq a_i \quad \forall v \in V, \forall i \in N \tag{22}$$

$$s_{iv} \leq b_i \quad \forall v \in V \ \forall i \in N \tag{23}$$

$$S_{iv} + ts_i + t_{ij} - M(1 - X_{ijv}) \leq S_{jv} \quad \forall v \in V, (i,j) \in A \tag{24}$$

$$S_{0v} + t_{0j} - M(1 - X_{0jv}) \leq S_{jv} \quad \forall v \in V, j \in N_c \tag{25}$$

$$X_{ijv} \in \{0,1\} \quad \forall (i,j) \in A; v \in V \tag{26}$$

The objective function (14) minimize the total routing cost for each period. Constraints (16) that a vehicle exit of customer i. Constraints (17) force that a only one vehicle enters to customer i. Constraints (18) state the exit vehicles of the depot. Constraints (19) represent the returning depot for the vehicles. Constraints (20) limit the capacity for each vehicle. Constraints (21) ensure the flow vehicles. Constraints (22) and (23) are the time windows constrains. Constraints (24) and (25) avoid the *subtours* and ensure the logic sequence for each path. Finally, constraints (26) stated the variable X_{ijv} as binary.

3.3   Rules to Select the Problematic Customer

Non-feasibility is able because other operative constraints such as maximum time or length of the route, time windows, etc. For this situation we design, a small procedure called Exit Rule that finds a problematic customer for a new assignation. If non-feasibility happens in last horizon planning day, Ending Inventory Rule is run. Both rules are described next:

Exit Rule
This is a procedure designed with the purpose of pointing out which customer could be the reason of non-feasibility in the solution. The objective is to ease the iterative process and converge faster to the final solution. As we present a CVRP-TW non-feasibility may happen in time windows constraints, so that's the reason we present this rule, however this is a subjective rule and may change in other problem circumstances. The Exit Rule we present is a generic one for a basic PVRP and we have no purpose in designing the most efficient.

$$CS_i = \sum_{j \in Nt|j \neq i} D_{ij} \quad \forall i \in Nt|i \neq 0 \tag{27}$$

In (1) Nt represents the set of nodes or customers to be visited in the non-feasible day including the depot, CS_i is the Exit Rule for customer i (can't be the depot) and points out the sum of the distances from customer i to all the set Nt; D_{ij} is the distance from node i to j. Then the maximum of all CS_i indicates that this customer is too far from the others and probably the reason of non-feasibility. This is communicated to phase 1 so the assignation cost of problematic customer is increased by a M factor and forcing to choose another day for him. It is important to notice that when Exit Rule is executed a new assignment schedule is generated and routing process begins from starting point (iteration happens).

Ending Inventory Rule
This rule is only used when the path for the last day (not fictitious) can't be found. For this situation the process is a little bit different: Exit Rule will be used to find the problematic customer and will be selected if and only if:

- The customer has met his minimum number of visits or in worst case, at least one.
- Quantity accumulated is less or equal to his Wished Quantity to Transport (explain in next section), so it can be hold until next visit.

Then the customer will be sent to the fictitious day, erased from the set of customers for last day and the path construction process begins again. When all routes were constructed for last day the PVRP has been successfully solved.

4 Example of Application

To show our method, we present an example with one depot (node 0), 6 customers geographically distributed, a planning horizon of 6 days, 2 vehicles with capacity of 300 units and no time windows constrains. Table 2 shows the parameters of the example of application.

Table 2. Parameters of example

i	$Cv_{ik}\backslash P_{ik}$												Cf_i	Ce_i	Q_i^*	II_i
k	1		2		3		4		5		6					
1	17	10	30	30	28	10	35	10	34	10	37	20	2	8	10	0
2	17	10	30	30	28	10	35	10	34	10	37	20	3	9	180	0
3	17	10	30	30	28	10	35	10	34	10	37	20	3	8	10	0
4	17	10	30	30	28	10	35	10	34	10	37	20	4	11	20	0
5	17	10	30	30	28	10	35	10	34	10	37	20	5	8	30	0
6	17	10	30	30	28	10	35	10	34	10	37	20	6	13	40	0

The example was performed in six iterations. Tables 3, 4, 5, 6, 7 and 8 shows the results for each iteration respectively. In the iteration 1, we find only one path for day 1, for day 2 the problem is not feasible, then we select the customer 6 as problematic and its visit cost is modified. For iteration 2, the day 1 is not feasible, then the customer 6 is again selected as problematic and its visit cost is modified.

Table 3. Example's results of iteration 1.

Iteration	1		Assignment cost	584			
Day	1		2	3	4	5	6
Assignment	1-3		1-3-4-6	1-3-5	1-3-4-6	1-3	1-2-3-4-5-6
Path			Day no feasible Exit criteria: $CS_1 = 58$ $CS_3 = 55$ $CS_4 = 50$ $CS_6 = 62$ Prob: 6. $CV_{6,2} = 100000$	-	-	-	-
Distance	A=24	B=26					

For iteration 3, days 1 and 2 are feasible, but day 3 is not feasible, then the customer 2 is selected as problematic and its visit cost is modified. The results of iteration 4 and 5 are presented in Tables 6 and 7, respectively. For both, the method stops until the last

Table 4. Example's results of iteration 2

Iteration	2		Assignment cost:	861		
Day	1	2	3	4	5	6
Assignment	1-3-6	1-3-4	1-3-5-6	1-3-4-6	1-3	1-2-3-4-5-6
Path	Day no feasible Exit criteria: $CS_1=38$ $CS_3=46$ $CS_6=48$ Prob: 6. $CV_{6,1}=100000$		-	-	-	-
Distance	-					

Table 5. Example's results of iteration3

Iteration	3		Assignment cost:	964		
Day	1	2	3	4	5	6
Assignment	1-3	1-3-4	1-3-5-6	1-3 -4	1-3-6	1-2-3-4-5-6
Path			Day no feasible Exit criteria: $CS_1=48.1$ $CS_3=65.1$ $CS_5=44.4$ $CS_6=56.1$ Prob: 3. $CV_{3,3}=100000$	-	-	-
Distance	A=24 B=26	A=26 B=28				

period. For the last iteration 6, the method finds feasible solution for periods 1 to 5. For day 6, there is not a feasible solution, then the criterion of ending inventory is performed. This determine the set of customers 1,3,4 and 5 as candidate. The first attempt finds the customer 1to leave inventory of 10 units. A new attempt finds the customer 5 with 30 units, and the method finds a feasible solution for the routing customers 2,3,4, and 6. The method stops here, with the solution described in Table 8. and the units as starting inventory for the next planning horizon.

Table 6. Example's results of iteration 4.

Iteration	4		Assignment cost:		1016	
Day	1		2		3	
Assignment	1-3		1-3-4		1-5-6	
Path						
Distance	A=24	B=26	A=26	B=28	A=30.2	B=22
Day	4		5		6	
Assignment	1-3-4-6		1-3		1-2-3-4-5-6	
Path	**Day no feasible** Exit criteria: $CS_1=58$ $CS_3=55$ $CS_4=50$ $CS_6=62$ *Prob*: 6. $CV_{6,4}=100000$		-		-	

Table 7. Example's results of iteration 5.

Iteration	5		Assignment cost:		1016	
Day	1		2		3	
Assignment	1-3		1-3-4		1-5-6	
Path						
Distance	A=24	B=26	A=26	B=28	A=30.2	B=22
Day	4		5		6	
Assignment	1-3-4		1-3-6		1-2-3-4-5-6	
Path			**Day no feasible** Exit criteria: $CS_1=38$ $CS_3=46$ $CS_6=48$ *Prob*: 6. $CV_{6,5}=100000$		-	
Distance	A=26	B=28				

Table 8. Example's results of iteration 6.

Iteration	6		Assignment cost:		1119
Day	1		2		3
Assignment	1-3		1-3-4		1-5-6
Path					
Distance	A=24	B=26	A=26	B=28	A=30.2	B=22
Day	4		5		6
Assignment	1-3-4		1-3		1-2-3-4-5-6
Path					Day no feasible.
Distance	A=26	B=28	A=26	B=24		
Last day rule	**Day no feasible** **Ending inventory rule.** : 1,3,4,5 CS_1=54.1 CS_3=51.1 CS_4=50.1 CS_5=50.4 *Prob*: 1. Ending inventory customer 1: 10		**Day no feasible** **Ending inventory rule.** :3,4,5. CS_3=40.1 CS_4=30.1 CS_5=40.3 *Prob*: 5. Ending inventory customer 5: 30		
Distance					A=28	B=32

5 Conclusions

This paper reviews a multi-period vehicle routing problem where a company has a set of vehicles and needs to deliver products or services to a set of customers in a planning horizon where not all customers need delivery on each period. This problem has two main sub-problems which need to be solved in an integrated way. The first sub problem consists that the customers must be allocated to periods on the planning horizon ensuring the frequency of service requested. The second sub-problem consist of determining the path of each vehicle on each period subject to operational constraints, like maximum length path.

It is common to use a set of schedules previously generated to ensure the frequency of service requested e.g. two or three times per period, as a parameter of the problem so the selection of the best schedules meets the allocation of customers to periods. The application of our proposed approach allows to solve the problem by avoiding using a set of schedules, i.e., a unique visit schedule is generated. Also, we allow deconsolidating the load, using non-regular periods of visits and variable frequencies in the method to make it robust and flexible tool for a real-world environment.

The novelty of our prosed approach consists in the integration of service models with scheduling and routing models. For future works, the development of new methodologies for the costs and parameter computation for the assignment model could be done. In addition, constrains as time windows could be involved, variants of the objective function as fractional objectives or multi-objective, and the use of heuristics and metaheuristics to solve larger problems.

Acknowledgments. We thank Fair Isaac Corporation (FICO) for providing us with Xpress-MP licenses under the Academic Partner Program subscribed with Universidad Distrital Francisco Jose de Caldas (Colombia). We thanks to Daniel Correa and Sebastian Rodriguez, students of Universidad Distrital for your help with the programming of the models.

References

1. Pinedo, M.L.: Planning and Scheduling in Manufacturing and Services. Springer, New York (2009). https://doi.org/10.1007/978-1-4419-0910-7
2. Böttcher, M., Fähnrich, K.-P.: Service systems modeling: concepts, formalized meta-model and technical concretion. In: Demirkan, H., Spohrer, J.C., Krishna, V. (eds.) The Science of Service Systems, pp. 131–149. Springer, US (2011). https://doi.org/10.1007/978-1-4419-8270-4_8
3. Spohrer, J., Maglio, P.P., Bailey, J., Gruhl, D., Spohrer, J., Maglio, P.P., Bailey, J., Gruhl, D.: Steps toward a science of service systems. In: The 2007 IEEE International Conference on Information Reuse, pp. 71–77. IEEE Computer Society (2007)
4. Demirkan, H., Spohrer, J.C., Krishna, V.: Introduction of the science of service systems. In: Demirkan, H., Spohrer, J.C., Krishna, V. (eds.) The Science of Service Systems, pp. 1–11. Springer, Boston (2011). https://doi.org/10.1007/978-1-4419-8270-4_1
5. López-Santana, E.R., Méndez-Giraldo, G.A.: A knowledge-based expert system for scheduling in services systems. In: Figueroa-García, J.C., López-Santana, E.R., Ferro-Escobar, R. (eds.) WEA 2016. CCIS, vol. 657, pp. 212–224. Springer, Cham (2016). https://doi.org/10.1007/978-3-319-50880-1_19
6. Beltrami, E.J., Bodin, L.D.: Networks and vehicle routing for municipal waste collection. Networks **4**, 65–94 (1974)
7. Russell, R., Igo, W.: An assignment routing problem. Networks **9**, 1–17 (1979)
8. Christofides, N., Beasley, J.E.: The period routing problem. Networks **14**, 237–256 (1984)
9. Tan, C.C.R., Beasley, J.E.: A heuristic algorithm for the period vehicle routing problem. Omega **12**, 497–504 (1984)
10. Fisher, M.L., Jaikumar, R.: A generalized assignment heuristic for vehicle routing. Networks **11**, 109–124 (1981)
11. Drummond, L.M.A., Ochi, L.S., Vianna, D.S.: An asynchronous parallel metaheuristic for the period vehicle routing problem. Future Gener. Comput. Syst. **17**, 379–386 (2001)

12. Mourgaya, M., Vanderbeck, F.: Column generation based heuristic for tactical planning in multi-period vehicle routing. Eur. J. Oper. Res. **183**, 1028–1041 (2007)
13. Cordeau, J.-F., Gendreau, M., Laporte, G.: A tabu search heuristic for periodic and multi-depot vehicle routing problems. Networks **30**, 105–119 (1997)
14. Hadjiconstantinou, E., Baldacci, R.: A multi-depot period vehicle routing problem arising in the utilities sector. J. Oper. Res. Soc. **49**, 1239 (1998)
15. Cordeau, J.-F., Laporte, G., Mercier, A.: A unified tabu search heuristic for vehicle routing problems with time windows. J. Oper. Res. Soc. **52**, 928–936 (2001)
16. Francis, P., Smilowitz, K., Tzur, M.: The period vehicle routing problem with service choice. Transp. Sci. **40**, 439–454 (2006)
17. Rodriguez, S., Correa, D., López-Santana, E.: An alternative iterative method to periodic vehicle routing problem. In: Cetinkaya, S., Ryan, J.K. (eds.) IIE Annual Conference and Expo 2015, pp. 2001–2010 (2015)
18. López-Santana, E.R., Romero Carvajal, J.: A hybrid column generation and clustering approach to the school bus routing problem with time windows. Ingeniería **20**, 111–127 (2015)
19. Patiño Chirva, J.A., Daza Cruz, Y.X., López-Santana, E.R.: A hybrid mixed-integer optimization and clustering approach to selective collection services problem of domestic solid waste. Ingeniería **21**, 235–247 (2016)

Study of Some Complex Systems by Using Numerical Methods

Dan Alexandru Iordache[1,2] and Paul Enache Sterian[1,2(✉)] (iD)

[1] Faculty of Applied Sciences, Physics Department, University "Politehnica" of Bucharest, 313 Splaiul Independentei, 060042 Bucharest, Romania
paulesterian@yahoo.com
[2] Academy of Romanian Scientists, Splaiul Independentei No. 54, 050094 Bucharest, Romania

Abstract. The study deals with the complex systems in Nature by using of some specific numerical methods. First the method of the physical similarity is used for the characterization of the fluids flow regimes. Then, the method of the power laws and some of its multiple uses in Physics and another related fields are analyzed. The method of phenomenological universality, applied to the description of the growth processes is also discussed. The authors results presented in the paper were mainly obtained by computer simulations using the finite difference (FD) method and the classical gradient method (CGM).

Keywords: Complex system · Method of similarity · Power law
Universality · Finite difference method · Gradient method

1 Introduction

As it is well known, the results of the experimental measurements are expressed by numbers but the obtainment of these numerical results and their organization in theoretical models is usually difficult in the case of the complex systems. That is why for the study of complex systems there are searched the efficient specific numerical methods. Given being the studied complex systems have often a physical nature, it is necessary to have a "bridge" towards the mathematical parameters (e.g. numbers, particularly) in order to ensure the use of the mathematical methods. Such a "bridge" is provided by the mathematical method of the physical similarity.

Consider a certain description of a physical state (or process) of a complex system, by means of n_U uniqueness parameters: $U_1, U_2, \ldots U_{n_U}$. If the physical dimension of a parameter (quantity) P specific to the studied state (or process) Σ is:

$$[P] = \prod_{i=1}^{n_U} [U_i]^{n_i},$$ (1)

then 2 states (processes) Σ' and Σ'' are named similar, if the values of the parameters (quantities) $\{U_i | i = 1, n\}$ and P corresponding to these states fulfill the condition [1, 6]:

© Springer International Publishing AG, part of Springer Nature 2018
O. Gervasi et al. (Eds.): ICCSA 2018, LNCS 10961, pp. 539–559, 2018.
https://doi.org/10.1007/978-3-319-95165-2_38

$$\frac{P'}{P''} = \prod_{i=1}^{n_U} \left(\frac{U_i'}{U_i''}\right)^{n_i}. \tag{2}$$

Some of the uniqueness parameters, could be called numbers (criteria) of similarity, if they are non-dimensional: $[s] = 1$, with equal values: $s' = s''$ in all similar states (or processes).

According to the first (Newton's) theorem of the mathematical theory (method) of the physical similarity, for any state or process of a physical system there are some specific similarity numbers (or criteria). E.g., it is very easy to check that the parameter:

$$s = \frac{P}{\prod_{i=1}^{n_U} U_i^{\alpha_i}} \tag{3}$$

is a similarity number (criterion) of the physical states (or processes) described by the relation (2).

The Buckingham's Π theorem of the similarity theory states that: "the number n_{is} of irreducible similarity numbers (criteria) corresponding to a state (or process) of a complex system is equal to the difference between the number n_U of its independent uniqueness parameters and the number n_a of the active fundamental (physical) quantities (e.g. $n_a = 2$ in kinematics, $n_a = 3$ in dynamics, etc.):

$$n_{is} = n_U - n_a. \tag{4}$$

In following, the 2nd (Federman's) theorem of the similarity theory states that: "any physical law of relation, can be expressed by means of some similarity numbers and only by means of some similarity numbers, exclusively".

Finally, the 3rd (Kirpichev-Gukhman's) theorem of the similarity theory states that: "if for two physical states (processes) Σ', Σ'', all the values of the irreducible similarity numbers (criteria) are equal:

$$s_1' = s_1'', \quad s_2' = s_2'', \quad \dots \quad s_{n_{is}}' = s_{n_{is}}'' \tag{5}$$

then the 2 considered states (or processes) are similar".

2 Fluids Flow Regimes by Physical Similarity

In following: (a) taking into account the resistant forces (e.g., those due to the fluid viscosity η) intervening in the fluid flows, which lead to turbulence (i.e. to the completely disordered displacements of the fluid micro-particles) and energy dissipation, and: (b) using the symbols $\tilde{f}$ and $\langle f \cdot g \rangle$ for the statistical averages of the parameter f, and of the product of parameters f and g, respectively, as well as the symbol $\delta f = f(\bar{r}, t) - \tilde{f}(\bar{r}, t)$ for the fluctuation of the parameter f, one finds [2–5, 75] that the system of flow equations in presence of strong fluctuations involve the following very intricate equations: *the flow equations; the continuity equation* and *the enthalpy correlation equation.*

Besides the similarity numbers (criteria) of Reynolds: (a, b) $\mathrm{Re} = \frac{\rho \cdot d \cdot v}{\eta} = \frac{4\dot{M}}{\eta \cdot P}$ (where P and $\dot{M}$ are the "wetted" parameter and the average mass flow rate) and Mach: $M = \frac{v}{c}$, there are frequently used the similarity numbers [5–7]: (c) the relative roughness $\frac{h}{d}$ (where h is the characteristic height of a roughness element), (d) the thermal conductivity λ, (e) the roughness Reynolds number:

$$\mathrm{Re}^+ = \frac{\rho \cdot h \cdot v_\tau}{\eta} = \frac{10\pi}{\sqrt{8}} \cdot \frac{h}{d} \tag{6}$$

(where $v_\tau = \sqrt{\frac{\tau}{\rho}}$ is the shear velocity, τ being the wall shear stress),

(f) the thickness of the boundary later:

$$\delta = \frac{10\pi \cdot d}{\mathrm{Re}\sqrt{f}}, \tag{7}$$

(g) the Darcy friction factor:

$$f = \frac{2d}{\rho \cdot \bar{v}^2} \cdot \frac{dp}{dl}, \tag{8}$$

where $\frac{dp}{dl}$ is the linear density of the pressure drop on the considered pipe, (h) the diffusion D coefficient,

(i) the Newton's coefficient of the convective heat transfer:

$$\alpha = \frac{J_W}{T_w - T_b} = \frac{J_W \cdot c_p}{i_w - i_b}, \tag{9}$$

where T_w, T_b, i_w, i_b are the values at the pipe wall surface and in the pipe bulk, of the thermodynamic temperature and mass density of the fluid enthalpy, respectively, j, (k) the Prandtl and the Nusselt numbers, respectively:

$$\mathrm{Pr} = \frac{v}{D} = \frac{c_p \cdot \eta}{\lambda}, Nu = \frac{\alpha \cdot L}{\lambda}. \tag{10}$$

3   Classical Similarity Models of Growth Processes

In the limits of certain accuracy, the growth processes can have a: (i) continuous, (ii) with frequent second type (fractal) discontinuous character, respectively. We can find some very good descriptions of the fractal growth processes in the frame of the works [8–10]. For this reason, our study will focus mainly on the principals models used for the description of the continuous (without too frequent discontinuities) growth processes.

Starting from the differential equation of the growth (accommodation) of an arbitrary physical parameter $Y(t)$:

$$\frac{dY}{dt} = \pi(t) \cdot Y(t), \text{ where: } [\pi(t)] = \frac{1}{T}, \tag{11}$$

hence $\pi(t)$ is the time density of the growth (accommodation) probability and introducing the similarity functional criteria:

$$\tau = \pi(0) \cdot t, \quad y(t) = \frac{Y(t)}{Y(0)} \quad \text{and: } p(t) = \frac{\pi(t)}{\pi(0)}, \tag{12}$$

one obtains *the similarity growth equation*:

$$\frac{dy}{d\tau} = p(\tau) \cdot y(\tau). \tag{13}$$

(a) *The particular case of the auto-catalytic growth processes (Universality class U0)*

If: $\pi(\tau) = const. = \frac{1}{\tau_{ac}}$, where τ_{ac} is the time constant of the auto-catalytic growth, one obtains *the auto-catalytic growth equation*:

$$Y(\tau) = \exp\left(\frac{\tau}{\tau_{ac}}\right). \tag{14}$$

(b) *Second particular case: the Gompertz's model [11–15] (Universality class U1)*

The Gompertz's model was proposed in 1825. In order to understand easier the basic hypotheses of this model, we will consider the optical pumping (with the probability time density $p_{de} = B_{ed}w_v$, where B_{ed} if the Einstein's coefficient for stimulated transitions, and w_v is the double bulk (volumetric) and spectral density of the energy of the optical pumping radiation) between 2 energy levels e (excited) and d (unexcited).

According to the hypotheses of the Einstein's semi-classical theory [16, 77–81], the increase of the population of the excited level in duration (time) dt is given by the expression:

$$dN_e(dt) = (N_u - N_e) \cdot p_{ue} \cdot dt, \tag{15}$$

hence:

$$\frac{d(N_e - N_u)}{N_u - N_e} = 2p_{ue} \cdot dt \quad \text{and: } N_u - N_e = \Delta N(0) \cdot e^{-\lambda \cdot t}. \tag{16}$$

It results that:

$$\frac{dN_e}{N_e} = \left(\frac{N_u - N_e}{N_e}\right) \cdot p_{ue} \cdot dt \cong R(0) \cdot e^{-\wp \cdot t} \cdot dt, \tag{17}$$

that can be written by means of the similitude expression (13), with:

$$p(t) \equiv a(t) = e^{-\tau}, \text{ hence } \Phi(p) \equiv \Phi(a) = -\frac{da}{d\tau} = a. \tag{18}$$

Integrating the Eq. (13) with the probability time density (18), one obtains:

$$\ln y = -\exp(-\tau) + C, \text{ hence: } y = \exp[C - \exp(-\tau)]; \tag{19}$$

from the condition: $y(0) = 1$, one finds the similitude expression of the growth equation, according to Gompertz's model:

$$y = \exp[1 - \exp(-\tau)]. \tag{20}$$

The Gompertz's model is valid for the description of some tumors growth processes [17–21, 72], as well as for those of some economical phenomena, of the population dynamics [22], etc.

(c) *The 3rd particular case: the Brown-West-Delsanto model (Universality class U2)*

The similarity expression of the Brown-West-Delsanto growths [23–26]:

$$y = [1 + b - b \cdot \exp(-\tau)]^{1/b} \tag{21}$$

leads to the similitude expression of the Gompertz's growth for $b \to 0$. Obviously, the growth rate is given in this case by the nonlinear expression:

$$\frac{dy}{d\tau} = \frac{1+b}{b} \cdot y^{1-b} - \frac{1}{b} \cdot y. \tag{22}$$

From Eq. (22) results the similarity plots of the growths of Brown-West-Delsanto's type for different values of the parameter b, the value $b = 0$ corresponding to the Gompertzian growths, while the value $b = +0.25$ corresponds to the original Brown-West's model [23–25, 74].

We consider as useful to point out that the West-Delsanto model:

(i) describes the growth processes of the living beings, in the range protozoa – plants – mammals, by means of the similarity equation:

$$m(\tau) = [M^b - b \cdot \exp(-\tau)]^{1/b}, \text{ where: } M = \lim_{\tau \to \infty} m(\tau) = (1+b)^{1/b}, \tag{23}$$

defining *the development remainder (rest)* by means of the expression:

$$z = 1 - \left(\frac{m}{M}\right)^{b}, \tag{24}$$

one finds that:

$$z = \exp(-\theta), \text{ where: } \theta = \tau + \ln b - b \cdot \ln M. \tag{25}$$

is the so-called *biological time*;

(ii) can be used for the tumors growth description, with values of the parameter p depending on the fractal nature of the biological channels (e.g. in angio-genesis) [19–21, 27].

(d) *The 4th particular case: the Delsanto's model* [19, 27] *(Universality class U3)*

Starting from the generalization of the similitude rate of the growth of the probability density:

$$\Phi(a) = a(1 + b \cdot a + c \cdot a^{2}), \tag{26}$$

one obtains:

$$-\ln y + K = \int \frac{da}{\Phi(a)} = \int \frac{da}{1 + b \cdot a + c \cdot a^{2}}. \tag{27}$$

It results the following expression of the growth rate:

$$\frac{dy}{d\tau} = \frac{d-c}{2c} \cdot y - \frac{K(d+c)}{2c} \cdot y^{p} + \frac{K}{1-d} \cdot \frac{dy^{p}}{d\tau}, \tag{28}$$

where:

$$d = \sqrt{b^{2} - 4ac} \text{ and: } K = \frac{d+b-2c}{d+b+2c}. \tag{29}$$

One finds that – the Delsanto's model involve an additional parameter (c) relative to the previous (Brown-West-Delsanto) model – the model expressed by the Eqs. (28), (29) presents important advantages for the detailed description of some particular features of the growth processes [28–36, 73].

4 Power Laws and Fractal Scaling

According to the Kenneth Wilson definition [35]: "Are complex the states of a system inside whom are concomitantly active strong *fluctuations* at several organization levels". The fluctuations are described by the volume (in the phases space) density of probability $\wp$ and this finding points out the prevalent role of *the Statistical Physics* for the complex systems. The same Kenneth Wilson's works point out also the prevalent role of the *Phase transitions*.

The same finding was obtained by Ettore Majorana by means of his study [36, 37], pointing out the validity also in social sciences of the laws of Statistical Physics. It results that the Complexity of some systems of different natures (physical, biological, social, economic, etc.) is strongly related to the Universality of their laws. Or, the unique possibility for an identical formal description of the complex systems of completely different natures is to use only *numbers* (remember also the "line" Pythagoras, and in following Archimede's and Newton's results in the frame of the physical similarity theory, etc.).

How could be possible to describe dimensional (physical, particularly) quantities only by numbers? Taking into account also the predictions of Philip Warren Anderson relative to the "explosive" auto-catalytic (exponential) growth following the spontaneous symmetry breaking inside the specific complex systems, one finds that a certain dimensional parameter p has to be described by its logarithm: $\ln p$. This finding is also supported by the Dalton's law of "defined proportions", intervening in the theory of chemical reactions (somewhat similar to the phase transforms) [38]:

$$d\xi = -\frac{dv_1}{v_1} = -\frac{dv_2}{v_2} = \ldots = +\frac{dv_N}{v_N} \tag{30}$$

where the sign "−" corresponds to substances that disappear during the considered chemical reaction, while the sign "+" corresponds to the appearing substances. One finds that the degree of advance ξ of the considered reaction can be expressed by means of $\ln v_j$, where v_j corresponds to the amount (e.g. number of moles) of one of the substances participating to the chemical reaction. It is obvious that the Dalton's relations lead also to the representation of some phase transforms (chemical reactions) by means of the typical numerical representation $\ln v_j$.

Ilya Prigogine pointed out [38], the crucial role of the energy dissipation processes for the complex systems evolutions. Or, these dissipation processes are characterized [35, 39] by the body (volume) density of the thermodynamic entropy S. Taking into account also the above findings referring to the prevalent role of: (a) statistical considerations and their associated probability density $\wp$, (b) numbers, in the description of complex systems, it is not at all surprising that the thermodynamic entropy is given by the (Planck-Boltzmann's) expression:

$$S = -k \cdot \ln \wp, \tag{31}$$

where k is a constant (the Boltzmann's one). Such an expression corresponds also (according to the Claude Shannon's information theory [39]) to the information quantity:

$$\Im = -a \cdot \ln \wp \ (a = constant), \tag{32}$$

finding that points out already the *strong connection between Complexity and Information*.

Consider now a pair of parameters p, q and their numerical correspondents $\ln p$, $\ln q$. Because the basic co-relations between different parameters are the linear ones, it results that in frame of the descriptions of complex systems, the typical relations will have the expression:

$$\ln p = \ln p_1 + s \cdot \ln q, \; i.e.: p = p_1 \cdot q^s. \tag{33}$$

One finds so that the typical relations between the parameters of the complex systems are given by some *power laws*, with irrational values of the exponent s, generally. This result was confirmed by the discovery (1897) of Vilfredo Pareto's power law [40, 41], describing the distribution of the individual wealth (Fig. 1).

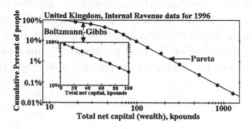

Fig. 1. Cumulative probability distribution of total net capital (wealth) shown in log-log, log-linear (inset) coordinates

Points: the actual data, solid lines: fits to the Boltzmann-Gibbs power law:

$$p(E) = C \cdot \exp\left(-\frac{E}{kT}\right) \quad \text{and} \quad \text{Pareto's } p(m) = A \cdot m^{-n} \tag{34}$$

We have to underline that many power laws of Physics correspond to some *phase transitions*. E.g. the Domb-Fisher (power law) relation [42]:

$$\frac{1}{\chi} = b(T - T_H)^n, \tag{35}$$

describing the temperature dependence of the magnetic susceptibility in the region between the Hopkinson's and Curie's temperatures, corresponds to the transition between the ferromagnetic and the paramagnetic phases [42, 43]

As examples of other power laws in Physics, we will mention:

(a) the dependence (for complex materials) of the nonlinear magnetization permeability [43, 44] on the magnetic field strength:

$$(a) \quad B - \mu_i H = a \cdot H^n, \quad \text{and: } \mu(H) - \mu_i = a \cdot H^{n-1}, \tag{36}$$

where n is a non-integer number, with values between 1 and 2,

(b) the frequency power law describing the dependence of the quality factor corresponding to the seismic waves propagation through different rocks on these waves frequency [45]:

$$Q = a \cdot \omega^\gamma, \tag{37}$$

(c) the similar frequency power law describing the dependence of the viscous coefficient of the oscillations of the magnetization domains walls of some complex magnetic materials on the magnetic field frequency [46]:

$$r = r_1 \cdot f^n. \tag{38}$$

These findings are valid not only in Physics and Social/Economic sciences, but also for various complex systems of different natures, e.g., for biologic systems. Consider as an example, the correlation between the (acoustic, light, etc.) sensation S and the stimulus intensity (excitation) I of a human being. Using at beginning the specific (logarithmic) complex description for the stimulus intensity, one obtains (without any other considerations) the Weber-Fechner law [46]:

$$S = k \cdot \log_{10} \frac{I}{I_o} \tag{39}$$

(k and I_o are specific constants), while using such logarithmic descriptions for both parameters [sensation S and stimulus (excitation) intensity I], one obtains *the Stevens' law* of Psychophysics [46, 47]:

$$S = S_1 \cdot I^n. \tag{40}$$

If q is the length of a specific size (length, width, height) of the considered system, then the power laws particularize in *fractal scaling*. A detailed mathematical study (Kolmogorov [7], Mandelbrot [48, 49]) of the geometry of complex systems described by fractal scaling pointed out the presence of some self-similarity properties of these systems geometry (structure), named *fractal structure*, while the corresponding systems themselves were called *fractals*.

5 Computer Simulations of Some Physical Processes

The frequent use of numerical simulations in different scientific and technical problems has 2 main causes: (a) the numerical simulations are considerably *cheaper* than the experimental determinations, (b) they can be used even in *inaccessible experimental conditions*.

Numerical simulations are implemented on computers, but *the computer errors* generate *numerical phenomena*, which can generate misleading results [50, 80–83].

5.1   The Finite Differences Method

While - for ideal media and some continuously variable inhomogeneous media – the differential equations for different physical processes [pulse (wave) propagation, in particular] have some analytical solutions, the presence of certain particular features (such as defects or of some arbitrary non-homogeneity) eliminates any possibility to obtain an analytical solution in the general case. Completely numerical procedures are often needed to solve problems without analytical solutions, or to test approximate solutions.

In order to identify - e.g. by means of ultrasounds - the location of some flaws inside a certain studied rather thick material piece, this piece can be divided in a very large number (of the magnitude order of millions, or even more) of very thin layers, of width ε. The Finite Differences (FD) method (Courant [50], Hildebrand [51]) starts from the Mc Laurin's series expansions of the functions depending on a unique variable (the coordinate along the perpendicular on the layers surfaces):

$$f(\varepsilon) = f(0) + \frac{f'(0)}{1!}\varepsilon + \frac{f''(0)}{2!}\varepsilon^2 + \frac{f'''(0)}{3!}\varepsilon^3 + \frac{f^{iv}}{4!}\varepsilon^4 + \ldots \qquad (41)$$

and:

$$f(-\varepsilon) = f(0) - \frac{f'(0)}{1!}\varepsilon + \frac{f''(0)}{2!}\varepsilon^2 - \frac{f'''(0)}{3!}\varepsilon^3 + \frac{f^{iv}(0)}{4!}\varepsilon^4 + \ldots \qquad (42)$$

It follows that - in the second order approximation (for a centered FD scheme with 2 initial time/space steps):

$$f'(0) = \frac{f(\varepsilon) - f(-\varepsilon)}{2\varepsilon} - \frac{1}{3!}f'''(0) \cdot \varepsilon^2 , \qquad (43)$$

and:

$$f''(0) = \frac{f(\varepsilon) - 2f(0) + f(\varepsilon)}{\varepsilon^2} - 2\frac{f^{iv}(0)}{4!}\varepsilon^2, \qquad (44)$$

while – *for a centered FD discretization scheme with 4 initial time/space steps*:

$$f'(0) = \frac{-f(2\varepsilon) + 8f(\varepsilon) - 8f(-\varepsilon) + f(-2\varepsilon)}{12\varepsilon}, \qquad (45)$$

and:

$$f''(0) = \frac{-f(2\varepsilon) + 16f(\varepsilon) - 30f(0) + 16f(-\varepsilon) - f(-2\varepsilon)}{12\varepsilon^2} \qquad (46)$$

In following, the time and space are discretized by means of finite difference (FD) elementary units (steps) τ ($\equiv\delta$) and ε, respectively, so that:

$$\tilde{t} = t \cdot \tau \quad and: \quad x = i \cdot \varepsilon, \; respectively. \tag{47}$$

By substituting the FD expressions (6.3) in the pulse (wave) equation:

$$\frac{\partial^2 w}{\partial x^2} = \frac{1}{v_\Phi^2} \cdot \frac{\partial^2 w}{\partial \tilde{t}^2} \tag{48}$$

one finds that – in the first approximation: $\dfrac{w_{i+1,t}-2w_{i,t}+w_{i-1,t}}{\varepsilon^2} = \dfrac{1}{v_\Phi^2} \cdot \dfrac{w_{i,t+1}-2w_{i,t}+w_{i,t-1}}{\delta^2}$,

therefore: $\quad w_{i,t+1} = c(w_{i+1,t}+w_{i-1,t}) + 2(1-c)w_{i,t} - w_{i,t-1} \tag{49}$

$$where: \; c = \left(\frac{v_\Phi}{v_{FD}}\right)^2 = C^2 \tag{50}$$

while $w_{i,t}$ is the wave displacement corresponding to the FD node i at time t, $v_{FD} = \varepsilon/\tau$ is the FD speed, and $C = v_\Phi/v_{FD}$ is the so-called Courant's (similarity) number.

In fact, the interaction - which corresponds to the pulse evolution (along the Ox axis) described by the second order differential equation - propagates with velocities $v_x = \pm v_\Phi$, hence the representative points associated with the pairs of space-time coordinates of the FD nodes which determine the pulse (oscillation) state in the node of coordinate x_I, at time t_{T+1} are located inside or on the sides of the triangle determined by the straight-lines of equations:

$$x = x_I + v_\Phi(\tilde{t} - \tilde{t}_{T+1}), \quad x = x_I - v_\Phi(\tilde{t} - \tilde{t}_{T+1}). \tag{51}$$

This triangle is called the cone (triangle) of the interaction propagation.

Taking into account that: $x = i\varepsilon$, $\; x_I = I \cdot \varepsilon$, $\tilde{t} = t \cdot \delta$ and : $\tilde{t}_{T+1} = (T+1)\delta$, the following FD expressions of the equations of straight-lines, which delineate the triangle of the interaction propagation, are obtained:

$$i = I \pm C(t - T - 1). \tag{52}$$

Let α and β be the segments between the intersections of the interaction straight-lines (52) with the lines $t = 0$ and: $t = 1$, respectively (see Fig. 2). Of course, the correct solution of the partial differential equation requires the knowledge of all initial data between the segments α and β from the internal part of the triangle (cone) of the interaction propagation.

If the Courant's number $C > 1$, the triangle of the interaction propagation includes the zigzag pentagonal line of the determination by means of the finite differences (FD) method (see Fig. 16). An important consequence follows: if in the case $C > 1$ one tends with $\tau \to 0$, then the solution of the FD equation *cannot converge* towards the solution of the differential equation.

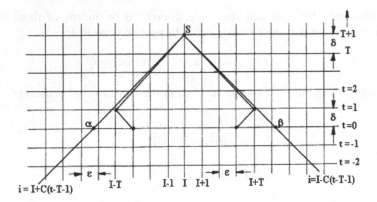

Fig. 2. Plot of the triangle (cone) of the interaction propagation

In this case, a modification of the initial values (required for the solution of the differential equation) in proximity of the marginal segments α and β (of the domain of interactions propagation) produces a change of itself this solution from node S(I, T+1). This last change is not presented also by the solution of the FD equation, equation. One finds that so that the Courant's triangle (cone) of the interaction propagation leads to the main types of FD numerical phenomena:

(a) *the accumulation of the errors of the finite differences (FD) equation for very large values of the number of FD "steps" will lead to the instability of the solution of the FD equation in the case $C > 1$.*

(b) Conversely, if $C < 1$ the zigzag pentagonal line of the determination by means of the finite differences (FD) method will involve also the triangle of the interactions propagation. In this case, *the solution of the finite differences (FD) equation: (i) takes in consideration all necessary initial data (which ensures its convergence towards the solution of the partial differential equation* [51]*), but: (ii) it involves also some pseudo-initial additional data (which are not necessary), fact which leads to some distortions of the FD solutions relative to the exact solutions of the partial differential equation, leading to the FD numerical phenomenon of pseudo-convergence.*

For the identification of flaws in industrial materials and of some additional numerical phenomena see also the LISA (Local Interaction Simulation Approach) method and the work [52–54].

Description of the Main FD Models Used to Smooth Sharp 1D-Interfaces
As it was pointed out before, one of the main causes of the impossibility to integrate the partial differential equations consists in the arbitrary non-homogeneity of the studied material, namely to the presence of some sharp interfaces inside. One finds that the main smoothing models of sharp 1D-interfaces differ upon: (i) the number and the positions of the transition FD nodes over which the sharp 1D-interface is spread, (ii) the

manner of deriving the mean values $\tilde{\rho}_i \equiv \langle\rho\rangle_i$, $\tilde{S}_i \equiv \langle S\rangle_i$ and: $\langle\frac{\partial S}{\partial x}\rangle_i$ of the densities and stiffness, required to use the FD discretized wave equation:

$$\tilde{\rho}_i\frac{w_{t+1}+w_{t-1}-2w}{\tau^2} = \left\langle\frac{\partial S}{\partial x}\right\rangle_i \cdot \frac{w_{i+1}-w_{i-1}}{2\varepsilon} + \tilde{S}_i\frac{w_{i+1}+w_{i-1}-2w}{\varepsilon^2}. \tag{53}$$

According to the number of transition nodes, we have models of the first (only one transition node), second or third type (2 or 3 transition nodes, respectively, see Fig. 3, models 1, 2 and 3). Similarly, while for models 1, 2b and 3a, the mean values are calculated starting from the values of the considered parameters (ρ, S) in the adjacent media, for models 2a (both $\tilde{\rho}_i$ and $\tilde{S}_i$) and 3b (only $\tilde{S}_i$) the same mean values are calculated starting from the averages of these parameters in the adjacent FD intervals (see Table 1, where the expressions of these averages are explicitly indicated).

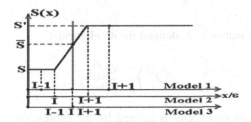

Fig. 3. Main FD smoothing models of sharp interfaces

Table 1. Definitions of the main FD smoothing models of sharp interfaces [50]

Para-meters	$\tilde{\rho}_i$			$\tilde{S}_i$			$\langle\frac{\partial S}{\partial x}\rangle_{I-1}$	$\langle\frac{\partial S}{\partial x}\rangle_I$	$\langle\frac{\partial S}{\partial x}\rangle_{I+1}$
i = MODEL	I − 1	I	I + 1	I − 1	I	I + 1			
1	ρ	$\frac{\rho+\rho'}{2}$	ρ'	S	$\frac{S+S'}{2}$	S'	0	$\frac{S'-S}{\varepsilon}$	0
2a	ρ	$\frac{\rho+\tilde{\rho}_{I,I+1}}{2}=\frac{3\rho+\rho'}{4}$	$\frac{\rho'+\tilde{\rho}_{I,I+1}}{2}=\frac{3\rho'+\rho}{4}$	S	$\frac{3S+S'}{4}$	$\frac{S'+\tilde{S}_{I,I+1}}{2}=\frac{3S'+S}{4}$	0	$\frac{S'-S}{2\varepsilon}$	$\frac{S'-S}{2\varepsilon}$
2b	ρ	ρ	ρ'	S	S	S'	0	$\frac{S'-S}{2\varepsilon}$	$\frac{S'-S}{2\varepsilon}$
3a	ρ	$\frac{\rho+\rho'}{2}$	ρ'	S	$\frac{S+S'}{2}$	S'	$\frac{S'-S}{4\varepsilon}$	$\frac{S'-S}{2\varepsilon}$	$\frac{S'-S}{4\varepsilon}$
3b	ρ	$\frac{\rho+\rho'}{2}$	ρ'	$\frac{S+\tilde{S}_{I-1,I}}{2}=\frac{7S+S'}{8}$	$\frac{S+S'}{2}$	$\frac{S'+\tilde{S}_{I,I+1}}{2}=\frac{7S'+S}{8}$	$\frac{S'-S}{4\varepsilon}$	$\frac{S'-S}{2\varepsilon}$	$\frac{S'-S}{4\varepsilon}$

5.2 The Classical Gradient Method

As it is known, the classical gradient method (Levenberg [55], Marquardt [56], Mei and Morris [57]) aims to find the values of the effective uniqueness parameters (described by the column-vector $\bar{u}$), by means of the minimization of the sum S of weighted squares of the deviations of the calculated values $\bar{t}_{calc}(\bar{u}, \bar{s})$ relative to the corresponding experimental values $\bar{t}_{exp}$:

$$S = \sum_{i=1}^{N} W_i(t_{calc.i} - t_{exp.i})^2 = (\bar{t}_{calc.} - \bar{t}_{exp.})^T \cdot \bar{\bar{W}}\cdot(\bar{t}_{calc.} - \bar{t}_{exp.}), \tag{54}$$

where $(\bar{t}_{calc.} - \bar{t}_{exp.})^T$ is the transposed of the difference of the column-vectors $\bar{t}_{calc.}$, $\bar{t}_{exp.}$, $\bar{\bar{W}}$ is the diagonal matrix of weights, and $\bar{s}$ is the vector of the state (or process) parameters.

The vector $\bar{C}^{(I)}$ of the corrections of the vector $\bar{u}$ of the uniqueness parameters in a certain successive approximation (iteration) I is obtained by means of the minimization condition of the sum S (exact if the functions $\bar{t}_{calc}(\bar{u}, \bar{p})$ would be linear):

$$\left[\frac{\partial(S^{(I)} + \delta S)}{\partial(\delta \bar{u})}\right]_{\delta \bar{u} = \bar{C}^{(I)}} = 0, \tag{55}$$

obtaining the expression (see e.g. [59]):

$$.\bar{C}^{(I)} = -\left(\bar{\bar{J}}^{(I)^T} \cdot \bar{\bar{W}} \cdot \bar{\bar{J}}^{(I)}\right)^{-1} \bar{\bar{J}}^{(I)^T} \cdot \bar{\bar{W}} \cdot \bar{D}^{(I)}, \tag{56}$$

where the Jacobean matrix $\bar{\bar{J}}^I$ is defined by its elements:

$$\left(\bar{\bar{J}}^{(I)}\right)_{ij} = \frac{\partial t_{calc.}^{(I)}}{\partial u_j}, \tag{57}$$

and the deviation (column) vector is defined by the expression:

$$\bar{D}^{(I)} = \bar{t}_{calc.}^{(I)} - \bar{t}_{exp}, \tag{58}$$

where $\bar{t}_{calc.}^{(I)}$ is the column-vector of the calculated values of the test parameters in the iteration I.

An important feature of the gradient method efficiency is the so-called relative standard deviation, defined starting from the weighted sum of the deviations,

$$\sigma(I) = \sqrt{\frac{S^{(I)}}{N}} = \sqrt{\frac{1}{N} \sum_{i=1}^{N} \left(t_{calc.i}^{(I)} - t_{exp.i}\right)^2} \tag{59}$$

where N is the number of the studied (independent) test parameters.

In the frame of the works [58–60], we studied the basic numerical phenomena met in the evaluation of the physical parameters of the charge-coupled devices (CCDs) (see [61, 62]) by means of the classical gradient method.

The accomplished studies [63, 64] pointed out the compatibility - with the existing experimental data for CCDs of the Hall [64], Shockley and Read [65] quantum theoretical model:

$$De^-(T) = De_{diff}^-(T) + De_{dep}^-(T)$$

$$= T^3 \exp\left(\ln De_{0,diff}^- - \frac{E_{g,eff.}}{kT}\right) + T^{3/2} \cdot \exp\left(\ln De_{0,dep}^- - \frac{E_{g,eff.}}{2kT}\right)$$

$$\cdot \ \text{sech}\left[\frac{E_t - E_i}{kT} + d\right]. \tag{60}$$

It was found also the following monotonic decreasing order of the 5 identified "effective" uniqueness parameters in respect with their relative strength on the dark current values: the energy gap E_g (the strongest), the natural logarithms of the diffusion $\ln D_{0,diff}^- \equiv \ln Diff$ and depletion $\ln D_{0,dep}^- \equiv \ln Dep$ pre-exponential factors of the dark current (in this order), the difference $|E_t - E_i|$ of the energies corresponding to the embedded traps and to the intrinsic Fermi level, and the polarization degree $d \equiv pdg$ (of weakest strength):

$$d \equiv pdg_n = \arg \tanh \frac{\sigma_n - \sigma_p}{\sigma_n + \sigma_p} \quad \left[= \frac{1}{2} \ln\left(\frac{\sigma_n}{\sigma_p}\right)\right], \tag{61}$$

of the capture cross-sections of electrons (σ_n) and holes (σ_p), respectively [66].

In order to start effectively the gradient method, some zero-order approximations are first of all necessary. Taking into account that: (a) the effective energy gap $E_{g,\ eff.}$ is the strongest uniqueness parameter intervening in the description of the temperature dependence of CCDs dark current [see e.g. (60)], (b) the best zero-order approximation of this parameter is the average value:

$$E_{g,Ave} = \frac{E_{go,Sze} + E_{g,Lin}}{2}, \tag{62}$$

of the Sze's [67] general estimation $E_{g,Sze}$ for silicon (1.17 eV) and of the modulus $E_{g,\ Lin}$ [the so-called linear approximation $E_{g,\ Lin}$ (specific to each pixel)] of the slope of the line joining the points corresponding to the extreme temperatures (222 and 291 K, for the experimental data [68, 69]) of the plot $\ln De^-(T) = f\left(\frac{1}{kT}\right)$, we will define the required successive neighbor zero-order approximations of the gap energy by means of the integer $m = \{-10, -8, -6, -4, -2, 0, 2, 4, 6, 8, 10\}$ and of the relation:

$$E_g^{(0)}(m) = E_{g,Ave} + \frac{m}{10}(E_{g,Sze} - E_{g,Ave}). \tag{63}$$

The convergence of the successive iterations of the gradient method towards the "true" values of the uniqueness parameters starting from different zero-order approximations was studied in the frame of the work [66, 68, 70], the obtained results being presented by Table 2.

The obtained numerical data synthesized by Table 2 point out a new numerical phenomenon: that of attractors, corresponding to the convergence of the first n figures of the main uniqueness parameters for some pixels. The properties of the attractors met in the frame of the applications of the classical gradient method were studied in detail by work [60].

Table 2. The values of the uniqueness parameters E_g, ln$Diff$, lnDep and $|E_t - E_{i\theta}|$ by means of the classical gradient method (for the experimental data see [68, 69])

Coordinates of the pixel	E_g Zero-order approximation m	$E_{g,eff}$ (eV)	ln$Diff$	lnDep	$|E_t - E_i|$, meV	Numerical phenomenon & Attractor
	-10	0.580869*	9.402933*	39.026176*	381.94396*	Pseudo-convergence
	-8	0.564653*	8.573753*	40.444841*	414.60294*	
	-6	1.072556	31.079047	17.52459	28.92168	
61, 140	-4	1.072556	31.079047	17.52459	28.92168	
	-2	1.072556	31.079047	17.52459	28.92168	Very strong attractor
	0	1.072556	31.079047	17.52459	28.92168	
	2	1.072556	31.079047	17.52459	28.92168	
	4	1.072556	31.079047	17.52459	28.92168	
	6; 8 & 10	Instability starting from iteration 4 (m = 6) and 2 (m = 8 and 10), respectively					
	-10	1.067221	30.865956	15.540974	13.31129	
	-8	1.067238	30.866604	15.567840	12.93887	
	-6	1.067272	30.867992	15.659601	13.543185	Weak attractor;
	-4	1.067263	30.867633	15.630247	13.350595	additionally,
121, 200	-2	1.067251	30.867136	15.596534	13.128485	medium
	0	1.067257	30.867372	15.611681	13.22839	amplitude
	2	1.067259	30.867458	15.617526	13.2669	oscillations
	4; 6; 8; 10	Instability starting from iteration 4 (m = 4) and 2 (m = 6; 8 and 10), respectively					
	-10	1.074871	31.172302	15.917362	11.094875	
	-8	1.075900	31.212400	16.033195	9.955040	
	-6	1.075840	31.210004	16.349191	6.748465	Extremely
	-4	1.075873	31.211324	16.765059	8.779725	Weak attractor;
241, 320	-2	1.075894	31.212169	15.976038	9.669870	additionally,
	0	1.075681	31.203713	15.338220	6.802035	large amplitude
	2	1.075685	31.203874	15.336640	6.792465	oscillations
	4; 6; 8; 10	Instability starting from iteration 3 (m = 4) and 2 (m = 6; 8 and 10), respectively					
	-10	0.587015*	10.54143*	44.932172*	406.378745*	Pseudo-convergence
	-8	Instability starting from iteration 9					
	-6	0.574936*	9.935104*	45.115503*	472.32972*	Pseudo-convergence
31, 247	-4	1.190187*	35.636207	19.734559	9.742655	
	-2	1.190174*	35.635711	19.830541	10.175875	Extremely
	0	1.190169*	35.635528	19.859227	10.302720	Weak pseudo-attractor;
	2	1.190204*	35.636852	19.641657	9.317010	additionally,
	4	1.190280*	35.639586	19.217493	7.276885	large amplitude
	6	1.190267*	35.639176	19.303182	7.692265	oscillations
	8; 10	Instability starting from iteration 2					

Given being that the usual single precision corresponds to 7 decimal places (for a 32-bit word machine [71, 78, 79], it is possible to define the *strength levels of an attractor relative to a certain uniqueness parameter* by means of the number of common first decimals for several neighbor zero-order approximations: 7 common first decimals (VS), 6 (S), 5 (MS), 4 (M), 3 (MW), 2 (W), 1 (VW), 0 but a certain weak convergence (VVW). Of course, *the general attractor's strength level* will be its strength level relative to the weakest studied uniqueness parameters, i.e. relative to $|E_t - E_i|$ for the charge coupled devices.

6 Conclusions

The accomplished study reveal some results obtained by authors using numerical methods to study some complex systems and their applications mainly in the physical sciences. Other theoretical contributions of the authors in the field of complex systems were concisely described also. All main results of the accomplished studies were scientifically analyzed.

The method of the physical similarity is used for the description of some fluids flow regimes. The method of the power laws and the method of phenomenological universality, applied to the description of the growth processes in biology and even in cosmology are illustrated also. The applications of the numerical methods used in the computer simulations of some physical processes in medine and bioengineering are also discussed.

Acknowledgements. The authors thank very much to Professor Pier Paolo Delsanto and to Dr. Marco Scalerandi from Dipartimento di Fisica di Politecnico di Torino for their valuable cooperation concerning the Finite Differences and LISA methods, as well as to Professors Erik Bodegom and Ralf Widenhorn from the Physics Department of the Portland State University for their important awarded information and suggestions concerning the field of Charge Coupled Devices.The conflict of InterestThe authors declare that there is no conflict of interest regarding the publication of this paper.

References

1. Gukhman, A.A.: Introduction to the Theory of Similarity. Academic Press, New York (1965)
2. Lyon, B.N.: Chem. Eng. Progr. **47**, 2 (1951)
3. Petukhov, B.S.: Heat transfer and friction in turbulent pipe flow with variable physical properties. Adv. Heat Transf. **6**, 503–564 (1970)
4. Landau, L., Lifshitz, E.M.: Mecanique des Fluides. MIR, Moscow (1971)
5. Iordache, D.A.: Selected Works of Numerical Physics. Printech, Bucuresti (2000)
6. Dobrescu, R., Iordache, D.: Complexity and Information. Romanian Academy Printing House, Bucharest (2010)
7. Kolmogorov, A.N.: A refinement of previous hypotheses concerning the local structure of turbulence in a viscous incompressible fluid at high reynolds number. J. Fluid Mech. **13**(1), 82–85 (1962)
8. Iordache, D.A., Iordache, V.: On the compatibility of the multi-fractal and similitude descriptions of the fracture parameters relative to the existing experimental data for concrete specimens. In: Proceedings of 1st South-East European Symposium on Interdisciplinary Approaches in Fractal Analysis (IAFA-3), Bucharest, 7–10 May, pp. 55–60 (2003)
9. Mandelbrot, B.B.: On the geometry of homogeneous turbulence, with stress on the fractal dimension of the iso-surfaces of scalars. J. Fluid Mech. **72**(3), 401–416 (1975)

10. Witten Jr., T.A., Sander, L.M.: Diffusion-limited aggregation, a kinetic critical phenomenon. Phys. Rev. Lett. **47**(19), 1400 (1981)

11. Bak, P., Tang, C., Wiesenfeld, K.: Self-organized criticality: an explanation of the 1/f noise. Phys. Rev. Lett. **59**(4), 381 (1987)

12. Petrescu, A.D., Sterian, A.R., Sterian, P.E.: Solitons propagation in optical fibers computer experiments for students training. In: Gervasi, O., Gavrilova, M.L. (eds.) ICCSA 2007. LNCS, vol. 4705, pp. 450–461. Springer, Heidelberg (2007). https://doi.org/10.1007/978-3-540-74472-6_36

13. Iordache, D.A., Pusca, S., Iordache, V.: Limit laws, frequency power laws and fractal scaling in technological series of ferrimagnetic materials. Rev. Non-conventional Technologies **4**, 7–12 (2005)

14. Gompertz, B.: On the nature of the function expressive of the law of human mortality, and on a new mode of determining the value of life contingencies. Phil. Trans. Roy. Soc. **115**, 513 (1825)

15. Einstein, A.: Strahlungs-emission und –absorption nach der Quantentheorie. Deutsche Physikalische Gesellchaft **18**, 318–323 (1916)

16. Steel, G.G.: Growth Kinetics of Tumors. Clarendon Press, Oxford (1974)

17. Weldom, T.E.: Mathematical model in Cancer Research. Adam Hilger, Briston (1988)

18. Delsanto, P.P., Griffa, M., Condat, C.A., Delsanto, S., Morra, L.: Phys. Rev. Lett. **94**(14), 148105 (2005)

19. Guiot, C., Pugno, N., Delsanto, P.P.: Elasto-mechanical model of tumor-invasion. Appl. Phys. Lett. **89**, 1 (2006)

20. Castorina, P., Delsanto, P.P., Guiot, C.: Phys. Rev. Lett. **96**(18), 188701 (2006)

21. Royama, T.: Analytic Population Dynamics. Chapman & Hall, London (1992)

22. Brown, J.H., West, G.B. (eds.): Scaling in Biology. Oxford University Press, New York (2000)

23. West, G.B., Brown, J.H., Enquist, B.J.: A general model for ontogenetic growth. Nature **413** (6856), 628 (2001)

24. West, G.B., Brown, J.H.: Life's universal scaling laws. Phys. Today **57**(9), 36–43 (2004)

25. Delsanto, P.P., Guiot, C., Degiorgis, P.G., Condat, C.A., Mansury, Y., Deisboeck, T.S.: Growth model for multicellular tumor spheroids. Appl. Phys. Lett. **85**(18), 4225–4227 (2004)

26. Guiot, C., Delsanto, P.P., Carpinteri, A., Pugno, N., Mansury, Y., Deisboeck, T.S.: The dynamic evolution of the power exponent in a universal growth model of tumors. J. Theor. Biol. **240**(3), 459–463 (2006)

27. Delsanto, P.P., Gliozzi, A.S., Guiot, C.: Scaling, growth and cyclicity in biology: a new computational approach. Theor. Biol. Med. Model. **5**, 5 (2008)

28. Hartung, K.: Healthy Child. In: Venzmer, G. (ed.) New Health Book. Bertelsmann, Ratgeberverlag, Reinhard Mohn (1965;1969)

29. Guth, A.H.: Inflationary universe: a possible solution to the horizon and flatness problems. Phys. Rev. D. **23**(2), 347 (1981)

30. Barontini, M., Dahia, P.L.: VHL disease. Best Pract. Res. Clin. Endocrinol. Metab. **24**(3), 401–413 (2010)

31. Linde, A.: Inflation and quantum cosmology. Phys. Scr. **1991**(T36), 30 (1991)

32. Iordache, D., Delsanto, P.P., Iordache, V.: Similitude models of some growth processes. In: Proceedings of 9th WSEAS International Mathematics and Computers in Biology and Chemistry (MCBC 2008), Bucharest, Romania, 54–59, 24 June 2008

33. Leibundgut, B., Sollerman, J.: A cosmological surprise: the universe accelerates. Europhys. News **32**(4), 121–125 (2001)

34. Dobrescu, R., Iordache, D.: Complexity Modeling (in Romanian). Politehnica Press, Bucharest (2007)
35. Wilson, K.G.: Re-normalization group and critical phenomena. Phys. Rev. B **4**, 3174–3184 (1971)
36. Majorana, E.: Il valore delle leggi statistiche nella fisica e nelle scienze sociali. Scientia, Febbraio-Marzo, p. 58 (1942)
37. Bodegom, E., Iordache, D.: Physics for Engineering students, vol. 1. Politehnica Press, Bucharest (2007)
38. Prigogine, I., Nicolis, G.: Self-Organization in Non-Equilibrium Systems: From Dissipative Structures to Order Through Fluctuations. Wiley, New York (1977)
39. Shannon, C.E.: A mathematical theory of communication. Bell Syst. Tech. J. **27**(4), 623–656 (1948)
40. Mantegna, R.N.: The tenth article of Ettore Majorana. Europhy. News **37**(4), 15–17 (2006)
41. Domb, C., Sykes, M.F.: On the susceptibility of a ferromagnetic above the Curie point. Proc. R. Soc. Lond. A **240**(1221), 214–228 (1957)
42. Zinn-Justin, J.: Quantum Field Theory and critical Phenomena, 4th edn. Oxford University Press, New York (2002)
43. Iordache, D.: L'étude de la courbe dynamique d'aimantation d'un ferrite mixte de manganèse et zinc, de haute perméabilité. Bull. Polytech. Insts. Bucharest, **29**(3) 25–41(1967)
44. Müller, G.: Rheological properties and velocity dispersion of a medium with power-law dependence of Q on frequency. J. Geophys. **54**, 20–29 (1983)
45. Daniello, L., Iordache, D., et al.: Study of the frequency dependence of the viscosity coefficient of the bloch wall oscillations. Rev. Roum. Phys. **25**(2), 193–198 (1980)
46. Stevens, S.S.: On the psychophysical law. Psychol. Rev. **64**(3), 153 (1957)
47. Kolmogorov, A.N.: J. Fluid Mech. **13**, 82 (1962)
48. Mandelbrot, B.B.: On the geometry of homogeneous turbulence, with stress on the fractal dimension of the iso-surfaces of scalars. J. Fluid Mech. **72**(3), 401–416 (1975)
49. Iordache, D.A.: Contributions to the study of Numerical Phenomena intervening in the Computer Simulations of some Physical Processes. Credis Printing House, Bucharest, 118 p. (2004)
50. Courant, R., Hilbert, D.: Methods of Mathematical Physics. Wiley Interscience Publishers, New York, London (1962)
51. Hildebrand, F.B.: Methods of Applied Mathematics, pp. 36–122. Prentice-Hall, New Jersey (1965)
52. Delsanto, P.P., Chaskelis, H.H., Whitcombe, T., Mignogna, R.: Connection machine simulation of boundary effects in ultrasonic NDE. In: Ruud, C.O., Bussière, J.F., Green, R.E. (eds.) Nondestructive Characterization of Materials IV. Springer, Boston, MA (1991). https://doi.org/10.1007/978-1-4899-0670-0_26
53. Iordache, D.A., Sterian, P., Sterian, A.R., Pop, F.: Complex computer simulations, numerical artifacts, and numerical phenomena. Int. J. Comput. Commun. Control **5**(5), 744–754 (2010)
54. Roșu, C., et al.: Mod. Phys. Lett. B **24**(01), 65–73 (2010)
55. Levenberg, K.: Quart. Appl. Math. 164(1941)
56. Marquardt, D.W.: An algorithm for least-squares estimation of non-linear parameters. J. Soc. Industr. Appl. Math. **11**, 431–441 (1963)
57. Mei, Z., Morris Jr., J.W.: Mössbauer spectrum curve fitting with a personal computer. Nucl. Instr. Meth. Phys. Res. Sect. B: Beam Interact. Mater. Atoms **47**(2), 181–186 (1990)
58. Bodegom, E., Mcclure, D.W., Delsanto, P.P., Gliozzi, A., Iordache, D.A., Pop, F., Rosu, C., Widemhorn, R.: Computational Physics Guide (2009)
59. Iordache, D.A., Sterian, P., Tunaru, I.: Study of the gradient method aided dark current spectroscopy of CCDs. Annal. Rom. Sci. Ser. Sci. Technol. Inf. **6**(2), 23–42 (2013)

60. Janesick, J.R.: Scientific charge-coupled devices. SPIE Press, Bellingham (2000). Appendices G1-G4, H1-H3
61. Widenhorn, R.: Charge Coupled Devices. VDM, Saarbruecken, Germany (2008)
62. Iordache, D.A., Sterian, P.E., Tunaru, I.: Charge coupled devices as particle detectors. Adv. High Energ. Phys. **2013**, 12 (2013)
63. Widenhorn, R., Bodegom, E., Iordache, D., Tunaru, I.: Computational Approach to Dark Current Spectroscopy in CCDs as complex systems. I. Experimental part and choice of the uniqueness parameters. Print at the Scientific Bull. Univ. "Politehnica" Bucharest, 1 January 2010
64. Hall, R.N.: Electron-hole recombination in germanium. Phys. Rev. **87**(2), 387 (1952)
65. Shockley, W., Read Jr., W.T.: Statistics of the recombinations of holes and electrons. Phys. Rev. **87**(5), 835 (1952)
66. Sze, S.M., Ng, K.K.: Physics of Semiconductor Devices. Willey, Hoboken (1981)
67. Widenhorn, R., Blouke, M.M., Weber, A., Rest, A., Bodegom, E.: Temperature dependence of dark current in a CCD. In: Sensors and Camera Systems for Scientific, Industrial, and Digital Photography Applications III, vol. 4669, pp. 193–202, 24 April 2002
68. Widenhorn, R., Blouke, M.M., Weber, A., Rest, A., Bodegom, E.: Temperature dependence of dark current in a CCD. In: Sensors and Camera Systems for Scientific, Industrial, and Digital Photography Applications III, vol. 4669, pp. 193–202, 24 April 2002
69. Rogojan, R., Sterian, P.E., Sterian, A.R., Elisa, M.: Spectral behavior and nonlinear optical properties of aluminophosphate semiconductor-doped glasses. In: 11th International School on Quantum Electronics: Laser Physics and Applications, vol. 4397, pp. 358–362, 9 April 2001
70. Landau, R.H., Paez, R.H.: Computational Physics: Problem Solving with Computers. Wiley, New York, Chichester (1997)
71. Dima M, et al.: The QUANTGRID project (RO)—quantum security in GRID computing applications. In: AIP Conference Proceedings, AIP, vol. 1203(1) (2010)
72. Iliescu, F.S., Sterian, A.P., Barbarini, E., Avram, M., Iliescu, C.: Continuous separation of white blood cell from blood in a microfluidic device. UPB Sci. Bull. Ser. A. **71**(4), 21–30 (2009)
73. Maciuc, F.C., Stere, C.I., Sterian, A.R.: Rate equations for an erbium laser system: a numerical approach. In: Sixth Conference on Optics, ROMOPTO 2000, 29 Jun, vol. 4430, pp. 136–147 (2001)
74. Lazar, B., et al.: Simulating delayed pulses in organic materials. Comput. Sci. Appl. **2006**, 779–784 (2006)
75. Sterian, A., Sterian, P.: Mathematical models of dissipative systems in quantum engineering. Math. Prob. Eng. **2012**, 12 (2012). Article ID 347674
76. Ninulescu, V., Sterian, A.-R.: Dynamics of a two-level medium under the action of short optical pulses. In: Gervasi, O., Gavrilova, M.L., Kumar, V., Laganà, A., Lee, H.P., Mun, Y., Taniar, D., Tan, Chih Jeng Kenneth (eds.) ICCSA 2005. LNCS, vol. 3482, pp. 635–642. Springer, Heidelberg (2005). https://doi.org/10.1007/11424857_70
77. Sterian, A., Ninulescu, V.: Nonlinear phenomena in erbium-doped lasers. In: Gervasi, O., Gavrilova, M.L., Kumar, V., Laganà, A., Lee, H.P., Mun, Y., Taniar, D., Tan, C.J.K. (eds.) ICCSA 2005. LNCS, vol. 3482, pp. 643–650. Springer, Heidelberg (2005). https://doi.org/10.1007/11424857_71
78. Dănilă, O., et al.: Perspectives on entangled nuclear particle pairs generation and manipulation in quantum communication and cryptography systems. Adv. High Energ. Phys. **2012**, 10 (2012)
79. Dima, M., et al.: Classical and quantum communications in grid computing. Optoelectron. Adv. Mater. Rapid Commun. **4**(1), 1840–1843 (2010)

80. Stefanescu, E., et al.: Study on the fermion systems coupled by electric dipol interaction with the free electromagnetic field. In: Proceedings of SPIE 5850, Advanced Laser Technologies 2004, 160 (2005)

81. Sterian, A.R.: Computer modeling of the coherent optical amplifier and laser systems. In: Gervasi, O., Gavrilova, M.L. (eds.) ICCSA 2007. LNCS, vol. 4705, pp. 436–449. Springer, Heidelberg (2007). https://doi.org/10.1007/978-3-540-74472-6_35

82. Anghel, D.A., et al.: Modeling quantum well lasers. Math. Prob. Eng. **2012**, 11 (2012)

83. Urquhart, P. (ed.): Advances in Optical Amplifiers. InTech, Rijeka, Croatia (2011)

Modeling the Nerve Conduction in a Myelinated Axon
A Brief Review

M. Filomena Teodoro[1,2](✉) (iD)

[1] CINAV, Portuguese Naval Academy, Portuguese Navy,
Base Naval de Lisboa, Alfeite, 2810-001 Almada, Portugal
`maria.alves.teodoro@marinha.pt`
[2] CEMAT - Center for Computational and Stochastic Mathematics,
Instituto Superior Técnico, Lisbon University,
Avenida Rovisco Pais, n. 1, 1048-001 Lisboa, Portugal

Abstract. In this paper it is done a brief review about the mathematical modeling of the nerve conduction in a myelinated axon considering the Fitzhugh-Nagumo equation, a forward-backward differential equation (FBDE). We look for a solution of this FBDE defined in $\mathbb{R}$, with known values at $\pm\infty$. Extending the idea initially presented in [1] and [2], was developed a numerical method to solve an autonomous linear FBDE using the method of steps and finite differences. Continuing this approach, the authors of [3–5] introduced some numerical schemes based on method of steps, collocation and finite element method. These schemes developed for linear FBDEs were adapted to solve the nonlinear boundary value problem, the Fitzhugh-Nagumo equation [6–8]. The homotopy analysis method, algorithm proposed Liao in 1991 [9], became in an important tool to solve non linear equations during the last two decades, was also applied to get the numerical solution of the equation under study [25]. Here, it is done a brief review of different aproaches to solve nunerically equations that models nerve conduction. Also is used a different data basis using radial functions [10, 11] to solve numerically the equation under study, similarly to the work presented in [12], where radial functions are considered to solve a nonlinear equation from acoustics. The results are computed and compared with the ones from other computational methods. The results are promising but it still necessary to continue with the experiments with another sets of basis funtions.

Keywords: Mixed-type functional forward-backward differential equation · Nonlinear boundary value problem · Nerve conduction
Method of steps · Collocation · Newton method
Continuation method · Fitzhugh-Nagumo equation · Radial functions

© Springer International Publishing AG, part of Springer Nature 2018
O. Gervasi et al. (Eds.): ICCSA 2018, LNCS 10961, pp. 560–569, 2018.
https://doi.org/10.1007/978-3-319-95165-2_39

1   Introduction

The objective of the present work is to model the nerve conduction in a myeli-nated[1] axon of a neuron. In [13] is presented some work about behavior of models of myelinated axons. The same author, in [14], studies some details about a diffusive model for a myelinated axon.

Detailing, in present work is taken into account a delay-advanced equation which models nerve conduction. The equation under study describes the potential propagation along a myelinated nerve axon, where the membrane has a fatty coat of myeline with spaced holes denominated the nodes of Ranvier. The typical struture of neuron can be consulted in Fig. 1. Dentrite, the receptive part, conduces the signal to the cell boby; the conducting zone is given by a single fiber, the axon, that conducts the signal from the cell to other neuron through the terminal branches that constitute the axon ending. A concise and visual description about nervous conduction can be found in Fig. 2.

On the computation of solution it is necessary to solve a nonlinear mixed type differential functional boundary value problem.

$$x'(t) = F(x(t)) + \beta(t)x(t - \tau) + \gamma(t)x(t + \tau), \tag{1}$$

where x is the unknown function, β, γ and F are known functions. τ is some positive constant.

In the aim of mathematical theory of optimal control, the author of [15] made important contribution for the analysis of FBDEs. In [16,17] is done a contribution to functional analysis of linear autonomous FBDEs.

We can found a interesting research on computation of mixed type functional differential boundary value problems in [18], in particular the modeling of the tails after truncation to a finite interval, in particular to the modeling of the tails where the original problem is transformed in a boundary value problem (BVP).

Similarly to the work presented in [8,19], where a FBDE from acoustics is solved numerically, the main interest of this work is the development, extension and adaptation of some methods which solve numerically Eq. (1), when $F(v(t)) = \alpha(t)x(t)$ and α, β and γ are smooth functions of t and τ is known. These methods were introduced initially for linear autonomous case in [3,20] and extended to the non-autonomous case at in [4], using collocation. This numerical approach was further developed in [5], where an numerical scheme, using the finite element method, was proposed for the solution of such linear boundary value problems and in [6,21] and [7] for nonlinear case.

In particular, the equation in study is the discrete FitzHugh–Nagumo equation given by (2)

$$RCv'(t) = F(v(t)) + v(t - \tau) + v(t + \tau), \quad t \in \mathbb{R}. \tag{2}$$

---

[1] Myelin is a fatty substance forming an electrically insulating sheath around many nerve fibers. The principal function of myelin is to increase the speed at which impulses are conducted.

The Eq. 2 is a boundary value problem (BVP) of first order. We look for for a solution defined in $\mathbb{R}$, which satisfies the nonlinear MTFDE (2) with boundary conditions (3)

$$\begin{cases} v(-\infty) = 0 \\ v(+\infty) = 1. \end{cases} \tag{3}$$

The unknown $v(t)$ represents the transmembrane potential at a node in a myelinated axon, in nerve conduction model. F reflects the current-voltage model. R and C are respectively the axomatic nodal resistivity and the nodal capacity. τ is the inverse of the wave potential speed propagation down the axon, it is unknown. A detailed derivation of the model (2) (3) can be found in [22].

This mathematical model is formulated from an equivalent electric circuit model which assumes pure saltatory conduction (PSC). When compared with the membrane, myelin has higher resistance and lower capacitance. So myeline decreases capacitance and increases electrical resistance across the axolemma (axon membrane), avoiding the electric current go out from axon. If the membrane is depolarized at a node (negative variation of membrane potential), potential tends to jump to the next node and excite the membrane there.

Also, it is supposed that nodes are equally spaced and electrically similar, potential cross-sectional variations in axon are negligible and the axon is infinite in extent. See Fig. 3.

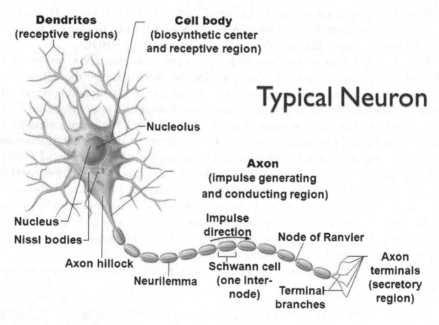

Fig. 1. Structure of a typical neuron. Source [23].

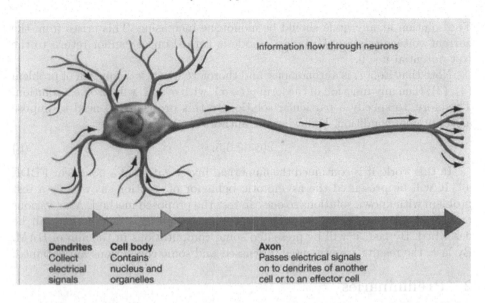

Fig. 2. Scheme about the information propagation through neurons. Source [24].

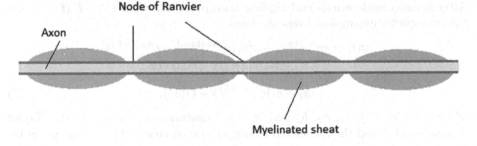

Fig. 3. Nervous conduction. Simplified scheme of the neuron. Source [25].

The Eq. (2) can be reduced to the non dimensional model:

$$v'(t) = f(v(t)) + v(t - \tau) + v(t + \tau) - 2v(t), \quad t \in \mathbb{R}, \tag{4}$$

where τ is the non dimensional time delay.

Several models can be obtained using different current-voltage expressions. Here it is used the FitzHugh–Nagumo dynamics for the nodal membrane, without a recovery term and assuming that a supra-threshold stimulus begins a propagated axon potential and consequently travels down the axon from node to node.

In this case, the function f is given by

$$f(v) = bv(v - a)(1 - v) \tag{5}$$

with a being the threshold potential in the non dimensional problem ($0 < a < 1$) and b a parameter related with the strength of the ionic current density ($b > 0$).

The solution at any node should be monotone increasing. This arises from the current-voltage relation $f(v)$ once a node is turned on, it cannot return to the rest potential $v = 0$.

Note that Eq. (4) is autonomous, and therefore if $v(t)$ is a solution of problem (4), (3), then any function of the form $v(t+\sigma)$, with $\sigma \in \mathbb{R}$, will also be a solution. Therefore, to specify a particular solution to this problem, we need to impose an additional condition. Following the authors of [22], we will set

$$v(0) = 0.5. \tag{6}$$

In this work, it is continued the numerical investigation of a nonlinear FBDE [6]. It will be presented the asymptotic behavior of solution, as well as a test problem with known solutions so one can test the proposed method. Also, various numerical schemes to get solution of problem of nervous conduction will be described. By last, it will be presented some computations in the aim of HAM. By last, the results are presented, discussed and some conclusions are obtained.

2   Preliminaries

2.1   Assymptotic Behaviour

After some considerations and algebric manipulation, when $t \leq -L$ $(t \to -\infty)$, the asymptotic expansion, takes the form

$$\begin{aligned} v(t) = \varepsilon e^{\lambda_+(t+L)} &+ \varepsilon^2 b_1(e^{2\lambda_+(t+L)} - e^{\lambda_+(t+L)}) \\ &+ \varepsilon^3(b_2 e^{2\lambda_+(t+L)} + b_3 e^{3\lambda_+(t+L)} \\ &- (b_2 + b_3)e^{\lambda_+(t+L)}) + O(\varepsilon^4), \end{aligned} \tag{7}$$

where $\varepsilon = v(-L)$, b_1, b_2, b_3 and λ_+ are constants depending on the Taylor expansion of f and the associated characteristic equation. The $b's$ are given by

$$\begin{aligned} b_1 &= \tfrac{a_2}{2\lambda_+ - a_1 + 2 - 2cosh(\lambda_+\tau)}, \\ b_2 &= -2b_1^2, \\ b_3 &= \tfrac{2a_1 b_1 + a_3}{3\lambda_+ - a_1 + 2 - 2cosh(3\lambda_+\tau)} \end{aligned} \tag{8}$$

Equally, when $t > L$ $(t \to \infty)$, we get the following asymptotic expression: takes the form

$$\begin{aligned} v(t) = 1 - \varepsilon_+ e^{\lambda_-(t-L)} &- \varepsilon^2 B_1(e^{2\lambda_-(t-L)} - e^{\lambda_-(t-L)}) \\ &- \varepsilon_+^3(B_2 e^{2\lambda_-(t-L)} + B_3 e^{3\lambda_-(t-L)} \\ &- (B_2 + B_3)e^{\lambda_-(t-L)}) + O(\varepsilon_+^4), \end{aligned} \tag{9}$$

where $\varepsilon_+ = 1 - v(L)$, B_1, B_2, B_3 and λ_- are constants depending on Taylor expansion of f and characteristic equation. The expressions of B_1, B_2, B_3 are given by

$$\begin{aligned} B_1 &= \tfrac{-A_2}{2\lambda_- + A_1 + 2 - 2cosh(\lambda_-\tau)}, \\ B_2 &= -2B_1^2, \\ B_3 &= \tfrac{-2A_1 B_1 - A_3}{3\lambda_- + A_1 + 2 - 2cosh(3\lambda_-\tau)}. \end{aligned} \tag{10}$$

2.2   Method of Steps

In this section is extended the formula (7) presented in Sect. 2 of [4] to this particular nonlinear case. It uses an adapted method of steps usually used to solve delay differential equations. In the linear case, one solves the equation over successive intervals of unitary length. In the actual case of Eq. (4), the side is similar, but for sequential intervals of length τ.

$$v(t + \tau) = v'(t) - v(t - \tau) + g(v(t)), t \in \mathbb{R} \tag{11}$$

where $g(u) = 2u - f(u)$.

We can use formula (11) to compute a solution for Eq. (3) on an interval $[a, a + k\tau]$, where $k \in \mathbb{Z}$, $a \in \mathbb{R}$, starting from its initial values on $[a - 2\tau, a]$; these values can be obtained from the asymptotic expansion (7).

When all the needed derivatives of f and v exist in $(a - 2\tau, a]$, we may obtain the following expressions for the solution in the first two intervals $(a, a + \tau]$ and $(a + \tau, a + 2\tau]$:

$$v(t + \tau) = v'(t) - v(t - \tau) + g(v(t)), \quad t \in (a, a + \tau];$$
$$v(t + 2\tau) = v'(t + \tau) - v(t) + g(v(t + \tau))$$
$$= v''(t) - v'(t - \tau) + g(v(t + \tau))$$
$$+ g'_v(v(t))v'(t) - v(t), \quad t \in (a + \tau, a + 2\tau]. \tag{12}$$

Continuing this process, we can extend the solution to any interval, provided that the initial functions in the first two intervals with length τ are smooth enough functions and satisfy some simple relationships.

3   Radial Basis Functions

Radial basis functions are those functions which have radial symmetry, that is, depend on only (beyond some known parameters) of the distance $r = \|x - x_j\|$, between the center of the function x_j, $j = 1, \ldots, N$, $N \in \mathbb{N}$ and the generic point x, and can be written generically in the form $\phi(r)$.

With such a general definition there will, therefore, be infinite functions of this kind. These functions can be classified as global (said to have global support) or local (Compact or local support) depending on whether they are defined in the entire domain or only partially of this [10].

The types of global support functions $\phi(r)$ include:

– Multiquadrics (MQ):

$$\sqrt{(x - x_j)^2 + (c_j^2)}, \qquad c_j \geq 0; \tag{13}$$

– Inverse Multiquadrics (IMQ):

$$((x - x_j)^2 + (c_j^2))^{-\frac{1}{2}}, \ c_j \geq 0; \tag{14}$$

- Inverse Multiquadratics (IMQT):

$$((x - x_j)^2 + (c_j^2))^{-1}, \ c_j \geq 0; \tag{15}$$

- Gaussians (G):

$$e^{(-c\ r^2)}, \ c > 0; \tag{16}$$

- Polyharmonic Splines (PS):

$$\phi(r) = r^k, \ k = 1, 3, 5, \ldots ; \tag{17}$$

$$\phi(r) = r^k \ln(r), \ k = 2, 4, 6, \ldots ; \tag{18}$$

- Thin plate splines (TPS): Particular case of PS, for $k = 2$,

$$r^{2\beta} lnr, \quad \beta \in \mathbb{N}. \tag{19}$$

Compact support radial basis functions are, for example, those of

- Wu and Wendland:

$$(1 - r)_+^n + P(r) \tag{20}$$

where $P(r)$ is a polynomial and $(1 - r)_+^n$ is 0 for r greater than the support;
- Buhmann:

$$\frac{1}{3} + r^2 - \frac{4}{3}r^3 + 2r^2 lnr. \tag{21}$$

Radial basis functions are typically used to build up function approximations of the form

$$y(x) = \sum_{j=1}^{N} w_j \, \phi(\|x - x_j\|), \tag{22}$$

where the approximating function $y(x)$ is represented as a sum of N radial basis functions, each associated with a different center x_i, and weighted by an appropriate coefficient w_i, $j = 1, \ldots, N$, $N \in \mathbb{N}$. The weights w_j, $j = 1, \ldots, N$, $N \in \mathbb{N}$ can be estimated [11] using the matrix methods of linear least squares, COLL, FEM (the approximating function is linear in the weights).

4   Numerical Scheme

The computational methods developed for the solution of presented problem are consequence of the work introduced before. Different issue in the previous works are the fact of the problem under investigation is defined in $\mathbb{R}$ and the value of τ is unknown. Summarizing the actual work, the BVP (4) and (3) defined in entire real axed is transformed in a problem defined in a limited interval, using the truncated asymptotic expressions (7) and (9) as boundary functions. In next stage, several ways can be applied. By one hand, we can manage a test problem which lets us to investigate the performance of the used methods. This test problem can also be used as an initial guess when it is applied a continuation method. By another hand, when we impose some regularity conditions we can estimate τ and use the method of steps to extend the boundary functions to the points of an regular partition of remaining interval. In next step, Newton method is the option to linearize the problem. After that, we can apply collocation, finite element method or other to the system of linearized equations. Initially, B-splines were considered as the basis functions when collocation and finite element method are applied. Recently, in [12], where considered radial basis functions to model a problem from human phonation. Here, we also have follow the same basis. The obtained results are similar to the ones obtained in [25].

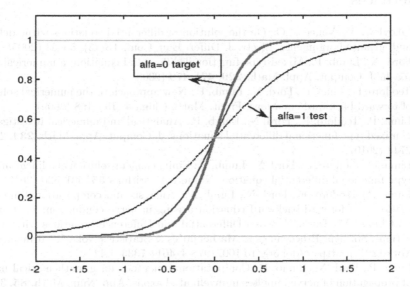

Fig. 4. Numerical approximation using approximation method. In black is the solution of test problem In red, is the numerical solution of problem (4) and (3). Source [25]. (Color figure online)

Another approach to take into consideration is the homotopy analysis method (HAM) proposed initially in [9]. HAM is an important method to solve non linear equations. We can find many applications of HAM in literature, e.g. in [26] where the HAM is applied to one specific form of Fitzhugh-Nagumo equation. Using the same idea, we tried to apply this technique to get the solution of the equation under study. The results are computed and compared with the ones obtained from other computational methods. The obtained results are promising, but it is still needed to do more experiments with different set of parameters.

5   Final Remarks

In present work, we revisit different aproaches to solve nunerically equations that models nerve conduction. Also we consider a different sent of basis functions, the radial basis functions. The results are discussed and compared. It is still necessary to proceed with the numerical analysis of the computational schemes used to solve numerically the proposed problem.

Acknowledgements. This work was supported by Portuguese funds through the *Center for Computational and Stochastic Mathematics* (CEMAT), *The Portuguese Foundation for Science and Technology* (FCT), University of Lisbon, Portugal, project UID/Multi/04621/2013, and *Center of Naval Research* (CINAV), Naval Academy, Portuguese Navy, Portugal.

References

1. Iakovleva, V., Vanegas, C.: On the solution of differential equations withe delayed and advanced arguments. Electr. J. Differ. Equ. Conf. **13**(13), 56–63 (2005)
2. Ford, N., Lumb, P.: Mixed type functional differential equation: a numerical approach. J. Comput. Appl. Math. **229**, 471–479 (2008)
3. Teodoro, F., Lima, P., Ford, N., Lumb, P.: New approach to the numerical solution of forward-backward equations. Front. Math. China **4**, 155–168 (2009)
4. Lima, P., Teodoro, F., Ford, N., Lumb, P.: Analytical and numerical investigation of mixed type functional differential equations. J. Comput. Appl. Math. **234**, 2732–2744 (2010)
5. Lima, P., Teodoro, F., Ford, N., Lumb, P.: Finite element solution of a linear mixed-type functional differential equation. Numer. Algorithms **55**, 301–320 (2010)
6. Lima, P., Teodoro, F., Ford, N., Lumb, P.: Analysis and computational approximation of a forward-backward equation arising in nerve conduction. In: Pinelas, S., Chipot, M., Dosla, Z. (eds.) Differential and Difference Equations with Applications. Springer Proceedings in Mathematics & Statistics, vol. 47. Springer, New York (2013). https://doi.org/10.1007/978-1-4614-7333-6_42
7. Lima, P., Ford, N., Lumb, P.: Computational methods for a mathematical model of propagation of nerve impulses in myelinated axons. App. Num. Math. **85**, 38–53 (2014)
8. Teodoro, M.F.: Numerical solution of a delay-advanced equation from acoustics. Int. J. Mech. **11**, 107–114 (2017)
9. Liao, S.: The proposed homotopy analysis technique for the solution of nonlinear problems. Ph.D. thesis, Shanghai Jiao Tong University (1992)
10. Buhmann, M.: Radial Basis Functions: Theory and Implementations. Cambridge University Press, Cambridge (2003)
11. Tiago, C., Leitão, V.: Utilização de funções de base radial em problemas unidimensionais de análise estrutural. In: Goicolea, J.M., Soares, C.M., Pastor, M., Bugeda, G. (eds.) Métodos Numéricos em Engenieria. No. V, SEMNI (2002). (in portuguese)
12. Teodoro, M.F.: Approximating a retarded-advanced differential equation using radial basis functions. In: Gervasi, O., Murgante, B., Misra, S., Borruso, G., Torre, C.M., Rocha, A.M.A.C., Taniar, D., Apduhan, B.O., Stankova, E., Cuzzocrea, A. (eds.) ICCSA 2017. LNCS, vol. 10408, pp. 33–43. Springer, Cham (2017). https://doi.org/10.1007/978-3-319-62404-4_3
13. Bell, J.: Behaviour of some models of myelinated axons. IMA J. Math. Appl. Med. Biol. **1**, 149–167 (1984)

14. Bell, J., Cosner, C.: Threshold conditions for a diffusive model of a myelinated axon. J. Math. Biol. **18**, 39–52 (1983)
15. Pontryagin, L.S., Gamkreledze, R.V., Mischenko, E.F.: The Mathematical Theory of Optimal Process. Interscience, New York (1962)
16. Rustichini, A.: Functional differential equations of mixed type: the linear autonomous case. J. Dyn. Differ. Equ. **1**, 121–143 (1989)
17. Rustichini, A.: Hopf bifurcation for functional differential equations of mixed type. J. Dyn. Differ. Equ. **1**, 145–177 (1989)
18. Abell, K.A., Elmer, C.E., Humphries, A.R., Vleck, E.S.V.: Computation of mixed type functional differential boundary value problems. SIADS - SIAM J. Appl. Dyn. Syst. **4**, 755–781 (2005)
19. Teodoro, M.F.: Numerical approximation of a delay-advanced equation from acoustics. In: Proceedings of International Conference on Mathematical Methods in Science and Engineering, Costa Ballena, Rota, Cadiz (Spain), 6–10 July 2015, CMMSE, Mathematical Methods in Science and Engineering (2015)
20. Teodoro, M.F., Lima, P., Ford, N., Lumb, P.: Numerical modelling of a functional differential equation with deviating arguments using a collocation method. In: Numerical Analysis and Applied Mathematics, Conference on Numerical Analysis and Applied Mathematics 2008, AIP Conference Proceedings (2008)
21. Teodoro, F., Lima, P., Ford, N., Lumb, P.: Numerical approximation of a nonlinear delay-advance functional differential equations by a finite element method. In: Numerical Analysis and Applied Mathematics: International Conference on Numerical Analysis and Applied Mathematics 2012, AIP Conference Proceedings (2012)
22. Chi, H., Bell, J., Hassard, B.: Numerical solution of a nonlinear advance-delay-differential equation from nerve conduction. J. Math. Biol. **24**, 5583–601 (1986)
23. Antranik: Fundamentals of the Nervous System and Nervous Tissue. https://antranik.org/fundamentals-of-the-nervous-system-and-nervous-tissue/. Accessed May 10th 2018
24. Essays: Conduction Physiology. UK. https://www.ukessays.com/essays/physiology/basic-physiology-of-nerve-conduction.php?vref=1. Accessed at May 10th 2018 (2013)
25. Teodoro, M.F.: Numerical solution of a forward-backward equation from physiology. Appl. Math. Inf. Sci. **11**(5), 287–1297 (2017)
26. Abbasbandy, S.: Soliton solutions for the fitzhugh-nagumo equation with the homotopy analysis method. Appl. Math. Model. **32**, 2706–2714 (2007)

Workshop Computational Optimization and Applications (COA 2018)

Optimization of Electro-Optical Performance and Material Parameters for a Tandem Metal Oxide Solar Cell

Constantin Dumitru[1], Vlad Muscurel[1], Ørnulf Nordseth[2],
Laurentiu Fara[1,3][✉] [iD], and Paul Sterian[1,3][✉] [iD]

[1] Univ. "Politehnica" of Bucharest, Spl. Independentei 313,
060042 Bucharest, Romania
lfara@renerg.pub.ro, paulesterian@yahoo.com
[2] Institute for Energy Technology, Instituttveien 18, 2007 Kjeller, Norway
[3] Academy of Romanian Scientists, Spl. Independentei 54,
030167 Bucharest, Romania

Abstract. In this work, investigation of a silicon-based tandem heterojunction solar cell was iterated via numerical modeling. The tandem cell was split into a top metal oxide and bottom c-Si subcell, and each subcell was analyzed and compared with experimental data. For the top subcell, Silvaco Atlas was used to ascertain optimum materials for the buffer layer and their impact on the cell performance. For the bottom subcell, a Quokka 2 model has be used to evaluate and compare current-voltage and quantum efficiency curves with experimental data. Transfer matrix algorithm was used to ascertain top subcell optical field characterization. The buffer layer materials for the ZnO/Cu_2O subcell that yielded best cell performance are presently TiO_2 and Ga_2O_3 while the Quokka 2 model presents a good fit with the experimental curves.

Keywords: Cuprous oxide · Tandem heterojunction ·
Modeling and simulation · Transfer matrix algorithm · Interface defect layer

1 Introduction and State of the Art

Tandem cells incorporating metal oxide heterojunctions are currently an important step in the technological development of high-efficiency solar cells. The unique properties of the p-type semiconductor Cu_2O, such as useful band gap, abundance, non-toxicity and inexpensive manufacturing, make it very attractive for implementation in a silicon-based tandem heterojunction solar cell. Copper oxide materials for photovoltaics have been well studied and their performance has improved in recent years.

For a regular cuprous oxide photovoltaic device the parameters are well known [1]. However, interface defect states pose a challenge in reaching efficiencies close to the theoretical maximum. Currently, the conversion efficiencies for cuprous oxide heterojunctions have the potential to reach 14% as reported by Takiguchi et al. [2] and a known theoretical maximum efficiency of around 19%. Methods of deposition and annealing conditions are presently studied for the optimum Cu_2O heterojunction to use

© Springer International Publishing AG, part of Springer Nature 2018
O. Gervasi et al. (Eds.): ICCSA 2018, LNCS 10961, pp. 573–582, 2018.
https://doi.org/10.1007/978-3-319-95165-2_40

in a photovoltaic device [3]. The current heterojunction tandem solar cell design used in this work [4] is presented in Fig. 1, consisting of a metal oxide top subcell and a Si bottom subcell. For the top subcell, a heterojunction between cuprous oxide and a buffer layer (n-type) is being used. This buffer layer is the focus of our top subcell electrical modeling, aiming to achieve an optimal material implementation [5, 6] for the metal oxide subcell with respect to the electrical performance of the heterojunction.

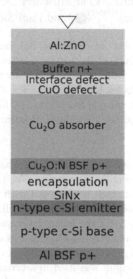

Fig. 1. Implemented design for the metal oxide heterojunction tandem solar cell

Moreover, we looked at the bottom subcell to ascertain how the model compares with the experimental data in regards to the current-voltage (I-V) and external quantum efficiency (QE) curves and the overall performance in full accord with theoretical researches [7, 14, 15]. The analysis has been carried out based on a numerical simulation in Silvaco Atlas, Matlab and Quokka.

2 Methodology and Simulation Approach

The adopted model for the solar cell follows closely the schematic in Fig. 1. Silvaco Atlas has been used to analyze the electronic properties of the metal oxide subcell. Atlas allows for precise tuning of the material properties, however, the main challenge was to correctly implement defects [7], mobilities and other material parameters that would assure convergence of the model. ZnO has been used as buffer layer but the conduction band offset is not optimal, and consequently, alternative materials are presently being investigated [8, 9]. Following the various published studies [10, 11, 21] on band offset for n-type contacts on cuprous oxides, several analyses have been made in Silvaco, based on a model developed by Takiguchi et al. [2, 16]. The model assumes the heterojunction as several layers where tabulated electronic properties and defects were implemented to correspond with experimental results for such heterojunctions. The transition between buffer and absorber layers is represented by the interface defect layer (IDL) and the CuO defective layer. Quokka 2 has been used to output I-V and QE curves for the silicon bottom subcell to compare with experimental data. Matlab was used for the transfer matrix implementation, given that the dimensions of the physical systems are on the order of the wavelength of light. Scattering effects were simplified, since we could extend the mathematical algorithm in order to introduce partial coherence, by modifying the Fresnel coefficients in the transfer-matrix formalism, but that method would not express and quantify the scattered light that leads to higher total absorbance which can be observed experimentally. Therefore the transfer-matrix algorithm has been used for multi-layer stacks to estimate the absorptance and reflectance inside the metal oxide subcell. The optical constants were measured using variable angle spectroscopic ellipsometry (VASE) and implemented in the model.

3   Results and Discussion

3.1   Metal Oxide Top Subcell

Using the Silvaco model for the top subcell, a comparison has been made between different buffer layer materials. The materials that are most interesting for our application are ZnO which yields the highest conversion efficiency along with TiO_2 and Ga_2O_3. CdS gives an efficiency close to 9% but is unfortunately a toxic material and thus is problematic to use. Another factor of importance in choosing a suitable buffer layer material is the conduction bandgap offset in regards to Cu_2O. Layer thickness has been studied for the Al:ZnO (AZO) layer, focusing on lateral charge collection. The AZO layer seems to benefit from increased thickness for proper charge carrier transport (Fig. 2), however, increased thickness results in reduced optical transparency. As such, 0.25 μm gave optimum results in the developed model. As for the Interface Defect Layer, the highly defective nature results in a decreased overall efficiency with increasing thickness (Fig. 3), and as such keeping with the physical implementation a 0.001 μm accurately simulate the defective interface between CuO transition layer and the buffer layer. The buffer layer electron mobility was also considered with respect to the subcell fill factor and efficiency. Data revealed that an electron mobility under 100 $cm^2/V \cdot s$ would greatly affect the fill factor and efficiency (Fig. 4). Defect densities are very important in the practical sense towards achieving desired performance, and while it does not pertain to the subject of this study, it is worth mentioning the relevance of the defects, especially in the absorber and defect layers. The optical analysis has been carried out using a script that computes absorption and interference in multi-layered stacks. The optical modeling approach is based on the transfer-matrix formalism, that yields the reflection and transmission at each interface. The calculation takes into account AM1.5 illumination, simplifies scattering and assumes an array of values for wavelengths (λ) from 300 to 800 nm.

The refractive index and absorption coefficients were checked against curves from literature. Calculation of J_{sc} assumes maximum internal quantum efficiency.

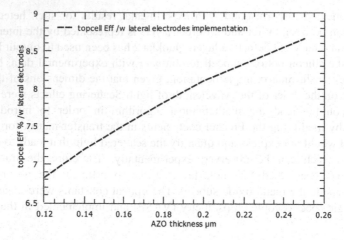

Fig. 2. AZO thickness vs topcell efficiency

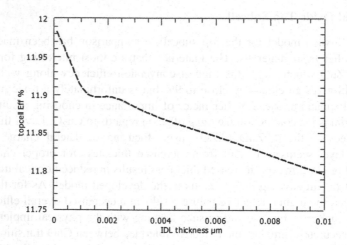

Fig. 3. IDL thickness vs topcell efficiency

Another comparison has been made between different affinities for the buffer and IDL materials (Fig. 5), keeping the bandgap fixed. We can see that for the buffer layer, the optimal affinity, from 3.4 to 3.6 eV, yields lower conduction band offset with the Cu_2O layer. In the case of IDL the optimal affinity interval is wider, from 2.95 to 3.4 eV.

In order to analyze the buffer material (see Table 1) behavior in the metal oxide heterojunction, a transfer matrix algorithm implementation in Matlab was used to ascertain the optical reflectance and absorption at the layer levels as it can be seen in Fig. 6, where ZnO yields good performance.

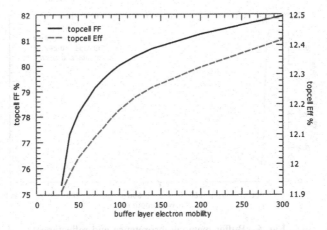

Fig. 4. Buffer electron mobility (cm^2/V·s) vs top subcell fill factor and efficiency

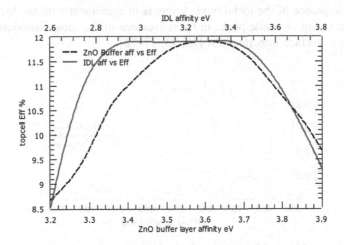

Fig. 5. Buffer and IDL affinity vs top subcell efficiency

Table 1. Buffer materials implemented in the simulation

Buffer material	Aff. eV	Eg eV	Eff %
ZnO	3.6	3.35	11.91
TiO$_2$	3.9	3.44	8.26
Ga$_2$O$_3$	4	5.18	8.92
CdS	4	2.40	8.45
Zn(O$_{0.25}$,S$_{0.75}$)	4.07	3.13	6.23
Zn(O$_{0.5}$,S$_{0.5}$)	4.45	2.83	2.8
Zn(O$_{0.75}$,S$_{0.25}$)	4.58	2.97	1.73
ZnS	4.5	3.50	3.97

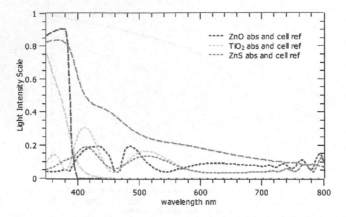

Fig. 6. Buffer material absorptance and reflectance

The absorptance of the metal oxide layers is in agreement with the literature, as it can be seen in Fig. 7, while peaks in the reflectance of the same materials could also exhibit due to surface imperfections [12, 13, 17–20].

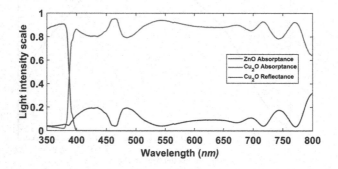

Fig. 7. Metal oxide subcell absorptance and reflectance

The effect of a rough interface can be approximated from a gradient in the input data. These inter-layers will reduce the overall reflectance of the interface layer following software interpolation. Even further improvements to the transfer matrix algorithm can be made by utilizing Effective Media Approximation, being able to take into account novel materials, like colloidal nanocrystals layers. While the deposition method can greatly influence the electronic behaviour and practical current density, the obtained current densities are good, as it can be seen in Fig. 8 where the thickness with respect to J_{SC} is shown for different materials [22–24] implemented in the buffer layer.

3.2 Silicon Bottom Subcell

For the bottom subcell, a model was adopted in the Quokka platform and used for evaluation of the electronic behavior.

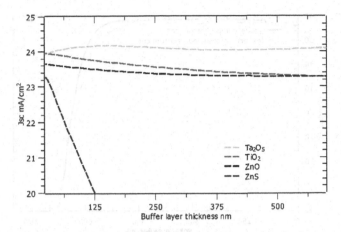

Fig. 8. Current density vs buffer layer thickness for different materials

While the Si subcell is very well studied, a model is still required to fit (see Table 2) to the experimental data for control and prediction.

Table 2. Experimental fit parameters for the c-Si subcell.

Sample c-Si subcell J-V fit parameters	
V_{OC} (mV)	625.16
Fill Factor (%)	76.83
R_S (ohm/cm^2):	0.196
R_{SH} (ohm/cm^2):	2382.8

Furthermore additional optimization can be adopted with user defined input spectrum, which is especially useful in a tandem design. The model yielded decently accurate results as it can be seen in Figs. 9 and 10 where a comparison between experimental data and model output for the J-V and EQE curves are shown. The model is subject to further improvements as can be seen in the EQE graph between 750 and 1000 nm.

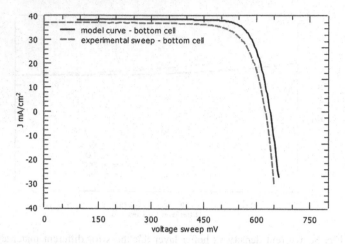

Fig. 9. Experimental vs Quokka modeled J-V curve.

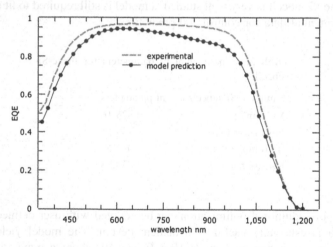

Fig. 10. Experimental vs Quokka modeled EQE curve.

4   Conclusions

In this work, a study for step by step optimization of a silicon tandem heterojunction solar cell has been presented. Cell design has been split into a ZnO/Cu$_2$O subcell and a c-Si bottom subcell, and each subcell has been investigated via numerical simulation together with comparison with experimental and literature data. Silvaco Atlas, Matlab and Quokka 2 were used for the modeling. The buffer layer affinity and mobility are important considering implementation in a ZnO/Cu$_2$O heterojunction solar cell. Zn(O, S), TiO$_2$, and Ga$_2$O$_3$ could be successfully implemented as buffer layer, while providing a low conduction band offset for the heterojunction. As the next step, in the future a full tandem implementation will be simulated after experimental top and bottom subcells get a final design pass.

The future demand for renewable energy requires efficient solar cells which are stable environmentally, so the materials selection and suitable fabrication methods are crucial.

Acknowledgements. This work was conducted under: (1) the research project SOLHET, 2016–2019, M-ERA.Net program, supported by the Research Council of Norway (RCN), project no. 251789 and the Romanian Executive Agency for Higher Education, Research, Development and Innovation Funding (UEFISCDI), project no. 34/2016; (2) the project MultiscaleSolar MP1406, 2015–2019, supported by the European Commission through COST program.

References

1. Wong, T.K., Zhuk, S., Masudy-Panah, S., Dalapati, G.K.: Current status and future prospects of copper oxide heterojunction solar cells. Materials **9**(4), 271 (2016)
2. Takiguchi, Y., Miyajima, S.: Device simulation of cuprous oxide heterojunction solar cells. Jpn. J. Appl. Phys. **54**, 112303 (2015)
3. Lindberg, P., Gorantla, S., Gunnæs, A., Svensson, B.G., Monakhov, E.: Electronic properties and morphology of copper oxide/n-type silicon heterostructures. J. Phys.: Condens. Matter **29**(31), 314701 (2017)
4. Nordseth, Ø., Kumar, R., Bergum, K., Fara, L., Foss Sean, S.E., Haug, H., Dragan, F., Craciunescu, D., Sterian, P., Chilibon, I., Vasiliu, C., Baschir, L., Savastru, D., Monakhov, E., Svensson, B.G.: Optical analysis of a ZnO/Cu$_2$O subcell in a silicon-based tandem heterojunction solar cell. Green Sustain. Chem. **7**, 57–69 (2017)
5. Minami, T., Nishi, Y., Miyata, T.: Relationship between the electrical properties of the n-oxide and p-Cu$_2$O layers and the photovoltaic properties of Cu$_2$O-based heterojunction solar cells. Sol. Energ. Mat. Sol. Cells **147**, 85–93 (2016)
6. Siol, S., Hellman, J.C., Tilley, D., Gratzel, M., Morasch, J., Deuermeier, J., Jaegermann, W., Klein, A.: Band Alignment Engineering at Cu2O/ZnO Heterointerfaces. ACS Appl. Mater. **8** (33), 21824–21831 (2016)
7. Lloyd, M.A., Siah, S.C., Brandt, R.E., Serdy, J., Johnson, S.W., Lee, Y.S., Buinassisi, T.: Intrinsic defect engineering of cuprous oxide to enhance electrical transport properties for photovoltaic applications. In: IEEE 40th Photovoltaic Specialists Conference (PVSC), vol. 2016, pp. 3443–3445, Denver, CO (2014)
8. Tolstova, Y., Omelchenko, S.T., Blackwell, R.E., Shing, A.M.: Polycrystalline Cu2O photovoltaic devices incorporating Zn(O, S) window layers. Sol. Energ. Mat. Sol. Cells **160**, 340–345 (2017)
9. Minami, T., Nishi, Y., Miyata, T.: High-efficiency Cu$_2$O-based heterojunction solar cells fabricated using a Ga$_2$O$_3$ thin film as n-type layer. Appl. Phys. Express **6**(4), 044101 (2013)
10. Robertson, J., Falabretti, B.: Band offsets of high K gate oxides on III-V semiconductors. J. Appl. Phys. **100**, 014111 (2006)
11. Brandt, R.E., Young, M., Hejin, H.P., Dameron, A., Chua, D., Lee, S.Y., Teeter, G., Gordon, R., Buonassisi, T.: Band offsets of n-type electron-selective contacts on cuprous oxide (Cu$_2$O) for photovoltaics. Appl. Phys. Lett. **105**, 263901 (2014)
12. Oku, T., Yamada, T., Fujimoto, K., Akiyama, T.: Microstructures and photovoltaic properties of Zn(Al)O/Cu$_2$O-based solar cells prepared by spin-coating and electrodeposition. Coatings **4**, 203–213 (2014)

13. Lee, S.W., Lee, Y.S., Heo, J., Siah, S.C., Chua, D., Brandt, R.E., Kim, S.B., Mailoa, J.P., Buonassisi, T., Gordon, R.: Improved Cu_2O-based solar cells using atomic layer deposition to control the Cu oxidation state at the p–n junction. Adv. Energy Mater. 4(11) (2014)

14. Sterian, A., Sterian, P.: Mathematical models of dissipative systems in quantum engineering. Math. Probl. Eng. 24, 2012 (2012)

15. Stefanescu, E., Sterian, A.R., Sterian, P.: Study on the fermion systems coupled by electric dipol interaction with the free electromagnetic field. Advanced Laser Technologies 2004, vol. 5850, pp. 160–166. International Society for Optics and Photonics, 7 June 2005

16. Sterian, A.R.: Computer modeling of the coherent optical amplifier and laser systems. In: Gervasi, O., Gavrilova, Marina L. (eds.) ICCSA 2007. LNCS, vol. 4705, pp. 436–449. Springer, Heidelberg (2007). https://doi.org/10.1007/978-3-540-74472-6_35

17. Rosu, C., Manaila-Maximean, D., Donescu, D., Frunza, S., Sterian, A.R.: Influence of polarizing electric fields on the electrical and optical properties of polymer-clay composite system. Mod. Phys. Lett. B 24(01), 65–73 (2010)

18. Lazar, B., Sterian, A., Pusca, S., Paun, V., Toma, C., Morarescu, C.: Simulating delayed pulses in organic materials. Comput. Sci. Appl.-ICCSA 2006, 779–784 (2006)

19. Ninulescu, V., Sterian, A.-R.: Dynamics of a two-level medium under the action of short optical pulses. In: Gervasi, O., Gavrilova, Marina L., Kumar, V., Laganà, A., Lee, H.P., Mun, Y., Taniar, D., Tan, C.J.K. (eds.) ICCSA 2005. LNCS, vol. 3482, pp. 635–642. Springer, Heidelberg (2005). https://doi.org/10.1007/11424857_70

20. Yang, X.J., Machado, J.T., Cattani, C., Gao, F.: On a fractal LC-electric circuit modeled by local fractional calculus. Commun. Nonlinear Sci. Numer. Simul. 30(47), 200–206 (2017)

21. Nordseth, Ø., Fara, L., Kumar, R., Foss, S.E., Dumitru, C., Muscurel, V., Dragan, F., Craciunescu, D., Bergum, K., Haug, H., Sterian, P., Chilibon, I., Vasiliu, C., Baschir, L., Savastru, D., Monakhov, E., Svensson, B.G.: Electro-optical modeling of a ZnO/Cu_2O subcell in a silicon-based tandem heterojunction solar cell. In: 33rd European Photovoltaic Solar Energy Conference and Exhibition (session 1CV.3.85), pp. 172–177 (2017)

22. Dumitru, C., Muscurel, V., Nordseth, Ø., Fara, L., Sterian, P.: Electrical modeling of the buffer layer for a Cu_2O/ZnO solar cell using Silvaco Atlas. U.P.B. Sci. Bull., Series B 79(2), 173–178 (2017)

23. Mitroi, R., Ninulescu, V., Fara, L.: Tandem solar cells based on Cu_2O and c-Si subcells in parallel configuration: numerical simulation. Int. J. Photoenergy, 2017, 6 p. (2017). Art. ID 7284367

24. Mitroi, R., Ninulescu, V., Fara, L.: Performance optimization of solar cells based on heterojunctions with Cu_2O: numerical analysis. J. Energy Eng. 143(4), 04017005 (2017)

The Huff Versus the Pareto-Huff Customer Choice Rules in a Discrete Competitive Location Model

Pascual Fernández[1]([✉]), Blas Pelegrín[1], Algirdas Lančinskas[2],
and Julius Žilinskas[2]

[1] Department Statistics and Operations Research, University of Murcia,
Murcia, Spain
{pfdez,pelegrin}@um.es
[2] Institute of Mathematics and Informatics, Vilnius University, Vilnius, Lithuania
{algirdas.lancinskas,julius.zilinskas}@mii.vu.lt

Abstract. An entering firm wants to compete for market share in a given area by opening some new facilities selected among a finite set of potential locations. Customers are spatially separated and other firms are already operating in that area. In this paper, we analyse the effect of two different customers' behavior over the optimal solutions, the Huff and the Pareto-Huff customer choice rules. In the first, the customer splits its demand among all competing facilities according to its attractions. In the second, the customer splits its demand among the facilities that are Pareto optimal with respect to the attraction (to be maximized) and the distance (to be minimized), proportionally to their attractions. So, a competitive facility location problem on discrete space is considered in which an entering firm wants to locate a fixed number of new facilities for market share maximization when both Huff and Pareto-Huff customer behavior are used. In order to solve these two models, a heuristic procedure is proposed to obtain the best solutions, and it is compared with a classical genetic algorithm for a set of real geographical coordinates and population data of municipalities in Spain.

1 Introduction

Probably, the most important decision for a firm that competes with other firms to provide goods or services to the customers in a given geographical area, is where to locate its facilities. Depending on location space, facility attraction, customer behavior, demand function, decision variables, etc., different location models and solution procedures have been proposed (see for instance survey papers [6,11]). The entering firm is focused in the determination of the optimal locations for the new facilities in order to maximize its market share or profit, taking into account the customers' behavior and that have to compete with other pre-existing facilities belonging to different firms for customers demand. Usually, it is assumed that the customers choose the nearest facility to be served, but

© Springer International Publishing AG, part of Springer Nature 2018
O. Gervasi et al. (Eds.): ICCSA 2018, LNCS 10961, pp. 583–592, 2018.
https://doi.org/10.1007/978-3-319-95165-2_41

on real problems, customers take into account some other characteristics of the facilities, in addition to the distance.

Since the attraction model proposed by Huff [9], different customer choice rules have been used to estimate the market share captured by the competing facilities. The attraction of a facility is defined as the quotient between facility quality (which depends on its characteristics) and a non-negative non-descending function of the distance between the customer and the facility. The most common customer choice rules are the Huff (or proportional or probabilistic) and the binary (or deterministic) (see [12]). In the Huff case, customers patronize all the facilities in proportion to facility attraction (see for instance [3,13]), and in the binary case, each customer patronizes the most attractive facility (see [1,7]).

When Huff customer choice rule is considered, customers will patronize very distant facilities even when more attractive facilities are much closer, although the captured demand by these facilities is small. To avoid these allocations and adjust the model more to reality, a modified Huff rule is considered, the so called Pareto-Huff customer choice rule [10], which has hardly been used in the literature. In this case, a customer will patronize a more distant facility only if it is more attractive, then distant facilities will be selected by customers only if no facility exists that is both closer and at least so attractive. So, on Pareto-Huff model, each customer splits its demand among the facilities that are Pareto optimal with respect to the attraction (to be maximized) and the distance (to be minimized), proportionally with their attractions.

In this paper we will consider these two customer choice rules, the Huff and the Pareto-Huff, will analyse its influence on the optimal solutions, and will propose a heuristic procedure to be solved them since these two models are not linear programming problems. To solve both problems, one of the algorithms proposed by Fernández et al. (2017) has been used, the one based on ranking and distance, because it can be used to solve any discrete competitive location problem, and since it do not require to have analytical expression of the objective function, but only be able to evaluate objective value at any solution candidate. To check performance of the proposed heuristic algorithm, it is necessary to know the optimal solution of the problems in order to compare it with the solution given by the heuristic algorithm. For small size data, a complete enumeration algorithm to obtain optimal solutions has been used for both models. For bigger size data, a classical genetic algorithm is used to obtain good solutions to be compared with solutions provided by the here proposed heuristic algorithm.

The reminder of the paper is organized as follows: Sect. 2 consists of description of the competitive location problems and its formulations, Sect. 3 is devoted to presentation of the heuristic algorithm, and Sect. 4 includes the description and discussion of the experimental investigation of the proposed algorithm; finally, conclusions are presented in Sect. 5.

2   Discrete Location Models

An entering firm wants to open new facilities in an area where similar facilities of other competing firms are already present. For simplicity, it is considered that all pre-existing facilities belong to the same firm, the competitor. Customers are aggregated to geographic demand points in order to make the problem computationally tractable (see [5] for demand aggregation), and its demand is fixed and known.

The following general notation is used:
Indices:

i, I index and set of demand points (customers)
j, k indeces of facilities

Data:

w_i demand at i
q_j quality of facility j
d_{ij} distance between demand point i and facility j
a_{ij} attraction that demand point i feels for facility j
L set of candidate locations for the new facilities
C set of pre-existing facilities of competetitor/s
r number of new facilities to be located

Variables:

X set of locations for the new facilities

2.1 Model with the Huff Customer Choice Rule

When Huff customer choice rule is considered, each customer splits his demand over all facilities in the market proportionally with his attraction to each facility (additive attraction). Note that in this model it is not necessary to know if the pre-existing facilities owns or not to different firms, since the demand of each customer i is split between all facilities, regardless of the firm to which they belong.

Usually, the attraction that a customer i feels for a facility j is defined as $a_{ij} = \frac{q_j}{g(d_{ij})}$, where $g(d_{ij})$ is a non-decreasing non-negative and convex function of the distance between customers and facilities. In this paper, it has been considered that $g(d_{ij}) = 1 + d_{ij}$ for simplicity.

If $M_H(X)$ denote the market share captured by the entering firm when Huff customer choice rule is used and its new facilities are located at X, the problem can be formulated as:

$$Max\{M_H(X) = \sum_{i \in I} w_i \frac{\sum_{j \in X} a_{ij}}{\sum_{j \in X} a_{ij} + \sum_{k \in C} a_{ik}} : |X| = r, X \subset L\}. \quad (1)$$

that is a nonlinear optimization problem.

2.2 Model with the Pareto-Huff Customer Choice Rule

In this new model, the demand of each customer i will be split between all Pareto optimal facilities PH_i with respect to quality and distance, proportionally with their attraction. For any customer i, facilities belonging to PH_i are non-dominated facilities with respect to quality and distance, i.e., for any $j \in PH_i$ there doesn't exist any other facility with at least quality q_j and closer to i than j (see Fig. 1 for an example).

If $M_{PH}(X)$ denote the market share captured by the entering firm when its new facilities are located at X, and the Pareto-Huff customer choice rule is considered, the problem can be formulated as:

$$Max\{M_{PH}(X) = \sum_{i \in I} w_i \frac{\sum_{j \in PH_i \cap X} a_{ij}}{\sum_{j \in PH_i} a_{ij}} : |X| = r, X \subset L\}. \tag{2}$$

which, as the Huff model, it is a nonlinear optimization problem.

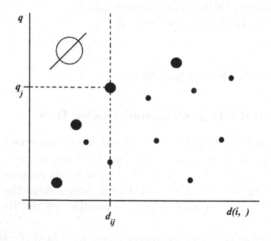

Fig. 1. Example of Pareto optimal facilities PH_i for customer i (big points).

3 Ranking-Based Discrete Optimization Algorithm

A heuristic algorithm has been developed to solve the location problems described in the previous section, which do not guarantee determination of the optimal solution, but rather its approximation. The algorithm is based on a single agent random search in the neighborhood of the best solution found so far, and its only requirement is to have availability to evaluate objective value at any possible solution. The Discrete Optimization Algorithm based on Ranking and Distance (RD) (see [4]) begins with a subset of location candidates X as an initial variable, which is considered as the best known (but not necessarily optimal) solution of the problem being solved. A new solution X' is generated by in turn taking location from X and changing them to another one with probability $\pi_c = 1/r$, thus ensuring that a single facility will be changed in average. The new facility l, in case of change, is selected from $L' = L \setminus (X \cup X')$ as

$$x_i' = \begin{cases} l \in L \setminus (X \cup X') & \text{if } \xi_i < 1/r \\ x_i & \text{otherwise} \end{cases} \tag{3}$$

where ξ_i is a random number uniformly generated over the interval $[0, 1]$, and $i = 1, 2, \ldots, r$.

Each candidate location $l_i \in L$, has different probability to be selected. This probability is based on the rank r_i of the candidate location l_i, and a geographical distance $d(l_i, x_z')$ between the candidate location l_i and the location x_z'; here x_z' is a location already forming solution X' and is expected to be changed $(z = 1, 2, \ldots, r)$, and can be expressed as

$$\pi_i^{rd} = \frac{r_i}{d(l_i, x_z') \sum_{j=1}^{|L|} \frac{r_j}{d(l_j, x_z')}} \tag{4}$$

At the beginning of the algorithm, all candidate solutions have unit ranks $r_i = 1$, forall $i = 1, 2, \ldots, |L|$. Later ranks are automatically adjusted according to the success and failures in improvement of the best known solution by selecting a particular candidate location. If the newly generated solution X' improves the best solution found so far X, i.e. $M(X') > M(X)$, where $M(\cdot)$ stands for the objective function, then

(1) the ranks of all candidate locations in X' are increased by one, and
(2) the ranks of all candidate locations that form X, but do not form X' are reduced by one.

Otherwise, if $M(X') \leq M(X)$, then the ranks of all candidate locations which form unsuccessfully generated solution X', but do not form the best known solution X, are reduced by one. If any of the ranks reaches zero, then ranks are increased by one.

If the new solution X' improves X, then X is changed by X'. Such a process is continued till a stopping criterion, which is usually based on the number of function evaluations, is satisfied.

4   Experimental Investigation

The proposed algorithm RD has been experimentally investigated by solving both considered models using real geographical data of coordinates and population of 6960 municipalities in Spain, numbered in decreasing order with respect to its population, which will be considered as demand points and its demand equal to the population, with total demand around 38,5 millions of inhabitants. The distances between demand points and facilities have been calculated in kilometers using Haversine distance [14], and the attraction that demand point i feels for facility j has been taken as $a_{ij} = \frac{q_j}{1+d_{ij}}$.

For all experiments, it has been considered that the number of pre-existing facilities is equal to 30 (the most populated, nodes from 1 to 30), and its quality values have been randomly generated in the interval [30, 70]. All new facilities for the entering firm is supposed to have the same quality equal to 35, 45, 55 and 65. Some combinations of parameters $(r, q, |L|)$ are considered when $r = 5, 10$, $q = 35, 45, 55, 65$, and $|L| = 500, 1000$.

The goodness of the proposed algorithm has been evaluated by the quality of the best solution X found. The best solution found by the proposed algorithm has been approximated using 10000 function evaluations for each instance. Due to its stochastic nature, the algorithm has been run for 100 independent runs and average results have been considered. The results obtained by RD have been compared with the results obtained by a Genetic Algorithm (GA) [2,8] with the population of 100 individuals, uniform crossover with the rate of 0.8 and mutation rate of $1/r$; GA has been run for 100 generations, thus performing 10000 function evaluations in total. All experiments have been run in a PC with Pentium IV Processor, 3.2 GHz and 3 GB RAM.

For the smaller data set, parameters $(5, q, 500)$, a Complete Enumeration Algorithm (CEA) has been used to obtain optimal solutions for both models. In this case, the quality of the best solution is the ratio between its objective value and the objective value of the optimal solutions provided by CEA, and to measure its quality, the probability to achieve the optimal solution with different error has been evaluated.

For the Huff model, the results show that RD provides better probability to achieve optimal solutions, independent of problem instance. The proposed heuristic algorithm guarantees to find the optimal solution with 1% error, independent of problem instance, whilst GA can provide a guarantee optimal solution with error of 4% for any instance (see Table 1).

Table 1. Huff model: results for parameters $(5, q, 500)$.

r	q	$|L|$	0%	1%	2%	3%	4%	5%
RD								
5	35	500	0,79	1,00	1,00	1,00	1,00	1,00
5	45	500	0,84	1,00	1,00	1,00	1,00	1,00
5	55	500	0,82	1,00	1,00	1,00	1,00	1,00
5	65	500	0,83	1,00	1,00	1,00	1,00	1,00
GA								
5	35	500	0,00	0,91	0,93	1,00	1,00	1,00
5	45	500	0,38	0,86	0,92	0,96	1,00	1,00
5	55	500	0,00	0,83	0,94	0,99	1,00	1,00
5	65	500	0,30	0,83	0,93	0,97	1,00	1,00

For Pareto-Huff model the results are similar. RD provides better probability to achieve optimal solution for all instances, guarantees to find the optimal solution with 2% error, while GA cannot guaranty optimal solution with error less than 5% for any instance (see Table 2).

Table 2. Pareto-Huff model: results for parameters $(5, q, 500)$.

r	q	$|L|$	0%	1%	2%	3%	4%	5%
RD								
5	35	500	0,76	1,00	1,00	1,00	1,00	1,00
5	45	500	0,98	0,98	1,00	1,00	1,00	1,00
5	55	500	0,77	1,00	1,00	1,00	1,00	1,00
5	65	500	0,95	1,00	1,00	1,00	1,00	1,00
GA								
5	35	500	0,00	0,17	0,68	0,99	1,00	1,00
5	45	500	0,03	0,28	0,45	0,85	0,97	0,97
5	55	500	0,10	0,80	0,90	0,93	0,96	0,99
5	65	500	0,03	0,16	0,64	0,73	0,91	0,98

For parameters $(5, q, 500)$, $(10, q, 500)$ and $(10, q, 1000)$, where $q = 35, 45, 55, 65$, solutions provide by RD and GA algorithms are compared (see Table 3). For the Huff model, the new facilities for all the parameters are located, in general, in points with greater demand, however, for the Pareto-Huff model, for $q = 34, 45$, the new facilities are not located in the points of greater demand, but in points with lower demand near the previous ones, and for $q = 55, 65$, the results are similar to the Huff model, although the locations for the new facilities are not the same. Regarding the total demand captured by the new facilities in both models, in the Huff model, greater market share is obtained for $q = 35$, 45, while for $q = 55$, 65, with the Pareto-Huff model, greater market share is captured.

The quality of the solution given by each algorithm has been measured by the ratio of average of utility function of the 100 runs, and the best known value of utility function obtained by any of the algorithms. Each experiment has also been ran for 10000 function evaluations and repeated 100 times. Results show that RD solves each instance better than GA independent on the parameters and the customers choice rule. Furthermore GA was more sensitive to the parameter of the problem. The quality of solutions obtained by RD for any set of parameters is always between 0,990 and 1, and by GA between 0,944 and 0,996 (see Table 4).

Table 3. Best solutions found by using RD algorithm.

	$(r, |L|)$	q	X	$M(X)$ (millions)
Huff	(5, 500)	35	1, 2, 3, 4, 6	5,38
		45	1, 2, 3, 4, 6	6,48
		55	1, 2, 3, 4, 6	7,46
		65	2, 3, 4, 5, 6	8,35
	(10, 500)	35	1, 2, 3, 4, 5, 6, 8, 14, 32, 35	8,36
		45	1, 2, 3, 4, 5, 6, 8, 14, 29, 32	9,95
		55	1, 2, 3, 4, 5, 6, 8, 14, 29, 32	11,3
		65	1, 2, 3, 4, 5, 6, 7, 8, 14, 29	12,6
	(10, 1000)	35	1, 2, 3, 4, 5, 6, 8, 14, 32, 35	8,36
		45	1, 2, 3, 4, 5, 6, 8, 14, 29, 32	9,95
		55	1, 2, 3, 4, 5, 6, 8, 14, 29, 32	11,3
		65	1, 2, 3, 4, 5, 6, 7, 8, 14, 29	12,6
Pareto-Huff	(5, 500)	35	21, 40, 55, 108, 112	2,55
		45	6, 14, 15, 55, 108	3,65
		55	1, 3, 4, 6, 12	10,2
		65	1, 3, 4, 12, 22	11,2
	(10, 500)	35	12, 21, 40, 53, 55, 101, 108, 112, 149, 377	4,26
		45	6, 12, 14, 15, 21, 55, 101, 108, 112, 149	5,78
		55	1, 3, 4, 5, 6, 8, 12, 14, 15, 23	14,6
		65	1, 3, 4, 5, 6, 7, 8, 12, 14, 22	16,6
	(10, 1000)	35	12, 21, 40, 53, 55, 101, 108, 112, 149, 377	4,26
		45	6, 12, 14, 15, 21, 55, 108, 112, 149, 621	5,78
		55	1, 3, 4, 5, 6, 8, 12, 14, 15, 23	14,6
		65	1, 3, 4, 5, 6, 7, 8, 12, 14, 22	16,6

Table 4. Results for parameters $(5, q, 500)$, $(10, q, 500)$ and $(10, q, 1000)$.

	$(r, |L|)$	$q = 35$		$q = 45$		$q = 55$		$q = 65$	
		RD	GA	RD	GA	RD	GA	RD	GA
Huff	(5,500)	0,999	0,996	0,999	0,995	0,999	0,995	1,000	0,994
	(10,500)	0,999	0,989	0,999	0,987	1,000	0,980	1,000	0,986
	(10,1000)	0,998	0,981	0,996	0,982	0,997	0,973	0,998	0,978
Pareto-Huff	(5,500)	0,999	0,984	1,000	0,981	0,999	0,991	1,000	0,980
	(10,500)	0,998	0,975	0,998	0,971	0,994	0,959	0,998	0,956
	(10,1000)	0,995	0,969	0,996	0,959	0,990	0,963	0,992	0,944

5   Conclusions

In this paper two discrete competitive facility location models for an entering firm have been considered depending if Huff or Pareto-Huff customers choice rule is considered. A heuristic algorithm has been proposed to solve these non-linear location problems, based on the ranking and the distance between candidate locations and customers [4]. To check the performance of the proposed algorithms we have used real geographical coordinates and population data of 6960 municipalities in Spain, and have compared the solutions generated with the best feasible solution found, and in the particular, for small size data, a complete enumeration algorithm has been used to obtain the optimal solution. Computational experiments prove that the proposed algorithm is always better than GA, and RD obtains always the best solution for all parameters of the problem. The quality of the solution obtained with RD is in average 0.998 when all the results for Huff and Pareto-Huff models are considered.

In conclusion, this heuristic algorithm, RD, can be a good option to solve discrete competitive facility location problems when an entering firm wants to locate new facilities in the market, and customer choice rule is Huff or Pareto-Huff.

Acknowledgments. This research has been supported by the Ministry of Economy and Competitiveness of Spain under the research project MTM2015-70260-P, and the Fundación Séneca (The Agency of Science and Technology of the Region of Murcia) under the research project 19241/PI/14, and also by a grant (No. MIP-051/2014) from the Research Council of Lithuania.

References

1. Campos, C.M., Santos-Peñate, D.R., Moreno, J.A.: An exact procedure and LP formulations for the leader-follower location problem. Top **18**(1), 97–121 (2010)
2. Davis, L.: Handbook of Genetic Algorithms. Van Nostrand Reinhold, New York (1991)
3. Drezner, T., Drezner, Z.: Finding the optimal solution to the Huff based competitive location model. Comput. Manag. Sci. **1**(2), 193–208 (2004)
4. Fernández, P., Pelegrín, B., Lančinskas, A., Žilinskas, J.: New heuristic algorithms for discrete competitive location problems with binary and partially binary customer behavior. Comput. Oper. Res. **79**, 12–18 (2017)
5. Francis, R.L., Lowe, T.J., Tamir, A.: Demand point aggregation for location models. In: Hamacher, H., Drezner, Z. (eds.) Facility Location: Application and Theory, pp. 207–232 (2002)
6. Friesz, T.: Competitive networks facility location models: a survey. Pap. Reg. Sci. **65**, 47–57 (1998)
7. Hakimi, L.: Location with spatial interactions: competitive locations and games. In: Drezner, Z. (ed.) Facility Location: A Survey of Applications and Methods, pp. 367–386 (1995)
8. Holland, J.H.: Adaptation in Natural and Artificial Systems. University of Michigan Press, Ann Arbor (1975)

9. Huff, D.: Defining and estimating a trade area. J. Mark. **28**, 34–38 (1964)
10. Peeters, P.H., Plastria, F.: Discretization results for the Huff and Pareto-Huff competitive location models on networks. TOP **6**, 247–260 (1998)
11. ReVelle, C., Eiselt, H., Daskin, M.: A bibliography for some fundamental problem categories in discrete location science. Eur. J. Oper. Res. **184**(3), 817–848 (2008)
12. Serra, D., Eiselt, H.A., Laporte, G., ReVelle, C.S.: Market capture models under various customer-choice rules. Environ. Plan. B: Plan. Des. **26**, 741–750 (1999)
13. Serra, D., Colomé, R.: Consumer choice and optimal location models: formulations and heuristics. Pap. Reg. Sci. **80**(4), 439–464 (2001)
14. Sinnott, R.W.: Virtues of the haversine. Sky Telescope **68**(2), 159 (1984)

Comparison of Combinatorial and Continuous Frameworks for the Beam Angle Optimization Problem in IMRT

Humberto Rocha[1,2]([✉])[ID], Joana Dias[1,2][ID], Tiago Ventura[3][ID],
Brígida Ferreira[4,5][ID], and Maria do Carmo Lopes[3,5][ID]

[1] CeBER and Faculdade de Economia, Universidade de Coimbra,
3004-512 Coimbra, Portugal
`hrocha@mat.uc.pt, joana@fe.uc.pt`
[2] INESC-Coimbra, 3030-290 Coimbra, Portugal
[3] Serviço de Física Médica, IPOC-FG, EPE, 3000-075 Coimbra, Portugal
`{tiagoventura,mclopes}@ipocoimbra.min-saude.pt`
[4] ESS.PP, Politécnico do Porto, 4400-330 Vila Nova de Gaia, Portugal
`bcf@ess.ipp.pt`
[5] I3N.UA, Universidade de Aveiro, 3810-193 Aveiro, Portugal

Abstract. Radiation therapy (RT) is used nowadays for the majority of cancer patients. A technologically advanced type of RT is IMRT – intensity-modulated radiation therapy. With this RT modality the cancerous cells of the patient can be irradiated using non-uniform radiation maps delivered from different beam directions. Although non-uniform radiation maps allow, by themselves, an enhanced sparing of the neighboring healthy organs while properly irradiating the tumor with the prescribed dose, selection of appropriate irradiation directions play a decisive role on these conflicting tasks: deliver dose to the tumor while preventing (too much) dose to be deposited in the surrounding tissues. This paper focus on the problem of choosing the best set of irradiation directions, known as beam angle optimization (BAO) problem. Two completely different mathematical formulations of this problem can be found in the literature. A combinatorial formulation, widely used and addressed by many different algorithms and strategies, and a continuous formulation proposed by the authors and addressed by derivative-free algorithms. In this paper, a comparison of two of the most successful strategies to address each one of these formulations is done resorting to a set of ten clinical nasopharyngeal tumor cases already treated at the Portuguese Institute of Oncology of Coimbra.

Keywords: IMRT · Beam angle optimization
Combinatorial optimization · Derivative-free optimization

1 Introduction

Cancer incidence and prevalence is continuously growing. The majority of the cancer patients is nowadays treated with radiation therapy (RT), either to kill

O. Gervasi et al. (Eds.): ICCSA 2018, LNCS 10961, pp. 593–606, 2018.
https://doi.org/10.1007/978-3-319-95165-2_42

the cancer cells or to palliate the symptoms. A technologically advanced type of RT is intensity-modulated radiation therapy (IMRT). A multileaf collimator is used in IMRT to transform the radiation beam into a number of discrete small sub-beams called beamlets. The optimal intensities of these beamlets are calculated independently, in a large-scale optimization problem called fluence map optimization (FMO) problem, leading to non-uniform radiation maps. Typically, a predefined number of non-uniform radiation maps intersects the tumor from different irradiation directions. Although non-uniform radiation maps allow, by themselves, an enhanced sparing of the neighboring healthy organs while properly irradiating the tumor with the prescribed dose, selection of appropriate irradiation directions play a decisive role on these conflicting tasks: deliver dose to the tumor while preventing (too much) dose to be deposited in the surrounding tissues. The optimal selection of beam irradiation directions, known as beam angle optimization (BAO) problem, is a very difficult optimization problem.

Two completely different mathematical formulations of the BAO problem can be found in the literature. A combinatorial formulation, widely used, considers a discrete sample of all continuous beam angle directions. This formulation leads to a NP-hard optimization problem [3]. A large number of different algorithms have been used to speed up the searches, including gradient search [7], neighborhood search [1], simulated annealing [9], response surface approaches [2], branch-and-prune [11] or hybrid approaches [4]. Iterative BAO is a successful combinatorial strategy used in practice that adds one beam at a time, sequentially, to a treatment plan, reducing the total number of possible combinations significantly [3]. Alternatively, a continuous formulation has been proposed by the authors, considering all continuous beam angle directions. This formulation leads to a highly non-convex optimization problem with many local minima on a continuous search space. Figure 1 illustrates the non-convex nature of a two-dimension BAO problem for a nasopharyngeal tumor case. Due to the curse of dimensionality, the number of local minima will increase exponentially for larger dimensions. The continuous search space of the BAO problem has been explored using derivative-free optimization frameworks [13–16].

This paper compares two of the most successful strategies used to address the continuous and the combinatorial BAO formulations: a parallel multistart derivative-free framework that explores thoroughly the BAO problem continuous search space is compared to an iterative BAO framework that would obtain a theoretical upper limit of the treatment plan quality [18]. A set of ten clinical cases of nasopharyngeal (intra-cranial) tumors treated at the Portuguese Institute of Oncology of Coimbra (IPOC) is used to test and discuss the benefits of our continuous approach against the benchmark combinatorial approach. The paper is organized as follows. In the next section we present a continuous and a combinatorial formulation of the BAO problem. In section three we describe a parallel multistart derivative-free framework for the BAO problem. Computational tests are presented in section four. In the last section we have the conclusions.

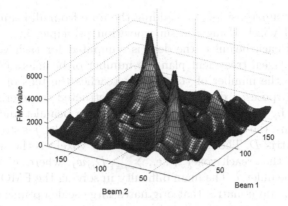

Fig. 1. BAO surface for a nasopharyngeal tumor case considering only two coplanar beam irradiation directions.

2 Mathematical Formulation of the BAO Problem

The aim of BAO is to determine the best ensemble of beam angle directions to irradiate the patient. Here, coplanar beams are considered, i.e. beam directions lay on the plane of rotation of the linear accelerator around the patient that lays in a fix positioned couch. It is assumed that the treatment planner defines, *a priori*, the number of beam irradiation directions to be n. In order to assess the quality of an n-beam angle ensemble, $\theta_1, \ldots, \theta_n$, the optimal value of the FMO problem obtained for that beam angle ensemble, $f(\theta_1, \ldots, \theta_n)$, is used. A mathematical formulation for the BAO problem can then consider that the best ensemble of beam directions is obtained for the (FMO) function's minimum:

$$\min f(\theta_1, \ldots, \theta_n)$$
$$s.t. \ \ \theta_1, \ldots, \theta_n \in \Theta, \text{ where } \Theta \text{ is the set of all possible beam angles.}$$

$$(1)$$

For a combinatorial BAO formulation, the interval of possible gantry angles, $[0°, 360°[$, is discretized into evenly spaced angles. For example, for an angle increment of one degree, the set of all candidate beam angles Θ of Eq. (1) corresponds to the set of 360 beam angles $\{0, 1, \ldots, 359\}$. For a continuous BAO formulation, the interval of possible gantry angles $[0°, 360°[$ is considered. Note that the beam angle directions $-10°$ and $350°$ are the same as well as beam angle directions $370°$ and $10°$. Thus, we can consider $\Theta = \mathbb{R}^n$ and avoid a bounded formulation.

Regardless of using a combinatorial or a continuous BAO formulation, the quality of each beam ensemble is assessed through the FMO optimal value. The resolution of the FMO problem requires the accurate assessment of the radiation dose distribution, measured in Gray (Gy), for each irradiated structure of the patient. The volume of each structure is discretized into small volume elements called voxels. The dose is calculated for each individual voxel using the principle of superposition, i.e., adding the dose from all beamlets that reach each individual voxel. Using the superposition principle, i.e., considering the contribution of each beamlet, the dose is computed for each voxel. Typically, for a nasopharyngeal treatment plan the number of beamlets (N_b) reaches the hundreds while the number of voxels (N_v) reaches the tens of thousands. For optimization purposes, a dose matrix D is constructed considering the beamlet intensities and by indexing each column to a given beamlet and each row to a given voxel. Thus, the dose deposited in voxel i by beamlet j is stored in row i and column j of matrix D. The total dose received by voxel i is the sum of the doses of all beamlets that reach voxel i, i.e., $\sum_{j=1}^{N_b} D_{ij}w_j$, where w_j is the intensity (or weight) of beamlet j. The main difficulty in solving the FMO problem is the dimension of the dose matrix that originates large-scale optimization problems.

Many different mathematical models and optimization procedures have been presented for the FMO problem, including linear models [17], nonlinear models [6], a priori multicriteria models [5], a posteriori multicriteria models [12], particle swarm optimization models [19] and fuzzy inference systems models [10]. Here, we use the following convex penalty function voxel-based nonlinear model [1]:

$$\min_w \sum_{i=1}^{N_v} \left[\underline{\lambda}_i \left(T_i - \sum_{j=1}^{N_b} D_{ij}w_j \right)_+^2 + \overline{\lambda}_i \left(\sum_{j=1}^{N_b} D_{ij}w_j - T_i \right)_+^2 \right]$$

$$s.t. \quad w_j \geq 0, \ j = 1, \dots, N_b,$$

where $\overline{\lambda}_i$ and $\underline{\lambda}_i$ are weights that penalize overdose and underdose of voxel i, T_i is the tolerance/prescribed dose for voxel i and $(\cdot)_+ = \max\{0, \cdot\}$. This model penalizes the square difference between the tolerance/prescribed dose and the received dose by each voxel, implying that small differences from the tolerance/prescribed dose (overdose or underdose) may be clinically tolerated while larger differences from the tolerance/prescribed dose are decreasingly accepted.

The discussion of the most appropriate FMO problem formulation/resolution to be embedded in a BAO framework is out of the scope of this study. Furthermore, the FMO model is used as a black-box function. Thus, the conclusions drawn regarding continuous or combinatorial BAO formulations/resolutions are valid regardless of the FMO formulation/resolution considered.

3   Parallel Multistart Derivative-Free Optimization Framework

The multistart strategy designed to address the continuous BAO formulation takes advantage of the peculiarities of this particular space. As the order of the irradiation directions of a beam ensemble is not important, the continuous BAO search space has symmetry features, which allows a large reduction of the space to be explored by simply keeping the beam directions sorted for each beam ensemble [16]. In order to sample this reduced search space in an appropriate manner, all possible combinations of sorted beam ensembles divided by the 4 quadrants will be considered as starting beam ensembles (iterates or points). E.g., for a continuous three-dimensional BAO search space, all possible three-beam directions distribution by the four quadrants are illustrated in Fig. 2(a). Each of these three-beam ensemble corresponds to a starting point placed in the different painted cubes illustrated in Fig. 2(b). For continuous tree-dimension BAO search space only $\frac{1}{4}$ of the entire search space $[0, 360]^3$ is explored. For n-beam angle ensembles, the total number of (hyper)cubes of the entire search space is 4^n while the number of (hyper)cubes of the reduced search space, which corresponds to the number of possible distributions of n sorted beam angles by the 4 quadrants is the combination with repetition of $\binom{n+4-1}{4} = \frac{(n+4-1)!}{4!(n-1)!}$. For continuous n-dimension BAO search space only $\frac{1}{2^n}$ of the entire search space $[0, 360]^n$ is explored.

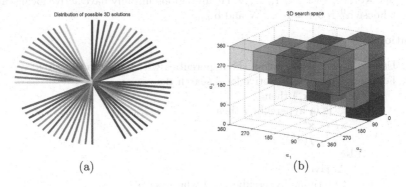

Distribution of possible 3D solutions   3D search space

(a)   (b)

Fig. 2. Three beam directions distribution by the four quadrants – (a) and the corresponding cubes in the search space $[0, 360]^3$ – (b).

After setting the starting points, $\mathbf{x}_i^0 \in [0, 360]^n, i = 1, \dots, N$, one for each hypercube of the reduced search space, the objective function value is evaluated at each of these initial beam ensembles. The best solutions and corresponding objective function values found so far for each region (hypercube) are assigned to these initial points and corresponding function values: $\mathbf{x}_i^* = \mathbf{x}_i^0, i = 1, \dots, N$; $f_i^* = f(\mathbf{x}_i^0), i = 1, \dots, N$. A local procedure is then used to locally improve that value. Two important aspects of a parallel multistart procedure in a multi-modal search space must be cautioned. First, as different search procedures coexist in time, the same region may end up being explored by different local search procedures wasting precious computational time. In order to avoid that, each hypercube can only be explored by a single local search procedure at a time. When the outcome of different local search procedures lay in the same hypercube, only the local search yielding the iterate with lowest function value remain active. Information of the regions that have active local searches is stored using a boolean vector, $\mathbf{Active}_{N \times 1}$, that is updated at the end of each iteration. Second, due to the highly non-convex nature of the search space, derivative-free local search algorithms are advisable. Pattern search methods (PSM) were previously selected for the resolution of the continuous BAO problem as they have the ability to avoid local entrapment and need a reduced number of function (FMO) evaluations to converge [13–15]. Pattern search methods as described in Rocha et al. [13–15] are used as local search procedure. Algorithm 1 displays the parallel multistart PSM algorithm.

Algorithm 1. Parallel multistart PSM algorithm

Initialization:

- Set $k \leftarrow 0$;
- Choose $\mathbf{x}_i^0 \in [0, 360]^n, i = 1, \ldots, N$;
- Compute $f(\mathbf{x}_i^0), i = 1, \ldots, N$ in parallel;
- Set $\mathbf{x}_i^* \leftarrow \mathbf{x}_i^0, i = 1, \ldots, N$ and $f_i^* \leftarrow f(\mathbf{x}_i^0), i = 1, \ldots, N$;
- Set $\mathbf{Active}_i \leftarrow 1, i = 1, \ldots, N$, i.e. all regions initially have active local searches;
- Choose $\alpha_i^0 > 0, i = 1, \ldots, N$ and α_{min};

Iteration:

1. Use PSM to locally explore the hypercubes with active local search;
2. For hypercubes i with active local search do
       If $f(\mathbf{x}_i^k) < f(\mathbf{x}_i^*)$ then
           If $\mathbf{x}_i^k$ is in hypercube i then
               $\mathbf{x}_i^* \leftarrow \mathbf{x}_i^k$;
               $f_i^* \leftarrow f(\mathbf{x}_i^k)$;
           Else
               $\mathbf{Active}_i \leftarrow 0$;
               Determine hypercube $j \neq i$ where $\mathbf{x}_i^k$ is;
               If $f(\mathbf{x}_i^k) < f(\mathbf{x}_j^*)$ then
                   $\mathbf{x}_j^* \leftarrow \mathbf{x}_i^k$;
                   $f_j^* \leftarrow f(\mathbf{x}_i^k)$;
                   $\mathbf{Active}_j \leftarrow 1$;
       Else
           $\alpha_i^{k+1} \leftarrow \frac{\alpha_i^k}{2}$;
           If $\alpha_i^{k+1} < \alpha_{min}$ then
               $\mathbf{Active}_i \leftarrow 0$;
3. If there exists active hypercubes go to first step and set $k \leftarrow k + 1$.

---

4 Computational Results

A set of ten clinical examples of nasopharyngeal tumor cases already treated at IPOC were used to test the different approaches. For the nasopharyngeal tumor cases in study, two different planning target volumes (PTVs) were considered, PTV_{70} and $PTV_{59.4}$, corresponding to two different levels of prescribed radiation doses. The organs at risk (OARs) considered were the brainstem, the spinal cord, the oral cavity and the parotid glands. OAR tolerance doses and prescribed doses for the PTVs are depicted at Table 1. The tolerance dose considered for

Table 1. Prescribed doses and tolerance doses for tumor volumes and OARs.

Structure	Mean dose	Max dose	Prescribed dose
PTV_{70}	–	–	70.0 Gy
$PTV_{59.4}$	–	–	59.4 Gy
Brainstem	–	54 Gy	–
Spinal cord	–	45 Gy	–
Oral cavity	30 Gy	–	–
Left parotid	26 Gy	–	–
Right parotid	26 Gy	–	–

the brainstem and the spinal cord is the maximum dose as these are serial type organs, i.e., organs whose function is jeopardized even if only a small portion is injured. The tolerance dose for the parotid glands, the larger salivary gland, and the oral cavity, that contains the remaining salivary glands, is the mean dose because the salivary glands are parallel type organs, i.e., organs whose function is not jeopardized if only a small portion is injured.

Our tests were performed on a 2.2 Ghz Intel Xeon 8-core computer workstation with 25 GB RAM. The nonlinear convex FMO formulation (Eq. (1)) was addressed using a trust-region-reflective algorithm (fmincon) from Optimization Toolbox of MATLAB (R2016a). CERR [8] was used to import the patients' computed tomography (CT) sets with the considered structures delineated. This freeware research software allows the computation of the necessary dosimetric data for treatment planning optimization as well as convenient visualization and analysis of the treatment plans obtained. QIB, the pencil beam algorithm of CERR, was used for dose calculations. An automated dose calculation procedure for each beam ensemble was developed instead of using the menu bar of CERR.

Typically, nasopharyngeal tumors are treated with five to nine equispaced coplanar beam ensembles. Since the importance of appropriate selection of beam directions increases for lower number of beam angles, we consider treatment plans with five coplanar beams. Thus, using the multistart PSM framework, five-beam treatment plans were obtained and denoted *MultistartBAO*. The initial step-size considered was $\alpha^0 = 2^5 = 32$ and the minimal value allowed was one, defining the stopping criteria. By choosing a power of two for initial step-size, as step-size remains the same at successful iterations and is halved at unsuccessful ones, the beam directions remain integer until the stopping criteria when the step-size becomes a rational number. Despite only integer irradiation directions are tested, it is worth to highlight that the continuous BAO space is explored which is fundamentally different from a combinatorial approach.

Iterative BAO is a successful strategy used in practice [5]. Furthermore, this strategy would obtain a theoretical upper limit of the treatment plan quality [18]. Treatment plans obtained by Wild et al. [18], called 4π and corresponding to a theoretical upper limit of a plan's quality, were obtained using iterative BAO considering noncoplanar beam orientations for a 5° angular spacing. In this study,

Table 2. Results of the beam angle optimization processes.

Case	Equi	IterativeBAO			MultistartBAO		
	FMO value	FMO value	%decrease	Fevals	FMO value	%decrease	Fevals
1	176,6	172,2	2,5	1790	162,9	7,7	718
2	168,7	159,2	5,6	1790	150,1	11,0	394
3	342,2	323,6	5,4	1790	320,8	6,3	418
4	370,9	346,6	6,6	1790	330,3	10,9	666
5	259,8	251,7	3,1	1790	236,9	8,8	884
6	213,5	188,5	11,7	1790	176,1	17,5	398
7	43,7	40,9	6,4	1790	36,8	15,8	192
8	118,2	103,3	12,6	1790	84,3	28,7	214
9	98,9	93,5	5,5	1790	84,2	14,9	228
10	75,2	67,1	10,8	1790	65,8	12,5	272

MultistartBAO plans were compared with five-beam treatment plans obtained using iterative BAO and denoted *IterativeBAO*. A discrete set of 360 beam directions, $\{0, 1, 2, \ldots, 359\}$, was used by considering a one degree angular spacing. In iterative BAO, beams are added sequentially one at a time to a treatment plan. The first beam is determined by computing the optimal FMO value of all one-beam ensembles for each possible beam direction. The one-beam ensemble leading to the lowest optimal FMO value is selected. Given a beam ensemble with $n - 1$ beam irradiation directions, the next beam direction, nth, is determined by computing the optimal FMO value of all n-beam ensembles obtained by adding each of the remaining beam directions to the $n - 1$-beam ensemble. The n-beam ensemble selected corresponds to the one yielding the lowest FMO value. Thus, obtaining a five-beam ensemble requires the computation of $360 + 359 + 358 + 357 + 356 = 1790$ FMO optimal values. Nevertheless, this greedy strategy reduces the number of FMO problem resolutions compared to other combinatorial BAO approaches.

Treatment plans obtained using optimized beam ensembles were also compared with five-beam coplanar equispaced treatment plans, denoted *Equi*. The objective of these comparisons is to benchmark the treatment plans with optimal beam angle ensembles with treatment plans commonly used in clinical practice. Table 2 displays the results of the BAO processes in terms of final FMO value, the measure considered for quality assessment of a beam ensemble. Compared to the FMO value of the *Equi* treatment plans, *MultistartBAO* obtained an average reduction of the FMO value of 13,4%, clearly outperforming *IterativeBAO* that obtained an average redution of 7,0%. Furthermore, *MultistartBAO* required an average of 438 function evaluations which is about four times less than the number required by *IterativeBAO*. Average computational time required by

Table 3. Target coverage obtained by treatment plans.

Case	Target coverage	MultistartBAO	IterativeBAO	Equi
1	PTV$_{70}$ at 95% volume	66.5 Gy	66.5 Gy	66.1 Gy
	PTV$_{70}$ % >93% of Rx (%)	99.1	98.9	98.0
	PTV$_{70}$ % >110% of Rx (%)	0.0	0.0	0.0
	PTV$_{59.4}$ at 95% volume	57.5 Gy	57.1 Gy	57.3 Gy
	PTV$_{59.4}$ % >93% of Rx (%)	97.4	96.7	97.0
	PTV$_{59.4}$ % >110% of Rx (%)	15.1	15.4	14.8
2	PTV$_{70}$ at 95% volume	67.5 Gy	67.1 Gy	67.3 Gy
	PTV$_{70}$ % >93% of Rx (%)	99.9	98.9	99.5
	PTV$_{70}$ % >110% of Rx (%)	0.0	0.0	0.0
	PTV$_{59.4}$ at 95% volume	54.7 Gy	54.7 Gy	53.5 Gy
	PTV$_{59.4}$ % >93% of Rx (%)	94.4	94.4	93.0
	PTV$_{59.4}$ % >110% of Rx (%)	5.3	5.3	5.6
3	PTV$_{70}$ at 95% volume	65.7 Gy	65.5 Gy	65.1 Gy
	PTV$_{70}$ % >93% of Rx (%)	96.6	95.9	94.9
	PTV$_{70}$ % >110% of Rx (%)	0.0	0.0	0.0
	PTV$_{59.4}$ at 95% volume	54.1 Gy	54.1 Gy	53.3 Gy
	PTV$_{59.4}$ % >93% of Rx (%)	93.9	93.7	93.3
	PTV$_{59.4}$ % >110% of Rx (%)	25.4	25.4	25.0
4	PTV$_{70}$ at 95% volume	68.3 Gy	68.3s Gy	68.3 Gy
	PTV$_{70}$ % >93% of Rx (%)	99.5	99.7	99.7
	PTV$_{70}$ % >110% of Rx (%)	0.0	0.0	0.0
	PTV$_{59.4}$ at 95% volume	53.5 Gy	53.5 Gy	51.3 Gy
	PTV$_{59.4}$ % >93% of Rx (%)	93.2	93.1	91.4
	PTV$_{59.4}$ % >110% of Rx (%)	18.5	18.7	19.5
5	PTV$_{70}$ at 95 % volume	67.5 Gy	67.3 Gy	67.1 Gy
	PTV$_{70}$ % >93% of Rx (%)	99.6	99.4	99.1
	PTV$_{70}$ % >110% of Rx (%)	0.0	0.0	0.0
	PTV$_{59.4}$ at 95% volume	52.7 Gy	51.9 Gy	51.5 Gy
	PTV$_{59.4}$ % >93% of Rx (%)	93.1	92.4	92.1
	PTV$_{59.4}$ % >110% of Rx (%)	7.7	7.8	8.0
6	PTV$_{70}$ at 95% volume	64.9 Gy	64.7 Gy	64.9 Gy
	PTV$_{70}$ % >93% of Rx (%)	99.4	94.2	94.3
	PTV$_{70}$ % >110% of Rx (%)	0.0	0.0	0.0
	PTV$_{59.4}$ at 95% volume	58.3 Gy	58.3 Gy	57.9 Gy
	PTV$_{59.4}$ % >93% of Rx (%)	98.2	98.2	97.7
	PTV$_{59.4}$ % >110% of Rx (%)	6.2	6.2	5.9

(continued)

Table 3. (*continued*)

Case	Target coverage	*MultistartBAO*	*IterativeBAO*	*Equi*
7	PTV_{70} at 95% volume	67.7 Gy	67.5 Gy	67.7 Gy
	PTV_{70} % >93% of Rx (%)	99.3	99.3	99.2
	PTV_{70} % >110% of Rx (%)	0.0	0.0	0.0
	$PTV_{59.4}$ at 95% volume	57.5 Gy	57.5 Gy	57.3 Gy
	$PTV_{59.4}$ % >93% of Rx (%)	98.2	97.9	97.9
	$PTV_{59.4}$ % >110% of Rx (%)	0.3	0.3	0.3
8	PTV_{70} at 95% volume	67.3 Gy	67.3 Gy	67.1 Gy
	PTV_{70} % >93% of Rx (%)	98.8	98.5	98.3
	PTV_{70} % >110% of Rx (%)	0.0	0.0	0.0
	$PTV_{59.4}$ at 95% volume	57.5 Gy	56.9 Gy	56.9 Gy
	$PTV_{59.4}$ % >93% of Rx (%)	98.0	97.0	97.0
	$PTV_{59.4}$ % >110% of Rx (%)	0.9	1.0	1.1
9	PTV_{70} at 95% volume	66.9 Gy	66.9 Gy	66.3 Gy
	PTV_{70} % >93% of Rx (%)	98.1	97.8	96.9
	PTV_{70} % >110% of Rx (%)	0.0	0.0	0.0
	$PTV_{59.4}$ at 95% volume	57.7 Gy	57.5 Gy	57.3 Gy
	$PTV_{59.4}$ % >93% of Rx (%)	97.9	97.7	97.7
	$PTV_{59.4}$ % >110% of Rx (%)	0.2	0.3	0.5
10	PTV_{70} at 95% volume	66.7 Gy	66.9 Gy	66.7 Gy
	PTV_{70} % >93% of Rx (%)	98.1	98.5	97.9
	PTV_{70} % >110% of Rx (%)	0.0	0.0	0.0
	$PTV_{59.4}$ at 95% volume	57.3 Gy	57.1 Gy	57.1 Gy
	$PTV_{59.4}$ % >93% of Rx (%)	97.4	97.4	97.2
	$PTV_{59.4}$ % >110% of Rx (%)	0.9	0.9	0.8

MultistartBAO was three hours while *IterativeBAO* spent an average of nine hours (also computed in parallel).

Despite the good results in terms of optimal FMO value improvement, treatment plan's quality can be acknowledged by different dose metrics. One of the most important target metrics is the tumor coverage, i.e. the percent of the tumor volume that receives at least 95% of the prescribed dose. Existence of coldspots, i.e. percentage of the tumor volume receiving less than 93% of the prescribed dose, and occurrence of hotspots, i.e. percentage of the tumor volume receiving more than 110% of the prescribed dose, are also metrics of interest. These three target metrics, displayed in Table 3, show that *MultistartBAO* outperforms both *IterativeBAO* and *Equi* treatment plans concerning tumor coverage metrics.

Table 4. OARs sparing obtained by treatment plans.

Case	OAR	Mean Dose (Gy)			Max Dose (Gy)		
		MultistartBAO	*IterativeBAO*	*Equi*	*MultistartBAO*	*IterativeBAO*	*Equi*
1	Spinal cord	–	–	–	38.7	42.1	39.1
	Brainstem	–	–	–	52.6	52.4	53.8
	Right parotid	22.3	23.7	24.4	–	–	–
	Left parotid	24.2	24.0	25.4	–	–	–
	Oral Cavity	25.6	27.1	28.6	–	–	–
2	Spinal cord	–	–	–	44.2	44.7	45.4
	Brainstem	–	–	–	53.8	53.6	54.3
	Right parotid	22.1	24.7	23.7	–	–	–
	Left parotid	21.6	23.2	25.5	–	–	–
	Oral Cavity	27.5	28.0	27.9	–	–	–
3	Spinal cord	–	–	–	40.9	40.5	44.4
	Brainstem	–	–	–	44.8	44.3	49.9
	Right parotid	25.9	26.3	25.1	–	–	–
	Left parotid	24.1	24.8	26.7	–	–	–
	Oral Cavity	30.3	31.6	34.3	–	–	–
4	Spinal cord	–	–	–	40.8	40.9	40.0
	Brainstem	–	–	–	49.6	49.5	49.2
	Right parotid	27.8	28.1	28.5	–	–	–
	Left parotid	23.9	26.3	26.9	–	–	–
	Oral Cavity	29.7	30.8	32.1	–	–	–
5	Spinal cord	–	–	–	38.5	38.6	38.6
	Brainstem	–	–	–	52.3	52.3	51.2
	Right parotid	28.7	29.0	28.2	–	–	–
	Left parotid	19.9	25.5	24.7	–	–	–
	Oral Cavity	23.4	25.8	26.4	–	–	–
6	Spinal cord	–	–	–	40.6	42.6	40.1
	Brainstem	–	–	–	52.6	53.8	52.9
	Right parotid	20.4	20.7	24.5	–	–	–
	Left parotid	21.5	22.3	25.4	–	–	–
	Oral Cavity	27.3	28.3	27.2	–	–	–
7	Spinal cord	–	–	–	41.3	42.8	39.9
	Brainstem	–	–	–	52.9	52.6	52.3
	Right parotid	25.6	26.5	28.6	–	–	–
	Left parotid	21.5	23.4	25.9	–	–	–
	Oral Cavity	24.9	26.1	28.2	–	–	–
8	Spinal cord	–	–	–	40.2	38.9	39.8
	Brainstem	–	–	–	53.6	54.6	55.0
	Right parotid	23.1	25.5	26.0	–	–	–
	Left parotid	22.6	25.4	24.0	–	–	–
	Oral Cavity	24.3	26.2	25.8	–	–	–
9	Spinal cord	–	–	–	40.3	45.1	39.5
	Brainstem	–	–	–	49.4	47.9	52.9
	Right parotid	21.6	23.2	25.0	–	–	–
	Left parotid	22.5	23.8	24.4	–	–	–
	Oral Cavity	22.8	24.0	26.4	–	–	–
10	Spinal cord	–	–	–	40.1	40.7	40.8
	Brainstem	–	–	–	53.5	53.9	54.6
	Right parotid	21.8	22.4	25.8	–	–	–
	Left parotid	23.8	24.2	25.5	–	–	–
	Oral Cavity	26.2	27.9	27.1	–	–	–

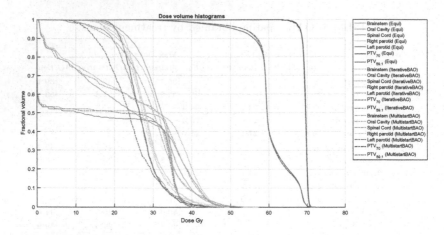

Fig. 3. Cumulative dose volume histogram comparing the results obtained by *Multi-startBAO*, *IterativeBAO* and *Equi* for the fourth case.

Metrics usually screened for OARs are mean and/or maximum doses, depending if the organ has a parallel or serial architecture, respectively. Table 4 depicts organ sparing results. For the brainstem and the spinal cord, serial organs, the maximum dose is displayed. It can be verified that treatment plans with optimized beam directions always comply with the prescribed maximum doses while *Equi* treatment plans fail to do so in some cases. For oral cavity and parotids, parallel organs, the mean dose is displayed. Improved sparing of oral cavity and parotids is clearly obtained by treatment plans with optimal five-beam ensembles. Compared to the *Equi* treatment plans, in average, *MultistartBAO* treatment plans achieve a mean dose irradiation reduction on the right parotid, left parotid and oral cavity of 2.1 Gy, 2.9 Gy and 2.2 Gy, respectively. Furthermore, *MultistartBAO* treatment plans double the mean dose irradiation reduction numbers of *IterativeBAO* treatment plans. Over-irradiation of salivary glands can lead to xerostomia, a common RT complication of nasopharyngeal cancer cases leading to swallow difficulties. Thus, the enhanced salivary glands sparing is of the utmost interest.

In clinical practice, results are typically judged by their dose-volume histogram (DVH). DVH are cumulative histograms that ideally would have 100% dose for the whole tumor volume dropping immediately to zero, while the curves for the remaining structures would be always zero meaning that no radiation was delivered to the healthy tissues. For illustration, DVH results for the fourth patient, a patient that obtained an average FMO value reduction, are displayed in Fig. 3. The DVH curves show enhanced tumor coverage and sparing by *MultistartBAO* treatment plans.

5   Conclusions

The BAO problem is a challenging highly non-convex optimization problem yet to be solved satisfactorily. Apart from iterative BAO, there is little or none commercial offer for beam direction selection. A parallel multistart PSM framework was presented and compared with iterative BAO using a set of clinical nasopharyngeal tumor cases. This multistart framework proved to be a competitive strategy to address the continuous BAO problem formulation. A global search scheme with a tailored sampling of the search space is combined with a procedure that locally improves the sampled ensembles. Despite the importance of the global strategy sketched, particularly for a search space with a peculiar shape due to symmetry properties, the choice of PSM, a derivative-free method, for locally improving the solutions is important to avoid local entrapment.

For the nasopharyngeal clinical cases retrospectively tested, the use of optimized directions obtained by the parallel multistart approach enhanced the quality of the treatment plans obtained. The high quality treatment plans obtained considering optimal beam ensembles were compared favorably with typical equispaced treatment plans. Furthermore, the presented multistart derivative-free framework for a continuous BAO formulation clearly outperforms an iterative approach for a combinatorial BAO formulation. Although iterative BAO reduces the number of comparisons required to achieve an improved solution compared to other combinatorial BAO approaches, it is a greedy strategy for the combinatorial BAO that truncates the search space at each iteration possibly disregarding the best ensembles with n-beam directions.

Several strategies for minimizing the number of function evaluations, and consequently decrease the computational time, were embedded in this multistart strategy including parallelization, searching in a reduced space and construction of hypercubes. In future work, further effort must be made to speed up even more this procedure maintaining the high quality results here detailed. One obvious strategy is to accelerate FMO computation as most of the BAO computational time is consumed for obtaining the optimal FMO values. Nevertheless, the computational burden of BAO will always decrease as future computer workstations will certainly become faster.

Acknowledgments. This work has been supported by project grant POCI-01-0145-FEDER-028030 and by the Fundação para a Ciência e a Tecnologia (FCT) under project grant UID/MULTI/00308/2013.

References

1. Aleman, D.M., Kumar, A., Ahuja, R.K., Romeijn, H.E., Dempsey, J.F.: Neighborhood search approaches to beam orientation optimization in intensity modulated radiation therapy treatment planning. J. Global Optim. **42**, 587–607 (2008)
2. Aleman, D.M., Romeijn, H.E., Dempsey, J.F.: A response surface approach to beam orientation optimization in intensity modulated radiation therapy treatment planning. INFORMS J. Comput. **21**, 62–76 (2009)

3. Bangert, M., Ziegenhein, P., Oelfke, U.: Characterizing the combinatorial beam angle selection problem. Phys. Med. Biol. **57**, 6707–6723 (2012)
4. Bertsimas, D., Cacchiani, V., Craft, D., Nohadani, O.: A hybrid approach to beam angle optimization in intensity-modulated radiation therapy. Comput. Oper. Res. **40**, 2187–2197 (2013)
5. Breedveld, S., Storchi, P., Voet, P., Heijmen, B.: iCycle: integrated, multicriterial beam angle, and profile optimization for generation of coplanar and noncoplanar IMRT plans. Med. Phys. **39**, 951–963 (2012)
6. Cheong, K., Suh, T., Romeijn, H., Li, J., Dempsey, J.: Fast nonlinear optimization with simple bounds for IMRT planning. Med. Phys. **32**, 1975–1975 (2005)
7. Craft, D.: Local beam angle optimization with linear programming and gradient search. Phys. Med. Biol. **52**, 127–135 (2007)
8. Deasy, J.O., Lee, E.K., Bortfeld, T., Langer, M., Zakarian, K., Alaly, J., Zhang, Y., Liu, H., Mohan, R., Ahuja, R., Pollack, A., Purdy, J., Rardin, R.: A collaboratory for radiation theraphy planning optimization research. Ann. Oper. Res. **148**, 55–63 (2006)
9. Dias, J., Rocha, H., Ferreira, B.C., Lopes, M.C.: Simulated annealing applied to IMRT beam angle optimization: a computational study. Phys. Med. **31**, 747–756 (2015)
10. Dias, J., Rocha, H., Ventura, T., Ferreira, B.C., Lopes, M.C.: Automated fluence map optimization based on fuzzy inference systems. Med. Phys. **43**, 1083–1095 (2016)
11. Lim, G.J., Cao, W.: A two-phase method for selecting IMRT treatment beam angles: Branch-and-Prune and local neighborhood search. Eur. J. Oper. Res. **217**, 609–618 (2012)
12. Monz, M., Kufer, K.H., Bortfeld, T.R., Thieke, C.: Pareto navigation Algorithmic foundation of interactive multi-criteria IMRT planning. Phys. Med. Biol. **53**, 985–998 (2008)
13. Rocha, H., Dias, J., Ferreira, B.C., Lopes, M.C.: Selection of intensity modulated radiation therapy treatment beam directions using radial basis functions within a pattern search methods framework. J. Glob. Optim. **57**, 1065–1089 (2013)
14. Rocha, H., Dias, J., Ferreira, B.C., Lopes, M.C.: Beam angle optimization for intensity-modulated radiation therapy using a guided pattern search method. Phys. Med. Biol. **58**, 2939–2953 (2013)
15. Rocha, H., Dias, J., Ferreira, B.C., Lopes, M.C.: Pattern search methods framework for beam angle optimization in radiotherapy design. Appl. Math. Comput. **219**, 10853–10865 (2013)
16. Rocha, H., Dias, J., Ventura, T., Ferreira, B.C., Lopes, M.C.: A derivative-free multistart framework for an automated noncoplanar beam angle optimization in IMRT. Med. Phys. **43**, 5514–5526 (2016)
17. Romeijn, H.E., Ahuja, R.K., Dempsey, J.F., Kumar, A., Li, J.: A novel linear programming approach to fluence map optimization for intensity modulated radiation therapy treatment planing. Phys. Med. Biol. **48**, 3521–3542 (2003)
18. Wild, E., Bangert, M., Nill, S., Oelfke, U.: Noncoplanar VMAT for nasopharyngeal tumors: Plan quality versus treatment time. Med. Phys. **42**, 2157–2168 (2015)
19. Yang, J., Zhang, P., Zhang, L., Shu, H., Li, B., Gui, Z.: Particle swarm optimizer for weighting factor selection in intensity-modulated radiation therapy optimization algorithms. Phys. Med. **33**, 136–145 (2017)

Approximation Algorithms for Packing Directed Acyclic Graphs into Two-Size Blocks

Yuichi Asahiro[1], Eiji Miyano[2], and Tsuyoshi Yagita[2(✉)]

[1] Kyushu Sangyo University, Fukuoka, Japan
asahiro@is.kyusan-u.ac.jp
[2] Kyushu Institute of Technology, Iizuka, Japan
miyano@ces.kyutech.ac.jp, yagita.tsuyoshi307@mail.kyutech.jp

Abstract. In this paper we consider the following variant of clustering or laying out problems of graphs: Given a directed acyclic graph (DAG for short) and an integer B, the objective is to find a mapping of its nodes into blocks of size at most B that minimizes the maximum number of external arcs during traversals of the acyclic structure by following paths from the roots to the leaves. An external arc is defined as an arc connecting two distinct blocks. This paper focuses on the case $B = 2$. Even if $B = 2$ and the height of the DAG is three, it is known that the problem is NP-hard, and furthermore, there is no $\frac{3}{2} - \varepsilon$ factor approximation algorithm for $B = 2$ and a small positive ε unless P = NP. On the other hand, the best approximation ratio previously shown is 3. In this paper we improve the approximation ratio into strictly smaller than 2. Also, we investigate the relationship between the height of input DAGs and the inapproximability, since the above inapproximability bound $\frac{3}{2} - \varepsilon$ is shown only for DAGs of height 3.

1 Introduction

Backgrounds. Large-scale graphs have recently emerged such as the web networks in the Internet, social networks like Twitter and Facebook, and genome databases, and their scales keep expanding rapidly. When working with such large-scale graphs on a computer, only a fraction of the graphs can be stored in the internal memory. Thus, the transfer of data between the internal memory and the external memory (or disk) is often the bottleneck in the computation time. In this paper we consider the graph processing on the *external memory model* [1,9], in which the memory hierarchy consists of an internal memory of limited space, and an arbitrarily large external memory divided into fixed contiguous *blocks* of size B. We assume that each external memory query or modification, called a *block transfer*, transfers one block of B objects from the external memory to the internal one.

This work is partially supported by JSPS KAKENHI Grant Numbers JP17K00016 and JP17K00024, and JST CREST JPMJR1402.

© Springer International Publishing AG, part of Springer Nature 2018
O. Gervasi et al. (Eds.): ICCSA 2018, LNCS 10961, pp. 607–623, 2018.
https://doi.org/10.1007/978-3-319-95165-2_43

One of the important data structures is the directed acyclic graph (DAG) which includes persistent (or multiversion) B-trees and ordered binary-decision diagrams (OBDDs). Hence many different kinds of information are modeled by DAGs. Using a DAG structure for the internal memory on the external one, we need to solve a laying out problem whose objective is to map the nodes of DAG to a set of disk blocks, minimizing the number of disk blocks transferred to the internal memory when we access a lot of nodes.

Our Problem and Previous Results. In this paper we consider the following laying out problem of DAGs, called the MINIMUM BLOCK TRANSFERS WITH B problem (MBT(B) for short): Given a DAG and an integer B as input, the objective of MBT(B) is to find a mapping of its nodes into blocks of size at most B that *minimizes the maximum number of external arcs* when we traverse the acyclic structure by following paths from the roots to the leaves. The number of external arcs on some path p is defined as the number of arcs connecting two distinct blocks on p, that is, it denotes the number of block transfers. In this paper we only focus on MBT(2), i.e., the input block size B is restricted to two.

The problem MBT(B) was previously considered by Diwan et al. [4]. Restricting the input graphs to trees, they provided a naive *bottom-up-packing greedy* algorithm. Indeed this algorithm is optimal for trees and runs in linear time. In addition, they presented a heuristic algorithm for DAGs based on the same bottom-up-packing idea. However, the approximation guarantee of this algorithm was not shown, and furthermore, the computational complexity of MBT(B) was not shown either. In [2], Asahiro, Furukawa, Ikegami, Miyano proved that MBT(2) remains NP-hard even if the height of each DAG is three, and furthermore there is no $(\frac{3}{2} - \varepsilon)$-approximation algorithm for any positive ε and $B = 2$ unless P $=$ NP. Note here that this inapproximability is shown for DAGs of height three. Hence, if the height of the input DAG is more than three, an algorithm having approximation ratio smaller than 3/2 may be designed. As for the approximability, they pointed out that the above bottom-up-packing greedy strategy in [4] achieves an approximation guarantee of 2 for MBT(2) although its proof has not been published yet. In the same paper [2], the authors claimed that a $\frac{3}{2}$-approximation algorithm can be designed for MBT(2). However, the proposed algorithm contains an error and its approximation ratio is actually at least $\frac{5}{3}$ since we can explicitly provide a counterexample as shown in Sect. 3. Hence, the previous best approximation ratio must be 3, which was recently shown by Donovan, Mkrtchyan, and Subramani in [5,6]. Moreover, they have shown the applications of MBT(B) to circuit layouts and the complexity for DAGs with node weights. Further related work can be found in [2].

Our Contributions. In this paper we consider the (in)approximability of MBT(2). Our main results are summarized in the following list:

(i) We first show that the $\frac{3}{2}$-approximation algorithm for MBT(2) proposed in [2] contains an error and thus its approximation ratio is actually at least $\frac{5}{3}$ by providing a counterexample.

(ii) Next, we revisit the naive bottom-up-packing greedy algorithm in [4], and give a detailed description of the algorithm and a full proof showing that it achieves the approximation ratio of 2.

(iii) Then, we provide a new simpler 2-approximation algorithm and furthermore an algorithm with approximation ratio strictly smaller than 2 for MBT(2).

(iv) Finally, we investigate the relationship between the height of input DAGs and the inapproximability of MBT(2), i.e., we show that MBT(2) cannot be approximated within a factor of $\frac{3}{2} - \varepsilon$ and $\frac{4}{3} - \varepsilon$ for any $\varepsilon > 0$ even if the input is restricted to DAGs of height at most five and DAGs of height at least six, respectively, unless P = NP.

Due to the page limitation, we omit some proofs from this extended abstract.

2   Preliminaries

Let $G = (V, A)$ be a simple directed acyclic graph, i.e., G does not include any directed cycle, any multiple arcs, or any self-loop. V and A denote the sets of nodes and arcs, respectively. $d^-(v)$ and $d^+(v)$ represent indegree and outdegree of node v, respectively. A node with no indegree and a node with no outdegree are called a *source* and a *sink* (or a *root* and a *leaf*), respectively. Let $N^-(v) = \{u \mid (u, v) \in A\}$ and $N^+(v) = \{u \mid (v, u) \in A\}$, then we define $A^-(v) = \{(u, v) \mid u \in N^-(v)\}$ and $A^+(v) = \{(v, u) \mid u \in N^+(v)\}$ in the following.

A (directed) *path* Q of *length* ℓ from a node v_0 to a node v_ℓ in G is a sequence $\langle v_0, v_1, \ldots, v_\ell \rangle$ of nodes such that $(v_{i-1}, v_i) \in A$ for $i = 1, 2, \ldots, \ell$. Consider two paths $Q_1 = \langle v_0, \ldots, v_i \rangle$ and $Q_2 = \langle v_i, \ldots, v_\ell \rangle$. Then, a path Q constituted by the two paths Q_1 and Q_2, i.e., $\langle v_0, \ldots, v_i, \ldots, v_\ell \rangle$, is denoted by $Q_1 \circ Q_2$. The length of the longest path from a source to a node v is the *depth* of v in G, denoted by $\delta(v)$. The *height* of a node in G is the number of arcs on the longest simple downward path from the node to a sink, and the *height of a DAG* G is the largest of all heights of its sources, denoted by $h(G)$. For a graph $G = (V, A)$ and a subset $V' \subseteq V$ of nodes and a subset $A' \subseteq A$ of arcs, $G[V'] = (V', A')$ denotes the *induced subgraph* of G such that its arc set A' consists of all arcs of G whose endpoints belong to V'.

If the fixed DAG structure G is stored in a disk and it is too large to access the entire objects, then G must be partitioned into small-sized *blocks* (or so-called *pages*) of size at most B, $\mathcal{P} = \{P_1, P_2, \ldots, P_k\}$ where $P_i \subseteq V$, $P_i \cap P_j = \emptyset$ for $i \neq j$, $\bigcup_{i=1}^{k} P_i = V$, $|P_i| \leq B$, and thus $k \geq \lceil |V|/B \rceil$, that is, we have to decide which nodes of G are loaded into which blocks in a main memory. We call $\mathcal{P}$ *packing* if the number of nodes partitioned into every block does not exceed the given block size B. An arc (u, v) is said to be *packed* (under a packing $\mathcal{P}$) if $\{u, v\} \subseteq P$ for some $P \in \mathcal{P}$. Given a packing $\mathcal{P}$, the *block transfer* $bt_{\mathcal{P}}(Q)$ of a path Q under $\mathcal{P}$ is the number of *external arcs* (u, v)'s on Q for which u and v are in different blocks, and furthermore, the *block transfer* $bt_{\mathcal{P}}(G)$ of a DAG G under $\mathcal{P}$ is the maximum block transfers $bt_{\mathcal{P}}(Q)$'s over all paths from sources to sinks.

The packing which an algorithm ALG outputs is denoted by $\mathcal{ALG}$. We sometimes use $bt_{\mathcal{ALG}}(G)$ as the block transfer of G under packing $\mathcal{ALG}$. The *block height* of a node v is the number of external arcs on the longest path from v to a sink. Now our problem MBT(B) is formulated as follows: Given a DAG $G = (V, A)$ and an integer B, the goal of MBT(B) is to find a packing $\mathcal{P}$ that minimizes the block transfer $bt_{\mathcal{P}}(G)$ such that the size of every block $P_i \in \mathcal{P}$ is bounded by B (this packing is denoted by $\mathcal{OPT}$, and termed an *optimal* packing).

An algorithm ALG is called a σ-approximation algorithm and ALG's approximation ratio is σ if $ALG(x)/OPT(x) \leq \sigma$ holds for every input x, where $ALG(x)$ and $OPT(x)$ are the values of solutions obtained by ALG and an optimal algorithm, respectively. A gap-introducing reduction from a NP-hard decision problem P_1 to a minimization problem P_2 with two functions f and α computes an instance y of P_2 from an instance x of P_1 in polynomial time such that (i) if x is yes for P_1, $OPT(y) \leq f(y)$, and (ii) if x is no for P_1, $OPT(y) > \alpha(|y|) \cdot f(y)$, where $OPT(y)$ is the value of an optimal solution for y of P_2, and $\alpha(|y|)$ is the inapproximability bound established by this gap-introducing reduction [8].

3   Previous Algorithms and Their Analyses

In this section, we briefly survey previous algorithms for MBT(2) introduced in [2]. In the following we assume that a set V of nodes of an input DAG $G = (V, A)$ is partitioned into layers $V_0, \ldots, V_{h(G)}$, i.e., $V = V_0 \cup \cdots \cup V_{h(G)}$ and $V_i \cap V_j = \emptyset$ for $i \neq j$, where V_0 contains all the sources in G and $v \in V_{\delta(v)}$. By this partition, there always exists an arc (u, v) for each node $v \in V_i$ ($1 \leq i \leq h(G)$) such that $u \in V_{i-1}$. This partition of V can be obtained in linear time $O(|V|+|A|)$ based on the topological sort [3]. Note that this definition of layering does not indicate the input DAG is a layered graph, since some arcs may connect non-consecutive layers.

3.1   Optimal Algorithms for DAGs of Height One and Two

It is shown in [2] that we can design polynomial-time exact algorithms, called HeightOne and HeightTwo, for MBT(2) on DAGs of height one and two, respectively. Here is a description of HeightOne, which tries to pack every connected component into one block:

Algorithm HeightOne
Input: DAG $G = (V, A)$ of height one **Output:** Packing $\mathcal{P}$
Step 1: Find all connected components in G. Let the set of nodes of the components be $C_1, \ldots, C_k$, where k is the number of connected components.
Step 2: If $|C_i| \leq B$ for all i, output $\mathcal{P} = \{C_1, \ldots, C_k\}$. Otherwise output $\mathcal{P} = \{\{v\} \mid v \in V\}$.

A connected component C_i such that $|C_i| \leq 2$ is one node or includes only two nodes and an arc between them. That is, if $B = 2$, HeightOne tries to pack all the isolated nodes and arcs.

Proposition 1 ([2]). *Algorithm* HeightOne *is a polynomial-time exact algorithm for MBT(2) on DAGs of height one.*

The algorithm HeightTwo for MBT(2) on DAGs of height at most two can obtain an optimal packing by reducing MBT(2) into the 2-CNF SATISFIABILITY problem (2-SAT), that is, given a Boolean formula in a conjunctive normal form with at most 2 variables per clause, the goal is to find a variable assignment that satisfies all the clauses [7].

Algorithm HeightTwo
  Input: DAG $G = (V, A)$ of height two **Output:** Packing $\mathcal{P}$
  Step 1: Transform G to a 2-CNF predicate f by the following manner:
    Step 1-1: Assign one variable x_i to each node $v_i \in V_1$.
    Step 1-2: Make the following clauses associated with $v_i \in V_1$ as follows.
      Rule A-(i): $(\overline{x_i})$ if $d^-(v_i) \geq 2$, and
      Rule A-(ii): (x_i) if $d^+(v_i) \geq 2$.
    Step 1-3: For each pair of v_i and $v_j \in V_1$, make the following clauses
      Rule B-(i): $(\overline{x_i} \vee \overline{x_j})$ if $d^-(v_i) = d^-(v_j) = 1$ and two arcs (u, v_i)
        and (u, v_j) exist for some $u \in V_0$, and
      Rule B-(ii): $(x_i \vee x_j)$ if $d^+(v_i) = d^+(v_j) = 1$ and two arcs (v_i, u)
        and (v_j, u) exist for some $u \in V_2$.
    Step 1-4: Construct f by adding the clauses made in Steps 1-2 and
      1-3 conjunctively.
  Step 2: Solve f by a polynomial-time algorithm for 2-SAT [8].
  Step 3: If f is unsatisfiable, then output $\{\{v\} \mid v \in V\}$ as a packing $\mathcal{P}$.
    If f is satisfiable, then output a packing according to the satisfying
    truth assignment in Step 2 as follows: For each variable x_i if $x_i = true$
    then add $\{v_i\} \cup N^-(v)$ to $\mathcal{P}$, otherwise add $\{v_i\} \cup N^+(v)$ to $\mathcal{P}$. For
    each node v not contained in such blocks, add $\{v\}$ to $\mathcal{P}$.

Proposition 2 ([2]). *Algorithm* HeightTwo *is a polynomial-time exact algorithm for MBT(2) on DAGs of height two.*

In [2], a DAG to which HeightTwo is applied is implicitly restricted to a subgraph (or connected component) to which HeightOne is already applied and it cannot reduce the block transfer. However, if we apply it to more general subgraphs (as will be seen in this paper), the above algorithm needs a more careful treatment and thus a small modification. If there exists a node v such that $d^-(v) = d^+(v) = 1$ in V_1, then the original HeightTwo cannot pack any of two arcs incident to v (i.e., one arc which goes into v and one arc which goes out from v), although the optimal solution reduces one block transfer by packing one of such arcs. Hereafter, the following modified algorithm is renamed HeightTwo:

Algorithm HeightTwo
  Input: DAG $G = (V, A)$ of height two **Output:** Packing $\mathcal{P}$
    Steps 1-1, 1-3, 1-4, 2, and 3: All the steps are the same as ones of
      HeightTwo, respectively.

Step 1-2: Make the following clauses associated with the node $v_i \in V_1$ as follows.
Rule A-(i): $(\overline{x_i})$ if $d^-(v_i) \geq 2$, and
Rule A-(ii): (x_i) if $d^+(v_i) \geq 2$.
Rule A-(iii): $(x_i \vee \overline{x_i})$ if $d^-(v_i) \leq 1$ and $d^+(v_i) \leq 1$

Namely, the difference from the original HeightTwo is the addition of **Rule A-(iii)** in **Step 1-2**. We can assign any value of *true* or *false* to the variables corresponding to the nodes in V_1 that satisfy **Rule A-(iii)** in order to make the block transfer 1, thus we add such a rule. By this rule we add the clause $(x_i \vee \overline{x_i})$ to the existing 2-CNF formula, which does not violate the correctness of the reduction.

3.2   Approximation Algorithms for DAGs of Height Three and Higher

In addition to the exact algorithms in Sect. 3.1, the authors in [2] propose two algorithms for MBT(2), called HeightThree and HeightFour, which work only for DAGs of height three and four, respectively (but details are omitted here).

Algorithm HeightThree
 Input: DAG $G = (V, A)$ of height three   **Output:** Packing $\mathcal{P}$
Step 1: Apply HeightOne first to $G[V_0 \cup V_1]$ and then $G[V_2 \cup V_3]$. Let the obtained packings be $\mathcal{P}_1$ and $\mathcal{P}_2$, respectively.
Step 2: If $bt_{\mathcal{P}_1}(G[V_0 \cup V_1]) = 0$ and $bt_{\mathcal{P}_2}(G[V_2 \cup V_3]) = 0$, then output $\mathcal{P} = \mathcal{P}_1 \cup \mathcal{P}_2$ and halt. If $bt_{\mathcal{P}_2}(G[V_2 \cup V_3]) = 1$, then output $\mathcal{P} = \{\{v\} \mid v \in V\}$ and halt.
Step 3: Let R be a set of nodes, each of which is reachable to nodes in V_3. If $R = V$, output $\mathcal{P} = \{\{v\} \mid v \in V\}$ and halt. Otherwise, first apply HeightTwo to $G[V - R]$, next HeightOne to $G[R \cap (V_0 \cup V_1)]$ and $G[R \cap (V_2 \cup V_3)]$, and then obtain packings, say, $\mathcal{P}_3$, $\mathcal{P}_4$ and $\mathcal{P}_5$, respectively. Output $\mathcal{P}_3 \cup \mathcal{P}_4 \cup \mathcal{P}_5$ and halt.

Algorithm HeightFour
 Input: DAG $G = (V, A)$ of height four   **Output:** Packing $\mathcal{P}$
Step 1: Apply HeightOne to $G[V_0 \cup V_1]$ and obtain a packing, say, $\mathcal{P}_1$. If $bt_{\mathcal{P}_1}(G[V_0 \cup V_1]) = 0$, then output $\mathcal{P} = \mathcal{P}_1 \cup \{\{v\} \mid v \in V_2 \cup V_3 \cup V_4\}$ and halt.
Step 2: Apply HeightTwo to $G[V_0 \cup V_1 \cup V_2]$ and obtain a packing, say, $\mathcal{P}_2$. If $bt_{\mathcal{P}_2}(G[V_0 \cup V_1 \cup V_2]) = 1$, then output $\mathcal{P} = \mathcal{P}_2 \cup \{\{v\} \mid v \in V_3 \cup V_4\}$ and halt.
Step 3: Output $\mathcal{P} = \{\{v\} \mid v \in V\}$ and halt.

Furthermore, in [2], the following approximation algorithm for DAGs of any height is presented, which uses HeightOne through HeightFour as subroutines:

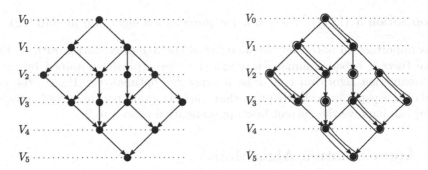

Fig. 1. (Left) A counterexample for `DAGPack`, and (Right) its optimal packing

Algorithm DAGPack

 Input: DAG $G = (V, A)$ **Output:** Packing $\mathcal{P}$

Step 1: Let $W_0 = V_0 \cup \cdots \cup V_4$, $W_1 = V_4 \cup \cdots \cup V_8$, ..., $W_k = V_{4k} \cup \cdots \cup V_{h(G)}$, where $k = \lfloor h(G)/4 \rfloor$.

Step 2: To each subgraph $G[W_i]$ for $0 \le i \le k - 1$, apply the algorithm `HeightFour`. Let the obtained packing for $G[W_i]$ be $\mathcal{P}_i$.

Step 3: Let $h' = h(G) - 4k$ $(1 \le h' \le 3)$ be the height of bottom layers included in $G[W_k]$. To the subgraph $G[W_k]$, apply the algorithms `HeightOne`, `HeightTwo`, and `HeightThree` if $h' = 1, 2$ and 3, respectively. Let the obtained packing is $\mathcal{P}_k$.

Step 4: Output $(\mathcal{P}_1 - \{\{v\} \mid v \in V_4\}) \cup (\mathcal{P}_2 - \{\{v\} \mid v \in V_8\}) \cup \cdots \cup \mathcal{P}_k$ and halt.

The authors in [2] claim that `DAGPack` achieves the following approximation ratio:

Claim 3 ([2]). Algorithm `DAGPack` is a $\frac{3}{2}$-approximation algorithm for the MBT(2).

However, the above claim is not correct; we can show a counterexample to the claim, which is one of the main contributions of this paper:

Theorem 4. *The approximation ratio of DAGPack is at least $\frac{5}{3}$.*

Proof. See Fig. 1, which illustrates the counterexample to Claim 3. For the DAG shown in Fig. 1(Left), `DAGPack` packs all the nodes singly, since `HeightOne` and `HeightTwo` used in `HeightFour` applied to $G[V_0 \cup \cdots \cup V_4]$, and `HeightOne` applied to $G[V_4 \cup V_5]$ cannot reduce any block transfers of the corresponding parts. Thus, the block transfer obtained by `DAGPack` is five. On the other hand, the block transfer can be reduced when the optimal solution packs like what is shown in Fig. 1(Right), under which the block transfer is 3. Therefore, the approximation ratio of `DAGPack` is at least $5/3$. □

Since Claim 3 is not correct and thus `DAGPack` contains an error, the previous best approximation ratio must be 3, which was recently shown in [5,6].

Proposition 5 ([5,6]). *There is a 3-approximation algorithm for MBT(2).*

It is important to note that the analysis of the 3-approximation ratio is tight since there is a bad example for which the block transfer obtained by the 3-approximation algorithm is at least 3 times the optimal one. Hence, the next goal of this paper is to clearly prove that the bottom-up-packing greedy strategy in [4] can improve the current best approximation ratio 3 to 2.

4   Approximation Algorithms

In this section, we first give a detailed description of the Bottom-Up-Packing Greedy algorithm for MBT(B), which was originally introduced for MBT(B) on trees in [4], and a full proof showing that the algorithm approximates MBT(2) within approximation ratio 2. Then, we slightly improve the ratio to strictly smaller than 2.

4.1   2-Approximation Algorithm

From now, we simply refer the following algorithm as Greedy:

> **Algorithm Greedy**
> **Input:** DAG $G = (V, A)$ **Output:** Packing $\mathcal{P}$
> **Step 1:** Initialize mapping $\mathcal{P}$ as an empty set, and obtain $\delta(v)$ for each node $v \in V$.
> **Step 2:** In the non-increasing order of $\delta(v)$, for each node, execute the following procedure:
> **(2-1)** If $d^+(v) = 0$, that is, v is a sink node, add a new block $P = \{v\}$ to $\mathcal{P}$. Otherwise,
> **(2-2)** Let $N^+(v) = \{v_1, \ldots, v_i\}$ and $P_1, \ldots, P_i$ be the blocks containing $v_1, \ldots, v_i$, respectively. Also, without loss of generality, let $\{v_1, \ldots, v_j\} \subseteq N^+(v)$ be nodes having the largest block height among nodes in $N^+(v)$. If v and all the nodes in $P_1, \ldots, P_j$ can be merged together in one block, i.e., $1 + \sum_{k=1}^{j} |P_k| \leq B$ holds, then merge all of them into a new block $P = \{v\} \cup P_1 \cup \cdots \cup P_j$, add P to $\mathcal{P}$, and delete $P_1, \ldots, P_j$ from $\mathcal{P}$. Otherwise, add a new block $P = \{v\}$ to $\mathcal{P}$.

In order to prove the approximation ratio of Greedy, we utilize the following propositions which give the lower bound of the block transfer.

Proposition 6 ([2]). *For a path Q of length ℓ, it holds that $bt_{\mathcal{OPT}}(Q) = \lfloor \ell/B \rfloor$.*

This proposition implies the following corollary which focuses on the case that the block size $B = 2$.

Corollary 7 ([2]). *For a path $Q = \langle v_0, v_1, \ldots, v_\ell \rangle$ of length ℓ, the optimal block transfer of Q for MBT(2) is $bt_{\mathcal{OPT}}(Q) = \lfloor \ell/2 \rfloor$. Moreover, if ℓ is even, then at least one of $\{v_0, v_1\} \in \mathcal{OPT}$ and $\{v_{\ell-1}, v_\ell\} \in \mathcal{OPT}$ holds. Otherwise, i.e., if ℓ is odd, then both of $\{v_0, v_1\} \in \mathcal{OPT}$ and $\{v_{\ell-1}, v_\ell\} \in \mathcal{OPT}$ hold.*

Based on Proposition 6, a lower bound of the block transfer is shown:

Proposition 8 ([2]). *For DAG G and the block size B, it holds that $bt_{\mathcal{OPT}}(G) \geq \lfloor h(G)/B \rfloor$.*

The next theorem shows the approximation ratio of Greedy:

Theorem 9. *Algorithm Greedy achieves the approximation ratio of 2 for MBT(2).*

Proof. From Proposition 8, it holds that $bt_{\mathcal{OPT}}(G) \geq \lfloor h(G)/2 \rfloor$. Note that $\lfloor h(G)/2 \rfloor < h(G)/2$ holds only when $h(G)$ is odd. Based on this observation, the following three cases are considered and we will see that the approximation ratio of Greedy is at most 2 for each case: (i) $h(G)$ is even, (ii) $h(G)$ is odd and $bt_{\mathcal{OPT}}(G) \geq \lfloor h(G)/2 \rfloor + 1$, and (iii) $h(G)$ is odd and $bt_{\mathcal{OPT}}(G) = \lfloor h(G)/2 \rfloor$. Let $\mathcal{P}$ denote the packing obtained by Greedy.

Case (i): $h(G)$ **is even.** It is clear that block transfer under any packing $\mathcal{P}$ is at most the height of the input graph, namely $bt_{\mathcal{P}}(G) \leq h(G)$ holds. Also, $\lfloor h(G)/2 \rfloor = h(G)/2$ holds since $h(G)$ is even. Combining these facts and $bt_{\mathcal{OPT}}(G) \geq \lfloor h(G)/2 \rfloor$ mentioned in the above, we have:

$$\frac{bt_{\mathcal{P}}(G)}{bt_{\mathcal{OPT}}(G)} \leq \frac{h(G)}{\lfloor \frac{h(G)}{2} \rfloor} = \frac{h(G)}{\frac{h(G)}{2}} = 2.$$

Case (ii): $h(G)$ **is odd and** $bt_{\mathcal{OPT}}(G) \geq \lfloor h(G)/2 \rfloor + 1$. Let $h(G) = 2k + 1$ for some non-negative integer k. Similarly to the above Case (i), the following can be shown:

$$\frac{bt_{\mathcal{P}}(G)}{bt_{\mathcal{OPT}}(G)} \leq \frac{h(G)}{\lfloor \frac{h(G)}{2} \rfloor + 1} = \frac{2k+1}{k+1} < 2.$$

Case (iii): $h(G)$ **is odd and** $bt_{\mathcal{OPT}}(G) = \lfloor h(G)/2 \rfloor$. We now need to show that Greedy surely outputs a packing $\mathcal{P}$ such that $bt_{\mathcal{P}}(G) \leq h(G) - 1$, because $h(G)/\lfloor h(G)/2 \rfloor > 2$ in this case. Let $h(G) = 2k + 1$ for some non-negative integer k. Since the target block transfer is $h(G) - 1$, we can ignore paths of length at most $h(G) - 1$.

Consider a path $Q = \langle s, t, \ldots, u, v \rangle$ of length $h(G)$. Let $Q' = \langle s, t, \ldots, u \rangle$ be the path which is obtained by removing v from Q. From Corollary 7, $\mathcal{OPT}$ must include $\{u, v\}$, where $u \in V_{h(G)-1}$ and $v \in V_{h(G)}$. This implies that $d^+(u) = |N^+(u) \cap V_{h(G)}| = 1$: Assume $d^+(u) \geq 2$ and there is an arc (u, v') for contradiction. Then, at most one of the two paths Q and $Q' \circ (u, v')$ can

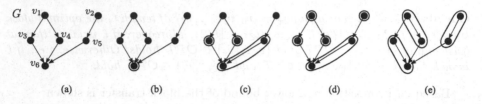

Fig. 2. Worst case example for Greedy: (a) input DAG; (b), (c) and (d) packing of Greedy; and (e) optimal packing

have block transfer $\lfloor h(G)/2 \rfloor$ since at most one of (u, v) and (u, v') can be packed. This contradicts the assumption that $bt_{\mathcal{OPT}}(G) = \lfloor h(G)/2 \rfloor$. Also, the assumption $d^-(v) = |N^-(v) \cap V_{h(G)-1}| \geq 2$ leads to a contradiction, since this condition means that there are two paths of length $h(G)$ ending at v and neither of them can have block transfer $\lfloor h(G)/2 \rfloor$ because of two arcs entering to v.

By this argument, we observe that every node in $V_{h(G)-1}$ has outdegree one and every node (sink) in $V_{h(G)}$ has indegree one in $G[V_{h(G)-1} \cup V_{h(G)}]$. Hence, Greedy works as follows: It first makes $\{v\}$ for every sink v in Step (2-1). Then in Step (2-2), for each node $u \in V_{h(G)-1}$ and its single child $v \in V_{h(G)}$, Greedy makes $\{u, v\}$. In other words, Greedy packs all the arcs between $V_{h(G)-1}$ and $V_{h(G)}$, as a result, $bt_{\mathcal{P}}(G) \leq h(G) - 1$ holds. Finally we have:

$$\frac{bt_{\mathcal{P}}(G)}{bt_{\mathcal{OPT}}(G)} \leq \frac{h(G) - 1}{\lfloor \frac{h(G)}{2} \rfloor} = \frac{2k}{\frac{2k}{2}} = 2.$$

□

As a remark, we can give a worst case example in Fig. 2. For the DAG G in Fig. 2(a) and block size 2, Greedy outputs a packing under which the block transfer is twice of that under $\mathcal{OPT}$. First Greedy makes a packing $\{v_6\}$ in Step (2-1), where $\delta(v_6) = 2$ (Fig. 2(b)). Since $\delta(v_3) = \delta(v_4) = \delta(v_5) = 1$, Greedy may choose v_5 as the first one to process in Step (2-2) and succeeds to pack v_6 and v_5 into $\{v_5, v_6\}$, followed by packing v_3 and v_4 singly (Fig. 2(c)). Then, neither of v_1 and v_2 can be packed with their children. Thus the output of Greedy is $\{\{v_5, v_6\}, \{v_4\}, \{v_3\}, \{v_1\}, \{v_2\}\}$ as shown in Fig. 2(d) and its block transfer is two. On the other hand, the optimal block transfer is one, by a packing $\{\{v_1, v_4\}, \{v_3, v_6\}, \{v_2, v_5\}\}$ as in Fig. 2(e).

4.2 Simpler 2-Approximation Algorithm

One can verify that packing arcs between $V_{h(G)-1}$ and $V_{h(G)}$ in the proof of Theorem 9 yields the approximation ratio 2 although Greedy tries to pack other arcs. This verification gives us a new simpler 2-approximation algorithm:

Algorithm LastArcs
 Input: DAG $G = (V, A)$ **Output:** Packing $\mathcal{P}$
 Step 1: Apply HeightOne to $G[V_{h(G)-1} \cup V_{h(G)}]$, and then outputs an obtained packing $\mathcal{P}$.

Theorem 10. *Algorithm LastArcs is a 2-approximation algorithm for MBT(2).*

Proof. The previous proof for the cases (i) $h(G)$ is even and (ii) $h(G)$ is odd and $bt_{OPT}(G) \geq \lfloor h(G)/2 \rfloor + 1$ are also valid for any algorithm. For the case (iii) $h(G)$ is odd and $bt_{OPT}(G) = \lfloor h(G)/2 \rfloor$, LastArcs can pack all the arcs between $V_{h(G)-1}$ and $V_{h(G)}$, since OPT packs them in this case. Hence, $bt_{\mathcal{P}}(G) = h(G) - 1$ holds, which implies the approximation ratio 2. Details are omitted. $\qquad\square$

4.3 Improved Approximation Algorithm

In this section, we show the approximation algorithm for MBT(2) with its approximation ratio strictly smaller than 2. To be concrete, for DAGs of height $h \geq 3$, our algorithm achieves the following approximation ratio: (i) $2 - 2/h$ for even $h \geq 4$, and $2 - 2/(h + 1)$ for odd $h \geq 3$. Note that if $h = 3$ or 4, then this approximation ratio is $3/2$ which matches the lower bound of the approximation ratio shown in [2] and Sect. 5. The basic idea of this algorithm is to apply the optimal algorithms, HeightOne and HeightTwo, to the top and bottom layers of an input DAG. Depending on whether the height of the DAG is even or odd, the algorithm decides which of the algorithms, Even or Odd, to apply.

Before describing the algorithm, we introduce notation only used in this section. For $0 \leq j \leq h(G)$, R_j denotes the set of nodes that are reachable to a node in V_j, where we define $R_j \supseteq V_j$. In order to simplify the following discussions, we define $R_{h(G)+1} = \emptyset$. Let $V_{i,j}$ be the set of nodes in V_i that are reachable to a node in V_j, but unreachable to any nodes in V_{j+1}, that is, $V_{i,j} = \{v \in V_i \mid v \in R_j \setminus R_{j+1}\}$ for $0 \leq i \leq j \leq h(G)$. Note that there may exist an arc from $V_{i,j}$ to $V_{i',j'}$ for some $i' > i$ and $j' < j$, however there is no arc from $V_{i,j}$ to $V_{i',j'}$ for $i' \leq i$ or $j \geq j'$. We can partition the node set of an input graph to $V_{0,1}, V_{0,2}, \dots, V_{0,h(G)}, V_{1,1}, \dots, V_{h(G),h(G)}$ in polynomial time. Let U_j denote a set of nodes that are reachable to V_j but unreachable to $V_{j'}$ for all $j' > j$, i.e., $U_j = \bigcup_{i=0}^{j} V_{i,j}$.

The below is an approximation algorithm for DAGs of even height ≥ 4.

Algorithm Even
 Input: DAG $G = (V, A)$ of even height $h \geq 4$ **Output:** Packing $\mathcal{P}$
 Step 1: Apply HeightTwo to $H = G[V_{0,h} \cup V_{1,h} \cup V_{2,h}]$ and obtain a packing $\mathcal{P}_1$.
 Step 2: Output $\mathcal{P} = \mathcal{P}_1 \cup \{\{v\} \mid v \in V(G) \setminus V(H)\}$.

The approximation ratio of Even is given in the next theorem.

Theorem 11. *Algorithm Even is a $(2 - \frac{2}{h})$-approximation algorithm for DAGs of even height $h \geq 4$.*

Proof. We divide this proof into two cases: (i) $bt_{\mathcal{OPT}}(G) = h/2$, and (ii) $bt_{\mathcal{OPT}}(G) \geq h/2 + 1$.

Case (i): $bt_{\mathcal{OPT}}(G) = h/2$. For the subgraph H in Step 1, we observe that $bt_{\mathcal{OPT}}(H) = 1$: assume for contradiction that $bt_{\mathcal{OPT}}(H) = 2$. This implies that there is a path Q_1 of block transfer 2 under any packing, which is from a node in $V_{0,h}$ to a node in $V_{2,h}$. Then there must be a path Q_2 of length $h-2$ from the end node of Q_1 to a node in $V_{h,h}$, based on the definition of $V_{2,h}$. Hence, the block transfer of the path $Q_1 \circ Q_2$ is at least $2 + (h-2)/2 = h/2 + 1$, where $h-2$ is even so that the block transfer of Q_2 is at least $(h-2)/2$ from Proposition 8. This contradicts the assumption that $bt_{\mathcal{OPT}}(G) = h/2$.

Since $bt_{\mathcal{OPT}}(H) = 1$, the algorithm HeightTwo finds an optimal packing $\mathcal{P}_1$ such that $bt_{\mathcal{P}_1}(H) = 1$ in Step 1. Hence, $bt_{\mathcal{P}_1}(G[U_h]) = h - 1$. In the input graph G, every path of length h exists only in $G[U_h]$. It follows that $bt_{\mathcal{P}}(G) = h - 1$. Therefore, it holds

$$\frac{bt_{\mathcal{P}}(G)}{bt_{\mathcal{OPT}}(G)} = \frac{h-1}{\frac{h}{2}} = 2 - \frac{2}{h}.$$

Case (ii): $bt_{\mathcal{OPT}}(G) \geq h/2 + 1$. In this case, we use a trivial upper bound h as the block transfer under $\mathcal{P}$ obtained by Even:

$$\frac{bt_{\mathcal{P}}(G)}{bt_{\mathcal{OPT}}(G)} \leq \frac{h}{\frac{h}{2} + 1} = 2 - \frac{4}{h+2}.$$

Hence the approximation ratio of Even is $2 - 2/h$, since $4/(h+2) > 2/h$. □

Next we describe an algorithm Odd for DAGs of odd height ≥ 3, which is more complicated than Even.

Algorithm Odd
  Input: DAG $G = (V, A)$ of odd height $h \geq 3$ **Output:** Packing $\mathcal{P}$
  Step 1: Apply HeightOne to $G[V_{0,h} \cup V_{1,h}]$ and obtain a packing $\mathcal{P}_1$.
  Step 2: Apply HeightOne to $G[V_{h-1,h} \cup V_{h,h}]$ and obtain a packing $\mathcal{P}_2$.
  Step 3: We define subsets of $V_{0,h}$, $V_{1,h-1}$, and $V_{2,h-1}$ as follows.
   - $V'_{0,h} = \{v \in V_{0,h} \mid N^+(v) \cap V_{1,h-1} \neq \emptyset\}$
   - $V'_{1,h-1} = \{v \in V_{1,h-1} \mid v \in N^+(u), u \in V'_{0,h}\}$ and $\overline{V'_{1,h-1}} = V_{1,h-1} \setminus V'_{1,h-1}$
   - $V'_{2,h-1} = \{v \in V_{2,h-1} \mid v \in N^+(u), u \in V'_{1,h-1}\}$ and $\overline{V'_{2,h-1}} = V_{2,h-1} \setminus V'_{2,h-1}$
  Apply HeightOne to $G[V'_{1,h-1} \cup V'_{2,h-1}]$ and obtain a packing $\mathcal{P}_3$.
  Then, apply HeightTwo to $G[V_{0,h-1} \cup \overline{V'_{1,h-1}} \cup \overline{V'_{2,h-1}}]$ and obtain a packing $\mathcal{P}_4$.
  Step 4: Construct a packing $\mathcal{P}_5 = \{\{v\} \mid v$ is not packed in $\mathcal{P}_1 \cup \mathcal{P}_2 \cup \mathcal{P}_3 \cup \mathcal{P}_4\}$.

Step 5: Output $\mathcal{P} = \mathcal{P}_1 \cup \mathcal{P}_2 \cup \mathcal{P}_3 \cup \mathcal{P}_4 \cup \mathcal{P}_5$.

The approximation ratio of Odd is given in the next theorem:

Theorem 12. *Algorithm* Odd *is a* $(2 - \frac{2}{h+1})$-*approximation algorithm for DAGs of odd height* $h \geq 3$.

Proof. We divide this proof into two cases: (i) $bt_{OPT}(G) = (h-1)/2$, and (ii) $bt_{OPT}(G) \geq (h-1)/2 + 1$.

Case (i): $bt_{OPT}(G) = (h-1)/2$. We show that $bt_{\mathcal{P}}(G) = h - 2$. In this case, it holds that $bt_{OPT}(G[V_{0,h} \cup V_{1,h}]) = 0$ and $bt_{OPT}(G[V_{h-1,h} \cup V_{h,h}]) = 0$ from the fact $bt_{OPT}(G) = (h-1)/2$ and Corollary 7. Hence Odd can also obtain packings $\mathcal{P}_1$ and $\mathcal{P}_2$ in Steps 1 and 2 such that $bt_{\mathcal{P}_1}(G[V_{0,h} \cup V_{1,h}]) = 0$ and $bt_{\mathcal{P}_2}(G[V_{h-1,h} \cup V_{h,h}]) = 0$, respectively, since HeightOne is an optimal algorithm for DAGs of height one. At this moment, $bt_{\mathcal{P}_1}(G[U_h]) = h-2$ holds. However there may exist a path of length $h-1$ in which any arc is not packed under $\mathcal{P}_1$ or $\mathcal{P}_2$. If such a path includes an arc from a node in $U_h \setminus V_{0,h}$ to a node in U_{h-1}[1], then the packing $\mathcal{P}_1$ has already reduced its block transfer to $h-2$; thus we need to consider a path of length $h-1$, which includes an arc from a node in $V_{0,h}$ to a node in $V_{1,h-1}$, or is constituted only by the nodes in U_{h-1}. We can handle such paths in $G[V'_{0,h} \cup U_{h-1}]$ in Step 3 of the the algorithm as below. The situation is illustrated in Fig. 3.

Consider the subgraph $H = G[V'_{0,h} \cup V_{0,h-1} \cup V_{1,h-1} \cup V_{2,h-1}]$. First we observe that $bt_{OPT}(H) = 1$: Assume for contradiction that $bt_{OPT}(H) = 2$. This implies that there is a path Q_1 of block transfer 2 under any packing such that Q_1 is from a node in $V'_{0,h} \cup V_{0,h-1}$ to a node in $V_{2,h-1}$. Then there must be a path Q_2 of length $h-3$ from the end node of Q_1 to a node in $V_{h-1,h-1}$, based on the definition of $V_{2,h-1}$. Hence, the block transfer of the path $Q_1 \circ Q_2$ is at least $2 + (h-3)/2 = (h+1)/2$, where $h-3$ is even and thus the lower bound of the block transfer of Q_2 is $(h-3)/2$ from Proposition 8. This contradicts the assumption that $bt_{OPT}(G) = (h-1)/2$.

It is seen that every node in $V'_{0,h}$ is packed under $\mathcal{P}_1$ with another node in $V_{1,h}$ in Step 1. From this viewpoint, in order to reduce the block transfer of a path of length 2 from a node in $V'_{0,h}$ to a node $V'_{2,h-1}$, the optimal algorithm must pack the arcs between $V'_{1,h-1}$ and $V'_{2,h-1}$, where Odd can also obtain such a packing $\mathcal{P}_3$ by HeightOne. Moreover, the optimal solution should include packings of arcs such that $bt_{OPT}(G[V_{0,h-1} \cup \overline{V'_{1,h-1}} \cup \overline{V'_{2,h-1}}]) = 1$. Such a packing can also be obtained by HeightTwo, i.e., it is also obtained in Step 3 of Odd. As a result, $bt_{\mathcal{P}_3 \cup \mathcal{P}_4}(H) = 1$ and thus $bt_{\mathcal{P}_3 \cup \mathcal{P}_4}(G[V'_{0,h} \cup U_h]) = h-2$. Note here that neither $\mathcal{P}_3$ nor $\mathcal{P}_4$ violates $\mathcal{P}_1$ and $\mathcal{P}_2$ since $\mathcal{P}_1$ is for $G[V_{0,h} \cup V_{1,h}]$ and $\mathcal{P}_2$ is for $G[V_{h-1,h} \cup V_{h,h}]$.

---

[1] Remind that there is no arc from U_{h-1} to U_h.

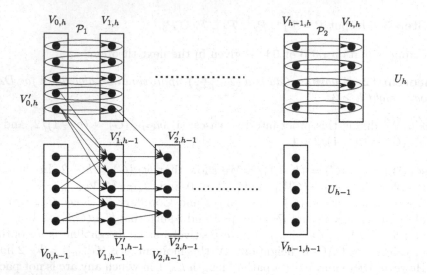

Fig. 3. Case (i) in the proof of Theorem 12, where only U_h and U_{h-1} are illustrated

Since the other paths except for paths in $G[U_h \cup U_{h-1}]$ have length at most $h-2$, their block transfers are also at most $h-2$. In summary, $bt_{\mathcal{P}}(G) = h-2$, and hence

$$\frac{bt_{\mathcal{P}}(G)}{bt_{\mathcal{OPT}}(G)} = \frac{h-2}{\frac{(h-1)}{2}} = 2 - \frac{2}{h-1}.$$

Case (ii) $bt_{\mathcal{OPT}}(G) \geq (h+1)/2$. In this case, we use a trivial upper bound h as the block transfer under $\mathcal{P}$ obtained by Odd:

$$\frac{bt_{\mathcal{P}}(G)}{bt_{\mathcal{OPT}}(G)} \leq \frac{h}{\frac{(h+1)}{2}} = 2 - \frac{2}{h+1}.$$

Hence the approximation ratio is $2 - 2/(h+1)$ since $2/(h-1) > 2/(h+1)$. □

5   Inapproximability for Height Greater Than Three

In [2], the $(3/2 - \varepsilon)$-inapproximability of MBT(2) is shown for DAGs of height three, while polynomial-time exact algorithms are designed for DAGs of height one and two. The main purpose of this section is to discuss whether DAGs of height greater than three are easier or harder for MBT(2) from the view point of inapproximability; we investigate the more accurate relationship between the height of input DAGs and the inapproximability of MBT(2).

The important points of the proof of the $(3/2 - \varepsilon)$-inapproximability are briefly summarized as follows:

– The gap-introducing reduction is from the 3-CNF SATISFIABILITY problem (3-SAT);

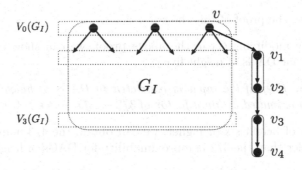

Fig. 4. Graph G_4 and a packing $\mathcal{P}$

- the reduced graph G_I from an instance I of 3-SAT has height three; and
- if the answer to I of 3-SAT is satisfiable (we say that I is yes), then $bt_{\mathcal{OPT}}(G_I) = 2$, otherwise, $bt_{\mathcal{OPT}}(G_I) = 3$, where $\mathcal{OPT}$ is an optimal packing. This condition is later referred as [C1].

Then the next proposition is shown based on the gap between two and three of the block transfer of G_I by the gap-introducing reduction: (i) if I is yes, $bt_{\mathcal{OPT}}(G_I) \leq 2$, and (ii) if I is no, $bt_{\mathcal{OPT}}(G_I) \geq 3$.

Proposition 13 ([2]). *Even if the input is restricted to DAGs of height three, MBT(2) cannot be approximated within a factor of $3/2 - \varepsilon$ for any $\varepsilon > 0$ unless $P = NP$.*

First we extend this result to the DAGs of height four and obtain a next theorem. We frequently use the above reduced graph G_I from an instance I of 3-SAT as a gadget in the following. For a graph G partitioned into layers, $V_i(G)$ denotes the subset of $V(G)$, which contains all nodes of depth i in $V(G)$.

Theorem 14. *Even if the input is restricted to DAGs of height four, MBT(2) cannot be approximated within a factor of $3/2 - \varepsilon$ for any $\varepsilon > 0$ unless $P = NP$.*

Proof. The new graph G_4 is constructed based on G_I as follows: See Fig. 4. Pick one node $v \in V_0(G_I)$ and then add new nodes v_1, v_2, v_3 and v_4 which constitute a path $Q = \langle v, v_1, v_2, v_3, v_4 \rangle$. By this construction, $h(G_4) = 4$. We show that the two conditions of the gap-introducing reduction hold: if I is yes, then $bt_{\mathcal{OPT}}(G_4) \leq 2$, otherwise, $bt_{\mathcal{OPT}}(G_4) \geq 3$.

The case I is yes. First an optimal packing $\mathcal{P}_I$ for G_I (which surely exists by [C1]) is applied to the part G_I of G_4, by which the block transfer of the part is 2. Then we add $\{v_1, v_2\}$ and $\{v_3, v_4\}$ to $\mathcal{P}_I$ and obtain a new packing $\mathcal{P} = \mathcal{P}_I \cup \{\{v_1, v_2\}, \{v_3, v_4\}\}$ by which $bt_{\mathcal{P}}(Q) = 2$. In summary, $bt_{\mathcal{P}}(G_4) = 2 \geq bt_{\mathcal{OPT}}(G_4)$.

The case I is no. Since $bt_{\mathcal{OPT}}(G_I) = 3$ and G_4 includes G_I as a subgraph, it holds that $bt_{\mathcal{OPT}}(G_4) \geq 3$.

This completes the proof of this theorem.   □

By slightly modifying G_4 in the above proof, we can show the same inapproximability for DAGs of height five:

Theorem 15. *Even if the input is restricted to DAGs of height five, MBT(2) cannot be approximated within a factor of $3/2 - \varepsilon$ for any $\varepsilon > 0$ unless $P = NP$.*

For DAGs of height six or higher, we can obtain the 4/3-inapproximability, which is smaller than the 3/2-inapproximability for DAGs of height 3, 4, and 5:

Theorem 16. *Even if the input is restricted to DAGs of height at least six, MBT(2) cannot be approximated within a factor of $4/3 - \varepsilon$ for any $\varepsilon > 0$ unless $P = NP$.*

6   Conclusion

We considered the problem MBT(2). The contribution of this paper is summarized as follows: (i) An error in [2] is pointed out; (ii) The approximation ratio 2 of the bottom-up-packing greedy algorithm in [4] is shown; (iii) A simpler 2-approximation algorithm, and a new algorithm with approximation ratio strictly smaller than 2 are designed; and (iv) Inapproximabilities 3/2 and 4/3 are shown, respectively for DAGs of height at most five and at least six. One important topic is to narrow the gap between the above approximability and inapproximability. Also, since little is known for MBT(B) with $B \geq 3$, considering the case $B \geq 3$ is another interesting subject.

References

1. Aggarwal, A., Vitter, J.S.: The input/output complexity of sorting and related problems. Commun. ACM **31**(9), 1116–1127 (1988). https://doi.org/10.1145/48529.48535
2. Asahiro, Y., Furukawa, T., Ikegami, K., Miyano, E.: How to pack directed acyclic graphs into small blocks. In: Calamoneri, T., Finocchi, I., Italiano, G.F. (eds.) CIAC 2006. LNCS, vol. 3998, pp. 272–283. Springer, Heidelberg (2006). https://doi.org/10.1007/11758471_27
3. Cormen, T.H., Leiserson, C.E., Rivest, R.L., Stein, C.: Introduction to Algorithms, 3rd ed. MIT Press, pp. 612–615 (2009). Section 22.4: Topological sort
4. Diwan, A.A., Rane, S., Seshadri, S., Sudarshan, S.: Clustering techniques for minimizing external path length. In: Proceedings of 22nd VLDB 1996, pp. 342–353 (1996)
5. Donovan, Z., Mkrtchyan, V., Subramani, K.: On clustering without replication in combinatorial circuits. In: Lu, Z., Kim, D., Wu, W., Li, W., Du, D.-Z. (eds.) COCOA 2015. LNCS, vol. 9486, pp. 334–347. Springer, Cham (2015). https://doi.org/10.1007/978-3-319-26626-8_25
6. Donovan, Z., Mkrtchyan, V., Subramani, K.: Complexity issues in some clustering problems in combinatorial circuits: when logic replication is not allowed. arXiv:1412.4051v2 (2017)

7. Even, S., Itai, A., Shamir, A.: On the complexity of timetable and multicommodity flow problems. SIAM J. Comput. **5**(4), 691–703 (1976). https://doi.org/10.1109/SFCS.1975.21

8. Vazirani, V.V.: Approximation Algorithms. Springer, Heidelberg (2003). https://doi.org/10.1007/978-3-662-04565-7

9. Vitter, J.S.: Algorithms and data structures for external memory. Found. Trends Theor. Comput Sci. **2**(4), 305–474 (2008). https://doi.org/10.1561/0400000014

Parameter Estimation of the Kinetic α-Pinene Isomerization Model Using the MCSFilter Algorithm

Andreia Amador[1], Florbela P. Fernandes[2](✉) ⓘ, Lino O. Santos[1] ⓘ,
Andrey Romanenko[1,3] ⓘ, and Ana Maria A. C. Rocha[4] ⓘ

[1] CIEPQPF, Department of Chemical Engineering,
Faculty of Sciences and Technology, University of Coimbra,
3030-790 Coimbra, Portugal
uc2010149251@student.uc.pt, lino@eq.uc.pt
[2] Research Centre in Digitalization and Intelligent Robotics (CeDRI),
Instituto Politécnico de Bragança, 5300-253 Bragança, Portugal
fflor@ipb.pt
[3] Ciengis, SA, Rua Pedro Nunes, Ed.E, Coimbra, Portugal
andrey.romanenko@ciengis.com
[4] Algoritmi Research Centre, University of Minho, 4710-057 Braga, Portugal
arocha@dps.uminho.pt

Abstract. This paper aims to illustrate the application of a derivative-free multistart algorithm with coordinate search filter, designated as the MCSFilter algorithm. The problem used in this study is the parameter estimation problem of the kinetic α-pinene isomerization model. This is a well known nonlinear optimization problem (NLP) that has been investigated as a case study for performance testing of most derivative based methods proposed in the literature. Since the MCSFilter algorithm features a stochastic component, it was run ten times to solve the NLP problem. The optimization problem was successfully solved in all the runs and the optimal solution demonstrates that the MCSFilter provides a good quality solution.

Keywords: MCSFilter · α-pinene isomerization model · Multistart
Derivative-free optimization

1 Introduction

The parameter estimation problem of the α-pinene isomerization model is one of the optimization problems that has been widely used as a benchmark problem to assess the performance of optimization algorithms. This is because of the challenges posed by the multivariable, complex and nonlinear nature of the kinetic model that describes the α-pinene isomerization phenomena. This system is described by the reaction scheme represented in Fig. 1. It comprises five

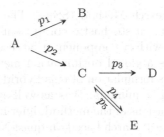

Fig. 1. α-pinene isomerization reaction scheme: A - α-pinene; B - dipentene; C - allo-ocimene; D - α and β-pironene; E - dimer.

reactions, one of them is reversible, and five chemical species: α-pinene (A), dipentene (B), allo-ocimene (C), α and β-pironene (D), and the dimer (E).

One of the earliest kinetic α-pinene isomerization models was proposed by Box and Drapper [1], and it was used to estimate the five kinetic rate constants of this reaction system, using the experimental data obtained by Fuguitt and Hawkins (see [1] and references therein). A later study [2] has demonstrated that there could exist linear dependencies between the experimental data on the concentration of the chemical species involved in the α-pinene isomerization. This was the cause of numerical difficulties to estimate the parameters and the consequent error estimates with respect to the experimental observations. For instance, the concentration of β-pironene was erroneously estimated by 3% of the total conversion of α-pinene [1]. Besides, these linear dependencies might be the root cause of some of the difficulties experienced by optimization methods in getting to the optimal value.

In the work of Ames [3] it is asserted that there are three linear relationships in the experimental chemical species concentration data. The first linear relationship concerns the mass balance to the mixture of the reacting system. The second one is due to the fact that the isomerization is an irreversible phenomenon. Finally, the third linear relationship arises from the fact that the sum of molar fractions of the chemical species in the reacting mixture has to be equal to one. Box et al. [2] solved this parameter estimation problem using a least square criterion. The objective function is defined as the sum of the squared deviation between the chemical species concentrations predicted by the model and the measurements obtained over a given time horizon. Tjoa and Biegler [4] have addressed this estimation problem by solving a constrained nonlinear optimization problem where a quadratic objective function is determined by invoking the numerical integration of the dynamic ODE model of the chemical reaction system. Their results are very similar to those obtained by [2]. In both works, the starting point to solve the optimization problem is very close to the optimal solution, which makes the optimizer convergence easier.

In a followup study based on the earlier works of [4,5], Dolan et al. [6] applies a search filter based method that lead to results similar to the ones obtained previously with the derivative based optimization methods. Egea-Larrosa [7,8]

has applied the Scatter Search Method (SSm). The SSm is a hybrid popula-
tional method that features a stochastic component made of a metaheuristic
scatter search associated with a component that uses the derivative function
information. It constitutes a global optimization method with a random local
search strategy. A previous formulation of this hybrid method by [9], where it is
assumed that the problem is unimodal, was as well as implemented by Egea et
al. [7]. The two implementations of the method differ in the local search strategy.
The method in [9] uses a local search based on quasi-Newton procedure, whereas
in [7] a direct search method is implemented based on a stochastic approach.

A recent work [10], in which the α-pinene system was also used for testing
purposes, details the development and implementation of the Firefly Algorithm.
This is a stochastic method for global optimization problems that mimics the
behavior of fireflies considering that the fireflies are unisex and usually attracted
to the brightest light. When applied to the optimization method, the "light
intensity" is measured according to the function value: the lower the value, the
brightest the light. This means that the points generated by the stochastic part
of the method will converge to lower values of the function. For further details
on this optimization strategy see [10].

The method used in this work to solve the α-pinene isomerization parameter
estimation problem is the Multistart Coordinate Search Filter Method (MCS-
Filter). It is a derivative-free method based on a multistart strategy coupled
with a local coordinate search filter procedure to find the global minimum. Further details on the underlying algorithm are given in Sect. 2 We demonstrate the
application of the MCSFilter to solve the α-pinene isomerization parameter estimation problem. Also, a comparison of the performance of the MCSFilter with
other optimization strategies is presented regarding the quality of the optimal
solution, as well as the influence of two parameters on the performance of the
algorithm.

The paper is organized as follows. The derivative-free multistart strategy
with coordinate search filter method (MCSFilter) is described in Sect. 2. The
kinetic model and the parameter estimation problem are presented in Sect. 3.
The numerical results and its discussion are presented in Sect. 4. Finally, some
remarks are given in Sect. 5.

2   The Multistart Coordinate Search Filter Method

The MCSFilter algorithm was initially developed by [11] to find multiple solutions of a nonconvex and nonlinear constrained optimization problems of the
following type:

$$\min f(x)$$
$$\text{subject to } g_j(x) \leq 0, \quad j = 1, ..., m \tag{1}$$
$$l_i \leq x_i \leq u_i, \, i = 1, ..., n$$

where, f is the objective function, $g_j(x) \, j = 1, ..., m$ are the constraint functions
and, at least, one of the functions $f, g_j : \mathbb{R}^n \longrightarrow \mathbb{R}$ is nonlinear; l and u are the
bounds and $\Omega = \{x \in \mathbb{R}^n : g(x) \leq 0, \, l \leq x \leq u\}$ is the feasible region.

This method does not use any derivative information and incorporate two major different parts: the multistart strategy related with the exploration feature of the method and a derivative-free local search related with the exploitation of promising regions.

The multistart strategy is a stochastic algorithm that repeatedly applies a local search to sampled points aiming to converge to all the solutions of a multimodal problem. When the direct search is repeatedly applied some minimizers can be found more than once. To avoid a previously computed minimizer, a clustering technique based on computing the regions of attraction of previously identified minimizers is used. In this way, if the sampled point belongs to the region of attraction of an already known minimizer the direct search procedure will not be performed since it would converge to this known minimizer.

Figure 2 illustrates the influence of the regions of attraction. The red/magenta lines between the initial approximation and the minimizer represents a local search that has been performed (red line is used to represent the first local search which converged to each minimum). The white dashed line between the two points represents a local search that was discarded, using the regions of attraction. A set of benchmark problems [11] as well as a small dimensional real problem [12] were used to test the algorithm and the results were very promising.

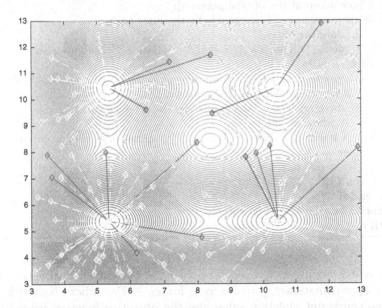

Fig. 2. Illustration of the Multistart strategy with regions of attraction.

The direct search used is a derivative-free local search that consists of a coordinate search combined with a filter methodology to generate a sequence of approximate solutions that improve either the constraint violation or the objective function relative to the previous approximation, called Coordinate Search Filter algorithm (CSFilter) [11].

A rough outline of the CSFilter algorithm is as follows and (Algorithm 1 displays the steps of the algorithm). At the beginning, the problem (1) is rewritten as a bi-objective optimization problem aiming to minimize both the objective function $f(x)$ and a nonnegative continuous aggregate constraint violation function $\theta(x)$ defined by

$$\theta(x) = \|g(x)_+\|^2 + \|(l - x)_+\|^2 + \|(x - u)_+\|^2 \qquad (2)$$

where $v_+ = \max\{0, v\}$. The filter is initialized to $\mathcal{F} = \{(\theta, f) : \theta \geq \theta_{\max}\}$, where $\theta_{\max} > 0$ is an upper bound on the acceptable constraint violation. The $\mathcal{D}_\oplus$ denotes the set of $2n$ coordinate directions, defined as the positive and negative unit coordinate vectors, $\mathcal{D}_\oplus = \{e_1, e_2, \ldots, e_n, -e_1, -e_2, \ldots, -e_n\}$.

Algorithm 1. CSFilter algorithm

Require: x and parameter values, $\alpha_{\min}$; set $\tilde{x} = x$, $x_{\mathcal{F}}^{inf} = x$, $z = \tilde{x}$;
1: Initialize the filter; Set $\alpha = \min\{1, 0.05\frac{\sum_{i=1}^{n} u_i - l_i}{n}\}$;
2: **repeat**
3:     Compute the trial approximations $z_a^i = \tilde{x} + \alpha e_i$, for all $e_i \in \mathcal{D}_\oplus$;
4:     **repeat**
5:         Check acceptability of trial points z_a^i;
6:         **if** there are some z_a^i acceptable by the filter **then**
7:             Update the filter;
8:             Choose z_a^{best}; set $z = \tilde{x}$, $\tilde{x} = z_a^{best}$; update $x_{\mathcal{F}}^{inf}$ if appropriate;
9:         **else**
10:            Compute the trial approximations $z_a^i = x_{\mathcal{F}}^{inf} + \alpha e_i$, for all $e_i \in \mathcal{D}_\oplus$;
11:            Check acceptability of trial points z_a^i;
12:            **if** there are some z_a^i acceptable by the filter **then**
13:                Update the filter;
14:                Choose z_a^{best}; Set $z = \tilde{x}$, $\tilde{x} = z_a^{best}$; update $x_{\mathcal{F}}^{inf}$ if appropriate;
15:            **else**
16:                Set $\alpha = \alpha/2$;
17:            **end if**
18:        **end if**
19:    **until** new trial z_a^{best} is acceptable
20: **until** $\alpha < \alpha_{\min}$

The search begins with a central point (the current approximation $\tilde{x}$), and $2n$ trial approximations $z_a^i = \tilde{x} + \alpha e_i$, for $e_i \in \mathcal{D}_\oplus$, where $\alpha > 0$ is a step size. The constraint violation value and the objective function value of all $2n$ points are computed. If some trial approximations improve over $\tilde{x}$, reducing θ or f and are acceptable by the filter, then the best of these non-dominated trial approximations, z_a^{best}, is selected, and the filter is updated (adding the corresponding entries to the filter and removing the dominated entries). This best approximation becomes the new central point in the next iteration, $\tilde{x} \leftarrow z_a^{best}$. On the other hand, if all trial approximations z_a^i are dominated by the current filter, then all z_a^i are rejected, and a restoration phase is invoked.

When it is not possible to find a non-dominated best trial approximation (before declaring the iteration unsuccessful) a restoration phase is invoked. In this phase, the most nearly feasible point in the filter, $x_{\mathcal{F}}^{inf}$, is recovered and the search along the $2n$ coordinate directions is carried out from it. If a non-dominated best trial approximation is found, this point becomes the new central point and the iteration is successful. Otherwise, the iteration is unsuccessful, the search returns back to the current $\tilde{x}$, the step size is reduced, $\alpha = \alpha/2$, and new $2n$ trial approximations z_a^i are generated from it. If a best non-dominated trial approximation is still not found, the step size is again reduced since another unsuccessful iteration has occurred. The search stops when α falls below $\alpha_{\min}$, a small positive tolerance. Further details about the multistart strategy and the CSFilter algorithm can be found in [11].

The MCSFilter algorithm was initially coded in MATLAB and, in this work, it was coded in Java language. Algorithm 2 shows the main steps of the MCS-Filter algorithm for finding a global solution to problem (1).

Algorithm 2. MCSFilter algorithm

Require: Parameter values; set $M^* = \emptyset$, $k = 1$, $t = 1$;
1: Randomly generate $x \in [l, u]$; compute $B_{\min} = \min_{i=1,\ldots,n}\{u_i - l_i\}$;
2: Compute $m_1 = \mathbf{CSFilter}(x)$, $R_1 = \|x - m_1\|$; set $r_1 = 1$, $M^* = M^* \cup m_1$;
3: **repeat**
4:     Randomly generate $x \in [l, u]$;
5:     Set $o = \arg\min_{j=1,\ldots,k} d_j \equiv \|x - m_j\|$;
6:     **if** $d_o < R_o$ **then**
7:         **if** the direction from x to y_o is ascent **then**
8:             Set $prob = 1$;
9:         **else**
10:            Compute $prob = \varrho\,\phi(\frac{d_o}{R_o}, r_o)$;
11:        **end if**
12:    **else**
13:        Set $prob = 1$;
14:    **end if**
15:    **if** $\zeta^{\ddagger} < prob$ **then**
16:        Compute $m = \mathbf{CSFilter}(x)$; set $t = t + 1$;
17:        **if** $\|m - m_j\| > \gamma^* B_{\min}$, for all $j = 1, \ldots, k$ **then**
18:            Set $k = k + 1$, $m_k = m$, $r_k = 1$, $M^* = M^* \cup m_k$; compute $R_k = \|x - m_k\|$;
19:        **else**
20:            Set $R_l = \max\{R_l, \|x - m_l\|\}$; $r_l = r_l + 1$;
21:        **end if**
22:    **else**
23:        Set $R_o = \max\{R_o, \|x - m_o\|\}$; $r_o = r_o + 1$;
24:    **end if**
25: **until** the stopping rule is satisfied

In this algorithm, M^* is the set containing the computed minimizers and ζ is a uniformly distributed number in $(0, 1)$. Moreover, line 17 means that $m \notin M^*$

and in lines 2 and 16, a call is made of the direct search coupled with the filter methodology, the CSFilter algorithm.

The stopping rule that is used in the MCSFilter algorithm is related to the number of initial points used in the multistart strategy. In this way, the algorithm stops when a maximum number of initial points is reached, $k \leq k_{\max}$.

3   Parameter Estimation Problem

As it is illustrated in Fig. 1, the isomerization of the α-pinene is characterized by the formation of dipentene and allo-ocimene, which in turn originates α and β-pironene through an irreversible process reaction, and a dimer through a reversible reaction. Let y_i, $i = 1, \ldots, 5$, denote the molar concentration of each component i, $i = 1, \ldots, 5$, in the mixture, respectively α-pinene, dipentene, allo-ocimene, α and β-pironene, and dimer. The partial mass balance to the mixture leads to the following ODE model:

$$\frac{dy_1}{dt} = -(p_1 + p_2)\, y_1, \tag{3a}$$

$$\frac{dy_2}{dt} = p_1\, y_1, \tag{3b}$$

$$\frac{dy_3}{dt} = p_2\, y_1 - (p_3 + p_4)\, y_3 + p_5\, y_5, \tag{3c}$$

$$\frac{dy_4}{dt} = p_3\, y_3, \tag{3d}$$

$$\frac{dy_5}{dt} = p_4\, y_3 - p_5\, y_5, \tag{3e}$$

with $t \in [0; 36420]$ and the following initial conditions: $y_1(0) = 100; y_2(0) = 0; y_3(0) = 0; y_4(0) = 0; y_5(0) = 0$. p_j represents the specific reaction rate of reaction j, $j = 1, \ldots, 5$. This is the set of kinetic parameters to be determined in order to fit the model to the experimental data (Table 1).

As mentioned before, because of its complex, nonlinear nature, this model has been used in several works as a benchmark problem to assess the performance of optimization algorithms (e.g., [4, 6, 8–10, 13–15]).

The parameter estimation problem can be formulated as an optimization problem that applies the least squares method with simple bounds [4]. Since (3) is a dynamic model, the calculation of the value of the objective function requires its numerical integration over the time horizon of interest (see Table 1). The kinetic model parameters, p, are the decision variables of the optimization problem which can be posed as follows:

$$\min_p \quad J(p) = \sum_{i=1}^{5} \sum_{k=1}^{9} (y_{\exp i,k} - y_{i,k})^2 \tag{4}$$

$$\text{subject to} \quad p_{\mathrm{L}} \leqslant p \leqslant p_{\mathrm{U}},$$

Table 1. Experimental data (e.g.,[7,10]).

k	t	α-pinene	dipentene	allo-ocimene	pyronene	dimer
		y_1	y_2	y_3	y_4	y_5
1	0	100.0	0.0	0.0	0.0	0.0
2	1230	88.35	7.3	2.3	0.4	1.75
3	3060	76.4	15.6	4.5	0.7	2.8
4	4920	65.1	23.1	5.3	1.1	5.8
5	7800	50.4	32.9	6.0	1.5	9.3
6	10680	37.5	42.7	6.0	1.9	12.0
7	15030	25.9	49.1	5.9	2.2	17.0
8	22620	14.0	57.4	5.1	2.6	21.0
9	36420	4.5	63.1	3.8	2.9	25.7

where $y_{\exp i,k}$ is the experimental concentration value and $y_{i,k}$ the concentration predicted by the model (3) for the chemical specie i at the time instant k. The subscripts U and L on p denote upper and lower limits, respectively.

The best known optimum value of the objective function for this problem is $J(p^*) = 19.872$ achieved at $p_1^* = 5.9256 \times 10^{-5}$, $p_2^* = 2.9632 \times 10^{-5}$, $p_3^* = 2.0450 \times 10^{-5}$, $p_4^* = 2.7473 \times 10^{-4}$, $p_5^* = 4.0073 \times 10^{-5}$ [7].

4   Numerical Results

In this section, the practical performance of the MCSFilter algorithm when solving problem (4) is analyzed. The computational tests were performed on a 2.6 GHz Core i7, with 8 GB of RAM and an operating system MacOs El Capitan laptop. The computational framework to solve the optimization problem (4) was implemented using Java programming language and a Java version of the MCSFilter. During the optimization process, the dynamic model (3) is solved with the explicit Adams-Bashforth integrator for ODEs in Java, from the Apache Commons Math 3.0 Library.

In the simulations done in this study, the absolute and relative tolerances for the integration were set to 1×10^{-8}. The upper and lower bounds on the parameter values were set to:

$$p_U = \begin{bmatrix} 1 \times 10^{-4} & 1 \times 10^{-4} & 1 \times 10^{-4} & 1 \times 10^{-3} & 1 \times 10^{-4} \end{bmatrix}^\top,$$

$$p_L = \begin{bmatrix} 1 \times 10^{-6} & 1 \times 10^{-6} & 1 \times 10^{-6} & 1 \times 10^{-5} & 1 \times 10^{-6} \end{bmatrix}^\top.$$

In order to evaluate the influence of the parameter values ($\alpha_{\min}$ and $k_{\max}$) on the quality of the solution, an experimental study was conducted to tune the stopping criteria parameters of the CSFilter and MCSFilter algorithms, in the context of the α-pinene problem. Nine combinations of $\alpha_{\min}$ and $k_{\max}$, using the values $\alpha_{\min} = \{10^{-5}, 10^{-6}\}$ and $k_{\max} = \{10, 15, 20, 50, 100\}$, were tested.

Table 2 presents the best (J_{best}), average (J_{avg}) and worst (J_{worst}) results produced by MCSFilter algorithm based on 10 executions, as well as the number of function evaluations for the best run, $n_{FE,best}$.

Table 2. Results obtained by MCSFilter, for different combinations of α_{min} and k_{max}.

α_{min}	k_{max}	J_{best}	J_{avg}	J_{worst}	$n_{FE,best}$
10^{-5}	10	29.5107	39.8377	75.8033	2933
10^{-5}	15	26.3374	39.6668	83.9623	4601
10^{-5}	20	23.6566	33.6128	52.1003	2729
10^{-5}	50	22.9355	30.6804	44.8241	14026
10^{-6}	10	20.0165	20.3306	20.9549	5304
10^{-6}	15	19.9517	20.1647	20.6374	5249
10^{-6}	20	19.9122	20.1013	20.3227	8486
10^{-6}	50	19.9157	20.0173	20.1143	20737
10^{-6}	100	19.9074	19.9798	20.1241	34241

Table 2 shows that MCSFilter algorithm converges to the known global minimum. The objective of this experimental study was to evaluate the performance of the MCSFilter algorithm for different values of α_{min} in order to obtain accurate solutions, but with a low number of function evaluations. However, despite the reduced number of evaluations of the function for $\alpha_{min} = 10^{-5}$ the obtained solutions are not good with a relative error of 16% or more of the global optimum known solution. It follows that an increase in the value of the parameter α_{min} leads to worst solutions since the global solution was never reached. In addition, we can also conclude that as k_{max} increases the number of evaluations of the function also increases. This is obvious, because if the number of points generated is greater, the number of evaluations of the function is also greater.

The best value of $J(p) = 19.9074$ is obtained for $\alpha_{min} = 10^{-6}$ and $k_{max} = 100$ with a relative error of $+0.17\%$ when compared with the best known solution in [7]. From Table 2 one may conclude that for smaller values of α_{min} the solution is better. Thus, increasing the value of α_{min} leads to a worse solution than reducing the number of initial points.

Finally, a last experiment with one execution of the MCSFilter algorithm was performed using $\alpha_{min} = 10^{-6}$, $k_{max} = 100$ and the following first initial point (in the multistart part):

$$p = \begin{bmatrix} 6.05 \times 10^{-5} & 3.60 \times 10^{-5} & 4.18 \times 10^{-5} & 4.79 \times 10^{-4} & 9.86 \times 10^{-5} \end{bmatrix}^{\top}.$$

The optimal objective function value found was $J(p) = 19.8828$. Since this result is very close to the best known optimum by Egea et al. [7], one can assert that an execution with a local search starting close to the optimum allows to obtain a very good solution, in the fastest way as stated by [5]. This means that, in all the experiments, the points sampled in the multistart stage are farther away from the known minimizer than the above initial point; in spite of that, and for $\alpha_{\min} = 10^{-6}$, the MCSFilter algorithm always obtained high quality solutions.

The results obtained with the MCSFilter were compared with those obtained with other methods [7,8,10]. Table 3 aggregates the published best found solution, J_{best}, the average solution (when existent), J_{avg}, and the average number of function evaluations, $n_{\text{FE,avg}}$, obtained for some methods in the literature. This table also presents the values for MCSFilter algorithm related with the 9 executions starting from a random initial point plus the execution with the first initial point close to the optimum, as described above. The average values presented for DE, SRES, SSm, FA, and MCSFilter are over 10 executions.

Table 3. α-pinene isomerization parameter estimation problem results reported in the literature.

Solver	J_{best}	J_{avg}	$n_{\text{FE,avg}}$
MCSFilter	19.8828	19.9703	40494
Global [7]	31638	35225	1277
DE [8]	34.856	22515	10000
SRES [8]	31251	32651	10000
DIRECT [8]	36218	-	9996
OQNLP [8]	31252	-	10000
SSm [8]	19.872	19.872	9518
SSm [7]	19.872	24.747	1163
FA [10]	19.8772	25.6777	5860[a]
fmincon [10]	19.929	-	217

[a] Number of function evaluations of the best solution.

The methods Global, DE, SRES, DIRECT and OQNLP fail to converge to the optimum value because of the limit (10000) on the maximum number of function evaluations [8] and, therefore, cannot be compared to the value obtained by the other methods. Besides that it is remarked that with $\alpha_{\min} = 10^{-6}$ and a smaller number of function evaluations (less than 10000 — see Table 2) the MCSFilter algorithm achieved a very good results.

Regarding the number of function evaluations, it can be observed that, in spite of the good quality of the solution and the MCSFilter consistency, the algorithm requires more function evaluations than the other methods listed in Table 3. Nevertheless, the MCSFilter presents better average values of the objective function than SSm [7] and FA [10], and with a relative error of +0.54%. This demonstrates that the MCSFilter has converged more often to the best solution than some other methods.

We remark that the best MCSFilter solution is close to its average solution (see Table 2), which are close to the known best minimum. These results assert the good quality of the solution presented by the MCSFilter and its consistency.

Table 4 shows the best and worst minimizers found by MCSFilter for $\alpha_{\min} = 10^{-6}$ and $k_{\max} = 100$ that corresponds to the J_{best} and J_{worst} solutions, respectively, presented in Table 2.

Table 4. Parameter values obtained by MCSFilter for $\alpha_{\min} = 10^{-6}$ and $k_{\max} = 100$.

Parameter	Best	Worst
p_1^*	5.936×10^{-5}	5.904×10^{-5}
p_2^*	2.965×10^{-5}	2.969×10^{-5}
p_3^*	2.067×10^{-5}	1.978×10^{-5}
p_4^*	2.776×10^{-4}	2.835×10^{-4}
p_5^*	4.090×10^{-5}	4.448×10^{-5}

Figure 3 illustrates the profiles obtained by solving the ODE model (3) using the parameter set, p^*, found by the MCSFilter algorithm, for the best solution in Table 4.

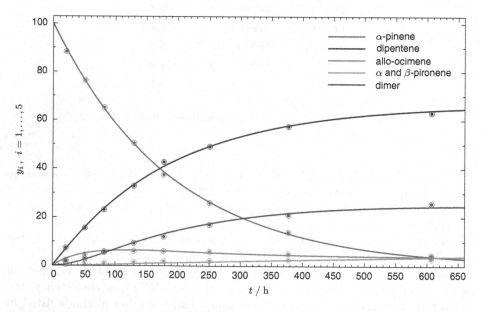

Fig. 3. Experimental data points and the profiles obtained from (3) with the kinetic model parameters determined by the MCSFilter.

As it can be observed, the obtained kinetic parameters provide a good fitting of the model to the experimental data.

5   Conclusions

The MSCFilter algorithm – a multistart strategy coupled with a coordinate search filter methodology – was implemented in the Java programming language and has successfully estimated the α-pinene isomerization optimal kinetic parameters.

Some preliminary experiments were carried out in order to tune the parameters of the stopping criteria of the CSFilter and MCSFilter algorithms. It is shown that this issue is crucial to the effective convergence of the algorithm when solving the α-pinene problem.

In comparison with the results reported in the literature, it is noticeable that the MCSFilter presents a much higher effort when 100 initial points are used. This is due to the higher number of function evaluations required by the MCSFilter method, namely by the CSFilter algorithm based on the set $\mathcal{D}_{\oplus}$ with $2n = 10$ coordinate directions when it is using 100 initial points. One may conclude that increasing $\alpha_{\min}$ has a big impact: CSFilter stops before reaching the best known solution. Despite this, the MCSFilter algorithm shows good performance by converging to the known solution of the problem — the experiments that were carried out show that (when $\alpha_{\min} = 10^{-6}$ is used) the best, worst and the average values of the objective function obtained by MCSFilter algorithm are closer to the best known in the literature.

The fitting of the model profiles to the experimental data demonstrate that the obtained solution is of very good quality.

As future work, a strategy of parallelization inside the MCSFilter algorithm, namely in the multistart strategy stage, should be implemented. The MCSFilter algorithm will also be applied in the context of dynamic systems where its ability to handle inequality constraints is of importance.

References

1. Box, G.E.P., Draper, N.R.: The Bayesian estimation of common parameters from several responses. Biometrika **52**(3–4), 355–365 (1965)
2. Box, G.E.P., Hunter, W.G., MacGregor, J.F., Erjavec, J.: Some problems associated with the analysis of multiresponse data. Technometrics **15**(1), 33–51 (1973)
3. Ames, W.F.: Canonical forms for non-linear kinetic differential equations. Ind. Eng. Chem. Fundam. **1**(3), 214–218 (1962)
4. Tjoa, I.-B., Biegler, L.T.: Simultaneous solution and optimization strategies for parameter estimation of differential-algebraic equation systems. Ind. Eng. Chem. **30**, 376–385 (1991)
5. Averick, B.M., Carter, R.G., Moré, J.J., Xue, G.: The minpack-2 test problem collection. Technical report, Mathematics and Computer Science Division, Argonne National Laboratory (1992)
6. Dolan, E.D., Moré, J.J., Munson, T.S.: Benchmarking optimization software with cops 3.0. Technical report, Argonne National Laboratory (2004)
7. Egea, J.A., Rodriguez-Fernandez, M., Banga, J.R., Martí, R.: Scatter search for chemical and bio-process optimization. J. Global Optim. **37**(3), 481–503 (2007)

8. Larrosa, J.A.E.: New Heuristics for Global Optimization of Complex Bioprocesses. Ph.D. thesis, University of Vigo (2008)
9. Csendes, T.: Non-linear parameter estimation by global optimization - efficiency and reliability. Acta Cybern. **8**(4), 361–370 (1988)
10. Rocha, A.M.A.C., Martins, M.C., Costa, M.F.P., Fernandes, E.M.G.P.: Direct sequential based firefly algorithm for the α-pinene isomerization problem. In: Gervasi, O., Murgante, B., Misra, S., Rocha, A.M.A.C., Torre, C., Taniar, D., Apduhan, B.O., Stankova, E., Wang, S. (eds.) ICCSA 2016. LNCS, vol. 9786, pp. 386–401. Springer, Cham (2016). https://doi.org/10.1007/978-3-319-42085-1_30
11. Fernandes, F.P., Costa, M.F.P., Fernandes, E.M.G.P.: Multilocal programming: a derivative-free filter multistart algorithm. In: Murgante, B., Misra, S., Carlini, M., Torre, C.M., Nguyen, H.-Q., Taniar, D., Apduhan, B.O., Gervasi, O. (eds.) ICCSA 2013. LNCS, vol. 7971, pp. 333–346. Springer, Heidelberg (2013). https://doi.org/10.1007/978-3-642-39637-3_27
12. Amador, A., Fernandes, F.P., Santos, L.O., Romanenko, A.: Application of MCS-Filter to estimate stiction control valve parameters. In: International Conference of Numerical Analysis and Applied Mathematics, AIP Conference Proceedings, vol. 1863, p. 270005 (2017)
13. Storn, R., Price, K.: Differential evolution — a simple and efficient heuristic for global optimization over continuous spaces. J. Global Optim. **11**, 341–359 (1997)
14. Runarsson, T.P., Yao, X.: Stochastic ranking for constrained evolutionary optimization. Inst. Electr. Electron. Eng. Trans. Evol. Comput. **4**(3), 284–294 (2000)
15. Jones, D.R.: Direct global optimization algorithm. In: Floudas, C.A., Pardalos, P.M. (eds.) Encyclopedia of Optimization, pp. 431–440. Springer, Boston (2001). https://doi.org/10.1007/0-306-48332-7

Mixed Integer Programming Models
for Fire Fighting

Filipe Alvelos[✉]

Centro Algoritmi, Universidade do Minho, Campus de Gualtar,
4710-057 Braga, Portugal
falvelos@dps.uminho.pt

Abstract. In this paper, a set of mixed integer programming (MIP) models to optimize the location of a set of resources when fighting fire is proposed. The MIP model integrates fire spread and the decisions relative to the resources location.

Four problems are considered: protecting specific areas, minimizing the total burned area, and two problems of fire containment (depending on the definition of fire containment: no new ignitions in a given time interval or resources located in all the fire perimeter). A small example is used to illustrate the solutions to these problems.

A transformation of the optimization problem of determining fire arrival times in a feasibility problem, based on linear programming duality, is also proposed. This transformation is used in all the MIP models, assuring the correctness of the fire arrival times in all the areas of the landscape.

Keywords: Optimization · Mixed integer programming · Fire spread
Fire containment

1 Introduction

We consider the general problem of locating resources (e.g. fire fighters) to fight wildland fire. Roughly speaking, this general problem consists in, given a fire ignition location in a known landscape, locate the set of available resources in such a way that the impact of the fire is minimized. We name this problem "fire fight problem" (FFP).

We address four specific problems, each one with a different objective: protect specific areas, minimize the total burned area, minimize new ignitions, and minimize the length of the fire perimeter not covered by a resource.

For each of these four problems, we formulate one mixed integer programming (MIP) model integrating decision variables and constraints related to the

F. Alvelos—This work has been supported by COMPETE: POCI-01-0145-FEDER-007043 and FCT - Fundação para a Ciência e Tecnologia within the Project Scope: UID/CEC/00319/2013.

minimum travel time (MTT) [4] fire spread model, to the resources locations and to the optimization objectives.

Although fire behaviour and spread models have been used since the 1920s, as surveyed in [10–12], few attempts have been made to integrate optimization. In particular, only a few models using MIP were proposed.

A problem related to the FFP which has received much more attention, is the fuel management problem (FMP). In the latter, it is intended to decide which fuel treatments (e.g. prescribed fire and thinning) should be applied in the areas of the landscape.

In modelling terms, the FMP and the FFP are closely related. In both problems, some locations in the landscape are used to delay the fire spread through fuel treatments (FMP case) or fire fight resources (FFP case). The main difference relies on the knowledge of the fire ignition location. In the FMP, a medium-to long-term problem, ignitions locations are uncertain, while in the FFP, a short-term problem, the present state of the fire is known. Still, running a FFP optimization model with different ignition locations may provide useful information for the FMP, e.g. burn probabilities for each area (modelling fuel treatments as resources). Inversely, running a fuel management model with a fire ignition may provide useful information for the FFP (modelling resources as fuel treatments).

We now review some literature where MIP is used to address the FMP or the FFP.

In [15], a MIP model for the FMP is proposed. The model is based on the burn risk of the areas of the landscape is presented. The fire risk of an area is decomposed in the ignition risk (in that area) and in a (linear) approximation of the fire risk of adjacent areas. This risk is then related with potential fuel treatments. The objective is to minimize the expected loss. Although incorporated in a MIP model, the way fire spread is modelled is considerably different from the one used here because it is based on probabilities and not on fire travel times.

In the MIP model of [17] to a FMP, fire spread is modelled with high hazard fuel patches. If two areas belong to the same patch fire will spread between them.

In [8], a MIP model that integrates fuel management and the location of resources for initial attack is presented. The objective is to maximize the number of areas that are treated or covered by a suppression resource. Fire spread is not modelled, but implicitly present in the covered areas.

In [7], a MIP model based on the fuel age (and not fire spread) is presented for the FMP. Objective functions are related with a graph representation of the landscape and the concepts of active nodes (high fuel load) and active edges (edges between two active nodes, which can propagate fire). For each time period, the graph of active nodes and edges depends of the fuel treatments and fuel load dynamics. One objective considered is to minimize the number of active edges overall in all time horizon, other is to maximize the total number of connected components. Given the complexity of the MIP model, a decomposition heuristic, consisting in solving a sequence of subproblems each one for a subset of time periods, is proposed.

In [3], a MIP model for fire containment is presented. No spatial information
are used but the length of the fire perimeter and the length of the line constructed
by the resources.

We now consider approaches which integrates MTT with resources location
as in the proposed MIP models. The advantage of modelling fire spread with
MIP is that the same model can include variables related to decisions on the
location of resources.

In [6], the objective is the protection of a given area from a fire ignited in
a known location. Therefore, the linear programming model maximizes the fire
arrival time at the protected area(s). Although published earlier, this model can
be seen as the linear programming version of the minimum travel time algorithm
(MTT) [4].

The MIP model proposed in Sect. 4 is closely related to [6], and has the
advantage of providing the correct fire arrival times in all areas.

In [16], a MIP model based on the duration of fires is presented. Following the
MTT algorithm, fire spread is modelled with continuous time decision variables
corresponding to the instant fire arrives at each node. A parameter corresponding
to an instant is defined in which the fire loss is minimized. Binary decision
variables are used to model the location of resources used in fighting the fire.
A budget constraint limits the number of resources used. Besides a MIP model,
the authors propose two iterative (heuristic) approaches for locating resources.

The MIP model proposed in Sect. 5 addresses a more general problem and
locates the resources optimally taking into account their time availability and
that they cannot be located in burned areas.

In [14] a version of the MIP model of [16] is extended for the fuel management
problem.

The major contribution of this paper is to integrate fire spread and its major
indicators (e.g. arrival times, burned areas, recent ignitions, fire perimeter) in the
optimization context. Furthermore, this integration is accomplished in a dynamic
setting: potential locations for the resources vary with fire spread. Resources may
have different instants for becoming available.

Another contribution is related with how the fire arrival times are modelled.
By using linear programming duality, an optimization problem is transformed
into a feasibility problem leading to the correctness of the arrival times for any
objective function.

This paper is organized as follows. In Sect. 2 the linear programming model of
MTT fire spread is described and its relation with the shortest path tree problem
clarified. This relation allows transforming the MTT optimization problem in
a feasibility problem. Section 3 introduces the components of the MIP models
(parameters, variables and constraints) related with resources locations.

The following four sections are devoted to four problems, for which a MIP
model is proposed and exemplified. Section 4 deals with the problem of assuring
some areas are protected from fire while minimizing the number of resources
used. Section 5 deals with the problem of minimizing the total burned area.
Both Sects. 6 and 7 describe MIP models to contain fire. In the former the fire

containment is evaluated by the number of new ignitions in some period. In the latter the fire containment is evaluated by the portion of the fire perimeter which is not covered by resources. In Sect. 8 the main conclusions of this work are drawn.

2   Fire Spread

2.1   Shortest Path Tree Problem

Let $G(N, A)$ be a graph representing the landscape. The set of nodes, denoted by N, correspond to areas and the set of arcs, denoted by A, represent fire spread between adjacent areas. Following the MTT approach, our model uses as input the fire travel time between adjacent nodes, i.e. associated with each arc ij there is a parameter $c_{ij}, \forall ij \in A$ corresponding to the fire travel time between the (center of) area i and the (center of) area j in that direction. The MTT approach relies on the equivalence of the fire arrival time at a node and the duration of the quickest path between the ignition node and that node. Therefore, estimating the fire spread corresponds to obtain the set of quickest paths from the ignition node to all the other nodes. These quickest paths can be obtained with a Dijkstra-like algorithm [1,2], as in [4], or with linear programming, as in [6,16].

A small example, which will be used throughout the paper, is given in Fig. 1. Each node has four adjacent nodes, but the proposed approaches can easily be extended to more, e.g. eight. The fire travel times of this small example were generated by considering three factors: wind (same velocity to east and to south and the three times slower for north and west), a slope of -90 degrees, and a random fuel influence on the fire speed. For each of these three components, values between 1 and 3 were attributed and summed up in order to obtain a fire travel time in each arc. In practice, fire travel times can be estimated in different ways, from fire behaviour models (using, for example, the software FlamMap [5]) to aerial thermal infrared and geographic information systems (as in [13]).

In networks terminology, obtaining how fire spreads (i.e. determining the fire arrival time at all nodes given an ignition node) corresponds to solve a shortest path tree problem, i.e. the shortest path from a root node to each of all the other nodes, whose set of arcs, form necessarily a tree (i.e. a set of $n-1$ arcs with no cycles, where n is the number of nodes). For a deep and comprehensive analysis of shortest path tree algorithms, see [1].

We obtain a linear programming model for the shortest path tree problem by defining decision variables x_{ij} as the number of paths (each one beginning in the root and ending in a different node) that include arc ij. Letting 1 be the root (ignition) node and n the total number of nodes, the model is

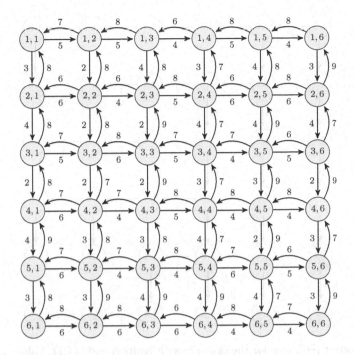

Fig. 1. Example of a network representing a landscape and fire travel times.

$$\text{Minimize} \qquad \sum_{ij \in A} c_{ij} x_{ij} \qquad\qquad (1)$$

Subject to:

$$-\sum_{1j \in A} x_{1j} = -n + 1 \qquad\qquad (2)$$

$$-\sum_{ij \in A} x_{ij} + \sum_{ji \in A} x_{ji} = 1 \qquad \forall i \in N \setminus \{1\} \qquad (3)$$

$$x_{ij} \geq 0 \qquad\qquad \forall ij \in A \qquad (4)$$

Constraints (2) state that there are $n-1$ paths leaving the root. Constraints (3) are flow conservation constraints forcing one path to arrive at each node (except node 1).

Figure 2 shows the optimal solution of this model with the data of Fig. 1.

It is well known that the dual variables of (1–4), $t_i, \forall i \in N$, are the length of the shortest path between the root and each node. Therefore, in the fire spread context, they are precisely the fire arrival times at each node. Their optimal

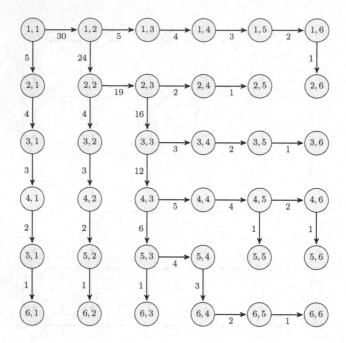

Fig. 2. Shortest path tree for the example with ignition node (1,1). Values next to the arcs correspond to the number of paths the arc belongs to.

values can also be obtained by solving the dual problem:

$$\text{Maximize} \quad \sum_{i \in N \setminus \{1\}} t_i \quad \quad (5)$$

Subject to:

$$t_j - t_i \leq c_{ij} \quad \quad \forall ij \in A \quad \quad (6)$$
$$t_1 = 0 \quad \quad (7)$$
$$t_i \text{ free} \quad \quad \forall i \in N \setminus \{1\} \quad \quad (8)$$

In an optimal primal-dual solution, the dual solution provides the arrival time at all the locations and the primal solution provides the fire paths.

Figure 3 shows the fire arrival times at each nodes for the example obtained, as all the other solutions presented in this paper, by IBM ILOG Cplex Optimization Studio [9].

2.2 Shortest Path Tree *Feasibility* Problem

We now present a transformation of the primal-dual linear optimization problem into a feasibility problem consisting in a set of constraints with no objective function. However, the feasibility of a solution x and t with respect to this set

0	5	10	14	19	23
3	7	11	16	22	26
7	9	13	18	22	27
9	11	15	20	24	28
13	14	18	22	26	31
16	17	22	26	30	34

Fig. 3. Fire arrival times at each node for the example with ignition node (1,1).

of constraints is a necessary and sufficient condition for x being optimal in the problem (1–4) and t being optimal in problem (5–8).

The purpose of this transformation is to obtain the correct time values for any objective function, even when additional decision variables and constraints are considered, as it will be clear in the next section where resources to fight fire are integrated in this model.

We consider constraints (2, 3, 4, 7, 8), and rewrite constraints (6) with slack variables, $s_{ij}, \forall ij \in A$.

$$t_j - t_i + s_{ij} = c_{ij} \qquad \forall ij \in A \qquad (9)$$

$$s_{ij} \geq 0 \qquad \forall ij \in A \qquad (10)$$

We further define the decision variables $q_{ij} = 1$ if arc ij belongs to the shortest path tree, $q_{ij} = 0$ otherwise, $\forall ij \in A$. Variables q and x are related through

$$x_{ij} \leq (n-1)q_{ij} \qquad \forall ij \in A \qquad (11)$$

$$q_{ij} \in \{0,1\} \qquad \forall ij \in A \qquad (12)$$

Note that $n-1$ is an upper bound to x_{ij}. An arc belonging to (at least) a fire path, must have slack 0 meaning that the arrival time of the destination node must be equal to the arrival time of the origin node plus the fire travel time between the two. Defining c^{max} as the maximum travel time of all arcs and noting that the maximum length of a path is $n-1$, variables q and s are related through

$$s_{ij} \leq (n-1)c^{max}(1-q_{ij}) \qquad \forall ij \in A \qquad (13)$$

Proposition 1. *Optimality of a primal-dual solution in problems (1–4) and (5–8) is equivalent to feasibility for the set of constraints (2–4, 7–10, 11–13).*

Proof. We use the necessary and sufficient optimality conditions of linear programming. These conditions state that, a primal-dual pair of solutions, is optimal if is primal feasible, dual feasible and satisfies the complementary slackness conditions. Primal feasibility is assured by (2–4). Dual feasibility is assured by (7–10). Complementary slackness conditions are the following:

$$s_{ij}.x_{ij} = 0 \qquad \forall ij \in A$$

By (11), binary variables q_{ij} can replace the x_{ij} variables:

$$s_{ij}.q_{ij} = 0 \qquad \forall ij \in A$$

These conditions can be stated as (i) $s_{ij} > 0$ implies $q_{ij} = 0$ and (ii) $q_{ij} = 1$ implies $s_{ij} = 0$. Both cases are assured by inequalities (13).   □

3   Locating Resources

We now introduce the use of resources to fire fight. We consider a set of K time instants, $K = \{b_1, b_2, ..., b_h\}$ and a set of resources R. In the kth instant, time b_k, a given number of resources, a_k, becomes available to be located in the unburned nodes of the network.

We define decision variables, $z_i^{kr} = 1$ if resource r is located at node i at instant b_k. Locating a resource in a node implies that the fire does not burn that node and its spread to adjacent nodes is delayed by a known value Δ.

Let o_k be the number of resources (available but) not used at instant k and therefore available at instant $k + 1$.

The following constraints are related to resources.

$$\sum_{i\in N}\sum_{k\in K} z_i^{kr} \leq 1 \qquad\qquad \forall r \in R \qquad (14)$$

$$\sum_{r\in R}\sum_{k\in N} z_i^{kr} \leq 1 \qquad\qquad \forall i \in N \qquad (15)$$

$$\sum_{i\in N}\sum_{r\in R} z_i^{1r} + o_1 = a_1 \qquad\qquad \forall i \in N \qquad (16)$$

$$\sum_{i\in N}\sum_{r\in R} z_i^{kr} + o_k = a_k + o_{k-1} \qquad\qquad k = 2,...,|K| \qquad (17)$$

$$z_i^{kr} \leq 1 + (t_j - b_k)/b_k \qquad\qquad \forall i \in N, \forall k \in K, \forall r \in R \qquad (18)$$

$$o_k \geq 0 \qquad\qquad \forall k \in K \qquad (19)$$

$$z_i^r \in \{0,1\} \qquad\qquad \forall i \in N, \forall k \in K, \forall r \in R \qquad (20)$$

Constraints (14) and (15) state that each resource can be located at most in one location and that each node can have at most one resource, considering all instants. Constraints (16) and (17) keep track of the number of resources available at each instant. Constraints (18) state that a resource can only be placed in an unburned location. Constraints (19) and (20) define the domain of the variables.

Constraints (9) and (13) become:

$$t_j - t_i + s_{ij} = c_{ij} + \Delta \sum_{r\in R, k\in K} z_i^{kr} \qquad\qquad \forall ij \in A \qquad (21)$$

$$s_{ij} \leq ((n-1)c^{max} + (|R| - 1)\Delta)(1 - q_{ij}) \qquad\qquad \forall ij \in A \qquad (22)$$

Constraints (21) take into account the delay in the fire travel time in all adjacent areas of the one where a resource is located. Constraints (22) update the upper bound (with respect to the one used in (13)) on the slack due to the delays implied by resources.

The inclusion of resources do not change the essence of Proposition 1. For each set of values of the z variables, the length of a set of arcs (the ones with a resource at their origin) becomes $c'_{ij} = c_{ij} + \Delta$. Therefore, for each set of values of the z variables, Proposition 1 remains valid because only the arc costs are changed. For each location of the resources, the arrival times and fire paths are correctly calculated, even when resources are located in any node of the network.

In modelling terms, the extension to different types of resources is straightforward.

With variables z associated with resources and the constraints just introduced, different models for fire fighting can be developed, as shown in the next sections.

In the following, constraints (2–4, 7–8, 10–12, 14–22) are referred to as base constraints as they are present in all models.

4 Protecting Areas

The first problem we consider has to do with nodes that must be protected. The objective is to minimize the number of resources used, assuring the fire arrival time at each of the nodes that must protected nodes (set P) is greater than a given value, g. The model is:

$$\text{Minimize} \qquad \sum_{i \in N} \sum_{k \in K} \sum_{r \in R} z_i^{kr} \qquad (23)$$

$$\text{Subject to:} \qquad t_i \geq g \qquad \forall i \in P$$
$$\text{(base constraints)} \qquad (24)$$

Figure 4 shows the optimal location of resources.

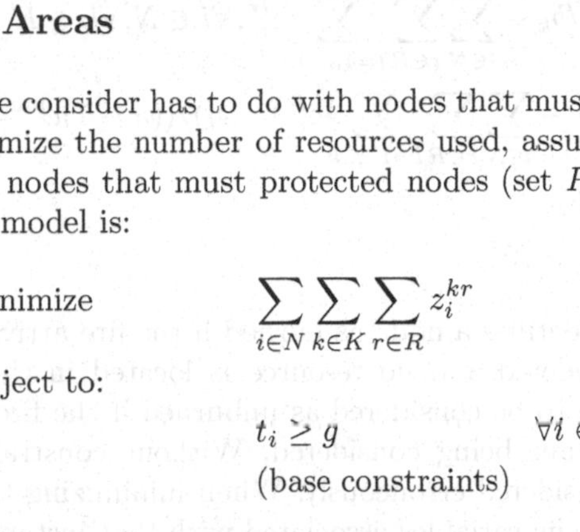

0	5	10	64	69	73
3	7	61	66	72	76
7	59	63	68	72	77
59	61	65	70	74	78
63	64	68	72	76	81
66	67	72	76	80	84

29	23	17	19	24	78
21	15	9	12	18	21
15	8	0	5	9	14
16	9	2	7	11	15
19	12	5	9	13	18
22	15	9	13	17	71

Fig. 4. Protecting nodes (1,6) and (6,6) with fire ignitions in (1,1) (left) and (3,3) (right). Resources are available at instant 6, and $\Delta = 50$ and $g = 50$. An optimal solution is to locate resources has at (3,1), (2,2) and (3,1) for ignition (1,1) (left) and to locate resources in (1,5), (2,6), (5,6) and (6,5) for ignition (3,3) (right).

It is worth noting that without the feasibility approach previously described, the optimal solution of this problem would not provide the correct fire arrival times for nodes not belonging to the fire paths to the protected nodes. This occurs because the slacks of the dual and the arc flows of the primal can be both positive if the complementary slackness conditions are not forced.

This issue (of not obtaining the correct arrival times) was first noted in [6] and addressed with a two step procedure in [16]. In our integrated approach, the right arrival times are correctly obtained with any additional decision variables or objectives.

5   Burned Area

For keeping the notation simple, we consider the same instants for when the model evaluates which nodes are burned and when resources become available. That is, we consider a set of K time instants, $K = \{b_1, b_2, ..., b_h\}$, and define decision variables $y_i^k = 1$ if node i is burned at instant k, $y_i^k = 0$, otherwise.

The relation between the arrival time and if a node is burned is the following:

$$y_i^k \geq (b_k - t_i)/b_k - \sum_{i \in N} \sum_{r \in R} \sum_{l=1,...,k} z_i^{lr}, \forall i \in N, \forall k \in K \tag{25}$$

$$y_i^k \leq 1 + (b_k(1 - \sum_{i \in N} \sum_{r \in R} \sum_{l=1,...,k} z_i^{lr}) - t_i)/((n-1)c^{max} + (|R|-1)\Delta)$$

$$\forall i \in N, \forall k \in K \tag{26}$$

$$y_i^k \in \{0, 1\}, \forall k \in K \tag{27}$$

Constraints (25) identifies a node as burned if the fire arrival time precedes the instant being considered and no resource is located in the node. Constraints (26) force the node to be considered as unburned if the fire arrival time occurs later than the instant being considered. Without constraints (26), unburned nodes could be considered erroneously. When minimizing the burned area at a given instant, only the variables associated with that instant and corresponding constraints need to be considered, as in the case of the objective function of the model below where instant h is considered as the instant where it is desired to minimize the burned area.

The model is

$$\text{Minimize} \qquad \sum_{i \in N} y_i^h + \epsilon(\sum_{i \in h} \sum_{k \in K} \sum_{r \in R} z_i^{kr}) \tag{28}$$

Subject to:

$$(25 - 27)$$

$$(\text{base constraints})$$

The second term of the objective function (28) can be seen as the price to pay to locate resources. Each resource has a cost of ϵ. For $\epsilon = 1/(\sum_{k \in K} a_k)$ a lexicographical optimization is conducted. Any solution with a lower value of $\sum_{i \in N} y_i^h$ is better independently of the price of the resources used. This avoids the location of resources with no use in terms of reducing the burned area.

Figure 5 shows fire spread and optimal location of resources when minimizing the burned area for the example.

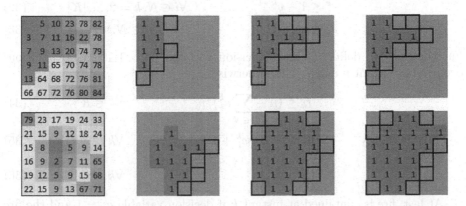

Fig. 5. Fire ignitions at $(1,1)$, top row, and $(3,3)$, bottom row. Four resources are available at instant 10 and more four at instant 20 all with $\Delta = 50$. An optimal solution is to locate resources in cells with bold border. First matrix is for the arrival times and the other three for burned cells in instants 10, 20 and 30.

It was assumed that the areas of the nodes are all equal. The extension to different areas is obtained with a coefficient for each variable y_i^k in the objective function representing the area of each node.

6   Fire Containment Based on New Ignitions

Fire containment can be evaluated by the number of new node ignitions in a given time interval. If there are no fire ignitions, the fire is contained. This definition includes the possibility of the fire being contained, at least in some front, by natural causes (e.g. a river) and not only by resources as assumed in the next section. Note, however, that fire can cross the frontier of the landscape under study. Therefore, we are assuming the area outside the landscape is non-burnable. Small modifications in the following can be made to consider, for example, that if (some) nodes of the frontier are burned, the fire is not contained. In the example, given the main fire direction is south-east, burned nodes in those frontiers could prevent the model to declare the fire contained.

We define decision variables $e_i^k = 1$ if the fire was ignited between instants $k - 1$ and k, for $k = 1, ..., h$ (with $e_i^0 = 0$), $\forall i \in N, \forall k \in K$. The following constraints assure the correct of values for these y and e variables.

$$e_i^1 = y_i^1 \qquad\qquad \forall i \in N \qquad (29)$$

$$e_i^k \geq y_i^k - y_i^{k-1} \qquad\qquad \forall i \in N, k = 2, ..., |K| \qquad (30)$$

$$e_i^k \leq y_i^k \qquad\qquad \forall i \in N, k = 2, ..., |K| \qquad (31)$$

$$e_i^k \leq 1 - y_i^{k-1} \qquad\qquad \forall i \in N, k = 2, ..., |K| \qquad (32)$$

$$e_i^k \in \{0, 1\} \qquad\qquad \forall i \in N, \forall k \in K \qquad (33)$$

Furthermore, we define a binary decision variable $f_k = 1$ if no fire ignitions occurred in instant k and $f_k = 0$, otherwise.

$$f_k \leq (n - \sum_{i \in N} e_i^k)/n \qquad\qquad \forall k \in K \qquad (34)$$

$$f_k \geq - \sum_{i \in N} e_i^k + 1 \qquad\qquad \forall k \in K \qquad (35)$$

$$f_k \in \{0, 1\} \qquad\qquad \forall k \in K \qquad (36)$$

At last, fire is contained at instant k if decision variable $c^k = 1$ and the fire was not contained if the binary decision α, is one.

$$c^1 = 0 \qquad\qquad (37)$$

$$c^k \geq f^k - f^{k-1} \qquad\qquad k = 2, ..., |K| \qquad (38)$$

$$c^k \leq f^k \qquad\qquad k = 2, ..., |K| \qquad (39)$$

$$c^k \leq 1 - f_{k-1} \qquad\qquad k = 2, ..., |K| \qquad (40)$$

$$\sum_{k \in K} c^k + \alpha = 1 \qquad\qquad (41)$$

$$c_k \in \{0, 1\} \qquad\qquad \forall k \in K \qquad (42)$$

$$\alpha \in \{0, 1\} \qquad\qquad (43)$$

The model is

Minimize
$$\sum_{k \in K} k c^k + (h + 1)\alpha + \epsilon(\sum_{i \in h} \sum_{k \in K} \sum_{r \in R} z_i^{kr}) \qquad (44)$$

Subject to:

(29 − 43)

(base constraints)

(25 − 27)

The objective function, (44), minimizes the earliest instant where containment can be reached using only the required resources (see discussion on the previous section for the ϵ value).

Figure 6 shows fire spread and optimal location of resources when minimizing the instant of fire containment.

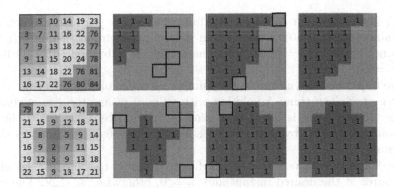

Fig. 6. In the top row, a fire ignition occurs at (1,1). In the bottom row, the fire ignition occurs at (3,3). Four resources are available at the first instant and more six at the second all with $\Delta = 50$. Time instants are $10, 20$, and 30. An optimal solution is to locate resources in cells with bold border. In both cases, fire is contained at the last instant.

7   Fire Containment Based on the Perimeter

The fire perimeter is a much relevant characteristic of fire as its length is an indicator to the possibility of fire containment. We assume that if, at a given instant, every node of the fire perimeter have a resource, the fire is contained.

In each instant of the set K, the fire perimeter is described by a set of decision variables, $w_i^k = 1$ if node i is in the fire frontier, $w_i^k = 0$, otherwise. A node is in the fire frontier, if it is not burned, at least an adjacent node is burned and not all adjacent nodes are burned. The set of adjacent incoming nodes of a node i is represented by $I(i)$. A node j belongs to $I(i)$ if and only if arc ji exists. The following auxiliary variables are used. $v_i^k = 1$ if at least one neighbor node of i is burned at instant k and $u_i^k = 1$ if all neighbors of i are burned at instant k.

$$v_i^k \geq \sum_{j \in I(i)} y_i^k / |I(i)| \qquad \forall i \in N, \forall k \in K \qquad (45)$$

$$v_i^k \leq \sum_{j \in I(i)} y_i^k \qquad \forall i \in N, \forall k \in K \qquad (46)$$

$$u_i^k \geq \sum_{j \in I(i)} y_i^k - (|I(i)| - 1) \qquad \forall i \in N, \forall k \in K \qquad (47)$$

$$u_i^k \leq \sum_{j \in I(i)} y_i^k / |I(i)| \qquad \forall i \in N, \forall k \in K \qquad (48)$$

$$w_i^k \geq v_i^k - y_i^k - u_i^k \qquad \forall i \in N, \forall k \in K \qquad (49)$$

$$w_i^k \leq (2 + v_i^k - y_i^k - u_i^k)/3 \qquad \forall i \in N, \forall k \in K \qquad (50)$$

$$v_i^k, u_i^k, w_i^k \in \{0, 1\} \qquad \forall k \in K$$

Constraints (45) and (46) force variables v_i^k to take value 1 if at least one neighbor of i at k is burned. Constraints (47) and (48) force variables u_i^k to take value 1 if all neighbours of i at k are burned. The fire perimeter is defined by constraints (49) and (50). A node i is in the fire perimeter at instant k ($w_i^k = 1$) if it is not burned ($y_i^k = 0$), at least one neighbour is burned ($v_i^k = 1$) but not all ($u_i^k = 1$).

The objective is to minimize the number of nodes of the perimeter with no resource at a given time. A solution with value 0 means the fire is contained because all perimeter is being controlled by a resource. One minus the value of a solution divided by the perimeter length provides a measure to the fire containment.

We define decision variables $\beta_i = 1$ if node i belongs to the perimeter and has no resource at the desired instant and $\beta_i = 0$, otherwise, $\forall i \in N$. The instant represented by b_h.

The model is

$$\text{Minimize} \qquad \sum_{i \in N} \beta_i + \epsilon(\sum_{i \in h} \sum_{k \in K} \sum_{r \in R} z_i^{kr}) \qquad (51)$$

Subject to:

$$\sum_{r in R} \sum_{k \in K} z_i^{kr} + \beta_i = w_i^h \qquad \forall i \in N \qquad (52)$$

$$(45 - 50)$$
$$\text{(base constraints)}$$
$$(25 - 27)$$
$$\beta_i \in \{0, 1\} \qquad \forall i \in N$$

Figure 7 shows fire spread and optimal location of resources when maximizing the perimeter covered by resources.

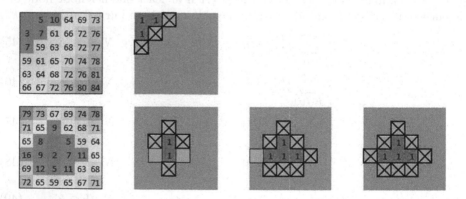

Fig. 7. Fire ignitions at (1,1), top row, and (3,3), bottom row. Four resources are available at instant the instant 5 and more six at the instant 10, all with $\Delta = 50$. The instant were the containment is evaluated is 15. An optimal solution is to locate resources in the crossed cells. In both ignitions the fire is contained.

8   Conclusions and Future Work

This paper addressed fire fighting through the use of mixed integer programming models. These models integrate fire spread and decisions, over time, about where to locate the fire fighting resources, and cover different objectives and fire spread measures. The components of these MIP models can be used to model variants and other problems.

Linear programming duality was used to transform an optimality problem into a feasibility one. A similar procedure may be helpful in other problems.

Obtaining good quality solutions for large instances of the fire fight problem is a challenging future work, for which the proposed MIP models represent a first step.

References

1. Ahuja, R.K., Magnanti, T.L., Orlin, J.B.: Networking Flows - Theory, Algorithms and Application (1993)
2. Dijkstra, E.W.: A note on two problems in connexion with graphs. Numerische mathematik **1**(1), 269–271 (1959)
3. Donovan, G.H., Rideout, D.B.: An integer programming model to optimize resource allocation for wildfire containment. For. Sci. **49**(2), 331–335 (2003)
4. Finney, M.A.: Fire growth using minimum travel time methods. Can. J. For. Res. **32**(8), 1420–1424 (2002)
5. Finney, M.A., Brittain, S., Seli, R.C., McHugh, C.W., Gangi, L.: FlamMap: Fire Mapping and Analysis System (Version 5.0) [Software] (2015). http://www.firelab. org/document/flammap-software
6. Hof, J., Omi, P.N., Bevers, M., Laven, R.D.: A timing-oriented approach to spatial allocation of fire management effort. For. Sci. **46**(3), 442–451 (2000)
7. Matsypura, D., Prokopyev, O.A., Zahar, A.: Wildfire fuel management: network-based models and optimization of prescribed burning. Eur. J. Oper. Res. **264**(2), 774–796 (2018)
8. Minas, J., Hearne, J., Martell, D.: An integrated optimization model for fuel management and fire suppression preparedness planning. Ann. Oper. Res. **232**(1), 201–215 (2015)
9. IBM, ILOG CPLEX Optimization Studio (version 12.6.2.0) [Software]. https:// www.ibm.com/products/ilog-cplex-optimization-studio
10. Sullivan, A.L.: Wildland surface fire spread modelling, 1990–2007. 1: physical and quasi-physical models. Int. J. Wildland Fire **18**(4), 349–368 (2009a)
11. Sullivan, A.L.: Wildland surface fire spread modelling, 1990–2007. 2: empirical and quasi-empirical models. Int. J. Wildland Fire **18**(4), 369–386 (2009b)
12. Sullivan, A.L.: Wildland surface fire spread modelling, 1990–2007. 3: simulation and mathematical analogue models. Int. J. Wildland Fire **18**(4), 387–403 (2009c)
13. Valero, M.M., Rios, O., Mata, C., Pastor, E., Planas, E.: An integrated approach for tactical monitoring and data-driven spread forecasting of wildfires. Fire Saf. J. **91**, 835–844 (2017)
14. Wei, Y.: Optimize landscape fuel treatment locations to create control opportunities for future fires. Can. J. For. Res. **42**(6), 1002–1014 (2012)

652   F. Alvelos

15. Wei, Y., Rideout, D., Kirsch, A.: An optimization model for locating fuel treatments across a landscape to reduce expected fire losses. Can. J. For. Res. **38**(4), 868–877 (2008)
16. Wei, Y., Rideout, D.B., Hall, T.B.: Toward efficient management of large fires: a mixed integer programming model and two iterative approaches. For. Sci. **57**(5), 435–447 (2011)
17. Wei, Y., Long, Y.: Schedule fuel treatments to fragment high fire hazard fuel patches. Math. Comput. For. Nat. Resour. Sci. **6**(1), 1 (2014)

On Parallelizing Benson's Algorithm:
Limits and Opportunities

H. Martin Bücker[1,4] (iD), Andreas Löhne[2,4] (iD), Benjamin Weißing[2(✉)],
and Gerhard Zumbusch[3]

[1] Institute for Computer Science, Friedrich Schiller University Jena, Jena, Germany
martin.buecker@uni-jena.de
[2] Institute for Mathematics, Friedrich Schiller University Jena, Jena, Germany
{andreas.loehne,benjamin.weissing}@uni-jena.de
[3] Institute for Applied Mathematics, Friedrich Schiller University Jena,
Jena, Germany
gerhard.zumbusch@uni-jena.de
[4] Michael Stifel Center Jena for Data-Driven and Simulation Science,
Friedrich Schiller University Jena, Jena, Germany

Abstract. Multiple objective linear programming problems frequently
arise in various applications of computational and data science. An
important class of iterative techniques for numerically solving these problems is based on Benson's algorithm. This algorithm starts with an initial outer approximation of a polyhedron and then iteratively refines
these outer approximations until a solution is found. This algorithm is
an archetype of a class of methods that have been extensively studied
serially. Today, however, there is hardly any discussion in the open literature on the difficulties encountered when executing this algorithm in
parallel. To fill this gap, we report on numerical experiences when parallelizing Benson's algorithm on two different shared-memory computers.
More precisely, we quantify the performance of a parallelized version of
this algorithm on two Intel systems (single socket Core i7-6700 with up to
4 threads and dual socket Xeon E5-2650v4 using up to 24 threads). We
show that parallelizing Benson's algorithm has its performance limitations caused by memory bandwidth saturation. We also sketch opportunities for future research directions on techniques that could improve the
performance of Benson-type algorithms on parallel computers.

Keywords: Mathematical programming · Parallel algorithms
Multiple objective linear programming.

1 Introduction

Benson's algorithm [1] is a cutting plane method for solving linear programs (LP)
involving more than one objective function. In contrast to other methods for

---

The computational experiments were performed on resources of Friedrich Schiller
University Jena supported in part by the Deutsche Forschungsgemeinschaft (DFG,
German Research Foundation) grant INST 275/334–1 FUGG.

© Springer International Publishing AG, part of Springer Nature 2018
O. Gervasi et al. (Eds.): ICCSA 2018, LNCS 10961, pp. 653–668, 2018.
https://doi.org/10.1007/978-3-319-95165-2_46

Multiple Objective Linear Programming (MOLP), this algorithm does not work in the variable space but in the objective space. It is therefore particularly interesting from a computational point of view if the dimension of the variable space is large compared to the dimension of the objective space. It offers the potential for reducing the computational cost for high-dimensional variable spaces.

Several modifications and extensions of the original algorithm have been developed; see e.g. [6,9,10,18]. Benson's algorithm has been proven to be a powerful tool for solving problems in various scientific areas, including information theory [5], medicine [17], and mathematical finance [9]. Moreover, it has been shown in [11] that MOLP is equivalent to the computation of projections of polyhedral convex sets. Consequently, an MOLP solver such as [12,13] can be used to efficiently implement polyhedral calculus [4].

The main idea of the Benson's algorithm is to approximate a particular convex polyhedron $\mathcal{P}$ by a sequence of iteratively refined convex polyhedral outer approximations $\mathcal{O}$. To this end, the algorithm starts with an initial polyhedral outer approximation $\mathcal{O} \supseteq \mathcal{P}$. By testing the extremal points and directions of $\mathcal{O}$ for membership in $\mathcal{P}$ it is determined whether or not $\mathcal{O}$ and $\mathcal{P}$ coincide. In case they do not, there exists an extremal point or direction of $\mathcal{O}$ that can be separated from $\mathcal{P}$ by a hyperplane defining a face of $\mathcal{P}$. The intersection of $\mathcal{O}$ with the corresponding halfspace results in a finer polyhedral outer approximation of $\mathcal{P}$. This procedure is repeated until $\mathcal{O}$ and $\mathcal{P}$ coincide.

The main tasks of a typical iteration of the algorithm are as follows: (i) Solve a single linear program that is parameterized by a vertex of the current outer approximation and (ii) apply vertex enumeration to obtain the vertices of the next outer approximation. In certain situations, the execution time of the algorithm is dominated by the time for solving the sequence of linear programs. Indeed, the number of linear programs that needs to be solved during the execution of the algorithm can become substantial. So, the overall resulting execution time becomes prohibitively large. This is where parallel computing enters the picture.

Surprisingly, today, Benson's algorithm is hardly ever discussed in the context of parallelism. It is used in [21] to solve a linear programming problem with two objectives representing the problem of allocating data sets to virtual machines in distributed heterogeneous clouds. Though it is used in this article to solve a problem modeling issues in parallel computing, it is executed on a serial computer. To the best of the authors' knowledge, there is only a single publication where Benson's algorithm is executed in parallel. In the thesis [19], an implementation of this algorithm in MATLAB is executed on a dual core Laptop equipped with an Intel Core i5-4210H CPU. However, the focus of the thesis is on the application where a proton therapy treatment plan is determined. There is only a short discussion of using MATLAB's `parfor` construct to parallelize the algorithm. A detailed analysis and an extensive set of numerical experiments are missing. While Benson's algorithm is an objective space based algorithm, an alternative approach for solving MOLPs is to search for *all* efficient points in the variable space. In [20] such an approach is parallelized. Usually, the variable space dimension of an MOLP is quite high and the number of efficient points may be intractably huge, while the objective space has a rather low dimension. The objective space based approach used in this paper substantially differs from the variable space approach.

The main contribution of the present article is to introduce a shared-memory parallelization of Benson's algorithm and to quantitatively asses its performance on two different parallel computers. The idea behind the proposed approach is to speed up the overall execution time by solving multiple linear programs concurrently.

This paper is organized as follows. In Sect. 2 the definition of an MOLP is presented and the meaning of an "optimal solution" is explained. Section 3 recalls a basic variant of Benson's algorithm in a serial environment. The shared-memory parallelization is introduced in Sect. 4. In Sect. 5, numerical experiments are reported assessing its parallel performance. Finally, options for future research directions on parallelizing Benson's algorithm are given in Sect. 6.

2 Multiple Objective Linear Programming

Given matrices $P \in \mathbb{R}^{q \times n}$, $A \in \mathbb{R}^{m \times n}$ and a vector $b \in \mathbb{R}^m$, we consider a *multiple objective linear program* (MOLP)

$$\min Px \quad \text{subject to} \quad x \in X, \tag{1}$$

where $X := \{x \in \mathbb{R}^n \mid Ax \leqslant b\} \subseteq \mathbb{R}^n$ is a polyhedral convex set. The rows of P can be seen as multiple linear objective functions. In case of $q = 1$, a linear program is obtained. Minimization in (1) is understood with respect to the partial order $\leq$ in $\mathbb{R}^q$ which is defined component-wise by the ordering $\leq$ in $\mathbb{R}$. For the sake of brevity and simplicity, we describe the problem of computing a solution of an MOLP in terms of commonly known concepts. For the same reason we consider bounded problems only. Further details can be found, for instance, in [9,10].

For a set $Y \subseteq \mathbb{R}^n$ we use the notation

$$P[Y] := \{Px \mid x \in Y\}$$

as an abbreviation for the image set resulting from applying the matrix P to the elements of the set Y. Problem (1) is said to be *bounded* if there is a lower bound $y \in \mathbb{R}^q$ such that

$$P[X] \subseteq \{y\} + \mathbb{R}^q_+,$$

or equivalently,

$$\forall z \in P[X] \colon y \leq z.$$

The problem of solving (1) can be expressed in terms of the *upper image* of (1), which is defined by

$$\mathcal{P} := P[X] + \mathbb{R}^q_+ = \{y \in \mathbb{R}^q \mid \exists x \in X \colon Px \leqslant y\}. \tag{2}$$

In case of a bounded problem, the goal is to compute all the vertices y of this polyhedron $\mathcal{P}$ together with corresponding *pre-images*, i.e. points $x \in X$ with $y = Px$. These pre-images form a set S which is called *solution* of (1). A solution S of (1) admits a finite representation of the upper image $\mathcal{P}$ by

$$\mathcal{P} = \operatorname{conv} P[S] + \mathbb{R}^q_+,$$

where $\operatorname{conv} P[S]$ denotes the convex hull of the finite set $P[S]$.

3   Benson's Algorithm

Benson's algorithm is a method for solving (1) that operates in the objective space $\mathbb{R}^q$ of the problem. The following explanation is used to explain the main idea of Benson's algorithm in order to keep the article self-contained and does not aim at being exhaustive. For further details the interested reader is referred to the original work of Benson [1], and to [9], where several improvements and extensions can be found. We note again that the following explanation of the algorithm refers to the case of (1) being bounded.

The algorithm computes a shrinking sequence of polyhedral outer approximations

$$\mathcal{O}^0 \supseteq \mathcal{O}^1 \supseteq \cdots \supseteq \mathcal{O}^{k-1} \supseteq \mathcal{O}^k = \mathcal{P}.$$

An initial approximation $\mathcal{O}^0$ is found by solving the following linear programs for $j \in \{1, \ldots, q\}$:

$$\min_{x \in \mathbb{R}^n} e^j Px \quad \text{s.t.} \quad x \in X, \tag{P_0^j}$$

where e^j denotes the j-th unit (row) vector, i.e. the j-th entry of e^j is equal to one, the remaining entries are all equal to zero. The dual solution of (P_0^j) provides a supporting half space H^j to $\mathcal{P}$, i.e., $H^j \supseteq \mathcal{P}$ and $\mathcal{P} \cap -H^j \neq \emptyset$. It should be noted that LP solvers usually provide a solution to the dual problem without additional computational effort. The initial outer approximation is the intersection of the q half spaces H^j:

$$\mathcal{O}^0 = \bigcap_{j=1,\ldots,q} H^j = \{y^0\} + \mathbb{R}^q.$$

The approximation $\mathcal{O}^0$ has a single vertex y^0, with component y_j^0 being equal to the optimal value of the LP (P_0^j).

After a certain number of iterations, say k, the algorithm eventually finds an outer approximation $\mathcal{O}^k$ that coincides with $\mathcal{P}$. In each iteration step, the set of vertices of the outer approximation $\mathcal{O}^i$ is updated. It is stored together with corresponding pre-image points. The pre-images of the vertices of the final outer approximation $\mathcal{O}^k = \mathcal{P}$ yield a solution of (1).

A pseudocode of a serial variant of Benson's algorithm is depicted in Algorithm 1. An initial, outer approximation $\mathcal{O}$ with vertices $\mathcal{O}^{\mathrm{poi}}$ and representation

$$\mathcal{O} = \operatorname{conv} \mathcal{O}^{\mathrm{poi}} + \mathbb{R}^q_+$$

serves as input. For example, $\mathcal{O}^0$ with $\mathcal{O}^{\mathrm{poi}} = \{y^0\}$ as described above can be used as initial outer approximation. Initially, the solution set S is empty. In every iteration step, either the solution set S is enlarged (line 7) or the outer approximation is reduced (line 9). After the reduction step, a face of $\mathcal{O}$ coincides with a face of $\mathcal{P}$. Based on the fact that $\mathcal{P}$ has only finitely many faces, one can prove that the exit condition of the loop (line 10) will be satisfied eventually.

In the i-th iteration step a vertex y of $\mathcal{O}^i$, which has not already been recognized as part of the solution (i.e. no $x \in S$ exists with $y = Px$), is chosen. Then, the following linear program needs to be solved:

$$\min_{z \in \mathbb{R},\, x \in \mathbb{R}^n} z \quad \text{s.t.} \quad x \in X,\ Px \le y + ze, \tag{P_y}$$

where e denotes the all-one vector in $\mathbb{R}^q$. Solving (P_y) can be interpreted geometrically: It describes how far, starting from the point y, one needs to move in direction e until the set $\mathcal{P}$ is reached. If the optimal value z of (P_y) equals zero, then y is a vertex of $\mathcal{P}$. In this case, the x-part of a solution to (P_y) is a pre-image for y which is added to the solution set S (line 7). The outer approximation is unchanged in this case: $\mathcal{O}^{i+1} = \mathcal{O}^i$. Otherwise, if $z > 0$, the dual of (P_y) provides a supporting half space H of $\mathcal{P}$ with $y \notin H$. This half space is used to refine the outer approximation: $\mathcal{O}^{i+1} = \mathcal{O}^i \cap H$. The computation of the vertex set of the updated outer approximation in line 9 is done by *vertex enumeration*, compare, for instance, [7]. The general idea of the vertex enumeration algorithm uses the fact that a vertex of $\mathcal{O}^{i+1}$ is (i) a vertex y of $\mathcal{O}^i$ with $y \in \mathrm{int}\, H$ or (ii) a point y on an edge of $\mathcal{O}^i$ with $y \in \mathrm{bd}\, H$, where $\mathrm{int}\, H$ denotes the interior of H, and $\mathrm{bd}\, H$ is the bounding hyperplane of H. Vertices of the first type simply remain in the vertex list $\mathcal{O}^{\mathrm{poi}}$, while vertices of the second type are possibly new and need to be computed. All vertices y of $\mathcal{O}^i$ with $y \in -\mathrm{int}\, H$ are discarded from the vertex list $\mathcal{O}^{\mathrm{poi}}$.

Algorithm 1. Pseudocode of a basic serial version of Benson's algorithm [9]

Input: Problem data X and P, initial outer approximation $\mathcal{O}$ of $\mathcal{P}$, and its vertex set $\mathcal{O}^{\mathrm{poi}}$

Output: a solution S of (1)

1: **begin**
2: $\quad S \leftarrow \emptyset$;
3: **repeat**
4: $\quad\quad$ choose $y \in \mathcal{O}^{\mathrm{poi}} \setminus P[S]$;
5: $\quad\quad (x, z, H) \leftarrow$ solve (P_y);
6: $\quad\quad$ **if** $z = 0$ **then**
7: $\quad\quad\quad S \leftarrow S \cup \{x\}$;
8: $\quad\quad$ **else**
9: $\quad\quad\quad \mathcal{O}^{\mathrm{poi}} \leftarrow$ vertenum $(\mathcal{O} \cap H)$;
10: **until** $\mathcal{O}^{\mathrm{poi}} \setminus P[S] = \emptyset$
11: **end**

---

4   A Shared-Memory Parallel Variant

Throughout this article, we consider a shared-memory parallelization [8]. In this parallel programming paradigm, a team of threads is communicating via a memory that can be accessed by all threads. From a software engineering point of view, we assume that there is a thread pool consisting of a fixed number of p threads at a time. We further assume that, conceptually, there is a master program (not shown here) that handles the allocation of tasks and the synchronization of threads. Algorithm 2 displays the pseudocode that is executed by some thread t. In that pseudocode, variables that are local to a thread t are labeled with the subscript t. In contrast, variables in the global scope are denoted without subscripts.

Conceptually, we assume that the master program correctly initializes the global variables: the outer approximation $\mathcal{O}$, its vertex set $\mathcal{O}^{\mathrm{poi}}$, and the solution set S. Moreover, the master program spawns threads as long as $\mathcal{O}^{\mathrm{poi}} \setminus P[S] \neq \emptyset$, takes a vertex y_t from the global vertex set $\mathcal{O}^{\mathrm{poi}} \setminus P[S]$ and passes it to thread t for local computations. The thread executes the code in Algorithm 2, and terminates upon completion.

The idea behind this parallelization is as follows. Since each thread t operates on a different vertex y_t, the parallelization is carried out by concurrently executing the tasks associated with the different vertices. More precisely, the task associated with a vertex y_t consists of the sequence of the following subtasks:

1. solve the LP (P_y) (line 2),
2. update either the solution set S (line 5) or the vertex set $\mathcal{O}^{\mathrm{poi}}$ (line 7).

Each such sequence is executed in parallel to sequences associated with different vertices. The polyhedral outer approximation $\mathcal{O}$, its vertex set $\mathcal{O}^{\mathrm{poi}}$, and the solution set S are shared between different threads. Thus, only atomic access is allowed in line 5 and line 7. This is necessary since the vertex enumeration may discard several vertices of the current outer approximation. In the parallel variant one thread t^0 might compute a new vertex y, which lies outside the cutting half space H_{t^1} computed by another thread t^1. Consequently, y would have to be discarded by the vertex enumeration process in thread t^1. However, this is not possible because y is not in the vertex list $\mathcal{O}^{\mathrm{poi}}$ of t^1 in this case. The solution set S needs to be kept as a global variable, because the master thread needs to know whether a vertex $y \in \mathcal{O}^{\mathrm{poi}}$ can be passed to a thread as y_t or it is identified as vertex of $\mathcal{P}$ already. Atomic access is enforced by critical sections indicated by a lock/unlock mechanism.

Suppose the master thread assigns the vertex $y \in \mathcal{O}^{\mathrm{poi}}$ of the current outer approximation to some thread t^0. While processing y, $\mathcal{O}^{\mathrm{poi}}$ may be altered by another thread t^1. This affects the vertex enumeration part of thread t^0. In the worst case, the half space H computed by t^0 is *redundant*, meaning $y \in H$ for all vertices $y \in \mathcal{O}^{\mathrm{poi}}$ of the updated outer approximation. In this case the LP solved by thread t^0 gives no new information, i.e. t^0 wasted resources. Whether, and how frequently, this case occurs is highly dependent on the structure of the upper image $\mathcal{P}$ of the problem. It also depends on the way the vertices y_t

for the threads are chosen: This worst case is much unlikelier to happen if the vertices y_{t^0} and y_{t^1} assigned to threads t^0 and t^1, respectively, are "far away" from each other instead of being adjacent. In the current implementations we use for numerical experiments, the vertices $\mathcal{O}^{poi}$ are maintained as a list with no specific order: the master thread simply chooses the next available vertex to pass onto the thread. A more sophisticated approach of distributing the available vertices to the different threads is an important subject of future research.

Another point to consider is the availability of vertices: The number of vertices of the intermediate outer approximations $\mathcal{O}^i$ may vary significantly. If the number of threads p exceeds the number available vertices of the current outer approximation $\mathcal{O}^i$, some threads are idle until new vertices become available in subsequent iterations. This inactivity highly affects the scalability of the parallel variant of Benson's algorithm. It is therefore a promising direction of future research to study how the number of available vertices of the intermediate outer approximations can be maintained large.

Algorithm 2. Pseudocode of the shared-memory parallel variant that is executed for vertex y_t by thread t

---

Input: Vertex $y_t \in \mathcal{O}^{poi} \setminus P[S]$
Shared: Solution set S, outer approximation $\mathcal{O}$, and its vertex set $\mathcal{O}^{poi}$

1: **begin**
2: $(x_t, z_t, H_t) \leftarrow$ solve (P_{y_t});
3: lock ();
4: **if** $z_t = 0$ **then**
5: $\quad S \leftarrow S \cup \{x_t\}$;
6: **else**
7: $\quad \mathcal{O}^{poi} \leftarrow$ vertenum $(\mathcal{O} \cap H_t)$;
8: unlock ();
9: **end**

---

5 Numerical Experiments

To demonstrate the feasibility of the parallelization approach, we consider the following numerical experiments. We implement the shared-memory parallel variant of Benson's algorithm (Algorithm 2) by modifying the open source Vector Linear Program (VLP) solver BENSOLVE [12], which is also capable of solving MOLPs. BENSOLVE is written in the programming language C, we use the pthreads library [2,3,15] to implement the parallel variant of the algorithm. The lock/unlock mechanism of the parallel variant (Algorithm 2) is implemented using mutexes. Threads waiting for available vertices are realized by using conditions and signals.

We apply this algorithm to an MOLP (1) described in [9], Example 6.2. This MOLP is based on a bi-criteria ($q = 2$) problem with $n = 3\,799$ variables and

Table 1. Characteristics of the Two Computer Systems

Machine name	PC4	Ara24
Processor number	Core i7-6700	Xeon E5-2650v4
Number of cores	4	$2 \cdot 12 = 24$
Base clock rate [GHz]	3.4	2.2
Max clock rate [GHz]	4.0	2.9
RAM [GB]	32	128
L3-Cache [MB]	8	30
Max memory bandwidth [GB/s]	34.1	$2 \cdot 76.8 = 153.6$

$m = 6\,161$ constraints, found in [16]. The constraint-matrix A is dense with 4 435 919 non-zero entries. Because this problem has only two objectives, the vertex enumeration problems occurring in line 7 of Algorithm 2 are rather easy to solve. Thus the main computational effort for this problem instance lies in solving the LPs (line 2). Each LP problem is solved using a (serial) reentrant version of the open source GNU Linear Programming Kit GLPK [14]. We compute ε-solutions (obtained by changing the condition $z = 0$ to $z < \varepsilon$ occurring in line 6/line 4 in Algorithm 1/Algorithm 2) to the problem with an approximation error of $\varepsilon = 10^{-7}$. For further details the interested reader is referred to [9].

All numerical experiments are carried out on one or both of the two different shared-memory systems PC4 and Ara24, whose characteristics are given in Table 1. The machine names of the single-socket system PC4 and the dual-socket system Ara24 are chosen to indicate the number of available cores. Comparing the two systems, we observe a larger clock rate for PC4 than for Ara24. However, the two memory channels of PC4 give rise to a lower maximal memory bandwidth than the four memory channels of Ara24. In all experiments, the clock rates are explicitly set to the base clock rates, deactivating the dynamic overclocking mechanism.

First of all, we consider the wall clock time of the sequential and the parallel codes as a function of the number of threads or processor cores denoted by t. More precisely, in Fig. 1, the parallel speedup is calculated with respect to the execution time of the parallel code executed with $t = 1$ thread. These reference times are given by 4803 s on Ara24 and 3427 s on PC4. We observe an almost uniform behavior of the speedup increasing up to about $S = 12.9$ for 24 threads on Ara24. This speedup corresponds to a decrease of the parallel efficiency down to $E = 54\%$ on that machine. A similar efficiency of $E \approx 60\%$ is obtained on PC4 with 4 threads. Notice that the efficiency on PC4 seems to descend rapidly. However, this visual impression is caused by the scaling of the axes.

To analyze the parallel code in more detail, we plot, for each thread on the vertical axis, the start and finish time of each call to the LP solver on the time axis. More precisely, Fig. 2 shows two scenarios on Ara24 with a different number of threads. In those two graphs, a grey horizontal bar denotes the time spent in

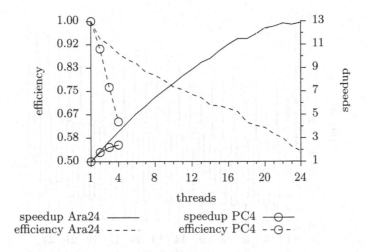

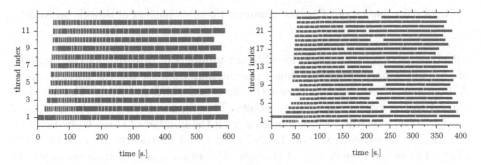

Fig. 1. Speedup and efficiency of Benson's algorithm on Ara24 and PC4

Fig. 2. The tasks of solving an LP, indicated by grey bars, plotted vs. time for $t = 12$ threads (left) and $t = 24$ threads (right) on Ara24

the LP solver routine. As we see, computing time consumed by the LP solver dominates the overall running time. One observes a start-up phase in the beginning, where there are fewer vertices than threads; leaving some of the threads idle. Synchronization and other parts of the algorithm have negligible execution time when $t = 12$ threads are used. We observe a similar behavior for all cases where $t < 18$. The corresponding graphs are omitted for the sake of brevity. However, for larger thread numbers, for instance $t = 24$ as displayed in the right of this figure, synchronization does play a role and there are algorithmic phases that involve an increasing number of idle threads for $t \geq 20$. The threshold of 18 threads depends on the test problem, but the effect in itself may be characteristic for this parallelized version of Benson's algorithm.

Another analysis of the algorithm is concerned with the execution times spent in the LP solver. For runs with different numbers of threads t, we show the distribution of LP solving times over all LPs solved in that run in a boxplot, see Fig. 3. We note that in our specific numerical example the number of LPs

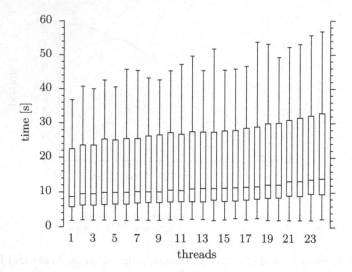

Fig. 3. Distribution of LP solver execution times vs. number of threads on Ara24

solved remains constant (347) for different numbers of threads. For each number of threads, a horizontal line shows the median value of the LP solving times. A box marks the region between the first and third quartiles. The whiskers extend to the most extreme data points. This figure shows that the median of the LP solver execution times increases with the number of threads. Notice that the median increases from roughly 8.7 s for $t = 1$ thread by a factor of 1.6 to about 14 s in the case of $t = 24$ threads. The other quartiles increase similarly. For a fixed number of threads t there is a large variation in the LP execution times. As the plot shows, the times vary by a factor of 20 to 25 for a fixed t.

The LP problems depend on the choice of the vertex $y_t \in \mathcal{O}^{\text{poi}} \setminus P[S]$, which is run time dependent. Consequently, the individual LPs to be solved during the course of the algorithm can differ for each number of threads t and each parallel program run. The LPs (P_y) are of the same size, but vary in the amount of work needed to solve them. However, we assume that the distribution of the amount of work of the LP solver remains the same with increasing numbers of threads t. The longer execution times for larger numbers of threads t mean that the LP solving routine becomes computationally less efficient. One way to explain this is memory bandwidth: For each thread one instance of the LP solver is executed by a dedicated processor core; however, the main memory system is shared. Running several LP solvers concurrently rather than executing a single LP solver may saturate the memory system. The individual available memory bandwidth per core decreases.

A further indication for memory saturation by multiple threads running at a time is shown in Table 2. In the following discussion, the term "job" is used to refer to the execution of one instance of the parallel variant of Benson's algorithm. For different numbers i, we run i jobs in parallel. Let $\tilde{t}$ denote the number of threads used to execute one job. We consider different numbers of jobs as well as different numbers of threads per job. This way we are capable of using up to 4 cores on PC4 or 16 cores on Ara24; but we use effectively just a fraction of the total memory bandwidth. Along a row indicating a fixed number of threads per job $\tilde{t}$, the values in that table vary the number of jobs i. Similarly, along a column indicating a fixed number of jobs i, the entries vary the number of threads per job $\tilde{t}$. Thus, a code performing independently of the maximum memory bandwidth would lead to execution times in a row that are constant. The reason is that these execution times are not influenced by whether one or several jobs are running at a time. A code with an execution time linearly dependent on memory bandwidth would lead to a doubling of the values along a table diagonal that leads from bottom-left to the top-right. The total number of threads summed over all jobs, $\tilde{t} \cdot i$, along that diagonal is constant. All these threads together share the total memory bandwidth. Each thread obtains the same amount of memory bandwidth. Its execution time is inverse proportional to the memory bandwidth, thus doubling the execution times along that table diagonal. In the left and right table we observe exactly this behavior. Therefore, the code is mainly memory bandwidth limited, presumably by the LP solvers involved.

Table 2. Execution times in seconds for multiple jobs on PC4 (left) and Ara24 (right)

threads per job	jobs		
	1	2	4
1	3427	3841	5609
2	1922	2814	
4	1419		

threads per job	jobs				
	1	2	4	8	16
1	4803	4771	5068	5052	6098
2	2508	2590	2798	3082	
4	1322	1421	1553		
8	732	818			
16	436				

6 Future Research

The performance results are reasonable given the simplicity of the parallelization approach. However, they indicate that there are still opportunities for future research aiming to increase the parallel performance further. One aspect of Benson's algorithm not considered in the parallel implementation we describe is the use of *warmstarts* for solving the LPs. To solve the LP (P_y) in line 5 of Algorithm 1, the LP solver needs to construct an initial basis and compute the corresponding basis factorization in every iteration. In the current implementation, the parameterized LPs (P_y) are initialized with the standard basis and the corresponding basis factorization is computed from scratch. An alternative way is to use the basis and the corresponding factorization associated with the

solution of a previously solved LP. Such a warmstart strategy can lead to a significant decline of computation times needed for solving the LPs, thus reducing
the overall computation time of Benson's algorithm. A straightforward warmstart strategy in the serial variant of Benson's algorithm (Algorithm 1) consists
in using the basis associated with the solution of the most recently solved LP as
initial basis for the current one.

One way to generalize the warmstart heuristic to the parallel version of the
algorithm (Algorithm 2) is that each thread t uses the basis associated with the
solution of the LP solved directly before in *that specific* thread as initial basis
for the current LP. We implement the warmstart strategy explained above, run
the example described in the previous section again and get a parallel speedup
of only ca. 5.3.

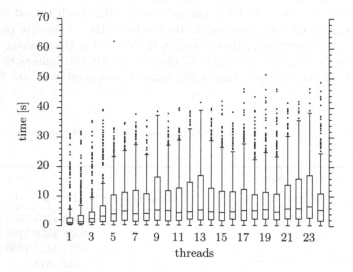

Fig. 4. Distribution of LP solver execution times for the warmstart version on Ara24,
with dots indicating outliers.

In the single thread case $t = 1$ the modification with warmstart heuristic
compared to coldstart is faster by a factor of about 4.6. The distribution of
solving times for the LPs changes dramatically. We plot the resulting distribution
of execution times of the LP solver in Fig. 4 against the different numbers of
threads t. The elements of this boxplot have the same meaning as discussed for
Fig. 3. Additionally, we plot outliers with dots, and the whiskers extend to the
most extreme data points not considered to be an outlier. Here, a data point
is considered to be an outlier, if it exceeds the third quartile plus 1.5 times
the range between the first and third quartile. In the implementation without
warmstarts, outliers do not occur (Fig. 3). The results show that in the sequential
case, $t = 1$, the average LP solving time is significantly lower compared to the
implementation without warmstarts (the median decreases from about 8.7 s in

Fig. 3 to ca. 1.0 s in Fig. 4). Compared to Fig. 3, the arithmetic average of the LP solver execution times in the warmstart version with a single thread is a factor of 4.6 lower, which coincides with the change of the total algorithm run time. Furthermore, for $t = 1$, the ratio of maximum to minimum LP solving times increases from 20 without warmstarts to 100 with warmstarts. At the same time, one sees several outliers, meaning the warmstart strategy does work well for most of the LPs, but for some LPs the basis chosen by the heuristic is not well suited.

Let us now consider the parallel case. With multiple threads, the assignment of initial bases to the corresponding LPs depends on the sequence of vertices y_t assigned to thread t, which is not deterministic for $t > 1$. The vertex selection we use leads to a sequence of vertices which are "close" to each other in the single-thread case. In the case of multiple threads, such a relationship between subsequently chosen vertices y_t clearly vanishes, which explains the quickly rising variation of the LP solving times for higher numbers of threads (Fig. 4). We see that the sequential version benefits more from warmstarts than the parallel versions do, especially for larger numbers of threads. In Fig. 4 the median LP solving time increases from 1.0 s for one thread to a maximum of 6.7 s for 23 threads. At the same time the minimum execution times remain comparable. The ratio of maximum to minimum solution times rises to 200 for $t = 24$ threads.

Thus, a first direction of future research is to develop more advanced warmstart heuristics, i.e. the assignment of initial bases to the LPs being solved.

We plot the start and finish time of each solved LP on the time axis for a 24 thread run with warmstarts on Ara24, see Fig. 5. There is a start-up phase, where there are fewer vertices than threads. In the warmstart case, this start-up is relatively longer, since the very first LP is solved with the standard basis, independent of whether warmstarts are enabled or not, but the LP solver can be accelerated when solving subsequent LPs. The warmstarts reduce the average time needed for solving an LP significantly, which may lead to a faster depletion of the pool of vertices available for computation. This effect can be observed in Fig. 5, the voids of the structure indicate that synchronization and dependencies between the different threads does play a greater role, compared to the implementation without warmstarts (see Fig. 2). There are longer algorithmic phases that leave a substantial number of threads idle. An interesting research direction is to develop warmstart heuristics, accompanied by vertex-selection rules, which avoid the observed problems.

Another closely related task is developing a good strategy for choosing the vertices y_t for the different threads t. This choice has an immediate effect on the sequence of LP problems. Thus, it heavily influences the serial execution times as well as the parallel performance. Also, the granularity of the parallelization is affected by this choice. A good parallelization strategy therefore requires a heuristic for choosing the vertices in a way such that a sufficient granularity is maintained. Thus, finding a heuristic for choosing a vertex y_t poses another promising direction of further research.

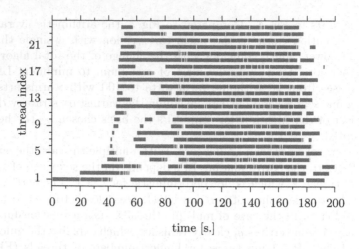

Fig. 5. The tasks of solving an LP plotted vs. time for the warmstart version using $t = 24$ threads on Ara24.

For further improvements of the parallel variant of Benson's algorithm, also the vertex enumeration part needs to be taken into account. The parallel efficiency of the presented algorithm depends significantly on the test problem. In the experiments reported in the present study we use a problem with two objectives. In a two-dimensional objective space the vertex enumeration does not need extensive computational effort, leading to negligible synchronization times between the different threads. In higher dimensions, however, vertex enumeration becomes more computationally expensive. As the vertex enumeration is an atomic operation in the parallel implementation, problem instances with higher objective space dimension may exhibit reduced scalability of the algorithm. We expect more difficulties to obtain a reasonable parallel performance when considering problems of higher dimensions. Thus it is imperative to explore possibilities to parallelize the vertex enumeration part of the algorithm. In addition, in higher objective space dimensions, multiple vertices of the current outer approximation may be associated with the same face of the upper image $\mathcal{P}$. In a parallel setting, multiple such vertices could be assigned to different threads at the same time, leading to redundantly solved LPs. This fact emphasizes the need for a "smart" vertex selection rule in a parallel setting.

Finally, to enable the use of a larger number of processors, it is necessary to consider computers with distributed memory. Our current shared-memory approach that uses a single global data structure is then no longer feasible. In particular, a large number of cores will cause a substantial synchronization and message passing overhead.

7   Concluding Remarks

The work described in the present article is concerned with solving linear programming problems that involve more than one objective function. This class of problems has a number of important applications in various scientific and engineering disciplines. Compared to the number of objectives, the number of free variables in problems arising in practical applications is often large. Here, Benson-type algorithms offer a computationally inexpensive alternative to other techniques. The reason is that Benson's algorithm is based on the objective space rather than on the variable space.

With the increase of the complexity and the sheer size of problems in real-world applications the need to cope with high requirements in terms of computation and storage is continuously increasing. Also, the ubiquity of multiple processing elements in today's computer architectures forces algorithm developers to pay attention to parallel algorithms. Unfortunately, the transition from serial to parallel computing is typically far from trivial. A mere parallelization of a given serial algorithm can sometimes work, but is often insufficient from a performance point of view. Therefore, serial algorithms need to be analyzed anew, with a focus on their potential for scalability to a large number of processors.

We introduced one of the first parallel implementations of Benson's algorithm. The approach is based on the shared-memory parallel programming model and is implemented using POSIX threads. The approach is direct and straightforward in the sense that the serial algorithm is parallelized. The parallelization is obtained from introducing a dynamic pool of tasks that are concurrently executed by a team of threads. Synchronization of threads is enforced by accessing a global data structure that is updated by each thread using an atomic operation. The contributions of the threads are accumulated in that data structure, eventually leading to the final result of the algorithm. The choice of vertices of the sequential and the parallel versions differ. So does the convergence history. It depends on the number of threads and the dynamic choice of vertices.

References

1. Benson, H.P.: Further analysis of an outcome set-based algorithm for multiple-objective linear programming. J. Optim. Theory Appl. **97**(1), 1–10 (1998). https://doi.org/10.1023/A:1022614814789
2. Butenhof, D.R.: Programming with Posix Threads. Addison-Wesley, Boston (1997)
3. Buttlar, D., Farrell, J., Nichols, B.: PThreads Programming. O'Reilly, Sebastopol (2013)
4. Ciripoi, D., Löhne, A., Weißing, B.: Bensolve tools - polyhedral calculus, global optimization and vector linear programming (2017). http://tools.bensolve.org
5. Csirmaz, L.: Using multiobjective optimization to map the entropy region. Comput. Optim. Appl. 1–23 (2015) https://doi.org/10.1007/s10589-015-9760-6
6. Ehrgott, M., Löhne, A., Shao, L.: A dual variant of Benson's "outer approximation algorithm" for multiple objective linear programming. J. Global Optim. **52**(4), 757–778 (2012). https://doi.org/10.1007/s10898-011-9709-y

7. Fukuda, K., Prodon, A.: Double description method revisited. In: Deza, M., Euler, R., Manoussakis, I. (eds.) CCS 1995. LNCS, vol. 1120, pp. 91–111. Springer, Heidelberg (1996). https://doi.org/10.1007/3-540-61576-8_77
8. Grama, A., Gupta, A., Karypis, G., Kumar, V.: Introduction to Parallel Computing, 2nd edn. Pearson, Harlow, UK (2003)
9. Hamel, A.H., Löhne, A., Rudloff, B.: Benson type algorithms for linear vector optimization and applications. J. Global Optim. 59(4), 811–836 (2014). https://doi.org/10.1007/s10898-013-0098-2
10. Löhne, A.: Vector Optimization with Infimum and Supremum. Springer, Heidelberg (2011). https://doi.org/10.1007/978-3-642-18351-5
11. Löhne, A., Weißing, B.: Equivalence between polyhedral projection, multiple objective linear programming and vector linear programming. Math. Methods Oper. Res. 84(2), 411–426 (2016). https://doi.org/10.1007/s00186-016-0554-0
12. Löhne, A., Weißing, B.: Bensolve - a free VLP solver (2017). http://bensolve.org
13. Löhne, A., Weißing, B.: The vector linear program solver Bensolve - notes on theoretical background. Eur. J. Oper. Res. 260(3), 807–813 (2017). https://doi.org/10.1016/j.ejor.2016.02.039
14. Makhorin, A.: GNU Linear Programming Kit: Reference Manual for GLPK version 4.64 (2017). http://www.gnu.org/software/glpk/glpk.html
15. IEEE/ANSI Std 1003.1: IEEE standard for information technology-portable operating system interface (POSIX)-Part 1: System application program interface (API) (C language). IEEE (1996)
16. Ruszczyński, A., Vanderbei, R.J.: Frontiers of stochastically nondominated portfolios. Econometrica 71(4), 1287–1297 (2003). https://doi.org/10.1111/1468-0262.t01-1-00448
17. Shao, L., Ehrgott, M.: Approximately solving multiobjective linear programmes in objective space and an application in radiotherapy treatment planning. Math. Methods Oper. Res. 68(2), 257–276 (2008). https://doi.org/10.1007/s00186-008-0220-2
18. Shao, L., Ehrgott, M.: Approximating the nondominated set of an MOLP by approximately solving its dual problem. Math. Methods Oper. Res. 68(3), 469–492 (2008) https://doi.org/10.1007/s00186-007-0194-5
19. Tyburec, M.: Multi-criteria optimization of proton therapy treatment plan. Bachelor thesis, Department of Mechanics, Faculty of Civil Engineering, Czech Technical University in Prague (2015)
20. Wiecek, M.M., Zhang, H.: A parallel algorithm for multiple objective linear programs. Comput. Optim. Appl. 8(1), 41–56 (1997). https://doi.org/10.1023/A:1008606530836
21. Yoon, M.S., Kamal, A.E.: Optimal dataset allocation in distributed heterogeneous clouds. In: 2014 IEEE Globecom Workshops, pp. 75–80 (2014). https://doi.org/10.1109/GLOCOMW.2014.7063389

Build Orientation Optimization Problem in Additive Manufacturing

Ana Maria A. C. Rocha[1]($\boxtimes$) (iD), Ana I. Pereira[2](iD), and A. Ismael F. Vaz[1](iD)

[1] Algoritmi Research Centre, University of Minho, 4710-057 Braga, Portugal
{arocha,aivaz}@dps.uminho.pt
[2] Research Centre in Digitalization and Intelligent Robotics (CeDRI),
Instituto Politécnico de Bragança, 5300-253 Bragança, Portugal
apereira@ipb.pt

Abstract. Additive manufacturing (AM) is an emerging type of production technology to create three-dimensional objects layer-by-layer directly from a 3D CAD model. AM is being extensively used by engineers and designers.

Build orientation is a critical issue in AM since it is associated with the object accuracy, the number of supports required and the processing time to produce the object. Finding the best build orientation in the AM will reduced significantly the building costs and will improve the object accuracy.

This paper presents an optimization approach to solve the part build orientation problem considering the staircase effect, support area characteristics and the build time. Two global optimization methods, the Electromagnetism-like and the Stretched Simulated Annealing algorithms, are used to study the optimal orientation of four models.

Preliminary experiments show that both optimization methods can effectively solve the build orientation problem in AM, finding several global solutions.

Keywords: Design tools · Additive manufacturing · 3D printing
Optimization · Build orientation

1 Introduction

Traditional manufacturing methods involve a solid block of material being carved, or shaped, into the desired product, where block parts are being successively removed in different ways.

Additive manufacturing (AM) has emerged in the last decades becoming an alternative to the traditional subtractive manufacturing. It is a technology that builds 3D objects by adding ultrathin layers of material, one by one, for fabricating the desired product.

Additive manufacturing processes involve the use of three-dimensional (3D) computer-aided design (CAD) data to create physical models. One of the greatest benefits of AM is the production of a wide range of shapes. Currently, AM is being used to make end-use products in aircraft, dental restorations, medical implants, automobiles, and even fashion products [7].

One of the current challenges faced by manufacturing industries is the reduction of prototype model development time through adoption of rapid prototyping technologies (techniques of fabricating a prototype model from a CAD file) in particular using the additive manufacturing process.

The performance of a rapid prototyping technology depends on the way parts are oriented on the build platform. Therefore, each part should be appropriately oriented to achieve better surface quality and either minimal support structure or lower build time [3]. Besides that, these strategies result in a process more environmental friendly since it will require less energy consumption and material waste.

A number of studies have been carried out in the problem of selecting a building direction given a 3D CAD model. A proposal based on the determination of the optimal part orientation when minimizing the build cost can be seen in [1]. Authors used various criteria like stair step error, build height, volume of supports, stability of object, among others, to determine the optimal part build orientation for any rapid prototyping process. Lan et al. [8] studied the best build orientation of a model part considering the surface quality, build time and the complexity of the support structure. Thrimurthulu et al. and Canellidis et al. [3,14] show methodologies addressing the optimal part orientation taking into account the surface quality, evaluate the surface roughness and build deposition time.

A presentation of methodologies for optimizing the build orientation problem based on the minimum volumetric error can be found in [9]. A part orientation optimization model using genetic algorithm that considers the build time, material usage, surface finish, interior geometry, strength characteristics and related parameters is presented in [15].

The literature suggests criteria to be considered for optimal build orientation such as the build height, staircase effect, volume of support structures and part area in contact with support structures [4,5,12,15].

In this study, we aim to analyse the behaviour of two multi-global optimization methods, named Electromagnetism-Like and Stretched Simulated Annealing algorithms, to solve the build orientation optimization problem in additive manufacturing.

This paper is organized as follows. Section 2 presents the build orientation optimization model as well as the mathematical formulation of the optimization problem. In Sect. 3, the optimizers used to solve the build orientation optimization problem are briefly described. The description of the models that will be analysed are presented in Sect. 4. Section 5 presents the results of the numerical experiments and Sect. 6 contains the conclusions of the present study and future work.

2   Build Orientation Optimization

In this section the build orientation model as well as the mathematical formulation of the build orientation optimization problem are presented.

2.1   Build Orientation Model

The surface finish of an object obtained through additive manufacturing process is highly important. Different measures to determine the best build orientation for an improvement of the surface finish can be considered taking into account factors as the part accuracy, building time, structure support and part stability. The general orientation characteristics for assessing the optimal build orientation include: the height of the part in the build direction; the total volume of support material used; the total area of contact of the object with the external support structure; the quality of selected faces that are subjected to the staircase effect and are in contact with the supports. These orientation characteristics can be individually used to rank a selection of possible orientations according to minimum build height, minimum volume of support structures, minimum area in contact with extra support structures or maximum accuracy of total surface area (staircase effect) or selected facets [5, 8, 15]. The best selection of the build orientation model will improve the surface accuracy of the object, minimize the supports needed and the production time, and, consequently, the build costs [1].

A major source of structure inaccuracy is due to the staircase effect. The staircase effect is used as the basis for developing an accuracy measure. The maximum deviation from layered part to the CAD surface measured in the normal direction to CAD surface is known as the cusp height, H_c (see Fig. 1).

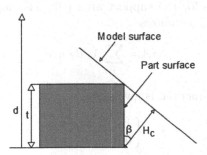

Fig. 1. Cusp height.

This depends on the angle β formed by the slicing direction d and the model surface normal, and on the layer thickness, t. Thicker layers and/or higher values of $\cos(\beta)$ will produce larger values for cusp height and consequently a more inaccurate surface will appear [1]. The cusp height is given by $H_c = t\cos(\beta)$. By using cusp height to measure the structure accuracy, the surface quality can be determined from the object geometry, build direction and layer thickness.

When the normal model surface is close to be collinear ($\beta \approx 0$) with the slicing direction, the volumetric difference (difference between CAD model and the slice volume) is very high, giving a low surface smoothness.

However if the normal of the model surface is close to be perpendicular to the slicing direction ($\beta \approx 90°$) the volumetric difference is very low, giving a high surface smoothness. In this context, an algorithm that slices the model along the slicing direction d can use the volumetric error to maximize the part smoothness. The volumetric error, VE, to be minimized in each layer stem from staircase effect is given by

$$VE = \sum_j \frac{t^2 |d \cdot n_j| A_j}{2}, \tag{1}$$

where t is the slicing height, n_j is the unit normal vector of the j triangle facet, A_j is its area, d is the unit normal vector of the building direction [16].

Another measure related to the optimal build orientation is the quantity of supports used, measured by the support area or support volume. The computation of the support volume is very complex. If the shape of the object is convex, the support volume is the volume of the region lying between the object solid of the part and the platform, the vertical polyhedral cylinder which is bounded below by the platform and above by the object facets whose outward normal point downward. But if the product shape is nonconvex, the problem is more complex, since the supports for some faces may actually be attached to other facets instead of to the platform [16]. The quantity of support area affects post-processing and surface finish. Thus, support area is the total area of the downward-facing facets. Note that the support area have more significant impact on the object accuracy than the support volume. So the part building direction optimization accounts for the support area [16]. The support area, SA, to be minimized is expressed as follows

$$SA = \sum_j A_j |d \cdot n_j| \delta \tag{2}$$

where δ, a threshold function, is given by

$$\delta = \begin{cases} 1 \text{ if } d \cdot n_j < 0 \\ 0 \text{ if } d \cdot n_j > 0. \end{cases}$$

Another measure that could be used to determine the optimal part build orientation is the build time without compromising the surface quality.

Canellidis et al. [3] considered that the build time includes the time required to manufacture the object as well as the time required for support removal and surface finishing. The major structure of the overall build time is the creation time of a designed object, whereas the time required for removal of supports and surface finishing is only a minor fraction of build time. It should be noted that different authors considered different definitions for the build time. For example, Lan et al. [8] only considered the build time as the time for creating a designed object while Zhao [16] considered the build time as the scanning time and the preparation time. The scanning time includes solid scanning time, contour scanning time and support scanning time, where the solid and contour scanning times are independent of the part building direction and the support scanning time depends on the volume of supports. The preparation time includes the time required to move down the platform during the re-coating, the scraping time and other preparation times. Moreover, the preparation time is dependent on the total number of layers, while the number of layers is dependent on the height of part building direction. Therefore, minimizing the height of the part building direction and, consequently, the total number of layers can reduce the part building time. The part building time, BT, to be minimized can be expressed as follows

$$BT = \max(d \cdot v_1, d \cdot v_2, \ldots, d \cdot v_n) - \min(d \cdot v_1, d \cdot v_2, \ldots, d \cdot v_n) \qquad (3)$$

where v_i are the vertex triangle facets.

2.2   Problem Formulation

Based on the part build orientation, the optimization problem will minimize the volumetric error, supporting area and build time defined in Eqs. (1)–(3). We aim to compute the optimal slicing direction d, which is a normalized vector (i.e. $\|d\| = 1$). An equivalent mathematical formulation is to compute the rotation along the x and y axis. In our case we considered $d = (0, 0, 1)^T$ as the slicing direction after a rotation along (x, y) angles, where each angle is between $0°$ and $180°$. Thus, the optimization problem is given by

$$\begin{aligned} \min \ & f(x, y) \\ \text{s.t.} \ \ & 0 \leq x \leq 180 \\ & 0 \leq y \leq 180 \end{aligned} \qquad (4)$$

where the objective function to be minimized, $f(x, y)$, is given by (1) for the volumetric error, (2) for the support area and (3) for the part building time.

3   Optimizers

In this section, two global optimization methods used to solve the build orientation problem are presented. First, the Electromagnetism-like algorithm is briefly described followed by a description of the Stretched Simulated Annealing algorithm.

3.1   Electromagnetism-Like Algorithm

The Electromagnetism-like (EM) algorithm, developed by Birbil and Fang [2], is a population-based stochastic search method for bound constrained global optimization problems that mimics the behaviour of electrically charged particles.

The method uses an attraction-repulsion mechanism to move a population of points towards optimality.

The EM algorithm simulates the electromagnetism theory of physics by considering each point in the population as an electrical charge that is released to the space. The charge of each point is related to the objective function value and determines the magnitude of attraction of the point over the others in the population. The better the objective function value, the higher the magnitude of attraction. The charges are used to find a direction for the movement of each point. The regions that have higher attraction will signal other points to move towards them. In addition, a repulsion mechanism is also introduced to explore new regions for even better solutions [2].

The EM algorithm comprises four main procedures: "Initialization", "Compute Force", "Move Points" and "Local Search". The main steps of the EM algorithm are presented in the Algorithm 1.

Initialization
while *stopping criterion in not satisfied* **do**
   | Compute Force
   | Move Points
end

Algorithm 1. EM algorithm

The "Initialization" procedure starts by randomly generating a sample of points. Each point is uniformly distributed between the lower and upper bounds. Then, the objective function value for each point is calculated and the best point of the population, x^{best}, is identified as well as its corresponding objective function value f^{best}.

In the "Compute Force" procedure, each particle charge that determines the power of attraction or repulsion for each point is calculated. In this way the points that have better objective function values possess higher charges. After the charge calculation, the total force vector on each point is then calculated by adding the individual component forces between any pair of points.

The "Move Points" procedure uses the total force vector to move each point in the direction of the force by a random step length λ. The best point, x^{best}, is not moved. To maintain feasibility, the force exerted on each point is normalized and scaled by the allowed range of movement towards the lower bound or the upper bound.

A fully description of the EM algorithm can be found in [13] as well as the used code.

3.2 Stretched Simulated Annealing Algorithm

Stretched Simulated Annealing (SSA) algorithm is a multilocal programming method that solves bound constrained optimization problems point-to-point. This stochastic method combines Simulated Annealing algorithm [6] with a stretching function technique [10].

SSA solves a sequence of global optimization problems in order to compute the global/local solutions of the original optimization problem. In each iteration, a new global optimization problem is generate combining the original objective function and the stretching function technique.

The mathematical formulation of the global optimization problem is as follows:

$$\min_{a \leq x \leq b} \Phi_l(x) \equiv \begin{cases} \hat{\phi}(x) \text{ if } x \in V_{\varepsilon^j}(x_j^*), \, j \in \{1, \ldots, N\} \\ f(x) \text{ otherwise} \end{cases} \tag{5}$$

where $V_{\varepsilon^j}(x_j^*)$ represents the neighborhood of the solution x_j^* with a ray ε^j.

The $\hat{\phi}(x)$ function is defined as

$$\hat{\phi}(x) = \bar{\phi}(x) + \frac{\delta_2[\text{sign}(f(x) - f(x_j^*)) + 1]}{2\tanh(\kappa(\bar{\phi}(x) - \bar{\phi}(x_j^*))} \tag{6}$$

and

$$\bar{\phi}(x) = f(x) + \frac{\delta_1}{2}\|x - x_j^*\|[\text{sign}(f(x) - f(x_j^*)) + 1] \tag{7}$$

where δ_1, δ_2 and κ are positive constants and N is the number of minimizers already detected.

The main steps of the SSA algorithm are presented in the Algorithm 2.

Initialization
while *stopping criterion in not satisfied* **do**
    Calculate a global solution x_j^* of problem (5)
    Calculate $V_{\varepsilon^j}(x_j^*)$
end

Algorithm 2. SSA algorithm

To solve the global optimization problems (5) the simulated annealing method is used [6]. The SSA algorithm stops when no new optimum is identified after l consecutive runs.

Details about the algorithm and its implementation can be found in [11].

4 Models Description

In this section, we present the 3D CAD models that will be used in our numerical testing of the global optimization algorithms.

First, CAD models are converted into STL (STereoLithography) that is the standard file type used by most common 3D printing file formats. STL files describe only the surface geometry of a three-dimensional object without any representation of color, texture or other common CAD model attributes. Figures 2, 3, 4 and 5 show the STL files of the models that will be used in the present study.

Fig. 2. Rear panel fixed 3D printing file.   **Fig. 3.** Air duct 3D printing file.

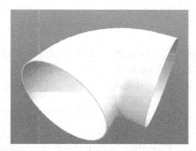

Fig. 4. Rocket shot 3D printing file.   **Fig. 5.** 45 degree short 3D printing file.

The STL file format approximates the surfaces of a solid model by a poly-hedral representation of a 3D object using triangular facets. The more complex the surface is more triangles are produced. Figure 2 shows a rear panel to replace the plexiglass panel on the rear of the Rostock Max v2 (a 3D printer) that has vents on either side. The rear panel is of a difference size of the side panels, but the side panels for left and right are the same. It was defined using 3008 triangles. Figure 3 shows an air duct splitter of 50 mm designed to direct the flow of two air vents into an air intake or to split the air from one into two places. It was defined using 6024 triangles. Figure 4 shows a rocket shot shaped cup. It was defined using 10616 triangles. Figure 5 shows a fan duct extension with 45 degree short radius elbow that was defined using 66888 triangles.

5   Numerical Experiments

In this section, a practical comparison of two optimizers, the EM and SSA des-cribed in Sect. 3, to solve the build orientation problem (4) is shown.

The numerical experiments involve the optimization of the build orientation problem using three different measures: the volumetric error, the support area and the part building time. The models used in the experiments are the ones presented in Sect. 4, namely the Rear panel, Air duct, Rocket shot and 45 degree short.

The numerical experiments were carried out on a PC Intel Core 2 Duo Processor E7500 with 2.9 GHz and 4 Gb of memory RAM. The algorithm was coded in MATLAB Version 9.2 (R2017a).

5.1 Details of Implementation

The stopping criterion used for each optimizer was the maximum number of function evaluations set to 500. Since the presented global methods are stochastic, 20 runs were performed for each problem. The population size used in the EM algorithm was set to 10.

Before optimization, the objects considered a slicing along the Z-axis with 5 mm height, resulting in 36 slices for the Rear panel fixed problem (see Fig. 6). Considering the same slicing, it was obtained 16 slices for the Rocket shot (see

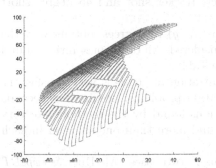

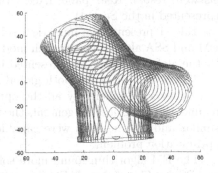

Fig. 6. Rear panel fixed with 5 mm of layer height.

Fig. 7. Air duct with with 2 mm of layer height.

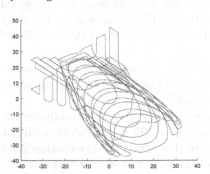

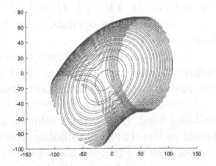

Fig. 8. Rocket shot with 5 mm of layer height.

Fig. 9. 45 degree short with 5 mm of layer height.

Fig. 8) and 25 slices for the 45 degree short problem (see Fig. 9). For the Air
duct problem a slicing along the Z-axis with 2 mm height was used resulting in
49 slices as shown at Fig. 7.

5.2 Comparative Results

In this section, we report the numerical results obtained with the
Electromagnetism-like and the Stretched Simulated Annealing algorithms.

In the following, we describe the numerical experiences to solve the build
orientation problem using the different measures:

- exp_VE - denotes optimizing problem (4) with $f(x, y) = VE$, the volumetric
  error given by (1);
- exp_SA - denotes optimizing problem (4) with $f(x, y) = SA$, the support
  area given by (2);
- exp_BT - denotes optimizing problem (4) with $f(x, y) = BT$, the build time
  given by (3).

In order to analyse the behaviour of the two global optimization methods in
solving the build orientation problem using the different measures, four models were tested: Rear panel fixed, Air duct, Rocket shot and 45 degree short
(presented in the Sect. 4).

Table 1 presents the numerical solutions, (x, y) in degrees, obtained by the
EM and SSA algorithms for each model considered. All different solutions found
by the global methods are presented in the Table 1.

The behaviour of the both global optimization methods is very satisfactory
since they solve efficiently all the optimization problems, needing few seconds
to find the solutions. In general, the solutions found by the methods are very
similar and the methods were capable to find more than one solution in each
optimization problem.

The EM algorithm found more solutions in two cases (Air Duct & exp_BT
and Rocket Shot & exp_VE) when compared with SSA algorithm. In some situations both algorithm identified different solutions (45 degree short & exp_BT).

To evaluate the impact of the different measures to identify the (x, y) on
the 3D printer, Figs. 10, 11 and 12 present the build orientation provided by
the algorithms when optimizing the build orientation problem of the Rear Panel
Fixed model).

The obtained solutions are consistent with the main idea of the measures
definition, since in the cases of exp_VE and exp_SA the objective is to minimize
volumetric error and the support area, respectively.

In the case of the measure exp_BT, where the objective is to minimize the
building time, the optimal solution $x = 0$ and $y = 135$ is consistent with the
height of the structure building direction. Note that when the orientation gives
the solution of $(180, 45)$ the representation of the object is similar to Fig. 12.

Next we will present the figures related to build orientation problem of the
Air duct model. Note that the obtained solutions for exp_VE and exp_SA are
the same, thus the figures of the four solutions are shown in Figs. 13 and 14.

Table 1. Solutions obtained by the EM and SSA algorithms (in degrees).

Problem	exp_VE			exp_SA			exp_BT		
	EM	SSA		EM	SSA		EM	SSA	
	(x^*,y^*)	(x^*,y^*)	$f(x^*,y^*)$	(x^*,y^*)	(x^*,y^*)	$f(x^*,y^*)$	(x^*,y^*)	(x^*,y^*)	$f(x^*,y^*)$
Rear panel	(90,0)	(90,0)	2.4×10^4	(90,0)	(90,0)	1.3×10^3	(0,135)	(0,135)	4.4×10^1
	(90,180)	(90,180)	2.5×10^4	(90,180)	(90,180)	8.6×10^2	(180,45)	(180,45)	4.4×10^1
Air duct	(0,0)	(0,0)	1.8×10^4	(0,0)	(0,0)	4.3×10^3	(90,90)	(90,90)	5.2×10^1
	(180,180)	(180,180)	1.8×10^4	(180,180)	(180,180)	4.3×10^3	(0,90)	-	5.2×10^1
	(0,180)	(0,180)	1.8×10^4	(0,180)	(0,180)	4.7×10^3	(160,90)	-	5.2×10^1
	(180,0)	(180,0)	1.8×10^4	(180,0)	(180,0)	4.7×10^3	(50,90)	-	5.2×10^1
	-	-	-	-	-	-	-	(120,90)	5.2×10^1
Rocket shot	(0,0)	(0,0)	2.7×10^4	(0,0)	(0,0)	9.2×10^2	(90,45)	(90,45)	4.5×10^1
	(180,180)	(180,180)	2.7×10^4	(180,180)	(180,180)	9.2×10^2	(90,135)	(90,135)	4.5×10^1
	(0,180)	-	2.7×10^4	(180,0)	(180,0)	1.3×10^3	-	-	-
	(180,0)	-	3.3×10^4	-	-	-	-	-	-
45 degree short	(90,135)	(90,135)	4.8×10^4	(90,135)	(90,135)	1.9×10^4	(0,0)	(0,0)	1.3×10^2
	-	-	-	-	-	-	(180,180)	(180,180)	1.3×10^2
	-	-	-	-	-	-	(180,0)	(180,0)	1.3×10^2
	-	-	-	-	-	-	(0,180)	-	1.3×10^2
	-	-	-	-	-	-	-	(25,25)	1.3×10^2

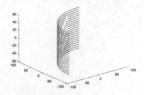

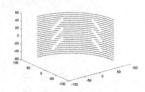

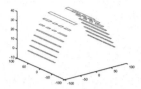

Fig. 10. Rear panel fixed of *exp_VE* and *exp_SA* for (90, 0).

Fig. 11. Rear panel fixed of *exp_VE* and *exp_SA* for (90, 180).

Fig. 12. Rear panel fixed of *exp_BT* (0, 135).

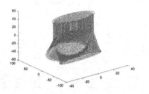

Fig. 13. Air duct of *exp_VE* and *exp_SA* for (180, 180) or (0, 0).

Fig. 14. Air duct of *exp_VE* and *exp_SA* for (0, 180) or (180, 0).

Fig. 15. Air duct of *exp_BT* for (90, 90) or (0, 90).

As expected, the algorithms found some solutions that have the same build orientation. It is the case of the (180, 180) or (0, 0) for the minimization of the volumetric error, *exp_VE*, and similar situations happen in the optimization of the support area and build time, experiments *exp_SA* and *exp_BT* (Fig. 15). As previously mentioned, the minimization of the total number of layers can reduce the part building time. Thus the optimal solutions of *exp_BT* are consistent regarding the structure building direction.

Next we will present the figures related to build orientation problem of the Rocket Shot model. Note that the obtained figures related to experiment *exp_VE* when the solution angles are (0, 0) and (180, 180) are the same (see Fig. 16) as well as for (0, 180) and (180, 0) (see Fig. 17). The solutions obtained by *exp_BT* are presented in Fig. 18.

Regarding the solution angles (0, 0) and (180, 180) seem to be the best direction (see Fig. 16). Since the solutions (0,180) and (180,0) have higher values of the objective function (see Table 1).

The build orientation directions produced by the global optimization algorithms for the 45 degree short model are depicted in Figs. 19, 20 and 21. The numerical results indicate that different angles x and y may result in the same direction of construction as had already occurred for the other models.

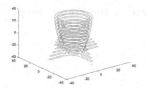

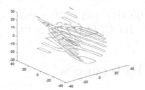

Fig. 16. Rocket shot of *exp_VE* and *exp_SA* for $(0,0)$ or $(180,180)$.

Fig. 17. Rocket shot of *exp_VE* for $(0,180)$ and $(180,0)$.

Fig. 18. Rocket shot of *exp_BT* for $(90,135)$ or $(90,45)$.

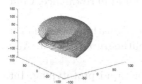

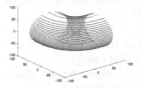

Fig. 19. 45 degree short of *exp_VE* and *exp_SA* for $(90,135)$.

Fig. 20. 45 degree short of *exp_BT* for $(180,0)$ or $(180,180)$.

Fig. 21. 45 degree short of *exp_BT* for $(0,0)$ or $(0,180)$.

6   Conclusions and Future Work

In this paper, it is presented a comparative study of two different global optimization methods, named the Electromagnetism-like and the Stretched Simulated Annealing algorithms, to solve the build orientation optimization problem. Numerical experiments have been carried out to analyse the behaviour of the EM and SSA algorithms when determining the best orientation to improve the surface accuracy of four 3D CAD models through three different measures, the volumetric error, the support area and the build time.

With this comparative study, we are able to conclude that both methods solve efficiently the optimization problem identifying different solutions in each model/measure. So, it is possible to conclude that for each presented model it is possible to build it with different orientations obtaining the same measure evaluation.

For future work we intend to solve the build orientation problem as a multiobjective problem and consider different and more complex models.

Acknowledgments. This work has been supported and developed under the FIBR3D project - Hybrid processes based on additive manufacturing of composites with long or short fibers reinforced thermoplastic matrix (POCI-01-0145-FEDER-016414), supported by the Lisbon Regional Operational Programme 2020, under the PORTUGAL 2020 Partnership Agreement, through the European Regional Development Fund (ERDF). This work was also supported by COMPETE: POCI-01-0145-FEDER-

007043 and FCT - Fundação para a Ciência e Tecnologia within the Project Scope: UID/CEC/00319/2013.

References

1. Alexander, P., Allen, S., Dutta, D.: Part orientation and build cost determination in layered manufacturing. Comput. Aided Des. **30**(5), 343–356 (1998)
2. Birbil, S.I., Fang, S.-C., Sheu, R.L.: On the convergence of a population-based global optimization algorithm. J. Global Optim. **30**, 301–318 (2004)
3. Canellidis, V., Dedoussis, V., Mantzouratos, N., Sofianopoulou, S.: Pre-processing methodology for optimizing stereolithography apparatus build performance. Comput. Ind. **57**(5), 424–36 (2006)
4. Canellidis, V., Giannatsis, J., Dedoussis, V.: Genetic-algorithm-based multi-objective optimization of the build orientation in stereolithography. Int. J. Adv. Manufact. Technol. **45**, 714–730 (2009)
5. Gogate, A.S., Pande, S.S.: Intelligent layout planning for rapid prototyping. Int. J. Prod. Res. **46**(20), 5607–5631 (2008)
6. Ingber, L.: Very fast simulated re-annealing. Math. Comput. Model. **12**, 967–973 (1989)
7. Khana, I., Mateus, A., Lorgerc, K., Mitchella, G.R.: Part specific applications of additive manufacturing. Procedia Manufact. **12**(2017), 89–95 (2017)
8. Lan, P., Chou, S., Chen, L., Gemmill, D.: Determining fabrication orientations for rapid prototyping with stereolithography apparatus. Comput. Aided Des. **29**(1), 53–62 (1997)
9. Masood, S., Rattanawong, W., Iovenitti, P.: Part build orientations based on volumetric error in fused deposition modelling. Int. J. Adv. Manufact. Technol. **16**, 162–168 (2000)
10. Parsopoulos, K., Plagianakos, V., Magoulas, G., Vrahatis, M.: Objective function stretching to alleviate convergence to local minima. Nonlinear Anal. **47**, 3419–3424 (2001)
11. Pereira, A.I., Ferreira, O., Pinho, S.P., Fernandes, E.M.G.P.: Multilocal programming and applications. In: Zelinka, I., Snášel, V., Abraham, A. (eds.) Handbook of Optimization. Intelligent Systems Reference Library, vol. 38. Springer, Heidelberg (2013). https://doi.org/10.1007/978-3-642-30504-7_7
12. Phatak, A.M., Pande, S.S.: Optimum part orientation in rapid prototyping using genetic algorithm. J. Manuf. Syst. **31**(4), 395–402 (2012)
13. Rocha, A.M.A.C., Silva, A., Rocha, J.G.: A new competitive implementation of the electromagnetism-like algorithm for global optimization. In: Gervasi, O., Murgante, B., Misra, S., Gavrilova, M.L., Rocha, A.M.A.C., Torre, C., Taniar, D., Apduhan, B.O. (eds.) ICCSA 2015. LNCS, vol. 9156, pp. 506–521. Springer, Cham (2015). https://doi.org/10.1007/978-3-319-21407-8_36
14. Thrimurthulu, K., Pandey, P.M., Reddy, N.V.: Optimum part deposition orientation in fused deposition modeling. Int. J. Mach. Tools Manuf **44**(6), 585–94 (2004)
15. Villalpando, L., Eiliat, H., Urbanic, R.J.: An optimization approach for components built by fused deposition modeling with parametric internal structures. Procedia CIRP **17**, 800–805 (2014)
16. Zhao J.: Determination of optimal build orientation based on satisfactory degree theory for RPT. In: Ninth International Conference on Computer Aided Design and Computer Graphics (CAD-CG 2005) (2005). p. 6

Modelling and Experimental Analysis Two-Wheeled Self Balance Robot Using PID Controller

Aminu Yahaya Zimit[1,2], Hwa Jen Yap[1], Mukhtar Fatihu Hamza[1,2(✉)],
Indrazno Siradjuddin[3], Billy Hendrik[4], and Tutut Herawan[3,5,6]

[1] Department of Mechanical Engineering, University of Malaya, Kuala Lumpur,
Malaysia
emukhtarfah@gmail.com
[2] Department of Mechatronics Engineering, Bayero University, Kano, Nigeria
[3] Politeknik Negeri Malang, Malang, Indonesia
[4] Universitas Putra Indonesia YPTK, Padang, Sumatera Barat, Indonesia
[5] Universitas Negeri Yogyakarta, Yogyakarta, Indonesia
[6] Universitas Teknologi Yogyakarta, Yogyakarta, Indonesia

Abstract. This research is aimed to design and implement Proportional Integral Derivative (PID) controller on Two-wheeled self-balance (TWSB) robot. The PID is used for the purpose of balancing the robot to stand still at upright position and to receive command via Bluetooth to follow the desired trajectory smoothly. The dynamic model of TWSB robot was developed using Lagrangian method. The PID gains were tuned until the optimum values are achieved. The Arduino based PID-controller was implemented on the TWSB robot in real world experiment. The experimental result shows the effectiveness of the proposed controller for stabilization and trajectory tracking control of TWSB robot.

Keywords: PID · Self-balanced robot · Mathematical model
Trajectory tracking control

1 Introduction

Nowadays, robots are more involved in many ways of human life. They are assigned to do many simple and complicated tasks easier, quicker and more precisely. The rationales behind this improvement in industries is to cut labor cost, achieve high productivity, maintain and improve familiarity among products, and eradicate negative human factors such as laziness, tiredness, absenteeism and so on [1, 2]. Over decades, there has been a rapid development in robotics, as a result of technological advancement in industries, military, health sectors and other ways of life [3]. Many types of materials are being used to develop robots so as to be fit and have the capability to tackle things that cannot be solved or are difficult or risky to be solved by human as a result of their limitations in terms of accuracy, speed, size, sense ability and many more [3]. Two wheeled self-balancing (TWSB) mobile robot is a special type of wheeled mobile robot. Signal processing and control techniques are the main factors in which robot performance and stability rely on [4]. In recent years, researchers found two

© Springer International Publishing AG, part of Springer Nature 2018
O. Gervasi et al. (Eds.): ICCSA 2018, LNCS 10961, pp. 683–698, 2018.
https://doi.org/10.1007/978-3-319-95165-2_48

wheeled self-balancing robots to be a good area of research due to its characteristics in terms of non-linearity, instability, having multiple variables, and strong coupling [5]. Main focus of this research project is to develop TWSB robot which is to be controlled by microcontroller based PID-controller to improve its robustness in terms of stability and navigation. The TWSB robot is inherently unstable and non-linear in nature, which makes it difficult to attain wheel stability by using its own mass is difficult [5]. Moreover, it is not easy to establish the reference tracking control system. Many different types of controllers have been proposed to solve the mentioned problems. However, to maintain the stability and at the same time achieve tracking control to follow the desired path remained an open research question. This states the driving force that motivates the present research. Self-balancing and navigation systems are the main focus in designing control system of TWSB robots including: (1) Achieving effective stability; (2) improving speed of response; (3) Maintaining steady state error; and (4) Preventing excessive oscillation, fluctuations, and vibration of the robot.

Many researches were conducted to come up with appropriate mathematical model, and to conduct practical work by developing prototype to improve the TWSV robot efficiency. Thus, this research proposed PID-controller for stabilizing and tracking reference control. The optimum gains of PID controller will be determined so as to achieve better performance. This because the excellent performance of PID controller defends on its gains. Two wheeled commercial human vehicles such as SEGWAY [6], NBot [7], JOE [8] are already in existence. However, high-tech and high quality sophisticated components were used to come up with these final products, making them scarce, costly and unaffordable. This research project seeks to develop a prototype from off-the-shelves components in order to cut down cost and make it available and affordable. The scope of this research is focused on the assembling of TWSB robot and its kinematics mathematical modelling. It also includes designing and running of Arduino-based PID controller on the assembled Robot.

The rest of this paper is organized as follow: Sect. 2 presents related works. Section 3 presents mathematical modelling and simulation. Section 4 presents proposed method. Section 5 presents obtained results and following by discussion. Finally, Sect. 6 concludes this work.

2   Related Works

The TWSV robot is an attractive mechanism made up of base which is referred to as cart, and wheels. It is characterized by rotating and translating on a plane surface, in some cases with a swinging member, in which it is center of mass situated just above its pivot axis and also it passes through the center of the wheel. Such kind of robots are employed as vehicle, e.g. Segway [6], telepresence Double, and also for testing techniques of unstable system as a research platform [9]. The basic idea for a TWSB robot is to drive the bikes, in the direction that the upper part of the robot is getting down. While that robot is moving, it can stay under its center of gravity, then the robot remains balanced [10]. The NBot was built by NASA in 2003, by using commercially available inertial sensor (piezo-electric gyroscope and ADXL202 accelerometer), and view information from the motor encoder to balance the system. The two wheels inverted pendulum models have drawn much attention in the area of control theory and engineering, due to been nonlinear and understated with inherent unstable dynamics [11]. Alternative techniques, including controlled Lagrangians [12], adaptive, and passivity-based techniques [13], are among the popular methods for controlling this under actuated mechanical systems.

The state observer based on adaptive fuzzy controller was proposed by [14], with robust techniques which ensure the asymptotic stability of the system. Fang et al. [15] presented fuzzy immune PD-controller for attainting stability of TWSB robot, Experimental results prove that it has higher performance in terms of low overshoot and low settling time than the conventional fuzzy PD-controller. Short et al. [16] studied the PID control algorithm for controlling two wheeled robot, by taking tilt angle and speed of the motors as the input parameters, in order to achieve stability and navigation. In conventional models of two wheeled self-balancing robot nonlinear terms are usually ignored, nevertheless it has significant effect on the dynamics of robot. The utilization of using accelerometer and gyroscope to measure tilt angle and fed into Kalman filter is investigated in [17]. The proposed controller is PID. The HC-05 Bluetooth module is used to navigate the robot wirelessly. Tsai and Tsai [18] presented a system using a technique of dividing the system into two subsystems, a rotation and inverted pendulum. Two intelligent adaptive fuzzy wavelet neural network (FWNN) controllers were proposed in achieving the stability, and tacking system. Through simulation FWNN proved to be robust and effective, but there is need for real time experiment to validate that. Goher and Tokhi [19] presented a unique system of two-wheel self-balancing robot with additional degree of freedom in vertical direction for the purpose of supporting things at different heights. Lagrangian method was used to derive the special equation of motion. Results from simulation show that stability can be achieved, but there is need for more improvement. Tsai et al. [20] also presents the technique of dividing the entire system into two subsystems, comprising of yaw control and inverted-pendulum. Two-intelligent adaptive fuzzy basis-function network controllers to attain asymptotic stability, achieve tracking and yaw motion control. These were achieved as shown by simulated results, but to validate the technique there is need to develop prototype, and conduct real-time experiment. Jamil et al. [21] aimed at developing an efficient controller for attaining asymptotic stability of TWSB robot in real time. Dual PID controller was proposed as a result of its simplicity and robustness. Simulink and Matlab were used for simulation to compare its performance and that of LQR controller and both proved to be capable of achieving stability and rejection of disturbance, with LQR controller having higher performance in position control. It is however difficult and cumbersome to conduct real-time experiment. Wasif et al. [22] studied and compared different types of PID-controller on a TWSB robot by simulation. Two-level adaptive PD-controller(tuned) was proposed, which proved to have superior performance than those compared with, including P, PD, PI, PID, 2-level adaptive PD (un-tuned). It has higher performance in terms of stability, low overshoot, and capability to resist opposite forces. All of these reviewed researches, have something in common, either in terms of costly materials used or complicated technology utilized. The present research uses affordable and simpler parts. Also an open-source Arduino program is utilized.

3 Mathematical Modelling and Simulation

The TWSB robot is made up of chassis section and wheels section. The chassis (main body) is attached to the motors, the main structure is simplified to modelling. The free-body diagram of TWSB robot is presented in Fig. 1.

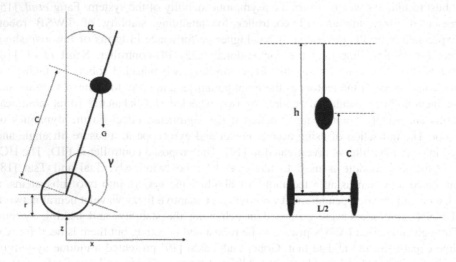

Fig. 1. Free-body diagram of TWSB robot

For ideal modelling of the TWSB robot the following assumptions are considered: (1) The robot chassis and the two wheels are rigid, (2) The left and the right wheels are having the same mass (m) and radius (r), (3) The distance between each wheel to the center of mass are equal ($l_r = l_l = l/2$), (4) There is a true rolling and no slipping during the motion, (5) Internal losses are neglected and (6) Inductance and frictions on the armature are not considered. The TWSB robot is considered to possess three degree of freedom, consisting of yaw angel (γ), tilt angle (α), and transitional motion (x). The two Lagrangian equations are as follows [23]:

$$L = T - V, \tag{1}$$

$$\frac{\partial}{\partial t}\left(\frac{\partial L}{\partial \dot{q}}\right) - \frac{\partial L}{\partial q} = F, \tag{2}$$

where L is the Lagrangian, T is the kinetic Energy, V is the potential energy, F is the forced function, q_x is the generalized coordinates. This robot has been controlled by two inputs torques applied to the motors produced by voltage.

$$T = T_C^L + T_C^R + T_W^L + T_W^R, \tag{3}$$

where T_C^L is the chassis kinetic energy due to linear displacement, T_C^R is the chassis' kinetic energy due to angular displacement, T_W^L is the wheel kinetic energy due to angular displacement, T_W^R wheel kinetic energy due to linear displacement.

$$T_c^R = \frac{1}{2}\left[I_x\dot{\alpha}^2 + I_y\dot{\gamma}_y^2 \sin \alpha^2 + I_z\gamma^2 \cos \alpha^2\right] \tag{4}$$

$$T_w^R = \frac{1}{2}Mr^2\left[\dot{\alpha}_r^2 + \dot{\alpha}_l^2\right] + \frac{1}{2}I\left[\dot{\alpha}_r^2 + \dot{\alpha}_l^2\right] \tag{5}$$

and,

$$\alpha_r = x + L\gamma, \alpha_l = x - L\gamma \tag{6}$$

$$\therefore T_w^R = \left(M + \frac{I}{r^2}\right)(\dot{x}^2 + L^2\gamma^2) \tag{7}$$

$$V = M_c g d \cos \alpha + M_c g r \tag{8}$$

From Eq. (1), the Lagrangian equation is as follows:

$$L = \left[M + 2M_w + \frac{2I}{r^2}\right]\ddot{x} - \left[Md^2 + \frac{I_x}{r^2}\right]\ddot{\alpha} + \left[\left(M + \frac{I}{r^2}\right)L^2 + \frac{1}{2}(I_z \cos$$

$$\alpha^2 + I_y \sin \alpha^2 + M_c d \sin \alpha^2)]\dot{\gamma} + M_c d \cos \alpha \dot{x}\dot{\alpha} - [M_c g d \cos \alpha + M_c g r] \tag{9}$$

For x-coordinate, we have the following equations:

$$\left(\frac{\partial L}{\partial \dot{x}}\right) = \left[M_c + 2M + \frac{2I}{r^2}\right]\dot{x} + M_c d\dot{\alpha} \cos \alpha \tag{10}$$

$$\frac{d}{dt}\left(\frac{\partial L}{\partial \dot{x}}\right) = \left[M_c + 2M + \frac{2I}{r^2}\right]\ddot{x} - M_c d\dot{\alpha}^2 \sin \alpha + M_c d\ddot{\alpha} \cos \alpha \tag{11}$$

$$\frac{\partial L}{\partial x} = 0 \tag{12}$$

$$\therefore \left[M_c + 2M + \frac{2I}{r^2}\right]\ddot{x} - M_c d\dot{\alpha}^2 \sin \alpha + M_c d\ddot{\alpha} \cos \alpha = \frac{\tau_r + \tau_l}{r} \tag{13}$$

$$\ddot{x} = \frac{\left[\frac{\tau_r + \tau_l}{r} - M_c d\ddot{\alpha} \cos \alpha + M_c d\dot{\alpha}^2 \sin \alpha\right]}{\left[M_c + 2M + \frac{2I}{r^2}\right]} \tag{14}$$

For α-coordinate, we have the following equations:

$$\left[M_c d^2 + I_x\right]\ddot{\alpha} + M_c d\ddot{x} \cos \alpha - \left[M_c d^2 + I_y - I_z\right]\dot{\gamma}^2 - M_c g d \sin \alpha = -[\tau_r + \tau_l] \quad (15)$$

From Eqs. 11 and 12, for the $\ddot{\alpha}$ can be the subject of the formula as:

$$\ddot{\alpha} = \left[\left(M_c + 2M + \frac{2I}{r^2}\right) + M_c d \cos \alpha\right][\tau_r + \tau_l] / \left\{\left[M_c + 2M + \frac{2I}{r^2}\right]\right.$$
$$[M_c d^2 + I_x] - M_c^2 d^2 \cos \alpha\} - M_c^2 d^2 \dot{\alpha}^2 \cos \alpha \sin \alpha /$$
$$\left\{\left[M_c + 2M + \frac{2I}{r^2}\right][M_c d^2 + I_x] - M_c^2 d^2 \cos \alpha\right\} + [M_c d^2 + I_y - I_z] / \left\{\left[M_c + 2M + \frac{2I}{r^2}\right]\right.$$
$$[M_c d^2 + I_x] - M_c^2 d^2 \cos \alpha\} - M_c g d \sin \alpha \left(M_c + 2M + \frac{2I}{r^2}\right) / \left\{\left[M_c + 2M + \frac{2I}{r^2}\right]\right.$$
$$[M_c d^2 + I_x] - M_c^2 d^2 \cos \alpha\}$$

$$(16)$$

Simplify to get:

$$\ddot{\alpha} = \frac{[M_c d^2 + I_y - I_z][M_c r^2 + 2M r^2 + 2I] \cos \alpha \sin \alpha}{[M_c rd \sin \alpha]^2 + ([M_c + 2M]r^2 + 2I)I_x + 2M_c d^2 (Mr^2 + I)}\dot{\gamma}^2$$
$$- \frac{M_c^2 d^2 r^2 \cos \alpha \sin \alpha}{[M_c rd \sin \alpha]^2 + ([M_c + 2M]r^2 + 2I)I_x + 2M_c d^2 (Mr^2 + I)}\dot{\alpha}^2$$
$$+ \frac{[M_c r^2 + 2M r^2 + 2I]M_c g d \sin \alpha)}{[M_c rd \sin \alpha]^2 + ([M_c + 2M]r^2 + 2I)I_x + 2M_c d^2 (Mr^2 + I)}$$
$$- \frac{[M_c r^2 + 2M r^2 + 2I]M_c dr \cos \alpha)}{[M_c rd \sin \alpha]^2 + ([M_c + 2M]r^2 + 2I)I_x + 2M_c d^2 (Mr^2 + I)}[\tau_r + \tau_l]$$

$$(17)$$

For x coordinate, the Lagrangian from Eq. (9) is as follows:

$$\ddot{\alpha} = \frac{\left[\frac{\tau_r + \tau_l}{r} + M_c d\dot{\alpha}^2 \sin \alpha - [M_c + 2M + \frac{2I}{r^2}]\right]\ddot{x}}{M_c d \cos \alpha} \quad (18)$$

By substituting Eqs. (16) in (12), then it gives Eq. (19) as follow:

$$[M_c d^2 + I_x]\frac{\left[\frac{\tau_r + \tau_l}{r} + M_c d\dot{\alpha}^2 \sin \alpha - [M_c + 2M + \frac{2I}{r^2}]\right]\ddot{x}}{M_c d \cos \alpha} + M_c d \cos \alpha \ddot{x}$$
$$- [M_c d^2 + I_y - I_z] \cos \alpha \sin \alpha \dot{\gamma}^2 - M_c g d \sin \alpha = -(\tau_r + \tau_l) \quad (19)$$

Collecting terms with $\ddot{x}$, and making it the subject of the following formula:

$$\ddot{x} = \frac{M_c dr \cos \alpha [M_c d^2 + I_y - I_z] \cos \alpha \sin \alpha}{[M_c d^2 + I_x][M_c r^2 + 2Mr^2 + 2I] - [M_c dr \cos \alpha]^2} \dot{\gamma}^2 - \frac{M_c^2 d^2 g r^2 \cos \alpha \sin \alpha}{[M_c d^2 + I_x][M_c r^2 + 2Mr^2 + 2I] - [M_c dr \cos \alpha]^2}$$

$$+ \frac{r^2 [M_c d^2 + I_x] M_c d \sin \alpha}{[M_c d^2 + I_x][M_c r^2 + 2Mr^2 + 2I] - [M_c dr \cos \alpha]^2} \dot{\alpha}^2 + \frac{r^2 [M_c d^2 + I_x + M_c dr \cos \alpha]}{[M_c d^2 + I_x][M_c r^2 + 2Mr^2 + 2I] - [M_c dr \cos \alpha]^2} (\tau_r + \tau_l)$$

$$(20)$$

For γ-coordinate: The Lagrangian is given in Eq. (21) as follow:

$$\left[2\left(M + \frac{I}{r^2} \right) L^2 + I_y \sin \alpha^2 + I_z (\cos \alpha)^2 + M_c d^2 \sin \alpha \right] \ddot{\gamma}$$

$$+ 2\left[[M_c d^2 + I_y - I_z] \cos \alpha \sin \alpha \right] \dot{\gamma} \dot{\alpha} = \frac{L}{r} (\tau_r + \tau_l) \tag{21}$$

Simplified further to make $\ddot{\gamma}$ the subject of the following formula:

$$\ddot{\gamma} = \frac{L}{2(r[M + \frac{I}{r^2}]L^2 + I_y \sin \alpha^2 + I_z(\cos \alpha)^2 + M_c d^2 \sin \alpha)} (\tau_r + \tau_l)$$

$$- \frac{2[[M_c d^2 + I_y - I_z] \cos \alpha \sin \alpha] \dot{\gamma} \dot{\alpha}}{2([M + \frac{I}{r^2}]L^2 + I_y \sin \alpha^2 + I_z(\cos \alpha)^2 + M_c d^2 \sin \alpha)} \tag{22}$$

To linearize the non-linear model, it is assumed that the robot conditions are stabilized at the zero tilt angle. For $\alpha = 0$, which implies that $\sin \alpha = \alpha, \cos \alpha = 1, \dot{\gamma} = 0,$ and $\dot{\alpha} = 0$ [24]. Therefore Eqs. (17), (20), and (22) become:

$$\ddot{x} = \frac{M_c^2 d^2 g r^2}{[M_c d^2 + I_x][M_c r^2 + 2Mr^2 + 2I] - [M_c dr]^2} \alpha + \frac{r(M_c d^2 + I_x + M_c dr)}{[M_c d^2 + I_x][M_c r^2 + 2Mr^2 + 2I] - [M_c dr]^2} (\tau_r + \tau_l) \tag{23}$$

$$\ddot{\alpha} = \frac{[M_c r^2 + 2Mr^2 2I] M_c g d}{[(M_c 2M)r^2 + 2I]I_x + 2M_c d^2 (Mr^2 + I)} \alpha$$

$$- \frac{[M_c r^2 + 2I] + M_c dr}{[(M_c 2M)r^2 + 2I]I_x + 2M_c d^2 (Mr^2 + I)} (\tau_r + \tau_l) \tag{24}$$

$$\ddot{\gamma} = \frac{L}{r(2[M + \frac{I}{r^2}]L^2 + I_z)} (\tau_r - \tau_l) \tag{25}$$

From Eqs. (23), (24), and (25) after substitution of robot parameters, Eqs. (26), (27), and (28) are obtained:

$$\ddot{x} = 0.188\alpha + 3.247(\tau_r + \tau_l) \tag{26}$$

$$\ddot{\alpha} = 5.1\alpha - 70(\tau_r + \tau_l) \tag{27}$$

$$\ddot{y} = 12.85(\tau_r - \tau_l) \tag{28}$$

Where

$$\begin{bmatrix} \dot{x} \\ \dot{\alpha} \\ \dot{y} \\ \ddot{x} \\ \ddot{\alpha} \\ \ddot{y} \end{bmatrix} = \begin{bmatrix} 0 & 0 & 0 & 1 & 0 & 0 \\ 0 & 0 & 0 & 0 & 1 & 0 \\ 0 & 0 & 0 & 0 & 0 & 1 \\ 0 & 0.188 & 0 & 0 & 0 & 0 \\ 0 & 5.1 & 0 & 0 & 0 & 0 \\ 0 & 0 & 0 & 0 & 0 & 0 \end{bmatrix} \begin{bmatrix} x \\ \alpha \\ y \\ \dot{x} \\ \dot{\alpha} \\ \dot{y} \end{bmatrix} + \begin{bmatrix} 0 & 0 \\ 0 & 0 \\ 0 & 0 \\ 3.247 & 3.247 \\ -70 & -70 \\ 12.85 & -12.85 \end{bmatrix} \begin{bmatrix} \tau_r \\ \tau_l \end{bmatrix} \tag{29}$$

These Eqs. (24), (25), and (26) are transformed into state-space form based on the TWSB robot parameters in Table 1.

Table 1. TWSB robot parameters

Parameter	Symbol	Quantity	Unit
Height of the chassis	h	0.08	m
Width of the chassis	w	0.147	m
Distance between wheels	L	0.082	m
Diameter of wheel	d	0.083	m
Mass of the chassis	M_c	0.305	kg
Mass of wheel	M	0.051	kg
Center of mass	C	0.04	m
Acceleration due to gravity	g	9.81	m/s
Moment of inertia of chassis wrt. x-axis	I_x	0.07124 E-3	kgm^2
Moment of inertia of chassis wrt. z-axis	I_z	0.725E-3	kgm^2
Moment of inertia of the wheel	I	0.044E-3	kgm^2

4 Proposed Method

This section presents PID controller methodology for TWSB robot development.

4.1 PID Controller

The main controlling system of the mobile robot adopts PID control. The mobile robot uses sensor feedback data as PID control variable to calculate an output response to do correction and follow the predefined trajectory. The equation of PID controller is as follow [25]:

$$\text{Output} = P + I + D = K_p e(t) + K_i \int e(t)dt + K_d \frac{d}{dt}e(t), \tag{30}$$

where P is proportional term which accounts for present error.

$$K_p e(t) = K_p * (\text{setpoint} - \text{input data}) \qquad (31)$$

The I is an integrate term that accounts the total error history.

$$K_i \int e(t)dt = K_i [(\text{error})_1 + (\text{error})_2 + (\text{error})_3 + \ldots \qquad (32)$$

The D stands for derivative which accounts for future error through differential/rate changes.

$$\text{Differential error} = K_d * \left[\frac{\partial}{\partial t} error \right], \qquad (33)$$

where K_p, K_i and K_d denotes the coefficients of the proportional, integral and derivative terms.

This equation is computed frequently through microcontroller at a very high frequency. Thus several addresses need to be made such as sampling time, derivative error, tuning, reset windup and on/off.

4.2   Methodology for TWSB Robot Development

There are two main electronic systems that were used to conduct this research, first one is the robot itself as an independent unit, sourcing its power from batteries embedded on its chassis, and second unit is an electronic system working also independently for measuring instantaneous coordinates and orientation in terms of degree/second and relative acceleration (g-force), it made up of Arduino Uno, MPU6050 and wiring system, connected directly to the PC. The parts that are procured and assembled to develop the TWSB are as follows: (1) Arduino Leonardo (Microcontroller), (2) MPU6050, (3) HC-60, (4) Arduino Uno, (5) A388, (6) Batteries, (7) Robot chassis, (8) Wheels and (9) Stepper motors. The Arduino Leonardo developed based on ATmega32U4 with hj344 electronic board that has the capabilities to handle routine operations required to achieve controlling and navigation of TWSB robot, processing data, communication between PC, sensors and actuators is used. It contains twenty-three digital Input/output pins for sending and receiving data, a 16 MHz crystal oscillator, a micro USB connection port, a power jack, an ICSP header, and a reset button. It has everything needed for supporting the controller.

The HJ board was used to provide a means for connecting stepper motors, H-bridges, power source, MPU6050, Bluetooth module (HC-06) with the microcontroller. The MPU 6050 used is a special sensor that integrates a MEMS accelerometer and a MEMS gyroscope in a single chip. It has so many advantages like been inexpensive, require low power, and having high efficiency. It incorporates 3-axis accelerometer and a 3-axis gyroscope, together with onboard digital motion processor (DMP), it processes 6-axis motion fusion algorithm. The MPU configuration is described in Fig. 2.

The Accelerometer is used to measure the acceleration relative to the free fall. Gyroscope is used to measure the rate of change of angle around a given axis, with respect to the orientation of world coordinate frame. The orientation of the Gyroscope and Accelerometer is shown in Fig. 3.

Fig. 2. MPU configuration

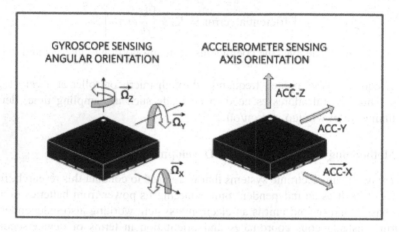

Fig. 3. Gyroscope/Accelerometer orientations

The chassis used is a robot frame made up of metal and plastic, upper part is cuboid in shape, used for mounting all the parts of the robot, consisting of Arduino board, power source (batteries), it also provides support for the mother board on which MPU6050, HC-06, and two H-bridges were mounted. Lower of it serve as a support to left and right stepper motors. The chassis make a robot rigid and one piece. The Nema 17 stepper motor is used to generate the required torque, for achieving stability and navigation, this stepper motor has the characteristics of holding torque of 16Ncm and step angle of 3.75°. The HC-06 is the Bluetooth module used to communicate between android and Arduino Leonardo. It serves as a serial device. Its working independently, but Arduino is the source of power. Pairing take place between Bluetooth module and android only, without Arduino been part of it. Therefore, there may be a scenario where by Bluetooth is connected to the android successful, but may code might not work.

The A0383 is a micro stepper driver is used for controlling the motors in this research project. It has built-in translator which enable motor to be control with just 2 pins from the controller, one pin for controlling the direction and the other for controlling the steps of the motor. The A4988 micro stepping driver gives the following step resolutions, full step, half step, quarter step, eight step, and sixteenth step, it also contains potentiometer for controlling output current, excessive temperature thermal shutdown, and crossover current protection. The picture of the developed TWSB robot is shown in Fig. 4.

Fig. 4. TWSB robot

5   Results and Discussion

This section presents the experimental results for stabilization and trajectory tracking controls. The experiment is divided into two parts. First part dealt with dynamic stability of the robot, aimed for attaining upright stability. While the second part dealt with navigation at the same time dynamic stability was achieved.

5.1   Stabilization

Optimum set of gains for dynamic stability of TWSB robot were determined here. The K_p and K_d gains play the dominant role in stabilizing the robot [15]. In this contest, at the range of $K_d = 20$ to 25, and $K_p = 0.1$ to 0.3, the TWSB robot can dynamically be stabilized with fluctuations, and generating vibration over time.

Both Figs. 5 and 6 show that robot cannot be stabilized with this sets of gains ($K_d = 23$ and $K_p = 0.22$, and $K_d = 25$ and $K_p = 0.22$ respectively) as there is reciprocating motion on the x-axis, which leads to vibration, and shock on the robot, making it difficult to maintain orientation.

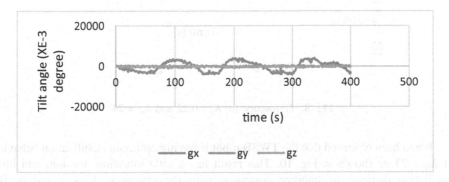

Fig. 5. Gyroscope for $K_d = 23$ and $K_p = 0.22$

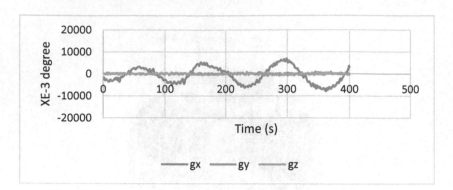

Fig. 6. Gyroscope for $K_d = 25$ and $K_p = 0.22$

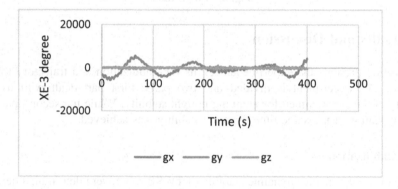

Fig. 7. Gyroscope for $K_p = 0.2$ and $K_d = 24$

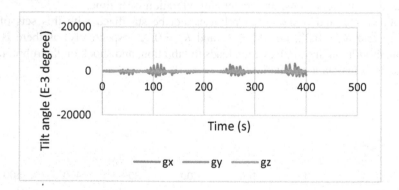

Fig. 8. Gyroscope for $K_p = 0.22$ and $K_d = 24$

It had been observed that the TWSB robot is having optimum stabilization behavior at $K_d = 24$ as shown in Fig. 10. This result has a little vibration, tension, and little oscillation distance to stabilize compared with the results in Figs. 5 and 6. By

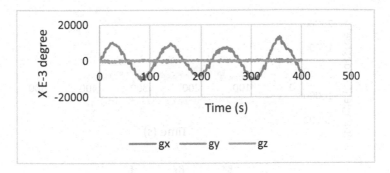

Fig. 9. Gyroscope for $K_p = 0.3$ and $K_d = 24$

comparing Figs. 7, 8 and 9 it can be seen that the optimum gains are $K_d = 24$ and $K_p = 0.22$, although all the other gains in Figs. 7 and 9 can stabilize the robot with fluctuation in orientation, tension, vibration, and large reciprocating displacement to keep it in upright position. The TWSB robot achieved dynamic stability with smooth navigation and less vibration as shown in Fig. 8. Also it demonstrates some level of robustness by withstanding a small external force (finger tap).

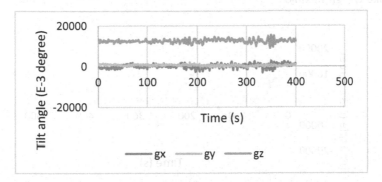

Fig. 10. Gyroscope for turning right

5.2   Navigation

Navigation was successfully run, using the optimum set of gains. The optimum gain values are $K_p = 0.22$, and $K_d = 24$ as indicated in Fig. 8. The robot can successfully run without any slipping or skidding of wheels. The three common navigation characteristics that are run are as follows: turning RIGHT, turning LEFT, and running FORWARD.

Figures 10 and 11 show the robot is stable on z-axis (at upright position), and gz shows the rate at which the robot is turning right and left respectively. Meanwhile there is no change of position along x and y-axes, which implies there no vibrations and tensions.

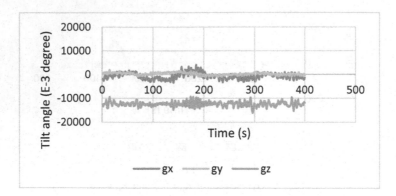

Fig. 11. Gyroscope for turning left

Robot runs forward with reasonable speed, while maintaining upright stability, as shown by Fig. 12. The fluctuation along x-axis shows the quantity and nature of its speed. The TWSB robot is speeding up, while balancing the mass on its center, which leads to fluctuation. With these presented results, we believed that developing TWSB robot, using PID-controller, based on Arduino technology is feasible, to cut down cost, and make design flexible.

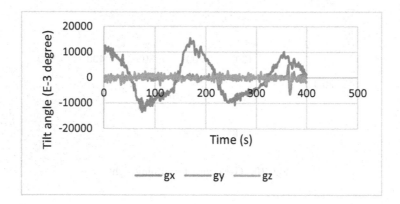

Fig. 12. Gyroscope for forward run

6   Conclusion

This paper has presented a design and implement Proportional Integral Derivative (PID) controller on Two-wheeled self-balance (TWSB) robot. It was illustrated that the TWSB robot that is capable of balancing on its two wheels and can follow desired trajectory is realized. This was done using Arduino, and other off-the-shelves parts to make it affordable, easier for maintenance and improvement. The robot is capable to maintain body's upright stability automatically and follow trajectory tracking path by receiving signal via Bluetooth successfully. The mathematical model was first developed using Lagrangian method. The PID controller was designed and developed in real-time. The importance of manipulating the PID gains to the performance of controller has been shown experimentally.

References

1. Raibert, M.H.: Legged Robots That Balance. MIT Press, Cambridge (1986)
2. Hamza, M.F., Yap, H.J., Choudhury, I.A.: Genetic algorithm and particle swarm optimization based cascade interval type 2 fuzzy PD controller for rotary inverted pendulum system. Math. Probl. Eng. **2015** (2015)
3. Tzafestas, S.G.: Introduction to Mobile Robot Control. Elsevier, New York (2013)
4. Ghani, N.A., Yatim, N.M., Azmi, N.A.: Comparative assessment for two wheels inverted pendulum mobile robot using robust control. In: 2010 International Conference on Control Automation and Systems (ICCAS), pp. 562–567. IEEE, October 2010
5. Wu, J., Zhang, W.: Design of fuzzy logic controller for two-wheeled self-balancing robot. In: 2011 6th International Forum on Strategic Technology (IFOST), vol. 2, pp. 1266–1270. IEEE, August 2011
6. Fierro, R., Lewis, F.L., Lowe, A.: Hybrid control for a class of underactuated mechanical systems. IEEE Trans. Syst. Man Cybern. Part A Syst. Hum. **29**(6), 649–654 (1999)
7. Juang, H.S., Lurrr, K.Y.: Design and control of a two-wheel self-balancing robot using the arduino microcontroller board. In: 2013 10th IEEE International Conference on Control and Automation (ICCA), pp. 634–639. IEEE, June 2013
8. Grasser, F.: D'arrigo, A., Colombi, S., Rufer, A.C.: JOE: a mobile, inverted pendulum. IEEE Trans. Ind. Electron. **49**(1), 107–114 (2002)
9. Akesson, J., Blomdell, A., Braun, R.: Design and control of YAIP—an inverted pendulum on two wheels robot. In: 2006 IEEE Conference on Computer Aided Control System Design, 2006 IEEE International Conference on Control Applications, 2006 IEEE International Symposium on Intelligent Control, pp. 2178–2183. IEEE, October 2006
10. Anderson, D.P.: NBot Balancing Robot, a two wheel balancing robot. 19 May 2003 [2000-07-10] (2003). http://www.geolog.smu.edu/~dpa-www/robo/nbot/index.html
11. Huang, J., Guan, Z.H., Matsuno, T., Fukuda, T., Sekiyama, K.: Sliding-mode velocity control of mobile-wheeled inverted-pendulum systems. IEEE Trans. Rob. **26**(4), 750–758 (2010)
12. Bloch, A.M., Leonard, N.E., Marsden, J.E.: Stabilization of the pendulum on a rotor arm by the method of controlled Lagrangians. In: Proceedings of the 1999 IEEE International Conference on Robotics and Automation, vol. 1, pp. 500–505. IEEE (1999)
13. Fantoni, I., Lozano, R., Spong, M.W.: Energy based control of the pendubot. IEEE Trans. Autom. Control **45**(4), 725–729 (2000)
14. Wu, T.S., Karkoub, M., Weng, C.C., Yu, W.S.: Trajectory tracking for uncertainty time delayed-state self-balancing train vehicles using observer-based adaptive fuzzy control. Inf. Sci. **324**, 1–22 (2015)
15. Fang, J., Liu, J.Y., Li, W.: Two-wheeled self-balancing robot systems using fuzzy immune algorithm. In: Advanced Materials Research, vol. 912, pp. 1037–1040. Trans Tech Publications (2014)
16. Short, A.R., Sayidmarie, O.K., Agouri, S.A., Tokhi, M.O., Goher, K.M., Almeshal, A.: Real time PID control of a two-wheeled robot. In: Adaptive Mobile Robotics, pp. 73–80. World Scientific (2012)

17. Valencia, J.A.B., Pasaye, J.J.R., Bernai, R.G.: Instrumentation and wireless control for the self-balancing mobile robot on two wheels. In: 2014 IEEE International Autumn Meeting on Power, Electronics and Computing (ROPEC), pp. 1–5. IEEE, November 2014
18. Tsai, C.C., Tsai, C.H.: Adaptive robust motion control using fuzzy wavelet neural networks for uncertain electric two-wheeled robotic vehicles. In: 2013 International Conference on System Science and Engineering (ICSSE), pp. 229–234. IEEE, July 2013
19. Goher, K.M., Tokhi, M.O.: Modeling and control of a two wheeled machine: a genetic algorithm-based optimization approach. J. Sel. Areas Robot. Control (JSRC), 17–22 (2010)
20. Tsai, C.C., Lin, S.C., Lin, B.C.: Intelligent adaptive motion control using fuzzy basis function networks for self-balancing two-wheeled transporters. In: 2010 IEEE International Conference on Fuzzy Systems (FUZZ), pp. 1–6. IEEE, July 2010
21. Jamil, O., Jamil, M., Ayaz, Y., Ahmad, K.: Modeling, control of a two-wheeled self-balancing robot. In: 2014 International Conference on Robotics and Emerging Allied Technologies in Engineering (iCREATE), pp. 191–199. IEEE, April 2014
22. Wasif, A., Raza, D., Rasheed, W., Farooq, Z., Ali, S.Q.: Design and implementation of a two wheel self-balancing robot with a two level adaptive control. In: ICDIM, pp. 187–193, September 2013
23. Isa, A.I., Hamza, M.F.: Effect of sampling time on PID controller design for a heat exchanger system. In: 2014 IEEE 6th International Conference on Adaptive Science and Technology (ICAST), pp. 1–8. IEEE, October 2014
24. Magaji, N., Hamza, M.F., Dan-Isa, A.: Comparison of GA and LQR tuning of static VAR compensator for damping oscillations. Int. J. Adv. Eng. Technol. 2, 594 (2012)
25. Hamza, M.F., Yap, H.J., Choudhury, I.A.: Recent advances on the use of meta-heuristic optimization algorithms to optimize the type-2 fuzzy logic systems in intelligent control. Neural Comput. Appl. 1–21 (2015)

PID Based Design and Development
of a Mobile Robot Using Microcontroller

Mukhtar Fatihu Hamza[1,2](✉), Joshua Lee Zhiyung[2],
Aminu Yahaya Zimit[1,2], Sani Danjuma[3], Erfan Rohadi[4],
Silfia Andini[5], and Tutut Herawan[4,6,7]

[1] Department of Mechatronics Engineering, Bayero University,
Kano 3011, Nigeria
emukhtarfah@gmail.com
[2] Department of Mechanical Engineering, University of Malaya,
Kuala Lumpur, Malaysia
[3] Department of Computer Science, Northwest University, Kano, Nigeria
[4] State Polytechnic of Malang, Malang, Indonesia
[5] Universitas Putra Indonesia YPTK, Padang, Sumatera Barat, Indonesia
[6] Universitas Negeri Yogyakarta, Yogyakarta, Indonesia
[7] Universitas Teknologi Yogyakarta, Yogyakarta, Indonesia

Abstract. Human labor work has been increasingly being replaced by robots to do works for decades, especially those that are tedious and risky. Moreover, works done by robotics have less error prone and higher efficiency. This paper presents a design and develops microcontroller based mobile robot (MR). The robot is based on a microcontroller, acting as the brain, which contain a series of programs that interpret its surrounding through input data from the sensors and maneuver through the limited data obtained while avoiding obstacle. The prototype was able to differentiate surrounding and maneuver to desired location smoothly according to predefined path while simultaneously sensing for obstacle to avoid. The Proportional–Integral–Derivative (PID) based program on the microcontroller was critical because it needs to handle the sensitive sensors feedback and sent correct command to respond to the surrounding while at the same time having the correct arrangement and format. The developed MR can be controlled autonomously, following the path by varying the current fed to the motor through error correction, towards desired location while simultaneously sensing for obstacle as far as 400 cm ahead. Through decision making the speed of the MR will adjust itself and will put stop moving when the obstacle was 5 cm ahead. Based on the experiment the advantage and disadvantage of the current development were realized for further development.

Keywords: Mobile robot · Microcontroller · PID controller · Sensor

1 Introduction

Over the years, development of the human society has been greatly improved with robotics as a dominant contributor. It is a field that requires combination of effort of a variety of scientific areas such as mechanical, electrical, control and software

© Springer International Publishing AG, part of Springer Nature 2018
O. Gervasi et al. (Eds.): ICCSA 2018, LNCS 10961, pp. 699–716, 2018.
https://doi.org/10.1007/978-3-319-95165-2_49

engineers [1, 2]. The mobile robot (MR) was firstly brought to market in 1950's by Barrett Electronics Corp (Northbrook, IL) and at the time it was simply a tow truck that follows a wire in the floor instead of a rail [3]. The earliest guided MR is line following MR. This is a type of MR that can follow a specific predetermined path by the user which acting as a guidance device where it can be simple physical line on the floor or complex invisible lines like a magnetic field embedded on the travelling horizon. This means the robot has the ability to follow path by sensing it and manoeuvre itself to stay on predefined path, correcting wrong moves constantly through embedded feedback mechanism to travel to its destination [4]. This type of MR may vary from simple low cost line sensing circuit to expansive vision systems. Although they may not be glamorous of robots, but their works are often essential to smooth running of factories, offices, hospitals and even houses. The usage of line following robot (LFR) is increasing day by day. From industrial point of view LFR has been implemented in semi and fully autonomous plants. The application in these environments usually functions as materials carrier to deliver products from one point to another where rail or conveyor solutions are not very suitable. The automation is very much desired due to the capability to always run non-stop while not getting tired in all sorts of environment as well as accelerate automatic transportation without any complaint [5, 6].

Punetha *et al.* developed MR in health care management system [7]. They described the techniques for analysing, designing, controlling and improving the health care management system using a LFR. In another side of health care services, MR has been proposed to be elderly-care. This research is done by Takuma *et al.* [8]. They proposed a MR that can detect human fall and respond by reporting to observers. Singh *et al.* [9] introduces a cell-phone detection based LFR. They presented a real time detection of mobile phone in restricted area using MR. The LFR uses mobile transmission detector to sense the presence of activated mobile phone from distance of one and a half metre and the robot will travel and stop at the location of the activated mobile phone. There are many reasons which yield to the creation of MR around the world. Most of them are to overcome the logistic problems that often occur in workplaces and to make improvement to the facilities provided in the workplaces [10]. In industries or factories, they can ease the physical strain on human workers by performing tiring tasks, such as lifting heavy materials, more efficiently with no signs of fatigue creeping in or dealing with continuous repetition of works without getting tired [4]. They can endure greater work load than human workers and their movements can be tracked and timed at all times. Moreover, they are being developed to be autonomous and being applied to be fit and forget as little supervision needed on them [10]. As a result, MRs have been increasingly replacing human labour to do their works. However, these MRs are not universal and bounded with limitations. Different types of MRs have been developed according to the working environment and their required work done. Meanwhile MRs are very well developed in industrial field and the like with similar environment, they are not very well developed in agricultural field. This is due to agriculture field having a completely different environment than factories and job scope. Thus, a study is needed to apply MRs to agricultural environment to perform works. This states the motivation of this work. Furthermore, the MR should always be in stable and functional condition.

This study develops a stable and useful guided MR, with proper study and accurate model regarding electronics and steering mechanism. After model design and improving performance, proper stability analysis was presented in this work. The line sensing process of the developed MR has a high resolution and high robustness. Despite the complexity of the LFR, the developed MR has the capability to sense tags to perform works accordingly, navigate junctions and decide or which junction to turn/ignore or having requirement to perform a 90° turn and also junction counting capabilities.

The rest of this paper is organized as follow: Sect. 2 presents proposed method. Section 3 presents obtained results and following by discussion. Finally, Sect. 4 concludes this work.

2 Proposed Method

Any embedded application generally involves a number of functions. The proposed smart and intelligent LFR consists of few basic parts which are sensors, comparator and actuators. Common LFRs use reflective optical infrared (IR) sensors to sense line which consist of an array of diodes in pair which one of them, light emitting diode (LED), sends ray while the other, light dependent resistor (LDR), receive the reflection ray. The output of the sensors is an analogue signal which depends on the amount of light reflected back to LDR due to the varying of the LDR resistance. The signal is given to the comparator to translate into digital binary system language which then fed to the logic circuit whose output is then passed through a diode matrix and then given to the driver circuits and finally generating instructions to driving motors. In this project, similar system is used, with the modification of orientation of the sensors, using raw data to differentiate colour and wireless output module for data collection. In addition,

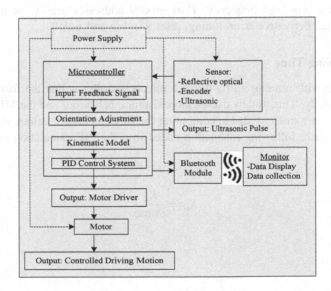

Fig. 1. Proposed system flow

ultrasonic sensor is added as added feature for obstacle detection and executes collision avoidance and rerouting the MR. The proposed system flow is shown in Fig. 1.

2.1 PID Controller

The main controlling system of the propose MR adopt PID control. The MR uses sensor feedback data as PID control variable to calculate an output response to do correction and follow the predefined path. The equation is given as follow [11]:

$$Output = P + I + D = K_p e(t) + K_i \int e(t)dt + K_d \frac{d}{dt}e(t) \tag{1}$$

where P is proportional term which accounts for present error.

$$K_p e(t) = K_p * (\text{setpoint} - \text{input data}) \tag{2}$$

The I is integrate term that accounts the total error history.

$$K_i \int e(t)dt = K_i[(\text{error})_1 + (\text{error})_2 + (\text{error})_3 + \ldots \tag{3}$$

The D stands for derivative which accounts for future error through differential/rate changes.

$$\text{differential error} = K_d * \left[\frac{\partial}{\partial t}\text{error}\right] \tag{4}$$

The K_p, K_i and K_d denotes the coefficients of the proportional, integral and derivative terms respectively. This equation is computed frequently through microcontroller at a very high frequency. Thus several addresses need to be made such as sampling time, derivative error, tuning, reset windup and on/off.

2.2 Sampling Time

The problem with running a PID through microcontroller is that the function will be called irregularly. This usually causes inconsistence behaviour and the MR will not be stable. Thus extra math needed in computing the time dependent values, derivative and integral. As such, following calculation added into the PID calculation [12].

$$K_i = K_i(\partial \text{time}) \tag{5}$$

$$K_d = \frac{K_d}{\partial \text{time}} \tag{6}$$

2.3 Debugging Derivative Error

Whenever there is a change in set point, especially during starting point from zero to a set point value, there will be a disturbance in the derivative, which causes instantaneous change in error, end up a very big undesired number. This can be debugged by removing the set point variable from the derivative equation [13].

$$\frac{\partial}{\partial t}error = \frac{\partial setpoint}{\partial t} - \frac{\partial input}{\partial t} = -\frac{\partial input}{\partial t} \qquad (7)$$

2.4 Tuning

It's crucial to be able to tune the PID coefficient to suits different situations. The PID will go wild when there are changes in parameter. The integral coefficient involves the summation of error history, a tune in K_i results in changes in the error history. Thus, modification of the calculation done by including each K_i into the integral instead of outside the integral [12].

$$K_i \int e(t)dt = (K_i * \text{error})_1 + (K_i * \text{error})_2 + (K_i * \text{error})_3 + \ldots \qquad (8)$$

where the desired yaw rate,

$$\gamma_d = \omega = \frac{V_o(1 + S_x) - V_i(1 + S_x)}{d} \qquad (9)$$

$$R_{\text{actual}} = \frac{V_o(1 + S_x) + V_i(1 + S_x)}{V_o(1 + S_x) - V_i(1 + S_x)} \cdot \frac{d}{2} \qquad (10)$$

while tuning the sampling time, the integral and differential coefficient scaled. Thus the coefficient needs to be resized by either multiplying or dividing according to the ratio of sampling time [13].

$$K_i = K_i(\partial \text{sample time}) \qquad (11)$$

$$K_d = \frac{K_d}{\partial \text{sample time}} \qquad (12)$$

2.5 Reset Windup

The microcontroller has no boundary, thus if the PID function runs incrementally, then at some point it will reach point which doesn't compatible with the hardware. Arduino PWM output ranged from 0–255 whereas the microcontroller has no boundary thus it will consider value higher than 255. This will results an unexpected lags in program and damage the microcontroller ports. The solution is to clamp the final output value to be at its max when it's over or min when it's lower by using microcontroller control structure.

Table 1. Comparison between conventional configuration and propose designed configuration

Situation	Conventional	Prototype	Explanation
			Sample design configuration
Cross junction			Sensor 1, 3/4, 6 detects paths, indicating it reached the centre of the cross junction and the control shifted towards decision making in either resuming straight path or self-rotate towards either left or right before resuming PID control. If the MR decision is to turn at the junction, the self-rotation will function until the sensor 1 and 6 detects the path again, indicating that the MR manoeuvred to the left or right path direction. Thus, PID can take over and resume its control over the MR. The conventional method however rely on either time delay which accuracy reduces with drop of battery charges or additional hardware to ratify it reaches the centre of the junction
T-junction (Minor road)			Sensor 2, 3, 4 and 5 detects path, indicating it reaches a split junction, while sensor 2 and 5 still detects path, eventually sensor 3 and 4 will not detect any path as the MR moving forward. This indicate that the MR approaching a T-junction, at the side of minor road, instead of a cross junction. The PID control edge sensing still functions with edge now shifted towards sensor 2 and 5, and later on 1 and 6, until the centre of the MR reaches the split point. Thus the control can be shifted to decision making on path selection and initiate self-rotation until the sensor 1 or 6 detects path, indicating the MR has reached the direction of T-junction main road. At initiation of PID, sensor 1 or 6 is set to temporary removed from the equation for PID to function normally. In conventional design, the sensors face the similar problem with cross junction. In addition, the sensors totally unable to rely on PID control as it approaching the

(*continued*)

Table 1. (*continued*)

Situation	Conventional	Prototype	Explanation
			junction as all the sensors unable to detect any path. This made the PID function unable to control the MR to approach the turning point. Alternative method needed to overcome this issue, with additional parts as a prerequisite
T-junction (main road)			The concept is similar to cross junction. Instead of detecting both side, it only detect one side, indicating the MR approaching a T-junction with the MR at the main road of the T-junction. In this condition, the PID function normally while the sensor 5 is to be temporary subtracted out of equation. When either sensor 1 or 6 detects, PID control is swapped with to decision making of either turning or continue following the main road. When the decision is to manoeuvre towards minor road, the self-rotate initiate and ends in the exact same method as cross junction. Therefore, simplifying the decision making program
Corner			In this situation, the concept adopts the combination of T-junction main and side road concept in detecting the corner path. In this condition, the program straight away jumps to self-rotating function and resumes PID control once sensor 3, 4 and 1 or 6 sensed the predefined path. While initiation of the PID, sensor 1 or 6 temporary removed from the equation

2.6 PID On/Off

At certain point the condition requires closing the PID control, such as the occurrence of multiple lines and junctions. When it resumes, the PID will have an unexpected bounce due to the integral and derivative equation. Thus when the PID equation needs to reset the integral and the derivative resets.

$$\partial \text{Input} = 0 \qquad (13)$$

$$K_i \int e(t)dt = 0 \qquad (14)$$

The PID equations are converted into Arduino code as a type function to be called, as shown in Appendix 1. The configurations of the sensors are carefully designed to enable detection junctions in addition of having conventional line sensing. Table 1 shows the comparison between conventional configuration and currently designed configuration at different situations, where the red dots represent single unit optical reflective IR sensors, labelled as sensor 1 to 6 from left to right, and the rectangle represent the MR body.

2.7 MR Design

The design focus more on the intelligence of the MR, mostly based on feedback system, embedded into a microcontroller [14, 15]. The design starts with the architect of the system to decide the parts and material needed. When the parts finalized, CAD software SolidWorks, as shown in Fig. 2, without wiring, used to model the MR for virtual inspection of the orientation and assembly. The MR modified from time to time until the final design is confirm.

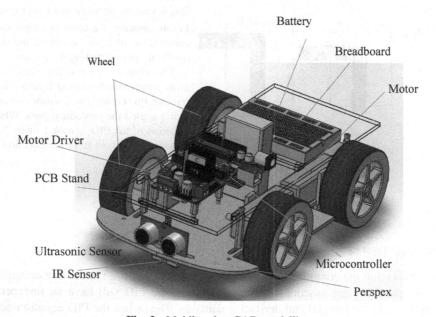

Fig. 2. Mobile robot CAD modelling

2.8   Communication Method

Stable and correct communication is needed especially when dealing with an operating MR [15]. Improper communication method would lead to data missing or programming standstill. The communication protocol involves both sender and receiver. The initial command starts from keyboard sending data to Arduino UNO which runs the function once using serial communication, as shown in Appendix 2, through Bluetooth module. The function is then while looped until reached destination or interrupted by central command, as shown in Appendix 3, when the serial communication is available.

Tuning parameter while operating is essential, to instantly fixing any unexpected change in environment. Thus, when entered the tuning function, the microcontroller will ask for new setting and stall until the there is an input of new parameter by an empty conditional loop as shown in Appendix 4.

Once the model is finalized, the process proceeds to fabrication. A prototype model fabricated shown in Fig. 3.

Fig. 3. Prototype model

3   Results and Discussion

After the completion of prototype fabrication, further development will involve the data extraction and computing reaction based on extracted data. The testing conducted breaks into several response starting with PID control, obstacle avoidance function and path selection. Since the MR, programming and setting made by hand on top of the limiting budget, the movement of the MR might have functional error and stability issues. However, the errors are covered by utilizing the microcontroller available software capacity. The whole program sketch thus far used 11,302 bytes (35%) of program storage space, out of maximum of 32,256 bytes and 547 bytes (26%) of dynamic memory for global variables, leaving 1,501 bytes for local variables. In order to design an autonomous MR, the environment must first be predefined. The testing field was designed according to a standard grid as shown in Fig. 4.

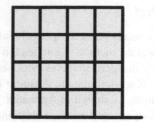

Fig. 4. Testing field

This test involves testing the MR PID program functionality in maneuvering according to predefined line. The test starts with the reaction test of the reflective optical IR sensors, placing the path under third and fourth sensor, and extraction of sensors feedback data which displayed in serial monitor to set the comparator program

Table 2. PID control result

Set point	Input	PID output	Error	Total error	Differential error	Left PWM	Right PWM
3.5	6	−217.49	−2.5	0.01	0.5	220	3
3.5	6	−219.99	−2.5	0.01	0	220	1
3.5	5.5	−178.5	−2	0	−0.5	220	42
3.5	5.5	−176	−2	0	0	220	44
3.5	5	−134.5	−1.5	0	−0.5	220	86
3.5	5	−132	−1.5	0	0	220	88
3.5	4.5	−90.5	−1	0	−0.5	220	130
3.5	4.5	−88	−1	0	0	220	132
3.5	4	−46.5	−0.5	0	−0.5	220	174
3.5	3.5	−2.5	0	0	−0.5	220	218
3.5	3.5	0	0	0	0	220	220
3.5	3	41.5	0.5	0	−0.5	179	220
3.5	3	44	0.5	0	0	177	220
3.5	2	127	1.5	0	−1	94	220
3.5	2	132	1.5	0	0	89	220
3.5	1.5	173.5	2	0	−0.5	47	220
3.5	1.5	176	2	0	0	45	220
3.5	1	217.5	2.5	0	−0.5	3	220
3.5	3	54	0.5	0	2	166	220
3.5	3	44	0.5	0	0	176	220
3.5	1	210	2.5	0	−2	10	220
3.5	1	220	2.5	0	0	0	220
3.5	1.5	178.5	2	0	0.5	42	220
3.5	1.5	176	2	0	0	44	220
3.5	1	217.5	2.5	0	−0.5	3	220
3.5	1.5	178.5	2	0	0.5	42	220
3.5	1	217.5	2.5	0	−0.5	3	220
3.5	2.33	109.34	1.17	0	1.33	111	220
3.5	2.5	88.84	1	0.01	0.17	132	220
3.5	1	212.51	2.5	0.01	−1.5	8	220
3.5	1	220	2.5	0.01	0	0	220

parameter, as Appendix 5. The data shows that the data fluctuate below 220 when sensing white region and above 800 when sensing the black path. Thus the comparator program can be defined as shown in Appendix 6. Afterwards, all the variable of the PID equation is verified and compared, as shown in Appendix 7, through serial monitor display, with the mathematical calculation. Table 2 which is extracted through processing program as shown in Appendix 8-show the results of deviation and PID response controlling the left and right motors of the MR.

In physical test, initially the MR placed in an orientation deviate from the center line before initiation, as shown in Fig. 5(a). Through PID calculation the MR detects the deviation and steer itself towards the center line, as shown in Fig. 5. The test was repeated with several different deviation orientations. The program is review and updated to debug unusual behavior of the MR, mainly due to non-precise handmade prototype and cheap standard part physical defect.

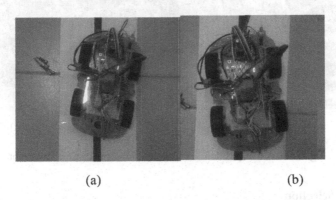

(a)   (b)

Fig. 5. MR (a) Before and (b) After initiation

3.1 Obstacle Avoidance

This test involves testing the MR proximity reaction. The test starts with the reaction test of the ultrasonic sensors. Obstacle placed twenty centimeters in front of the MR and moving towards it. The sensor feedback data extracted and displayed in the serial monitor, as shown in Fig. 6, together with post processed data in unit centimeter. A graph of actual obstacle distance against sensor input distance plotted as shown in Appendix 9. The graph compares the actual distance and distance computed by microcontroller based on ultrasonic sensor feedback data. It is shown that the computed data is quite stable with a slight ±1 cm fluctuation. At the end it is shown that there is a limit towards accuracy as starts from 2 cm and nearer the computation went wild. After that, test run is conducted to observe the relationship between proximity function and the PID response. Figure 7(a) show the MR still collide even though it sensed obstacle ahead before stopping. This is due to the delay in reaction time from looping a long list of program. Thus timer interrupt function, which interrupt the loop in a constant 50 μs, to check for obstacle is added for improvement. A success in avoiding collision is shown in Fig. 7(b).

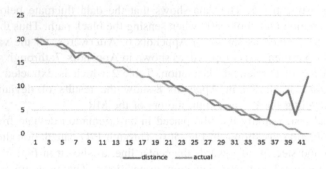

Fig. 6. Comparison between actual distance and sensor computed distance

(a)   (b)

Fig. 7. MR halt position (a) without and (b) with timer interrupt

3.2 Path Selection

The final destination is predefined in central command and tested in testing field. The MR is set to turn left on first junction, then turn right on the third junction before reaching final junction as destination using PID control on straight path and junction selection at junctions. The result shows that the MR able to reach its destination correctly, as shown in Fig. 8.

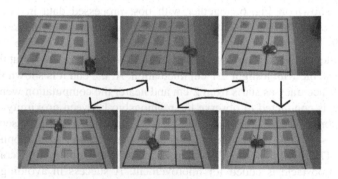

Fig. 8. MR field test

3.3   Colour Sensing

A test is conducted for the reflective optical IR sensor to sense red, green, blue (RGB), Cyan, Yellow and Magenta (CYM) colour. The range for each colour is determined and a graph, as shown in Fig. 9, of the feedback data against time is plotted.

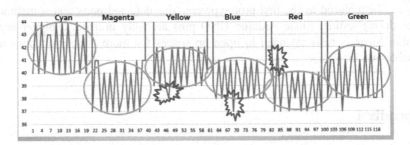

Fig. 9. Graph of data vs time (static) (Color figure online)

The range overlaps each other and the data differs from time to time due to environmental factor. Fortunately the pattern is consistent as the maximum and minimum range for each color is different. Thus, the color can be recognized by comparing with a default color, through determining with its maximum and minimum range value. This method requires a MR to be static for a short moment as moving MR unable to obtain a consistent range, as shown in Fig. 10.

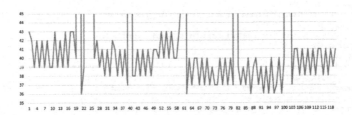

Fig. 10. Graph of data vs time (moving)

4   Conclusion

In this paper, a prototype of an autonomous guided MR based on microcontroller has been successfully fabricated. The feedback control was designed and tested able to follow the predefined path and perform path selection at junctions and reach designated location at a grid pattern field and best settling at $K_p = 88$, $K_i = 0.015$ while K_d have minor influences.

The prototype was able to achieve a 90° self-rotation will minimal skidding effect. The range of raw data from the reflective optical IR sensor for standard RGB and CYM color was also determined. Though, the MR also have some solvable handmade flaw issues. The stability of the prototype was tested and the result is acceptable. Still there are a lot of further improvement can be done to enhance the stability and functionality of the MR. The design of the MR can be further customized and studied for better performance. Some parts can be replaced as the first prototype contains defected parts that sometimes are issues during testing. Since Arduino UNO pins are fully utilized, a bigger capacity Arduino Mega is recommended to open up spaces for more added functions as the available pins increases.

Appendix 1

```
sketch_may29a §

void pid(){   bw();senseline();currenttime=millis();
    timechange=currenttime-lasttime;
    if(timechange>=sampletime){sampletimeinsec= sampletime/1000;Ki=Ki*sampletimeinsec;Kd=Kd/sampletimeinsec;}
    error = setpoint- ro_input; totalError += Ki*error;
    if(totalError>speedlimit){totalError=speedlimit;}
    if(totalError<Nspeedlimit){totalError=Nspeedlimit;}
    dError=ro_input-previousRo_input;
    pid_output = (Kp*error) + totalError+ (Kd*dError);previousRo_input = ro_input;
    if( pid_output>speedlimit ) { pid_output = speedlimit; }
    if( pid_output<Nspeedlimit ) { pid_output = Nspeedlimit;}
    if (distance<10 && distance >=0){
    if(pid_output<0)
    { rightspeed = speedlimit;leftspeed = speedlimit - abs(int(pid_output));}
    if(pid_output>0)
    { rightspeed = speedlimit - abs(int(pid_output));leftspeed = speedlimit;}
    if(pid_output==0)
    {rightspeed = speedlimit;
      leftspeed = speedlimit;}}
      else{    if(pid_output>0)
    { rightspeed = speedlimit;leftspeed = speedlimit - abs(int(pid_output));}
    if(pid_output<0) // Turn right
    { rightspeed = speedlimit - abs(int(pid_output));leftspeed = speedlimit;}
    if(pid_output==0)
    {rightspeed = speedlimit;leftspeed = speedlimit;}}
      leftspeedscaled=leftspeed/1.9,rightspeedscaled=rightspeed/1.9;drive();
      for(int x=1;x<=6;x++){prevro[x]=ro[x];}}
```

Appendix 2: Serial Communication Program

```
if(Serial.available()>0){ data=Serial.read();
switch(data)
    { case 'a': movetoA();break;case 'b': movetoB();break;case 'c': movetoC();break;
      case 'd': movetoD();break;case 'e': movetoE();break;case 'f': movetoF();break;
      case 'g': movetoG();break;case 'h': movetoH();break;case 'i': movetoI();break;
      case 'j': movetoJ();break;case 'k': movetoK();break;case 'l': movetoL();break;
      case 'm': movetoM();break;case 'n': movetoN();break;case 'o': movetoO();break;
      case 'p': movetoP();break;case 'q': tunesampletime();break;case 'r':pidtunning();break;
      case 's': tunespeedlimit();break;
      default : break;}}}
```

Appendix 3: Conditional Looping Program

```
void movetoA()
{do{ ////////////////
    ///functions///
    ////////////////
} while(Serial.available()==0)
}
```

Appendix 4: Tuning Program

```
Serial.print("new Kp=");
while(Serial.available()==0){}
Kp=Serial.parseFloat();
Serial.println(Kp),Serial.print("new Ki=");
while(Serial.available()==0){}
Ki=Serial.parseFloat();
Serial.println(Ki),Serial.print("new Kd=");
while(Serial.available()==0){}
Kd=Serial.parseFloat();
Serial.println(Kd);}
```

Appendix 5: Serial Monitor Display of IR Sensor Raw Data

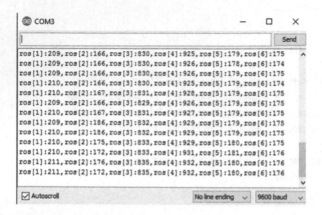

Appendix 6: Comparator Program

```
if (ros[1]>300)      { ro[1] = HIGH;}
        else                              { ro[1] = LOW;}
        if (ros[2]>300)     { ro[2] = HIGH;}
        else                              { ro[2] = LOW;}
        if (ros[3]>300)     { ro[3] = HIGH;}
        else                              { ro[3] = LOW;}
        if (ros[4]>300)     { ro[4] = HIGH;}
        else                              { ro[4] = LOW;}
        if (ros[5]>300)     { ro[5] = HIGH;}
        else                              { ro[5] = LOW;}
        if (ros[6]>300)     { ro[6] = HIGH;}
          else                            { ro[6] = LOW;}
```

Appendix 7: PID Feedback Parameter

```
COM3                                                    —   □   ×
[                                                    ] [Send]
setpoint:3.50
Input:5.00
Kp: 88.00,Ki :0.00,Kd :5.00
pid output: -132.00
error: -1.50,totalError: -0.00,differential error: 0.00
speed:(left)220.00, (right)88.00
setpoint:3.50
Input:4.00
Kp: 88.00,Ki :0.00,Kd :5.00
pid output: -49.00
error: -0.50,totalError: -0.00,differential error: -1.00
speed:(left)220.00, (right)171.00
setpoint:3.50
Input:4.00
Kp: 88.00,Ki :0.00,Kd :5.00
pid output: -44.00
error: -0.50,totalError: -0.00,differential error: 0.00
speed:(left)220.00, (right)176.00
setpoint:3.50
Input:3.50
Kp: 88.00,Ki :0.00,Kd :5.00
pid output: -2.50
error: 0.00,totalError: -0.00,differential error: -0.50
speed:(left)220.00, (right)218.00
setpoint:3.50
☑ Autoscroll              No line ending  ∨   9600 baud  ∨
```

Appendix 8: Processing Program

```
fyp_pptx
import processing.serial.*;
Serial port;
String reading="";
PrintWriter output;
String fname = "pid.csv";
void setup() {
  size(400,200);
  port = new Serial(this, "COM3", 9600);
  port.bufferUntil('\n');
  output = createWriter(fname);
  writeText("data visualization");
  output.println("input,kp,ki,kd,pidoutput,error,totalerror,differentialerror,left speed,right speed,setpoint");}
void draw() {}
void serialEvent (Serial port){
  reading = port.readStringUntil('\n');
  if(reading != null){
    println(reading);
    reading=trim(reading); }
  writeText("Sensor Reading: " + reading);
  output.println(reading);}
void writeText(String textToWrite){
  background(255);
  fill(0);
  text(textToWrite, width/20, height/2);  }
void keyPressed() {
  output.flush();  // Writes the remaining data to the file
  output.close();  // Finishes the file
  exit(); } // Stops the program
```

Appendix 9: Ultrasonic Processed Feedback

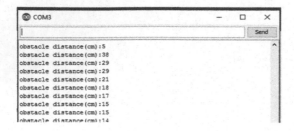

References

1. Spong, M.W., Vidyasagar, M.: Robot Dynamics and Control. Wiley, Hoboken (2008)
2. Hamza, M.F., Yap, H.J., Choudhury, I.A., Isa, A.I.: Application of kane's method for dynamic modeling of rotary inverted pendulum system
3. Tzafestas, S.G.: Introduction to Mobile Robot Control. Elsevier, Amsterdam (2013)
4. Hassan, Z.Z.: Automated guided vehicle (AGV) using 68HC11 microcontroller, Universiti Malaysia Pahang (2006)
5. Chapman, T.: Lab automation and robotics: automation on the move. Nature **421**, 661–666 (2003)
6. Royakkers, L., van Est, R.: A literature review on new robotics: automation from love to war. Int. J. Soc. Robot. **7**, 549–570 (2015)
7. Punetha, D., Kumar, N., Mehta, V.: Development and applications of line following robot based health care management system. Adv. Res. Comput. Eng. Technol. (IJARCET) **2**, 2446–2450 (2013)
8. Sumiya, T., Matsubara, Y., Nakano, M., Sugaya, M.: A mobile robot for fall detection for elderly-care. Procedia Comput. Sci. **60**, 870–880 (2015)
9. Singh, K., Singh, M., Gupta, N.: Design and implementation of cell-phone detection based line follower robot. Int. J. Electron. Comput. Sci. Eng.
10. Denei, S., Mastrogiovanni, F., Cannata, G.: Towards the creation of tactile maps for robots and their use in robot contact motion control. Robot. Auton. Syst. **63**, 293–308 (2015)
11. Normey-Rico, J.E., Alcala, I., Gómez-Ortega, J., Camacho, E.F.: Mobile robot path tracking using a robust PID controller. Control Eng. Pract. **9**, 1209–1214 (2001)
12. Durand, S., Marchand, N.: Further results on event-based PID controller. In: 2009 European Control Conference (ECC), pp. 1979–1984 (2009)
13. Smith, J., Campbell, S., Morton, J.: Design and implementation of a control algorithm for an autonomous lawnmower. In: 48th Midwest Symposium on Circuits and Systems, 2005, pp. 456–459 (2005)
14. Arduino, L.: Arduino Introduction, Arduino (2015). http://arduino.cc/en/guide/introduction
15. Schmidt, M.: Arduino. Pragmatic Bookshelf (2011)

Workshop Computational Astrochemistry (CompAstro 2018)

A Theoretical Investigation of the Reaction H+SiS$_2$ and Implications for the Chemistry of Silicon in the Interstellar Medium

Dimitrios Skouteris[1]($\boxtimes$) (iD), Marzio Rosi[2,3] (iD), Nadia Balucani[4,5,6] (iD),
Luca Mancini[4], Noelia Faginas Lago[4] (iD), Linda Podio[5] (iD),
Claudio Codella[5] (iD), Bertrand Lefloch[6], and Cecilia Ceccarelli[6] (iD)

[1] Scuola Normale Superiore, 56126 Pisa, Italy
dimitrios.skouteris@sns.it
[2] Dipartimento di Ingegneria Civile e Ambientale,
Università degli Studi di Perugia, 06125 Perugia, Italy
marzio.rosi@unipg.it
[3] CNR-ISTM, 06123 Perugia, Italy
[4] Dipartimento di Chimica, Biologia e Biotecnologie,
Università degli Studi di Perugia, 06123 Perugia, Italy
{nadia.balucani, noelia.faginaslago}@unipg.it
[5] INAF, Osservatorio Astrofisico di Arcetri, 50125 Florence, Italy
{lpodio, codella}@arcetri.inaf.it
[6] Université Grenoble Alpes, IPAG, 38000 Grenoble, France
{bertrand.lefloch,
cecilia.ceccarelli}@univ-grenoble-alpes.fr

Abstract. Silicon sulfide, SiS, has been recently detected in a shocked region around a Sun-like protostar (L1157-B1) with an anomalously high abundance with respect to the more common SiO. This has challenged our comprehension of silicon chemistry in the interstellar medium. In this paper, the reaction H+SiS$_2$ has been computationally investigated by means of electronic structure and kinetic calculations to establish its role in the conversion of interstellar SiS$_2$ into SiS by the abundant H atoms. The calculated reaction rate coefficients between 70–100 K are high enough to conclude that SiS$_2$ cannot be considered a reservoir species of silicon or sulphur in interstellar objects and that, if formed, SiS$_2$ is rapidly converted into SiS+HS by the reaction with atomic hydrogen.

Keywords: Electronic structure calculations · Kinetic calculations
Astrochemistry · Silicon chemistry

1 Introduction

Silicon is the seventh most abundant element in the universe (after H, He, O, C, N, and Ne) with an atom fraction of 30 parts per million. Sulfur is also relatively abundant with an atom fraction of 16 parts per million. Numerous gaseous molecular species including Si or S have been detected in the interstellar medium, and their size ranges from 2 to 8 atoms [1]. Concerning interstellar silicon, most of it is actually found in the

© Springer International Publishing AG, part of Springer Nature 2018
O. Gervasi et al. (Eds.): ICCSA 2018, LNCS 10961, pp. 719–729, 2018.
https://doi.org/10.1007/978-3-319-95165-2_50

form of silicates in interstellar dust particles and can only be transferred back in the gas phase when high intensity shocks are able to sputter the refractory core of interstellar dust grains, releasing gaseous silicon. Star forming regions are particularly vivid examples of such environments, where the violently ejected material encounters the surrounding quiescent zone (see [2] and references therein). As soon as silicon is released in the gas phase, it is largely transformed into the diatomic molecule SiO, which is indeed the most abundant gaseous silicon compound [3, 4]. In addition to SiO, silicon monosulfide (SiS) has also been detected in a number of sources, such as Orion KL [5–7], SgrB2 [8, 9], and, more recently, in L1157-B1 [2], a shocked region driven by a fast jet ejected from a Sun-like protostar. In the last case, a surprisingly high abundance of SiS has been inferred in a well-localized region around the protostar: while typical SiO/SiS abundance ratios are around 200, in that small region this ratio diminishes to values as low as 25 [2]. The reason for such diversity is unknown, but cannot be related to a local overabundance of sulphur as the abundance of other common sulphur species (*e.g.* SO) were seen to remain constant [2]. While a high abundance of SiS has been inferred also for Orion KL and SgrB2 (in Orion KL SiO/SiS $\sim$ 40–80), what is surprising in L1157-B1 is the strong gradient across the shock, where no SiS is detected at the shock impact region (SiO/SiS > 180) and "high" SiS abundance at the head of the shock (SiO/SiS $\sim$ 25).

To understand the cause of such high abundance of silicon sulfide is a challenge to our comprehension of the chemistry of interstellar Si species. As a matter of fact, very little was known about the formation mechanisms of SiS until the recent work by the present authors on the reactions SiH+S and SiH+S$_2$ [10]. Previously, the only process considered to give rise to interstellar SiS was the dissociative ion-electron recombination reaction [11, 12] of the HSiS$^+$ ion

$$HSiS^+ + e^- \rightarrow H + SiS$$

However, the HSiS$^+$ forming reactions included in astrochemical models have been demonstrated to be extremely inefficient in laboratory experiments [13, 14].

Possible gas-phase neutral-neutral reactions leading to SiS had previously been neglected, because of the common belief that such reactions are slow at the temperatures involved (10–100 K). However, in recent work we proved that the reactions SiH+S and SiH+S$_2$ are barrierless processes possibly leading to SiS or, in the case of SiH+S$_2$, to SiS$_2$ [10].

In this contribution we analyze from a theoretical and computational point of view the potential energy surface (PES) and kinetics properties of the related reaction H+SiS$_2$. The interest for this reaction arises from the fact that, as already suggested by Rosi *et al.* [10], if it is confirmed that the H+SiS$_2$ reaction is fast and efficient, SiS$_2$ cannot be considered a reservoir of silicon or sulphur in the interstellar medium because it is rapidly converted into SiS+HS by the abundant hydrogen atoms. This is at variance with the case of the isovalent reaction H+SiO$_2$, which is known to be slightly endothermic and, therefore, inefficient in the conditions of the interstellar medium [15, 16]. The different chemical behavior of SiS$_2$ and SiO$_2$ in the presence of H atoms could ultimately lead to the abundance anomalies observed in L1157-B1.

2 Computational Details

DFT calculations with the B3LYP hybrid functional [17, 18] were performed, using the Gaussian09 suite of programs [19]. The aug-cc-pV(T + d)Z basis set was used throughout the calculations [20, 21]. Structures were optimized at the DFT level, identifying the stationary points (intermediates and transition states). Subsequently, vibrational frequencies were calculated at the stationary points using the Hessian matrix (second derivatives) of the energy. The natures of the stationary points identified were determined according to the number of imaginary frequencies (no imaginary frequency implies a minimum, one and only one imaginary frequency implies a saddle point along the mode corresponding to that frequency). The transition states were characterized performing IRC (intrinsic reaction coordinate) calculations [22, 23] and using Molekel [24, 25]. Finally, coupled cluster (CCSD(T)) calculations were performed at the B3LYP optimized geometries of all stationary points (reactants, products, intermediates and transition states) in order to determine a more accurate value of the energy [26–28]. It is assumed that the reaction takes place on the ground electronic state but, otherwise, all possible paths have been taken into account.

Having determined the characteristics of the transition states associated with the two possible addition mechanisms of H to SiS$_2$ (see later), we have employed Transition State Theory (TST) to determine the global rate coefficients associated with the two additions of H to one of the terminal S atoms or to the central Si atom. The sum of these two rate constants represents an upper bound on the actual rate constants of the formation of the SiS+HS products because of the possibility of back-dissociation towards the reactants. Given the energetics of the reaction scheme, however, such a possibility is deemed rather improbable and therefore we believe that the association rate constant is a good estimate of the reactive one. As done in previous works [29–35], we use TST at a constant energy (assuming the energy is completely randomized in the reactant degrees of freedom), deriving bimolecular microcanonical association rate constants according to the formula

$$k(E) = \frac{N(E)}{h\rho(E)}$$

where $N(E)$ is the number of microstates available in the transition state, $\rho(E)$ is the density of states per unit volume of the reactants and h is Planck's constant. Subsequently, the rate constants are Boltzmann averaged to yield temperature-dependent ones. Tunnelling is taken account of by simulating each transition state by an Eckart barrier of the same energy and imaginary frequency.

3 Results

According to the present electronic structure calculations, the addition of an H atom to SiS$_2$ can occur in two different ways, that is, H can interact with one of the terminal sulphur atoms or with the central Si atom. In this way, two different addition intermediates can be formed that can then evolve into the products following different pathways. The situation is rather similar to that observed in the isovalent reactions H+SiO$_2$ [15, 16] and H+CO$_2$ [36, 37]. In the following we will describe separately the two possible initial attacks leading to the intermediates MIN1 and MIN2 (see Fig. 1) and the chemical rearrangements up to the products of MIN1 and MIN2. The numerical values obtained for the enthalpy changes and barrier heights (with respect to the reactant energy taken as 0) are summarized in Table 1 as they were obtained at the B3LYP/aug-cc-pV(T + d)Z and CCSD(T)/aug-cc-pV(T + d)Z levels of theory.

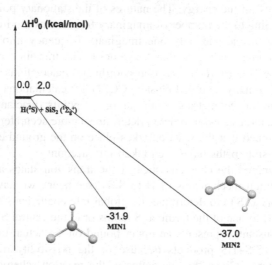

Fig. 1. The entrance region of the H+SiS$_2$ potential energy surface. Enthalpy changes (kcal/mol, 0 K) computed at the CCSD(T)/aug-cc-pV(T + d)Z levels of theory

Table 1. Enthalpy changes (kcal/mol, 0 K) computed at the B3LYP/aug-cc-pV(T + d)Z and CCSD(T)/aug-cc-pV(T + d)Z levels of theory for selected steps in the H+SiS$_2$ reaction

	ΔH_0^0		Barrier height	
	B3LYP	CCSD(T)	B3LYP	CCSD(T)
H (^{2}S)+SiS$_2$ ($^1\Sigma_g^+$) → MIN1	−36.8	−31.9		
H (^{2}S)+SiS$_2$ ($^1\Sigma_g^+$) → MIN2	−30.1	−37.0	0.6	2.0
MIN1 → MIN3	−3.7	−6.2	23.1	20.3
MIN2 → MIN3	−1.3	−1.1	4.8	4.6
MIN2 → SiS ($^1\Sigma^+$) + HS ($^2\Pi$)	30.5	30.0		
MIN3 → SiS ($^1\Sigma^+$) + HS ($^2\Pi$)	31.8	31.1		
MIN1 → MIN4	18.5	14.2	32.7	27.3
MIN4 → MIN5	15.0	18.4	16.6	20.2
MIN5 → MIN6	2.7	2.6	3.9	4.3
MIN5 → SiH ($^2\Pi$) + S$_2$ ($^3\Sigma_g^-$)	45.8	48.1		
MIN6 → SiH ($^2\Pi$) + S$_2$ ($^3\Sigma_g^-$)	43.1	45.5		
MIN6 → MIN7	−8.0	−7.9	8.2	7.1
MIN7 → MIN8	−0.5	−0.8	−0.1	−0.1
MIN8 → SiS ($^1\Sigma^+$) + HS ($^2\Pi$)	0.4	−1.4		

3.1 The Addition of H to SiS$_2$

When approaching an SiS$_2$ molecule, H atoms can interact either with a lone pair of one of the terminal sulphur atoms or with the central Si atom. SiS$_2$ is a linear molecule, but the H addition has the effect, in both cases, to change the relative position of the S-Si-S skeleton which now forms an angle of 113.6° in the case of the intermediate resulting from central addition (MIN1 in Fig. 1) or an angle of 124.0° in the case of the intermediate resulting from terminal addition (MIN2 in Fig. 1). According to our calculations the energy barrier associated with the central addition is lower than that associated with the terminal addition. In the former case, a transition state was located at the same energy level of the reactant asymptote and, therefore, this channel can be considered to be barrierless. In the latter case, instead, a transition state located at +2.0 kcal/mol is present. Given the presence of lone pairs on sulphur, this result might be somewhat surprising because the electrophilic H atomic radical is expected to easily interact with the lone pair electrons. Nevertheless, the situation is totally similar in the case of the reaction H+SiO$_2$ as verified by two independent sets of calculations by Hao *et al.* [15] and Yang *et al.* [16]. Furthermore, also for the isovalent H+CO$_2$ reaction the entrance barrier associated with the central addition is lower in energy with respect to the one associated with terminal addition. This is confirmed in the recent PES derived by Xie *et al.* [36] which has proved to be accurate by a detailed comparison with sensitive experimental quantities [37].

3.2 The Evolution of the Central Addition Intermediate MIN1

Once formed, the central addition intermediate MIN1 can isomerize to MIN3 by an H migration from Si to S, producing a *trans*-SSiSH species, which can, in turn, dissociate into the SiS+HS products in a barrierless process. In this case, the energy associated with the MIN1 → MIN3 transition state is well below the entrance energy and, therefore, can be easily surmounted by the system.

Alternatively, MIN1 can undergo a ring-closure process to MIN4 and then, through an additional ring-opening, can rearrange into the species *trans/cis*-HSiSS (MIN5 and MIN6 in Fig. 2). *cis*-HSiSS can fragment into the SiS+HS products by overcoming an exit barrier of +10.2 kcal/mol with respect to the reactant asymptote. Other, high energy rearrangements lead, instead, to the SiH+S$_2$ products in a very endothermic channel. Given the very low energy conditions of the interstellar medium (typical temperatures in star-forming regions are between 10 and 100 K), this part of the HSiS$_2$ PES cannot play any role.

3.3 The Evolution of the Terminal Addition Intermediate MIN2

Once formed, the terminal addition intermediate MIN2 can directly dissociate into the SiS+HS products in a barrierless process (see Fig. 3). Alternatively, by overcoming a small barrier it can isomerize to its *trans* isomer, MIN3, that then fragments into the same set of products.

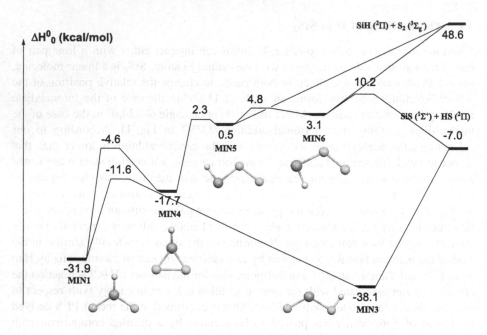

Fig. 2. The evolution of the central addition intermediate MIN1. Enthalpy changes (kcal/mol, 0 K) computed at the CCSD(T)/aug-cc-pV(T + d)Z levels of theory

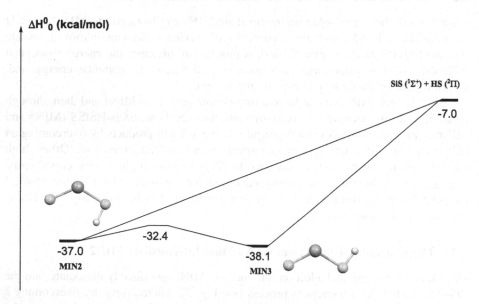

Fig. 3. The evolution of the terminal addition intermediate MIN1. Enthalpy changes (kcal/mol, 0 K) computed at the CCSD(T)/aug-cc-pV(T + d)Z levels of theory

3.4   The Global Rate Coefficients for the Two Possible Addition Reactions

The rate constants for both additions at three different temperatures (10 K, 70 K and 100 K) are shown in Table 2.

Table 2. Rate coefficients for the two addition reactions at three different temperatures representative of typical values for interstellar objects. The units of all rate constants are $cm^3 \, s^{-1}$.

T	Central	Terminal
10 K	5.97 (−16)	7.21 (−20)
70 K	2.97 (−10)	6.73 (−15)
100 K	6.48 (−10)	1.66 (−13)

In all three cases, the terminal addition rate is lower than the central one by 3 to 5 orders of magnitude, despite the fact that terminal addition is favored by a statistical factor of 2 (as reflected in the corresponding transition state symmetry numbers). The obvious reason for this is the barrier for terminal addition, whose effect is most important at low temperatures. Also the barrierless central addition reaction has a very low rate constant at low temperatures, both because of the sparsity of transition state microstates and because of the relatively high reactant density of states associated with translational motion. As the temperature rises to 70 K, both rate constants increase by around 6 orders of magnitude as the number of states available increases. However, the terminal addition rate constant remains rather low because of its energy barrier. Between 70 K and 100 K the two reactions behave rather differently. The terminal addition barrier becomes easier to overcome, with a consequent increase of 1–2 orders of magnitude of the rate constant. On the other hand, the increase of the central addition rate constant is much more modest, as there is no barrier.

4   Implications for the Chemistry of Interstellar Silicon

As already mentioned in the Introduction, the theoretical investigation on the reaction H+SiS$_2$ reported here belongs to a systematic study that we have undertaken to understand the chemistry of interstellar silicon and, more specifically, the possible formation routes of SiS. Silicon chemistry is mainly associated with shocked regions where elemental silicon is liberated in the gas phase. If we conclude that SiS is totally formed by neutral-neutral gas phase reactions, its presence and distribution in interstellar objects could become a kind of signpost for that type of chemistry being dominant in the above mentioned regions. Indeed, the observed chemical complexity of molecules in interstellar objects (more than 200 molecular species have been observed with many of them encompassing more than 5 atoms) can be explained by gas phase chemistry, or surface chemistry on the icy mantles of interstellar grains or a combination of the two [38, 39]. In the last decade, because of supposedly missing formation routes in the gas phase, ice-induced chemistry has been invoked to be responsible for most of the observed complexity. However, recent work by some of the present authors [29–31, 40] have clearly demonstrated that previously overlooked gas phase processes can account for the formation of many detected molecules. The same can be true for silicon-bearing species like SiS, especially if one considers that, as also recent work demonstrated, elemental silicon is preferentially converted into SiO or SiH_4 in the icy mantles [41].

In previous work, we demonstrated that SiH+S and $SiH+S_2$ are viable routes of SiS formation [10]. The SiH radical is produced by silane photodissociation or by other high energy processes involving silane [16]. Atomic sulphur and disulphur are also relatively abundant and, therefore, their reactions could account for the observed amount of SiS. Still, the mystery of why SiS is overabundant in the L1157-B1 region remains. In this contribution, by analyzing the title reaction, we have added another piece to this complex puzzle. We have, indeed, demonstrated that SiS_2 cannot be considered a stable reservoir of silicon because it is rapidly converted by H atoms into SiS. Therefore, every process that leads to SiS_2 is actually a step toward SiS formation. For instance, the already mentioned reaction $SiH+S_2$ can either produce SiS+HS or SiS_2+ H with probably similar branching ratio (the determination of the exact branching ratio is currently being pursued by some of the present authors). Yang *et al.* [16], indeed, have recently demonstrated that both SiO_2+H and SiO+OH are formed in the analogous reaction $SiH+O_2$. Now, as both SiO_2 and SiS_2 are linear molecules with null dipole moment, their presence cannot be easily determined by the usual rotational spectroscopy and their abundance in most interstellar objects is unknown. As a consequence, if in regions with a very active chemistry like L1157-B1 SiO (easily detectable) can be converted into SiO_2 (non detectable) by several reactions like SiO +OH, SiS cannot be transformed into the non detectable equivalent species SiS_2 in a stable way. We plan to use the derived rate coefficients in astrochemical models, as recently done for other cases [29–31], to verify whether these processes are at work in the ISM and can account for the observed overabundance of SiS in L1157-B1.

Acknowledgments. DS wishes to thank the Italian Ministero dell'Istruzione, Università e Ricerca (MIUR_FFABR17_SKOUTERIS) and the Scuola Normale Superiore (SNS_RB_SKOUTERIS) for financial support. N. F-L acknowledges financial support from Fondazione Cassa di Risparmio di Perugia (P2014/1255, ACT2014/6167). This work has been supported by the project PRIN-INAF 2016 The Cradle of Life - GENESIS-SKA (General Conditions in Early Planetary Systems for the rise of life with SKA). This project has received funding from the European Research Council (ERC) under the European Union's Horizon 2020 research and innovation programme, for the Project "The Dawn of Organic Chemistry" (DCO), grant agreement No 741002. This work has also been supported by MIUR "PRIN 2015" funds, project "STARS in the CAOS (Simulation Tools for Astrochemical Reactivity and Spectroscopy in the Cyberinfrastructure for Astrochemical Organic Species)", Grant Number 2015F59J3R.

References

1. The Cologne database. http://www.astro.uni-koeln.de/cdms/molecules. Accessed 26 Feb 2008
2. Podio, L., Codella, C., Lefloch, B., Balucani, N., Ceccarelli, C., Bachiller, R., Benedettini, M., Cernicharo, J., Faginas-Lago, N., Fontani, F., Gusdorf, A., Rosi, M.: Silicon-bearing molecules in the shock L1157-B1: first detection of SiS around a Sun-like protostar. Mon. Not. R. Astron. Soc. Lett. **470**(1), L16–L20 (2017)
3. Herbst, E., Millar, T.J., Wlodek, S., Bohme, D.K.: The chemistry of silicon in dense interstellar clouds. Astron. Astrophys. **222**, 205–210 (1989)
4. MacKay, D.D.S.: The chemistry of silicon in hot molecular cores. Mon. Not. R. Astron. Soc. **274**, 694–700 (1995)
5. Ziurys, L.M.: SiS in Orion KL – Evidence for outflow chemistry. Astrophys. J. **324**, 544–552 (1988)
6. Ziurys, L.M.: SiS in outflow regions – more high-temperature silicon chemistry. Astrophys. J. **379**, 260–266 (1991)
7. Tercero, B., Vincent, L., Cernicharo, J., Viti, S., Marcelino, N.: A line-confusion limited millimeter survey of Orion KL II. Silicon-bearing species. Astron. Astrophys. **528**, A26 (2011)
8. Morris, M., Gilmore, W., Palmer, P., Turner, B.E., Zuckerman, B.: Detection of interstellar SiS and a study of IRC+10216 molecular envelope. Astrophys. J. **199**, L47–L51 (1975)
9. Dickinson, D.F., Kuiper, E.N.R.: Inter-stellar silicon sulfide. Astrophys. J. **247**, 112–115 (1981)
10. Rosi, M., Mancini, L., Skouteris, D., Ceccarelli, C., Faginas Lago, N., Podio, L., Codella, C., Lefloch, B., Balucani, N.: Possible scenarios for SiS formation in the interstellar medium: electronic structure calculations of the potential energy surfaces for the reactions of the SiH radical with atomic sulphur and S_2. Chem. Phys. Lett. **695**, 87–93 (2018)
11. Wakelam, V., Loison, J.-C., Herbst, E., Pavone, B., Bergeat, A., Beroff, K., Chabot, M., Faure, A., Galli, D., Geppert, W.D., Gerlich, D., Gratier, P., Harada, N., Hickson, K.M., Honvault, P., Klippenstein, S.J., Le Picard, S.D., Nyman, G., Ruaud, M., Schlemmer, S., Sims, I.R., Talbi, D., Tennyson, J., Wester, R.: The 2014 KIDA network for interstellar chemistry. Astrophys. J. Suppl. Ser. **217**(2), 20 (2015)
12. McElroy, D., Walsh, C., Markwick, A.J., Cordiner, M.A., Smith, K., Millar, T.J.: The UMIST database for astrochemistry 2012. Astron. Astrophys. **550**, A36 (2013)
13. Wlodek, S., Bohme, D.K.: Gas-phase oxidation and sulfidation of $Si^+(^2P)$, SiO^+ and SiS^+. J. Chem. Soc., Faraday Trans. 2(85), 1643–1654 (1989)
14. Wlodek, S., Fox, A., Bohme, D.K.: Gas-phase reactions of Si^+ and $SiOH^+$ with molecules containing hydroxyl groups – possible ion molecule reaction pathways toward silicon monoxide, silanoic acid, and trihydroxy-silane, trimethoxysilane and triethoxysilane. J. Am. Chem. Soc. **109**, 6663–6667 (1987)
15. Hao, Y., Xie, Y., Schaefer III, H.F.: Features of the potential energy surface for the SiO +OH→SiO_2+H reaction: relationship to oxygen isotopic partitioning during gas phase SiO_2 formation. RSC Adv. **4**, 47163–47168 (2014)
16. Yang, T., Thomas, A.M., Dangi, B.B., Kaiser, R.I., Mebel, A.M., Millar, T.J.: Directed gas phase formation of silicon dioxide and implications for the formation of interstellar silicates. Nat. Commun. **9**, 774 (2018)
17. Becke, A.D.: Density functional thermochemistry. III. The role of exact exchange. J. Chem. Phys. **98**, 5648–5652 (1993)

18. Stephens, P.J., Devlin, F.J., Chablowski, C.F., Frisch, M.J.: Ab Initio calculation of vibrational absorption and circular dichroism spectra using density functional force fields. J. Phys. Chem. **98**, 11623–11627 (1994)
19. Frisch, M.J., Trucks, G.W., Schlegel, H.B., Scuseria, G.E., Robb, M.A., Cheeseman, J.R., Scalmani, G., Barone, V., Mennucci, B., Petersson, G.A., Nakatsuji, H., Caricato, M., Li, X., Hratchian, H.P., Izmaylov, A.F., Bloino, J., Zheng, G., Sonnenberg, J.L., Hada, M., Ehara, M., Toyota, K., Fukuda, R., Hasegawa, J., Ishida, M., Nakajima, T., Honda, Y., Kitao, O., Nakai, H., Vreven, T., Montgomery, Jr., J.A., Peralta, J.E., Ogliaro, F., Bearpark, M., Heyd, J.J., Brothers, E., Kudin, K.N., Staroverov, V.N., Kobayashi, R., Normand, J., Raghavachari, K., Rendell, A., Burant, J.C., Iyengar, S.S., Tomasi, J., Cosi, M., Rega, N., Milla, J.M., Klene, M., Knox, J.E., Cross, J.B., Bakken, V., Adamo, C., Jaramillo, J., Gomperts, R., Stratmann, R.E., Yazyev, O., Austin, A.J., Cammi, R., Pomelli, C., Ochterski, J.W., Martin, R.L., Morokuma, K., Zakrzewski, V.G., Voth, G.A., Salvador, P., Dannenberg, J.J., Dapprich, S., Daniels, A.D., Farkas, O., Foresman, J.B., Ortiz, J.V., Cioslowski, J., Fox, D. J.: Gaussian 09, Revision A.02. Gaussian, Inc., Wallingford CT (2009)
20. Dunning Jr., T.H.: Gaussian basis sets for use in correlated molecular calculations. I. The atoms boron through neon and hydrogen. J. Chem. Phys. **90**, 1007–1023 (1989)
21. Woon, D.E., Dunning Jr., T.H.: Gaussian basis sets for use in correlated molecular calculations. III. The atoms aluminum through argon. J. Chem. Phys. **98**, 1358–1371 (1983)
22. Gonzalez, C., Schlegel, H.B.: An improved algorithm for reaction path following. J. Chem. Phys. **90**, 2154–2161 (1989)
23. Gonzalez, C., Schlegel, H.B.: Reaction path following in mass-weighted internal coordinates. J. Phys. Chem. **94**, 5523–5527 (1990)
24. Flükiger, P., Lüthi, H.P., Portmann, S., Weber, J.: MOLEKEL 4.3. Swiss Center for Scientific Computing, Manno (Switzerland), (2000–2002)
25. Portmann, S., Lüthi, H.P.: MOLEKEL: an interactive molecular graphics tool. Chimia **54**, 766–769 (2000)
26. Bartlett, R.J.: Many-body perturbation theory and coupled cluster theory for electron correlation in molecules. Annu. Rev. Phys. Chem. **32**, 359–401 (1981)
27. Raghavachari, K., Trucks, G.W., Pople, J.A., Head-Gordon, M.: Quadratic configuration interaction. A general technique for determining electron correlation energies. Chem. Phys Lett. **157**, 479–483 (1989)
28. Olsen, J., Jorgensen, P., Koch, H., Balkova, A., Bartlett, R.J.: Full configuration–interaction and state of the art correlation calculations on water in a valence double-zeta basis with polarization functions. J. Chem. Phys. **104**, 8007–8015 (1996)
29. Barone, V., Latouche, C., Skouteris, D., Vazart, F., Balucani, N., Ceccarelli, C., Lefloch, B.: Gas-phase formation of the prebiotic molecule formamide: insights from new quantum computations. Mon. Not. R. Astron. Soc. Lett. **453**, L31–L35 (2015)
30. Skouteris, D., Vazart, F., Ceccarelli, C., Balucani, N., Puzzarini, C., Barone, V.: New quantum chemical computations of formamide deuteration support gas-phase formation of this prebiotic molecule. Mon. Not. R. Astron. Soc. Lett. **468**, L1–L5 (2017)
31. Skouteris, D., Balucani, N., Ceccarelli, C., Vazart, F., Puzzarini, C., Barone, V., Codella, C., Lefloch, B.: The genealogical tree of ethanol: gas-phase formation of glycolaldehyde, acetic acid and formic acid. Astrophys. J. **854**, 135 (2018)
32. Vazart, F., Latouche, C., Skouteris, D., Balucani, N., Barone, V.: Cyanomethanimine isomers in cold interstellar clouds: insights from electronic structure and kinetic calculations. Astrophys. J. **810**, 111 (2015)

33. Leonori, F., Petrucci, R., Balucani, N., Casavecchia, P., Rosi, M., Skouteris, D., Berteloite, C., Le Picard, S.D., Canosa, A., Sims, I.R.: Crossed-beam dynamics, low-temperature kinetics, and theoretical studies of the reaction $S(^1D)+C_2H_4$. J. Phys. Chem. A **113**, 15328–15345 (2009)

34. Balucani, N., Skouteris, D., Leonori, F., Petrucci, R., Hamberg, M., Geppert, W.D., Casavecchia, P., Rosi, M.: Combined crossed beam and theoretical studies of the $N(^2D)+C_2H_4$ reaction and implications for atmospheric models of Titan. J. Phys. Chem. A **116**, 10467–10479 (2012)

35. Leonori, F., Skouteris, D., Petrucci, R., Casavecchia, P., Rosi, M., Balucani, N.: Combined crossed beam and theoretical studies of the $C(^1D)+CH_4$ reaction. J. Chem. Phys. **138**(2), 024311 (2013)

36. Xie, C., Li, J., Xie, D., Guo, H.: Quasi-classical trajectory study of the $H+CO_2{\rightarrow}HO+CO$ reaction on a new ab initio based potential energy surface. J. Chem. Phys. **137**, 024308 (2012)

37. Caracciolo, A., Lu, D., Balucani, N., Vanuzzo, G., Stranges, D., Wang, X., Li, J., Guo, G., Casavecchia, P.: A combined experimental-theoretical study of the $OH+CO{\rightarrow}H+CO_2$ reaction dynamics. J. Phys. Chem. Lett. **9**, 1229–1236 (2018). https://doi.org/10.1021/acs.jpclett.7b03439

38. Caselli, P., Ceccarelli, C.: Our astrochemical heritage. Astron. Astrophys. Rev. **20**, 56 (2012)

39. Ceccarelli, C., Caselli, P., Fontani, F., Neri, R., López-Sepulcre, A., Codella, C., Feng, S., Jiménez-Serra, I., Lefloch, B., Pineda, J.E., Vastel, C., Alves, F., Bachiller, R., Balucani, N., Bianchi, E., Bizzocchi, L., Bottinelli, S., Caux, E., Chacón-Tanarro, A., Choudhury, R., Coutens, A., Dulieu, F., Favre, C., Hily-Blant, P., Holdship, J., Kahane, C., Jaber Al-Edhari, A., Laas, J., Ospina, J., Oya, Y., Podio, L., Pon, A., Punanova, A., Quenard, D., Rimola, A., Sakai, N., Sims, I.R., Spezzano, S., Taquet, V., Testi, L., Theulé, P., Ugliengo, P., Vasyunin, A.I., Viti, S., Wiesenfeld, L., Yamamoto, S.: Astrophys. J. **850**, 176 (2017)

40. Balucani, N., Ceccarelli, C., Taquet, V.: Formation of complex organic molecules in cold objects: the role of gas-phase reactions. Mon. Not. R. Astron. Soc. **449**, L16–L20 (2015)

41. Ceccarelli, C., Viti, S., Balucani, N., Taquet, V.: The evolution of grain mantles and silicate dust growth at high redshift. Mon. Not. R. Astron. Soc. **476**, 1371–1383 (2018). https://doi.org/10.1093/mnras/sty313/4848281

The Ethanol Tree: Gas-Phase Formation Routes for Glycolaldehyde, Its Isomer Acetic Acid and Formic Acid

Fanny Vazart[1]([✉]), Dimitrios Skouteris[2], Nadia Balucani[3,4],
Eleonora Bianchi[1,4], Cecilia Ceccarelli[1], Claudio Codella[4],
and Bertrand Lefloch[1]

[1] Univ. Grenoble Alpes, CNRS, IPAG, 38000 Grenoble, France
fanny.vazart@univ-grenoble-alpes.fr
[2] Scuola Normale Superiore, piazza dei Cavalieri 7, 56126 Pisa, Italy
[3] Dipartimento di Chimica, Biologia e Biotechnologie,
Università degli Studi di Perugia, via Elce di Sotto 8, 06123 Perugia, Italy
[4] INAF-Osservatorio Astrofisico di Arcetri, Largo E. Fermi 5,
50125 Florence, Italy

Abstract. In the field of astro- and prebiotic chemistry, the building blocks of life, which are molecules containing C atoms and composed of more than 6 atoms, are called Complex Organic Molecules (COMs). Their appearances on the early inorganic Earth is therefore one of the major issues faced by researchers interested in the origin of life. In this paper, new insights into the formation of several interstellar species of great relevance in prebiotic chemistry (glycolaldehyde, acetic acid and formic acid) are provided by electronic structure and kinetic calculations. The precursors $O(^3P)$ and both hydroxyethyl radicals ($^{\bullet}CH_2CH_2OH$ and $CH_3\,^{\bullet}CHOH$) were considered. Two reaction paths were obtained and the resulting rate constants show not only that they are viable in interstellar medium (ISM), but also that when included in an astro-chemical model, the obtained abundances for glycolaldehyde match well the observed ones. Unfortunately, in the case of acetic acid and formic acid, the predicted abundances are found around one order of magnitude higher than the observed ones.

Keywords: Astrochemistry · Computational chemistry · Gas-phase

1 Introduction

Glycolaldehyde $HOCH_2CHO$, as the simplest sugar-related molecule, and its isomer acetic acid CH_3COOH are of large importance in the field of prebiotic chemistry, which aims at figuring out how life appeared on an originally inorganic Earth. Indeed, while the first is itself very important in biochemistry as the simplest sugar-related compound, the second is able to act as a precursor for the synthesis of glycine, one of the most important amino acid [1]. Both isomers have been detected in the interstellar medium (ISM) by means of micro-wave spectroscopy. The first detection of acetic acid in 1997 towards the galactic center source Sgr B2 was presented by Mehringer et al. [2]. After

© Springer International Publishing AG, part of Springer Nature 2018
O. Gervasi et al. (Eds.): ICCSA 2018, LNCS 10961, pp. 730–745, 2018.
https://doi.org/10.1007/978-3-319-95165-2_51

that, it has also been observed towards several hot molecular cores [3, 4]. Glyco-laldehyde, as far as it is concerned, has been also originally detected towards Sgr B2 [5] and then towards hot cores outside the Galactic Center [6, 7].

More recently, it has been observed towards a low-mass binary protostellar system IRAS 16293–2422 [8]. So far, glycolaldehyde has been detected in a lower abundance than acetic acid.

The gas-phase formation routes for glycolaldehyde and acetic acid proposed up to now have not been able to successfully reproduce their estimated abundances. There-fore, they have been suspected to be formed through grain surface chemistry [5, 9–12].

In order to verify if the formation of glycolaldehyde and acetic acid could not be also explained thanks to gas-phase chemistry, new radical formation paths in the gas-phase involving the atomic oxygen and hydroxyethyl radicals were computationally studied. All the investigated compounds present in the schemes are shown in Figs. 1 and 2.

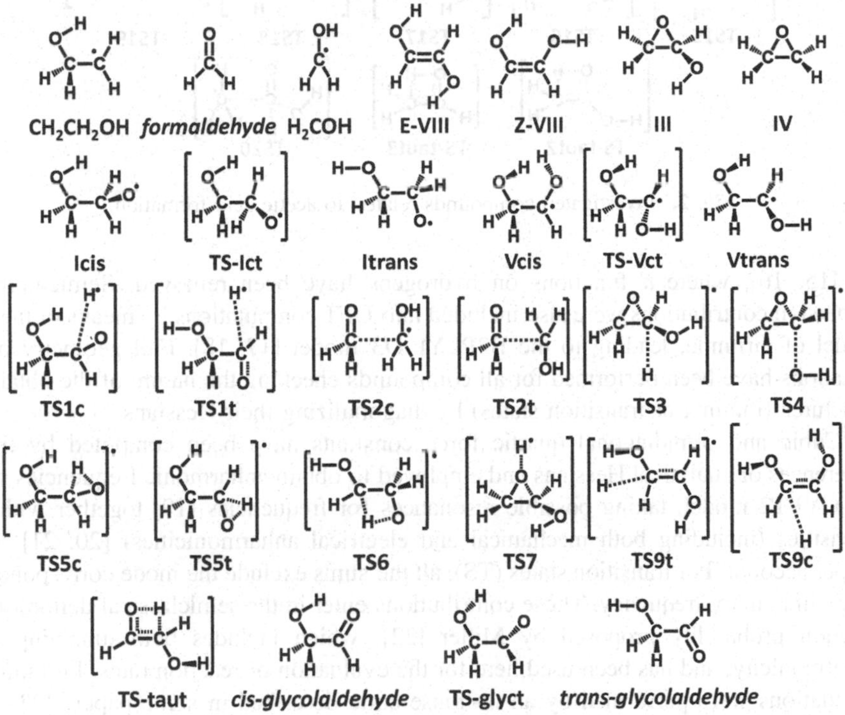

Fig. 1. Investigated compounds related to glycolaldehyde formation.

2   Computational Details

All DFT calculations have been carried out with a development version of the Gaussian suite of programs [13]. Most of the computations were performed with the double hybrid B2PLYP functional [14] in conjunction with the m-aug-cc-pVTZ triple-ξ basis

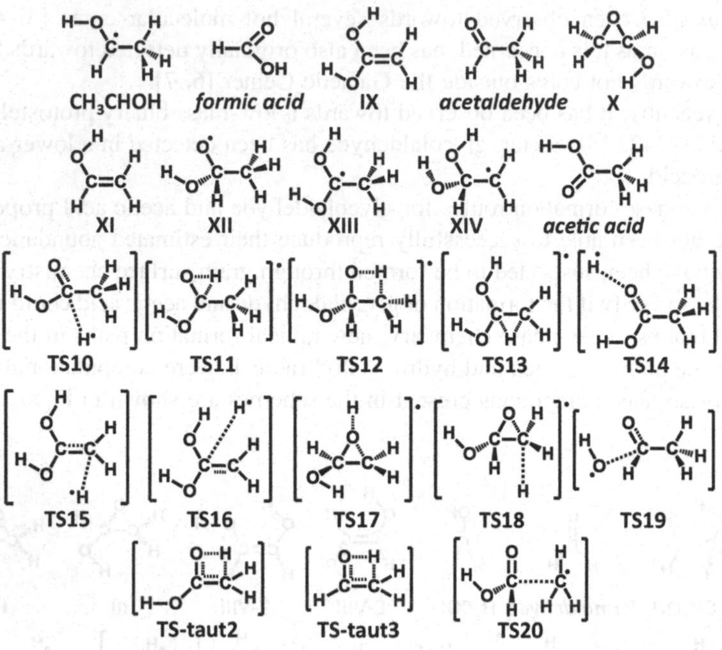

Fig. 2. Investigated compounds related to acetic acid formation.

set [15, 16], where d functions on hydrogens have been removed. Semiempirical dispersion contributions were also included into DFT computations by means of the D3 model of Grimme, leading to the B2PLYP-D3 model [17, 18]. Full geometry optimizations have been performed for all compounds checking the nature of the obtained structures (minima or transition states) by diagonalizing their Hessians.

Cubic and semidiagonal quartic force constants have been computed by finite differences of analytical Hessians and employed to obtain anharmonic frequencies with the GVPT2 model, taking possible resonances for frequencies [19] together with IR intensities (including both mechanical and electrical anharmonicities) [20, 21], into proper account. For transition states (TS), all the sums exclude the mode corresponding to the imaginary frequency. Those contributions enter in the semiclassical definition of reaction probability proposed by Miller [22], which includes both tunneling and anharmonicity, and has been used here for the evaluation of reaction rates. Full kinetic calculations were performed by an in-house code described in some papers [23–25], following the approach described in Ref. [26].

All the spectra have been generated and managed by the VMS-draw graphical user interface [27].

3 Results and Discussion

3.1 Vibrational Study of Glycolaldehyde and Acetic Acid

In order to further check the reliability of the computational model (*i.e.*, B2PLYP-D3/m-aug-cc-pVTZ) the simulated and experimental infrared (IR) spectra of cis-glycolaldehyde and acetic acid were compared (see Figs. 3 and 4) [28, 29].

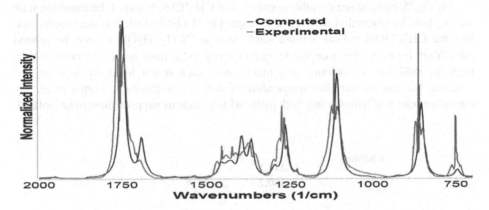

Fig. 3. Computed (black, B2PLYP-D3/m-aug-cc-pVTZ anharmonic treatment) vs. experimental (red, taken from Ref. [28]) infrared spectrum of cis-glycolaldehyde. (Color figure online)

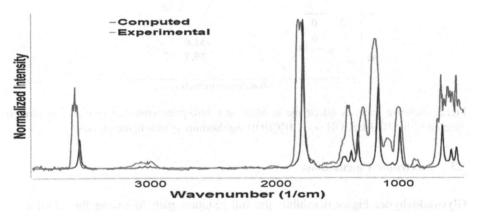

Fig. 4. Computed (black, B2PLYP-D3/m-aug-cc-pVTZ anharmonic treatment) vs. experimental (red, taken from Ref. [29]) infrared spectrum of acetic acid. (Color figure online)

It is noticeable that the simulated spectra fit nicely the experimental ones. Such a good agreement gives us further confidence to investigate the reaction path concerning the formation of glycolaldehyde and acetic acid with this method.

3.2 Hydroxyethyl Radicals

Both studied reactions involve an addition of oxygen $O(^3P)$ on a hydroxyethyl radical, easily obtained from ethanol and radicals $^\bullet OH/^\bullet Cl$ in ISM. In the case of the formation of glycolaldehyde, the oxygen atom is added on the 2-hydroxyethyl radical $^\bullet CH_2CH_2OH$, while in the case of the acetic acid formation, the oxygen atom is added on the 1-hydroxyethyl radical $CH_3{}^\bullet CHOH$. It is therefore interesting to figure out how accessible the transformation from one into the other is.

On Fig. 5, one can see the relative energies of $CH_3{}^\bullet CHOH$ and of the transition state linking both hydroxyethyl radicals, with respect to $^\bullet CH_2CH_2OH$. It is noteworthy first that the $CH_3^\bullet CHOH$ radical is more stable than its $^\bullet CH_2CH_2OH$ isomer, by around 30 kJ/mol. From another side, the required energy to go from one to the other is very high for ISM (*ca.* 170 kJ/mol) and makes this reaction not likely to occur in this medium, because the very low temperature of such an environment. Furthermore, any transition state was found to link both paths, which made us suppose them to be isolated.

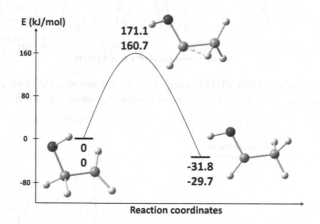

Fig. 5. Relative energies (electronic in black and zero-point corrected in green, in kJ/mol) diagram of the $^\bullet CH_2CH_2OH \leftrightarrow CH_3^\bullet CHOH$ equilibrium. (Color figure online)

3.3 Electronic Calculations

Glycolaldehyde. Figure 6 exhibits the full reaction path following the addition of atomic oxygen $O(^3P)$ on the 2-hydroxyethyl radical $^\bullet CH_2CH_2OH$. While both fragments are approaching, the H atom belonging to the OH moiety on the $^\bullet CH_2CH_2OH$ radical stabilizes the oxygen atom. Indeed, the barrier-less addition of oxygen leads to the **Icis** compound, which is *ca.* 400 kJ/mol more stable than the reactants. Its *trans*

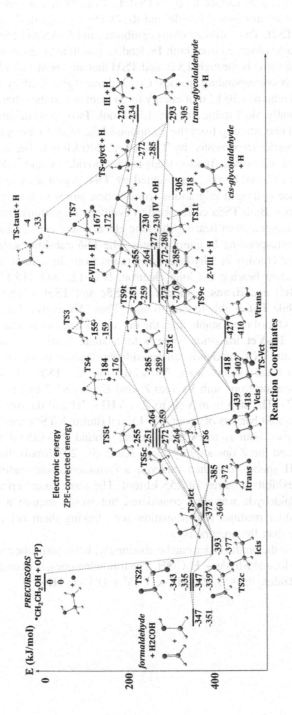

Fig. 6. Proposed path for the addition of O(^{3}P) on $^\bullet$CH$_2$CH$_2$OH reaction. Relative electronic energies (black) are issuing from B2PLYP-D3/m-aug-cc-pVTZ calculations while the applied ZPE corrections (green) come from anharmonic vibrational calculations at the same level. All the energies are given in kJ/mol. (Color figure online)

counterpart, the slightly less stable (by 8 kJ/mol) intermediate **Itrans**, can easily be reached from the *cis*, through a 20 kJ/mol barrier (**TS-Ict**). Both **Ix** species are then able to undergo a dissociation into formaldehyde and the $^\bullet CH_2OH$ radical, thanks to transition states **TS2c** and **TS2t**. These dissociations exhibit around 55 kJ/mol barriers. Other dissociations can also be observed from both **Ix**, leading this time to *cis*- or *trans*-glycolaldehyde, and $^\bullet H$, respectively through **TS1c** and **TS1t** that are about 115 kJ/mol higher in energy than their **Ix** corresponding species. *Cis*- and *trans*-glycolaldehyde are connected by **TS-glyct** and require a 30 kJ/mol energy to go from one to the other. The *cis* conformer is the marginally most stable one, by 15 kJ/mol. Two epoxidations can also be envisaged. The first one, starting from the compound **Icis**, leads to the epoxide **III** and $H^\bullet$ and exhibits a barrier (represented by **TS3**) of *ca.* 240 kJ/mol. The second one, as far as it is concerned, starts from **Itrans**, leads to the epoxide **IV** and $^\bullet OH$ and has to go through a *ca.* 110 kJ/mol barrier, represented by **TS4**. Again starting from both **Ix** species, one can see hydrogen migrations from carbon atoms to the oxygen atom bearing the lone electron. Both **TS5x** correspond to hydrogen migrations from the carbon atom linked to the oxygen atom bearing the lone electron and are 128 kJ/mol more energetic than their corresponding **Ix** intermediates. The **TS6** transition state can be reached from both **Ix** and consists in a hydrogen migration from the carbon that is not linked to the oxygen atom bearing the lone electron. It is 122 and 115 kJ/mol energetically higher than **Icis** and **Itrans**, respectively. **TS5c** and **TS5t** respectively lead to **Vcis** and **Vtrans** while **TS6** is able to lead to both. These **Vx** intermediates are found to be more than 430 kJ/mol more stable than the precursors and can be linked to each other thanks to the **TS-Vct** transition state with a small barrier of around 25 kJ/mol. Starting from both **Vx** compounds, an epoxidation leading to the epoxide **III** and $^\bullet H$ can be envisaged and exhibits a *ca.* 280 kJ/mol barrier (**TS7**). The other possible reaction is a dissociation from both **Vx** into *Z*- and *E*-ethene-1,2-diol isomers (**Z-VIII** and **E-VIII**) and $^\bullet H$. The step from **Vcis** to $Z - VIII + ^\bullet H$ and the one from **Vtrans** to $E - VIII + ^\bullet H$ exhibit barriers of about 175 kJ/mol (through **TS9c** and **TS9t** transition states, respectively), both isomers being found around 270 kJ/mol more stable than the precursors and the *Z* one slightly more stable (by 20 kJ/mol) than its *E* counterpart. This **E-VIII** species can then undergo a tautomerization leading to *trans*-glycolaldehyde that exhibits a barrier of 255 kJ/mol. The same tautomerization from **Z-VIII** to *cis*-glycolaldehyde was also considered but would require a non-available energy in interstellar medium (the transition state linking them being *ca.* 40 kJ/mol higher in energy than the precursors).

If we look more carefully at the products that can be obtained with this path, one can see that the most stable ones are formaldehyde + H_2COH. The following ones, in decreasing order of stability, are glycolaldehyde + H, **Z-VIII** + H, **IV** + OH and **III** + H.

The proposed radical mechanism based on this path is given in Fig. 7.

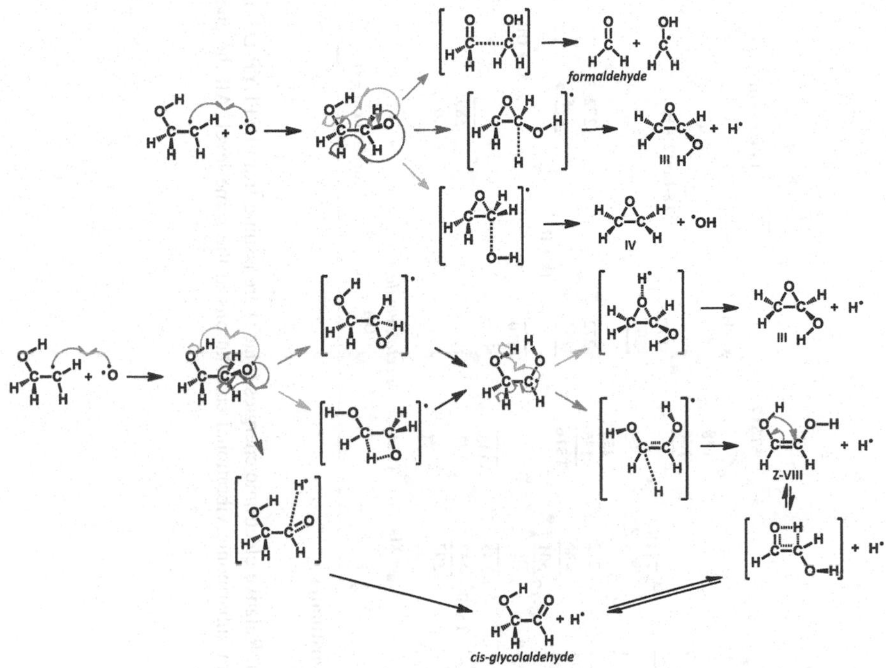

Fig. 7. Possible radical mechanism for glycolaldehyde formation, focused on cis species.

Acetic Acid. Figure 8 exhibits the full reaction path following the addition of atomic oxygen $O(^3P)$ on the 1-hydroxyethyl radical $CH_3^{\bullet}CHOH$. The barrier-less addition of oxygen leads to the **XII** compound, which is *ca.* 410 kJ/mol more stable than the reactants. This **XII** species is then able to undergo a dissociation into formic acid and the $^{\bullet}CH$ radical, through the transition state **TS20**. This dissociation exhibits a *ca.* 45 kJ/mol barrier. Other dissociations can also be observed, leading this time to acetaldehyde and $^{\bullet}OH$ or to acetic acid and $^{\bullet}H$, respectively through **TS19** and **TS10** that are about 100 and 60 kJ/mol higher in energy than **XII**. Thanks to a keto-enol tautomerism, acetaldehyde can turn into its **XI** enol form, through a 285 kJ/mol barrier (**TS-taut3**). Starting again from **XII**, a *ca.* 250 kJ/mol barrier (**TS18**) epoxidation is possible, leading to epoxide **X** and $^{\bullet}H$. One can envisage also two types of hydrogen migration. The first one would be a migration from the carbon atom in the carboxylic acid moiety and the second one from the carbon atom in the CH_3 moiety, both to the oxygen atom bearing the lone electron.

These two migrations respectively lead to compounds **XIII** and **XIV** and exhibit 105 (**TS11**) and 135 (**TS12**) kJ/mol barriers. The intermediates **XIII** and **XIV** are found to be respectively *ca.* 460 and 410 kJ/mol more stable than the precursors and are connected to each other thanks to **TS13** which is 215 kJ/mol less stable than **XIII**. This compound **XIII** can also undergo two types of hydrogen loss. The first one

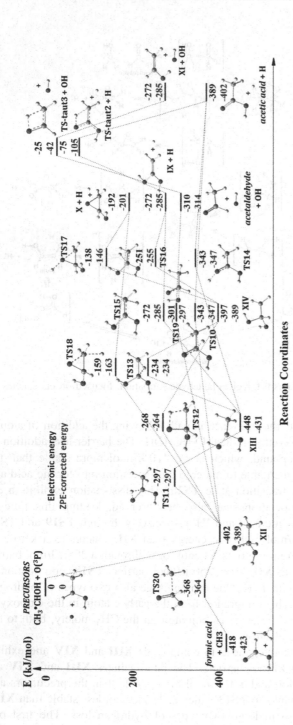

Fig. 8. Proposed path for the addition of O(3P) on CH₃•CHOH reaction. Relative electronic energies (black) are issuing from B2PLYP-D3/m-aug-cc-pVTZ calculations while the applied ZPE corrections (green) come from anharmonic vibrational calculations at the same level. All the energies are given in kJ/mol. (Color figure online)

concerns the hydrogen linked to an oxygen atom and results in acetic acid and $^{\bullet}$H through a 117 kJ/mol barrier (**TS14**) while the second one concerns a hydrogen atom on the CH$_3$ moiety. This second possibility leads to the enol **IX** and $^{\bullet}$H and requires an energy of 178 kJ/mol to overcome the barrier (**TS15**). Starting from intermediate **XIV**, it is feasible to obtain again the epoxide **X** and $^{\bullet}$H through a 271 kJ/mol barrier (**TS17**) or the enol **IV** and $^{\bullet}$H through a 154 kJ/mol barrier (**TS16**). Through a *ca.* 200 kJ/mol barrier (**TS-taut2**), this enol **IX** can give acetic acid thanks to a keto-enol tautomerism. If we take a closer look to the possible reaction products, it is noticeable that the most stable ones are formic acid and $^{\bullet}$CH3. Following in decreasing order of stability are acetic acid + H, acetaldehyde + OH, and their enol forms (**IX** + H, **XI** + OH).

The proposed radical mechanism based on this path is given in Fig. 9.

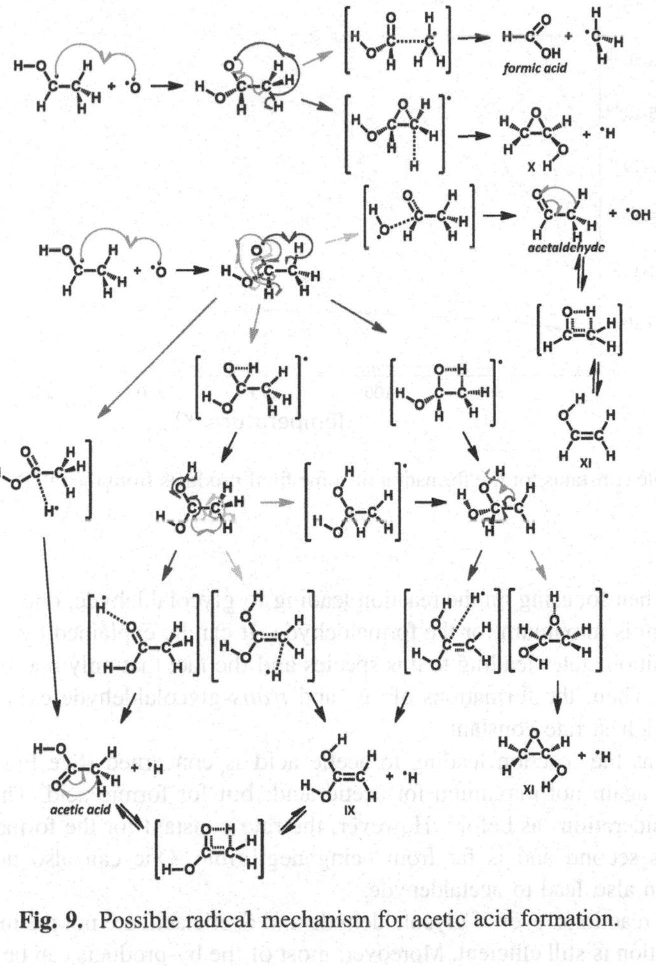

Fig. 9. Possible radical mechanism for acetic acid formation.

3.4 Kinetics Study

Figures 10 and 11 exhibit the rate constants for the formation of some final products issuing from the reactions leading to glycolaldehyde and acetic acid, respectively. In both cases, the formation of some products was found negligible and therefore not shown on the figures.

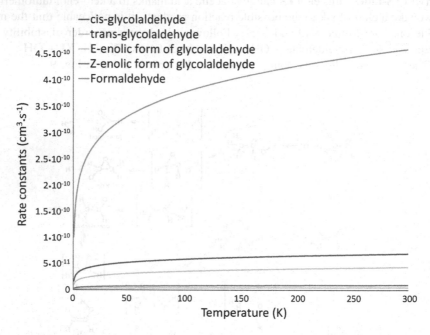

Fig. 10. Rate constants for the formation of some final products from the $O(^3P) + {}^\bullet CH_2CH_2OH$ reaction.

First, when focusing on the reaction leading to glycolaldehyde, one can see that the rate constant is maximum for the formaldehyde. It can be explained by the low energy of the transition states leading to this species and the fact that only one step is required to reach it. Then, the formations of *cis*- and *trans*-glycolaldehyde exhibit the second and third highest rate constant.

As far as the reaction leading to acetic acid is concerned (See Fig. 11), the rate constant is again not maximum for acetic acid, but for formic acid. This is for analogous considerations as before. However, the rate constant for the formation of acetic acid comes second and is far from being negligible. One can also notice that this reaction can also lead to acetaldehyde.

In both reactions, even if glycolaldehyde and acetic acid are not the major products, their formation is still efficient. Moreover, most of the by-products can be considered of interest in prebiotic chemistry and have been detected in ISM.

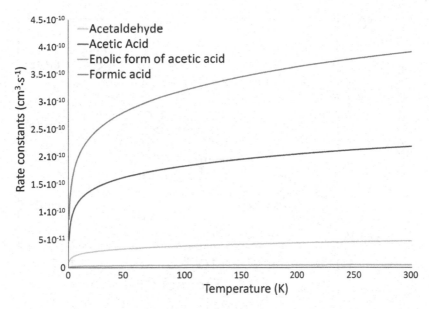

Fig. 11. Rate constants for the formation of some final products from the $O(^3P) + CH_3^\bullet CHOH$ reaction.

3.5 Astrochemical Modeling

In order to understand whether the proposed new reaction schemes and rates can explain the observations towards the hot corinos, an astrochemical model that simulates the conditions of the hot cores/corinos was used. In the conditions assumed by this model, the injected ethanol is all consumed in about 2000 yr. Formic acid is the one that benefits most, followed by acetic acid and, finally, glycolaldehyde. Before ethanol is fully burned, the abundance ratios are $HCOOH/CH_3COOH \sim 1.5$ and $CH_3COOH/HCOCH_2OH \sim 10$, and are mostly governed by the branching ratios of the first two steps of the proposed reaction paths (Figs. 6 and 8).

The comparison of the model predictions with measurements of the glycolaldehyde abundance for generic hot corino conditions gives very encouraging agreement, as shown in Fig. 12. In addition, the proposed schemes to synthesize glycolaldehyde and acetic acid from ethanol naturally explains the correlation seen by Lefloch et al. [30] between the abundance of these two species. On the contrary, the abundance of acetic acid and formic acid is predicted to be about one order of magnitude larger than the ones measured. However, the measurement of the acetic acid abundance and an upper limit to that of formic acid is L1157-B1, which is not a hot corino, so a more specific modelling is necessary before firmly conclude that there is a problem.

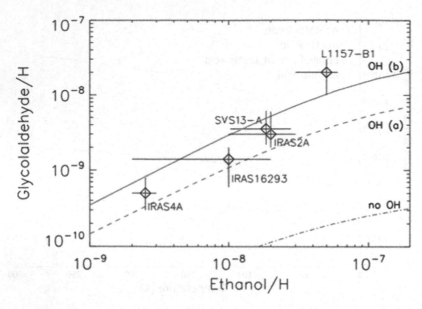

Fig. 12. Abundance of glycolaldehyde as a function of ethanol abundance in the gas phase, which can be different from the one injected from the mantles. The computations for the model refer to a gas with temperature equal to 100 K, H nuclei density 2.108 cm^{-3}, cosmic ray ionisation rate 3.10^{-1} s^{-1} and time $1.5.10^3$ yr. The three curves refer to models with different reactions to get the hydroxyethyl radicals: adopting the reactions $CH_3CH_2OH + OH \longrightarrow CH_3CHOH + H_2O$ and $CH_3CH_2OH + OH \longrightarrow CH_2CH_2OH + H_2O$ (solid line and dashed line, depending on the value of branching ratios that has been considered, in light of the different ones reported in literature) and excluding the reaction with the OH radicals (dotted dashed line). The atomic chlorine abundance (used for the $CH_3CH_2OH + Cl \longrightarrow CH_3CHOH + HCl$ and $CH_3CH_2OH + Cl \longrightarrow CH_2CH_2OH + HCl$ reactions) is $2.2.10^{-8}$ in the computations. Measured abundances towards NGC1333, IRAS4A and IRAS2A, IRAS16293-2422, L1157-B1 and SVS13-A are also reported with their uncertainties. For the latter observation, the abundance of atomic hydrogen being uncertain, it was considered that $n(H) = 5.10^{23}$cm^{-2} based on its upper limit [31].

4 Conclusion

New insights into the formation of glycolaldehyde and acetic acid in the ISM were provided. Electronic structure and kinetics calculations demonstrated that the reactions $O(^3P) + CH_2CH_2OH$ and $O(^3P + CH_3{}^\bullet CHOH)$ are viable formations route of glycolaldehyde and acetic acid, respectively, even under the extreme conditions of density and temperature typical of ISM. The difficult interconversion between both hydroxyethyl radicals and the absence of transition states leading to one path to the other assures that both of them are separate. The obtained rate constants were inserted in an updated chemical network to produce predicted abundances of glycolaldehyde, acetic acid and formic acid as a function of that of ethanol. The predictions match extremely well with the measured abundance of glycolaldehyde in solar type hot corinos and shock sites. On the contrary, acetic acid and formic acid are predicted to be about ten times more abundant than the extremely sparse detections so far available towards hot corinos and shock sites (only one in each case). This might point to a lack of important routes of destruction of these two molecules in our network, possibly via reactions involving radicals and leading to larger molecules. However, since observations are published towards only two sources and the model presented here contain a very generic description of hot corinos conditions, more observations and source-dedicated modelling are necessary to confirm this discrepancy.

Acknowledgements. This project has received funding from the European Research Council (ERC) under the European Union's Horizon 2020 research and innovation programme, for the Project "The Dawn of Organic Chemistry" (DOC), grant agreement No 741002.

References

1. Sorrell, W.H.: Origin of amino acids and organic sugars in interstellar clouds. Astrophys. J. Lett. **555**(2), L129 (2001)
2. Mehringer, D.M., Snyder, L.E., Miao, Y., Lovas, F.J.: Detection and confirmation of interstellar acetic acid. Astrophys. J. Lett. **480**(1), L71 (1997)
3. Remijan, A., Snyder, L.E., Liu, S.-Y., Mehringer, D., Kuan, Y.-J.: Acetic acid in the hot cores of sagitarrius B2(N) and W51. Astrophys. J. **576**(1), 264 (2002)
4. Shiao, Y.-S.J., Looney, L.W., Remijan, A.J., Snyder, L.E., Friedel, D.N.: First acetic acid survey with CARMA in hot molecular cores. Astrophys. J. **716**(1), 286 (2010)
5. Hollis, J.M., Lovas, F.J., Jewell, P.R.: Interstellar glycolaldehyde: the first sugar. Astrophys. J. Lett. **540**(2), L107 (2000)
6. Beltrán, M.T., Codella, C., Viti, S., Neri, R., Cesaroni, R.: First detection of glycolaldehyde outside the galactic center. Astrophys. J. Lett. **690**(2), L93 (2009)
7. Calcutt, H., Viti, S., Codella, C., Beltrán, M.T., Fontani, F., Woods, P.M.: A high-resolution study of complex organic molecules in hot cores. Mon. Not. R. Astron. Soc. **443**(4), 3157–3173 (2014)
8. Jørgensen, J.K., Favre, C., Bisschop, S.E., Bourke, T.L., van Dishoeck, E.F., Schmalzl, M.: Detection of the simplest sugar, glycolaldehyde, in a solar-type protostar with ALMA. Astrophys. J. Lett. **757**(1), L4 (2012)
9. Garrod, R.T., Herbst, E.: Formation of methyl formate and other organic species in the warm-up phase of hot molecular cores. A&A **457**(3), 927–936 (2006)
10. Occhiogrosso, A., Viti, S., Modica, P., Palumbo, M.E.: A study of methyl formate in astrochemical environments. Mon. Not. R. Astron. Soc. **418**(3), 1923–1927 (2011)
11. Woods, P.M., Slater, B., Raza, Z., Viti, S., Brown, W.A., Burke, D.J.: Glycolaldehyde Formation via the Dimerisation of the Formyl Radical. ArXiv e-prints (2013)
12. Burke, D.J., Puletti, F., Brown, W.A., Woods, P.M., Viti, S., Slater, B.: Glycolaldehyde, methyl formate and acetic acid adsorption and thermal desorption from interstellar ices. Mon. Not. R. Astron. Soc. **447**(2), 1444–1451 (2015)

13. Frisch, M.J., Trucks, G.W., Schlegel, H.B., Scuseria, G.E., Robb, M.A., Cheeseman, J.R., Scalmani, G., Barone, V., Mennucci, B., Petersson, G.A., Nakatsuji, H., Caricato, M., Li, X., Hratchian, H.R., Izmaylov, A.F., Bloino, J., Zheng, G., Sonnenberg, J.L., Hada, M., Ehara, M., Toyota, K., Fukuda, R., Hasegawa, J., Ishida, M., Nakajima, T., Honda, Y., Kitao, O., Nakai, H., Vreven, T., Montgomery Jr., J.A., Peralta, J.R., Ogliaro, F., Bearpark, M., Heyd, J.J., Brothers, E., Kudin, K.N., Staroverov, V.N., Kobayashi, R., Normand, J., Raghavachari, K., Rendell, A., Burant, J.C., Iyengar, S.S., Tomasi, J., Cossi, M., Rega, N., Millam, J.M., Klene, M., Knox, J.E., Cross, J.B., Bakken, V., Adamo, C., Jaramillo, J., Gomperts, R., Stratmann, R.E., Yazyev, O., Austin, A.J., Cammi, R., Pomelli, C., Ochterski, J.W., Martin, R.L., Morokuma, K., Zakrzewski, V.G., Voth, G.A., Salvador, P., Dannenberg, J.J., Dapprich, S., Daniels, A.D., Farkas, O., Foresman, J.B., Ortiz, J.V., Cioslowski, J., Fox, D. J.: GDVH37p (2014)

14. Grimme, S.: Semiempirical hybrid density functional with perturbative second-order correlation. J. Chem. Phys. **124**(3), 34108 (2006)

15. Papajak, E., Leverentz, H.R., Zheng, J., Truhlar, D.G.: Efficient diffuse basis sets: Cc-pVxZ+ and Maug-Cc-pVxZ. J. Chem. Theory Comput. **5**(5), 1197–1202 (2009)

16. Dunning, T.H.: Gaussian basis sets for use in correlated molecular calculations. I. the atoms boron through neon and hydrogen. J. Chem. Phys. **90**(2), 1007 (1989)

17. Grimme, S., Antony, J., Ehrlich, S., Krieg, H.: A consistent and accurate ab initio parametrization of density functional dispersion correction (DFT-D) for the 94 elements H-Pu. J. Chem. Phys. **132**(15), 154104 (2010)

18. Goerigk, L., Grimme, S.: Efficient and accurate double-hybrid-meta-GGA density functionals-evaluation with the extended GMTKN30 database for general main group thermochemistry, kinetics, and noncovalent interactions. J. Chem. Theor. Comput. **7**(2), 291–309 (2011)

19. Barone, V.: Anharmonic vibrational properties by a fully automated second-order perturbative approach. J. Chem. Phys. **122**, 14108 (2005)

20. Bloino, J., Biczysko, M., Barone, V.: General perturbative approach for spectroscopy, thermodynamics, and kinetics: methodological background and benchmark studies. J. Chem. Theory Comput. **8**(3), 1015–1036 (2012)

21. Barone, V., Biczysko, M., Bloino, J.: Fully anharmonic IR and raman spectra of medium-size molecular systems: accuracy and interpretation. Phys. Chem. Chem. Phys. **16**(5), 1759–1787 (2014)

22. Miller, W.H., Hernandez, R., Handy, N.C., Jayatilaka, D., Willetts, A.: Ab initio calculation of anharmonic constants for a transition state, with application to semiclassical transition state tunneling probabilities. Chem. Phys. Lett. **172**(1), 62–68 (1990)

23. Leonori, F., Skouteris, D., Petrucci, R., Casavecchia, P., Rosi, M., Balucani, N.: Combined crossed beam and theoretical studies of the $C(^1D) + CH_4$ reaction. J. Chem. Phys. **138**, 24311 (2013)

24. Leonori, F., Petrucci, R., Balucani, N., Casavecchia, P., Rosi, M., Skouteris, D., Berteloite, C., Le Picard, S.D., Canosa, A., Sims, I.R.: Crossed-beam dynamics, low-temperature kinetics, and theoretical studies of the reaction $S(^1D) + C_2H_4$. J. Phys. Chem. A **113**, 15328–15345 (2009)

25. Vazart, F., Latouche, C., Skouteris, D., Balucani, N., Barone, V.: Cyanomethanimine isomers in cold interstellar clouds: insights from electronic structure and kinetic calculations. Astrophys. J. **810**(2), 111 (2015)

26. Vazart, F., Calderini, D., Puzzarini, C., Skouteris, D., Barone, V.: State-of-the-art thermochemical and kinetic computations for astrochemical complex organic molecule: formamide formation in cold interstellar clouds as a case study. J. Chem. Theor. Comput. **12** (11), 5385–5397 (2016)

27. Licari, D., Baiardi, A., Biczysko, M., Egidi, F., Latouche, C., Barone, V.: Implementation of a graphical user interface for the virtual multifrequency spectrometer: the vms-draw tool. J. Comput. Chem. **36**(5), 321–334 (2014)
28. Johnson, T.J., Sams, R.L., Profeta, L.T.M., Akagi, S.K., Burling, I.R., Yokelson, R.J., Williams, S.D.: Quantitative IR spectrum and vibrational assignments for glycolaldehyde vapor: glycolaldehyde measurements in biomass burning plumes. J. Phys. Chem. A **117**(20), 4096–4107 (2013)
29. IR-Acetic Acid NIST, visited on 25th of January 2016
30. Lefloch, B., Ceccarelli, C., Codella, C., Favre, C., Podio, L., Vastel, C., Viti, S., Bachiller, R.: L1157-B1, a factory of complex organic molecules in a solar-type star forming region. Mon. Not. R. Astron. Soc. **469**, L73–L77 (2017)
31. Codella, C., Ceccarelli, C., Cabrit, S., Podio, L., Bachiller, R., Fontani, F., Gusdorf, A., Lefloch, B., Leurini, S., Tafalla, M.: Water and acetaldehyde in HH212: The first hot corino in Orion. A&A Lett. https://doi.org/10.1051/0004-6361/201527424

Double Photoionization of Simple Molecules of Astrochemical Interest

Stefano Falcinelli[1(✉)] ⓘ, Marzio Rosi[1,2], Franco Vecchiocattivi[1],
Fernando Pirani[3], Michele Alagia[4], Luca Schio[4], Robert Richter[5],
and Stefano Stranges[4,6]

[1] Department of Civil and Environmental Engineering, University of Perugia,
Via G. Duranti 93, 06125 Perugia, Italy
{stefano.falcinelli,marzio.rosi}@unipg.it,
franco@vecchio.it
[2] ISTM-CNR, 06123 Perugia, Italy
[3] Department of Chemistry, Biology and Biotechnologies, University of Perugia,
Via Elce di Sotto 8, 06123 Perugia, Italy
fernando.pirani@unipg.it
[4] IOM CNR Laboratorio TASC, 34012 Trieste, Italy
alagiam@elettra.trieste.it
[5] Sincrotrone Trieste, Area Science Park, 34149 Basovizza, Trieste, Italy
robert.richter@elettra.trieste.it
[6] Department of Chemistry and Drug Technology,
University of Rome Sapienza, 00185 Rome, Italy
stefano.stranges@uniroma1.it

Abstract. An experimental and computational investigation characterizing the processes following the double photoionization of the methyloxirane and N-methylformamide molecules has been reported. The double photoionization experiments have been performed at the Elettra Synchrotron Facility of Trieste (Italy). Preliminary data show: (i) in the case of methyloxirane, six different two-body fragmentation processes leading to $CH_2^+/C_2H_4O^+$, $CH_3^+/C_2H_3O^+$, $O^+/C_3H_6^+$, $OH^+/C_3H_5^+$, $C_2H_3^+/CH_3O^+$, $C_2H_4^+/CH_2O^+$ pairs of final ions; (ii) in the case of N-methylformamide, two main two-body fragmentation processes, leading to $CH_3^+ + CH_2NO^+$ and $H^+ + C_2H_4NO^+$. The threshold's energy for each dissociation channel is determined with the relative cross sections as a function of the investigated photon energy range. A careful analysis of recorded electron-ion-ion coincidence spectra mainly based on a Monte Carlo trajectory simulation is able to provide also the kinetic energy released (KER) distribution for the final ions of the investigated fragmentation reactions. These important experimental data are mandatory information to unravel the physical chemistry of the elementary processes induced by the interaction of photons, with simple relevant organic molecules: (i) the methyloxirane of astrochemical interest, being the first chiral molecule recently discovered in interstellar cloud Sagittarius B2; (ii) the N-methylformamide, being an important simple molecule containing the peptide bond, recently detected in the interstellar medium, in order to investigate its selective cleavage induced by UV photons. In the latter case, this can improve a deeper definition of formation/destruction routes in astrochemical environments of the more abundant formamide molecule.

© Springer International Publishing AG, part of Springer Nature 2018
O. Gervasi et al. (Eds.): ICCSA 2018, LNCS 10961, pp. 746–762, 2018.
https://doi.org/10.1007/978-3-319-95165-2_52

Keywords: Double photoionization · Molecular dications
Synchrotron radiation · Monte carlo simulation
Peptide bond · Astrochemistry

1 Introduction

The present paper represents an effort to unravel the physical chemistry of the elementary processes induced by the interaction of ionizing vacuum ultraviolet VUV photons with model molecules of astrochemical interest having the following peculiarity: (i) a simple chiral molecules, the methyloxirane, being the first chiral molecule detected by astronomers using highly sensitive radio telescopes in interstellar space [1]; (ii) one of the simplest organic molecule containing the peptide bond, as the N-methylformamide, in order to investigate its selective cleavage induced by UV photons, and to obtain deeper understanding in the photo-degradation mechanism of proteins. Furthermore, N-methylformamide has been recently detected in interstellar medium [2].

It is well known that the left-right dissymmetry, both at macroscopic and microscopic scales, plays a fundamental role in life science. Investigation of molecular enantiomeric nature has therefore a strong impact in chemistry in various subareas such as, heterogeneous enantioselective catalysis, photochemical asymmetric synthesis, drug activity, enzymatic catalysis, and chiral surface science involving supramolecular assemblies [3, 4]. The interaction of polarized light with chiral systems has been extensively studied since Pasteur's pioneering experiments on optical activity leading to the enantiomer recognition [5]. Although techniques involving optical rotation and circular dichroism in photoabsorption with visible/UV light are routinely used as well established analytical methods, studies of chiral systems using ionizing photons are instead very limited to date (see Ref. [6] and references therein). Progresses in synchrotron radiation techniques allowed intense photon sources with high degree of both linearly and circularly polarized light of both helicities to be used in experiments like that one concerning the present paper.

In particular, in the present paper we intended to study the fragmentation dynamics following the double photoionization of methyloxirane whose importance from an astrochemical point of view has been already mentioned above. In fact, this chiral molecule has been detected in the gas phase in a cold extended molecular shell around the embedded, massive protostellar clusters in the Sagittarius B2 star-forming region, being a material representative of the earliest stage of solar system evolution in which a chiral molecule has been found [1]. To characterize the ionizing VUV interaction with such a molecule, we started by the use of a linearly polarized synchrotron radiation, as that one available at the "Circular Polarization (CiPo)" Beamline at the Elettra Synchrotron Facility of Trieste (Italy), to perform a double photoionization experiment using the same ARPES (Angle Resolved Photo-Emission Spectroscopy) apparatus successfully employed in previous studies, performed by our research team [7–11]. In such an experiment, the double photoionization of methyloxirane molecules in a racemic mixture, has been performed in order to measure: (i) the threshold energy for the different ionic products formation; (ii) the related branching ratios, and (iii) the kinetic energy released (KER) distribution of fragment ions at different photon energies.

This preliminary study is important to provide unavailable data on dication energetics and nuclear dissociation dynamics, this being mandatory information for further experimental and theoretical investigations of the interaction between chiral molecules and circularly polarized radiation. For such a reason, we are planning to switch in next future to use the circularly polarized light, as available at "CiPo" Beamline, using the two enantiomers of methyloxirane with the aim to investigate possible differences on the angular and energy distribution of fragment ions and ejected photoelectrons at different photon energies.

On the other hand, concerning the study of the radiation damage on a biological system, it has to be noted that it is triggered by processes occurring at the microscopic level on its elementary constituents and the use of gas phase techniques is particularly suited to elucidate the mechanisms of damage in a variety of systems of biological relevance. The approach used in the present experimental study, where the interaction of molecules containing a peptide bond with an external probe as the UV synchrotron radiation is studied in a controlled environment, leads to a deep understanding of the role of the initial excitation process, the structural reorganization of the molecular system and the chemical reactions occurring in the early stages of the induced photo-degradation damage. To achieve these objectives, this work aims to bring together an experimental and theoretical effort, with complementary skills encompassing several fields of gas-phase chemistry, like mass spectrometry, spectroscopy, reaction dynamics, and theoretical chemistry [12–15].

2 Experimental

The data reported and discussed in this paper were recorded in experiments performed at the ELETTRA Synchrotron Facility of Basovizza, Trieste (Italy). The ARPES end station was employed at the "Circular Polarization (CiPo)" (in the case of the double photoionization of methyloxirane) and "Gas Phase" (in the case of N-methylformamide) beamlines.

For the present experiment we used a 3D-ion-imaging TOF spectrometer schematized in Fig. 1 that we have successfully applied recently to N_2O [16, 17], CO_2 [18, 19], C_6H_6 [20, 21], and C_2H_2 [22, 23] double photoionization experiments. In particular, this device consists in a time of flight (TOF) spectrometer equipped with an ion position sensitive detector (stack of three micro-channel-plates with a multi-anode array arranged in 32 rows and 32 columns). It has been especially designed in order to properly measure the spatial momentum components of the dissociation ionic products [24]. The data were accumulated using the same method previously employed, and the analysis has been carried out by using the codes and computational procedure already well tested (see Sect. 3). The energy selected synchrotron light beam operating in the 18–37 eV (in the case of methyloxirane) and 26–45 eV (N-methylformamide) photon energy ranges crosses at right angle an effusive molecular beam of the neutral precursor molecule, and the ion products are detected in coincidence with photoelectrons coming out from the same double photoionization event under study.

Both methyloxirane and N-methylformamide molecular beams were prepared by effusion from a glass bottle containing a commercial sample (with a 99% nominal

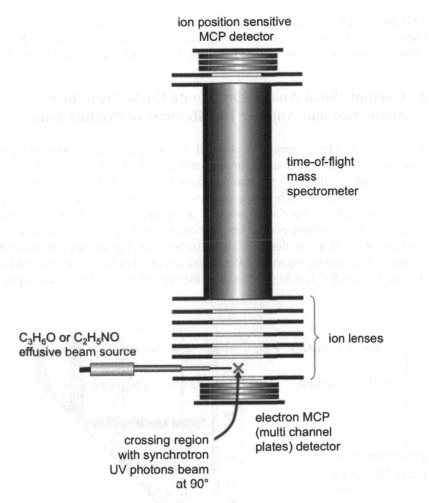

Fig. 1. A schematic view of the electron-ion-ion coincidence device used in our 3D-ion-imaging TOF mass spectrometry determinations.

purity), and were supplied by a needle effusive beam source taking advantage of their relatively high vapor pressure at a room temperature. For such a purpose we worked also using a closed system having a forced ventilation hood. In the double photoionization experiment of methyloxirane ("CiPo" beamline) has been used a Normal Incidence Monochromator (NIM), equipped with two different holographic gratings, allowing to cover the 18–37 eV energy range by means of a Gold (2400 l/mm) and an Aluminum (1200 l/mm) coated grating. spurious effects, due to ionization by photons from higher orders of diffraction, are reduced by the use of the NIM geometry.

In the double photoionization of N-mehyl formamide performed at the "GasPhase" beamline in the 26–45 eV photon energy range a monochromator using a 400 l/mm spherical grating in first diffraction order was employed with a magnesium film filter placed in the synchrotron radiation beam path in order to avoid spurious effects due to ionization by photons from higher orders of diffraction. In both experiments the resolution in the investigated photon energy range was about 1.5–2.0 meV. More details about the used experimental techniques have been detailed elsewhere [25–27].

3 Computational Analysis by Monte Carlo Trajectory Simulation and Angular Distributions of Product Ions

A typical coincidence spectrum obtained in our photoelectron-photoion-photoion coincidence measurements, using the apparatus described in Sect. 2, has been reported in Fig. 2 and is related to the double photoionization of N-methylformamide at a photon energy of 35 eV. The lower panel, in Fig. 2 shows the mass spectrum of ions produced in such an experiment, whereas in the upper panel of the same figure the related ion–ion coincidences diagram is reported. The latter is an example of a typical spectrum obtained in our double photoionization experiments using the electron-ion-ion coincidence device reported in Fig. 1 and discussed in Sect. 2. In this kind of plot, any point, inside the areas highlighted with the two red ovals in Fig. 2, corresponds to a

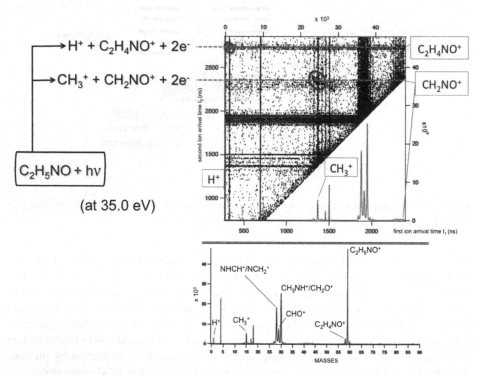

Fig. 2. The coincidence spectrum (upper panel) and the relative mass spectrum (lower panel) recorded in the double photoionization experiment of N-methylformamide at a photon energy of 35 eV. In the Figure the two possible two-body fragmentation channels observed in our experiments are also reported. In red color are the dotted regions used for the evaluation of the relative cross sections of recorded dissociation channels.

couple of time-of-flight values of a pair of ions produced in the same photoionization event (see for instance Ref. [28]).

In the mass spectrum (see Fig. 2 - lower panel) all product ions obtained in the single and double ionization of the neutral molecular precursor (in this case the N-methylformamide) are evident together with some background peaks. In the coincidence plot of the same figure (see the upper panel) are clearly indicated the ionic products detected in coincidence, with their relative traces (see the blue lines in the figure), and produced by the two two-body dissociation processes in the double photoionization of N-methylformamide. In our experiment they are the two $H^+ + C_2H_4NO^+$ and $CH_3^+ + CH_2NO^+$ pairs of fragment ions. The points in the figure represent the coincidence events as a function of the arrival time of the first ion, t_1, and of the second ion, t_2 (both times are reported in ns).

The analysis of coincidence spectra recorded at each investigated photon energy (as the one shown in Fig. 2) allows the following: (i) the evaluation of the relative cross section for each investigated two-body fragmentation channel, by counting the density of coincidences inside the related areas in the recorded experimental plots (as for example, the two red oval regions of Fig. 2 – upper panel); (ii) the KER of the two ionic fragments by a simple analysis based on the method suggested by Lundqvist et al. [29]; (iii) the determination of the lifetime τ of the intermediate molecular dication formed in the double ionization of the neutral molecular precursor by the analysis of coincidence dot distributions as a function of the arrival time differences $(t_2 - t_1)$ of the fragment ions to the ion-position-sensitive MCP detector as suggested by Field and Eland [30].

By using a proper computational procedure developed in our laboratory, applaying a Monte Carlo trajectory simulation already discussed in previous papers [31–34], the experimental distribution of the coincidences dot density $I(t_2 - t_1)$ is performed, adjusting KER and τ and evaluating the standard deviation as a reliability level of the simulation.

In our experiments concerning both methyloxirane and N-methylformamide molecules no clear evidence for the formation of stable $C_3H_6O^{2+}$ and $C_2H_5NO^{2+}$ molecular dications, respectively has been detected. All recorded coincidence spectra, in the whole investigated photon energy range, indicated that the lifetime of both $C_3H_6O^{2+}$ and $C_2H_5NO^{2+}$ dications should be shorter than ~ 50 ns, being the characteristic time window of our electron-ion-ion coincidence apparatus [35–39].

4 Discussion

The investigated molecules are of interest because the methyloxirane is the first chiral molecule detected in interstellar space [1], and the N-methylformamide is a prototype simple molecule containing the peptide bond recently found in space [2]. The data here reported and discussed concern: (i) the KER distributions recorded for each investigated two-body fragmentation channels observed in the 18–37 eV double photoionization of methyloxirane; (ii) the relative cross sections for the two-body dissociation channels observed in a preliminar double photoionization experiment of N-methylformamide performed in the 26–45 eV photon energy range.

4.1 Kinetic Energy Released Distributions of Product Ions in the Double Photoionization of Methyloxirane

In a recent double photoionization experiment of methyloxirane in a photon energy range of 18–37 eV [6] we found the following six two-body fragmentation channels accessible in the Coulomb explosion of the $(C_3H_6O^{2+})^*$ intermediate molecular dication with the measured relative abundances:

$$C_3H_6O + h\nu \rightarrow (C_3H_6O^{2+})^* + 2e^- \rightarrow C_2H_4^+ + CH_2O^+ \quad 66.70\% \tag{1}$$

$$\rightarrow CH_2^+ + C_2H_4O^+ \quad 7.84\% \tag{2}$$

$$\rightarrow CH_3^+ + C_2H_3O^+ \quad 5.00\% \tag{3}$$

$$\rightarrow O^+ + C_3H_6^+ \quad 1.59\% \tag{4}$$

$$\rightarrow C_2H_3^+ + CH_6O^+ \quad 18.70\% \tag{5}$$

$$\rightarrow OH^+ + C_3H_5^+ \quad 0.17\% \tag{6}$$

The measured threshold for the double ionization of methyloxirane was 28.3 ± 0.1 eV [6]. In this paper we present the KER distributions of product ions obtained as a function of the investigated photon energy for each reaction (1)–(6) above. Such KER distributions are reported in Figs. 3, 5, 6 and 7. It was not possible to determine KER distributions related to product ions of reaction (6) because the too low intensity of recorded signals for $OH^+ + C_3H_5^+$ coincidences. All recorded KER distributions of Figs. 3, 5, 6 and 7 do not change appreciably with the photon energy. In particular, they appear rather symmetric and can be easily fitted by a simple Gaussian function. It has to be noted that in such Figures the peaks position and relative shapes, for each analyzed dissociation channel, are practically the same for all investigated photon energies. This could be an indication that each fragmentation channel involves one specific region of the multidimensional potential energy surface, associated to the effective intramolecular interaction within the $(C_3H_6O)^{2+}$ dication frame and responsible of the opening of the various two body fragmentation channels, at all investigated energies. Therefore, for all investigated fragmentation channels the excess of the used photon energy respect to the double ionization threshold energy should be released as electron recoil energy. The only exception is constituted by the recorded total KER distribution for the two $CH_3^+ + C_2H_3O^+$ product ions of reaction (3) shown in the right panel of Fig. 7 as a function of the investigated photon energy. It is evident that such total KER distributions are characterized by a bimodal behavior depending on the two possible microscopic mechanisms for the two body fragmentation of $(C_3H_6O)^{2+}$ dication producing $CH_3^+ + C_2H_3O^+$. In fact, reaction (3) may occurs by two different pathways: in one case (probably the most important one) a direct fragmentation of the $(C_3H_6O)^{2+}$ dication into $CH_3^+ + C_2H_3O^+$ products can occurs, while in a second case the Coulomb explosion of the $(C_3H_6O)^{2+}$ dication takes place by means of a hydrogen migration from the methyl group of propylene oxide molecule to the end carbon atom

$$C_3H_6O + h\nu \longrightarrow C_2H_4^+ + CH_2O^+ + 2\ e^-$$

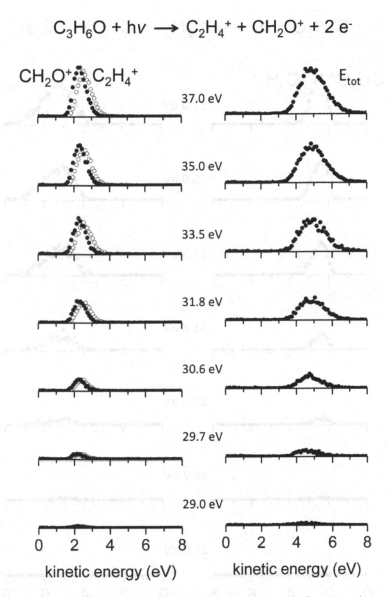

Fig. 3. The kinetic energy released (KER) distribution of the $C_2H_4^+ + CH_2O^+$ products of reaction (1) formed in the double photoionization experiment of methyloxirane at different photon energies: in the left panel are reported the KER for each fragment ion, whereas in right panel the total KER distributions are shown.

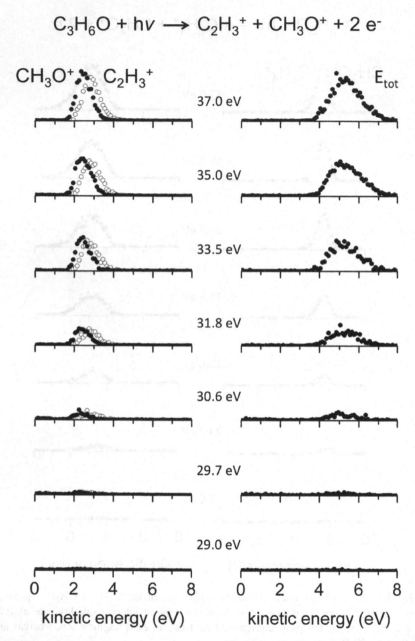

Fig. 4. The kinetic energy released (KER) distribution of the $C_2H_3^+ + CH_3O^+$ products of reaction (5) formed in the double photoionization experiment of methyloxirane at different photon energies: in the left panel are reported the KER for each fragment ion, whereas in right panel the total KER distributions are shown.

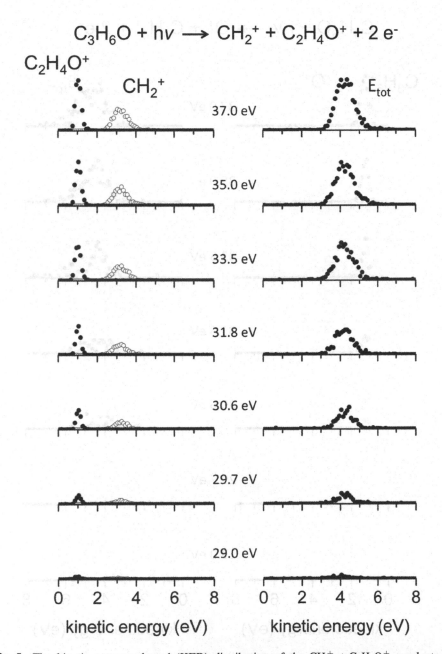

Fig. 5. The kinetic energy released (KER) distribution of the $CH_2^+ + C_2H_4O^+$ products of reaction (2) formed in the double photoionization experiment of methyloxirane at different photon energies: in the left panel are reported the KER for each fragment ion, whereas in right panel the total KER distributions are shown.

756 S. Falcinelli et al.

$$C_3H_6O + h\nu \longrightarrow O^+ + C_3H_6^+ + 2\,e^-$$

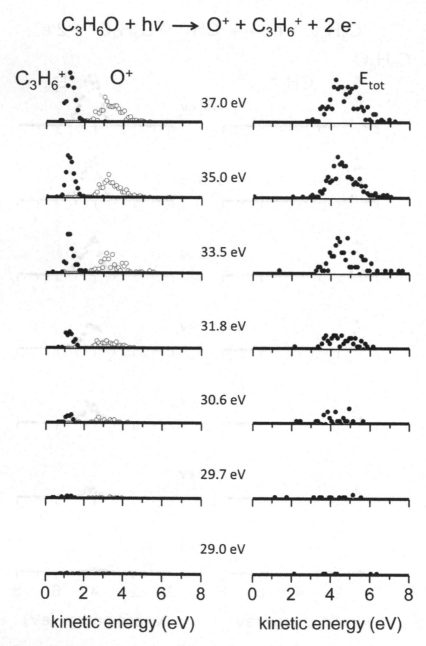

Fig. 6. The kinetic energy released (KER) distribution of the $O^+ + C_3H_6^+$ products of reaction (4) formed in the double photoionization experiment of methyloxirane at different photon energies: in the left panel are reported the KER for each fragment ion, whereas in right panel the total KER distributions are shown.

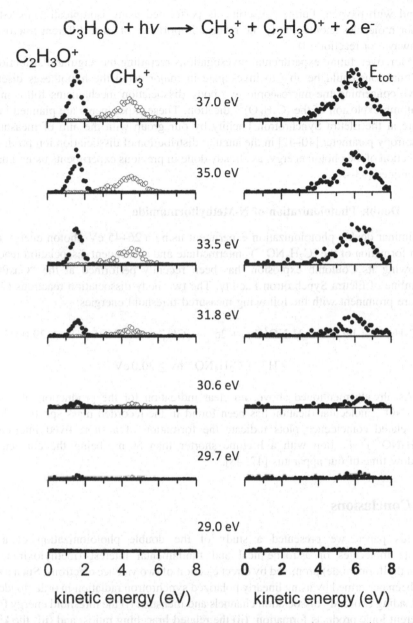

$$C_3H_6O + h\nu \longrightarrow CH_3^+ + C_2H_3O^+ + 2\,e^-$$

Fig. 7. The kinetic energy released (KER) distribution of the $CH_3^+ + C_2H_3O^+$ products of reaction (3) formed in the double photoionization experiment of methyloxirane at different photon energies: in the left panel are reported the KER for each fragment ion, whereas in right panel the total KER distributions are shown.

bound with oxygen. Further experiments performed using isotopically labeled precursor molecules should clarify the relative importance of such different microscopic pathways for reaction (3).

Moreover, future experimental investigations recording the angular distributions of the final ions could be able to investigate in major detail the hypotheses discussed above concerning the microscopic two body dissociation mechanisms following the Coulomb explosion of the $(C_3H_6O)^{2+}$ dication. These experiments are planned in next future at the Elettra Synchrotron Facility by our group with the aim of measure the anisotropy parameter [40–42] in the angular distribution of dissociation ion products as a function of the photon energy, as already done in previous experiments using imaging techniques [43–46].

4.2 Double Photoionization of N-Methylformamide

Preliminar double photoionization experiment using a 26–45 eV photon energy range with formation of the $(C_2H_5NO^{2+})^*$ intermediate and subsequent dissociation reactions following its Coulomb explosion, has been recently performed at the "GasPhase" beamline of Elettra Synchrotron Facility. The two-body dissociation reactions (7) and (8) are prominent with the following measured threshold energies:

$$C_2H_5NO + h\nu \rightarrow \left(C_2H_5NO^{2+}\right)^* + 2e^- \rightarrow CH_3^+ + CH_2NO^+ \quad h\nu \geq 29.0\,eV \quad (7)$$

$$\rightarrow H^+ + C_2H_4NO^+ \quad h\nu \geq 30.0\,eV \quad (8)$$

As already mentioned above, no clear indication for the production of a stable $C_2H_5NO^{2+}$ molecular dication has been found in the recorded mass spectra, whereas the related coincidence plots indicate the formation of a short lived intermediate $(C_2H_5NO^{2+})^*$ dication with a lifetime shorter than 50 ns, being the characteristic window time of our apparatus [47, 48].

5 Conclusions

In this paper, we presented a study of the double photoionization of a two simple molecules of astrochemical and fundamental interest (methyloxirane and N-methylformamide) promoted by direct ejection of two valence electrons. Such a study has been performed by using linearly polarized synchrotron radiation in order to identify the leading two-body dissociation channels and measure: (i) the threshold energy for the different ionic products formation; (ii) the related branching ratios, and (iii) the kinetic energy released distribution of fragment ions at different photon energies. This preliminary study is important to provide unavailable data on $C_3H_6O^{2+}$ and $C_2H_5NO^{2+}$ dications energetics, and nuclear dissociation dynamics, being mandatory information for further experimental and theoretical investigations of the interaction between chiral and peptide bond containing molecules and linearly or circularly polarized light. In our experiment we were able to directly measure the threshold energies for each open dissociation channels. Besides, for all investigated fragmentation channels, in the case of the double photoionization of methyloxirane, the recorded KER distributions indicate that the excess of the used photon energy, respect to the double ionization threshold energy, should be released as electron recoil energy [49–51]. The CH_3^+ formation by reaction (3) could involve two different carbon atoms of the precursor molecule: in one case the carbon atom of the methyl end of the propylene oxide molecule, while in a second case there is the possibility of a hydrogen migration from this methyl group to the end carbon atom bound with oxygen. This is confirmed by the observation of a bimodality in the total KER distribution for the $CH_3^+ + C_2H_3O^+$ product ions of reaction (3). Further experiments performed using isotopically labeled precursor molecules should clarify the relative importance of such different microscopic pathways. In the case of the N-methylformamide the preliminar reported results indicate two main two-body fragmentation reactions for the Coulomb explosion of the intermediate molecular dication. These data are mandatory for a fully description of the microscopic dynamics following the peptide bond cleavage by UV radiations and can help to better define its destruction pathways which can improve also a deeper definition of formation/destruction routes in astrochemical environments of the much more abundant formamide [52]. For such a purpose, further experiments are planned to investigate a set of isotopically labeled molecules (D, C13, N15, and O18 isotopically labeld N-methylformamides), to distinguish possible competitive microscopic mechanisms forming the same final ion products.

Furthermore, at the same time, theoretical efforts will be done by our group, by using the same methodology already applied for different investigated systems [53–58] in order to calculate the energy and structure of dissociation product ions to provide further information on the dynamics of the charge separation reactions following the photoionization event.

Acknowledgments. This work has been supported by MIUR "PRIN 2015" funds, project "STARS in the CAOS (Simulation Tools for Astrochemical Reactivity and Spectroscopy in the Cyberinfrastructure for Astrochemical Organic Species)", Grant Number 2015F59J3R. Financial contributions from the "Fondazione Cassa di Risparmio di Perugia" is gratefully acknowledged.

References

1. McGuire, B.A., Carroll, P.B., Loomis, R.A., et al.: Science **352**, 1449–1452 (2016)
2. Belloche, A., Meshcheryakov, A.A., Garrod, R.T., et al.: A&A **601**, A49 (2017)
3. Wan, T.A., Davies, M.E.: Nature (London), **370**, p. 449 (1994)
4. Riviera, J.M., Martin, T., Rebek Jr., J.: Science **279**, 1021 (1998)
5. Pasteur, L.: Ann. Chim. Phys. **24**, 442 (1848)
6. Falcinelli, S., Vecchiocattivi, F., Alagia, M., Schio, L., Richter, R., Stranges, S.P., et al.: J. Chem. Phys. **148**, 114302 (2018)
7. Rosi, M., Falcinelli, S., Balucani, N., Casavecchia, P., Leonori, F., Skouteris, D.: Theoretical study of reactions relevant for atmospheric models of titan: interaction of excited nitrogen atoms with small hydrocarbons. In: Murgante, B., Gervasi, O., Misra, S., Nedjah, N., Rocha, A.M.A.C., Taniar, D., Apduhan, B.O. (eds.) ICCSA 2012, Part 1. LNCS, vol. 7333, pp. 331–344. Springer, Heidelberg (2012). https://doi.org/10.1007/978-3-642-31125-3_26
8. Falcinelli, S., Pirani, F., Vecchiocattivi, F.: Atmosphere **6**(3), 299–317 (2015)

9. Alagia, M., Balucani, N., Candori, P., Falcinelli, S., Richter, R., Rosi, M., Pirani, F., Stranges, S., Vecchiocattivi, F.: Rendiconti Lincei Scienze Fisiche e Naturali **24**, 53–65 (2013)
10. Falcinelli, S.: Acta Phys. Pol., A **131**(1), 112–116 (2017)
11. Falcinelli, S., Candori, P., Pirani, F., Vecchiocattivi, F.: Phys. Chem. Chem. Phys. **19**(10), 6933–6944 (2017)
12. Falcinelli, S., Pirani, F., Alagia, M., Schio, L., Richter, R., et al.: Chem. Phys. Lett. **666**, 1–6 (2016)
13. Falcinelli, S., Capriccioli, A., Pirani, F., Vecchiocattivi, F., Stranges, S., Martì, C., et al.: Fuel **209**, 802–811 (2017)
14. Kalogerakis, K.S., Matsiev, D., Cosby, P.C., et al.: Ann. Geophys. **36**, 13–24 (2018)
15. Sebastiani, B., Falcinelli, S.: Environments **5**(3), 33 (2018)
16. Alagia, M., Candori, P., Falcinelli, S., Lavollée, M., Pirani, F., Richter, R., Stranges, S., Vecchiocattivi, F.: J. Chem. Phys. **126**(20), 201101 (2007)
17. Alagia, M., Candori, P., Falcinelli, S., Lavollée, M., Pirani, F., Richter, R., Stranges, S., Vecchiocattivi, F.: Chem. Phys. Lett. **432**, 398–402 (2006)
18. Alagia, M., Candori, P., Falcinelli, S., Lavollée, M., Pirani, F., Richter, R., Stranges, S., Vecchiocattivi, F.: J. Phys. Chem. A **113**, 14755–14759 (2009)
19. Alagia, M., Candori, P., Falcinelli, S., Lavollèe, M., Pirani, F., Richter, R., Stranges, S., Vecchiocattivi, F.: Phys. Chem. Chem. Phys. **12**, 5389–5395 (2010)
20. Alagia, M., Candori, P., Falcinelli, S., Pirani, F., Pedrosa Mundim, M.S., Richter, R., Rosi, M., Stranges, S., Vecchiocattivi, F.: Phys. Chem. Chem. Phys. **13**(18), 8245–8250 (2011)
21. Alagia, M., Candori, P., Falcinelli, S., Mundim, M.S.P., Pirani, F., Richter, R., Rosi, M., Stranges, S., Vecchiocattivi, F.: J. Chem. Phys. **135**(14), 144304 (2011)
22. Alagia, M., Callegari, C., Candori, P., Falcinelli, S., Pirani, F., Richter, R., Stranges, S., Vecchiocattivi, F.: J. Chem. Phys. **136**, 204302 (2012)
23. Falcinelli, S., Alagia, M., Farrar, J.M., Kalogerakis, K.S., Pirani, F., Richter, R., et al.: J. Chem. Phys. **145**(11), 114308 (2016)
24. Lavollée, M.: Rev. Sci. Instr. **70**, 2968 (1990)
25. Schio, L., Li, C., Monti, S., Salén, P., Yatsyna, V., Feifel, R., Alagia, M., et al.: Phys. Chem. Chem. Phys. **17**(14), 9040–9048 (2015)
26. Falcinelli, S., Pirani, F., Alagia, M., Schio, L., Richter, R., Stranges, S., Balucani, N., Vecchiocattivi, F.: Atmosphere **7**(9), 112 (2016)
27. Falcinelli, S., Rosi, M., Cavalli, S., Pirani, F., Vecchiocattivi, F.: Chem. Eur. J. **22**(35), 12518–12526 (2016)
28. Falcinelli, S., Rosi, M., Candori, P., Vecchiocattivi, F., Farrar, J.M., Pirani, F., Balucani, N., Alagia, M., Richter, R., Stranges, S.: The escape probability of some ions from mars and titan ionospheres. In: Murgante, B., Misra, S., Rocha, A.M.A.C., Torre, C., Rocha, J.G., Falcão, M.I., Taniar, D., Apduhan, B.O., Gervasi, O. (eds.) ICCSA 2014, Part I. LNCS, vol. 8579, pp. 554–570. Springer, Cham (2014). https://doi.org/10.1007/978-3-319-09144-0_38
29. Lundqvist, M., Baltzer, P., Edvardsson, D., et al.: Phys. Rev. Lett. **75**, 1058 (1995)
30. Field, T.A., Eland, J.H.D.: Chem. Phys. Lett. **211**, 436 (1993)
31. Candori, P., Falcinelli, S., Pirani, F., Tarantelli, F., Vecchiocattivi, F.: Chem. Phys. Lett. **436**, 322–326 (2007)
32. Alagia, M., Bodo, E., Decleva, P., Falcinelli, S., Ponzi, A., Richter, R., Stranges, S.: Phys. Chem. Chem. Phys. **15**(4), 1310–1318 (2013)
33. Falcinelli, S., Bartocci, A., Cavalli, S., Pirani, F., Vecchiocattivi, F.: Chem. Eur. J. **22**(2), 764–771 (2016)

34. Falcinelli, S., Rosi, M., Candori, P., Vecchiocattivi, F., Farrar, J.M., Kalogerakis, K.S., Pirani, F., Balucani, N., Alagia, M., Richter, R., Stranges, S.: Angular distributions of fragment ions produced by coulomb explosion of simple molecular dications of astrochemical interest. In: Gervasi, O., Murgante, B., Misra, S., Gavrilova, M.L., Rocha, A.M.A.C., Torre, C., Taniar, D., Apduhan, B.O. (eds.) ICCSA 2015, Part II. LNCS, vol. 9156, pp. 291–307. Springer, Cham (2015). https://doi.org/10.1007/978-3-319-21407-8_22

35. Falcinelli, S., Rosi, M., Candori, P., Farrar, J.M., Vecchiocattivi, F., Pirani, F., Balucani, N., Alagia, M., Richter, R., Stranges, S.: Planet. Space Sci. **99**, 149–157 (2014)

36. Pirani, F., Falcinelli, S., Vecchiocattivi, F., Alagia, M., Richter, R., Stranges, S.: Rendiconti Lincei Scienze Fisiche e Naturali **29**(1), 179–189 (2018)

37. Alagia, M., Candori, P., Falcinelli, S., Mundim, K.C., Mundim, M.S.P., Pirani, F., et al.: Chem. Phys. **398**, 134–141 (2012)

38. Biondini, F., Brunetti, B.G., Candori, P., De Angelis, F., Falcinelli, S., Tarantelli, F., Teixidor, M.M., Pirani, F., Vecchiocattivi, F.: J. Chem. Phys. **122**(16), 164307 (2005)

39. Biondini, F., Brunetti, B.G., Candori, P., De Angelis, F., Falcinelli, S., Tarantelli, F., Pirani, F., Vecchiocattivi, F.: J. Chem. Phys. **122**(16), 164308 (2005)

40. Zare, R.N.: Mol. Photochem. **4**, 1 (1972)

41. Alagia, M., Brunetti, B.G., Candori, P., Falcinelli, S., Teixidor, M.M., Pirani, F., et al.: J. Chem. Phys. **120**(15), 6980–6984 (2004)

42. Alagia, M., Brunetti, B.G., Candori, P., Falcinelli, S., Teixidor, M.M., Pirani, F., et al.: J. Chem. Phys. **120**(15), 6985–6991 (2004)

43. Alagia, M., Biondini, F., Brunetti, B.G., Candori, P., Falcinelli, S., Teixidor, M.M., Pirani, F., et al.: J. Chem. Phys. **121**(21), 10508–10512 (2004)

44. Teixidor, M.M., Pirani, F., Candori, P., Falcinelli, S., Vecchiocattivi, F.: Chem. Phys. Lett. **379**, 139–146 (2003)

45. Alagia, M., Brunetti, B.G., Candori, P., et al.: J. Chem. Phys. **124**(20), 204318 (2006)

46. Pei, L., Carrascosa, E., Yang, N., Falcinelli, S., Farrar, J.M.: J. Phys. Chem. Lett. **6**(9), 1684–1689 (2015)

47. Schio, L., Li, C., Monti, S., Salen, P., Yatsyna, V., et al.: Phys. Chem. Chem. Phys. **17**(14), 9040–9048 (2015)

48. Ben Arfa, M., Lescop, B., Cherid, M., Brunetti, B., Candori, P., et al.: Chem. Phys. Lett. **308**, 71–77 (1999)

49. Brunetti, B., Candori, P., Falcinelli, S., Lescop, B., et al.: Eur. Phys. J. D **38**, 21–27 (2006)

50. Lombardi, A., Lago, N.F., Laganà, A., Pirani, F., Falcinelli, S.: A bond-bond portable approach to intermolecular interactions: simulations for N-methylacetamide and carbon dioxide dimers. In: Murgante, B., Gervasi, O., Misra, S., Nedjah, N., Rocha, A.M.A.C., Taniar, D., Apduhan, B.O. (eds.) ICCSA 2012. LNCS, vol. 7333, pp. 387–400. Springer, Heidelberg (2012). https://doi.org/10.1007/978-3-642-31125-3_30

51. Falcinelli, S., et al.: Modeling the intermolecular interactions and characterization of the dynamics of collisional autoionization processes. In: Murgante, B., et al. (eds.) ICCSA 2013, Part 1. LNCS, vol. 7971. Springer, Heidelberg (2013). https://doi.org/10.1007/978-3-642-39637-3_6

52. Barone, V., Latouche, C., Skouteris, D., et al.: MNRAS Letters **453**, L31–L35 (2015)

53. Falcinelli, S., Fernandez-Alonso, F., Kalogerakis, K., Zare, R.N.: Mol. Phys. **88**(3), 663–672 (1996)

54. Alagia, M., Boustimi, M., Brunetti, B.G., Candori, P., et al.: J. Chem. Phys. **117**(3), 1098–1102 (2002)

55. Alagia, M., Furlani, F., Pirani, F., Lavollée, M., Richter, R., Stranges, S., et al.: Rendiconti Lincei Scienze Fisiche e Naturali **19**, 215–221 (2008)

56. Balucani, N., Bartocci, A., Brunetti, B., Candori, C., et al.: Chem. Phys. Lett. **546**, 34–39 (2012)
57. Skouteris, D., Balucani, N., Faginas-Lago, N., et al.: A&A **584**, A76 (2015)
58. Rosi, M., Falcinelli, S., Balucani, N., Faginas-Lago, N., Ceccarelli, C., Skouteris, D.: A theoretical study on the relevance of protonated and ionized species of methanimine and methanol in astrochemistry. In: Gervasi, O., Murgante, B., Misra, S., Rocha, A.M.C., Torre, C., Taniar, D., Apduhan, B.O., Stankova, E., Wang, S. (eds.) ICCSA 2016, PArt 1. LNCS, vol. 9786, pp. 296–308. Springer, Cham (2016). https://doi.org/10.1007/978-3-319-42085-1_23

A Theoretical Investigation of the Reaction N(^{2}D) + C$_6$H$_6$ and Implications for the Upper Atmosphere of Titan

Nadia Balucani$^{1(\boxtimes)}$ ⓘ, Leonardo Pacifici^1, Dimitrios Skouteris^2 ⓘ,
Adriana Caracciolo^1, Piergiorgio Casavecchia^1 ⓘ,
and Marzio Rosi^{3,4} ⓘ

^{1} Dipartimento di Chimica, Biologia e Biotecnologie,
Università degli Studi di Perugia, 06123 Perugia, Italy
{nadia.balucani, piergiorgio.casavecchia}@unipg.it,
adriana.caracciolo@studenti.unipg.it
^{2} Scuola Normale Superiore, 56126 Pisa, Italy
dimitrios.skouteris@sns.it
^{3} Dipartimento di Ingegneria Civile e Ambientale,
Università degli Studi di Perugia, 06125 Perugia, Italy
marzio.rosi@unipg.it
^{4} CNR-ISTM, 06123 Perugia, Italy

Abstract. The reaction between nitrogen atoms in their first electronically excited state ^{2}D with benzene has been characterized by electronic structure calculations of the stationary points along the minimum energy path. According to this study, there are six open channels leading to C$_6$H$_5$N (phenylnitrene) + H, C$_6$H$_4$ + NH$_2$, C$_5$H$_5$ (cyclopentadienyl) + HNC, C$_5$H$_5$CN + H, C$_5$H$_4$ + HCNH and C$_5$H$_5$N (pyridine) + CH. There is no barrier in the entrance channel, so that the N(^{2}D) + C$_6$H$_6$ reaction is expected to be very fast also under the low temperature conditions of Titan, the massive moon of Saturn. The possible impact of the title reaction in the chemistry of the upper atmosphere of Titan, where benzene is present and atomic nitrogen in ^{2}D state can be efficiently produced by a series of high-energy processes, is also discussed.

Keywords: Electronic structure calculations · Kinetics calculations
Chemistry of planetary atmosphere · Prebiotic chemistry

1 Introduction

Titan is a massive moon of Saturn with the characteristics of a real planet. In particular, it does possess an atmosphere, which is actually thicker than the terrestrial one. Similarly to the case of the terrestrial atmosphere, the composition of atmosphere of Titan is dominated by dinitrogen, N$_2$, with a mole fraction of 0.97. The second most abundant species, with an average amount of 2.7%, is methane, CH$_4$. Minor components include H$_2$, Ar, higher hydrocarbons (C$_2$H$_6$, C$_2$H$_2$, C$_2$H$_4$) and nitriles (HCN, HCCCN). The NASA/ESA/ASI Cassini-Huygens mission provided us with a plethora of information about this interesting object of our Solar System, which revealed itself as the body with

O. Gervasi et al. (Eds.): ICCSA 2018, LNCS 10961, pp. 763–772, 2018.
https://doi.org/10.1007/978-3-319-95165-2_53

the most chemically active atmosphere, in spite of the global low temperature (94 K at the surface and up to *ca.* 200 K at high altitudes) [1, 2]. Unexpectedly, the richest chemistry occurs in the upper part of the atmosphere, from the stratosphere up to the thermosphere where the first haze layer is located. The first measurements of Titan's ionosphere revealed a totally unexpected complex composition with positive ions as large as $m/z \sim 350$ [3–5] and negatively charged ions with m/z up to 4000 [6]. In recent years, the atmosphere of Titan has become the object of further ground-based observations with the ALMA interferometer [7].

Among the species identified by Cassini Ion Neutral Mass Spectrometer (INMS), benzene is characterized by a significant mole fraction (for instance, at 950 km the mole fraction of benzene is 1.3×10^{-6} [8]). In the same range of altitude, molecular nitrogen is converted into atomic nitrogen or N^{+}/N_2^{+} ions by the interaction with extreme ultra-violet (EUV) photons or by other energetic processes [9]. In particular, N atoms are produced by N_2 dissociation induced by electron impact/EUV photons or dissociative photoionization, galactic cosmic ray absorption, and N_2^{+} dissociative recombination [9]. All these processes lead to the formation of atomic nitrogen in its ground electronic state $^{4}S_{3/2}$ and, in a similar amount, in the first electronically excited $^{2}D_{3/2,5/2}$ states [9]. The radiative lifetimes of the metastable $^{2}D_{3/2,5/2}$ states are long enough (6.1×10^{4} s and 1.4×10^{5} s for the $^{2}D_{3/2}$ and $^{2}D_{5/2}$ state, respectively) to make possible their chemical reactions in binary collisions with other constituents of the upper atmosphere [10–14]. This specific aspect is rather important because it is known that nitrogen is significantly incorporated into the large N-containing organic molecules that form the orange aerosol covering the moon [15]. The reactions of $N(^{2}D)$ with various hydrocarbons (CH_4, C_2H_2, C_2H_4, C_2H_6) have been characterized in laboratory experiments [16–21] and are known to be rather efficient, while the same reactions involving the ground state ^{4}S atoms are very slow [9, 16]. Interestingly, in all the above mentioned cases, the formation of product species containing a novel C-N bond has been observed [17–22]. Nitrogen atoms in the $^{2}D_{3/2,5/2}$ states can also react with molecular hydrogen and water vapor, other species observed in Titan's atmosphere [23–26].

In this contribution, we report on a theoretical characterization of the reaction involving $N(^{2}D)$ and benzene. The aim is to determine the chemical behavior of $N(^{2}D)$ with aromatic species after the previous investigation with aliphatic molecules [17–22]. In particular, we wish to establish whether the aromatic ring is preserved in this reaction (as already observed in other cases [27–31]) and whether the N atom is incorporated in the ring of carbon atoms [32], forming pyridine or its less stable isomers. Remarkably, by the analysis of the spectra recorded by the Cassini-INMS in the Open Source Ion mode the presence of a species with general formula C_5H_5N was inferred, indicating that either pyridine or one of its isomers are actually formed in the upper atmosphere of Titan starting from active forms of nitrogen [5].

With this aim, we have performed electronic structure calculations of the stationary points along the minimum energy path. These calculations will complement crossed molecular beam (CMB) experiments which are currently under way and will also be completed by kinetics calculations.

2 Computational Details

The potential energy surface (PES) of the N(^{2}D) + C$_6$H$_6$ system was investigated by locating the lowest stationary points at the B3LYP level of theory [33, 34]. The 6-311 +G** basis set [35, 36] is used, which implies the following functions: (12s6p1d)/ [5s4p1d] for C and N and (5s1p)/[3s1p] for H. At the same level of theory we have computed the harmonic vibrational frequencies in order to check the nature of the stationary points, i.e. minimum if all the frequencies are real, saddle point if there is only one imaginary frequency. The assignment of the saddle points was performed using intrinsic reaction coordinate (IRC) calculations [37, 38]. The geometry of all the species was optimized without any symmetry constraints. For comparison purposes, the energy of selected stationary points was computed also at the higher level of calculation CCSD(T) [39–41] using the aug-cc-pVTZ basis set [42] at the B3LYP optimized geometries, following a well-established computational scheme [43]. Both the B3LYP and the CCSD(T) energies were corrected to 0 K by adding the zero-point energy correction computed using the scaled harmonic vibrational frequencies evaluated at B3LYP/6-311+G** level. All calculations were done using Gaussian 09 [44] while the analysis of the vibrational frequencies was performed using Molekel [45, 46].

3 Results

Figure 1 reports the minimum energy path for the reaction N(^{2}D) + C$_6$H$_6$ computed at the B3LYP/6-311+G** level, while Table 1 shows for the same process the enthalpy changes and the barrier heights computed at the same level of calculation for selected dissociation and isomerization processes for the investigated system.

Table 1. Enthalpy changes and barrier heights (kcal/mol, 0 K) computed at the B3LYP/6-311 +G** level of theory for selected dissociation and isomerization processes for the system N (^{2}D) + C$_6$H$_6$. When indicated, the superscript represents the spin multiplicity.

	ΔH_0^0	Barrier height
N(^{2}D) + C$_6$H$_6$ → C$_6$H$_6$N (1)	−30.1	
C$_6$H$_6$N (1) → C$_6$H$_6$N (2)	−22.0	2.5
C$_6$H$_6$N (2) → C$_6$H$_6$N (3)	−25.4	0.1
C$_6$H$_6$N (3) → C$_6$H$_5$NH (4)	−51.8	48.4
C$_6$H$_5$NH (4) → ^{3}C$_6$H$_5$N + H (5)	85.7	
C$_6$H$_5$NH (4) → C$_5$H$_5$CNH (6)	51.4	57.3
C$_5$H$_5$CNH (6) → C$_5$H$_5$CNH (7)	−6.0	14.2
C$_5$H$_5$CNH (7) → ^{1}C$_5$H$_5$CN + H (8)	20.4	25.2
^{1}C$_5$H$_5$CN (8) → C$_5$H$_5$ + CN	94.9	
C$_5$H$_5$CNH (7) → C$_5$H$_5$ + HNC (15)	2.4	17.1
HNC → HCN	−14.0	30.4

(continued)

Table 1. (*continued*)

	ΔH_0^0	Barrier height
C$_6$H$_6$N (3) → C$_6$H$_6$N (9)	12.2	17.3
C$_6$H$_6$N (9) → C$_6$H$_5$NCH (10)	7.9	20.1
C$_6$H$_5$NCH (10) → C$_6$H$_5$NCH (11)	−15.4	22.8
C$_6$H$_5$NCH (11) → C$_6$H$_5$N + CH (12)	56.4	
C$_6$H$_5$NH (4) → C$_6$H$_4$NH$_2$ (13)	22.4	62.2
C$_6$H$_4$NH$_2$ (13) → C$_6$H$_4$ + NH$_2$ (14)	70.0	
C$_6$H$_5$NH (4) → C$_6$H$_5$ + NH	101.2	
C$_5$H$_5$CNH (7) → C$_5$H$_4$C(H)NH (16)	−23.6	33.3
C$_5$H$_4$C(H)NH(16) → C$_5$H$_4$ + cis-HCNH (17)	105.5	
C$_5$H$_4$C(H)NH(16) → C$_5$H$_4$ + trans-HCNH (17)	101.0	

The interaction of a nitrogen atom in its excited ^{2}D state with a benzene molecule gives rise to an electrostatic adduct (species (1) in Fig. 1) in a process which shows no barrier. In this species the nitrogen interacts with a carbon atom of the benzene ring. This species is more stable than the reactants by 30.1 kcal/mol, but, through a barrier as low as 2.5 kcal/mol, can isomerize to the more stable species (2) which is 22.0 kcal/mol lower in energy. Species (2) isomerizes very easily, the barrier height being only 0.1 kcal/mol, to

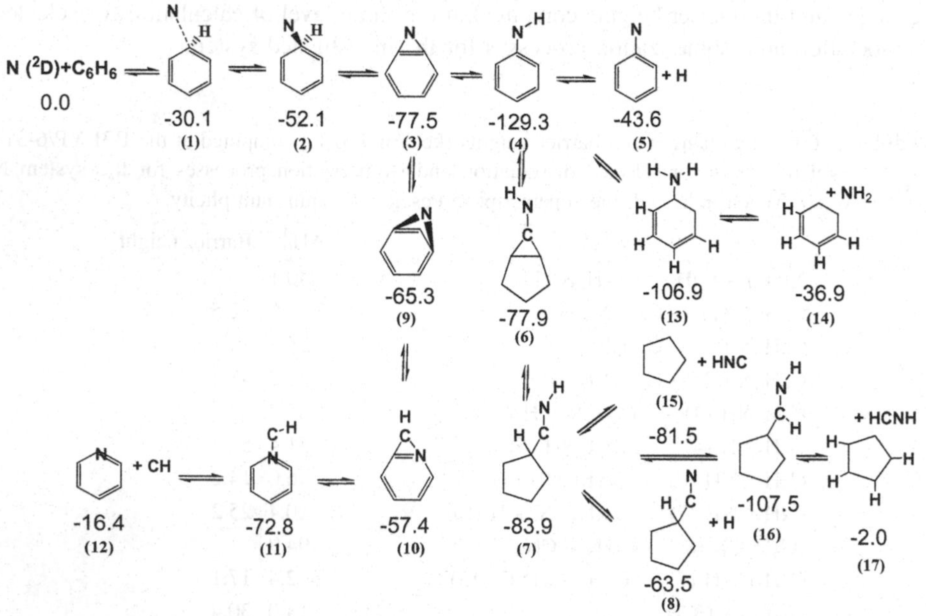

Fig. 1. Main steps along the minimum energy path for the reaction N + C$_6$H$_6$. Relative energies (kcal/mol, 0 K) with respect to N + C$_6$H$_6$.

species (3) more stable by 25.4 kcal/mol. Species (3), which shows the nitrogen atom bridging two carbon atoms of the ring, can isomerize in two different ways: it can give species (4) in an exothermic reaction or (9) in an endothermic process, which shows however a reasonably low barrier. The formation of (9) is very interesting, because (9), through the isomerization to (10) and (11), gives rise to the formation of pyridine (12). Species (4) can evolve in three different ways: it can lose one hydrogen atom giving rise to phenylnitrene in a reaction endothermic by 85.7 kcal/mol, it can isomerize to species (13) which can then lose a NH$_2$ group or it can isomerize to species (6). This last molecule is particularly interesting because, after the isomerization to (7), can produce HNC in conjunction with the C$_5$H$_5$ (cyclopentadienyl) radical (15). Alternatively, species (7) can lose a hydrogen atom giving rise to (8) which in turn can lose a CN radical, but this reaction is much more endothermic and requires an energy larger than that of the initial reactants. Finally, species (7) can also isomerize to (16) which can then dissociate to C$_5$H$_4$ and HCNH (17).

4 Discussion and Implications for the Atmospheric Chemistry of Titan

According to our electronic structure calculations, the title reaction has several open channels that can be summarized as follows:

$$
\begin{aligned}
N(^2D) + C_6H_6 &\rightarrow C_6H_5N \text{ (phenylnitrene)} + H & \Delta H^\circ_0 &= -43.6 \text{ kcal/mol} & \text{(a)}\\
&\rightarrow C_6H_4 + NH_2 & \Delta H^\circ_0 &= -36.9 \text{ kcal/mol} & \text{(b)}\\
&\rightarrow C_5H_5 \text{ (cyclopentadienyl)} + HNC & \Delta H^\circ_0 &= -81.5 \text{ kcal/mol} & \text{(c)}\\
&\rightarrow C_5H_5CN + H & \Delta H^\circ_0 &= -63.5 \text{ kcal/mol} & \text{(d)}\\
&\rightarrow C_5H_4 + HCNH & \Delta H^\circ_0 &= -2.0 \text{ kcal/mol} & \text{(e)}\\
&\rightarrow C_5H_5N \text{ (pyridine)} + CH & \Delta H^\circ_0 &= -16.4 \text{ kcal/mol} & \text{(f)}
\end{aligned}
$$

The preliminary analysis of the CMB experiments currently under way in our laboratory clearly indicates that molecular products with a mass-to-charge ratio (m/z) of 91 (C$_6$H$_5$N$^+$), 65 (C$_5$H$_5$$^+$) and, possibly, 64 (C$_5H_4$$^+$) are formed. Detection of pyridine or its isomers at m/z = 79 is hampered by the elastic scattering interference of the benzene reactant, because of the natural abundance of ^{13}C. Experimental results, therefore, confirm the occurrence of one or both H-displacement channels (a) and (d) and of the HNC elimination channel (c). A more detailed analysis will furnish the product branching ratios as already done for several reactive systems [17, 25, 31, 47–52]. Furthermore, RRKM calculations will be performed to derive the product branching ratio from the present electronic structure calculations also for the channels that cannot be investigated experimentally (for instance, see [17, 20, 21, 53–56]). The experimental/RRKM calculations will allow establishing which of the possible (a)–(f) channels is/are the dominant one.

In all cases, important conclusions can be drawn about the possible impact of the title reaction on the chemistry of the atmosphere of Titan. There is no barrier in the entrance channel, so that the N(^{2}D) + C$_6$H$_6$ reaction is expected to be very fast (in the gas-kinetics range) also under the low temperature conditions of Titan. In addition, this study demonstrates that the formation of species with m/z from 65 to 91 is possible. In particular, N atoms can be directly incorporated in the aromatic ring forming pyridine or substitute one H atom forming phenylnitrene or one of its isomers. Radical species with rings of 5/6 C atoms can also be formed in conjunction with HNC, NH_2 or HCNH. Radical species can further react in the conditions of the upper atmosphere of Titan thus contributing to the growing up of the large N-rich organic macromolecules constituting the haze aerosols of the moon. The present reaction can also be the missing formation route of pyridine, the presence of which was inferred by INMS results. Pyridine is currently the subject of a dedicated observational campaign with ALMA [56].

Acknowledgments. This work has been supported by MIUR "PRIN 2015" funds, project "STARS in the CAOS (Simulation Tools for Astrochemical Reactivity and Spectroscopy in the Cyberinfrastructure for Astrochemical Organic Species)", Grant Number 2015F59J3R. DS wishes to thank the Italian Ministero dell'Istruzione, Università e Ricerca (MIUR_F-FABR17_SKOUTERIS) and the Scuola Normale Superiore (SNS_RB_SKOUTERIS) for financial support.

References

1. Brown, R., Lebreton, J.P., Waite, J. (eds.): Titan from Cassini-Huygens. Springer, Netherlands (2010). https://doi.org/10.1007/978-1-4020-9215-2
2. Vuitton, V., Dutuit, O., Smith, M.A., Balucani, N.: Chemistry of Titan's atmosphere. In: Mueller-Wodarg, I., Griffith, C., Lellouch, E., Cravens, T. (eds.) Titan: Surface, Atmosphere and Magnetosphere. Cambridge University Press, Cambridge (2013)
3. Vuitton, V., Yelle, R.V., Anicich, V.G.: The nitrogen chemistry of Titan's upper atmosphere revealed. Astrophys. J. **647**, L175–L178 (2006)
4. Waite Jr., J.H., Young, D.T., Cravens, T.E., Coates, A.J., Crary, F.J., Magee, B., Westlake, J.: The process of tholin formation in Titan's upper atmosphere. Science **316**, 870–875 (2007)
5. Vuitton, V., Yelle, R.V., McEwan, M.J.: Ion chemistry and N-containing molecules in Titan's upper atmosphere. Icarus **191**, 722–742 (2007)
6. Coates, A.J., Wellbrock, A., Lewis, G.R., Jones, G.H., Young, D.T., Crary, F.J., Waite Jr., J. H., Johnson, R.E., Hill, T.W., Sittler Jr., E.C.: Negative ions at Titan and Enceladus: recent results. Faraday Discuss. **147**, 293–305 (2010)
7. Lai, J.C.-Y., Cordiner, M.A., Nixon, C.A., Achterberg, R.K., Molter, E.M., Teanby, N.A., Palmer, M.Y., Charnley, S.B., Lindberg, J.E., Kisiel, Z., Mumma, M.J., Irwin, P.G.: Mapping vinyl cyanide and other nitriles in Titan's atmosphere using ALMA. Astron. J. **154** (206), 1–10 (2017)
8. Vuitton, V., Yelle, R.V., Cui, J.: Formation and distribution of benzene on Titan. J. Geophys. Res. **113**, E05007 (2008)
9. Lavvas, P., Galand, M., Yelle, R.V., Heays, A.N., Lewis, B.R., Lewis, G.R., Coates, A.J.: Energy deposition and primary chemical products in Titan's upper atmosphere. Icarus **213**, 233–251 (2011)

10. Dutuit, O., Carrasco, N., Thissen, R., Vuitton, V., Alcaraz, C., Pernot, P., Balucani, N., Casavecchia, P., Canosa, A., Le Picard, S., Loison, J.-C., Herman, Z., Zabka, J., Ascenzi, D., Tosi, P., Franceschi, P., Price, S.D., Lavvas, P.: Critical review of N, N$^+$, N$_2^+$, N^{++} and N$_2^{++}$ main production processes and reactions of relevance to Titan's atmosphere. Astrophys. J. Suppl. Ser. **204**, 20 (2013)

11. Balucani, N.: Nitrogen fixation by photochemistry in the atmosphere of Titan and implications for prebiotic chemistry. In: Trigo-Rodriguez, J., Raulin, F., Muller, C., Nixon, C. (eds.) The Early Evolution of the Atmospheres of Terrestrial Planets. Astrophysics and Space Science Proceedings, vol. 35, pp. 155–164. Springer, New York (2013). https://doi.org/10.1007/978-1-4614-5191-4_12

12. Balucani, N.: Elementary reactions of N atoms with hydrocarbons: first steps towards the formation of prebiotic N-containing molecules in planetary atmospheres. Chem. Soc. Rev. **41**, 5473–5483 (2012)

13. Balucani, N.: Elementary reactions and their role in gas-phase prebiotic chemistry. Int. J. Mol. Sci. **10**, 2304–2335 (2009)

14. Imanaka, H., Smith, M.A.: Formation of nitrogenated organic aerosols in the Titan upper atmosphere. PNAS **107**, 12423–12428 (2010)

15. Israel, G., Szopa, C., Raulin, F., Cabane, M., Niemann, H.B., Atreya, S.K., Bauer, S.J., Brun, J.F., Chassefiere, E., Coll, P., Conde, E., Coscia, D., Hauchecorne, A., Millian, P., Nguyen, M.J., Owen, T., Riedler, W., Samuelson, R.E., Siguier, J.M., Steller, M., Sternberg, R., Vidal-Madjar, C.: Complex organic matter in Titan's atmospheric aerosols from in situ pyrolysis and analysis. Nature **438**, 796 (2005)

16. Herron, J.T.: Evaluated chemical kinetics data for reactions of N(^{2}D), N(^{2}P), and N$_2$(A$^3\Sigma_u^+$) in the gas phase. J. Phys. Chem. Ref. Data **28**, 1453 (1999)

17. Balucani, N., Bergeat, A., Cartechini, L., Volpi, G.G., Casavecchia, P., Skouteris, D., Rosi, M.: Combined crossed molecular beam and theoretical studies of the N(^{2}D) + CH$_4$ reaction and implications for atmospheric models of Titan. J. Phys. Chem. A **113**, 11138–11152 (2009)

18. Balucani, N., Alagia, M., Cartechini, L., Casavecchia, P., Volpi, G.G., Sato, K., Takayanagi, T., Kurosaki, Y.: Cyanomethylene formation from the reaction of excited nitrogen atoms with acetylene: a crossed beam and ab initio study. J. Am. Chem. Soc. **122**, 4443–4450 (2000)

19. Balucani, N., Cartechini, L., Alagia, M., Casavecchia, P., Volpi, G.G.: Observation of nitrogen-bearing organic molecules from reactions of nitrogen atoms with hydrocarbons: a crossed beam study of N(^{2}D) + ethylene. J. Phys. Chem. A **104**, 5655–5659 (2000)

20. Balucani, N., Leonori, F., Petrucci, R., Stazi, M., Skouteris, D., Rosi, M., Casavecchia, P.: Formation of nitriles and imines in the atmosphere of Titan: combined crossed-beam and theoretical studies on the reaction dynamics of excited nitrogen atoms N(^{2}D) with ethane. Faraday Discuss. **147**, 189–216 (2010)

21. Balucani, N., Skouteris, D., Leonori, F., Petrucci, R., Hamberg, M., Geppert, W.D., Casavecchia, P., Rosi, M.: Combined crossed beam and theoretical studies of the N(^{2}D) + C$_2$H$_4$ reaction and implications for atmospheric models of Titan. J. Phys. Chem. A **116**, 10467–10479 (2012)

22. Rosi, M., Falcinelli, S., Balucani, N., Casavecchia, P., Skouteris, D.: A theoretical study of formation routes and dimerization of methanimine and implications for the aerosols formation in the upper atmosphere of Titan. In: Murgante, B., et al. (eds.) Computational Science and Its Applications – ICCSA 2013, ICCSA 2013. Lecture Notes in Computer Science, vol. 7971, pp. 47–56. Springer, Heidelberg (2013). https://doi.org/10.1007/978-3-642-39637-3_4

23. Balucani, N., Alagia, M., Cartechini, L., Casavecchia, P., Volpi, G.G., Pederson, L.A., Schatz, G.C.: Dynamics of the $N(^2D)+D_2$ reaction from crossed-beam and quasiclassical trajectory studies. J. Phys. Chem. A **105**, 2414–2422 (2001)

24. Balucani, N., Casavecchia, P., Banares, L., Aoiz, F.J., Gonzalez-Lezana, T., Honvault, P., Launay, J.M.: Experimental and theoretical differential cross sections for the $N(^2D)+H_2$ reaction. J. Phys. Chem. A **110**, 817–829 (2006)

25. Homayoon, Z., Bowman, J.M., Balucani, N., Casavecchia, P.: Quasiclassical trajectory calculations of the $N(^2D) + H_2O$ reaction elucidating the formation mechanism of HNO and HON seen in molecular beam experiments. J. Phys. Chem. Lett. **5**, 3508–3513 (2014)

26. Balucani, N., Cartechini, L., Casavecchia, P., Homayoon, Z., Bowman, J.M.: A combined crossed molecular beam and quasiclassical trajectory study of the Titan-relevant $N(^2D) + D_2O$ reaction. Mol. Phys. **113**, 2296–2301 (2015)

27. Balucani, N., Asvany, O., Chang, A.H.H., Lin, S.H., Lee, Y.T., Kaiser, R.I., Bettinger, H.F., Schleyer, P.V.R., Schaefer III, H.F.: Crossed beam reaction of cyano radicals with hydrocarbon molecules. I. Chemical dynamics of cyanobenzene (C6H5CN; X 1A1) and perdeutero cyanobenzene (C6D5CN; X 1A1) formation from reaction of CN (X 2Σ+) with benzene C6H6 (X 1A1g), and d6-benzene C6D6 (X 1A1g). J. Chem. Phys. **111**, 7457–7471 (1999)

28. Zhang, F., Guo, Y., Gu, X., Kaiser, R.I.: A crossed molecular beam study on the reaction of boron atoms, $B(^2P_j)$, with benzene, C_6H_6 (X^1A_{1g}), and D6-benzene $C_6D_6(X^1A_{1g})$. Chem. Phys. Lett. **440**, 56–63 (2007)

29. Balucani, N., Zhang, F., Kaiser, R.I.: Elementary reactions of boron atoms with hydrocarbons - toward the formation of organo-boron compounds. Chem. Rev. **110**, 5107–5127 (2010)

30. Parker, D.S.N., Dangi, B.B., Balucani, N., Stranges, D., Mebel, A.M., Kaiser, R.I.: Gas-phase synthesis of phenyl oxoborane (C_6H_5BO) via the reaction of boron monoxide with benzene. J. Org. Chem. **78**, 11896–11900 (2013)

31. Caracciolo, A., Balucani, N., Vanuzzo, G., Minton, T.K., Casavecchia, P.: In Preparation

32. Bettinger, H.F., Schleyer, P.V.R., Schaefer III, H.F., Schreiner, P.R., Kaiser, R.I., Lee, Y.T.: The reaction of benzene with a ground state carbon atom, $C(^3P_j)$. J. Chem. Phys. **113**, 4250–4264 (2000)

33. Becke, A.D.: Density functional thermochemistry. III. The role of exact exchange. J. Chem. Phys. **98**, 5648–5652 (1993)

34. Stephens, P.J., Devlin, F.J., Chablowski, C.F., Frisch, M.J.: Ab initio calculation of vibrational absorption and circular dichroism spectra using density functional force fields. J. Phys. Chem. **98**, 11623–11627 (1994)

35. Krishnan, R., Binkley, J.S., Seeger, R., Pople, J.A.: Self-consistent molecular orbital methods. XX. A basis set for correlated wave functions. J. Chem. Phys. **72**, 650–654 (1980)

36. Frisch, M.J., Pople, J.A., Binkley, J.S.: Self-consistent molecular orbital methods 25. Supplementary functions for Gaussian basis sets. J. Chem. Phys. **80**, 3265–3269 (1984)

37. Gonzalez, C., Schlegel, H.B.: An improved algorithm for reaction path following. J. Chem. Phys. **90**, 2154–2161 (1989)

38. Gonzalez, C., Schlegel, H.B.: Reaction path following in mass-weighted internal coordinates. J. Phys. Chem. **94**, 5523–5527 (1990)

39. Bartlett, R.J.: Many-body perturbation theory and coupled cluster theory for electron correlation in molecules. Annu. Rev. Phys. Chem. **32**, 359–401 (1981)

40. Raghavachari, K., Trucks, G.W., Pople, J.A., Head-Gordon, M.: Quadratic configuration interaction. A general technique for determining electron correlation energies. Chem. Phys. Lett. **157**, 479–483 (1989)

41. Olsen, J., Jorgensen, P., Koch, H., Balkova, A., Bartlett, R.J.: Full configuration–interaction and state of the art correlation calculations on water in a valence double-zeta basis with polarization functions. J. Chem. Phys. **104**, 8007–8015 (1996)
42. Dunning Jr., T.H.: Gaussian basis sets for use in correlated molecular calculations. I. The atoms boron through neon and hydrogen. J. Chem. Phys. **90**, 1007–1023 (1989)
43. de Petris, G., Cacace, F., Cipollini, R., Cartoni, A., Rosi, M., Troiani, A.: Experimental detection of theoretically predicted N$_2$CO. Angew. Chem. **117**, 466–469 (2005)
44. Frisch, M.J., Trucks, G.W., Schlegel, H.B., Scuseria, G.E., Robb, M.A., Cheeseman, J.R., Scalmani, G., Barone, V., Mennucci, B., Petersson, G.A., Nakatsuji, H., Caricato, M., Li, X., Hratchian, H.P., Izmaylov, A.F., Bloino, J., Zheng, G., Sonnenberg, J.L., Hada, M., Ehara, M., Toyota, K., Fukuda, R., Hasegawa, J., Ishida, M., Nakajima, T., Honda, Y., Kitao, O., Nakai, H., Vreven, T., Montgomery, J.A., Jr., Peralta, J.E., Ogliaro, F., Bearpark, M., Heyd, J.J., Brothers, E., Kudin, K.N., Staroverov, V.N., Kobayashi, R., Normand, J., Raghavachari, K., Rendell, A., Burant, J.C., Iyengar, S.S., Tomasi, J., Cosi, M., Rega, N., Milla, J.M., Klene, M., Knox, J.E., Cross, J.B., Bakken, V., Adamo, C., Jaramillo, J., Gomperts, R., Stratmann, R.E., Yazyev, O., Austin, A.J., Cammi, R., Pomelli, C., Ochterski, J.W., Martin, R.L., Morokuma, K., Zakrzewski, V.G., Voth, G.A., Salvador, P., Dannenberg, J.J., Dapprich, S., Daniels, A.D., Farkas, O., Foresman, J.B., Ortiz, J.V., Cioslowski, J., Fox, D. J.: Gaussian 09, Revision A.02. Gaussian, Inc., Wallingford (2009)
45. Flükiger, P., Lüthi, H.P., Portmann, S., Weber, J.: MOLEKEL 4.3, Swiss Center for Scientific Computing, Manno, Switzerland, 2000–2002
46. Portmann, S., Lüthi, H.P.: MOLEKEL: an interactive molecular graphics tool. Chimia **54**, 766–769 (2000)
47. Leonori, F., Skouteris, D., Petrucci, R., Casavecchia, P., Rosi, M., Balucani, N.: Combined crossed beam and theoretical studies of the C(^{1}D) + CH$_4$ reaction. J. Chem. Phys. **138**(2), 024311 (2013)
48. Leonori, F., Petrucci, R., Balucani, N., Casavecchia, P., Rosi, M., Skouteris, D., Berteloite, C., Le Picard, S.D., Canosa, A., Sims, I.R.: Crossed-beam dynamics, low-temperature kinetics, and theoretical studies of the reaction S(^{1}D)+C$_2$H$_4$. J. Phys. Chem. A **113**, 15328–15345 (2009)
49. Leonori, F., Balucani, N., Capozza, G., Segoloni, E., Volpi, G.G., Casavecchia, P.: Dynamics of the O(^{3}P) + C$_2$H$_2$ reaction from crossed molecular beam experiments with soft electron ionization detection. Phys. Chem. Chem.- Phys. **16**, 10008–10022 (2014)
50. Casavecchia, P., Leonori, F., Balucani, N.: Reaction dynamics of oxygen atoms with unsaturated hydrocarbons from crossed molecular beam studies: primary products, branching ratios and role of intersystem crossing. Int. Rev. Phys. Chem. **34**, 161–204 (2015)
51. Balucani, N., Leonori, F., Casavecchia, P., Fu, B., Bowman, J.M.: Crossed molecular beams and quasiclassical trajectory surface hopping studies of the multichannel nonadiabatic O(^{3}P) +ethylene reaction at high collision energy. J. Phys. Chem. A **119**, 12498–12511 (2015)
52. Cavallotti, C., Leonori, F., Balucani, N., Nevrly, V., Bergeat, A., Falcinelli, S., Vanuzzo, G., Casavecchia, P.: Relevance of the channel leading to formaldehyde + triplet ethylidene in the O(^{3}P) + propene reaction under combustion conditions. J. Phys. Chem. Lett. **5**, 4213–4218 (2014)
53. Vanuzzo, G., Balucani, N., Leonori, F., Stranges, D., Nevrly, V., Falcinelli, S., Bergeat, A., Casavecchia, P., Cavallotti, C.: Reaction dynamics of O(^{3}P)+propyne: I. Primary products, branching ratios and role of intersystem crossing from crossed molecular beam experiments. J. Phys. Chem. A **120**, 4603–4618 (2016)
54. Balucani, N., Leonori, F., Petrucci, R., Wang, X., Casavecchia, P., Skouteris, D., Albernaz, A.F., Gargano, R.: A combined crossed molecular beams and theoretical study of the reaction CN + C$_2$H$_4$. Chem. Phys. **449**, 34–42 (2015)

55. Vazart, F., Latouche, C., Skouteris, D., Balucani, N., Barone, V.: Cyanomethanimine isomers in cold interstellar clouds: insights from electronic structure and kinetic calculations. Astrophys. J. **810**, 111 (2015)
56. Nixon, C.A., Cordiner, M.A., Greathouse, T.K., Richter, M., Kisiel, Z., Irwin, P.G.J., Teanby, N.A., Kuan, Y.T., Charnley, S.B.: Multi-wavelength search for complex molecules in Titan's Atmosphere, American Geophysical Union, Fall Meeting 2017, abstract #P13D-2589 (2017)

Formation of Nitrogen-Bearing Organic Molecules in the Reaction NH + C$_2$H$_5$: A Theoretical Investigation and Main Implications for Prebiotic Chemistry in Space

Marzio Rosi[1,2(✉)], Dimitrios Skouteris[3], Piergiorgio Casavecchia[4], Stefano Falcinelli[1], Cecilia Ceccarelli[5], and Nadia Balucani[4,5]

[1] Dipartimento di Ingegneria Civile e Ambientale, Università degli Studi di Perugia, 06125 Perugia, Italy
{marzio.rosi,stefano.falcinelli}@unipg.it
[2] CNR-ISTM, 06123 Perugia, Italy
[3] Scuola Normale Superiore, 56126 Pisa, Italy
dimitrios.skouteris@sns.it
[4] Dipartimento di Chimica, Biologia e Biotecnologie, Università degli Studi di Perugia, 06123 Perugia, Italy
{piergiorgio.casavecchia,nadia.balucani}@unipg.it
[5] Université Grenoble Alpes, IPAG, 38000 Grenoble, France
cecilia.ceccarelli@univ-grenoble-alpes.fr

Abstract. The synthesis of nitrogen-containing organic molecules is a crucial step in prebiotic chemistry, as they are potential precursors of important biological molecules such as nucleobases and amino acids. In this respect, unsaturated species like nitriles (containing a –CN group) or imines (containing a carbon–nitrogen double bond) are particularly interesting because the presence of an unsaturated bond allows for further evolution. Interestingly, simple species belonging to both nitrile and imine families have been detected in the interstellar medium and in the upper atmosphere of Titan. In this contribution, the reaction between the imidogen radical (NH) and ethyl radical (C$_2$H$_5$) is investigated from a theoretical point of view to establish whether it can form product species with a novel C-N bond. According to the present electronic structure calculations of the stationary points of the C$_2$H$_6$N potential energy surface, the NH + C$_2$H$_5$ reaction is a viable route of formation of methanimine and ethanimine, that is, two N-containing molecules already detected in the interstellar medium.

Keywords: Ab initio methods · Astrochemistry Electronic structure calculations · Kinetic calculations

1 Introduction

Simple organic molecules containing a carbon atom bound to a nitrogen atom are widely spread in our galaxy, having been detected in various regions of the interstellar medium, in comets and in the atmospheres of planets and moons [1]. Some of them, like HCCCN or NH$_2$CHO, have been detected in many different extraterrestrial environments dominated by various density and temperature conditions (for recent detections see Refs [2, 3] and references therein).

In general, space detection of small unsaturated species like nitriles (containing a – CN group) or aldimines (containing a carbon–nitrogen double bond) is particularly interesting because they are molecules simple enough to be formed in totally abiotic environments but contain multiple bonds that can allow further chemical evolution in denser and chemically active environments. In other words, these species might be the link between interstellar matter and the complex molecules from which life emerged on primitive Earth [4–9]. In particular, both nitriles and imines are known to polymerize and hydrolyze leading to important biological molecules such as nucleobases and amino-acids (see [7] and references therein).

The smallest member of the aldimine family, methanimine (CH_2NH), has been widely detected in the interstellar medium with its first detection dating back to 1973 [10]. Its presence in the upper atmosphere of Titan (the massive moon of Saturn), has also been inferred by the detection of its protonated form by the Cassini Ion Neutral Mass Spectrometer (INMS) [11]. In the upper atmosphere of Titan, CH_2NH is mainly produced by reactions involving the first electronically excited ^2D state of atomic nitrogen with methane or ethane [12–14], or via the $NH + CH_3$ reaction [15]. Photochemical models derived a larger abundance of CH_2NH with respect to the estimated values [16, 17], thus implying that its chemistry is not well-defined yet. Interestingly, methanimine has been considered as the precursor of hexahydro-1,3,5- triazine, which has been observed upon UV irradiation of a $H_2O:CH_3OH:CO:NH_3$ ice mixture at 12 K simulating cometary ice [18] or as a source of aerosol formation in the upper atmosphere of Titan [16]. A dedicated study to characterize methanimine polymerization, however, could not confirm the assumed behavior [19], unless ionized methanimine is involved [20].

In addition to methanimine, other imines have been recently detected in interstellar objects: ketenimine ($CH_2=C=NH$) [21], ethanimine ($CH_3CH=NH$) [22] and cyanomethanimine ($HN=CHCN$) [23]. Because of the very low number density of those environments, however, $N(^2D)$ reactions cannot be invoked in their formation (the excited ^2D state has a very long radiative lifetime of $ca.$ 48 h [24], but the collision frequency is very low in interstellar clouds). Indeed, while the formation of nitriles has been widely explored and their formation routes are well-established [25–35], more uncertain is the mechanism of formation of imines [36–38] with the exception of cyanomethanimine, for which a well-established formation route is available [39]. Concerning the ethanimine formation route, the reaction $NH + C_2H_5$ seems to be the best candidate among the gaseous processes considered by Quan et al. [37]. In the absence of any information about this reaction, however, Quan et al. used the rate coefficient determined by Stief et al. [40] for the reaction $N + C_2H_5$ and partitioned its global value with the branching ratio derived by Yang et al. [41]. However, atomic nitrogen is not isoelectronic with NH and, therefore, there is no reason to expect a similar reactivity. In addition, the rate coefficient employed by Quan et al. [37] was reduced by one order of magnitude with respect to the value measured by Stief et al. [40] for no apparent reason.

In this contribution we present a theoretical characterization of the reaction $NH + C_2H_5$. To the best of our knowledge, this is the first study ever of this reactive system.

2 Computational Details

The potential energy surface (PES) of the lowest doublet state of the $[C_2H_6N]$ system has been calculated using a computational scheme successfully employed in several cases (see for instance [42]) which implies an optimization of the minima and saddle points at the density functional method (DFT) level, using the hybrid B3LYP functional [43, 44], followed by an energy refinement of all the stationary points at the coupled-cluster single and double excitation method with a perturbational estimate of the triple excitations (CCSD(T)) level [45–47]. For both methods the correlation consistent aug-cc-pVTZ basis set has been employed [48]. Transition states were located on the PES using the synchronous transit-guided quasi-Newton method of Schlegel and coworkers [49, 50]. At the optimized geometries, vibrational frequencies were computed using the B3LYP/auc-cc-pVTZ method in order to check the nature of the stationary point, i.e. minimum if all the frequencies are real and saddle point if there is one, and only one, imaginary frequency. Intrinsic reaction coordinate (IRC) calculations [51, 52] were performed to connect all the transition states with the corresponding reactants and products. Zero-point energy corrections evaluated at the B3LYP/aug-cc-pVTZ level were added to both the B3LYP and CCSD(T) energies. All calculations were performed using Gaussian 09 [53] while the analysis of the vibrational frequencies was performed using Molekel [54, 55].

Kinetics calculations were performed as detailed below. The initial NH + CH_3CH_2 association rate constant is calculated using capture theory [56], after fitting the long-range interaction potential of the two molecules to a

$$V(r) = -\frac{C}{r^6}$$

Equation, where r stands for the intermolecular distance. Typically it can be taken to be the distance between the centers of mass or between two heavy atoms. C stands for the proportionality constant between the potential and $1/r^6$ and it is determined by fitting of long-range ab initio data. We have verified using the detailed balance principle that back-dissociation from the initial adduct to the reactants does not occur, given the large depth of the potential energy well. As a result, the initial capture rate constant is equal to the overall reaction rate constant, i.e. the sum of all product-specific rate constants. The raw capture rate constant has been divided by a statistical factor of 3 in order to account for the non-reactive spin states of the reactants. We remind that CH_3CH_2 and NH are found in a doublet and a triplet state respectively. Out of the six overall spin states, two are reactive (the ones that correspond to a singlet configuration of the two electrons of the newly formed bond and the two possible configurations of the remaining lone electron).

3 Results

3.1 Electronic Structure Calculations of Minima Along the Minimum Energy Path

Figure 1 reports the minimum energy path for the reaction NH + C$_2$H$_5$ computed at the CCSD(T)/aug-cc-pVTZ level, while Table 1 shows for the same process the enthalpy changes and the barrier heights computed both at the B3LYP/aug-cc-pVTZ and CCSD (T)/aug-cc-pVTZ level. The agreement between the two methods is reasonably good. For simplicity, in the following discussion we will consider only the more accurate CCSD(T) energies.

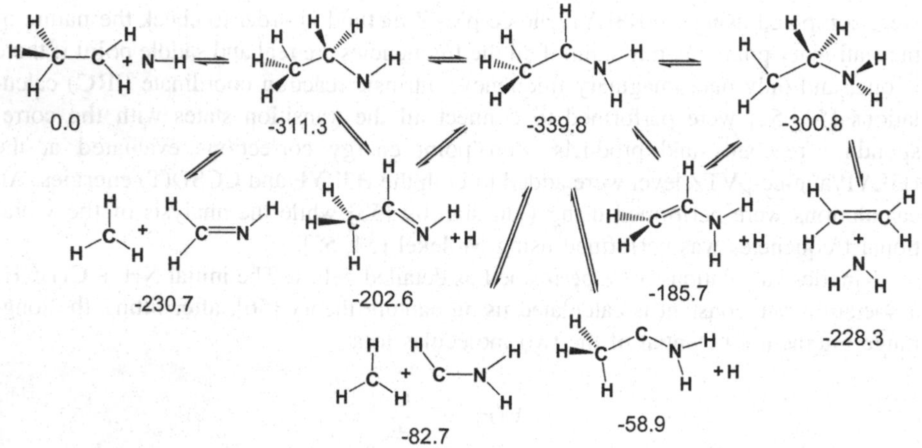

Fig. 1. Main steps along the minimum energy path for the reaction NH + C$_2$H$_5$. Relative energies (kJ/mol, 0 K) computed at CCSD(T)/aug-cc-pVTZ level with respect to NH + C$_2$H$_5$.

Table 1. Enthalpy changes and barrier heights (kJ/mol, 0 K) computed at the B3LYP/aug-cc-pVTZ and CCSD(T)/aug-cc-pVTZ levels of theory for selected reactions of the system NH + CH$_3$CH$_2$.

	ΔH_0^0		Barrier height	
	B3LYP	CCSD(T)	B3LYP	CCSD(T)
NH ($^3\Sigma^-$) + CH$_3$CH$_2$ → CH$_3$CH$_2$NH	−309.0	−311.3		
CH$_3$CH$_2$NH → CH$_3$CHNH$_2$	−34.8	−28.5	143.9	146.2
CH$_3$CHNH$_2$ → CH$_2$CH$_2$NH$_2$	46.7	39.0	190.8	193.6
CH$_3$CH$_2$NH → CH$_3$CHNH + H	114.6	108.7	131.2	131.0
CH$_3$CH$_2$NH → CH$_3$ + CH$_2$NH	72.7	80.6	104.7	113.5
CH$_3$CHNH$_2$ → CH$_3$CHNH + H	149.4	137.2	152.2	148.3
CH$_3$CHNH$_2$ → CH$_2$CHNH$_2$ +H	158.3	154.1	158.6	154.2
CH$_3$CHNH$_2$ → CH$_3$ + CHNH$_2$	251.4	257.1	255.2	258.9
CH$_3$CHNH$_2$ → CH$_3$CNH$_2$ + H	286.6	280.9	286.8	280.9
CH$_2$CH$_2$NH$_2$ → C$_2$H$_4$ + NH$_2$	63.8	72.5	82.5	93.7
CH$_2$CH$_2$NH$_2$ → CH$_2$CHNH$_2$ + H	111.6	115.1	126.3	140.0

The interaction of NH in its triplet $^3\Sigma^-$ ground state with the radical C$_2$H$_5$ gives rise to the formation of the species CH$_3$CH$_2$NH, more stable than the reactants by 311.3 kJ/mol, without any barrier. This species, through the transfer of an H atom from the central carbon atom to the nitrogen one, isomerizes to the CH$_3$CHNH$_2$ species more stable by 28.5 kJ/mol; however, this reaction implies the overcoming of an energy barrier of 146.2 kJ/mol. CH$_3$CH$_2$NH can also dissociate losing a hydrogen atom or a methyl radical giving rise to the formation of ethanimine or methanimine, respectively. Both these reactions are endothermic (108.7 and 80.6 kJ/mol, respectively) and show barriers slightly higher than the endothermicity (131.0 and 113.5 kJ/mol, respectively). CH$_3$CHNH$_2$, once formed, can isomerize to the species CH$_2$CH$_2$NH$_2$, less stable by 39.0 kJ/mol, through a barrier as high as 193.6 kJ/mol or can dissociate giving rise to ethanimine or other products; all of these reactions are endothermic and shows energy barriers which are, however, only slightly higher than the endothermicity of the reactions. CH$_2$CH$_2$NH$_2$, once formed, can dissociate giving rise to ethylene in a reaction endothermic by only 72.5 kJ/mol which shows a barrier of 93.7 kJ/mol. Otherwise CH$_2$CH$_2$NH$_2$ can lose a hydrogen atom in a more endothermic reaction.

In summary, we can notice, as reported in Fig. 1, that methanimine can be formed only by CH$_3$CH$_2$NH, while ethanimine can be formed by CH$_3$CH$_2$NH or CH$_3$CHNH$_2$.

3.2   The Global Rate Coefficient

The global rate coefficient as a function of the temperature is reported in Fig. 2. As expected for a barrier-less reaction, the rate coefficient is very high in the gas-kinetics limit. In addition, as visible in Fig. 2, the capture rate coefficient rises steeply at low temperatures, rapidly reaching a plateau as the temperature rises. By fitting the trend with the temperature with the usual dependence k = α(T/300)$^\beta$exp($-\gamma$/T), we obtain for the global reaction $\alpha = 5.768 \times 10^{-10}$ cm^3 s^{-1}, $\beta = 0.172$ and $\gamma = 0.517$ K.

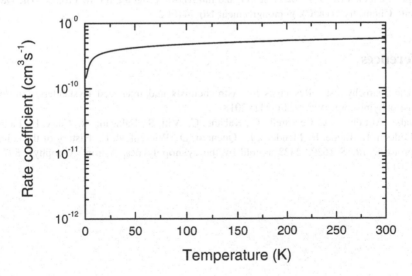

Fig. 2. Global rate coefficient as a function of the temperature of the reaction NH + C$_2$H$_5$

4 Astrophysical Implications

In this contribution, we have reported on a theoretical investigation of the title reaction up to the estimate of the global rate coefficient which falls in the gas-kinetics value in the entire range of analyzed temperatures, as expected for a radical-radical reaction. However, our calculations clearly demonstrate that ethanimine formation is not the sole reaction channel, as assumed by Quan *et al.* [37], and also other product channels are open. In particular, the methyl elimination channel leading to methanimine seems to be favored because it is formed starting from the initial addition intermediate with an exit barrier lower in energy than that associated to the H-elimination channel with ethanimine formation. The present results are going to affect the astrochemical models designed to reproduce the ethanimine abundance in Sagittarius B2(N) [22, 37]. In particular, while the global rate coefficient is larger by one order of magnitude with respect to the one used by Quan *et al.* [37], the inclusion of the appropriate product branching ratio can further affect the model predictions. For this reason, we are envisaging a more thorough study to derive also the product branching ratio and the actual astrochemical models.

In all cases, the present investigation clearly demonstrates that the title reaction is a viable route to the synthesis of aldimines, namely $CH_2=NH$ and $CH_3CH=NH$. Both molecules have a strong prebiotic potential, as aldimines are important intermediate in the Strecker synthesis of amino acids (see, for instance, [57–59]).

Acknowledgments. This work has been supported by MIUR "PRIN 2015" funds, project "STARS in the CAOS (Simulation Tools for Astrochemical Reactivity and Spectroscopy in the Cyberinfrastructure for Astrochemical Organic Species)", Grant Number 2015F59J3R. DS wishes to thank the Italian Ministero dell'Istruzione, Università e Ricerca (MIUR_F-FABR17_SKOUTERIS) and the Scuola Normale Superiore (SNS_RB_SKOUTERIS) for financial support. Partially supported also by the European Research Council (ERC) under the European Union's Horizon 2020 research and innovation program, for the Project "The Dawn of Organic Chemistry" (DOC), grant agreement No 741002.

References

1. The Astrochymist - Resources for Astrochemists and Interested Bystanders. http://www.astrochymist.org. Accessed 6 Mar 2018
2. Jaber Al-Edhari, A., Ceccarelli, C., Kahane, C., Viti, S., Balucani, N., Caux, E., Faure, A., Lefloch, B., Lique, F., Mendoza, E., Quenard, D., Wiesenfeld, L.: History of the solar-type protostar IRAS 16293-2422 as told by the cyanopolyynes. Astron. Astrophys. **597**, A40 (2017)

3. Codella, C., Ceccarelli, C., Caselli, P., Balucani, N., Barone, V., Fontani, F., Lefloch, B., Podio, L., Viti, S., Feng, S., Bachiller, R., Bianchi, E., Dulieu, F., Jiménez-Serra, I., Holdship, J., Neri, R., Pineda, J.E., Pon, A., Sims, I., Spezzano, S., Vasyunin, A.I., Alves, F., Bizzocchi, L., Bottinelli, S., Caux, E., Chacón-Tanarro, A., Choudhury, R., Coutens, A., Favre, C., Hily-Blant, P., Kahane, C., Jaber Al-Edhari, A., Laas, J., López-Sepulcre, A., Ospina, J., Oya, Y., Punanova, A., Puzzarini, C., Quenard, D., Rimola, A., Sakai, N., Skouteris, D., Taquet, V., Testi, L., Theulé, P., Ugliengo, P., Vastel, C., Vazart, F., Wiesenfeld, L., Yamamoto, S.: Seeds of Life in Space (SOLIS). II. Formamide in protostellar shocks: evidence for gas-phase formation. Astron. Astrophys. **605**, 7 (2017)
4. Caselli, P., Ceccarelli, C.: Our astrochemical heritage. Astron. Astrophys. Rev. **20**, 56 (2012)
5. Ehrenfreund, P., Charnley, S.B.: Organic molecules in the interstellar medium, comets, and meteorites: a voyage from dark clouds to the early earth. Ann. Rev. Astron. Astrophys. **38**, 427–483 (2000)
6. Balucani, N.: Elementary reactions of N atoms with hydrocarbons: first steps towards the formation of prebiotic N-containing molecules in planetary atmospheres. Chem. Soc. Rev. **41**, 5473–5483 (2012)
7. Balucani, N.: Elementary reactions and their role in gas-phase prebiotic chemistry. Int. J. Mol. Sci. **10**, 2304–2335 (2009)
8. Balucani, N.: Gas-phase prebiotic chemistry in extraterrestrial environments. In: Corbett, I.F. (ed.) Highlights of Astronomy, Proceedings of the International Astronomical Union, vol. 5, no. H15. Cambridge University Press (2009)
9. Balucani, N.: Nitrogen fixation by photochemistry in the atmosphere of Titan and implications for prebiotic chemistry. In: Trigo-Rodriguez, J., Raulin, F., Muller, C., Nixon, C. (eds.) The Early Evolution of the Atmospheres of Terrestrial Planets, Astrophysics and Space Science Proceedings, vol. 35. Springer, New York (2013). https://doi.org/10.1007/978-1-4614-5191-4_12
10. Godfrey, P.D., Brown, R.D., Robinson, B.J., Sinclair, M.W.: Discovery of interstellar methanimine (formaldimine). Astrophys. Lett. **13**, 119 (1973)
11. Vuitton, V., Yelle, R.V., Anicich, V.G.: The nitrogen chemistry of Titan's upper atmosphere revealed. Astrophys. J. **647**, L175–L178 (2006)
12. Casavecchia, P., Balucani, N., Cartechini, L., Capozza, G., Bergeat, A., Volpi, G.G.: Crossed beam studies of elementary reactions of N and C atoms and CN radicals of importance in combustion. Faraday Discuss. **119**, 27–49 (2001)
13. Balucani, N., Bergeat, A., Cartechini, L., Volpi, G.G., Casavecchia, P., Skouteris, D., Rosi, M.: Combined crossed molecular beam and theoretical studies of the N(^{2}D) + CH$_4$ reaction and implications for atmospheric models of Titan. J. Phys. Chem. A **113**, 11138–11152 (2009)
14. Balucani, N., Leonori, F., Petrucci, R., Stazi, M., Skouteris, D., Rosi, M., Casavecchia, P.: Formation of nitriles and imines in the atmosphere of Titan: combined crossed-beam and theoretical studies on the reaction dynamics of excited nitrogen atoms N(^{2}D) with ethane. Faraday Discuss. **147**, 189–216 (2010)
15. Redondo, P., Pauzat, F., Ellinger, Y.: Theoretical survey of the NH + CH$_3$ potential energy surface in relation to Titan atmospheric chemistry. Planet. Space Sci. **54**, 181–187 (2006)
16. Lavvas, P.P., Coustenis, A., Vardavas, I.M.: Coupling photochemistry with haze formation in Titan's atmosphere. Part II: results and validation with Cassini/Huygens data. Planet. Space Sci. **56**, 67–99 (2008)
17. Loison, J.C., Hébrard, E., Dobrijevic, M., Hickson, K.M., Caralp, F., Hue, V., Gronoff, G., Venot, O., Bénilan, Y.: The neutral photochemistry of nitriles, amines and imines in the atmosphere of Titan. Icarus **247**, 218–247 (2015)

18. Bernstein, M.P., Sandford, S.A., Allamandola, L.J., Chang, S., Scharberg, M.A.: Organic compounds produced by photolysis of realistic interstellar and cometary ice analogs containing methanol. Astrophys. J. **454**, 327–344 (1995)

19. Rosi, M., Falcinelli, S., Balucani, N., Casavecchia, P., Skouteris, D.: A Theoretical study of formation routes and dimerization of methanimine and implications for the aerosols formation in the upper atmosphere of Titan. In: Murgante, B., Misra, S., Carlini, M., Torre, Carmelo M., Nguyen, H.-Q., Taniar, D., Apduhan, Bernady O., Gervasi, O. (eds.) ICCSA 2013. LNCS, vol. 7971, pp. 47–56. Springer, Heidelberg (2013). https://doi.org/10.1007/978-3-642-39637-3_4

20. Skouteris, D., Balucani, N., Faginas-Lago, N., Falcinelli, S., Rosi, M.: Dimerization of methanimine and its charged species in the atmosphere of Titan and interstellar/cometary ice analogs. Astron. Astrophys. **584**, A76 (2015)

21. Lovas, F.J., Hollis, J.M., Remijan, A.J., Jewell, P.R.: Detection of ketenimine (CH_2CNH) in sagittarius B2(N) hot cores. Astrophys. J. **645**, L137–L140 (2006)

22. Loomis, R.A., Zaleski, D.P., Steber, A.L., Neill, J.L., Muckle, M.T., Harris, B.J., Hollis, J. M., Jewell, P.R., Lattanzi, V., Lovas, F.J., Martinez Jr., O., McCarthy, M.C., Remijan, A.J., Pate, B.H., Corby, J.F.: The detection of interstellar ethanimine (CH_3CHNH) from observations taken during the GBT PRIMOS survey. Astrophys. J. **765**, L9 (2013)

23. Zaleski, D.P., Seifert, N.A., Steber, A.L., Muckle, M.T., Loomis, R.A., Corby, J.F., Martinez Jr., O., Crabtree, K.N., Jewell, P.R., Hollis, J.M., Lovas, F.J., Vasquez, D., Nyiramahirwe, J., Sciortino, N., Johnson, K., McCarthy, M.C., Remijan, A.J., Pate, B.H.: Detection of e-cyanomethanimine toward sagittarius B2(N) in the green bank telescope PRIMOS survey. Astrophys. J. **765**, L10 (2013)

24. Dutuit, O., Carrasco, N., Thissen, R., Vuitton, V., Alcaraz, C., Pernot, P., Balucani, N., Casavecchia, P., Canosa, A., Le Picard, S., Loison, J.-C., Herman, Z., Zabka, J., Ascenzi, D., Tosi, P., Franceschi, P., Price, S.D., Lavvas, P.: Critical review of N, N^+, N_2^+, N^{++} and N_2^{++} main production processes and reactions of relevance to Titan's atmosphere. Astrophys. J. Suppl. Ser. **204**, 20 (2013)

25. Balucani, N., Asvany, O., Chang, A.H.H., Lin, S.H., Lee, Y.T., Kaiser, R.I., Bettinger, H.F., Schleyer, P.V.R., Schaefer III, H.F.: Crossed beam reaction of cyano radicals with hydrocarbon molecules. I. Chemical dynamics of cyanobenzene (C_6H_5CN; X $^1A_1$) and perdeutero cyanobenzene (C_6D_5CN; X $^1A_1$) formation from reaction of CN (X $^2\Sigma^+$) with benzene C_6H_6 (X $^1A_{1g}$), and d6-benzene C_6D_6 (X $^1A_{1g}$). J. Chem. Phys. **111**, 7457–7471 (1999)

26. Balucani, N., Asvany, O., Chang, A.H.H., Lin, S.H., Lee, Y.T., Kaiser, R.I., Bettinger, H.F., Schleyer, P.V.R., Schaefer III, H.F.: Crossed beam reaction of cyano radicals with hydrocarbon molecules. II. Chemical dynamics of 1-cyano-1-methylallene ($CNCH_3CCCH_2$; X $^1A'$) formation from reaction of CN (X $^2\Sigma^+$) with dimethylacetylene CH_3CCCH_3 (X $^1A_1'$). J. Chem. Phys. **111**, 7472–7479 (1999)

27. Huang, L.C.L., Balucani, N., Lee, Y.T., Kaiser, R.I., Osamura, Y.: Crossed beam reaction of the cyano radical, CN (X $^2\Sigma^+$), with methylacetylene, CH_3CCH (X$^1A_1$): Observation of cyanopropyne, CH_3CCCN (X$^1A_1$), and cyanoallene, $H_2CCCHCN$ (X$^1A'$). J. Chem. Phys. **111**, 2857–2860 (1999)

28. Balucani, N., Asvany, O., Chang, A.H.H., Lin, S.H., Lee, Y.T., Kaiser, R.I., Osamura, Y.: Crossed beam reaction of cyano radicals with hydrocarbon molecules. III. Chemical dynamics of vinylcyanide (C_2H_3CN; X $^1A'$) formation from reaction of CN (X $^2\Sigma^+$) with ethylene, C_2H_4 (X ^1A_g). J. Chem. Phys. **113**, 8643–8655 (2000)

29. Balucani, N., Asvany, O., Kaiser, R.I., Osamura, Y.: Formation of three C_4H_3N isomers from the reaction of $CN(X^2\Sigma^+)$ with allene, H_2CCCH_2 (X $^1A_1$), and methylacetylene, CH_3CCH (X $^1A_1$): a combined crossed beam and ab initio study. J. Phys. Chem. A **106**, 4301–4311 (2002)

30. Leonori, F., Hickson, K.M., Le Picard, S.D., Wang, X., Petrucci, R., Foggi, P., Balucani, N., Casavecchia, P.: Crossed-beam universal-detection reactive scattering of radical beams characterized by laser-induced fluorescence: the case of C_2 and CN. Mol. Phys. **108**, 1097–1113 (2010)

31. Balucani, N., Leonori, F., Petrucci, R., Wang, X., Casavecchia, P., Skouteris, D., Albernaz, A.F., Gargano, R.: A combined crossed molecular beams and theoretical study of the reaction CN + C_2H_4. Chem. Phys. **449**, 34–42 (2015)

32. Leonori, F., Petrucci, R., Wang, X., Casavecchia, P., Balucani, N.: A crossed beam study of the reaction CN + C_2H_4 at a high collision energy: the opening of a new reaction channel. Chem. Phys. Lett. **553**, 1–5 (2012)

33. Sleiman, C., El Dib, G., Rosi, M., Skouteris, D., Balucani, N., Canosa, A.: Low temperature kinetics and theoretical studies of the reaction CN + CH_3NH_2: a potential source of cyanamide and methyl cyanamide in the interstellar medium. Phys. Chem. Chem. Phys. **20**, 5478–5489 (2018)

34. Kaiser, R.I., Balucani, N.: The formation of nitriles in hydrocarbon rich atmospheres of planets and their satellites: laboratory investigations by the crossed molecular beam technique. Acc. Chem. Res. **34**, 699 (2001)

35. Balucani, N., Asvany, O., Huang, L.C.L., Lee, Y.T., Kaiser, R.I., Osamura, Y., Bettinger, H.F.: Neutral-neutral reactions in the interstellar medium iii: formation of nitriles via reaction of cyano radicals, $CN(X^2\Sigma^+)$, with unsaturated hydrocarbons. Astrophys. J. **545**, 892 (2000)

36. Woon, D.E.: Pathways to glycine and other amino acids in ultraviolet-irradiated astrophysical ices determined via quantum chemical modelling. Astrophys. J. **571**, L177–L180 (2002)

37. Quan, D., Herbst, E., Corby, J.F., Durr, A., Hassel, G.: Chemical simulations of prebiotic molecules: interstellar ethanimine isomers. Astrophys. J. **824**, 129–142 (2016)

38. Sil, M., Gorai, P., Das, A., Bhat, B., Etim, E.E., Chakrabarti, S.K.: Chemical modeling for predicting the abundances of certain aldimines and imines in hot cores. Astrophys. J. **853**, 139–158 (2018)

39. Vazart, F., Latouche, C., Skouteris, D., Balucani, N., Barone, V.: Cyanomethanimine isomers in cold interstellar clouds: insights from electronic structure and kinetic calculations. Astrophys. J. **810**, 111 (2015)

40. Stief, L.J., Nesbitt, F.L., Payne, W.A., Kuo, S.C., Tao, W., Klemm, R.B.: Rate constant and reaction channels for the reaction of atomic nitrogen with the ethyl radical. J. Chem. Phys. **102**, 5309–5317 (1995)

41. Yang, Y., Zhang, W., Pei, S., Shao, J., Huang, W., Gao, X.: Theoretical study on the mechanism of the $N(^4S)$ + C_2H_5 reaction. J. Mol. Struc.: THEOCHEM **725**, 133–138 (2005)

42. de Petris, G., Cacace, F., Cipollini, R., Cartoni, A., Rosi, M., Troiani, A.: Experimental detection of theoretically predicted N_2CO. Angew. Chem. **117**, 466–469 (2005)

43. Becke, A.D.: Density functional thermochemistry. III. The role of exact exchange. J. Chem. Phys. **98**, 5648–5652 (1993)

44. Stephens, P.J., Devlin, F.J., Chablowski, C.F., Frisch, M.J.: Ab initio calculation of vibrational absorption and circular dichroism spectra using density functional force fields. J. Phys. Chem. **98**, 11623–11627 (1994)

45. Bartlett, R.J.: Many-body perturbation theory and coupled cluster theory for electron correlation in molecules. Annu. Rev. Phys. Chem. **32**, 359–401 (1981)

46. Raghavachari, K., Trucks, G.W., Pople, J.A., Head-Gordon, M.: Quadratic configuration interaction. A general technique for determining electron correlation energies. Chem. Phys. Lett. **157**, 479–483 (1989)
47. Olsen, J., Jorgensen, P., Koch, H., Balkova, A., Bartlett, R.J.: Full configuration–interaction and state of the art correlation calculations on water in a valence double-zeta basis with polarization functions. J. Chem. Phys. **104**, 8007–8015 (1996)
48. Dunning Jr., T.H.: Gaussian basis sets for use in correlated molecular calculations. I. The atoms boron through neon and hydrogen. J. Chem. Phys. **90**, 1007–1023 (1989)
49. Peng, C., Schlegel, H.B.: Combining synchronous transit and Quasi-Newton methods to find transition states. Isr. J. Chem. **33**, 449–454 (1993)
50. Peng, C., Ayala, P.Y., Schlegel, H.B., Frisch, M.J.: Using redundant internal coordinates to optimize geometries and transition states. J. Comput. Chem. **17**, 49–56 (1996)
51. Gonzalez, C., Schlegel, H.B.: An improved algorithm for reaction path following. J. Chem. Phys. **90**, 2154–2161 (1989)
52. Gonzalez, C., Schlegel, H.B.: Reaction path following in mass-weighted internal coordinates. J. Phys. Chem. **94**, 5523–5527 (1990)
53. Frisch, M.J., Trucks, G.W., Schlegel, H.B., Scuseria, G.E., Robb, M.A., Cheeseman, J.R., Scalmani, G., Barone, V., Mennucci, B., Petersson, G.A., Nakatsuji, H., Caricato, M., Li, X., Hratchian, H.P., Izmaylov, A.F., Bloino, J., Zheng, G., Sonnenberg, J.L., Hada, M., Ehara, M., Toyota, K., Fukuda, R., Hasegawa, J., Ishida, M., Nakajima, T., Honda, Y., Kitao, O., Nakai, H., Vreven, T., Montgomery, J.A., Jr., Peralta, J.E., Ogliaro, F., Bearpark, M., Heyd, J.J., Brothers, E., Kudin, K.N., Staroverov, V.N., Kobayashi, R., Normand, J., Raghavachari, K., Rendell, A., Burant, J.C., Iyengar, S.S., Tomasi, J., Cosi, M., Rega, N., Milla, J.M., Klene, M., Knox, J.E., Cross, J.B., Bakken, V., Adamo, C., Jaramillo, J., Gomperts, R., Stratmann, R.E., Yazyev, O., Austin, A.J., Cammi, R., Pomelli, C., Ochterski, J.W., Martin, R.L., Morokuma, K., Zakrzewski, V.G., Voth, G.A., Salvador, P., Dannenberg, J.J., Dapprich, S., Daniels, A.D., Farkas, O., Foresman, J.B., Ortiz, J.V., Cioslowski, J., Fox, D. J.: Gaussian 09, Revision A.02. Gaussian, Inc., Wallingford (2009)
54. Flükiger, P., Lüthi, H.P., Portmann, S., Weber, J.: MOLEKEL 4.3, Swiss Center for Scientific Computing, Manno, Switzerland, 2000–2002
55. Portmann, S., Lüthi, H.P.: MOLEKEL: an interactive molecular graphics tool. Chimia **54**, 766–769 (2000)
56. Levine, R.D.: Molecular Reaction Dynamics. Cambridge University Press, Cambridge (2005)
57. Rimola, A., Sodupe, M., Ugliengo, P.: Computational study of interstellar glycine formation occurring at radical surfaces of water-ice dust particles. Astrophys. J. **754**, 24 (2012)
58. Rimola, A., Sodupe, M., Ugliengo, P.: In silico study of the interstellar prebiotic formation and delivery of glycine. Rend. Fis. Acc. Lincei **22**, 137 (2011)
59. Koch, D.M., Toubin, C., Peslherbe, G.H., Hynes, H.T.: A theoretical study of the formation of the aminoacetonitrile precursor of glycine on icy grain mantles in the interstellar medium. J. Phys. Chem. C **112**, 2972–2980 (2008)

Author Index

Printed in the United States
By Bookmasters

Printed in the United States
By Bookmasters